Qualitatively *and* quantitatively speaking . . .

this Babbie is revolutionary.

In the eighth edition of Earl Babbie's best-seller, Babbie brings together methodological shifts in the field, new technologies that add richness to the research, and combines all this with his proven ability to *connect* with students. The result is an aggressive revision that gives you the excellence you'd expect from Babbie plus the material that anticipates your classroom needs as the field evolves into the 21st century.

You'll find:

- **Masterful, class-tested coverage of theory and its symbiotic connection to "doing" actual research**
- **Balanced—and uniquely integrated—coverage of qualitative and quantitative approaches**
- **A student-friendly writing style that brings abstract theory to life**
- **New coverage of ethics, postmodernism, and the field's latest research**
- **Emphasis throughout on the Internet and other technology as a research tool**

For full details about this revision and its expanded collection of teaching and learning materials, please turn the page.

Babbie's ability to clarify material and motivate students is unprecedented

What hasn't changed in this edition is Babbie's engaging exposition of the theoretical principles that are the foundation of scientific research, and his proven ability to demonstrate how these principles are translated into "doing" research.

The Premodern View This view of reality has guided most of human history. Our early ancestors all assumed that they saw things as they really were. In fact, this assumption was so fundamental that they didn't even see it as an assumption. No cavemom said to her cavekid, "Our tribe makes an assumption that evil spirits reside in the Old Twisted Tree." No, they said, "STAY OUT OF THAT TREE OR YOU'LL TURN INTO A TOAD!"

As humans evolved and became aware of their diversity, they came to recognize that others did not always share their views of things. Thus, they may have discovered that another tribe didn't buy the wicked tree thing; in fact, the second tribe felt the spirits in the tree were holy and beneficial. The discovery of this diversity in views led members of the first tribe to conclude that "some tribes I could name are pretty stupid." For them, the tree was still wicked, and they expected some misguided people were going to be moving to Toad City.

Why do students respond so positively? For starters, Babbie engages them with humor and down-to-earth metaphors. His many well-placed examples often elicit chuckles and nods of appreciation. He touches students' academic and social lives, shows them how theory makes sense, how it leads to practice and, how, suddenly, the abstractions become real. No other social research text connects with your students at so many levels to promote retention.

There are other ways of knowing things, however. In contrast to knowing things through agreement, it is also possible to know them through direct experience—through observation. If you dive into a glacial stream flowing down through the Canadian Rockies, you don't need anyone to tell you it's cold. You notice that all by yourself. The first time you stepped on a thorn, you knew that hurt even before anyone told you.

When your experience conflicts with what everyone else knows, there's a good chance you'll surrender your experience in favor of the agreement.

Let's take an example. Imagine you've come to a party at my house. It's a high-class affair, and the drinks and food are excellent. In particular, you are taken by one of the appetizers I bring around on a tray. It's a breaded, deep-fried appetizer with an especially zesty taste. You have a couple—they are so delicious! You have more. Soon you are subtly moving around the room to be wherever I am when I arrive with a tray of these nibblies.

Finally, you can't contain yourself any more. "What are they?" you ask. "How can I get the recipe?" And I let you in on the secret: "You've been eating breaded, deep-fried *worms*!" Your response is dramatic: Your stomach rebels, and you promptly throw up all over the living room rug. Awful! What a terrible thing to serve guests!

The point of the story is that both feelings about the appetizer would be very real. Your initial liking for them was certainly real, but so was the feeling you had when you found out what you'd been eating. It should be evident, however, that the feeling of disgust you had when you discovered you were eating worms was strictly a product of the agreements you have with those around you that worms aren't fit to eat. That's an agreement you began the first time your parents found you sitting in a pile of dirt with half of a wriggling worm dangling from your lips. You learned worms are not acceptable in our society when they pried your mouth open and reached down your throat in search of the other half of the worm.

Aside from the agreements, what's wrong with worms? They are probably high in protein and low in calories. Bite-sized and easily packaged, they are a distributor's dream. They are also a delicacy for some people who live in societies that lack our agreement that worms are disgusting. Some people might love the worms but would be turned off by the deep-fried breading.

Here's a question you might consider: Are worms "really" good or "really" bad to eat? And here's a more interesting question: *How would you know* which was really so? This book is about answering the second kind of question.

Innovative, <u>integrated</u> coverage of qualitative material throughout

This eighth edition does much more than simply expand its coverage of qualitative methods. Babbie incorporates qualitative material into the fabric and flow of every chapter, juxtaposing qualitative and quantitative methods so students can see the advantages and disadvantages of each for a given situation.

CHAPTER ONE has been completely revised and now includes a section that introduces qualitative and quantitative approaches. He enriches this discussion by also including idiographic/nomothetic and inductive/deductive distinctions.

I have a young friend, Ray Zhang, who was responsible for communications at the 1989 Freedom demonstrations at Tiananmen Square in Beijing. Following the Army clamp-down, Ray fled south, was arrested and then released with orders to return to Beijing. Instead, he escaped from China and made his way to Paris. Eventually, he came to the United States, where he resumed the graduate studies he had to abandon in fleeing his homeland. I have seen him deal with the difficulties of getting enrolled in school without any transcripts from China, studying in a foreign language, meeting his financial needs—doing all this on his own, thousands of miles from his family. Through all this, Ray still speaks of one day returning to China to build a system of democracy.

Ray strikes me as someone "older than his years." You'll probably agree. This qualitative description, while it fleshes out the meaning of the phrase, still does not equip us to say *how much older* or even to compare two people in these terms without the risk of disagreeing as to which one is more "worldly."

It might be possible to quantify this concept, however. For example, we might establish a list of life experiences that would contribute to what we mean by *worldliness*:

Getting married
Getting divorced
Having a parent die
Seeing a murder committed
Being arrested
Being exiled
Being fired from a job
Running away with the circus, and so forth

We might quantify people's worldliness as the number of such experiences they've had: the more such experiences, the more worldly we'd say they were. If we thought that some experiences were more powerful than others, we could give those experiences more points. Once we had made our list and point system, scoring people and comparing their worldliness would be pretty straightforward. We should have no difficulty agreeing on who had more points than whom.

To quantify a concept like worldliness, we need to be explicit about what we mean. By focusing specifically on what we will include in our measurement of the concept, however, we also exclude the other possible meanings. Inevitably, then, We face a trade-off. Any explicated, quantitative measure will be more superficial than the corresponding qualitative description.

So, rather than viewing qualitative and quantitative methods as competitive choices, students learn that both these methods are "good science" and that both are valid approaches in the researcher's arsenal.

Cyberspace, new technologies... and their impact on research methods

T*he all-encompassing changes to research methods brought about by technology are well represented throughout this eighth edition.*

A *NEW full service Web site dedicated to you and your students*
http://sociology.wadsworth.com

3. Using one of the many search engines (such as Lycos, WebCrawler, Excite, Yahoo, and Infoseek), find information on the Web concerning at least three of the following paradigms. Give the Web locations and report on the theorists discussed in connection with the discussions you found.

Functionalism	Feminism
Conflict theory	Positivism
Interactionism	Exchange theory
Ethnomethodology	Postmodernism

3. Go to Holocaust Studies: Prejudice(http://www.socialstudies.com:80/12/126items.html) and browse through the materials described there. Make a list of the various dimensions.

B*ABBIE'S* **The Practice of Social Research,** *together with this full-service Web resource center, offers you a truly interactive learning system. There are news groups, a career center, surfing lessons, surfing information specific to social research, and many other selections.*

And when you click on the Research icon, you will be connected to Wadsworth research titles, and, in particular, to the Home Page for Babbie's **The Practice of Social Research.** *The Babbie site includes many important resources for you and your students:*

- ***For the instructor:*** links to other relevant social research sites, on-line access to Earl Babbie, and a forum for airing and discussing issues and ideas for teaching social research.
- ***For the student:*** additional 'Net exercises for every chapter, links to relevant social research sites, a hyperglossary, on-line access to Earl Babbie, a news page linking the text to current research and events, interactive quizzes, an ongoing student discussion group, and Web-based resources to help students improve their study skills.

- **INTERNET EXERCISES ARE NOW INCLUDED IN EVERY CHAPTER** to encourage students to practice searching and other research techniques on the Web.

- **A NEW APPENDIX, SOCIAL RESEARCH IN CYBERSPACE,** offers a tantalizing and practical glimpse of the many advantages Internet offers the researcher.

Plus new and updated coverage in every chapter

GREATLY EXPANDED COVERAGE OF THE ETHICAL ISSUES RELATED TO RESEARCH—In addition to Chapter 18, which is dedicated to ethics in research, the book now includes an introduction to ethical issues in Chapter 1 and integrated coverage of ethics as it relates to discussion of specific research topics.

A COMPLETELY REVISED AND UPDATED CHAPTER 8, SAMPLING, that now begins with a discussion of nonprobability sampling techniques with special attention to how they fit into many qualitative research designs.

INTERESTING AND PRAGMATIC COVERAGE OF POSTMODERNISM that makes a good case for the inevitability of subjectivity no matter how hard the researcher strives for objectivity.

THE ETHICS OF SOCIAL RESEARCH

By devoting most of this book to the logic and skills of doing social research I hope you will come to understand the various techniques preferred by social researchers, and why they value them. There are, however, some vital nonscientific concerns that shape the activities of social researchers.

Though Chapter 18 of this book deals extensively with research ethics, I would like to introduce you to the topic now. If you keep these ethical considerations in mind as you learn the logic and techniques of social research, you will better understand the discussion in Chapter 18.

No Harm to Subjects

The foremost ethical rule of social research is that it bring *no harm to research subjects*. While social researchers usually do not intend to hurt people, they can cause inadvertent harm if they are not careful. If you revealed damaging information about the people you interview, you would have violated this ethical rule.

Surely no one would disagree with this rule in principle. You will see, however, that it is sometimes difficult to follow this rule absolutely. Suppose some of the people you are interviewing about their religious views realize for the first time their doubts. Or perhaps your study of women's rights will cause some women to become unhappy with their jobs or marriages.

You are going to see that abiding by this seemingly simple ethical rule requires vigilance on your part. As you design your study, you should continue asking yourself whether your research will harm the people you are studying. Since everything you do in life *could possibly* harm someone else, you will have to weigh the relative danger against the importance of the research activity.

Voluntary Participation

Another basic ethical rule of social research is that *participation should be voluntary*. Again, in principle, this appears a pretty simply rule to follow. An experimenter who forced people to participate in the experiment would be roundly criticized. When someone calls and asks you to participate in a telephone survey, you are free to refuse.

Yet when we formally observe a campus demonstration, we do not ask permission of all the participants. When a researcher pretends to join a religious cult to do research on it, those being observed have not really volunteered for the research project. Social scientists often debate whether a particular research design did or did not violate established research ethics.

As we continue with our examination of research, you will see the great complexity of research ethics. And it certainly deserves your attention.

These, then, are some of the foundations of social scientific research. I don't know your preconceptions of this course, I hope you can now see clearly that social science research is a vibrant and exciting activity. All you need is an open mind and a sense of adventure to keep it from ever being routine or boring.

A COMPLETELY REVISED CHAPTER 11, FIELD RESEARCH, that now begins with a glossary of terms commonly associated with qualitative research. The chapter's discussion of qualitative interviewing has been expanded, as has the discussion of qualitative data analysis, and Babbie also includes a new illustration of field research (Daniel Wolf's study of outlaw bikers) and a new section on field research ethics.

IN ADDITION, EVERY CHAPTER IN THE BOOK HAS BEEN UPDATED, revised, and further strengthened for clarity and currency. See the author's preface for full details.

An expanded collection of carefully prepared teaching and learning materials

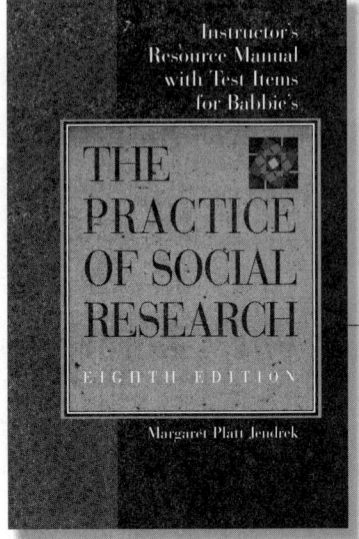

INSTRUCTOR'S RESOURCE MANUAL WITH TEST ITEMS
by Margaret Platt Jendrek
Chapter outlines, behavioral objectives, in-class lecture materials and projects, and exam questions, plus solutions and guidelines to selected activities in the study guide.
0-534-50471-X

COMPUTERIZED TESTING
The test questions are also available on disk so you can easily edit, delete, and add your own questions for customized testing. Available in the following formats:
DOS: 0-534-50462-0
Macintosh: 0-534-50467-1
Windows: 0-534-50466-3

AUTHOR'S VIDEO
In ten-to-fifteen-minute segments, Earl Babbie helps students understand five challenging concepts: theory, conceptualization, indexes and scales, sampling, and field research. Available upon adoption.
0-534-18755-2

GSS DATA DISK
by Jeff Jacques
From the National Opinion Research Center's General Opinion Survey. Includes data from 1,500 respondents around the country over the last 25 years.
Windows: 0-534-50472-8
Macintosh: 0-534-50465-5

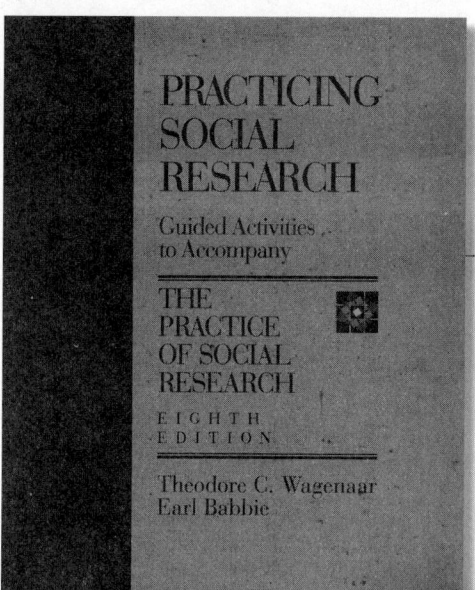

PRACTICING SOCIAL RESEARCH: GUIDED ACTIVITIES TO ACCOMPANY THE PRACTICE OF SOCIAL RESEARCH
by Theodore C. Wagenaar & Earl Babbie
Guides students through the actual processes of gathering and analyzing data while reinforcing material learned in the text. Contains chapter objectives, summaries, terms, review questions, discussion questions, exercises, and other helpful study aids.
0-534-50469-8

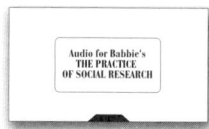

AUTHOR AUDIO TAPE
Earl Babbie introduces students to each chapter in the book and reinforces main concepts. Available for shrink-wrapping to the text or study guide. **0-534-50498-1**

HYPERGLOSSARY
Terms, definitions, and exercises organized into an interactive format to reinforce vocabulary appearing in the text.

A SPECIAL OFFER TO HELP YOUR STUDENTS SAVE MONEY ON TEXTBOOKS:

The items listed at the right can be shrink-wrapped with Babbie's **The Practice of Social Research** and sold to your students at a lower cost than purchasing the items separately.

Contact your Wadsworth/ITP representative for details and other possible combinations.

Practicing Social Research: Guided Activities (study guide)
  Bundle ISBN **0–534–83420–5**
GSS Data Disk Bundle   ISBN **0–534–83429–9** (Mac)
GSS Data Disk Bundle   ISBN **0–534–83438–8** (IBM)
Kardas/Milford, *Using the Internet for Social Research and Practice*
  Bundle ISBN **0–534–83447–7**
Kurland/John, *The Internet Guide for Sociology*
  Bundle ISBN **0–534–83456–6**
Frey/First, *Investigating Change in American Society*
  Macintosh Bundle ISBN **0–534–52345–5**
Frey/First, *Investigating Change in American Society*
  IBM Bundle ISBN **0–534–83483–3**
Stata Corporation/Anagnoson/DeLeon, *StataQuest 4 for Windows 95*
  Bundle ISBN **0–534–52138–X**
Stata Corporation/Anagnoson/DeLeon, *StataQuest 4 for Windows, 2nd Edition*   Bundle ISBN **0–534–83501–5**
Ferrante, *Let's Go Sociology*   Bundle ISBN **0–534–83465–5**

In-text study aids to enhance your students' understanding

A unique 12-page chapter-by-chapter **Holographic Overview** *of the entire book appears at the front of the book to give students a macroscopic view that they can refer to during the course.*

What You'll Learn in This Chapter *and outlines of the chapter organization give a quick overview of the chapter's main directions.*

 Holographic Overview

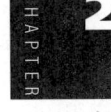

CHAPTER 2 Paradigms, Theory, and Research

What You'll Learn in this Chapter
You'll see some of the theoretical points of view that structure social scientific inquiry. This chapter will lay the groundwork for your understanding of the specific reserach techniques discussed throughout the rest of the book.

INTRODUCTION

SOME SOCIAL SCIENCE PARADIGMS
Macrotheory and Microtheory
Early Positivism
Social Darwinism
Conflict Paradigm
Symbolic Interactionism
Role Theory
Ethnomethodology
Structural Functionalism
The Feminist Paradigm
The Exchange Paradigm
Rational Objectivity Reconsidered

THE STRUCTURE OF SOCIAL THEORY
Terms Used in Theory Construction

TWO LOGICAL SYSTEMS
The Traditional Model of S
Deduction and Induction C

DEDUCTIVE THEORY CONSTRUCTION
Getting Started
Constructing Your Theory
An Example of Deductive Theory

INDUCTIVE THEORY CONSTRUCTION
Why Do People Smoke Marijuana?

THE LINKS BETWEEN THEORY AND RESERACH

MAIN POINTS

REVIEW QUESTIONS AND EXERCISES

ADDITIONAL READINGS

Substantial introductions to each part give an overview of the material covered within that part.

Main Points, Review Questions and Exercises, and Additional Readings conclude each chapter.

Instructive tables and figures throughout reinforce main points.

THE WHOLE THING: HOLOGRAM 4

Chapter 1. Human Inquiry and Science

Observing and trying to interpret what we observe is a native human activity. It's the foundation for our survival. In everyday life, however, we are often casual and semiconscious in both our observations and our interpretations, so that we make mistakes in both. Scientists make observation and interpretation conscious, deliberate acts.

Because there is no single way of doing social research, we'll examine some of the different approaches used by social researchers. Sometimes they seek a general, albeit partial, understanding of social patterns of behavior; other times they are more intent on probing deeply into the idiosyncracies of a particular case. Sometimes, researchers begin with a general theory and test it through controlled observations; other times they choose to discern general patterns among what has been observed in a more open-ended and unstructured inquiry. Finally, while *objectivity* is an important aspect of all science, we'll see that *subjectivity* can also be a critical tool for social scientists.

changing the way the world learns[SM]

To get extra value from this book for no additional cost, go to:

http://www.thomson.com/wadsworth.html

thomson.com is the World Wide Web site for Wadsworth/ITP and is your direct source to dozens of on-line resources. *thomson.com* helps you find out about supplements, experiment with demonstration software, search for a job, and send e-mail to many of our authors. You can even preview new publications and exciting new technologies.

thomson.com It's where you'll find us in the future.

A Note from the Author

Writing is my joy, sociology my passion. I delight in putting words together in a way that makes people learn or laugh or both. Sociology shows up as a set of words, also. It represents our last, best hope for planet-training our race and finding ways for us to live together. I feel a special excitement at being present when sociology, at last, comes into focus as an idea whose time has come.

I grew up in small-town Vermont and New Hampshire. When I announced I wanted to be an auto-body mechanic, like my dad, my teacher told me I should go to college instead. When Malcolm X announced he wanted to be a lawyer, his teacher told him a colored boy should be something more like a carpenter. The difference in our experiences says something powerful about the idea of a level playing field. The inequalities among ethnic groups runs deep.

I ventured into the outer world by way of Harvard, the USMC, U.C. Berkeley, and twelve years teaching at the University of Hawaii. Along the way, I married Sheila two months after our first date, and we created Aaron three years after that: two of my wisest acts. I resigned from

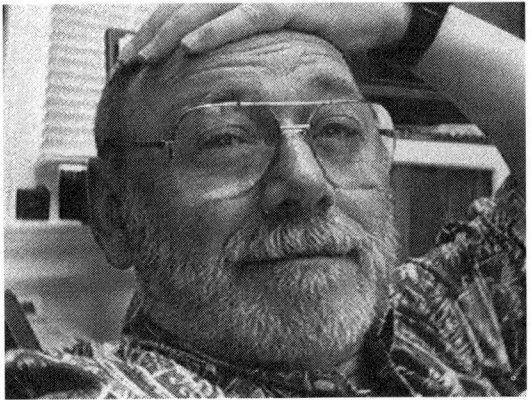

teaching in 1980 and wrote full-time for seven years, until the call of the classroom became too loud to ignore. For me, teaching is like playing jazz. Even if you perform the same number over and over, it never comes out the same twice and you don't know exactly what it'll sound like until you hear it. Teaching is like writing with your voice.

At last, I have matured enough to rediscover and appreciate my roots in Vermont each summer. Rather than a return to the past, it feels more like the next turn in a widening spiral. I can't wait to see what's around the next bend.

THE PRACTICE OF SOCIAL RESEARCH

EIGHTH EDITION

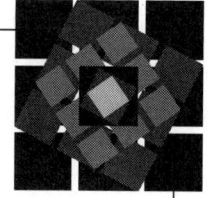

EARL BABBIE

Chapman University

Wadsworth Publishing Company
I(T)P® An International Thomson Publishing Company

Belmont, CA • Albany, NY • Bonn • Boston • Cincinnati • Detroit • Johannesburg • London • Madrid
Melbourne • Mexico City • New York • Paris • Singapore • Tokyo • Toronto • Washington

Sociology Editor: Eve Howard
Assistant Editor: Jennifer Burke
Editorial Assistant: Barbara Yien
Marketing Manager: Chaunfayta Hightower
Production: Greg Hubit Bookworks
Print Buyer: Karen Hunt

Permissions Editor: Robert Kauser
Text and Cover Designer: Norman Baugher
Copy Editor: Molly D. Roth
Compositor: G & S Typesetters, Inc.
Printer: Courier, Westford, MA

COPYRIGHT © 1998 by Wadsworth Publishing Company
A Division of International Thomson Publishing Inc.
I(T)P® The ITP logo is a registered trademark under license.
Duxbury Press and the leaf logo are trademarks used under license.

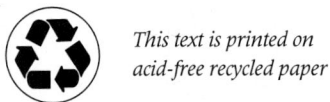

This text is printed on acid-free recycled paper

Printed in the United States of America
1 2 3 4 5 6 7 8 9 10

For more information, contact Wadsworth Publishing Company, 10 Davis Drive, Belmont, CA 94002, or electronically at http://www.thomson.com/wadsworth.html

International Thomson Publishing Europe
Berkshire House 168–173
High Holborn
London WC1V 7AA, England

Thomas Nelson Australia
102 Dodds Street
South Melbourne 3205
Victoria, Australia

Nelson Canada
1120 Birchmount Road
Scarborough, Ontario
Canada M1K 5G4

International Thomson Publishing GmbH
Königswinterer Strasse 418
53227 Bonn, Germany

International Thomson Editores
Seneca 53
Col. Polanco
11560 México D.F., México

International Thomson Publishing Asia
221 Henderson Road
#05–10 Henderson Building
Singapore 0315

International Thomson Publishing Japan
Hirakawacho Kyowa Building, 3F
2-2-1 Hirakawacho
Chiyoda-ku, Tokyo 102, Japan

International Thomson Publishing Southern Africa
Building 18, Constantia Park
240 Old Pretoria Road
Halfway House, 1685 South Africa

All rights reserved. No part of this work covered by the copyright hereon may be reproduced or used in any form or by any means—graphic, electronic, or mechanical, including photocopying, recording, taping, or information storage and retrieval systems—without the written permission of the publisher.

Library of Congress Cataloging-in-Publication Data
Babbie, Earl R.
   The Practice of Social Research / Earl Babbie—8th ed.
     p. cm.
   Includes bibliographical references and index.
   ISBN 0-534-50468-X
   1. Social Sciences—Research. 2. Social Sciences—Methodology.
I. Title
H62.B2   1998
300'.72—dc21   97-25892

Dedication

Sheila Babbie

ACCOMPANYING THIS TEXTBOOK—

Practicing Social Research: Guided Activities to Accompany The Practice of Social Research, Eighth Edition, by Theodore C. Wagenaar and Earl Babbie

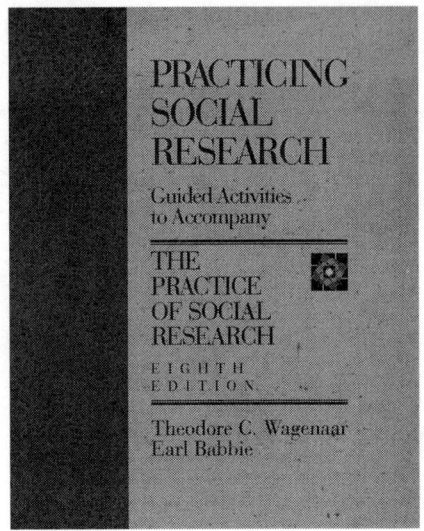

This practical book of activities is designed to help reinforce and extend your understanding of the material in The Practice of Social Research. *For each chapter this study guide contains objectives, a summary, key terms, multiple-choice review questions, discussion questions, and exercises that engage you in actual research and involve the analysis of data from the 1973 through 1993 General Social Surveys.*

To order a copy of this book, contact your bookstore.

Also by Earl Babbie and available from Wadsworth Publishing Company

SOCIAL RESEARCH FOR CONSUMERS

SURVEY RESEARCH METHODS, Second Edition

OBSERVING OURSELVES: Essays in Social Research

RESEARCH METHODS FOR SOCIAL WORK (with Allen Rubin), Third Edition

THE SOCIOLOGICAL SPIRIT: Critical Essays in a Critical Science, Second Edition

APPLE LOGO FOR TEACHERS

RESEARCH METHODS FOR CRIMINAL JUSTICE AND CRIMINOLOGY, Second Edition (with Michael Maxfield)

Contents in Brief

Preface xv
Acknowledgments xx
Prologue xxi
Holographic Overview 1

PART 1
AN INTRODUCTION TO INQUIRY 14

1. Human Inquiry and Science 16
2. Paradigms, Theory, and Research 41
3. The Nature of Causation 68

PART 2
THE STRUCTURING OF INQUIRY 86

4. Research Design 88
5. Conceptualization and Measurement 115
6. Operationalization 138
7. Indexes, Scales, and Typologies 166
8. The Logic of Sampling 191

PART 3
MODES OF OBSERVATION 230

9. Experiments 232
10. Survey Research 254
11. Field Research 279
12. Unobtrusive Research 307
13. Evaluation Research 333

PART 4
ANALYSIS OF DATA 356

14. Quantifying Data 358
15. Elementary Analyses 369
16. The Elaboration Model 388
17. Social Statistics 404

PART 5
THE SOCIAL CONTEXT OF RESEARCH 434

18. The Ethics and Politics of Social Research 436
19. The Uses of Social Research 457

APPENDIXES A1

A: Using the Library A2
B: Social Research in Cyberspace A8
C: The Research Report A15
D: GSS Household Enumeration Questionnaire A22
E: Random Numbers A32
F: Distribution of Chi Square A34
G: Normal Curve Areas A36
H: Estimated Sampling Error A37
I: A Learner's Guide to SPSS A38
J: Twenty Questions a Journalist Should Ask about Poll Results A139

Contents in Detail

Preface   xv
Prologue   xxi

Holographic Overview   1

PART 1
AN INTRODUCTION TO INQUIRY   14

CHAPTER 1
Human Inquiry and Science   16

Introduction   17
Looking for Reality   18
   Ordinary Human Inquiry   18
   Tradition   19
   Authority   19
   Errors in Inquiry and Some Solutions   20
   What's Really Real?   21
The Foundations of Social Science   24
   Theory, Not Philosophy or Belief   25
   Social Regularities   25
   Aggregates, Not Individuals   28
   A Variable Language   29
Some Dialectics of Social Science   34
   Idiographic and Nomothetic Explanation   34
   Inductive and Deductive Theory   35
   Qualitative and Quantitative Data   36
The Ethics of Social Research   38
   No Harm to Subjects   38
   Voluntary Participation   38
Main Points   39
Review Questions and Exercises   39
Additional Readings   40

CHAPTER 2
Paradigms, Theory, and Research   41

Introduction   42
Some Social Science Paradigms   42
   Macrotheory and Microtheory   43
   Early Positivism   43
   Social Darwinism   44
   Conflict Paradigm   44
   Symbolic Interactionism   45
   Role Theory   45
   Ethnomethodology   46
   Structural Functionalism   47
   Feminist Paradigms   47
   The Exchange Paradigm   48
   Rational Objectivity Reconsidered   49
The Structure of Social Theory   51
   Terms Used in Theory Construction   51
Two Logical Systems   52
   The Traditional Model of Science   52
   Deduction and Induction Compared   54
Deductive Theory Construction   60
   Getting Started   60
   Constructing Your Theory   60
   An Example of Deductive Theory   61
Inductive Theory Construction   63
   Why Do People Smoke Marijuana?   63
The Links Between Theory and Research   64
Main Points   65
Review Questions and Exercises   66
Additional Readings   66

CHAPTER 3
The Nature of Causation   68

Introduction   69
Determinism and Social Science   69
   Causation in the Natural Sciences   69
   Finding Causes in Social Science   69
   Reasons Have Reasons   70
   Determinism in Perspective   71
Idiographic and Nomothetic Models
   of Explanation   71

Contents in Detail ix

Criteria for Causality 73
   Necessary and Sufficient Causes 76

Errors of Reasoning 77
   Provincialism 78
   Hasty Conclusion 79
   Questionable Cause 79
   Suppressed Evidence 79
   False Dilemma 79

Linking Measurement and Association 79
   The Traditional Deductive Model 80
   An Example of Measurement and Association 82

Main Points 83

Review Questions and Exercises 83

Additional Readings 84

PART 2
THE STRUCTURING OF INQUIRY 86

CHAPTER 4
Research Design 88

Introduction 89

Purposes of Research 90
   Exploration 90
   Description 91
   Explanation 92

Units of Analysis 92
   Individuals 93
   Groups 93
   Organizations 94
   Social Artifacts 94
   Units of Analysis in Review 95
   The Ecological Fallacy 96
   Reductionism 97

Points of Focus 97
   Characteristics 97
   Orientations 100
   Actions 100

The Time Dimension 100
   Cross-Sectional Studies 100
   Longitudinal Studies 101
   Approximating Longitudinal Studies 103

How to Design a Research Project 105
   Getting Started 106
   Conceptualization 108

   Choice of Research Method 108
   Operationalization 109
   Population and Sampling 109
   Observations 109
   Data Processing 109
   Analysis 110
   Application 110
   Review 110

The Research Proposal 111
   Elements of a Research Proposal 112

Main Points 112

Review Questions and Exercises 113

Additional Readings 113

CHAPTER 5
Conceptualization and Measurement 115

Introduction 116

Measuring Anything That Exists 116
   How Do You Know? 116
   Conceptions and Concepts 118
   Conceptualization 120
   Indicators and Dimensions 120
   The Interchangeability of Indicators 121
   The Confusion over Definitions and Reality 122
   Creating Conceptual Order 122
   An Example of Conceptualization 122

Definitions and Research Purposes 128

Criteria for Measurement Quality 129
   Reliability 129
   Validity 133
   Who Decides What's Valid? 134
   Tension between Reliability and Validity 135

Main Points 136

Review Questions and Exercises 136

Additional Readings 137

CHAPTER 6
Operationalization 138

Introduction 139

Operationalization Choices 139
   Range of Variation 139
   Variations between the Extremes 140
   A Note on Dimensions 141

Contents in Detail

  Levels of Measurement 141
  Single or Multiple Indicators 145

Some Operationalization Illustrations 146

Guidelines for Asking Questions 147
  Questions and Statements 147
  Open-Ended and Closed-Ended Questions 148
  Make Items Clear 148
  Avoid Double-Barreled Questions 149
  Respondents Must Be Competent to Answer 149
  Respondents Must Be Willing to Answer 149
  Questions Should Be Relevant 151
  Short Items Are Best 151
  Avoid Negative Items 152
  Avoid Biased Items and Terms 152

Questionnaire Construction 153
  General Questionnaire Format 153
  Formats for Respondents 154
  Contingency Questions 155
  Matrix Questions 156
  Ordering Items in a Questionnaire 157
  Instructions 158
  Pretesting the Questionnaire 159
  A Composite Illustration 159

Operationalization Goes On and On 163

Main Points 163

Review Questions and Exercises 164

Additional Readings 164

CHAPTER 7
Indexes, Scales, and Typologies 166

Introduction 167

Indexes versus Scales 167

Index Construction 170
  Item Selection 170
  Bivariate Relationships among Items 171
  Multivariate Relationships among Items 174
  Index Scoring 176
  Handling Missing Data 177
  Index Validation 178
  Indexing the Status of Women 181

Scale Construction 182
  Bogardus Social Distance Scale 182
  Thurstone Scales 183
  Likert Scaling 183
  Semantic Differential 184
  Guttman Scaling 185

Typologies 187

Main Points 189

Review Questions and Exercises 189

Additional Readings 190

CHAPTER 8
The Logic of Sampling 191

Introduction 192

The History of Sampling 192
  President Alf Landon 192
  President Thomas E. Dewey 193
  Two Types of Sampling Methods 194

Nonprobability Sampling 194
  Reliance on Available Subjects 194
  Purposive or Judgmental Sampling 195
  Snowball Sampling 195
  Quota Sampling 196
  Selecting Informants 196

The Logic of Probability Sampling 197
  Conscious and Unconscious Sampling Bias 198
  Representativeness and Probability
    of Selection 200

Sampling Concepts and Terminology 200

Probability Sampling Theory and Sampling
    Distribution 202
  Probability Sampling Theory 202
  The Sampling Distribution of Ten Cases 203
  Binomial Sampling Distribution 205

Populations and Sampling Frames 210
  Review of Populations and Sampling Frames 212

Types of Sampling Designs 213
  Simple Random Sampling 213
  Systematic Sampling 213
  Stratified Sampling 216
  Implicit Stratification in
    Systematic Sampling 218

Illustration: Sampling University Students 219
  Study Population and Sampling Frame 219
  Stratification 219
  Sample Selection 219
  Sample Modification 219

Multistage Cluster Sampling   219
   Multistage Cluster Sampling, Stratification   222
   Probability Proportionate to Size (PPS) Sampling   222
   Disproportionate Sampling and Weighting   224

Illustration: Sampling Churchwomen   226
   Selecting the Churches   226
   Selecting the Churchwomen   226

Probability Sampling in Review   227

Main Points   227

Review Questions and Exercises   229

Additional Readings   229

PART 3
MODES OF OBSERVATION   230

CHAPTER 9
Experiments   232

Introduction   233

Topics Appropriate to Experiments   233

The Classical Experiment   233
   Independent and Dependent Variables   234
   Pretesting and Posttesting   234
   Experimental and Control Groups   235
   The Double-Blind Experiment   236

Selecting Subjects   237
   Probability Sampling   237
   Randomization   237
   Matching   238

Variations on Experimental Design   239
   Sources of Internal Invalidity   240
   Sources of External Invalidity   244

An Illustration of Experimentation   245

Focus Groups   248

"Natural" Experiments   249

Strengths and Weaknesses of the Experimental Method   251

Main Points   252

Review Questions and Exercises   252

Additional Readings   253

CHAPTER 10
Survey Research   254

Introduction   255

Topics Appropriate to Survey Research   256

Self-Administered Questionnaires   257
   Mail Distribution and Return   258
   Electronic Surveys   259
   Monitoring Returns   260
   Follow-up Mailings   261
   Acceptable Response Rates   261
   A Case Study   262

Interview Surveys   264
   The Role of the Survey Interviewer   264
   General Rules for Survey Interviewing   265
   Coordination and Control   267

Telephone Surveys   268
   Computer Assisted Telephone Interviewing (CATI)   270

Comparison of the Three Methods   271

Strengths and Weaknesses of Survey Research   272

Secondary Analysis   274

Main Points   276

Review Questions and Exercises   276

Additional Readings   277

CHAPTER 11
Field Research   279

Introduction   280

Some Terminology of Qualitative Inquiry   280
   Phenomenology   281
   Interpretivism   281
   Hermeneutics   281
   Participant Observation   282
   In-depth Interview   282
   Case Study   282
   Ethnography   282
   Grounded Theory   283

Topics Appropriate to Field Research   283

The Various Roles of the Observer   286

Relations to Subjects   287

Preparing for the Field   289

Qualitative Interviewing   290
Recording Observations   293
Qualitative Data Processing   294
   Rewriting Your Notes   294
   Creating Files   295
   Using Computers   296
Qualitative Data Analysis   297
Illustrations of Field Research   299
   Studying the Satanists   299
   Life in the Streets   300
   Observing Outlaw Bikers   301
Research Ethics in Field Research   302
Strengths and Weaknesses of Field Research   303
   Validity   303
   Reliability   304
Main Points   305
Review Questions and Exercises   305
Additional Readings   306

CHAPTER 12
Unobtrusive Research   307

Introduction   308
A Comment on Unobtrusive Measures   308
Topics Appropriate to Content Analysis   309
Sampling in Content Analysis   310
   Units of Analysis   310
   Sampling Techniques   312
Coding in Content Analysis   313
   Manifest and Latent Content   313
   Conceptualization and the Creation of Code Categories   314
   Counting and Record Keeping   315
   Qualitative Data Analysis   315
An Illustration of Content Analysis   317
Strengths and Weaknesses of Content Analysis   318
Analyzing Existing Statistics   319
   Studying Suicide   319
   Units of Analysis   320
   Problems of Validity   322
   Problems of Reliability   322
   Sources of Existing Statistics   323
Historical/Comparative Analysis   325
   Examples of Historical/Comparative Analysis   325
   Sources of Historical/Comparative Data   328
   Analytical Techniques   329
Main Points   330
Review Questions and Exercises   331
Additional Readings   332

CHAPTER 13
Evaluation Research   333

Introduction   334
Topics Commonly Subjected to Evaluation Research   335
Formulating the Problem   336
   Measurement   337
   Experimental Designs   339
   Quasi-Experimental Designs   340
   Operationalizing Success/Failure   345
   Qualitative Evaluations   345
The Social Context   346
   Logistical Problems   346
   Some Ethical Issues   348
   Use of Research Results   348
Social Indicators Research   352
   The Death Penalty and Deterrence   352
   Computer Simulation   353
Main Points   354
Review Questions and Exercises   354
Additional Readings   354

PART 4
ANALYSIS OF DATA   356

CHAPTER 14
Quantifying Data   358

Introduction   359
Computers in Social Research   359
   Enter Computers   360
   Microcomputers   361
Coding   362
   Developing Code Categories   362

Codebook Construction   363
Coding and Data Entry Options   364
Transfer Sheets   364
Edge-Coding   365
Direct Data Entry   365
Data Entry by Interviewers   365
Coding to Optical Scan Sheets   365
Direct Use of Optical Scan Sheets   366
Connecting with a Data Analysis Program   366
Data Cleaning   366
Possible-Code Cleaning   366
Contingency Cleaning   367
Main Points   367
Review Questions and Exercises   367
Additional Readings   368

CHAPTER 15
Elementary Analyses   369

Introduction   370
Univariate Analysis   370
Distributions   370
Central Tendency   370
Dispersion   374
Continuous and Discrete Variables   374
Detail versus Manageability   374
Subgroup Comparisons   375
"Collapsing" Response Categories   376
Handling "Don't Knows"   377
Numerical Descriptions in Qualitative Research   378
Bivariate Analysis   378
Percentaging a Table   381
Constructing and Reading Tables   382
Bivariate Table Formats   383
Introduction to Multivariate Analysis   383
Main Points   386
Review Questions and Exercises   386
Additional Readings   387

CHAPTER 16
The Elaboration Model   388

Introduction   389
History of the Elaboration Model   389

The Elaboration Paradigm   393
Replication   394
Explanation   396
Interpretation   397
Specification   398
Refinements to the Paradigm   399
Elaboration and Ex Post Facto Hypothesizing   401
Main Points   402
Review Questions and Exercises   403
Additional Readings   403

CHAPTER 17
Social Statistics   404

Introduction   405
The Danger of Success in Math   405
Descriptive Statistics   406
Data Reduction   406
Measures of Association   407
Regression Analysis   411
Other Multivariate Techniques   415
Path Analysis   415
Time-Series Analysis   417
Factor Analysis   418
Inferential Statistics   420
Univariate Inferences   421
Tests of Statistical Significance   422
The Logic of Statistical Significance   422
Chi Square   427
Main Points   431
Review Questions and Exercises   433
Additional Readings   433

PART 5
THE SOCIAL CONTEXT OF RESEARCH   434

CHAPTER 18
The Ethics and Politics of Social Research   436

Introduction   437
Ethical Issues in Social Research   438
Voluntary Participation   438
No Harm to the Participants   439

Anonymity and Confidentiality 440
Deceiving Subjects 442
Analysis and Reporting 443
Institutional Review Boards 444
A Professional Code of Ethics 445

Two Ethical Controversies 447
Trouble in the Tearoom 447
Observing Human Obedience 448

Discussion Examples 449

The Politics of Social Research 450
Objectivity and Ideology 450
Politics with a Little "p" 453
Politics in Perspective 454

Main Points 456

Review Questions and Exercises 456

Additional Readings 456

CHAPTER 19
The Uses of Social Research 457

Introduction 458

Theory—Data Collection—Analysis 458

Everyday Uses of Social Research Skills 459

A Consumer's Guide to Social Research 461
Research Design 461
Measurement 462
Sampling 462
Experiments 462
Survey Research 463
Field Research 463
Analyzing Existing Statistics 464
Evaluation Research 464
Data Analysis 464
Data Reporting 465

Conclusion 465

APPENDIXES A1

A: Using the Library A2
B: Social Research in Cyberspace A8
C: The Research Report A15
D: GSS Household Enumeration Questionnaire A22
E: Random Numbers A32
F: Distribution of Chi Square A34
G: Normal Curve Areas A36
H: Estimated Sampling Error A37
I: A Learner's Guide to SPSS A38
J: Twenty Questions a Journalist Should Ask about Poll Results A139

Bibliography B1
Glossary G1
Index I1

Preface

In 1968, I began teaching social research methods for the first time, at the University of Hawaii. The course focused specifically on survey research methods, and I had only six students in the class that first semester. It was my first real teaching experience, and the small class size didn't keep me from planting myself behind a desk on a platform down front, while the students scattered themselves around the large lecture hall.

As the semester progressed, I became more relaxed as a teacher, came to like and appreciate my students, and eventually moved out from behind the platform at the head of the lecture hall. Before long, my students and I began meeting in my office, where I could grab and loan books from my own library as their relevance occurred to me during class meetings. (By the way, if any of those first six students are reading this, would you please return my books?)

The problem that continued to nag at me in the course, however, was the lack of a good textbook on survey research. Books I considered seemed to fall into one of two groups. Some books presented the theoretical logic of research methods in such abstract terms that I didn't think students would be able to apply any of the general principles to the practical, real world of "doing" research. The other books were just the opposite. Often termed "cookbooks," they presented detailed, step-by-step instructions on how to conduct a survey. Unfortunately, this approach only prepared students to conduct surveys very much like the one described by the authors. Neither the abstract nor the "cookbook" approach seemed truly useful to students or to their instructors.

One day I found myself jotting down the table of contents for the ideal research methods textbook. It was organized around three principles: theoretical principles on which scientific research was based.

1. Understanding the *theoretical* principles on which scientific research was based.
2. Seeing how those principles were reflected in the established techniques for *doing* research.
3. Being prepared to make appropriate *compromises* whenever field conditions didn't permit the routine application of established techniques.

The next day, I received an unexpected letter from the sociology editor at Wadsworth Publishing Company, asking if I would be interested in writing a textbook on survey research methods. Enclosing a table of contents by return mail, I said I would, and I was soon at work on my first textbook.

Survey Research Methods was published in 1973. My editors and I immediately discovered some good news, some bad news, and some additional good news. The first good news was that all survey research instructors seemed to love the book, and it seemed as though our book was being used in virtually every survey research course in the country. The bad news was that there weren't all that many survey research courses.

The final good news, however, was that many instructors who taught more general social research courses—covering survey research alongside other research methods—were inclined to use our book and supplement it with other books dealing with field research, experiments, and so on. While adjusting to our specialized book, however, many instructors suggested that Wadsworth have "that same guy" write a more general social research text.

By this time, Steve Rutter was the sociology editor at Wadsworth, and he and I began working together to design a general social research textbook that would serve the needs of students and instructors. Although it's probably polite for an author to speak of having a partnership with an editor, the partnership Steve and I forged was as real and solid as any profound friendship I've had in life. He's like a brother to me.

One of Steve's particular jobs in the partnership was to sample the needs, opinions, and practices of instructors around the country. The Preface of the first edition of *The Practice of Social Research* (1975) acknowledged the assistance of a dozen social research instructors from California to Florida. The resulting book, then, was a collaboration in a very real sense, even though only my name was on the cover and I was ultimately responsible for it.

The Practice of Social Research was an immediate success. It was initially written for sociology courses, but subsequent editions have been increasingly used in fields such as political science, social work, marketing research, and so forth. Moreover, it is being used by teachers and researchers in numerous countries around the world, including China and Russia.

I've laid out this lengthy history of the book for a couple of reasons. First, when I was a student, I suppose I thought of textbooks the same way I thought about government buildings: They were just *there*. I never really thought about them being written by human beings. I certainly never thought about textbooks *evolving:* being updated, getting better, having errors corrected. As a student, I would have been horrified by the thought that any of my textbooks might contain mistakes!

Second, pointing out the evolution of the book sets the stage for a preview of the changes that have gone into this eighth edition. As with previous revisions, changes have been prompted by several factors. For example, because social research technology and practices are continually changing, the book must be updated to remain current and useful. In my own teaching, I frequently find improved ways to present standard materials. Colleagues also frequently share their ideas for ways to teach specific topics. Some of these appear as boxed inserts in the book. Both students and instructors often suggest that various topics be reorganized, expanded, clarified, shrunk, or—gasp—deleted.

■ THE EIGHTH EDITION

In a previous edition of this book, I said, "Revising a textbook such as this is a humbling experience. No matter how good it seems to be, there is no end of ideas about how it could be improved." That observation still holds true. When we asked instructors what could be improved, they thought of things once more, and I have considered all their suggestions, have followed many of them, and have chosen to "think some more" about others. I also receive a lot of comments and suggestions from students who've been assigned the book; many of the changes come from them.

The most noticeable change in this edition has to do with the presentation of qualitative and quantitative orientations in social science. When I first wrote this book, quantitative methods dominated social research, having eclipsed the historical and field methods so popular in earlier decades. While quantitative methods are still widely and powerfully used throughout the social sciences, there has been a resurgent interest in qualitative methods. I believe this edition reflects the current balance of interest and use.

My chief intention in this regard is to have students feel comfortable with and inclined to use both approaches. Though practicing social scientists tend to identify themselves as primarily qualitative or quantitative in orientation, I would like students to see these different approaches to inquiry as two parts of a seamless whole. I have taken this approach in the Holographic Overview and have talked about this issue theoretically in

Chapters 1 and 2. Both approaches are represented throughout the rest of the book.

Chapter 1 has been extensively revised. I have reorganized and expanded the discussion of "reality" and have trimmed the discussion of errors in ordinary human reasoning. (Some, I think, were more interesting to me than they were useful to students.) I've also added a section, "Some Dialectics of Social Science," in which I introduce and relate (1) idiographic and nomothetic explanations, (2) inductive and deductive theory, and (3) qualitative and quantitative data. Finally, I've added an introduction to social research ethics, although the extensive treatment of it is still presented in Chapter 18.

Chapter 2 treats the issue of objectivity/subjectivity in more depth and less positivistically than in earlier editions. In the same vein, Chapter 3 provides a more evenhanded treatment of idiographic and nomothetic models of explanation.

In Chapters 4 to 7, I have included more qualitative examples to illustrate the fundamentals of study design. My preference is to show how both qualitative and quantitative methods are fundamental to social research inquiry, rather than create a qualitative ghetto.

I've made several changes in Chapter 8. Following a short history of sampling in social research, the chapter begins with a discussion of nonprobability sampling techniques, with special attention to how they fit into many qualitative research designs. The discussion of snowball sampling has been moved here from the chapter on field research, and I've added comments on the use of deviant cases.

In the discussion of probability sampling, I've shortened and clarified the discussion of probability proportionate to size (PPS) sampling. I've deleted the sections on "Degrees of Precision In Weighting" and "Methods for Weighting," having been persuaded that students can live full and productive lives without being exposed to these topics in their first brush with social research methods.

There are no major structural changes to Chapter 9, although I've revised earlier materials, and I've beefed up the discussion of focus groups with the National Issues Convention in Austin. I have revised Figure 9-5, to clarify the comparisons you might make in analyzing the results of a Solomon Four-Group Design.

Given the general increase in mischief being done in the name of polling, Chapter 10 discusses "push-polls," which feed phony or biased information to respondents, presumably for the purpose of learning the impact of such disinformation. In fact, the chief intent is simply to mislead voters. I've also added a new box ("A Candy Poll") to the chapter, prompted by a communication from an instructor in San Diego. I hope this will demonstrate to students how social science techniques are widely applicable. The chapter also has an expanded discussion of electronic surveys that goes beyond CATI to its cousins. I am grateful here for the work of Bill Nicholls and his colleagues at the census bureau.

Chapter 11 has been substantially restructured and revised. It begins with a glossary of terms commonly associated with qualitative research. I've abbreviated the roles of the observer to "complete participant" and "complete observer," noting there are degrees of variations in between. I'm not sure it's vital for students to know the difference between a "participant-as-observer" and "observer-as-participant." I've tried to enliven the discussion a bit by including Fred Davis's typology of the "Martian" and the "Convert."

Then, I have expanded the discussion with a new section, "Relations to Subjects." This discussion goes beyond technique to consider the objectivity/subjectivity dialectic and ethical issues as well.

The discussion of qualitative interviewing has been expanded and made more rigorous. I've expanded the discussion of qualitative data analysis and the computer programs available for it. I've also added a new illustration of field research—Daniel Wolf's study of outlaw bikers—and the chapter ends with a new section, "Research Ethics in Field Research."

In Chapter 12, I've added qualitative and feminist examples of content analysis, and there is a new section on "Qualitative Data Analysis." I've also included several Web sites where students can get data for analysis.

Chapter 13 now begins with a report on the Population Communication International's work in Tanzania and elsewhere to fight overpopulation and AIDS through radio soap operas. A recent evaluation of the project offers an excellent example of this research purpose. I've added a new section on qualitative evaluations, and the discussion of ethical issues describes the Tuskegee syphilis experiments.

Every edition of the book calls for an updating of the computer technology. Although this is a chore, it's always exciting to look at the new advances that have become available in the past three years. Chapter 14 now has a short section on getting data into a data analysis program. I've replaced the codebook example (Figure 14-1) with data from the General Social Survey, and I've replaced some of the hypothetical examples with real data from the GSS.

While Chapter 15 is primarily a quantitative chapter, I've added a section on the use of numerical data in qualitative research. Once again I hope this will break down the perceived barrier between the two approaches. Hypothetical examples have been replaced by real ones.

There are no major changes in Chapter 16. You may be pleased to know that Chapter 17 now begins with a different joke. I've also provided new explanations of gamma and lambda and have provided a table by Peter Nardi that helps students pick the right statistic based on the level of measurement of the independent and dependent variables. There's an expanded discussion of the misuses of statistical significance, reporting a study of how they are used by journals.

The main change regarding ethics is that I've put more examples and discussions throughout the book. In Chapter 18, there is more discussion of informed consent and IRBs, and I've included the example of Rik Scarce as an illustration of how researchers protect their subjects. To illustrate the influence of politics on research, I've given an example of legislation introduced to regulate the techniques of survey research.

In Chapter 19, I've changed the language from earlier editions that said the three bases of social research were theory, methods, and statistics, since that's not accurate. Instead, this edition talks of theory, data collection, and data analysis, some of which is statistical and some of which is not. The summaries now have more qualitative research examples.

Appendix A ("Using the Library") has more on electronic storage and retrieval, and Appendix B ("Social Research in Cyberspace") is new. Appendix I ("A Learner's Guide to SPSS") has been rewritten for use with SPSS 7.0.

As with each edition, I've updated technical materials. (I love all the new changes in computer technology, but it always means more revisions to the book.) In this edition, you will find expanded discussions of the Internet, World Wide Web, and other electronic aids to social research. The new Appendix B addresses these topics specifically. Moreover, the publishers and I have developed a Web site for the book, which offers continually updated support for instructors and students. You can find us at http://tposr.wadsworth.com.

As an instructor, I am always searching for new and more effective ways of explaining social research to my own students; many of those new explanations take the form of diagrams. You'll find a number of new graphic illustrations in this edition. Once again, I've sought to replace aging research examples (except for the classics) with more recent ones. I've also dropped some sections that I don't think do much for students any more. There are no major structural changes in this edition, however—no chapters moved, added, or deleted.

As with each new edition, I would appreciate any comments you have about how the book can be improved. Its evolution over the past 23 years has reflected countless inputs from students and faculty, and I am grateful for your partnership in the book.

SUPPLEMENTS

Practicing Social Research

The student study guide and workbook Ted Wagenaar and I have prepared continues to be a mainstay in my own teaching. Students tell me they use it heavily as a review of the text, and I count the exercises as half their grade in the course. I specify a certain number of points for each exercise—depending on how hard it is and how much I want them to do it—and give a deadline for each exercise, typically right after we've covered the materials in class. Most exercises rate between 5 and 25 points.

Finally, I specify the total number of points that will rate an *A* on the exercises, the range of points representing a *B*, and so forth. From there on, it's up to the students. They can do whichever exercises they want and as many as they want, as long as they complete each by its deadline. Every exercise they submit gets them some fraction of the maximum points assigned to it.

Though I end up with a fair amount of grading during the course, my experience is that those who do the exercises also do better on exams and papers.

In this edition, Ted and I have once again sorted through the exercises and added new ones we've created in our own teaching or heard about from colleagues. In particular, we have provided exercises for students who have access to SPSS, as well as kept plenty for those who don't.

Data Disk

Over the years, we have sought to provide up-to-date computer—particularly, microcomputer—support for students and instructors. Because there are now many excellent programs for analyzing data, we have provided data to be used with them. Specifically, Jeff Jacques, author of the SPSS appendix, has pulled together a set of data from the National Opinion Research Center's *General Social Survey,* offering students data from 1,500 respondents around the country in 1973, 1978, 1983, 1988, and 1993. As you'll see, I've used this data set for many of the examples in the textbook.

Instructor's Manual

As with past editions, Margaret Jendrek has prepared an excellent instructor's manual to help instructors write examinations. In addition to the usual multiple choice, true-false, and essay questions, the manual provides resources for planning lectures and gives suggested answers for some of the student problems in the study guide. Although students may not appreciate examinations as a general principle, I know that they benefit from the clarity Marty brings to that task.

Acknowledgments

It would be impossible to acknowledge adequately all the people who have influenced this book. My earlier methods text, *Survey Research Methods,* was dedicated to Samuel Stouffer, Paul Lazarsfeld, and Charles Glock. I would like to again acknowledge my debt to them.

I would like to repeat my thanks to those colleagues acknowledged for their comments during the writing of the first, second, and third editions of this book. Though revised, the present book still reflects their contributions. Many other colleagues helped me revise the book. I particularly want to thank the instructors who reviewed the manuscript of this edition and made helpful suggestions: Roland Chilton, University of Massachusetts, Amherst; M. Richard Cramer, University of North Carolina, Chapel Hill; Shaul Gabbay, University of Illinois, Chicago; Marcia Ghidina, University of North Carolina, Asheville; Jeffrey Jacques, Florida A&M University; Wanda Kosinski, Ramapo College, New Jersey; Manfred Kuechler, CUNY Hunter College; Joan Morris, University of Central Florida; Beth Anne Shelton, University of Texas, Arlington; Ron Stewart, SUNY Buffalo; Randy Stoecker, University of Toledo; Theodore Wagenaar, Miami University, Ohio; and Jerome Wolfe, University of Miami.

Over the years, I have become more and more impressed by the important role played by editors in books like this. While an author's name appears on the book's spine, much of its backbone derives from the strength of its editors. Since 1973, I've worked with six sociology editors at Wadsworth, which has involved the kinds of adjustments you might need to make in six successive marriages. Happily, this edition of the book has greatly profited from my partnership with Eve Howard. While Eve brings a wealth of publishing experience to the project, she also knows the cutting edge of new technologies and pedagogies and how to take advantage of them.

Ted Wagenaar has contributed extensively to this book. Ted and I coauthor the accompanying workbook, *Practicing Social Research,* but that's only the tip of the iceberg. Ted is a cherished colleague, welcomed critic, good friend, and altogether decent human being. I am grateful also for the SPSS appendix prepared by Jeffrey M. Jacques, Florida A&M University.

I would like to thank Winston Moore for the use of his camp on Walton Pond: a perfect place to write about research methods or anything else. Also, my thanks to Kay Orlandi for making us feel so welcome back home in Vermont.

I have dedicated this book to my wife, Sheila, who has contributed greatly to its origin and evolution. Sheila and I first met when she was assigned to assist me on a project I was supervising at U.C. Berkeley's Survey Research Center.* We have worked on numerous research projects during a third of a century of marriage, and I suppose we'll do more in the future. My gratitude to Sheila, however, extends well beyond our research activities. She is a powerful partner in life. Her insight and support take me always to the horizon of my purpose and allow me to look beyond. There's no way to thank her adequately for that.

---

*This means Sheila married her boss, no matter what she says today.

Prologue: The Importance of Social Research

In many ways, the twentieth century hasn't been one of our better periods. Except for the relatively carefree twenties, we've moved from World War I to the Great Depression to World War II to the Cold War and its threat of thermonuclear holocaust and the tragedy of Vietnam. The thawing of the Cold War and the opening of Eastern Europe was a welcome relief, though it has in many ways heightened concern over the environmental destruction of our planet.

A case could be made that these are not the best of times. Many sage observers have written about the insecurity and malaise that characterize this century. All the same, the twentieth century has generated countless individual efforts and social movements aimed at creating humane social affairs, and most of those have arisen on college campuses. Perhaps you find these kinds of concerns and commitments in yourself.

As you look at the flow of events in the world, you can see the broad range of choices available if you want to make a significant contribution to future generations. Environmental problems are many and varied. Prejudice and discrimination are with us still. Millions die of hunger, and wars large and small circle the globe. There is, in short, no end to the ways you could demonstrate to yourself that your life matters, that you make a difference.

Given all the things you could choose from—things that really *matter*—why should you spend your time learning social research methods? I want to address this question at the start, because I'm going to suggest that you devote some of your time and attention to learning about such things as social theory, sampling, interviewing, experiments, computers, and so forth—things that can seem pretty distant from solving the world's pressing problems. Social science, though, is not only relevant to the major problems I've just listed, but it also holds answers to them.

Many of the *big* problems we've faced and still face in this century have arisen out of our increasing technological abilities. The threat of nuclear terrorism is an example. Not unreasonably, we have tended to look to technology and technologists for solutions to those problems. Unfortunately, every technological solution so far has turned out to create new problems. At the beginning of this century, for example, many people worried about the danger of horse manure piling up in city streets. That problem was averted with the invention of the automobile. Now, no one worries about manure in the streets; we worry instead about a new and deadlier kind of pollutant in the air we breathe.

Similarly, in years past, we attempted to avoid nuclear attack by building better bombs and missiles of our own—so that no enemy would dare attack. But that only prompted our potential enemies to build ever bigger and more powerful weapons. Now, although the United States and Russia are exhibiting far less nuclear belligerence, similar contests elsewhere in the world could escalate. There is no technological end in sight for the insane nuclear weapons race.

The simple fact is that technology alone will never save us. It will never make the world work. You and I are the only ones who can do that. *The only real solutions lie in the ways we orga-*

nize and run our social affairs. This becomes evident when you consider all the social problems that persist today despite the clear presence of viable, technological solutions.

Overpopulation, for example, is a pressing problem in the world today. The number of people currently living on earth severely taxes our planet's life support systems, and this number is rapidly increasing year after year. If you study the matter you'll find that we already possess all the technological developments needed to stem population growth. It is technologically possible and feasible for us to stop population growth on the planet at whatever limit we want. Yet, overpopulation worsens each year.

Clearly, the solution to overpopulation is social. The causes of population growth lie in the forms, values, and customs that make up organized social life, and that is where the solutions are hidden. Those causes include beliefs about what it takes to be a "real woman" or a "real man," the perceived importance of perpetuating a family name, cultural tradition, and so forth. Ultimately, only social science can save us from overpopulation.

Or consider the problem of hunger on the planet. Some 13 to 15 million people die as a consequence of hunger each year. That amounts to 28 people a minute, every minute of every day, with 21 of them children. Everyone would agree that this condition is deplorable; all would prefer it otherwise. But we tolerate this level of starvation in the belief that it is currently inevitable. We hope that perhaps one day someone will invent a method of producing food that will defeat starvation once and for all.

When you study the issue of starvation in the world, however, you learn some astounding facts. First, you learn that the earth currently produces *more than enough food* to feed everyone. Moreover, this level of production does not even take into account farm programs that pay farmers not to plant and produce all the food they could.

Second, you learn that there are carefully planned and tested methods for ending starvation. In fact, since World War II, more than 30 countries have actually faced and ended their own problems of starvation. Some did it through food distribution programs. Others focused on land reform. Some collectivized; others developed agribusiness. Many applied the advances of the Green Revolution. Taken together, these proven solutions make it possible to eliminate starvation totally.

Why then haven't we ended hunger altogether on the planet? The answer, again, lies in the organization and operation of our social life. New developments in food production will not end starvation any more than earlier ones have. People will continue to starve until we can *command* our social affairs rather than be enslaved by them.

Possibly, the problems of overpopulation and hunger seem distant to you, occurring somewhere "over there," on the other side of the globe. To save space, I'll simply remind you of the conclusion, increasingly reached, that there is no "over there" anymore: There is only "over here" in today's world. And regardless of how you view world problems, there is undeniably no end to the social problems in your own backyard—possibly even in your front yard: crime, inflation, unemployment, homelessness, cheating in government and business, child abuse, prejudice and discrimination, pollution, drug abuse, increased taxes, and reduced public services.

We can't solve our social problems until we understand how they come about and persist. Social science research offers a way to examine and understand the operation of human social affairs. It provides points of view and technical procedures that uncover things that would otherwise escape our awareness. Often, as the cliche goes, things are not what they seem; social science research can make that clear. One example illustrates this fact.

Poverty is a persistent problem in the United States, and none of its intended solutions is more controversial than *welfare*. Although the program is intended to give the poor a helping hand while they reestablish their financial viability, many complain that it has the opposite effect.

Part of the public image of welfare in action was crystallized by Susan Sheehan (1976) in her book, *A Welfare Mother*, which describes the situation of a three-generation welfare family, suggesting that the welfare system trapped the poor rather than liberating them. Martin Anderson (1978:56) agreed with Sheehan's assessment and charged that the welfare system had established a caste system in America, "perhaps as much as one-tenth of this nation—a caste of people almost totally dependent on the state, with little hope or prospect of breaking free. Perhaps we should call them the Dependent Americans."

George Gilder (1990) has spoken for many who believe the poor are poor mainly because they refuse to work, saying the welfare system saps their incentive to take care of themselves. Ralph Segalman and David Marsland (1989) support the view that welfare has become an intergenerational way of life for the poor in welfare systems around the world. Children raised in welfare families, they assert, will likely live their adult lives on welfare.

■ This conflict between the intent of welfare as a temporary aid (as so understood by most of the public) and welfare as a permanent right (as understood by the welfare bureaucracy and welfare state planners) has serious implications. The welfare state nations, by and large, have given up on the concept of client rehabilitation for self-sufficiency, an intent originally supported by most welfare state proponents. What was to have been a temporary condition has become a permanent cost on the welfare state. As a result, welfare discourages productivity and self-sufficiency and establishes a new mode of approved behaviour in the society—one of acceptance of dependency as the norm.

(SEGALMAN AND MARSLAND 1989:6–7)

These negative views of the effects of the welfare system are widely shared by the general public, even among those basically sympathetic to the aims of the program. Greg Duncan at the University of Michigan's Survey Research Center points out that census data would seem to confirm the impression that a hard core of the poor have become trapped in their poverty. Speaking of the percentage of the population living in poverty at any given time, he says:

■ Year-to-year changes in these fractions are typically less than 1 percent, and the Census survey's other measures show little change in the characteristic of the poor from one year to the next. They have shown repeatedly that the individuals who are poor are more likely to be in families headed by a woman, by someone with low education, and by blacks.

Evidence that one-eighth of the population was poor in two consecutive years, and that those poor shared similar characteristics, is consistent with an inference of absolutely no turnover in the poverty population. Moreover, the evidence seems to fit the stereotype that those families that are poor are likely to remain poor, and that there is a hard-core population of poor families for whom there is little hope of self-improvement.

(DUNCAN 1984:2–3)

Duncan continues, however, to warn that such snapshots of the population can conceal changes taking place. Specifically, an unchanging percentage of the population living in poverty does not necessarily mean the *same* families are poor from year to year. Theoretically, it could be a totally different set of families each year.

To determine the real nature of poverty and welfare, the University of Michigan undertook a "Panel Study of Income Dynamics" in which they followed the economic fate of 5,000 families from 1969 to 1978, or ten years, the period supposedly typified by Sheehan's "welfare mother." At the beginning, the researchers found that in 1978, 8.1 percent of these families were receiving some welfare benefits and 3.5 percent depended on welfare for more than half their income. Moreover, these percentages did not differ drastically over the ten-year period. (Duncan 1984:75)

Looking beyond these surface data, however, the researchers found something you might not have expected. During the ten-year period, about one-fourth of the 5,000 families received welfare benefits at least once. However, only 8.7 percent of the families were ever dependent on welfare for more than half their income.

"Only a little over one-half of the individuals living in poverty in one year are found to be poor in the next, and considerably less than one-half of those who experience poverty remain persistently poor over many years" (Duncan 1984:3; emphasis original).

Only 2 percent of the families received welfare each of the 10 years, and less than 1 percent were continuously dependent on welfare for the 10 years. Table P-1 summarizes these findings.

These data paint a much different picture of poverty than people commonly assume. In a summary of his findings, Duncan says:

■ While nearly one-quarter of the population received income from welfare sources at least once in the decade, only about 2 percent of all the population could be characterized as dependent upon this income for extended periods of time. Many families receiving welfare benefits at any given time were in the early stages of recovering from an economic crisis caused by the death, departure, or disability of a husband, a recovery that often lifted them out of welfare when they found full-time employment, or remarried, or both. Furthermore, most of the children raised in welfare families did not themselves receive welfare benefits after they left home and formed their own households.

(DUNCAN 1984:4–5)

Many of the things social scientists study—including all the social problems you've just read about—generate deep emotions and firm convictions in most people. This makes effective inquiry into the facts difficult at best; all too often, researchers manage only to confirm their initial prejudices. The special value of social science research methods is that they offer a way to address such issues with logical and observational rigor. They let us all pierce through our personal viewpoints and take a look at the world that lies beyond our own perspective. And it is that "world beyond" that holds the solutions to the social problems we face today.

At a time of increased depression and disillusionment, we are continually tempted to turn away from confronting social problems and retreat into the concerns of our own self-interest. Social science research offers an opportunity to take on those problems and discover the experience of making a difference after all. The choice is yours; I invite you to take on the challenge. Your instructor and I would like to share the excitement of social science with you.

TABLE P-1
Incidence of Short- and Long-Run Welfare Receipt and Dependence, 1969–78

	Percent of U.S. Population: Receiving Any Welfare Income	Percent of U.S. Population: Dependent on Welfare for More Than 50% of Family Income
Welfare in 1978	8.1%	3.5%
Welfare in 1 or more years, 1969–78	25.2	8.7
Welfare in 5 or more years, 1969–78	8.3	3.5
Welfare in all 10 years, 1969–78	2.0	0.7
"Persistent welfare" (welfare in 8 or more years), 1969–78	4.4	2.0

Source: Greg J. Duncan, *Years of Poverty, Years of Plenty: the Changing Fortunes of American Workers and Families* (Ann Arbor: University of Michigan, 1984), 75.

The Practice of Social Research

Holographic Overview

SOCIAL RESEARCH is made up of many parts, which cannot easily be laid out in a neat chronological order. Over the years of teaching research methods in the classroom and writing textbooks on the subject, I have never stopped grappling with the order in which to present topics. By and large, I have tried to organize lectures and chapters according to the steps involved in doing research, though not every topic fits consistently into one point in the process. Research ethics is a good example.

I'd like you to consider social research as a *hologram,* which, you may know, is an image resulting from a rather odd photographic process. If we were to take an ordinary picture of you and me, we could make a print from the negative and there we'd be in the picture. If we were to cut the negative in half and make a print from one of the pieces, however, only one of us would show up. A holographic negative is strangely different, though. If we were to cut it in half and make a print from one of the pieces, the resulting print would show the whole picture: It would just be a little fainter. If we cut that piece in half and made a print, we'd still get the whole picture, but it would be even fainter.

This textbook—especially as represented in this preview—has been constructed after the model of a hologram. Shortly, I will give you the entire subject in one sentence. I'll give you the whole thing very quickly, but you need to know that your understanding of the subject will be a bit faint.

Following that first, very brief overview, I will give you the whole thing in a paragraph, then again in a few pages. Next, I'll present the whole thing again, in a little more detail. Finally, the rest of the book will present the whole topic once more—with all the details you need for a well-rounded knowledge of social research.

I anticipate that this kind of holographic presentation of the topic will serve you in several ways. Your first reading of this overview chapter can create a context in which you can hold and make sense of the specific topics that follow. There are so many details on the subject of social research that you will not be able to remember them all without some organizing scheme to help you. That's one way to use this overview. You might also want to review parts of this overview from time to time as you proceed through the book. This can help you keep the forest in focus as you become familiar with the individual trees.

This overview can also serve you well later, as a review of the book. It should put all the pieces back into context for you, pointing out again how they are all linked to each other.

Finally, you can use parts of this chapter to satisfy family and friends when they ask what a nice person like you is doing in a course like this.

■ THE WHOLE THING: HOLOGRAM 1

Social research is the systematic observation of social life for the purpose of finding and understanding patterns among what is observed.

■ THE WHOLE THING: HOLOGRAM 2

People interact with one another and create structures for those interactions. Social scientists seek to discover the nature of human relations, just as biologists seek to understand the functioning of physical organisms or astronomers the motions of heavenly bodies. When people normally observe what is going on around them and seek to understand it, their observations and explanations are often clouded by (1) their opinions about the way things *should* be, (2) the misconceptions and superstitions they learned growing up, and (3) sloppy and erroneous observations. In contrast, social researchers make observation a conscious and deliberate act—often a team activity, in fact. The results of their observations are then analyzed carefully and objectively to determine what *is*, regardless of the researcher's feelings about what *ought* to be.

■ THE WHOLE THING: HOLOGRAM 3

Social research (in fact, all science) is organized around two activities: measurement and interpretation. Social researchers measure aspects of social reality and then draw conclusions about the meaning of what they have measured.

Throughout this book, I will use the terms *measurement* and *observation* somewhat interchangeably, as measurement is really a special form of observation. Whereas all of us are observing all the time, measurement refers to something more deliberate and rigorous: The scientist makes a conscious decision to observe, is equally deliberate about what will be observed, takes precautions against erroneous observation, and records those observations *carefully*. Sometimes measurements are numerical or *quantitative* ("Students went to the bathroom an average of 2.4 times during the exam."); sometimes they are *qualitative* ("The motorist expressed annoyance on being told the emergency road service closed at 5 P.M.").

Whereas physical scientists use calipers, spectrographs, and other such equipment for measurement, social researchers use a variety of techniques, some of which you'll see in Part 3 of this book. Sometimes they administer questionnaires in surveys. Experimenters create controlled situations and note subjects' behaviors; participant observers immerse themselves in the real-life situations they want to study and observe from the inside. Content analysts may use tally sheets, sitting in front of a television set and noting the frequency of various occurrences. As you'll discover, there's an almost limitless variety of measurement techniques available for rigorous social research. The only limit, really, is your imagination.

Measurements begin with observations, but these raw materials must often be refined and clarified. In Chapters 5 and 6, we'll look at the initial structuring of systematic observations (in the design of questionnaires, for example). We'll return to the topic later in Chapter 7, when we examine ways of creating complex measures such as indexes, scales, and typologies. You'll see that you can often combine several specific pieces of information about people so as to characterize them in terms of general tendencies, such as prejudice, intellectual sophistication, alienation, or political orientations.

In the social sciences, more than in the natural sciences, *what* is measured is as important as *how* it is measured. In a political poll, for example, one needs to ask for voters' opinions in a manner that does not bias their responses; however, it is also vital to choose the right voters for the poll. Simply polling people in a wealthy suburb won't produce an accurate prediction of how the whole electorate will vote, nor will polling only people in an impoverished urban ghetto. *Sampling* is a precise science that allows pollsters to interview 1,500 or so voters and predict quite accurately how some 100,000,000 will vote. You'll learn how to do that in Chapter 8. Similarly, a participant observer seeking guidance from informants must be sure to pick those who can and will offer relevant points of views on the situation under study.

Measurement, then, is one of the keys to social research. The other is *interpretation,* sometimes referred to as *data analysis*. Part 4 of the book is devoted exclusively to data analysis. You will see how logic and, sometimes, mathematics are brought to bear on a body of observations in order to discover meaningful patterns. Sometimes it is important to uncover simple descriptive patterns: What percentage of the voters will vote for a particular candidate? Which cities have the highest crime rates?

Social research analysis proceeds through what has been called a "variable language." While social researchers study *people,* they are interested in understanding the *variables* that characterize or describe those people and the groups they live in. For example, "gender" is a variable, in that some people are male and others female. Thus, researchers might be interested in learning the "gender distribution" of juvenile delinquents in a particular city: What proportion are boys, what proportion girls? Or they may pay special attention to the behaviors of campus demonstration leaders so as to distinguish and understand different "leadership styles"—another social variable.

In addition to describing people merely in terms of variables, social researchers often want to discover the *relationships among variables.* Thus, for example, political researchers discovered a relationship between religious affiliation and voting behavior in U.S. politics. Specifically, Roman Catholics and Jews are more likely to vote for Democratic party candidates than are Protestants. In another realm, researchers sometimes speak of the different leadership styles typical of men and women.

As you'll see, the interpretation of observations involves more than measurement; it also rests on a logical understanding of *why* variables should be related. This is the realm of *theory,* which we'll consider early in the book and will return to throughout our journey.

Ultimately, social research is about discovering the patterns and rules governing the ways people interact with one another in society. It differs in that regard from religions or other moral systems that prescribe what *ought to be.* At the same time, social research is a powerful tool for shaping a better society: Learning the causes of prejudice, for example, can point to ways of eliminating it. Thus, while social research itself is neither moral nor immoral, it leads to several ethical considerations, which we'll consider in Chapter 18.

■ THE WHOLE THING: HOLOGRAM 4

Chapter 1. Human Inquiry and Science

Observing and trying to interpret what we observe is a native human activity. It's the foundation of our survival. In everyday life, however, we are often casual and semiconscious in both our observations and our interpretations, so that we make mistakes in both. Scientists make observation and interpretation conscious, deliberate acts.

Because there is no single way of doing social research, we'll examine different approaches used by social researchers. Sometimes they seek a general, albeit partial, understanding of social patterns of behavior; other times they are more intent on probing deeply into the idiosyncracies of a particular case. Sometimes, researchers begin with a general theory and test it through controlled observations; other times they choose to discern general patterns among what has been observed in a more open-ended and unstructured inquiry. Finally, while *objectivity* is an important aspect of all science, you'll see that *subjectivity* can also be a critical tool for social scientists.

Chapter 2. Paradigms, Theory, and Research

While discussions of research methods typically focus on techniques of measurement and analysis, all such techniques are employed within logical systems called **paradigms.*** These models or frames of reference direct our attention in making measurements and shape the **theories** we develop for purposes of general understanding.

For example, the **functionalist** paradigm has us regard society as a system, made up of components, each of which serves a function for the whole. A symphony orchestra offers a good illustration of this view in action. Each member of

---

*Boldface indicates terms that are in the glossary.

the orchestra has a specific job to do: the conductor, the percussionist, the cellist, the first violin. When we listen to the composite result, we can understand *why* each person is doing what he or she is doing. Imagine trying to understand the behavior of the conductor in isolation. They lock people up for behaving like that.

The **interactionist paradigm,** by contrast, focuses our attention on the ways people interact and communicate with each other, how the actions of one affect the responses of another. In observing a jazz combo, for example, we might be interested in how the alto sax solo was grounded in the beat laid down by the rhythm section (drums, bass, and piano) and how themes emerging from the soloist were picked up by the other musicians. This would seem a more productive way to listen to Charlie Parker and Miles Davis trade improvisations than simply to examine the functions of the alto sax and trumpet, respectively.

Social scientists can ground their inquiries in any number of paradigms. None is right or wrong, merely more or less useful in particular situations. They each shape the kind of theory created for general understanding. Thus, for example, Karl Marx's theories about the relations among social classes were grounded in a **conflict paradigm,** which focuses on the attempts of one group to dominate others and to avoid being dominated. In this context, Marx talked a great deal about "class struggle," a concept that would have much less importance in a functionalist theory about how social classes play different roles in the functioning of the whole society.

The relationship between research and theory can be seen in terms of two different, though interrelated, models. The *inductive method* begins with concrete, specific observations and aims at identifying general principles governing what is being observed. We might begin with an intention of determining what kinds of people are more likely to jaywalk, and which are less likely as we watch people at a traffic intersection.

The *deductive* method, on the other hand, begins with general principles (theory), then turns to observation to test the validity of theoretical expectations. Beginning with a theory of gender-role expectations in U.S. society, for example, we might conclude that men should be more likely to jaywalk than women; then we would set about observing pedestrian patterns to determine whether our theoretical conclusion was correct. This is called *hypothesis testing.*

Both inductive and deductive methods are legitimate in science. In fact, the study of specific topics will typically involve alternation between the two: observations may result in theoretical explanations; those explanations suggest other patterns that should be present; further observations test those expectations; and the results will lead to modifications in the theory and in subsequent expectations.

Chapter 3. The Nature of Causation

While some social research is devoted mainly to *describing* aspects of social life, social scientists are often very much interested in *explanatory* or *causal* analyses: Why are things the way they are?

The logic and discussion of causation in research is in the language of variables: We say that some variables cause or determine others. In this sense, increased education causes a reduction in prejudice. Religious affiliation determines voting behavior. Gender determines attitudes about the Equal Rights Amendment, aimed at guaranteeing equal rights for women.

If you balked at the seemingly absolute nature of the preceding statements, your instincts are right. After all, education is not the only thing affecting prejudice; voting reflects more than just religion; and some women oppose the ERA while some men favor it.

In the causal language of social research, it is seldom the case that one variable absolutely and completely causes another. Voting behavior, for example, is influenced by party affiliation and political philosophy, of course, but it is also influenced by education, income, region of the country, religion, and other variables. Social scientific explanations, then, frequently involve several causal variables. This is not all that different from the many factors that may lead to your catching a cold (sitting in a draft, being sneezed on, being overtired, and so on).

Chapter 4. Research Design

If the basic purposes of social research are to observe and to make sense out of those observations, there are many options available in the pursuit of those ends. One of the first steps in designing a research project involves a clarification of the *unit of analysis*—the object of our attention. Typically, the unit of analysis in social research is the individual human being, though we may need to specify that we are interested only in U.S. citizens, college students, church members, California voters, or some other subset of humanity. At the same time, the units of analysis for research can also be families, corporations, cities, nations, movies, poems, or anything else that has some social relevance and can be observed. We might, for example, observe a large number of rock music videos, noting the genders of the performers and measuring the degree of violence or hostility portrayed. We could then determine whether the two variables were related.

Chapter 5. Conceptualization and Measurement

Measurement, you'll recall, is one of the fundamental pillars of social research. Three chapters in this book are devoted exclusively to this topic. This first one deals with the intellectual roots of measurement. *Conceptualization* refers to the process of identifying and clarifying concepts: ideas we have about the nature of things. We've already been trafficking in such concepts throughout this overview: prejudice, education, religion, and so on.

If we wished to study bigotry, for example, it might be appropriate to distinguish *stereotypes* (beliefs), *discrimination* (actions), and *prejudice* (feelings). Not only that, we would need to specify the objects of bigotry that interested us: racial or ethnic groups, women, religious minorities, gays, and so on. This degree of specificity would be necessary for creating a research project; it also would allow us to discover, later on, that the factors causing discrimination are not necessarily the same as those causing discrimination against women. We also could discover some common patterns.

In the course of this chapter, you are going to learn that none of the concepts we identify and study have "true" definitions, only those we agree to assign them. In an important sense, the term *prejudice* can mean whatever we choose to have it mean; the challenge is to specify observations that we can gather usefully under that same term.

Chapter 6. Operationalization

Whereas conceptualization concerns the intellectual clarification of concepts for measurement, *operationalization* is the construction of actual, concrete measurement techniques. Literally, it is the creation of "operations" that will result in the desired measurements.

In a survey of attitudes regarding feminist issues, for example, we should probably measure respondents' genders, because men and women are likely to have somewhat different views on the issue. Conceptualization is not terribly difficult in this instance, and operationalization is pretty straightforward as well. We might operationalize this measurement in the questionnaire as follows:

Gender

☐ Male
☐ Female

A good way to measure age in a questionnaire is with an item like this:

Age: _____

Or, we might ask people to indicate their approximate age within specified ranges, as follows:

Age

☐ Under 21
☐ 21–34
☐ 35–49
☐ 50–64
☐ 65 or older

Sometimes attitudes and opinions can be measured effectively with a single question in a questionnaire. Here's a straightforward way of learning attitudes toward capital punishment: "Do you favor or oppose the death penalty for persons convicted of murder?" (That's how the variable is measured in the General Social Survey, a national survey conducted every year or two by the National Opinion Research Center at the University of Chicago.) Chapter 6 will discuss in detail some of the considerations involved in designing questions that elicit attitudes and opinions without unconsciously biasing respondents in one direction or the other.

As a quite different example, suppose you were doing a historical/comparative study of the relationship between military expenditures and poverty, with nation-states as the units of analysis. You'd need to specify precisely how you would measure each of these variables, as well as other variables such as population size and gross domestic product. Perhaps you would use official statistics from the countries under study or data from the United Nations.

Chapter 7. Indexes, Scales, and Typologies

Most social scientific variables require much thought and ingenuity in conceptualization and operationalization. Consider attitudes toward feminism, for example. In our conceptualization of the variable, we might decide to limit our attention to "political equality for men and women." We could operationalize the variable in a number of ways. For example, we might ask respondents to agree or disagree with each of the following statements:

1. I would like to see a woman elected president.
2. I would be willing to vote for a qualified woman candidate for Congress.
3. Frankly, I'm not sure that women are physically and psychologically equipped for political office.
4. All things considered, we would probably be better off if women left polities to men.

Note that each of these statements reflects an attitude about women in politics. The first two statements are stated positively (in support of women in politics), the last two negatively. We might operationalize in terms of respondents' answers to the four statements, giving them one "point" for each feminist answer, for example. Thus, respondents would get one point each for agreeing with statements (1) and (2) and for *dis*agreeing with statements (3) and (4).

The combination of the several indicators I've just described would constitute an *index*. Alternatively, we could create a *scale*, which takes into account the fact that some indicators of a variable seem more extreme than others. Saying you were against women voting, for example, would be a pretty strong indicator of antifeminism. We'll examine several types of scales in Chapter 7.

Chapter 8. The Logic of Sampling

A fundamental element in social research that is not always so important in physical science concerns how we select from the infinite observations we might make. That is, since we can't observe everything, how do we pick what to observe?

When physical scientists set out to study the properties of oxygen, for example, they can't study all oxygen, even though they want to draw conclusions about oxygen in general. By the same token, when political scientists want to draw conclusions about voters' preferences among candidates, they can't question all voters. So how do these scientists each decide precisely what to study?

In the case of oxygen, one molecule's as good as any other. Physicists simply send research assistants to Neiman-Marcus, the K-Mart hardware department, or wherever they shop for supplies to buy a liter of oxygen. Nobody worries about *which* liter. Political scientists who study any voters who happen to be handy will be in trouble, however, because all voters are definitely not alike. Imagine shopping for voters to study at Neiman-Marcus, at K-Mart, at a union meeting, or at a corporate stockholders' meeting. It would make a *big* difference which voters you chose to interview.

As you will see, however, it is possible to select a relatively small sample of voters in such a way that their responses represent the intentions of tens of millions of voters across the country. It's worth noting that one of the chief criticisms of political polling these days is that it "takes all the fun out of elections" by telling us how the voting will turn out even before the votes are cast. In a similar vein, some worry that poll predictions may have an impact on whether people even go to the polls and/or how they vote if they do.

In Chapter 8, you will learn about the simplest techniques of random and systematic sampling. You will also get a taste of the more complex forms of stratified, multistage sampling used in major national surveys. Even if you never conduct a survey on your own, you will be able to understand and evaluate reports of sampling techniques in media accounts of polls and reported margins of sampling error, for example.

Even when we cannot select random samples from a known population, the logic of sampling still applies. In field research on juvenile gangs, it would be important to interview and observe a variety of members from a variety of gangs in order to avoid a narrowly biased picture. Or if we would like to develop an in-depth understanding of the life of a professional politician, what we learned would depend heavily on *which* politicians we studied.

Even if we intended to provide a fully detailed description of a single case (a particular community, for example), with no concern for speaking about a broader class of individuals or groups, we would have to sample among the possible observations we might make of that one case. What we observe and what we do not observe should be a matter of deliberate choice rather than chance.

Chapter 9. Experiments

Probably most laypeople's image of science involves experiments, typically conducted by scientists wearing long, white coats—with or without demonic sneers and leers. While social scientists use a variety of techniques, one of these is the *controlled experiment,* often conducted in a laboratory setting, though they seldom wear white coats (or sneer and leer). In addition to being a commonly used technique for doing research, the controlled experiment is also a useful model for understanding the *logic* of causal social research.

In simplest terms, researchers often investigate causal relationships among variables, speaking of *independent* variables that cause *dependent* variables. For example, it might be the case that studying this book for eight hours on the night before the midterm will improve your exam grade, but how would you know?

We might design a simple experiment in which some students would study eight hours the night before the exam and others would watch TV. Then we'd compare the grades of the two groups and see if those who studied did better. In this example, by the way, studying or not studying would be the independent variable and grades would be the dependent variable. Imagine the following results:

	Average grade
Studied............................	80
Watched TV.....................	70

This would certainly seem to vouch for the value of studying all night before the midterm, but there are a number of reasons you might want to question the validity of the conclusion. Maybe the better students studied the night before the exam, while the weaker students watched TV. That might account for differences in the exam grades. As you'll see, there are sampling and matching techniques in experimentation that can guard against this possibility of *internal invalidity* in the experimental design.

As you think about this hypothetical experiment, you may wonder whether the results of an experiment like this, where students knew they were being studied, would really reflect what happens in normal life. That's a good question, a matter of *external invalidity* that we'll examine in Chapter 9, along with several other matters of internal and external invalidity.

Perhaps you were surprised at the relatively small difference in average scores—only ten points—in the hypothetical example. Does studying all night really make all that much difference? In fact, could the observed, modest difference be just a matter of chance?

If we conducted the experiment again, the results might go in just the opposite direction. Questions such as these will be dealt with later on in the book, in the context of statistical analyses, when we look at the *statistical* and *substantive significance* of differences. My purpose is to protect you from being misled into thinking that trivial differences are important. You may even find yourself responding to certain advertising claims more critically.

Chapter 10. Survey Research

One of the most common research methods used in the social sciences these days involves the administration of a questionnaire—either by interview or through the mail—to a sample of respondents. Political polls and government censuses are examples of survey research.

A central element in survey research is the *standardized questionnaire*. In terms of the fundamental issue of measurement, this kind of questionnaire insures that exactly the same observation technique is used with each and every respondent in the study. If the question addressed which presidential candidate people planned to vote for, everyone surveyed would be asked exactly the same question, such as, "If the election for president were held today, who would you vote for: Tweedledee or Tweedledum?" While there are questions as to whether respondents will answer honestly, whether they have truly reached a decision about the election, and so forth, at least we know exactly what question they were responding to. Whereas Chapter 6, on operationalization, deals with techniques of question wording in the creation of a questionnaire, Chapter 10 explains the options for administering a questionnaire: in a face-to-face interview, over the telephone, or through the mail or other self-administered formats. We'll also look at how computers are being used to administer survey questionnaires.

Chapter 11. Field Research

Perhaps the most natural technique for doing social research involves simply going where the action is and observing it, not unlike newspaper reporting. This is, in fact, a well-established social research method called *field research*. In one form of this technique—*participant observation*—the researcher actually joins in the events under study and examines the phenomenon from the inside. Suppose you were interested in studying about the nature of political discussions among punk rockers in Los Angeles. You'd dig out your guitar and go underground.

While you've been doing this kind of research all your life, you'll see in Chapter 11 that social researchers have developed effective techniques for observing, taking notes, and analyzing their observations. You'll also have a chance to review some of the more interesting studies social researchers have undertaken in this fashion.

Chapter 12. Unobtrusive Research

Most social research involves some interaction with the people under study: asking them questions in a survey, giving them tasks to perform in an experiment, or rubbing shoulders with them in field research. There is a concomitant danger that accompanies such intrusions into the flow of social life: The act of research may influence the subject of study itself. By asking people about their voting intentions, we probably influence those intentions in some degree, perhaps making respondents more definite in their choices by getting them to commit themselves out loud.

Many social research techniques can be called *unobtrusive* in that they have no impact on what is being studied. Chapter 12 will detail several of these. For example, social scientists can study many phenomena through the reanalysis of existing statistics. Emile Durkheim, the great French sociologist, examined differential suicide rates for different countries and different regions within those countries to gain insights into the causes of self-destruction. Sometimes, historical documents can provide data for analysis, as in Max Weber's classic study of the rise of capitalism in connection with the asceticism of Calvinism. Content analysis is another example, involving the study of recorded communications—anything from books, speeches, and poems to paintings, songs, or television commercials. Once again, you are going to see that the possibilities for social research are virtually endless.

Chapter 13. Evaluation Research

Much social research is conducted specifically to evaluate programs of social intervention. Let's say a state legislature allocates several million dollars to institute a new *rehabilitation* program for convicts in the state prison. It would be nice to know whether the program ultimately has the intended result: Does anyone get rehabilitated? This is just one opportunity for social researchers to make an important contribution to society.

If you were called on to evaluate a prison rehabilitation program, you would need to begin by clarifying the specific intentions of the program. What is meant by *rehabilitation?* How could you determine whether a prisoner was rehabilitated or not? Having reached agreement on that issue, you'd probably want to determine the "normal" rates of rehabilitation; that would give you something against which to compare the impact of the new program. Then you could design an evaluation of the rehabilitation program pretty much in accord with the logic of the controlled experiment. As you'll see in Chapter 13, however, evaluation research is never quite as logically pure as it may sound. Evaluation researchers often have to cope with more complex ethical, political, and administrative issues than in other forms of social research.

Chapter 14. Quantifying Data

So far we've been talking about making observations and measurements, collecting data, and similar activities. One of the key characteristics of any science is that it is empirically based—grounded in facts. Sometimes the facts (in the form of observations) come first and set off an inquiry into understanding why things are the way they are. Sometimes a theory is generated first and must then be tested against the reality of what can be observed.

Sometimes, the collection of facts through observation results in the creation of data files suitable for *quantitative* (that is, numerical) analyses. These days this usually means the creation of data files suitable for statistical manipulation by computers. In Chapter 14, we'll take a look at the development of computers and how they've influenced social research. Then we'll see how data are transformed into the raw materials for computer analyses.

You are going to see how the computer—especially the microcomputer—has become for the social sciences what the microscope was for biology and the telescope for astronomy. The microcomputer allows researchers to analyze a set of social data from a variety of perspectives, focusing in on special subsets, testing causal processes, and so forth. It's almost as though you are able to hold a portion of society in your hands and turn it around for a variety of inspections.

Chapter 15. Elementary Analyses

The most exciting part of social research comes when your efforts at data collection bring you to the point of analyzing those data, or looking at descriptive patterns and causal relationships among variables. Ultimately, this comes down to the patterns of distribution of attributes on one or more variables.

In the simplest form of analysis—*univariate analysis*—we examine the distribution of attributes within a single variable. In 1996, for example, the General Social Survey asked a sample of American adults to identify their political views as liberal, conservative, or moderate. (This variable is labelled POLVIEWS in the GSS data set, Table I-29.) Here's how they replied:

2%	Extremely liberal
11	Liberal
13	Slightly liberal
38	Moderate
16	Slightly conservative
16	Conservative
3	Extremely conservative

We can simplify this univariate analysis further by noting that 26 percent identified themselves as liberal (combining the first three categories) and 35 percent said they were conservative. (Notice, by the way, that sets of percentages like this don't always add up to exactly 100%, because of rounding off.) In and of itself, you may find these data interesting. It might be more interesting, however, to explore how different kinds of people identify themselves. Consider gender, for example.

Political views

	Men	Women
Liberal	24%	29%
Moderate	35	40
Conservative	40	31

As these data indicate, the main difference is that women in the sample tended to identify themselves as middle-of-the-road, whereas men were more likely to be conservative. About the same percentages of women considered themselves liberal as conservative.

What variable is more likely to be associated with certain political views? One that comes to mind is political party. In recent decades, the Republican party has tended to be more conservative than the Democratic party. Let's see if that pattern appeared among the GSS sample. We'll also look at those who identified themselves as Independents.

Political views

	Democrats	Independents	Republicans
Liberal	41%	26%	10%
Moderate	36	44	31
Conservative	23	29	59

The political views held by Democrats, Independents, and Republicans reflect the general pattern we expected, although the differences may not be as strong as you might have expected. In particular, we can see that Democrats are spread across the political spectrum, whereas the Republicans are more concentrated on the conservative side.

These latest two tables are examples *of bivariate analysis:* the analysis of two variables at one time in an attempt to discover the relationship between them.

Chapter 16. The Elaboration Model

The *elaboration model* is the name associated with a logical model used in the analysis of multivariate relationships in social research. Specifically, it involves the introduction of a *control variable* as a mechanism for understanding a relationship discovered between two other variables.

Sometimes the elaboration model is used to discover the mechanisms whereby two variables are related to one another. We'll discover, for example, that children from broken homes are more likely to become juvenile delinquents than children living with both a mother and a father. Elaboration analysis allows us to discover the reason for this: the amount of adult supervision the children receive. Supervised children are less likely to become delinquent, and those in broken homes are more likely to lack supervision. If they *are* supervised, however, they are no more likely to become delinquent than other children.

Sometimes the elaboration model can uncover misleading relationships; other times it will reveal the specific conditions under which relationships occur; and sometimes it merely confirms the **generalizability** of observed relationships. For example, the relationship between party and political ideology exists for both men and women, as the following data indicate:

Political Views: MEN

	Democrats	Independents	Republicans
Liberal	38%	26%	9%
Moderate	38	40	27
Conservative	24	34	65

Political views: WOMEN

	Democrats	Independents	Republicans
Liberal	42%	26%	11%
Moderate	35	48	35
Conservative	23	25	54

An examination of the elaboration model will show some of the ways social research resembles detective work, as we try to track down the meaningful patterns embedded in our social life.

Chapter 17. Social Statistics

The simple percentage tables I've been presenting offer examples of statistical analyses of quantitative data. I have a personal affinity for such analyses, because most people can understand the meaning of percentage descriptions and comparisons. Sometimes, however, the relationships that exist among variables cannot be viewed this simply. Social scientists have therefore developed complex analytical techniques for probing into and revealing such relationships. In Chapter 17, you will get a look at the logic of some of these techniques.

The advanced statistical techniques used by social scientists are so complex that you would need to study them in some depth before you could use them effectively. My purpose is to acquaint you with the fundamental logic of some techniques you are likely to encounter in social scientific journals so you will understand the results of such analyses even if you do not undertake them on your own. Of course, I also plan to give you the grounding you'll need to go on to master these techniques through further study, if you wish to do that.

Chapter 18. The Ethics and Politics of Social Research

For the most part, this book will introduce you to the logic and skills of doing social research. I want you to understand how social research would be conducted if conditions for it were perfect; then I want you to see how social scientists cope with the constraints of the real world: what to do when there are no lists to sample from, when people won't return questionnaires, and so on.

Equally important as your understanding of the logistical constraints of the "real world" on doing research are the constraints imposed by ethical and political considerations. For example, it is not acceptable to conduct social research that will injure the subjects of study in the process; most of us are horrified by the way these constraints were violated by Nazi doctors during World War II. While social science would seldom threaten people's lives, it can often cause them embarrassment, worry, self-doubt, and other forms of psychological distress; further, publicly revealing what has been learned about them could cause them severe harm. Social researchers have a number of strict principles to ensure ethical research, which you'll learn about in Chapter 18. By no means should you consider ethical concerns unimportant just because they are discussed late in the book. I have delayed the discussion only in the belief that it will mean more to you once you are more familiar with the logic and techniques of social research.

Political issues establish another set of constraints on the practice of social research. More than once, social researchers have been stopped short in the execution of a study. Imagine conducting a study of the honesty and effectiveness of government officials during an election campaign, for example. It's unlikely that you'd be free to operate according to scientific principles alone. Some of the political candidates would refuse to participate and might even attempt to block the study. Research into sensitive topics such as sex education, homosexuality, abortion, or AIDS is often conducted within a context of popular controversy. Evaluation research, designed to test the success of particular programs, typically must deal with the personal and professional interests of those responsible for the programs.

Research in the physical sciences is also constrained by ethical and political considerations, but the topics studied by social scientists make such constraints more common for them. In any event, I want to help you become sensitive to the ethics and politics of social research so you can deal with these real-world factors and, in the case of ethics, protect yourself from unconsciously slipping into research activities that violate accepted principles for ethical behavior.

Chapter 19. The Uses of Social Research

I end this book by recognizing that you may not be in training for a career in social research. I know most readers will not become professional social researchers, and that's fine. If everyone who took a course in social research methods chose this as a career, most of us would be unemployed.

At the same time, there are a couple of special ways this course (and the book, I hope) can serve interests outside a career in social research. First, you will be reading and hearing about social research for the rest of your life, and a basic understanding of the principles involved constitutes part of a Civilization Survival Kit. I'll show you how to use what you've learned to be an effective consumer of social research.

Second, much of what you are going to learn in this book can be applied to the nonresearch parts of your life. I've pointed out, for example, that what you learn about questionnaire construction applies equally well to the design of forms for other administrative purposes. Participant observer skills can assist you as a newspaper reporter, a detective, or a spy (though the discussion of ethics may be problematic there).

I arranged the comments of Chapter 19 to provide a general review of the book, just in case you're asked to say something about it on an examination. (Good luck, by the way.)

This completes Hologram 4. The rest of the book constitutes another holographic presentation of social research. Feel free to come back to this overview anytime you find yourself losing the overall context for whatever is being discussed; I'll be here 24 hours a day. I hope you'll enjoy learning about social research as much as I do.

PART 1
An Introduction to Inquiry

1 Human Inquiry and Science
2 Paradigms, Theory, and Research
3 The Nature of Causation

SCIENCE is a familiar word used by everyone. Yet images of science differ greatly. For some, science is mathematics; for others, it is white coats and laboratories. It is often confused with technology or equated with tough high school or college courses.

Science is, of course, none of these things per se. It is difficult, however, to specify exactly what science is. Scientists, in fact, disagree on the proper definition. For the purposes of this book, however, we shall look at science as a method of inquiry—a way of learning and knowing things about the world around us. Contrasted with other ways of learning and knowing about the world, science has some special characteristics. We'll examine these traits in this opening set of chapters.

Dr. Benjamin Spock, the renowned author and pediatrician, begins his books on child care by assuring new parents that they already know more about child care than they think they do. I want to begin this book on a similar note. It will become clear to you before you've read very far that you already know a great deal about the practice of scientific social research. In fact, you've been conducting scientific research all your life. From that perspective, the purpose of this book is to help you sharpen skills you already have and perhaps to show you some tricks that may not have occurred to you.

Part 1 of this book is intended to lay the groundwork for the discussions that follow in the rest of the book—to examine the fundamental characteristics and issues that make science different from other ways of knowing things. In Chapter 1, we'll begin with a look at native human inquiry, the sort of thing you've been doing all your life. In the course of that examination, we'll see some of the ways people go astray in trying to understand the world around them, and I'll summarize the primary characteristics of scientific inquiry that guard against those errors.

Chapter 2 deals with social scientific theories, as well as the links between theory and research. We'll look at some of the theoretical paradigms that shape the nature of inquiry, largely determining what scientists look for and how they interpret what they see.

In their attempt to develop generalized understanding, scientists seek to discover patterns of interrelationships among variables. Very often these interrelationships take a cause-and-effect form. Chapter 3 addresses the nature and logic of causation as appropriate to social scientific research. This theoretical chapter forms the basis for the chapters on analytical techniques.

The overall purpose of Part 1 is to construct a backdrop against which to view more specific aspects of research design and execution. By the time you complete Part 1, you should be ready to look at some of the more concrete aspects of social research.

CHAPTER 1
Human Inquiry and Science

What You'll Learn in This Chapter
We'll examine the way people learn about their world and the mistakes they make along the way. We'll also begin to see what makes science different from other ways of knowing things.

INTRODUCTION

LOOKING FOR REALITY
Ordinary Human Inquiry
Tradition
Authority
Errors in Inquiry and Some Solutions
What's Really Real?

THE FOUNDATIONS OF SOCIAL SCIENCE
Theory, Not Philosophy or Belief
Social Regularities
Aggregates, Not Individuals
A Variable Language

SOME DIALECTICS OF SOCIAL SCIENCE
Idiographic and Nomothetic Explanation
Inductive and Deductive Theory
Qualitative and Quantitative Data

THE ETHICS OF SOCIAL RESEARCH
No Harm to Subjects
Voluntary Participation

MAIN POINTS

REVIEW QUESTIONS AND EXERCISES

ADDITIONAL READINGS

■ INTRODUCTION

This book is about knowing things. Although you will probably come away from the book knowing some things you don't know right now, my primary purpose is to help you look at *how* you know things, not *what* you know. Let's start by examining a few things you probably know already.

You know the world is round. You probably also know it's cold on the dark side of the moon, and you know people speak Chinese in China. You know that vitamin C prevents colds and that unprotected sex can result in AIDS.

How do you know? If you reflect on it for a minute, you'll see you know these things because somebody told them to you, and you believed what you were told. You may have read in *National Geographic* that people speak Chinese in China, and that made sense to you, so you didn't question it. Perhaps your physics or astronomy instructor told you it was cold on the dark side of the moon, or maybe you read it in *Newsweek*. That's how you know.

Some of the things you know seem absolutely obvious to you. If I asked you how you know the world is round, you'd probably say, "Everybody knows that." There are a lot of things everybody knows. Of course, at one time, everyone "knew" the world was flat.

Most of what you know is a matter of agreement and belief. Little of it is based on personal experience and discovery. A big part of growing up in any society, in fact, is the process of learning to accept what everybody around you "knows" is so. If you don't know those same things, you can't really be a part of the group. If you were to question seriously that the world is really round, you'd quickly find yourself set apart from other people. You might be sent to live in a hospital with other people who ask questions like that.

Although it's important for you to see that most of what you know is a matter of believing what you've been told, I also want you to see that there's nothing wrong with you in that respect. That's simply the way human societies are structured. The basis of knowledge is agreement. Because you can't learn through personal experience and discovery alone all you need to know, things are set up so you can simply believe what others tell you. You know some things through tradition, others from "experts."

There are other ways of knowing things, however. In contrast to knowing things through agreement, you can know them through direct experience—through observation. If you dive into a glacial stream flowing through the Canadian Rockies, you don't need anyone to tell you it's cold. You notice that all by yourself. The first time you stepped on a thorn, you knew it hurt even before anyone told you.

When your experience conflicts with what everyone else knows, though, there's a good chance you'll surrender your experience in favor of the agreement.

Let's take an example. Imagine you've come to a party at my house. It's a high-class affair, and the drinks and food are excellent. In particular, you are taken by one of the appetizers I bring around on a tray: a breaded, deep-fried appetizer that's especially zesty. You have a couple—they're so delicious! You have more. Soon you are subtly moving around the room to be wherever I am when I arrive with a tray of these nibblies.

Finally, you can't contain yourself any more. "What are they?" you ask. "How can I get the recipe?" And I let you in on the secret: "You've been eating breaded, deep-fried *worms*!" Your response is dramatic: Your stomach rebels, and you promptly throw up all over the living room rug. Awful! What a terrible thing to serve guests!

The point of the story is that both feelings about the appetizer would be quite real. Your initial liking for them was certainly real, but so was the feeling you had when you found out what you'd been eating. It should be evident, however, that the feeling of disgust you had when you discovered you were eating worms was strictly a product of the agreements you have with those around you that worms aren't fit to eat. That's an agreement you began the first time your parents found you sitting in a pile of dirt with half of a wriggling worm dangling from your lips. You learned that worms are not acceptable food in our society when they pried your mouth open and reached down your throat in search of the other half of the worm.

Aside from these agreements, what's wrong with worms? They are probably high in protein and low in calories. Bite-sized and easily packaged, they are a distributor's dream. They are also a delicacy for some people who live in societies that lack our agreement that worms are disgusting. Some people might love the worms but would be turned off by the deep-fried breading.

Here's a question you might consider: "Are worms "really" good or "really" bad to eat?" And here's a more interesting question: "*How could you know* which was really so?" This book is about answering the second kind of question.

■ LOOKING FOR REALITY

Reality is a tricky business. You've probably already gotten the suspicion that some of the things you "know" may not be true, but how can you really know what's real? People have grappled with this question for thousands of years.

One answer that has arisen out of that grappling is science, which offers an approach to both agreement reality and experiential reality. Scientists have certain criteria that must be met before they will accept the reality of something they haven't personally experienced. In general, an assertion must have both *logical* and *empirical* support: It must make sense, and it must not contradict actual observation. Why do earthbound scientists accept the assertion that it's cold on the dark side of the moon? First, it makes sense, because the surface heat of the moon comes from the sun's rays. Second, the scientific measurements made on the moon's dark side confirm the expectation. So, scientists accept the reality of things they don't personally experience—they accept an agreement reality—but they have special standards for doing so.

More to the point of this book, however, science offers a special approach to the discovery of reality through personal experience. It offers a special approach to the business of inquiry. *Epistemology* is the science of knowing; *methodology* (a subfield of epistemology) might be called the science of finding out. This book is an examination and presentation of social science methodology, or how social scientists find out about human social life.

In the remainder of this chapter, we're going to look at inquiry as an activity. We'll begin by examining inquiry as a natural human activity. It is something you and I have engaged in every day of our lives. Next, we'll look at some kinds of errors we make in normal inquiry, and we'll conclude by examining what makes science different. We'll see some of the ways in which science guards against the common human errors in inquiry.

Ordinary Human Inquiry

Practically all people, and many other animals as well, exhibit a desire to predict their future circumstances. We seem quite willing, moreover, to undertake this task using *causal* and *probabilistic* reasoning. First, we generally recognize that future circumstances are somehow caused or conditioned by present ones. We learn that getting an education will affect how much money we earn later in life and that swimming beyond the reef may bring an unhappy encounter with a shark. Sharks, on the other hand, may learn that hanging around the reef may bring a happy encounter with unhappy swimmers. As students we learn that studying hard will result in better examination grades.

Second, people, and seemingly other animals, also learn that such patterns of cause and effect are *probabilistic* in nature: The effects occur more often when the causes occur than when the causes are absent—but not always. Thus, students learn that studying hard produces good grades in most instances, but not every time. We recognize the danger of swimming beyond the reef without believing that every such swim will be fatal. We'll return to these concepts of causality and probability throughout the book. As you'll see, science makes them more explicit and provides techniques for dealing with them more rigorously than does casual human inquiry. What I want to do is sharpen the skills you already have, making you more conscious, rigorous, and explicit in your inquiries.

In looking at ordinary human inquiry, we need to distinguish prediction and understanding. Often, we can make predictions without understanding—perhaps you can predict rain when your trick knee aches. And often, even if we don't understand why, we are willing to act on the basis of a demonstrated predictive ability. The race track buff who finds that the third-ranked horse in the third race of the day always wins will probably keep betting without knowing, or caring, why it works out that way.

Whatever the primitive drives or instincts that motivate human beings and other animals, satisfying them depends heavily on the ability to predict future circumstances. For people, however, the attempt to predict is often placed in a context of knowledge and understanding. If you can understand why things are related to one another, why certain regular patterns occur, you can predict even better than if you simply observe and remember those patterns. Thus, human inquiry aims at answering both "what" and "why" questions, and we pursue these goals by observing and figuring out.

As I suggested earlier in the chapter, our attempts to learn about the world are only partly linked to direct, personal inquiry or experience. Another, much larger, part comes from the agreed-on knowledge that others give us. This agreement reality both assists and hinders our attempts to find out for ourselves. Two important sources of our secondhand knowledge—tradition and authority—deserve brief consideration here.

Tradition

Each of us inherits a culture made up, in part, of firmly accepted knowledge about the workings of the world. We may learn from others that planting corn in the spring will gain the greatest assistance from the gods, that eating too much candy will decay our teeth, that the circumference of a circle is approximately twenty-two sevenths of its diameter, or that masturbation will blind us. We may test a few of these "truths" on our own, but we simply accept the great majority of them. These are the things that "everybody knows."

Tradition, in this sense of the term, offers some clear advantages to human inquiry. By accepting what everybody knows, you are spared the overwhelming task of starting from scratch in your search for regularities and understanding. Knowledge is cumulative, and an inherited body of information and understanding is the jumping-off point for the development of more knowledge. We often speak of "standing on the shoulders of giants," that is, of previous generations.

At the same time, tradition may be detrimental to human inquiry. If you seek a fresh understanding of something everybody already understands and has always understood, you may be marked the fool for your efforts. More to the point, however, it will probably never occur to you to seek a different understanding of something already understood and obvious.

Authority

Despite the power of tradition, new knowledge appears every day. Quite aside from your own personal inquiries, throughout your life you will benefit from new discoveries and understandings produced by others. Often, acceptance of these new acquisitions will depend on the status of the discoverer. You're more likely to believe the epidemiologist who declares that the common cold can be transmitted through kissing, for example, than to believe your uncle Pete.

Like tradition, authority can both assist and hinder human inquiry. We do well to trust in the judgment of the person who has special training, expertise, and credentials in a given matter, especially in the face of controversy. At the same time, inquiry can be greatly hindered by the legitimate authority who errs within his or her own special province. Biologists, after all, do make mistakes in the field of biology. Biological knowledge changes over time.

Inquiry is also hindered when we depend on the authority of experts speaking outside their realm of expertise. For example, consider the political or religious leader with no biochemical expertise who declares that marijuana is a dangerous drug. The advertising industry plays heavily on this misuse of authority by having popular athletes discuss the nutritional value of breakfast cereals, having movie actors evaluate the performance of automobiles, and using other similar tactics.

Both tradition and authority, then, are double-edged swords in the search for knowledge about the world. Simply put, they provide us with a starting point for our own inquiry, but they may lead us to start at the wrong point and push us off in the wrong direction.

Errors in Inquiry and Some Solutions

Quite aside from the potential dangers of tradition and authority, you and I often stumble and fall when we set out to learn for ourselves. I'm going to mention some of the common errors we make in our casual inquiries and look at the ways science guards against those errors.

Inaccurate Observations Quite frequently, you and I make mistakes in our observations. What color shoes was your methodology instructor wearing the first time you were together, for example? If you have to guess, that's because most of our daily observations are casual and semiconscious. That's why we often disagree about what really happened.

In contrast to casual human inquiry, scientific observation is a *conscious* activity. Simply making observation more deliberate helps reduce error. You probably don't recall, for example, what your instructor was wearing on the first day of class. If you had to guess now, you'd probably make a mistake. If you had gone to the first class meeting with a conscious plan to observe and record what your instructor was wearing, however, you'd be more accurate.

In many cases, both simple and complex measurement devices help guard against inaccurate observations. Moreover, they add a degree of precision well beyond the capacity of the unassisted human senses. Suppose, for example, that you had taken color photographs of your instructor that day.

Overgeneralization When we look for patterns among the specific things we observe around us, we often assume that a few similar events are evidence of a general pattern. Probably the tendency to overgeneralize is greatest when the pressure to arrive at a general understanding is high. Yet it also occurs without such pressure. Whenever overgeneralization does occur, it can misdirect or impede inquiry.

Imagine you are a reporter covering an animal-rights demonstration. You have orders to turn in your story in just two hours, and you need to know why people are demonstrating. Rushing to the scene, you start interviewing them, asking for their reasons. If the first two demonstrators you interview give you essentially the same reason, you may simply assume that the other 3,000 are also there for that reason.

Scientists guard against overgeneralization by committing themselves in advance to a sufficiently large sample of observations. The **replication** of inquiry provides another safeguard. Basically, this means repeating a study, checking to see if the same results are produced each time. Then the study may be repeated under slightly varied conditions.

Selective Observation One danger of overgeneralization is that it may lead to selective observation. Once you have concluded that a particular pattern exists and have developed a general understanding of why it does, you will tend to focus on future events and situations that fit the pattern and ignore those that don't. Racial and ethnic prejudices depend heavily on selective observation for their persistence.

Sometimes, a research design will specify in advance the number and kind of observations to be made as a basis for reaching a conclusion. If you and I wanted to learn whether women were more likely than men to support freedom to choose an abortion, we'd commit ourselves to making a specified number of observations on that question in a research project. We might select a thousand people to be interviewed on the issue. Alternately, when making direct observations of an event, such as attending the animal-rights demonstration, social scientists make a special effort to find "deviant cases"—precisely those who do not fit into the general pattern.

Illogical Reasoning There are other ways of handling observations that contradict our conclusions about the way things are in daily life. Surely one of the most remarkable creations of the human mind is "the exception that proves the rule." That idea doesn't make any sense at all. An exception can draw attention to a rule or to a supposed rule, but in no system of logic can it prove the rule it contradicts. Yet, we often use this pithy saying to brush away contradictions with a simple stroke of illogic.

What statisticians have called the *gambler's fallacy* is another illustration of illogic in day-to-day reasoning. A consistent run of either good or bad luck is presumed to foreshadow its opposite. An evening of bad luck at poker may kindle the belief that a winning hand is just around the corner, so that many a poker player has stayed in a game much too long because of that mistaken belief. Conversely, an extended period of good weather may lead you to worry that it is certain to rain on the weekend picnic.

Although all of us sometimes fall into embarrassingly illogical reasoning in day-to-day life, scientists avoid this pitfall by using systems of logic consciously and explicitly. Chapter 2 will examine the logic(s) of science in more depth. For now, it is sufficient to note that logical reasoning is a conscious activity for scientists, and they always have their colleagues around to keep them honest in that regard as in others.

These, then, are a few of the ways you and I go astray in our attempts to know and understand the world and some of the ways that science protects its inquiries from these pitfalls. Scientific inquiry is more conscious and careful than our casual efforts. In scientific inquiry, we are more wary of making mistakes and take special precautions to avoid error.

I hope the preceding comments make it clear that the observation and understanding of reality is not an obvious or trivial matter. Indeed, it's more complicated than have I suggested so far.

What's Really Real?

Philosophers sometimes use the phrase "naive realism" to describe the way most of us operate in our daily lives. When you sit at a table to write, you probably don't spend a lot of time thinking about whether the table is really made up of atoms, which in turn are mostly empty space. When you step into the street and see a city bus hurtling down on you, it's not the best time to reflect on methods for testing whether the bus really exists. We all live with a view that what's real is pretty obvious—and that view usually gets us through the day.

I don't want this book to interfere with your ability to deal with everyday life. I hope, however, that the preceding discussions have demonstrated that the nature of "reality" is perhaps more complex than we tend to assume in our everyday functioning. Here are three views on reality that will provide a philosophical backdrop for the discussions of science to follow. Let's look at what are sometimes called *premodern, modern,* and *postmodern* views of reality (Anderson 1990).

The Premodern View This view of reality has guided most of human history. Our early ancestors all assumed that they saw things as they really were. In fact, this assumption was so fundamental that they didn't even see it as an assumption. No cavemom said to her cavekid, "Our tribe makes an assumption that evil spirits reside in the Old Twisted Tree." No, she said, "STAY OUT OF THAT TREE OR YOU'LL TURN INTO A TOAD!"

As humans evolved and became aware of their diversity, they came to recognize that others did not always share their views of things. Thus, they may have discovered that another tribe didn't buy the wicked tree thing; in fact, the second tribe felt the spirits in the tree were holy and beneficial. The discovery of this diversity led members of the first tribe to conclude that "some tribes I could name are pretty stupid." For them, the tree was still wicked, and they expected some misguided people were going to be moving to Toad City.

The Modern View What philosophers call the *modern* view accepts such diversity as legitimate, a philosophical "different strokes for different folks." As a modern thinker, you would say, "I regard the spirits in the tree as evil, but I know others regard them as good. Neither of us is right or wrong. There are simply spirits in the tree. They are neither good nor evil, but different people have different ideas about them."

It's probably pretty easy for you to adopt the modern view. Some might regard a dandelion as a beautiful flower while others only see an

FIGURE 1-1
A Book

A.
B.
C.
D.

FIGURE 1-2
Wife's Point of View

annoying weed. To the premoderns, a dandelion has to be either one or the other. If you think it is a weed, it is *really* a weed, though you may admit that some people have a warped sense of beauty. In the modern view, a dandelion is simply a dandelion. It is a plant with yellow petals and green leaves. The concepts "beautiful flower" and "annoying weed" are subjective points of view imposed on the plant by different people. Neither is a quality of the plant itself, just as "good" and

FIGURE 1-3
Husband's Point of View

"evil" were concepts imposed on the spirits in the tree.

The Postmodern View Increasingly, philosophers speak of a *postmodern* view of reality. In this view, the spirits don't exist. Neither does the dandelion. All that's "real" are the images we get through our points of view. Put differently, there's nothing *out there*, it's all *in here*. As Gertrude Stein said of Oakland, "There's no there, there."

No matter how bizarre the postmodern view may seem to you on first reflection, it has a certain ironic inevitability. Take a moment to notice the book you are reading; notice specifically what it looks like. Since you are reading these words, it probably looks something like Figure 1-1A.

But does Figure 1-1A represent the way your book "really" looks? Or does it merely represent what the book looks like from your current point of view? Surely, Figures 1-1B, C, and D are equally valid representations. But these views of the book are so different from one another. Which is the "reality"?

As this example should illustrate, there is no answer to the question, "What does the book *really* look like?" All we can offer is the different ways it looks from different points of view. Thus, according to the postmodern view, there is no "book," only various images of it from different points of view. And all the different images are equally "true."

Now let's apply this logic to a social situation. Imagine a husband and wife arguing. When she looks over at her quarreling husband, Figure 1-2 is what the wife sees. Take a minute to imagine what you would feel and think if you were the woman in this drawing. How would you explain later to an outsider, to your best friend, what had happened? What solutions to the conflict would seem appropriate if you were this woman? Perhaps you have been in similar situations, and your memories of those events can help you answer these questions.

Now let's shift gears dramatically. What the woman's husband sees is another matter altogether, as shown in Figure 1-3.

Take a minute to imagine experiencing the situation from his point of view. What thoughts and feelings would you have? How would you tell your best friend what had happened? What solutions would seem appropriate for resolving the conflict?

Now, consider a third point of view. Suppose you are an outside observer, watching this interaction between a wife and husband. What would it look like to you now? Unfortunately, we can't easily portray the third point of view without knowing something about the personal feelings, beliefs, past experiences, and so forth that you would bring to your task as "outside" observer. (Though I call you an *outside* observer, you are, of course, observing from *inside* your own mental system.)

To take an extreme example, if you were a confirmed male chauvinist, you'd probably see the fight pretty much the same way that the husband saw it. Or, on the other hand, if you were committed to the view that men are generally unreasonable bums, you'd see things the way the wife saw them in the earlier picture.

But consider this. Imagine that you look at this situation and see two unreasonable people, quarreling irrationally with one another. Can you get the feeling that they are equally responsible for the conflict?

Or, imagine that you see two people facing a difficult human situation, each doing the best he or she could to resolve it. Imagine feeling compassion for them and noticing how each of them attempts to end the hostility, even though the gravity of the problem keeps them fighting.

Notice how different these last two views are. Which is a "true" picture of what is happening between the wife and the husband? You win the prize if you notice that the personal baggage you brought along to the observational task would again color your perception of what is happening here.

The postmodern view represents a critical dilemma for scientists. While their task is to observe and understand what is "really" happening, they are all human and, as such, bring along personal orientations that will color what they observe and how they explain it. There is ultimately no way people can totally step outside their humanness to see and understand the world as it "really" is.

Whereas the modern view acknowledges the inevitability of human subjectivity, the postmodern view suggests there is actually no "objective" reality to be observed in the first place. There are only our several subjective views.

I am going to let you ponder these views on your own for awhile. We'll return to this discussion in Chapter 2 when we focus in on more specific scientific paradigms. In particular, we'll trace the progress of social scientific thinking from *positivism* to *post-positivism*.

What you will see, ultimately, is that (1) established scientific procedures sometimes allow you to deal effectively with this dilemma—that is, you can study people and help them through their difficulties without being able to view "reality" directly—and (2) the philosophical stances I've presented suggest a powerful range of possibilities for structuring your research.

Let's turn now to the foundations of the social scientific approaches to understanding. Then we'll be able to go on to the specific research techniques social scientists use.

■ THE FOUNDATIONS OF SOCIAL SCIENCE

Science is sometimes characterized as *logico-empirical*. This ugly term carries an important message: The two pillars of science are logic and observation. A scientific understanding of the world must (1) make sense and (2) correspond with what we observe. Both elements are essential to science and relate to three major aspects of the overall scientific enterprise: *theory, data collection,* and *data analysis*.

As a gross generalization, scientific theory deals with the logical aspect of science, data collection deals with the observational aspect, and data analysis looks for patterns in what is observed and, where appropriate, compares what is logically expected with what is actually observed. Though most of this textbook deals primarily with data collection and data analysis—demonstrating how to conduct empirical research—you must recognize that social *science* involves all three elements. As such, Chapters 2 and 3 of this book deal with the theoretical context of research; Parts 2 and 3 focus on data collection; Part 4 offers an introduction to the analysis of data; and Chapter 19 brings it all together once more. Figure 1-4 offers a schematic view of how the book addresses these three aspects of social science.

Let's turn now to some of the fundamental issues that distinguish social science—theory, data collection, and analysis—from other ways of looking at social phenomena.

Theory, Not Philosophy or Belief

Social scientific theory has to do with what *is*, not with what *should be*. I point this out at the start because social theory for many centuries has combined these two orientations. Social philosophers mixed liberally their observations of what happened around them, their speculations about why, and their ideas about how things ought to be. Although modern social scientists may do the same from time to time, it is important to realize that social *science* has to do with how things are and why.

This means that scientific theory—and, more broadly, science itself—cannot settle debates on value. Science cannot determine whether capitalism is better or worse than socialism except in terms of some set of agreed-on criteria. We could only determine scientifically whether capitalism or socialism most supported human dignity and freedom if we could agree on some definition of dignity and freedom; our conclusion in that case would depend totally on this agreement. The conclusions would have no general meaning beyond that.

By the same token, if we could agree that suicide rates, say, or giving to charity were good measures of a religion's quality, then we could determine scientifically whether Buddhism or Christianity is the better religion. Again, our conclusion would be inextricably tied to the given criterion. As a practical matter, people seldom agree on criteria for determining issues of value, so science is seldom useful in settling such debates.

We'll consider this issue in more detail in Chapter 13, when we look at *evaluation research*. As you'll see, social scientists have become increasingly involved in studying programs that reflect ideological points of view, so that one of the biggest problems faced by researchers is getting people to agree on criteria of success and failure. Yet, such criteria are essential if social scientific research is to tell us anything useful about matters of value. By analogy, a stopwatch cannot tell us if one sprinter is better than another unless we can agree that speed is the critical criterion.

Thus, social science can help us know only what is and why. We can use it to determine what ought to be only when people agree on the criteria for deciding what's better than something else. Furthermore, this agreement seldom occurs. With that understood, let's turn now to some of the fundamental bases on which social science allows us to develop theories about what is and why.

Social Regularities

In large part, social scientific theory aims to find patterns of regularity in social life. That aim, of course, applies to all science, but it is sometimes a barrier for people when they first approach *social* science.

Certainly at first glance the subject matter of the physical sciences seems more regular than that of the social sciences. A heavy object, after all, falls to earth every time we drop it, but a person may vote for a particular candidate in one election and against that same candidate in the next. Similarly, ice *always* melts when heated enough, but habitually honest people sometimes steal. Although true, such examples can lead us to lose sight of the high degree of regularity in social affairs.

To begin, a vast number of formal norms in society create a considerable degree of regularity. For example, only people who have reached a certain age can vote in elections. In the U.S. military, until recently only men could participate in combat. Such formal prescriptions, then, regulate, or regularize, social behavior.

Aside from formal prescriptions, we can observe other social norms that create more regularities. Registered Republicans are more likely to vote for Republican candidates than are registered Democrats. University professors tend to

FIGURE 1-4
Social Science = Theory + Data Collection + Data Analysis

THEORY

Religious affiliation
Prejudice
Education
Voting behavior
Social class

Chapters 2–3

DATA COLLECTION

Planning to do research	Sampling	Observation	Data processing
Chapters 4–7	Chapter 8	Chapters 9–13	Chapter 14

DATA ANALYSIS

$Y = a + x_1 + x_2 + x_3 + x_4 + e$

	x	$\bar{x}$
y	34%	78%
$\bar{y}$	66%	22%

Part 4

earn more money than unskilled laborers. Men earn more than women. The list of regularities could go on and on.

Three objections are sometimes raised in regard to such social regularities. First, some of the regularities may seem trivial: So Republicans vote for Republicans; everyone knew that. Second, contradictory cases may be cited, indicating that the "regularity" isn't totally regular anyway. Some laborers make more money than some professors. And third, it may be argued that the people involved in the regularity could upset the whole thing if they wanted to.

Let's handle the business of triviality first, those things that "everybody knows."

The Charge of Triviality During World War II, Samuel Stouffer, one of the greatest social science researchers, organized a research branch in the U.S. Army to conduct studies in support of the war effort (Stouffer 1949, 1950). Many of the studies concerned the morale among soldiers. Stouffer and his colleagues found there was a great deal of "common wisdom" regarding the bases of military morale. Much of their research was devoted to testing the "obvious."

For example, it had been recognized for a long time that promotions affect morale in the military. When people get promotions and the promotion system seems fair, morale rises. Moreover, it makes sense that people who are getting promoted will tend to think the system is fair, whereas those passed over will likely think the system is unfair. By extension, it seems sensible that soldiers in units with slow promotion rates will tend to think the system is unfair, and those in units with rapid promotions will think the system is fair. Was this the way they really felt though?

Stouffer and his colleagues focused their studies on two units: the Military Police (MPs), which had the slowest promotions in the Army, and the Army Air Corps (forerunner of the U.S. Air Force), which had the fastest promotions. It stood to reason that MPs would say the promotion system was unfair, and the air corpsmen would say it was fair. The studies, however, showed just the opposite.

Notice the dilemma faced by a researcher in a situation such as this. On the one hand, the observations don't make any sense. On the other hand, an explanation that makes obvious good sense isn't supported by the facts.

A lesser person would have set the problem aside "for further study." Stouffer, however, looked for an explanation for this observation, and eventually he found it. Robert Merton and some other sociologists at Columbia University had begun thinking and writing about something they called *reference group theory*. This theory says that people judge their lot in life less by objective conditions than by comparing themselves with others around them—their reference group. For example, if you lived among poor people, a salary of $50,000 a year would make you feel like a millionaire. But if you lived among people who earned $500,000 a year, "only" $50,000 would make you feel impoverished.

Stouffer applied this line of reasoning to the soldiers he had studied. Even if a particular MP had not been promoted for a long time, it was unlikely he knew some less deserving person who had gotten promoted faster. Nobody got promoted in the MPs. Had he been in the Air Corps—even if he had gotten several promotions in rapid succession—he would probably be able to point to someone less deserving who had gotten even faster promotions. An MP's reference group, then, was his fellow MPs, and the air corpsman compared himself with fellow corpsmen. Ultimately, then, Stouffer reached an understanding of soldiers' attitudes toward the promotion system that (1) made sense and (2) corresponded to the facts.

This story shows that documenting the obvious is a valuable function of any science, physical or social. All too often, the obvious turns out to be wrong; thus, apparent triviality is not a legitimate objection to any scientific endeavor. (Darwin coined the phrase *fool's experiment* in ironic reference to much of his own research—research in which he tested things that everyone else already knew.)

What about Exceptions? The objection that there are always exceptions to any social regularity is also inappropriate. It is not important that a particular woman earns more money than a particular man if men earn more than women overall. The pattern still exists. Social regularities represent probabilistic patterns, and a general pattern need not be reflected in 100 percent of the observable cases.

This rule applies in physical science as well as social science. In genetics, for example, the mating of a blue-eyed person with a brown-eyed person will *probably* result in a brown-eyed offspring. The birth of a blue-eyed child does not challenge the observed regularity, however, since the geneticist states only that the brown-eyed offspring is more likely and, further, that brown-eyed offspring will be born in a certain percentage of the cases. The social scientist makes a similar, probabilistic prediction—that women overall are likely to earn less than men. And the social scientist has grounds for asking why that is the case.

People Could Interfere Finally, the objection that observed social regularities could be upset through the conscious will of the actors is not a serious challenge to social science, even though there does not seem to be a parallel situation in the physical sciences. (Presumably an object cannot resist falling to earth "because it wants to.") There is no denying that a religious, right-wing bigot could go to the polls and vote for an agnostic, left-wing radical African American if he or she wanted to upset the political scientist studying the election. All voters in an election could suddenly switch to the underdog just to frustrate the pollster. Similarly, workers could go to work early or stay home from work and thereby prevent the expected rush-hour traffic. But these things do not happen often enough to threaten seriously the observation of social regularities.

The facts remain that social norms do exist and that the social scientist can observe their effects. When norms change over time, the social scientist can observe and explain those changes. Ultimately, social regularities persist because they tend to make sense for the people they affect. When the social scientist suggests that it is logical to expect a given type of person to behave in a certain manner, that type of person may very well agree with the logical basis for the expectation. Thus, although a religious, right-wing bigot could vote for an agnostic, left-wing radical African American, such a voter would be the first to consider it foolish to do so.

Aggregates, Not Individuals

Social regularities do exist, then; further, they are both susceptible to and worthy of theoretical and empirical study. As such, social scientists primarily study social patterns rather than individual ones. All the regular patterns I've mentioned have reflected the *aggregate* or collective actions and situations of many individuals. Although social scientists often study motivations that affect individuals, the individual per se is seldom the subject of social science. We create theories about the nature of group, rather than individual, life.

Sometimes the collective regularities are amazing. Consider the birthrate, for example. People have babies for an incredibly wide range of personal reasons. Some do it because their own parents want them to. Some feel it's a way of completing their womanhood or manhood. Others want to hold their marriages together. Still others have babies by accident.

If you have had a baby, you could probably tell a much more detailed, idiosyncratic story. Why did you have the baby when you did, rather than a year earlier or later? Maybe your house burned down and you had to delay a year before you could afford to have the baby. Maybe you felt that being a family person would demonstrate maturity, which would support a promotion at work.

Everyone who had a baby last year had a different set of reasons for doing so. Yet, despite this vast diversity, despite the idiosyncrasy of each individual's reasons, the overall birthrate in a society (the number of live births per 1,000 population) is remarkably consistent from year to year. Here are some recent birthrates for the United States.

1980	16
1985	16
1990	17
1995	15
1996	15

Source: U.S. Bureau of the Census, *Statistical Abstract of the United States*, 1995, CD-ROM, CD-SA-95, Table No. 89 and Population Reference Bureau, *World Population Data Sheet*, 1995 and 1996.

If the U.S. birthrate were 15.9, 35.6, 7.8, 28.9, and 16.2 in five successive years, demographers would begin dropping like flies.

Social scientific theories deal then, typically, with aggregated, not individual, behavior. Their purpose is to explain why aggregated patterns of behavior are so regular even when the individuals participating in them may change over time. It could be said that social scientists don't even seek to explain *people*. They try to understand the *systems* in which people operate, the systems that explain why people do what they do. The elements in such a system are not people but *variables*.

A Variable Language

Our most natural attempts at understanding usually take place at the level of the concrete and idiosyncratic. That's just the way we think.

Imagine that someone says to you, "Women ought to get back into the kitchen where they belong." You are likely to hear that comment in terms of what you know about the speaker. If it's your old uncle Harry who, you recall, is also strongly opposed to daylight saving time, zip codes, and electricity, you are likely to think his latest pronouncement simply fits into his rather dated point of view about things in general.

If, on the other hand, the statement issues forth from a politician who is trailing a female challenger and who has also begun making statements about women being emotionally unfit for public office, not understanding politics, and the like, you may hear his latest comment in the context of this political challenge.

In both examples, you're trying to understand the thoughts of a particular individual. In social science, however, researchers go beyond that level of understanding to seek insights into classes or types of individuals. Regarding the two examples just described, they might use terms such as "old-fashioned" or "bigot" to describe the kind of person who made the comment. In other words, they try to identify the concrete individual with some set of similar individuals, and that identification operates on the basis of abstract concepts.

One implication of this approach is that when this venture into understanding and explanation ends, social scientists will be able to make sense out of more than one person. In understanding what makes the bigoted politician think the way he does, then, they'll also learn about other people who are "like him." This is possible because, in an important sense, they have not been studying bigots as much as we have been studying *bigotry*. They observe bigots because that is the best place to find bigotry.

Bigotry is spoken of as a *variable* because it varies. Some people are more bigoted than others. Social scientists are interested in understanding the system of variables that causes bigotry to be high in one instance and low in another.

Because the idea of a system composed of variables may be foreign to you, here's another analogy to demonstrate what I mean. The subject of a physician's attention is the patient. If the patient is ill, the physician's purpose is to help that patient get well. By contrast, a medical researcher's subject matter is different: a disease, for example. The medical researcher may study the physician's patient, but for the researcher that patient is relevant only as a *carrier* of the disease.

That is not to say that medical researchers don't care about real people. They certainly do. Their ultimate purpose in studying diseases is to protect people from them. But in their actual research, patients are directly relevant only for what they reveal about the disease under study. In fact, when they can study a disease meaningfully without involving actual patients, medical researchers do so.

Social science involves the study of variables and the attributes that compose them. Social scientific theories are written in a language of variables, and people get involved only as the carriers of those variables. Here's a closer look at what social scientists mean by variables and attributes.

Attributes or values are characteristics or qualities that describe an object—in this case, a person. Examples include *female, Asian, alienated, conservative, dishonest, intelligent,* and *farmer.* Anything you might say to describe yourself or someone else involves an attribute.

Variables, on the other hand, are logical groupings of attributes. Thus, for example, *male* and *female* are attributes, and *sex* or *gender* are the variables composed of those two attributes. The variable *occupation* is composed of attributes such

FIGURE 1-5
Variables and Attributes

A.

Some Common Social Concepts
Female Young Gender Upper class Asian Religion Plumber Race/ethnicity Middle-aged Male Occupation Social class

B.

Two Different Kinds of Concepts	
Variables	Attributes
Gender	Female Young
Religion	Upper class Asian
Race/ethnicity	Plumber
Occupation Social class	Middle-aged Male

C.

The Relationship between Variables and Attributes	
Variables	Attributes
Gender	Female, male
Age	Young, middle-aged, old . . .
Race/ethnicity	Caucasian, African American, Asian, Latino(a) . . .
Social class	Lower class, middle class, upper class. . .
Occupation	Plumber, carpenter, sociologist, lawyer. . .

as *farmer, professor,* and *truck driver. Social class* is a variable composed of a set of attributes such as *upper class, middle class,* and *lower class.* Sometimes it helps to think of attributes as the "categories" that make up a variable. (See Figure 1-5 for a schematic review of what social scientists mean by variables and attributes.)

The relationship between attributes and variables lies at the heart of both description and explanation in science. For example, we might describe a college class in terms of the variable *gender* by reporting the observed frequencies of the attributes *male* and *female:* "The class is 60 percent men and 40 percent women." An unemployment rate can be thought of as a description of the variable *employment status* of a labor force in terms of the attributes *employed* and *unemployed.* Even the report of family income for a city is a summary of attributes composing that variable: $3,124; $10,980; $35,000; and so forth.

Sometimes the meanings of the concepts that lie behind social science concepts are pretty clear. Other times they aren't. This is discussed in the box "The Hardest Hit Was . . ."

The relationship between attributes and variables is more complicated in the case of *explanation* and gets to the heart of the variable language of scientific theory. Here's a simple example, in-

The Hardest Hit Was...

In early 1982, a deadly storm ravaged the San Francisco Bay Area, leaving an aftermath of death, injury, and property damage. As the mass media sought to highlight the most tragic results of the storm, they sometimes focused on several people who were buried alive in a mud slide in Santa Cruz. Other times, they covered the plight of the 2,900 made homeless in Marin County.

Implicitly, everyone wanted to know where the worst damage was done, but the answer was not clear. Here are some data describing the results of the storm in two counties: Marin and Santa Cruz. Look over the comparisons and see if you can determine which county was "hardest hit."

	Marin	Santa Cruz
Businesses destroyed	$15.0 million	$56.5 million
People killed	5	22
People injured	379	50
People displaced	370	400
Homes destroyed	28	135
Homes damaged	2,900	300
Businesses destroyed	25	10
Businesses damaged	800	35
Private damages	$65.1 million	$50.0 million
Public damages	$15.0 million	$56.5 million

Certainly, in terms of the loss of life, Santa Cruz was the "hardest hit" of the two counties. Yet more than seven times as many people were injured in Marin as in Santa Cruz; certainly, Marin County was "hardest hit" in that regard. Or consider the number of homes destroyed (worse in Santa Cruz) or damaged (worse in Marin): It matters which you focus on. The same dilemma holds true for the value of the damage done: Should we pay more attention to private damage or public damage?

So which county was "hardest hit"? Ultimately, the question as posed has no answer. While you and I both have images in our minds about communities that are "devastated" or communities that are only "lightly touched," these images are not precise enough to permit rigorous measurements.

The question can be answered only if we can specify what we mean by "hardest hit." If we measure it by death toll, then Santa Cruz was the hardest hit. If we choose to define the variable in terms of people injured and/or displaced, then Marin was the bigger disaster. The simple fact is that we cannot answer the question without specifying exactly what we mean by the term *hardest hit*. This is a fundamental requirement that will arise again and again as we attempt to measure social science variables.

Data source: San Francisco Chronicle, January 13, 1982, p. 16.

---

volving two variables, *education* and *prejudice*. For the sake of simplicity, let's assume that the variable *education* has only two attributes: *educated* and *uneducated*. (Chapters 5 and 6 will address the issue of how such things are defined and measured.) Similarly, let's give the variable *prejudice* two attributes: *prejudiced* and *unprejudiced*.

Now let's suppose that 90 percent of the uneducated are prejudiced, and the other 10 percent are unprejudiced. And let's suppose that 30 percent of the educated people are prejudiced, and the other 70 percent are unprejudiced. This is illustrated graphically in Figure 1-6A.

Figure 1-6A illustrates a *relationship* or *association* between the variables *education* and *prejudice*. This relationship can be seen in terms of the pairings of attributes on the two variables. There are two predominant pairings: (1) those who are educated and unprejudiced and (2) those who are uneducated and prejudiced. Here are two other useful ways of viewing that relationship.

First, let's suppose that we play a game in which we bet on your ability to guess whether a person is prejudiced or unprejudiced. I'll pick the people one at a time (not telling you which ones I've picked), and you have to guess whether each

FIGURE 1-6
Illustration of Relationship between Two Variables (Two Possibilities)

A. The uneducated are more prejudiced than the educated.

B. There is no apparent relationship between education and prejudice.

person is prejudiced. We'll do it for all 20 people in Figure 1-6A. Your best strategy in this case would be to guess *prejudiced* each time, since 12 out of the 20 are categorized that way. Thus, you'll get 12 right and 8 wrong, for a net success of 4.

Now let's suppose that when I pick a person from the figure, I have to tell you whether the person is educated or uneducated. Your best strategy now would be to guess *prejudiced* for each uneducated person and *unprejudiced* for each educated person. If you followed that strategy, you'd get 16 right and 4 wrong. Your improvement in guessing prejudice by knowing education is an illustration of what I mean by the variables being related. (This procedure, by the way, provides the basis for the statistical calculation *lambda*, to be discussed in Chapter 17.)

Second, by contrast, let's consider how the 20 people would be distributed if education and prejudice were *unrelated* to one another. This is illustrated in Figure 1-6B. Notice that half the people are educated, and half are uneducated. Also notice that 12 of the 20 (60 percent) are prejudiced. If 6 of the 10 people in each group were prejudiced, we would conclude that the two variables were unrelated to each other. Then knowing a person's education would not be of any value to you in guessing whether that person was prejudiced.

You'll be looking at the nature of relationships between variables in some depth in Part 4 of this book. In particular, you'll see some of the ways relationships can be discovered and interpreted in research analysis. You need a general understanding of relationships now, however, to appreciate the logic of social scientific theories.

Theories describe the relationships we might logically expect among variables. Often, the expectation involves the idea of *causation*. A person's attributes on one variable are expected to cause, predispose, or encourage a particular attribute on another variable. In the example just illustrated, it appeared that a person's being educated or uneducated caused that person to be unprejudiced or prejudiced, respectively. It seems that there is something about being educated that leads people to be less prejudiced than if they are uneducated.

As I'll discuss in more detail later in the book, education and prejudice in this example would be regarded as independent and dependent variables, respectively. These two concepts are implicit in deterministic, causal models (see Chapter 3). In this example, we assume that levels of prejudice are determined or caused by something; prejudice depends on something, hence it is called the dependent variable, which depends on an independent variable, in this case on education. Although the educational levels of the people being studied vary, that variation is independent of prejudice.

Notice, at the same time, that educational variations can be found to depend on something else—such as our subjects' parents' educational levels. People whose parents have a lot of education are more likely to get a lot of education than those whose parents have little education. In this relationship, the subject's education is the dependent variable, the parents' education the independent variable. We can say the independent variable is the cause, the dependent variable the effect.

Returning to our first example, the discussion of Figure 1-6 has involved the interpretation of data. We looked at the distribution of the 20 people in terms of the two variables. In constructing a social scientific theory, we would derive an expectation regarding the relationship between the two variables based on what we know about each. We know, for example, that education exposes people to a wide range of cultural variation and to diverse points of view—in short, it broadens their perspectives. Prejudice, on the other hand, represents a narrower perspective. Logically, then, we would expect that education and prejudice would be somewhat incompatible. We might arrive at an expectation, therefore, that increasing education would reduce prejudice, an expectation that would be supported by the observations to be made later.

Whereas Figure 1-6 illustrates two possibilities—(A) that education reduces prejudice or (B) that it has no effect—you might be interested in knowing what's actually the case. As one measure of prejudice, the 1996 General Social Survey asked a national sample of adults in the United States how they felt about the opinion, "White people have a right to keep Blacks out of their neighborhoods if they want to and Blacks should respect that right." Only 6 percent of the sample agreed strongly with the statement, with another 5 percent agreeing slightly. The majority—71 percent—strongly disagreed.

Table 1-1 presents an analysis of those data, grouping respondents according to their levels of educational attainment.

The easiest way to read this table is to focus on the last line of percentages: those disagreeing strongly with the statement. Strong opposition to segregation increases steadily from 62 percent among those who hadn't completed high school to 85 percent among college graduates. This clearly supports the view that education reduces prejudice.

Notice that the theory has to do with the two variables education and prejudice, not with people per se. People are, as I indicated before, the carriers of those two variables, so the relationship

TABLE 1-1
Education and Support for Segregation

	Educational Level of Respondents			
	Less than HS Graduate	HS Graduate	Some College	College Graduate
Agree strongly	10%	7%	6%	1%
Agree slightly	8	5	5	4
Disagree slightly	19	26	18	10
Disagree strongly	62	62	70	85
	100% = (98)	(189)	(190)	(193)

between the variables can only be seen when we observe people. Ultimately, however, the theory uses a language of variables. It describes the associations that we might logically expect to exist between particular attributes of different variables.

■ SOME DIALECTICS OF SOCIAL RESEARCH

There is no one way to do social research. (If there were, this would be a much shorter book.) In fact, much of the power and potential of social research lies in the many valid approaches it comprises.

Three broad and interrelated distinctions, however, underlie these approaches. Though these distinctions can be seen as competing choices, a good social researcher masters each of the orientations I am about to describe.

Idiographic and Nomothetic Explanation

All of us go through life explaining things. We do it every day. You explain why you did poorly or well on an exam, why your favorite team is winning or losing, why you may be having trouble getting dates you enjoy. In our everyday explanations, we engage in two distinct forms of causal reasoning, though we do not ordinarily distinguish them.

Sometimes we attempt to explain a single situation exhaustively. Thus, for example, you may have done poorly on an exam because (1) you had forgotten there was an exam that day, (2) it was in your worst subject, (3) a traffic jam made you late for class, (4) your roommate had kept you up the night before the exam with loud music in your dorm room, (5) the police kept you up until dawn demanding to know what you had done with your roommate's stereo—and what you had done with your roommate for that matter—and (6) a wild band of coyotes ate your textbook. Given all these circumstances, it is no wonder that you did poorly.

This type of causal reasoning is called an **idiographic** explanation. *Idio-* in this context means unique, separate, peculiar, or distinct, as in the word *idiosyncracy*. When we have completed an idiographic explanation, we feel that we fully understand the causes of what happened in this particular instance. At the same time, the scope of our explanation is limited to the case at hand. While parts of the idiographic explanation might apply to other situations, our intention is to explain one case fully.

Now consider a different kind of explanation. (1) Every time you study with a group, you do better on the exam than if you study alone. (2) Your favorite team does better at home than on the road. (3) Athletes get more dates than members of the biology club. This type of explanation—labelled **nomothethic**—seeks to explain a class of situations or events rather than a single one. Moreover, it seeks to explain "economically," using only one or just a few explanatory factors. Finally, it settles for a partial rather than a full explanation.

In each of these examples, you might qualify your causal statements with such words or phrases as "on the whole," "usually," or "all else being equal." Thus, you usually do better on exams when you've studied in a group, but not always. Similarly, your team has won some games on the road and lost some at home. And the wealthy head of the biology club may get lots of dates, while the defensive lineman Pigpen-the-Terminator may spend a lot of Saturday nights alone punching heavy farm equipment. Such exceptions are an acceptable price to pay for a broader range of overall explanation.

Both the idiographic and the nomothetic approaches to understanding can be useful to you in your daily life. The nomothethic patterns you discover might offer a good guide for planning your study habits, but the idiographic explanation is more convincing for your parents or parole officer.

By the same token, both idiographic and nomothetic reasoning are powerful tools for social research. The researcher who seeks an exhaustive understanding of the inner workings of a particular juvenile gang or the corporate leadership of a particular multinational conglomerate engages in idiographic research: She or he tries to understand that particular group as fully as possible.

Thus, in undertaking an in-depth analysis of class consciousness among Local 10 of San Francisco's Longshoremen's and Warehousemen's Union (ILWU), David Wellman (1995) recognized that this particular union did not typify the U.S. labor movement. While Wellman was interested in gaining insights into labor unionism generally and into the nature of capitalism, his immediate goal was to understand the history of Local 10 fully.

Sometimes, however, researchers aim at a more generalized understanding across a class of events, even though the level of understanding is inevitably more superficial. For example, those who seek to uncover the chief factors leading to juvenile delinquency are pursuing a nomothetic inquiry. They might discover, for example, that children from broken homes were more likely to be delinquent than those from intact families. Though this explanation would extend well beyond any single child, it would do so at the expense of a complete explanation.

In contrast to the Wellman study of Local 10, Susan Tiano (1994) sought to understand the overall impact of Third-World industrialization on the status of women. Does their movement into the industrial labor force signify liberation or oppression? Her survey of women factory workers in Mexico illustrates the nomothetic approach to understanding.

As you can see then, social scientists can access two distinct kinds of explanation. Just as the physicists sometimes treat light as a particle and other times as a wave, so social scientists can search for relatively superficial universals today and probe the narrowly particular tomorrow. Both are good science, both are rewarding, and both can be fun.

Inductive and Deductive Theory

Though I'll have more to say about inductive and deductive theory in Chapter 2, I want to introduce you to the distinction here. Again, these ways of thinking exist in your daily life, and they represent an important variation in social research.

There are two routes to the conclusion that you do better on exams if you study with others. On the one hand, you might find yourself puzzling, halfway through your college career, why you do so well on exams sometimes but poorly at other times. You might list all the exams you've taken, noting how well you did on each. Then you might try to recall any circumstances shared by all the good exams and by all the poor ones. Did you do better on multiple-choice exams or essay exams? Morning exams or afternoon exams? Exams in the natural sciences, the humanities, or the social sciences? Times when you studied alone or . . . SHAZAM! It occurs to you that you have almost always done best on exams when you studied with others. This mode of inquiry is known as **induction**.

Inductive reasoning moves from the particular to the general, from a set of specific observations to the discovery of a pattern that represents some degree of order among all the given events. Notice, incidentally, that your discovery doesn't necessarily tell you why the pattern exists—just that it does.

Here's a very different way you might have arrived at the same conclusion about studying for exams. Imagine approaching your first set of exams in college. You wonder about the best ways to study—how much you should review the readings, how much you should focus on your class notes. You learn that some students prepare by rewriting their notes in an orderly fashion.

Then you consider if you should study at a measured pace or else pull an all-nighter just before the exam. Among these kinds of musings, you might ask whether you should get together with other students in the class or just study on your own. You could evaluate the pros and cons of both options.

Studying with others might not be as efficient, because a lot of time might be spent on things you already understand. On the other hand, you can understand something even better when you've explained it to someone else. And other students might understand parts of the course that you haven't gotten yet. Several minds can reveal perspectives that might have escaped you. Also, making a commitment to study with others makes it more likely that you'll study rather than deciding to watch the special *Brady Bunch* retrospective.

In this fashion, you might add up the pros and the cons and conclude, logically, that you'd benefit from studying with others. It seems reasonable to you, the way it seems reasonable that you'll do better if you study rather than not. Sometimes, we say things like this are true "in theory." To complete the process, we test whether they are true in practice. For a complete test, you might study alone for half your exams and study with others for the other exams. This procedure would test your logical reasoning. This second mode of inquiry is known as **deduction**.

Deductive reasoning moves from the general to the specific. It moves from (1) a pattern that might be logically or theoretically expected to (2) observations that test whether the expected pattern actually occurs. Notice that deduction begins with "why" and moves to "whether," while induction moves in the opposite direction.

As you'll see later in this book, these two very different approaches are both valid avenues for science. Moreover, you'll see how they work together to provide ever more powerful and complete understandings.

Notice, by the way, that the deductive/inductive distinction is not necessarily linked to the nomothetic and idiographic modes. They represent four possibilities, in your own life as much as in social research.

For example, idiographically and deductively, you might prepare for a particular date by taking into account everything you know about the person you're dating, trying to anticipate logically how you can prepare—what kinds of garb, behavior, hairstyle, oral hygiene, and so forth are likely to produce a successful date. Or, idiographically and inductively, you might try to figure out what it was exactly that caused your date to call 911.

A nomothetic, deductive approach arises when you coach others on your "rules of dating," when you wisely explain why their dates will be impressed to hear them expound on the dangers of satanic messages concealed in rock and roll lyrics. When you later review your life and wonder why you didn't date more musicians, you might engage in nomothetic induction.

We'll return to induction and deduction later in the book. At this point, let's turn to the third broad distinction generating the rich variations in social research.

Quantitative and Qualitative Data

Most simply put, the distinction between quantitative and qualitative data in social research is the distinction between numerical and nonnumerical data. When you say someone is beautiful, you've made a qualitative assertion. When you say he or she is a "9" on a scale from 1 to 10, you are attempting to quantify your qualitative assessment.

Every observation is qualitative at the outset, whether it be your experience of someone's beauty, the location of a pointer on a measuring scale, or a check mark entered in a questionnaire. None of these things is inherently numerical or quantitative, but sometimes it is useful to *convert* them to a numerical form.

Joel Smith (1991:3) describes the distinction between qualitative and quantitative data in terms of uniqueness and categorization:

■ No one seriously argues that events or groups or people are not unique in at least some minor detail. Rather, the issue is whether objects share attributes so important *for one's concerns* that their unique features can be ignored. The real issue is whether we can categorize. After all, categorizing permits grouping, grouping permits case enumeration, and counts are intrinsically quantitative.

Quantification often makes our observations more explicit. It also can make it easier to aggregate and summarize data. Further, it opens up the possibility of statistical analyses, ranging from simple averages to complex formulas and mathematical models.

Thus a social researcher might ask whether you tend to date people older or younger than yourself. A quantitative answer to this seems easily attained. The researcher asks how old each of your dates has been, calculates an average, and sees whether it's older or younger than you. Case closed.

Or is it? While "age" here represents the number of years people have been alive, sometimes people use the term differently; perhaps for some "age" really means "maturity." Though your dates may tend to be a little older than you, they may act more immature and thus represent the same "age." Or someone might see "age" as how young or old your dates look or maybe the degree of variation in their life experiences, their worldliness. These latter meanings would be lost in the quantitative calculation of average age.

In addition to greater detail, qualitative data seem richer in meaning than quantified data. This is implicit in the cliché, "He is older than his years." The somewhat poetic meaning of this expression would be lost in attempts to specify *how much* older.

The richness of meaning I've mentioned is partly a function of ambiguity. If the expression meant something to you when you read it, that meaning arises from your own experiences, from people you have known who might fit the description of being "older than their years" or perhaps the times you have heard others use that expression. Two things are certain: (1) You and I probably don't mean exactly the same thing, and (2) you don't know exactly what I meant.

I have a young friend, Ray Zhang, who was responsible for communications at the 1989 freedom demonstrations in Tiananmen Square, Beijing. Following the Army clampdown, Ray fled south, was arrested and then released with orders to return to Beijing. Instead, he escaped from China and made his way to Paris. Eventually, he came to the United States, where he resumed the graduate studies he had been forced to abandon in fleeing his homeland. I have seen him deal with the difficulties of getting enrolled in school without any transcripts from China, studying in a foreign language, meeting his financial needs—all on his own, thousands of miles from his family. Ray still speaks of one day returning to China to build a system of democracy.

Ray strikes me as someone "older than his years." You'll probably agree. This qualitative description, while it fleshes out the meaning of the phrase, still does not equip us to say *how much older* or even to compare two people in these terms without the risk of disagreeing as to which one is more "worldly."

It might be possible to quantify this concept, however. For example, we might establish a list of life experiences that would contribute to what we mean by *worldliness:*

Getting married
Getting divorced
Having a parent die
Seeing a murder committed
Being arrested
Being exiled
Being fired from a job
Running away with the circus, and so forth

We might quantify people's worldliness as the number of such experiences they've had: the more such experiences, the more worldly we'd say they were. If we thought of some experiences as more powerful than others, we could give those experiences more points. Once we had made our list and point system, scoring people and comparing their worldliness would be pretty straightforward. We would have no difficulty agreeing on who had more points than whom.

To quantify a concept like worldliness, we need to be explicit about what we mean. By focusing specifically on what we will include in our measurement of the concept, however, we also exclude any other meanings. Inevitably, then, we face a trade-off: Any explicated, quantitative measure will be more superficial than the corresponding qualitative description.

What a dilemma! Which approach should you choose? Which is better? Which is more appropriate to social research?

The good news is that you don't need to choose. In fact, you shouldn't. Both qualitative and quantitative methods are useful and legitimate in social research; you should master both. You will discover that some research situations and topics are most amenable to qualitative examination, others to quantification.

At the same time, you will find that these two approaches call for different skills and procedures. As a result, you may feel more comfortable and become more adept in one mode than the other. You will be a stronger researcher, however, to the extent that you can master both approaches. At the very least, you should recognize the legitimacy of both.

Finally, you may have noticed that the qualitative approach seems more aligned with idiographic explanations, while nomothetic explanations are more easily achieved through quantification. Though this is true, these relationships are not absolute. Moreover, both approaches present considerable "gray area." Thus, while these terms alert you to and validate different ways of doing social research, you need not identify your activities in such terms.

■ THE ETHICS OF SOCIAL RESEARCH

By devoting most of this book to the logic and skills of doing social research, I hope you will come to understand the various techniques preferred by social researchers, and why they value them. There are, however, some vital nonscientific concerns that shape the activities of social researchers.

Though Chapter 18 of this book deals extensively with research ethics, I would like to introduce you to the topic now. If you keep these ethical considerations in mind as you learn the logic and techniques of social research, you will better understand the discussion in Chapter 18.

No Harm to Subjects

The foremost ethical rule of social research is that it bring *no harm to research subjects*. While social researchers usually do not intend to hurt people, they can cause inadvertent harm if they are not careful. If you revealed damaging information about the people you interview, you would have violated this ethical rule.

Surely no one would disagree with this rule in principle. You will see, however, that it is sometimes difficult to follow this rule absolutely. Suppose some of the people you are interviewing about their religious views realize for the first time their doubts. Or perhaps your study of women's rights will cause some women to become unhappy with their jobs or marriages.

You are going to see that abiding by this seemingly simple ethical rule requires vigilance on your part. As you design your study, you should continue asking yourself whether your research will harm the people you are studying. Since everything you do in life *could possibly* harm someone else, you will have to weigh the relative danger against the importance of the research activity.

Voluntary Participation

Another basic ethical rule of social research is that *participation should be voluntary*. Again, in principle, this appears a pretty simple rule to follow. Any experimenter who forced people to participate in the experiment would be roundly criticized. When someone calls and asks you to participate in a telephone survey, you are free to refuse.

Yet when we formally observe a campus demonstration, we do not ask for permission from all the participants. When a researcher pretends to join a religious cult to do research on it, those being observed have not really volunteered for the research project. Social scientists often debate whether a particular research design did or did not violate established research ethics.

As we continue with our examination of research, you will see the great complexity of research ethics. And it certainly deserves your attention.

These, then, are some of the foundations of social scientific research. Though I don't know your preconceptions of this course, I hope you can now see clearly that social science research is a vibrant and exciting activity. All you need is an open mind and a sense of adventure to keep it from being routine or boring.

■ MAIN POINTS

- Inquiry is a natural human activity.
- People seek general understanding about the world around them.
- Much of what we know, we know by agreement rather than by experience.
- Tradition and authority are important sources of understanding.
- When we understand through experience, we make observations and seek patterns of regularities in what we observe.
- In day-to-day inquiry, we often make mistakes. Science offers protection against such mistakes.
- Whereas people often observe inaccurately, such errors are avoided in science by making observation a careful and deliberate activity.
- Sometimes we jump to general conclusions on the basis of only a few observations. Scientists avoid overgeneralization through replication, or repeating studies.
- Once a conclusion has been reached, we sometimes ignore evidence that contradicts that conclusion, paying attention only to evidence that confirms it. Scientists commit themselves in advance to a set of observations to be made regardless of apparent patterns.
- Sometimes people reason illogically. Scientists avoid this by being as careful and deliberate in their reasoning as in their observations. Moreover, the public nature of science means that scientists have their colleagues looking over their shoulders.
- Social scientific theory addresses what is, not what should be. Theory should not be confused with philosophy or belief.
- Social science looks for regularities in social life.
- Social scientists are interested in explaining human aggregates, not individuals.
- An attribute is a characteristic, such as *male* or *young*.
- A variable is a logical set of attributes. *Gender*, for example, is a variable made up of the attributes *male* and *female*.
- Although social scientists observe people, they are primarily interested in finding relationships that connect variables.
- Idiographic explanations seek to understand specific cases fully.
- Nomothetic explanations seek a generalized, though superficial understanding of many cases.
- Inductive theories find general patterns within specific observations.
- Deductive theories predict specific events based on general theories.
- Quantitative data are numerical; qualitative data are not.
- Social research ethics prohibit bringing harm to subjects.
- Participation in social research should be voluntary.

■ REVIEW QUESTIONS AND EXERCISES

1. Review the common errors of human inquiry discussed in this chapter. Find a magazine or newspaper article, or perhaps a letter to the editor, that illustrates one of these errors. Discuss how a scientist would avoid it.
2. List five social variables and the attributes they comprise.
3. Go to one of the following Web sites and find examples of both qualitative and quantitative data.

a. UN High Commissioner for Refugees
   http://www.unhcr.ch/
b. US Centers for Disease Control and Prevention
   http://www.cdc.gov/
c. National Library of Australia
   http://www.nla.gov.au/

■ ADDITIONAL READINGS

Babbie, Earl. *Observing Ourselves: Essays in Social Research*. Belmont, CA: Wadsworth, 1986. A collection of essays that expand some of the philosophical issues you will see in the following chapters, including objectivity, paradigms, determinism, concepts, reality, causation, and values.

Babbie, Earl. *The Sociological Spirit*. Belmont, CA: Wadsworth, 1994. This book is a primer in some sociological points of view. It introduces you to many of the concepts commonly used in the social sciences.

Cole, Stephen. *Making Science: Between Nature and Society*. Cambridge, MA: Harvard University Press, 1992. If you are interested in a deeper examination of science as a social enterprise, you may find this a fascinating analysis.

Gallup, George Jr., Burns Roper, Daniel Yankelovich, et al. "Polls that Made a Difference." *The Public Perspective*, May/June 1990, pp. 17–21. Several public opinion researchers talk about social research polls that have had an important impact on everyday life.

Hoover, Kenneth R. *The Elements of Social Scientific Thinking*. New York: St. Martin's Press, 1992. Hoover presents an excellent overview of the key elements in social scientific analysis.

CHAPTER 2: Paradigms, Theory, and Research

What You'll Learn in This Chapter
You'll see some of the theoretical points of view that structure social scientific inquiry. This chapter will lay the groundwork for your understanding of the specific research techniques discussed throughout the rest of the book.

INTRODUCTION

SOME SOCIAL SCIENCE PARADIGMS
Macrotheory and Microtheory
Early Positivism
Social Darwinism
Conflict Paradigm
Symbolic Interactionism
Role Theory
Ethnomethodology
Structural Functionalism
The Feminist Paradigm
The Exchange Paradigm
Rational Objectivity Reconsidered

THE STRUCTURE OF SOCIAL THEORY
Terms Used in Theory Construction

TWO LOGICAL SYSTEMS
The Traditional Model of Science
Deduction and Induction Compared

DEDUCTIVE THEORY CONSTRUCTION
Getting Started
Constructing Your Theory
An Example of Deductive Theory

INDUCTIVE THEORY CONSTRUCTION
Why Do People Smoke Marijuana?

THE LINKS BETWEEN THEORY AND RESEARCH

MAIN POINTS

REVIEW QUESTIONS AND EXERCISES

ADDITIONAL READINGS

INTRODUCTION

There are restaurants in the United States fond of conducting political polls among their diners whenever an election is in the offing. Some take these polls very seriously because of their uncanny history of predicting winners. By the same token, there are movie theaters that have achieved similar success by offering popcorn in bags picturing either donkeys or elephants. Years ago, granaries in the Midwest offered farmers a chance to indicate their political preferences through the bags of grain they selected.

Such oddities are of some interest to us all. All have the same pattern over time, however. They work for a while, and then they fail. Moreover, we can't predict when or why they will fail.

These unusual polling techniques point to the shortcoming of "research findings" based only on the observation of patterns. Unless we can offer logical explanations for such patterns, the regularities we've observed may be mere flukes, chance occurrences. If you flip coins long enough, you'll get ten heads in a row. Scientists might adapt a street expression to describe this situation: "Patterns happen."

Theory functions three ways in research. First, it prevents our being taken in by flukes. If we can't explain *why* Ma's Diner has been so successful in predicting elections, we run the risk of supporting a fluke. If we know why it has happened, we can anticipate whether it will be successful in the future.

Second, theories make sense of observed patterns in a way that can suggest other possibilities. If we understand the reasons why broken homes produce more juvenile delinquency than intact homes—lack of supervision, for example—we can take effective action, such as after-school youth programs in this case.

Finally, theories can shape and direct research efforts, pointing toward likely discoveries through empirical observation. If you were looking for your lost keys on a dark street, you could whip your flashlight around randomly, hoping to chance upon the errant keys—or you could use your memory of where you had been to limit your search to more likely areas. Theory, by analogy, directs researchers' flashlights where they are most likely to observe interesting patterns of social life.

In this chapter, we are going to explore some specific ways theory and research work hand in hand during the adventure of inquiry into social life. We'll begin with a brief introduction to several theoretical paradigms.

SOME SOCIAL SCIENCE PARADIGMS

Because theories organize our observations and make sense of them, there is usually more than one way to make sense of things. Different points of view usually yield different explanations. This is true in daily life: Liberals and conservatives, for example, often explain the same phenomenon quite differently; so do atheists and fundamentalists.

We begin our examination, then, with some of the major points of view social scientists have taken in the search for meaning. Thomas Kuhn (1970) refers to the fundamental points of view characterizing a science as its *paradigms*. In the history of the natural sciences, major paradigms include Newtonian mechanics, Einsteinian relativism, Darwin's evolutionary theory, and Copernicus's heliocentric theory of heavenly motion, to name a few.

While we sometimes think of science as developing gradually over time, marked by important discoveries and inventions, Kuhn says it was typical for one paradigm to become entrenched, resisting any substantial change. Eventually, however, as the shortcomings of that paradigm became obvious, a new paradigm would emerge and supplant the old one. Thus, the view that the sun revolves around the earth was supplanted by the view that the earth revolves around the sun. Kuhn's classic book on this subject is titled, appropriately enough, *The Structure of Scientific Revolutions*.

Social scientists have developed several paradigms for understanding social behavior. The fate of supplanted paradigms in the social sciences has differed from what Kuhn has observed in the natural sciences, however. Natural scientists generally believe that the succession from one paradigm to another represents progress from a false view to a true one. No modern astronomer believes that the sun revolves around the earth, for example.

In the social sciences, on the other hand, theoretical paradigms may gain or lose popularity, but they are seldom discarded. As you'll see shortly, the paradigms of the social sciences offer a variety of views, each of which offers insights the others lack—but ignores aspects of social life that the others reveal.

Thus, each of the paradigms we are about to examine offers a different way of looking at human social life. Each makes certain assumptions about the nature of social reality. I advise you to examine each as to how it might open up new understandings for you, rather than to try to decide which is true and which false. Ultimately, paradigms cannot be true or false; as ways of looking, they can only be more or less useful. Try to find ways these paradigms might be useful to you.

Macrotheory and Microtheory

Let's begin with a difference of focus that stretches across many of the paradigms to be discussed. Some theorists focus their attention on society at large or at least on large portions of it. Topics of study for such **macrotheory** include the struggle between economic classes in a society, international relations, or the interrelations among major institutions in society, such as government, religion, and family. Macrotheory deals with large, aggregate entities of society or even whole societies.

Some scholars have taken a more intimate view of social life. **Microtheory** deals with issues of social life at the level of individuals and small groups. Dating behavior, jury deliberations, and student-faculty interactions are apt subjects for a microtheory perspective. As you may have anticipated, such studies often come close to the realm of psychology, but whereas psychologists typically focus on what goes on inside humans, social scientists study what goes on *between* them.

The distinction between macro- and microtheory crosscuts the paradigms we'll examine below. While some of them, such as symbolic interactionism and ethnomethodology, are more often limited to the microlevel, others, such as the conflict paradigm, can be pursued at either the micro- or the macrolevel.

Early Positivism

When the French philosopher Auguste Comte (1798–1857) coined the term *sociologie* in 1822, he launched an intellectual adventure that is still unfolding today. Most important, Comte identified society as a phenomenon that can be studied scientifically. (Initially, he wanted to label his enterprise "social physics," but that term was co-opted by another scholar.)

Prior to Comte's time, society simply *was*. To the extent that people recognized different kinds of societies or changes in society over time, religious paradigms generally predominated in explanations of the differences. The state of social affairs was often seen as a reflection of God's will. Alternatively, people were challenged to create a "City of God" on earth to replace sin and godlessness.

Comte separated his inquiry from religion. He felt that society could be studied scientifically, that religious belief could be replaced with scientific objectivity. His "positive philosophy" postulated three stages of history. A "theological stage" predominated throughout the world until about 1300. During the next five hundred years, a "metaphysical stage" replaced God with ideas such as "nature" and "natural law."

Finally, Comte felt he was launching the third stage of history, in which science would replace religion and metaphysics—basing knowledge on observations through the five senses rather than on belief. Comte felt that society could be studied and understood logically and rationally, that sociology could be as scientific as biology or physics.

Comte's view came to form the foundation for subsequent development of the social sciences. In his optimism for the future, he coined the term *positivism* to describe this scientific approach—in contrast to what he regarded as negative elements in the Enlightenment. Only in recent decades has the idea of positivism come under serious challenge, as you'll see later in this discussion.

Social Darwinism

Comte's major work on his positivist philosophy was published between 1830 and 1842. One year after the publication of the first volume in that series, a young British naturalist set sail on the HMS *Beagle*, beginning a cruise that would profoundly affect the way we have come to think of ourselves and our place in the world.

In 1858, when Charles Darwin published his *Origin of the Species*, he set forth the idea of *evolution* through the process of *natural selection*. Simply put, the theory states that as a species coped with its environment, those individuals most suited to success would be the most likely to survive long enough to reproduce. Those less well suited would perish; therefore the former group would come to dominate the species.

As scholars began to study society analytically, it was perhaps inevitable that Darwin's ideas would be applied to the changes that had taken place in the structure of human affairs. The journey from simple hunting-and-gathering tribes to large, industrial civilizations was easily seen as the evolution of progressively "fitter" forms of society.

Herbert Spencer (1820–1903) was one who concluded that society was getting better and better. Indeed, his native England had profited greatly from the development of industrial capitalism, and Spencer favored a system of free competition, which he felt would insure continued progress and improvement. Spencer may even have coined the phrase, "the survival of the fittest." In any event, he believed it was a primary force in shaping the nature of society. *Social Darwinism* or *social evolution* was a popular view in Spencer's time, although it was not universally accepted.

This excerpt from a social science methods textbook published in 1950 illustrates the long-term popularity of the notion that things are getting better and better.

■ The use of atomic energy as an explosive offers most interesting prospects in the civil as in the military field. Atomic explosives may be used for transforming the landscape. They may be used for blasting great holes and trenches in the earth, which can be transformed into lakes and canals. In this way, it may become possible to produce lakes in the midst of deserts, and thus convert some of the worst places in the world into oases and fertile countries. It may also be possible to make the Arctic regions comfortable by providing immense and constant sources of heat. The North Pole might be converted into a holiday resort.

(GEE 1950: 339–340).

Quite aside from the widespread disenchantment with nuclear power, the contemporary concerns over global warming and the threat of rising sea levels illustrate a growing consciousness that "progress" is often a two-edged sword.

Conflict Paradigm

One of Spencer's contemporaries took a sharply different view of the evolution of capitalism. Karl Marx (1818–1883) suggested that social behavior could best be seen as the process of conflict: the attempt to dominate others and to avoid being dominated. Marx primarily focused on the struggle among economic classes. Specifically, he examined the way capitalism produced the oppression of workers by the owners of industry. As you know, Marx's interest in this topic did not end with analytical study: He was also ideologically committed to restructuring economic relations to end the oppression he observed.

The contrast in the views set forth by Spencer and Marx indicates the influence that paradigms have on research. These fundamental viewpoints shape the kinds of observations we are likely to make, the facts we will seek to discover, and the conclusions we draw from those facts. Whereas economic classes were essential to Marx's analysis, for example, Spencer was more interested in the relationship between individuals and society—particularly, the amount of freedom individuals had to surrender for society to work.

The conflict paradigm is not limited to economic analyses. Georg Simmel (1858–1918) was particularly interested in small-scale conflict, in contrast to the class struggle that interested Marx. Simmel noted, for example, that conflicts among members of a tightly knit group tended to be more intense than those among people who did not share feelings of belonging and intimacy.

Where it is perhaps natural to see conflict as a threat to organized society, Lewis Coser (1956) pointed out that conflict can sometimes promote social solidarity. Conflict between two groups tends to increase cohesion within each. Or, the expression of conflict within a group can often serve the function of "letting off steam" before stresses become too great to be resolved.

These few examples should illustrate some of the ways you might view social life if you were taking your lead from the conflict paradigm. To explore the applicability of this paradigm, you might take a minute to skim through a daily newspaper or news magazine and identify events that you could interpret in terms of individuals and groups attempting to dominate each other and avoid being dominated. The theoretical concepts and premises of the conflict paradigm might help you make sense out of these events.

Symbolic Interactionism

In his overall focus, Georg Simmel differed from both Spencer and Marx. Whereas they were chiefly concerned with macrotheoretical issues—large institutions and whole societies in their evolution through the course of history—Simmel, by contrast, was more interested in the ways in which individuals interacted with one another. He began by examining dyads (two people) and triads (three people), for example. Similarly, he wrote about "the web of group affiliations."

Simmel was one of the first European sociologists to influence the development of U.S. sociology. His focus on the nature of interactions particularly influenced George Herbert Mead (1863–1931), Charles Horton Cooley (1864–1929), and others who took up the cause and developed it into a powerful paradigm for research.

Cooley, for example, introduced the idea of the "primary group," those intimate associates with whom we share a sense of belonging, such as our family, friendship cliques, and so forth. Cooley also wrote of the "looking-glass self" we form by looking into the reactions of people around us. If everyone treats us as beautiful, for example, we conclude that we are. See how fundamentally this paradigm differs from the society-level concerns of Spencer and Marx.

Mead emphasized the importance of our human ability to "take the role of the other," imagining how others feel and how they might behave in certain circumstances. As we gain an idea of how people in general see things, we develop a sense of what Mead called the "generalized other." See how this relates to Cooley's "looking-glass self."

Mead also had a special interest in the role of communications in human affairs. Most interactions, he felt, revolved around the process of individuals reaching common understanding through the use of language and other symbol systems, hence the term *symbolic* interactionism.

Here's one way you might apply this paradigm to an examination of your own life. The next time you meet someone new, pay attention to how you get to know each other. To begin, what assumptions do you make about the other person based merely on how they look, how they talk, and the circumstances under which you've met. ("What's someone like you doing in a place like this?") Then watch how your knowledge of each other unfolds through the process of interaction. Notice also any attempts you make to manage the image you are creating in the other person's mind.

Role Theory

In *As You Like It*, Shakespeare penned some very social scientific lines:

■ All the world's a stage
And all the men and women merely players:
They have their exits and their entrances;
And one man in his time plays many parts.
(ACT 2, SCENE 7)

The insights of Mead, Cooley, and others regarding the nature of interaction yielded some fundamental social scientific concepts. Ralph

Linton (1895–1953) specified the ideas of status and role. *Status* is a position we occupy in society (such as daughter, lawyer, Republican, American), and a *role* is a set of expected behaviors. When a professor and a student meet to discuss a term paper assignment, there are numerous expectations about the way each will behave in the interaction: The student will plead for an extension, the professor will heartlessly refuse, and so on.

Some social scientists have focused their analysis on how people deal with their various role expectations. This approach yields a variety of new concepts, such as "role strain" (too many expectations for one person to manage) and "role conflict" (my role as professor calls for one thing, my role as the student's son, as it so happens, calls for another).

To get a better idea of this paradigm, you might pay special attention to the ways you and others present yourselves in different situations. Do you speak differently to your professors than to your friends? When you need to deal with the college administration, what role do you assume? How about the roles you assume at worship services, in a supermarket, at a sports event, at a party? After reflecting on your repertoire of roles, you might want to consider how they relate to who you "really" are. What would *you* be like if you weren't acting out any social role?

Ethnomethodology

While some social scientific paradigms emphasize the impact of social structure (such as norms, values, control agents) on human behavior, others do not. Thus, while our social statuses establish expectations for our behavior, everyone deals with these expectations somewhat differently.

Harold Garfinkel, a contemporary sociologist, takes the point of view that people are continually creating social structure through their actions and interactions—that they are, in fact, creating their realities. Thus, when you and I meet to discuss your term paper, even though there are myriad expectations about how we should act, our conversation will be somewhat different from any of those that have occurred before, and how we act will somewhat modify our expectations in the future. That is, discussing your term paper will impact our interactions with other professors/students in the future.

Given the tentativeness of reality in this view, Garfinkel suggests that people are continuously trying to make sense of the life they experience. In a sense, he suggests that everyone is acting like a social scientist: hence the term *ethnomethodology,* or "methodology of the people."

How would you go about learning about people's expectations and how they make sense out of their world? One technique ethnomethodologists use is to *break the rules,* to violate people's expectations. Thus, if you try to talk to me about your term paper and I keep talking about football, that might reveal the expectations you had for my behavior. We might also see how you make sense out of my behavior. ("Maybe he's using football as an analogy for understanding social systems theory.")

In another example of ethnomethodology, Johen Heritage and David Greatbatch (1992) examined the role of applause in British political speeches: How did the speakers evoke applause, and what function did it serve (e.g., to complete a topic)? Communications have often been the focus of research within the ethnomethodological paradigm.

There is no end to the opportunities you have for trying on the ethnomethodological paradigm. For instance, the next time you get on an elevator, spend your ride facing the rear of the elevator. Don't face front and watch the floor numbers whip by (that's the norm). Just stand quietly facing the rear. See how others react to this behavior. Just as important, notice how *you* feel about it. If you do this experiment a few times, you should begin to develop a feel for the ethnomethodological paradigm.*

---

*I am grateful to my colleague, Bernard McGrane, for this experiment. Barney also has his students eat dinner with their hands, watch TV without turning it on, and engage in other strangely enlightening behavior (McGrane 1994).

Structural Functionalism

Structural functionalism, sometimes also known as "social systems theory," grows out of a notion introduced by Comte and Spencer: that a social entity, such as an organization or a whole society, can be viewed as an *organism*. Like other organisms, a social system is made up of parts, each of which contributes to the functioning of the whole.

By analogy, consider the human body. Each component—such as the heart, lungs, kidneys, skin, and brain—has a particular job to do. The body as a whole cannot survive unless each of these parts does its job, and none of the parts can survive except as a part of the whole body. Or consider an automobile. It is composed of the tires, the steering wheel, the gas tank, the spark plugs, and so forth. Each of the parts serves a function for the whole; taken together, that system can get us across town. None of the individual parts would be of much use to us by itself, however.

The view of society as a social system, then, looks for the "functions" served by its various components. We might consider a football team as a social system—one in which the quarterback, running backs, offensive linemen, and others each have their jobs to do for the team as a whole. Or, we could look at a symphony orchestra and examine the functions served by the conductor, the first violinist, and the other musicians.

Social scientists using the structural functional paradigm might note that the function of the police, for example, is to exercise social control—encouraging people to abide by the norms of society and bringing to justice those who do not. We could just as reasonably ask what functions criminals serve in society, however. Within the functionalist paradigm, we'd see that criminals serve as job security for the police. In a related observation, Emile Durkheim (1858–1917) suggested that crimes and their punishment provided an opportunity for the reaffirmation of a society's values. By catching and punishing a thief, we reaffirm our collective respect for private property.

To get a sense of the structural-functional paradigm, you might thumb through your college or university catalog and begin assembling a list of the administrators (such as president, deans, registrar, campus security, maintenance personnel). Figure out what each of them does. To what extent do these roles relate to the chief functions of your college or university, such as teaching or research? Suppose you were studying some other kind of organization. How many of the school administrators' functions would also be needed in, say, an insurance company?

Feminist Paradigms

When Ralph Linton concluded his anthropological classic, *The Study of Man,* (1937:490), speaking of "a store of knowledge that promises to give man a better life than any he has known," no one complained that he had left *women* out. Linton was using the linguistic conventions of his time; he implicitly included women in all his references to men. Or did he?

When feminists (of both genders) first began questioning the use of the third-person masculine whenever gender was ambiguous, their concerns were often viewed as petty, even silly. At most, many felt the issue was one of women having their feelings hurt, their egos bruised.

In fact, feminism has established important theoretical paradigms for social research. In part it has focused on gender differences and how they relate to the rest of social organization. These paradigms have drawn attention to the oppression of women in a great many societies, which has in turn shed light on general oppression.

Because men and women have had very different social experiences throughout history, they have come to see things differently, with the result that their conclusions about social life differ in many ways. In perhaps the most general example, feminist paradigms have challenged the prevailing notions concerning consensus in society. Most descriptions of the predominant beliefs, values, and norms of a society are written by people representing only portions of society. In the United States, for example, such analyses have typically been written by middle-class white men—not surprisingly, they have written about the beliefs, values, and norms they themselves share. Though George Herbert Mead spoke of the "generalized other" that each of us becomes aware of and can "take the role of," feminist paradigms question whether such a *generalized* other even exists.

Where Mead used the example of learning to play baseball to illustrate how we learn about the generalized other, Janet Lever's research suggests that understanding the experience of boys may tell us little about girls.

■ Girls' play and games are very different. They are mostly spontaneous, imaginative, and free of structure or rules. Turn-taking activities like jumprope may be played without setting explicit goals. Girls have far less experience with interpersonal competition. The style of their competition is indirect, rather than face to face, individual rather than team affiliated. Leadership roles are either missing or randomly filled.

(LEVER 1986:86)

Our growing recognition of the intellectual differences between men and women generally, led the psychologist Mary Field Belenky and her colleagues to speak of *Women's Ways of Knowing* (1986). In-depth interviews with 45 women led the researchers to distinguish five perspectives on knowing that should challenge the view of inquiry as obvious and straightforward:

Silence: Some women, especially early in life, feel themselves isolated from the world of knowledge, their lives largely determined by external authorities.

Received knowledge: From this perspective, women feel themselves capable of taking in and holding knowledge originating with external authorities.

Subjective knowledge: This perspective opens up the possibility of personal, subjective knowledge, including intuition.

Procedural knowledge: Some women feel they have mastered the ways of gaining knowledge through objective procedures.

Constructed knowledge: The authors describe this perspective as "a position in which women view all knowledge as contextual, experience themselves as creators of knowledge, and value both subjective and objective strategies for knowing" (Belenky et al. 1986:15).

"Constructed knowledge" is particularly interesting in the context of our previous discussions. The positivistic paradigm of Comte would have a place neither for "subjective knowledge" nor for the idea that truth might vary according to its context. The ethnomethodological paradigm, on the other hand, would accommodate these notions.

To try out feminist paradigms, you might want to look into the possibility of discrimination against women at your college or university. Are the top administrative positions held equally by men and women? How about secretarial and clerical positions? Are men's and women's sports supported equally? Read through the official history of your school; is it a history that includes men and women equally? (If you attend an all-male or all-female school, of course, some of these questions won't apply.)

The Exchange Paradigm

George Homans, a contemporary social scientist, has suggested that all human behavior can be seen to reflect people's calculations of costs and benefits. More than any of the previously mentioned theorists, Homans consciously states his views as explicit propositions, such as these:

■ The more often a particular action of a person is rewarded, the more likely the person is to perform that action.

(HOMANS 1974:16)

■ The more valuable to a person is the result of his action, the more likely he is to perform the action.

(HOMANS 1974:25)

■ The more often in the recent past a person has received a particular reward, the less valuable any further unit of that reward becomes for him.

(HOMANS 1974:29)

Notice that Homans, a sociologist, approaches *social* relations from a fundamentally *psychological* starting point, grounded in how individuals see things, how they reason, and how they draw conclusions. Other theorists, such as Peter Blau (1975), have shown that the basic notion of *exchange*, however, can also be applied to groups and organizations: companies, departments within companies, or countries dealing with one another.

To get a sense of this paradigm, you might review your decision to attend the college or university you are now attending. Did you have alternative schools to choose from? At the very least, you had the choice not to attend college. What were the pluses and minuses of each possible choice? Can you see any ways your deliberations conformed with Homans's propositions?

Notice that the exchange paradigm contains the implicit assumption that human beings are basically *rational* in their life choices. For this reason, the exchange paradigm is often included within a larger paradigm, labeled *rational-choice paradigm*. Some contemporary scholars, however, question the links between rationality and social science.

Rational Objectivity Reconsidered

We began with Comte's assertion that we can study society rationally and objectively. Since his time, the growth of science, the relative decline of superstition, and the rise of bureaucratic structures all seem to put rationality more and more in the center of social life. As fundamental as rationality is to most of us, however, some contemporary scholars have raised questions about it.

For example, positivistic social scientists have sometimes erred in assuming that humans will always act rationally. I'm sure your own experience offers ample evidence to the contrary. And yet, many modern economic models fundamentally assume that people will make rational choices in the economic sector: They will choose the highest-paying job, pay the lowest price, and so forth. However, this assumption ignores the power of such matters as tradition, loyalty, and image that compete with reason in the determination of human behavior.

FIGURE 2-1
The Asch Experiment

A more sophisticated positivism would assert that we can rationally understand even nonrational human behavior. Here's an example. In the famous "Asch Experiment" (Asch 1958), a group of subjects is presented with a set of lines on a screen and asked to identify the two lines of equal length.

Imagine yourself a subject in such an experiment. You are sitting in the front row of a classroom in a group of six subjects. A set of lines (see Figure 2-1) is projected on the wall in front of you. The experimenter asks you, one at a time, to identify the line to the right (A, B, or C) that matches the length of line X. The correct answer (B) is pretty obvious to you. To your surprise, however, you find that all the other subjects agree on a different answer!

The experimenter announces that all but one of the group has gotten the correct answer; that is, you've gotten it *wrong*. Then a new set of lines is presented, and you have the same experience. The obviously correct answer is wrong, and everyone but you seems to understand that.

As it turns out, of course, you are the only *real* subject in the experiment—all the others are working with the experimenter—and the purpose is to see whether you would be swayed by public pressure and go along with the incorrect answer. In one-third of the initial experiments, Asch found that his subjects did just that.

Giving in to public pressure is an example of nonrational behavior. Nonetheless, experimenters can examine the various circumstances that lead more or fewer subjects to go along with the incorrect answer. Thus, it is possible to study nonrational behavior rationally and scientifically.

More radically, we can question whether social life abides by rational principles at all. In the physical sciences, developments such as *chaos theory, fuzzy logic,* and *complexity* have suggested that we may need to rethink fundamentally the orderliness of events on our planet.

The contemporary challenge to positivism, however, goes beyond the question of whether people behave rationally. In part, the criticism of positivism challenges the idea that scientists can be as objective as the scientific ideal assumes. Most scientists would agree that personal feelings can and do influence the problems scientists choose to study, what they choose to observe, and the conclusions they draw from their observations.

As with rationality, there is a more radical critique of objectivity. Whereas scientific objectivity has long stood as an unquestionable ideal, some contemporary researchers suggest that subjectivity might actually be preferred in some situations, as we glimpsed in the discussions of feminism and ethnomethodology. Let's take a moment to return to the dialectic of subjectivity and objectivity.

To begin, all our *experiences are inescapably subjective.* There is no way out. You can only see through your own eyes, and anything peculiar to *your* eyes will shape what you see. You can only hear things the way your particular ears and brain transmit and interpret sound waves.

Despite the inescapable subjectivity of our experience, we humans seem to be wired to seek an agreement on what is *really real,* what is *objectively* so. Objectivity is a *conceptual* attempt to get beyond our individual views. It is ultimately a matter of communication, as you and I attempt to find a common ground in our subjective experiences. Whenever we succeed in our search, we say we are dealing with objective reality. This is the *agreement reality* discussed in Chapter 1.

While our subjectivity is individual, our search for objectivity is social. This is true in all aspects of life, not just in science. While you and I prefer different foods, we must agree to some extent on what is fit to eat and what is not, or else there could be no restaurants, no grocery stores. There could be no food industry. The same argument could be made regarding every other form of consumption. There could be no movies or television, no sports.

Social scientists as well have found benefits in the concept of objective reality. As people seek to impose order on their experience of life, they find it useful to pursue this goal as a collective venture. What are the causes and cures of prejudice? Working together, social researchers have uncovered some answers that hold up to **intersubjective** scrutiny. Whatever your subjective experience of things, for example, you can discover for yourself that as education increases, prejudice generally tends to decrease. Because each of us can discover this independently, we say that it is objectively true.

From the seventeenth century through the middle of the twentieth, the belief in an objective reality that people could see ever more clearly predominated in science. For the most part, it was not simply held as a useful paradigm but as *The Truth.* The term *positivism* has generally represented the belief in a logically ordered, objective reality that we can come to know. This is the view challenged today by the postmodernists and others.

Some say that the ideal of objectivity conceals as much as it reveals. As we saw earlier, much of what was agreed on as scientific objectivity in years past was actually an agreement primarily among white, middle-class European men. Subjective experiences common to women, to ethnic minorities, or to the poor, for example, were not necessarily represented in that reality.

The early anthropologists are now criticized for often making modern, Westernized "sense" out of the beliefs and practices of nonliterate tribes around the world—sometimes portraying their subjects as superstitious savages. We often call nonliterate tribal beliefs about the distant past "creation myth," whereas we speak of our own beliefs as "history." Increasingly today, there is a demand to find the native logic by which various peoples make sense out of life.

Ultimately, we'll never know whether there is an objective reality that we experience subjectively or whether our concepts of an objective reality are illusory. So desperate is our need to know just what is going on, however, that both the positivists and the postmodernists are sometimes drawn into the belief that their view is real and true. There is a dual irony in this. On the one hand, the positivist's belief in the reality of the objective world must ultimately be based on faith; it cannot be proven by "objective" science, since that's precisely what's at issue. And the postmodernists, who say nothing is objectively so, do at least feel the absence of objective reality is *really* the way things are.

Rather than align yourself with either of these approaches as a religion, I encourage you to treat them as two distinct arrows in your quiver. Each approach brings special strengths, and each compensates for the weaknesses of the other. Why choose, therefore? Work both sides of the street.

These brief remarks on the critique of positivism are intended to illustrate the rich variety of theoretical perspectives that can be brought to bear on the study of human social life. While the attempt to establish formal theories of society has been closely associated with the belief in a discoverable, objective reality, the issues involved in theory construction are of interest and use to all social researchers, from the positivists to the postmodernists—and all those in between.

■ THE STRUCTURE OF SOCIAL THEORY

Whereas the terms *paradigm* and *theory* are sometimes used interchangeably, I want to distinguish them more clearly in the remainder of this chapter. Paradigms are general frameworks or viewpoints: literally "points from which to view." They provide ways of looking at life and are grounded in sets of assumptions about the nature of reality.

A theory, by contrast, is a systematic set of interrelated statements intended to explain some aspect of social life. Thus, theories flesh out and specify paradigms. Whereas a paradigm offers a way of looking, a theory aims at explaining what we see. Earlier, in the discussion of the exchange paradigm, we saw examples of statements that might make up a theory of interaction. Thus, the exchange *paradigm* suggests that we analyze social situations in terms of the perceived costs and benefits of various behaviors, whereas exchange *theory* asserts, among other things, that "the more often a particular action of a person is rewarded, the more likely the person is to perform that action." (Homans 1974:16)

Let's look a little more deliberately now at some of the elements of a theory.

Terms Used in Theory Construction

Observation In the previous discussions, the "experience" of whatever may or may not really exist typically refers to the operation of the human senses. In the case of social research, this is typically limited to seeing, hearing, and—less commonly—touching. The term *observation* is generally used in reference to such information gathering. (Part 3 of this book is devoted to the many modes of observation employed by social scientists.)

Fact Although for philosophers "fact" is as complex a notion as "reality," social scientists generally use it to mean some phenomenon that has been observed. It is a fact, for example, that Bill Clinton defeated George Bush in the 1992 presidential election.

Law Abraham Kaplan (1964:91) defines laws as universal generalizations about classes of facts. The law of gravity is a classic example: Bodies are attracted to each other in proportion to their masses and inversely proportionate to the distance separating them.

Laws must be truly universal, however, not merely accidental patterns found among a specific set of facts. It is a fact, Kaplan points out (1964:92), that in each of the U.S. presidential elections from 1920 to 1960, the major candidate with the longest name won. That is not a law, however, as shown by the next three elections. The earlier pattern was a coincidence.

Sometimes called *principles,* laws are important statements about what is so. We speak of them as being "discovered," that is, scientists do not create laws. Also, laws in and of themselves do not explain anything. They just summarize the way things are. Explanation is a function of theory, and theories are created, as we'll see shortly.

There are no social scientific laws that have the universal certainty of those of the natural sciences. In fact, as I've hinted, social scientists debate among themselves as to whether we will ever discover such laws. Perhaps social life essentially does not abide by invariant laws. This does not mean that social life is so chaotic as to defy prediction and explanation. As we saw in Chapter 1, social behavior falls into patterns, and those patterns very often make perfect sense, although you may have to look below the surface to find the logic.

Theory A theory is a systematic explanation for the observations that relate to a particular aspect of life: juvenile delinquency, for example, or perhaps social stratification or political revolution.

Concepts Jonathan Turner (1989:5) calls concepts the "basic building blocks of theory." They are abstract elements representing classes of phenomena within the field of study. The concepts relevant to a theory of juvenile delinquency, for example, include juvenile and delinquency, for starters. A peer group—the people you hang around with and identify with—is another relevant concept. Social class and ethnicity are undoubtedly relevant concepts in a theory of juvenile delinquency. School performance might also be relevant.

Variables A variable is a special kind of concept, as we saw in Chapter 1. Each variable comprises a set of attributes; thus, *delinquency*, in the simplest case, is made up of *delinquent* and *not delinquent*. A theory of delinquency would aim at explaining why some juveniles are delinquent and others are not.

Axioms or Postulates are fundamental assertions, taken to be true, on which a theory is grounded. In a theory of juvenile delinquency, we might begin with axioms such as "Everyone desires material comforts" and "The ability to obtain material comforts legally is greater for the wealthy than for the poor."

Propositions are conclusions drawn about the relationships among concepts, derived from the axiomatic groundwork. From our beginning axioms about juvenile delinquency, for example, we might reasonably conclude that poor youths are more likely to break the law to gain material comforts than rich youths.

This proposition, incidentally, accords with Robert Merton's classic attempt to account for deviance in society. Merton (1957:139–57) spoke of the agreed-on *means* and *ends* of a society. In Merton's model, nondeviants are those who share the societal agreement as to desired ends (such as a new car) and the means prescribed for achieving them (such as to buy it). One type of deviant—whom Merton called the "innovator"—agrees on the desired end but does not have access to the prescribed means for achieving it. That person finds another method of getting the desired end—and crime is one of them.

Hypotheses are specified expectations about empirical reality, derived from propositions. In our present example, a theory might contain the hypothesis, "Poor youths have higher delinquency rates than rich youths." Such a hypothesis could then be tested through research.

Let's look now at how theory and research come together.

■ TWO LOGICAL SYSTEMS

In Chapter 1, I introduced deductive and inductive theory, with a promise that we would return to them later. It's later.

The Traditional Model of Science

In my experience as a teacher, I've found that university instruction in "the scientific method"—especially in the physical sciences—tends to create in students' minds a particular picture of how science operates. Although this traditional model of science tells only a part of the story, it is important that you understand its logic.

There are three main elements in the traditional model of science, and they are typically presented in a chronological order of execution: *theory, operationalization,* and *observation*. Let's look at each in turn.

Theory According to the traditional model of science, scientists begin with an interest in some aspect of the real world. As we've just discussed, they might be interested in the causes of juvenile delinquency. Let's assume they've arrived at a hypothesis about social class and delinquency.

Operationalization To test any hypothesis, we must specify the meanings of all the variables involved in it: social class and delinquency in the present case. For example, delinquency might be specified as "being arrested for a crime," "being convicted of a crime," or some other meaning. Wealth (rich versus poor) might be specified as family income for this particular study.

Moving beyond the specific definition, we need to specify how we'll measure it. **Operationalization** literally means the operations involved in measuring a variable. There are many ways we can pursue this topic, each of which allows for different ways of measuring our variables.

For simplicity, let's assume we are planning to conduct a survey of high school students. We might operationalize delinquency in the form of the question: "Have you ever stolen anything?" Those who answer "yes" will be classified as delinquents in our study; those who say "no" will be classified as nondelinquents. Similarly, we might operationalize family income by asking respondents, "What was your family's income last year?" and providing them with a set of family income categories: under $10,000; $10,000–$24,999; $25,000–$49,999; and $50,000 and above.

Notice that the way we have operationalized our variables in this simplistic example may cause problems. Perhaps some respondents will lie about stealing, in which cases we'll misclassify them as nondelinquent. Some respondents will not know their family incomes and will give mistaken answers; others may be embarrassed and lie. Chapters 5, 6, and 7 will deal with such issues in depth. For the purposes of this introductory example, though, let's use the operationalizations described here.

Our operationalized hypothesis now is that the highest incidence of delinquents will be found among respondents who select the lowest family income category (under $10,000); a lower percentage of delinquents will be found in the $10,000–$24,999 category; still fewer delinquents will be found in the $25,000–$49,999 category; and the lowest percentage of delinquents will be found in the $50,000 and above category.

Observation The final step in the traditional model of science involves actual observation, looking at the world and making measurements of what is seen. Having developed theoretical clarity and expectations and having created a strategy for looking, all that remains is to look at the way things are.

Let's suppose our survey produced the following data:

	Percentage delinquent
Under $10,000	20
$10,000–$24,999	15
$25,000–$49,999	10
$50,000 and above	5

Observations producing such data would confirm our hypothesis. But suppose our findings were as follows:

	Percentage delinquent
Under $10,000	15
$10,000–$24,999	15
$25,000–$49,999	15
$50,000 and above	15

These findings would disconfirm our hypothesis regarding family income and delinquency. *Disconfirmability* is an essential quality in any hypothesis.

Figure 2-2 provides a schematic diagram of the traditional model of scientific inquiry. In it we see the researcher beginning with an interest in something or an idea about it. Next comes the development of a theoretical understanding. The theoretical considerations result in a **hypothesis,** or an expectation about the way things ought to be in the world if the theoretical expectations are

FIGURE 2-2
The Traditional Image of Science

correct. The notation $Y = f(x)$ is a conventional way of saying that Y (for example, delinquency) is a function of (is in some way caused by) X (for example, poverty). At that level, however, X and Y have general rather than specific meanings.

In the operationalization process, general concepts are translated into specific indicators and procedures. The lowercase x, for example, is a concrete indicator of capital X. This operationalization process results in the formation of a testable hypothesis: for example, increasing family income reduces self-reported theft. Observations aimed at finding out are part of what is typically called **hypothesis testing**. (See the box "Hints for Stating Hypotheses" for more on this.)

Deduction and Induction Compared

As you will have recognized, the traditional model of science just discussed uses deductive logic (see Chapter 1). In this section, we are going to look more deeply into deductive logic as it fits into social scientific research and contrast it with inductive logic. W. I. B. Beveridge, a philosopher of science, describes these two systems of logic in a way that should already seem familiar to you:

■ Logicians distinguish between inductive reasoning (from particular instances to general principles, from facts to theories) and deductive reasoning (from the general to the particular, applying a theory to a particular case). In induction one starts from observed data and develops a generalization which explains the relationships between the objects observed. On the other hand, in deductive reasoning one starts from some general law and applies it to a particular instance.

(BEVERIDGE 1950:113)

The classical illustration of deductive logic is the familiar syllogism "All men are mortal; Socrates is a man; therefore Socrates is mortal." This syllogism presents a theory and its operationalization. To prove it, you might then perform an empirical test of Socrates' mortality. That is essentially the approach discussed as the traditional model.

Using inductive logic, you might begin by noting that Socrates is mortal and observing a number of other men as well. You might then note that all the observed men were mortals, thereby arriving at the tentative conclusion that all men are mortal.

Now let's consider a real research example as a vehicle for comparing the deductive and inductive linkages between theory and research.

A Deductive Illustration Years ago, Charles Glock, Benjamin Ringer, and I (1967) set out to discover what caused differing levels of church involvement among U.S. Episcopalians. A number of theoretical or quasitheoretical positions suggested possible answers. I'll focus on only one here: what we came to call the "Comfort Hypothesis."

In part, we took our lead from the Christian injunction to care for "the halt, the lame, and the blind" and those who are "weary and heavy laden." At the same time, ironically, we noted the Marxist assertion that religion is an "opiate for the masses." On both bases, then, it made sense to expect the following, which was our hypothesis: "Parishioners whose life situations most deprive them of satisfaction and fulfillment in the secular society turn to the church for comfort and substitute rewards" (Glock et al., 1967:107–8).

Having framed this general hypothesis, we set about testing it. Were those deprived of satisfaction in the secular society in fact more religious than those who got more satisfaction from the secular society? To answer this, we needed to distinguish who was deprived. The questionnaire, which was constructed for the purpose of testing the Comfort Hypothesis, included items that seemed to offer indicators of whether parishioners were relatively deprived or gratified in the secular society.

To start, we reasoned that men enjoyed more status than women in our generally male-dominated society. Though hardly a novel conclusion in itself, it laid the groundwork for testing the Comfort Hypothesis. If we were correct in our hypothesis, women should appear more religious than men. Once the survey data had been collected and analyzed, our expectation about gender and religion was clearly confirmed. On three separate measures of religious involvement—*ritual* (for example, church attendance), *organizational* (for example, belonging to church organizations), and *intellectual* (for example, reading church publications)—women were more religious than men. On our overall measure, women scored 50 percent higher than men.

In another test of the Comfort Hypothesis, we reasoned that in a youth-oriented society, old people would be more deprived of secular gratification than the young. Once again, our expectation was confirmed by the data. The oldest parishioners were more religious than the middle-aged, who were more religious than the young adults.

Social class—measured by education and income—afforded another test of the Comfort Hypothesis. Once again, the test was successful. Those with low social status were more involved in the church than those with high social status.

The hypothesis was even confirmed in a test that went against everyone's commonsense expectations. Despite church posters showing worshipful young families and bearing the slogan, "The Family that Prays Together Stays Together," the Comfort Hypothesis suggested that parishioners who were married and had children—the clear American ideal at that time—would enjoy secular gratification in that regard. As a consequence, they should be *less* religious than those who lacked one or both family components. Thus, we hypothesized that parishioners who were both single and childless should be the most religious; those with either spouse or child should be somewhat less religious; and those married with children—representing the ideal pictured on all those posters—should be least religious of all. That's exactly what we found!

Finally, the Comfort Hypothesis would suggest that the various kinds of secular deprivation should be cumulative: Those with all the characteristics associated with deprivation should be the most religious; those with none should be the least. When we combined the four individual

Hints for Stating Hypotheses

By Riley E. Dunlap
Department of Sociology, Washington State University

A hypothesis is the basic statement that is tested in research. Typically a hypothesis states a relationship between two variables. (Although it is possible to use more than two variables, you should stick to two for now.) Because a hypothesis makes a *prediction* about the relationship between the two variables, it must be *testable* so you can determine if the prediction is right or wrong when you examine the results obtained in your study. A hypothesis must be stated in an unambiguous manner to be clearly testable. What follows are suggestions for developing testable hypotheses.

Assume you have an interest in trying to predict some phenomenon such as "attitudes toward women's liberation," and that you can measure such attitudes on a continuum ranging from "opposed to women's liberation" to "neutral" to "supportive of women's liberation." Also assume that, lacking a theory, you'll rely on "hunches" to come up with variables that might be related to attitudes toward women's liberation.

In a sense, you can think of hypothesis construction as a case of filling in the blank: "_____ is related to attitudes toward women's liberation." Your job is to think of a variable that might plausibly be related to such attitudes, and then to word a hypothesis that states a relationship between the two variables (the one that fills in the "blank" and "attitudes toward women's liberation"). You need to do so in a precise manner so that you can determine clearly whether the hypothesis is supported or not when you examine the results (in this case, most likely the results of a survey).

The key is to word the hypothesis carefully so that the prediction it makes is quite clear to you as well as others. If you use age, note that saying "Age is related to attitudes toward women's liberation" does not say precisely *how* you think the two are related (in fact, the only way this hypothesis could be falsified is if you fail to find a statistically significant relationship of any type between age and attitudes toward women's liberation). In this case a couple of steps are necessary. You have two options:

1. "Age is related to attitudes toward women's liberation, with younger adults being more supportive than older adults." (Or, you could state the opposite, if you believed older people are likely to be more supportive.)
2. "Age is *negatively* related to *support* for women's liberation." Note here that I specify "support" for women's liberation (SWL) and then predict a

measures of deprivation into a composite measure (see Chapter 7 for methods of doing this), the theoretical expectation was exactly confirmed. Comparing the two extremes, we found that single, childless, old, lower-class female parishioners scored more than three times as high on the measure of church involvement than did young, married, upper-class fathers. Thus was the Comfort Hypothesis confirmed.

I like this research example because it so clearly illustrates the logic of the deductive model. Beginning with general, theoretical expectations about the impact of social deprivation on church involvement, I've shown how it was possible to derive concrete hypotheses linking specific measurable variables, such as age and church attendance. The actual empirical data could then be analyzed to determine whether the deductive expectations were supported by empirical reality.

I say this example shows how it was *possible* to do it that way, but, alas, I've been fibbing a little bit just now.

An Inductive Illustration To tell the truth, although we began with an interest in discovering what negative relationship—that is, as age goes up, I predict that SWL will go down.

In this hypothesis, note that both of the variables (*age*, the independent variable or likely "cause," and *SWL*, the dependent variable or likely "effect") range from low to high. This feature of the two variables is what allows you to use "negatively" (or "positively") to describe the relationship.

Notice what happens if you hypothesize a relationship between gender and SWL. Since *gender* is a *nominal variable* (as you'll learn in Chapter 6), it does not range from low to high—people are either *male* or *female* (the two attributes of the variable *gender*). Consequently, you must be careful in stating the hypothesis unambiguously:

1. "Gender is positively (or negatively) related to SWL" is *not* an adequate hypothesis, because it doesn't specify *how* you expect gender to be related to SWL—that is, whether you think men or women will be more supportive of women's liberation.
2. It is tempting to say something like "Women are positively related to SWL," but this really doesn't work because *female* is only an attribute, not a full variable (*gender* is the variable).
3. "Gender is related to SWL, with women being more supportive than men" would be my recommendation. Or, you could say, "with men being less supportive than women," which makes the identical prediction. (Of course, you could also make the opposite prediction, that men are more supportive than women are, if you wished.)
4. Equally legitimate would be "Women are more likely to support women's liberation than are men." (Note the need for the second "are," or you could be construed as hypothesizing that women support women's liberation more than they support men—not quite the same idea.)

The above examples hypothesized relationships between a "characteristic" (age or gender) and an "orientation" (attitudes toward women's liberation), as described in Chapter 4. Because the causal order is pretty clear (obviously age and gender come before attitudes, and are less alterable), we could state the hypotheses as I've done, and everyone would assume that we were stating *causal* hypotheses.

Finally, you may run across references to the **null hypothesis,** especially in statistics. Such a hypothesis predicts no relationship (technically, no statistically significant relationship) between the two variables, and it is always implicit in testing hypotheses. Basically, if you have hypothesized a positive (or negative) relationship, you are hoping that the results will allow you to *reject the null hypothesis* and verify your hypothesized relationship.

---

caused variations in church involvement among Episcopalians, we didn't actually begin with a Comfort Hypothesis, or any other hypothesis for that matter. (In the interest of further honesty, Glock and Ringer initiated the study, and I joined it years after the data had been collected.)

A questionnaire was designed to collect information from parishioners that *might* shed some light on why some participated in the church more than others, but questionnaire construction was not guided by any precise, deductive theory. Once the data were collected, the task of explaining differences in religiosity began with an analysis of variables that have a wide impact on people's lives, including gender, age, social class, and family status. Each of these four variables was found to relate strongly to church involvement—in the ways already described. Indeed, they had a cumulative effect, also already described. Rather than being good news, this presented a dilemma.

Glock recalls discussing his findings with colleagues over lunch at the Columbia faculty club. Once he had displayed the tables illustrating the impact of each individual variable as well as their

FIGURE 2-3
Deductive and Inductive Methods

1. Deductive Method

(a) Hypothesis

(b) Observations

(c) Accept or reject hypothesis?

2. Inductive Method

(a) Observations

(b) Finding a pattern

(c) Tentative conclusion

powerful composite effect, a colleague asked, "What does it all mean, Charlie?" Glock was at a loss. Why were those variables so strongly related to church involvement?

That question launched a process of reasoning about what the several variables had in common, aside from their impact on religiosity. (The composite index was originally labeled "Predisposition to Church Involvement.") Eventually we saw that each of the four variables also reflected differential status in the secular society and *then* had the thought that perhaps the issue of comfort was involved. Thus, the inductive process had moved from concrete observations to a general theoretical explanation.

A Graphic Contrast Figure 2-3 shows a graphic comparison of the deductive and inductive methods. In both cases, we are interested in the rela-

FIGURE 2-4
The Wheel of Science

```
                    → Theories ─
                  ╱              ╲
    Empirical                      Hypotheses
    Generalizations
                  ╲              ╱
                    ← Observations
   INDUCTION                      DEDUCTION
```

Source: Adapted from Walter Wallace, *The Logic of Science in Sociology* (New York: Aldine deGruyter, 1971). Copyright © 1971 by Walter L. Wallace. Used by permission.

tionship between the number of hours spent studying for an exam and the grade earned on that exam. Using the deductive method, we would begin by examining the matter logically. Doing well on an exam reflects a student's ability to recall and manipulate information. Both of these abilities should be increased by exposure to the information before the exam. In this fashion, we would arrive at a hypothesis suggesting a positive relationship between the number of hours spent studying and the grade earned on the exam. We say positive because we expect grades to increase as the hours of studying increase. If increased hours produced decreased grades, that would be called a negative relationship. The hypothesis is represented by the line in part 1(a) of Figure 2-3.

Our next step, using the deductive method, would be to make observations relevant to testing our hypothesis. The shaded area in part 1(b) of the figure represents perhaps hundreds of observations of different students, noting how many hours they studied and what grades they got. Finally, in part 1(c), we compare the hypothesis and the observations. Because observations in the real world seldom if ever match our expectations perfectly, we must decide whether the match is close enough to consider the hypothesis confirmed. Put differently, can we conclude that the hypothesis describes the general pattern that exists, granting some variations in real life?

Now let's turn to addressing the same research question, using the inductive method. In this case, we would begin—as in part 2(a) of the figure—with a set of observations. Curious about the relationship between hours spent studying and grades earned, we might simply arrange to collect some relevant data. Then we'd look for a pattern that best represented or summarized our observations. In part 2(b) of the figure, the pattern is shown as a curved line running through the center of the curving mass of points.

The pattern found among the points in this case suggests that with 1 to 15 hours of studying, each additional hour generally produces a higher grade on the exam. With 15 to about 25 hours, however, more study seems to slightly lower the grade. Studying more than 25 hours, on the other hand, results in a return to the initial pattern: More hours produce higher grades. Using the inductive method, then, we end up with a *tentative* conclusion about the pattern of the relationship between the two variables. The conclusion is tentative because the observations we have made cannot be taken as a test of the pattern—those observations are the *source* of the pattern we've created.

In actual practice, theory and research interact through a never ending alternation of deduction, induction, deduction, and so forth. Walter Wallace (1971) has represented this process nicely as a circle, which is presented in a modified form in Figure 2-4.

When Emile Durkheim ([1897] 1951) pored through table after table of official statistics on suicide rates in different areas, he was struck by the fact that Protestant countries consistently had higher suicide rates than Catholic ones. Why should that be the case? His initial observations led him to create a theory of religion, social integration, anomie, and suicide. His theoretical explanations led to further hypotheses and further observations.

In summary, the scientific norm of logical reasoning provides a bridge between theory and research—a two-way bridge. Scientific inquiry in practice typically involves an alternation between deduction and induction. During the deductive phase, we reason *toward* observations; during the inductive phase, we reason *from* observations. Both logic and observation are essential. In practice, both deduction and induction are routes to the construction of social theories. Let's look a little more closely at how each of the two methods operates in that regard.

While both inductive and deductive methods are valid in scientific inquiry, individuals may feel more comfortable with one approach than the other. Consider this exchange in Sir Arthur Conan Doyle's "A Scandal in Bohemia," as Sherlock Holmes answers Dr. Watson's inquiry (Doyle [1891] 1892:13):

■ "What do you imagine that it means?"
"I have no data yet. It is a capital mistake to theorise before one has data. Insensibly one begins to twist facts to suit theories, instead of theories to suit facts."

Some social scientists would more or less agree with this inductive position, while others would take a deductive stance. Most, however, concede the legitimacy of both approaches. Having gotten an overview of the deductive and inductive linkages between theory and research, let's look just a little deeper into how theories are constructed using these two different approaches.

■ DEDUCTIVE THEORY CONSTRUCTION

What's involved in deductive theory construction and hypothesis testing? To begin, here's an overview of some of the terminology associated with deductive theory construction. Then we'll look at how you might go about constructing such a theory.

Getting Started

The first step in deductive theory construction is to pick a topic that interests you. It can be broad, such as "What's the structure of society?" or narrower, as in "Why do people support or oppose a woman's right to an abortion?" Whatever the topic, it should be something you're interested in understanding and explaining.

Once you've picked your topic, you should undertake an inventory of what is known or thought about it. In part, this means writing down your own observations and ideas about it. Beyond that, you'll want to learn what other scholars have said about it. You can talk to other people, and you'll want to read what others have written about it. Appendix A provides guidelines for using the library—you'll probably spend a lot of time there.

By the same token, your preliminary research will probably uncover consistent patterns discovered by prior scholars. For example, religious and political variables will stand out as important determinants of attitudes about abortion. Findings such as these will be very useful to you in creating your own theory.

In this context, I want to say a word or two on the value of introspection. If you are able to look at your own personal processes—including reactions, fears, and prejudices you aren't especially proud of—you may be able to gain important insights into human behavior in general. I don't mean to say that everyone thinks like you, but introspection can be a useful source of insights.

Constructing Your Theory

Although theory construction is not a lockstep affair, the following list of elements in theory construction should organize the activity for you.

1. Specify the topic.
2. Specify the range of phenomena your theory addresses. Will your theory apply to all of human social life, will it apply only to U.S. citizens, only to young people, or what?

3. Identify and specify your major concepts and variables.
4. Find out what is known (propositions) about the relationships among those variables.
5. Reason logically from those propositions to the specific topic you are examining.

We've already discussed items (1) through (3), so let's focus now on (4) and (5). As you identify the relevant concepts and discover what has already been learned about them, you can begin to create a propositional structure that explains the topic under study. For the most part, social scientists have not created formal, propositional theories. Still, it is useful to look at a well-reasoned example.

That's enough discussion of the building blocks. Let's look now at an example of how they fit together in actual deductive theory construction and empirical research.

An Example of Deductive Theory

A topic of central interest to scholars using the exchange paradigm (discussed earlier) is that of *distributive justice,* your perception of whether you're being treated fairly by life, whether you are getting "your share." Guillermina Jasso describes the theory of distributive justice more formally, as follows:

■ The theory provides a mathematical description of the process whereby individuals, reflecting on their holdings of the goods they value (such as beauty, intelligence, or wealth), compare themselves to others, experiencing a fundamental instantaneous magnitude of the justice evaluation (J), which captures their sense of being fairly or unfairly treated in the distributions of natural and social goods.

(JASSO 1989:11)

Notice that Jasso has assigned a symbolic representation for her key variable: J will stand for distributive justice. She does this to support her intention of stating her theory in mathematical formulas. Though theories are often expressed mathematically, we'll not delve too deeply into that practice here.

Jasso indicates that there are three kinds of postulates in her theory. "The first makes explicit the fundamental axiom which represents the substantive point of departure for the theory." She elaborates as follows:

■ The theory begins with the received *Axiom of Comparison,* which formalizes the long-held view that a wide class of phenomena, including happiness, self-esteem, and the sense of distributive justice, may be understood as the product of a comparison process.

(JASSO 1989:11)

Thus, your sense of whether you are receiving a "fair" share of the good things of life comes from comparing yourself with others. If this seems obvious to you, that's not a shortcoming of the axiom. Remember, axioms are the take-for-granted beginnings of theory.

Jasso continues to do the groundwork for her theory. First, she indicates that our sense of distributive justice is a function of "Actual Holding (A)" and "Comparison Holdings (C)" of some good. Let's consider money, for example. My sense of justice in this regard is a function of how much I actually have compared with how much others have. By specifying the two components of the comparison, Jasso can use them as variables in her theory.

Jasso then offers a "measurement rule" that further specifies how the two variables, A and C, will be conceptualized. This step is needed because some of the goods to be examined are concrete and commonly measured (such as money) whereas others are less tangible (such as respect). The former kind, she says, will be measured conventionally, whereas the latter will be measured "by the individual's relative rank . . . within a specially selected comparison group" and provide a formula for making that measurement (Jasso 1988:13).

Jasso continues in this fashion to introduce additional elements, weaving them into mathematical formulas to be used in deriving predictions about the workings of distributive justice in a variety of social settings. Here is just a sampling of where her theorizing takes her.

1. Persons who are blind or deaf have fewer dimensions of self-evaluation, per unit of time, than otherwise comparable persons....
3. Other things the same, a person will prefer to steal from a fellow group member rather than from an outsider.
4. The preference to steal from a fellow group member is more pronounced in poor groups than in rich groups.
5. In the case of theft, informants arise only in cross-group theft, in which case they are members of the thief's group....
9. Persons who arrive a week late at summer camp or for freshman year of college are more likely to become friends of persons who play games of chance than of persons who play games of skill.
10. An immigrant's propensity to learn the language of the host country is an increasing function of the ratio of the origin-country's per capita GNP to the host-country's per capita GNP....
12. If both spouses work full-time, marital cohesiveness increases with the ratio of the smaller to the larger earnings....
14. In wartime, the favorite leisure-time activity of soldiers is playing games of chance....
17. A society becomes more vulnerable to deficit spending as its wealth increases....
22. Societies in which population growth is welcomed must be societies in which the set of valued goods includes at least one quantity-good, such as wealth.

(Jasso 1988:14–15)

These propositions should provide a good sense of where deductive theorizing can take you. While we aren't going to trace all the theoretical and mathematical reasoning that produced each of the propositions shown, let's look briefly at the logic involved in the propositions relating to theft within and outside one's group, specifically Propositions 3 and 5.

Beginning with the assumption that thieves want to maximize their relative wealth, take a minute to ask whether that goal would be best served by stealing from those you compare yourself with or from outsiders. In each case, stealing will increase your Actual Holdings, but what about your Comparison Holdings? If you think about it, you'll see that stealing from people in your comparison group will *lower* their holdings, further increasing your *relative* wealth.

To simplify, imagine there are only two people in your comparison group: you and me. Suppose we each have $100. If you steal $50 from someone outside our group, you will have increased your relative wealth by 50 percent compared with me: $150 versus $100. But if you steal $50 from me, you will have increased your relative wealth 200 percent: $150 to my $50. Your goal is best served by stealing from within the comparison group; hence, Proposition 3.

Regarding Proposition 5, can you see why it would make sense for informants (1) to arise only in the case of cross-group theft and (2) to come from the thief's comparison group? To understand this, we must consider the fundamental assumption that everyone wants to increase his or her relative standing. Suppose you and I are in the same comparison group, which in this instance contains additional people.

If you steal from someone else in our comparison group, my relative standing does not change. While your wealth has increased, the average wealth in the group remains the same (since someone else's wealth has decreased by the same amount), so my relative standing remains the same.

If you steal from someone outside our comparison group, your nefarious income increases the total wealth in our group, so my own wealth relative to that total is diminished. Since my relative wealth has suffered, I am more likely to bring an end to your stealing.

This latest deduction also begins to explain why informants are more likely to arrive from within the thief's comparison group. We've just seen how my relative standing was decreased by your theft. How about other members of the other group? Each of them would actually profit from the theft, since you would have reduced the total with which they compare themselves. Hence, the theory of distributive justice predicts that informants arise from the thief's comparison group.

This brief and selective peek into Jasso's derivations should give you some sense of the enterprise of deductive theory. Realize, of course, that the theory guarantees none of the given predictions. The role of research is to test each of them empirically to determine whether what makes sense (theory) occurs in practice (research).

There are two important elements in science, then: logical integrity and empirical verification. Both are essential to scientific inquiry and discovery. Logic alone is not enough, but on the other hand, the mere observation and collection of empirical facts does not provide understanding—the telephone directory, for example, is not a scientific conclusion. Observation, however, can be the springboard for the construction of a social scientific theory, as we now see in the case of inductive theory.

■ INDUCTIVE THEORY CONSTRUCTION

Quite often, social scientists begin constructing a theory through the inductive method by observing aspects of social life, and then seeking to discover patterns that may point to relatively universal principles. Barney Glaser and Anselm Strauss (1967) coined the term *grounded theory* in reference to this method.

Field research—the direct observation of events in progress (discussed in depth in Chapter 11)—is frequently used to develop theories through observation. A long and rich anthropological tradition has seen this method used to good advantage.

Among contemporary social scientists, no one was more adept at seeing the patterns of human behavior through observation than Erving Goffman:

■ A game such as chess generates a habitable universe for those who can follow it, a plane of being, a cast of characters with a seemingly unlimited number of different situations and acts through which to realize their natures and destinies. Yet much of this is reducible to a small set of interdependent rules and practices. If the meaningfulness of everyday activity is similarly dependent on a closed, finite set of rules, then explication of them would give one a powerful means of analyzing social life.

(1974:5)

In a variety of research efforts, Goffman uncovered the rules of such diverse behaviors as living in a mental institution (1961) and managing the "spoiled identity" of disfiguration (1963). In each case, Goffman observed the phenomenon in depth and teased out the rules governing behavior. Goffman's research provides an excellent example of qualitative field research as a source of grounded theory.

As indicated by the search for causes of church involvement, qualitative field research is not the only method of observation appropriate to the development of inductive theory. Here's another detailed example to illustrate further the construction of inductive theory using quantitative methods. During the 1960s and 1970s, marijuana use on America's college campuses was a subject of considerable discussion in the popular press. Some people were troubled by marijuana's popularity; others welcomed it. What interests us here is why some students smoked marijuana and others didn't. A survey of students at the University of Hawaii (Takeuchi 1974) provided the data to answer that question.

Why Do People Smoke Marijuana?

At the time of the study, countless explanations were being offered for drug use. People who opposed drug use, for example, often suggested that marijuana smokers were academic failures trying to avoid the rigors of college life. Those in favor of marijuana, on the other hand, often spoke of the search for new values: Marijuana smokers, they said, were people who had seen through the hypocrisy of middle-class values.

David Takeuchi's (1974) analysis of the data gathered from University of Hawaii students, however, did not support any of the explanations being offered. Those who reported smoking marijuana had essentially the same academic records as those who didn't smoke it, and both groups were equally involved in traditional "school spirit" activities. Both groups seemed to feel equally well integrated into campus life.

There were differences, however:

1. Women were less likely than men to smoke marijuana.
2. Asian students (a large proportion of the student body) were less likely to smoke marijuana than non-Asians.
3. Students living at home were less likely to smoke marijuana than those living in apartments.

As in the case of religiosity, the three variables independently affected the likelihood of a student's smoking marijuana. About 10 percent of the Asian women living at home had smoked marijuana, as contrasted with about 80 percent of the non-Asian men living in apartments. And, as in the religiosity study, the researchers discovered a powerful pattern of drug use before they had an explanation for that pattern.

In this instance, the explanation took a peculiar turn. Instead of explaining why some students smoked marijuana, the researchers explained why some *didn't*. Assuming that all students had some motivation for trying drugs, the researchers suggested that students differed in the degree of "social constraints" preventing them from following through on that motivation.

U.S. society is, on the whole, more permissive with men than with women when it comes to deviant behavior. Consider, for example, a group of men getting drunk and boisterous. We tend to dismiss such behavior with references to "camaraderie" and "having a good time," whereas a group of women behaving similarly would probably be regarded with great disapproval. We have an idiom, "Boys will be boys," but no comparable idiom for girls. The researchers reasoned, therefore, that women would have more to lose by smoking marijuana than men would. Being female, then, provided a constraint against smoking marijuana.

Students living at home had obvious constraints against smoking marijuana, compared with students living on their own. Quite aside from differences in opportunity, those living at home were seen as being more dependent on their parents—hence more vulnerable to additional punishment for breaking the law.

Finally, the Asian subculture in Hawaii has traditionally placed a higher premium on obedience to the law than other subcultures, so Asian students would have more to lose if they were caught violating the law by smoking marijuana.

Overall, then, a "social constraints" theory was offered as the explanation for observed differences in the likelihood of smoking marijuana. The more constraints a student had, the less likely he or she would be to smoke marijuana. It bears repeating that the researchers had no thoughts about such a theory when their research began. The theory came from an examination of the data.

■ THE LINKS BETWEEN THEORY AND RESEARCH

Throughout this chapter, we have seen various aspects of the links between theory and research in social scientific inquiry. In the deductive model, research is used to test theories. And in the inductive model, theories are developed from the analysis of research data. In this final section, we look more closely into the ways theory and research are related in actual social scientific inquiry.

Whereas we have discussed two logical models for the linking of theory and research, actual social scientific inquiries have developed a great many variations on these themes. Sometimes theoretical issues are introduced merely as a background for empirical analyses. Other studies cite selected empirical data to bolster theoretical arguments. In neither case is there really an interaction between theory and research for the purpose of developing new explanations. And some studies make no use of theory at all, aiming specifically at an ethnographic description of a particular social situation, for example.

Rather than simply discuss the possible relationships between theory and research, let's take a look at the ways social scientists have actually linked them in their studies. To do this, we're going to examine four decades of articles published in the *American Sociological Review* (ASR), the main research journal for U.S. sociologists.

To find out how theory has figured in sociological research, Richard H. Wells and J. Steven Picou (1981) conducted a content analysis—the rigorous examination of communications (see Chapter 12)—of a sample of 707 articles from the 2,619 published in the ASR between 1936 and 1978. One of the first things Wells and Picou discovered was that sociologists have increasingly employed theory in their research articles. Between 1936 and 1949, only 34 percent of the ASR articles included any use of theory, with the percentage increasing to 66 percent in the period from 1965 to 1978 (1981:103). Table 2-1 reports the various uses made of theory during the entire period from 1936 to 1978.

Among the many different uses made of theory in connection with sociological research, notice that only 24.5 percent of the articles involved the testing of theoretically derived hypotheses: the traditional model of scientific inquiry. Of these, 22.5 percent presented findings in support of the hypotheses, and 2 percent refuted the hypotheses. Taken together, these two items amount to 38 percent of those articles that used theory at all.

When Wells and Picou examined the uses of theory over time, they found a substantial increase in the traditional hypothesis-testing model. During the period 1936–49, this model was used for only 16 percent of the articles making any use of theory; 36 percent used it during the period 1950–64; and 54 percent during 1965–78 (1981:106).

In the decades since the Wells-Picou analysis, there appears to have been something of a returned interest in and use of qualitative and inductive approaches, as I've suggested earlier in this chapter. Realize that I report this as a subjective, qualitative observation rather a contention supported by quantified data.

The various discussions of this chapter should make you realize that there is no simple recipe for conducting social science research. It is far more open-ended than the traditional view of science would suggest. Ultimately, science rests on two pillars: logic and observation. As you'll see throughout this book, they can be fit together in many patterns.

TABLE 2-1
How Theory Was Utilized in the ASR, 1936–78

Primary Theory Utilization	Percent
No theoretically related research	35.8%
Theory used to support author's idea	1.9
Theory used to focus research problem	3.3
Concepts used to discuss and interpret findings	20.8
Theory used to discuss and interpret findings	0.9
Modification or extension of existing theory	4.5
Development of theory	2.1
Theory used to develop testable hypotheses and findings support the hypotheses	22.5
Theory used to develop testable hypotheses and findings refute the hypotheses	2.0
Unfavorable discussion of theory	2.7
Favorable discussion of theory	3.8
TOTAL	**100.0**
	(707)

Source: Richard H. Wells and J. Steven Picou, *American Sociology: Theoretical and Methodological Structures* (Washington, DC: University Press of America, 1981), 105. Used by permission.

■ MAIN POINTS

- A paradigm is a fundamental model or scheme that organizes our view of something.
- Social scientists use a variety of paradigms to organize how they understand and inquire into social life.
- Positivism assumes we can scientifically discover the rules governing social life.
- Social Darwinism sees a progressive evolution in social life.
- The conflict paradigm focuses on the attempt of one person or group to dominate others and to avoid being dominated.
- The symbolic interactionist paradigm examines how shared meanings and social patterns are developed in the course of social interactions.

- Role theory uses the metaphor of the theater for understanding the roles played by social actors and the scripts governing their behavior.
- Ethnomethodology focuses on the ways people make sense out of life in the process of living it, as though each were a researcher engaged in an inquiry.
- The structural functionalist (or social systems) paradigm seeks to discover what functions the many elements of society perform for the whole system—for example, the functions of mothers, labor unions, radio talk shows.
- The feminist paradigm, in addition to drawing attention to the oppression of women in most societies, highlights how previous images of social reality have often come from and reinforced the experiences of men.
- The exchange paradigm suggests that we analyze social situations in terms of the perceived costs and benefits of various behaviors.
- The longstanding belief in an objective reality that abides by rational rules has been challenged by some contemporary theorists and researchers.
- The traditional image of science includes theory, operationalization, and observation.
- The traditional image of science is not a very accurate picture of how scientific research is actually done.
- Social scientific theory and research are linked through two logical methods:
  - *Deduction* involves the derivation of expectations or hypotheses from theories.
  - *Induction* involves the development of generalizations from specific observations.
- Science is a process involving an alternation of deduction and induction.
- A fact usually refers to something that has been observed.
- A law is a universal generalization about a class of facts.
- A theory is a systematic explanation for a set of facts and laws.
- Grounded theory refers to theory based more on observation than on deduction.

■ REVIEW QUESTIONS AND EXERCISES

1. Consider the possible relationship between education and prejudice (mentioned in Chapter 1). Describe how that relationship might be examined through (a) deductive and (b) inductive methods.
2. Review the relationships between theory and research described in Table 2-1. Select a research article from an academic journal and classify the relationship between theory and research you find there.
3. Using one of the many search engines (such as Lycos, WebCrawler, Excite, Yahoo, and Infoseek), find information on the Web concerning at least three of the following paradigms. Give the Web locations and report on the theorists discussed in connection with the discussions you found.

Functionalism	Feminism
Conflict theory	Positivism
Interactionism	Exchange theory
Ethnomethodology	Postmodernism

■ ADDITIONAL READINGS

Berger, Joseph, Morris Zelditch, Jr., and Bo Anderson, eds. *Sociological Theories in Progress.* Newbury Park, CA: Sage, 1989. Several authors develop parts of a theory of social interaction, many of which focus on how we create expectations for each other's behavior.

Chavetz, Janet. *A Primer on the Construction and Testing of Theories in Sociology.* Itasca, IL: Peacock, 1978. One of the few books on theory construction written expressly for undergraduates. Chavetz provides a rudimentary understanding of the philosophy of science through simple language and everyday examples. She describes the nature of explanation, the role of assumptions and concepts, and the building and testing of theories.

Denzin, Norman K., and Yvonna S. Lincoln. *Handbook of Qualitative Research.* Newbury Park, CA: Sage, 1994. Various authors discuss the process of qualitative research from the perspective of various paradigms, showing how they influence the nature of inquiry. The editors also critique positivism from a postmodern perspective.

Kuhn, Thomas. *The Structure of Scientific Revolutions.* Chicago: University of Chicago Press, 1970. An exciting and innovative recasting of the nature of scientific development. Kuhn disputes the notion of gradual change and modification in science, arguing instead that established "paradigms" tend to persist until the weight of contradictory evidence brings their rejection and replacement by new paradigms. This short book is at once stimulating and informative.

Lofland, John, and Lyn H. Lofland. *Analyzing Social Settings: A Guide to Qualitative Observation and Analysis.* Belmont, CA: Wadsworth, 1995. An excellent text on how to conduct qualitative inquiry with an eye toward discovering the rules of social life. Includes a critique of postmodernism.

McGrane, Bernard. *The Un-TV and 10 mph Car: Experiments in Personal Freedom and Everyday Life.* Fort Bragg, CA: The Small Press, 1994. Some excellent and imaginative examples of an ethnomethodological approach to society and to the craft of sociology. The book is useful for both students and faculty.

Reinharz, Shulamit. *Feminist Methods in Social Research.* New York: Oxford University Press, 1992. This book explores several social research techniques (such as interviewing, experiments, and content analysis) from a feminist perspective.

Ritzer, George. *Sociological Theory.* New York: Knopf, 1988. This is an excellent overview of the major theoretical traditions in sociology.

Turner, Jonathan H., ed. *Theory Building in Sociology: Assessing Theoretical Cumulation.* Newbury Park, CA: Sage, 1989. This collection of essays on sociological theory construction focuses specifically on the question posed by Turner's introductory chapter, "Can Sociology Be a Cumulative Science?"

Turner, Stephen Park, and Jonathan H. Turner. *The Impossible Science: An Institutional Analysis of American Sociology.* Newbury Park, CA: Sage, 1990. Two authors bring two very different points of view to the history of U.S. sociologists' attempt to establish a *science* of society.

CHAPTER 3: The Nature of Causation

What You'll Learn in This Chapter
Here you'll see how the notions of cause and effect relate to explanatory social science. You'll learn about both the technical and the philosophical aspects of the issue.

INTRODUCTION

DETERMINISM AND SOCIAL SCIENCE
Causation in the Natural Sciences
Finding Causes in Social Science
Reasons Have Reasons
Determinism in Perspective

IDIOGRAPHIC AND NOMOTHETIC MODELS OF EXPLANATION

CRITERIA FOR CAUSALITY
Necessary and Sufficient Causes

ERRORS OF REASONING
Provincialism
Hasty Conclusion
Questionable Cause
Suppressed Evidence
False Dilemma

LINKING MEASUREMENT AND ASSOCIATION
The Traditional Deductive Model
An Example of Measurement and Association

MAIN POINTS

REVIEW QUESTIONS AND EXERCISES

ADDITIONAL READINGS

■ INTRODUCTION

Implicit in much of what you've read so far in this book are the ideas of cause and effect. One of the chief goals of the scientist—social or other—is to explain why things are the way they are. Typically, they do that by specifying the causes for the way things are: Some things are caused by other things.

In our discussion of the idiographic and nomothetic approaches, we've already begun to look at causation. Now we'll delve more deeply into this concept.

The general notion of causation is at once simple and complex. I imagine, on the one hand, that I could have ignored the issue altogether in this book—simply using the terms *cause* and *effect*—and you would have easily understood them. On the other hand, an adequate discourse on causation would require a whole book in its own right, or even a series of books. However, let me aim at the middle ground, providing something more than a commonsense perspective on causation without attempting to be definitive.

We'll begin with the subject of determinism in social science. After that, we'll return briefly to the topic of deductive and inductive logic, with deterministic assumptions added. Next we'll consider some appropriate and inappropriate criteria for causality. The chapter will conclude with a discussion of the links between measurement and association.

■ DETERMINISM AND SOCIAL SCIENCE

The deterministic perspective to be discussed now contrasts the idea of *free will,* which you and I take for granted in our daily lives. The fundamental issue is this: Is your behavior the product of your personal willpower or the product of forces and factors in the world that you cannot control and may not even recognize? Once we have completed our examination of this issue, we'll be in a position to look at the place of causation in social scientific research. Let's start with an example outside the social sciences altogether.

Causation in the Natural Sciences

The deterministic model of explanation is exemplified throughout the natural sciences. Growth, for example, is caused by several factors. We can affect the growth of plants by varying the amount of light, water, and nutrients they receive. We also know that the growth rate of human beings is affected by the nutrients they receive. The desire to grow or not to grow is irrelevant—for humans just as for plants. We acknowledge that nutrition greatly overshadows our free will in the matter.

The point of this example is to show that the natural sciences operate on the basis of a cause-and-effect, deterministic model, and that model is often applied to human beings as well as to plants and inanimate objects. For the most part, moreover, we accept the deterministic model as appropriate in such cases. We recognize that our free will is limited by certain constraints.

Finding Causes in Social Science

Essentially the same model is used in the social sciences. It is usually so implicit that we may forget the nature of the model we are using, so let me illustrate how social science might proceed with that model. Imagine that you have managed to obtain a million-dollar grant from the National Science Foundation to find out the causes of prejudice. That's certainly a laudable aim, and various government and private foundations are often willing to support such research. Let's suppose you receive the money and spend it doing your research. Now you are ready to send your project report to the foundation. Here's how the report reads:

■ After an exhaustive examination of the subject, we have discovered that some people are prejudiced, and the reason is that they want to be prejudiced. Other people are not prejudiced, and the reason is that they don't want to be prejudiced.

Obviously, this paragraph would not be a satisfactory conclusion for a research project aimed at finding out what causes prejudice. When we look for the causes of prejudice, we look for the reasons, the things that make some people prejudiced and others not. Satisfactory reasons would include economic competition, religious ideology, political views, childhood experiences, and amount and kind of education. We know, for example, that education tends to reduce prejudice. That's the kind of causal explanation we accept as the end product of social research.

Now let's look at the logic of such an explanation a little more closely. What does it say about the people involved in the research conclusion—the subjects of study? Fundamentally, it says that they turned out prejudiced or unprejudiced as a result of something they did not control or choose. It's as though they came to a fork in the road—one turn prejudice and the other no prejudice—and they were propelled down one or the other by forces such as childhood experiences, inherited religious affiliation, and similar factors they neither controlled nor even recognized. That is, they turned out prejudiced or unprejudiced for reasons beyond their control.

When social scientists study juvenile delinquency, the basic model is the same: Delinquency is caused by factors other than the delinquent's free choice. It is further assumed that those factors can be discovered and perhaps modified, regardless of whether the delinquent wants to change or not.

The same model applies when social scientists study "nice" behaviors. What are the factors that cause a person to be altruistic, considerate, responsible? If we knew the answer, we could make more people that way—so the implicit reasoning goes.

Reasons Have Reasons

Sometimes people protest this reasoning by arguing that individuals personally choose those things that determine how prejudiced, delinquent, or altruistic they are. For example, let's say you are quite unprejudiced, and researchers conclude that your lack of prejudice is probably a function of all the education you've received. Didn't you choose to go to school? Aren't you, therefore, the source of your being unprejudiced?

The problem with this view is that reasons have reasons. Why did you go to school? If you and I were discussing this subject, I know you'd be able to give me reasons for having continued going to school up to this point. Let's say you wanted to learn about the world around you, and you thought college would be a good way to do it. That makes sense.

It makes so much sense in fact that we might even say your desire to learn about the world *caused* you to continue going to school. It's as if your desire *forced* you to go to school. Given that you had such a desire, how could you *not* go to school?

"I might not have gone if I hadn't had enough money," you might say. That's true. If you hadn't had enough money to go to school, that factor would have *forced* you to stay out of school. But then suppose your desire to learn about the world around you was so powerful that you overcame the lack of money—maybe you got a scholarship or went to work for a while. In that case, we are back to your powerful desire forcing you to go to school.

Ah, but why did you have such a strong desire to go to school? Perhaps you grew up in a family where everyone had gone to college generation after generation, and you'd have felt you were letting your family down if you didn't go to college. Or perhaps you come from a family where nobody had ever gone to college before, and they were all proud of the fact that you might be the first. In both cases, we can see that factors *forced* you to have the powerful desire to go to college, and that powerful desire *forced* you to go to college, and going to college *forced* you to be unprejudiced.

Clearly I can't—through a book—deal with all the particular reasons you had for doing something like going to college, but I think you'll be able to see that you did it for reasons and that those reasons caused you to go. Moreover, no matter what reason you had at any specific step in the process, your reason would have a reason. The ultimate implication of this discussion is that your being prejudiced or unprejudiced can be traced back through a long and complex chain of reasons that explain why you turned out the way you did.

Whenever we undertake explanatory social science research—when we set out to discover the causes of prejudice, for example—we adopt a model of human behavior that assumes people have little individual freedom of choice. Of course, we don't *say* that, but if you look at the implications of asking "Why are people prejudiced?" you'll see that it's so.

Determinism in Perspective

As you no doubt know, the issue of determinism and freedom is a complex one that philosophers have debated for thousands of years and will probably debate for thousands more. It is perhaps one of those "open questions" that are more valuable asked than answered. Certainly, we are not going to resolve the issue here.

My purpose in raising the issue of determinism is to engage you in the question and to alert you to its place in social research. I have observed that when people set out to learn the skills of explanatory social research, the implicit assumption of determinism disturbs them. New researchers often harbor a concern about whether they are learning to demonstrate that *they* themselves have no free will, no personal freedom in determining the course of their own lives. To the extent that this concern grows and festers, it interferes with the learning of analytic skills and techniques. Therefore I think it's best to confront the issue head-on rather than leaving it for you to discover later.

Having said all this, let me clarify what is not part of the model. First, social scientists do not believe all human actions, thoughts, and feelings are determined, nor do they lead their lives as though they believed it. Second, the deterministic model does not assume that causal patterns are simple, as I've already suggested. Nor does the model assume we are all controlled by the same factors and forces: Your reasons for going to college surely differed somewhat from mine. Moreover, the deterministic model at the base of explanatory social science does not suggest that we now know all the answers about what causes what or that we ever will.

Finally, as you'll see later, social science typically operates on the basis of a *probabilistic* causal model. Rather than predicting, for example, that a particular person will attend college, we say that certain factors make attending college more or less likely within groups of people. Thus, high school students whose parents attended college are more likely to attend college themselves than those students whose parents didn't attend college. This does not mean that all of the former and none of the latter will attend college.

To summarize, the kind of understanding we seek as we analyze social research data inevitably involves a deterministic model of human behavior. In looking for the reasons why people are the way they are and do the things they do, we implicitly assume that their characteristics and actions are determined by forces and factors operating on them. You do not need to *believe* that human beings are totally determined, nor do you have to lead your life as though you were, but you must be willing to use deterministic logic in looking for explanations when you engage in social science research.

■ IDIOGRAPHIC AND NOMOTHETIC MODELS OF EXPLANATION

You've probably recognized that the preceding discussions, which probe the multiplicity of reasons that can account for a specific behavior, illustrate the *idiographic model of explanation*. This model aims at explanation through the enumeration of the numerous, perhaps unique, considerations that lie behind a given action. Though we never truly exhaust such reasons in practice, the idiographic model is employed frequently in many different contexts.

Traditional historians, for example, tend to use the idiographic model, enumerating all the special causes of the French Revolution or World War II. Clinical psychologists may employ this model in seeking an explanation for the aberrant behavior of a patient. A criminal court, in response to a plea of extenuating circumstances, may seek to examine all the various considerations that have resulted in the crime in question.

When Charles Payne (1995) detailed the processes leading to 33 Mississippi lynchings between

1930 and 1950, he intended more to have the reader fully understand each case on its own merits rather than to develop a generalized theory of race violence. While the separate accounts contain common themes, the researcher's focus was more idiographic than nomothetic.

Or consider the events of May 13, 1985, in Philadelphia. The city's police force had been attempting to serve arrest warrants on activist members of the MOVE civil rights group. Finally, having evacuated the neighborhood and surrounded the organization's headquarters with 500 heavily armed officers, the police launched their attack. Beginning with automatic weapons, water canons, and tear gas, the police assault culminated with a helicopter dropping explosives on the roof, killing 11 people and destroying two urban blocks.

In shocked tones that would be echoed later regarding Waco and Ruby Ridge, people asked how such a tragedy could have occurred. Robin Wagner-Pacifici (1995) undertook research to find the causes, using a technique known as **discourse analysis,** which involves dissecting the underlying meanings found in various forms of communications. In this case, the police pronouncements can be best understood as a "discourse of war." Hence, the resulting battle makes sense.

While the idiographic model of explanation is often used in daily life and in social research, other situations and purposes call for a different approach, one I have previously noted: the *nomothetic model of explanation.* This model does not involve an exhaustive enumeration of all the considerations that result in a *particular* action or event. Rather, as we've seen, the nomothetic model is consciously designed to discover those considerations that are most important in explaining general classes of actions or events.

Suppose we wanted to find out why people voted the way they did in the 1996 presidential election. Each individual we talked to could give a great many reasons why he or she voted for either Clinton or Dole. Suppose someone gave us 99 different reasons for voting for Clinton. We'd probably feel we had a pretty complete explanation for that person's vote. In fact, if we found someone else with those same 99 reasons, we would feel pretty confident in predicting that *that* person also voted for Clinton. This approach represents the idiographic model of explanation.

The nomothetic model of explanation, on the other hand, involves the isolation of those *relatively few* considerations that will provide a partial explanation for the voting behavior of many or all people. For example, political orientation—liberal or conservative—would probably be a consideration of great *general* importance in determining the voting behavior of the electorate as a whole. Most of those sharing the attribute *liberal* probably voted for Clinton, and most of those sharing the attribute *conservative* probably voted for Dole. Realize, however, that this single consideration would not provide a complete explanation for all voting behavior. Some liberals voted for Dole; some conservatives for Clinton. The nomothetic model of explanation aims at providing the greatest amount of explanation with the fewest number of causal variables to uncover general patterns of cause and effect.

The nomothetic model of explanation is inevitably *probabilistic* in its approach to causation. Naming a few considerations seldom if ever provides a complete explanation. For example, we might discover that everyone who believed Dole was the best man voted for him, but that would not be a very satisfying explanation. In the best of all practical worlds, the nomothetic model indicates a very high (or very low) probability that a given action will occur whenever a limited number of specified considerations are present. Adding more specified considerations to the equation typically increases the degree of explanation, but the basic simplicity of the model calls for a balancing of a high degree of explanation with a small number of considerations.

Thus, when Eric Plutzer and John Zipp (1996) set out to understand the number of votes feminist political candidates received in the 1992 elections, they looked for variables that would make a difference *in general* rather than in specific cases. As you might expect, for example, women were more likely than men to vote for the 14 feminist candidates. But the researchers were also interested in seeing how and to what extent gender-based voting conflicted with party loyalty, with some Democratic men deserting their party's feminist candidates and some Republican women supporting them.

In another illustration of nomothetic explanation, listen to the language of causation when Jeremy Hein [1993:55] reviews the body of research aimed at distinguishing the experiences of refugees from other immigrants.

■ The same demographic variables predict employment status and earnings for immigrants and refugees. Both populations adapt as households and obtain income from multiple sources. Women perform the central function of bridging social networks and economic arenas. However, state intervention once again produces some important differences, particularly of access to the social welfare system. [Refugees are entitled to welfare immediately, while other immigrants must wait five years.]

Social scientists are sometimes criticized for *dehumanizing* the people they study. This charge is lodged specifically against the nomothetic model of explanation; the severity of the charge increases when social scientists analyze matters of great human concern. Religious people, for example, often feel robbed of their human individuality when a social scientist reports that their religiosity is largely a function of their gender, age, marital status, and social class. Any religious person will quickly report there is much more than that to the strength of his or her convictions. And indeed there is, as the use of the idiographic model in the case of any individual person would reveal. Is the idiographic model, though, any less dehumanizing than the nomothetic model?

If everything—including being religious—is a product of prior considerations, is it any more dehumanizing to seek partial but general explanations using only a few of those considerations than to seek a total explanation using them all? I suspect the true source of concern, underlying the charges of dehumanization, is based on the more direct confrontation with determinism that the nomothetic model represents. Realize, however, that a careful listing of all the private individual reasons for being religious, or for voting for Candidate X, or for any other action, involves the acknowledgment of a deterministic perspective: one that is logically no different from the deterministic perspective that permits us to specify the four variables most important in causing religiosity.

In summary, social researchers have and use two distinct modes of causal explanation. Both are legitimate and useful. What we learn in individual cases, moreover, can suggest general, causal relationships among variables, just as those general relationships can help to focus analyses of a particular case. Most useful of all, of course, is a combination of the two approaches—if not in the same study, by the research community collectively.

■ CRITERIA FOR CAUSALITY

Nothing in the preceding discussion provides much practical guidance to the discovery of causality in scientific research. Regarding idiographic explanation, Joseph Maxwell (1996:87–88) speaks of the validity of an explanation and says the main criteria are (1) its credibility or believability and (2) whether alternative explanations ("rival hypotheses") were seriously considered and found wanting. The first criterion relates to earlier comments about logic as one of the foundations of science: We demand that our explanations make sense, even if the logic is sometimes complex. The second criterion reminds us of Sherlock Holmes's dictum that when all other possibilities have been eliminated, the remaining explanation must be the truth.

Regarding nomothetic explanation, we'll examine three specific criteria for causality among variables as suggested by Paul Lazarsfeld (1959). Chapter 16 will illustrate the actual use of these criteria in research practice.

The first requirement in a causal relationship between two variables is that the cause precede the effect in time. It makes no sense in science to imagine something being caused by something else that

Correlation and Causality

by Charles Bonney
Department of Sociology, Eastern Michigan University

Having demonstrated a statistical relationship between a hypothesized "cause" and its presumed "effect," many people (sometimes including researchers who should know better) are only too eager to proclaim "proof" of causation. Let's take an example to see why "it ain't necessarily so."

Imagine you have conducted a study on college students and have found an inverse correlation between marijuana smoking (variable M) and grade point average (variable G)—that is, those who smoke tend to have lower GPAs than those who do not, and the more smoked, the lower the GPA. You might therefore claim that smoking marijuana lowers one's grades (in symbolic form, M→G), giving as an explanation, perhaps, that marijuana adversely affects memory, which would naturally have detrimental consequences on grades.

However, if an inverse correlation is all the evidence you have, a second possibility exists. Getting poor grades is frustrating; frustration often leads to escapist behavior; getting stoned is a popular means of escape; ergo, low grades cause marijuana smoking (G→M)! Unless you can establish which came first, smoking or low grades, this explanation is supported by the correlation just as plausibly as the first.

Let's introduce another variable into the picture: the existence and/or extent of emotional problems (variable E). It could certainly be plausibly argued that having emotional problems may lead to escapist behavior, including marijuana smoking. Likewise it seems reasonable to suggest that emotional problems are likely to adversely affect grades. That correlation of marijuana smoking and low grades may exist for the same reason that runny noses and sore throats tend to go together—*neither* is the cause of the other, but rather, both are the consequences of some third variable ($E \underset{G}{\overset{M}{\lessgtr}}$). Unless you can rule out such third variables, this explanation too is just as well supported by the data as is the first (or the second).

Then again, perhaps students smoke marijuana primarily because they have friends who happened later on. A bullet leaving the muzzle of a gun does not cause the gunpowder to explode; it works the other way around.

As simple and obvious as this criterion may seem, you'll discover endless problems in this regard in the analysis of social science data. Often, the order of two variables is simply unclear. Which comes first: authoritarianism or prejudice? Even when the time order seems essentially clear, exceptions can often be found. For example, we would normally assume that the educational level of parents would be a cause of the educational level of their children. Yet, some parents may return to school as a result of the advanced education of their own children.

The second requirement in a causal relationship is that the two variables be empirically correlated with one another. It would make no sense to say that exploding gunpowder causes bullets to leave muzzles of guns if, in observed reality, bullets did not come out after the gunpowder exploded.

Again, social science research has difficulties in regard to this apparently obvious requirement. At least in the probabilistic world of nomothetic explanations, there are few perfect correlations. Most conservatives voted for Dole, but some didn't. We are forced to ask, therefore, how great the empirical relationship must be for that relationship to be considered causal.

The third requirement for a causal relationship is that the observed empirical correlation between two variables cannot be explained in terms of some third variable that causes both of them. For example, there is a positive correlation between ice cream sales smoke, and get low grades because they are simply not as bright or well prepared or industrious as their classmates, and the fact that it's the same students in each case in your sample is purely coincidental. Unless your correlation is so strong and so consistent that mere coincidence becomes highly unlikely, this last possibility, while not supported by your data, is not precluded either. Incidentally, this particular example was selected for two reasons. First of all, *every one* of the above explanations for such an inverse correlation has appeared in a national magazine at one time or another. And second, *every one* of them is probably doomed to failure because it turns out that, among college students, most studies indicate a direct correlation, that is, it is those with higher GPAs who are more likely to be marijuana smokers! Thus, with tongue firmly in cheek, we may reanalyze this finding:

1. Marijuana relaxes a person, clearing away other stresses, thus allowing more effective study; hence, M→G.

or

2. Marijuana is used as a reward for really hitting the books or doing well ("Wow, man! An 'A'! Let's go get high!"); hence, G→M.

or

3. A high level of curiosity (E) is definitely an asset to learning and achieving high grades and may also lead one to investigate "taboo" substances; hence, $E \rightrightarrows_G^M$.

or

4. Again coincidence, but this time the samples just happened to contain a lot of brighter, more industrious students whose friends smoke marijuana!

The obvious conclusion is this: If *all* of these are possible explanations for a relationship between two variables, then no *one* of them should be too readily singled out. Establishing that two variables tend to occur together is a *necessary* condition for demonstrating a causal relationship, but it is not by itself a *sufficient* condition. It is a fact, for example, that human birthrates are higher in areas of Europe where there are lots of storks, but as to the meaning of that relationship . . . !

and deaths due to drowning: the more ice cream sold, the more drownings, and vice versa. The third variable at work here is *season* or *temperature*. Most drowning deaths occur during summer—the peak period for ice cream sales. There is no direct link between ice cream and drowning, however. (See Chapter 16 for more on this third requirement.)

The box entitled "Correlation and Causality" illustrates the point that correlation does not necessarily point to a particular causal relationship.

As John and Lyn Lofland (1995:138–139) caution, it is important to distinguish the testing of causal relationships from *conjecture* about it. While it is perfectly acceptable to report your hunches or untested hypotheses about the causal processes at work in what you have observed, you should keep such suspicions separate from proven conclusions.

To review, most social researchers consider two variables to be causally related—that is, one causes the other—if (1) the cause precedes the effect in time, (2) there is an empirical correlation between them, and (3) the relationship is not found to be the result of some third variable. Any relationship satisfying *all* these criteria is causal, and these are the only criteria.

To emphasize this point more strongly, let's briefly examine some inappropriate criteria sometimes employed, especially by nonscientists. In this discussion, I am indebted to Travis Hirschi and Hanan Selvin for an excellent article on this subject and its later expansion in their book *Principles of Survey Analysis* (1973:114–36).

FIGURE 3-1
Necessary Cause

Necessary and Sufficient Causes

First, to review a point made earlier, a *perfect* correlation between variables is not a criterion of causality in social science research (or in science generally for that matter). Put another way, exceptions, although they do not prove the rule, do not necessarily deny the rule either. In probabilistic models, there are almost always exceptions to the posited relationship. If a few liberals voted for Dole and a few conservatives voted for Clinton, that would not deny the general causal relationship between political orientations and voting in the election.

Within this probabilistic model, it is useful to distinguish two types of causes: necessary and sufficient causes. A *necessary cause* represents a condition that must be present for the effect to follow. For example, it is necessary for you to take college courses in order to get a degree, but simply taking the courses is not sufficient. (You need to take the right ones and pass them.)

Or, consider the relationship between gender and pregnancy: Being female is a necessary condition for pregnancy. Figure 3-1 illustrates that relationship.

A *sufficient cause*, on the other hand, represents a condition that, if it is present, will pretty much guarantee the effect in question. Thus, for example, getting married is a sufficient cause for becoming sex partners, though it's not the only way. Or, skipping an exam in this course would be a sufficient cause for failing it, though you could fail it other ways as well. Figure 3-2 illustrates the latter state of affairs.

The discovery of a *necessary and sufficient cause* is, of course, the most satisfying outcome in research. If juvenile delinquency were the effect under examination, it would be nice to discover a single condition that (1) had to be present for delinquency to develop and (2) always resulted in delinquency. In such a case, you would surely feel that you knew precisely what caused juvenile delinquency.

Unfortunately, we never discover single causes that are absolutely necessary *and* absolutely sufficient when analyzing the nomothetic relationships among variables. It is not uncommon, however, to find causal factors that are *either* 100 percent necessary (you must be female to become pregnant) or 100 percent sufficient (pleading guilty will result in your conviction).

In the idiographic analysis of single cases, you may reach a depth of explanation from which it is reasonable to assume that things could not have turned out differently, suggesting you have determined the sufficient conditions for something. (Anyone with all the same details of your up-

FIGURE 3-2
Sufficient Cause

	Took the exam	Didn't take the exam
Failed the exam	F F F F F	F F F F F F F F F
Passed the exam	A C A D A B C A D B C B C B C B C B D D D A C A	

bringing and subsequent experiences would have ended up with the same view you have on abortion.) By definition, such idiographic explanations do not posit single causes, and there could always be other causal paths to the same result. Thus, the explanation is not a necessary one.

In social science, either necessary or sufficient causes—even imperfect ones—can be the basis for concluding there is a causal relationship.

■ ERRORS OF REASONING

Cause and effect, as we've seen, is essential to scientific explanation and more complex than meets the eye. It is also fundamental to our day-to-day lives, where we commonly make errors in our assessment of causation. It will be useful, therefore, to look at some examples from daily life. See if you can detect the error before reading my explanation. Where appropriate, I've also indicated the issues of causal relationships that we'll be pursuing later in the book.

Early in the history of the AIDS epidemic, the *San Francisco Chronicle* carried an article reporting research that claimed a link between AIDS and fluoridation of the water. In part, the claim hinged on the assertion that "while half the country's communities have fluoridated water supplies and half do not, 90 percent of AIDS cases are coming from fluoridated areas and only 10 percent are coming from nonfluoridated areas." Can you see any flaws in this reasoning? Think about it for a minute before continuing.

To begin, you should always beware when data about communities are used to draw conclusions about individuals. (We'll examine this further in Chapter 4.) In this instance, "half the communities" may not contain half the population. Indeed, we might imagine that large cities would be more likely to fluoridate their water than small, rural towns. Logically, it would be possible for the fluoridated communities to have 90 percent of the nation's population, in which case they should have 90 percent of the AIDS cases even if there were no relationship between AIDS and fluoridation.

Second, it's possible that "cosmopolitan/progressive" social values more common to cities than to small towns might affect both (1) lifestyles associated with AIDS and (2) the decision to fluoridate the water supply. In that case, AIDS and fluoridation could be statistically correlated without being causally linked. (We'll explore this possibility further in Chapter 16.)

The problems of faulty causal reasoning are not limited to statistical analyses. The examination of historical processes (see Chapter 11) is equally vulnerable. Consider this example: At a news conference on August 5, 1985, then-President Ronald Reagan noted the fortieth anniversary of the atomic bombing of Hiroshima by saying that that terrible example of nuclear destruction had served as "a deterrent that kept us at peace for the longest stretch we've ever known, 40 years of peace." Many people who supported an immediate end to the nuclear arms race were quick to deny the causal relationship asserted by the president, saying it was not the bombing of Hiroshima that had kept the peace. Can you spot another flaw in the causal assertion?

What seems most subject to question was not the causes of the "40 years of peace" but its *existence*. The period in question included the Korean War from 1950 to 1953 as well as the Vietnam War from 1959 to 1973! It is difficult to maintain that the bombing of Hiroshima caused a period of peace when there was no consistent peace.

Sometimes it's possible to detect failures of causal reasoning on logical grounds alone—when there is no possibility of examining empirical data. Again, concern about AIDS offers an example. It has been argued by some that the AIDS epidemic represents God's displeasure with certain human behaviors: specifically, homosexuality and drug use. The evangelist Don Boys spoke on the sexual issue in a guest editorial in *USA Today* (October 7, 1985):

■ The AIDS epidemic indicates that morality has broken its mooring and drifted into a miasmic swamp, producing disease, degeneracy, and death. . . . God's plan is for each man to have one woman—his wife—for a lifetime, and be faithful to her.

The flaw in this case is not that AIDS has become increasingly common among heterosexual, married couples or that some hemophiliac young people have contracted AIDS through tainted blood transfusions. It is legitimate to use a probabilistic model of causation in this context, and homosexual men are, in fact, more likely to contract AIDS than heterosexual men. However, if AIDS is an indication of "God's plan," then lesbians must be the most favored of all, because AIDS is rarest among them.

None of these illustrations of faulty causal reasoning is intended as an indictment of the perpetrators. All of us fall into such errors. It has been said that the problem with "common sense" is that it's not all that common. My purpose in these examples has been twofold. First, I want to sensitize you to faulty causal reasoning by showing some of the ways it shows up in daily life. Perhaps that alone will help you avoid some errors and recognize them in others' reasoning. Second, I want to use such examples as a backdrop for understanding the power of careful, scientific reasoning. Although scientists are not immune to logical error, the procedures of science offer some degree of protection. I want to make that protection available to you.

Although no one can give you a neat set of rules for logical reasoning, I want to draw your attention to an excellent book—Howard Kahane's *Logic and Contemporary Rhetoric* (1992)—which outlines many of the errors people commonly make. Here are some of the pitfalls Kahane discusses.

Provincialism

All of us look at the world through glasses framed by our particular histories and current situations. There is always a danger, then, that researchers will interpret people's behavior so that it makes sense from the researchers' own points of view. For example, a Christian researcher may see things in Christian terms, a socialist within socialist terms, and so forth. This problem is particularly evident in cross-cultural research.

At the same time, Harry Wolcott (1995:164–165), in discussing "the art of fieldwork," suggests that our personal and cultural biases can work for the good. They can lend focus to an inquiry and provide insights by involving a point of view different from that of the participants being observed. The key is to be conscious of your particular views and not to assume they are more valid than other views.

Hasty Conclusion

Researchers as well as other people are susceptible to drawing hasty conclusions. Whenever the researcher offers an interpretation of data, be sure to evaluate the "weight" of evidence leading to that interpretation. Is the conclusion essentially inevitable given the data lying behind it, or are other conclusions just as reasonable?

Questionable Cause

Whenever it seems to you that X caused Y, ask yourself if that is necessarily the case. What else could have caused Y? Kahane (1992:63) gives several economic examples. If a business goes bankrupt, people often conclude that the company's president lacked business skills—even when the bankruptcy occurred during a severe recession, marked by a great many business failures.

Suppressed Evidence

Field researchers amass a great deal of information through direct observations, interviews, library work, and so on. To reach conclusions requires dismissing information as much as selecting it. On the whole, the researcher will dismiss information that is "not relevant"; however, that in itself is obviously a matter of judgment.

In particular, take note of observations you've noted that do not figure in the conclusions, as well as observations not mentioned that you can reasonably assume were made. If a researcher concludes that members of a neo-Nazi group opposed African Americans out of a fear of economic competition, for example, we would expect that most members were working class or lower middle class. But if the researcher has not indicated the occupations of the members, you might well wonder about the conclusion.

False Dilemma

Research conclusions, like nonscientific opinions, often represent the selection of one position from among alternatives. Selecting one often seems to rule out all others, but this need not be the case. Kahane offers this example: "Economics, not biology, may explain male domination." This bold assertion seems to rule out the influence of politics, education, custom, religion, and a host of other possibilities.

■ This statement suggests that there are just two possibilities: either biology explains male dominance (note the begged question!), or economic success does. And it suggests that the second possibility, economic success, "may" (weasel word) be the true explanation of male domination. Yet there are many other possibilities, such as social custom, religious conviction, and various *combinations* of economic and biological factors. By tempting us to think of the cause of male domination as either economics or biology, the quote leads us to overlook other possibilities and thus to commit the fallacy of *false dilemma*.

(1992:42)

This warning is echoed by David Silverman (1993:205), in saying a basic rule in the analysis of qualitative data is "never appeal to a single element as an explanation." Always look for alternative or additional causes. Be wary of this pitfall in reading the works of others, but also be wary of falling into it yourself.

I suspect these few examples of logical pitfalls will have sharpened your critical faculties somewhat, and I encourage you to read Kahane's book for more guidance and insights. The box entitled "Are Black Children Undernourished?" gives you another opportunity to sharpen your critical reasoning skills.

■ LINKING MEASUREMENT AND ASSOCIATION

As we have seen, one of the key elements determining causation in science is an empirical correlation between the *cause* and the *effect*. All too often, however, the process of measuring variables is seen as separate from that of determining the *associations* between variables. This view is incorrect, I think, or at least misleading.

Are Black Children Undernourished?

Here's an example of faulty reasoning to help you refine your analytical skills. In the midst of national concern over the persistence of hunger in the United States, then-President Reagan appointed a 13-member Task Force on Food Assistance to determine the nature and extent of the problem and to recommend government action. One of the panel's members, Dr. George Graham, attracted considerable attention by indicating his belief that the problem of malnutrition among children had been exaggerated—especially with regard to black children. He was quoted as follows:

■ "National data show that black children are now taller than white children—obviously, they must be getting more to eat," he said yesterday, echoing comments he made Wednesday. "If you think that blacks as a group are undernourished, look around at the black athletes on television—they're a pretty hefty bunch."

As you can see, Dr. Graham cites two pieces of evidence—one statistical, one impressionistic—to support his thesis that black people in the United States are no more likely to suffer malnutrition than other U.S. citizens. Are you convinced by his arguments? If not, how would you respond? Think about it, and then continue reading.

First, Graham says black children are taller, on the average, than white children. But does this mean "they must be getting more to eat"? What other factors might affect height? If you said "genetics," you can go to the head of the class. Racial and ethnic groups differ in average height. Consider the African Watusi tribes, for example. These poor cattleherders of Burundi and Rwanda are noted for their spectacular height, commonly over seven feet. It would be absurd to conclude that they must eat more than do people in the United States.

Second, how about the black athletes on television? Does their heftiness mean that U.S. blacks as a whole must be getting a lot to eat? In this instance, you might have asked whether the black athletes are typical of all U.S. blacks. Of course not. They are no more typical of blacks in general than white athletes are typical of all U.S. whites. Otherwise, we would need to look at Japanese sumo wrestlers and conclude that the Japanese people in general must be bigger and better fed than U.S. citizens.

Source: "Big Changes Made in Hunger Report," *San Francisco Chronicle*, December 30, 1983, p. 10.

This section addresses the intimate links between measurement and association within the context of nomothetic, causal inference. To do that, we'll review the traditional, deductive model of science. Then we'll examine some alternative images of science.

The Traditional Deductive Model

The traditional perspective on the scientific method, as you'll recall, is based on a series of steps, summarized as follows:

1. Theory construction
2. Derivation of theoretical hypotheses
3. Operationalization of concepts
4. Collection of empirical data
5. Empirical testing of hypotheses

Let's explore this view of the scientific research process through an example.

Theory Construction Faced with an aspect of the natural or social world that interests them, scientists create an abstract deductive theory to describe it. This is a largely logical exercise. Let's assume for the moment that a social scientist is interested in deviant behavior. A theory of deviant behavior would be constructed on the basis of existing sociological theory, such as social control theory, which focuses on the coercive and persuasive forces that establish and maintain social order. Among other things, this theory includes a variety of concepts relevant to the causes of deviant behavior.

Derivation of Theoretical Hypotheses On the basis of this total theory of deviant behavior, the scientist derives hypotheses relating to the various concepts composing the theory. Following the previous example, let us suppose that the scientist logically derives the hypothesis that juvenile delinquency is a function of supervision: As supervision increases, juvenile delinquency decreases.

Operationalization of Concepts The next step is to specify empirical indicators that represent the theoretical concepts. Although theoretical concepts must be somewhat abstract and perhaps vague, the empirical **indicators** must be precise and specific (as we'll examine in detail in Chapters 5 and 6). Thus, in our example, the scientist might operationalize the concept *juvenile* as anyone under 18 years of age; *delinquency* as being arrested for a criminal act; and *supervision* as the presence of a nonworking adult in the home.

The effect of operationalization is to convert the theoretical hypothesis into an empirical one. In the present case, the empirical hypothesis would be that among people under 18 years of age, those living in homes with a nonworking adult will be less likely to be arrested for a criminal act than will those without a nonworking adult in the home.

Collection of Empirical Data Based on the operationalization of theoretical concepts, the researcher collects data relating to the empirical indicators. In the present example, he or she might conduct a survey of people under 18 years of age. Among other things, the survey questionnaire would ask them whether they lived in a home with a nonworking adult and whether they had ever been arrested for a criminal act.

Empirical Testing of Hypotheses Once the data have been collected, the final step is the statistical testing of the hypothesis. The scientist determines, empirically, whether those juveniles with a nonworking adult in the home are less likely to have been arrested for criminal acts than those with no nonworking adult. The confirmation or disconfirmation of the empirical hypothesis is then used toward accepting or rejecting the theoretical hypothesis.

Practical Problems Although this traditional image of scientific research can be useful to keep in mind, it tends to conceal some of the practical problems that crop up in most actual research. In particular, there are two basic problems that prevent the easy application of this model in practice.

First, theoretical concepts seldom, if ever, permit unambiguous operationalization. Because concepts are abstract and general, every specification of empirical indicators must be an approximation. In the previous example, it is unlikely that the general concept of *supervision* is adequately represented by the presence of a nonworking adult in the home. The presence of such an adult does not assure supervision of the juvenile; in some homes lacking such an adult, other arrangements may be made for the juvenile's supervision.

Being arrested for a criminal act cannot be equated with the abstract concept of *delinquency*. Some juveniles may engage in delinquent behavior without being arrested. Others may be arrested falsely. Moreover, the specification of *juvenile* as a person under 18 years of age is arbitrary. Other specifications might have been made, and probably none would be unambiguously correct. Every empirical indicator has some defects; all could be improved on, and the search for better indicators is endless.

Second, the empirical associations among variables are almost never perfect. In the previous example, if all juveniles with nonworking adults in the home had never been arrested and all those without such adults had been arrested, we might conclude that the hypothesis had been confirmed. Or if both groups had exactly the same records, we might conclude that the hypothesis had been rejected. Neither eventuality is likely in practice, however. Nearly all variables are related empirically to one another to some extent. Specifying the extent that represents acceptance of the hypothesis and the extent that represents rejection, however, is also an arbitrary act. (See Chapter 17 for a discussion of tests of statistical significance.)

Ultimately, then, scientists use imperfect indicators of theoretical concepts to discover imperfect associations. And these imperfections conspire with one another against us. Suppose that you specify a degree of association that will constitute acceptance of the hypothesis, and the empirical analysis falls short. You will quite naturally ask yourself whether different indicators of the concepts might have produced the specified extent of association. If you measured *juvenile delinquency* as being convicted of a crime, for example, perhaps the analysis would have turned out differently if you had used arrests rather than convictions as your indicator.

Measurement and association are interrelated concepts. The scientist must handle both simultaneously and logically. Rather than moving through a fixed set of steps, the scientist moves back and forth through them endlessly. Often theoretical constructions are built around the previously observed associations between empirical indicators. Partial theoretical constructions may suggest new empirical data to be examined, and so forth. After each activity, you hope to understand your subject matter a little better. The "critical experiment" that ultimately determines the fate of an entire theory is rare indeed.

Scientific research, then, is a never ending enterprise aimed at the understanding of some phenomenon. To that end, you continually measure and examine associations, and you must constantly be aware of the relationships among them.

An Example of Measurement and Association

Several years ago, a controversy brewed in the sociology of religion concerning the relationship between religiosity and prejudice. A book by Charles Glock and Rodney Stark entitled *Christian Beliefs and Anti-Semitism* (1967) reported empirical data indicating that Christian church members holding orthodox beliefs (in God, Jesus, the Bible, and so on) were more likely to be anti-Semitic than were less orthodox members. The book's findings stirred considerable discussion within the churches, and other researchers did follow-up projects on the same topic.

One of these research projects arrived at a conclusion directly opposite that of Glock and Stark. The researchers reported that as orthodoxy increased, prejudice decreased. On closer examination, however, it was noted that orthodoxy in that study was measured by acceptance of questionnaire statements of the traditional Christian doctrines of "All men are brothers" and "Love thy neighbor." Not surprisingly, survey respondents who accepted the statements based on these doctrines appeared less prejudiced than those who rejected them. Normally, these research findings would be (and were) challenged on the grounds of "contamination": The indicators used to operationalize religious orthodoxy and prejudice actually measured the same or similar qualities. Calling one set of indicators "orthodoxy" and the other "prejudice" does not prove that prejudice decreases with increasing orthodoxy in a general sense. (Of course, measuring orthodoxy in terms of brotherly love and equality might be extremely useful in some other context.)

The discussions of this chapter suggest a somewhat different reaction to the two kinds of research findings. Asking *how* orthodoxy and prejudice are associated with each other rather than *whether* they are associated, we would conclude that orthodoxy measured in terms of the Glock-Stark indicators is positively associated with prejudice, and orthodoxy measured as commitment to the norms of brotherly love and equality is negatively associated with prejudice. Both conclusions are empirically correct; neither conclusion answers the more general question of *whether* religion and prejudice are related. The final remaining step, of course, is to evaluate the relative utility of the conclusions. The finding that orthodoxy and prejudice are negatively associated in this instance would probably be disregarded as a *tautology*, a statement that is true by definition: "People who believe in brotherly love believe in brotherly love."

The various discussions of this chapter should have given you a sense of the explanatory purpose of social research. Though it's not the only purpose of research, we very often wish to explain why people think and act as they do. Typically, we ask what causes what. Sometimes we seek an in-depth, idiographic explanation that lets us fully understand a particular case; sometimes we look for a more general, though partial explanation that applies to a broad class of cases. Both are legitimate approaches in social science that support each other.

I have introduced the notion of causation early in the book so that you can hold it as a backdrop for the technical discussions that follow.

■ MAIN POINTS

- Explanatory scientific research depends implicitly on the idea of cause and effect.
- Explanatory social scientific research depends implicitly on a deterministic image of human behavior, at least in part.
- The idiographic model of explanation aims at a complete understanding of a particular phenomenon, using all relevant causal factors.
- The nomothetic model of explanation aims at a general understanding—not necessarily complete—of a *class* of phenomena, using the smallest number of most relevant causal factors.
- Most explanatory social research uses a probabilistic model of causation. X may be said to cause Y if it is seen to have some influence on Y.
- There are two important types of causes: *necessary* and *sufficient*. X is a necessary cause of Y if Y cannot happen without X having happened. X is a sufficient cause of Y if Y always happens when X happens. The scientifically most satisfying discovery is a necessary *and* sufficient cause.
- There are three basic criteria for the determination of causation in the nomothetic analysis of relationships among variables: (1) The independent (cause) and dependent (effect) variables must be empirically related to one another, (2) the independent variable must occur earlier in time than the dependent variable, and (3) the observed relationship cannot be explained away as the effect of another, earlier variable. (This final criterion will be discussed more fully in Chapter 16.)
- A perfect statistical relationship between two variables is *not* an appropriate criterion for causation in social research. We may say that a causal relationship exists between X and Y, then, even though X is not the *total* cause of Y.
- Contamination of indicators means that the operational measure of one of two variables may be construed as a measure of the other variable as well. For example, it would be an inappropriate test of the relationship between religiosity and prejudice if the measure of religiosity might be seen as a measure of prejudice as well.

■ REVIEW QUESTIONS AND EXERCISES

1. Several times we have discussed the relationship between education and prejudice. Describe the conditions that would lead us to conclude that education was
   a. a necessary cause
   b. a sufficient cause
   c. a necessary and sufficient cause
2. Women earn roughly 70 percent as much as men in U.S. society. What do you suppose "causes" that difference? Describe the procedures by which you might test your conjectures.
3. Why did you choose to attend the college you are now attending? Create an idiographic explanation by detailing all the factors that led to your choice.
4. Find at least three Web sites dealing with the issue of free will and determinism. Identify the sites and give a one- or two-sentence description of each.

ADDITIONAL READINGS

Beck, E. M., and Stewart E. Tolnay. "The Killing Fields of the Deep South: The Market for Cotton and the Lynching of Blacks, 1882–1930." *American Sociological Review* 55 (August 1990): 526–39. This analysis of the structural causes of lynchings in the South illustrates the type of causal analysis that social scientists often undertake. Some of the variables examined are inflation, the price of cotton, and the proportion of blacks in the population.

Davis, James A. *The Logic of Causal Order.* Beverly Hills, CA: Sage, 1985. Davis examines the logical and statistical dimensions of causality in social research.

Hirschi, Travis, and Hanan Selvin. *Principles of Survey Analysis.* New York: Free Press, 1973, especially Part II. Excellent statements on causation within a practical framework. I can think of no better discussions of causation within the context of particular research findings than these. The book is readable, stimulating, and generally just plain excellent.

Lazarsfeld, Paul. Foreword. In Herbert Hyman, *Survey Design and Analysis.* New York: Free Press, 1955. A classic and still valid statement of causation in social science. In the context of the elaboration model, Lazarsfeld provides a clear statement of the criteria for determining causation.

Shaver, Kelly G. *The Attribution of Blame: Causality, Responsibility, and Blameworthiness.* New York: Springer-Verlag, 1985. Shaver discusses many of the aspects of causality presented in this chapter and shows how they relate to the notions of responsibility and blame.

Wallace, William A. *Causality and Scientific Explanation.* Ann Arbor: University of Michigan Press, 1972. In case you developed an interest in the question of causality, this two-volume work provides a full examination of the history of the concept within science, from medieval times to the present.

PART 2: The Structuring of Inquiry

4 Research Design
5 Conceptualization and Measurement
6 Operationalization
7 Indexes, Scales, and Typologies
8 The Logic of Sampling

POSING problems properly is often more difficult than answering them. Indeed, a properly phrased question often seems to answer itself. You may have discovered the answer to a question just in the process of making the question clear to someone else.

Part 2 deals with what should be observed, that is, Part 2 considers the posing of proper scientific questions, the structuring of inquiry. Part 3 goes on to describe some of the specific methods of social scientific observation.

Chapter 4 addresses the beginnings of research. It examines some of the purposes of inquiry, the units of analysis and points of focus in social scientific research, and the reasons scientists get involved in research projects.

Chapter 5 deals with the specification of what it is you want to study—a process called *conceptualization*. We're going to look at some of the terms that you and I use quite casually in everyday life—*prejudice, liberalism,* and *happiness,* and so forth—and we're going to see how essential it is to clarify what we really mean by such terms when we do research.

Chapter 6 is an extension of Chapter 5. Once we clarify what we mean by certain terms, we can then measure the referents of those terms. The process of devising steps or operations for measuring what we want to study is called *operationalization*. Chapter 6 deals with the topic of operationalization in general, paying special attention to the framing of questions for interviews and questionnaires.

To complete this lengthy introduction to measurement, Chapter 7 breaks with the chronological discussion of how research is conducted. In this chapter, we'll examine techniques for measuring variables in quantitative research through the combination of several indicators: *indexes, scales,* and *typologies.* As an example, we might ask survey respondents five different questions about their attitudes toward gender equality and then combine the answers to all five questions into a composite measure of gender-based egalitarianism. Such composite measures are constructed during the analysis of data (see Part 4), though the raw materials for them must be provided for in the design and execution of data collection.

Finally, we'll look at how social scientists select people or things for observation. Chapter 8, on *sampling,* addresses the fundamental scientific issue of *generalizability.* As you'll see, we can select a few people or things for observation and then apply what we observe to a much larger group of people or things. For example, by surveying 1,000 U.S. citizens about whom they favor for president of the United States, we can accurately predict how tens of millions will vote. In this chapter, we'll examine techniques that increase the generalizability of what we observe.

What you learn in Part 2 will bring you to the verge of making controlled social scientific observations. Part 3 will then show you how to take that next step.

CHAPTER 4: Research Design

What You'll Learn in This Chapter

Here you'll learn the wide variety of research designs available to social science researchers: variations concerning who or what is to be studied when, how, and for what purpose.

INTRODUCTION

PURPOSES OF RESEARCH
Exploration
Description
Explanation

UNITS OF ANALYSIS
Individuals
Groups
Organizations
Social Artifacts
Units of Analysis in Review
The Ecological Fallacy
Reductionism

POINTS OF FOCUS
Characteristics
Orientations
Actions

THE TIME DIMENSION
Cross-Sectional Studies
Longitudinal Studies
Approximating Longitudinal Studies

HOW TO DESIGN A RESEARCH PROJECT
Getting Started
Conceptualization
Choice of Research Method
Operationalization
Population and Sampling
Observations
Data Processing
Analysis
Application
Review

THE RESEARCH PROPOSAL
Elements of a Research Proposal

MAIN POINTS

REVIEW QUESTIONS AND EXERCISES

ADDITIONAL READINGS

INTRODUCTION

Science is an enterprise dedicated to "finding out." No matter what you want to find out, though, there will likely be a great many ways of doing it. That's true in life generally. Suppose, for example, that you want to find out whether a particular automobile—say, the new Burpo-Blasto—would be a good car for you. You could, of course, buy one and find out that way. You could talk to a lot of B-B owners or to people who considered buying one and didn't. You might check the classified ads to see if there are a lot of B-Bs being sold cheap. You could read a consumer magazine evaluation of Burpo-Blastos, or you could find out in a number of other ways. The same situation occurs in scientific inquiry.

Research design, the topic of this chapter, addresses the planning of scientific inquiry—designing a strategy for finding out something. Although the special details vary according to what you wish to study, there are two major aspects of research design. First, you must specify as clearly as possible what you want to find out. Second, you must determine the best way to do it. Interestingly, if you can handle the first consideration fully, you'll probably handle the second in the same process. As mathematicians say, a properly framed question contains the answer.

Ultimately, scientific inquiry comes down to making observations and interpreting what you've observed. (Parts 3 and 4 of this book deal with these two major aspects of social research.) Before you can observe and analyze, however, you need a plan. You need to determine what you're going to observe and analyze: why and how. That's what research design is all about.

Let's say you're interested in studying corruption in government. That's certainly a worthy and appropriate topic for social research. But what *specifically* are you interested in? What do you mean by *corruption*? What kinds of behavior do you have in mind? And what do you mean by *government*? Whom do you want to study: all public employees? only civilian employees? elected officials? civil servants? Finally, what is your purpose? Do you want to find out *how much* corruption there is? Do you want to learn *why* corruption exists? These are the kinds of questions that need to be answered in the course of research design.

This chapter provides a general introduction to research design, while the other chapters in Part 2 elaborate on specific aspects. In practice, all aspects of research design are interrelated. I have separated them here only to permit a reasonably coherent picture of research. In this chapter, I want to lay out the various possibilities for social research. As you read, the interrelationships among parts will become clearer.

We'll start by briefly examining the main *purposes* of social research. Then, we'll consider *units of analysis*—the what or whom you want to study, further covered in Chapter 8.

Next, we'll look at some of the *points of focus* you might take in studying those units of analysis; Chapters 5 and 6 elaborate on this topic. As you'll see, this aspect of research design is inextricably tied to the method of observation you'll use.

There are two additional topics covered in this chapter. First, I consider alternative ways of handling *time* in social research. As you'll see, it is sometimes appropriate to examine a static cross section of social life, but other studies follow social processes across time.

Next, a brief overview of the overall research process serves two purposes: (1) it gives you a map to the remainder of this book, and (2) it helps you see how you might go about designing a study. In this latter regard, I've suggested some inexpensive research projects you could undertake.

Finally, I've said a little about *research proposals*. Often the actual conduct of research needs to be preceded by this detailing of your intentions—to obtain funding for a major project or perhaps to get your instructor's approval for a class project. You'll see that this offers an excellent excuse and forum for ensuring you have considered all aspects of your research in advance.

So, let's get started. We'll begin with the various purposes of social research.

■ PURPOSES OF RESEARCH

Social research, of course, serves many purposes. Three of the most common and useful purposes are *exploration, description,* and *explanation.* Although a given study can have more than one of these purposes—and most do—examining them separately is useful because each has different implications for other aspects of research design.

Exploration

Much of social research is conducted to explore a topic, or to provide a beginning familiarity with that topic. This approach is typical when a researcher examines a new interest or when the subject of study itself is relatively new.

As an example, let's suppose that widespread taxpayer dissatisfaction with the government erupts into a taxpayers' revolt. People begin refusing to pay their taxes, and they organize themselves around that issue. You might like to learn more about the movement: How widespread is it? What levels and degrees of support are there within the community? How is the movement organized? What kinds of people are active in it? You might undertake an exploratory study to obtain at least approximate answers to some of these questions. You might check figures with tax-collecting officials, collect and study the literature of the movement, attend meetings, and interview leaders.

Exploratory studies are also appropriate for more persistent phenomena. Suppose you are unhappy with your college's graduation requirements and want to help change them. You might study the history of such requirements at the college and meet with college officials to learn the reasons for the current standards. You could talk to several students to get a rough idea of their sentiments on the subject. Though this last activity would not necessarily yield a precise and accurate picture of student opinion, it could suggest what the results of a more extensive study might be.

Sometimes exploratory research is pursued through the use of *focus groups,* or guided small-group discussions. This technique is frequently used in market research; we'll examine it further in Chapter 9.

Exploratory studies are most typically done for three purposes: (1) to satisfy the researcher's curiosity and desire for better understanding, (2) to test the feasibility of undertaking a more extensive study, and (3) to develop the methods to be employed in any subsequent study.

Not long ago, for example, I became aware of the growing popularity of something called "channeling," in which a person known as a *channel* or *medium* enters a trance state and begins speaking with a voice that claims it originates outside the channel. Some of the voices say they come from a spirit world of the dead; some say they are from other planets; and still others say they exist on dimensions of reality difficult to explain in ordinary human terms. You may be familiar with channeling through the "Seth" books of Jane Roberts (1974) or more recent books by Shirley MacLaine (1983).

The channeled voices, often referred to as *entities,* sometimes use the metaphor of radio or television for the phenomenon they represent. "When you watch the news," one told me in the course of an interview, "you don't believe Dan Rather is really inside the television set. The same is true of me. I use this medium's body the way Dan Rather uses your television set."

The idea of channeling interested me from a number of perspectives, not the least of which was the methodological question of how to study scientifically something that violates so much of what we take for granted, including scientific staples such as space, time, causation, and individuality.

Lacking any rigorous theory or precise expectations, I merely set out to learn more. Using some of the techniques of field research discussed in Chapter 11, I began amassing information and forming categories for making sense of what I observed. I read books and articles about the phenomenon and talked to people who had attended channeling sessions. I then attended channeling sessions myself, observing those who attended as well as the channel and entity. Subsequently, I conducted personal interviews with numerous channels and entities.

In most interviews, I began by asking the human channels questions about how they first began channeling, what it was like, and why they continued, as well as standard biographical questions. The channel would then go into a trance, whereby the interview continued with the entity speaking. "Who are you?" I might ask. "Where do you come from?" "Why are you doing this?" "How can I tell if you are real or a fake?" Although I went into these interview sessions with several questions prepared in advance, each of the interviews followed whatever course seemed appropriate in the light of answers given.

This example of exploration illustrates where social research often begins. Whereas researchers working from deductive theories have the key variables laid out in advance, one of my first tasks was to identify some of the possibly relevant variables. For example, I noted a channel's gender, age, education, religious background, regional origins, and previous participation in things metaphysical. I also noted differences in the circumstances of channeling sessions. Some channels said they must go into deep trances, some use light trances, and others remain conscious. Most sit down while channeling, but others stand and walk about. Some channels operate under pretty ordinary conditions; others seem to require metaphysical props such as dim lights, incense, and chanting. Many of these differences became apparent to me only in the course of my initial observations.

Regarding the entities, I have been interested in classifying where they say they come from. Over the course of my interviews, I've developed a set of questions about specific aspects of "reality," attempting to classify the answers they give. Similarly, I ask each to speak about future events.

Over the course of this research, my examination of specific topics has become increasingly focused as I've identified variables that seem worth pursuing. Note, however, that I began with a reasonably blank slate.

Exploratory studies are quite valuable in social scientific research. They are essential whenever a researcher is breaking new ground, and they can almost always yield new insights into a topic for research. Exploratory studies are also a source of grounded theory, as discussed in Chapter 2.

The chief shortcoming of exploratory studies is that they seldom provide satisfactory answers to research questions, though they can hint at the answers and can give insights into the research methods that could provide definitive answers. The reason exploratory studies are seldom definitive in themselves has to do with representativeness, discussed at length in Chapter 8. Once you understand representativeness, you will be able to know whether a given exploratory study actually answered its research problem or only pointed the way toward an answer.

Description

A major purpose of many social scientific studies is to describe situations and events. The researcher observes and then describes what was observed. Because scientific observation is careful and deliberate, however, scientific descriptions are typically more accurate and precise than casual ones.

The U.S. Census is an excellent example of descriptive social research. The goal of the **census** is to describe accurately and precisely a wide variety of characteristics of the U.S. population, as well as the populations of smaller areas such as states and counties. Other examples of descriptive studies are the computation of age-gender profiles of populations done by demographers and the computation of crime rates for different cities.

A Gallup Poll conducted during a political election campaign describes the voting intentions of the electorate. A product marketing survey normally describes the people who use, or would use, a particular product. A researcher who carefully chronicles the events that take place on a labor union picket line has, or at least serves, a descriptive purpose. A researcher who computes and reports the number of times individual legislators voted for or against organized labor also fulfills descriptive purpose.

Many qualitative studies aim primarily at description. An anthropological ethnography, for example, may try to detail the particular culture of some preliterate society. At the same time, such studies are seldom limited to a merely descriptive purpose. Researchers usually go on to examine *why* the observed patterns exist and their implications.

Explanation

The third general purpose of social scientific research is to explain things. So when William Sanders (1994) set about describing the varieties of gang violence, he also wanted to reconstruct the process that brought about violent episodes among the gangs of different ethnic groups.

Reporting the voting intentions of an electorate is a descriptive activity, but reporting *why* some people plan to vote for Candidate A and others for Candidate B is an explanatory activity. Reporting *why* some cities have higher crime rates than others involves explanation, but simply reporting the different crime rates is a case of description. A researcher has an explanatory purpose if he or she wishes to know why an anti-abortion demonstration ended in a violent confrontation with police, as opposed to simply describing what happened.

What factors do you suppose might shape people's attitudes toward the legalization of marijuana? Do you think men and women might differ in their opinions? Which group do you think would be the most supportive? An explanatory analysis of the 1993 GSS data indicates that 28 percent of the men and 15 percent of the women said marijuana should be legalized: While strong majorities of both genders oppose legalization, men are nearly twice as supportive as women.

In 1993, political orientations also correlate with attitudes about marijuana legalization. Among liberals, 37 percent say marijuana should be legalized, compared with 15 percent each of moderates and conservatives. When we consider political party, we find that 39 percent of the Democrats, 18 percent of the Independents, and 15 percent of the Republicans support legalization.

These abbreviated analyses should give you an indication of what the statistics of nomothetic explanation can look like. We'll get much deeper into this in Part 4 of the book.

Although it is useful to distinguish the three purposes of research, it bears repeating that most studies will have elements of all three. Suppose, for example, that you have set out to evaluate a new form of psychotherapy. Your study will have exploratory aspects, as you map out the impacts of the therapy. You will want to describe recovery rates, and you will undoubtedly seek to explain why the therapy works better for some types of people than for others.

You will see these several purposes at work in the following discussions of other aspects of research design. Let's turn now to a consideration of whom or what you want to explore, describe, and explain.

■ UNITS OF ANALYSIS

In social scientific research, there is virtually no limit to what or whom can be studied, or the **units of analysis.** This topic is relevant to all forms of social research, although its implications are clearest in the case of nomothetic, quantitative studies.

Social scientists perhaps most typically choose individual people as their units of analysis. You may note the characteristics of individual people—gender, age, region of birth, attitudes, and so forth. You can then combine these descriptions to provide a composite picture of the group the individuals represent, whether a street-corner gang or a whole society.

For example, you may note the age and gender of each student enrolled in Political Science 110 and then characterize the group of students as being 53 percent men and 47 percent women and as having a mean age of 18.6 years, or a descriptive analysis. Although the final description would be of the class as a whole, the individual characteristics are aggregated for purposes of describing some larger group.

The same aggregation would occur in an explanatory study. Suppose you wished to discover whether students with a high grade point average (GPA) received better grades in Political Science 110 than did students with a low GPA. You would measure the GPAs and the course grades of individual students. You might then aggregate students with a high GPA and those with a low GPA and see which group received the best grades in the course. The purpose of the study would be to explain why some students do better in the course than others (looking at overall grade point averages as a possible explanation), but individual students would still be the units of analysis.

Units of analysis in a study are typically also the *units of observation*. Thus, to study voting intentions, we would interview ("observe") individual voters. Sometimes, however, we "observe" our units of analysis indirectly. For example, we might ask husbands and wives their individual voting intentions, for the purpose of distinguishing couples who agree and disagree politically. We might want to find out whether political disagreements tend to cause divorce, perhaps. In this case, our units of analysis would be families, though the *units of observation* would be the individual wives and husbands.

Units of analysis, then, are those things we examine in order to create summary descriptions of all such units and to explain differences among them. This concept should be clarified further as we now consider several common social science units of analysis.

Individuals

As mentioned previously, individual human beings are perhaps the most typical units of analysis for social scientific research. We tend to describe and explain social groups and interactions by aggregating and manipulating the descriptions of individuals.

Any type of individual may be the unit of analysis for social scientific research. This point is more important than it may seem at first reading. The norm of *generalized understanding* in social science should suggest that scientific findings are most valuable when they apply to *all* kinds of people. In practice, however, social scientists seldom study all kinds of people. At the very least, their studies are typically limited to the people living in a single country, though some comparative studies stretch across national boundaries. Often, though, studies are quite circumscribed.

Examples of specific groups whose members may be units of analysis—at the individual level—include students, gays and lesbians, auto workers, voters, single parents, and faculty members. Note that each of these terms implies some population of individual persons. (See Chapter 8 for more on populations.) At this point, it is enough to realize that descriptive studies with individuals as their units of analysis typically aim to describe the population that comprises those individuals, whereas explanatory studies aim to discover the social dynamics operating within that population.

As the units of analysis, individuals may be characterized in terms of their membership in social groupings. Thus, an individual may be described as belonging to a rich family or to a poor one, or a person may be described as having a college-educated mother or not. We might examine in a research project whether people with college-educated mothers are more likely to attend college than those with non-college-educated mothers or whether high school graduates in rich families are more likely to attend college than those in poor families. In each case, the individual would be the unit of analysis—not the mother or the family.

Groups

Social groups themselves may also be the units of analysis for social scientific research. Realize how this differs from studying the individuals within a group. If you were to study the members of a criminal gang to learn about criminals, for example, the individual (criminal) would be the unit of analysis; but if you studied all the gangs in a city to learn the differences, say, between big gangs and small ones, between "uptown" and "downtown" gangs, and so forth, the unit of analysis would be the *gang*, a social group.

Here's another example. You might describe families in terms of total annual income and according to whether or not they had computers. You could aggregate families and describe the mean income of families and the percentage with computers. You would then be in a position to determine whether families with higher incomes were more likely to have computers than those with lower incomes. The individual *family* in such a case would be the unit of analysis.

Other units of analysis at the group level could be friendship cliques, married couples, census blocks, cities, or geographic regions. Each of these terms also implies some population. *Street gangs* implies some population that includes all street gangs. The population of street gangs could be described, say, in terms of its geographical distribution throughout a city, and an explanatory study of street gangs might discover, say, whether large gangs were more likely than small ones to engage in intergang warfare.

Organizations

Formal social organizations may also be the units of analysis in social scientific research. An example would be corporations, implying, of course, a population of all corporations. Individual corporations might be characterized in terms of their number of employees, net annual profits, gross assets, number of defense contracts, percentage of employees from racial or ethnic minority groups, and so forth. We might determine whether large corporations hire a larger or smaller percentage of minority group employees than small corporations. Other examples of formal social organizations suitable as units of analysis would be church congregations, colleges, army divisions, academic departments, and supermarkets.

As with other units of analysis, we can derive the characteristics of social groups from those of their individual members. Thus, we might describe a family in terms of the age, race, or education of its head. In a descriptive study, then, we might find the percentage of all families that have a college-educated head of family. In an explanatory study, we might determine whether such families have, on the average, more or fewer children than families headed by people who have not graduated from college. In each of these examples, however, the *family* would be the unit of analysis. Had we asked whether college graduates—college-educated *individuals*—have more or fewer children than their less educated counterparts, then the individual *person* would have been the unit of analysis.

Social groups may be characterized in other ways, such as according to their environments or their membership in larger groupings. Families, for example, might be described in terms of their dwelling: We might want to determine whether rich families are more likely to reside in single-family houses (as opposed to, say, apartments) than poor families. The unit of analysis would still be the family.

If all this seems unduly complicated, be assured that in most research projects you are likely to undertake, the unit of analysis will be relatively clear to you. When the unit of analysis is not so clear, however, it is absolutely essential to determine what it is; otherwise, you cannot determine what observations are to be made about whom or what.

Some studies try to describe or explain more than one unit of analysis. In these cases, the researcher must anticipate what conclusions she or he wishes to draw with regard to which units of analysis.

Social Artifacts

Another unit of analysis is the social artifact, or any product of social beings or their behavior. One class of artifacts includes concrete objects such as books, poems, paintings, automobiles, buildings, songs, pottery, jokes, student excuses for missing exams, and scientific discoveries. In the Robin Wagner-Pacifici (1995) examination of the Philadelphia police attack on MOVE, official pronouncements were the units of analysis.

Each social object implies a set of all such objects: all books, all novels, all biographies, all introductory sociology textbooks, all cookbooks, all press conferences. An individual book might be characterized by its size, weight, length, price, content, number of pictures, number sold, or description of its author. The population of all books or of a particular kind of book could be analyzed for the purpose of description or explanation.

A social scientist could analyze whether paintings by Russian, Chinese, or U.S. artists showed the greatest degree of working-class consciousness, taking paintings as the units of analysis and describing each, in part, by the nationality of its creator. You might examine a local newspaper's editorials regarding a local university for purposes of describing, or perhaps explaining, changes in the newspaper's editorial position on the university over time; individual editorials would be the units of analysis.

Social interactions form another class of social artifacts suitable for social scientific research. For example, we might characterize weddings as racially or religiously mixed or not, as religious or secular in ceremony, as resulting in divorce or not, or by descriptions of one or both of the marriage partners (such as, "previously married, Oakland Raider fan, wanted by the FBI"). Realize that when a researcher reports that weddings between partners of different religions are more likely to be performed by secular authorities than those between partners of the same religion, the weddings are the units of analysis, not the individuals involved.

Other examples of such units of analysis are friendship choices, court cases, traffic accidents, divorces, fistfights, ship launchings, airline hijackings, race riots, final exams, student demonstrations, and congressional hearings. The congressional hearings could be characterized by whether they occurred during an election campaign or not, whether the committee chairs were running for a higher office and/or had been convicted of a felony, and so forth.

Units of Analysis in Review

The purpose of this section has been to stretch your imagination somewhat regarding possible units of analysis for social scientific research. Although individual human beings are typical units of analysis, this need not be the case. Indeed, many research questions can be answered more appropriately through the examination of other units of analysis. (This discussion should point out once more that social scientists can study absolutely anything.)

Realize further that the units of analysis I've named and discussed here are not the only possibilities. Morris Rosenberg (1968:234-48), for example, speaks of individual, group, organizational, institutional, spatial, cultural, and societal units of analysis. John and Lyn Lofland (1995:103-13) speak of practices, episodes, encounters, roles, relationships, groups, organizations, settlements, social worlds, lifestyles, and subcultures as suitable units of study. Grasping the logic of units of analysis is more important than repeating a particular list.

The concept of the unit of analysis may seem more complicated than it needs to be. What you *call* a given unit of analysis—a group, a formal organization, or a social artifact—is irrelevant. You must, however, be clear as to what your unit of analysis *is*. You must decide whether you are studying marriages or marriage partners, crimes or criminals, corporations or corporate executives. Unless you keep this point in mind, you run the risk of making assertions about one unit of analysis based on the examination of another.

To test your grasp of the concept of units of analysis, here are some examples of real research topics. See if you can determine the unit of analysis in each. (The answers are at the end of this chapter.)

■ [1] Women watch TV more than men because they are likely to work fewer hours outside the home than men. . . . Black people watch an average of approximately three-quarters of an hour more television per day than white people.

(Hughes 1980:290)

■ [2] Of the 130 incorporated U.S. cities with more than 100,000 inhabitants in 1960, 126 had at least two short-term nonproprietary general hospitals accredited by the American Hospital Association.

(Turk 1980:317)

■ [3] The early TM [transcendental meditation] organizations were small and informal. The Los Angeles group, begun in June 1959, met at a member's house where, incidentally, Maharishi was living.

(JOHNSTON 1980:337)

■ [4] However, it appears that the nursing staffs exercise strong influence over . . . a decision to change the nursing care system. . . . Conversely, among those decisions dominated by the administration and the medical staffs . . .

(COMSTOCK 1980:77)

■ [5] In 1958, there were 13 establishments with 1,000 employees or more, accounting for 60 percent of the industry's value added. In 1977, the number of this type of establishment dropped to 11, but their share of industry value added had fallen to about 48 percent.

(YORK AND PERSIGEHL 1981:41)

■ [6] Though 667,000 out of 2 million farmers in the United States are women, women historically have not been viewed as farmers, but rather, as the farmer's wife.

(VOTAW 1979:8)

■ [7] The analysis of community opposition to group homes for the mentally handicapped . . . indicates that deteriorating neighborhoods are most likely to organize in opposition, but that upper-middle class neighborhoods are most likely to enjoy private access to local officials.

(GRAHAM AND HOGAN 1990:513)

■ [8] Some analysts during the 1960s predicted that the rise of economic ambition and political militancy among blacks would foster discontent with the "otherworldly" black mainline churches.

(ELLISON AND SHERKAT 1990:551)

■ [9] This analysis explores whether propositions and empirical findings of contemporary theories of organizations directly apply to both private product producing organizations (PPOs) and public human service organizations (PSOs).

(SCHIFLETT AND ZEY 1990:569)

■ [10] This paper examines variations in job title structures across work roles. Analyzing 3,173 job titles in the California civil service system in 1985, we investigate how and why lines of work vary in the proliferation of job categories that differentiate ranks, functions, or particular organizational locations.

(STRANG AND BARON 1990:479)

Figure 4-1 on pages 98–99 gives you a graphic illustration of some different units of analysis and the statements that might be made about them.

The Ecological Fallacy

At this point I should introduce two important concepts related to units of analysis: the **ecological fallacy** and **reductionism**. First *ecological* in this context refers to groups or sets or systems: something larger than individuals. The fallacy is to assume that something learned about such an ecological unit says something about the individuals making up that unit. Let's consider a hypothetical illustration of this fallacy.

Suppose we are interested in learning something about the nature of electoral support received by a female political candidate in a recent citywide election. Let's assume that we have the vote tally for each precinct so that we can tell which precincts gave her the greatest support and which the least. Assume also that we have census data describing some characteristics of these precincts. Our analysis of such data might show that precincts with relatively young voters gave the female candidate a greater proportion of their votes than precincts with older voters. We might be tempted to conclude from these findings that young voters are more likely to vote for female candidates than older voters—that age affects support for the woman. In reaching such a conclusion, we run the risk of committing the *ecological fallacy* because it may have been the older voters in those "young" precincts who voted for the woman. Our problem is that we have examined *precincts* as our units of analysis but wish to draw conclusions about *voters*.

The same problem would arise if we discovered that crime rates were higher in cities having large African-American populations than in those with few African Americans. We would not know if the crimes were actually committed by African Americans. Or if we found suicide rates higher in Protestant countries than in Catholic ones, we still could not know for sure that more Protestants than Catholics committed suicide.

Very often the social scientist must address a particular research question through an ecological analysis. Perhaps the most appropriate data are simply not available. For example, the precinct vote tallies and the precinct characteristics mentioned in our initial example might be easy to obtain, but we may not have the resources to conduct a post-election survey of individual voters. In such cases, we may reach a *tentative* conclusion, recognizing and noting the risk of an ecological fallacy.

Don't let these warnings against the ecological fallacy lead you into committing what we might call an *individualistic fallacy*. Some students approaching social research for the first time have trouble reconciling general patterns of attitudes and actions with individual exceptions they know of. Your knowing a rich Democrat, for example, doesn't deny the fact that most rich people vote Republican—as a general pattern. Similarly, if you know someone who has gotten rich without any formal education, that doesn't deny the general pattern of higher education relating to higher income.

The ecological fallacy deals with something else altogether—drawing conclusions about individuals based solely on the observation of groups. Although the patterns observed among variables may be genuine, the danger here lies in drawing unwarranted assumptions about the cause of those patterns—assumptions about the individuals making up the groups.

Reductionism

The second concept I want to introduce here is *reductionism*, or seeing and explaining everything in terms of a particular, narrow set of concepts. Thus, sociologists may tend to consider only sociological variables (such as values, norms, roles), economists only economic variables (such as supply and demand, marginal value), and psychologists only psychological variables (such as personality types, traumas). For example, what caused the American Revolution? A shared commitment to the value of individual liberty? The economic plight of the colonies in relation to Britain? The megalomania of the founding fathers? Scientists from different disciplines tend to look at different types of answers and ignore the others. Explaining all or most human behavior in terms of economic factors is called *economic reductionism;* explaining all or most human behavior in terms of psychological factors is called *psychological reductionism;* and so forth. Note how this issue relates to the discussion of theoretical paradigms in Chapter 2.

Reductionism of any type tends to suggest that particular units of analysis or variables are more relevant than others. If we were to regard shared values as the cause of the American Revolution, our unit of analysis would be the individual colonist. An economist, though, might choose the 13 colonies as units of analysis and examine the economic organizations and conditions of each. A psychologist might choose individual leaders as the units of analysis for purposes of examining their personalities.

Like the ecological fallacy, reductionism can occur when we use inappropriate units of analysis. The appropriate unit of analysis for a given research question, however, is not always clear. Social scientists, especially across disciplinary boundaries, often debate this issue

■ POINTS OF FOCUS

In the preceding discussion of different possible units of analysis, I've frequently mentioned ways of describing or characterizing them. These ways represent aspects of those units of analysis that might be researched.

In the following overview of this topic, we'll consider three points of focus: *characteristics, orientations,* and *actions*. These three are not rigidly separate from each other. Certainly, they hardly exhaust the possibilities for research—I'll expand the list in Chapter 11. Nonetheless, the present discussion should broaden your view of what social scientists can and do choose to research.

Characteristics

To begin, we can describe units of analysis in terms of their characteristics or their states of being. Individuals might be characterized by gender, age, height, marital status, deformities, region of

FIGURE 4-1
Illustrations of Units of Analysis

Units of Analysis
Individuals

Sample Statements

60% of the sample are women
10% of the sample are wearing an eye patch
10% of the sample have pigtails

Families

20% of the families have a single parent
40% of the families have two children
20% of the famillies have no children

The mean number of children per family is 1.2

FIGURE 4-1
Illustrations of Units of Analysis (*continued*)

Units of Analysis
Households

Sample Statements

20% of the households are occupied by more than one family

30% of the households have holes in their roofs

10% of the households are occupied by aliens

Notice also that 33% of the families live in multiple-family households with family as the unit of analysis origin, or hearing ability. Social groups and formal organizations might be characterized by size, structure, location, and aggregated descriptions of their members. Physical social artifacts might be described physically—by size, weight, and color, for example—or by the characteristics of the people associated with them. Social interactions might be characterized in terms of where they occur, when they occur, or what the people involved are like.

These examples do not represent an exhaustive list of possibilities. Nevertheless, they should suggest some of the ways to characterize units of analysis.

Orientations

When individual people are the units of analysis, we frequently investigate what are called *orientations:* attitudes, beliefs, personality traits, prejudices, predispositions, and the like. Individuals might be characterized as religious, politically liberal, anti-Semitic, intellectually sophisticated, superstitious, or scientific. Orientations, then, are general tendencies, inclinations, or predilections.

Social groups and formal organizations, similarly, might be characterized in terms of their purposes, policies, regulations, or procedures, or in terms of the aggregated orientations of their members.

Social interactions might be similarly characterized. For example, we could see airline hijackings as politically or nonpolitically motivated; we could also characterize court cases and congressional hearings this way.

Actions

Sometimes social *action* is the focus of research. We may observe directly or accept secondhand accounts of individual human actions such as voting, bond buying, investing, striking, dropping out of school, going to church, or buying Brand X toothpaste. Secondhand accounts of actions may come from the participants themselves or from other sources. Thus, to find out whether people have registered to vote, we might ask them or check the list of registered voters.

Social groups and formal organizations act as well. Families may go on picnics, pray together, fight over money, or move to another city. Fraternities may sponsor concerts; sororities may collect money to send girls to camp. Corporations may contribute to political campaigns, merge with other corporations, fix prices, or go bankrupt.

Because social interactions are actions themselves, it is a little more difficult to imagine them engaging in actions. Nevertheless, marriages succeed or fail, court cases result in conviction or acquittal, and fistfights cool off or get out of hand.

Like the earlier discussion of units of analysis, the present section is intended as a mind-expanding exercise, not as a definitive statement of all the possible or legitimate focal points. It matters little at this point whether you regard a person's score on an IQ test as a characteristic, an orientation, or an action—only that you recognize it as something available for study.

Chapters 5 and 6 will return to these issues with a more rigorously analytical perspective.

■ THE TIME DIMENSION

Time plays many roles in the design and execution of research, quite aside from the time it takes to do research. When we examine causation in Part 4, we'll find that the time sequence of events and situations is critical to determining causation. Time also affects the generalizability of research findings. Do the descriptions and explanations resulting from a particular study accurately represent the situation of ten years ago, ten years from now, or only the present?

So far in this chapter, we have regarded research design as a process for deciding *what aspects* we shall observe, *of whom,* and *for what purpose.* Now we must consider a set of time-related options that cuts across each of these earlier considerations. We can choose to make observations more or less at one time or over a long period.

Cross-Sectional Studies

Many research projects are designed to study some phenomenon by taking a cross section of it at one time and analyzing that cross section carefully. Exploratory and descriptive studies are often cross-sectional. A single U.S. Census, for instance, is a study aimed at describing the U.S. population at a given time.

Many explanatory studies are also cross-sectional. A researcher conducting a large-scale national survey to examine the sources of racial and religious prejudice would, in all likelihood, be dealing with a single time frame in the ongoing process of prejudice.

Explanatory cross-sectional studies have an inherent problem. Though they typically aim at understanding causal processes that occur over time, their conclusions are based on observations made at only one time. This problem is somewhat akin to that of determining the speed of a moving object on the basis of a high-speed, still photograph that freezes the movement of the object.

Yanjie Bian, for example, conducted a survey of workers in Tianjin, China, for the purpose of studying stratification in contemporary, urban Chinese society. In undertaking the survey in 1988, however, he was conscious of the important changes brought about by a series of national campaigns, such as the Great Proletarian Cultural Revolution, dating from the 1949 revolution and continuing into the present.

■ These campaigns altered political atmospheres and affected people's work and nonwork activities. Because of these campaigns, it is difficult to draw conclusions from a cross-sectional social survey, such as the one presented in this book, about *general* patterns of Chinese workplaces and their effects on workers. Such conclusions may be limited to one period of time and are subject to further tests based on data collected at other times.

(1994:19)

The problem of speaking about social life in general, based on a snapshot in time, is one we will address repeatedly throughout the book. One solution is suggested by Bian's final comment—about data collected "at other times."

Longitudinal Studies

Some research projects, called **longitudinal studies,** are designed to permit observations over an extended period. For example, a researcher can participate in and observe the activities of a radical political group from its inception to its demise. In analyses of newspaper editorials or Supreme Court decisions over time, it would be irrelevant whether the researcher's actual observations and analyses were made at one time or over the course of the actual events under study; however, the studies would still be considered longitudinal.

Most field research projects, involving direct observation and perhaps in-depth interviews, are naturally longitudinal. Thus, for example, when Ramona Asher and Gary Fine (1991) studied the life experiences of the wives of alcoholic men, they were in a position to examine the evolution of their troubled marital relationships over time, sometimes even including the reactions of the subjects to the research itself.

In the classic study, *When Prophecy Fails* (1956), Leon Festinger, Henry Reicker, and Stanley Schachter were specifically interested in learning what happened to a flying saucer cult when their predictions of an alien encounter failed to come true. Would they close down the group or would they become all the more committed to their beliefs? A longitudinal study was required to provide an answer. (They redoubled their efforts to get new members.)

Longitudinal studies can be more difficult for quantitative studies such as large-scale surveys. Nonetheless, they are often undertaken; three special types of longitudinal studies should be noted here.

Trend Studies When we study changes within some general population over time, we engage in a **trend study.** Examples include a comparison of U.S. Censuses over time, showing growth in the national population, and a series of Gallup Polls during the course of an election campaign, showing trends in the relative strengths and standing of different candidates.

Michael Carpini and Scott Keeter (1991) wanted to know whether U.S. citizens today are better or more poorly informed about politics than those of an earlier generation. To find out, they compared the results of several Gallup Polls conducted during the 1940s and 1950s with a 1989 survey that asked several of the same questions tapping political knowledge.

Overall, the analysis suggests that current citizens are slightly better informed. In 1989, for example, 74 percent of the sample could name the vice president of the United States, compared with 67 percent in 1952. In 1989, substantially higher percentages could explain presidential vetoes and congressional overrides of vetoes than could people in 1947. On the other hand, more of the 1947 sample could identify their U.S. representative (38 percent) than could the 1989 sample (29 percent).

An in-depth analysis, however, indicates that the slight increase in political knowledge resulted from the fact that the people in the 1989 sample were more highly educated than those from earlier samples. When educational levels were taken into account, the researchers concluded that political knowledge has actually declined (within specific educational groups).

Cohort Studies When we examine relatively specific subpopulations or *cohorts* as they change over time, we engage in a **cohort study**. Typically, a cohort is an age group, such as those people born during the 1920s, but it can also be based on some other time grouping, such as people born during the Vietnam War, people who got married in 1964, and so forth. An example of a cohort study would be a series of national surveys, conducted perhaps every 20 years, to study the economic attitudes of the cohort born during the depression of the early 1930s. A sample of people 15–20 years of age might be surveyed in 1950, another sample of those 35–40 years of age in 1970, and another sample of those 55–60 years of age in 1990. Although the specific set of people studied in each survey would differ, each sample would represent the survivors of the cohort born between 1930 and 1935.

James Davis (1992) turned to a cohort analysis in an attempt to understand shifting political orientations during the 1970s and 1980s in America. Overall, he found a liberal trend on issues such as race, gender, religion, politics, crime, and free speech. But did this trend represent people in general getting a bit more liberal, or did it merely reflect more liberal younger generations replacing the conservative older ones?

To answer this question, Davis examined national surveys conducted in four time periods, five years apart. In each survey, he grouped the respondents into age groups, also five years apart. This strategy allowed him to compare different age groups at any given point in time, as well as follow the political development of each age group over time.

One of the questions he examined was whether a person who admitted to being a communist should be allowed to speak in the respondents' communities. Consistently, the younger respondents in each period of time were more willing to let the communist speak than were the older ones. Among those aged 20–40 in the first set of the survey, for example, 72 percent took this liberal position, contrasted with 27 percent among respondents 80 and older. What Davis found when he examined the youngest cohort over time is shown in Table 4-1.

This pattern of a slight, conservative shift in the 1970s, followed by a liberal rebound in the 1980s, typifies the several cohorts Davis analyzed (Davis 1992:269).

Panel Studies Though similar to trend and cohort studies, **panel studies** examine the same set of people each time. For example, we could interview the same sample of voters every month during an election campaign, asking for whom they intended to vote. Though such a study would allow us to to analyze overall trends in voter preferences for different candidates, it would also show the precise patterns of persistence and change in intentions. For example, a trend study that showed that Candidates A and B each had exactly half of the voters on September 1 and on October 1 as well could indicate that none of the electorate had changed voting plans, that all of the voters had changed their intentions, or something in between. A panel study would eliminate this confusion by showing what kinds of voters switched from A to B and what kinds switched from B to A, as well as other facts.

Joseph Veroff, Shirley Hatchett, and Elizabeth Douvan (1992) wanted to learn about marital adjustment among newlyweds, looking for differences between white and African-American

TABLE 4-1
Age and Political Liberalism

Survey Dates	1972 to 1974	1977 to 1980	1982 to 1984	1987 to 1989
Age of Cohort	20–24	25–29	30–34	35–39
Percent who would let the communist speak	72%	68%	73%	73%

couples. To get subjects for study, they selected a sample of couples who applied for marriage licenses in Wayne County, Michigan, April through June 1986.

Concerned about the possible impact their research might have on the couples' marital adjustment, the researchers divided their sample in half at random: an *experimental* group and a *control* group (concepts we'll explore further in Chapter 9). Couples in the former group were intensively interviewed over a four-year period, whereas the latter group was contacted only briefly each year.

By studying the same couples over time, the researchers could follow the specific problems that arose and the way the couples dealt with them. As a by-product of their research, they found that those studied the most intensely seemed to achieve a somewhat better marital adjustment. The researchers felt that the interviews may have forced couples to discuss matters they may have otherwise buried.

The Three Types Contrasted Because the distinctions between trend, cohort, and panel studies are sometimes difficult to grasp at first, let's contrast the three study designs in terms of the same variable: political party affiliation. A trend study might look at shifts in the affiliations of the U.S. electorate over time, as the Gallup Poll does on a regular basis. A cohort study might follow shifts in party affiliations among "the Depression generation," specifically, say, people who were between 20 and 30 in 1932. We could study a sample of people 30–40 years old in 1942, a new sample of people aged 40–50 in 1952, and so forth. A panel study could start with a sample of the whole population or of some special subset and study those specific individuals over time. Notice that only the panel study would give a full picture of the shifts in party affiliations: from Democrat to Republican, from Republican to Democrat, and so forth. Cohort and trend studies would uncover only net changes.

Longitudinal studies have an obvious advantage over cross-sectional ones in providing information describing processes over time. But this advantage often comes at a heavy cost in both time and money, especially in a large-scale survey. Observations may have to be made at the time events are occurring, and the method of observation may require many research workers.

Panel studies, which offer the most comprehensive data on changes over time, face a special problem: *panel attrition*. Some of the respondents studied in the first wave of the survey may not participate in later waves. (This is comparable to the problem of experimental mortality discussed in Chapter 9.) The danger is that those who drop out of the study may not be typical, thereby distorting the results of the study. Thus, when Carol S. Aneshensel et al. conducted a panel study of adolescent girls (comparing Latinas and non-Latinas), they looked for and found differences in characteristics of survey dropouts among Latinas born in the United States and those born in Mexico. These differences needed to be taken into account to avoid misleading conclusions about differences between Latinas and non-Latinas (Aneshensel et al. 1989).

Approximating Longitudinal Studies

Often we can draw approximate conclusions about processes that take place over time, even when only cross-sectional data are available. Here are some ways to do that.

Sometimes, cross-sectional data imply processes over time on the basis of simple logic. For example, in the study of student drug use conducted at the University of Hawaii that I mentioned in Chapter 2, students were asked to report whether they had ever tried each of several illegal drugs. Regarding marijuana and LSD, it was found that some students had tried both drugs, some had tried only one, and others had not tried either. Because these data were collected at one time, and because some students presumably would experiment with drugs later on, it would appear that such a study could not tell whether students were more likely to try marijuana or LSD first.

A closer examination of the data showed, however, that although some students reported having tried marijuana but not LSD, there were no students in the study who had tried only LSD. From this finding it was inferred—as common sense suggested—that marijuana use preceded LSD use. If the process of drug experimentation occurred in the opposite time order, then a study at a given time should have found some students who had tried LSD but not marijuana, and it should have found no students who had tried only marijuana.

Logical inferences may also be made whenever the time order of variables is clear. If we discover in a cross-sectional study of college students that those educated in private high schools received better college grades than those educated in public high schools, we would conclude that the type of high school attended affected college grades, not the other way around. Thus, even though our observations were made at only one time, we would feel justified in drawing conclusions about processes taking place across time.

Very often, age differences discovered in a cross-sectional study form the basis for inferring processes across time. Suppose you are interested in the pattern of worsening health over the course of the typical life cycle. You might do so by studying the results of annual checkups in a large hospital. You could group health records according to the ages of those examined and rate each age group in terms of several health conditions—sight, hearing, blood pressure, and so forth. By reading across the age-group ratings for each health condition, you would have something approximating the health history of individuals. Thus, you might conclude that the average person develops vision problems earlier in life than hearing problems, for example. You would need to be cautious in this assumption, however, since the differences might reflect societywide trends. Perhaps improved hearing examinations instituted in the schools had affected only the young people in your study.

Asking people to *recall* their pasts is another common way of approximating observations over time. We use that method when we ask people where they were born or when they graduated from high school or whom they voted for in 1988. Qualitative researchers often conduct in-depth "life history" interviews.

The danger in this technique is evident. Sometimes people have faulty memories; sometimes they lie. When people are asked in postelection polls whom they voted for, the results inevitably show more people voting for the winner than actually did so on election day. As part of a series of in-depth interviews, such a report can be validated in the context of other reported details; however, results based on a single question in a survey must be regarded with caution.

These, then, are some of the ways time figures into social research and some of the ways social scientists have learned to cope with them. In designing any study, you need to look at both the explicit and the implicit assumptions you are making about time. Are you interested in describing some process that occurs over time, or are you simply going to describe what exists now? If you want to describe a process occurring over time, will you be able to make observations at different points in the process, or will you have to approximate such observations—drawing logical inferences from what you can observe now? Unless you pay attention to questions like these, you'll probably end up in trouble. The box entitled "The Time Dimension and Aging" explores this issue further.

The Time Dimension and Aging

by Joseph J. Leon
Behavioral Science Department,
California State Polytechnic University, Pomona

One way to identify the type of time dimension used in a study is to imagine a number of different research projects on growing older in the American society. If we studied a sample of individuals in 1990 and compared the different age groups, the design would be termed *cross-sectional*. If we drew another sample of individuals using the same study instrument in the year 2000 and compared the new data with the 1990 data, the design would be termed *trend*.

Suppose we wished to study only those individuals who were 51–60 in the year 2000 and compare them with the 1990 sample of 41–50-year old persons (the 41–50 age cohort); this study design would be termed *cohort*. The comparison could be made for the 51–60 and 61–70 age cohorts as well. Now, if we desired to do a *panel* study on growing older in America, we would draw a sample in the year 1990 and, using the same sampled individuals in the year 2000, do the study again. Remember, there would be fewer people in the year 2000 study because all the 41–50-year-old people in 1990 are 51–60 and there wold be no 41–50-year-old individuals in the year 2000 study. Furthermore, some of the sampled individuals in 1990 would no longer be alive in the year 2000.

CROSS-SECTIONAL STUDY
1990
41– 50
51– 60
61– 70
71– 80

COHORT STUDY
1990   2000
41– 50   41– 50
51– 60   51– 60
61– 70   61– 70
71– 80   71– 80

TREND STUDY
1990   2000
41– 50 ⟷   41– 50
51– 60 ⟷   51– 60
61– 70 ⟷   61– 70
71– 80 ⟷   71– 80

PANEL STUDY
1990   2000
41– 50*   41– 50
51– 60*   51– 60*
61– 70*   61– 70*
71– 80*   71– 80*
              +81*

⟷ Denotes comparison
*Denotes same individuals

■ HOW TO DESIGN A RESEARCH PROJECT

You've now seen some of the options available to social researchers in designing projects. I know there are a lot of pieces, and the relationships among them may not be totally clear, so here's a way of pulling the parts together. Let's assume *you* were to undertake research. Where would you start? Then, where would you go?

Although research design occurs at the beginning of a research project, it involves all the steps of the subsequent project. The comments that follow, then, should (1) give you some guidance on how to start a research project and (2) provide an overview of the topics that follow in later chapters of the book. Ultimately, you need to grasp the research process as a *whole* to create a research design. (The Holographic Overview at the beginning of the book should reduce this problem somewhat.) Unfortunately, both textbooks and human cognition operate on the basis of sequential *parts*.

Figure 4-2 presents a schematic view of the social science research process. I present this view reluctantly, since it may suggest more of a step-by-step order to research than actual practice bears out. Nonetheless, as I've said, it should be useful to you to have some overview of the whole process before we launch into the specific details of particular components of research.

At the top of the diagram are interests, ideas, and theories, the possible beginning points for a line of research. The letters (A, B, X, Y, and so forth) represent variables or concepts such as prejudice or alienation. Thus, you might have a general *interest* in finding out what causes some people to be more prejudiced than others, or you might want to know some of the consequences of alienation, say. Alternatively, your inquiry might begin with a specific *idea* about the way things are. You might have the idea that working on an assembly line causes alienation, for example. I have put a question mark in the diagram to indicate that you aren't sure things are the way you suspect they are. Finally, I have represented a *theory* as a complex set of relationships among several variables.

Notice, moreover, that there is often a movement back and forth across these several possible beginnings. An initial interest may lead to the formulation of an idea, which may be fit into a larger theory, and the theory may produce new ideas and create new interests.

Any or all of these three may suggest the need for empirical research. The purpose of such research can be to explore an interest, test a specific idea, or validate a complex theory. Whatever the purpose, a variety of decisions needs to be made, as indicated in the remainder of the diagram.

To make this discussion more concrete, let's take a specific research example. Suppose you are concerned with the issue of abortion and have a special interest in learning why some college students support abortion rights, whereas others oppose them. Going a step further, let's say you have formed the impression that students in the humanities and social sciences seem generally more inclined to support the idea of abortion rights than those in the natural sciences. (That kind of thinking often leads people to design and conduct social research.)

In terms of the options we've discussed earlier in this chapter, your research would pretty much be exploratory. You probably have both descriptive and explanatory interests: What percentage of the student body supports a woman's right to an abortion, and what causes some to support it and others to oppose it? The units of analysis are individuals: college students. You might decide that a cross-sectional study would suit your purposes. Let's assume you'd be satisfied to learn something about the way things are now. Although this would provide you with no direct evidence of processes taking place over time, you might be able to approximate some longitudinal analyses.

Getting Started

The topmost portion of Figure 4-2 contains several possible activities. In pursuing your interest in student attitudes about abortion rights, you would undoubtedly want to read something about the issue. If you have a hunch that attitudes are somehow related to a college major, you might want to find out what other researchers may have written about that. Appendix A of this book will help you make use of your college library. In addition, you would probably want to talk to some people who support abortion rights and some who don't. You would probably want to attend meetings of abortion-related groups. All these activities can prepare you to handle the various decisions of research design we are about to examine. As you review the previous research literature regarding abortion rights, you should note the design decisions other researchers have made, always asking whether the same decisions would satisfy your purpose.

FIGURE 4-2
The Research Process

```
┌─────────────────────────────────────────────────────────────────┐
│   INTEREST              IDEA                 THEORY             │
│   ? → Y                 X →?→ Y              A → B → E → F      │
│   Y → ?                 A →?→ B              ↘C ↔ D↗↘X→Y        │
└─────────────────────────────────────────────────────────────────┘
           │                  │                      │
           ▼                  ▼                      ▼
   ┌───────────────┐  ┌─────────────────┐  ┌──────────────────────┐
   │CONCEPTUALIZATION│ │ CHOICE OF       │  │POPULATION AND SAMPLING│
   │Specify the meaning│ RESEARCH METHOD │  │Whom do we want to be │
   │of the concepts and│ Experiments     │  │able to draw conclusions│
   │variables to be    │ Survey research │  │about? Who will be observed│
   │studied            │ Field research  │  │for that purpose?     │
   └───────────────┘  │ Content analysis│  └──────────────────────┘
           │          │ Existing data research│
           ▼          │ Comparative research│
   ┌───────────────┐  │ Evaluation research│
   │OPERATIONALIZATION│└─────────────────┘
   │How will we actually│
   │measure the variables│
   │under study?       │
   └───────────────┘
                      ▼
              ┌────────────────┐
              │  OBSERVATIONS  │
              │Collecting data for│
              │analysis and interpretation│
              └────────────────┘
                      ▼
              ┌────────────────┐
              │ DATA PROCESSING│
              │Transforming the data│
              │collected into a form│
              │appropriate to manipulation│
              │and analysis    │
              └────────────────┘
                      ▼
              ┌────────────────┐
              │    ANALYSIS    │
              │Analyzing data and│
              │drawing conclusions│
              └────────────────┘
                      ▼
              ┌────────────────┐
              │  APPLICATION   │
              │Reporting results and│
              │assessing their implications│
              └────────────────┘
```

What *is* your purpose, by the way? It's important that you clarify that before designing your study. Do you plan to write a paper based on your research to satisfy a course requirement or as an honors thesis? Is your purpose to gain information that will support you in arguing for or against abortion rights? Do you want to write an article for the campus newspaper or for an academic journal?

Usually, your purpose for undertaking research can be expressed in the form of a *report*. Appendix C of this book will help you with the organization of research reports, and I would recommend that you outline such a report as the first step in the design of your project. Specifically, you should be clear about the kinds of statements you want to make when the research is complete. Here are some examples of such statements: "Students frequently mentioned abortion rights in the context of discussing social issues that concerned them personally." "*X* percent of State U. students favor a woman's right to choose an abortion." "Engineers are (more/less) likely than sociologists to favor abortion rights."

Although your final report may not look much like your initial image of it, this exercise will give you something against which to test the appropriateness of different research designs.

Conceptualization

We often talk pretty casually about social science concepts such as prejudice, alienation, religiosity, and liberalism, but it's necessary to clarify what we mean by these concepts in order to draw meaningful conclusions about them. Chapter 5 examines this process of **conceptualization** in depth. For now, let's see what it might involve in the case of our hypothetical example.

If you are going to study how college students feel about abortion and why, the first thing you'll have to specify is what you mean by "the right to an abortion." Specifically, you will want to pay attention to the different conditions under which people might approve or disapprove of abortion: for example, when the woman's life is in danger, in the case of rape or incest, or simply because the woman wants to have an abortion. You will find that overall support for abortion varies according to the circumstances.

You will, of course, need to specify all the concepts you plan to study. If you want to study the possible effect of a college major, you'll have to decide whether you want to consider only officially declared majors or to include students' intentions as well. What will you do with those who have no major?

If you are conducting a survey or an experiment, you will need to specify such concepts in advance. If you are planning less tightly structured research, such as open-ended interviews, an important part of your research may involve the discovery of different dimensions, aspects, or nuances of concepts. Thus you will be able to uncover and report aspects of social life that are not accessible through the more casual or less rigorous use of language.

Choice of Research Method

As you'll see in Part 3 of this book, there are a variety of research methods available to the social scientist. Each of those methods has strengths and weaknesses, and certain concepts are more appropriately studied by some methods than by others.

In terms of our hypothetical study of attitudes toward abortion rights, a survey might be the most appropriate method: either interviewing students or asking them to fill out a questionnaire. As you'll see in Chapter 10, surveys are particularly well suited to the study of mass public opinion. This is not to say that you couldn't make good use of the other methods presented in Part 3. For example, through *content analysis* (see Chapter 12), you might examine letters to the editor and analyze the different images letter writers have of abortion. *Field research* (Chapter 11) would provide an avenue to understanding how people interact with one another regarding the issue of abortion, how they discuss it, and how they change their minds. As you read Part 3, you'll see how you could use other research methods in studying this topic. Usually, the best study design uses more than one research method, taking advantage of their different strengths.

Operationalization

Having specified the concepts to be studied and chosen a research method, we must decide on our measurement techniques or operations (see Chapter 6). In some cases, this requires a concrete delineation of techniques, such as the wording of questionnaire items. In any event, we must decide how desired data will be collected: direct observation, review of official documents, a questionnaire, or some other technique.

If you decided to use a survey to study attitudes toward abortion rights, you might operationalize your main variable by asking respondents whether they would approve a woman's right to have an abortion under the variety of conditions you've conceptualized: in the case of rape or incest, if her life were threatened by the pregnancy, and so forth. You'd ask respondents to approve or disapprove separately for each situation.

Population and Sampling

In addition to refining concepts and measurements, you must decide *whom* or *what* to study. The *population* for a study is that group (usually of people) about whom we want to draw conclusions. We are almost never able to study all the members of the population that interests us, however, and we can never make every possible observation of them. In every case, then, we will select a *sample* from among the data that might be collected and studied. The sampling of information, of course, occurs in everyday life and often produces biased observations. (Recall the discussion of "selective observation" in Chapter 1). Social researchers are more deliberate in their sampling of what will be observed.

Chapter 8 describes methods for selecting samples that give an adequate reflection of the whole population that interests us. Notice in Figure 4-2 that decisions about population and sampling are related to decisions about the research method to be used. Whereas probability sampling techniques would be relevant to a large-scale survey or a content analysis, a field researcher might need to select only those informants who will yield a balanced picture of the situation under study and an experimenter might assign subjects to experimental and control groups in a manner that creates comparability.

In our hypothetical study of abortion attitudes, the relevant population would be the student population of your college. As you'll discover in Chapter 8, however, selecting a sample will require you to get more specific than that. Will you include part-time as well as full-time students? Only degree candidates or everyone? International students as well as U.S. citizens? Undergraduates, graduate students, or both? There are many such questions—each of which must be answered in terms of your research purpose. If your purpose is to predict how students would vote in a local referendum on abortion, you might want to limit your population to those eligible and likely to vote.

Observations

Having decided what to study among whom by what method, you're now ready to make observations—to collect empirical data. The chapters of Part 3, which describe the various research methods, give the different observation methods appropriate to each.

In the case of the abortion survey, you might want to print questionnaires and mail them to a sample selected from the student body, or you could arrange to have a team of interviewers conduct the survey over the telephone. The relative advantages and disadvantages of these and other possibilities are discussed in Chapter 10.

Data Processing

Depending on the research method chosen, you'll have amassed a volume of observations in a form that probably isn't immediately interpretable. If you've spent a month observing a street-corner gang firsthand, you will now have enough field notes to fill a book. In a historical study of ethnic diversity at your school, you may have amassed volumes of official documents, interviews with administrators and others, and so forth. Chapter 14 describes some of the ways social scientific data are processed or transformed for quantitative or qualitative analysis.

In the case of a survey, the "raw" observations are typically in the form of questionnaires with boxes checked, answers written in spaces, and the like. The data-processing phase for a survey typically involves the classification (*coding*) of written-in answers and the transfer of all information to a computer.

Analysis

Finally, we interpret the collected data for the purpose of drawing conclusions that reflect on the interests, ideas, and theories that initiated the inquiry. Chapters 11 and 15 through 17 describe a few of the many options available to you in analyzing data. Notice that the results of your analyses feed back into your initial interests, ideas, and theories. In practice, this feedback may very well represent the beginning of another cycle of inquiry.

In the survey of student attitudes about abortion rights, the analysis phase would pursue both descriptive and explanatory aims. You might begin by calculating the percentages of students who favored or opposed each of the several different versions of abortion rights. Taken together, these several percentages would provide a good picture of student opinion on the issue.

Moving beyond simple description, you might describe the opinions of different subsets of the student body: men versus women; frosh, sophomores, juniors, seniors, graduate students; engineering majors, sociology majors, English majors, and so forth. The description of subgroups could then lead you into an explanatory analysis, as explained in Chapter 15.

Application

The final stage of the research process involves the uses made of the research you've conducted and the conclusions you've reached. To start, you'll probably want to communicate your findings, so that others will know what you've learned. It may be appropriate to prepare—and even publish—a written report. Perhaps you will make oral presentations, such as papers delivered to professional and scientific meetings. Other students would also be interested in hearing what you have learned about them.

You may want to go beyond simply reporting what you have learned to discuss the implications of your findings. Do they say anything about actions that might be taken in support of policy goals? Both the proponents and the opponents of abortion rights would be interested.

Finally, you should consider what your research suggests in regard to further research on your subject. What mistakes should be corrected in future studies? What avenues—opened up slightly in your study—should be pursued further in later investigations? This aspect of the research process will be discussed in Chapter 19.

Review

As this overview shows, research design involves a set of decisions regarding *what topic* is to be studied among *what population* with *what research methods* for *what purpose*. Whereas the earlier sections of this chapter—dealing with research purposes, units of analysis, points of focus—aimed at broadening your perspective in all these regards, research design is the process of narrowing, of focusing, your perspective for the purposes of a particular study.

If you're doing a research project for one of your courses, many aspects of research design may have been specified for you in advance. If you must do a project for a course in experimental methods, the method of research will have been specified for you. If the project is for a course in voting behavior, the research topic will have been somewhat specified. Because it would not be feasible for me to anticipate all such constraints, the following discussion will assume there are none.

In designing a research project, you will find it useful to begin by assessing three things: your interests, abilities, and available resources. Each of these considerations will suggest a large number of possible studies.

Simulate the beginning of a somewhat conventional research project: Ask yourself what you are interested in understanding. Surely you have several questions about social behavior and attitudes. Why are some people politically liberal and others politically conservative? Why are some people more religious than others? Why do people join militia groups? Do colleges and universities still discriminate against minority faculty members? Why would a woman stay in an abusive relationship? Sit for a while and think about the kinds of questions that interest and concern you.

Once you have a few questions you would be interested in answering for yourself, think about the kind of information needed to answer them. What research units of analysis would provide the most relevant information: college students, corporations, voters, cities, or what? This question will probably be inseparable in your thoughts from the question of research topics. Then ask which *aspects* of the units of analysis would provide the information you need to answer your research question.

Once you have some ideas about the kind of information relevant to your purpose, ask yourself how you might go about getting that information. Are the relevant data likely to be already available somewhere (say, in a government publication), or would you have to collect them yourself? If you think you would have to collect them, how would you go about doing it? Would you need to survey a large number of people or interview a few people in depth? Could you learn what you need to know by attending meetings of certain groups? Could you glean the data you need from books in the library?

As you answer these questions, you will find yourself well into the process of research design. Keep in mind your own research abilities and the resources available to you, however. Do not design the perfect study that you cannot carry out. You may want to try a research method you have not used before so you can learn that much more, but you should not put yourself at too great a disadvantage.

Once you have a general idea of what you want to study and how, carefully review previous research in journals and books to see how other researchers have addressed the topic and what they have learned about it. Your review of the literature may lead you to revise your research design: Perhaps you will decide to use a previous researcher's method or even *replicate* an earlier study. The independent replication of research projects is a standard procedure in the physical sciences, and it is just as important in the social sciences, although social scientists tend to overlook that. Or, you might want to go beyond replication and study some aspect of the topic that you feel previous researchers have overlooked.

Here's another approach you might take. Suppose a topic has been studied previously using field research methods. Can you design an experiment that would test the findings those earlier researchers produced? Or, can you think of existing statistics that could be used to test their conclusions? Did a mass survey yield results that you'd like to explore in greater detail through some on-the-spot observations and in-depth interviews? The use of several different research methods to test the same finding is sometimes called *triangulation,* and you should always keep it in mind as a valuable research strategy. Because each research method has particular strengths and weaknesses, there is always a danger that research findings will reflect, at least in part, the method of inquiry. In the best of all worlds, your own research design should bring more than one research method to bear on the topic.

■ THE RESEARCH PROPOSAL

Quite often, in the design of a research project, you will have to lay out the details of your plan for someone else's review and/or approval. In the case of a course project, for example, your instructor might very well want to see a "proposal" before you set off to work. Later in your career, if you wanted to undertake a major project, you might need to obtain funding from a foundation or governmental agency, who would most definitely want a detailed proposal that described how you would spend their money.

I'll conclude this chapter with a brief discussion of how you might prepare such a proposal. This will give you one more overview of the whole research process that the rest of this book details.

Elements of a Research Proposal

Although some funding agencies (or your instructor, for that matter) may have specific requirements for the elements and/or structure of a research proposal, here are some basic elements you should discuss.

Problem or Objective   What exactly do you want to study? Why is it worth studying? Does the proposed study have practical significance? Does it contribute to the construction of social theories, for example?

Literature Review   What have others said about this topic? What theories address it and what do they say? What research has been done previously? Are there consistent findings, or do past studies disagree? Are there flaws in the body of existing research that you feel you can remedy?

Subjects for Study   Whom or what will you study in order to collect data? Identify the subjects in general, theoretical terms; in specific, more concrete terms, identify who is available for study and how you will reach them. Will it be appropriate to select a sample? If so, how will you do that? If there is any possibility that your research will affect those you study, how will you insure that the research does not harm them?

Measurement   What are the key variables in your study? How will you define and measure them? Do your definitions and measurement methods duplicate (that's okay, incidentally) or differ from those of previous research on this topic? If you have already developed your measurement device (a questionnaire, for example) or will be using something previously developed by others, it might be appropriate to include a copy in an appendix to your proposal.

Data-Collection Methods   How will you actually collect the data for your study? Will you conduct an experiment or a survey? Will you undertake field research or will you focus on the reanalysis of statistics already created by others? Perhaps you will use more than one method.

Analysis   Indicate the kind of analysis you plan to conduct. Spell out the purpose and logic of your analysis. Are you interested in precise description? Do you intend to explain why things are the way they are? Do you plan to account for variations in some quality: for example, why some students are more liberal than others? What possible explanatory variables will your analysis consider, and how will you know if you've explained variations adequately?

Schedule   It is often appropriate to provide a schedule for the various stages of research. Even if you don't do this for the proposal, do it for yourself. Unless you have a timeline for accomplishing the several stages of research and keeping in touch with how you're doing, you may end up in trouble.

Budget   When you ask someone to cover the costs of your research, you need to provide a budget that specifies where the money will go. Large, expensive projects include budgetary categories such as personnel, equipment, supplies, telephones, and postage. Even for a project you will pay for yourself, it's a good idea to spend some time anticipating expenses: office supplies, photocopying, computer disks, telephone calls, transportation, and so on.

As you can see, if you were interested in conducting a social science research project, it would be a good idea to prepare a research proposal for your own purposes, even if you weren't required to do so by your instructor or a funding agency. If you are going to invest your time and energy in such a project, you should do what you can to insure a return on that investment.

Now that you've had a broad overview of social research, let's move on to the remaining chapters in this book and learn exactly how to design and execute each specific step. If you've found a research topic that really interests you, you'll want to keep it in mind as you see how you might go about studying it.

■ MAIN POINTS

- Exploration is the attempt to develop an initial, rough understanding of some phenomenon.
- Description is the precise measurement and reporting of the characteristics of some population or phenomenon under study.

- Explanation is the discovery and reporting of relationships among different aspects of the phenomenon under study. Whereas descriptive studies answer the question "What's so?" explanatory ones tend to answer the question "Why?"
- Units of analysis are the people or things the characteristics of which social researchers observe, describe, and explain. Typically, the unit of analysis in social research is the individual person, but it may also be a group or a social artifact.
- The ecological fallacy involves conclusions drawn from the analysis of groups (e.g., corporations) that are then assumed to apply to individuals (e.g., the employees of corporations).
- Reductionism is the attempt to understand some phenomenon in terms of (arguably) inappropriate concepts, such as attempting to explain the American Revolution as a consequence of George Washington's toilet training.
- Whatever the units of analysis in research, they offer numerous points of focus that might be subjected to research: characteristics, orientations, and actions, for example.
- Cross-sectional studies are based on observations made at one time. Although such studies are limited by this characteristic, inferences can be made about processes that occur over time.
- In longitudinal studies, observations are made at many times. Such observations may be made of samples drawn from general populations (trend studies), samples drawn from more specific subpopulations (cohort studies), or the same sample of people each time (panel studies).
- Conceptualization is the process of clarifying what is meant by the concepts being used in a study.
- Operationalization is the specification of how variables are to be measured—an extension of the process begun with conceptualization.
- A research proposal provides a preview of why a study will be undertaken and how it will be conducted. A useful device for planning, it may be required in some circumstances.

■ REVIEW QUESTIONS AND EXERCISES

1. Make up a research example—different from those discussed in the text—that would illustrate a researcher falling into the trap of the ecological fallacy. Then modify the example to avoid this trap.
2. Look through an academic research journal until you find examples of at least three different units of analysis. Identify each and present quotations from the journal to justify your conclusions.
3. Drop in at the Russell Sage Foundation (http://www.epn.org/sage.html) and look at their publications. Select one and identify the units of analysis and the key variables dealt with in that publication.

■ ADDITIONAL READINGS

Bart, Pauline, and Linda Frankel. *The Student Sociologist's Handbook.* Morristown, NJ: General Learning Press, 1986. A handy little reference book to help you get started on a research project. Written from the standpoint of a student term paper, this volume offers a particularly good guide to the periodical literature of the social sciences that's waiting for you in your campus library.

Casley, D. J., and D. A. Lury. *Data Collection in Developing Countries.* Oxford: Clarendon Press, 1987. We've mostly talked about designing social research in the United States or similar countries. This book discusses the special problems of research in the developing world.

Cooper, Harris M. *Integrating Research: A Guide for Literature Reviews.* Newbury Park, CA: Sage, 1989. The author leads you through each step in the literature review process.

Hunt, Morton. *Profiles of Social Research: The Scientific Study of Human Interactions.* New York: Basic Books, 1985. An engaging and informative series of project biographies: James Coleman's study of segregated schools is presented, as well as several other major projects that illustrate the elements of social research in actual practice.

Iversen, Gudmund R. *Contextual Analysis.* Newbury Park, CA: Sage, 1991. Contextual analysis examines the impact of socioenvironmental factors on individual behavior. Durkheim's study of suicide offers a good example of this, identifying social contexts that affect the likelihood of self-destruction.

Maxwell, Joseph A. *Qualitative Research Design: An Interactive Approach.* Newbury Park, CA: Sage, 1996. Maxwell covers many of the same topics as this chapter does but with attention devoted specifically to qualitative research projects.

Menard, Scott. *Longitudinal Research.* Newbury Park, CA: Sage, 1991. Beginning by explaining why we conduct longitudinal research, the author goes on to detail a variety of study designs as well as suggestions for the analysis of longitudinal data.

Miller, Delbert. *Handbook of Research Design and Social Measurement.* Newbury Park, CA: Sage, 1991. A useful reference book for introducing or reviewing numerous issues involved in design and measurement. In addition, the book contains a wealth of practical information relating to foundations, journals, and professional associations.

■ ANSWERS TO UNITS OF ANALYSIS EXERCISE (PAGES 95–96)

1. Individuals (men and women, black and white people)
2. Groups (incorporated U.S. cities)
3. Groups (transcendental meditation organizations)
4. Groups (nursing staffs)
5. Groups (establishments)
6. Individuals (farmers)
7. Groups (neighborhoods)
8. Individuals (African Americans)
9. Organizations (service and production organizations)
10. Artifacts (job titles)

CHAPTER 5: Conceptualization and Measurement

What You'll Learn in This Chapter

You'll discover that most of the words used in everyday language communicate vague, unspecified meanings. In science, however, it's essential to specify exactly what we mean (and don't mean) by the terms we use.

INTRODUCTION

MEASURING ANYTHING THAT EXISTS
How Do You Know?
Conceptions and Concepts
Conceptualization
Indicators and Dimensions
The Interchangeability of Indicators
The Confusion over Definitions and Reality
Creating Conceptual Order
An Example of Conceptualization

DEFINITIONS AND RESEARCH PURPOSES

CRITERIA FOR MEASUREMENT QUALITY
Reliability
Validity
Who Decides What's Valid?
Tension between Reliability and Validity

MAIN POINTS

REVIEW QUESTIONS AND EXERCISES

ADDITIONAL READINGS

INTRODUCTION

This chapter is the first of three dealing with the process of moving from vague ideas about what you want to study to recognizing it and measuring it in the real world. In this chapter we deal with the general issue of *conceptualization,* which sets up a foundation for the discussions of *operationalization* in Chapter 6. The issues raised in Chapters 5 and 6 will be concluded in Chapter 7, which deals with more complex types of measurements.

I want to begin this chapter with a frontal attack on the hidden concern people sometimes have about whether it's possible to measure the stuff of life: love, hate, prejudice, radicalism, alienation, and things like that. The answer is yes, but it will take a few pages for me to make that point. Once you see that we can measure anything that exists, we'll turn to the steps involved in doing just that.

MEASURING ANYTHING THAT EXISTS

It seems altogether possible to me that you may have some reservations about the ability of science to measure the really important aspects of human social existence. You may have read research reports dealing with something like liberalism or religion or prejudice, and you may have been dissatisfied with the way the researchers measured whatever they were studying. You may have felt they were too superficial, that they missed the aspects that really matter most. Maybe they measured *religiosity* as the number of times a person went to church, or maybe they measured *liberalism* by how people voted in a single election. Your dissatisfaction would surely have been increased if you found yourself being misclassified by the measurement system. People often have that experience.

Or, you may have looked up the definition of a word like *compassionate* in the dictionary and found the definition wanting. You may have heard yourself muttering, "There's more to it than that." In fact, whenever you look up the definition of something you already understand well, you can probably see ways people might misunderstand the term if they had only that definition to go on.

Earlier in this book, I said that one of the two pillars of science is *observation.* Because this word can suggest a rather casual, passive activity, scientists often use *measurement* instead, meaning careful, deliberate observations of the real world for the purpose of describing objects and events in terms of the attributes composing a variable. If the variable under study were *political party affiliation,* we might consult the list of registered voters to note whether the people we were studying were registered as Democrats or Republicans. In this fashion, we would have measured their political party affiliation. Or in an in-depth interview about political matters, we might simply ask someone what party they identify with and take their response as our measure. There is usually more than one way to measure a variable. If it exists, we can measure it.

How Do You Know?

To demonstrate to you that social scientists can measure anything that exists, I'd like you to imagine that we are discussing the matter. I'll write the script, but feel free to make substitutions for your side of the dialogue as you see fit.

ME: Social scientists can measure anything that exists.
YOU: Hah! Betcha can't.
ME: Tell me something that exists, and I'll tell you how to measure it.
YOU: Okay, let's see you measure prejudice.
ME: Good choice. Now, I'm not willing to waste our time trying to measure something that doesn't exist. So, tell me if it exists.
YOU: Yes, of course it exists. Everybody knows that prejudice exists. Everybody knows that. If you're so smart, I would have thought you'd know that. Even stupid people know that.
ME: Everybody used to "know" the world was flat, too. I want to know *how* you know prejudice really exists.

Measuring Anything That Exists

YOU: Okay, okay. Since you seem to get off on "observation," how about: "I've *seen* prejudice."

ME: What have you seen that proves prejudice exists?

YOU: Well, a businessman told me that he'd never hire a woman for an executive position because he thought all women were flighty and irrational. How's that?

ME: Great! That sounds like prejudice to me, so I guess we can assume prejudice exists. I am now prepared to measure prejudice. Ready?

YOU: Ready.

ME: You and I will circulate quietly through the business community, talking to businessmen about hiring. Whenever a businessman tells us that he would never hire a woman for an executive position because he thinks all women are flighty and irrational, we'll count that as a case of prejudice. Whenever we are not told that, we'll count the conversation as a case of nonprejudice. When we finish, we'll be able to classify all the businessmen we've talked to as either prejudiced or nonprejudiced.

YOU: Wait a minute! That's not a very good measure of prejudice. We're going to miss a lot of prejudice that way. All we'll measure is blatant prejudice against women in hiring. That's precisely why I doubt that you can really measure prejudice.

ME: I see what you mean. But your comment also means that the situation you described before proves only that blatant prejudice against women in hiring exists. We'd better reconsider whether prejudice exists. Does it?

YOU: Of course it does. I was just giving you one example of prejudice. There are hundreds of other examples.

ME: Give me one that proves prejudice exists.

YOU: Okay, try this for size. I was in on campus the other night, and two guys—one white and one African American—were arguing about politics. Finally, the white guy got so angry, he started using ugly racist language and yelled, "All you people ought to be sent back to Africa." Is that prejudiced enough for you?

ME: Suits me. That would seem to prove that prejudice exists, so I'm ready again to measure prejudice. You and I will split up and start touring the campus every night. We'll keep our ears open and listen for a white person using ugly racial epithets and saying, "All you people. . . ."

YOU: Hold it! I see where this is headed, and that's not going to do it either. A person who said that would be prejudiced, but we're going to classify a lot of prejudiced people as nonprejudiced just because they don't happen to get carried away and use racial epithets.

ME: All of which brings me back to my original question. Does prejudice really exist, or have you been just stringing me along?

YOU: Yes, it exists!

ME: Well, I'm not sure any longer. You persuaded me that businessmen who discriminate against women in hiring exist, because you saw that, and I believe you. You persuaded me that there are people who call African-American people ugly names and say they should all go back to Africa. But I'm not so sure *prejudice* exists. I'd sure like to track it down so I can show you that I can measure it. To be honest, though, I'm beginning to doubt that it really exists. I mean, have you ever seen a prejudice? What color is it? How much does it weigh? Where is it located?

YOU: What are you talking about? Hello. Earth to Babbie. E.B., phone home.

The point of this dialogue, as you may have guessed, is to demonstrate that *prejudice doesn't exist*. We don't know what a prejudice looks like, how big it is, or what color. None of us has ever touched a prejudice or ridden in one. But we do talk a lot about prejudice. Here's how that came about.

As you and I wandered down the road of life, we observed a lot of things and knew they were real through our observations. We heard about a lot of other things that other people said they observed, and those other things seemed to have existed. Someone reported seeing a lynching and described the whole thing in great detail.

With additional experience, we noticed something more. People who participate in lynchings are also quite likely to call African Americans ugly names. A lot of them, moreover, seem to want women to "stay in their place." Eventually, we began to get the feeling that there was a certain kind of person who had those several tendencies. When we discussed the people we'd met, it was sometimes appropriate to identify someone in terms of those tendencies. We used to say a person was "one of those who participate in lynchings, call African Americans ugly names, and won't hire a woman for an executive position." After a while, however, it got pretty clumsy to say all of that, and you had a bright idea: "Let's use the word *prejudiced* as a shorthand notation for people like that. We can use the term even if they don't do all those things—as long as they're pretty much like that."

Being basically agreeable and interested in efficiency, I agreed to go along with the system. That's where *prejudice* came from. It never really existed. We never saw it. We just made it up as a shortcut for talking behind people's backs. Ultimately, *prejudice* is merely a term we have agreed to use in communication: a name we use to represent a whole collection of apparently related phenomena that we've each observed in the course of life. Each of us developed his or her own mental image of what the set of real phenomena we've observed represent in general and what they have in common.

When I say the word *prejudice*, I know it evokes a mental image in your mind, just as it evokes one in mine. It's as though file drawers in our minds contain thousands of sheets of paper, with each sheet of paper labeled in the upper right-hand corner. A sheet of paper in each of your file drawers has the term *prejudice* on it. On your sheet are all the things you were told about prejudice and everything you've observed that seemed to be an example of it. My sheet has what I was told about it plus all the things I've observed that seemed to be examples of it.

Conceptions and Concepts

The technical term for those mental images, those sheets of paper in our mental file drawers, is *conception*. That is, each sheet of paper is a conception. Now, we cannot communicate these mental images directly. There is no way I can directly reveal to you what's written on mine. So we use the terms written in the upper right-hand corner as a way of communicating about our conceptions and the things we observe that are related to those conceptions. The terms associated with the conceptions in our separate minds make it possible for us to communicate and eventually agree on specifically what we will mean by those terms. The process of coming to an agreement is *conceptualization* and the result is called a *concept*.

Let's suppose that I'm going to meet someone named Pat whom you already know. I ask you what Pat is like. Now suppose that you have seen Pat help lost children find their parents and put a tiny bird back in its nest. Pat got you to take turkeys to poor families on Thanksgiving and to visit a children's hospital on Christmas. You've seen Pat weep in a movie about a mother overcoming adversities to save and protect her child. As you search through your mental file drawer, you may find all or most of those phenomena recorded on a single sheet labeled *compassionate*. You look over the other entries on the page, and you find they seem to provide an accurate description of Pat. So, you say, "Pat is compassionate."

Now I leaf through my own mental file drawer until I find a sheet marked *compassionate*. I then look over the things written on my sheet, and say, "Oh, that's nice." I now feel I know what Pat is like, but my expectations in that regard reflect the entries on *my* file sheet, not yours. Later, when I meet Pat, I happen to find that my own experiences correspond to the entries I have on my *compassionate* file sheet, and I say that you sure were right. But say my observations of Pat contradict the things I have on my file sheet. I tell you that I don't think Pat is very compassionate, and we begin to compare notes.

You say, "I once saw Pat weep in a movie about a mother overcoming adversity to save and protect her child." I look at my *compassionate* sheet and can't find anything like that. Looking elsewhere in my file, I locate that sort of phenomenon on a sheet labeled *sentimental.* I retort, "That's not compassion. That's just sentimentality."

To further strengthen my case, I tell you that I saw Pat refuse to give money to an organization dedicated to saving the whales from extinction. "That represents a lack of compassion," I argue. You search through your files and find saving the whales on two sheets— *environmental activism* and *cross-species dating*—and you say so. Eventually, we set about comparing the entries we have on our respective sheets labeled *compassionate.* We may discover that we have quite different mental images represented by that term.

In the big picture, language and communication work only to the extent that you and I have considerable overlap in the kinds of entries we have on our corresponding mental file sheets. The similarities we have on those sheets represent the agreements existing in our society. As we grow up, we're told approximately the same thing when we're first introduced to a particular term. Dictionaries formalize the agreements our society has about such terms. Each of us, then, shapes his or her mental images to correspond with such agreements, but because all of us have different experiences and observations, no two people end up with exactly the same set of entries on any sheet in their file systems. Returning to the assertion made at the outset of this chapter, we can measure anything that's real. We can measure, for example, whether Pat actually puts the little bird back in its nest, visits the hospital on Christmas, weeps at the movie, or refuses to contribute to saving the whales. All of those things exist, so we can measure them. But is Pat really compassionate? We can't answer that question; we can't measure compassion in that sense, because compassion doesn't exist the way those things I just described exist.

Compassion as a *term* does exist. We can measure the number of letters it contains and agree that there are ten. We can agree that it has three syllables and that it begins with the letter *C.* In short, we can measure those aspects of it that are real.

Some aspects of our conceptions are real also. Whether or not you have a mental image associated with the term *compassion* is real. When an elementary school teacher asks a class how many know what *compassion* means, those who raise their hands can be counted. The presence of particular entries on the sheets bearing a given label is also real, and that can be measured. We could measure how many people do or do not associate giving money to save the whales with their conception of compassion. About the only thing we cannot measure is what compassion really means, because compassion isn't real. Compassion exists only in the form of the agreements we have about how to use the term in communicating *about* things that are real.

If you recall our earlier discussions of postmodernism, you'll recognize that some people would object to the degree of "reality" I've allowed in the preceding comments. Though we are not going to be radically postmodern in this chapter, I think you will recognize the importance of an intellectually tough view of what's real and what's not. (When the intellectual going gets tough, the tough become social scientists.)

In this context, Abraham Kaplan (1964) distinguishes three classes of things that scientists measure. The first class is *direct observables:* those things we can observe rather simply and directly, like the color of an apple or the check mark made in a questionnaire. *Indirect observables* require "relatively more subtle, complex, or indirect observations" (1964:55). We note a person's check mark beside *female* in a questionnaire and have indirectly observed that person's gender. History books or minutes of corporate board meetings provide indirect observations of past social actions. Finally, *constructs* are theoretical creations based on observations but which cannot be observed directly or indirectly. IQ is a good example. It is constructed mathematically from observations of the answers given to a large number of questions on an IQ test. (Chapter 7 offers other examples of constructs.)

Kaplan (1964:49) defines *concept* as a "family of conceptions." A concept is, as Kaplan notes, a construct. The concept of *compassion*, then, is a construct created from your conception of it, my conception of it, and the conceptions of all those who have ever used the term. It cannot be observed directly or indirectly, because it doesn't exist. We made it up.

Conceptualization

Day-to-day communication usually occurs through a system of vague and general agreements about the use of terms. Usually, others do not understand exactly what we wish to communicate, but they get the general drift of our meaning. Although you and I do not agree completely about the use of the term *compassionate*, I'm probably safe in assuming that Pat won't pull the wings off flies. A wide range of misunderstandings and conflict—from the interpersonal to the international—is the price we pay for our imprecision, but somehow we muddle through. Science, however, aims at more than muddling; it cannot operate in a context of such imprecision.

Catherine Marshall and Gretchen Rossman (1995:18) speak of a "conceptual funnel" through which a researcher's interest becomes increasingly focused. Thus, a general interest in social activism could narrow to "individuals who are committed to empowerment and social change" and further focus on discovering "what experiences shaped the development of fully committed social activists." This focussing process is inescapably linked to the language we use.

As you've seen, *conceptualization* is the process through which we specify what we will mean when we use particular terms. Suppose we want to find out, for example, whether women are more compassionate than men. I suspect many people assume that is the case, but it might be interesting to find out if it's really so. We can't meaningfully study the question, let alone agree on the answer, without some working agreements about the meaning of *compassion*. They are *working* agreements in the sense that they allow us to work on the question. We don't need to agree or even pretend to agree that a particular specification is ultimately the best one.

Indicators and Dimensions

The product of this conceptualization process is the specification of one or more *indicators* of what we have in mind, indicating the presence or absence of the concept we are studying. Here's a fairly simple example.

We might agree that visiting children's hospitals during Christmas and Hanukkah is an indicator of compassion. Putting little birds back in their nests might be agreed on as another indicator, and so forth. If the unit of analysis for our study were the individual person, we could then observe the presence or absence of each indicator for each person under study. Going beyond that, we could add up the number of indicators of compassion observed for each individual. We might agree on ten specific indicators, for example, and find six present in our study of Pat, three for John, nine for Mary, and so forth.

Returning to our original question, we might calculate that the women we studied had an average of 6.5 indicators of compassion, the men an average of 3.2. We might therefore conclude on the basis of our quantitative analysis of group difference that women are, on the whole, more compassionate than men. Usually, though, it's not that simple.

Imagine you're interested in understanding a small fundamentalist Christian cult, particularly their harsh views about various groups: gays, atheists, feminists, and others. In fact, they suggest that anyone who refuses to join their group will burn in hell. In the context of your continuing interest in compassion, they don't seem to have much. And yet, the group's literature often speaks of their compassion for others.

To explore this research interest, you might arrange to interact with cult members, getting to know them and learning more about their views. You could tell them you were a social researcher interested in learning about their group, or perhaps you'd just express an interest in learning more without saying why.

In the course of your conversations with group members and perhaps in attending religious services, you would have put yourself in a situation where you could come to understand what the cult members meant by *compassion*. You might learn, for example, that members of the group were so deeply concerned about sinners burning in hell that they were willing to be aggressive, even violent, to make people change their sinful ways. Within this paradigm, then, cult members would see beating up gays, prostitutes, and abortion doctors as an act of compassion.

Social scientists often focus their attention on the meanings given to words and actions by the people under study. While this can clarify the behaviors observed, it almost always complicates the concepts they're interested in.

Whenever we take our concepts seriously and set about specifying what we mean by them, we discover disagreements and inconsistencies. Not only do you and I disagree, but each of us is likely to find a good deal of muddiness within our own mental images. If you take a moment to look at what *you* mean by compassion, you'll probably find that your image contains several *kinds* of compassion. The entries on your file sheet can be combined into groups and subgroups, and you'll even find several different strategies for making the combinations. For example, you might group the entries into feelings and actions.

The technical term for such groupings is **dimension:** a specifiable aspect or facet of a concept. Thus, we might speak of the "feeling dimension" of compassion and the "action dimension" of compassion. In a different grouping scheme, we might distinguish "compassion for humans" from "compassion for animals." Or, we might see compassion as helping people have what *we* want for them versus what *they* want for themselves. Still differently, we might distinguish "compassion as forgiveness" from "compassion as pity."

Thus, we could subdivide *compassion* according to several sets of dimensions. Conceptualization involves both specifying dimensions and identifying the various indicators for each.

Specifying the different dimensions of a concept often paves the way for a more sophisticated understanding of what we're studying. We might observe, for example, that women are more compassionate in terms of feelings, and men more so in terms of actions—or vice versa. Whichever the case, we would not be able to say whether men or women are really more compassionate. Our research, in fact, would have shown that there is no single answer to the question.

The Interchangeability of Indicators

Suppose, for the moment, that you and I have compiled a list of 100 indicators of *compassion* and its various dimensions. Suppose further that we disagree widely on which indicators give the clearest evidence of compassion or its absence. If we pretty much agree on some indicators, we could focus our attention on those, and we would probably agree on the answer they provided. But suppose we don't really agree on any of the possible indicators. We can still reach an agreement on whether men or women are the more compassionate.

If we disagree totally on the value of the indicators, one solution would be to study all of them. Now, suppose that women turn out to be more compassionate than men on all 100 indicators—on all the indicators you favor and on all of mine. Then we would be able to agree that women are more compassionate than men even though we still disagree on what compassion means in general.

The **interchangeability of indicators** means that if several different indicators all represent, to some degree, the same concept, then all of them will behave the same way that the concept would behave if it were real and could be observed. Thus, if women are generally more compassionate than men, we should be able to observe that difference by using any reasonable measure of compassion.

You have now seen the fundamental logic of conceptualization and measurement. The discussions that follow in this chapter and the next are mainly refinements and extensions of what I've just presented. Before turning to more technical elaborations on the main framework, however, I want to cover a few useful general topics.

First, I know the previous discussions may not fit exactly with your previous understanding of the meaning of such terms as *prejudice* and *compassion*. We tend to operate in daily life as though such terms have real, ultimate meanings. In the next subsection, then, I want to comment briefly on how we came to that understanding.

Second, lest this whole discussion create a picture of anarchy in the meanings of words, I will describe some of the ways social researchers have organized the confusion so as to provide standards, consistency, and commonality in the meaning of terms. You should come away from this latter discussion with a recaptured sense of order—but one based on a conscious understanding rather than on a casual acceptance of common usage.

The Confusion over Definitions and Reality

First, here's a brief review. Concepts are derived from the mental images (conceptions) that summarize collections of seemingly related observations and experiences. Although the observations and experiences are real, at least subjectively, concepts are only mental creations. The terms associated with concepts are merely devices created for the purposes of filing and communication. For example, *prejudice* is only a collection of letters and has no intrinsic meaning.

Usually, however, we fall into the trap of believing that terms have real meanings. That danger seems to grow stronger when we begin to take terms seriously and attempt to use them precisely. Further, the danger is all the greater in the presence of experts who appear to know more than you do about what the terms really mean: It's very easy to yield to authority in such a situation.

Once we have assumed that terms have real meanings, we begin the tortured task of discovering what those real meanings are and what constitutes a genuine measurement of them. Figure 5-1 illustrates the history of this process. We make up conceptual summaries of real observations because the summaries are convenient. They prove to be so convenient, however, that we begin to think they are real. Regarding as real those things that are not is called **reification**, and the reification of concepts in day-to-day life is quite common.

The design and execution of social research requires us to clear away the confusion over concepts and reality. To this end, logicians and scientists have found it useful to distinguish three kinds of definitions: *real, nominal,* and *operational*. The first of these reflects the reification of terms. As Carl Hempel has cautioned,

■ A "real" definition, according to traditional logic, is not a stipulation determining the meaning of some expression but a statement of the "essential nature" or the "essential attributes" of some entity. The notion of essential nature, however, is so vague as to render this characterization useless for the purposes of rigorous inquiry.

(1952:6)

The specification of concepts in scientific inquiry depends on nominal and operational definitions. A *nominal* definition is one that is assigned to a term. In the midst of disagreement and confusion over what a term really means, we can specify a working definition for the purposes of an inquiry. Wishing to examine socioeconomic status (SES) in a study, for example, we may simply specify that we are going to treat it as a combination of income and educational attainment. In this decision, we rule out other possible aspects of SES: occupational status, money in the bank, property, lineage, lifestyle, and so forth.

Creating Conceptual Order

The clarification of concepts is a continuing process in social research. In some forms of qualitative research, concept clarification is a key element in data collection. Suppose you were conducting interviews and observations in a radical political group devoted to combating oppression in U.S. society. Imagine how the meaning of *oppression* would shift as you delved more and more deeply into the members' experiences and worldviews.

In the analysis of textual materials, social researchers sometimes speak of the "hermeneutic circle," a cyclical process of ever deeper understanding.

FIGURE 5-1
The Process of Conceptual Entrapment

1. Many of our observations in life seem to have something in common. We get the sense that they represent something more general than the simple content of any single observation. We find it useful, moreover, to communicate about the general concept.

2. It is inconvenient to keep describing all the specific observations whenever we want to communicate about the general concept they seem to have in common, so we give a name to the general concept— to stand for whatever it is the specific observations have in commmon.

3. As we communicate about the general concept, using its term, we begin to think that the concept is some *thing* that really exists, not just a summary reference for several concrete observations in the world.

4. The belief that the concept itself is real results in irony. We now begin discussing and debating whether specific observations are "really" sufficient indicators of the concept.

■ The understanding of a text takes place through a process in which the meaning of the separate parts is determined by the global meaning of the text as it is anticipated. The closer determination of the meaning of the separate parts may eventually change the originally anticipated meaning of the totality, which again influences the meaning of the separate parts, and so on.

(KVALE 1996:47)

The continual refinement of concepts occurs in all social research methods, however; you will find yourself refining their meanings even as you write up your final report.

Although conceptualization is a continuing process, it is vital that you specifically address it at the beginning of any study design, especially rigorously structured research designs such as surveys and experiments. In a survey, for example, operationalization results in a commitment to a specific set of questionnaire items that will represent the concepts under study. Without that commitment, the study could not proceed further.

In less structured research methods, however, you must also begin with an initial set of anticipated meanings you can refine during data collection and interpretation. No one seriously believes we can observe life with no preconceptions; thus the scientific observer must be conscious and explicit about those starting points.

Let's explore initial conceptualization the way it applies to structured inquiries such as surveys and experiments. Though specifying nominal definitions focuses our observational strategy, it does not allow us to observe. As a next step we must specify exactly what we are going to observe, how we will do it, and what interpretations we are going to place on various possible observations. All these further specifications make up what is called the **operational definition** of the concept—a definition that spells out precisely how the concept will be measured. Strictly speaking, an operational definition is a description of the "operations" that will be undertaken in measuring a concept.

Pursuing the case of SES, we might decide to ask survey respondents two questions:

1. What was your total family income during the past 12 months?
2. What is the highest level of school you completed?

Here, we would probably want to specify a system for categorizing the answers people give us. For income, we might use categories such as "under $5,000" or "$5,000 to $10,000." Educational attainment might be similarly grouped in categories. Finally, we would specify the way a person's responses to these two questions would be combined in creating a measure of SES. (Chapter 7 will present some methods for doing this.)

Ultimately, we would create a working and workable definition of SES. Though others might disagree with our conceptualization and operationalization, the definition would have one essential scientific virtue: It would be absolutely specific and unambiguous. Even if someone disagreed with our definition, that person would have a good idea how to interpret our research results, because what we meant by SES—reflected in our analyses and conclusions—would be clear.

Here is a diagram showing the progression of measurement steps from our vague sense of what a term means to specific measurements in a fully structured scientific study:

Conceptualization
↓
Nominal Definition
↓
Operational Definition
↓
Measurements in the Real World

An Example of Conceptualization

I want to bring the preceding discussions together now in a brief history of a social scientific concept. Researchers studying urban riots are often interested in the part played by feelings of powerlessness. Social scientists sometimes use the word *anomie* in this context. This term was first introduced into social science by Emile Durkheim, the great French sociologist, in his classic 1897 study, *Suicide*.

Using only government publications on suicide rates in different regions and countries, Durkheim produced a work of analytical genius. To determine the effects of religion on suicide, he compared the suicide rates of predominantly Protestant countries with those of predominantly Catholic ones, Protestant regions of Catholic countries with Catholic regions of Protestant countries, and so forth. To determine the possible effects of the weather, he compared suicide rates in northern and southern countries and regions, and he examined the different suicide rates across the months and seasons of the year. Thus, he could draw conclusions about a supremely individualistic and personal act without having any data about the individuals engaging in it.

At a more general level, Durkheim suggested that suicide also reflected the extent to which a society's agreements were clear and stable. Noting that times of social upheaval and change often present the individual with grave uncertainties about what is expected of him or her, Durkheim suggested that such uncertainties cause confusion, anxiety, and even self-destruction. To describe this societal condition of normlessness, Durkheim chose the term *anomie*. It is worth noting that Durkheim did not make this word up out of thin air. Used in both German and French, it meant, literally, *without law*, and the English term *anomy* had been used for at least three centuries before Durkheim to mean *disregard for divine law*. Still, Durkheim created anomie as a social scientific concept.

In the years that have followed the publication of *Suicide*, social scientists have found *anomie* a useful concept, and many have expanded on Durkheim's use. Robert Merton, in a classic article entitled "Social Structure and Anomie" (1938), concluded that anomie results from a disparity between the goals and means prescribed by a society. Monetary success, for example, is a widely shared goal in our society, yet not all individuals have the resources to achieve it through acceptable means. An emphasis on the goal itself, Merton suggested, produces normlessness, because those denied the traditional avenues to wealth go about getting it through illegitimate means. Merton's discussion, then, could be considered a further conceptualization of the concept of anomie.

Although Durkheim originally used the concept of *anomie* as a characteristic of societies, as did Merton after him, other social scientists have used it to describe individuals. (To clarify this distinction, some scholars have chosen to use the term in its original, societal meaning and to use *anomia* in reference to the individual characteristic.) In a given society, then, some individuals experience anomia, and others do not. Elwin Powell, writing 20 years after Merton, provided the following conceptualization of anomia (though using the term *anomie*) as a characteristic of individuals:

■ When the ends of action become contradictory, inaccessible or insignificant, a condition of anomie arises. Characterized by a general loss of orientation and accompanied by feelings of "emptiness" and apathy, anomie can be simply conceived as meaninglessness.

(1957:132)

Powell went on to suggest there were two distinct kinds of anomia and to examine how the two rose out of different occupational experiences to result, sometimes, in suicide. In his study, however, Powell did not measure anomia per se; he studied the relationship between suicide and occupation, making inferences about the two kinds of anomia. Thus, the study did not provide an operational definition of anomia, only a further conceptualization.

Though many researchers have offered operational definitions, one name stands out over all. Two years before Powell's article appeared, Leo Srole (1956) published a set of questionnaire items that he said provided a good measure of anomia as experienced by individuals. It consists of five statements that subjects are asked to agree or disagree with.

1. In spite of what some people say, the lot of the average man is getting worse.
2. It's hardly fair to bring children into the world with the way things look for the future.
3. Nowadays a person has to live pretty much for today and let tomorrow take care of itself.

The Origins of Anomia

by Leo Srole
Center for Geriatrics and Gerontology, Columbia University

My career-long fixation on anomie began with reading Durkheim's *Le Suicide* as a Harvard undergraduate. Later, as a graduate student at Chicago, I studied under two Durkheimian anthropologists: William Lloyd Warner and Alfred Radcliffe-Brown. Radcliffe-Brown had carried on a lively correspondence with Durkheim, making me a collateral "descendant" of the great French sociologist.

For me, the early impact of Durkheim's work on suicide was mixed but permanent. On the one hand, I had serious reservations about his strenuous, ingenious, and often awkward efforts to force the crude, bureaucratic records on suicide rates to fit with his unidirectional sociological determinism. On the other hand, I was moved by Durkheim's unswerving preoccupation with the moral force of the interpersonal ties that bind us to our time, place, and past, and also his insights about the lethal consequences that can follow from shrinkage and decay in those ties.

My interest in anomie received an eyewitness jolt at the finale of World War II, when I served with the United Nations Relief and Rehabilitation Administration, helping to rebuild a war-torn Europe. At the Nazi concentration camp of Dachau, I saw first-hand the depths of dehumanization that macro-social forces, such as those that engaged Durkheim, could produce in individuals like Hitler, Eichmann, and the others serving their dictates at all levels in the Nazi death factories.

Returning from my UNRRA post, I felt most urgently that the time was long overdue to come to an understanding of the dynamics underlying disintegrated social bonds. We needed to work

---

4. These days a person doesn't really know who he can count on.
5. There's little use writing to public officials because they aren't really interested in the problems of the average man.

(1956:713)

In the decades following its publication, the Srole scale has become a research staple for social scientists. You'll likely find this particular operationalization of anomie used in many of the research projects reported in academic journals. Srole touches on this in the accompanying box, "The Origins of Anomia," which he prepared for this book before his death.

In case you're interested in *anomia,* here are some data from a 1994 national survey conducted by the National Opinion Research Center at the University of Chicago as part of its ongoing General Social Survey (See GSS web site: http://www.icpsr.umich.edu/gss/subject/anomia.htm.). For each of the items shown, I've indicated the percentage who agree among those who have an opinion.

	Percent who agree
In spite of what some people say, the lot of the average man is getting worse, not better.	69%
It's hardly fair to bring children into the world with the way things look for the future.	45%
Most public officials (people in public office) are not really interested in the problems of the average man.	76%

I've presented this greatly abbreviated history of anomie and anomia as social scientific concepts for several reasons. First, they illustrate the process through which general concepts become operationalized measurements, though I wouldn't want you to think that the issue of anomie/anomia has been resolved once and for all. Scholars will surely continue to reconceptualize and reoperationalize them for years to come, continually seeking more useful measures.

expeditiously, deemphasizing proliferation of macro-level theory in favor of a direct exploratory encounter with individuals, using newly developed state-of-the-art survey research methodology. Such research, I also felt, should focus on a broader spectrum of behavioral pathologies than suicide.

My initial investigations were a diverse effort. In 1950, for example, I was able to interview a sample of 401 bus riders in Springfield, Mass. Four years later, the Midtown Manhattan Mental Health Study provided a much larger population reach. These and other field projects gave me scope to expand and refine my measurements of that quality in individuals which reflected the macro-social quality Durkheim had called *anomie*.

While I began by using Durkheim's term in my own work, I soon decided that it was necessary to limit the use of that concept to its macro-social meaning and to sharply segregate it from its individual manifestations. For the latter purpose, the cognate but hitherto obsolete Greek term, *anomie*, readily suggested itself.

I first published the anomie construct in a 1956 article in the *American Sociological Review*,* describing ways of operationalizing it, and presenting the results of its initial field application research. By 1982, the Science Citation Index and Social Science Citation Index had listed some 400 publications in political science, psychology, social work, and sociology journals here and abroad that had cited use of that article's instruments or findings, warranting the American Institute for Scientific Information to designate it a "citation classic."

---

*Leo Srole, "Social Integration and Certain Corollaries: An Exploratory Study," *American Sociological Review* 21 (1956): 709–16.

I've ended the story with the Srole scale, however, because it illustrates another important point. Letting conceptualization and operationalization be open-ended does not necessarily produce anarchy and chaos as you might expect. Order often emerges. There are several elements in this order. First, although you *could* define anomia any way you chose—in terms of, say, shoe size—you're likely to define it in ways not too different from other people's mental images. If you were to use a really offbeat definition, people would probably ignore you.

Second, as researchers discover the *utility* of a particular conceptualization and operationalization of a concept, they're likely to adopt it, which leads to standardized definitions of concepts. Besides the Srole scale, examples include IQ tests and a whole host of demographic and economic measures developed by the U.S. Census Bureau. Using such established measures has two advantages: They have been extensively pretested and debugged, and studies using the same scales can be compared. If you and I do separate studies of two different groups and use the Srole scale, we can compare our two groups on the basis of anomia.

Thus, social scientists can measure anything that's real; they can even do a pretty good job of measuring things that aren't. Granting that such concepts as socioeconomic status, prejudice, compassion, and anomia aren't real ultimately, we've now seen that social scientists can create order in handling them. It is an order based on utility, however, not on ultimate truth.

I devote the rest of this chapter to some considerations and alternatives involved in the creation of useful definitions and measurements. First, we're going to look at the relationship between definitions and research purposes; then the chapter concludes with an examination of some criteria used in determining the *quality* of the measurements we create.

DEFINITIONS AND RESEARCH PURPOSES

Recall from Chapter 4 that two of the general purposes of research are *description* and *explanation*. The distinction between them has important implications for definition and measurement. If you have formed the opinion that description is a simpler task than explanation, you will be surprised to learn that definitions are more problematic for descriptive research than for explanatory research. Before we turn to other aspects of measurement, you'll need a basic understanding of why this is so, though I will discuss this point more fully in Part 4.

The importance of definitions for descriptive research should be clear. If we want to describe and report the unemployment rate in a city, our definition of *being unemployed* is critical. That definition will depend on our definition of another term: the *labor force*. If it seems patently absurd to regard a three-year-old child as being unemployed, it is because such a child is not considered a member of the labor force. Thus, we might follow the U.S. Census Bureau's convention and exclude all people under 14 years of age from the labor force.

This convention alone, however, would not give us a satisfactory definition, because it would count as unemployed such people as high school students, the retired, the disabled, and homemakers. We might follow the census convention further by defining the labor force as "all persons 14 years of age and over who are employed, looking for work, or waiting to be called back to a job from which they have been laid off or furloughed." Unemployed people, then, would be those members of the labor force who are not employed. If a student, homemaker, or retired person is not looking for work, such a person would not be included in the labor force.

But what does "looking for work" mean? Must a person register with the state employment service or go from door to door asking for employment? Or would it be sufficient to want a job or be open to an offer of employment? Conventionally, "looking for work" is defined operationally as saying yes in response to an interviewer's asking "Have you been looking for a job during the past seven days?" (Seven days is the period most often specified, but for some research purposes it might make more sense to shorten or lengthen it.)

I have spelled out these considerations in some detail so you can see that the conclusion of a descriptive study about the unemployment rate, for example, depends directly on how each issue is resolved. Increasing the period of time during which people are counted as looking for work would have the effect of adding more unemployed people to the labor force as defined, thereby increasing the reported unemployment rate. If we follow another convention and speak of the *civilian* labor force and the *civilian* unemployment rate, we are excluding military personnel; that, too, increases the reported unemployment rate, because military personnel would be employed—*by definition.*

Thus the descriptive statement that the unemployment rate in a city is 3 percent, or 9 percent, or whatever it might be, depends directly on the operational definitions used. This example is relatively clear because there are several accepted conventions relating to the labor force and unemployment. Consider how difficult it would be to get agreement about the definitions you'd need to say, "45 percent of the students are politically conservative." This percentage, like the unemployment rate, would depend directly on your definition of what is being measured. A different definition might result in the conclusion "5 percent of the student body are politically conservative."

Ironically, definitions are less problematic in the case of explanatory research. Let's suppose we are interested in explaining political conservatism. Why are some people conservative and others not? More specifically, let's suppose we are interested in whether old people are generally more conservative than young people. What if you and I have 25 different operational definitions of *conservative,* and we can't agree on which definition is the best one? As we've already seen, this is not necessarily an insurmountable obstacle to our research. Suppose, for example, that we found old people more conservative than young people in terms of *all 25 definitions!* (Recall the earlier discussion of compassion in men and women.) Suppose we found old people more conservative than young people by *every* reasonable definition of conservatism we could think of. It wouldn't matter what our definition was. We would conclude that old people are generally more conservative than young people—even though we couldn't agree about what a conservative really was.

In practice, explanatory research seldom results in findings quite as unambiguous as this example suggests; nonetheless, the general pattern is quite common in actual research. There *are* consistent patterns of relationships in human social life that result in consistent research findings; however, such consistency does not appear in a descriptive situation. Changing definitions almost inevitably result in different descriptive conclusions.

The box "The Importance of Variable Names" explores this issue in connection with the variable *citizen participation.*

■ CRITERIA FOR MEASUREMENT QUALITY

This chapter has come some distance. It began with the bald assertion that social scientists can measure anything that exists. Then we discovered that most of the things we might want to measure and study don't really exist. Next we learned that it is possible to measure them anyway. I want to conclude the chapter with a discussion of some of the yardsticks against which we judge our relative success or failure in measuring things—even things that don't exist.

To begin, measurements can be made with varying degrees of *precision,* representing the fineness of distinctions made between attributes composing a variable. The description of a woman as "43 years old" is more precise than "in her forties." Saying a streetcorner gang was formed in the summer of 1996 is more precise than saying "during the 1990s."

As a general rule, precise measurements are superior to imprecise ones, as common sense would dictate. There are no conditions under which imprecise measurements would be intrinsically superior to precise ones. Even so, precision is not always necessary or desirable. If knowing that a woman is in her forties satisfies your research requirements, then any additional effort invested in learning her precise age is wasted. The operationalization of concepts, then, must be guided partly by an understanding of the degree of precision required. If your needs are not clear, be more precise rather than less.

Don't confuse precision with *accuracy,* however. Describing someone as "born in Stowe, Vermont," is more precise than "born in New England"—but suppose the person in question was actually born in Boston. The less precise description, in this instance, is more accurate, a better reflection of the real world.

Precision and accuracy are obviously important qualities in research measurement, and they probably need no further explanation. When social scientists construct and evaluate measurements, however, they pay special attention to two technical considerations: **reliability** and **validity.**

Reliability

In the abstract, *reliability* is a matter of whether a particular technique, applied repeatedly to the same object, would yield the same result each time. Let's say you want to know how much I weigh. (No, I don't know why.) As one technique, you might ask two different people to estimate my weight. If the first person estimated 150 pounds and the other estimated 300, we would have to conclude the technique of having people estimate my weight wasn't very reliable.

Suppose, as an alternative, that we use a bathroom scale as our measurement technique. I step on the scale twice, and we note the result each time. The scale would presumably report the same weight for me both times, indicating that the scale provided a more reliable technique for measuring a person's weight than did asking people to estimate it.

Reliability, however, does not ensure accuracy any more than precision does. Suppose I've set my bathroom scale to shave five pounds off my

The Importance of Variable Names

by Patricia Fisher
Graduate School of Planning, University of Tennessee

Operationalization is one of those things that's easier said than done. It is quite simple to explain to someone the purpose and importance of operational definitions for variables, and even to describe how operationalization typically takes place. However, until you've tried to operationalize a rather complex variable, you may not appreciate some of the subtle difficulties involved. Of considerable importance to the operationalization effort is the particular name that you have chosen for a variable. Let's consider an example from the field of Urban Planning.

A variable of interest to planners is citizen participation. Planners are convinced that participation in the planning process by citizens is important to the success of plan implementation. Citizen participation is an aid to planners' understanding of the real and perceived needs of a community, and such involvement by citizens tends to enhance their cooperation with and support for planning efforts. Although many different conceptual definitions might be offered by different planners, there would be little misunderstanding over what is meant by citizen participation. The name of the variable seems adequate.

However, if we asked different planners to provide very simple operational measures for citizen participation, we are likely to find a variety among their responses that does generate confusion. One planner might keep a tally of attendance by private citizens at city commission and

---

weight just to make me feel better. Although you would (reliably) report the same weight for me each time, you would always be wrong. This new element, called **bias**, is discussed in Chapter 8. For now, just be warned that reliability does not ensure accuracy.

Let's suppose we're interested in studying morale among factory workers in two different kinds of factories. In one set of factories, workers have specialized jobs, reflecting an extreme division of labor. Each worker contributes a tiny part to the overall process performed on a long assembly line. In the other set of factories, each worker performs many tasks, and small teams of workers complete the whole process.

How should we measure morale? Following one strategy, we could observe the workers in each factory, noticing such things as whether they joke with one another, whether they smile and laugh a lot, and so forth. We could ask them how they like their work and even ask them whether they think they would prefer their current arrangement or the other one being studied. By comparing what we observed in the different factories, we might reach a conclusion about which assembly process produced the higher morale.

Now let's look at some reliability problems inherent in this method. First, how you and I are feeling when we do the observing will likely color what we see. We may misinterpret what we see. We may see workers kidding each other but think they're having an argument. Or, maybe we'll catch them on an off day. If we were to observe the same group of workers several days in a row, we might arrive at different evaluations on each day. If several observers evaluated the same behavior, on the other hand, they too might arrive at different conclusions about the workers' morale.

Here's another strategy for assessing morale. Suppose we check the company records to see how many grievances have been filed with the union during some fixed period of time. Presumother local government meetings; another might maintain a record of the different topics addressed by private citizens at similar meetings; while a third might record the number of local government meeting attendees, letters, and phone calls received by the mayor and other public officials, and meetings held by special interest groups during a particular time period. As skilled researchers, we can readily see that each planner would be measuring (in a very simplistic fashion) a different dimension of citizen participation: extent of citizen participation, issues prompting citizen participation, and form of citizen participation. Therefore, the original *naming* of our variable, citizen participation, which was quite satisfactory from a conceptual point of view, proved inadequate for purposes of operationalization.

The precise and exact naming of variables is important in research. It is both essential to and a result of good operationalization. Variable names quite often evolve from an iterative process of forming a conceptual definition, then an operational definition, then renaming the concept to better match what can or will be measured. This looping process continues (our example above illustrates only one iteration), resulting in a gradual refinement of the variable name and its measurement until a reasonable fit is obtained. Sometimes the concept of the variable that you end up with is a bit different from the original one that you started with, but at least you are measuring what you are talking about, if only because you are talking about what you are measuring!

---

ably this would be an indicator of morale: the more grievances, the lower the morale. This measurement strategy would appear to be more reliable: Counting up the grievances over and over, we should keep arriving at the same number.

If you find yourself saying "Wait a minute" over the second measurement strategy, you're worrying about *validity,* not reliability. Let's complete the discussion of reliability, and then we'll handle validity.

In social research, reliability problems crop up in many forms. Reliability is a concern every time a single observer is the source of data, because we have no certain guard against the impact of that observer's subjectivity. We can't tell for sure how much of what's reported originated in the situation observed and how much in the observer. This is not only a problem with single observers, however.

Survey researchers have known for a long time that because of their own attitudes and demeanors, different interviewers get different answers from respondents. Or, if we were to conduct a study of editorial positions on some public issue, we might create a team of coders to take on the job of reading hundreds of editorials and classifying them in terms of their position on the issue. Different coders would code the same editorial differently. Or, we might want to classify a few hundred specific occupations in terms of some standard coding scheme, say a set of categories created by the Department of Labor or by the Census Bureau. You and I would not place all those occupations in the same categories.

Each of these examples illustrates problems of reliability. Similar problems arise whenever we ask people to give us information about themselves. Sometimes we ask questions that people don't know the answers to: How many times have you been to church? Sometimes we ask people about things they consider totally irrelevant: Are you satisfied with China's current relationship with Albania? And sometimes we explore issues so complicated that a person who had a clear opinion in the matter might arrive at a different interpretation of the question when asked a second time.

How do you create reliable measures? There are several techniques. First, in asking people for information—if your research design calls for that—be careful to ask only about things the respondents are likely to know the answer to. Ask about things relevant to them, and be clear in what you're asking. The danger in these instances is that people *will* give you answers—reliable or not. People will tell you how they feel about China's relationship with Albania even if they haven't the foggiest idea what that relationship is.

Fortunately, social researchers have developed a number of techniques for dealing with the basic problem of reliability.

Test-Retest Method Sometimes it is appropriate to make the same measurement more than once. If you do not expect the information sought to change, then you should expect the same response both times. If answers vary, the measurement method may, to the extent of that variation, be unreliable. Here's an illustration.

In their research on Health Hazard Appraisal (HHA), a part of preventive medicine, Jeffrey Sacks, W. Mark Krushat, and Jeffrey Newman (1980) wanted to determine the risks associated with various background and lifestyle factors, making it possible for physicians to counsel their patients appropriately. By knowing patients' life situations, physicians could advise them on their potential for survival and on how to improve it. This purpose, of course, depended heavily on the accuracy of the information gathered about each subject in the study.

To test the reliability of their information, Sacks and his colleagues had all 207 subjects complete a baseline questionnaire that asked about their characteristics and behavior. Three months later, a follow-up questionnaire asked the same subjects for the same information, and the results of the two surveys were compared. Overall, only 15 percent of the subjects reported the same information in both studies.

Sacks and his colleagues report (1980:730) the following:

■ Almost 10 percent of subjects reported a different height at follow-up examination. Parental age was changed by over one in three subjects. One parent reportedly aged 20 chronologic years in three months. One in five ex-smokers and ex-drinkers have apparent difficulty in reliably recalling their previous consumption pattern.

Some subjects erased all trace of previously reported heart murmur, diabetes, emphysema, arrest record, and thoughts of suicide. One subject's mother, deceased in the first questionnaire, was apparently alive and well in time for the second. One subject had one ovary missing in the first study but present in the second. In another case, an ovary present in the first study was missing in the second study—and had been for ten years! One subject was reportedly 55 years old in the first study and 50 years old three months later. You have to wonder if the physician-counselors could ever have nearly the impact on their patients that their patients' memories did. Thus, the data-collection method was not especially reliable.

Split-Half Method As a general rule, it is always good to make more than one measurement of any subtle or complex social concept, such as prejudice, alienation, or social class. This procedure lays the groundwork for another check on reliability. Let's say you've created a questionnaire that contains ten items you believe measure prejudice against women. Using the split-half technique, you would randomly (see Chapter 8) assign those ten items to two sets of five. As we saw in the discussion of Lazarsfeld's "interchangeability of indicators," each set should provide a good measure of prejudice against women, and the sets should correspond in the way they classify the respondents to the study. If the two sets of items measure people differently, that, again, points to a problem in the reliability of how you're measuring the variable.

Using Established Measures Another way to help insure reliability in getting information from people is to use measures that have proven their reliability in previous research. If you want to measure anomia, for example, you might want to follow Srole's lead.

The heavy use of measures, though, does not guarantee their reliability. For example, the Scholastic Aptitude Tests and the Minnesota Multiphasic Personality Inventory (MMPI) have been accepted as established standards in their respective domains for decades. In recent years, though, they've needed fundamental overhauling to reflect changes in society.

Reliability of Research Workers It is also possible for measurement unreliability to be generated by research workers: interviewers and coders, for example. There are several solutions. To guard against interviewer unreliability, it is common practice in surveys to have a supervisor call a subsample of the respondents on the telephone and verify selected pieces of information.

Replication works in other situations also. If you are worried that newspaper editorials or occupations may not be classified reliably, why not have each independently coded by several coders? Those that generate disagreement should be evaluated more carefully and resolved.

Finally, clarity, specificity, training, and practice will avoid a great deal of unreliability and grief. If you and I spent some time reaching a clear agreement on how to evaluate editorial positions on an issue—discussing various positions and reading through several together—we could probably do a good job of classifying them in the same way independently.

The reliability of measurements is a fundamental issue in social research, and we'll return to it more than once in the chapters ahead. For now, however, let's recall that even total reliability doesn't ensure that our measures measure what we think they measure. Now let's plunge into the question of validity.

Validity

In conventional usage, the term *validity* refers to the extent to which an empirical measure adequately reflects the *real meaning* of the concept under consideration. Whoops! I've already committed us to the view that concepts don't have real meanings. How can we ever say whether a particular measure adequately reflects the concept's meaning, then? Ultimately, of course, we can't. At the same time, as we've already seen, all of social life, including social research, operates on *agreements* about the terms we use and the concepts they represent. There are several criteria regarding our success in making measurements appropriate to these agreements.

First, there's something called **face validity.** Particular empirical measures may or may not jibe with our common agreements and our individual mental images concerning a particular concept. You and I might quarrel about the adequacy of measuring worker morale by counting the number of grievances filed with the union, but we'd surely agree that the number of grievances has something to do with morale. If I were to suggest that we measure morale by finding out how many books the workers took out of the library during their off-duty hours, you'd undoubtedly raise a more serious objection: That measure wouldn't have much face validity.

Second, I've already pointed to many of the more formally established agreements that define some concepts. The Census Bureau, for example, has created operational definitions of such concepts as family, household, and employment status that seem to have a workable validity in most studies using these concepts.

Edward Carmines and Richard Zeller (1979) discuss three more types of validity: *criterion-related validity, construct validity,* and *content validity.*

Criterion-related validity, sometimes called *predictive validity,* is based on some external criterion. For example, the validity of the college board is shown in its ability to predict the college success of students. The validity of a written driver's test is determined, in this sense, by the relationship between the scores people get on the test and their subsequent driving records. In these examples, college success and driving ability are the *criteria.*

To test your understanding of this concept, see if you can think of behaviors that might be used to validate each of the following attitudes:

Is very religious
Supports equality of men and women
Supports far-right militia groups
Is concerned about the environment

Sometimes it is difficult to find behavioral criteria that can be taken to validate measures as directly as in such examples. In those instances, however, we can often approximate such criteria by considering how the variable in question ought, theoretically, to relate to other variables. **Construct validity** is based on the logical relationships among variables.

Let's suppose, for example, that you want to study marital satisfaction—its sources and consequences. As part of your research, you develop a measure of marital satisfaction, and you want to assess its validity.

In addition to developing your measure, you will have also developed certain theoretical expectations about the way the variable *marital satisfaction* relates to other variables. For example, you might reasonably conclude that satisfied husbands and wives will be less likely than dissatisfied ones to cheat on their spouses. If your measure relates to marital fidelity in the expected fashion, that constitutes evidence of your measure's construct validity. If satisfied marriage partners were as likely to cheat on their spouses as the dissatisfied ones, however, that would challenge the validity of your measure.

Tests of construct validity, then, can offer a *weight of evidence* that your measure either does or doesn't tap the quality you want it to measure, without providing definitive proof. Though I have suggested here that tests of construct validity are less compelling than those of criterion validity, you should realize there is room for disagreement as to which kind of test a particular variable represents in a given situation. It is less important that you distinguish these two types than that you understand the logic of validation that they have in common: If we have been successful in measuring some variable, then our measures should relate in some logical fashion to other measures.

Finally, **content validity** refers to how much a measure covers the range of meanings included within the concept. For example, Carmines and Zeller (1979) point out that a test of mathematical ability cannot be limited to addition alone but would also need to cover subtraction, multiplication, division, and so forth. Or, if we say we are measuring prejudice *in general,* do our measurements reflect prejudice against racial and ethnic groups, religious minorities, women, the elderly, and so on?

Figure 5-2 presents a graphic portrayal of the difference between validity and reliability. If you can think of measurement as analogous to hitting the bull's-eye on a target, you'll see that reliability looks like a "tight pattern," regardless of where it hits, because reliability is a function of consistency. Validity, on the other hand, is a function of shots being arranged around the bull's-eye. The failure of reliability in the figure can be seen as a random error; the failure of validity is a systematic error. Notice that neither an unreliable nor an invalid measure is likely to be very useful.

Who Decides What's Valid?

I began the preceding comments on validity by reminding you that we depend on agreements to determine what's real, and we've just seen some of the ways social scientists can agree among themselves that they have made valid measurements. There is yet another way of looking at validity.

Social researchers sometimes criticize themselves and each other for implicitly assuming they are somewhat superior to those they study. Indeed, we often seek to uncover motivations that the social actors themselves are unaware of. *You think* you bought that new Burpo-Blaster because of its high performance and good looks, but *we know* you are really trying to establish a higher social status for yourself.

Though this implicit sense of superiority would fit comfortably with a totally positivistic approach (the biologist feels superior to the frog on the lab table), it clashes with the more humanistic and typically qualitative approach taken by many social scientists. Thus, for example, David Silverman (1993:94–95) says this of validity in the context of in-depth interviews:

■ If interviewees are to be viewed as subjects who actively construct the features of their cognitive world, then one should try to obtain intersubjective depth be-

FIGURE 5-2
An Analogy to Validity and Reliability

Reliable but not valid   Valid but not reliable   Valid *and* reliable

tween both sides so that a deep mutual understanding can be achieved.

In seeking to understand the way ordinary people conceptualize and make sense of their worlds, ethnomethodologists have urged all social scientists to pay more respect to these natural social processes. At the very least, behavior that may seem irrational from the scientist's paradigm may make logical sense when viewed from the actor's paradigm.

As you know, I've spent years studying trance channelling, in which the channeller goes into a trance and speaks with a voice that says it belongs to someone else: the spirit of someone dead, a being from another planet, and so forth. From the beginning, it was clear to me that I would never "make sense" of what I was observing as long as I required it to abide by the rules of the worldview I had grown up with. Thus, for example, when I probed the issue of "good spirits" and "bad spirits," I sought to discover the agreements that existed among the spirits themselves and among those who channelled them.

Ultimately, social researchers should look both to their colleagues and to their subjects as sources of agreement on the most useful meanings and measurements of the concepts they study. Sometimes one source will be more useful, sometimes the other. Neither should be dismissed, however.

Tension between Reliability and Validity

In a footnote to these discussions, I want to point out that a tension often exists between the criteria of reliability and validity, a trade-off between the two.

If you'll recall for a moment the example of measuring morale in different factories, I think you'll see that the strategy of immersing yourself in the day-to-day routine of the assembly line, observing what goes on, and talking to the workers seems to provide a more valid measure of morale than counting grievances. It just seems obvious that you'd get a clearer sense of whether the morale was high or low.

As I pointed out earlier, however, the counting strategy would be more reliable. This situation reflects a more general strain in research measurement. Most of the really interesting concepts we want to study have many subtle nuances, and it's hard to specify precisely what we mean by them. Researchers sometimes speak of such concepts as having a "richness of meaning." Though scores of books and articles have been written on the topic of anomie/anomia, they still haven't exhausted it.

Very often, then, the specification of reliable operational definitions and measurements seems to rob such concepts of their richness of meaning. After all, morale is much more than a lack of grievances filed with the union; anomie is much more than the five items created by Leo Srole. Yet, the more variation and richness we allow for a concept, the more opportunity there is for disagreement on how it applies to a particular situation, thus reducing reliability.

To some extent, this dilemma explains the persistence of two quite different approaches to social research: quantitative, nomothetic, structured techniques such as surveys and experiments versus qualitative, idiographic methods such as field research and historical studies.

By being forewarned, you'll be effectively forearmed against this persistent and inevitable dilemma. Be prepared for it, and deal with it. If there is no clear agreement on how to measure a concept, measure it several different ways. If the concept has several dimensions, measure them all. Above all, know that the concept does not have any meaning other than what you and I give it. The only justification for giving any concept a particular meaning is utility. Measure concepts in ways that help us understand the world around us.

■ MAIN POINTS

- Conceptions are idiosyncratic mental images we use as summary devices for bringing together observations and experiences that seem to have something in common. We use terms or labels to reference these conceptions.
- Concepts are the agreed-on meanings we assign to terms, thereby facilitating communication, measurement, and research.
- Our concepts do not exist in the real world, so they can't be measured directly.
- It *is* possible to measure the things that our concepts summarize.
- Conceptualization is the process of specifying the vague mental imagery of our concepts, sorting out the kinds of observations and measurements that will be appropriate for our research.
- The interchangeability of indicators permits us to study and draw conclusions about concepts even when we can't agree on how those concepts should be defined.
- Precision refers to the exactness of the measure used in an observation or description of an attribute. For example, the description of a person as being "six feet, one and three-quarters inches tall" is more precise than "about six feet tall."
- Reliability refers to the likelihood that a given measurement procedure will yield the same description of a given phenomenon if that measurement is repeated. For example, estimating a person's age by asking his or her friends would be less reliable than asking the person or checking the birth certificate.
- Validity refers to the extent to which a specific measurement provides data that relate to commonly accepted meanings of a particular concept. There are numerous yardsticks for determining validity: face validity, criterion-related validity, content validity, and construct validity.
- The creation of specific, reliable measures often seems to diminish the richness of meaning our general concepts have. This problem is inevitable. The best solution is to use several different measures, tapping the different aspects of the concept.

■ REVIEW QUESTIONS AND EXERCISES

1. Pick a social science concept such as liberalism or alienation, and then specify that concept so that it could be studied in a research project. Be sure to specify the dimensions you wish to include and those you wish to exclude in your conceptualization.
2. In a newspaper or magazine, find an instance of invalid and/or unreliable measurement. Justify your choice.
3. Go to Holocaust Studies: Prejudice (http://www.socialstudies.com:80/12/126items.html) and browse through the materials described there. Make a list of the various dimensions of prejudice that are dealt with.

ADDITIONAL READINGS

Bohrnstedt, George W. "Measurement." Pp. 70–121 in *Handbook of Survey Research,* edited by Peter H. Rossi, James D. Wright, and Andy B. Anderson. New York: Academic Press, 1983. This essay offers the logical and statistical grounding of reliability and validity in measurement.

Carmines, Edward G., and Richard A. Zeller. *Reliability and Validity Assessment.* Beverly Hills, CA: Sage, 1979. In this chapter, we've examined the basic logic of validity and reliability in social science measurement. Carmines and Zeller explore these issues in more detail and examine some of the ways to calculate reliability mathematically.

Gould, Julius, and William Kolb. *A Dictionary of the Social Sciences.* New York: Free Press, 1964. A primary reference to the social scientific agreements on various concepts. Although the terms used by social scientists do not have ultimately "true" meanings, this reference book lays out the meanings social scientists have in mind when they use those terms.

Grimes, Michael D. *Class in Twentieth-Century American Sociology: An Analysis of Theories and Measurement Strategies.* New York: Praeger, 1991. This book provides an excellent, long-term view of conceptualization as the author examines a variety of theoretical views of social class and the measurement techniques appropriate to those theories.

Lazarsfeld, Paul F., and Morris Rosenberg, eds. *The Language of Social Research.* New York: Free Press of Glencoe, 1955, Section I. An excellent and diverse classic collection of descriptions of specific measurements in past social research. These 14 articles present useful and readable accounts of actual measurement operations performed by social researchers as well as more conceptual discussions of measurement in general.

Silverman, David. *Interpreting Qualitative Data: Methods for Analyzing Talk, Text, and Interaction.* Newbury Park, CA: Sage, 1993, Chapter 7. This chapter deals with the issues of validity and reliability specifically in regard to qualitative research.

U.S. Department of Health and Human Services. *Survey Measurement of Drug Use.* Washington, DC: Government Printing Office, 1992. An extensive review of techniques devised and used for measuring various kinds of drug use.

Wallace, Walter. *The Logic of Science in Sociology.* Chicago: Aldine-Atherton, 1971, Chapter 3. A brief and lucid presentation of concept formation within the context of other research steps. This discussion relates conceptualization to observation on the one hand and to generalization on the other.

CHAPTER 6 Operationalization

What You'll Learn in This Chapter
Now we'll go from conceptualization to the next step in measurement—seeing how social scientists find concepts reflected in the real world. In particular, we'll look at some of the skills involved in asking questions.

INTRODUCTION

OPERATIONALIZATION CHOICES
Range of Variation
Variations between the Extremes
A Note on Dimensions
Levels of Measurement
Single or Multiple Indicators

SOME OPERATIONALIZATION ILLUSTRATIONS

GUIDELINES FOR ASKING QUESTIONS
Questions and Statements
Open-Ended and Closed-Ended Questions
Make Items Clear
Avoid Double-Barreled Questions
Respondents Must Be Competent to Answer
Respondents Must Be Willing to Answer
Questions Should Be Relevant
Short Items Are Best
Avoid Negative Items
Avoid Biased Items and Terms

QUESTIONNAIRE CONSTRUCTION
General Questionnaire Format
Formats for Respondents
Contingency Questions
Matrix Questions
Ordering Items in a Questionnaire
Instructions
Pretesting the Questionnaire
A Composite Illustration

OPERATIONALIZATION GOES ON AND ON

MAIN POINTS

REVIEW QUESTIONS AND EXERCISES

ADDITIONAL READINGS

INTRODUCTION

The preceding chapter discussed and described various aspects of the conceptualization process. In the course of that discussion, I frequently talked about operationalization, for the two are intimately linked. I have distinguished them as follows: *Conceptualization* is the refinement and specification of abstract concepts, and *operationalization* is the development of specific research procedures (operations) that will result in empirical observations representing those concepts in the real world.

While the measurement issues to be dealt with in this chapter are relevant to all forms of social research, many of the techniques discussed relate specifically to the construction of questionnaires, commonly used in survey research and experiments. In Part 3, we'll examine operationalization techniques that apply to other specific methods.

We'll begin with an overview of some of the operationalization choices you have in organizing the business of observation and measurement: what range of variation to consider, what levels of measurement to use, and whether to depend on a single indicator or several. Then, I'll illustrate some different ways to measure a given variable, which I hope will broaden your imagination and vision.

Next, because social research often involves asking people for information—in surveys, experiments, and field research—I'll present some general guidelines and concrete techniques for doing that in a useful way. As you'll see, there are many styles of questions, only some of which will give you useful information about how human social life operates. One danger in observation is that your magnifying glass can turn into a mirror, so that all you see is yourself.

The chapter ends with a discussion of operationalization as a process that continues throughout a research project. Although I've discussed it in the context of research design—gearing up for the collection of data—you'll see that concepts are also operationalized when these data are analyzed. This concluding discussion, then, should round out your introduction to how social scientists measure things. We'll conclude the discussion of measurement in Chapter 7.

OPERATIONALIZATION CHOICES

As I've indicated, the social researcher has a wide variety of options available when it comes to measuring a concept. Most obvious are the several methods of data collection: surveys, experiments, field research, content analysis, historical research, and so on, which will be discussed in depth in Part 3. As you'll see in this section, however, researchers have many other options as well. Although the several choices are intimately interconnected, I've separated them for the sake of discussion. Please realize, however, that operationalization does not proceed through a systematic checklist.

Range of Variation

In operationalizing any concept, you must be clear about the range of variation that interests you in your research. To what extent are you willing to combine attributes in fairly gross categories?

Let's suppose you want to measure people's incomes in a study—collecting the information from either records or interviews. The highest annual incomes people receive run into the millions of dollars, but not many people get that much. Unless you are studying the very rich, it probably wouldn't be worth much to allow for and keep track of extremely high categories. Depending on whom you study, you'll probably want to establish a highest income category with a much lower floor—maybe $100,000 or more. Although this decision will lead you to throw together people who earn a trillion dollars a year with paupers earning a mere $100,000, they'll survive it, and that mixing probably won't hurt your research any, either. The same decision faces you at the other end of the income spectrum. In studies of the general U.S. population, a cutoff of $5,000 or less usually works just fine.

In the study of attitudes and orientations, the question of range of variation has another dimension. Unless you're careful, you may end up measuring only half an attitude without really meaning to. Here's an example of what I mean.

Suppose you're interested in people's attitudes toward the expanded use of nuclear power generators. You'd anticipate in advance that some people consider it the greatest thing since the wheel, whereas other people have absolutely no interest in it whatever. Given that anticipation, it would seem to make sense to ask people how much they favor expanding the use of nuclear energy. You might give them answer categories ranging from "Favor it very much" to "Don't favor it at all."

This operationalization, however, conceals half the attitudinal spectrum regarding nuclear energy. Many people have feelings that go beyond simply not favoring it: They are absolutely *opposed* to it. In this instance, there is considerable variation on the left side of zero. Some oppose it a little, some quite a bit, and others a great deal. To measure the full range of variation, then, you'd want to operationalize attitudes toward nuclear energy with a range from favoring it very much, through no feelings one way or the other, to opposing it very much.

This consideration applies to many of the variables social scientists study. Virtually any public issue involves both support and opposition, each in varying degrees. Political orientations range from very liberal to very conservative, and depending on the people you are studying, you may want to allow for radicals on one or both ends. People are not just more or less religious; some are antireligious.

I don't mean that you must measure the full range of variation in every case. You should, however, consider whether you need to, given your research purpose. If the difference between *not religious* and *antireligious* isn't relevant to your research, forget it. Someone has defined pragmatism as "any difference that makes no difference is no difference." Be pragmatic.

Finally, your decision on the range of variation should be governed by the expected distribution of attributes among your subjects of study. That is what I meant earlier when I said range depends on whom you are studying. In a study of college professors' attitudes toward the value of higher education, you could probably stop at *no value* and not worry about those who might consider higher education dangerous to students' health. (If you were studying students, however . . .)

Variations between the Extremes

In Chapter 5, I briefly discussed precision as a criterion of quality in measurement. It arises again as a consideration in operationalizing variables. What it boils down to is how fine you will make distinctions among the various possible attributes composing a given variable. Does it really matter whether a person is 17 or 18 years old, or could you conduct your inquiry by throwing them together in a group labeled 10 to 19 years old? Don't answer too quickly. If you wanted to study rates of voter registration and participation, you'd definitely want to know whether the people you studied were old enough to vote.

If you're going to measure age, then, you must look at the purpose and procedures of your study and decide whether fine or gross differences in age are important to you. If you measure political affiliation, will it matter to your inquiry whether a person is a conservative Democrat rather than a liberal Democrat, or will it be sufficient to know the party? In measuring religious affiliation, is it enough to know that a person is a Protestant, or do you need to know the denomination? Do you simply need to know whether a person is married or not, or will it make a difference to know if he or she has never married or is separated, widowed, or divorced?

There is, of course, no general answer to such questions. The answers come out of the purpose of your study, or why you're making a particular measurement. I can mention a useful guideline, though. Whenever you're not sure how much detail to get in a measurement, get too much rather than too little. During the analysis of data, you can always combine precise attributes into more general categories, but you can never separate out any variations you lumped together during observation and measurement.

A Note on Dimensions

When people get down to the business of creating operational measures of variables, they often discover—or worse, never notice—that they're not exactly clear about which dimensions of a variable they're really interested in. In Chapter 5, I dealt with this to some degree, but now I want to look at it more closely. Here's an example to illustrate what I mean.

Let's suppose you and I are studying people's attitudes toward government, and we want to include an examination of how people feel about corruption. Here are just a few of the dimensions we might examine:

- Do people think there is corruption in government?
- How much corruption do they think there is?
- How certain are they in their judgment of how much corruption there is?
- How do they feel about corruption in government as a problem in society?
- What do they think causes it?
- Do they think it's inevitable?
- What do they feel should be done about it?
- What are they willing to do personally to eliminate corruption in government?
- How certain are they that they would be willing to do what they say they would do?

The list could go on and on—how people feel about corruption in government has many dimensions. It's essential that you be clear about which ones are important in your inquiry; otherwise, you may measure how people feel about it when you really wanted to know how much they think there is, or vice versa.

Once you have determined how you are going to collect your data (for example, survey, field research) and have decided on the relevant range of variation, the degree of precision needed between the extremes of variation, and the specific dimensions of the variables that interest you, you may have another choice: a mathematical-logical one. That is, you may need to decide what level of measurement to use. To discuss this we need to take another look at attributes and their relationship to variables. (See Chapter 1 for the first discussion of this topic.)

Levels of Measurement

An attribute, you'll recall, is a characteristic or quality of something. *Female* would be an example. So would *old* or *student*. Variables, on the other hand, are logical sets of attributes. Thus, *gender* is a variable composed of the attributes *female* and *male*.

The conceptualization and operationalization processes can be seen as the specification of variables and the attributes composing them. Thus, in one of the examples given in the preceding chapter, *employment status* would be a variable having the attributes *employed* and *unemployed;* the list of attributes could also be expanded to include the other possibilities discussed.

Every variable must have two important qualities. First, the attributes composing it should be *exhaustive*. For the variable to have any utility in research, you must be able to classify every observation in terms of one of the attributes composing the variable. You'll run into trouble if you conceptualize the variable *political party affiliation* in terms of the attributes *Republican* and *Democrat,* because some of the people you set out to study will identify with Ross Perot's "United We Stand" movement, the Green Party, or some other organization, and some (often a large percentage) will tell you they have no party affiliation. You could make the list of attributes exhaustive by adding *other* and *no affiliation.* Whatever you do, you must be able to classify every observation.

At the same time, attributes composing a variable must be *mutually exclusive*. You must be able to classify every observation in terms of *one and only one* attribute. Thus, for example, you need to define *employed* and *unemployed* in such a way that nobody can be both at the same time. That means being able to handle the person who is working at a job *and* is looking for work. (You might run across a fully employed soldier of fortune who is looking for the glamour and excitement of being a social researcher.) In this case, you might define your attributes so that *employed* takes precedence over *unemployed,* and anyone working at a job is employed regardless of whether he or she is looking for something better.

Attributes operationalized as mutually exclusive and exhaustive may be related in other ways as well. For example, the attributes composing variables may represent different *levels of measurement.* In this section, we'll examine four levels of measurement: nominal, ordinal, interval, and ratio.

Nominal Measures Variables whose attributes have *only* the characteristics of exhaustiveness and mutual exclusiveness are **nominal measures.** Examples include *gender, religious affiliation, political party affiliation, birthplace, college major,* and *hair color.* Although the attributes composing each of these variables—*male* and *female* composing the variable *gender*—are distinct from one another (and exhaust the possibilities of gender among people), they have no additional structures. Nominal measures merely offer names or labels for characteristics.

It might be useful to imagine a group of people being characterized in terms of one such variable and physically grouped by the applicable attributes. Imagine asking a large gathering of people to stand together in groups according to the states in which they were born: all those born in Vermont in one group, those born in California in another, and so forth. The variable would be *place of birth;* the attributes would be *born in California, born in Vermont,* and so on. All the people standing in a given group would have at least one thing in common and would differ from the people in all other groups in that same regard. Where the individual groups formed, how close they were to one another, or how the groups were arranged in the room would be irrelevant. All that would matter would be that all the members of a given group share the same state of birth and that each group have a different shared state of birth.

Ordinal Measures Variables with attributes we can logically *rank-order* are **ordinal measures.** The different attributes represent relatively more or less of the variable. Variables of this type are social class, conservatism, alienation, prejudice, intellectual sophistication, and the like.

In the physical sciences, *hardness* is the most frequently cited example of an ordinal measure. We may say that one material (for example, diamond) is harder than another (say, glass) if the former can scratch the latter and not vice versa (that is, diamond scratches glass, but glass does not scratch diamond). By attempting to scratch various materials with other materials, we might eventually be able to arrange several materials in a row, ranging from the softest to the hardest. We could never say how hard a given material was in absolute terms, but only in relative terms—which materials it was harder than and which it was softer than.

Let's pursue the earlier example of grouping the people at a social gathering and imagine that we asked all the people who had graduated from college to stand in one group, all those with only a high school diploma to stand in another group, and all those who had not graduated from high school to stand in a third group. This manner of grouping people would satisfy the requirements for exhaustiveness and mutual exclusiveness discussed earlier. In addition, however, we might logically arrange the three groups in terms of the relative amount of formal education (the shared attribute) each had. We might arrange the three groups in a row, ranging from most to least formal education. This arrangement would provide a physical representation of an ordinal measure. If we knew which groups two individuals were in, we could determine that one had more, less, or the same formal education as the other. In a similar way, one individual object could be ranked as harder, softer, or of the same hardness as another object.

It is important to note that in this example it would be irrelevant how close or far apart the educational groups were from one another. The college and high school groups could be 5 feet apart, and the less-than-high-school group might be 500 feet farther down the line. These actual distances would not have any meaning. The high school group, however, should be between the less-than-high-school group and the college group, or else the rank order would be incorrect.

Interval Measures For the attributes composing some variables, the actual distance separating those attributes does have meaning. Such variables are **interval measures.** For these, the logical distance between attributes can be expressed in meaningful standard intervals. For example, in the Fahrenheit temperature scale, the difference, or distance, between 80 degrees and 90 degrees is the same as that between 40 degrees and 50 degrees in the Celsius scale. However, 80 degrees Fahrenheit is not twice as hot as 40 degrees, since the zero point in the Fahrenheit and Celsius scales is arbitrary; zero degrees does not really mean lack of heat, nor does −30 degrees represent 30 degrees less than no heat. (The Kelvin scale is based on an absolute zero, which does mean a complete lack of heat.)

About the only interval measures commonly used in social scientific research are constructed measures such as standardized intelligence tests that have been more or less accepted. The interval separating IQ scores of 100 and 110 may be regarded as the same as the interval separating scores of 110 and 120 by virtue of the distribution of observed scores obtained by many thousands of people who have taken the tests over the years. (A person who received a score of 0 on a standard IQ test could not be regarded, strictly speaking, as having no intelligence, although we might feel he or she was unsuited to be a college professor or even a college student. But perhaps a dean . . . ?)

Ratio Measures Most of the social scientific variables meeting the minimum requirements for interval measures also meet the requirements for **ratio measures.** In ratio measures, the attributes composing a variable, besides having all the structural characteristics mentioned previously, are based on a true zero point. I have already mentioned the Kelvin temperature scale in contrast to the Fahrenheit and Celsius scales. Examples from social scientific research would include *age, length of residence in a given place, number of organizations belonged to, number of times attending church during a particular period of time, number of times married, and number of Arab friends.*

Returning to the illustration of methodological party games at a social gathering, we might ask people to group themselves by age. All the one-year-olds would stand (or sit or lie) together, the two-year-olds together, the three-year-olds, and so forth. The fact that members of a single group share the same age and that each different group has a different shared age satisfies the minimum requirements for a nominal measure. Averaging the several groups in a line from youngest to oldest meets the additional requirements of an ordinal measure and lets us determine if one person is older than, younger than, or the same age as another. If we space the groups equally far apart, we satisfy the additional requirements of an interval measure and will be able to say *how much* older one person is than another. Finally, because one of the attributes included in age represents a true zero (babies carried by women about to give birth), the phalanx of hapless party goers also meets the requirements for a ratio measure, permitting us to say that one person is twice as old as another.

To review this discussion, Figure 6-1 presents a graphic illustration of the four levels of measurement.

Implications of Levels of Measurement Because it is unlikely you will undertake the physical grouping of people described above (try it once, and you won't be invited to many parties), I should draw your attention to some of the practical implications of the differences that have been distinguished. Primarily, these implications appear in the analysis of data (discussed in Part 4), but those analytical implications should be anticipated in the structuring of your research project.

Certain quantitative analysis techniques require variables that meet certain minimum levels of measurement. To the extent that the variables to be examined in your research project are limited to a particular level of measurement—say, ordinal—you should plan your analytical techniques accordingly. More precisely, you should anticipate drawing research conclusions appropriate

FIGURE 6-1
Levels of Measurement

Nominal Measure Example: Gender

Female   Male

Ordinal Measure Example: Religiosity "How important is religion to you?"

Not very important   Fairly important   Very important   Most important thing in my life

Low   High

Interval Measure Example: IQ

95   100   105   110   115

Ratio Measure Example: Income

0    $10,000 $20,000 $30,000 $40,000 $50,000

to the levels of measurement used in your variables. For example, you might reasonably plan to determine and report the mean age of a population under study (add up all the individual ages and divide by the number of people), but you should not plan to report the mean religious affiliation, since that is a nominal variable, and the mean requires ratio-level data. (You could report the *modal*—the most common—religious affiliation.)

At the same time, you can treat some variables as representing different levels of measurement. Ratio measures are the highest level, descending through interval and ordinal to nominal, the lowest level of measurement. A variable representing a given level of measurement—say, ratio—may also be treated as representing a lower level of measurement—say, ordinal. Recall, for example, that age is a ratio measure. If you wished to examine only the relationship between age and some ordinal-level variable—say, self-perceived religiosity: high, medium, and low—you might choose to treat age as an ordinal-level variable as well. You might characterize the subjects of your study as being *young, middle-aged,* and *old,* specifying what age range composed each of these groupings. Finally, *age* might be used as a nominal-level variable for certain research purposes. People might be grouped as being born during the depression of the 1930s or not. Another nominal measurement, based on birth date rather than just age, would be the grouping of people by astrological signs.

The analytical uses planned for a given variable, then, should determine the level of measurement to be sought, with the realization that some variables are inherently limited to a certain level. If a variable is to be used in a variety of ways, requiring different levels of measurement, the study should be designed to achieve the highest level required. For example, if the subjects in a study are asked their exact ages, they can later be organized into ordinal or nominal groupings.

You need not necessarily measure variables at their highest level of measurement, however. If you're sure to have no need for ages of people at higher than the ordinal level of measurement, you may simply ask people to indicate their age range, such as 20 to 29, 30 to 39, and so forth. In a study of the wealth of corporations, you may use Dun & Bradstreet data to rank corporations rather than seek more precise information. Whenever your research purposes are not altogether clear, however, you should seek the highest level of measurement possible. Again, although ratio measures can later be reduced to ordinal ones, you cannot convert an ordinal measure to a ratio one. More generally, you cannot convert a lower-level measure to a higher-level one. That is a one-way street worth remembering.

Single or Multiple Indicators

With so many alternatives for operationalizing social scientific variables, you may find yourself worrying about whether you will make the right choices. To counter this feeling, let me add a momentary dash of certainty and stability.

Many social scientific variables have pretty obvious, straightforward measures. No matter how you cut it, gender usually turns out to be a matter of male or female: a nominal-level variable that can be measured by a single observation—either looking or asking a question. Although you'll want to think about adopted and foster children, it's usually pretty easy to find out how many children a family has. And although some fine-tuning is possible, for most research purposes, the resident population of a country is the resident population of that country—you can look it up in an almanac and know the answer. A great many variables, then, have obvious single indicators. If you can get one piece of information, you have what you need.

Sometimes, however, there is no single indicator that will give you the measure of a variable you really want. As discussed in Chapter 5, many concepts are subject to varying interpretations—each with several possible indicators. In these cases, you'll want to make several observations for a given variable. You can then combine the several pieces of information you've collected to create a *composite* measurement of the variable in question. Because all of Chapter 7 is devoted to ways of doing that, I'll give you only a simple illustration here.

Consider the concept *college performance.* All of us have noticed that some students do well in college and others don't do so well in terms of their performance in courses. In studying this, we might ask what characteristics and experiences are related to high levels of performance; many researchers have done just that. How should we measure overall performance? Each grade in any single course is a potential indicator of college performance, but in using any single course grade, we run a risk that the one used will not typify the student's general performance. The solution to this problem is so firmly established that it is, of course, obvious to you: the *grade point average* (GPA). We assign numerical scores to each letter grade, total the points earned by a given student, and divide by the number of courses taken to obtain a composite measure. (If the courses vary in number of credits, adjustments are made in that regard.) It is often appropriate to create such composite measures in social research.

Here's another example of variables being measured as calculations from more than one variable, taken from Larry Isaac and Larry Griffin (1989: 879) in their analysis of historical patterns in unionization:

■ Union GROWTH is operationalized as the annual percent change in the number of union members. Strike frequency is defined as the number of strikes per 10,000 employed nonagricultural labor force participants.

■ SOME OPERATIONALIZATION ILLUSTRATIONS

To bring together all the operationalization choices available to the social researcher and to show the potential in those possibilities, I want to take a little time to illustrate some of the ways you might address certain research problems. My purpose here is to stretch your imagination just a bit further and demonstrate the challenge that social research can present to your ingenuity. To simplify matters, I have not attempted to describe all the research conditions that would make one alternative superior to the others, though you should realize that in a given situation they would not all be equally appropriate. Let's look at specific research questions, then, and some of the ways you could address them. We'll begin with an example discussed at length in Chapter 5. It has the added advantage that one of the variables is reasonably straightforward.

1. *Are women more compassionate than men?*
    a. Select a group of subjects for study. Present them with hypothetical situations that involve someone's being in trouble. Ask them what *they* would do if they were confronted with that situation. What would they do, for example, if they came across a small child who was lost and crying for his or her parents? Consider any answer that involves helping the child or comforting him or her to be compassionate, and count whether men or women are more likely to indicate they would be compassionate.
    b. Set up an experiment in which you pay a small child to pretend that he or she is lost. Put the kid to work on a busy sidewalk, and *observe* whether men or women are more likely to offer assistance. Be sure to count how many men and women walk by, also, since there may be more of one than the other. If that's the case, simply calculate the percentage of men and the percentage of women who help.
    c. Select a sample of people and do a survey in which you ask them what organizations they belong to. Calculate whether women or men are more likely to belong to those that seem to reflect compassionate feelings. To take account of men belonging to more organizations than women in general—or vice versa—do this: For each person you study, calculate the *percentage* of his or her organizational memberships that reflect compassion. See if men or women have a higher average percentage.
    d. Watch your local newspaper for a special feature on some issue involving compassion—the slaughter of baby seals, for example. In the days that follow, keep a record of all letters to the editor on the subject. See whether men or women are the more likely to express their compassion in the matter—making the necessary adjustments for one gender writing more letters to the editor than the other in general.
2. *Are sociology students or accounting students better informed about world affairs?*
    a. Prepare a short quiz on world affairs and arrange to administer it to the students in a sociology class and in a comparable accounting class. If you want to compare sociology and accounting *majors,* be sure to ask students what they are majoring in.
    b. Get the instructor of a course in world affairs to give you the average grades of sociology and accounting students in the course.

c. Take a petition to sociology and accounting classes that urges that "the United Nations headquarters be moved to New York City." Keep a count of how many in each class sign the petition and how many inform you that the UN headquarters is already located in New York City.

3. *Do people consider New York or California the better place to live?*
   a. Consulting the *Statistical Abstract of the United States* or a similar publication, check the migration rates into and out of each state. See if you can find the numbers moving directly from New York to California and vice versa.
   b. The national polling companies—Gallup, Harris, Roper, and so forth—often ask people what they consider the best state to live in. Look up some recent results in the library or through your local newspaper.
   c. Compare suicide rates in the two states.

4. *Who are the most popular instructors on your campus: those in the social sciences, the natural sciences, or the humanities?*
   a. If your school has a provision for student evaluation of instructors, review some recent results and compute the average ratings given the three groups.
   b. Begin visiting the introductory courses given in each group of disciplines and count the numbers of students attending classes. Get the enrollment figures for the classes you study, and calculate the average absentee rates.
   c. In December, select a group of faculty in each of the three divisions and ask them to keep a record of the numbers of holiday greeting cards and presents they receive from admiring students. See who wins.
   d. Read the obituary column in your campus newspaper every day, and keep a record of all the faculty who are lynched after class by mobs of irate students—taking care to always note their departmental affiliation. Be sure to adjust your figures to take account of the total number of faculty in each division: The percentages lynched are more appropriate than the numbers lynched.

We could continue moving from the ridiculous to the more ridiculous, but the point of these illustrations has been to broaden your vision of the many ways variables can be operationalized, not necessarily to suggest respectable research projects. When you think about it, absolutely everything you see around you is already an operationalized measure of some variable. Most are measures of more than one variable, so all you have to do is pick the ones you want and decide what they will represent in your particular study. Usually, you'll want to use more than one measure for each variable in the inquiry.

■ GUIDELINES FOR ASKING QUESTIONS

In the previous illustrations—and in the actual practice of social research—variables are often operationalized when researchers ask people questions as a way of getting data for analysis and interpretation. That is always the case in survey research, and such "self-report" data are often collected in experiments, field research, and other modes of observation. Sometimes the questions are asked by an interviewer; sometimes they are written down and given to respondents for completion (these are called *self-administered questionnaires*).

Because questionnaires represent a common and concrete illustration of the operationalization process, they are a fit topic for completing our general examination. As you'll see, several general guidelines can help you frame and ask questions that serve as excellent operationalizations of variables. There are also pitfalls that can result in useless and even misleading information; this section should help you distinguish the two. Let's begin with some of the options available to you in creating questionnaires.

Questions and Statements

Though the term **questionnaire** suggests a collection of questions, an examination of a typical questionnaire will probably reveal as many statements as questions. This is not without reason. Often, the researcher is interested in determining the extent to which respondents hold a particular attitude or perspective. If you can summarize the attitude in a fairly brief statement, you can present that statement and ask respondents whether they agree or disagree with it. Rensis Likert has greatly formalized this procedure through the creation of the Likert scale, a format in which respondents are asked to strongly agree, agree, disagree, or strongly disagree, or perhaps strongly approve, approve, and so forth.

Both questions and statements may be used profitably. Using both in a given questionnaire gives you more flexibility in the design of items and can make the questionnaire more interesting as well.

Open-Ended and Closed-Ended Questions

In asking questions, researchers have two options. They may ask *open-ended questions,* in which case the **respondent** is asked to provide his or her own answer to the question. For example, the respondent may be asked, "What do you feel is the most important issue facing the United States today?" and be provided with a space to write in the answer (or be asked to report it verbally to an interviewer).

In the other case, *closed-ended questions,* the respondent is asked to select an answer from among a list provided by the researcher. Closed-ended questions are very popular because they provide a greater uniformity of responses and are more easily processed. Open-ended responses must be coded before they can be processed for computer analysis, as will be discussed in Chapter 14. This coding process often requires that the researcher interpret the meaning of responses, opening the possibility of misunderstanding and researcher bias. There is also a danger that some respondents will give answers that are essentially irrelevant to the researcher's intent. Closed-ended responses, on the other hand, can often be transferred directly into a computer format.

The chief shortcoming of closed-ended questions lies in the researcher's structuring of responses. When the relevant answers to a given question are relatively clear, there should be no problem. In other cases, however, the researcher's structuring of responses may overlook some important responses. In asking about "the most important issue facing the United States," for example, your checklist of issues might omit certain issues that respondents would have said were important.

In the construction of closed-ended questions, you should be guided by the two structural requirements discussed earlier. The response categories provided should be *exhaustive:* They should include all the possible responses that might be expected. Often, researchers ensure this by adding a category labeled something like Other (Please specify: _____).

Second, the answer categories must be *mutually exclusive:* The respondent should not feel compelled to select more than one. (In some cases, you may wish to solicit multiple answers, but these may create difficulties in data processing and analysis later on.) To insure that your categories are mutually exclusive, carefully consider each combination of categories, asking yourself whether a person could reasonably choose more than one answer. In addition, it is useful to add an instruction to the question asking the respondent to select the one best answer, but this technique is not a satisfactory substitute for a carefully constructed set of responses.

Make Items Clear

It should go without saying that questionnaire items should be clear and unambiguous, but the broad proliferation of unclear and ambiguous questions in surveys makes the point worth stressing here. Often you can become so deeply involved in the topic under examination that opinions and perspectives are clear to you but not to your respondents—many of whom have paid little or no attention to the topic. Or if you have only a superficial understanding of the topic, you may fail to specify the intent of your question sufficiently. The question "What do you think about the proposed peace plan?" may evoke in the respondent a counterquestion: "*Which* proposed peace plan?" Questionnaire items should be precise so that the respondent knows exactly what the researcher is asking.

The possibilities for misunderstanding are endless and no researcher is immune (Polivka and Rothgeb 1993). One of the most established research projects in the United States is the Census Bureau's ongoing "Current Population Survey" or CPS, which measures, among other critical data, the nation's unemployment rate.

A part of the measurement of employment patterns focuses on a respondent's activities during "last week," by which the Census Bureau means Sunday through Saturday. Studies undertaken to determine the accuracy of the survey found that more than half the respondents took "last week" to include only Monday through Friday. By the same token, whereas the Census Bureau defines "working full-time" as 35 or more hours a week, the same evaluation studies showed respondents using the more traditional definition of 40 hours per week. As a consequence, the wording of these questions in the CPS was modified in 1994 to specify the Census Bureau's definitions.

The use of the term "Native American" to mean "American Indian" often produces an overrepresentation of that ethnic group in surveys. Clearly, many respondents understand the term to mean "born in the United States."

Avoid Double-Barreled Questions

Frequently, researchers ask respondents for a single answer to a combination of questions. That seems to happen most often when the researcher has personally identified with a complex question. For example, you might ask respondents to agree or disagree with the statement "The United States should abandon its space program and spend the money on domestic programs." Although many people would unequivocally agree with the statement and others would unequivocally disagree, still others would be unable to answer. Some would want to abandon the space program and give the money back to the taxpayers. Others would want to continue the space program but also put more money into domestic programs. These latter respondents could neither agree nor disagree without misleading you.

As a general rule, whenever the word *and* appears in a question or questionnaire statement, you should check whether you are asking a *double-barreled* question. See the box entitled "Double-Barreled and Beyond" for some imaginative variations on this theme.

Respondents Must Be Competent to Answer

In asking respondents to provide information, you should continually ask yourself whether they are able to do so reliably. In a study of child rearing, you might ask respondents to report the age at which they first talked back to their parents. Quite aside from the problem of defining *talking back to parents*, it is doubtful if most respondents would remember with any degree of accuracy.

As another example, student government leaders occasionally ask their constituents to indicate the manner in which students' fees ought to be spent. Typically, respondents are asked to indicate the percentage of available funds that should be devoted to a long list of activities. Without a fairly good knowledge of the nature of those activities and the costs involved in them, the respondents cannot provide meaningful answers. (*Administrative costs* will receive little support although they may be essential to the program as a whole.)

One group of researchers examining the driving experience of teenagers insisted on asking an open-ended question concerning the number of miles driven since receiving a license. Although consultants argued that few drivers would be able to estimate such information with any accuracy, the question was asked nonetheless. In response, some teenagers reported driving hundreds of thousands of miles.

Respondents Must Be Willing to Answer

Often, we would like to learn things from people that they are unwilling to share with us. For example, Yanjie Bian indicates that it has often been

Double-Barreled and Beyond

Even established, professional researchers have sometimes created double-barreled questions and worse. Consider this question, asked of U.S. citizens in April 1986, at a time when the country's relationship with Libya was at an especially low point. Some observers suggested the United States might end up in a shooting war with the small North African nation. The Harris Poll sought to find out what U.S. public opinion was.

■ If Libya now increases its terrorist acts against the U.S. and we keep inflicting more damage on Libya, then inevitably it will all end in the U.S. going to war and finally invading that country which would be wrong.

Respondents were given the opportunity of answering "Agree," "Disagree," or "Not sure."

Notice the elements contained in the complex statement:

1. Will Libya increase its terrorist acts against the U.S.?
2. Will the U.S. inflict more damage on Libya?
3. Will the U.S. inevitably or otherwise go to war against Libya?
4. Would the U.S. invade Libya?
5. Would that be right or wrong?

These several elements offer the possibility of numerous points of view—far more than the three alternatives offered respondents to the survey. Even if we were to assume hypothetically that Libya would "increase its terrorist attacks" and the U.S. would "keep inflicting more damage" in return, you might have any one of at least seven distinct expectations about the outcome:

---

difficult to get candid answers from people in China

■ where people are generally careful about what they say on nonprivate occasions in order to survive under authoritarianism. During the Cultural Revolution between 1966 and 1976, for example, because of the radical political agenda and political intensity throughout the country, it was almost impossible to use survey techniques to collect valid and reliable data inside China about the Chinese people's life experiences, characteristics, and attitudes towards the Communist regime.

(1994:19–20)

Sometimes, U.S. respondents may say they are undecided when, in fact, they have an opinion but think they are in a minority. Under that condition, they may be reluctant to tell a stranger (the interviewer) what that opinion is. Given this problem, the Gallup Organization, for example, has used a "secret ballot" format, which simulates actual election conditions, in that the "voter" enjoys complete anonymity. In an analysis of the Gallup Poll election data from 1944 to 1988, Andrew Smith and G. F. Bishop (1992) have found that this technique substantially reduced the percentage saying they were undecided about how they would vote.

This problem is not limited to survey research, however. Richard Mitchell (1991:100) faced a similar problem in his field research among U.S. survivalists:

■ Survivalists, for example, are ambivalent about concealing their identities and inclinations. They realize that secrecy protects then from the ridicule of a disbelieving majority, but enforced separatism diminishes opportunities for recruitment and information exchange. . . .

"Secretive" survivalists eschew telephones, launder their mail through letter exchanges, use nicknames and aliases, and carefully conceal their addresses from strangers. Yet once I was invited to group meetings, I found them cooperative respondents.

	U.S. will not go to war	War is probable but not inevitable	War is inevitable
U.S. will not invade Libya	1	2	3
U.S. will invade Libya but it would be wrong		4	5
U.S. will invade Libya and it would be right		6	7

The examination of prognoses about the Libyan situation is not the only example of double-barrelled questions sneaking into public opinion research. Here are some questions the Harris Poll asked in an attempt to gauge U.S. public opinion about then Soviet General Secretary Gorbachev:

■ He looks like the kind of Russian leader who will recognize that both the Soviets and the Americans can destroy each other with nuclear missiles so it is better to come to verifiable arms control agreements.

He seems to be more modern, enlightened, and attractive, which is a good sign for the peace of the world.

Even though he looks much more modern and attractive, it would be a mistake to think he will be much different from other Russian leaders.

How many elements can you identify in each of the questions? How many possible opinions could people have in each case? What does a simple "agree" or "disagree" really mean in such cases?

Source: Reported in *World Opinion Update*, October 1985 and May 1986, respectively.

Questions Should Be Relevant

Similarly, questions asked in a questionnaire should be relevant to most respondents. When attitudes are requested on a topic that few respondents have thought about or really care about, the results are not likely to be very useful. Of course, because the respondents may express attitudes even though they have never given any thought to the issue, you run the risk of being misled.

This point is illustrated occasionally when researchers ask for responses relating to fictitious people and issues. In one political poll I conducted, I asked respondents whether they were familiar with each of 15 political figures in the community. As a methodological exercise, I made up a name: Tom Sakumoto. In response, 9 percent of the respondents said they were familiar with him. Of those respondents familiar with him, about half reported seeing him on television and reading about him in the newspapers.

When you obtain responses to fictitious issues, you can disregard those responses. But when the issue is real, you may have no way of telling which responses genuinely reflect attitudes and which reflect meaningless answers to an irrelevant question.

Ideally, we would like respondents to simply report that they don't know, have no opinion, or are undecided in those instances where that is the case. As we've seen, however, they often make up answers.

Short Items Are Best

In the interest of being unambiguous and precise and pointing to the relevance of an issue, the researcher is often led into long and complicated items. That should be avoided. Respondents are often unwilling to study an item in order to understand it. The respondent should be able to read an item quickly, understand its intent, and select or provide an answer without difficulty. In general, you should assume that respondents *will* read items quickly and give quick answers; therefore, you should provide clear, short items that will not be misinterpreted under those conditions.

Avoid Negative Items

The appearance of a negation in a questionnaire item paves the way for easy misinterpretation. Asked to agree or disagree with the statement "The United States should *not* recognize Cuba," a sizable portion of the respondents will read over the word not and answer on that basis. Thus, some will agree with the statement when they are in favor of recognition, and others will agree when they oppose it. And you may never know which is which.

In a study of civil liberties support, respondents were asked whether they felt "the following kinds of people should be prohibited from teaching in public schools," and were presented with a list including such items as a communist, a Ku Klux Klansman, and so forth. The response categories "yes" and "no" were given beside each entry. A comparison of the responses to this item with other items reflecting support for civil liberties strongly suggested that many respondents gave the answer "yes" to indicate willingness for such a person to teach, rather than to indicate that such a person should be prohibited from teaching. (A later study in the series giving as answer categories "permit" and "prohibit" produced much clearer results.)

Avoid Biased Items and Terms

Recall from the earlier discussion of conceptualization and operationalization that there are no ultimately true meanings for any of the concepts we typically study in social science. *Prejudice* has no ultimately correct definition, and whether a given person is prejudiced depends on our definition of that term. This same general principle applies to the responses we get from people completing a questionnaire.

The meaning of someone's response to a question depends in large part on its wording. This is true of every question and answer. Some questions seem to encourage particular responses more than other questions do. Questions that encourage respondents to answer in a particular way are *biased*.

Most researchers recognize the likely effect of a question that begins, "Don't you agree with the President of the United States that . . ." and no reputable researcher would use such an item. Unhappily, the biasing effect of items and terms is far subtler than this example suggests.

The mere identification of an attitude or position with a prestigious person or agency can bias responses. The item "Do you agree or disagree with the recent Supreme Court decision that . . ." would have a similar effect. I'm not suggesting, however, that such wording will necessarily produce consensus or even a majority in support of the position identified with the prestigious person or agency, only that support would likely be increased over what would have been obtained without such identification.

Sometimes the impact of different forms of question wording is relatively subtle. For example, when Kenneth Rasinski (1989) analyzed the results of several General Social Survey studies of attitudes toward government spending, he found that the way programs were identified had an impact on the amount of public support they received. Here are some comparisons:

More Support	Less Support
"Assistance to the poor"	"Welfare"
"Halting rising crime rate"	"Law enforcement"
"Dealing with drug addiction"	"Drug rehabilitation"
"Solving problems of big cities"	"Assistance to big cities"
"Improving conditions of blacks"	"Assistance to blacks"
"Protecting social security"	"Social security"

In 1986, for example, 62.8 percent of the respondents said too little money was being spent on "assistance to the poor," while in a matched survey that year, only 23.1 percent said we were spending too little on "welfare."

In this context, you need to be generally wary of what researchers call the *social desirability* of questions and answers. Whenever you ask people for information, they answer through a filter of what will make them look good. That is especially true if they are being interviewed face-to-face. Thus, for example, a particular man may feel that things would be a lot better if women were kept in the kitchen, not allowed to vote, forced to be quiet in public, and so forth. Asked whether he supports equal rights for women, however, he may want to avoid looking like a male chauvinist pig. Recognizing that his views might have been progressive in the fifteenth century but are out of step with current thinking, he may choose to say "yes." The main guidance I can offer you in relation to this problem is to suggest that you imagine how you would feel giving each of the answers you offered to respondents. If you'd feel embarrassed, perverted, inhumane, stupid, irresponsible, or anything like that, you should give some serious thought to whether others will be willing to give those answers.

The biasing effect of particular wording is often difficult to anticipate. In surveys and in experiments, it is sometimes useful to ask respondents to consider hypothetical situations and say how they think they would behave. Because those situations often involve other people, the names used can affect responses. For example, researchers have long known that male names for the hypothetical people may produce different responses than female names do. Research by Joseph Kasof (1993) points to the importance of what the specific names are: whether they generally evoke positive or negative images in terms of attractiveness, age, intelligence, and so forth. Kasof's review of past research suggests there has been a tendency to use more positively valued names for men than for women.

As in all other examples, you must carefully examine the purpose of your inquiry and construct items that will be most useful to it. You should never be misled into thinking there are ultimately "right" and "wrong" ways of asking the questions. When you are in doubt about the best question to ask, moreover, remember that you should ask more than one.

These, then, are some general guidelines for writing questions to elicit data for analysis and interpretation. Next we look at questionnaire construction. (There also is more about administering questionnaires in Chapter 10.)

■ QUESTIONNAIRE CONSTRUCTION

While there are many ways of operationalizing variables in social research, as we've already seen, questionnaires are used in connection with many modes of observation in social research. Though questionnaires are essential to and most directly associated with survey research, they are also widely used in experiments, field research, and other data-collection activities.

Given the widespread use of questionnaires in social research, we're going to turn our attention now to some of the established techniques for questionnaire construction. You should read the following sections not just as a continuation of our theoretical discussions of conceptualization and measurement but also in terms of learning a practical skill.

As in the earlier discussion of question wording, I may run the risk of offending you by presenting some nitty-gritty details that seem unworthy of scientific attention and other details that seem too obvious to mention. I take the risk, however, because I have made each of the mistakes I'll warn against and have seen others do the same. Let's begin with some issues of questionnaire format.

General Questionnaire Format

The format of a questionnaire is just as important as the nature and wording of the questions asked. An improperly laid out questionnaire can lead respondents to miss questions, confuse them about the nature of the data desired, and even lead them to throw the questionnaire away.

As a general rule, the questionnaire should be spread out and uncluttered. Inexperienced researchers tend to fear that their questionnaire will look too long; as a result, they squeeze several questions onto a single line, abbreviate questions, and try to use as few pages as possible. All these efforts are ill-advised and even dangerous. Putting more than one question on a line will cause some respondents to miss the second question altogether. Some respondents will misinterpret abbreviated questions. And more generally, respondents who find they have spent considerable time on the first page of what seemed a short questionnaire will be more demoralized than respondents who quickly completed the first several pages of what initially seemed a rather long form. Moreover, the latter will have made fewer errors and will not have been forced to reread confusing, abbreviated questions. Nor will they have been forced to write a long answer in a tiny space.

The desirability of spreading out questions in the questionnaire cannot be overemphasized. Squeezed-together questionnaires are disastrous, whether they are to be completed by the respondents themselves or to be administered by trained interviewers. And the processing of such questionnaires is another nightmare. I'll have more to say about that in Chapter 14.

Formats for Respondents

In one of the most common questionnaire formats, the respondent is expected to check one response from a series. Of the variety of methods available, it has been my experience that *boxes* adequately spaced apart are the best. Modern word-processing computers make the use of boxes a practical technique these days; setting boxes in type can also be accomplished easily and neatly. You can even approximate boxes on a typewriter.

If the questionnaire is typed on a typewriter with brackets, excellent boxes can be produced by a left bracket, a space, and a right bracket: [ ]. If brackets are not available, parentheses work reasonably well in the same fashion: ( ). I'd discourage the use of slashes and underscores, however. First, this technique requires considerably more typing effort; and second, the result is not very neat, especially if the response categories must be single-spaced. Figure 6-2 provides a comparison of the different methods.

FIGURE 6-2
Three Answer Formats

```
[ ] Yes        ( ) Yes        /_/ Yes
[ ] No         ( ) No         /_/ No
[ ] Don't      ( ) Don't      /_/ Don't
    know           know           know
```

Of the three methods shown, the brackets and the parentheses are clearly the neatest; the slash-and-underscore method simply looks sloppy. Because every typewriter at least has parentheses, there is no excuse for using slashes and underscores. The worst method of all is to provide open blanks for check marks, because respondents will often enter rather large check marks, and it will not be possible to determine which response was intended.

If you are creating a questionnaire on a computer, you should take the few extra minutes to create genuine boxes that will give your questionnaire a more professional look. Here are some easy examples:

☐   ○   ❑

Rather than providing boxes to be checked, the researcher might print a code number beside each response and ask the respondent to *circle* the appropriate number (see Figure 6-3). This method has the added advantage of specifying the code number to be entered later in the processing stage (see Chapter 14). If numbers are to be circled, however, you should provide clear and prominent instructions to the respondent, because many will be tempted to cross out the appropriate number, which makes data-processing

FIGURE 6-3
Circling the Answer

```
    1. Yes
   (2.) No
    3. Don't know
```

FIGURE 6-4
Contingency Question Format

```
        23. Have you ever smoked marijuana?
            [ ] Yes
            [ ] No

                    If yes: About how many times have
                            you smoked marijuana?
                            [ ] Once
                            [ ] 2 to 5 times
                            [ ] 6 to 10 times
                            [ ] 11 to 20 times
                            [ ] More than 20 times
```

even more difficult. (Note that the technique can be used more safely when interviewers administer the questionnaires, for they can specially instruct and supervise the respondents.)

Contingency Questions

Quite often in questionnaires, certain questions will be relevant to some of the respondents and irrelevant to others. In a study of birth control methods, for instance, you would probably not want to ask men if they take birth control pills.

This sort of situation often arises when you wish to ask a series of questions about a certain topic. You may want to ask whether your respondents belong to a particular organization and, if so, how often they attend meetings, whether they have held office in the organization, and so forth. Or, you might want to ask whether respondents have heard anything about a certain political issue and then learn the attitudes of those who have heard of it.

The subsequent questions in series such as these are called **contingency questions:** Whether they are to be asked and answered is contingent on responses to the first question in the series. The proper use of contingency questions can facilitate the respondents' task in completing the questionnaire because they are not faced with trying to answer questions irrelevant to them.

There are several formats for contingency questions. The one shown in Figure 6-4 is probably the clearest and most effective. Note two key elements in this format. First, the contingency question is isolated from the other questions by being set off to the side and enclosed in a box. Second, an arrow connects the contingency question to the answer on which it is contingent. In the illustration, only those respondents answering yes are expected to answer the contingency question. The rest of the respondents should simply skip it.

Note that the questions shown in Figure 6-4 could have been dealt with in a single question. The question might have read, "How many times, if any, have you smoked marijuana?" The response categories, then, might have read: "Never," "Once," "2 to 5 times," and so forth. Such a single question would apply to all respondents, and each would find an appropriate answer category. Such a question, however, might put some pressure on respondents to report having smoked marijuana, since the main question asks how many times they have smoked it, even though it allows for those *exceptional cases* who have *never smoked marijuana even once*. (The emphases used in the previous sentence give a fair indication of how respondents might read the question.) The contingency question format illustrated in Figure 6-4 should reduce the subtle pressure on respondents to report having smoked marijuana. The foregoing discussion should show how seemingly theoretical issues of *validity* and *reliability* are involved in so mundane a matter as how to put questions on a piece of paper.

FIGURE 6-5
Complex Contingency Question

```
14. Have you ever heard anything about
    the Neighborhood Watch Program?
    [ ] Yes ─────┐
    [ ] No       │
                 ▼
        ┌────────────────────────────────────────────┐
        │ If yes:                                    │
        │                                            │
        │ a. Do you generally approve or             │
        │    disapprove of that program?             │
        │    [ ] Approve                             │
        │    [ ] Disapprove                          │
        │    [ ] No opinion                          │
        │                                            │
        │ b. Have you ever attended a Neighborhood   │
        │    Watch resident meeting?                 │
        │    [ ] Yes ─────┐                          │
        │    [ ] No       │                          │
        │                 ▼                          │
        │        ┌──────────────────────────────┐   │
        │        │ If yes: When did you last    │   │
        │        │         attend a meeting?    │   │
        │        │                              │   │
        │        │  ─────────────────────       │   │
        │        └──────────────────────────────┘   │
        └────────────────────────────────────────────┘
```

Used properly, even rather complex sets of contingency questions can be constructed without confusing the respondent. Figure 6-5 illustrates a more complicated example.

Sometimes a set of contingency questions is long enough to extend over several pages. Suppose you are studying political activities of college students, and you wish to ask a large number of questions of those students who had voted in a national, state, or local election. You could separate out the relevant respondents with an initial question such as "Have you ever voted in a national, state, or local election?" but it would be confusing to place the contingency questions in a box stretching over several pages. It would make more sense to enter instructions in parentheses after each answer telling respondents to answer or skip the contingency questions. Figure 6-6 provides an illustration of this method.

In addition to these instructions, it would be worthwhile to place an instruction at the top of each page containing only the contingency questions. For example, you might say, "This page is only for respondents who have voted in a national, state, or local election." Clear instructions such as these spare respondents the frustration of reading and puzzling over questions that are irrelevant to them as well as increasing the likelihood of responses from those for whom the questions are relevant.

Matrix Questions

Quite often, you will want to ask several questions that have the same set of answer categories. This is typically the case whenever the Likert response categories are used. In such cases, it is often possible to construct a matrix of items and answers as illustrated in Figure 6-7.

This format offers several advantages over other formats. First, it uses space efficiently. Second, respondents will probably find it faster to complete a set of questions presented in this fashion. In addition, this format may increase the comparability of responses given to different questions for the respondent as well as for the researcher. Because respondents can quickly review their answers to earlier items in the set, they might choose between, say, "strongly agree" and "agree"

FIGURE 6-6
Instructions to Skip

```
13. Have you ever voted in a national, state, or local election?
    [ ] Yes (Please answer questions 14-25.)
    [ ] No  (Please skip questions 14-25. Go directly to question 26 on page 8.)
```

FIGURE 6-7
Matrix Question Format

```
17. Beside each of the statements presented below, please indicate whether you Strongly
    Agree (SA), Agree (A), Disagree (D), Strongly Disagree (SD), or are Undecided (U).

                              SA      A       D      SD      U
                              ──      ──      ──     ──      ──
    a. What this country needs
       is more law and order....... [ ]    [ ]    [ ]    [ ]    [ ]
    b. The police should be
       disarmed in America........ [ ]    [ ]    [ ]    [ ]    [ ]
    c. During riots, looters
       should be shot on sight.... [ ]    [ ]    [ ]    [ ]    [ ]
    etc.
```

on a given statement by comparing the strength of their agreement with their earlier responses in the set.

There are some dangers inherent in using this format, however. Its advantages may encourage you to structure an item so that the responses fit into the matrix format when a different, more idiosyncratic, set of responses might be more appropriate. Also, the matrix question format can foster a *response-set* among some respondents: They may develop a pattern of, say, agreeing with all the statements. That would be especially likely if the set of statements began with several that indicated a particular orientation (for example, a liberal political perspective) with only a few later ones representing the opposite orientation. Respondents might assume that all the statements represented the same orientation and, reading quickly, misread some of them, thereby giving the wrong answers. This problem can be reduced somewhat by alternating statements representing different orientations and by making all statements short and clear.

Ordering Items in a Questionnaire

The order in which questionnaire items are presented can also affect responses. First, the appearance of one question can affect the answers given to later ones. For example, if several questions have been asked about the dangers of communism to the United States and then a question asks respondents to volunteer (open-ended) what they believe to represent dangers to the United States, communism will receive more citations than would otherwise be the case. In this situation, it is preferable to ask the open-ended question first.

If respondents are asked to assess their overall religiosity ("How important is your religion to you in general?"), their responses to later questions concerning specific aspects of religiosity will be aimed at consistency with the prior assessment. The converse would be true as well. If respondents are first asked specific questions about different aspects of their religiosity, their subsequent overall assessment will reflect the earlier answers.

The impact of item order is not uniform. When J. Edwin Benton and John Daly (1991) conducted a local government survey, they found that the less educated respondents were more influenced by the order of questionnaire items than those with more education.

Some researchers attempt to overcome this effect by randomizing the order of items. That is usually a futile effort. To begin, a randomized set of items will probably strike respondents as chaotic and worthless. It will be difficult to answer, moreover, since they must continually switch their attention from one topic to another. And, finally, even a randomized ordering of items will have the effect discussed previously—except that you will have no control over the effect.

The safest solution is sensitivity to the problem. Although you cannot avoid the effect of item order, try to estimate what that effect will be. Thus, you will be able to interpret results meaningfully. If the order of items seems an especially important issue in a given study, you might construct more than one version of the questionnaire containing the different possible ordering of items. You would then be able to determine the effects. At the very least, you should pretest your questionnaire in the different forms.

The desired ordering of items differs somewhat between interviews and self-administered questionnaires. In the latter, it is usually best to begin the questionnaire with the most interesting set of items. The potential respondents who glance casually over the first few items should *want* to answer them. Perhaps the items will ask for attitudes they are aching to express. At the same time, however, the initial items should not be threatening. (It might be a bad idea to begin with items about sexual behavior or drug use.) Requests for duller, demographic data (age, gender, and the like) should generally be placed at the end of a self-administered questionnaire. Placing these items at the beginning, as many inexperienced researchers are tempted to do, gives the questionnaire the initial appearance of a routine form, and the person receiving it may not be motivated to complete it.

Just the opposite is generally true for interview surveys. When the potential respondent's door first opens, the interviewer must begin gaining rapport quickly. After a short introduction to the study, the interviewer can best begin by enumerating the members of the household, getting demographic data about each. Such items are easily answered and generally nonthreatening. Once the initial rapport has been established, the interviewer can then move into the area of attitudes and more sensitive matters. An interview that began with the question "Do you believe in witchcraft?" would probably end rather quickly.

Instructions

Every questionnaire, whether it is to be completed by respondents or administered by interviewers, should contain clear instructions and introductory comments where appropriate.

It is useful to begin every self-administered questionnaire with basic instructions for completing it. Although many people these days are pretty familiar with forms and questionnaires, you should begin by telling them exactly what you want: that they are to indicate their answers to certain questions by placing a check mark or an X in the box beside the appropriate answer or by writing in their answer when asked to do so. If many open-ended questions are used, respondents should be given some guidelines about whether brief or lengthy answers are expected. If you wish to encourage your respondents to elaborate on their responses to closed-ended questions, that should be noted.

If a questionnaire is arranged into content subsections—political attitudes, religious attitudes, background data—introduce each section with a short statement concerning its content and purpose. For example, "In this section, we would like to know what people around here consider the most important community problems." Demographic items at the end of a self-administered questionnaire might be introduced thus: "Finally, we would like to know just a little about you so we can see how different types of people feel about the issues we have been examining."

Short introductions such as these help the respondent make sense of the questionnaire. They make the questionnaire seem less chaotic, especially when it taps a variety of data. And they help put the respondent in the proper frame of mind for answering the questions.

Some questions may require special instructions to facilitate proper answering. This is especially true if a given question varies from the general instructions pertaining to the whole questionnaire. Some specific examples will illustrate this situation.

Despite the desirability for mutually exclusive answer categories in closed-ended questions, more than one answer often will apply for respondents. If you want a single answer, you should make this perfectly clear in the question. An example would be, "From the list below, please check the *primary* reason for your decision to attend college." Often the main question can be followed by a parenthetical note: "Please check the one best answer." If, on the other hand, you want the respondent to check as many answers as apply, that should be made clear as well.

When a set of answer categories are to be rank-ordered by the respondent, the instructions should indicate as much, and a different type of answer format should be used (for example, blanks instead of boxes). These instructions should indicate how many answers are to be ranked (for example, all, first and second, first and last, most important and least important) and the order of ranking (for example, "Place a 1 beside the most important, a 2 beside the next most important, and so forth"). Rank-ordering of responses is often difficult for respondents, however, since they may have to read and reread the list several times, so this technique should only be used in those situations where no other method will produce the desired result.

In multiple-part matrix questions, it is useful to give special instructions unless the same format is used throughout the questionnaire. Sometimes respondents will be expected to check one answer in each *column* of the matrix; in other questionnaires they will be expected to check one answer in each *row*. Whenever the questionnaire contains both types, it will be useful to add an instruction clarifying which is expected in each case.

Pretesting the Questionnaire

No matter how carefully you design a data-collection instrument such as a questionnaire, there is always the possibility—indeed the certainty—of error. You are certain to make some mistake: an ambiguous question, one that people cannot answer, or some other violation of the rules just discussed.

The surest protection against such errors is to *pretest* the questionnaire in full and/or in part. Give the questionnaire to the ten people in your bowling league, for example. It's not usually essential that the pretest subjects comprise a representative sample, although you should use people to whom the questionnaire is at least relevant.

By and large, you'll do better to ask people to complete the questionnaire rather than reading through it looking for errors. All too often, a question will seem to make sense when you first look at it, but you may later discover you can't exactly *answer* it.

Stanley Presser and Johnny Blair (1994) describe several different pretesting strategies and report on the effectiveness of each technique. They also provide data on the cost of the various methods.

If I gave you all the tips and guidelines I could for questionnaire construction, this section would be longer than the rest of the book. Somewhat reluctantly, I'll complete this discussion with an illustration of a real questionnaire, showing how some of these comments find substance in practice.

Before turning to the illustration, however, I want to mention a critical aspect of questionnaire design that I discuss in Chapter 14: *precoding*. Because the information collected by questionnaires is typically transformed into some type of computer format, it is usually appropriate to include data-processing instructions on the questionnaire itself. These instructions indicate where specific pieces of information will be stored in the machine-readable data files. In Chapter 14, I'll discuss the nature of such storage and point out appropriate questionnaire notations. As a preview, however, notice that the following illustration has been precoded with the mysterious numbers that appear near questions and answer categories.

A Composite Illustration

Figure 6-8 is part of a questionnaire used by the University of Chicago's National Opinion Research Center in its widely used General Social Survey. The questionnaire deals with people's attitudes toward the government and is designed to be self-administered.

FIGURE 6-8
A Sample Questionnaire

10. Here are some things the government might do for the economy. Circle one number for each action to show whether you are in favor of it or against it.

> 1. Strongly in favor of
> 2. In favor of
> 3. Neither in favor of nor against
> 4. Against
> 5. Strongly disagree

PLEASE CIRCLE A NUMBER

a. Control of wages by legislation	1	2	3	4	5	28/
b. Control of prices by legislation	1	2	3	4	5	29/
c. Cuts in government spending	1	2	3	4	5	30/
d. Government financing of projects to create new jobs	1	2	3	4	5	31/
e. Less government regulation of business	1	2	3	4	5	32/
f. Support for industry to develop new products and technology	1	2	3	4	5	33/
g. Supporting declining industries to protect jobs	1	2	3	4	5	34/
h. Reducing the work week to create more jobs	1	2	3	4	5	35/

11. Listed below are various areas of government spending. Please indicate whether you would like to see more or less government spending in each area. Remember that if you say "much more," it might require a tax increase to pay for it.

> 1. Spend much more
> 2. Spend more
> 3. Spend the same as now
> 4. Spend less
> 5. Spend much less
> 8. Can't choose

PLEASE CIRCLE A NUMBER

a. The environment	1	2	3	4	5	8	36/
b. Health	1	2	3	4	5	8	37/
c. The police and law enforcement	1	2	3	4	5	8	38/
d. Education	1	2	3	4	5	8	39/
e. The military and defense	1	2	3	4	5	8	40/
f. Retirement benefits	1	2	3	4	5	8	41/
g. Unemployment benefits	1	2	3	4	5	8	42/
h. Culture and the arts	1	2	3	4	5	8	43/

12. If the government *had* to choose between keeping down inflation or keeping down unemployment, to which do you think it should give highest priority?
    Keeping down inflation 1   44/
    Keeping down unemployment 2
    Can't choose 8

13. Do you think that labor unions in this country have too much power or too little power?
    Far too much power 1   45/
    Too much power 2
    About the right amount of power 3
    Too little power 4
    Far too little power 5
    Can't choose 8

FIGURE 6-8
A Sample Questionnaire (*continued*)

14. How about business and industry, do they have too much power or too little power?
    - Far too much power 1   46/
    - Too much power 2
    - About the right amount of power 3
    - Too little power 4
    - Far too little power 5
    - Can't choose 8

15. And what about the federal government, does it have too much power or too little power?
    - Far too much power 1   47/
    - Too much power 2
    - About the right amount of power 3
    - Too little power 4
    - Far too little power 5
    - Can't choose 8

16. In general, how good would you say labor unions are for the country as a whole?
    - Excellent 1   48/
    - Very good 2
    - Fairly good 3
    - Not very good 4
    - Not good at all 5
    - Can't choose 8

17. What do you think the government's role in each of these industries should be?

    > 1. Own it
    > 2. Control prices and profits but not own it
    > 3. Neither own it nor control its prices and profits
    > 8. Can't choose

	PLEASE CIRCLE A NUMBER				
a. Electric power	1	2	3	8	49/
b. The steel industry	1	2	3	8	50/
c. Banking and insurance	1	2	3	8	51/

18. On the whole, do you think it should or should not be the government's responsibility to . . .

    > 1. Definitely should be
    > 2. Probably should be
    > 3. Probably should not be
    > 4. Definitely should not be
    > 8. Can't choose

	PLEASE CIRCLE A NUMBER					
a. Provide a job for everyone who wants one....	1	2	3	4	8	52/
b. Keep prices under control...................	1	2	3	4	8	53/
c. Provide health care for the sick.............	1	2	3	4	8	54/
d. Provide a decent standard of living for the old...	1	2	3	4	8	55/

FIGURE 6-8
A Sample Questionnaire (*continued*)

    e. Provide industry with the help it needs to grow 1   2   3   4   8   56/
    f. Provide a decent standard of living for the unemployed 1   2   3   4   8   57/
    g. Reduce income differences between the rich and poor 1   2   3   4   8   58/
    h. Give financial assistance to college students from low-income families 1   2   3   4   8   59/
    i. Provide decent housing for those who can't afford it 1   2   3   4   8   60/

19. How interested would you say you personally are in politics?
    Very interested 1   61/
    Fairly interested 2
    Somewhat interested 3
    Not very interested 4
    Not at all interested 5
    Can't choose 8

20. Here are some other areas of government spending. Please indicate whether you would like to see more or less government spending in each area. Remember that if you say "much more," it might require a tax increase to pay for it.

    1. Spend much more
    2. Spend more
    3. Spend the same as now
    4. Spend less
    5. Spend much less
    8. Can't choose

                                              PLEASE CIRCLE A NUMBER

    a. Prenatal care for pregnant mothers who can't afford it 1   2   3   4   5   8   62/
    b. Health care for children whose families don't have insurance 1   2   3   4   5   8   63/
    c. Preschool programs like Head Start for poor children 1   2   3   4   5   8   64/
    d. Child care for poor children 1   2   3   4   5   8   65/
    e. Child care for all children with working parents 1   2   3   4   5   8   66/
    f. Housing for poor families with children 1   2   3   4   5   8   67/
    g. Services for disabled and chronically ill children 1   2   3   4   5   8   68/
    h. Drug abuse prevention and treatment for children and youth 1   2   3   4   5   8   69/
    i. Nutrition programs for poor children and families, such as food stamps and school lunches 1   2   3   4   5   8   70/
    j. Contraceptive services for teenagers 1   2   3   4   5   8   71/

THANK YOU VERY MUCH FOR COMPLETING THE QUESTIONNAIRE

■ OPERATIONALIZATION GOES ON AND ON

Although I've discussed conceptualization and operationalization as activities that precede data collection and analysis—that is, you must design questionnaire items before you send out the questionnaire—you should realize that these two processes continue throughout any research project, even if the data have been collected in a structured, mass survey. As you've seen, in less structured methods such as field research, the identification and specification of relevant concepts is inseparable from the ongoing process of observation.

In study designs that require you to commit yourself to standardized measures of concepts, it is usually wise to tap several different indicators of each, particularly if they are at all open to different interpretations and definitions. By measuring the variable in several different ways, you'll be able to examine alternative operational definitions during your analysis. Because you'll have several single indicators to choose from and many ways of creating different composite measures, you'll be able to experiment with different measures—each representing a somewhat different conceptualization and operationalization—to decide which gives the clearest and most useful answers to your research questions.

The ultimate purpose of social research is to clarify the nature of social life. The validity and utility of what you learn in this regard doesn't depend on when you first figured out how to look at things any more than it matters whether you got the idea from a learned textbook, a dream, or your brother-in-law.

■ MAIN POINTS

- Operationalization is an extension of the conceptualization process.
- In operationalization, we specify concrete empirical procedures that will result in measurements of variables.
- Operationalization is the final specification of how we would recognize the different attributes of a given variable in the real world.
- While operationalization as discussed in this chapter is essential to questionnaire construction, the logic involved is useful to all other modes of observation as well.
- In determining the range of variation for a variable, be sure to consider the opposite of the concept. Will it be sufficient to measure *religiosity* from "very much" to "none," or should you go past "none" to measure "anti-religiosity" as well?
- Nominal measures describe variables with attributes that are simply different from one another, such as *gender*.
- Ordinal measures refer to variables with attributes we can rank-order along some progression from more to less. One example is the variable *prejudice* as composed of the attributes *very prejudiced, somewhat prejudiced, slightly prejudiced,* and *not at all prejudiced.*
- Interval measures refer to those variables with attributes not only rank-ordered but also separated by a uniform distance. One example is IQ.
- Ratio measures are the same as interval measures except that ratio measures are also based on a true zero point. Age is an example of a ratio measure, since that variable contains the attribute *zero years old.*
- A given variable can sometimes be measured at different levels of measurement. Thus, age, potentially a ratio measure, may also be treated as interval, ordinal, or even nominal. The most appropriate level of measurement used depends on the purpose of the measurement.
- Questionnaires provide a method of collecting data by (1) asking people questions or (2) asking them to agree or disagree with statements representing different points of view.
- Questions may be open-ended (respondents supply their own answers) or closed-ended (they select from a list of provided answers).
- Usually, short items in a questionnaire are better than long ones.
- Negative items and terms should be avoided in questionnaires because they may confuse respondents.

- Bias is the quality in questionnaire items that encourages respondents to answer in a particular way or to support a particular point of view. Avoid it.
- Question wording *and* questionnaire formats can influence the quality of data collected.
- Contingency questions are those to be answered only by some respondents, based on answers to previous questions.
- The matrix question is an efficient format for presenting several items sharing the same response categories.
- The order of items in a questionnaire can influence the responses given.
- Clear instructions are important for getting appropriate responses in a questionnaire.
- Operationalization begins in study design and continues throughout the research project, including the analysis of data.

■ REVIEW QUESTIONS AND EXERCISES

1. What level of measurement—nominal, ordinal, interval, or ratio—describes each of the following variables:
   a. Race (white, African American, Asian, and so on)
   b. Order of finish in a race (first, second, third, and so on)
   c. Number of children in families
   d. Populations of nations
   e. Attitudes toward nuclear energy (strongly approve, approve, disapprove, strongly disapprove)
   f. Region of birth (Northeast, Midwest, and so on)
   g. Political orientation (very liberal, somewhat liberal, somewhat conservative, very conservative)
2. For each of the following open-ended questions, construct a closed-ended question that could be used in a questionnaire.
   a. What was your family's total income last year?
   b. How do you feel about the space shuttle program?
   c. How important is religion in your life?
   d. What was your main reason for attending college?
   e. What do you feel is the biggest problem facing your community?
3. Find a questionnaire on the Web (*hint:* search for "questionnaire"). Critique at least five of the questions contained in it—either positively or negatively. Be sure to give the Web address (URL) for the questionnaire and the exact wording of the questions you critique.

■ ADDITIONAL READINGS

Feick, Lawrence F. "Latent Class Analysis of Survey Questions That Include Don't Know Responses." *Public Opinion Quarterly* 53, no. 4 (Winter 1989): 525–47. *Don't know* can mean a variety of things, as this analysis indicates.

Fowler, Floyd J., Jr. *Improving Survey Questions: Design and Evaluation.* Thousand Oaks, CA: Sage, 1995. Discusses the logic of obtaining information through survey questions and gives numerous guidelines for being effective. Offers several examples of questions you might use.

Miller, Delbert. *Handbook of Research Design and Social Measurement.* Newbury Park, CA: Sage, 1991. A powerful reference work. This book, especially Part 6, cites and describes a wide variety of operational measures used in earlier social research. In a number of cases, the questionnaire formats used are presented. Though the quality of these illustrations is uneven, they provide excellent examples of the variations possible.

Schwartz, Norman, et al. "Rating Scales: Numeric Values May Change the Meaning of Scale Labels." *Public Opinion Quarterly* (Winter 1991): 570–82. German researchers experimented with different scale formats and found that the changes affected the responses.

Sheatsley, Paul F. "Questionnaire Construction and Item Writing." Pp. 195–230 in *Handbook of Survey Research,* edited by Peter H. Rossi, James D. Wright, and Andy B. Anderson. New York: Academic Press, 1983. An excellent examination of the topic by an expert in the field.

Smith, Eric R. A. N., and Peverill Squire, "The Effects of Prestige Names in Question Wording." *Public Opinion Quarterly* 54 (Spring 1990): 97–116. Not only do prestigious names affect the overall responses given to survey questionnaires, they also affect such things as the correlation between education and the number of don't know answers.

Tourangeau, Roger, et al. "Carryover Effects in Attitude Surveys." *Public Opinion Quarterly* 53 (Winter 1989): 495–524. The authors asked six target questions in a telephone survey of 1,100 respondents, varying the questions immediately preceding the target questions. They found substantial differences.

CHAPTER 7
Indexes, Scales, and Typologies

What You'll Learn in This Chapter
Now we conclude the discussion of measurement, begun in Chapters 5 and 6. You'll learn the logic and skills of constructing composite measures from among several indicators of variables.

INTRODUCTION

INDEXES VERSUS SCALES

INDEX CONSTRUCTION
Item Selection
Bivariate Relationships among Items
Multivariate Relationships among Items
Index Scoring
Handling Missing Data
Index Validation
Indexing the Status of Women

SCALE CONSTRUCTION
Bogardus Social Distance Scale
Thurstone Scales
Likert Scaling
Semantic Differential
Guttman Scaling

TYPOLOGIES

MAIN POINTS

REVIEW QUESTIONS AND EXERCISES

ADDITIONAL READINGS

INTRODUCTION

As we've seen in the last two chapters, many social scientific concepts have complex and varied meanings. Making measurements that capture such concepts can be a challenge. In particular, I'd like you to recall the discussion of content validity, which concerns whether we have captured all the different dimensions of a concept.

To achieve broad coverage, we usually need to make multiple observations pertaining to a given concept. Thus, for example, Bruce Berg (1989:21) advises in-depth interviewers to prepare *essential questions*, which are "geared toward eliciting specific, desired information." In addition, the researcher should prepare *extra questions:* "questions roughly equivalent to certain essential ones, but worded slightly differently."

Multiple indicators are used with quantitative data as well. Though you can sometimes construct a single questionnaire item that captures the variable of interest— "Gender: ☐ Male ☐ Female" is a simple example— other variables are less straightforward and may require you to use several questionnaire items to measure them adequately.

Quantitative data analysts have developed specific techniques for combining indicators into a single measure. This chapter discusses the construction of **indexes** and **scales** as composite measures of variables. While scales and indexes can be used in any form of social research, they are more common to survey research and other quantitative methods. A short section at the end of the chapter considers **typologies,** which are relevant to both qualitative and quantitative research.

Composite measures are frequently used in quantitative research, for several reasons. First, despite the care taken in designing studies to provide valid and reliable measurements of variables, the researcher can seldom develop in advance single indicators of complex concepts. This is especially true with regard to attitudes and orientations. Rarely can the survey researcher, for example, devise single questionnaire items that adequately tap respondents' degrees of prejudice, religiosity, political orientations, alienation, and the like. More likely, you will devise several items, each of which provides some indication of the variables. Each of these, however, is likely to prove invalid or unreliable for many respondents.

Some variables are rather easily measured through single indicators. We may determine a survey respondent's age by asking: "How old are you?" We may determine a newspaper's circulation by merely looking at the figure the newspaper reports. The number of times an experimental stimulus is administered to an experimental group is clearly defined in the design of the experiment. Nonetheless, social scientists, using a variety of research methods, frequently wish to study variables that have no clear and unambiguous single indicators.

Second, you may wish to employ a rather refined ordinal measure of your variable, arranging cases in several ordinal categories from—for example—very low to very high on a variable such as *alienation*. A single data item might not have enough categories to provide the desired range of variation, but an index or scale formed from several items would.

Finally, indexes and scales are efficient devices for data analysis. If considering a single data item gives us only a rough indication of a given variable, considering several data items may give us a more comprehensive and more accurate indication. For example, a single newspaper editorial may give us some indication of the political orientations of that newspaper. Examining several editorials would probably give us a better assessment, but the manipulation of several data items simultaneously could be very complicated. Indexes and scales (especially scales) are efficient *data-reduction devices:* Several indicators may be summarized in a single numerical score, while sometimes nearly maintaining the specific details of all the individual indicators.

INDEXES VERSUS SCALES

The terms *index* and *scale* are typically used imprecisely and interchangeably in social research literature. Before considering the distinctions this book will make between indexes and scales, let's first see what they have in common.

Both scales and indexes are typical *ordinal* measures of variables. Both rank-order the units of analysis in terms of specific variables such as *religiosity, alienation, socioeconomic status, prejudice,* or *intellectual sophistication.* A person's score on a scale or index of religiosity, for example, gives an indication of his or her relative religiosity vis-à-vis other people.

In this book, both scales and indexes are *composite measures of variables:* measurements based on more than one data item. Thus, a survey respondent's score on an index or scale of religiosity would be determined by the specific responses given to several questionnaire items, each of which would provide some indication of his or her religiosity. Similarly, a person's IQ score is based on answers to a large number of test questions. The political orientation of a newspaper might be represented by an index or scale score reflecting the newspaper's editorial policy on various political issues.

In this book we'll distinguish indexes and scales through the manner in which scores are assigned. An *index* is constructed through the simple accumulation of scores assigned to individual attributes. We might measure prejudice, for example, by adding up the number of prejudiced statements each respondent agreed with. A *scale* is constructed through the assignment of scores to *patterns* of responses, recognizing that some items reflect a relatively weak degree of the variable while others reflect something stronger. Agreeing that "Women are different from men" is certainly weak evidence of sexism compared with agreeing that "Women should not be allowed to vote." Thus, a scale takes advantage of any *intensity structure* that may exist among attributes. Another simple example should clarify this distinction.

Figure 7-1 provides a graphic illustration of the difference between indexes and scales. Let's assume we want to develop a measure of political activism, distinguishing those people who are very active in political affairs, those who don't participate much at all, and those who are somewhere in between.

The first part of Figure 7-1 illustrates the logic of indexes. I've represented six different political actions. Although you and I might disagree on some specifics, I think we could agree that the six actions represent roughly the same degree of political activism. Although some people might give money more easily than write letters to the editor—or vice versa—the six actions are probably more or less equal if we consider the population as a whole.

We could construct an index of political activism, using the six items, by giving each person 1 point for each of the actions he or she has taken. So if you wrote to a public official and signed a petition, you'd get a total of 2 points. If I gave money to a candidate and persuaded someone to change their vote, I'd get the same score as you. Using this approach, we'd conclude that you and I had the same degree of political activism, even though we had taken different actions.

The second part of Figure 7-1 describes the logic of scale construction. In this case, the actions clearly represent *different* degrees of political activism—ranging from simply voting to running for office. Moreover, it seems safe to assume a *pattern* of actions in this case. For example, all those who contributed money probably also voted. Those who worked on a campaign probably also gave some money and voted. This suggests that most people will fall into only one of five "ideal" action patterns, represented by the small illustrations at the bottom of the figure. The discussion of scales, later in this chapter, describes ways of identifying people with the type they most closely represent.

Scales are generally superior to indexes because scales take into consideration the *intensity* with which different items reflect the variable being measured. Also, as the example in Figure 7-1 shows, scale scores convey more information than index scores. Still, you should be wary of the common misuse of the term *scale;* clearly, calling a given measure a scale rather than an index does not make it better.

FIGURE 7-1
Indexes versus Scales

Index-Construction Logic

Here are several types of political actions people may have taken. By and large, the different actions seem to represent similar *degrees* of political activism. To create an *index* of overall political activism, we might give people 1 point for each of the actions they've taken.

- Wrote a letter to a public official
- Signed a political petition
- Gave money to a political cause
- Gave money to a political candidate
- Wrote a political letter to the editor
- Persuaded someone to change their voting plans

Scale-Construction Logic

Here are some political actions that represent very different degrees of activism: e.g., running for office represents a higher degree of activism than simply voting. It seems likely, moreover, that anyone who has taken one of the more demanding actions would have taken all the easier ones as well. To construct a *scale* of political activism, we might score people on the basis of which of the following "ideal" patterns comes closest to describing them.

- Ran for office
- Worked on a political campaign
- Contributed money to a political campaign
- Voted

0 1 2 3 4

You should also be cautioned against two other misconceptions about scaling. First, whether the combination of several data items results in a scale almost always depends on the particular sample of observations under study. Because certain items may form a scale among one sample but not among another, you should not assume that a given set of items is a scale because it has formed a scale among a given sample. Second, the use of certain *scaling techniques* to be discussed does not assure the creation of a scale any more than the use of items that have previously formed scales does.

An examination of the substantive literature based on social science data will show that indexes are used much more frequently than scales. Ironically, however, the methodological literature contains little if any discussion of index construction, but discussions of scale construction abound. There appear to be two reasons for this disparity.

First, indexes are more frequently used because scales are often difficult or impossible to construct from the data at hand. Second, methods of index construction seem so obvious and straightforward that they aren't discussed much.

Index construction is not a simple undertaking, however. The general failure to develop index construction techniques has resulted in the creation of many bad indexes in social research. With this in mind, I've devoted over half of this chapter to the methods of index construction. Once you fully understand the logic of this activity, you will be better equipped to attempt the construction of scales. Indeed, a carefully constructed index may turn out to be a scale.

■ INDEX CONSTRUCTION

Let's look now at the several steps involved in the creation of an index: selecting possible items, examining their empirical relationships, combining some items into an index, and validating it. Because they're not all obvious, I've presented these steps in some detail. You should come away from this section able to create a composite measure that will fully support your subsequent analyses.

Item Selection

Face Validity The first step in creating an index is selecting items for a composite index, which is created to measure some variable. The first criterion for selecting items to be included in the index is *face validity* (or logical validity). If you want to measure political conservatism, for example, each of your items should appear *on its face* to indicate conservatism (or its opposite, liberalism). Political party affiliation would be one such item. If people were asked to approve or disapprove of the views of a well-known conservative public figure, their responses might logically provide another indication of their conservatism. In constructing an index of religiosity, you might consider items such as church attendance, acceptance of certain religious beliefs, and frequency of prayer; each of these appears to offer some indication of religiosity.

Unidimensionality The methodological literature on conceptualization and measurement stresses the need for *unidimensionality* in scale and index construction: A composite measure should represent only one dimension. Thus, items reflecting religiosity should not be included in a measure of political conservatism, even though the two variables might be empirically related to one another.

General or Specific At the same time, you should be aware of nuances that may exist within the general dimension you're attempting to measure. Thus in the example of religiosity, the indicators mentioned previously represent different *types* of religiosity—ritual participation, belief, and so on. If you wished to focus on ritual participation in religion, you should choose items specifically indicating this type of religiosity: church attendance, communion, confession, and the like. If you wished to measure religiosity in a more general way, you would include a balanced set of items, representing each of the different types of religiosity. Ultimately, the nature of the items included will determine how specifically or generally the variable is measured.

Variance In selecting items for an index, you must also be concerned with the amount of *variance* they provide. If an item is intended to indicate political conservatism, for example, you should note what proportion of respondents was identified as conservatives by the item. If a given item identified no one as a conservative or everyone as a conservative—for example, if nobody indicated approval of a radical right political figure—that item would not be very useful in the construction of an index.

To guarantee variance, you have two options. First, you may select several items the responses to which divide people about equally in terms of the variable; for example, about half conservative and half liberal. Although no single response would justify the characterization of a person as very conservative, a person who responded as a conservative on all items might be so characterized.

The second option is to select items differing in variance. One item might identify about half the subjects as conservative, while another might identify few of the respondents as conservatives.

Note that this second option is necessary for scaling, and it is reasonable for index construction as well.

Bivariate Relationships among Items

The second step in index construction is to examine the *bivariate relationships* among the items being considered for inclusion. In this, we are anticipating a discussion that will be pursued more fully in Chapter 15; you might want to review the Holographic Overview of that chapter. The basic issue involved is whether respondents' answers to one question—in a questionnaire, for example—give us any clue as to how they will answer other questions.

Suppose we want to measure respondents' support for U.S. participation in the United Nations. One indicator of different levels of support might be the question: "Do you feel the U.S. financial support of the UN is ☐ Too high ☐ About right ☐ Too low?"

Another indicator of support for the United Nations might be the question: "Should the United States contribute military personnel to UN peace-keeping actions? ☐ Strongly approve ☐ Mostly approve ☐ Mostly disapprove ☐ Strongly disapprove."

Both of these questions, on their face, seem to reflect different degrees of support for the United Nations. Nonetheless, some people might feel the United States should give more money but not provide troops. Others might favor sending troops but cutting back on financial support.

If the two items both reflect degrees of the same thing, however, we should expect responses to the two items to generally correspond with one another. Specifically, those who approve of military support should be more likely to favor financial support than those who disapprove of military support would do. Conversely, those who favor financial support should be more likely to favor military support than those disapproving of financial support would. If these expectations are met, we say there is a *bivariate relationship* between the two items.

Here's another example. Suppose we want to determine the degree to which respondents feel women have the right to an abortion. We might ask (1) "Do you feel a woman should have the right to an abortion when her pregnancy was the result of rape?" and (2) "Do you feel a woman should have the right to an abortion if continuing her pregnancy would seriously threaten her life?"

Granted, some respondents might agree with item (1) and disagree with item (2); others will do just the reverse. If both items tap into some general opinion people have about the issue of abortion, then the responses to these two items should be related to one another. Those who support the right to an abortion in the case of rape should be more likely to support it if the woman's life is threatened than those who disapproved of abortion in the case of rape would. This would be another example of a bivariate relationship between the two items.

You should examine all the possible bivariate relationships among the several items being considered for inclusion in an index to determine the relative strengths of relationships among the several pairs of items. Percentage tables, correlation coefficients (see Chapter 17), or both may be used for this purpose. The primary criterion for evaluating these several relationships is the strength of the relationships. The use of this criterion, however, is rather subtle. The box entitled "'Cause' and 'Effect' Indicators" examines some of these subtleties.

Be wary of items that are not related to one another empirically: It is unlikely that they measure the same variable. You should probably drop any item that is not related to several other items.

At the same time a very strong relationship between two items presents a different problem. If two items are perfectly related to one another, then only one is necessary for inclusion in the index, since it completely conveys the indications provided by the other. (This problem will become even clearer in the next section.)

Here's an example to illustrate the testing of bivariate relationships in index construction. I once conducted a survey of medical school faculty members to find out about the consequences of a "scientific perspective" on the quality of patient care provided by physicians. The primary intent was to determine whether more scientifically

"Cause" and "Effect" Indicators

by Kenneth Bollen
Department of Sociology, University of North Carolina, Chapel Hill

While it often makes sense to expect indicators of the same variable to be positively related to one another, as discussed in the text, this is not always the case.

Indicators should be related to one another if they are essentially "effects" of a variable. For example, to measure self-esteem, we might ask a person to indicate whether he or she agrees or disagrees with the statements (1) "I am a good person" and (2) "I am happy with myself." A person with high self-esteem should agree with both statements while one with low self-esteem would probably disagree with both. Since each indicator depends on or "reflects" self-esteem, we expect them to be positively correlated. More generally, indicators that depend on the same variable should be associated with one another if they are valid measures.

But, this is not the case when the indicators are the "cause" rather than the "effect" of a variable. In this situation the indicators may correlate positively, negatively, or not at all. For example, we could use gender and race as indicators of the variable *exposure to discrimination*.

---

inclined doctors treated patients more impersonally than other doctors.

The survey questionnaire offered several possible indicators of respondents' scientific perspectives. Of those, three items appeared to provide especially clear indications of whether the doctors were scientifically oriented:

■ 1. As a medical school faculty member, in what capacity do you feel you can make your greatest *teaching* contribution: as a practicing physician or as a medical researcher?

■ 2. As you continue to advance your own medical knowledge, would you say your ultimate medical interests lie primarily in the direction of total patient management or the understanding of basic mechanisms? [The purpose of this item was to distinguish those who were mostly interested in overall patient care from those mostly interested in biological processes.]

■ 3. In the field of therapeutic research, are you generally more interested in articles reporting evaluations of the effectiveness of various treatments or articles exploring the basic rationale underlying the treatments? [Similarly, I wanted to distinguish those more interested in articles dealing with patient care from those more interested in biological processes.]

(BABBIE 1970:27–31)

For each of these items, we might conclude that those respondents who chose the second answer are more scientifically oriented than respondents who chose the first answer. Though this *comparative* conclusion is reasonable, we should not be misled into thinking that respondents who chose the second answer to a given item are scientists in any absolute sense. They are simply *more scientific* than those who chose the first answer to the item. To see this point more clearly, let's examine the distribution of responses to each item. From the first item—best teaching role—only about one-third of the respondents appeared scientifically oriented. (Approximately one-third said they could make their greatest teaching contribution as medical researchers.) In response to the second item—ultimate medical interests—approximately two-thirds chose the scientific answer, saying they were more interested in learning about basic mechanisms than learning about total patient management. In response to the third item—reading preferences—about 80 percent chose the scientific answer.

So these three questionnaire items cannot tell us how many "scientists" there are in the sample, for none of them is related to a set of criteria for what constitutes being a scientist in any absolute

Being nonwhite or female increases the likelihood of experiencing discrimination, so both are good indicators of the variable. But we would not expect the race and gender of individuals to be strongly associated.

Or, we may measure *social interaction* with three indicators: time spent with friends, time spent with family, and time spent with coworkers. Though each indicator is valid, they need not be positively correlated. Time spent with friends, for instance, may be inversely related to time spent with family. Here, the three indicators "cause" the degree of social interaction.

As a final example, *exposure to stress* may be measured by whether a person recently experienced divorce, death of a spouse, or loss of a job. Though any of these events may indicate stress, they need not correlate with one another.

In short, we expect an association between indicators that depend on or "reflect" a variable, that is, if they are the "effects" of the variable. But if the variable depends on the indicators—if the indicators are the "causes"—those indicators may be either positively or negatively correlated, or even unrelated. Therefore, we should decide whether indicators are causes or effects of a variable before using their intercorrelations to assess their validity.

---

sense. Using the items for this purpose would present us with the problem of three quite different estimates of how many scientists there were in the sample.

However, these items do provide us with three independent indicators of respondents' *relative* inclinations toward science in medicine. Each item separates respondents into the *more* scientific and the *less* scientific. But each grouping of more or less scientific respondents will have a somewhat different membership from the others. Respondents who seem scientific in terms of one item will not seem scientific in terms of another. Nevertheless, to the extent that each item measures the same general dimension, we should find some correspondence among the several groupings. Respondents who appear scientific in terms of one item should be more likely to appear scientific in their response to another item than those who appeared nonscientific in their response to the first. We should find an association or correlation between the responses given to two items.

Figure 7-2 shows the associations among the responses to the three items. Three bivariate tables are presented, showing the distribution of responses for each pair of items. Although each single item produces a different grouping of "scientific" and "nonscientific" respondents, we see in Figure 7-2 that the responses given to each of the items correspond, to a degree, to the responses given to each of the other items.

An examination of the three bivariate relationships presented in Figure 7-2 supports the suggestion that the three items all measure the same variable: *scientific orientations*. To see why this is so, let's begin by looking at the first bivariate relationship in the table. The table shows that faculty who responded that "researcher" was their best teaching role were more likely to identify their ultimate medical interests as "basic mechanisms" than those who answered "physician." The data show that 87 percent of the "researchers" also chose the scientific response to the second item, as opposed to 51 percent of the "physicians." (*Note:* The fact that the "physicians" are about evenly split in their ultimate medical interests is irrelevant. It is only relevant that they are less scientific in their medical interests than the "researchers.") The strength of this relationship may be summarized as a 36 percentage point difference.

The same general conclusion applies to the other bivariate relationships. The strength of the relationship between reading preferences and

FIGURE 7-2
Bivariate Relationships among Scientific Orientation Items

A.

Ultimate Medical Interest

	Best Teaching Role	
	Physician	Researcher
Total patient management	49%	13%
Basic mechanisms	51%	87%
	100% (268)	100% (159)

B.

Ultimate Medical Interest

	Reading Preferences	
	Effectiveness	Rationale
Total patient management	68%	30%
Basic mechanisms	32%	70%
	100% (78)	100% (349)

C.

Best Teaching Role

	Reading Preferences	
	Effectiveness	Rationale
Physician	85%	64%
Researcher	15%	36%
	100% (78)	100% (349)

ultimate medical interests may be summarized as a 38 percentage point difference, and the strength of the relationship between reading preferences and the two teaching roles as a 21 percentage point difference.

Initially, the three items were selected on the basis of face validity—each appeared to give some indication of faculty members' orientations to science. By examining the bivariate relationship between the pairs of items, we have found support for the expectation that they all measure basically the same thing. However, that support does not sufficiently justify including the items in a composite index.

Multivariate Relationships among Items

Before combining them in a single index, we need to examine the *multivariate relationships* among the several variables. Whereas a bivariate relationship deals with two variables at a time, a multivariate one uses more than two variables.

Recall that the primary purpose of index construction is to develop a method of classifying subjects in terms of some variable such as *political conservatism, religiosity, scientific orientation,* or whatever. An index of political conservatism should identify those who are very conservative, moderately conservative, not very conservative, and not

FIGURE 7-3
Trivariate Relationships among Scientific Orientation Items

Percentage Interested in Basic Mechanisms

		Best Teaching Role	
		Physician	Researcher
Reading Preferences	Effectiveness	27% (66)	58% (12)
	Rationale	58% (219)	89% (130)

at all conservative (or moderately liberal and very liberal, respectively, in place of the last two categories). The several gradations of the variable are provided by the combination of responses given to the several items included in the index. Thus, the respondent who appeared conservative on all items would be considered very conservative overall.

For an index to provide meaningful gradations in this sense, each item must add something to the evaluation of each respondent. Recall from the preceding section that two items perfectly related to one another should not be included in the same index. If one item were included, the other would add nothing to our evaluation of respondents. The examination of multivariate relationships among the items is another way of eliminating deadwood. It also determines the overall power of the particular collection of items in measuring the variable under consideration.

The purposes of this multivariate examination will become clearer if we return to the earlier example of measuring scientific orientations among medical school faculty members. Figure 7-3 presents the trivariate relationships among the three items.

Presented somewhat differently from Figure 7-2, Figure 7-3 categorizes the sample respondents into four groups according to (1) their best teaching roles and (2) their reading preferences. The numbers in parentheses indicate the number of respondents in each group. (Thus 66 of the faculty members who said they could best teach as physicians also said they preferred articles dealing with the effectiveness of treatments.) For each of the four groups, the percentage that say they are ultimately more interested in basic mechanisms has been presented. (Of the 66 faculty mentioned, 27 percent are primarily interested in basic mechanisms.)

The arrangement of the four groups is based on a previously drawn conclusion regarding scientific orientations. The group in the upper left corner of the table is presumably the least scientifically oriented, based on best teaching role and reading preference. The group in the lower right corner is presumably the most scientifically oriented in terms of those items.

Recall that expressing a primary interest in basic mechanisms was also taken as an indication of scientific orientations. As we should expect, then, those in the lower right corner are the most likely to give this response (89 percent), and those in the upper left corner are the least likely (27 percent). The respondents who gave mixed responses in terms of teaching roles and reading preferences have an intermediate rank in their concern for basic mechanisms (58 percent in both cases).

This table tells us many things. First, we may note that the original relationships between pairs of items are not significantly affected by the presence of a third item. Recall, for example, that the relationship between teaching role and ultimate medical interest was summarized as a 36 percentage point difference. Looking at Figure 7-3, we see that among only those respondents who are most interested in articles dealing with the effectiveness of treatments, the relationship between

FIGURE 7-4
Hypothetical Trivariate Relationship among Scientific Orientation Items

Percentage Interested in Basic Mechanisms

		Best Teaching Role	
		Physician	Researcher
Reading Preferences	Effectiveness	51% (66)	87% (12)
	Rationale	51% (219)	87% (130)

teaching role and ultimate medical interest is 31 percentage points (58 percent minus 27 percent: first row), and the same is true among those most interested in articles dealing with the rationale for treatments (89 percent minus 58 percent: second row). The original relationship between teaching role and ultimate medical interest is essentially the same as in Figure 7-2, even among those respondents judged as scientific or nonscientific in terms of reading preferences.

We can draw the same conclusion from the columns in Figure 7-3. Recall that the original relationship between reading preferences and ultimate medical interests was summarized as a 38 percentage point difference. Looking only at the "physicians" in Figure 7-3, we see that the relationship between the other two items is now 31 percentage points. The same relationship is found among the "researchers" in the second column.

The importance of these observations becomes clearer when we consider what might have happened. In Figure 7-4, hypothetical data tell a much different story than do the actual data in Figure 7-3. As you can see, Figure 7-4 shows that the original relationship between teaching role and ultimate medical interest persists, even when reading preferences are introduced into the picture. In each row of the table the "researchers" are more likely to express an interest in basic mechanisms than the "physicians." Looking down the columns, however, we note that there is no relationship between reading preferences and ultimate medical interest. If we know whether a respondent feels he or she can best teach as a physician or as a researcher, knowing the respondent's reading preference adds nothing to our evaluation of his or her scientific orientation. If something like Figure 7-4 resulted from the actual data, we would conclude that reading preference should not be included in the same index as teaching role, since it contributes nothing to the composite index.

This example used only three questionnaire items. If more were being considered, then more complex multivariate tables would be in order, constructed of four, five, or more variables. The purpose of this step in index construction, again, is to discover the simultaneous interaction of the items to determine which should be included in the same index.

Index Scoring

When you have chosen the best items for the index, you next assign scores for particular responses, thereby creating a single composite index out of the several items. There are two basic decisions to be made in this step.

First, you must decide the desirable range of the index scores. Certainly a primary advantage of an index over a single item is the range of gradations it offers in the measurement of a variable. As noted earlier, *political conservatism* might be measured from "very conservative" to "not at all conservative" (or "very liberal"). How far to the extremes, then, should the index extend?

In this decision, the question of variance enters once more. Almost always, as the possible extremes of an index are extended, fewer cases are to be found at each end. The researcher who wishes to measure political conservatism to its greatest extreme may find there is almost no one in that category.

The first decision, then, concerns the conflicting desire for (1) a range of measurement in the index and (2) an adequate number of cases at each point in the index. You'll be forced to reach some kind of compromise between these conflicting desires.

The second decision concerns the actual assignment of scores for each particular response. Basically you must decide whether to give each item an equal weight in the index or to give them different weights. Although there are no firm rules, I suggest—and practice tends to support this method—that items be weighted equally unless there are compelling reasons for differential weighting. That is, the burden of proof should be on differential weighting; equal weighting should be the norm.

Of course, this decision must be related to the earlier issue regarding the balance of items chosen. If the index is to represent the composite of slightly different aspects of a given variable, then you should give each aspect the same weight. In some instances, however, you may feel that, say, two items reflect essentially the same aspect, and the third reflects a different aspect. If you wished to have both aspects equally represented by the index, you might decide to give the different item a weight equal to the combination of the two similar ones. In such a situation, you might want to assign a maximum score of 2 to the different item and a maximum score of 1 to each of the similar ones.

Although the rationale for scoring responses should take such concerns as these into account, you'll typically experiment with different scoring methods, examining the relative weights given to different aspects but at the same time worrying about the range and distribution of cases provided. Ultimately, the scoring method chosen will represent a compromise among these several demands. Of course, as in most research activities, such a decision is open to revision on the basis of later examinations. Validation of the index, to be discussed shortly, may lead you to recycle your efforts toward constructing a completely different index.

In the example taken from the medical school faculty survey, I decided to weight the items equally, since I'd chosen them, in part, because they represented slightly different aspects of the overall variable *scientific orientation*. On each of the items, the respondents were given a score of 1 for choosing the "scientific" response to the item and a score of 0 for choosing the "nonscientific" response. Each respondent, then, could receive a score of 0, 1, 2, or 3. This scoring method provided what was considered a useful range of variation—four index categories—and also provided enough cases for analysis in each category.

Here's a similar example of index scoring, from a recent study of work satisfaction. One of the key variables was *job-related depression*, measured by an index composed of the following four items, which asked workers how they felt when thinking about themselves and their jobs:

- "I feel downhearted and blue."
- "I get tired for no reason."
- "I find myself restless and can't keep still."
- "I am more irritable than usual."

The researchers, Amy Wharton and James Baron, report, "Each of these items was coded: 4 = often, 3 = sometimes, 2 = rarely, 1 = never" (Wharton and Baron 1987:578). They go on to explain how they measured other variables examined in the study:

■ Job-related self-esteem was based on four items asking respondents how they saw themselves in their work: happy/sad; successful/not successful; important/not important; doing their best/not doing their best. Each item ranged from 1 to 7, where 1 indicates a self-perception of not being happy, successful, important, or doing one's best.

(P. 578)

As you look through the social research literature, you will find numerous similar examples of cumulative indexes being used to measure variables.

Handling Missing Data

Regardless of your data-collection method, you'll frequently face the problem of missing data. In a content analysis of the political orientations of newspapers, for example, you may discover that a particular newspaper has never taken an editorial position on one of the issues being studied—it may never have taken a stand on the United Nations, for example. In an experimental design involving several retests of subjects over time, some subjects may be unable to participate in some of the sessions. In virtually every survey, some respondents fail to answer some questions (or choose a "don't know" response). Although missing data present problems at all stages of analysis, they're especially troublesome in index construction. There are, however, several methods of dealing with these problems.

First, if there are relatively few cases with missing data, you may decide to exclude them from the construction of the index and the analysis. (I did this in the medical school faculty example.) The primary concerns in this instance are whether the numbers available for analysis will remain sufficient and whether the exclusion will result in a biased sample whenever the index is used in the analysis. The latter possibility can be examined through a comparison—on other relevant variables—of those who would be included and excluded from the index.

Second, you may sometimes have grounds for treating missing data as one of the available responses. For example, if a questionnaire has asked respondents to indicate their participation in a number of activities by checking "yes" or "no" for each, many respondents may have checked some of the activities "yes" and left the remainder blank. In such a case, you might decide that a failure to answer meant "no," and score missing data in this case as though the respondents had checked the "no" space.

Third, a careful analysis of missing data may yield an interpretation of their meaning. In constructing a measure of political conservatism, for example, you may discover that respondents who failed to answer a given question were generally as conservative on other items as those who gave the conservative answer. As another example, a recent study measuring religious beliefs found that people who answered "don't know" about a given belief were almost identical to the "dis-believers" in their answers about other beliefs. (*Note:* You should not take these examples as empirical guides in your own studies, but only as suggesting general ways to analyze your own data.) Whenever the analysis of missing data yields such interpretations, then, you may decide to score such cases accordingly.

There are many other ways of handling this problem. If an item has several possible values, you might assign the middle value to cases with missing data; for example, you could assign a 2 if the values are 0, 1, 2, 3, and 4. For a continuous variable such as age, you could similarly assign the mean to cases with missing data. Or, missing data can be supplied by assigning values at random. All of these are conservative solutions in that they work against any relationships you may expect to find.

If you're creating an index out of several items, you can sometimes handle missing data by using proportions based on what is observed. Suppose your index is composed of six indicators, and you only have four observations for a particular subject. If the subject has earned 4 points out of a possible 4, you might assign an index score of 6; if the subject has 2 points (half the possible score on four items), you could assign a score of 3 (half the possible score on six observations).

The choice of a particular method to be used depends so much on the research situation that I can't reasonably suggest a single "best" method or rank the several I have described. Excluding all cases with missing data can bias the representativeness of the findings, but including such cases by assigning scores to missing data can influence the nature of the findings. The safest and best method is to construct the index using alternative methods and see whether the same findings follow from each. Understanding your data is the final goal of analysis anyway.

Index Validation

Up to this point, we've discussed all the steps in the selection and scoring of items that result in a composite index purporting to measure some variable. If each of the preceding steps is carried out carefully, the likelihood of the index actually measuring the variable is enhanced. To demonstrate success, however, there must be *validation* of the index. In the basic logic of validation, we assume that the composite index provides a measure of some variable; that is, the successive scores on the index arrange cases in a rank order in terms of that variable. An index of political conservatism rank-orders people in terms of their relative conservatism. If the index does that successfully, then people scored as relatively conservative on the index should appear relatively conservative in all other indications of political orientation, such as questionnaire items. There are several methods for validating a composite index.

Item Analysis The first step in index validation is an **internal validation** called *item analysis*. In item analysis, you examine the extent to which the composite index is related to (or predicts responses to) the individual items it comprises. Here's an illustration of this step.

In the index of scientific orientations among medical school faculty, for example, index scores ranged from 0 (most interested in patient care) to 3 (most interested in research). Now let's consider one of the items in the index: whether respondents wanted to advance their own knowledge more with regard to total patient management or more in the area of basic mechanisms. The latter were treated as being more scientifically oriented than the former. The following empty table shows how we would examine the relationship between the index and the individual item.

	Index of Scientific Orientations			
	0	1	2	3
Percentage who said they were more interested in basic mechanisms	??	??	??	??

If you take a minute to reflect on the table, you may see that we already know the numbers that go in two of the cells. To get a score of 3 on the index, respondents had to say "basic mechanisms" in response to this question and give the "scientific" answers to the other two items as well. Thus, 100 percent of the 3's on the index said "basic mechanisms." By the same token, all the 0's had to answer this item with "total patient management." Thus, 0 percent of those respondents said "basic mechanisms." Here's how the table looks with the information we already know.

	Index of Scientific Orientations			
	0	1	2	3
Percentage who said they were more interested in basic mechanisms	0	??	??	100

If the individual item is a good reflection of the overall index, we should expect the 1's and 2's to fill in a progression between 0 percent and 100 percent. More of the 2's should choose "basic mechanisms" than 1's. This is not guaranteed by the way the index was constructed, however; it is an empirical question—one we answer in an item analysis. Here's how this particular item analysis turned out.

	Index of Scientific Orientations			
	0	1	2	3
Percentage who said they were more interested in basic mechanisms	0	16	91	100

As you can see, in accord with our assumption that the 2's are more scientifically oriented than the 1's, we find that a higher percentage of the 2's (91 percent) say "basic mechanisms" than the 1's (16 percent).

An item analysis of the other two components of the index yields similar results, as shown below.

	Index of Scientific Orientations			
	0	1	2	3
Percentage who said they were more interested in basic mechanisms	0	4	14	100
Percentage who said they preferred reading about rationales	0	80	97	100

Each of the items, then, seems an appropriate component in the index. Each seems to reflect the same quality that the index as a whole measures.

In a complex index containing many items, this step provides a convenient test of the independent contribution of each item to the index. If a given item is found to be poorly related to the index, it may be assumed that other items in the index cancel out the contribution of that item. If the item in question contributes nothing to the index's power, it should be excluded.

Although item analysis is an important first test of the index's validity, it is scarcely a sufficient test. If the index adequately measures a given variable, it should successfully predict other indications of that variable. To test this, we must turn to items not included in the index.

External Validation People scored as politically conservative on an index should appear conservative in their responses to other items in the questionnaire. Of course, we're talking about relative conservatism, because we can't make a final absolute definition of what constitutes conservatism. However, those respondents scored as the most conservative on the index should be the most conservative in answering other questions. Those scored as the least conservative on the index should be the least conservative on other items. Indeed, the ranking of groups of respondents on the index should predict the ranking of those groups in answering other questions dealing with political orientations.

In our example of the scientific orientation index, several questions in the questionnaire offered the possibility of such **external validation**. Table 7-1 presents some of these items, which provide several lessons regarding index validation. First, we note that the index strongly predicts the responses to the validating items in the sense that the rank order of scientific responses among the four groups is the same as the rank order provided by the index itself. At the same time, each item gives a different *description* of scientific orientations overall. For example, the last validating item indicates that the great majority of *all* faculty were engaged in research during the preceding year. If this were the only indicator of scientific orientation, we would conclude that nearly all faculty were scientific. Nevertheless, those scored as more scientific on the index are more likely to have engaged in research than those who were scored as relatively less scientific. The third validating item provides a different descriptive picture: Only a minority of the faculty overall say they would prefer duties limited exclusively to research. Nevertheless, the percentages giving this answer correspond to the scores assigned on the index.

Bad Index versus Bad Validators Nearly every index constructor at some time must face the apparent failure of external items to validate the index. If the internal item analysis shows inconsistent relationships between the items included in the index and the index itself, something is wrong with the index. But if the index fails to predict strongly the external validation items, the conclusion to be drawn is more ambiguous. You must choose between two possibilities: (1) the index does not adequately measure the variable in question, or (2) the validation items do not adequately measure the variable and thereby do not provide a sufficient test of the index.

The researcher who has worked long and conscientiously on the construction of an index will find the second conclusion compelling. Typically, you will feel you have included the best indicators of the variable in the index; the validating items are, therefore, second-rate indicators. Nevertheless, you should recognize that the index is purportedly a very powerful measure of the variable; thus, it should be somewhat related to any item that taps the variable even poorly.

When external validation fails, you should reexamine the index before deciding that the validating items are insufficient. One way to do this is to examine the relationships between the validating items and the individual items included in the index. If you discover that some of the index items relate to the validators and others do not, you'll have improved your understanding of the index as it was initially constituted.

There is no cookbook solution to this dilemma; it is an agony serious researchers must learn to survive. Ultimately, the wisdom of your decision to accept an index will be determined by the usefulness of that index in your later analyses. Perhaps you will initially decide that the index is a

TABLE 7-1
Validation of Scientific Orientation Index

	Index of Scientific Orientation			
	Low 0	1	2	High 3
Percentage interested in attending scientific lectures at the medical school	34	42	46	65
Percentage who say faculty members should have experience as medical researchers	43	60	65	89
Percentage who would prefer faculty duties involving research activities only	0	8	32	66
Percentage who engaged in research during the preceding academic year	61	76	94	99

good one and that the validators are defective, and later find that the variable in question (as measured by the index) is not related to other variables in the ways you expected. Then you may have to compose a new index.

Indexing the Status of Women

For the most part, I've talked about index construction in the context of survey research, but other types of research also lend themselves to this kind of composite measure. For example, when the United Nations (1995) set about examining the status of women in the world, they chose to create two indexes, reflecting two different dimensions.

The Gender-related Development Index (GDI) compared women to men in terms of three indicators: life expectancy, education, and income. These indicators are commonly used in monitoring the status of women in the world. The Scandinavian countries of Norway, Sweden, Finland, and Denmark ranked highest on this measure.

The second index, the Gender Empowerment Measure (GEM), aimed more at power issues and comprised three different indicators:

- The proportion of parliamentary seats held by women
- The proportion of administrative, managerial, professional, and technical positions held by women
- A measure of access to jobs and wages

Once again, the Scandinavian countries ranked high but were joined by Canada, New Zealand, the Netherlands, the United States, and Austria. Having two different measures of gender equality allowed the researchers to make more sophisticated distinctions. For example, in several countries, most notably Greece, France, and Japan, women fared relatively well on the GDI but quite poorly on the GEM; thus while they were doing fairly well in terms of income, education, and life expectancy, they were still denied access to power. And while the GDI scores were higher in the wealthier nations than in the poorer ones, GEM scores showed that women's empowerment was less dependent on national wealth, with many poor, developing countries outpacing some rich, industrial ones in regard to such empowerment.

By examining several different dimensions of the variables involved in their study, the UN researchers also uncovered an aspect of women's earnings that generally goes unnoticed. Population Communications International (1996:1) has summarized the finding nicely:

■ Every year, women make an invisible contribution of eleven trillion U.S. dollars to the global economy, the UNDP report says, counting both unpaid work and the underpayment of women's work at prevailing market prices. This "undervaluation" of women's work not only undermines their purchasing power, says the 1995 HDR, but also reduces their already low social status and affects their ability to own property and use credit. Mahbub ul Haq, the principal author of the report, says that, "if women's work were accurately reflected in national statistics, it would shatter the myth that men are the main breadwinner of the world." The UNDP report finds that women work longer hours than men in almost every country, including both paid and unpaid duties. In developing countries, women do approximately 53% of all work and spend two-thirds of their work time on unremunerated activities. In industrialized countries, women do an average of 51% of the total work, and—like their counterparts in the developing world—perform about two-thirds of their total labor without pay. Men in industrialized countries are compensated for two-thirds of their work.

Now we'll turn our attention from the creation of cumulative indexes to an examination of scaling techniques. Although many methods of scaling are available, I'm going to limit our discussion primarily to four—the Bogardus, Thurstone, Likert, and Guttman scales—along with a discussion of the semantic differential.

■ SCALE CONSTRUCTION

Good indexes provide an ordinal ranking of cases on a given variable. All indexes are based on this kind of assumption: A senator who voted for seven conservative bills is considered to be more conservative than one who only voted for four of them. What an index may fail to take into account, however, is that not all indicators of a variable are equally important or equally strong. The first senator might have voted in favor of seven mildly conservative bills, whereas the second senator might have voted in favor of four extremely conservative bills. (The second senator might have considered the other seven bills too liberal and voted against them.)

Scales offer more assurance of ordinality by tapping *structures* among the indicators. The several items going into a composite measure may have different *intensities* in terms of the variable. The four scaling procedures described will illustrate the variety of techniques available.

Bogardus Social Distance Scale

Let's suppose you're interested in the extent to which Americans are willing to associate with, say, Albanians. You might ask the following questions:

1. Are you willing to permit Albanians to live in your country?
2. Are you willing to permit Albanians to live in your community?
3. Are you willing to permit Albanians to live in your neighborhood?
4. Would you be willing to let an Albanian live next door to you?
5. Would you let your child marry an Albanian?

Note that the several questions increase in terms of the closeness of contact the respondents may or may not want with Albanians. Beginning with the original concern to measure willingness to associate with Albanians, we have developed several questions indicating differing degrees of intensity on this variable. The kinds of items presented constitute a **Bogardus social distance scale.**

The clear differences of intensity suggest a structure among the items. Presumably if a person is willing to accept a given kind of association, he or she would be willing to accept all those preceding it in the list—those with lesser intensities. For example, the person who is willing to permit Albanians to live in the neighborhood will surely accept them in the community and the nation but may or may not be willing to accept them as next-door neighbors or relatives. This, then, is the logical structure of intensity inherent among the items.

Empirically, one would expect to find the largest number of people accepting co-citizenship and the fewest accepting intermarriage. In this sense, we speak of "easy items" (for example, residence in the United States) and "hard items" (for example, intermarriage). More people agree to the easy items than to the hard ones. With some inevitable exceptions, logic demands that once a person has refused a relationship presented in the scale, he or she will also refuse all the harder ones that follow it.

The Bogardus social distance scale illustrates the important economy of scaling as a data-reduction device. By knowing *how many* relationships with Albanians a given respondent will accept, we know *which* relationships were accepted. Thus, a single number can accurately summarize five or six data items without a loss of information.

Thurstone Scales

Often the inherent structure of the Bogardus social distance scale is not appropriate to the variable being measured. Indeed, such a logical structure among several indicators is seldom apparent. **Thurstone scaling** is an attempt to develop a format for generating groups of indicators of a variable that have at least an *empirical* structure among them. One of the basic formats is that of "equal-appearing intervals."

A group of judges is given perhaps a hundred items felt to be indicators of a given variable. Each judge is then asked to estimate how strong an indicator of a variable each item is—by assigning scores of perhaps 1 to 13. If the variable were *prejudice,* for example, the judges would be asked to assign the score of 1 to the very weakest indicators of prejudice, the score of 13 to the strongest indicators, and intermediate scores to those felt to be somewhere in between.

Once the judges have completed this task, the researcher examines the scores assigned to each item by all the judges to determine which items produced the greatest agreement among the judges. Those items on which the judges disagreed broadly would be rejected as ambiguous. Among those items producing general agreement in scoring, one or more would be selected to represent each scale score from 1 to 13.

The items selected in this manner might then be included in a survey questionnaire. Respondents who appeared prejudiced on those items representing a strength of 5 would then be expected to appear prejudiced on those having lesser strengths, and if some of those respondents did not appear prejudiced on the items with a strength of 6, it would be expected that they would also not appear prejudiced on those with greater strengths.

If the Thurstone scale items were adequately developed and scored, the economy and effectiveness of data reduction inherent in the Bogardus social distance scale would appear. A single score might be assigned to each respondent (the strength of the hardest item accepted), and that score would adequately represent the responses to several questionnaire items. And as is true of the Bogardus scale, a respondent scored 6 might be regarded as more prejudiced than one scored 5 or less.

Thurstone scaling is not often used in research today, primarily because of the tremendous expenditure of energy and time required to have 10 to 15 judges score the items. Because the quality of their judgments would depend on their experience with the variable under consideration, professional researchers might be needed. Moreover, the meanings conveyed by the several items indicating a given variable tend to change over time. Thus an item having a given weight at one time might have quite a different weight later on. For a Thurstone scale to be effective, it would have to be periodically updated.

Likert Scaling

You may sometimes hear people refer to a questionnaire item containing response categories such as "strongly agree," "agree," "disagree," and "strongly disagree" as a **Likert scale.** This is technically a misnomer, although Rensis Likert (pronounced 'LICK-ert') did create this commonly used question format.

The particular value of this format is the unambiguous *ordinality* of response categories. If respondents were permitted to volunteer or select such answers as "sort of agree," "pretty much agree," "really agree," and so forth, the researcher would find it impossible to judge the relative strength of agreement intended by the various respondents. The Likert format resolves this problem.

Likert had something more in mind, however. He created a method by which this question format could be used to determine the *relative intensity* of different items. As a simple example, suppose we wished to measure prejudice against women. To do this, we created a set of 20 statements, each of which reflected that prejudice. One of the items might be "Women can't drive as well as men." Another might be "Women shouldn't be allowed to vote." The relative intensity of these two items is probably clear to you, and Likert's scaling technique would demonstrate that difference as well as pegging the intensity of the other 18 statements.

Let's suppose we ask a sample of people to agree or disagree with each of the 20 statements. Simply giving one point for each of the indicators of prejudice against women would yield the possibility of index scores ranging from 0 to 20. Likert scaling goes one step beyond that and calculates the *average index* score for those agreeing with each of the individual statements. Let's say that all those who agreed that women are poorer drivers than men had an average index score of 1.5 (out of a possible 20). Those who agreed that women should be denied the right to vote might have an average index score of, say, 19.5—indicating the greater degree of prejudice reflected in that response.

As a result of this item analysis, respondents could be rescored to form a scale: 1.5 points for agreeing that women are poorer drivers, 19.5 points for saying women shouldn't vote, and points for other responses reflecting how those items related to the initial, simple index. If those who *disagreed* with the statement, "I might vote for a woman for president," had an average index score of 15, then the scale would give 15 points to people disagreeing with that statement.

In practice, Likert scaling is seldom used today. I don't know why; maybe it seems too complex. The item format devised by Likert, however, is one of the most commonly used in contemporary questionnaire design. Typically, it is now used in the creation of simple indexes. With, say, five response categories, scores of 0 to 4 or 1 to 5 might be assigned, taking the direction of the items into account (for example, assign a score of 5 to "strongly agree" for positive items and to "strongly disagree" for negative items). Each respondent would then be assigned an overall score representing the summation of the scores he or she received for responses to the individual items.

Semantic Differential

Like the Likert format, the **semantic differential** asks respondents to choose between two opposite positions. Here's how it works.

Suppose you are evaluating the effectiveness of a new music appreciation lecture on subjects' appreciation of music. As a part of your study, you want to play some musical selections and have the subjects report their feelings about them. A good way to tap those feelings would be to use a semantic differential format.

To begin, you must determine the *dimensions* along which each selection should be judged by subjects. Then you need to find two *opposite* terms, representing the polar extremes along each dimension. Let's suppose one dimension that interests you is simply whether subjects enjoyed the piece or not. Two opposite terms in this case could be "enjoyable" and "unenjoyable." Similarly, you might want to know whether they regarded the individual selections as "complex" or "simple," "harmonic" or "discordant," and so forth.

Once you have determined the relevant dimensions and have found terms to represent the extremes of each, you might prepare a rating sheet each subject would complete for each piece of music. Figure 7-5 shows what it might look like.

On each line of the rating sheet, the subject would indicate how he or she felt about the piece of music: whether it was enjoyable or unenjoyable, for example, and whether it was "somewhat" that way or "very much" so. To avoid creating a biased pattern of responses to such items, it's a good idea to vary the placement of terms that are likely to be related to each other. Notice, for example, that "discordant" and "traditional" are on the left side of the sheet, with "harmonic" and "modern" on the right. Most likely, those selections scored as "discordant" would also be scored as "modern" as opposed to "traditional."

Both the Likert and semantic differential formats have a greater rigor and structure than other question formats. As I've indicated earlier,

FIGURE 7-5
Semantic Differential: Feelings about Musical Selections

	Very Much	Some-what	Neither	Some-what	Very Much	
Enjoyable	☐	☐	☐	☐	☐	Unenjoyable
Simple	☐	☐	☐	☐	☐	Complex
Discordant	☐	☐	☐	☐	☐	Harmonic
Traditional	☐	☐	☐	☐	☐	Modern
			etc.			

these formats produce data suitable to both indexing and scaling.

Guttman Scaling

Researchers today often use the scale developed by Louis Guttman. Like Bogardus, Thurstone, and Likert scaling, Guttman scaling is based on the fact that some items under consideration may prove to be more extreme indicators of the variable than others. One example should suffice to illustrate this pattern.

In the earlier example of measuring scientific orientations among medical school faculty members, you'll recall that a simple index was constructed. As it happens, however, the three items included in the index essentially form a **Guttman scale.**

The construction of a Guttman scale would begin with some of the same steps that initiate index construction. You would begin by examining the face validity of items available for analysis. Then, you would examine the bivariate and perhaps multivariate relations among those items. In scale construction, however, you would also look for relatively "hard" and "easy" indicators of the variable being examined.

Earlier, when we talked about attitudes regarding a woman's right to have an abortion, we discussed several conditions that can affect people's opinions: whether the woman is married, whether her health is endangered, and so forth. These differing conditions provide an excellent illustration of Guttman scaling.

Here are the percentages of the people in the 1996 GSS sample who supported a woman's right to an abortion, under three different conditions:

Woman's health is seriously endangered	92%
Pregnant as a result of rape	86%
Woman is not married	48%

The different percentages supporting abortion under the three conditions suggest something about the different *levels* of support that each item indicates. For example, if someone would support abortion when the mother's life is seriously endangered, that's not a very strong indicator of general support for abortion, because almost everyone agreed with that. Supporting abortion for unmarried women seems a much stronger indicator of support for abortion in general—fewer than half the sample took that position.

Guttman scaling is based on the notion that anyone who gives a strong indicator of some variable will also give the weaker indicators. In this case, we would assume that anyone who supported abortion for unmarried women would also support it in the case of rape or of the woman's health being threatened. Table 7-2 tests this assumption by presenting the number of respondents who gave each of the possible response patterns.

The first four response patterns in the table compose what we would call the *scale types:* those patterns that form a scalar structure. Following those respondents who supported abortion under all three conditions (line 1), we see (line 2) that those with only two pro-choice responses have chosen the two easier ones; those with only one such response (line 3) chose the easiest of the three (the woman's health being endangered). And finally, there are some respondents who opposed abortion in all three circumstances (line 4).

TABLE 7-2
Scaling Support for Choice of Abortion

	Women's Health	Result of Rape	Woman Unmarried	Number of Cases
Scale Types	+	+	+	612
	+	+	−	448
	+	−	−	92
	−	−	−	79
				Total = 1231
Mixed Types	−	+	−	15
	+	−	+	5
	−	−	+	2
	−	+	+	5
				Total = 27

+ = favors woman's right to choose; − = opposes woman's right to choose

The second part of the table presents those response patterns that violate the scalar structure of the items. The most radical departures from the scalar structure are the last two response patterns: those who accepted only the hardest item and those who rejected only the easiest one.

The final column in the table indicates the number of survey respondents who gave each of the response patterns. It's immediately apparent that the great majority (98 percent) of the respondents fit into one of the scale types. The presence of mixed types, however, indicates that the items do not form a *perfect* Guttman scale.

We should recall at this point that one of the chief functions of scaling is efficient data reduction. Scales provide a technique for presenting data in a summary form while maintaining as much of the original information as possible.

When the scientific orientation items were formed into an index in our earlier discussion, respondents were given one point for each scientific response they gave. If these same three items were scored as a Guttman scale, some respondents would be assigned scale scores that would permit the most accurate reproduction of their original responses to all three items.

Respondents fitting into the scale types would receive the same scores as were assigned in the index construction. Persons selecting all three pro-choice responses would still be scored 3, those who selected pro-choice responses to the two easier items and were opposed on the hardest item would be scored 2, and so on. For each of the four scale types we could predict accurately all the actual responses given by all the respondents based on their scores.

The mixed types in the table present a problem, however. The first mixed type (− + −) was scored 1 on the index to indicate only one pro-choice response. But, if 1 were assigned as a scale score, we would predict that the 15 respondents in this group had chosen only the easiest item (approving abortion when the woman's life was endangered), and we would be making two errors for each such respondent. Scale scores are assigned, therefore, with the aim of minimizing the errors that would be made in reconstructing the original responses.

Table 7-3 illustrates the index and scale scores that would be assigned to each of the response patterns in our example. Note that one error is made for each respondent in the mixed types. This is the minimum we can hope for in a mixed type pattern. In the first mixed type, for example, we would erroneously predict a pro-choice response to the easiest item for each of the 15 respondents in this group, making a total of 15 errors.

The extent to which a set of empirical responses form a Guttman scale is determined by the accuracy with which the original responses can be reconstructed from the scale scores. For each of the 1,258 respondents in this example, we will predict three questionnaire responses, for a total of 3,774 predictions. Table 7-3 indicates that

TABLE 7-3
Index and Scale Scores

	Response Pattern	Number of Cases	Index Scores	Scale Scores*	Total Scale Errors
Scale Types	+ + +	612	3	3	0
	+ + −	448	2	2	0
	+ − −	92	1	1	0
	− − −	79	0	0	0
Mixed Types	− + −	15	1	2	15
	+ − +	5	2	3	5
	− − +	2	1	0	2
	− + +	5	2	3	5

Total Scale Errors = 27

$$\text{Coefficient of reproducibility} = 1 - \frac{\text{number of errors}}{\text{number of guesses}}$$

$$= 1 - \frac{27}{1258 \times 3} = \frac{27}{3774}$$

$$= .993 = 99.3\%$$

*This table presents one common method for scoring mixed types, but you should be advised that other methods are also used.

we will make 27 errors using the scale scores assigned. The percentage of *correct* predictions is called the coefficient of reproducibility: the percentage of original responses that could be *reproduced* by knowing the scale scores used to summarize them. In the present example, the coefficient of reproducibility is 3,747/3,774 or 99.3 percent.

Except for the case of perfect (100 percent) reproducibility, there is no way of saying that a set of items does or does not form a Guttman scale in any absolute sense. Virtually all sets of such items *approximate* a scale. As a general guideline, however, coefficients of 90 or 95 percent are the commonly used standards in this regard. If the observed reproducibility exceeds the level you've set, you'll probably decide to score and use the items as a scale.

The decision concerning criteria in this regard is, of course, arbitrary. Moreover, a high degree of reproducibility does not insure that the scale constructed in fact measures the concept under consideration, although it increases confidence that all the component items measure the same thing. Also, you should realize that a high **coefficient of reproducibility** is most likely when few items are involved.

One concluding remark should be made with regard to Guttman scaling: It is based on the structure observed among the *actual data under examination*. This is an important point that is often misunderstood. It does not make sense to say that a set of questionnaire items (perhaps developed and used by a previous researcher) constitutes a Guttman scale. Rather, we can say only that they form a scale within a given body of data being analyzed. Scalability, then, is a sample-dependent, empirical matter. Although a set of items may form a Guttman scale among one sample of survey respondents, for example, there is no guarantee that this set will form such a scale among another sample. In this sense, then, a set of questionnaire items in and of themselves never forms a scale, but a set of empirical observations may.

■ TYPOLOGIES

We'll conclude this chapter with a short discussion of typology construction and analysis. Recall that indexes and scales are constructed to provide ordinal measures of given variables. We attempt to assign index or scale scores to cases in such a

TABLE 7-4
A Political Typology of Newspapers

		Foreign Policy	
		Conservative	Liberal
Domestic Policy	Conservative	A	B
	Liberal	C	D

way as to indicate a rising degree of prejudice, religiosity, conservatism, and so forth. In such cases, we're dealing with single dimensions.

Often, however, the researcher wishes to summarize the intersection of two or more variables, thereby creating a set of categories or types, which we call a *typology*. You may, for example, wish to examine the political orientations of newspapers separately in terms of domestic issues and foreign policy. The fourfold presentation in Table 7-4 describes such a typology.

Newspapers in cell A of the table are conservative on both foreign policy and domestic policy; those in cell D are liberal on both. Those in cells B and C are conservative on one and liberal on the other.

Frequently, you arrive at a typology in the course of an attempt to construct an index or scale. The items that you felt represented a single variable appear to represent two. We might have been attempting to construct a single index of political orientations for newspapers but discovered—empirically—that foreign and domestic politics had to be kept separate.

In any event, you should be warned against a difficulty inherent in typological analysis. Whenever the typology is used as the **independent variable,** there will probably be no problem. In the preceding example, you might compute the percentages of newspapers in each cell that normally endorse Democratic candidates; you could then easily examine the effects of both foreign and domestic policies on political endorsements.

It is extremely difficult, however, to analyze a typology as a **dependent variable.** If you want to discover why newspapers fall into the different cells of typology, you're in trouble. That becomes apparent when we consider the ways you might construct and read your tables. Assume, for example, that you want to examine the effects of community size on political policies. With a single dimension, you could easily determine the percentages of rural and urban newspapers that were scored conservative and liberal on your index or scale.

With a typology, however, you would have to present the distribution of the urban newspapers in your sample among types A, B, C, and D. Then you would repeat the procedure for the rural ones in the sample and compare the two distributions. Let's suppose that 80 percent of the rural newspapers are scored as type A (conservative on both dimensions) as compared with 30 percent of the urban ones. Moreover, suppose that only 5 percent of the rural newspapers are scored as type B (conservative only on domestic issues) as compared with 40 percent of the urban ones. It would be incorrect to conclude from an examination of type B that urban newspapers are more conservative on domestic issues than rural ones, since 85 percent of the rural newspapers, compared with 70 percent of the urban ones, have this characteristic. The relative sparsity of rural newspapers in type B is due to their concentration in type A. It should be apparent that an interpretation of such data would be very difficult for anything other than description.

In reality, you'd probably examine two such dimensions separately, especially if the dependent variable has more categories of responses than the example given.

Don't think that typologies should always be avoided in social research; often they provide the most appropriate device for understanding the data. You should be warned, however, against the special difficulties involved in using typologies as dependent variables.

■ MAIN POINTS

- Single indicators of variables seldom have sufficiently clear validity to warrant their use.
- Composite measures, such as scales and indexes, solve this problem by including several indicators of a variable in one summary measure.
- Both scales and indexes are intended as ordinal measures of variables, though scales typically satisfy this goal better than indexes.
- Indexes are based on the simple cumulation of indicators of a variable.
- Scales take advantage of any logical or empirical intensity structures that exist among a variable's indicators.
- Face validity is the first criterion indicators must meet to be included in a composite measure; that is, an indicator must seem, on face value, to provide some measure of the variable.
- If different items are indeed indicators of the same variable, then they should be related empirically to one another. If, for example, frequency of church attendance and frequency of prayer are both indicators of religiosity, then those people who attend church frequently should be found to pray more than those who attend church less frequently.
- Once an index or a scale has been constructed, it must be validated. Internal validation refers to the relationship between individual items included in the composite measure and the measure itself. External validation refers to the relationships between the composite measure and other indicators of the variable—indicators *not* included in the measure.
- The Bogardus social distance scale is a device for measuring the varying degrees to which a person would be willing to associate with a given class of people, such as an ethnic minority. Subjects are asked to indicate whether or not they would be willing to accept different kinds of association. The several responses produced by these questions can be adequately summarized by a single score, representing the closest association that is acceptable, because those willing to accept a given association also would be willing to accept more distant ones.
- Thurstone scaling is a technique for creating indicators of variables that have a clear intensity structure among them. Judges determine the intensities of different indicators.
- Likert scaling is a measurement technique based on the use of standardized response categories (for example, "strongly agree," "agree," "disagree," "strongly disagree") for several questionnaire items. Likert-format items may be used appropriately in the construction of either indexes or scales.
- The semantic differential is a question format that asks respondents to make ratings that lie between two extremes, such as "very positive" and "very negative."
- Probably the most popular scaling technique in social research today, Guttman scaling is a method of discovering and using the empirical intensity structure among several indicators of a given variable.
- A coefficient of reproducibility is a measure of the extent to which all the particular responses given to the individual items included in a scale can be reproduced from the scale score alone.
- A typology is a nominal composite measure often used in social research. Typologies may be used effectively as independent variables, but interpretation is difficult when they are used as dependent variables.

■ REVIEW QUESTIONS AND EXERCISES

1. In your own words, describe the difference between an index and a scale.
2. Make up three questionnaire items that measure attitudes toward nuclear power and that would probably form a Guttman scale.

3. Economists often use indexes to measure economic variables, such as the cost of living. Go to the Bureau of Labor Statistics (http://stats.bls.gov) and find the Consumer Price Index survey. What are some of the dimensions of living costs included in this measure?

■ ADDITIONAL READINGS

Anderson, Andy B., Alexander Basilevsky, and Derek P. J. Hum. "Measurement: Theory and Techniques." Pp. 231–87 in *Handbook of Survey Research,* edited by Peter H. Rossi, James D. Wright, and Andy B. Anderson. New York: Academic Press, 1983. The logic of measurement is analyzed in the context of composite measures.

Bobo, Lawrence, and Frederick C. Licari. "Education and Political Tolerance: Testing the Effects of Cognitive Sophistication and Target Group Effect." *Public Opinion Quarterly* 53 (Fall 1989): 285–308. The authors use a variety of techniques for determining how best to measure tolerance toward different groups in society.

Glock, Charles, Benjamin B. Ringer, and Earl Babbie. *To Comfort and to Challenge: A Dilemma of the Contemporary Church.* Berkeley: University of California Press, 1967. An empirical study illustrating composite measures. Since the construction of scales and indexes can be most fully grasped through concrete examples, this might be a useful study to examine. The authors use a variety of composite measures, and they are relatively clear about the methods used in constructing them.

Lazarsfeld, Paul, Ann Pasanella, and Morris Rosenberg, eds. *Continuities in the Language of Social Research.* New York: Free Press, 1972, especially Section 1. An excellent collection of conceptual discussions and concrete illustrations. The construction of composite measures is presented within the more general area of conceptualization and measurement.

McIver, John P. and Edward G. Carmines. *Unidimensional Scaling.* Newbury Park, CA: Sage, 1981. Here's an excellent way to pursue Thurstone, Likert, and Guttman scaling in further depth.

Miller, Delbert. *Handbook of Research Design and Social Measurement.* Newbury Park, CA: Sage, 1991. An excellent compilation of frequently used and semistandardized scales. The many illustrations reported in Part 4 of the Miller book may be directly adaptable to studies or at least suggestive of modified measures. Studying the several different illustrations, moreover, may also give you a better understanding of the logic of composite measures in general.

CHAPTER 8: The Logic of Sampling

What You'll Learn in This Chapter

Now you'll see how it's possible for social scientists to select a few people for study—and discover things that apply to hundreds of millions of people not studied.

INTRODUCTION

THE HISTORY OF SAMPLING
President Alf Landon
President Thomas E. Dewey
Two Types of Sampling Methods

NONPROBABILITY SAMPLING
Reliance on Available Subjects
Purposive or Judgmental Sampling
Snowball Sampling
Quota Sampling
Selecting Informants

THE LOGIC OF PROBABILITY SAMPLING
Conscious and Unconscious Sampling Bias
Representativeness and Probability of Selection

SAMPLING CONCEPTS AND TERMINOLOGY

PROBABILITY SAMPLING THEORY AND SAMPLING DISTRIBUTION
Probability Sampling Theory
The Sampling Distribution of Ten Cases
Binomial Sampling Distribution

POPULATIONS AND SAMPLING FRAMES
Review of Populations and Sampling Frames

TYPES OF SAMPLING DESIGNS
Simple Random Sampling
Systematic Sampling
Stratified Sampling
Implicit Stratification in Systematic Sampling

ILLUSTRATION: SAMPLING UNIVERSITY STUDENTS
Study Population and Sampling Frame
Stratification
Sample Selection
Sample Modification

MULTISTAGE CLUSTER SAMPLING
Multistage Cluster Sampling, Stratification
Probability Proportionate to Size (PPS) Sampling
Disproportionate Sampling and Weighting

ILLUSTRATION: SAMPLING CHURCHWOMEN
Selecting the Churches
Selecting the Churchwomen

PROBABILITY SAMPLING IN REVIEW

MAIN POINTS

REVIEW QUESTIONS AND EXERCISES

ADDITIONAL READINGS

Chapter 8: The Logic of Sampling

■ INTRODUCTION

In November 1996, Bill Clinton was reelected president of the United States with 49 percent of the popular vote, versus 41 percent for the former-Senator Robert Dole and 9 percent for the third-party candidate, Ross Perot. Prior to the election, many political polls had predicted the Clinton victory.

Here are the results of several national polls conducted near the election, in late October and early November (Table 8-1). For purposes of comparability, I've distributed those who were "undecided" in the polls among the three candidates proportionate to the votes they received from those who *did* give a preference. Though the polls tended to overestimate the Clinton vote in 1996, most, as you'll see, came within two or three percentage points of the actual vote.

Now, how many interviews do you suppose it took each of these pollsters to come within a couple of percentage points in estimating the behavior of about ninety million voters? Fewer than 2,000! In this chapter, we are going to find out how social researchers can pull off such wizardry.

Though we've been talking a lot about observation in recent chapters, our discussions have omitted the question of what or who will be observed. When you think about it, you'll see that a social researcher has a whole world of potential observations. Yet, nobody can observe everything. A critical part of social research, then, is the decision about what to observe and what not. If you want to study voters, for example, which voters should you study? That's the subject of this chapter.

Sampling is the process of selecting observations. After a brief history of social scientific sampling, the key section of this chapter discusses the logic and the skills of probability sampling. As you'll see, probability sampling techniques—involving *random sampling*—allow a researcher to make relatively few observations and generalize from those observations to a much wider population. We'll examine the requirements for generalizability.

As you'll discover, random selection is a precise, scientific procedure; there's nothing haphazard about it. Specific sampling techniques allow us to determine and/or control the likelihood of specific individuals being selected for study. In the simplest example, flipping a coin to choose between two individuals gives each one exactly the same probability of selection—50 percent. Complex techniques also guarantee an equal probability of selection when substantial samples are selected from large populations.

You will find sampling more rigorous and precise than some topics in this book. Where social research as a whole is both art and science, sampling leans toward science. Because sampling is more "technical," some students find it more difficult than other aspects of social research. At the same time, other students say the logical neatness of sampling actually makes it easier for them to comprehend it than, say, conceptualization or causation.

Although probability sampling is central to social research today, we'll take some time to examine a variety of nonprobability methods as well. Although not based on random selection, these methods have their own logic and can provide useful samples for social inquiry. We'll examine both the advantages and the shortcomings of such methods, and we'll see where they fit within the social scientific enterprise.

■ THE HISTORY OF SAMPLING

Sampling in social research has developed hand in hand with political polling. This is the case, no doubt, because political polling is one of the few opportunities social researchers have to discover the accuracy of their estimates. On election day, they find out how well or how poorly they did.

President Alf Landon

You may have heard about the *Literary Digest* in connection with political polling. The *Digest* was a popular news magazine published between 1890 and 1938 in America. In 1920, *Digest* editors mailed postcards to people in six states, asking them whom they were planning to vote for in the presidential campaign between Warren Harding

TABLE 8-1
Polls Predicting Presidential Election Outcomes

		Percent of Votes for			
Dates	Agency	Clinton	Dole	Perot	Other
10/28–31	Hotline/Battleground	49	40	9	2
10/30–11/2	CBS/New York Times	54	35	9	2
10/31–11/3	Pew Research Center	52	38	8	2
11/1–3	Reuter/Zogby	49	41	8	2
11/1–3	Harris	51	39	9	1
11/2–3	ABC	52	39	7	2
11/2–3	NBC/Wall St. Journal	51	38	9	2
11/3–4	Gallup/CNN/USA Today	51	38	9	2
	Election Results	**49**	**41**	**9**	**2**

Source: Robert M. Worcester, "Reporting the Polls: You can Do Better," *The Public Perspective*, December–January 1997, p. 54.

and James Cox. Names were selected for the poll from telephone directories and automobile registration lists. Based on the postcards sent back, the *Digest* correctly predicted that Harding would be elected. In the elections that followed, the *Literary Digest* expanded the size of its poll and made correct predictions in 1924, 1928, and 1932.

In 1936, the *Digest* conducted its most ambitious poll: Ten million ballots were sent to people listed in telephone directories and on lists of automobile owners. Over two million responded, giving the Republican contender, Alf Landon, a stunning 57 to 43 percent landslide over the incumbent, President Franklin Roosevelt. The editors modestly cautioned,

■ We make no claim to infallibility. We did not coin the phrase "uncanny accuracy" which has been so freely applied to our Polls. We know only too well the limitations of every straw vote, however enormous the sample gathered, however scientific the method. It would be a miracle if every State of the forty-eight behaved on Election Day exactly as forecast by the Poll.
(1936A:6)

Two weeks later, the *Digest* editors knew the limitations of straw polls even better: Voters gave Roosevelt a second term in office by the largest landslide in history, with 61 percent of the vote. Landon won only 8 electoral votes to Roosevelt's 523. The editors were puzzled by their unfortunate turn of luck.

A part of the problem surely lay in the 22 percent return rate garnered by the poll. The editors asked,

■ Why did only one in five voters in Chicago to whom the *Digest* sent ballots take the trouble to reply? And why was there a preponderance of Republicans in the one-fifth that did reply? . . . We were getting better cooperation in what we have always regarded as a public service from Republicans than we were getting from Democrats. Do Republicans live nearer to mailboxes? Do Democrats generally disapprove of straw polls?
(1936B:7)

A part of the answer to these questions lay in the sampling frame used by the *Digest:* telephone subscribers and automobile owners. Such a design selected a disproportionately wealthy sample, especially coming on the tail end of the worst economic depression in the nation's history. The sample effectively excluded poor people, and the poor people predominantly voted for Roosevelt's New Deal recovery program.

President Thomas E. Dewey

The 1936 election also saw the emergence of a young pollster whose name would become synonymous with public opinion. In contrast to the *Literary Digest,* George Gallup correctly predicted that Roosevelt would beat Landon. Gallup's success in 1936 hinged on his use of quota sampling, which I'll have more to say about later in the chapter. For now, you need know only that quota sampling is based on a knowledge of the characteristics of the population being sampled: what proportion are men, what proportion are women, what proportions are of various incomes, ages, and so on. People are selected to match the population characteristics: the right number of poor, white, rural men; the right number of rich, African-American, urban women; and so on. The quotas are based on those variables most relevant to the study. By knowing the numbers of people with various incomes in the nation, Gallup selected his sample so as to ensure the right proportion of respondents at each income level.

Gallup and his American Institute of Public Opinion used quota sampling to good effect in 1936, 1940, and 1944—correctly picking the presidential winner each of those years. Then, in 1948, Gallup and most political pollsters suffered the embarrassment of picking New York Governor Thomas Dewey over incumbent President Harry Truman. Several factors accounted for the 1948 failure. First, most of the pollsters stopped polling in early October despite a steady trend toward Truman during the campaign. In addition, many voters were undecided throughout the campaign, and they went disproportionately for Truman when they stepped in the voting booth. More important, Gallup's failure rested on the unrepresentativeness of his samples.

Quota sampling—which had been effective in earlier years—was Gallup's undoing in 1948. This technique requires that the researcher know something about the total population (of voters in this instance). For national political polls, such information came primarily from census data. By 1948, however, World War II had produced a massive movement from country to city, radically changing the character of the U.S. population from what the 1940 census showed, and Gallup relied on 1940 census data. City dwellers, moreover, tended to vote Democratic; hence the over-representation of rural voters also underestimated the number of Democratic votes.

Two Types of Sampling Methods

In 1948, some academic researchers had been experimenting with **probability sampling** methods. Basically this technique involves the selection of a "random sample" from a list containing the names of everyone in the population you are interested in studying. By and large, the probability sampling methods used in 1948 were far more accurate than quota sampling techniques.

Today, probability sampling remains the primary method for selecting large, representative samples for social science research, such as the political polls described earlier. The bulk of this chapter will be addressed to the logic and techniques of probability sampling.

At the same time, many research situations often make probability sampling impossible or inappropriate. **Nonprobability sampling** techniques are often the most appropriate. We'll begin now with a discussion of some nonprobability sampling techniques used in social research, and then we'll examine the logic and techniques of probability sampling techniques.

■ NONPROBABILITY SAMPLING

Social research is often conducted in situations where you can't select the kinds of probability samples used in large-scale social surveys. Suppose you wanted to study homelessness: There is no list of all homeless individuals, nor are you likely to create such a list. Moreover, as you'll see, there are times when probability sampling wouldn't be appropriate even if it were possible. Many such situations call for nonprobability sampling. We'll examine four types in this section: reliance on available subjects, **purposive or judgmental sampling, snowball sampling,** and **quota sampling.** Then, we'll examine techniques for selecting **informants.**

Reliance on Available Subjects

Relying on available subjects, such as stopping people at a street corner or some other location, is an extremely risky sampling method, although it is used all too frequently. It is justified only if the researcher wants to study the characteristics of people passing the sampling point at specified times or if less risky sampling methods are not feasible. Even when use of this method is justified on grounds of feasibility, you must exercise great caution in generalizing from your data. Also, you should alert readers to the risks associated with this method.

University researchers frequently conduct surveys among the students enrolled in large lecture classes. The ease and inexpense of such a method explains its popularity, but it seldom produces data of any general value. It may be useful for pretesting a questionnaire, but such a sampling method should not be used for a study purportedly describing students as a whole.

Consider this report on the sampling design in an examination of knowledge and opinions about nutrition and cancer among medical students and family physicians:

■ The fourth-year medical students of the University of Minnesota Medical School in Minneapolis comprised the student population in this study. The physician population consisted of all physicians attending a "Family Practice Review and Update" course sponsored by the University of Minnesota Department of Continuing Medical Education.

(COOPER-STEPHENSON AND THEOLOGIDES 1981:472)

After all is said and done, what will the results of this study represent? They do not provide a meaningful comparison of medical students and family physicians in the United States or even in Minnesota. Who were the physicians who attended the course? We can guess that they were probably more concerned about their continuing education than other physicians, but we can't say that for sure. While such studies can be the source of useful insights, we must take care not to overgeneralize from them.

Purposive or Judgmental Sampling

Sometimes it's appropriate for you to select your sample on the basis of your own knowledge of the population, its elements, and the nature of your research aims: in short, based on your judgment and the purpose of the study. Especially in the initial design of a questionnaire, you might wish to select the widest variety of respondents to test the broad applicability of questions. Although the study findings would not represent any meaningful population, the test run might effectively uncover any peculiar defects in your questionnaire. This situation would be considered a pretest, however, rather than a final study.

In some instances, you may wish to study a small subset of a larger population in which many members of the subset are easily identified, but the enumeration of all of them would be nearly impossible. For example, you might want to study the leadership of a student protest movement; many of the leaders are easily visible, but it would not be feasible to define and sample all leaders. In studying all or a sample of the most visible leaders, you may collect data sufficient for your purposes.

Or let's say you want to compare left-wing and right-wing students. Because you may not be able to enumerate and sample from all such students, you might decide to sample the memberships of the Green Party and Young Americans for Freedom. Although such a sample design would not provide a good description of either left-wing or right-wing students as a whole, it might suffice for general comparative purposes.

Field researchers are often particularly interested in studying *deviant cases.* Often, their understanding of fairly regular patterns of attitudes and behaviors is further improved by examining those cases that do not fit into the regular pattern. You might gain important insights into the nature of school spirit as exhibited at a pep rally by interviewing people who did not appear to be caught up in the emotions of the crowd or by interviewing students who did not attend the rally at all.

Snowball Sampling

Another nonprobability sampling technique, one that some consider to be a form of accidental sampling, is called snowball sampling. Because this procedure is most commonly used in qualitative field research, we'll discuss it further in Chapter 11. Snowball sampling is appropriate when the members of a special population are difficult to locate. It thus might be appropriately used to find a sample of homeless individuals, migrant workers, undocumented immigrants, and so on. This procedure is implemented by collecting data on the few members of the target population you can locate, and then asking those individuals to provide the information needed to locate other members of that population whom they happen to know. *Snowball* refers to the process of accumulation as each located subject suggests other subjects. Because this procedure also results in samples with questionable representativeness, it's used primarily for exploratory purposes.

If you wish to learn, say, the pattern of recruitment to a community organization over time, you might begin by interviewing fairly recent recruits, asking them who introduced them to the group. You might then interview the people named, asking them who introduced *them* to the group. You might then interview those people named, asking, in part, who introduced *them*. In studying a loosely structured political group, you might ask one of the participants who he or she believes to be the most influential members of the group. You might interview those people and, in the course of the interviews, ask who *they* believe to be the most influential. In each of these examples, your sample would "snowball" as each of your interviewees suggested others.

Quota Sampling

As you know, quota sampling is the method that helped George Gallup avoid disaster in 1936—and set up the disaster of 1948. Like probability sampling, quota sampling addresses the issue of representativeness, although the two methods approach the issue quite differently.

Quota sampling begins with a *matrix*, or table, describing the characteristics of the target population. You need to know what proportion of the population is male and what proportion female, for example, and what proportions of each gender fall into various age categories, educational levels, ethnic groups, and so forth. In establishing a national quota sample, you would need to know what proportion of the national population is urban, eastern, male, under 25, white, working class, and the like, and all the other permutations of such a matrix.

Once such a matrix has been created and a relative proportion assigned to each cell in the matrix, you collect data from people having all the characteristics of a given cell. All the people in a given cell are then assigned a weight appropriate to their portion of the total population. When all the sample elements are so weighted, the overall data should provide a reasonable representation of the total population.

Quota sampling has several inherent problems. First, the *quota frame* (the proportions that different cells represent) must be accurate, and it is often difficult to get up-to-date information for this purpose. The Gallup failure to predict Truman as the presidential victor in 1948 was due partly to this problem. Second, biases may exist in the selection of sample elements within a given cell—even though its proportion of the population is accurately estimated. Instructed to interview five people who meet a given, complex set of characteristics, an interviewer may still avoid people living at the top of seven-story walk-ups, having particularly run-down homes, or owning vicious dogs.

In recent years, attempts have been made to combine probability and quota sampling methods, but the effectiveness of this effort remains to be seen. At present, you would be advised to treat quota sampling warily if your purpose is statistical description.

At the same time, the logic of quota sampling can sometimes be applied usefully to a field research project. In the study of a formal group, for example, you might wish to interview both leaders and nonleaders. In studying a student political organization, you might want to interview both radical and more moderate members of that group. In general, whenever representativeness is desired, you should use quota sampling and interview both men and women, young people and old, and so forth.

Selecting Informants

When field research involves the researcher's attempt to understand some social setting—a juvenile gang or local neighborhood, for example—much of that understanding will come from a collaboration with some members of the group being studied. Whereas social researchers speak of *respondents* as people who provide information about themselves, allowing the researcher to construct a composite picture of the group those respondents represent, *informants* are members of the group who can talk directly about the group per se.

Especially important to anthropologists, informants are important to other social researchers as well. If you wanted to learn about informal social networks in a local public housing project, for example, you would do well to locate individuals who could understand what you were looking for and help you find it.

When Jeffrey Johnson (1990) set out to study a salmon fishing camp, he evaluated potential informants regarding several criteria. Did their positions allow them to interact regularly with other members of the camp, for example, or were they isolated? (He found the carpenter had a wider range of interactions than the boat captain.) Was their information about the camp pretty much limited to their specific jobs, or did it cover many aspects of the operation? These and other criteria affected how useful different potential informants might be.

Usually, you'll want to select informants who are somewhat typical of the groups you are studying. Otherwise, their observations and opinions may be misleading. Interviewing only physicians will not give you a well-rounded view of how a community medical clinic is working, for example. Along the same lines, an anthropologist who interviewed only men (in a society where women were sheltered from outsiders) would get a biased view. Similarly, while Westernized informants, fluent in English, would be desirable in some obvious respects, they would not typify the members of an isolated, preliterate society.

Simply because they're the ones willing to work with outside investigators, informants will almost always be somewhat "marginal" or atypical within their group. Sometimes this is obvious. Other times, however, you'll learn about their marginality only in the course of your research.

In Jeffrey Johnson's study of a North Carolina fishing community, the county agent identified one fisherman who seemed squarely in the mainstream of the community. Moreover, he was cooperative and helpful to Johnson's research. The more Johnson worked with the fisherman, however, the more he found the man to be a marginal member of the fishing community.

■ First, he was a Yankee in a southern town. Second, he had a pension from the Navy [so he was not seen as a "serious fisherman" by others in the community].... Third, he was a major Republican activist in a mostly Democratic village. Finally, he kept his boat in an isolated anchorage, far from the community harbor.

(1990:56)

Informants' marginality may not only bias the view you get, but their marginal status may also limit their access (and hence yours) to the different sectors of the community you wish to study.

These comments should give you some sense of the concerns involved in nonprobability sampling, typically used in qualitative research projects. I conclude with the following injunction (Lofland and Lofland 1995:16):

■ Your overall goal is to collect the *richest possible data*. Rich data mean, ideally, a wide and diverse range of information collected over a relatively prolonged period of time. Again, ideally, you achieve this through direct, face-to-face contact with, and prolonged immersion in, some social location or circumstance. [emphasis original]

Let's shift gears now and look at sampling in large-scale surveys, aimed at precise, statistical descriptions of large populations. Sometimes we want to know the percentage of the population who are unemployed, plan to vote for Candidate X, or feel a rape victim should have the right to an abortion. These tasks are typically accomplished through the logic and techniques of probability sampling.

■ THE LOGIC OF PROBABILITY SAMPLING

If all members of a population were identical in all respects—all demographic characteristics, attitudes, experiences, behaviors, and so on—there would be no need for careful sampling procedures. In such a case, any sample would indeed

FIGURE 8-1
A Population of 100 Folks

44 white women
44 white men
6 African-American women
6 African-American men

be sufficient. In this extreme case of homogeneity, in fact, *one* case would suffice as a sample to study characteristics of the whole population.

In fact, of course, the human beings who compose any real population are quite heterogeneous, varying in many ways. Figure 8-1 offers a simplified illustration of a heterogeneous population: The 100 members of this small population differ by gender and race. We'll use this hypothetical micropopulation to illustrate various aspects of sampling through the chapter.

To provide useful descriptions of the total population, a sample of individuals from a population must contain essentially the same variations that exist in the population. This isn't as simple as it might seem, however.

Let's take a minute to look at some of the ways researchers might go astray. Then we'll see how probability sampling provides an efficient method for selecting a sample that should adequately reflect variations that exist in the population.

Conscious and Unconscious Sampling Bias

At first glance, it may look as though sampling is a pretty straightforward matter. To select a sample of 100 university students, you might simply go to campus and interview the first 100 students you find walking around campus. This kind of sampling method is often used by untrained researchers, but it has serious problems.

Figure 8-2 illustrates what can happen when you simply select people who are convenient for study. Although women are only 50 percent of our micropopulation, those closest to the researcher (in the upper-right corner) happen to be 70 percent women; and although the population is 12 percent black, none were selected into the sample.

Beyond the risks inherent in simply studying people who are convenient, other problems can arise. To begin, your own personal leanings may affect the sample to the point where it would not truly represent the student population. Suppose

The Logic of Probability Sampling 199

FIGURE 8-2
A Sample of Convenience:
Easy, but Not Representative

you're a little intimidated by students who look particularly "cool," feeling they might ridicule your research effort. You might consciously or unconsciously avoid interviewing such people. Or, you might feel that the attitudes of "super-straight-looking" students would be irrelevant to your research purposes, and so avoid interviewing them.

Even if you sought to interview a "balanced" group of students, you wouldn't know the exact proportions of different types of students making up such a balance, and you wouldn't always be able to identify the different types just by watching them walk by.

And even if you made a conscientious effort to interview every tenth student entering the university library, you could not be sure of a *representative* sample, since different types of students visit the library with different frequencies. Your sample would overrepresent students who visit the library more often.

When we speak of *bias* in connection with sampling, this simply means those selected are not "typical" or "representative" of the larger populations they have been chosen from. This kind of bias is virtually inevitable when you pick people by the seat of your pants.

Similarly, the "public-opinion call-in polls"— in which radio stations or newspapers ask people to call specified telephone numbers to register their opinions—cannot be trusted to represent general populations. At the very least, not everyone in the population will even be aware of the poll. This problem also invalidates polls by magazines and newspapers who publish coupons for readers to complete and mail in. Even among those who are aware of such polls, not all will express an opinion, especially if doing so will cost them a stamp, an envelope, or a telephone charge.

Ironically, the failure of such polls to represent all opinions equally was inadvertently acknowledged by Philip Perinelli (1986), a staff manager of AT&T Communications' DIAL-IT 900 Service, which offers a call-in poll facility to organizations. Perinelli attempted to counter criticisms by saying, "The 50-cent charge assures that only interested parties respond and helps assure also that no individual 'stuffs' the ballot box." We cannot determine general public opinion while considering "only interested parties." This excludes those who don't care 50-cents' worth, as well as those who recognize that such polls are not valid. Both types of people may have opinions and may even vote on election day. Perinelli's assertion that the 50-cent charge will prevent ballot stuffing actually means that only the wealthy can afford to engage in that practice.

The possibilities for inadvertent sampling bias are endless and not always obvious. Fortunately there are techniques that let us avoid bias.

Representativeness and Probability of Selection

Although the term **representativeness** has no precise, scientific meaning, it carries a common-sense meaning that makes it useful here. For our purpose, a sample will be representative of the population from which it is selected if the aggregate characteristics of the sample closely approximate those same aggregate characteristics in the population. (Samples need not be representative in all respects; representativeness is limited to those characteristics that are relevant to the substantive interests of the study, though you may not know which are relevant at first.) If the population, for example, contains 50 percent women, then a representative sample would also contain "close to" 50 percent women. Later, we'll discuss "how close" in detail.

A basic principle of probability sampling is that *a sample will be representative of the population from which it is selected if all members of the population have an equal chance of being selected in the sample.* (We'll see shortly that the size of the sample selected also affects the *degree* of representativeness.) Samples that have this quality are often labeled **EPSEM** samples (equal probability of selection method). Later I'll discuss variations of this principle, which forms the basis of probability sampling.

Moving beyond this basic principle, we must realize that samples—even carefully selected EPSEM samples—seldom if ever *perfectly* represent the populations from which they are drawn. Nevertheless, probability sampling offers two special advantages.

First, probability samples, although never perfectly representative, are typically *more representative* than other types of samples because the biases previously discussed are avoided. In practice, a probability sample is more likely to be representative of the population from which it is drawn than a nonprobability sample is.

Second, and more important, probability theory permits us to estimate the accuracy or representativeness of the sample. Conceivably, an uninformed researcher might, through wholly haphazard means, select a sample that nearly perfectly represents the larger population. The odds are against doing so, however, and we would be unable to estimate the likelihood that he or she has achieved representativeness. The probability sampler, on the other hand, can provide an accurate estimate of success or failure.

Following a brief glossary of sampling terminology, we'll examine the means the probability sampler uses to estimate the representativeness of the sample.

■ SAMPLING CONCEPTS AND TERMINOLOGY

The following discussions of sampling theory and practice use many technical terms, which I'll quickly define here. For the most part, I'll employ terms commonly used in sampling and statistical textbooks so that you may better understand those other sources.

In presenting this glossary, I would like to acknowledge a debt to Leslie Kish and his excellent textbook *Survey Sampling*. Although I've modified some of the conventions used by Kish, his presentation is easily the most important source of this discussion.

Element An *element* is that unit about which information is collected and that provides the basis of analysis. Typically, in survey research, elements are people or certain types of people. However, other kinds of units can constitute the elements for social research: Families, social clubs, or corporations might be the elements of a study. (*Note:* Elements and units of analysis are often the same in a given study, though the former refer to sample selection, the latter to data analysis.)

Population A *population* is the theoretically specified aggregation of study elements. Whereas the vague term *Americans* might be the target for a study, the delineation of the population would include the definition of the element *Americans* (for example, citizenship, residence) and the time referent for the study (Americans as of when?). Translating the abstract *adult New Yorkers* into a workable population would require a specification of the age defining *adult* and the boundaries of *New York*. Specifying the term *college student* would include a consideration of full- and part-time students, degree candidates and nondegree candidates, undergraduate and graduate students, and so forth.

Although researchers must begin with careful specification of their population, poetic license usually permits them to phrase their reports in terms of the hypothetical universe. For ease of presentation, even the most conscientious researcher normally speaks of "Americans" rather than "resident citizens of the United States of America as of November 12, 1985." The primary guide in this matter, as in most others, is that you should not mislead or deceive your readers.

Study Population A study population is that aggregation of elements from which the sample is actually selected. As a practical matter, you are seldom in a position to guarantee that every element meeting the theoretical definitions laid down actually has a chance of being selected in the sample. Even where lists of elements exist for sampling purposes, the lists are usually somewhat incomplete. Some students are always omitted, inadvertently, from student rosters. Some telephone subscribers request that their names and numbers be unlisted.

Often researchers decide to limit their study populations more severely than indicated in the preceding examples. National polling firms may limit their national samples to the 48 adjacent states, omitting Alaska and Hawaii for practical reasons. A researcher wishing to sample psychology professors may limit the study population to those who are serving in psychology departments, omitting those serving in other departments. (In a sense, we might say that these researchers have redefined their universes and populations, in which case they must make the revisions clear to their readers.)

Sampling Unit A *sampling unit* is that element or set of elements considered for selection in some stage of sampling. In a simple single-stage sample, the sampling units are the same as the elements and are probably the units of analysis. In more complex samples, however, different levels of sampling units may be employed. For example, you might select a sample of census blocks in a city, then select a sample of households on the selected blocks, and finally select a sample of adults from the selected households. The sampling units for these three stages of sampling are, respectively, census blocks, households, and adults, of which only the last of these are the elements. More specifically, the phrases *primary sampling units, secondary sampling units,* and *final sampling units* designate the successive stages.

Sampling Frame A *sampling frame* is the actual list of sampling units from which the sample, or some stage of the sample, is selected. In single-stage sampling designs, the sampling frame is simply a list of the study population, defined earlier. If a simple sample of students is selected from a student roster, the roster is the sampling frame. If the primary sampling unit for a complex population sample is the census block, the list of census blocks composes the sampling frame—in the form of a printed booklet, a magnetic tape file, or some other computerized record.

In a single-stage sample design, the sampling frame is a list of the elements composing the study population. In practice, existing sampling frames often define the study population rather than the other way around. We often begin with a population in mind for our study; then we search for possible sampling frames. The frames available for our use are examined and evaluated, and we decide which frame presents a study population most appropriate to our needs.

Though the relationship between populations and sampling frames is critical, it has not received sufficient attention. A later section will pursue this issue in greater detail.

Observation Unit An *observation unit*, or unit of data collection, is an element or aggregation of elements from which information is collected. Again, the unit of analysis and unit of observation are often the same—the individual person—but that need not be the case. Thus the researcher may interview heads of households (the observation units) to collect information about all members of the households (the units of analysis).

Our task is simplified when the unit of analysis and the observation unit are the same. Often this isn't possible or feasible, however, and in such situations we need to exercise some ingenuity in collecting data relevant to our units of analysis without actually observing those units.

Variable As discussed earlier, a *variable* is a set of mutually exclusive attributes: gender, age, employment status, and so forth. The elements of a given population may be described in terms of their individual attributes on a given variable. Often social research aims at describing the distribution of attributes composing a variable in a population. Thus a researcher may describe the age distribution of a population by examining the relative frequency of different ages among members of the population.

A variable, by definition, must possess *variation*; if all elements in the population have the same attribute, that attribute is a *constant* in the population, rather than part of a variable.

Parameter A *parameter* is the summary description of a given variable in a population. The mean income of all families in a city and the age distribution of the city's population are parameters. An important portion of social research involves the estimation of population parameters on the basis of sample observations.

Statistic A *statistic* is the summary description of a given variable in a sample. Thus the mean income computed from a sample and the age distribution of that sample are statistics. Sample statistics are used to make estimates of population parameters.

Sampling Error Probability sampling methods seldom, if ever, provide statistics exactly equal to the parameters they are to estimate. Probability theory, however, permits us to estimate the degree of error to be expected for a given sample design. *Sampling error* is discussed in more detail later.

Confidence Levels and Confidence Intervals The two key components of sampling error estimates are *confidence levels* and *confidence intervals*. We express the accuracy of our sample statistics in terms of a level of confidence that the statistics fall within a specified interval from the parameter. For example, we may say we are 95 percent confident that our sample statistics (for example, 50 percent favor Candidate X) are within plus or minus 5 percentage points of the population parameter. As the confidence interval is expanded for a given statistic, our confidence increases, and we may say we are 99.9 percent confident that our statistic falls within ±7.5 percentage points of the parameter. In the next section, I'll describe how sampling intervals and levels are calculated, making these two concepts even clearer.

■ PROBABILITY SAMPLING THEORY AND SAMPLING DISTRIBUTION

With definitions presented, we can now examine the basic theory of probability sampling as it applies to social research. We'll also consider the logic of sampling distribution and sampling error with regard to a **binomial variable**—a variable composed of two attributes.

Probability Sampling Theory

The ultimate purpose of sampling is to select a set of elements from a population in such a way that descriptions of those elements (statistics) accurately portray the parameters of the total population from which the elements are selected. Probability sampling enhances the likelihood of accomplishing this aim and also provides methods for estimating the degree of probable success.

FIGURE 8-3
A Population of Ten People with $0–$9

Random selection is the key to this process. In random selection, each element has an equal chance of selection independent of any other event in the selection process. Flipping a perfect coin is the most frequently cited example: The "selection" of a head or a tail is independent of previous selections of heads or tails. Rolling a perfect set of dice is another example. Such images of random selection seldom apply directly to social research sampling methods, however. The social researcher more typically uses tables of random numbers or computer programs that provide a random selection of sampling units. In Chapter 10, on survey research, we'll see how computers are used to select random telephone numbers for interviewing—called *random-digit dialing*.

The reasons for using random selection methods—random-number tables or computer programs—are twofold. First, this procedure serves as a check on conscious or unconscious bias on the part of the researcher. The researcher who selects cases on an intuitive basis might very well select cases that would support his or her research expectations or hypotheses. Random selection erases this danger. More important, random selection offers access to the body of probability theory, which provides the basis for estimates of population parameters and estimates of error. Let's now examine this probability theory in greater detail.

The Sampling Distribution of Ten Cases

To introduce the statistics of probability sampling, let's begin with a simple example of only ten cases.* Suppose there are ten people in a group, and each has a certain amount of money in his or her pocket. To simplify, let's assume that one person has no money, another has one dollar, another has two dollars, and so forth up to the person with nine dollars. Figure 8-3 presents the population of ten people.

Our task is to determine the average amount of money one person has: specifically, the **mean** number of dollars. If you simply add up the money shown in Figure 8-3, you'll find that the total is $45, so the mean is $4.50. Our purpose in the rest of this exercise is to estimate that mean

---
*I want to thank Hanan Selvin for suggesting this method of introducing probability sampling.

Chapter 8: The Logic of Sampling

FIGURE 8-4
The Sampling Distribution of Samples of 1

[Graph: Number of samples (Total = 10) on y-axis from 1 to 10; Estimate of mean (Sample size = 1) on x-axis from $0 to $9. True mean = $4.50 indicated with an arrow. Ten dots, one at each value from $0 through $9.]

without actually observing all ten individuals. We'll do that by selecting random samples from the population and using the means of those samples to estimate the mean of the whole population.

To start, suppose we were to select—at random—a sample of only *one* person from the ten. Depending on which person we selected, we'd estimate the group's mean as anywhere from $0 to $9. Figure 8-3 displays the ten possible samples.

The ten dots shown on the graph in Figure 8-4 represent the ten "sample" means we would get as estimates of the population. The distribution of the dots on the graph is called the *sampling distribution*. Obviously, it wouldn't be a very good idea to select a sample of only one, since we stand a very good chance of missing the true mean of $4.50 by quite a bit.

But what if we take samples of two each? As you can see from Figure 8-5, increasing the sample size improves our estimations. There are now 45 possible samples: [$0 $1], [$0 $2], . . . [$7 $8], [$8 $9]. Moreover, some of those samples produce the same means. For example, [$0 $6], [$1 $5], and [$2 $4] all produce means of $3. In Figure 8-5, the three dots shown above the $3 mean represent those three samples.

The 45 sample means are not evenly distributed, as you can see. Rather, they are somewhat clustered around the true value of $4.50. Only two samples deviate by as much as four dollars from the true value ([$0 $1] and [$8 $9]), whereas five of the samples would give the true estimate of $4.50; another eight samples miss the mark by only fifty cents (plus or minus).

Now suppose we select even larger samples. What do you suppose that will do to our estimates of the mean? Figure 8-6 presents the sampling distributions of samples of 3, 4, 5, and 6.

The progression of sampling distributions is clear. Every increase in sample size improves the distribution of estimates of the mean. The limiting case in this procedure, of course, is to select a

FIGURE 8-5
The Sampling Distribution of Samples of 2

True mean = $4.50

Number of samples (Total = 45)

Estimate of mean (Sample size = 2)

sample of ten. There would be only one possible sample (everyone) and it would give us the true mean of $4.50.

Binomial Sampling Distribution

Let's turn now to a more realistic sampling situation and see how the notion of sampling distribution applies, using a simple example involving a population much larger than ten. Let's assume for the moment that we wish to study the student population of State University (SU) to determine approval or disapproval of a student conduct code proposed by the administration. The study population will be that aggregation of, say, 20,000 students contained in a student roster: the sampling frame. The elements will be the individual students at SU. The variable under consideration will be attitudes toward the code, a binomial variable: approve and disapprove. We'll select a random sample of, say, 100 students for the purposes of estimating the entire student body.

The horizontal axis of Figure 8-7 presents all *possible* values of this parameter in the population—from 0 percent to 100 percent approval. The midpoint of the axis—50 percent—represents half the students approving of the code and the other half disapproving.

To choose our sample, we give each student on the student roster a number and select 100 random numbers from a table of random numbers. Then we interview the 100 students whose numbers have been selected and ask for their attitudes toward the student code: whether they approve or disapprove. Suppose this operation gives us 48 students who approve of the code and 52 who disapprove. We present this statistic by placing a dot on the *x* axis at the point representing 48 percent.

Now let's suppose we select another sample of 100 students in exactly the same fashion and measure their approval or disapproval of the student code. Perhaps 51 students in the second sample

FIGURE 8-6
The Sampling Distributions of Samples of 3, 4, 5, and 6

FIGURE 8-7
Range of Possible Sample Study Results

|_____|_____|_____|
0   50   100
Percent of students approving of the student code

approve of the code. We place another dot in the appropriate place on the x axis. Repeating this process once more, we may discover that 52 students in the third sample approve of the code.

Figure 8-8 presents the three different sample statistics representing the percentages of students in each of the three random samples who approved of the student code. The basic rule of random sampling is that such samples drawn from a population give estimates of the parameter that pertains in the total population. Each of the random samples, then, gives us an estimate of the percentage of students in the total student body who approve of the student code. Unhappily, however, we have selected three samples and now have three separate estimates.

To retrieve ourselves from this problem, let's draw more and more samples of 100 students each, question each of the samples concerning their approval or disapproval of the code, and plot the new sample statistics on our summary graph. In drawing many such samples, we discover that some of the new samples provide duplicate estimates, as in the illustration of ten cases. Figure 8-9 shows the sampling distribution of, say, hundreds of samples. This is often referred to as a *normal curve*.

Note that by increasing the number of samples selected and interviewed, we have also increased the range of estimates provided by the sampling operation. In one sense we have increased our dilemma in attempting to guess the parameter in the population. Probability theory, however, provides certain important rules regarding the sampling distribution presented in Figure 8-9.

First, if many independent random samples are selected from a population, the sample statistics provided by those samples will be *distributed around the population parameter* in a known way. Thus, although Figure 8-9 shows a wide range of estimates, more of them are in the vicinity of 50 percent than elsewhere in the graph. Probability theory tells us, then, that the true value is in the vicinity of 50 percent.

Second, probability theory gives us a formula for estimating *how closely* the sample statistics are clustered around the true value. This formula contains three factors: the parameter, the sample size, and the *standard error* (a measure of sampling error):

$$s = \sqrt{\frac{P \times Q}{n}}$$

The symbols P and Q in the formula equal the population parameters for the binomial: If 60 percent of the student body approve of the code and 40 percent disapprove, P and Q are 60 percent

FIGURE 8-8
Results Produced by Three Hypothetical Studies

Sample 1 (48%) Sample 2 (51%) Sample 3 (52%)

|_____|_____|_____|
0   50   100
Percent of students approving of the student code

FIGURE 8-9
The Sampling Distribution

and 40 percent, respectively, or .6 and .4. Note that $Q = 1 - P$ and $P = 1 - Q$. The symbol n equals the number of cases in each sample, and s is the standard error.

Let's assume that the population parameter in the student example is 50 percent approving of the code and 50 percent disapproving. Recall that we've been selecting samples of 100 cases each. When these numbers are put into the formula, we find that the standard error equals .05, or 5 percent.

In probability theory, the standard error is a valuable piece of information because it indicates the extent to which the sample estimates will be distributed around the population parameter. If you are familiar with the *standard deviation* in statistics, you may recognize that the standard error, in this case, is the standard deviation of the sampling distribution.

Specifically, probability theory indicates that certain proportions of the sample estimates will fall within specified increments—each equal to one standard error—from the population parameter. Approximately 34 percent (.3413) of the sample estimates will fall within one standard error increment above the population parameter, and another 34 percent will fall within one standard error below the parameter. In our example, the standard error increment is 5 percent, so we know that 34 percent of our samples will give estimates of student approval between 50 percent (the parameter) and 55 percent (one standard error above); another 34 percent of the samples will give estimates between 50 percent and 45 percent (one standard error below the parameter). Taken together, then, we know that roughly two-thirds (68 percent) of the samples will give estimates within ±5 percent of the parameter.

Moreover, probability theory dictates that roughly 95 percent of the samples will fall within plus or minus two standard errors of the true value, and 99.9 percent of the samples will fall within plus or minus three standard errors. In our present example, then, we know that only one sample out of a thousand would give an estimate lower than 35 percent approval or higher than 65 percent.

The proportion of samples falling within one, two, or three standard errors of the parameter is constant for any random sampling procedure such as the one just described, providing that a large number of samples are selected. The size of the standard error in any given case, however, is a function of the population parameter and the sample size. If we return to the formula for a moment, we note that the standard error will increase as a function of an increase in the quantity P times Q. Note further that this quantity reaches its maximum in the situation of an even split in the population. If $P = .5$, $PQ = .25$; if $P = .6$, $PQ =$

.24; if $P = .8$, $PQ = .16$; if $P = .99$, $PQ = .0099$. By extension, if P is either 0.0 or 1.0 (either 0 percent or 100 percent approve of the student code), the standard error will be 0. If everyone in the population has the same attitude (no variation), then every sample will give exactly that estimate.

The standard error is also a function of the sample size—an *inverse* function. As the sample size increases, the standard error decreases. As the sample size increases, the several samples will be clustered nearer to the true value. Another general guideline is evident in the formula: Because of the square root formula, the standard error is reduced by half if the sample size is *quadrupled*. In our present example, samples of 100 produce a standard error of 5 percent; to reduce the standard error to 2.5 percent, we must increase the sample size to 400.

All of this information is provided by established probability theory in reference to the selection of large numbers of random samples. (If you have taken a statistics course, you may know this as the "Central Tendency Theorem.") If the population parameter is known and many random samples are selected, we can predict how many of the samples will fall within specified intervals from the parameter. Be clear that this discussion only illustrates the *logic* of probability sampling; it does not describe the way research is actually conducted. Usually, we do not know the parameter: We conduct a sample survey to estimate that value. Moreover, we don't actually select large numbers of samples: We select only one sample. Nevertheless, the preceding discussion of probability theory provides the basis for inferences about the typical social research situation. Knowing what it would be like to select thousands of samples allows us to make assumptions about the one sample we do select and study.

Whereas probability theory specifies that 68 percent of that fictitious large number of samples would produce estimates falling within one standard error of the parameter, we turn the logic around and infer that any single random sample has a 68-percent chance of falling within that range. In this regard we speak of *confidence levels*:

We are 68 percent confident that our sample estimate is within one standard error of the parameter. Or we may say that we are 95 percent confident that the sample statistic is within two standard errors of the parameter, and so forth. Quite reasonably, our confidence increases as the margin for error is extended. We are virtually positive (99.9 percent) that we are within three standard errors of the true value.

Although we may be confident (at some level) of being within a certain range of the parameter, we have already noted that we seldom know what the parameter is. To resolve this problem, we substitute our sample estimate for the parameter in the formula; that is, lacking the true value, we substitute the best available guess.

The result of these inferences and estimations is that we can estimate a population parameter and also the expected degree of error on the basis of one sample drawn from a population. Beginning with the question, "What percentage of the student body approves of the student code?" you could select a random sample of 100 students and interview them. You might then report that your best estimate is that 50 percent of the student body approves of the code and that you are 95 percent confident that between 40 and 60 percent (plus or minus two standard errors) approve. The range from 40 to 60 percent is called the *confidence interval*. (At the 68 percent confidence level, the confidence interval would be 45–55 percent.)

The logic of confidence levels and confidence intervals also provides the basis for determining the appropriate sample size for a study. Once you have decided on the degree of sampling error you can tolerate, you'll be able to calculate the number of cases needed in your sample. Thus, for example, if you want to be 95 percent confident that your study findings are accurate within ±5 percentage points of the population parameters, you should select a sample of at least 400. (Appendix H is a convenient guide in this regard.)

This then is the basic logic of probability sampling. Random selection permits the researcher to link findings from a sample to the body of probability theory so as to estimate the accuracy of those findings. All statements of accuracy in sampling must specify both a confidence level and a confidence interval. The researcher must report that he or she is *x* percent confident that the population parameter is between two specific values.

Here's how George Gallup (1984:7) described his sampling error in a newspaper report of a recent Gallup Poll regarding attitudes of children and parents:

■ The adult findings are based on in-person interviews with 1520 adults, 18 and older, conducted in more than 300 scientifically selected localities across the nation during the period October 26–29. For results based on samples of this size, one can say with 95 percent confidence that the error attributable to sampling and other random effects could be three percentage points in either direction.

Or hear what the *New York Times* ("How the Poll Was Conducted," 1995:15) had to say about a poll it conducted on religious opinions:

■ In theory, in 19 cases out of 20 the results based on such samples will differ by no more than three percentage points in either direction, from what would have been obtained by seeking out all American adults.

The next time you read statements like these in the newspaper, they should make more sense to you. Be wary, however, that such statements are sometimes made when they are not warranted, but you are now able to make that determination.

The foregoing discussion has considered only one type of statistic: the percentages produced by a *binomial* or **dichotomous variable.** The same logic, however, would apply to the examination of other statistics, such as mean income. Because the computations are somewhat more complicated in such a case, I have chosen to consider only binomials in this introduction.

You should be cautioned that the survey uses of probability theory as discussed previously are technically not wholly justified. The theory of sampling distribution makes assumptions that almost never apply in survey conditions. The number of samples contained within specified increments of standard errors, for example, assumes an infinitely large population, an infinite number of samples, and sampling with replacement. Moreover, the inferential jump from the distribution of several samples to the probable characteristics of one sample has been grossly oversimplified here.

These cautions are offered to give you perspective. Researchers often appear to overestimate the precision of estimates produced by use of probability theory in connection with social research. As I'll mention elsewhere in this chapter and throughout the book, variations in sampling techniques and nonsampling factors may further reduce the legitimacy of such estimates. Nevertheless, the calculations discussed in this section can be extremely valuable to you in understanding and evaluating your data. Although the calculations do not provide as precise estimates as some researchers might assume, they can be quite valid for practical purposes. They are unquestionably more valid than less rigorously derived estimates based on less rigorous sampling methods.

Most important, you should be familiar with the basic *logic* underlying the calculations. If you are so informed, you will be able to react sensibly to your own data and to those reported by others.

■ POPULATIONS AND SAMPLING FRAMES

The immediately preceding section has dealt with the theoretical model for social research sampling. Although the research consumer, student, and researcher need to understand that theory, it is no less important that they appreciate the less-than-perfect conditions that exist in the field. The present section is devoted to a discussion of one aspect of field conditions that requires a compromise with regard to theoretical conditions and assumptions. Here we'll consider the congruence of or disparity between populations of sampling frames.

Simply put, a sampling frame is the list or quasi list of elements from which a probability sample is selected. Here are some reports of sampling frames appearing in research journals:

■ The data for this research were obtained from a random sample of parents of children in the third grade in public and parochial schools in Yakima County, Washington.

(PETERSEN AND MAYNARD 1981:92)

■ The sample at Time 1 consisted of 160 names drawn randomly from the telephone directory of Lubbock, Texas.

(TAN 1980:242)

■ The data reported in this paper . . . were gathered from a probability sample of adults aged 18 and over residing in households in the 48 contiguous United States. Personal interviews with 1,914 respondents were conducted by the Survey Research Center of the University of Michigan during the fall of 1975.

(JACKMAN AND SENTER 1980:345)

Properly drawn samples provide information appropriate for describing the population of elements composing the sampling frame—nothing more. I emphasize this point in view of the all-too-common tendency for researchers to select samples from a given sampling frame and then make assertions about a population similar to, but not identical to, the population defined by the sampling frame.

For example, take a look at this report, which discusses the drugs most frequently prescribed by U.S. physicians:

■ Information on prescription drug sales is not easy to obtain. But Rinaldo V. DeNuzzo, a professor of pharmacy at the Albany College of Pharmacy, Union University, Albany, NY, has been tracking prescription drug sales for 25 years by polling nearby drugstores. He publishes the results in an industry trade magazine, *MM&M*.

DeNuzzo's latest survey, covering 1980, is based on reports from 66 pharmacies in 48 communities in New York and New Jersey. Unless there is something peculiar about that part of the country, his findings can be taken as representative of what happens across the country.

(MOSKOWITZ 1981:33)

The main thing that should strike you is the casual comment about whether there is anything peculiar about New York and New Jersey. There is. The lifestyle in these two states hardly typifies the other 48. We cannot assume that residents in these large, urbanized, Eastern seaboard states necessarily have the same drug-use patterns as residents of Mississippi, Nebraska, or Vermont.

Does the survey even represent prescription patterns in New York and New Jersey? To determine that, we would have to know something about the manner in which the 48 communities and the 66 pharmacies were selected. We should be wary in this regard, in view of the reference to "polling nearby drugstores." As we'll see, there are several methods for selecting samples that insure representativeness, and unless they are used, we should not generalize from the study findings.

Studies of organizations are often the simplest from a sampling standpoint because organizations typically have membership lists. In such cases, the list of members constitutes an excellent sampling frame. If a random sample is selected from a membership list, the data collected from that sample may be taken as representative of all members—if all members are included in the list.

Populations that can be sampled from good organizational lists include elementary school, high school, and university students and faculty; church members; factory workers; fraternity or sorority members; members of social, service, or political clubs; and members of professional associations.

The preceding comments apply primarily to local organizations. Often statewide or national organizations do not have a single membership list. There is, for example, no single list of Episcopalian church members. However, a slightly more complex sample design could take advantage of local church membership lists by first sampling churches and then subsampling the membership lists of those churches selected. (More about that later.)

Other lists of individuals may be especially relevant to the research needs of a particular study. Government agencies maintain lists of registered voters, for example, that might be used if you wanted to conduct a preelection poll or an in-depth examination of voting behavior—but you must insure that the list is up-to-date. Similar lists contain the names of automobile owners, welfare recipients, taxpayers, business permit holders, licensed professionals, and so forth. Although it may be difficult to gain access to some of these lists, they provide excellent sampling frames for specialized research purposes.

Realizing that the sampling elements in a study need not be individual persons, we may note that the lists of other types of elements also exist: universities, businesses of various types, cities, academic journals, newspapers, unions, political clubs, professional associations, and so forth.

Telephone directories are frequently used for "quick and dirty" public opinion polls. Undeniably they are easy and inexpensive to use—no doubt the reason for their popularity. And, if you want to make assertions about telephone subscribers, the directory is a fairly good sampling frame. (Realize, of course, that a given directory will not include new subscribers or those who have requested unlisted numbers. Sampling is further complicated by the directories' inclusion of nonresidential listings.) Unfortunately, telephone directories are all too often used as a listing of a city's population or of its voters. Of the many defects in this reasoning, the chief one involves a social-class bias. Poor people are less likely to have telephones; rich people may have more than one line. A telephone directory sample, therefore, is likely to have a middle- or upper-class bias.

The class bias inherent in telephone directory samples is often hidden. Preelection polls conducted in this fashion are sometimes quite accurate, perhaps because of the class bias evident in voting itself: Poor people are less likely to vote. Frequently, then, these two biases nearly coincide, so that the results of a telephone poll may come very close to the final election outcome. Unhappily, you never know for sure until after the election. And sometimes, as in the case of the 1936 *Literary Digest* poll, you may discover that the voters have not acted according to the expected class biases. The ultimate disadvantage of this method, then, is the researcher's inability to estimate the degree of error to be expected in the sample findings. Street directories and tax maps are often used for easy samples of households, but they may also suffer from incompleteness and possible bias. For example, in strictly zoned urban regions, illegal housing units are unlikely to appear on official records. As a result, such units could not be selected, and sample findings could not be representative of those units, which are often poorer and more overcrowded than the average.

Though most of these comments apply to the United States, the situation is quite different in some other countries. In Japan, for example, the government maintains quite accurate population registration lists. Moreover, citizens are required by law to keep their information up-to-date, such as changes in residence or births and deaths in the household. As a consequence, you can select simple random samples of the Japanese population more easily. Such a registration list in the United States would conflict directly with this country's norms regarding individual privacy.

Review of Populations and Sampling Frames

Because social research literature gives surprisingly little attention to the issues of populations and sampling frames, I've devoted special attention to them here. Here is a summary of the main guidelines to remember:

1. Findings based on a sample can be taken as representing only the aggregation of elements that compose the sampling frame.
2. Often, sampling frames do not truly include all the elements their names might imply. Omissions are almost inevitable. Thus a first concern of the researcher must be to assess the extent of the omissions and to correct them if possible. (Realize, of course, that the researcher may feel he or she can safely ignore a small number of omissions that cannot easily be corrected.)
3. To be generalized even to the population composing the sampling frame, all elements must have equal representation in the frame: Typically, each element should appear only once.

Elements that appear more than once will have a greater probability of selection, and the sample will, overall, overrepresent those elements.

Other, more practical matters relating to populations and sampling frames will be treated elsewhere in this book. For example, the form of the sampling frame—such as a list in a publication, a 3-by-5 cardfile, computer disks, or magnetic tapes—can affect how easy it is to use. And ease of use may often take priority over scientific considerations: An "easier" list may be chosen over a "harder" one, even though the latter is more appropriate to the target population. We should not take a dogmatic position in this regard, but every researcher should carefully weigh the relative advantages and disadvantages of such alternatives.

■ TYPES OF SAMPLING DESIGNS

Up to this point, we've focused on simple random sampling (SRS). And, indeed, the body of statistics typically used by social researchers assumes such a sample. As you'll see shortly, however, you have several options in choosing your sampling method, and you'll seldom if ever choose simple random sampling. There are two reasons for this. First, with all but the simplest sampling frame, simple random sampling is not feasible. Second, and probably surprisingly, simple random sampling may not be the most accurate method available. Let's turn now to a discussion of simple random sampling and the other options available.

Simple Random Sampling

As noted, **simple random sampling** is the basic sampling method assumed in the statistical computations of social research. Because the mathematics of random sampling are especially complex, we'll detour around them in favor of describing the ways of employing this method in the field.

Once a sampling frame has been properly established, to use simple random sampling the researcher assigns a single number to each element in the list, not skipping any number in the process. A table of random numbers (Appendix E) is then used to select elements for the sample. The box entitled "Using a Table of Random Numbers" explains its use.

If your sampling frame is in a machine-readable form, such as computer disk or magnetic tape, a simple random sample can be selected automatically by computer. (In effect, the computer program numbers the elements in the sampling frame, generates its own series of random numbers, and prints out the list of elements selected.)

Figure 8-10 offers a graphic illustration of simple random sampling. Note that the members of our hypothetical micropopulation have been numbered from 1 to 100. Moving to Appendix E, we decide to use the last two digits of the first column and to begin with the third number from the top. This yields person number 30 as the first one selected into the sample. Number 67 is next, and so forth. (Person 100 would have been selected if "00" had come up in the list.)

Systematic Sampling

Simple random sampling is seldom used in practice. As you'll see, it's not usually the most efficient method, and it can be laborious if done manually. SRS typically requires a list of elements. When such a list is available, researchers usually employ systematic sampling rather than simple random sampling.

In **systematic sampling,** every *k*th element in the total list is chosen (systematically) for inclusion in the sample. If the list contains 10,000 elements and you want a sample of 1,000, you select every tenth element for your sample. To insure against any possible human bias in using this method, you should select the first element at random. Thus, in the preceding example, you would begin by selecting a random number between one and ten. The element having that number is included in the sample, plus every tenth element following it. This method is technically referred to as a *systematic sample with a random start.* Two terms are frequently used in connection with systematic sampling. The **sampling interval** is the standard distance between elements selected

Using a Table of Random Numbers

IN SOCIAL research, it's often appropriate to select a set of random numbers from a table such as the one in Appendix E. Here's how to do that.

Suppose you want to select a simple random sample of 100 people (or other units) out of a population totaling 980.

1. To begin, number the members of the population: in this case, from 1 to 980. Now the problem is to select 100 random numbers. Once you've done that, your sample will consist of the people having the numbers you've selected. (*Note:* It's not essential to actually number them, as long as you're sure of the total. If you have them in a list, for example, you can always count through the list after you've selected the numbers.)

2. The next step is to determine the number of digits you'll need in the random numbers you select. In our example, there are 980 members of the population, so you'll need three-digit numbers to give everyone a chance of selection. (If there were 11,825 members of the population, you'd need to select five-digit numbers.) Thus, we want to select 100 random numbers in the range from 001 to 980.

3. Now turn to the first page of Appendix E. Notice there are several rows and columns of five-digit numbers, and there are several pages. The table represents a series of random numbers in the range from 00001 to 99999. To use the table for your hypothetical sample, you have to answer these questions:
   a. How will you create three-digit numbers out of five-digit numbers?
   b. What pattern will you follow in moving through the table to select your numbers?
   c. Where will you start?

   Each of these questions has several satisfactory answers. The key is to create a plan and follow it. Here's an example.

4. To create three-digit numbers from five-digit numbers, let's agree to select five-digit numbers from the table but consider only the left-most three digits in each case. If we picked the first number on the first page—10480—we would only consider the 104. (We could agree to take the digits furthest to the right, 480, or the middle

---

in the sample: ten in the preceding sample. The sampling ratio is the proportion of elements in the population that are selected: 1/10 in the example.

$$\text{sampling interval} = \frac{\text{population size}}{\text{sample size}}$$

$$\text{sampling ratio} = \frac{\text{sample size}}{\text{population size}}$$

In practice, systematic sampling is virtually identical to simple random sampling. If the list of elements is indeed randomized before sampling, one might argue that a systematic sample drawn from that list is in fact a simple random sample. By now, debates over the relative merits of simple random sampling and systematic sampling have been resolved largely in favor of the latter, simpler method. Empirically, the results are virtually identical. And, as you'll see in a later section, systematic sampling, in some instances, is slightly more accurate than simple random sampling.

There is one danger involved in systematic sampling. The arrangement of elements in the list can make systematic sampling unwise. Such an arrangement is usually called *periodicity*. If the list of elements is arranged in a cyclical pattern that coincides with the sampling interval, a grossly biased sample may be drawn. Two examples will illustrate this.

In a classic study of soldiers during World War II, the researchers selected a systematic sample from unit rosters. Every tenth soldier on the roster was selected for the study. The rosters, how-three digits, 048, and any of these plans would work.) They key is to make a plan and stick with it. For convenience, let's use the left-most three digits.

5. We can also choose to progress through the tables any way we want: down the columns, up them, across to the right or to the left, or diagonally. Again, any of these plans will work just fine so long as we stick to it. For convenience, let's agree to move down the columns. When we get to the bottom of one column, we'll go to the top of the next; when we exhaust a given page, we'll start at the top of the first column of the next page.

6. Now, where do we start? You can close your eyes and stick a pencil into the table and start wherever the pencil point lands. (I know it doesn't sound scientific, but it works.) Or, if you're afraid you'll hurt the book or miss it altogether, close your eyes and make up a column number and a row number. ("I'll pick the number in the fifth row of column 2.") Start with that number.

7. Let's suppose we decide to start with the fifth number in column 2. If you look on the first page of Appendix E, you'll see that the starting number is 39975. We have selected 399 as our first random number, and we have 99 more to go. Moving down the second column, we select 069, 729, 919, 143, 368, 695, 409, 939, and so forth. At the bottom of column 2, we select number 104 and continue to the top of column 3: 015, 255, and so on.

8. See how easy it is? But trouble lies ahead. When we reach column 5, we are speeding along, selecting 816, 309, 763, 078, 061, 277, 988 . . . Wait a minute! There are only 980 students in the senior class. How can we pick number 988? The solution is simple: Ignore it. Any time you come across a number that lies outside your range, skip it and continue on your way: 188, 174, and so forth. The same solution applies if the same number comes up more than once. If you select 399 again, for example, just ignore it the second time.

9. That's it. You keep up the procedure until you've selected 100 random numbers. Returning to your list, your sample consists of person number 399, person number 69, person number 729, and so forth.

ever, were arranged in a table of organizations: sergeants first, then corporals and privates, squad by squad. Each squad had ten members. As a result, every tenth person on the roster was a squad sergeant. The systematic sample selected contained only sergeants. It could, of course, have been the case that no sergeants were selected for the same reason.

As another example, suppose we select a sample of apartments in an apartment building. If the sample is drawn from a list of apartments arranged in numerical order (for example, 101, 102, 103, 104, 201, 202, and so on), there is a danger of the sampling interval coinciding with the number of apartments on a floor or some multiple thereof. Then the samples might include only northwest-corner apartments or only apartments near the elevator. If these types of apartments have some other particular characteristic in common (for example, higher rent), the sample will be biased. The same danger would appear in a systematic sample of houses in a subdivision arranged with the same number of houses on a block.

In considering a systematic sample from a list, then, you should carefully examine the nature of that list. If the elements are arranged in any particular order, you should figure out whether that order will bias the sample to be selected and take steps to counteract any possible bias (for example, take a simple random sample from cyclical portions).

In summary, however, systematic sampling is usually superior to simple random sampling, in

FIGURE 8-10
A Simple Random Sample

	Appendix E Table of Random Numbers	
10480	15011	01536
22368	46573	25595
241	30	48360	22527
421	67	93093	06243
375	70	39975	81837
779	21	06907	11008
995	62	72905	56420
963	01	91977	05463
895	79	14342	63661
854	75	36857	53342
289	18	69578	88231
635	53	40961	48235
09429	93969	52636

The sample: 30, 67, 70, 21, 62, 01, 79, 75, 18, 53

convenience if nothing else. Problems in the ordering of elements in the sampling frame can usually be remedied quite easily.

Stratified Sampling

In the two preceding sections, we discussed two methods of sample selection from a list: random and systematic. **Stratification** is not an alternative to these methods; rather, it represents a possible modification in their use.

Simple random sampling and systematic sampling both ensure a degree of representativeness and permit an estimate of the error present. Stratified sampling is a method for obtaining a greater degree of representativeness—decreasing the probable sampling error. To understand this method, we must return briefly to the basic theory of sampling distribution.

Recall that sampling error is reduced by two factors in the sample design. First, a large sample produces a smaller sampling error than a small sample. Second, a homogeneous population produces samples with smaller sampling errors than does a heterogeneous population. If 99 percent of the population agrees with a certain statement, it's extremely unlikely that any probability sample will greatly misrepresent the extent of agreement. If the population is split 50–50 on the statement, then the sampling error will be much greater.

Stratified sampling is based on this second factor in sampling theory. Rather than selecting your sample from the total population at large, you ensure that appropriate numbers of elements are drawn from homogeneous subsets of that population. To get a stratified sample of university students, for example, you would first organize your population by college class and then draw appropriate numbers of frosh, sophomores, juniors, and seniors. In a nonstratified sample, representation by class would be subjected to the same sampling error as other variables. In a sample stratified by class, the sampling error on this variable is reduced to zero.

Even more complex stratification methods are possible. In addition to stratifying by class, you might also stratify by gender, by GPA, and so forth. In this fashion you might be able to insure that your sample would contain the proper numbers of male sophomores with a 4.0 average, of female sophomores with a 4.0 average, and so forth.

The ultimate function of stratification, then, is to organize the population into homogeneous subsets (with heterogeneity between subsets) and to select the appropriate number of elements from each. To the extent that the subsets are homogeneous on the stratification variables, they may be homogeneous on other variables as well. Because age is related to college class, a sample stratified by class will be more representative in terms of age as well. Because occupational aspirations still seem to be related to gender, a sample stratified by gender will be more representative in terms of occupational aspirations.

The choice of stratification variables typically depends on what variables are available. Gender can often be determined in a list of names. University lists are typically arranged by class. Lists of faculty members may indicate their departmental affiliation. Government agency files may be arranged by geographical region. Voter registration lists are arranged according to precinct.

In selecting stratification variables from among those available, however, you should be concerned primarily with those that are presumably related to variables you want to represent accurately. Because gender is related to many variables and is often available for stratification, it is often used. Education is related to many variables, but it is often not available for stratification. Geographical location within a city, state, or nation is related to many things. Within a city, stratification by geographical location usually increases representativeness in social class, ethnic group, and so forth. Within a nation, it increases representativeness in a broad range of attitudes as well as in social class and ethnicity.

When you're working with a simple list of all elements in the population, two methods of stratification predominate. In one method, you sort the population elements into discrete groups based on whatever stratification variables are being used. On the basis of the relative proportion of the population represented by a given group, you select—randomly or systematically—several elements from that group constituting the same proportion of your desired sample size. For example, if sophomore men with a 4.0 average compose 1 percent of the student population and you desire a sample of 1,000 students, you would select 10 sophomore men with a 4.0 average.

The other method is to group students as described and then put those groups together in a continuous list, beginning with all frosh men with a 4.0 average and ending with all senior women with a 1.0 or below. You would then select a systematic sample, with a random start, from the entire list. Given the arrangement of the list, a systematic sample would select proper numbers (within an error range of 1 or 2) from each subgroup. (*Note:* A simple random sample drawn from such a composite list would cancel out the stratification.)

Figure 8-11 offers a graphic illustration of stratified, systematic sampling. As you can see, we lined up our micropopulation according to gender and race. Then, beginning with a random start of "3," we've taken every tenth person thereafter: 3, 13, 23, . . . , 93.

FIGURE 8-11
A Stratified, Systematic Sample with a Random Start

Stratified sampling insures the proper representation of the stratification variables to enhance representation of other variables related to them. Taken as a whole, then, a stratified sample is likely to be more representative on several variables than a simple random sample. Although the simple random sample is still regarded as somewhat sacred, it should now be clear that you can often do better.

Implicit Stratification in Systematic Sampling

I mentioned that systematic sampling can, under certain conditions, be more accurate than simple random sampling. This is the case whenever the arrangement of the list creates an implicit stratification. As already noted, if a list of university students is arranged by class, then a systematic sample provides a stratification by class where a simple random sample would not.

In a study of students at the University of Hawaii, after stratification by school class, the students were arranged by their student identification numbers. These numbers, however, were their social security numbers. The first three digits of the social security number indicate the state in which the number was issued. As a result, within a class, students were arranged by the state in which they were issued a social security number, providing a rough stratification by geographical origin.

You should realize, therefore, that an ordered list of elements may be more useful to you than an unordered, randomized list. This point has been stressed here in view of an unfortunate belief that lists should be randomized before systematic sampling. Only if the arrangement presents the problems discussed earlier should the list be rearranged.

ILLUSTRATION: SAMPLING UNIVERSITY STUDENTS

Let's put these principles into practice by looking at an actual sampling design used to select a sample of university students. The purpose of the study was to survey, with a mail-out questionnaire, a representative cross section of students attending the main campus of the University of Hawaii. The following sections will describe the steps and decisions involved in selecting that sample.

Study Population and Sampling Frame

The obvious sampling frame available for use in this sample selection was the computerized file maintained by the university administration. The tape contained students' names, local and permanent addresses, social security numbers, and a variety of other information such as field of study, class, age, and gender.

The computer database, however, contained files on all people who could, by any conceivable definition, be called students, many of whom seemed inappropriate to the purposes of the study. As a result, it was necessary to define the *study population* in a somewhat more restricted fashion. The final definition included those 15,225 day program degree candidates registered for the fall semester on the Manoa campus of the university, including all colleges and departments, both undergraduate and graduate students, and both U.S. and foreign students. The computer program used for sampling, therefore, limited consideration to students fitting this definition.

Stratification

The sampling program also permitted stratification of students before sample selection. The researchers decided that stratification by college class would be sufficient, although the students might have been further stratified within class, if desired, by gender, college, major, and so forth.

Sample Selection

Once the students had been arranged by class, a systematic sample was selected across the entire rearranged list. The sample size for the study was initially set at 1,100. To achieve this sample, the sampling program was set for a $\frac{1}{14}$ **sampling ratio**. The program generated a random number between 1 and 14; the student having that number and every fourteenth student thereafter was selected in the sample.

Once the sample had been selected, the computer was instructed to print each student's name and mailing address on self-adhesive mailing labels. These labels were then simply transferred to envelopes for mailing the questionnaires.

Sample Modification

This initial design of the sample had to be modified. Before the mailing of questionnaires, the researchers discovered that unexpected expenses in the production of the questionnaires made it impossible to cover the costs of mailing to all 1,100 students. As a result, one-third of the mailing labels were systematically selected (with a random start) for exclusion from the sample. The final sample for the study was thereby reduced to about 770.

This modification to the sample is mentioned here to illustrate the frequent necessity to change aspects of the study plan in midstream. Because the excluded students were systematically omitted from the initial systematic sample, the remaining 770 students could still be taken as reasonably representing the study population. The reduction in sample size did, of course, increase the range of sampling error.

MULTISTAGE CLUSTER SAMPLING

The preceding sections have dealt with reasonably simple procedures for sampling from lists of elements. Such a situation is ideal. Unfortunately, however, much interesting social research requires the selection of samples from populations that cannot be easily listed for sampling purposes. Examples would be the population of a city, state, or nation; all university students in the United States; and so forth. In such cases, the sample design must be much more complex. Such a design typically involves the initial sampling of groups of elements—*clusters*—followed by the selection of elements within each of the selected clusters.

Cluster sampling may be used when it is either impossible or impractical to compile an exhaustive list of the elements composing the target population. All church members in the United States would be an example of such a population. Often, however, the population elements are already grouped into subpopulations, and a list of those subpopulations either exists or can be created practically. In our example, church members in the United States belong to discrete churches, which are either listed or could be. Following a cluster sample format, then, you could sample the list of churches in some manner (for example, a stratified, systematic sample). Next, you would obtain lists of members from each of the selected churches. Each of the lists would then be sampled, to provide samples of church members for study. (For an example, see Glock et al. 1967.)

Another typical situation concerns sampling among population areas such as a city. Although there is no single list of a city's population, citizens reside on discrete city blocks or census blocks. You can, therefore, select a sample of blocks initially, create a list of persons living on each of the selected blocks, and subsample persons on each block.

In a more complex design, you might sample blocks, list the households on each selected block, sample the households, list the persons residing in each household, and, finally, sample persons within each selected household. This multistage sample design would lead to the ultimate selection of a sample of individuals but would not require the initial listing of all individuals in the city's population.

Multistage cluster sampling, then, involves the repetition of two basic steps: listing and sampling. The list of primary sampling units (churches, blocks) is compiled and, perhaps, stratified for sampling. Then a sample of those units is selected. The selected primary sampling units are then listed and perhaps stratified. The list of secondary sampling units is then sampled, and so forth.

Multistage cluster sampling makes possible those studies otherwise impossible. Consider, for example, the "Santa Claus" survey described in the box entitled "Sampling Santa's Fans."

Though cluster sampling is highly efficient, the price of that efficiency is a less accurate sample. A simple random sample drawn from a population list is subject to a single sampling error, but a two-stage cluster sample is subject to two sampling errors. First, the initial sample of clusters will represent the population of clusters only within a range of sampling error. Second, the sample of elements selected within a given cluster will represent all the elements in that cluster only within a range of sampling error. Thus, for example, you run a certain risk of selecting a sample of disproportionately wealthy city blocks, plus a sample of disproportionately wealthy households within those blocks. The best solution to this problem lies in the number of clusters selected initially and the number of elements selected within each.

Typically, you'll be restricted to a total sample size; for example, you may be limited to conducting 2,000 interviews in a city. Given this broad limitation, however, you have several options in designing your cluster sample. At the extremes you might choose one cluster and select 2,000 elements within that cluster, or else select 2,000 clusters with one element selected within each. Of course, neither is advisable, but a broad range of choices lies between them. Fortunately, the logic of sampling distributions provides a general guideline for this task.

Recall that sampling error is reduced by two factors: an increase in the sample size and increased homogeneity of the elements being sampled. These factors operate at each level of a multistage sample design. A sample of clusters will best represent all clusters if a large number are selected and if all clusters are very much alike. A sample of elements will best represent all elements in a given cluster if a large number are selected from the cluster and if all the elements in the cluster are very much alike.

With a given total sample size, however, if the number of clusters is increased, the number of ele-

Sampling Santa's Fans

WITH the approach of Christmas 1985, the *New York Times* thought it would be interesting to survey the nation's children regarding their beliefs in Santa Claus. There being no national registry of those who've been naughty and nice, the *Times* had to use some ingenuity. Here's their description of what they did:

The latest New York Times Poll is based on telephone interviews conducted Dec. 14–18 with 261 children ages 3 through 10 around the United States, excluding Alaska and Hawaii.

The sample of telephone exchanges called was selected by a computer from a complete list of exchanges in the country. The exchanges were chosen to ensure that each region of the country was represented in proportion to its population. For each exchange, the telephone numbers were formed by random digits, thus permitting access to both listed and unlisted residential numbers.

After interviews with 1,358 adults were completed, parents were asked if their children could be interviewed on the subject of Christmas. The results have been weighted to take account of household size and number of residential telephones and to adjust for variations in the sample relation to region, race, sex, age and education.

By the way, 87 percent of the children said they believed in Santa Claus: ranging from 96 percent among those 3–5 down to 69 percent among the 9–10-year-olds.

Source: Sara Rimer, "Poll Sees Landslide for Santa: Of U.S. Children, 87% Believe," *New York Times,* December 24, 1985.

---

ments within a cluster must be decreased. In this respect, the representativeness of the clusters is increased at the expense of more poorly representing the elements composing each cluster, or vice versa. Fortunately, the factor of homogeneity can be used to ease this dilemma.

Typically, the elements composing a given natural cluster within a population are more homogeneous than are all elements composing the total population. The members of a given church are more alike than are all church members; the residents of a given city block are more alike than are the residents of a whole city. As a result, relatively fewer elements may be needed to represent a given natural cluster adequately, although a larger number of clusters may be needed to represent adequately the diversity found among the clusters. This fact is most clearly seen in the extreme case of very different clusters composed of identical elements within each. In such a situation, a large number of clusters would adequately represent all its members. Although this extreme situation never exists in reality, it is closer to the truth in most cases than its opposite: identical clusters composed of grossly divergent elements.

The general guideline for cluster design, then, is to maximize the number of clusters selected while decreasing the number of elements within each cluster. However, this scientific guideline must be balanced against an administrative constraint. The efficiency of cluster sampling is based on the ability to minimize the listing of population elements. By initially selecting clusters, you need only list the elements composing the selected clusters, not all elements in the entire population. Increasing the number of clusters, however, goes directly against this efficiency factor in cluster sampling. A small number of clusters may be listed more quickly and more cheaply than a large number. (Remember that all the elements in a selected cluster must be listed even if only a few are to be chosen in the sample.)

The final sample design will reflect these two constraints. In effect, you'll probably select as many clusters as you can afford. Lest this issue be left too open-ended at this point, here is one general guideline. Population researchers conventionally aim at the selection of 5 households per census block. If a total of 2,000 households are to be interviewed, you would aim at 400 blocks with 5 household interviews on each. Figure 8-12 presents a graphic overview of this process.

Before turning to other, more detailed procedures available to cluster sampling, I'll repeat that this method almost inevitably involves a loss of accuracy. The manner in which this appears, however, is somewhat complex. First, as noted earlier, a multistage sample design is subject to a sampling error at each stage. Because the sample size is necessarily smaller at each stage than the total sample size, the sampling error at each stage will be greater than would be the case for a single-stage random sample of elements. Second, sampling error is estimated on the basis of observed variance among the sample elements. When those elements are drawn from among relatively homogeneous clusters, the estimated sampling error will be too optimistic and must be corrected in the light of the cluster sample design.

Multistage Cluster Sampling, Stratification

Thus far, we've looked at cluster sampling as though a simple random sample were selected at each stage of the design. In fact, stratification techniques can be used to refine and improve the sample being selected.

The basic options here are essentially the same as those in single-stage sampling from a list. In selecting a national sample of churches, for example, you might initially stratify your list of churches by denomination, geographical region, size, rural or urban location, and perhaps by some measure of social class.

Once the primary sampling units (churches, blocks) have been grouped according to the relevant, available stratification variables, either simple random or systematic sampling techniques can be used to select the sample. You might select a specified number of units from each group, or *stratum*, or you might arrange the stratified clusters in a continuous list and systematically sample that list.

To the extent that clusters are combined into homogeneous strata, the sampling error at this stage will be reduced. The primary goal of stratification, as before, is homogeneity.

There's no reason why stratification couldn't take place at each level of sampling. The elements listed within a selected cluster might be stratified before the next stage of sampling. Typically, however, this is not done. (Recall the assumption of relative homogeneity within clusters.)

Probability Proportionate to Size (PPS) Sampling

In this section, I want to introduce you to a more sophisticated form of cluster sampling, used in many large-scale survey sampling projects. In the preceding discussion, I talked about selecting a random or systematic sample of clusters and then a random or systematic sample of elements within each cluster selected. Notice that this produces an overall sampling scheme in which every element in the whole population has the same probability of selection.

Let's say we're selecting households within a city. If there are 1,000 city blocks and we initially select a sample of 100, that means that each block has a 100/1,000 or .1 chance of being selected. If we next select 1 household in 10 from those residing on the selected blocks, each household has a .1 chance of selection within its block. To calculate the overall probability of a household being selected, we simply multiply the probabilities at the individual steps in sampling. That is, each household has a 1/10 chance of its block being selected and a 1/10 chance of that specific household being selected if the block is one of those chosen. Each household, in this case, has a $1/10 \times 1/10 = 1/100$ chance of selection overall. Because each household would have the same chance of selection, the sample so selected should be representative of all households in the city.

There are dangers in this procedure, however. In particular, the varying sizes of blocks (measured in numbers of households) present a problem. Let's suppose that half the city's population resides in 10 densely packed blocks filled with high-rise apartment buildings, and suppose that the rest

FIGURE 8-12
Multistage Cluster Sampling

Stage One: Identify blocks and select a sample. (Selected blocks are shaded.)

Stage Two: Go to each selected block and list all households in order. (Example of one listed block.)

1. 491 Rosemary Ave.
2. 487 Rosemary Ave.
3. 473 Rosemary Ave.
4. 455 Rosemary Ave.
5. 437 Rosemary Ave. **
6. 423 Rosemary Ave.
7. 411 Rosemary Ave.
8. 403 Rosemary Ave.
9. 1101 4th St.
10. 1123 4th St.
11. 1137 4th St. **
12. 1157 4th St.
13. 1169 4th St.
14. 1187 4th St.
15. 402 Thyme Ave.
16. 408 Thyme Ave.
17. 424 Thyme Ave. **
18. 446 Thyme Ave.
19. 458 Thyme Ave.
20. 480 Thyme Ave.
21. 498 Thyme Ave.
22. 1186 5th St.
23. 1174 5th St. **
24. 1160 5th St.
25. 1140 5th St.
26. 1122 5th St.
27. 1118 5th St.
28. 1116 5th St.
29. 1104 5th St. **
30. 1102 5th St.

Stage Three: For each list, select sample of households. (In this example, every sixth household has been selected starting with #5, which was selected at random.)

of the population lives in single-family dwellings spread out over the remaining 900 blocks. When we first select our sample of 1/10 of the blocks, it's quite possible that we'll miss all of the 10 densely packed high-rise blocks. No matter what happens in the second stage of sampling, our final sample of households will be grossly unrepresentative of the city, comprising only single-family dwellings.

Whenever the clusters sampled are of greatly differing sizes, it is appropriate to use a modified sampling design called *probability proportionate to size*—**PPS.** This design (1) guards against the problem I've just described and (2) still produces a final sample in which each element has the same chance of selection.

As the name suggests, each cluster is given a chance of selection proportionate to its size. Thus, a city block with 200 households has twice the chance of selection as one with only 100 households. (We'll look at how this is done in the section on sampling churchwomen, to follow shortly.) Within each cluster, however, a fixed *number* of elements is selected, say, 5 households per block. Notice how this procedure results in each household having the same probability of selection overall.

Let's look at households of two different city blocks. Block A has 100 households, Block B has only 10. In PPS sampling, we would give Block A ten times as good a chance of being selected as Block B. So if, in the overall sample design, Block A has a 1/20 chance of being selected, that means Block B would only have a 1/200 chance. Notice that this means that all the households on Block A would have a 1/20 chance of having their block selected; Block B households have only a 1/200 chance.

If Block A is selected and we are taking 5 households from each selected block, then the households on Block A have a 5/100 chance of being selected into the block's sample. Since we can multiply probabilities in a case like this, we see that every household on Block A had an overall chance of selection equal to $1/20 \times 5/100 = 5/2000 = 1/400$.

If Block B happens to be selected, on the other hand, its households stand a much better chance of being among the 5 chosen there: 5/10. When this is combined with their relatively poorer chance of having their block selected in the first place, however, they end up with the same chance of selection as those on Block A: $1/200 \times 5/10 = 5/2000 = 1/400$.

Further refinements to this design make it a very efficient and effective method for selecting large cluster samples. For now, however, it's enough for you to understand the basic logic involved.

Disproportionate Sampling and Weighting

Ultimately, a probability sample is representative of a population if all elements in the population have an equal chance of selection in that sample. Thus, in each of the preceding discussions we've noted that the various sampling procedures result in an equal chance of selection—even though the ultimate selection probability is the product of several partial probabilities.

More generally, however, a probability sample is one in which each population element has a *known nonzero* probability of selection—even though different elements may have different probabilities. If controlled probability sampling procedures have been used, any such sample may be representative of the population from which it is drawn if each sample element is assigned a weight equal to the inverse of its probability of selection. Thus, where all sample elements have had the same chance of selection, each is given the same weight: 1. This is called a *self-weighting* sample.

Disproportionate sampling and **weighting** come into play in two basic ways. First, you may sample subpopulations disproportionately to insure sufficient numbers of cases from each for analysis. For example, a given city may have a suburban area containing one-fourth of its total population. Yet you might be especially interested in a detailed analysis of households in that area and may feel that one-fourth of this total sample size would be too few. As a result, you might decide to select the same number of households from the suburban area as from the remainder of the city. Households in the suburban area, then, are given a disproportionately better chance of selection than those located elsewhere in the city.

As long as you analyze the two area samples separately or comparatively, you need not worry about the differential sampling. If you want to combine the two samples to create a composite picture of the entire city, however, you must take the disproportionate sampling into account. If n is the number of households selected from each area, then the households in the suburban area had a chance of selection equal to n divided by one-fourth of the total city population. Because the total city population and the sample size are the same for both areas, the suburban-area households should be given a weight of $\frac{1}{4}n$, and the remaining households should be given a weight of $\frac{3}{4}n$. This weighting procedure could be simplified by merely giving a weight of 3 to each of the households selected outside the suburban area. (This procedure gives a proportionate representation to each sample element. The population figure would have to be included in the weighting if population estimates were desired.)

Here's an example of the problems that can be created when disproportionate sampling is not accompanied by a weighting scheme. When the *Harvard Business Review* decided to survey its subscribers on the issue of sexual harassment at work, for example, it seemed appropriate to oversample women. Here's how G. C. Collins and Timothy Blodgett explained the matter:

■ We also skewed the sample another way: to ensure a representative response from women, we mailed a questionnaire to virtually every female subscriber, for a male/female ratio of 68% to 32%. This bias resulted in a response of 52% male and 44% female (and 4% who gave no indication of gender)—compared to HBR's U.S. subscriber proportion of 93% male and 7% female.

(1981:78)

You should have noticed a couple of things in this quotation. First, it would be nice to know a little more about what "virtually every female" means. Evidently, they didn't send questionnaires to all female subscribers, but there's no indication of who was omitted and why. Second, they didn't use the term *representative* in its normal social science usage. What they mean, of course, is that they want to get a substantial or "large enough" response from women, and oversampling is a perfectly acceptable way of accomplishing that.

By sampling more women than a straightforward probability sample would have produced, they've gotten enough women (812) to compare with the men (960). Thus, when the authors report, for example, that 32 percent of the women and 66 percent of the men agree that "the amount of sexual harassment at work is greatly exaggerated," we know that the female response is based on a substantial number of cases. That's good. There are problems, however.

To begin, subscriber surveys are always problematic. In this case, the best the researchers can hope to talk about is "what subscribers to *Harvard Business Review* think." In a loose way, it might make sense to think of that population as representing the more sophisticated portion of corporate management. Unfortunately, the overall response rate was 25 percent. Although that is quite good for subscriber surveys, it is a low response rate in terms of generalizing from probability samples.

Beyond that, however, the disproportionate sample design creates a further problem. When the authors state that 73 percent favor company policies against harassment (Collins and Blodgett, 1981:78), that figure is undoubtedly too high, since the sample contains a disproportionately high percentage of women—who are more likely to favor such policies. And, when the researchers report that top managers are more likely to feel that claims of sexual harassment are exaggerated than are middle- and lower-level managers (1981:81), that finding is also suspect. As the researchers report, women are disproportionately represented in lower management. That alone might account for the apparent differences in different levels of management. In short, the failure

Chapter 8: The Logic of Sampling

to take account of the oversampling of women confounds all survey results that don't separate findings by gender.

■ ILLUSTRATION: SAMPLING CHURCHWOMEN

Let's complete the discussion of cluster sampling with a research example. The example that follows is not as complex as the area probability samples that are employed in studies of geographic areas such as cities, states, or the nation. Nonetheless, it should illustrate the various principles of cluster sampling.

The purpose of this study was to examine the religious and social attitudes of women members of churches in a diocese of the Episcopal church. A representative sample of all churchwomen in the diocese was desired. Because there was no single list of such women, a multistage sample design was created. In the initial stage of sampling, churches were selected with probability proportionate to size (PPS), and then women were selected from each.

Selecting the Churches

The diocese in question publishes an annual report that lists the 100 or so diocesan churches and their membership sizes. This listing constituted the sampling frame for the first stage of sampling.

A total of approximately 500 respondents was desired for the study, so the decision was made to select 25 churches with probability proportionate to size and take 20 women from each of those selected. To accomplish this, the list of churches was arranged geographically, and then a table was created similar to the partial listing shown in Table 8-2.

Beside each church in the table, its membership was entered, and that figure was used to compute the cumulative total running through the list. The final total came to approximately 200,000. The object at this point was to select a sample of 25 churches in such a way that each would have a chance of selection proportionate

TABLE 8-2
Form Used in Listing of Churches

Church	Membership	Cumulative Membership
Church A	3,000	3,000
Church B	5,000	8,000
Church C	1,000	9,000

to the number of its members. To accomplish this, the cumulative totals were used to create ranges of numbers for each church equaling the number of members in that church. Church A in the table was assigned the numbers 1 through 3,000; Church B was assigned 3,001 through 8,000; Church C was assigned 8,001 through 9,000; and so forth.

By selecting 25 numbers ranging between 1 and 200,000, it was possible to select 25 churches for the study. The 25 numbers were selected in a systematic sample as follows. The sampling interval was set at 8,000 (200,000/25), and a random start was selected between 1 and 8,000. Let us say the random number was 4,538. Because that number fell within the range of numbers assigned to Church B (3,001–8,000), Church B was selected.

Increments of 8,000 (the sampling interval) were then added to the random start, and every church within whose range one of the resultant numbers appeared was selected into the sample of churches. It should be apparent that in this fashion, each church in the diocese had a chance of selection directly proportionate to its membership size. A church with 4,000 members had twice the chance of selection as a church of 2,000 and 10 times the chance of selection as one with only 400 members.

Selecting the Churchwomen

Once the sample of churches was selected, arrangements were made to get lists of the women members of each. It is worth noting here that in practice the lists varied greatly in their form and content. In some cases, lists of all members (men and women) were provided, and it was necessary to sort out the women before sampling the lists.

The form of the lists varied from typed lists to 3-by-5 cards printed from mailing address plates.

As the list arrived from a selected church, a sampling interval for that church was computed on the basis of the number of women members and the number desired (20). If a church had 2,000 women members, the sample interval was set at 100. A random number was selected and incremented by the sampling interval to select the sample of women from that church. This procedure was repeated for each church.

Note that this sample design ultimately gives every woman in the diocese an equal chance of selection *only* if the assumption is made that each church has the same ratio of men to women. That is due to the fact that churches were given a chance of selection based on their *total* membership with an assumption that half the members of each church were women. In fact, of course, women made up more than half the members of some churches and less than half of others. Given the aims of this particular study, the slight inequities of selection were considered insignificant.

A more sophisticated sample design for the second stage would have resolved this possible problem. Because each church was given a chance of selection based on an assumed number of women (assuming 1,000 women in a church of 2,000), the sampling interval could have been computed on the basis of that assumption rather than on the actual number of women listed. If it were assumed in the first stage of sampling that a church had 1,000 women (out of a membership of 2,000), the sampling interval could have been set at 50 (1,000/20). Then this interval could have been used in the selection of respondents regardless of the actual number of women listed for that church. If 1,000 women were in fact listed, then their church had the proper chance of selection and 20 women would be selected from it. If 1,200 women were listed, that would mean that the church had too small a chance of selection, but this would have been remedied through the selection of 24 women using the preestablished sampling interval. If only 800 women were listed, on the other hand, only 16 would have been selected.

■ PROBABILITY SAMPLING IN REVIEW

The preceding discussions have been devoted to the key sampling method used in controlled survey research: probability sampling. In each of the variations examined, we've seen that elements are chosen for study from a population on a basis of random selection with known nonzero probabilities.

Depending on the field situation, probability sampling can be either very simple or extremely difficult, time consuming, and expensive. Whatever the situation, however, it remains the most effective method for the selection of study elements. There are two reasons for this.

First, probability sampling avoids researchers' conscious or unconscious biases in element selection. If all elements in the population have an equal (or unequal and subsequently weighted) chance of selection, there is an excellent chance that the sample so selected will closely represent the population of all elements.

Second, probability sampling permits estimates of sampling error. Although no probability sample will be perfectly representative in all respects, controlled selection methods permit the researcher to estimate the degree of expected error in that regard.

In this lengthy chapter, we've taken on a basic issue in much social research: selecting observations that will tell us something more general than the specifics we have actually observed. This issue confronts field researchers, who face more action and more actors than they can note in their totalities, as well as political pollsters who want to predict an election but cannot interview all voters. This is an issue social scientists have devoted a good deal of attention to and have developed several techniques for dealing with.

■ MAIN POINTS

- It is never possible to observe all the actions and actors relevant to the social phenomenon under study.

- Social researchers must select observations that will allow them to generalize to people and events not observed. Often this involves a selection of people to observe.
- A sample is a special subset of a population observed in order to make inferences about the nature of the total population itself.
- Sampling has often centered on the ability of researchers to gauge public opinion, such as voting intentions. Despite a history of errors, current techniques are quite accurate.
- Social researchers have developed several sampling techniques appropriate to different research situations.
- Sometimes you can and should select probability samples using precise statistical techniques, but other times nonprobability techniques are more appropriate.
- Sometimes you must rely on available subjects, or on an accidental sample, but it is difficult to know how representative such subjects are.
- Purposive sampling is a type of nonprobability sampling method in which the researcher uses his or her own judgment in the selection of sample members. It is sometimes called a judgmental sample.
- Quota sampling is another nonprobability sampling method. You begin with a detailed description of the characteristics of the total population (quota matrix) and then select your sample members so that they include different composite profiles that exist in the population. The representativeness of a quota sampling depends in large part on how accurately the quota matrix reflects the characteristics of the population.
- Snowball sampling is a technique often used in rare populations; each subject interviewed is asked to identify others.
- When informants are used, they should be selected in such a way as to provide a broad, diverse view of the group under study.
- Probability sampling methods provide an excellent way of selecting representative samples from large, known populations.
- The most carefully selected sample will never provide a perfect representation of the population from which it was selected. There will always be some degree of sampling error.
- Probability sampling methods make it possible to estimate the amount of sampling error expected in a given sample.
- The chief principle of probability sampling is that every member of the total population must have some known nonzero probability of being selected into the sample.
- An EPSEM sample is one in which every member of a population has the same probability of being selected.
- A sampling frame is a list or quasi list of the members of a population. It is the resource used in the selection of a sample. A sample's representativeness depends directly on the extent to which a sampling frame contains all the members of the total population that the sample is intended to represent.
- Simple random sampling is logically the most fundamental technique in probability sampling, though it is seldom used in practice.
- Systematic sampling involves the selection of every kth member from a sampling frame. This method is functionally equivalent to simple random sampling, with a few exceptions; systematic sampling is more practical, however.
- Stratification is the process of grouping the members of a population into relatively homogeneous strata before sampling. This practice improves the representativeness of a sample by reducing the degree of sampling error.
- Multistage cluster sampling is a relatively complex sampling technique frequently used when a list of all the members of a population does not exist. An initial sample of groups of members (clusters) is selected first. Then, all the members of the selected cluster are listed, often through direct observation in the field. Finally, the members listed in each of the selected clusters are subsampled, thereby providing the final sample of members.
- Probability proportionate to size (PPS) is a special, efficient method for multistage cluster sampling.
- If the members of a population have unequal probabilities of selection into the sample, re-

searchers must assign weights to the different observations made in order to provide a representative picture of the total population. Basically, the weight assigned to a particular sample member should be the inverse of its probability of selection.

■ REVIEW QUESTIONS AND EXERCISES

1. Review the discussion of the 1948 Gallup Poll that predicted that Thomas Dewey would defeat Harry Truman for president. Discuss some ways in which Gallup could have modified his quota sample design to avoid the error.
2. Using Appendix E of this book, select a simple random sample of 10 numbers in the range from 1 to 9,876. Describe each step in the process.
3. In a paragraph or two, describe the steps involved in selecting a multistage cluster sample of students taking first-year English in the nation's colleges and universities.
4. The General Social Survey is a mainstay of modern social research, one that employs careful sampling methods. Use the World Wide Web to find out the sizes of the original samples for the three most recent surveys—and the number of completed interviews ("completed cases") achieved each of those years. Start at the GSS home page (http://www.icpsr.umich.edu/gss/) and go to the Codebook Appendices.

■ ADDITIONAL READINGS

Kalton, Graham. *Introduction to Survey Sampling*. Newbury Park, CA: Sage, 1983. Kalton goes into more of the mathematical details of sampling than the present chapter without attempting to be as definitive as Kish, described next.

Kish, Leslie. *Survey Sampling*. New York: Wiley, 1965. Unquestionably the definitive work on sampling in social research. Kish's coverage ranges from the simplest matters to the most complex and mathematical, both highly theoretical and downright practical. Easily readable and difficult passages intermingle as Kish exhausts everything you could want or need to know about each aspect of sampling.

Sudman, Seymour. "Applied Sampling." Pp. 145–94 in *Handbook of Survey Research*, edited by Peter H. Rossi, James D. Wright, and Andy B. Anderson. New York: Academic Press, 1983. An excellent, practical guide to survey sampling.

PART 3 Modes of Observation

9 *Experiments*
10 *Survey Research*
11 *Field Research*
12 *Unobtrusive Research*
13 *Evaluation Research*

I HAVE a hunch that you may have grown impatient. If you began this book with a view that doing research means making observations and analyzing what you've observed, the preceding discussions of various aspects of research design may have seemed overlong. It bears repeating, however, that the structuring of inquiry is an integral part of research. With this point firmly in mind, let's dive into the various observational techniques available to social scientists.

Experiments are usually thought of in connection with the physical sciences. In Chapter 9 we'll see how social scientists use experiments. This is the most rigorously controllable of the methods we'll examine. You should come away from this chapter with a better understanding of the general logic of social scientific research.

Chapter 10 will describe survey research, one of the most popular of methods in social science. As you'll see, this type of research involves collecting data through asking people questions—either in self-administered questionnaires or through interviews, which, in turn, can be conducted face-to-face or over the telephone.

Chapter 11, on field research, examines perhaps the most natural form of data collection used by social scientists: the direct observation of social phenomena in natural settings. As you'll see, some researchers go beyond mere observation to participate in what they are studying, because they want a more intimate view and fuller understanding.

Chapter 12 discusses three forms of unobtrusive data collection that take advantage of some of the data available all around us. *Content analysis* is a method of collecting social data through carefully specifying and counting social artifacts such as books, songs, speeches, and paintings. Without making any personal contact with people, you can use this method to examine a wide variety of social phenomena. The analysis of existing statistics offers another way of studying people without having to talk to them. Governments and a variety of private organizations regularly compile great masses of data, which you often can use with little or no modification to answer properly posed questions. Finally, historical documents are a valuable resource for social scientific analysis.

Chapter 13, on evaluation research, looks at a rapidly growing subfield in social science, involving the application of experimental and quasi-experimental models to the testing of social interventions in real life. You might use evaluation research, for example, to test the effectiveness of a drug rehabilitation program or the efficiency of a new school cafeteria. In the same chapter, we'll look briefly at social indicators as a way of assessing broader social processes.

Before we turn to the actual descriptions of the several methods, two points should be made. First, you'll probably discover that you have been using these scientific methods casually in your daily life for as long as you can remember. You use some form of field research every day. You are employing a crude form of content analysis every time you judge an author's motivation or orientation from her or his writings. You engage in at least casual experiments frequently. The chapters in Part 3 will show you how to improve your use of these methods so as to avoid the pitfalls of casual, uncontrolled observation.

Second, none of the data-collection methods described in the following chapters is appropriate to all research topics and situations. I've tried to give you some ideas, early in each chapter, of when a given method might be appropriate. Still, I could never anticipate all the possible research topics that may one day interest you. As a general guideline, you should always use a variety of techniques in the study of any topic. Because each method has its weaknesses, the use of several methods can help fill in any gaps; if the different, independent approaches to the topic all yield the same conclusion, you've achieved a form of replication.

CHAPTER 9 *Experiments*

What You'll Learn in This Chapter
This chapter examines the experimental method. Besides learning about a specific mode of observation, you'll see a logic of inquiry that you can apply to other modes as well.

INTRODUCTION

TOPICS APPROPRIATE TO EXPERIMENTS

THE CLASSICAL EXPERIMENT
Independent and Dependent Variables
Pretesting and Posttesting
Experimental and Control Groups
The Double-Blind Experiment

SELECTING SUBJECTS
Probability Sampling
Randomization
Matching

VARIATIONS ON EXPERIMENTAL DESIGN
Sources of Internal Invalidity
Sources of External Invalidity

AN ILLUSTRATION OF EXPERIMENTATION

FOCUS GROUPS

"NATURAL" EXPERIMENTS

STRENGTHS AND WEAKNESSES OF THE EXPERIMENTAL METHOD

MAIN POINTS

REVIEW QUESTIONS AND EXERCISES

ADDITIONAL READINGS

■ INTRODUCTION

This chapter addresses that research method probably most frequently associated with structured science in general. Here we'll discuss the *experiment* as a mode of scientific observation. At base, experiments involve (1) taking action and (2) observing the consequences of that action. Social scientific researchers typically select a group of subjects, do something to them, and observe the effect of what was done. In this chapter, we'll examine both the logic and the various techniques of social scientific experiments.

It is worth noting at the outset that experiments also are used often in nonscientific human inquiry. In preparing a stew, for example, we add salt, taste, add more salt, and taste again. In defusing a bomb, we clip a wire, observe whether the bomb explodes, clip another, and . . .

We also experiment copiously in our attempt to develop generalized understanding about the world we live in. All skills are learned through experimentation: eating, walking, talking, riding a bicycle, swimming, and so forth. Through experimentation, students discover how much studying is required for academic success. Through experimentation, professors learn how much preparation is required for successful lectures. This chapter will discuss some ways social scientists use experiments to develop generalized understandings. We'll see that, like other methods available to the social scientist, experimenting has its special strengths and weaknesses.

■ TOPICS APPROPRIATE TO EXPERIMENTS

Experiments are especially well suited to research projects involving relatively limited and well-defined concepts and propositions. The traditional image of science, discussed earlier in this book, and the *experimental model* are closely related to each other. Experimentation, then, is especially appropriate for hypothesis testing. It's also better suited to explanatory than to descriptive purposes. Let's assume, for example, that we want to study prejudice against African Americans and to discover ways of reducing it. We hypothesize that learning about the contribution of African Americans to U.S. history will have the effect of reducing prejudice, and we can test this hypothesis experimentally. To begin, we might test a group of experimental subjects to determine their levels of prejudice against African Americans. Next, we might show them a documentary film depicting the many ways African Americans have contributed importantly to the scientific, literary, political, and social development of the nation. Finally, we'd measure our subjects' levels of prejudice against African Americans to determine whether the film has actually reduced prejudice.

Experimentation is also appropriate and has been successful in the study of small group interaction. Thus, we might bring together a small group of experimental subjects and assign them a task, such as making recommendations for popularizing carpools. We observe, then, the manner in which the group organizes itself and deals with the problem. Over the course of several such experiments, we might vary the nature of the task or the rewards for handling the task successfully. By observing differences in the way groups organize themselves and operate under these varying conditions, we can learn a great deal about the nature of small group interaction.

We typically think of experiments as being conducted in laboratories. Indeed, most of the examples to be used in this chapter will involve such a setting. This need not be the case, however. As you'll see, social scientists often study what are called *natural experiments:* "experiments" that occur in the regular course of social events. The latter portion of this chapter will deal with such research.

■ THE CLASSICAL EXPERIMENT

The most conventional type of experiment, in the natural as well as the social sciences, involves three major pairs of components: (1) independent and dependent variables, (2) pretesting and posttesting, and (3) experimental and control groups.

This section of the chapter will deal with each of these and the way they are put together in the execution of the experiment.

Independent and Dependent Variables

Essentially, an experiment examines the effect of an independent variable on a dependent variable. Typically, the independent variable takes the form of an experimental stimulus, which is either present or absent: that is, a *dichotomous variable*, having two attributes. (This need not be the case, however, as later sections of this chapter will indicate.) In the example concerning prejudice against African Americans, *prejudice* is the dependent variable and *exposure to African-American history* is the independent variable. The researcher's hypothesis suggests that prejudice depends, in part, on a lack of knowledge of African-American history. The purpose of the experiment is to test the validity of this hypothesis. The independent and dependent variables appropriate to experimentation are nearly limitless. Moreover, a given variable might serve as an independent variable in one experiment and as a dependent variable in another. For example, *prejudice* would be the dependent variable in the previous example, whereas it might be the independent variable in an experiment examining the effect of prejudice on voting behavior.

In other terms, the independent variable is the cause and the dependent variable is the effect. Thus, we might say that watching the film caused a change in prejudice or that reduced prejudice was an effect of watching the film.

Both independent and dependent variables must be operationally defined for purposes of experimentation. Such operational definitions might involve a variety of observation methods. Responses to a questionnaire, for example, might be the basis for defining prejudice. Speaking to African-American subjects, agreeing with African-American subjects, disagreeing with African-American subjects, or ignoring the comments of African-American subjects might be elements in the operational definition of interaction with African Americans in a small group setting.

Conventionally, in the experimental model, dependent and independent variables must be operationally defined before the experiment begins. However, as you'll see in connection with survey research and other methods, it's sometimes appropriate to make a wide variety of observations during data collection first and then determine the most useful operational definitions of variables during later analyses. Ultimately, however, experimentation, like other quantitative methods, requires specific and standardized measurements and observations.

Pretesting and Posttesting

In the simplest experimental design, subjects are measured in terms of a dependent variable (pretested), exposed to a stimulus representing an independent variable, and then remeasured in terms of the dependent variable (posttested). Differences noted between the first and last measurements on the dependent variable are then attributed to the independent variable.

In the example of prejudice and exposure to African-American history, we'd begin by pretesting the extent of prejudice among our experimental subjects. Using a questionnaire asking about attitudes toward African Americans, for example, we could measure the extent of prejudice exhibited by each individual subject and the average prejudice level of the whole group. After exposing the subjects to the African-American history film, we could administer the same questionnaire again. Responses given in this posttest would permit us to measure the later extent of prejudice for each subject and the average prejudice level of the group as a whole. If we discovered a lower level of prejudice during the second administration of the questionnaire, we might conclude that the film had indeed reduced prejudice.

In the experimental examination of attitudes such as prejudice, we face a special practical problem relating to *validity*. As you may already have imagined, the subjects might respond differently to the questionnaires the second time even if their attitudes remained unchanged. During the first administration of the questionnaire, the sub-

FIGURE 9-1
Diagram of Basic Experimental Design

```
         Experimental                                    Control
            Group                                         Group

    ┌──────────────────┐                          ┌──────────────────┐
    │ Measure dependent│──── Compare: Same? ─────│ Measure dependent│
    │     variable     │                          │     variable     │
    └──────────────────┘                          └──────────────────┘
            │                                              │
            ▼                                              │
    ┌──────────────────┐                                   │
    │    Administer    │                                   │
    │    experimental  │                                   │
    │   stimulus (film)│                                   │
    └──────────────────┘                                   │
            │                                              │
            ▼                                              ▼
    ┌──────────────────┐                          ┌──────────────────┐
    │Remeasure dependent│──── Compare: Different? ─│Remeasure dependent│
    │     variable     │                          │     variable     │
    └──────────────────┘                          └──────────────────┘
```

jects may have been unaware of its purpose. By the time of the second measurement, they might have figured out that the researchers were interested in measuring their prejudice. Because no one wishes to seem prejudiced, the subjects might have "cleaned up" their answers the second time around. Thus, the film would seem to have reduced prejudice although, in fact, it had not.

This is an example of a more general problem that plagues many forms of social scientific research. The very act of studying something may change it. The techniques for dealing with this problem in the context of experimentation will be discussed in various places throughout the chapter.

Experimental and Control Groups

The foremost method of offsetting the effects of the experiment itself is the use of a **control group.** Laboratory experiments seldom if ever involve only the observation of an experimental group to which a stimulus has been administered. In addition, the researchers also observe a control group, which does not receive the experimental stimulus.

In the example of prejudice and African-American history, two groups of subjects might be examined. To begin, each group is administered a questionnaire designed to measure their prejudice against African Americans. Then, the experimental group is shown the film. Later, the researcher administers a posttest of prejudice to *both* groups. Figure 9-1 illustrates this basic experimental design.

Using a control group allows the researcher to detect any effects of the experiment itself. If the posttest shows that the overall level of prejudice exhibited by the control group has dropped as much as that of the experimental group, then the apparent reduction in prejudice must be a function of the experiment or of some external factor rather than a function of the film. If, on the other hand, prejudice were reduced *only* in the experimental group, such reduction would seem to be a consequence of exposure to the film, because that's the only difference between the two groups. Alternatively, if prejudice were reduced *more* in the experimental group than in the control group, that, too, would be grounds for assuming that the film reduced prejudice.

The need for control groups in social research became clear in connection with a series of studies of employee satisfaction conducted by F. J. Roethlisberger and W. J. Dickson (1939) in the late 1920s and early 1930s. These two researchers studied working conditions in the telephone "bank wiring room" of the Western Electric Works in the Chicago suburb of Hawthorne, Illinois, attempting to discover what changes in working conditions would improve employee satisfaction and productivity.

To the researchers' great satisfaction, they discovered that making working conditions better consistently increased satisfaction and productivity. As the workroom was brightened up through better lighting, for example, productivity went up. Lighting was further improved, and productivity went up again. To further substantiate their scientific conclusion, the researchers then dimmed the lights: *Productivity again improved!*

It became evident then that the wiring room workers were responding more to the *attention* given them by the researchers than to improved working conditions. As a result of this phenomenon, often called the **Hawthorne effect,** social researchers have become more sensitive to and cautious about the possible effects of experiments themselves. The use of a proper control group—studied intensively without any of the working conditions changed otherwise—would have pointed to the existence of this effect in the wiring room study.

The need for control groups in experimentation has been nowhere more evident than in medical research. Time and again, patients who participate in medical experiments have appeared to improve, and it has been unclear how much of the improvement has come from the experimental treatment and how much from the experiment. In testing the effects of new drugs, then, medical researchers frequently administer a *placebo* (for example, sugar pills) to a control group. Thus, the control group patients believe they, like the experimental group, are receiving an experimental drug. Often, they improve. If the new drug is effective, however, those receiving that drug will improve more than those receiving the placebo.

In social scientific experiments, control groups are important as a guard against not only the effects of the experiments themselves but also the effects of any events outside the laboratory during the experiments. In the example of the study of prejudice, suppose that a very popular African-American leader were assassinated in the middle of, say, a week-long experiment. Such an event might very well horrify the experimental subjects, requiring them to examine their own attitudes toward African Americans, with the result of reduced prejudice. Because such an effect should happen about equally for members of the control and experimental groups, a *greater* reduction of prejudice among the experimental group would, again, point to the impact of the experimental stimulus: the documentary film.

Sometimes an experimental design will require more than one experimental or control group. In the case of the documentary film, for example, you might also want to examine the impact of reading a book on African-American history. In that case, you might have one group see the film *and* read the book; another group would only see the movie; still another group would only read the book; and the control group would do neither. With this kind of design, you could determine the impact of each stimulus separately, as well as their combined effect.

The Double-Blind Experiment

Like patients who improve when they merely *think* they are receiving a new drug, sometimes experimenters tend to prejudge results. In medical research, the experimenters may be more likely to "observe" improvements among patients receiving the experimental drug than among those receiving the placebo. (This would be most likely, perhaps, for the researcher who developed the drug.) A double-blind experiment eliminates this possibility, because neither the subjects nor the experimenters know which is the experimental group and which the control. In the medical case, those researchers who were responsible for administering the drug and for noting improvements would not be told which subjects were receiving the drug and which the placebo. Conversely, the researcher who knew which subjects were in which group would not administer the experiment.

In social scientific experiments, as in medical experiments, the danger of experimenter bias is further reduced to the extent that the operational definitions of the dependent variables are clear and precise. Thus, medical researchers would be less likely to unconsciously bias their reading of a patient's temperature than they would be to bias their assessment of how lethargic the patient was. For the same reason, the small group researcher would be less likely to misperceive which subject spoke, or to whom he or she spoke, than whether the subject's comments sounded cooperative or competitive.

As I've indicated several times, seldom can we devise operational definitions and measurements that are wholly precise and unambiguous. It may be appropriate sometimes, therefore, to employ a double-blind design in social research experiments.

■ SELECTING SUBJECTS

It seems likely that most social scientific laboratory experiments are conducted with college undergraduates as subjects. Typically, the experimenter asks students enrolled in his or her classes to participate in experiments or advertises for subjects in a college newspaper. Subjects may or may not be paid for participating in such experiments. (Chapter 18 will discuss the ethical issues involved in asking students to participate in such studies.)

In relation to the norm of *generalizability* in science, this tendency clearly represents a potential defect in social scientific research. Simply put, college undergraduates are not typical of the public at large. There is a danger, therefore, that we may learn much about the attitudes and actions of college undergraduates but not about social attitudes and actions in general.

However, this potential defect is less significant in explanatory research than it would be in descriptive research. True, having noted the level of prejudice among a group of college undergraduates, we would have little confidence that the same level existed among the public at large. If a documentary film, on the other hand, were found to reduce prejudice among those undergraduates, we would have more confidence—without being certain—that it would have a similar effect in the community at large. Social processes and *patterns* of causal relationships appear to be more generalizable and more stable than *specific* characteristics.

Aside from the question of generalizability, the cardinal rule of subject selection and experimentation concerns the comparability of experimental and control groups. Ideally, the control group represents what the experimental group would have been like had it not been exposed to the experimental stimulus. It is essential, therefore, that experimental and control groups be as similar as possible. There are several ways to accomplish this.

Probability Sampling

The earlier discussions of the logic and techniques of probability sampling provide one method for selecting two groups of people similar to each other. Beginning with a sampling frame composed of all the people in the population under study, the researcher might select two probability samples. If two probability samples each resemble the total population from which they are selected, they will also resemble each other.

Recall also, however, that the degree of resemblance (representativeness) achieved by probability sampling is largely a function of the sample size. As a general guideline, probability samples of less than 100 are not likely to be terribly representative, and social scientific experiments seldom involve that many subjects in either experimental or control groups. As a result, then, probability sampling is seldom used in experiments to select subjects from a larger population. The logic of random selection is used in a modified fashion, however.

Randomization

Having recruited, by whatever means, a total group of subjects, the experimenter may randomly assign those subjects to either the experimental or the control group. Such **randomization** might be accomplished by numbering all of the subjects serially and selecting numbers by means of a random number table, or the experimenter might assign the odd-numbered subjects to the experimental group and the even-numbered subjects to the control group.

Let's return again to the basic concept of probability sampling. If the experimenter has recruited 40 subjects altogether, in response to a newspaper advertisement, for example, there's no reason to believe that the 40 subjects represent the entire population from which they have been drawn. Nor can we assume that the 20 subjects randomly assigned to the experimental group represent that larger population. We may have greater confidence, however, that the 20 subjects randomly assigned to the experimental group will be reasonably similar to the 20 assigned to the control group.

Within the logic of our earlier discussions of sampling, it is as though the 40 subjects in this instance are a population from which we select two probability samples—each consisting of half the population. Because each sample will reflect the characteristics of the total population, so the two samples will mirror each other. And, as we saw in Chapter 8, the *number* of subjects involved is important. In the extreme, if we recruited only two subjects and assigned, by the flip of a coin, one as the experimental subject and one as the control, there would be no reason to assume that the two subjects are similar to each other. With larger numbers of subjects, however, randomization makes good sense.

Matching

The comparability of experimental and control groups can sometimes be achieved more directly through a **matching** process similar to the *quota sampling* methods discussed in Chapter 8. If 12 of your subjects are young white men, you might assign 6 of those at random to the experimental group and the other 6 to the control group. If 14 are middle-aged African-American women, you might assign 7 to each group. The overall matching process could be most efficiently achieved through the creation of a *quota matrix* constructed of all the most relevant characteristics. (Figure 9-2 provides a simplified illustration of such a matrix.) Ideally, the quota matrix would be constructed to result in an even number of subjects in each cell of the matrix. Then, half the subjects in each cell would go into the experimental group and half into the control group.

Alternatively, you might recruit more subjects than your experimental design requires. You might then examine many characteristics of the large initial group of subjects. Whenever you discover a pair of quite similar subjects, you might assign one at random to the experimental group and the other to the control group. Potential subjects unlike anyone else in the initial group might be left out of the experiment altogether.

Whatever method you employ, the desired result is the same. The overall average description of the experimental group should be the same as that of the control group. For example, they should have about the same average age, the same gender composition, the same racial composition, and so forth. This same test of comparability should be used whether the two groups are created through probability sampling or through randomization.

Thus far, I have referred to the "important" variables without saying clearly what those variables are. Of course, I can't give a definite answer to this question, any more than I could specify, earlier, which variables should be used in stratified sampling. The answer ultimately depends on the nature and purpose of an experiment. As a general rule, however, the two groups should be comparable in terms of those variables most likely to be related to the dependent variable under study. In a study of prejudice, for example, the two groups should be alike in terms of education, ethnicity, and age, among others. In some cases, moreover, you may delay assigning subjects to experimental and control groups until you have initially measured the dependent variable. Thus, for example, you might administer a questionnaire measuring subjects' prejudice and then match the experimental and control groups to assure yourself that the two groups exhibited the same overall level of prejudice.

When assigning subjects to the experimental and control groups, you should be aware of two arguments in favor of randomization over matching. First, you may not be in a position to know in advance what the relevant variables are for the matching process. Second, most of the statistics

FIGURE 9-2
Quota Matrix Illustration

	Men		Women	
	African American	White	African American	White
Under 30 years	8	12	10	16
30 to 50 years	18	30	14	28
Over 50 years	12	20	12	22

Experimental group
6
7
etc.

Control group
6
7
etc.

used to evaluate the results of experiments assume randomization. Failure to design your experiment that way, then, makes your later use of those statistics less meaningful.

Sometimes you can combine matching and randomization. When conducting an experiment in the educational enrichment of young adolescents, Milton Yinger and his colleagues (1977) needed to assign a large number of students, aged 13 and 14, to several different experimental and control groups to ensure the comparability of students composing each of the groups. They achieved this goal by the following method.

Beginning with a pool of subjects, the researchers first created strata of students nearly identical to one another in terms of some 15 variables. From each of the strata, students were randomly assigned to the different experimental and control groups. In this fashion, the researchers actually improved on conventional randomization. Essentially, they had used a stratified sampling procedure (recall Chapter 8), except that they had employed far more stratification variables than are typically used in, say, survey sampling.

Thus far I've described the classical experiment—the experimental design that best represents the logic of causal analysis in the laboratory. In practice, however, social researchers use a great variety of experimental designs. Let's look at some now.

■ VARIATIONS ON EXPERIMENTAL DESIGN

Donald Campbell and Julian Stanley (1963), in an excellent little book on research design, describe some 16 different experimental and quasi-experimental designs. In this section, I'm going to describe some of them briefly to give you a broader view of the potential for experimentation in social research.

To begin, Campbell and Stanley discuss three preexperimental designs, not to recommend them but because they are frequently used in less-than-professional research. In the first such design—*the one-shot case study*—a single group of subjects is measured on a dependent variable following the administration of some experimental stimulus. Suppose, for example, that we show the African-American history film mentioned earlier to a group of people and then administer a questionnaire that seems to measure prejudice against

African Americans. Suppose further that the answers given to the questionnaire seem to represent a low level of prejudice. We might be tempted to conclude that the film reduced prejudice. Lacking a pretest, however, we can't be sure. Perhaps the questionnaire doesn't really represent a very sensitive measure of prejudice, or perhaps the group we're studying was low in prejudice to begin with. In either case, the film might have made no difference, though our experimental results might have misled us into thinking it did.

The second preexperimental design discussed by Campbell and Stanley adds a pretest for the experimental group but lacks a control group. This design—which the authors call the *one-group pretest-posttest design*—suffers from the possibility that some factor other than the independent variable might cause a change between the pretest and posttest results, such as the assassination of a respected African-American leader. Thus, although we can see that prejudice has been reduced, we can't be sure the film caused that reduction.

To round out the possibilities for preexperimental designs, Campbell and Stanley point out that some research is based on experimental and control groups but has no pretests. They call this design the *static-group comparison*. In the case of the African-American history film, we might show the film to one group and not to another and then measure prejudice in both groups. If the experimental group had less prejudice at the conclusion of the experiment, we might assume the film was responsible. But unless we had randomized our subjects, we would have no way of knowing that the two groups had the same degree of prejudice initially; perhaps the experimental group started out with less.

Figure 9-3 graphically illustrates these three preexperimental research designs, using a different research question: *Does exercise cause weight reduction?* To make the several designs clearer, I've used individuals rather than groups, but you should realize that the same logic pertains to group comparisons. Let's review the three preexperimental designs with this new example.

The one-shot study design represents a common form of logical reasoning. Asked whether exercise causes weight-reduction, we may bring to mind an example that would seem to support the proposition: someone who exercises and is thin. There are problems with this reasoning, however. Perhaps the person was thin long before beginning to exercise. Or, perhaps he became thin for some other reason, like eating less or getting sick. The observations shown in the diagram do not guard against these other possibilities. Moreover, the observation that the man in the diagram is in trim shape depends on our intuitive idea of what constitutes trim and overweight body shapes. All told, this is very weak evidence for testing the relationship between exercise and weight loss.

The one-group pretest-posttest design offers somewhat better evidence that exercise produces weight-loss. Specifically, we have ruled out the possibility that the man was thin before beginning to exercise. However, we still have no assurance that it was his exercising that caused him to lose weight.

Finally, the static-group comparison eliminates the problem of our questionable definition of what constitutes trim or overweight body shapes. In this case, we can compare the shapes of the man who exercises and the one who does not. This design, however, reopens the possibility that the man who exercises was thin to begin with.

At this point I want to present in a more systematic way the factors that affect experimental research—those I've already discussed as well as additional factors. We're going to look at what Campbell and Stanley call the sources of internal invalidity, reviewed and expanded in a follow-up book by Thomas Cook and Donald Campbell (1979). Later, we'll look at the problem of generalizing experimental results to the "real" world, referred to as *external invalidity*. Having examined these, we'll be in a position to appreciate the advantages of some of the more sophisticated experimental and quasi-experimental designs social science researchers sometimes use.

Sources of Internal Invalidity

The problem of **internal invalidity** refers to the possibility that the conclusions drawn from experimental results may not accurately reflect what

FIGURE 9-3
Three Preexperimental Research Designs

One-Shot Case Study

A man who exercises is observed to be in trim shape

Comparison → Some intuitive standard of what constitutes a trim shape

Time 1   Time 2   Time 3

One-Group Pretest-Posttest Design

An overweight man who exercises is later observed to be in trim shape

Comparison

Time 1   Time 2   Time 3

Static-Group Comparison

A man who exercises is observed to be in trim shape while one who doesn't is observed to be overweight

Comparison

Time 1   Time 2   Time 3

---

has gone on in the experiment itself. The threat of internal invalidity is present whenever anything other than the experimental stimulus can affect the dependent variable. Campbell and Stanley (1963:5–6) and T. Cook and Campbell (1979: 51–55) point to several sources of the problem. Here are twelve:

1. *History.* Historical events may occur during the course of the experiment that will confound the experimental results. The assassination of an African-American leader during the course of an experiment on reducing anti–African-American prejudice would be an example.

2. *Maturation.* People are continually growing and changing, whether in an experiment or not, and such changes affect the results of the experiment. In a long-term experiment, the fact that the subjects grow older (and wiser?) may have an effect.

In shorter experiments, they will grow tired, sleepy, bored, or hungry, or change in other ways that may affect their behavior in the experiment.

3. *Testing.* Often the process of testing and retesting will influence people's behavior, thereby confounding the experimental results. Suppose we administer a questionnaire to a group as a way of measuring their prejudice. Then we administer an experimental stimulus and remeasure their prejudice. By the time we conduct the posttest, the subjects will probably have gotten more sensitive to the issue of prejudice and will be more thoughtful in their answers. In fact, they may have figured out that we are trying to find out how prejudiced they are, and, because few people like to appear prejudiced, they will be on their best behavior and give answers that they think we want or that will make them look good.

4. *Instrumentation.* Thus far, I haven't said very much about the process of measurement in pretesting and posttesting, but I'd like to remind you of the problems of conceptualization and operationalization discussed earlier. If we use different measures of the dependent variable (say, different questionnaires about prejudice), how can we be sure they're comparable to one another? Perhaps prejudice will seem to have decreased simply because the pretest measure was more sensitive than the posttest measure. Or if the measurements are being made by the experimenters, their standards or their abilities may change over the course of the experiment.

5. *Statistical regression.* Sometimes it's appropriate to conduct experiments on subjects who start out with extreme scores on the dependent variable. If you were testing a new method for teaching math to hardcore failures in math, you'd want to conduct your experiment on people who have done extremely poorly in math previously. But consider for a minute what is likely to happen to the math achievement of such people over time without any experimental interference. They're starting out so low that they can only stay at the bottom or improve: They can't get worse. Even without any experimental stimulus, then, the group as a whole is likely to show some improvement over time. Referring to a *regression to the mean,* statisticians often point out that extremely tall people as a group are likely to have children shorter than themselves, and extremely short people as a group are likely to have children taller than themselves. There is a danger, then, that changes occurring by virtue of subjects starting out in extreme positions will be attributed erroneously to the effects of the experimental stimulus.

6. *Selection biases.* We discussed bias in selection earlier when we examined different ways of selecting subjects for experiments and assigning them to experimental and control groups. Comparisons don't have any meaning unless the groups are *comparable.*

7. *Experimental mortality.* Although some social experiments could, I suppose, kill subjects, this problem refers to a more general and less extreme form of mortality. Often, experimental subjects will drop out of the experiment before it is completed, and this can affect statistical comparisons and conclusions. In the classical experiment involving an experimental and a control group, each with a pretest and posttest, suppose that the bigots in the experimental group are so offended by the African-American history film that they tell the experimenter to forget it, and they leave. Those subjects sticking around for the posttest will have been less prejudiced to start with, so the group results will reflect a substantial "decrease" in prejudice.

8. *Causal time-order.* Though rare in social research, ambiguity about the time-order of the experimental stimulus and the dependent variable can arise. Whenever this occurs, the research conclusion that the stimulus caused the dependent variable can be challenged with the explanation that the "dependent" variable actually caused changes in the stimulus (see Chapter 3).

9. *Diffusion or imitation of treatments.* When experimental and control-group subjects can communicate with each other, experimental subjects could pass on some elements of the experimental stimulus to the control group. Members of the exper-

FIGURE 9-4
Another Look at the Classical Experiment

Experimental group → Pretest → Stimulus → Posttest
Control group → Pretest → Posttest
COMPARISONS (between posttests, and between pretest and posttest of experimental group)
TIME →

imental group might tell control-group subjects about the African-American history film. In that case, the control group becomes affected by the stimulus and is not a real control. Sometimes we speak of the control group as having been "contaminated."

10. *Compensation.* As you'll see in Chapter 13, in experiments in real-life situations—such as a special educational program—subjects in the control group are often deprived of something considered to be of value. In such cases, there may be pressures to offer some form of compensation. For example, hospital staff might feel sorry for medical control group patients and give them extra "tender loving care." In such a situation, the control group is no longer a genuine control group.

11. *Compensatory rivalry.* In real-life experiments, the subjects deprived of the experimental stimulus may try to compensate for the missing stimulus by working harder. Suppose an experimental math program is the experimental stimulus; the control group may work harder than before on their math in the attempt to beat the "special" experimental subjects.

12. *Demoralization.* On the other hand, feelings of deprivation within the control group may result in their giving up. In educational experiments, demoralized control group subjects may stop studying, act up, or get angry.

These, then, are some of the sources of internal invalidity cited by Campbell, Stanley, and Cook. Aware of these, experimenters have devised designs aimed at handling them. The classical experiment, discussed earlier in the chapter, if coupled with proper subject selection and assignment, addresses each of these problems. Let's look again at that study design, presented graphically in Figure 9-4.

Pursuing the example of the African-American history film as an attempt to reduce anti–African-American prejudice, if we use the experimental design shown in Figure 9-4, we should expect two findings. For the experimental group, the level of prejudice measured in their posttest should be less than was found in their pretest. In addition, when the two posttests are compared, less prejudice should be found in the experimental group than in the control.

This design also guards against the problem of history in that anything occurring outside the experiment that might affect the experimental group should also affect the control group. There should still be a difference in the two posttest results. The same comparison guards against problems of maturation as long as the subjects have been randomly assigned to the two groups. Testing and instrumentation can't be problems, since both the experimental and control groups are subject to the same tests and experimenter effects. If the subjects have been assigned to the two groups randomly, statistical regression should affect both equally, even if people with extreme scores on prejudice (or whatever the dependent variable is) are being studied. Selection bias is ruled out by the random assignment of subjects.

Experimental mortality is more complicated to handle, but the data provided in this study design offer several ways to deal with it. Slight modifications to the design—administering a placebo (such as a film having nothing to do with African Americans) to the control group, for example—can make the problem even easier to manage.

The remaining five problems of internal invalidity are avoided through the careful administration of a controlled experimental design. The experimental design we've been discussing facilitates the clear specification of independent and dependent variables. Experimental and control subjects can be kept separate, reducing the possibility of diffusion or imitation of treatments. Administrative controls can avoid compensations given to the control group, and compensatory rivalry can be watched for and taken into account in evaluating the results of the experiment, as can the problem of demoralization.

Sources of External Invalidity

Internal invalidity accounts for only some of the complications faced by experimenters. In addition, there are problems of what Campbell and Stanley call **external invalidity,** which relates to the *generalizability* of experimental findings to the "real" world. Even if the results of an experiment are an accurate gauge of what happened during that experiment, do they really tell us anything about life in the wilds of society?

Campbell and Stanley describe four forms of this problem; I'll present one of them to you as an illustration. The generalizability of experimental findings is jeopardized, as the authors point out, if there is an interaction between the testing situation and the experimental stimulus (1963:18). Here's an example of what they mean.

Staying with the study of prejudice and the African-American history film, let's suppose that our experimental group—in the classical experiment—has less prejudice in its posttest than in its pretest and that its posttest shows less prejudice than that of the control group. We can be confident that the film actually reduced prejudice among our experimental subjects. But would it have the same effect if the film were shown in theaters or on television? We can't be sure, since the film might only be effective when people have been sensitized to the issue of prejudice, as the subjects may have been in taking the pretest. This is an example of interaction between the testing and the stimulus. The classical experimental design cannot control for that possibility. Fortunately, experimenters have devised other designs that can.

The *Solomon four-group design* (Campbell and Stanley 1963:24–25) addresses the problem of testing interaction with the stimulus. As the name suggests, it involves four groups of subjects, assigned randomly from a pool. Figure 9-5 presents this design graphically.

Notice that Groups 1 and 2 in Figure 9-5 compose the classical experiment. Group 3 is administered the experimental stimulus without a pretest, and Group 4 is only posttested. This latest experimental design permits four meaningful comparisons. If the African-American history film really reduces prejudice—unaccounted for by the problem of internal validity *and* unaccounted for by an interaction between the testing and the stimulus—we should expect four findings:

1. In Group 1, posttest prejudice should be less than pretest prejudice.
2. There should be less prejudice evident in the Group 1 posttest than in the Group 2 posttest.
3. The Group 3 posttest should show less prejudice than the Group 2 pretest.
4. The Group 3 posttest should show less prejudice than the Group 4 posttest.

Notice that findings (3) and (4) rule out any interaction between the testing and the stimulus. And remember that these comparisons are meaningful only if subjects have been assigned randomly to the different groups, thereby providing groups of equal prejudice initially, even though their preexperiment prejudice is only measured in Groups 1 and 2.

There is a side benefit to this research design, as the authors point out. Not only does the Solomon four-group design rule out interactions between testing and the stimulus, it also provides data for comparisons that will reveal the amount

FIGURE 9-5
The Solomon Four-Group Design

Group 1   Pretest   Stimulus   Posttest
Group 2   Pretest   Posttest
Group 3   Stimulus   Posttest
Group 4   Posttest

———— TIME ————→

① Posttest should show less prejudice than the pretest.
② Posttest and pretest should show the same amount of prejudice.
③ Group 1 should show less prejudice than Group 2.
④ Group 3 should show less prejudice than Group 4.

of such interaction that occurs in the classical experimental design. This knowledge would allow a researcher to review and evaluate the value of any prior research that used the simpler design.

The last experimental design I want to mention is what Campbell and Stanley (1963:25–26) call the *posttest-only control group design;* it consists of the second half—Groups 3 and 4—of the Solomon design. As the authors argue persuasively, with proper randomization, only Groups 3 and 4 are needed for a true experiment that controls for the problems of internal invalidity as well as for the interaction between testing and stimulus. With randomized assignment to experimental and control groups (which distinguishes this design from the static-group comparison discussed earlier), the subjects will be initially comparable on the dependent variable—comparable enough to satisfy the conventional statistical tests used to evaluate the results—so it is not necessary to measure them. Indeed, Campbell and Stanley suggest the only justification for pretesting in this situation is tradition. Experimenters have simply grown accustomed to pretesting and feel more secure with research designs that include it. Be clear, however,

that this applies only to experiments in which subjects have been assigned to experimental and control groups *randomly,* since that's what justifies the assumption that the groups are equivalent—without actually measuring them to find out.

I trust this discussion has given you a sense of the intricacies of experimental design, its problems, and some solutions. There are, of course, a great many other possible experimental designs in use. Some involve more than one stimulus and combinations of stimuli. Others involve several tests of the dependent variable over time and the administration of the stimulus at different times for different groups. If you're interested in pursuing this topic, look at the Campbell and Stanley book, since such variations go beyond the scope of this discussion.

■ AN ILLUSTRATION OF EXPERIMENTATION

Experiments have been used to study a wide variety of topics in the social sciences. Some experiments have been conducted within laboratory situations; others occur out in the "real world." The following discussion will give you a glimpse of both, while focusing on a single topic.

In George Bernard Shaw's well-loved play, *Pygmalion*—the basis for the long-running Broadway musical, *My Fair Lady*—Eliza Doolittle speaks of the powers others have in determining our social identity. Here's how she distinguishes the way she's treated by her tutor, Professor Higgins, and by Higgins' friend, Colonel Pickering:

■ You see, really and truly, apart from the things anyone can pick up (the dressing and the proper way of speaking, and so on), the difference between a lady and a flower girl is not how she behaves, but how she's treated. I shall always be a flower girl to Professor Higgins, because he always treats me as a flower girl, and always will, but I know I can be a lady to you, because you always treat me as a lady, and always will.

The sentiment Eliza expresses here is basic social science, addressed more formally by sociologists such as Charles Horton Cooley ("Looking-glass self") and George Herbert Mead ("the generalized other"). The basic point is that who we think we are—our *self-concept*—and how we behave is largely a function of how others see and treat us. Related to this, the way others perceive us is largely conditioned by expectations they may have in advance. If they've been told we're stupid, for example, they're likely to see us that way—and we may come to see ourselves that way and actually act stupidly.

If you've begun thinking this set of ideas would be nicely suited to controlled experiments, you're absolutely correct. Moreover, this topic has generally been called the *Pygmalion effect*.

In one of the best-known experiments on this topic, Robert Rosenthal and Lenore Jacobson (1968) administered what they called a "Harvard Test of Inflected Acquisition" to students in a West Coast school. Subsequently, they met with the students' teachers to present the results of the test. In particular, Rosenthal and Jacobson identified certain students as very likely to exhibit a sudden spurt in academic abilities during the coming year, based on the results of the test.

When IQ test scores were compared later, the researchers' predictions proved accurate. The students identified as "spurters" far exceeded their classmates during the following year, suggesting that the predictive test was a powerful one. In fact, the test was a hoax! The researchers had made their predictions randomly among both good and poor students. What they told the teachers did not really reflect students' test scores at all. The progress made by the "spurters" was simply a result of the teachers expecting the improvement and paying more attention to those students, encouraging them, and rewarding them for achievements. Notice the similarity between this situation and the Hawthorne effect, mentioned earlier.

The Rosenthal-Jacobson study attracted a lot of popular as well as scientific attention. Subsequent experiments have focused on specific aspects of what has become known as the *attribution process*, or the *expectations communication model*. This research, largely conducted by psychologists, parallels research primarily by sociologists, which takes a slightly different focus and is often gathered under the label *expectations-states theory*. The former studies focus on situations in which the expectations of a dominant individual affect the performance of subordinates—as in the case of a teacher and students, or a boss and employees. The sociological research has tended to focus more on the role of expectations among equals in small, task-oriented groups. In a jury, for example, how do jurors initially evaluate each other and how do those initial assessments affect later interactions?

Here's an example of an experiment conducted to examine the way our perceptions of our abilities and those of others affect our willingness to accept the other person's ideas. Martha Foschi, G. Keith Warriner, and Stephen Hart (1985) were particularly interested in the role "standards" played in that respect.

■ In general terms, by "standards" we mean how well or how poorly a person has to perform in order for an ability to be attributed or denied him/her. In our view, standards are a key variable affecting how evaluations are processed and what expectations result. For example, depending on the standards used, the same level of success may be interpreted as a major accomplishment or dismissed as unimportant.

(1985:108–109)

To begin examining the role of standards, the researchers designed an experiment involving four experimental groups and a control. Subjects were told the experiment involved something called "pattern recognition ability," which was an innate ability some people had and others didn't. The researchers said subjects would be working in pairs on pattern recognition problems. As you've guessed, there is no such thing as "pattern recognition ability."

The first stage of the experiment was to "test" each subject's abilities at pattern recognition. If you had been a subject in the experiment, you would have been shown a geometrical pattern for 8 seconds, followed by two more patterns, each of which was similar to but not the same as the first one. Your task would be to choose which of the subsequent set had a pattern closest to the first one you saw. You would be asked to do this 20 times, and a computer printout would print out your "score." Half the subjects were told they had gotten 14 correct; the other half were told they had only gotten 6 correct—regardless of which patterns they matched with which. Depending on the luck of the draw, you would either think you had done quite well or quite badly. Notice, however, that you wouldn't really have any standard for judging your performance—since 4 correct might be considered a great performance.

At the same time you were given your score, however, you would also be given your "partner's score," although both the "partners" and their "scores" were also computerized fictions. (Subjects were told they would be communicating with their partners via computer terminals but would not be allowed to see each other.) If you were assigned a score of 14, you'd be told your partner had a score of 6; if you were assigned 6, you'd be told your partner had 14.

This procedure meant that you would enter the teamwork phase of the experiment believing either (1) you had done better than your partner or (2) you had done worse than your partner. This constituted part of the "standard" you would be operating under in the experiment. In addition, half of each group was told that a score of between 12 and 20 meant the subject *definitely* had pattern recognition ability; the other subjects were told that a score of 14 wasn't really high enough to prove anything definite. Thus, you would emerge from this with one of the following beliefs:

1. You are *definitely better* at pattern recognition than your partner.
2. You are *possibly better* than your partner.
3. You are *possibly worse* than your partner.
4. You are *definitely worse* than your partner.

The control group for this experiment was told nothing about their own abilities or their partners'. In other words, they had no expectations.

The final step in the experiment was to set the "teams" to work. As before, each subject would be given an initial pattern, followed by a comparison pair to choose from. When you entered your choice in this round, however, you would be told what your partner had answered; then you would be asked to choose again. In your final choice, you could either stick with your original choice or switch. The "partner's" choice was, of course, created by the computer, and as you can guess, there was often a disagreement in the team: 16 out of 20 times, in fact.

The dependent variable in this experiment was the extent to which subjects would switch their choices to match those of their partners. The researchers hypothesized that "the *definitely better* group would switch least often, followed by the *probably better* group, followed by the *control group*, followed by the *probably worse* group, followed by the *definitely worse* group, who would switch most often."

The number of times subjects in the five groups switched their answers follows. Realize that each had 16 opportunities to do so. These data indicate that each of the researchers' expectations was correct—with the exception of the *possibly/definitely worse* comparison. The latter group was in fact the more likely to switch, but the difference is too small to be taken as a confirmation of the hypothesis. (Chapter 17 will discuss the statistical tests that let you make decisions like this.)

Group	Mean Number of Switches
Definitely better	5.05
Possibly better	6.23
Control Group	7.95
Possibly worse	9.23
Definitely worse	9.28

In more detailed analyses, it was found that the same basic pattern held for both men and women, though it was somewhat clearer for women than for men. Here are the actual data:

	Mean Number of Switches	
	Women	Men
Definitely better	4.50	5.66
Possibly better	6.34	6.10
Control Group	7.68	8.34
Possibly worse	9.36	9.09
Definitely worse	10.00	8.70

Because specific research efforts like this one sometimes seem extremely focused in their scope, you might wonder about their relevance to anything. As part of a larger research effort, however, studies like this one add concrete pieces to our understanding of more general social processes.

It's worth taking a minute or so to consider some of the life situations where "expectation states" might have very real and important consequences. I've mentioned the case of jury deliberations. How about all forms of prejudice and discrimination? Or, consider how expectation states figure into job interviews or meeting your heartthrob's parents. Think about it, and you'll see other situations where these laboratory concepts apply in real life.

■ FOCUS GROUPS

Sometimes subjects are brought into a laboratory setting for less rigorously structured explorations than characterize the controlled experiment. Particularly in the field of market research, social scientists may use focus groups to probe various aspects of an issue.

Imagine that you're thinking about introducing a new product—a new computer, for example. Let's suppose, in fact, that you've invented a new computer that not only does word processing, spreadsheets, data analysis, and the like, but also contains a fax machine, AM/FM/TV tuner, CD player, dual-cassette unit, microwave oven, denture cleaner, and coffee maker. To highlight its computing and coffee-making features, you're thinking of calling it *The Compulator*. You figure the new computer will sell for about $28,000, and you want to know whether people are likely to buy it. Your prospects might be well served by focus groups.

In a focus group, typically 12 to 15 people are brought together in a room to engage in a guided discussion of some topic—in this case, the acceptability and salability of *The Compulator*. These subjects are selected on the basis of relevancy to the topic under study. Given the likely cost of *The Compulator*, your focus group participants would probably be limited to upper-income groups, for example. Other, similar considerations might figure into the selection, although participants are not likely to be chosen through rigorous, probability sampling methods. This means that participants do not statistically represent any meaningful population. However, the purpose of the study is to explore rather than to describe or explain in any definitive sense.

Typically, more than one focus group is convened in a given study, because there is a serious danger that a single group of 7 to 12 people would be too atypical to offer any generalizable insights.

Richard Krueger points to five advantages of focus groups:

1. the technique is a socially oriented research method capturing real-life data in a social environment
2. it has flexibility
3. it has high face validity
4. it has speedy results; and
5. it is low in cost.

(1988:47)

The group dynamics that occur in focus groups frequently bring out aspects of the topic that would not have been anticipated by the researcher and would not have emerged from interviews with individuals. In a side conversation, for example, a couple of the participants might start joking about the risk of leaving out one letter from the product's name. This realization might save us from great embarrassment later on. Similar research might have spared Chevrolet an unsuccessful attempt to sell its Nova in Spanish-speaking countries, where the name translates roughly as "no go."

Krueger also notes some disadvantages of the method:

- 1. focus groups afford the researcher less control than individual interviews
- 2. data are difficult to analyze
- 3. moderators require special skills
- 4. difference between groups can be troublesome
- 5. groups are difficult to assemble; and
- 6. the discussion must be conducted in a conducive environment.

(1988:44–45)

William Gamson (1992) has used focus groups to examine how U.S. citizens frame their views of political issues. Having picked four issues—affirmative action, nuclear power, troubled industries, and the Arab-Israeli conflict—Gamson undertook a content analysis of press coverage to get an idea of the media context within which we think and talk about politics. Then the focus groups were convened for a first-hand observation of the process of people discussing issues with their friends.

In addition, David Morgan (1993) suggests focus groups are an excellent device for generating questionnaire items for a subsequent survey.

An interesting variation on the idea of a focus group was conducted at the University of Texas at Austin in January 1996. Organizers selected a national, random sample of 459 "delegates" to attend a National Issues Convention. Over one weekend, attendees heard from several political figures on a variety of issues. They had a chance to question Vice President Al Gore and Republican presidential candidates Phil Gramm, Richard Lugar, Steve Forbes, and Lamar Alexander (Beniger 1996).

The researchers who organized the convention were especially interested in measuring opinions at the beginning and the end of it to see how an intensive political educational experience would change voters' views. For example, about two-thirds believed there had been a breakdown in the traditional family in the United States, and the deliberations didn't change this percentage. Those attributing the breakdown to economic pressure increased from 36 to 51 percent, while those saying it was due to a breakdown in values fell from 58 to 48 percent. In foreign affairs, the percentage agreeing with the statement, "The United States should continue to engage in military cooperation with other nations to address trouble spots in the world" increased from 72 to 82.

Consistently, the percentage saying "don't know" decreased, and a definite shift occured in response to the statement, "I have opinions about politics that are worth listening to."

	Before	After	Difference
Strongly agree	41.0%	68.1%	+27.1
Agree somewhat	43.4	25.8	−17.6
Disagree somewhat	8.4	3.6	−4.8
Disagree strongly	4.1	1.4	−2.7
Don't know	3.2	1.1	−2.1

Whereas laboratory experiments are often criticized for being too alien to everyday life, an attempt is made in focus groups to simulate the kinds of bull-session discussion people commonly have when they discuss some topic. Some experiments, as you'll see next, actually occur in the midst of real life, making the importance of experimental logic all the more apparent to our living together in society.

■ "NATURAL" EXPERIMENTS

Although we tend to equate the terms *experiment* and *laboratory experiment,* many important social scientific experiments occur outside controlled settings, often in the course of normal social events. Sometimes nature designs and executes experiments that we can observe and analyze; sometimes social and political decision makers serve this natural function.

Let's imagine, for example, that a hurricane has struck a particular town. Some residents of the town suffer severe financial damages, and others escape relatively lightly. What, we might ask, are the behavioral consequences of suffering a natural disaster? Are those who suffer most more likely to take precautions against future disasters than those who suffer least? To answer these questions, we might interview residents of the town some time after the hurricane. We might question them regarding their precautions before the hurricane and precautions they are currently taking, comparing those who suffered greatly from the hurricane with those who suffered relatively little. In this fashion, we might take advantage of a natural experiment, which we could not have arranged even if we were perversely willing to do so.

A similar example comes from the annals of social research concerning World War II. After the war ended, social researchers undertook retrospective surveys of wartime morale among civilians in several German cities. Among other things, they wanted to determine the effect of mass bombing on the morale of civilians. They compared the reports of wartime morale of residents in heavily bombed cities and cities that received relatively little bombing. (Bombing did not reduce morale.)

Because the researcher must take things pretty much as they occur, natural experiments raise many of the validity problems discussed earlier. Thus when Stanislav Kasl, Rupert Chisolm, and Brenda Eskenazi (1981) chose to study the impact of the Three Mile Island (TMI) nuclear accident on plant workers, they had to be especially careful in the study design:

■ Disaster research is necessarily opportunistic, quasi-experimental, and after-the-fact. In the terminology of Campbell and Stanley's classical analysis of research designs, our study falls into the "static-group comparison" category, considered one of the weak research designs. However, the weaknesses are potential and their actual presence depends on the unique circumstances of each study.

(1981:474)

The foundation of this study was a survey of the people who had been working at Three Mile Island on March 28, 1978, when the cooling system failed in the number 2 reactor and began melting the uranium core. The survey was conducted five to six months after the accident. Among other things, the survey questionnaire measured workers' attitudes toward working at nuclear power plants. If they had measured only the TMI workers' attitudes after the accident, the researchers would have had no idea whether attitudes had changed as a consequence of the accident. But they improved their study design by selecting another, nearby—seemingly comparable—nuclear power plant (abbreviated as PB) and surveyed workers there as a control group: hence their reference to a static-group comparison.

Even with an experimental and a control group, the authors were wary of potential problems in their design. In particular, their design was based on the idea that the two sets of workers were equivalent to one another, except for the single fact of the accident. The researchers could have assumed this if they had been able to assign workers to the two plants randomly, but of course that was not the case. Instead, they needed to compare characteristics of the two groups and infer whether they were equivalent. Ultimately, the researchers concluded that the two sets of workers were very much alike, and the plant they worked at was merely a function of where they lived.

Even granting that the two sets of workers were equivalent, the researchers faced another problem of comparability. They could not contact all the workers who had been employed at TMI at the time of the accident. The researchers discuss the problem as follows:

■ One special attrition problem in this study was the possibility that some of the no-contact nonrespondents among the TMI subjects, but not PB subjects, had permanently left the area because of the accident. This biased attrition would, most likely, attenuate the estimated extent of the impact. Using the evidence of disconnected or "not in service" telephone numbers, we estimate this bias to be negligible (1 percent).

(KASL ET AL. 1981:475)

The TMI example points both to the special problems involved in natural experiments and to the possibility for taking those problems into account. Social research generally requires ingenuity and insight; natural experiments call for a little more than the average.

Earlier in this chapter, I introduced a hypothetical example of using an African-American history film to reduce prejudice. Sandra Ball-Rokeach, Joel Grube, and Milton Rokeach (1981) were able to address that topic in real life through a natural experiment. In 1977, the television dramatization of Alex Haley's *Roots* was presented by ABC on eight consecutive nights. It garnered the largest audiences in television history up to that time. Ball-Rokeach and her colleagues wanted to know if *Roots* changed white Americans' attitudes toward African Americans. Their opportunity arose in 1979, when a sequel—*Roots: The Next Generation*—was televised. Although it would have been nice (from a researcher's point of view) to assign random samples of Americans to either watch or not watch the show, that wasn't possible. Instead, the researchers selected four samples in Washington State and mailed questionnaires that measured attitudes toward African Americans. Following the last episode of the show, respondents were called and asked how many, if any, episodes they had watched. Subsequently, questionnaires were sent to respondents, remeasuring their attitudes toward African Americans.

By comparing attitudes before and after for both those who watched the show and those who didn't, the researchers reached several conclusions. For example, they found that people with already egalitarian attitudes were much more likely to watch the show than those who were more prejudiced toward African Americans: a self-selection phenomenon. Comparing the before and after attitudes of those who watched the show, moreover, suggested the show itself had little or no effect. Those who watched it were no more egalitarian afterward than they had been before.

This example anticipates the subject of Chapter 13, *evaluation research*, which can be seen as a special type of natural experiment. As you'll see, it involves taking the logic of experimentation into the field to observe and evaluate the effects of stimuli in real life. Because it is an increasingly important form of social research, I'll devote a whole chapter to it.

■ STRENGTHS AND WEAKNESSES OF THE EXPERIMENTAL METHOD

The chief advantage of a controlled experiment lies in the isolation of the experimental variable and its impact over time. This is seen most clearly in terms of the basic experimental model. A group of experimental subjects are found, at the outset of the experiment, to have a certain characteristic; following the administration of an experimental stimulus, they are found to have a different characteristic. To the extent that subjects have experienced no other stimuli, we may conclude that the change of characteristics is attributable to the experimental stimulus.

Further, since individual experiments are often rather limited in scope, requiring relatively little time and money and relatively few subjects, we often can replicate a given experiment several times using several different groups of subjects. (This isn't always the case, of course, but it's usually easier to repeat experiments than, say, survey research.) As in all other forms of scientific research, replication of research findings strengthens our confidence in the validity and generalizability of those findings.

Chapter 9: Experiments

The greatest weakness of laboratory experiments lies in their artificiality. Social processes that occur in a laboratory setting might not necessarily occur in more natural social settings. For example, an African-American history film might genuinely reduce prejudice among a group of experimental subjects. This would not necessarily mean, however, that the same film shown in neighborhood movie theaters throughout the country would reduce prejudice among the general public. Artificiality is not as much of a problem, of course, for natural experiments as for those conducted in the laboratory.

In discussing several of the sources of internal and external invalidity mentioned by Campbell, Stanley, and Cook, we saw that we can create experimental designs that logically control such problems. This possibility points to one of the great advantages of experiments: They lend themselves to a logical rigor that is often much more difficult to achieve in other modes of observation.

■ MAIN POINTS

- Experiments are an excellent vehicle for the controlled testing of causal processes.
- The classical experiment tests the effect of an experimental stimulus on some dependent variable through the pretesting and post-testing of experimental and control groups.
- It is generally less important that a group of experimental subjects be representative of some larger population than that experimental and control groups be similar to one another.
- Randomization is the generally preferred method for achieving comparability in the experimental and control groups.
- Campbell and Stanley describe three forms of preexperiments: the one-shot case study, the one-group pretest-posttest design, and the static-group comparison.
- There are 12 sources of internal invalidity in experimental design:
  1. History
  2. Maturation
  3. Testing
  4. Instrumentation
  5. Statistical regression
  6. Selection biases
  7. Experimental mortality
  8. Causal time-order
  9. Diffusion or imitation of treatments
  10. Compensation
  11. Compensatory rivalry
  12. Demoralization
- The classical experiment with random assignment of subjects guards against each of these sources of internal invalidity.
- Experiments also face problems of external invalidity: Experimental findings may not reflect real life.
- The interaction of testing with the stimulus is an example of external invalidity; the classical experiment does not guard against it.
- The Solomon four-group design and other variations on the classical experiment can safeguard against external invalidity.
- Campbell and Stanley suggest that, given proper randomization in the assignment of subjects to the experimental and control groups, there is no need for pretesting in experiments.
- Natural experiments often occur in the course of social life in the real world, and social researchers can implement them in somewhat the same way they would design and conduct laboratory experiments.

■ REVIEW QUESTIONS AND EXERCISES

1. Pick 6 of the 12 sources of internal invalidity discussed in the book and make up examples (not discussed in the book) to illustrate each.
2. Think of a recent natural disaster you've witnessed or read about. Frame a research question that might be studied by treating that disaster as a natural experiment. In two or three paragraphs, outline how the study might be done.
3. In this chapter, we looked briefly at the problem of "placebo effects." On the Web, find a study in which the placebo effect figured im-

portantly. Write a brief report on the study, including the source of your information. (*Hint:* you might want to do a net search of *placebo*.)

■ ADDITIONAL READINGS

Campbell, Donald, and Julian Stanley. *Experimental and Quasi-Experimental Designs for Research*. Chicago: Rand McNally, 1963. An excellent analysis of the logic and methods of experimentation in social research. This book is especially useful in its application of the logic of experiments to other social research methods. Though fairly old, this book has attained the status of a classic and is still frequently cited.

Cook, Thomas D., and Donald T. Campbell. *Quasi-Experimentation: Design and Analysis Issues for Field Settings*. Chicago: Rand McNally, 1979. An expanded and updated version of Campbell and Stanley.

Jones, Stephen R. G. "Worker Independence and Output: The Hawthorne Studies Reevaluated." *American Sociological Review* 55 (April 1990): 176–90. This article reviews these classical studies and questions the traditional interpretation (which was presented in this chapter).

Martin, David W. *Doing Psychology Experiments*. Monterey, CA: Brooks/Cole, 1991. Thorough explanations of the logic behind research methods, often in a humorous style. The book emphasizes ideas of particular importance to the beginning researcher, such as getting an idea for an experiment or reviewing the literature.

Morgan, David L., ed. *Successful Focus Groups: Advancing the State of the Art*. Newbury Park, CA: Sage, 1993. This collection of articles on the uses of focus groups points to many aspects not normally considered.

Ray, William, and Richard Ravizza. *Methods toward a Science of Behavior and Experience*. Belmont, CA: Wadsworth, 1993. A comprehensive examination of social science research methods, with a special emphasis on experimentation. This book is especially strong in the philosophy of science.

CHAPTER 10 *Survey Research*

What You'll Learn in This Chapter

Here you'll learn how to do mail, interview, and telephone surveys. You'll need to recall the earlier discussions of sampling and question wording.

INTRODUCTION

TOPICS APPROPRIATE TO SURVEY RESEARCH

SELF-ADMINISTERED QUESTIONNAIRES
Mail Distribution and Return
Electronic Surveys
Monitoring Returns
Follow-up Mailings
Acceptable Response Rates
A Case Study

INTERVIEW SURVEYS
The Role of the Survey Interviewer
General Rules for Survey Interviewing
Coordination and Control

TELEPHONE SURVEYS
Computer Assisted Telephone Interviewing (CATI)

COMPARISON OF THE THREE METHODS

STRENGTHS AND WEAKNESSES OF SURVEY RESEARCH

SECONDARY ANALYSIS

MAIN POINTS

REVIEW QUESTIONS AND EXERCISES

ADDITIONAL READINGS

■ INTRODUCTION

Survey research is a very old research technique. In the Old Testament, for example, we find the following:

■ After the plague the Lord said to Moses and to Eleazar the son of Aaron, the priest, "Take a census of all the congregation of the people of Israel, from twenty old and upward...."

(NUMBERS 26:1–2)

Ancient Egyptian rulers conducted censuses to help them administer their domains. Jesus was born away from home because Joseph and Mary were journeying to Joseph's ancestral home for a Roman census.

A little-known survey was attempted among French workers in 1880. A German political sociologist mailed some 25,000 questionnaires to workers to determine the extent of their exploitation by employers. The rather lengthy questionnaire included items such as these:

■ Does your employer or his representative resort to trickery in order to defraud you of a part of your earnings?

If you are paid piece rates, is the quality of the article made a pretext for fraudulent deductions from your wages?

The survey researcher in this case was not George Gallup but Karl Marx ([1880] 1956: 208). Though 25,000 questionnaires were mailed out, there is no record of any being returned.

Tom Smith has traced the history of U.S. political polling back to within 50 years of the nation's founding:

■ The election of 1824 marked the end of the first American party system, formed in the 1790s when the national unity government of George Washington began to split into the Federalists, led by Vice President John Adams, and the Democratic-Republicans of Secretary of State Thomas Jefferson.

(1990:22)

Smith indicates that many of the straw polls were conducted at public gatherings, such as military musters. He quotes a report in the August 5, 1824, edition of the *Carolina Observer*.

■ At a company muster held at Maj. Wm. Watfard's, Bertie County, on the 17th July, in the afternoon it was proposed to take the sentiments of the company on the Presidential question, when the vote stood as follows:

Jackson	102
Crawford	30
Adams	1
Clay	0

(T. SMITH, 1990:26)

Today, survey research is perhaps the most frequently used mode of observation in the social sciences. As we saw in Table 4-1, it is far and away the most common method reported in recent articles of the *American Sociological Review*. I'm certain that you've been a respondent in a survey more than once; you may have even done a survey of your own. In a typical survey, the researcher selects a sample of respondents and administers a standardized questionnaire to them.

Because several of the fundamental elements of survey research have already been covered in detail in this book, you're already partially trained in this important research method. In Chapter 6, we examined the logic and techniques of questionnaire construction, so I won't repeat that in this chapter. Also, Chapter 8 has already covered sampling, referring most often to survey situations.

Given that you already know how to prepare a questionnaire and select a sample of people to answer it, this chapter will focus on the options available to you for administering the questionnaire. How do you go about getting questionnaires answered? As you'll see, sometimes it's appropriate to have respondents complete questionnaires themselves, but other times it's more appropriate to have interviewers ask the questions and record the answers given. This latter technique can be used in face-to-face **interviews** or over the telephone. We'll examine all these possibilities and then compare their relative advantages and disadvantages.

The chapter concludes with a short discussion of **secondary analysis,** the analysis of survey data collected by someone else, perhaps for some purpose other than that of subsequent analyses. This use of survey results has become an important aspect of survey research in recent years, and it's especially useful for students and others with scarce research funds.

Let's begin by looking at the kinds of topics you could study using survey research.

■ TOPICS APPROPRIATE TO SURVEY RESEARCH

Surveys may be used for descriptive, explanatory, and exploratory purposes. They are chiefly used in studies that have individual people as the units of analysis. Although this method can be used for other units of analysis, such as groups or interactions, some individual persons must serve as respondents or informants. Thus, we could undertake a survey in which divorces were the unit of analysis, but we would need to administer the survey questionnaire to the participants in the divorces (or to some other informants).

Survey research is probably the best method available to the social scientist interested in collecting original data for describing a population too large to observe directly. Careful probability sampling provides a group of respondents whose characteristics may be taken to reflect those of the larger population, and carefully constructed standardized questionnaires provide data in the same form from all respondents. The U.S. Decennial Census differs from surveys primarily in that all members of the U.S. population are studied rather than a sample. (The Census Bureau also conducts numerous sample surveys in addition to the decennial censuses, including the Current Population Survey of 60,000 households a month, used to measure unemployment.)

Surveys are also excellent vehicles for measuring attitudes and orientations in a large population. Public opinion polls—for example, Gallup, Harris, Roper, Yankelovich—are well-known examples of this use.

The popularity of public opinion polling—particularly political polling—has often made the research technique itself a subject of public discussion, as indicated in this sampling of newspaper headlines:

- "Polls' Divergence Puzzles Experts"
- "Why Trust the Polls?"
- "Networks Criticized on Polls"
- "First, You Take a Poll—Not Always"
- "Are Restraints Needed on Election Day Polls?"
- "Dilemma of Voter Polls: Suspense or Knowledge"
- "Pollsters Bicker on Why Landslide Caught Them"

Perhaps my favorite story in this genre appeared on May 20, 1985, in the *New York Times* under the headline "Pollsters Cite Surveys Indicating Confidence in Their Work." Adam Clymer began his report on the meetings of the American Association for Public Opinion Research this way:

■ Two of the nation's leading polltakers say their surveys show that the public is pretty well satisfied with the accuracy and usefulness of public opinion polls. But as they discussed their findings with their colleagues, they sounded as if they did not trust their own results.

The public's opinion of public opinion research is further complicated by scientifically unsound "surveys" that nonetheless capture our attention because of the topics they cover and/or their "findings." A good recent example may be found in the "Hite Reports" on human sexuality. While enjoying considerable attention in the popular press, the writer Shere Hite was roundly criticized by the research community for her data-collection methods. For example, a 1987 Hite report was based on questionnaires completed by women around the country—but which women? Hite reported that she distributed some 100,000 questionnaires through various organizations, and around 4,500 were returned.

Now 4,500 and 100,000 are large numbers in the context of survey sampling. However, given Hite's research methods, her 4,500 respondents didn't necessarily represent U.S. women any more than the *Literary Digest*'s enormous 1936 sample represented the U.S. electorate when their 2 million sample ballots indicated Alf Landon would bury FDR in a landslide.

Sometimes, people use the pretense of survey research for quite different purposes. For example, you may have received a telephone call indicating you've been selected for a survey, only to find the first question was "How would you like to make thousands of dollars a week right there in your own home?" Or you may have been told you could win a prize if you could name the president whose picture is on the penny. (Tell them it's Elvis.) Unfortunately, a few unscrupulous telemarketers do try to prey on the general cooperation people have given to survey researchers.

By the same token, the political parties and charitable organizations have begun conducting phony "surveys." Often under the guise of collecting public opinion about some issue, callers ultimately ask respondents for a monetary contribution.

Recent political campaigns have produced another form of bogus survey, called the "push poll." Here's what the American Association for Public Opinion Polling had to say in condemning this practice:

■ A "push poll" is a telemarketing technique in which telephone calls are used to canvass potential voters, feeding them false or misleading "information" about a candidate under the pretense of taking a poll to see how this "information" affects voter preferences. In fact, the intent is not to measure public opinion but to manipulate it—to "push" voters away from one candidate and toward the opposing candidate. Such polls defame selected candidates by spreading false or misleading information about them. The intent is to disseminate campaign propaganda under the guise of conducting a legitimate public opinion poll.

(BEDNARZ 1996)

A letter signed jointly by 34 polling companies pointed to another distinction between survey research and push polls:

■ Survey research firms only interview a limited sample of people that attempts to mirror the entire population being studied, frequently as low as 300 interviews in a congressional district to a high of 800 or 1000 interviews in a major statewide study. Push-polls contact thousands of people per hour with an objective of reaching sometimes hundreds of thousands of households.

(THOMPSON 1996)

In short, the term "survey" or "poll" does not necessarily mean you should put your trust in what follows. Despite the misuses of the technique, however, survey research can be a useful tool of social inquiry as the accompanying box, "A Candy Poll," indicates. The key is for you to be able to separate the wheat from the chaff. This chapter aims at assisting you in that task. Let's turn now to the three major methods for getting responses to questionnaires.

■ SELF-ADMINISTERED QUESTIONNAIRES

There are three main methods of administering survey questionnaires to a sample of respondents. This section will deal with the method in which respondents are asked to complete the questionnaires themselves—*self-administered questionnaires*. The following sections will deal with surveys administered by staff interviewers in face-to-face encounters or by telephone.

Although the mail survey is the typical method used in self-administered studies, there are several other common methods. At times, it may be appropriate to administer the questionnaire to a group of respondents gathered at the same place at the same time. A survey of students taking introductory psychology might be conducted in this manner during class. High school students might be surveyed during homeroom period.

A Candy Poll

Paul T. Melevin, who teaches research methods in San Diego, told me about one of his students, Jocelyn Valencia, who felt it would help her mastery of the subject if she could put it to work in her job: teaching third-grade mathematics.

When Ms. Valencia started telling her class about the research class she was taking, they became unexpectedly interested in it. In particular, they wanted to know more about survey research as a means of assessing public opinion.

It seems the San Diego third-graders had a problem. It was the general consensus in one of Ms. Valencia's classes that the school candy machine was understocking Snickers bars. They were convinced that most students wanted more Snickers bars in the machine, but they felt powerless to bring about a change. The idea of measuring student candy preferences appealed to them.

Before you could say probability-proportionate-to-size, the students had selected a random sample of the student body and had drafted a questionnaire to measure candy preferences. Realizing that the kindergarten children wouldn't be able to complete the questionnaire, Ms. Valencia's third-graders drafted an interview schedule for face-to-face interviews with the littlest kids.

Throughout the whole process, she warned her young researchers against the impact of researcher bias—especially in the case of the interviews. This was particularly important, since a lot of the youngest respondents were a little weak on brand recognition, often giving a preference for "Halloween candy" or something equally ambiguous.

When all the data had been tabulated, Snickers did emerge as the most popular specific candy bar (hypothesis confirmed), although Ms. Valencia had to keep pointing out that most respondents chose something else. Now there's a group of third-graders who know the difference between a majority and a plurality.

Some recent experimentation has been conducted with regard to the home delivery of questionnaires. A research worker delivers the questionnaire to the home of sample respondents and explains the study. Then the questionnaire is left for the respondent to complete, and the researcher picks it up later.

Home delivery and the mail can be used in combination as well. Questionnaires are mailed to families, and then research workers visit homes to pick up the questionnaires and check them for completeness. In just the opposite method, questionnaires have been hand delivered by research workers with a request that the respondents mail the completed questionnaires to the research office.

On the whole, when a research worker either delivers the questionnaire, picks it up, or both, the completion rate seems higher than for straightforward mail surveys. Additional experimentation with this method is likely to point to other techniques for improving completion rates while reducing costs. Mail surveys are the typical form of self-administered survey, however, and the remainder of this section is devoted specifically to this type of study.

Mail Distribution and Return

The basic method for data collection through the mail has been transmittal of a questionnaire, accompanied by a letter of explanation and a self-addressed, stamped envelope for returning the questionnaire. I imagine you have received one or two in your lifetime. As a respondent, you are expected to complete the questionnaire, put it in the envelope, and return it. If, by any chance, you've received such a questionnaire and failed to return it, it would be extremely valuable for you to recall the reasons you had for not returning it—and keep them in mind any time you plan to send questionnaires to others.

One big reason for not returning questionnaires is that it's too much trouble. To overcome this problem, researchers have developed several ways to make returning them easier. For instance, the *self-mailing* questionnaire requires no return envelope: When the questionnaire is folded a particular way, the return address appears on the outside; the respondent doesn't have to worry about losing the envelope.

Use this method with caution, however. One of the first surveys I conducted was an enormous one with some 70,000 respondents. To save money and simplify the logistics, I had the questionnaire printed on a long sheet of paper and had it prefolded so that my return address and business-reply permit showed on the outside. To facilitate several follow-up mailings (discussed later), I had nearly a quarter of a million questionnaires printed. Because we were going to be receiving a lot of mail, we decided to warn the local post office and see if we could arrange to have the questionnaires delivered to us in mailbags. When the postal officials saw the questionnaire, however, they announced that it violated postal regulations! Because I had made no provisions for the folded questionnaire to be sealed (required for first-class mail), the local officials indicated they couldn't handle it. Only an inspirational discussion of social research and a tearful appeal to save my graduate career got the questionnaires into the mail.

More elaborate designs are available also. The university student questionnaire described later in this chapter was bound in a booklet with a special, two-panel back cover. Once the questionnaire was completed, the respondent needed only to fold out the extra panel, wrap it around the booklet, and seal the whole thing with the adhesive strip running along the edge of the panel. The foldout panel contained my return address and postage. When I repeated the study a couple of years later, I improved on the design. Both the front and back covers had foldout panels: one for sending the questionnaire out and the other for getting it back—thus avoiding the use of envelopes altogether.

The point here is that anything you can do to make the job of completing and returning the questionnaire easier will improve your study. Imagine receiving a questionnaire that made no provisions for its return to the researcher. Suppose you had to (1) find an envelope, (2) write the address on it, (3) figure out how much postage it required, and (4) put the stamps on it. How likely is it that you would return the questionnaire?

A few brief comments on postal options are in order. You have options for mailing questionnaires out and for getting them returned. On outgoing mail, your choices are essentially between first-class postage and bulk rate. First is more certain, but bulk rate is far cheaper. (Check your local post office for rates and procedures.) On return mail, your choice is between postage stamps and business-reply permits. Here, the cost differential is more complicated. If you use stamps, you pay for them whether people return their questionnaires or not. With the business-reply permit, you pay for only those that are used, but you pay an additional surcharge of about a nickel. This means that stamps are cheaper if a lot of questionnaires are returned, but business-reply permits are cheaper if fewer are returned (and you won't know in advance how many will be returned).

There are many other considerations involved in choosing among the several postal options. Some researchers, for example, feel that the use of postage stamps communicates more "humanness" and sincerity than bulk rate and business-reply permits. Others worry that respondents will steam off the stamps and use them for some purpose other than returning the questionnaires. Because both bulk rate and business-reply permits require establishing accounts at the post office, you'll probably find stamps much easier in small surveys.

Electronic Surveys

The newest innovations in self-administered questionnaires make use of the computer. Several techniques have emerged and are being tested (Nicholls, Baker, and Martin 1996):

CATI (computer assisted telephone interviewing): A telephone survey interviewer reads questions as they appear on a computer screen and types in the respondent's answers. (We'll examine this technique later in the chapter.)

CAPI (computer assisted personal interviewing): Similar to CATI but in face-to-face interviews rather than over the phone.

CASI (computer assisted self-interviewing): A research worker brings a computer to the respondent's home, and the respondent reads questions on the computer screen and enters his or her own answers.

CSAQ (computerized self-administered questionnaire): The respondent receives the questionnaire via floppy disk, bulletin board, or other means and runs the software, which asks questions and accepts the respondent's answers. Following this, the respondent returns the data file.

TDE (touchtone data entry): The respondent initiates the process by calling a number at the research organization. This prompts a series of computerized questions, which the respondent answers by pressing keys on the telephone keypad.

VR (voice recognition): Instead of asking the respondent to use the telephone keypad as in TDE above, this system accepts spoken responses.

Nicholls et al. report that such techniques are more efficient than conventional techniques, and they do not appear to result in a reduction of data quality. You should expect to see more use of computerized techniques in the future.

Monitoring Returns

The mailing of questionnaires sets up a new research question that may prove valuable to a study. As questionnaires are returned, you should not sit back idly but should undertake a careful recording of the varying rates of return among respondents.

An invaluable tool in this activity will be a return rate graph. The day on which questionnaires were mailed should be labeled Day 1 on the graph, and every day thereafter the number of returned questionnaires should be logged on the graph. Because this is a minor activity, it is usually best to compile two graphs. One should show the number returned each day—rising, then dropping. Another should report the *cumulative* number or percentage. In part, this activity provides you with gratification, as you get to draw a picture of your successful data collection. More important, however, it is your guide to how the data collection is going. If you plan follow-up mailings, the graph provides a clue about when such mailings should be launched. (The dates of subsequent mailings should be noted on the graph.)

As completed questionnaires are returned, each should be opened, scanned, and assigned an identification number. These numbers should be assigned serially as the questionnaires are returned—even if other identification (ID) numbers have already been assigned. Two examples should illustrate the important advantages of this procedure.

Let's assume you're studying attitudes toward a political figure. In the middle of the data collection, let's say the politician is discovered to be sleeping around. By knowing the date of that public disclosure and the dates when questionnaires were received, you'll be in a position to determine the effects of the disclosure. (Recall the discussion of history in connection with experiments.)

In a less sensational way, serialized ID numbers can be valuable in estimating nonresponse biases in the survey. Barring more direct tests of bias, you may wish to assume that those who failed to answer the questionnaire will be more like respondents who delayed answering than like those who answered right away. An analysis of questionnaires received at different points in the data collection might then be used for estimates of sampling bias. For example, if the grade point averages (GPAs) reported by student respondents decrease steadily through the data collection, with those replying right away having higher GPAs and those replying later having lower GPAs, then you might tentatively conclude that those who failed to answer at all have lower GPAs yet. Although it would not be advisable to make statistical estimates of bias in this fashion, you could take advantage of approximate estimates.

If respondents have been identified for purposes of follow-up mailing, then preparations for those mailings should be made as the questionnaires are returned. The case study later in this chapter will discuss this process in greater detail.

Follow-up Mailings

Follow-up mailings may be administered in several ways. In the simplest, nonrespondents are simply sent a letter of additional encouragement to participate. A better method, however, is to send a new copy of the survey questionnaire with the follow-up letter. If potential respondents have not returned their questionnaires after two or three weeks, the questionnaires probably have been lost or misplaced. Receiving a follow-up letter might encourage them to look for the original questionnaire, but if they can't find it easily, the letter may go for naught.

The methodological literature on follow-up mailings strongly suggests that it is an effective method for increasing return rates in mail surveys. In general, the longer a potential respondent delays replying, the less likely he or she is to do so at all. Properly timed follow-up mailings, then, provide additional stimuli to respond.

The effects of follow-up mailings will be seen in the response rate curves recorded during data collection. The initial mailings will be followed by a rise and subsequent subsiding of returns; the follow-up mailings will spur a resurgence of returns; and more follow-ups will do the same. In practice, three mailings (an original and two follow-ups) seem the most efficient.

The timing of follow-up mailings is also important. Here the methodological literature offers less precise guides, but it has been my experience that two or three weeks is a reasonable space between mailings. (This period might be increased by a few days if the mailing time—out and in—is more than two or three days.)

When researchers conduct several surveys of the same population over time, they can develop more specific guidelines in this regard. The Survey Research Office at the University of Hawaii conducts frequent student surveys and has been able to refine the mailing and remailing procedure considerably. Indeed, a consistent pattern of returns has been found, which appears to transcend differences of survey content, quality of instrument, and so forth. Within two weeks of the first mailing, approximately 40 percent of the questionnaires are returned; within two weeks of the first follow-up, an additional 20 percent are received; and within two weeks of the final follow-up, an additional 10 percent are received. (These response rates all involved the sending of additional questionnaires, not just letters.) There are no grounds for assuming that a similar pattern would appear in surveys of different populations, but this illustration should indicate the value of carefully tabulating return rates for every survey conducted.

If the individuals in the survey sample are not identified on the questionnaires, it may not be possible to remail only to nonrespondents. In such a case, you should send your follow-up mailing to all members of the sample, thanking those who may have already participated and encouraging those who have not to do so. (The case study reported in a later section of this chapter describes another method you can use in an anonymous mail survey.)

Acceptable Response Rates

A question that new survey researchers frequently ask concerns the percentage return rate that should be achieved in a mail survey. The body of inferential statistics used in connection with survey analysis assumes that *all* members of the initial sample complete and return their questionnaires. Since this almost never happens, response bias becomes a concern, with the researcher testing (and hoping for) the possibility that the respondents look essentially like a random sample of the initial sample, and thus a somewhat smaller random sample of the total population. (For more detailed discussions of response bias, you might want to read Donald [1960] and Brownlee [1975].)

Nevertheless, overall **response rate** is one guide to the representativeness of the sample respondents. If a high response rate is achieved, there is less chance of significant response bias than in a low rate. But what is a *high* response rate?

Conversely, a low response rate is a danger signal, because the nonrespondents are likely to differ from the respondents in ways other than just their willingness to participate in your survey. Richard Bolstein (1991), for example, found that those who did not respond to a preelection political poll were less likely to vote that those who did participate. Estimating the turnout rate from the survey respondents, then, would have overestimated the number who would show up at the polls.

A quick review of the survey literature will uncover a wide range of response rates. Each of these may be accompanied by a statement like "This is regarded as a relatively high response rate for a survey of this type." (A U.S. senator made this statement regarding a poll of constituents that achieved a 4-percent return rate.) Even so, it's possible to state some rules of thumb about return rates. I feel that a response rate of 50 percent is *adequate* for analysis and reporting. A response of 60 percent is *good*. And a response rate of 70 percent is *very good*. You should bear in mind, however, that these are only rough guides; they have no statistical basis, and a demonstrated lack of response bias is far more important than a high response rate. If you want to pursue this matter further, Delbert Miller (1991:145–55) has reviewed several specific surveys to offer a better sense of the variability of response rates.

As you can imagine, one of the more persistent discussions among survey researchers concerns ways of increasing response rates. You'll recall that this was a chief concern in the earlier discussion of options for mailing out and receiving questionnaires. Survey researchers have developed a number of ingenious techniques addressing this problem. Some have experimented with novel formats. Others have tried paying respondents to participate. The problem with paying, of course, is that it's expensive to make meaningfully high payment to hundreds or thousands of respondents, but some imaginative alternatives have been used. Some researchers have said, "We want to get your two-cents' worth on some issues, and we're willing to pay"—enclosing two pennies. Another enclosed a quarter, suggesting that the respondent make some little child happy. Still others have enclosed paper money.

Don Dillman (1978) provides an excellent review of the various techniques survey researchers have used to increase return rates on mail surveys, and he evaluates the impact of each. More important, Dillman stresses the necessity of paying attention to *all* aspects of the study—what he calls the "Total Design Method"—rather than one or two special gimmicks.

More recently, Francis Yammarino, Steven Skinner, and Terry Childers (1991) have undertaken an in-depth analysis of the response rates achieved in many studies using different techniques. Their findings are too complex to summarize easily, but you might find some guidance there for effective survey design.

A Case Study

The steps involved in the administration of a mail survey are many and can best be appreciated in a walk-through of an actual study. I'll conclude this section, then, with a detailed description of one student survey. As you'll see shortly, the study did not represent the theoretical ideal for such studies, but in that regard it serves present purposes all the better. The study was conducted by the students in my graduate seminar in survey research methods.

Approximately 1,100 students were selected from the university registration tape through a stratified, systematic sampling procedure. For each student selected, six self-adhesive mailing labels were printed by the computer.

By the time we were ready to distribute the questionnaires, it became apparent that our meager research funds wouldn't cover several mailings to the entire sample of 1,100 students (questionnaire printing costs were higher than anticipated). As a result, a systematic two-thirds sample of the mailing labels was chosen, yielding a subsample of 770 students.

Earlier, we had decided to keep the survey anonymous in the hope of encouraging more candid responses to some sensitive questions. (Later surveys of the same issues among the same population indicated this anonymity was unnecessary.) Thus, the questionnaires would carry no identification of students on them. At the same time, we hoped to reduce the follow-up mailing costs by mailing only to nonrespondents.

To achieve both of these aims, a special postcard method was devised. Each student was mailed a questionnaire that carried no identifying marks, plus a postcard addressed to the research office—with one of the student's mailing labels affixed to the reverse side of the card. The introductory letter asked the student to complete and return the questionnaire—assuring anonymity—and to return the postcard simultaneously. Receiving the postcard would tell us that the student had returned his or her questionnaire—without indicating which questionnaire it was. This procedure would then facilitate follow-up mailings.

The 32-page questionnaire was printed in booklet form (photo-offset and saddle-stitched). A three-panel cover—described earlier in this chapter—permitted the questionnaire to be returned without an additional envelope.

A letter introducing the study and its purposes was printed on the front cover of the booklet. It explained why the study was being conducted (to learn how students feel about a variety of issues), how students had been selected for the study, the importance of each student's responding, and the mechanics of returning the questionnaire.

Students were assured that their responses to the survey were anonymous, and the postcard method was explained. A statement followed about the auspices under which the study was being conducted, and a telephone number was provided for those who might want more information about the study. (About five students called for information.)

By printing the introductory letter on the questionnaire, we avoided the necessity of enclosing a separate letter in the outgoing envelope, thereby simplifying the task of assembling mailing pieces.

The materials for the initial mailing were assembled in the following steps. (1) One mailing label for each student was stuck on a postcard. (2) Another label was stuck on an outgoing manila envelope. (3) One postcard and one questionnaire were placed in each envelope—with a glance to insure that the name on the postcard and on the envelope were the same in each case.

These steps were accomplished in an assembly line involving several members of the research team. Although the procedure was somewhat organized in advance, it took a certain amount of actual practice before the best allocation of tasks and people was discovered.

It's also worth noting that the entire process was delayed several days while the initial batch of manila envelopes was exchanged for larger ones. This delay could have been avoided if we had walked through the assembly process in advance.

The distribution of the survey questionnaires had been set up for a bulk rate mailing. Once the questionnaires had been stuffed into envelopes, they were grouped by zip codes, tied in bundles, and delivered to the post office.

Shortly after the initial mailing, questionnaires and postcards began arriving at the research office. Questionnaires were opened, scanned, and assigned identification numbers as described earlier in this chapter. For every postcard received, a search was made for that student's remaining labels, and they were destroyed.

After a period of two or three weeks, the remaining mailing labels were used to organize a follow-up mailing. The assembly procedures described previously were repeated with one exception. A special, separate letter of appeal was included in the mailing piece. The new letter indicated that many students had returned their questionnaires already, but that it was very important for all others to do so as well.

The follow-up mailing stimulated a resurgence of returns, as expected, and the same logging procedures were continued. The returned postcards told us which additional mailing labels to destroy. Unfortunately, time and financial pressures made it impossible to undertake a third mailing, as had been initially planned, but the two mailings resulted in an overall return rate of 62 percent.

I trust this illustration will give you a fairly good sense of what's involved in the execution of mailed self-administered questionnaires—a very popular survey method. Let's turn now to another method of conducting surveys.

■ INTERVIEW SURVEYS

The interview is an alternative method of collecting survey data. Rather than asking respondents to read questionnaires and enter their own answers, researchers send interviewers to ask the questions orally and record respondents' answers. Interviewing is typically done in a face-to-face encounter, but telephone interviewing, as you'll see, follows most of the same guidelines. Also, most interview surveys require more than one interviewer, although you might undertake a small-scale interview survey yourself. Portions of this section will discuss methods for training and supervising a staff of interviewers assisting you on the survey.

This section deals specifically with *survey* interviewing. In Chapter 11, we'll talk about the less structured, in-depth interviews often conducted in field research.

The Role of the Survey Interviewer

There are several advantages to having a questionnaire administered by an interviewer rather than the respondent. To begin, interview surveys typically attain higher response rates than mail surveys. A properly designed and executed interview survey ought to achieve a completion rate of at least 80 to 85 percent. (Federally funded surveys often require one of these response rates.) Respondents seem more reluctant to turn down an interviewer standing on their doorstep than to throw away a mailed questionnaire.

The presence of an interviewer also generally decreases the number of "don't knows" and "no answers." If minimizing such responses is important to the study, the interviewer can be instructed to probe for answers ("If you had to pick one of the answers, which do you think would come closest to your feelings?").

Interviewers can also serve as a guard against confusing questionnaire items. If the respondent clearly misunderstands the intent of a question or indicates that he or she does not understand, the interviewer can clarify matters, thereby obtaining relevant responses. (Such clarifications must be strictly controlled, however, through formal *specifications,* as you'll soon see.)

Finally, the interviewer can observe respondents as well as ask questions. For example, the interviewer can note the respondent's race if this is considered too delicate a question to ask. Similar observations can be made regarding the quality of the dwelling, the presence of various possessions, the respondent's ability to speak English, the respondent's general reactions to the study, and so forth. In one survey of students, respondents were given a short, self-administered questionnaire to complete—concerning sexual attitudes and behavior—during the course of the interview. While a student completed the questionnaire, the interviewer made detailed notes regarding the dress and grooming of the respondent.

This raises an ethical issue. Some researchers have objected that such practices violate the spirit of the agreement by which the respondent has allowed the interview. Although ethical issues seldom are open and shut in social research, it is important for you to be sensitive to that aspect of research. We'll examine ethical issues in detail in Chapter 18.

Survey research is of necessity based on an unrealistic *stimulus-response* theory of cognition and behavior. It must be assumed that a questionnaire item will mean the same thing to every respondent, and every given response must mean the same when given by different respondents. Although this is an impossible goal, survey questions are drafted to approximate the ideal as closely as possible.

The interviewer must also fit into this ideal situation. The interviewer's presence should not affect a respondent's perception of a question or the answer given. The interviewer, then, should be a *neutral* medium through which questions and answers are transmitted.

If this goal is successfully accomplished, different interviewers will obtain exactly the same responses from a given respondent. (Recall earlier discussions of reliability.) This neutrality has a special importance in area samples. To save time and money, a given interviewer is typically assigned to complete all the interviews in a particular geographical area—a city block or a group of nearby blocks. If the interviewer does anything to affect the responses obtained, the bias thus interjected might be interpreted as a characteristic of that area.

Let's suppose that a survey is being done to determine attitudes toward low-cost housing, to help in the selection of a site for a new government-sponsored development. An interviewer assigned to a given neighborhood might—through word or gesture—communicate his or her own distaste for low-cost housing developments. Respondents might therefore tend to give responses in general agreement with the interviewer's own position. The results of the survey would indicate that the neighborhood in question strongly resisted construction of the development in its area whereas their apparent resistance might only reflect the interviewer's attitudes.

General Rules for Survey Interviewing

The manner in which interviews ought to be conducted will vary somewhat by survey population and will be affected somewhat by the nature of the survey content as well. Nevertheless, some general guidelines apply to most if not all interviewing situations.

Appearance and Demeanor As a general rule, the interviewer should dress in a fashion similar to that of the people he or she will be interviewing. A richly dressed interviewer will probably have difficulty getting good cooperation and responses from poorer respondents. And a poorly dressed interviewer will have similar difficulties with richer respondents.

To the extent that the interviewer's dress and grooming differ from those of the respondents, it should be in the direction of cleanliness and neatness in modest apparel. If cleanliness is not next to godliness, it appears to be next to neutrality. Although middle-class neatness and cleanliness may not be accepted by all sectors of U.S. society, they remain the primary norm and are the most likely to be acceptable to the largest number of respondents.

Dress and grooming are typically regarded as signs of a person's attitudes and orientations. At the time this is being written, torn jeans, green hair, and a razor-blade earring may communicate—correctly or incorrectly—that you are politically radical, sexually permissive, favorable to drug use, and so forth.

In demeanor, interviewers should be pleasant if nothing else. Because they will be prying into the respondent's personal life and attitudes, they must communicate a genuine interest in getting to know the respondent without appearing to spy. They must be relaxed and friendly without being too casual or clinging. Good interviewers also have the ability to determine very quickly the kind of person the respondent will feel most comfortable with, the kind of person the respondent would most enjoy talking to. Clearly, the interview will be more successful if the interviewer can become the kind of person the respondent is comfortable with. Further, because respondents are asked to volunteer a portion of their time and to divulge personal information, they deserve the most enjoyable experience the researcher and interviewer can provide.

Familiarity with Questionnaire If an interviewer is unfamiliar with the questionnaire, the study suffers and an unfair burden is placed on the respondent. The interview is likely to take more time than necessary and be unpleasant. Moreover, the interviewer cannot acquire familiarity by skimming through the questionnaire two or three times. It must be studied carefully, question by question, and the interviewer must practice reading it aloud.

Ultimately, the interviewer must be able to read the questionnaire items to respondents without error, without stumbling over words and phrases. A good model for interviewers is the actor reading lines in a play or motion picture. The lines must be read as naturally as though they constituted a natural conversation, but that conversation must follow exactly the language set down in the questionnaire.

By the same token, the interviewer must be familiar with the specifications prepared in conjunction with the questionnaire. Inevitably some questions will not exactly fit a given respondent's situation, and the interviewer must determine how the question should be interpreted in that situation. The specifications provided to the interviewer should give adequate guidance in such cases, but the interviewer must know the organization and contents of the specifications well enough to refer to them efficiently. It would be better for the interviewer to leave a given question unanswered than to spend five minutes searching through the specifications for clarification or trying to interpret the relevant instructions.

Following Question Wording Exactly In Chapter 6, I discussed the significance of question wording for the responses obtained. A slight change in the wording of a given question may lead a respondent to answer "yes" rather than "no."

Even though you have very carefully phrased your questionnaire items to obtain the information you need and to insure that respondents will interpret items precisely as you intend, all this effort will be wasted if interviewers rephrase questions in their own words.

Recording Responses Exactly Whenever the questionnaire contains open-ended questions, those soliciting the respondent's own answer, it is very important that the interviewer record that answer exactly as given. No attempt should be made to summarize, paraphrase, or correct bad grammar.

This exactness is especially important because the interviewer will not know how the responses are to be coded before processing. Indeed, the researchers may not know the coding until they have read a hundred or so responses. For example, the questionnaire might ask respondents how they feel about the traffic situation in their community. One respondent might answer that there are too many cars on the roads and that something should be done to limit their numbers. Another might say that more roads are needed. If the interviewer recorded these two responses with the same summary—"congested traffic"—the researchers would not be able to take advantage of the important differences in the original responses.

Sometimes, the respondent may be so inarticulate that the verbal response is too ambiguous to permit interpretation. However, the interviewer may be able to understand the intent of the response through the respondent's gestures or tone. In such a situation, the exact verbal response should still be recorded, but the interviewer should add marginal comments giving both the interpretation and the reasons for arriving at it.

More generally, researchers can use any marginal comments explaining aspects of the response not conveyed in the verbal recording, such as the respondent's apparent uncertainty in answering, anger, embarrassment, and so forth. In each case, however, the exact verbal response should also be recorded.

Probing for Responses Sometimes respondents will give an inappropriate answer. For example, a question may present an attitudinal statement and ask the respondent to strongly agree, agree somewhat, disagree somewhat, or strongly disagree. The respondent, however, may reply: "I think that's true." The interviewer should follow this reply with: "Would you say you strongly agree or agree somewhat?" If necessary, interviewers can explain that they must check one or the other of the categories provided. If the respondent adamantly refuses to choose, the interviewer should write in the exact response given by the respondent.

Probes are more frequently required in eliciting responses to open-ended questions. For example, in response to a question about traffic conditions, the respondent might simply reply, "Pretty bad." The interviewer could obtain an elaboration on this response through a variety of probes. Sometimes the best probe is silence; if the interviewer sits quietly with pencil poised, the respondent will probably fill the pause with additional comments. (This technique is used effectively by newspaper reporters.) Appropriate verbal probes might be "How is that?" or "In what ways?" Perhaps the most generally useful probe is "Anything else?"

Often, interviewers need to probe for answers that will be sufficiently informative for analytical purposes. In every case, however, it is imperative that such probes be completely *neutral*. The probe must not in any way affect the nature of the subsequent response. Whenever you anticipate that a given question may require probing for appropriate responses, you should present one or more useful probes next to the question in the questionnaire. This practice has two important advantages. First, you will have more time to devise the best, most neutral probes. Second, all interviewers will use the same probes whenever they are needed. Thus, even if the probe is not perfectly neutral, all respondents will be presented with the same stimulus. This is the same logical guideline discussed for question wording. Although a question should not be loaded or biased, it is essential that every respondent be presented with the same question, even a biased one.

Coordination and Control

Most interview surveys require the assistance of several interviewers. In the large-scale surveys, of course, such interviewers are hired and paid for their work. As a student researcher, you might find yourself recruiting friends to help you interview. Whenever more than one interviewer is involved in a survey, efforts must be carefully controlled. There are two aspects of this control: training interviewers and supervising them after they begin work.

The interviewers' training session should begin with the description of what the study is all about. Even though the interviewers may be involved only in the data-collection phase of the project, it will be useful to them to understand what will be done with the interviews they conduct and what purpose will be served. Morale and motivation are usually low when interviewers don't know what's going on.

The training on how to interview should begin with a discussion of general guidelines and procedures, such as those discussed earlier in this chapter. Then the whole group should go through the questionnaire together—question by question. Don't simply ask if anyone has any questions about the first page of the questionnaire. Read the first question aloud, explain the purpose of the question, and then entertain any questions or comments the interviewers may have. Once all their questions and comments have been handled, go on to the next question in the questionnaire.

It's always a good idea to prepare *specifications* to accompany an interview questionnaire. Specifications are explanatory and clarifying comments about handling difficult or confusing situations that may occur with regard to specific questions in the questionnaire. When drafting the questionnaire, you should try to think of all the problem cases that might arise—the bizarre circumstances that might make a question difficult to answer. The survey specifications should provide detailed guidelines on how to handle such situations. For example, even as simple a matter as age might present problems. Suppose a respondent says he or she will be 25 next week. The interviewer might not be sure whether to take the respondent's current age or the nearest one. The specifications for that question should explain what should be done. (Probably, you would specify that age as of last birthday should be recorded in all cases.)

If you've prepared a set of specifications, you should go over them with the interviewers when you go over the individual questions in the questionnaire. Make sure your interviewers fully understand the specifications as well as the questions themselves and the reasons for them.

This portion of the interviewer training is likely to generate many troublesome questions from your interviewers. They'll ask, "What should I do if . . . ?" In such cases, you should never give a quick answer. If you have specifications, be sure to show how the solution to the problem could be determined from the specifications. If you do not have specifications prepared, show how the preferred handling of the situation fits within the general logic of the question and the purpose of the study. Giving offhand, unexplained answers to such questions will only confuse the interviewers, and they will probably not take their work seriously. If you do not know the answer to such a question when it is asked, admit it and ask for some time to decide on the best answer. Then think out the situation carefully and be sure to give all the interviewers your answer, explaining your reasons.

Once you have gone through the whole questionnaire, you should conduct one or two demonstration interviews in front of everyone. Preferably, you should interview someone else. Realize that your interview will be a model for those you are training, and make it good. It would be best, moreover, if the demonstration interview were done as realistically as possible. Do not pause during the demonstration to point out how you have handled a complicated situation: Handle it, and then explain later. It is irrelevant if the person you are interviewing gives real answers or takes on some hypothetical identity for the purpose, just as long as the answers are consistent.

After the demonstration interviews, you should pair off your interviewers and have them practice on each other. When they have completed the questionnaire, have them reverse roles and do it over again. Interviewing is the best training for interviewing. As your interviewers are practicing on each other, you should wander around, listening in on the practice so you'll know how well they're doing. Once the practice is completed, the whole group should discuss their experiences and ask any other questions they may have.

The final stage of the training for interviewers should involve some "real" interviews. Have them conduct some interviews under the actual conditions that will pertain to the final survey. You may want to assign them people to interview, or perhaps they may be allowed to pick people themselves. Do not have them practice on people you've selected in your sample, however. After each interviewer has completed three to five interviews, have him or her check back with you. Look over the completed questionnaires for any evidence of misunderstanding. Again, answer any questions that the interviewers may have. Once you're convinced that a given interviewer knows what to do, assign some actual interviews—using the sample you have selected for the study.

It is essential that you continue supervising the work of interviewers over the course of the study. It is probably unwise to let them conduct more than 20 or 30 interviews without seeing you. You might assign 20 interviews, have the interviewer bring back those questionnaires when they are completed, look them over, and assign another 20 or so. Although this may seem overly cautious, you must continually protect yourself against misunderstandings that may not be evident early in the study.

If you're the only interviewer in your study, these comments may not seem relevant to you. However, you would be advised, for example, to prepare specifications for potentially troublesome questions in your questionnaire. Otherwise, you run the risk of making ad hoc decisions during the course of the study that you'll later regret or forget. Also, the emphasis on practice applies equally to the one-person project and to the complex funded survey with a large interviewing staff.

■ TELEPHONE SURVEYS

Throughout the early history of survey research, interview surveys were always conducted face-to-face, typically in the respondent's household. As the telephone became more omnipresent in U.S. society, however, researchers began experimenting with it for survey interviewing.

For years telephone surveys had a rather bad reputation among professional researchers. Telephone surveys are limited by definition to people who have telephones. Years ago, then, this method produced a substantial social-class bias by excluding poor people from the surveys. This was vividly demonstrated by the *Literary Digest* fiasco of 1936. Even though voters were contacted by mail, the sample was partially selected from telephone subscribers—who were hardly typical in a nation just recovering from the Great Depression.

Over time, however, the telephone has become a standard fixture in almost all U.S. homes. The Census Bureau (1996: Table 1224) estimated that 93.4 percent of all housing units had telephones in 1993, so the earlier form of class bias has been substantially reduced.

A related sampling problem involved unlisted numbers. If the survey sample were selected from the pages of a local telephone directory, it would totally omit all those people—typically richer—who requested that their numbers not be published. This potential bias has been erased through a technique that has advanced telephone sampling substantially: *random-digit dialing*, which we'll examine in the following section.

Telephone surveys have many advantages that underlie the growing popularity of this method. Probably the greatest advantages are money and time, in that order. In a face-to-face, household interview, you may drive several miles to a respondent's home, find no one there, return to the research office, and drive back the next day—possibly finding no one there again. It's cheaper and quicker to let your fingers make the trips.

Interviewing by telephone, you can dress any way you please without affecting the answers respondents give. And, sometimes respondents will be more honest in giving socially disapproved answers if they don't have to look you in the eye. Similarly, it may be possible to probe into more sensitive areas, though this isn't necessarily the case. (People are, to some extent, more suspicious when they can't see the person asking them questions—perhaps a consequence of "surveys" aimed at selling magazine subscriptions and time-share condominiums.)

You should realize, however, that people can communicate a lot about themselves over the phone, even though they can't be seen, as indicated in the box "Subtle Telephone Cues." For example, researchers worry about the impact of an interviewer's name (particularly if ethnicity is relevant to the study) and debate the ethics of having all interviewers use bland "stage names" such as Smith or Jones. (Female interviewers sometimes ask permission to do this, to avoid subsequent harrassment from men they interview.)

Telephone surveys can give you greater control over data collection if several interviewers are engaged in the project. If all the interviewers are calling from the research office, they can get clarification from the person in charge whenever problems occur, as they inevitably do. Alone in the boondocks, an interviewer may have to wing it between weekly visits with the interviewing supervisor.

Finally, another important factor involved in the growing use of telephone surveys has to do with personal safety. Don Dillman (1978:4) describes the situation this way:

■ Interviewers must be able to operate comfortably in a climate in which strangers are viewed with distrust and must successfully counter respondents' objections to being interviewed. Increasingly, interviewers must be willing to work at night to contact residents in many households. In some cases, this necessitates providing protection for interviewers working in areas of a city in which a definite threat to the safety of individuals exists.

Concerns for safety, thus, work two ways to hamper face-to-face interviews. Potential respondents may refuse to be interviewed, fearing the stranger-interviewer. And the interviewers themselves may be in danger. All this is made even worse by the possibility of the researchers being sued for huge sums if anything goes wrong.

There are still problems involved in telephone interviewing. As I've already mentioned, the method is hampered by the proliferation of bogus "surveys," which are actually sales campaigns disguised as research. If you have any questions about any such call you receive, by the way, ask the interviewer directly whether you've been selected for a survey only or if a sales "opportunity" is involved. It's also a good idea, if you have any doubts, to get the interviewer's name, phone number, and company. Hang up if they refuse to provide any of these.

The ease with which people can hang up is, of course, another shortcoming of telephone surveys. Once you've been let inside someone's home for an interview, they are unlikely to order you out of the house in midinterview. It's much easier to terminate a telephone interview abruptly, saying something like, "Whoops! Someone's at the door. I gotta go." or "OMIGOD! The pigs are eating my Volvo!" (That sort of thing is much harder to fake when you're sitting in their living room.)

Another potential problem for telephone interviewing is the continuing spread of telephone answering machines. Peter Tuckel and Barry Feinberg (1991:201) estimate that as of spring

Subtle Telephone Cues

The telephone does not eliminate all interviewer effects, because you can often tell something about the person you are talking to just by the sound of his or her voice. You can usually tell gender and perhaps age—and sometimes you can tell more.

In 1989, Douglas Wilder, an African American, was running for governor of Virginia (a race he won) against a white opponent. We might well imagine that the race of interviewers in face-to-face pre-election polls might have influenced the responses of voters when they were asked about their voting intentions.

In one pre-election poll, for example, the stated voting intentions of white voters interviewed by white interviewers were about evenly divided between the two candidates. White voters interviewed by African-American interviewers, however, appeared much more supportive of Wilder: 52 percent, versus 33 percent for his white opponent.

What makes this particularly interesting is that the survey was conducted over the telephone! It gives powerful evidence of the extent to which we reveal ourselves in the ways we talk.

Source: Steven E. Finkel, Thomas M. Guterbok, and Marian J. Borg, "Race-of-Interviewer Effects in a Preelection Poll: Virginia 1989," *Public Opinion Quarterly,* Fall 1991, pp. 313–30.

1988, approximately one-fourth to one-fifth of U.S. households had telephone answering machines. A study conducted by Walker Research (1988), moreover, found that half of owners acknowledged using their machines to "screen" calls at least some of the time. Tuckel and Feinberg's research, however, shows that answering machines have not yet had a significant effect on the ability of telephone researchers to contact prospective respondents. The researchers conclude that as the proliferation of answering machines continues to grow, "the sociodemographic characteristics of owners will change." This fact makes it likely that "different behavior patterns associated with the utilization of the answering machine" could emerge (1991:216).

Reflecting a related technological development, Jeffery Walker (1994) has explored the possibility of conducting surveys by fax machine. Questionnaires are faxed to respondents, who are asked to fax their answers back. Of course, such surveys can only represent that part of the population that has fax machines. Walker reports that fax surveys don't achieve as high response rates as face-to-face interviews, but, because of the perceived urgency, they do produce higher response rates than mail or telephone surveys. In one test case, all those who had ignored a mail questionnaire were sent a fax followup, and 83 percent responded.

Computer Assisted Telephone Interviewing (CATI)

In Chapter 14, we'll be looking at some of the ways computers have influenced the conduct of social research—particularly data processing and analysis. Computers are also changing the nature of telephone interviewing. In the years to come, you'll hear a great deal about *CATI,* which I've already mentioned. Though there are variations in practice, here's what it can look like.

Imagine an interviewer wearing a telephone-operator headset, sitting in front of a computer terminal and its video screen. The central computer has been programmed to select a telephone number at random and dials it. (*Random digit dialing* avoids the problem of unlisted telephone numbers.) On the video screen is an introduction ("Hello, my name is . . .") and the first question to be asked ("Could you tell me how many people live at this address?").

When the respondent answers the phone, the interviewer says hello, introduces the study, and asks the first question displayed on the screen. When the respondent answers the question, the interviewer types that answer into the computer terminal—either the verbatim response to an open-ended question or the code category for the appropriate answer to a closed-ended question. The answer is immediately stored in the central computer. The second question appears on the video screen, is asked, and the answer is entered into the computer. Thus, the interview continues.

This is not science fiction but a method used increasingly by academic, government, and commercial survey researchers. Much of the development work for this technique has occurred at the University of California's Survey Research Center in Berkeley, sometimes in collaboration with the U.S. Department of Agriculture and other governmental agencies.

J. Merrill Shanks and Robert Tortora (1985:4) have reviewed some of the ways computers are integrated into the survey process. In addition to the benefits you saw in the preceding scenario, the computer is a valuable tool in the development of questionnaires: drafting, testing, revising, and formatting. The logistics of the interviewing process (for example, training, scheduling, and supervising interviewers) can be managed by computer. As you'll see in Chapter 14, coding open-ended responses is also well suited to the computer, as is the prevention and/or correction of errors.

In addition to the obvious advantages in terms of data collection, CATI automatically prepares the data for analysis; in fact, the researcher can begin analyzing the data before the interviewing is complete, thereby gaining an advanced view of how the analysis will turn out.

The development of computer technology in connection with data collection is one of the most exciting things happening today in survey research. Although it is particularly relevant to telephone interviewing, its potential extends much farther, as the box, "Voice Capture,™" illustrates.

■ COMPARISON OF THE THREE METHODS

We've now seen several ways to collect survey data. Although I've touched on some of the relative advantages and disadvantages of each, let's take a minute to compare them more directly. Self-administered questionnaires are generally cheaper and quicker than face-to-face interview surveys. These considerations are likely to be important for an unfunded student wishing to undertake a survey for a term paper or thesis. Moreover, if you use the self-administered mail format, it costs no more to conduct a national survey than a local one; a national interview survey (either face-to-face or by telephone) would cost far more than a local one. Also, mail surveys typically require a small staff: One person can conduct a reasonable mail survey alone, although you shouldn't underestimate the work involved.

Further, respondents are sometimes reluctant to report controversial or deviant attitudes or behaviors in interviews but are willing to respond to an anonymous self-administered questionnaire.

Interview surveys also offer many advantages. For example, they generally produce fewer incomplete questionnaires. Although respondents may skip questions in a self-administered questionnaire, interviewers are trained not to do so. The computer offers a further check on this in CATI surveys. Interview surveys, moreover, have typically achieved higher completion rates than self-administered ones.

Although self-administered questionnaires may be more effective for sensitive issues, interview surveys are definitely more effective for complicated ones. Prime examples would be the enumeration of household members and the determination of whether a given address corresponds to more than one housing unit. Although the concept *housing unit* has been refined and standardized by the Bureau of the Census and interviewers can be trained to deal with the concept, it is extremely difficult to communicate in a self-administered questionnaire. This advantage of interview surveys pertains generally to all complicated contingency questions.

With interviewers, you can conduct a survey based on a sample of addresses or phone numbers rather than on names. An interviewer can arrive at an assigned address or call the assigned number, introduce the survey, and even—following instructions—choose the appropriate person at that address to respond to the survey.

Voice Capture™

by James E. Dannemiller
SMS Research, Honolulu

THE development of various CATI techniques has been a boon to survey and marketing research, though mostly it has supported the collection, coding, and analysis of "data as usual." The Voice Capture™ technique developed by Survey Systems, however, offers quite unusual possibilities, which we are only beginning to explore.

In the course of a CATI-based telephone interview, the interviewer can trigger the computer to begin digitally recording the conversation with the respondent. Having determined that the respondent has recently changed his or her favorite TV news show, for example, the interviewer can ask, "Why did you change?" and begin recording the verbatim response. (Early in the interview, the interviewer has asked permission to record parts of the interview.)

Later on, coders can play back the responses and code them—much as they would do with the interviewer's typescript of the responses. This offers an easier and more accurate way of accomplishing a conventional task. But that's a tame use of the new capability.

It is also possible to incorporate such oral data as parts of a cross-tabulation during analysis. We may create a table of gender by age by reasons for switching TV news shows. Thus, we can hear,

---

By contrast, self-administered questionnaires addressed to "occupant" receive a notoriously low response.

Finally, as we've seen, interviewers questioning respondents face-to-face can make important observations aside from responses to questions asked in the interview. In a household interview, they may note the characteristics of the neighborhood, the dwelling unit, and so forth. They may also note characteristics of the respondents or the quality of their interaction with the respondents—whether the respondent had difficulty communicating, was hostile, seemed to be lying, and so forth.

The chief advantages of telephone surveys over those conducted face-to-face center primarily on time and money. Telephone interviews are much cheaper and can be mounted and executed quickly. Also, interviewers are safer when interviewing in high-crime areas. Moreover, we've seen that the impact of the interviewers on responses is somewhat lessened when they can't be seen by the respondents. As only one indicator of the popularity of telephone interviewing, when Johnny Blair and his colleagues (1995) compiled a bibliography on sample designs for telephone interviews, they listed over 200 items.

Ultimately, you must balance all these advantages and disadvantages of the three methods in relation to (1) your research needs and (2) your resources.

■ STRENGTHS AND WEAKNESSES OF SURVEY RESEARCH

Like other modes of observation in social scientific research, surveys have special strengths and weaknesses. You should keep these in mind when determining whether the survey format is appropriate to your research goals.

Surveys are particularly useful in describing the characteristics of a large population. A carefully selected probability sample in combination with a standardized questionnaire offers the possibility of making refined descriptive assertions about a student body, a city, a nation, or any other large population. Surveys determine unemployment rates, voting intentions, and the like with uncanny accuracy. Although the examination of official documents—such as marriage, birth, or death records—can provide equal accuracy for a few topics, no other method of observation can provide this general capability.

in turn, the responses of the young men, young women, middle-aged men, and so forth. In one such study we found the younger and older men tending to watch one TV news show, while the middle-aged men watched something else. Listening to the responses of the middle-aged men, one after another, we heard a common comment: "Well, now that I'm older . . ." This kind of aside might have been lost in the notes hastily typed by interviewers, but such comments stood out dramatically in the oral data. The middle-aged men seemed to be telling us they felt "maturity" required them to watch a particular show, while more years under their belts let them drift back to what they liked in the first place.

These kinds of data are especially compelling to clients, particularly in customer satisfaction studies. Rather than summarize what we feel a client's customers like and don't like, we can let the respondents speak directly to the client in their own words. It's like a focus group on demand. Going one step further, we have found that letting line employees (bank tellers, for example) listen to the responses has more impact than having their supervisors tell them what they are doing right or wrong.

As exciting as these experiences are, I have the strong feeling that we have scarcely begun to tap into the possibilities for such unconventional forms of data.

Surveys—especially self-administered ones—make large samples feasible. Surveys of 2,000 respondents are not unusual. A large number of cases is very important for both descriptive and explanatory analyses, especially wherever several variables are to be analyzed simultaneously.

In one sense, surveys are flexible. Many questions may be asked on a given topic, giving you considerable flexibility in your analyses. Although experimental design may require you to commit yourself in advance to a particular operational definition of a concept, surveys let you develop operational definitions from actual observations.

Finally, standardized questionnaires have an important strength in regard to measurement generally. Earlier chapters have discussed the ambiguous nature of most concepts: They have no ultimately *real* meanings. One person's religiosity is quite different from another's. Although you must be able to define concepts in those ways most relevant to your research goals, you may not find it easy to apply the same definitions uniformly to all subjects. The survey researcher is bound to this requirement by having to ask exactly the same questions of all subjects and having to impute the same intent to all respondents giving a particular response.

Survey research also has several weaknesses. First, the requirement for standardization just mentioned often seems to result in the fitting of round pegs into square holes. Standardized questionnaire items often represent the least common denominator in assessing people's attitudes, orientations, circumstances, and experiences. By designing questions that will be at least minimally appropriate to all respondents, you may miss what is most appropriate to many respondents. In this sense, surveys often appear superficial in their coverage of complex topics. Although this problem can be partly offset through sophisticated analyses, it is inherent in survey research.

Similarly, survey research can seldom deal with the *context* of social life. Although questionnaires can provide information in this area, the survey researcher rarely develops the feel for the total life situation in which respondents are thinking and acting that, say, the participant observer can (see Chapter 11).

In many ways, surveys are inflexible. Studies involving direct observation can be modified as field conditions warrant, but surveys typically require that an initial study design remain unchanged throughout. As a field researcher, for example, you can become aware of an important new variable operating in the phenomenon you are studying and begin making careful observations of it. The survey researcher would probably be unaware of the new variable's importance and could do nothing about it in any event.

Finally, surveys are subject to the artificiality mentioned earlier in connection with experiments. Finding out that a person gives conservative answers to a questionnaire does not necessarily mean the person is conservative; finding out that a person gives prejudiced answers to a questionnaire does not necessarily mean the person is prejudiced. This shortcoming is especially salient in the realm of action. Surveys cannot measure social action; they can only collect self-reports of recalled past action or of prospective or hypothetical action.

This problem has two aspects. First, the topic of study may not be amenable to measurement through questionnaires. Second, the act of studying that topic—an attitude, for example—may affect it. A survey respondent may have given no thought to whether the governor should be impeached until asked for his or her opinion by an interviewer. He or she may, at that point, form an opinion on the matter.

Survey research is generally weak on validity and strong on reliability. In comparison with field research, for example, the artificiality of the survey format puts a strain on validity. As an illustration, people's opinions on issues seldom take the form of strongly agreeing, agreeing, disagreeing, or strongly disagreeing with a specific statement. Their survey responses in such cases, then, must be regarded as approximate indicators of what researchers have in mind initially in framing the questions. This comment, however, needs to be held in the context of earlier discussions of the ambiguity of *validity* itself. To say something is a valid or an invalid measure assumes the existence of a "real" definition of what is being measured, and many scholars now reject that assumption.

Reliability is a clearer matter. By presenting all subjects with a standardized stimulus, survey research goes a long way toward eliminating unreliability in observations made by the researcher. Moreover, careful wording of the questions can also reduce significantly the subject's own unreliability.

As with all methods of observation, a full awareness of the inherent or probable weaknesses of survey research can partially resolve them in some cases. Ultimately, though, you are on the safest ground when you can employ several research methods in studying a given topic.

■ SECONDARY ANALYSIS

As a mode of observation, survey research involves the following steps: (1) questionnaire construction, (2) sample selection, and (3) data collection, through either interviewing or self-administered questionnaires. As you will have gathered, surveys are usually major undertakings. It's not unusual for a large-scale survey to take several months or even more than a year to progress from conceptualization to data in hand. (Smaller-scale surveys can, of course, be done more quickly.) Through *secondary analysis*, however, you can pursue your particular social research interests—analyzing survey data from, say, a national sample of 2,000 respondents—while avoiding the enormous expenditure of time and money such a survey entails.

With the development of computer-based analyses in social research, it has become easy for social researchers to *share* their data with one another. Suppose, for example, that I've obtained the money and time to conduct large-scale surveys on political socialization and the nature of political participation in five different nations. Perhaps I want to learn something about the various faces of democracy as a form of political organization in the United States, Germany, Mexico, England, and Italy. It has taken me a few years and a very large international staff to design and execute such a set of surveys. Once the interviews are complete, I process the data (see Chapter 14) and analyze them, answering the research questions that led to the study in the first place.

Now suppose further that you have some research interests in the same general area as mine.

You have questions you would have addressed had you been able to get the resources necessary for the five-nation survey I conducted. Unfortunately, you couldn't get the money to do such a survey. But here's what you *can* do. For very little money—and with my cooperation—you can get a copy of the data collected in my study. If I've collected the data appropriate to answering your research questions, you're off and running.

The hypothetical situation I've just described is not hypothetical at all. In the late 1950s and early 1960s, Gabriel Almond and Sidney Verba designed and executed the five-nation study I've been describing. They reported their research results in 1963 in a book called *The Civic Culture*. Once their own analyses were completed, the researchers made the data available to others for secondary analysis. Since then, the Almond-Verba data have probably become the most analyzed set of data in existence. Individual researchers have pursued particular research interests, and the data have also been used for teaching purposes in research methods classes. Let me illustrate this use with a short personal example.

As a graduate student at Berkeley, I became interested in Charles Glock's notions about the causes of religious involvement (recall Chapter 2's discussion of the Comfort Hypothesis). As you'll recall, Glock had suggested that people who saw, and felt capable of achieving, secular solutions to social problems would seek those means. Those who did not see secular solutions would turn to the church. I wanted to test that notion, though I didn't have the resources necessary to conduct a large-scale survey. The Almond-Verba data, however, contained information about both religious and political activities—and about people's perceptions of political solutions to problems. As a result, I was able to examine whether people who did not see political solutions were more religiously involved than those who did see political solutions. Because the data set had been purchased for use in my research methods class, I could undertake my study at absolutely no cost to me.

By now the Almond-Verba data have taken on historical interest, and you could undertake your own analysis of the political cultures prevailing among the citizens of five nations during the late 1950s. This is possible because of the creation of a network of *data archives,* in which survey data files (magnetic disks or tapes) are collected and distributed the way books are handled in a conventional library. Whereas library books are loaned, however, the data sets are reproduced and sold. You get to keep your copy and use it again and again for as long as you find new things to study.

E. Jill Kiecolt and Laura Nathan (1985) have compiled an annotated listing of the several U.S. and international archives available to social researchers. It provides data on a wide variety of topics. If your interests run to Scandinavian societies, for example, you might want to contact the Norwegian Social Science Data Services in Bergen, the Karolinska Institute in Stockholm, or the Danish Data Archives in Odense. If you are more interested in American studies, you have a number of U.S. archives, such as the Inter-University Consortium for Political and Social Research (University of Michigan), the Roper Center for Public Opinion Research (University of Connecticut), and the National Opinion Research Center (University of Chicago). In these and other archives across the country, you can get access to a wide variety of data sets, including the wealth of data available from decades of Gallup, Harris, Roper, and Yankelovich polls.

The advantages of secondary analysis are obvious and enormous: It is cheaper and faster than doing original surveys, and, depending on who did the original survey, you may benefit from the work of top-flight professionals. There are disadvantages, however. The key problem involves the recurrent question of validity. When one researcher collects data for one particular purpose, you have no assurance that those data will be appropriate for *your* research interests. Typically, you'll find that the original researcher asked a question that "comes close" to measuring what you're interested in, but you'll wish the question had been asked just a little differently—or that another, related question had also been asked. Your question, then, is whether the question that was asked provides a valid measure of the variable you want to analyze. Kiecolt and Nathan offer some useful guidelines for making the most of secondary analysis.

In this book, the discussion of secondary analysis has a special purpose. As we continue our examination of modes of observation in social research, you're probably developing a full appreciation of the range of possibilities available in finding the answers to questions about social life. There is no single method that unlocks all puzzles. Yet there is no limit to the ways you can find out about things. And when you zero in on an issue from several independent directions, you gain that much more expertise.

■ MAIN POINTS

- Survey research, a popular social research method, is the administration of questionnaires to a sample of respondents selected from some population.
- Survey research is especially appropriate for making descriptive studies of large populations; survey data may be used for explanatory purposes as well.
- Questionnaires may be administered in three basic ways: Self-administered questionnaires may be completed by the respondents themselves; interviewers may administer questionnaires in face-to-face encounters, reading the items to respondents and recording the answers; or interviewers may conduct telephone surveys.
- It is generally advisable to plan follow-up mailings in the case of self-administered questionnaires, sending new questionnaires to those respondents who fail to respond to the initial appeal.
- Properly monitoring questionnaire returns will provide a good guide to when a follow-up mailing is appropriate.
- The essential characteristic of interviewers is that they be neutral; their presence in the data-collection process must not have any effect on the responses given to questionnaire items.
- Interviewers must be carefully trained to be familiar with the questionnaire, to follow the question wording and question order exactly, and to record responses exactly as they are given.
- A probe is a neutral, nondirective question designed to elicit an elaboration on an incomplete or ambiguous response, given in an interview in response to an open-ended question. Examples include "Anything else?" "How is that?" "In what ways?"
- The advantages of a self-administered questionnaire over an interview survey are economy, speed, lack of interviewer bias, and the possibility of anonymity and privacy to encourage candid responses on sensitive issues.
- Surveys conducted over the telephone have become more common and more effective in recent years, and computer-assisted telephone interviewing (CATI) techniques are especially promising.
- The advantages of an interview survey over a self-administered questionnaire are fewer incomplete questionnaires and fewer misunderstood questions, generally higher return rates, and greater flexibility in terms of sampling and special observations.
- Survey research in general offers advantages in terms of economy and the amount of data that can be collected. The standardization of the data collected represents another special strength of survey research.
- Survey research has the weaknesses of being somewhat artificial and potentially superficial. It is difficult to gain a full sense of social processes in their natural settings through the use of surveys.
- Secondary analysis refers to the analysis of data collected earlier by another researcher for some purpose other than the topic of the current study.

■ REVIEW QUESTIONS AND EXERCISES

1. Construct a set of contingency questions for use in a self-administered questionnaire that would solicit the following information:

a. Is the respondent employed?
   b. If unemployed, is the respondent looking for work?
   c. If the unemployed respondent is not looking for work, is he or she retired, a student, or a homemaker?
   d. If the respondent is looking for work, how long has he or she been looking?
2. Find a questionnaire printed in a magazine or newspaper (for a reader survey, for example). Bring the questionnaire to class and critique it. Critique other aspects of the survey design.
3. Locate a survey being conducted on the Web. Briefly describe the survey and discuss its strengths and weaknesses.

ADDITIONAL READINGS

Babbie, Earl. *Survey Research Methods.* Belmont, CA: Wadsworth, 1990. A comprehensive overview of survey methods. (You thought I'd say it was lousy?) This textbook, although overlapping the present one somewhat, covers aspects of survey techniques omitted here.

Bradburn, Norman M., and Seymour Sudman. *Polls and Surveys: Understanding What They Tell Us.* San Francisco: Jossey-Bass, 1988. These veteran survey researchers answer questions about their craft the general public commonly ask.

Converse, Jean M. *Survey Research in the United States: Roots and Emergence, 1890–1960.* Berkeley: University of California Press, 1987. Here's a history of the several faces of survey research: academic, commercial, and governmental. You'll meet the major players involved and see the unfolding of this research specialty over the course of seven decades.

Converse, Jean M., and Stanley Presser. *Survey Questions: Handcrafting the Standardized Questionnaire.* Newbury Park, CA: Sage, 1986. This is a useful book for the questionnaire designer. It's very readable and contains many helpful tips.

Dillman, Don A. *Mail and Telephone Surveys: The Total Design Method.* New York: Wiley, 1978. An excellent review of the methodological literature on mail and telephone surveys. Dillman makes many good suggestions for improving response rates.

Elder, Glen H., Jr., Eliza K. Pavalko, and Elizabeth C. Clipp. *Working with Archival Data: Studying Lives.* Newbury Park, CA: Sage, 1993. This book discusses the possibilities and techniques for using existing data archives in the United States, especially those providing longitudinal data.

Fowler, Floyd J., Jr. *Improving Survey Questions: Design and Evaluation.* Thousand Oaks, CA: Sage, 1995. A comprehensive discussion of questionnaire construction, including a number of suggestions for pretesting questions.

Groves, Robert M. "Theories and Methods of Telephone Surveys." Pp. 221–40 in *Annual Review of Sociology.* Vol. 16, edited by W. Richard Scott and Judith Blake. Palo Alto, CA: Annual Reviews, 1990. An attempt to place telephone surveys in the context of sociological and psychological theories and to address the various kinds of errors common to this research method.

Hyman, Herbert H., with Eleanor Singer. *Taking Society's Measure: A Personal History of Survey Research.* New York: Russell Sage Foundation, 1991. Here's an opportunity to witness the development of survey research from the eyes of one of its chief participants.

Kiecolt, E. Jill, and Laura E. Nathan. *Secondary Analysis of Survey Data.* Beverly Hills, CA: Sage, 1985. An excellent overview of the major sources of data for secondary analysis and guidelines for taking advantage of them.

Smith, Tom W. "The First Straw? A Study of the Origins of Election Polls." *Public Opinion Quarterly* 54 (Spring 1990): 21–36. The article examines the early history of U.S. political polling, with special attention to the media reactions to the polls.

Swafford, Michael. "Soviet Survey Research: The 1970's vs. the 1990's." *AAPOR News* 19, no. 3 (Spring 1992): 3–4. The author contrasts the general repression of survey research during his first visit in 1973–74 with the renewed use of the method in more recent times. He notes, for example, that the Soviet government commissioned a national survey to determine public opinion on the possible reunification of Germany.

Williams, Robin M., Jr. "The American Soldier: An Assessment, Several Wars Later." *Public Opinion Quarterly* 53 (Summer 1989): 155–74). One of the classic studies in the history of survey research is reviewed by one of its authors.

CHAPTER 11 Field Research

What You'll Learn in This Chapter

You'll improve your ability to observe social life in its natural habitat: going where the action is and watching. You'll learn how to prepare for the field, how to observe, how to take notes, and how to analyze what you observe.

INTRODUCTION

SOME TERMINOLOGY OF QUALITATIVE INQUIRY
Phenomenology
Interpretivism
Hermeneutics
Participant Observation
In-depth Interview
Case Study
Ethnography
Grounded Theory

TOPICS APPROPRIATE TO FIELD RESEARCH

THE VARIOUS ROLES OF THE OBSERVER

RELATIONS TO SUBJECTS

PREPARING FOR THE FIELD

QUALITATIVE INTERVIEWING

RECORDING OBSERVATIONS

QUALITATIVE DATA PROCESSING
Rewriting Your Notes
Creating Files
Using Computers

QUALITATIVE DATA ANALYSIS

ILLUSTRATIONS OF FIELD RESEARCH
Studying the Satanists
Life in the Streets
Observing Outlaw Bikers

RESEARCH ETHICS IN FIELD RESEARCH

STRENGTHS AND WEAKNESSES OF FIELD RESEARCH
Validity
Reliability

MAIN POINTS

REVIEW QUESTIONS AND EXERCISES

ADDITIONAL READINGS

INTRODUCTION

Several chapters ago, I said that you've been doing social research all your life. This should become even clearer to you as we turn now to what probably seems like the most obvious method of making observations: field research. If you want to know about something, why not just go where it's happening and watch it happen, experience it, perhaps even participate in it? While these are "natural" activities, you'll see that they're also skills to be learned and honed. That's what this chapter is all about. I have used the term *field research* to include methods of research sometimes referred to as *participant observation, direct observation,* and *case studies.*

Many of the observation methods discussed in this book are designed to produce data appropriate for *quantitative* (statistical) analysis. Thus, surveys provide data from which to calculate the percentage unemployed in a population, mean incomes, and so forth. Field research more typically yields *qualitative* data: observations not easily reduced to numbers. Thus, for example, a field researcher may note the "paternalistic demeanor" of leaders at a political rally or the "defensive evasions" of a public official at a public hearing without trying to express either the paternalism or the defensiveness as numerical quantities or degrees. This is not to say, however, that field research cannot also be used to collect quantitative data: noting the number of interactions of various specified types within a field setting, for example. (I'll delay the discussion of content analysis until the following chapter, since it can be approached both qualitatively and quantitatively.)

Field research is at once very old and very new in social science. Many of the techniques discussed in this chapter have been used by social researchers for centuries. Within the social sciences, anthropologists are especially associated with this method and have contributed to its development as a scientific technique. Moreover, something similar to this method is employed by many people who might not, strictly speaking, be regarded as social science researchers. Newspaper reporters are one example; welfare department case workers are another.

It bears repeating that field research is constantly used in everyday life, by all of us. In a sense, we do field research whenever we observe or participate in social behavior and try to understand it, whether in a college classroom, in a doctor's waiting room, or an airplane. Whenever we report our observations to others, we are reporting our field research efforts. In this chapter I'll discuss this method in some detail, providing a logical overview and suggesting some of the specific skills and techniques that make scientific field research more useful than the casual observation we all engage in.

Field observation differs from some other models of observation in that it is not just a data-collecting activity. Frequently, perhaps typically, it is a theory-generating activity as well. As a field researcher you'll seldom approach your task with precisely defined hypotheses to be tested. More typically, you'll attempt to make sense out of an ongoing process that cannot be predicted in advance—making initial observations, developing tentative general conclusions that suggest particular types of further observations, making those observations and thereby revising your conclusions, and so forth. The alternation of induction and deduction discussed in Part 1 of this book is perhaps nowhere more evident and essential than in good field research.

Though the theoretical and logical discussions presented earlier apply in varying degrees to field research, I want to begin this chapter with a brief introduction to some of the special concepts associated with qualitative inquiry.

SOME TERMINOLOGY OF QUALITATIVE INQUIRY

If you read much of the literature on qualitative inquiry—either reports of qualitative research or texts on how to do it—you're likely to encounter a "terminological jungle" (Lofland and Lofland 1995:6). In this jungle, authors often use different labels for research approaches that can seem confusingly similar. As such, let's briefly examine some important terms here before moving on to the field research techniques that tend to cut across these labels.

Phenomenology

Phenomenology is a philosophical term, mostly associated with Edmund Husserl, that refers to a consideration of all perceived phenomenon, both the "objective" and "subjective." It's also associated with the eminent Flip Wilson, who said, "What you see is what you get."

Qualitative researchers often attempt to make comprehensive observations at the outset and then to winnow out any elements that originated in their own worldview rather than in the worldview of the people being observed and/or interviewed. They aim at discovering subjects' experiences and how subjects make sense of them, for example.

Interpretivism

Akin to phenomenology, *interpretivism* aims at discovering how the subject of study understands his or her life. Steinar Kvale (1996:11) contrasts this with a more positivistic approach:

■ There is a move away from obtaining knowledge primarily through external observation and experimental manipulation of human subjects, toward an understanding by means of conversations with the human beings to be understood. The subjects not only answer questions prepared by an expert, but themselves formulate in a dialogue their own conceptions of their lived world.

Recalling the terms of an earlier discussion, Kvale is speaking in favor of a more *idiographic* than *nomothetic* approach. In the nomothetic approach, we might ask a random sample of U.S. citizens:

Have you ever felt you were the victim of racial or ethnic discrimination?

This would allow us to calculate the percentage of U.S. citizens who feel they've been discriminated against. If we also asked them to identify their own ethnicity, we could compare different ethnic groups in the degrees to which they feel discriminated against.

In a more idiographic, interpretivist approach, we might ask a smaller number of individuals:

What would you consider examples of racial or ethnic discrimination in today's society? Have you ever experienced such discrimination? Can you say something about that experience?

This latter approach would yield a greater, in-depth understanding of the subjects' experiences and how the subjects interpreted them, but it would be more difficult to draw conclusions about the feelings of the general public.

Hermeneutics

Originally referring to the interpretation of religious texts, Jurgen Habermas (1971) and others have adapted the process of hermeneutics to the understanding of social life. As used in the social sciences, *hermeneutics* aims at understanding the process of understanding. Whereas the interpretivist seeks to discover how the subject interprets his or her experience of life, the hermeneuticist is more interested in the interpretivist's process of discovery.

Recall the earlier discussion of the "hermeneutic circle" (Chapter 5) through which the meaning of a text is sought. Our initial, overall understanding of a text gives us a place from which to examine and interpret the meaning of the parts it comprises. The examination of the parts, however, may lead us to reframe our overall assessment—which gives us a new ground from which to evaluate those parts.

Thus, for example, we may begin with the understanding that a woman is staying with her abusive husband for reasons of economic security. This initial, overall interpretation should lead us to focus on economic elements in the specifics of her conversation. That focused examination, however, may draw our attention to comments indicating that she actually has independent, economic resources. This discovery would cause us to reconsider whether her motivations are really based in economics or whether she has underestimated her own economic resources.

Participant Observation

Participant observation is a specific form of field research in which the researcher participates as an actor in the events under study. To study the experiences of taxi drivers, you might get a license to drive a taxi. To study taxi dancers, you could bone up on your two-step and start hoofing it.

A later section of this chapter will delve more deeply into the various roles that participant observers may play within the context of interactions being studied, roles that vary mainly in how far they participate and how much they reveal their research identity.

In-depth Interview

In the preceding chapter, we discussed the techniques of survey interviewing. In this chapter we'll examine a different type of interviewing, one that is less structured and gives the subject of the interview more freedom to direct the flow of conversation.

In-depth interviewing is a mainstay of participant observation, used both by participant observers and by researchers who make no pretense of being a part of what is being studied. As you have for many of the techniques we've already discussed, you'll see that (1) you already engage in in-depth interviews in your daily life and (2) there are special techniques that move this activity from a casual form of interaction to a powerful scientific tool.

Case Study

A *case study* is an idiographic examination of a single individual, group, or society. Its chief purpose is description, although attempts at explanation are also acceptable. Examples include an anthropological depiction of a specific, preliterate tribe; a sociological analysis of the organizational structure of a modern corporation; and a political scientist's examination of a particular political movement.

Ethnography

Often associated with anthropological studies, *ethnography* typically refers to naturalistic observations and holistic understandings of cultures or subcultures. Thus, when you read Elliot Liebow's description of *Tally's Corner* (1967), you come away with an intimate feel for the way of life he observed. While ethnography has traditionally emphasized description rather than explanation, however, this need not be the case.

John Lofland (1995) speaks more specifically of *analytic ethnography,* in an article aimed at delineating the key elements in a research strategy used by many field researchers.

Generic Propositions Lofland argues that analytic ethnographers are committed ultimately to establishing general propositions regarding the patterns of human social life. Some of these patterns are descriptive (such as the frequency of certain events) and some explanatory (such as what causes certain kinds of behavior).

Unfettered Inquiry Despite diverse views about what is or is not a "proper" subject for social science inquiry, Lofland suggests that field researchers basically hold the view that anything is fair game.

Deep Familiarity To the extent possible you place yourself in the position of those you wish to understand. Lofland quotes (1995:45) Erving Goffman describing this process:

■ You are close to them while they are responding to what life does to them. I feel that the way this is done is not, of course, just to listen to what they talk about, but to pick up their minor grunts and groans as they respond to their situation.

Goffman suggests such researchers are not so much interviewers or listeners as they are *witnesses.*

Emergent Analysis Lofland indicates that theory emerges in the course of analyzing observations rather than preceding observation in the form of hypotheses, as you saw way back in Chapter 1.

True Content Confronting postmodern suggestions that there is no "true" reality, Lofland says that analytic ethnographers proceed nonetheless as though it existed, developing and using techniques that will accurately capture what is "really" going on.

New Content In contrast to the natural sciences' tradition of replicating findings, Lofland says that analytic ethnographers aim at creating new observations and/or new analyses with each research effort.

Developed Treatment Here Lofland speaks of a balance between the presentation of data from observations and the elaboration of theoretical concepts that can represent and make sense of those data.

Lofland recognizes that some field researchers would quibble with certain details in his characterization of analytic ethnography, and some would even disagree with some fundamentals. Nonetheless, his description provides a good sense of what is typically meant by ethnography in field research.

Grounded Theory

Grounded theory, a phrase coined by Barney Glaser and Anselm Strauss (1967), was mentioned in Chapter 1's discussion of the *inductive* approach to understanding. Let's look a little more deeply into this concept now, as it is frequently associated with field research.

In sharp contrast to the deductive approach, which begins with a general theory and derives hypotheses for empirical testing, grounded theory begins with observations and then proposes patterns, themes, or common categories. This does not mean that researchers have no preconceived ideas or expectations; in fact, what has been previously learned will shape the new search for generalities. However, the analysis is not set up to confirm or disconfirm specific hypotheses.

By the same token, the openness of the grounded theory approach allows a greater latitude for discovering the unexpected—some regularity or disparity totally unanticipated by the concepts that might compose a particular theory or hypothesis.

Please recall that there's no need to choose between inductive and deductive approaches. You can design research to test specific hypotheses and undertake an inductive analysis of the data collected in that endeavor. Your ability to engage the grounded theory approach would depend chiefly on the richness of the data collected. Thus, a bare-bones experiment that measured only two or three variables would not lend itself to this approach.

■ TOPICS APPROPRIATE TO FIELD RESEARCH

One of the key strengths of field research is the comprehensiveness of perspective it gives researchers. By going directly to the social phenomenon under study and observing it as completely as possible, they can develop a deeper and fuller understanding of it. This mode of observation, then, is especially, though not exclusively, appropriate to research topics and social studies that appear to defy simple quantification. Field researchers may recognize several nuances of attitude and behavior that might escape researchers using other methods.

Field research is especially appropriate to the study of those attitudes and behaviors best understood within their natural setting, as opposed to the somewhat artificial settings of experiments and surveys. For example, field research provides a superior method for studying the dynamics of religious conversion at a revival meeting, just as a statistical analysis of membership rolls would be a better way of discovering whether men or women were more likely to convert.

Finally, field research is well suited to the study of social processes over time. Thus, the field researcher might be in a position to examine the rumblings and final explosion of a riot as events actually occur rather than afterward in a reconstruction of the same.

Other good places to apply field research methods would include campus demonstrations, courtroom proceedings, labor negotiations, public hearings, or similar events taking place within a relatively limited area and time. Several such observations must be combined in a more comprehensive examination over time and space.

In their *Analyzing Social Settings* (1995:101–13), John and Lyn Lofland discuss several elements of social life appropriate for field research. They call them *thinking topics*.

1. *Practices*. This refers to various kinds of behavior.
2. *Episodes*. Here the Loflands include a variety of events such as divorce, crime, and illness.
3. *Encounters*. This involves two or more people meeting and interacting in immediate proximity with one another.
4. *Roles*. Field research is also appropriate to the analysis of the positions people occupy and the behavior associated with those positions: occupations, family roles, ethnic groups.
5. *Relationships*. Much social life can be examined in terms of the kinds of behavior appropriate to pairs or sets of roles: mother-son relationships, friendships, and the like.
6. *Groups*. Moving beyond relationships, field research can also be used to study small groups, such as friendship cliques, athletic teams, and work groups.
7. *Organizations*. Beyond small groups, field researchers also study formal organizations, such as hospitals or schools.
8. *Settlements*. It is difficult to study large societies such as nations, but field researchers often study smaller-scale "societies" such as villages, ghettos, and neighborhoods.
9. *Social Worlds*. Ambiguous social entities with vague boundaries and populations can nonetheless be proper subjects for social scientific study: "the sports world," "Wall Street," and the like.
10. *Lifestyles* or *Subcultures*. Finally, social scientists sometimes focus on how large numbers of people adjust to life: groups such as a "ruling class" or an "urban underclass."

In all these social settings, field research can reveal things that would not otherwise be apparent. Let me give you a concrete example.

One issue I'm particularly interested in (Babbie 1985) is the nature of responsibility for public matters: Who's responsible for making the things that we share work? Who's responsible for keeping public spaces—parks, malls, buildings, and so on—clean? Who's responsible for seeing that broken street signs get fixed? Or, if a strong wind knocks over garbage cans and rolls them around the street, who's responsible for getting them out of the street?

On the surface, the answer to these questions is pretty clear. We have formal and informal agreements in our society that assign responsibility for these activities. Government custodians are responsible for keeping public places clean. Transportation department employees are responsible for the street signs, and perhaps the police are responsible for the garbage cans rolling around the street on a windy day. And when these responsibilities are not fulfilled, we tend to look around for someone to blame.

What fascinates me is the extent to which the assignment of responsibility for public things to specific individuals not only relieves others of the responsibility but actually *prohibits them from taking responsibility*. It's my notion that it has become unacceptable for someone like you or me to take personal responsibility for public matters that haven't been assigned to us.

Let me illustrate what I mean. If you were walking through a public park and you threw down a bunch of trash, you'd discover that your action was unacceptable to those around you. People would glare at you, grumble to each other, and perhaps someone would say something to you about it. Whatever the form, you'd be subjected to definite, negative sanctions for littering. Now here's the irony. If you were walking through that same park, came across a bunch of trash that someone else had dropped, and cleaned it up, it's likely that your action would also be unacceptable to those around you. You'd probably be subjected to definite, negative sanctions for cleaning it up.

When I first began discussing this pattern with students, most felt the notion was absurd. Although we would be negatively sanctioned for littering, cleaning up a public place would obviously bring positive sanctions. People would be pleased with us for doing it. Certainly, all my students said they would be pleased if someone cleaned up a public place. It seemed likely that everyone else would be pleased, too, if we asked them how they would react to someone's cleaning up litter in a public place or otherwise taking personal responsibility for fixing some social problem.

To settle the issue, I suggested that my students start fixing the public problems they came across in the course of their everyday activities. As they did so, I asked them to note the answers to two questions:

1. How did they feel while they were fixing a public problem they had not been assigned responsibility for?
2. How did others around them react?

My students picked up litter, fixed street signs, put knocked-over traffic cones back in place, cleaned and decorated communal lounges in their dorms, trimmed trees that blocked visibility at intersections, repaired public playground equipment, cleaned public restrooms, and took care of a hundred other public problems that weren't "their responsibility."

Most reported feeling very uncomfortable doing whatever they did. They felt foolish, goody-goody, conspicuous, and all the other feelings that keep us from performing these activities normally. In almost every case, their personal feelings of discomfort were increased by the reactions of those around them. One student was removing a damaged and long-unused newspaper box from the bus stop where it had been a problem for months, when the police arrived, having been summoned by a neighbor. Another student decided to clean out a clogged storm drain on his street and found himself being yelled at by a neighbor who insisted that the mess should be left for the street cleaners. Everyone who picked up litter was sneered at, laughed at, and generally put down. One young man was picking up litter scattered around a trash can when a passerby sneered, "Clumsy!" It became clear to us that there are only three acceptable explanations for picking up litter in a public place:

1. You did it and got caught—somebody forced you to clean up your mess.
2. You did it and felt guilty.
3. You're stealing litter.

In the normal course of things, it's simply not acceptable for people to take responsibility for public things.

Clearly, we could not have discovered the nature and strength of agreements about taking personal responsibility for public things except through field research. Social norms suggest that taking responsibility is a good thing—sometimes referred to as *good citizenship*. Asking people what they thought about it would have produced a solid consensus that it was good. Only going out into life, doing it, and watching what happened gave us an accurate picture.

As an interesting footnote to this story, my students and I found that whenever people could get past their initial reactions and discover that the students were simply taking responsibility for fixing things for the sake of having them work, the tendency was for the passersby to assist. Although there are some very strong agreements making it "unsafe" to take responsibility for public things, the willingness of one person to rise above those agreements seemed to make it safe for others to do so, and they did.

In summary, then, field research offers the advantage of probing social life in its natural habitat. Although some things can be studied adequately in questionnaires or in the laboratory, others cannot. And direct observation in the field lets you observe subtle communications and other events that might not be anticipated or measured otherwise.

■ THE VARIOUS ROLES OF THE OBSERVER

The students who fixed public things were definitely *participating* in what they wanted to observe. In this chapter, I have used the term *field research* rather than the frequently used term *participant observation*, since field researchers need not always participate in what they are studying, though they usually will study it directly at the scene of the action. As Catherine Marshall and Gretchen Rossman (1995:60) point out,

■ The researcher may plan a role that entails varying degrees of "participantness"—that is, the degree of actual participation in daily life. At one extreme is the full participant, who goes about ordinary life in a role or set of roles constructed in the setting. At the other extreme is the complete observer, who engages not at all in social interaction and may even shun involvement in the world being studied. And, of course, all possible complementary mixes along the continuum are available to the researcher.

The complete participant, in this sense, may be a genuine participant in what he or she is studying (for example, a participant in a campus demonstration) or may pretend to be a genuine participant. In any event, if you are acting as the complete participant, you let people see you *only* as a participant, not as a researcher. For instance, if you're studying a group made up of uneducated and inarticulate people, it would not be appropriate for you to talk and act like a university professor or student.

Here let me draw your attention to an ethical issue, one on which social researchers themselves are divided. Is it ethical to deceive the people you are studying in the hope that they will confide in you as they will not confide in an identified researcher? Do the interests of science—the scientific values of the research—offset such considerations? Although many professional associations have addressed this issue, the norms to be followed remain somewhat ambiguous when applied to specific situations. (We'll examine such ethical issues more deeply in Chapter 18.)

Related to this ethical consideration is a scientific one. No researcher deceives his or her subjects solely for the purpose of deception. Rather, it is done in the belief that the data will be more valid and reliable, that the subjects will be more natural and honest if they do not know the researcher is doing a research project. If the people being studied know they are being studied, they might modify their behavior in a variety of ways. First, they might expel the researcher. Second, they might modify their speech and behavior to appear more respectable than would otherwise be the case. Third, the social process itself might be radically changed. Students making plans to burn down the university administration building, for example, might give up the plan altogether once they learn that one of their group is a social scientist conducting a research project.

On the other side of the coin, if you are a complete participant, you may affect what you are studying. To play the role of participant, you must *participate*. Yet, your participation may importantly affect the social process you're studying. Suppose, for example, that you're asked for your ideas about what the group should do next. No matter what you say, you will affect the process in some fashion. If the group follows your suggestion, your influence on the process is obvious. If the group decides not to follow your suggestion, the process whereby the suggestion is rejected may importantly affect what happens next. Finally, if you indicate that you just don't know what should be done next, you may be adding to a general feeling of uncertainty and indecisiveness in the group.

Ultimately, *anything* the participant-observer does or does not do will have some effect on what is being observed; it is simply inevitable. More seriously, what you do or do not do may have an *important* effect on what happens. There is no complete protection against this effect, though sensitivity to the issue may provide a partial protection. (This influence, called the Hawthorne effect, was discussed more fully in Chapter 9.)

Because of these several considerations, ethical and scientific, the field researcher frequently chooses a different role from that of complete participant. You could participate fully with the group under study but make it clear that you were also undertaking research. As a member of the volleyball team, for example, you might use your position to launch a study in the sociology of sports, letting your teammates know what you were doing. There are dangers in this role also, however. The people being studied may shift much of their attention to the research project rather than focus on the natural social process, making the process being observed no longer typical. Or, conversely, you yourself may come to identify too much with the interests and viewpoints of the participants. You may begin to "go native" and lose much of your scientific detachment.

The *complete observer*, at the other extreme, observes a social process without becoming a part of it in any way. Quite possibly, the subjects of study might not realize they are being studied, because of the researcher's unobtrusiveness. Sitting at a bus stop to observe jaywalking at a nearby intersection would be an example. Although the complete observer is less likely to affect what's being studied and less likely to "go native" than the complete participant, she or he is also less likely to develop a full appreciation of what's being studied. Observations may be more sketchy and transitory.

Fred Davis (1973) characterizes the extreme roles that observers might play as "the Martian" and "the Convert." The latter involves the observer delving deeper and deeper into the phenomenon under study, running the risk of "going native." We'll examine this further in the next section.

On the other hand, you may be able to grasp most fully the "Martian" approach by imagining that you were sent to observe some new-found life on Mars. Probably you would feel yourself inescapably separate from the Martians. Some social scientists adopt this degree of separation when observing cultures or social classes different from their own.

Marshall and Rossman (1995:60–61) also note that the researcher can vary the amount of time spent in the setting being observed: You can be a full-time presence on the scene or just show up now and then. Moreover, you can focus your attention on a limited aspect of the social setting or seek to observe all of it—framing an appropriate role to match your aims.

Different situations ultimately require different roles for the researcher. Unfortunately, there are no clear guidelines for making this choice— you must rely on your understanding of the situation and your own good judgment. In making your decision, however, you must be guided by both methodological and ethical considerations. Because these often conflict, your decision will frequently be difficult, and you may find sometimes that your role limits your study.

■ RELATIONS TO SUBJECTS

Having introduced the different roles you might play in connection with your field research observations, we're now going to focus more specifically on how you may relate to the subjects of your study and to their points of view. In the previous section, I introduced the possibility of pretending to occupy social statuses you don't really occupy. Now let's consider how you would think and feel in such a situation.

Suppose you've decided to study a religious cult that has enrolled many people in your neighborhood. You might study the group by joining it or pretending to join it. Take a moment to ask yourself what the difference is between "really" joining and "pretending" to join. The main difference is whether you actually take on the beliefs, attitudes, and other points of view shared by the "real" members. If the cult members believe that Jesus will come next Thursday night to destroy the world and save the members of the cult, do you believe it or do you simply pretend to believe it?

Traditionally, social scientists have tended to emphasize the importance of "objectivity" in such matters. In this example, that injunction would be to avoid getting swept up in the beliefs of the group. Without denying the advantages associated with such objectivity, social scientists today also recognize the benefits gained by immersing themselves in the points of view they are studying, what Lofland and Lofland (1995:61) refer to as "insider understanding." Ultimately, you will not be able to understand the thoughts and actions of the cult members unless you can *adopt their points of view as true*—even only temporarily. To fully appreciate the phenomenon you've set out to study, you need to *believe* that Jesus is coming Thursday night.

Adopting an alien point of view is an uncomfortable prospect for most people. It's one thing to learn about the strange views that others may hold. Sometimes you probably find it hard just to tolerate certain views. But to take them on as your own is ten times worse. Robert Bellah (1970, 1974) has offered the term *symbolic realism* in this regard, indicating the need for social researchers to treat the beliefs they study as worthy of respect rather than as objects of ridicule. If you seriously entertain this prospect, you may appreciate why William Shaffir and Robert Stebbins (1991:1) conclude that "fieldwork must certainly rank with the more disagreeable activities that humanity has fashioned for itself."

There is, of course, a danger in adopting the points of view of the people you're studying. When you abandon your objectivity in favor of adopting such views, you lose the possibility of seeing and understanding the phenomenon within frames of reference unavailable to your subjects. On the one hand, accepting the belief that the world will end Thursday night allows you to appreciate aspects of that belief available only to believers; stepping outside that view, however, makes it possible for you to consider some reasons why people might adopt such a view. You may discover some did so as a consequence of personal traumas (such as unemployment or divorce) while others were brought into the fold through their participation in particular social networks (for example, their whole bowling team joined the cult). Notice that the cult members might disagree with those "objective" explanations, and you might not come up with them to the extent that you had operated legitimately within the group's views.

There is, of course, an apparent dilemma here: There are important advantages in both postures, even though they seem mutually exclusive. It is, in fact, possible to assume both postures. Sometimes you can simply shift viewpoints at will. When appropriate, you can fully assume the beliefs of the cult; later, you can step outside those beliefs (more accurately, you step inside the viewpoints associated with social science). As you become more adept at this kind of research, you may come to hold contradictory viewpoints simultaneously, rather than switch back and forth.

During my study of trance channelers—people who allow spirits to occupy their bodies and speak through them—I found I could participate fully in channeling sessions without becoming alienated from conventional social science. Rather than "believing" in the reality of channeling, I found it possible to suspend beliefs in that realm: neither believing it to be genuine (like most of the other participants) nor disbelieving it (like most scientists). Put differently, I was open to either possibility. Notice how this differs from our normal need to "know" whether such things are legitimate or not.

The problem we've just been discussing could be seen as psychological, occuring mostly inside the researcher's head. There is a corresponding problem at a social level, however. When you become deeply involved in the lives of the people you're studying, you're likely to be moved by their personal problems and crises. Imagine, for example, that one of the cult members becomes ill and needs a ride to the hospital. Should you provide transportation? Sure. Suppose someone wants to borrow money to buy a stereo. Should you loan it? Probably not. Suppose they need the money for food?

There are no black-and-white rules for resolving situations such as these. However, you should be warned that such problems arise and you will need to deal with them, regardless of whether you've revealed yourself to be a researcher or not. Such problems do not tend to arise in other types of research—surveys and experiments, for example—but they are part and parcel of participant observation.

■ PREPARING FOR THE FIELD

Suppose for the moment that you've decided to undertake field research on a campus political organization. Let's assume further that you're not a member of that group, that you do not know a great deal about it, and that you will identify yourself to the participants as a researcher. This section will discuss some of the ways you might prepare yourself before undertaking direct observation of the group.

As is true of all research methods, you would be well advised to begin with a search of the relevant literature, filling in your knowledge of the subject and learning what others have said about it. Because library research is discussed at length in Appendix A, I won't say anything further about it at this point.

In the next phase of your research, you may wish to make use of informants (discussed in Chapter 8). You might wish to discuss the student political group with others who have already studied it or with anyone else likely to be familiar with it. In particular, you might find it useful to discuss the group with one of its members. Perhaps you have a friend who is a member, or you can meet someone who is. This aspect of your preparation is likely to be more effective if your relationship with the informant extends beyond your research role. In dealing with members of the group as informants, you should take care that your initial discussions do not compromise or limit later aspects of your research. Realize that the impression you make on the informant, the role you establish for yourself, may carry over into your later effort. For example, creating the initial impression that you may be an undercover FBI agent is unlikely to facilitate later observations of the group.

You should also be wary about the information you get from informants. Although they may have more direct, personal knowledge of the subject under study than you do, what they "know" is probably a mixture of fact and point of view. Members of the political group in our example would not likely give you completely unbiased information (nor would members of opposing political groups). Before making your first contact with the student group, then, you should already be quite familiar with it, and you should understand its general philosophical context.

There are a variety of ways to establish your initial contact with the people you plan to study. How you do it will depend, in part, on the role you intend to play. Especially if you decide to take on the role of complete participant, you must find a way to develop an identity with the people to be studied. If you wish to study dishwashers in a restaurant, the most direct method would be to get a job as a dishwasher. In the case of the student political group, you might simply join the group.

Many of the social processes appropriate to field research are sufficiently open to make your contact with the people to be studied rather simple and straightforward. If you wish to observe a mass demonstration, just be there. If you wish to observe patterns in jaywalking, hang around busy streets.

Whenever you wish to make more formal contact with the people, identifying yourself as a researcher, you must establish a certain rapport with them. You might contact a participant with whom you feel comfortable and gain that person's assistance. In studying a formal group, you might approach the group leaders. Or you may find that one of your informants who has studied the group can introduce you.

While you'll probably have many options in making your initial contact with the group, you should realize that your choice can influence your subsequent observations. Suppose, for example, that you're studying a university and begin with high-level administrators. First, your initial impressions of the university are going to be shaped by the administrators' views, which will be quite different from those of students or faculty. This initial impression may influence the way you will observe and interpret subsequently—even if you are unaware of the influence.

Second, if the administrators approve of your research project and encourage students and faculty to cooperate with you, the latter groups will probably look on you as somehow aligned with the administration, which can affect what they say to you. Faculty might be reluctant to tell you about plans to organize through the teamsters' union.

In making a direct, formal contact with the people you want to study, you'll be required to give them some explanation of the purpose of your study. Here again, you face an ethical dilemma. Telling them the complete purpose of your research might eliminate their cooperation altogether or importantly affect their behavior. On the other hand, giving only what you believe would be an acceptable explanation may involve outright deception. Realize in all this that your decisions—in practice—may be largely determined by the purpose of your study, the nature of what you're studying, observations you wish to use, and other such factors.

Previous field research offers no fixed rule—methodological or ethical—to follow in this regard. Your appearance as a researcher, regardless of your stated purpose, may result in a warm welcome from people who are flattered that a scientist finds them important enough to study. Or, it may result in your being totally ostracized or worse. (Do not, for example, burst into a meeting of an organized crime syndicate and announce that you're writing a term paper on organized crime.)

■ QUALITATIVE INTERVIEWING

In part, field research is a matter of going where the action is and simply watching and listening. You can learn a lot merely by paying attention to what's going on. At the same time, as I've already indicated, field research can involve more active inquiry. Sometimes it's appropriate to ask people questions and record their answers. Your on-the-spot observations of a full-blown riot will lack something if you don't know why people are rioting. Ask somebody.

We've already discussed interviewing in Chapter 10, on survey research. The interviewing you'll do in connection with field observation, however, is different enough to demand a separate treatment here. In surveys, questionnaires are rigidly structured; however, less structured interviews are more appropriate to field research.

Herbert and Riene Rubin (1995:43) make this distinction: "Qualitative interviewing design is *flexible, iterative,* and *continuous,* rather than prepared in advance and locked in stone."

■ Design in qualitative interviewing is iterative. That means that each time you repeat the basic process of gathering information, analyzing it, winnowing it, and testing it, you come closer to a clear and convincing model of the phenomenon you are studying. . . .

The continuous nature of qualitative interviewing means that the questioning is redesigned throughout the project.

(RUBIN AND RUBIN 1995:46, 47)

A qualitative interview is an interaction between an interviewer and a respondent in which the interviewer has a general plan of inquiry but not a specific set of questions that must be asked in particular words and in a particular order. A qualitative interview is essentially a conversation in which the interviewer establishes a general direction for the conversation and pursues specific topics raised by the respondent. Ideally, the respondent does most of the talking.

Steinar Kvale (1996:3–5) offers two metaphors for interviewing: the interviewer as a "miner" or as a "traveler." The first model assumes that the subject possesses specific information and that the interviewer's job is to dig it out. By contrast, in the second model, the interviewer

■ wanders through the landscape and enters into conversations with the people encountered. The traveler explores the many domains of the country, as unknown territory or with maps, roaming freely around the territory. . . . The interviewer wanders along with the local inhabitants, asks questions that lead the subjects to tell their own stories of their lived world.

Asking questions and noting answers is a natural process for us all, and it seems simple enough to add it to your bag of tricks as a field researcher. Be a little cautious, however. As I've already discussed in Chapter 6, wording questions is a tricky business. All too often, the way we ask questions subtly biases the answers we get. Sometimes we put our respondent under pressure to look good. Sometimes we put the question in a particular context that omits altogether the most relevant answers.

Pursuing the previous example of student political action, suppose you want to find out why a group of students is rioting and pillaging on campus. You might be tempted to focus your questioning on how students feel about the dean's recent ruling that requires students always to carry *The Practice of Social Research* with them on campus. (Makes sense to me.) Although you may collect a great deal of information about students' attitudes toward the infamous ruling, they may be rioting for some other reason. Or perhaps most are simply joining in for the excitement. Properly done, field research interviewing would enable you to find out.

Although you may set out to conduct interviews with a pretty clear idea of what you want to ask, one of the special strengths of field research is its flexibility in the field. The answers evoked by your initial questions should shape your subsequent ones. It doesn't work, in this situation, merely to ask preestablished questions and record the answers. You need to ask a question, hear the answer, interpret its meaning for your general inquiry, frame another question either to dig into the earlier answer in more depth or to redirect the person's attention to an area more relevant to your inquiry. In short, you need to be able to listen, think, and talk almost at the same time.

The discussion of probes in Chapter 10 provides a useful guide to getting answers in more depth without biasing later answers. Learn the skills of being a good listener. Be more interested than interesting. Learn to say things like "How is that?" "In what ways?" "How do you mean that?" "What would be an example of that?" Learn to look and listen expectantly, and let the person you're interviewing fill in the silence.

At the same time, you can't afford to be a totally passive receiver in the interaction. You'll go into your interviews with some general (or specific) questions you want answered and some topics you want addressed, and you will have to learn the skills of subtly directing the flow of conversation.

There's something you can learn here from the martial arts. The aikido master never resists an opponent's blow but instead accepts it, joins with it, and then subtly redirects it in a more appropriate direction. You should master a similar skill for interviewing. Don't try to halt your respondent's line of discussion, but learn to take what he or she has just said and branch that comment back in the direction appropriate to your purposes. Most people love to talk to anyone who's really interested. Stopping their line of conversation tells them you aren't interested; asking them to elaborate in a particular direction tells them you are. Consider this hypothetical example in which you are interested in why college students chose their majors.

YOU: What are you majoring in?
RESP: Engineering.
YOU: I see. How did you come to choose engineering?
RESP: I have an uncle who was voted the best engineer in Arizona in 1981.
YOU: Gee, that's great.
RESP: Yeah. He was the engineer in charge of developing the new civic center in Tucson. It was written up in most of the engineering journals.
YOU: I see. Did you talk to him about your becoming an engineer?
RESP: Yeah. He said that he got into engineering by accident. He needed a job when he graduated from high school, so he went to work

as a laborer on a construction job. He spent eight years working his way up from the bottom, until he decided to go to college and come back nearer the top.

You: So is your main interest civil engineering, like your uncle, or are you more interested in some other branch of engineering?

Resp: Actually, I'm leaning more toward electrical engineering—computers, in particular. I started messing around with microcomputers when I was in high school, and my long-term plan is . . .

Notice how the interview first begins to wander off into a story about the respondent's uncle. The first attempt to focus things back on the student's own choice of major failed. The second attempt succeeded. Now the student is providing the kind of information you're looking for. It's important for you to develop the ability to "control" conversations in that fashion.

Herbert and Riene Rubin offer several ways to control a "guided conversation," such as the following:

■ If you can limit the number of main topics, it is easier to maintain a conversational flow from one topic to another. Transitions should be smooth and logical. "We have been talking about mothers, now let's talk about fathers," sounds abrupt. A smoother transition might be, "You mentioned your mother did not care how you performed in school—was your father more involved?" The more abrupt the transition, the more it sounds like the interviewer has an agenda that he or she wants to get through, rather than wanting to hear what the interviewee has to say.

(Rubin and Rubin 1995:123)

Because field research interviewing is so much like normal conversation, you must keep reminding yourself that you are *not* having a normal conversation. In normal conversations, each of us wants to come across as an interesting, worthwhile person. If you watch yourself the next time you chat with someone you don't know too well, I think you'll find that much of your attention is spent on thinking up interesting things to *say*—contributions to the conversation that will make a good impression. Often, we don't really hear each other, because we're too busy thinking of what we'll say next. As an interviewer, the desire to appear interesting is counterproductive to your job. You need to make the *other* person seem interesting, by being interested. (Do this in ordinary conversations, by the way, and people will actually regard you as a great conversationalist.)

John and Lyn Lofland (1995:56–57) suggest that investigators adopt the role of the "socially acceptable incompetent" when interviewing. You should offer yourself as someone who does not understand the situation you find yourself in and must be helped to grasp even the most basic and obvious aspects of that situation.

■ A naturalistic investigator, almost by definition, is one who does not understand. She or he is "ignorant" and needs to be "taught." This role of watcher and asker of questions is the quintessential *student* role.

(Lofland and Lofland 1995:56)

Interviewing needs to be an integral part of your whole field research process. Later, I'll stress that you need to review your notes every night—making sense out of what you've observed, getting a clearer feel for the situation you're studying, and finding out what you should pay more attention to in further observations. In this same fashion, you need to review your notes on interviews, detecting all those questions you should have asked but didn't. Start asking such questions the next time you interview.

Steinar Kvale (1996:88) details seven stages in a complete interviewing process, which I describe here:

1. *Thematizing:* clarifying the purpose of the interviews and the concepts to be explored
2. *Designing:* laying out the process through which you'll accomplish your purpose, including a consideration of the ethical dimension
3. *Interviewing:* doing the actual interviews
4. *Transcribing:* creating a written text of the interviews

5. *Analyzing:* determining the meaning of gathered materials in relation to the purpose of the study
6. *Verifying:* checking the reliability and validity of the materials
7. *Reporting:* telling others what you've learned

As with all other aspects of field research, interviewing improves with practice. Fortunately, it's something you can practice any time you want. Practice on your friends.

■ RECORDING OBSERVATIONS

In both direct observation and interviewing, it is vital that you make full and accurate notes of what went on. Even tape recorders and cameras cannot capture all the relevant aspects of social processes. The greatest advantage of the field research method is the presence of an observing, thinking researcher on the scene of the action. If possible, you should take notes on your observations *as you observe*. When that's not feasible, you should write down your notes as soon as possible afterward.

Your notes should include both your empirical observations and your interpretations of them. You should record what you "know" has happened and what you "think" has happened. Further, you must identify these different kinds of notes for what they are. For example, you might note that Person X spoke out in opposition to a proposal made by a group leader, that you *think* this represents an attempt by Person X to take over leadership of the group, and that you *think* you heard the leader comment to that effect in response to the opposition.

Just as you cannot hope to observe everything, neither can you record everything you do observe. Just as your observations represent a *de facto* sample of all possible observations, your notes represent a sample of your observations. Rather than recording a random sample of your observations, you should, of course, record the most important ones.

Some of the most important observations can be anticipated before you begin the study; others will become apparent as your observations progress. Sometimes your note taking can be made easier if you prepare standardized recording forms in advance. In a study of jaywalking, for example, you might anticipate the characteristics of pedestrians the most likely to be useful for analysis—age, gender, social class, ethnicity, and so forth—and prepare a form in which actual observations can be recorded easily. Or, you might develop a symbolic shorthand in advance to speed up recording. For studying audience participation at a mass meeting, you might want to construct a numbered grid representing the different sections of the meeting room; then you could record the location of participants easily, quickly, and accurately.

None of this advance preparation should limit your recording of unanticipated events and aspects of the situation. Quite the contrary, speedy handling of anticipated observations can give you more freedom to observe the unanticipated.

I know you're familiar with the process of taking notes. Every student is. And as I've said earlier, everybody is somewhat familiar with field research in general. Like *good* field research, however, *good* note taking requires careful and deliberate attention and involves some specific skills. Some guidelines follow. (You can learn more from John and Lyn Lofland's *Analyzing Social Settings* [1995:91–96].)

First, don't trust your memory any more than you have to; it's untrustworthy. If I'm being too unkind to your mind, try this experiment. Recall the last few movies you saw that you really liked. Now, name five of the actors or actresses. Who had the longest hair? Who was the most likely to start conversations? Who was the most likely to make suggestions that others followed? Now, if you didn't have any trouble answering any of those questions, how *sure* are you of your answers? Would you be willing to bet a hundred dollars that a panel of impartial judges would observe what you recall?

Even if you pride yourself on having a photographic memory, it's a good idea to take notes either during the observation or as soon afterward as possible. If you take notes during observation, do it unobtrusively, since people are likely to behave differently if they see you taking down everything they say or do.

Second, it's usually a good idea to take notes in stages. In the first stage, you may need to take sketchy notes (words and phrases) in order to keep abreast of what's happening. Then go off by yourself and rewrite your notes in more detail. If you do this soon after the events you've observed, the sketchy notes should allow you to recall most of the details. The longer you delay, the less likely you'll be able to recall things accurately and fully.

I know this method sounds logical, and you've probably made a mental resolve to do it that way if you're ever involved in field research. Let me warn you, however, that you'll need some self-discipline to keep your resolution. Careful observation and note taking can be tiring, especially if it involves excitement or tension and if it extends over a long period. If you've just spent eight hours straight observing and making notes on how people have been coping with a disastrous flood, your first desire afterward will likely be getting some sleep, dry clothes, or a drink. You may need to take some inspiration from newspaper reporters who undergo the same sorts of hardships, then write their stories to meet their deadlines.

Third, you'll inevitably wonder *how much* you should record. Is it really worth the effort to write out all the details you can recall right after the observation session? The general guideline here is *yes*. Generally, in field research you can't be really sure of what's important and what's unimportant until you've had a chance to review and analyze a great volume of information, so you should even record things that don't seem important at the outset. They may turn out to be significant after all. Also, the act of recording the details of something "unimportant" may jog your memory on something that is important.

You should realize that most of your field notes will not be reflected in your final report on the project. Put more harshly, most of the notes you take will be "wasted." But take heart: Even the richest gold ore yields only about 30 grams of gold per metric ton, meaning that 99.997 percent of the ore is wasted. Yet, that 30 grams of gold can be hammered out to cover an area 18 feet square—the equivalent of about 685 book pages. So take a ton of notes, and plan to select and use only the gold.

Like other aspects of field research (and all research for that matter), proficiency comes with practice. The nice thing about field research is you can begin practicing now and can continue practicing in almost any situation. You don't have to be engaged in an organized research project to practice observation and recording. You might start by volunteering to take the minutes at committee meetings, for example.

■ QUALITATIVE DATA PROCESSING

The preceding section of this chapter dealt with the ways you, as a field researcher, would make observations and record them. Now, we're going to look at what you might do with those recorded observations afterward. In large part, this discussion will focus on the process of *filing* and organizing. I'll give you a brief overview of the process, but before actually undertaking a project, you'd do well to study some of the specific techniques field researchers have developed. Again, an excellent source of nitty-gritty, detailed suggestions is John and Lyn Lofland's *Analyzing Social Settings* (1995:181–203).

Rewriting Your Notes

Hot on the trail of some social phenomenon, you are likely to end a day of observations with a mass of scribbled notes. Depending on how late in the day or night you complete your observations, you may be tempted to set the notes aside and sleep on them. Don't! Field researchers can't work on a 9-to-5 schedule, and it's vital that you rewrite your notes as soon as possible after making a set of observations.

It's far better to type your full notes than to write them longhand. They'll be more legible, and as your typing improves it will be faster than longhand. If you can use a computer for this purpose, better yet. I'll discuss the possibilities computers offer, but first let's see what you can do with a typewriter and paper.

Use your notes as a stimulus to recreate as many details of the day's experiences as possible. Your goal should be to produce typed notes as comprehensive and detailed as you would have taken in the first place if you could have recorded everything that seemed potentially relevant. If you regard your scribbled on-the-spot notes as a trigger for your memory, then you'll see the importance of retyping each night, and you'll have a clear sense of how to proceed.

Also, you should make at least two copies of your notes—so make a photocopy. When you analyze your data and prepare your report, you'll need to be able to cut and paste without losing information. With at least two copies, you can cut up one and have the other as a backup. Now let's see how you'll use the multiple copies of your typed notes.

Creating Files

Your typed notes will probably represent a more or less chronological record of your observations in the project, so you should be sure to note the dates and times you made them. You should keep one complete set of notes in this form. It will serve as a master file you can fall back on to establish the chronological order of events later on and to get more copies of certain notes if you need them. You don't need to store your master file in a bank safe-deposit box (unless you're studying organized crime), but you should take care of it.

The copies of your typed notes are for cutting up, underlining, scribbling on, circling, and filing. So far in this chapter, we've focused on making observations. A mass of raw observations, however, doesn't tell us much of general value about social life. Ultimately, you must analyze and interpret your observations, discerning *patterns* of behavior, finding the underlying *meaning* in the things you observed. The organization and filing of your notes is the first step in discovering that meaning.

Files can be organized in endless ways, so I'll just suggest some possibilities you might otherwise overlook. As you undertake your own research project, however, you'll find that deciding what files to create is a part of your analysis of the data.

As a start, you should create some background files. If you're studying a social movement, for example, it would be useful to have a separate file on its history. You'll probably begin the file with notes from your initial reading about the movement: When and where did it begin? How many people were in it initially? What have been the major events in the history of the movement? What were the dates? Although you'll probably begin this file before making observations in the field, you should plan to add to it over the course of your study, since you'll be continually learning more about the history of your subject.

You'll probably want to create a biographical file, too. Who are the key figures in the movement? You may want to have separate files for the most important figures. In any event, you should keep all the information on a particular individual together, which will allow you to get a fuller sense of the person. It may also help you understand the links between diverse events.

Lest you forget, you should also create a bibliographical file to keep track of all the things you will have read in the course of your study. When you write your report, you'll want to make references to what other people have written, and it will be both wasteful and frustrating if you have to return continually to the library to relocate sources.

The creation of background files represents a pretty straightforward housekeeping function, but the creation of *analytical* files depends more on the nature of what you're studying and what you "see" in what you observe. As you begin to develop a sense of the different aspects of what you're observing, you'll want to establish files to deal with them.

Suppose, for example, that you begin to sense that the political movement you're studying has a religious or quasi-religious significance for the people participating in it. You'll want to establish a file for data relating to that aspect, perhaps as follows. Write "Religious Significance" on a manila file folder. Every time you find an entry in your notes that's relevant to the religious aspect of the movement—say a participant has told you that the movement has provided a new meaning to life—you should cut out that entry (recall the multiple copies?) and stick it in the file folder.

Perhaps one of your interests in the political movement concerns the varying degrees of violence considered, proposed, or engaged in by movement members. Sometimes they seem peaceful and willing to compromise; other times they are more oriented toward hard-line aggression. Perhaps you'll want to explain why those differences occur. Create a file on "Degrees of Violence" and clip and file all relevant entries from your notes.

I could continue endlessly with illustrations of the kinds of analytical files you might want to create, but I think you've gotten a sense of what's involved. I can't give you a blueprint of what files will be appropriate in your project—you get to do that. I should add, however, that the creation of analytical files is a continuous process. Do not create a filing system at the beginning of the project and stick doggedly to it throughout. Stay flexible and keep modifying the system as new topics appear to be relevant.

The flexibility of your filing system suggests another important step in the data processing of field research notes and other materials. As you modify your view of how best to organize your files, you should frequently review the materials already filed to see if certain notes should be moved to a newly created file. Sometimes, it will work merely to *cross-reference* your notes. You can jot a note to yourself indicating that the notes on X in File A are also relevant to the topic in File G. Stick the jotted note in File G.

Using Computers

You may think of computers primarily in connection with the statistical analysis of quantitative data. However, computers have made a powerful contribution to field research and other forms of qualitative research. Although this potential is just now being realized, I'd like to give you some sense of what you can expect as well as what you can do right now.

To begin, any standard word-processing system is a vast improvement over the cut-and-paste technology of the typewriter. Once you've entered your field notes into the computer, you can make complete or partial copies effortlessly, excerpting and reorganizing your notes any number of ways.

Word-processing systems will search through your notes for specific words and phrases. Enter the word *shout* in such a search routine, and the computer will show you each time that string of letters appears in your notes: *shout, shouting, shouted,* and so on. If you anticipate this tactic when you enter your notes, in fact, you can be even more effective. In addition to the narratives and analyses you might normally write, jot in key code words relevant to your study. For example, you might type in the word *demographics* every time your notes discuss the makeup of the groups you're observing.

Once you've entered your notes into the computer, you can review and reprocess them endlessly. Let's say you didn't take my advice about entering code words when you first typed up the notes, or perhaps you didn't anticipate some of the variables you now wish you had noted. You can go back and enter such codes easily.

In addition to the benefits you can get from standard word-processing systems, there are now numerous computer programs designed specifically for use in qualitative research. The first popular program for this purpose was Ethnograph; in more recent years Nudist has become extremely popular. Other programs used by qualitative researchers include Aspects, ATLAS/ti, Cofta, Computer-Mediated Dialog Simulation, Context, DragonDictate, Graphics COPE, HyperResearch, Intext, Kurzweil Voice, Kwalitan, SALT (Systemic Analysis of Language Transactions), Sonar Professional, Textpack, Top Grade, VBPro, and WinWord. My purpose in providing this list is to document the fact that computers are no longer seen as appropriate only for quantitative research.

There is, in fact, an Internet *listserv* (electronic discussion group) established to "increase awareness and debate about Computer Assisted Qualitative Data Analysis Software": qual-software@mailbase.ac.uk. If you have access to the Internet, you can subscribe to this listserv, originating in the United Kingdom, and keep up to date on new developments. (See Appendix B, "Social Research in Cyberspace.") Given the pace of technological change, the discussion in this book will inevitably be somewhat out of date by the time you read it. You can also explore this topic further in Eben Weitzman and Matthew Miles's book *Computer Programs for Qualitative Data Analysis* (1995).

Many of the programs, such as Ethnograph, can be applied to field notes entered in a standard word-processing system. Once you've created a file of your notes using a word-processing system, you can ask Ethnograph to number all the lines of that file. On a printed copy of the numbered notes, you'd make marginal notations coding portions in terms of the variables you're interested in. You could mark each of the places that contain demographic descriptions, for example, or those that deal with the emotional states of those you observed. You could mark all the places that have to do with group leadership, social action, or gender discrimination, for example.

As I've indicated, the creation and use of analytical files is part and parcel of the interpretation of your data. Let's turn now to that topic specifically.

■ QUALITATIVE DATA ANALYSIS

Throughout the previous discussions, I've omitted a direct discussion of the two most critical aspects of field research: how you determine what is important to observe and how you formulate your analytical conclusions on the basis of those observations. I've indicated that observations and analysis are interwoven processes in field research. Now it's time to say something about that interweaving. In addressing this **qualitative analysis**, we return to an early discussion of inductive logic. Field research is one place where this mode of reasoning is especially evident and important.

As perhaps the most general guide, you look especially for *similarities* and *dissimilarities*. (That just about covers everything you're likely to see.) On the one hand, you look for those patterns of interaction and events that are generally common to what you are studying. In sociological terms, you look for *norms* of behavior. What behavior patterns do all the participants in a situation share? Do all jaywalkers check for police officers before darting across the street? Do all the participants in a campus political rally join in the same forms of supportive behavior during speeches? Do all the participants in a religious revival meeting shout "amen" at the appropriate times? Do all prostitutes dress seductively? In this sense, then, the field researcher is especially attuned to the discovery of *universals*. As you first notice these, you become more deliberate in observing whether they are truly universal in the situation you're observing. If they are essentially universal, you ask why that should be the case. What function do they serve, for example? This explanation may suggest conditions under which the universals would not appear, and you may look around for those conditions in order to test your expectations.

On the other hand, the field researcher is constantly alert to *differences*. You should be on the watch for deviation from the general norms you may have noted. Although most of the participants in a religious revival meeting murmur "amen" throughout the leader's sermon, you may note a few who don't. Why do they deviate from the norm? In what other ways do they differ from the other participants?

Sometimes you'll find aspects of behavior for which there is no easily identifiable norm. How do different people handle the problem of standing in a line for tickets at a movie theater? Some stare into space, some strike up conversations with strangers, some talk to themselves, some keep standing on tiptoes to see if the line is really moving, some keep counting their money, some read, and so forth. In such situations, an important part of your initial task as a field researcher is to create a classification of behaviors: an organized list of the variety of types. Having done that, you then seek to discover other characteristics associated with those different types of behavior. Are the "rich-looking" or "poor-looking" moviegoers more likely to recount their money? Do men strike up more conversations with strangers than women do? Do old people talk to themselves more than young people do? Your purpose is to discover general patterns.

John and Lyn Lofland (1995:127–45) suggest six different ways of looking for patterns in the topic of your research. Let's suppose you're interested in analyzing child abuse in a particular neighborhood. Here are some of the ways you might make sense out of your observations.

1. *Frequencies:* How often does child abuse occur among families in the neighborhood under study? Realize that there may be a difference between the frequency and what people are willing to tell you.
2. *Magnitudes:* What are the levels of abuse? How brutal are they?
3. *Structures:* What are the different types of abuse: physical, mental, sexual? Are they related in any particular manner?
4. *Processes:* Is there any order among the elements of structure? Do abusers begin with mental abuse and move on to physical and sexual abuse, or does the order of elements vary?
5. *Causes:* What are the causes of child abuse? Is it more common in particular social classes, different religious or ethnic groups? Does it occur more often during good times or bad?
6. *Consequences:* How does child abuse affect the victims, in both the short and the long term? What changes does it cause in the abusers?

To the field researcher, the formulation of theoretical propositions, the observation of empirical events, and the evaluation of theory are typically all part of the same ongoing process. Although your actual field observations may be preceded by deductive theoretical formulas, you seldom if ever merely test a theory and let it go at that. Rather, you develop theories, or generalized understandings, over the course of your observations. You ask what each new set of empirical observations represents in terms of general social scientific principles. Your tentative conclusions, so arrived at, then provide the conceptual framework for further observations. In the course of your observations of jaywalking, for example, it may strike you that whenever a well-dressed and important-looking person jaywalks, others tend to follow suit. Having noticed this apparent pattern, you might pay more attention to this aspect of the phenomenon, thereby testing more carefully your initial impression. You might later observe that your initial impression held true only when the jaywalking "leader" was also middle-aged, for example, or perhaps only when he or she was white. These more specific impressions would simultaneously lead you to pay special attention to the new variables and require that you consider what general principle might be underlying the new observations.

An inherent advantage of field research is that interaction between data collection and data analysis affords a greater flexibility than is typical for other research methods. Survey researchers, for example, must at some point commit themselves to a questionnaire, thus limiting the kind of data that will be collected. If subsequent analyses indicate that they have overlooked the most important variable of all, they're out of luck. The field researcher, on the other hand, can continually modify the research design according to observations, the developing theoretical perspective, or changes in what he or she is studying.

This advantage in field research comes at the price of a particular danger. As you develop a theoretical understanding of what you're observing, there's a constant risk that you'll observe only those things that support your theoretical conclusions. You'll recall that this problem has already been discussed in connection with selective perception.

You can, at least partially, avoid this danger in several ways. First, you can augment your qualitative observations with quantitative ones. If you expect religious proselytization to be greater under some conditions than others, you might formulate a concrete operational definition of proselytization and begin counting under the different conditions. For example, you might note the number of group members who raised this topic, the number of members assigned to the task, or perhaps the number of new converts added to the group. Even rough quantifications such as these might provide a safeguard against selective perception and misinterpretation.

Second, recall that one of the norms of science is its *intersubjectivity*. As a field researcher, then, you might enlist the assistance of others as you begin to refine your theoretical conclusions. In the case of religious conversion, for example, you might ask colleagues to attend several meetings of the group over time and indicate their observations about the relative stress placed on proselytization in each of the meetings.

Finally, as with all such problems, sensitivity and awareness may provide sufficient safeguards. By merely being aware of the problem, you may be able to avoid it.

This last comment points to a more general aspect of field research analysis. *Introspection*—examining your own thoughts and feelings—is a natural and crucial process for understanding what you observe. Because you'll have observed social life close up in all its details, you should be able to put yourself in the place of those you are studying—George Herbert Mead called this "taking the role of the other"—and ask yourself how you would have felt and behaved. Can you imagine yourself acting the way the person you observed acted? Why do you suppose you would have done that?

Introspection, then, can protect against many of the pitfalls of inquiry. And, when leavened with some role taking, it can give you insights into what you see going on around you. And as you'll recall from an earlier discussion, sometimes participant observation put you in a position to experience directly the phenomenon under study, rather than have to imagine how others might think or feel.

In all social science research methods, a large gap lies between understanding the skills of data analysis and actually using those skills effectively. Typically, experience is the only effective bridge across the gap. This situation applies more to field research than to any other method. It is worth recalling the parallel between the activities of the scientist and those of the investigative detective. Although fledgling detectives can be taught technical skills and can be given general guidelines, insight and experience separate good detectives from mediocre ones. The same is true of field researchers.

ILLUSTRATIONS OF FIELD RESEARCH

The creative, malleable, and open-ended nature of qualitative research makes it harder to be as precise about how to gather and interpret data as quantitative research allows. In qualitative research, there are fewer strict rules to determine whether it's being done appropriately or whether the data are being interpreted correctly. Books on qualitative methodology often refer to qualitative inquiry as a craft or a mindset and suggest that the best way to learn about the many ways of doing it may be involvement in several differing qualitative studies. Therefore, let's now examine some lengthier illustrations of qualitative inquiry in action. I hope these descriptions will give you a clearer sense of the diverse and creative ways you might undertake field research in your own inquiries.

Studying the Satanists

As a part of a broad-based study of the "new religious consciousness," a sociology graduate student, Randall Alfred (1976), was given the task of studying and reporting on the Church of Satan. Pronouncing itself in league with Satan and opposed to Christ, the church is headquartered in San Francisco and operates under the charismatic leadership of Anton LaVey. You can probably imagine how you'd handle an assignment to study the local Methodist or Episcopalian congregation, but how would you go about studying the Satanists? Here's what Alfred did:

■ I approached the group in April 1968 as an outsider and indicated an immediate interest in joining. My feigned conversion to Satanism was accepted as genuine and I made rapid progress in the group, as measured by my advancement in ritual rank, my being given administrative as well as magical responsibilities, and my appointment to the "ruling" body of the church.

From April 1968 to August 1969 I attended fifty-two of the group's weekly rituals, participating in all but eight of these early on. I was also present at twelve meetings of the ruling council, at twelve classes on various aspects of Satanism, and at six parties.

(1976:183–84)

Alfred studied the church until 1973, having some 100 contacts with members, lasting a total of perhaps 600 hours and resulting in about as many pages of notes. In addition, he read books and articles about the group, including publications of the church itself. Right up to the end, he played the role of complete participant, concealing his research identity from those he was studying.

Alfred's total immersion in church life gave him insights into the nature of Satanism that would have been hard to gain from the outside. He was able to discover and distinguish many different motivations that led people to the group. Some were attracted by the prospect of sexual indulgence, others by the powers they might gain from magic, and others by the chance to rebel against convention, religious and otherwise. Still others saw Satanism as a wave of the future, a new millennium.

Through his *participation* in the church—he ultimately became the official church historian—Alfred could learn details of rituals and other practices that would have been kept secret from outsiders. He observed LaVey and other church leaders close up and studied the dynamics of interpersonal relations in the church. There simply would have been no other way of gaining such information.

In reading Alfred's report, I also had the sense that many of his analytical insights would have escaped an outsider. For example, the popular view of Satanism is one of total self-indulgence: Freed from all conventional social norms, Satanists are completely hedonistic, indulging their every urge and desire. This is not what Alfred observed, however. In the case of sex, for example, Satanists limit sexual indulgence to acts that don't hurt others against their will. LaVey further distinguishes between indulgence freely chosen and compulsive acts. Satanists should be free to indulge their desires, but they should not be run by those desires. By the same token, Satanists have a negative view of drug use. Even more unexpectedly, perhaps, LaVey strongly urges his followers to work hard at their jobs and succeed.

As a closing note, Alfred reported that he eventually found himself regretting the initial decision to conceal his research identity: He felt increasingly unethical. After all, he had been admitted to the inner circles of the church and been given a position of trust and responsibility. As he approached the final stages of wrapping up and reporting the project, he went to LaVey to tell him the truth and to request permission to publish an article about what he had learned. LaVey indicated that he had suspected all along that Alfred was doing research. Did he feel Alfred had been unethical in attempting deception? Not at all: It was an appropriately satanic thing to do!

Life in the Streets

Elliot Liebow's modern classic study *Tally's Corner* (1967) differs from Alfred's study in many ways. There is an initial similarity, however. Like Alfred, Liebow was assigned to his task as part of a larger research project. In this instance, Liebow, an anthropology graduate student, was hired to work on an ongoing study of childrearing practices among low-income families in the District of Columbia. Liebow's task was to do field work among low-income adult men to fill out the picture created by numerous interviews with families.

Liebow prepared for the field work through a series of meetings with the project staff, learning the kinds of materials that were needed. He read the reports already written on the project. Then, one day,

■ having partially digested the project literature, I told the director that I was ready to get started. He suggested a neighborhood that might be "a good place to get your feet wet." His instructions were: "Get out there and make like an anthropologist."

(1967:245)

Arriving in the suggested neighborhood, Liebow discovered a white police detective scuffling with an angry African-American woman. Approaching two African-American male onlookers, Liebow asked them what happened. They answered cautiously. The conversation continued, warming somewhat as each expressed negative feelings about the police. Eventually convinced that Liebow was not himself a policeman, one of the men spent the next several hours talking to him over coffee.

Unlike Alfred, Liebow revealed his identity as a researcher and the purpose of his research from the start. Though recognized as an "outsider," he was accepted as a friend, and he became more and more a part of the street-corner life as the research progressed. Like Alfred, Liebow soon found himself deeply involved in the lives of his subjects. He reports,

■ I went to three different jails during this time, sat through one murder trial and two hearings in judges' chambers, testifying at one of them. I went to bondsmen's offices, to the United Employment Services, to the Blessed Martin de Porres Hostel (for homeless men) and into several private homes.

(1967:245)

Whenever his new friends ran afoul of the law, Liebow's legal advice was sought and respected. He reports that he stayed in close touch with the project director about this participation, weighing the consequences of his actions for his research. There was certainly a danger that his own participation would change the character of the events and situations he had set out to study in the first place.

Liebow's description of his record keeping nicely illustrates the procedures described earlier in this chapter:

■ Throughout this period, my field observations were focused on individuals: what they said, what they did, and the contexts in which they said them or did them. I sought them out and was sought out by them.

My field notes contain a record of what I saw when I looked at Tally, Richard, Sea Cat and the others. I have only a small notion—and one that I myself consider suspect—of what they saw when they looked at me.

(1967:248)

Ultimately, Liebow gained a personal experience of street-corner life in an African-American, urban ghetto that few other white people have experienced. To an unusual extent, he could see and understand the men as they saw and understood themselves. He learned their views and experiences of family life, employment, and—more to the point—unemployment.

Though two short accounts scarcely do justice to the projects they describe, they should give you a more concrete view of what field research entails. Both original reports are interesting and eminently readable, so you might like to read them for yourself.

Observing Outlaw Bikers

Daniel Wolf (1990) was a graduate student in Alberta, Canada, when he decided to engage in field research among an outlaw motorcycle club. He understood how the bikers were perceived by the general society, but he wanted to learn about their own worldview: How did they see themselves and how did they collectively create their subculture?

Though he bought an appropriate motorcycle and biker clothing, Wolf found it particularly difficult to gain access to a club.

■ In Calgary, I met several members of the Kings Crew MC in a motorcycle show and expressed an interest in "hanging around." But I lacked patience and pushed the situation by asking too many questions. I found out quickly that outsiders, even bikers, do not rush into a club, and that anyone who doesn't show the proper restraint will be shut out.

(WOLF 1991:213)

Notice that while his attempt to join up with the Kings Crew was unsuccessful, Wolf learned something about biker clubs nonetheless. His rapport with the club was not helped, however, when he got into a barroom fight with a club member days later.

■ He flattened my nose and began choking me. Unable to get air down my throat and breathing only blood through my nostrils, I managed a body punch that luckily found his solar plexus and loosened his grip. I then grabbed one of his hands and pulled back on the thumb until I heard the joint break. Mistake number two. It was time to move on.

(WOLF 1991:213)

Eventually, Wolf made a successful contact with the Rebels, beginning with a casual conversation about motorcycles with a gang member. He was invited to drink with the club, then to ride with them. Gradually, he became friends with more and more club members, and his participation increased steadily.

For three years, Wolf became more involved with the Rebels and came to grasp their worldview more fully. He experienced his friendship with club members as genuine; they became more his brothers than research subjects.

■ Brotherhood, I came to learn, is the foundation of the outlaw club community. It establishes among members a sense of moral, emotional, and material interdependence and commitment. The enduring emotion of brotherhood is comradeship. To a patch holder, brotherhood means being there when needed; its most dramatic expression occurs when brothers defend each other from outside threats.

(WOLF 1991:216)

As he felt himself more and more a full participant in the Rebels, his role as researcher became increasingly problematic, similar to Alfred's experience with the Satanists. Doing secret research was a blatant betrayal of the men he now regarded as his friends. Moreover, Wolf knew that three police officers who had attempted to infiltrate the club previously had been murdered. He wanted to tell the club members about his research but was afraid to do so.

Then one day, he got a lucky break. Club members knew that Wolf was an anthropology graduate student, and one asked if he had ever considered doing research on the club. Wolf said he would be interested in doing that and now had an excuse for making a proposal to the club leadership and members. After some heated disagreements, the club agreed, and Wolf could conduct his research openly.

Wolf eventually completed his thesis and gave a copy to the club. His desire to publish his thesis as a book, however, raised more disagreements among club members. Ultimately, he worked with club members to create fictional names that would protect them as individuals. The club itself was well-known, however, and Wolf made no attempt to disguise it.

While Wolf continued to feel a personal friendship with members of the Rebels, his emergence as a researcher steadily eroded that relationship.

■ I continued to ride with the Rebels for another year and a half, during which time I carried out formal data procedures—structured interviews. As my role as an ethnographer became more evident, my role as a biker became more contrived and I began to be excluded from the brotherhood. My contact with members became less frequent and less intense. As an ethnographer, my relationship with the club lost its substance and meaning and I lost touch with the innermost core of Rebel reality; I simply faded away.

(WOLF 1991:222)

■ RESEARCH ETHICS IN FIELD RESEARCH

When I introduced the topic of research ethics in Chapter 1, I pointed out that all forms of social research raise a wide range of ethical issues. By bringing researchers into direct and often intimate contact with their subjects, field research raises these concerns in a particularly dramatic way.

As a reminder of the importance of ethical concerns in social research, I've reported here some of the problems mentioned by John and Lyn Lofland (1995:63):

- Is it ethical to talk to people when they do not know you will be recording their words?
- Is it ethical to get information for your own purposes from people you hate?

- Is it ethical to see a severe need for help and not respond to it directly?
- Is it ethical to be in a setting or situation but not commit yourself wholeheartedly to it?
- Is it ethical to develop a calculated stance toward other humans, that is, to be strategic in your relations?
- Is it ethical to take sides or to avoid taking sides in a factionalized situation?
- Is it ethical to "pay" people with trade-offs for access to their lives and minds?
- Is it ethical to "use" people as allies or informants in order to gain entree to other people or to elusive understandings?

We'll continue our discussion of research ethics in field research and other techniques in Chapter 18.

■ STRENGTHS AND WEAKNESSES OF FIELD RESEARCH

It's time now to wrap up the discussion of field research and move on to some of the other methods available to social researchers. I want to conclude this chapter by assessing the relative strengths and weaknesses of this particular method. This examination will be somewhat longer than those of earlier chapters because I want to spend part of the time comparing field research with experiments and surveys.

As I've already indicated, field research is especially effective for studying the subtle nuances of attitudes and behaviors and for examining social processes over time. As such, the chief strength of this method lies in the depth of understanding it may permit. Although other research methods may be challenged as "superficial," this charge is seldom lodged against field research.

Flexibility is another advantage of field research. In this method, you may modify your research design at any time, as discussed earlier. Moreover, you're always prepared to engage in field research, whenever the occasion should arise, whereas you could not as easily initiate a survey or an experiment.

Field research can be relatively inexpensive. Other social scientific research methods may require expensive equipment or an expensive research staff, but field research typically can be undertaken by one researcher with a notebook and a pencil. This is not to say that field research is never expensive. The nature of the research project, for example, may require a large number of trained observers. Expensive recording equipment may be needed. Or you may wish to undertake participant observation of interactions in expensive Paris nightclubs.

Field research has a number of weaknesses as well. First, being qualitative rather than quantitative, it is not an appropriate means to arriving at statistical descriptions of a large population. Observing casual political discussions in Laundromats, for example, would not yield trustworthy estimates of the future voting behavior of the total electorate. Nevertheless, the study could provide important insights into the process of political attitude formation.

To assess field research further, let's focus on the issues of validity and reliability. You'll recall that validity and reliability are both qualities of measurements. Validity concerns whether measurements actually measure what they're supposed to rather than measuring something else. Reliability, on the other hand, is a matter of dependability: If you made the same measurement again and again, would you get the same result? Let's see how field research stacks up in these respects.

Validity

Field research seems to provide more valid measures than survey and experimental measurements, which are often criticized as superficial and not really valid. Let's review a couple of field research examples to see why this is so.

"Being there" is a powerful technique for gaining insights into the nature of human affairs. Listen, for example, to what this nurse reports about the impediments to patients' coping with cancer:

■ Common fears that may impede the coping process for the person with cancer can include the following:

—Fear of death—for the patient, and the implications his or her death will have for significant others.

—Fear of incapacitation—because cancer can be a chronic disease with acute episodes that may result in periodic stressful periods, the variability of the person's ability to cope and constantly adjust may require a dependency upon others for activities of daily living and may consequently become a burden.

—Fear of alienation—from significant others and health care givers, thereby creating helplessness and hopelessness.

—Fear of contagion—that cancer is transmissible and/or inherited.

—Fear of losing one's dignity—losing control of all bodily functions and being totally vulnerable.

(GARANT 1980:2167)

Observations and conceptualizations such as these are valuable in their own right. In addition, they can provide the basis for further research—both qualitative and quantitative.

Now listen to what Joseph Howell has to say about "toughness" as a fundamental ingredient of life on Clay Street, a white, working-class neighborhood in Washington, D.C.

■ Most of the people on Clay Street saw themselves as fighters in both the figurative and literal sense. They considered themselves strong, independent people who would not let themselves be pushed around. For Bobbi, being a fighter meant battling the welfare department and cussing out social workers and doctors upon occasion. It meant spiking Barry's beer with sleeping pills and bashing him over the head with a broom. For Barry it meant telling off his boss and refusing to hang the door, an act that led to his being fired. It meant going through the ritual of a duel with Al. It meant pushing Bubba around and at times getting rough with Bobbi.

June and Sam had less to fight about, though if pressed they both hinted that they, too, would fight. Being a fighter led Ted into near conflict with Peg's brothers, Les into conflict with Lonnie, Arlene into conflict with Phyllis at the bowling alley, etc.

(1973:292)

Even without having heard the episodes Howell refers to in this passage, you have the distinct impression that Clay Street is a tough place to live in. That "toughness" comes through far more powerfully here than it would in a set of statistics on the median number of fistfights occurring during a specified period.

These examples point to the superior validity of field research, as compared with surveys and experiments. The kinds of comprehensive measurements available to the field researcher tap a depth of meaning in our concepts, such as liberal and conservative, that are generally unavailable to surveys and experiments. Instead of specifying concepts, field researchers commonly give detailed illustrations.

Reliability

Field research has, however, a potential problem with reliability, as defined earlier in this book. Suppose you were to characterize your best friend's political orientations based on everything you know about him or her. There's certainly no question that your assessment of your friend's politics would be superficial. The measurement you arrived at would appear to have considerable validity. We couldn't be sure, however, that someone else would characterize your friend's politics the same way you did, even with the same amount of observation.

Field research measurements—although in-depth—are also often very personal. How I judge your friend's political orientation depends very much on my own, just as your judgment depends on your political orientation. Conceivably, then, you could describe your friend as middle-of-the-road, although I might have felt I'd been observing a fire-breathing radical.

Be wary, therefore, of any purely descriptive measurements in field research. If a researcher reports that the members of a club are pretty conservative, know that such a judgment is unavoidably linked to the researcher's own politics. You can be more trusting, however, of comparative evaluations: identifying who is more conservative than whom, for example. Even if you and I had different political orientations, we would probably agree pretty much in ranking the *relative* conservatism of the members of a group.

As I've suggested earlier, those researchers who use qualitative techniques are conscious of this issue and take pains to address it. Not only can individual researchers often sort out their own biases and points of view, but the communal nature of science means that their colleagues will help them in that regard.

As we've seen, field research is a potentially powerful tool for social scientists, one that provides a useful balance to the strengths and weaknesses of experiments and surveys. These are not the only modes of observation available, however, as you'll see in the remaining chapters of Part 3.

■ MAIN POINTS

- Field research is a social research method that involves the direct observation of social phenomena in their natural settings.
- Phenomenology is a philosophical term that refers to a consideration of all perceived phenomena, both the "objective" and "subjective."
- Interpretivism seeks to understand how the subjects of study make sense of their own lives.
- Hermeneutics aims at understanding (and improving) the process of understanding.
- Participant observation is a form of field research in which the researcher participates as an actor in the events under study.
- Field researchers often conduct in-depth interviews that are much less structured than those conducted in survey research.
- A case study is an idiographic examination of a single individual, group, or society.
- Ethnography involves naturalistic observations and holistic understandings of cultures or subcultures.
- Grounded theory refers to the attempt to derive theories from an analysis of the patterns, themes, and common categories discovered among observational data.
- Appropriate topics for field research include practices, episodes, encounters, roles, relationships, groups, organizations, settlements, social worlds, lifestyles, and subcultures.
- You may or may not identify yourself as a researcher to the people you're observing. Identifying yourself as a researcher may have some effect on the nature of what you're observing, but concealing your identity may involve deceit.
- Because field research takes you into close contact with subjects, you must negotiate your relationship with them, and there are several options for doing so.
- Qualitative interviewing is more of a guided conversation than a search for specific information.
- The field journal is the backbone of field research, for that is where the researcher records his or her observations. Journal entries should be detailed, yet concise. If possible, observations should be recorded as they're made; otherwise, they should be recorded as soon afterward as possible.
- Computers are now widely used in the creation of field notes and in data analysis.
- In field research, observation, data processing, and analysis are interwoven and cyclical processes.
- The process of data analysis is largely a search for patterns of similarities and differences—followed by an interpretation of those patterns.
- Compared with surveys and experiments, field research measurements generally have more validity but less reliability.

■ REVIEW QUESTIONS AND EXERCISES

1. Think of some group or activity you participate in or are very familiar with. In two or three paragraphs, describe how an outsider might effectively go about studying that group or activity. What should he or she read, what contacts should be made, and so on?
2. To show that you appreciate the various strengths and weaknesses of experiments, surveys, and field research, give brief descriptions of two studies especially appropriate to each method. Be sure each one would be

most appropriately studied by the method you identify it with.
3. Using the Web, compile a bibliography of at least ten works on the subject of grounded theory.

■ ADDITIONAL READINGS

Emerson, Robert M., ed. *Contemporary Field Research.* Boston: Little, Brown, 1988. A diverse and interesting collection of articles on how field research contributes to understanding, the role of theory in such research, personal and relational issues that emerge, and ethical and political issues.

Gubrium, Jaber F., and David Silverman, eds. *The Politics of Field Research: Sociology beyond Enlightenment.* Newbury Park, CA: Sage, 1989. A set of essays dealing with the issue of bias in scientific observation "against the commonplace view that Science, Reason, and enlightened intervention are the straightforward hallmarks of Progress in the resolution of social problems" (p. 1).

Johnson, Jeffrey C. *Selecting Ethnographic Informants.* Newbury Park, CA: Sage, 1990. The author discusses the various strategies that apply to the task of sampling in field research.

Kelle, Udo, ed. *Computer-Aided Qualitative Data Analysis: Theory, Methods, and Practice.* Thousand Oaks, CA: Sage, 1995. An international group of scholars report on their experiences with a variety of computer programs used in the analysis of qualitative data.

Kvale, Steinar. *InterViews: An Introduction to Qualitative Research Interviewing.* Thousand Oaks, CA: Sage, 1996, An in-depth presentation on in-depth interviewing. Besides presenting techniques, Kvale places interviewing in the context of postmodernism and other philosophical systems.

Lofland, John, and Lyn Lofland. *Analyzing Social Settings,* 3rd ed. Belmont, CA: Wadsworth, 1995. An unexcelled presentation of field research methods from beginning to end. This eminently readable book manages successfully to draw the links between the logic of scientific inquiry and the nitty-gritty practicalities of observing, communicating, recording, filing, reporting, and everything else involved in field research. In addition, the book contains a wealth of references to field research illustrations.

Shaffir, William B., and Robert A. Stebbins, eds. *Experiencing Fieldwork: An Inside View of Qualitative Research.* Newbury Park, CA: Sage, 1991. Several practicing field research practitioners discuss the nature of the craft and recall experiences in the field. Here's an opportunity to gain a "feel" for the method as well as learn some techniques.

Shostak, Arthur, ed. *Our Sociological Eye: Personal Essays on Society and Culture.* Port Washington, NY: Alfred, 1977. An orgy of social scientific introspection, this delightful collection of first-person research accounts offers concrete, inside views of the thinking process in sociological research, especially field research.

Silverman, David. *Interpreting Qualitative Data.* Newbury Park, CA: Sage, 1993. This book brings together theoretical concerns, data-collection techniques, and the process of making sense of what is observed.

CHAPTER 12 *Unobtrusive Research*

What You'll Learn in This Chapter

This chapter will present overviews of three unobtrusive research methods: content analysis, the analysis of existing statistics, and historical/comparative analysis. Each of these methods allows researchers to study social life from afar, without influencing it in the process.

INTRODUCTION

A COMMENT ON UNOBTRUSIVE MEASURES

TOPICS APPROPRIATE TO CONTENT ANALYSIS

SAMPLING IN CONTENT ANALYSIS
Units of Analysis
Sampling Techniques

CODING IN CONTENT ANALYSIS
Manifest and Latent Content
Conceptualization and the Creation
  of Code Categories
Counting and Record Keeping
Qualitative Data Analysis

ILLUSTRATIONS OF CONTENT ANALYSIS
Coding Commercials
Understanding the Underground

STRENGTHS AND WEAKNESSES OF CONTENT ANALYSIS

ANALYZING EXISTING STATISTICS
Studying Suicide
Units of Analysis
Problems of Validity
Problems of Reliability
Sources of Existing Statistics

HISTORICAL/COMPARATIVE ANALYSIS
Examples of Historical/Comparative Analysis
Sources of Historical/Comparative Data
Analytical Techniques

MAIN POINTS

REVIEW QUESTIONS AND EXERCISES

ADDITIONAL READINGS

INTRODUCTION

With the exception of the complete observer in field research, each of the modes of observation discussed so far requires the researcher to intrude to some degree on whatever he or she is studying. This is most obvious in the case of experiments, followed closely by survey research. Even the field researcher, as we've seen, can change things in the process of studying them.

At least one previous example in this book, however, was totally exempt from that danger. Durkheim's analysis of suicide did nothing to affect suicides one way or the other (see Chapter 2).

For most of this chapter, we'll examine three different research methods: content analysis, analysis of existing statistics, and historical/comparative analysis. In *content analysis,* researchers examine a class of social artifacts, typically written documents (recall Chapter 4). Suppose, for example, you wanted to contrast the relative importance of foreign versus domestic problems for U.S. citizens in the 1930s and the 1980s. One way, as we saw in Chapter 10, would be to examine the results of public opinion polls in those two periods. Another method would be to analyze, say, newspaper articles during the two periods. This latter design would be an example of content analysis: the analysis of communications.

The Durkheim study is an example of the *analysis of existing statistics,* another form of unobtrusive research to be examined in this chapter. As you'll see, there are great masses of data all around you, awaiting your use in the understanding of social life.

Finally, we'll consider *historical/comparative analysis,* a form of research with a venerable history in the social sciences and one that is enjoying a resurgence of popularity at present. Like field research, historical/comparative analysis is a qualitative method, one in which the researcher attempts to master many subtle details. The main resources for observation and analysis are historical records. Although a historical/comparative analysis might include content analysis, it is not limited to communications. The method's name includes the word *comparative* because social scientists—in contrast to historians who may simply describe a particular set of events—seek to discover common patterns that recur in different times and places.

To set the stage for our examination of these three research methods, I want to draw your attention to an excellent book that should sharpen your senses about the potential for unobtrusive measures in general. It is, among other things, the book from which I take the term *unobtrusive measures.*

A COMMENT ON UNOBTRUSIVE MEASURES

In 1966, Eugene Webb and three colleagues published an ingenious little book on social research (revised in 1981) that has become a classic. It focuses on the idea of *unobtrusive* or *nonreactive* research. Webb and his colleagues have played freely with the task of learning about human behavior by observing what people inadvertently leave behind them. Want to know what exhibits are the most popular at a museum? You could conduct a poll, but people might tell you what they thought you wanted to hear or what might make them look more intellectual and serious. You could stand by different exhibits and count the viewers that came by, but people might come over to see what you were doing. Webb and his colleagues suggest you check the wear and tear on the floor in front of various exhibits. Those where the tiles have been worn down the most are probably the most popular. Want to know which exhibits are popular with little kids? Look for mucus on the glass cases. To get a sense of the most popular radio stations, you could arrange with an auto mechanic to check the radio dial settings for cars brought in for repair.

The possibilities are limitless. Like an investigative detective, the social researcher looks for clues. If you stop to notice, you'll find that clues of social behavior are all around you. In a sense, everything you see represents the answer to some important social scientific question—all you have to do is think of the question.

Although problems of validity and reliability crop up in unobtrusive measures, a little ingenuity can either handle them or put them in perspective. I encourage you to look at Webb's book. It's enjoyable reading, and it can be a source of stimulation and insight in taking on social inquiry through the use of the data that already exist. For now, let's turn our attention to three unobtrusive methods often employed by social scientists.

■ TOPICS APPROPRIATE TO CONTENT ANALYSIS

Content analysis methods may be applied to virtually any form of communication. Among the possible artifacts for study are books, magazines, poems, newspapers, songs, paintings, speeches, letters, laws, and constitutions, as well as any components or collections thereof. Are popular French novels more concerned with love than American ones? Was the popular American music of the 1960s more politically cynical than the popular German music during that period? Do political candidates who primarily address "bread and butter" issues get elected more often than those who address issues of high principle? Each of these questions addresses a social scientific research topic: The first might address national character, the second political orientations, and the third political process. Although such topics might be studied through observation of individual people, content analysis provides another approach.

The best-selling *Megatrends 2000* (Naisbitt and Aburdene, 1990) used content analysis to determine the major trends in modern U.S. life. The authors regularly monitored thousands of local newspapers a month in order to discover local and regional trends for publication in a series of quarterly reports. Their book examined some of the trends they observed in the nation at large.

Shulamit Reinharz (1992:146–47) points out that feminist researchers have used this technique to study

■ children's books, fairy tales, billboards, feminist nonfiction and fiction books, children's art work, fashion, fat-letter postcards, Girl Scout Handbooks, works of fine art, newspaper rhetoric, clinical records, research publications, introductory sociology textbooks, and citations, to mention only a few.

In 1891, Ida B. Wells, whose parents had been slaves, wanted to test the widely held assumption that black men were being lynched in the South primarily for raping white women. As a research method, she examined newspaper articles on the 728 lynchings reported during the previous ten years. In only a third of the cases were the lynching victims even accused of rape, much less proven guilty. Primarily, they were charged with being insolent, not staying in "their place" (cited in Reinharz 1992:146).

Some topics are more appropriately addressed by content analysis than by any other method of inquiry. Suppose for a moment that you're interested in violence on television. Maybe you suspect that the manufacturers of men's products are more likely to sponsor violent TV shows than other kinds of sponsors are. Content analysis would be the best way of finding out if it's true.

Briefly, here's what you would do. First, you'd develop operational definitions of the two key variables in your inquiry: *men's products* and *violence*. The section on coding, later in this chapter, will discuss some of the ways you could do that. Ultimately, you'd need a plan that would allow you to watch TV, classify sponsors, and rate the degree of violence on particular shows.

Next, you'd have to decide what to watch. Probably you'd decide (1) what stations to watch, (2) for what days or period, and (3) at what hours. Then, you'd stock in some beer and potato chips and start watching, classifying, and recording. Once you had completed your observations, you'd be able to analyze the data you collected and determine whether men's product manufacturers sponsored more blood and gore than other sponsors.

Content analysis, then, is particularly well suited to the study of communications and to answering the classic question of communications research: "Who says what, to whom, why, how, and with what effect?" As a mode of observation, content analysis requires a considered handling of the *what*, and the analysis of data collected in this mode, as in others, addresses the *why* and *with what effect*.

■ SAMPLING IN CONTENT ANALYSIS

In the study of communications, as in the study of people, you often can't observe directly all you're interested in. In your study of TV violence and sponsorship, I'd advise against attempting to watch everything that's broadcast. It wouldn't be possible, and your brain would probably short-circuit before you got close to discovering that for yourself. Usually, then, it's appropriate to sample. Let's begin by looking again at units of analysis and then review some of the sampling techniques that might be applied to them in content analysis.

Units of Analysis

You'll recall from Chapter 4 that determining appropriate units of analysis, the individual units about which or whom descriptive and explanatory statements are to be made, can be a complicated task. For example, if we wished to compute the average family income, the individual family would be the unit of analysis. But we would have to ask individual members of families how much money they make. Thus individuals would be the units of observation, and the individual family would still be the unit of analysis. Similarly, we may wish to compare crime rates of different cities in terms of their sizes, geographical regions, racial composition, and other differences. Even though the characteristics of these cities are partly a function of the behaviors and characteristics of their individual residents, the cities would ultimately be the units of analysis.

The complexity of this issue is often more apparent in content analysis than in other research methods, especially when the units of observation differ from the units of analysis. A few examples should clarify this distinction.

Let's suppose we want to find out whether criminal law or civil law makes the most distinctions between men and women. In this instance, individual laws would be both the units of observation and the units of analysis. We might select a sample of a state's criminal and civil laws and then categorize each law by whether it makes a distinction between men and women. In this fashion, we would be able to determine whether criminal or civil law distinguishes most by gender.

Somewhat differently, we might wish to determine whether states that enact laws distinguishing between different racial groups are also more likely than other states to enact laws distinguishing between men and women. Although the examination of this question would also involve the coding of individual acts of legislation, the unit of analysis in this latter case is the individual state, not the law.

Or, changing topics radically, let's suppose we're interested in representationalism in painting. If we wish to compare the relative popularity of representational and nonrepresentational paintings, the individual paintings would be our units of analysis. If, on the other hand, we wish to discover whether representationalism in painting is more characteristic of wealthy or impoverished painters, of educated or uneducated painters, of capitalist or socialist painters, the individual painters would be our units of analysis.

It is essential that this issue be clear, because sample selection depends largely on what the unit of analysis is. If individual writers are the units of analysis, the sample design should select all or a sample of the writers appropriate to the research question. If books are the units of analysis, we should select a sample of books, regardless of their authors. Bruce Berg (1989:112–13) points out that even if you plan to analyze some body of textual materials, the units of analysis might be words, themes, characters, paragraphs, items (such as a book or letter), concepts, semantics, or combinations of these.

I'm not suggesting that sampling should be based solely on the units of analysis. Indeed, we may often subsample—select samples of subcategories—for each individual unit of analysis. Thus, if writers are the units of analysis, we might (1) select a sample of writers from the total population of writers, (2) select a sample of books writ-

FIGURE 12-1
Example of Recording Sheet for TV Violence

Sponsor	Men's Product?			Number of Instances of Violence	
	Yes	No	?	Before	After
Grunt Aftershave	✓			6	4
Brute Jock Straps	✓			6	4
Roperot Cigars	✓			4	3
Grunt Aftershave	✓			3	0
Snowflake Toothpaste		✓		3	0
Godliness Cleanser		✓		3	0
Big Thumb Hammers			✓	0	1
Snowflake Toothpaste		✓		1	0
Big Thumb Hammers			✓	1	0
Buttercup Bras		✓		0	0

ten by each writer selected, and (3) select portions of each selected book for observation and coding.

Finally, let's look at a trickier example: the study of TV violence and sponsors. What's the unit of analysis for the research question, "Are the manufacturers of men's products more likely to sponsor violent shows than other sponsors?" Is it the TV show? The sponsor? The instance of violence? In the simplest study design, it would be none of these.

Though you might structure your inquiry in various ways, the most straightforward design would be based on the *commercial* as the unit of analysis. You would use two kinds of observational units: the commercial and the program (the show that gets squeezed in between commercials). You'd want to observe both units. You would classify commercials by whether they advertised men's products and the programs by their violence. The program classifications would be transferred to the commercials occurring near them. Figure 12-1 provides an example of the kind of record you might keep.

Notice that in the research design illustrated in Figure 12-1, all the commercials occurring together are bracketed and get the same scores. Also, the number of violent instances recorded as following one commercial is the same as the number preceding the next commercial. This simple design allows us to classify each commercial by its sponsorship and the degree of violence associated with it. Thus, for example, the first Grunt Aftershave commercial is coded as being a men's product and as having 10 instances of violence associated with it. The Buttercup Bra commercial is coded as not being a men's product and as having no violent instances associated with it.

In the illustration, we have four men's product commercials with an average of 7.5 violent instances each. The four commercials classified as definitely not men's products have an average of 1.75, and the two that might or might not be considered men's products have an average of 1 violent instance each. If this pattern of differences persisted across a much larger number of observations, we'd probably conclude that men's products manufacturers are more likely to sponsor TV violence than other sponsors.

The point of this illustration is to demonstrate how units of analysis figure into the data collection and analysis. You need to be clear about your unit of analysis before planning your sampling strategy, but in this case you can't sample commercials. Unless you have access to the stations' broadcasting logs, you won't know when the commercials are going to occur. Moreover, you need to observe the programming as well as the commercials. As a result, you must set up a sampling design that will include everything you need to observe.

In designing the sample, you would need to establish the universe to be sampled from. In this case, what TV stations will you observe? What will be the period of the study—number of days? And what hours of each day will you observe? Then, how many commercials do you want to observe and code for analysis? Watch television for a while and find out how many commercials occur each hour; then you can figure out how many hours of observation you'll need.

Now you're ready to design the sample selection. As a practical matter, you wouldn't have to sample among the different stations if you had assistants—each of you could watch a different channel during the same time period. But let's suppose you're working alone. Your final sampling frame, from which a sample will be selected and watched, might look something like this:

Jan. 7, Channel 2, 7–9 P.M.
Jan. 7, Channel 4, 7–9 P.M.
Jan. 7, Channel 9, 7–9 P.M.
Jan. 7, Channel 2, 9–11 P.M.
Jan. 7, Channel 4, 9–11 P.M.
Jan. 7, Channel 9, 9–11 P.M.
Jan. 8, Channel 2, 7–9 P.M.
Jan. 8, Channel 4, 7–9 P.M.
Jan. 8, Channel 9, 7–9 P.M.
Jan. 8, Channel 2, 9–11 P.M.
Jan. 8, Channel 4, 9–11 P.M.
Jan. 8, Channel 9, 9–11 P.M.
Jan. 9, Channel 2, 7–9 P.M.
Jan. 9, Channel 4, 7–9 P.M.
etc.

Notice that I've made several decisions for you in the illustration. First, I've assumed that channels 2, 4, and 9 are the ones appropriate to your study. I've assumed that you found the 7 to 11 P.M. prime-time hours to be the most relevant and that two-hour periods would do the job. I picked January 7 out of the hat for a starting date. In practice, of course, all these decisions should be based on your careful consideration of what would be appropriate to your particular study.

Once you have become clear about your units of analysis and the observations appropriate to those units and have created a sampling frame like the one I've illustrated, sampling is simple and straightforward. The alternative procedures available to you are the same ones described in Chapter 8: random, systematic, stratified, and so on.

Sampling Techniques

As you've seen, in the content analysis of written prose, sampling may occur at any or all of several levels, including the contexts relevant to the works. Other forms of communication may also be sampled at any of the conceptual levels appropriate to them.

In content analysis, we could employ any of the conventional sampling techniques discussed in Chapter 8. We might select a *random* or *systematic* sample of French and U.S. novelists, of laws passed in the state of Mississippi, or of Shakespearean soliloquies. We might select (with a random start) every 23rd paragraph in Tolstoy's *War and Peace*. Or, we might number all of the songs recorded by the Beatles and select a random sample of 25.

Stratified sampling is also appropriate to content analysis. To analyze the editorial policies of U.S. newspapers, for example, we might first group all newspapers by region of the country, size of the community in which they are published, frequency of publication, or average circulation. We might then select a stratified random or systematic sample of newspapers for analysis. Having done so, we might select a sample of editorials from each selected newspaper, perhaps stratified chronologically.

Cluster sampling is equally appropriate to content analysis. Indeed, if individual editorials were to be the unit of analysis in the previous example, then the selection of newspapers at the first stage of sampling would be a cluster sample. In an analysis of political speeches, we might begin by selecting a sample of politicians; each politician would represent a cluster of political speeches. The TV commercial study described previously is another example of cluster sampling.

It should be repeated that sampling need not end when we reach the unit of analysis. If novels are the unit of analysis in a study, we might select a sample of novelists, subsamples of novels written by each selected author, and a sample of paragraphs within each novel. We would then analyze the content of the paragraphs for the purpose of describing the novels themselves.

Let's turn now to that more direct examination of analysis I've mentioned frequently in the previous discussions—*content analysis*. At this point, it will refer to the coding or classification of material being observed. Part 4 will deal with the manipulation of such classifications to draw descriptive and explanatory conclusions.

■ CODING IN CONTENT ANALYSIS

Content analysis is essentially a **coding** operation. Communications—oral, written, or other—are coded or classified according to some conceptual framework. Thus, for example, newspaper editorials may be coded as liberal or conservative. Radio broadcasts might be coded as propagandistic or not, novels as romantic or not, paintings as representational or not, and political speeches as containing character assassinations or not. Recall that terms such as these are subject to many interpretations, and the researcher must specify definitions clearly.

Coding in content analysis involves the logic of conceptualization and operationalization as discussed in Chapters 5 and 6. In content analysis, as in other research methods, you must refine your conceptual framework and develop specific methods for observing in relation to that framework.

Manifest and Latent Content

In the earlier discussions of field research, we found that the researcher faces a fundamental choice between *depth* and *specificity* of understanding. Often, this represents a choice between *validity* and *reliability,* respectively. Typically, field researchers opt for depth, preferring to base their judgments on a broad range of observations and information, even at the risk that another observer might reach a different judgment of the same situation. But survey research—through the use of standardized questionnaires—represents the other extreme: total specificity, even though the specific measures of variables may not be fully satisfactory as valid reflections of those variables. The content analyst has some choice in this matter, however.

Coding the **manifest content**—the visible, surface content—of a communication is analogous to using a standardized questionnaire. To determine, for example, how erotic certain novels are, you might simply count the number of times the word *love* appears in each novel or the average number of appearances per page. Or, you might use a list of words, such as *love, kiss, hug,* and *caress,* each of which might serve as an indicator of the erotic nature of the novel. This method would have the advantage of ease and *reliability* in coding and of letting the reader of the research report know precisely how eroticism was measured. It would have a disadvantage, on the other hand, in terms of *validity.* Surely the phrase *erotic novel* conveys a richer and deeper meaning than the number of times the word *love* is used.

Alternatively, you may code the **latent content** of the communication: its underlying meaning. In the present example, you might read an entire novel or a sample of paragraphs or pages and make an overall assessment of how erotic the novel was. Although your total assessment might very well be influenced by the appearance of words such as *love* and *kiss,* it would not depend fully on their frequency.

Clearly, this second method seems better designed for tapping the underlying meaning of communications, but its advantage comes at a cost of reliability and specificity. Especially if more than one person is coding the novel, somewhat different definitions or standards may be employed. A passage that one coder regards as erotic may not seem erotic to another. Even if you do all of the coding yourself, there is no guarantee that your definitions and standards will remain constant throughout the enterprise. Moreover, the reader of your research report would be generally uncertain about the definitions you've employed.

Wherever possible, the best solution to this dilemma is to use *both* methods. For example, Carol Auster was interested in changes in the socialization of young women in Girl Scouts. To explore this, she undertook a content analysis of the Girl Scout manuals as revised over time. In particular, Auster was interested in the view that women should be limited to homemaking. Her analysis of the manifest content suggested a change: "I found that while 23% of the badges in 1913 centered on home life, this was true of only 13% of the badges in 1963 and 7% of the badges in 1980" (1985:361).

An analysis of the latent content also pointed to an emancipation of Girl Scouts, similar to that occuring in U.S. society at large. The change of uniform was one indicator: "The shift from skirts to pants may reflect an acknowledgement of the more physically active role of women as well as the variety of physical images available to modern women" (Auster 1985:362). Supporting evidence was found in the appearance of badges such as "Science Sleuth," "Aerospace," and "Ms. Fix-It."

Conceptualization and the Creation of Code Categories

For all research methods, conceptualization and operationalization typically involve the interaction of theoretical concerns and empirical observations. If, for example, you believe some newspaper editorials to be liberal and others to be conservative, ask yourself why you think so. Read some editorials, asking yourself which ones are liberal and which ones are conservative. Was the political orientation of a particular editorial most clearly indicated by its manifest content or by its tone? Was your decision based on the use of certain terms (for example, *pinko, fascist,* and so on) or on the support or opposition given to a particular issue or political personality?

Both inductive and deductive methods should be used in this activity. If you are testing theoretical propositions, your theories should suggest empirical indicators of concepts. If you begin with specific empirical observations, you should attempt to derive general principles relating to them and then apply those principles to the other empirical observations.

Bruce Berg (1989:111) places code development in the context of grounded theory and likens it to solving a puzzle:

■ Coding and other fundamental procedures associated with grounded theory development are certainly hard work and must be taken seriously, but just as many people enjoy finishing a complicated jigsaw puzzle, many researchers find great satisfaction in coding and analysis. As researchers . . . begin to see the puzzle pieces come together to form a more complete picture, the process can be downright thrilling.

Throughout this activity, you should remember that the operational definition of any variable is composed of the attributes included in it. Such attributes, moreover, should be mutually exclusive and exhaustive. A newspaper editorial, for example, should not be described as both liberal and conservative, though you should probably allow for some to be middle-of-the-road. It may be sufficient for your purposes to code novels as erotic or nonerotic, but you may also want to consider that some could be antierotic. Paintings might be classified as representational or not, if that satisfied your research purpose, or you might wish to further classify them as impressionistic, abstract, allegorical, and so forth.

Realize further that different levels of measurement may be used in content analysis. You may, for example, use the *nominal* categories of liberal and conservative for characterizing newspaper editorials, or you might wish to use a more refined ordinal ranking, ranging from extremely liberal to extremely conservative. Bear in mind, however, that the level of measurement implicit in your coding methods—nominal, ordinal, interval, or ratio—does not necessarily reflect the nature of your variables. If the word *love* appeared 100 times in Novel A and 50 times in Novel B, you would be justified in saying that the word *love* appeared twice as often in Novel A, but not that Novel A was twice as erotic as Novel B. Similarly, agreeing with twice as many anti-Semitic statements in a questionnaire does not make one twice as anti-Semitic, necessarily.

Counting and Record Keeping

If you plan to evaluate your content analysis data quantitatively, your coding operation must be amenable to data processing.

First, the end product of your coding must be *numerical*. If you're counting the frequency of certain words, phrases, or other manifest content, this will necessarily be the case. Even if you're coding latent content on the basis of overall judgments, it will be necessary to represent your coding decision numerically: 1 = very liberal, 2 = moderately liberal, 3 = moderately conservative, and so on.

Second, your record keeping must clearly distinguish between your units of analysis and your units of observation, especially if these two are different. The initial coding, of course, must relate to your units of observation. If novelists are your units of analysis, for example, and you wish to characterize them through a content analysis of their novels, your primary records will represent novels. You may then combine your scoring of individual novels to characterize each novelist.

Third, when counting, it will normally be important to record the *base* from which the counting is done. It would probably be useless to know the number of realistic paintings produced by a given painter without knowing the number he or she had painted all together; the painter would be regarded as *realistic* if a high percentage of paintings were of that genre. Similarly, it would tell us little that the word *love* appeared 87 times in a novel if we did not know about how many words there were in the novel all together. The issue of observational base is most easily resolved if *every* observation is coded in terms of one of the attributes making up a variable. Rather than simply counting the number of liberal editorials in a given collection, for example, code each editorial by its political orientation, even if it must be coded "no apparent orientation."

Let's suppose we want to describe and explain the editorial policies of different newspapers. Figure 12-2 presents part of a tally sheet that might result from the coding of newspaper editorials. Note that newspapers are the units of analysis. Each newspaper has been assigned an identification number to facilitate mechanized processing. The second column has a space for the number of editorials coded for each newspaper. This will be an important piece of information, since we want to be able to say, for example, "Of all the editorials, 22 percent were pro–United Nations," not just "There were eight pro–United Nations editorials."

One column in Figure 12-2 is for assigning a subjective overall assessment of the newspapers' editorial policies. (Such assignments might later be compared with the several objective measures.) Other columns provide space for recording numbers of editorials reflecting specific editorial positions. In a real content analysis, there would be spaces for recording other editorial positions plus noneditorial information about each newspaper, such as the region in which it is published, its circulation, and so forth.

Qualitative Data Analysis

Not all content analysis results in counting. Sometimes a qualitative assessment of the materials is most appropriate. Carol Auster's examination of changes in Girl Scout uniforms and handbook language (previously discussed) offers one example.

Bruce Berg (1989:123–25) discusses "negative case testing" as a technique for qualitative hypothesis testing. First, in the grounded theory tradition, you begin with an examination of the

FIGURE 12-2
Sample Tally Sheet (Partial)

Newspaper ID	Number of editorials evaluated	SUBJECTIVE EVALUATION 1. Very liberal 2. Moderately liberal 3. Middle-of-road 4. Moderately conservative 5. Very conservative	Number of "anticommunist" editorials	Number of "pro-UN" editorials	Number of "anti-UN" editorials
001	37	2	0	8	0
002	26	5	10	0	6
003	44	4	2	1	2
004	22	3	1	2	3
005	30	1	0	6	0

data, which may yield a general hypothesis. Let's say that you're examining the leadership of a new community association by reviewing the minutes of meetings to see who made motions that were subsequently passed. Your initial examination of the data suggests that the wealthier members are the most likely to assume this leadership role.

The second stage in the analysis is to search your data to find all the cases that would contradict the initial hypothesis. In this instance, you would look for poorer members who made successful motions and wealthy members who never did. Third, you must review each of the disconfirming cases and either (1) give up the hypothesis or (2) see how it needs to be fine-tuned.

Let's say that in your analysis of disconfirming cases, you notice that each of the unwealthy leaders is quite highly educated—with graduate degrees; each of the wealthy nonleaders has very little formal education. You may revise your hypothesis to consider both education and wealth as routes to leadership in the association. Perhaps you will discover some threshold (a white-collar job/income and a college degree) for leadership—beyond that, those with the most money and/or education are the most active leaders.

This process is an example of what Barney Glaser and Anselm Strauss (1967) call *analytic induction*. It is inductive in that it primarily begins with observations, and it is analytic because it goes beyond description to find patterns and relationships among variables.

There are, of course, dangers in this form of analysis, as in all others. The chief risk here is that you will misclassify observations so as to support your emerging hypothesis. You may erroneously conclude that a nonleader didn't graduate from college or you may decide that the job of factory foreman is close enough to being white-collar.

Berg (1989:124) offers techniques for avoiding these errors. (1) If there are sufficient cases, for example, you should select some at random from each category—to avoid merely picking those that best support the hypothesis. (2) Give at least three examples in support of every assertion you make about the data. (3) Have your analytic interpretations carefully reviewed by others uninvolved in the research project to see if they agree. (4) Finally, report whatever inconsistencies you do discover—any cases that simply do not fit your hypotheses. Realize that few social patterns are 100 percent consistent, so you may have discovered something important even if it doesn't apply to absolutely all of social life. However, you should be honest with your reader in that regard.

■ AN ILLUSTRATION OF CONTENT ANALYSIS

Several studies have indicated that women are stereotyped in traditional roles on television. R. Stephen Craig (1992) took this line of inquiry one step further to examine the portrayal of both men and women during different periods of television programming.

To study gender stereotyping in television commercials, Craig selected a sample of 2,209 network commericials during several periods between January 6 and 14, 1990.

■ The weekday day part (in this sample, Monday–Friday, 2–4 P.M.) consisted exclusively of soap operas and was chosen for its high percentage of women viewers. The weekend day part (two consecutive Saturday and Sunday afternoons during sports telecasts) was selected for its high percentage of men viewers. Evening "prime time" (Monday–Friday, 9–11 P.M.) was chosen as a basis for comparison with past studies and the other day parts.

(1992:199)

Each of the commercials was coded in several ways. "Characters" were coded as:

All male adults
All female adults
All adults, mixed gender
Male adults with children or teens (no women)
Female adults with children or teens (no men)
Mixture of ages and genders

In addition, Craig's coders noted which character was on the screen longest during the commercial—the "primary visual character"—as well as the roles played by the characters (such as spouse, celebrity, parent), the type of product advertised (such as body product, alcohol), the setting (such as kitchen, school, business), and the voice-over narrator.

Table 12-1 indicates the differences in the times when men and women appeared in commercials. Women were more common during the daytime (with its soap operas), men predominated during the weekend commercials (with its sports programming), and men and women were equally represented during evening prime time.

Craig found other differences in the ways men and women were portrayed.

■ Further analysis indicated that male primary characters were proportionately more likely than females to be portrayed as celebrities and professionals in every day part, while women were proportionately more likely to be portrayed as interviewer/demonstrators, parent/spouses, or sex object/models in every day part.... Women were proportionately more likely to appear as sex object/models during the weekend than during the day.

(1992:204)

The research also showed that different products were advertised during different time periods. As you might have imagined, almost all the daytime commercials dealt with body, food, or home products. These products accounted for only one in three on the weekends. Instead, weekend commercials stressed automotive (29 percent), business products or services (27 percent), or alcohol

TABLE 12-1
Percentages of Adult Primary Visual Characters by Sex Appearing in Commercials in Three Day Parts

	Daytime	Evening	Weekend
Adult male	40	52	80
Adult female	60	48	20

Source: R. Stephen Craig, "The Effect of Television Day Part on Gender Portrayals in Television Commercials: A Content Analysis," *Sex Roles* 26, nos. 5/6 (1992): 204.

(10 percent). There were virtually no alcohol ads during evenings and daytime.

As you might suspect, women were most likely to be portrayed in home settings, men most likely to be shown away from home. Other findings dealt with the different roles played by men and women.

■ The women who appeared in weekend ads were almost never portrayed without men and seldom as the commercial's primary character. They were generally seen in roles subservient to men (e.g., hotel receptionist, secretary, or stewardess), or as sex objects or models in which their only function seemed to be to lend an aspect of eroticism to the ad.

(1992:208)

Though some of Craig's findings may not surprise you, remember that "common knowledge" does not always correspond with reality. Also, it's useful to know more specific details about the nature of the situation—details such as those provided by a content analysis like this one.

■ STRENGTHS AND WEAKNESSES OF CONTENT ANALYSIS

Probably the greatest advantage of content analysis is its economy in terms of both time and money. A single college student could undertake a content analysis, whereas undertaking a survey, for example, might not be feasible. There is no requirement for a large research staff; no special equipment is required. As long as you have access to the material to be coded, you can undertake content analysis.

Safety is another advantage of content analysis. If you discover you have botched up a survey or an experiment, you may be forced to repeat the whole research project with all its attendant costs in time and money. If you botch up your field research, it may be impossible to redo the project; the event under study may no longer exist. In content analysis, it is usually easier to repeat a portion of the study than for other research methods. You might be required, moreover, to recode only a portion of your data rather than all of it.

Also important, content analysis permits you to study processes occurring over long periods of time. You might focus on the imagery of African Americans conveyed in U.S. novels of 1850 to 1860, for example, or you might examine changing imagery from 1850 to the present.

Finally, content analysis has the advantage, mentioned at the outset of this chapter, of being *unobtrusive*. That is, the content analyst seldom has any effect on the subject being studied. Because the novels have already been written, the paintings already painted, the speeches already presented, content analyses can have no effect on them.

Content analysis has disadvantages as well. For one thing, it's limited to the examination of *recorded* communications. Such communications may be oral, written, or graphic, but they must be recorded in some fashion to permit analysis.

As we've seen, content analysis has both advantages and disadvantages in terms of validity and reliability. Problems of validity are likely unless you happen to be studying communication processes per se. For example, did the appearance of expressive/instrumental values in the underground press represent the most valid measure of those values in the hippie movement in general? Probably not. Even if the researchers achieved a high degree of validity in their coding of value orientations in the underground press and mainstream magazines, there's still a question of whether they had a valid measure of the *cultures* those media were taken to represent. This is a common problem with content analysis.

On the other side of the ledger, the concreteness of materials studied in content analysis strengthens the likelihood of reliability. You can always code and recode and even recode again if you want, making certain that the coding is consistent. In field research, by contrast, there's probably nothing you can do after the fact to insure greater reliability in observation and categorization.

Let's move from content analysis now and turn to a related research method: the analysis of existing data. Although numbers rather than communications are the substance analyzed in this case, I think you'll see the similarity to content analysis.

■ ANALYZING EXISTING STATISTICS

Frequently you can or must undertake social scientific inquiry through the use of official or quasi-official statistics. This differs from secondary analysis, in which you obtain a copy of someone else's data and undertake your own statistical analysis. In this section, we're going to look at ways of using the data analyses others have already done.

Before getting into the nuts and bolts of this research method, I'd like to point out that existing statistics should always be considered at least a *supplemental* source of data. If you were planning a survey of political attitudes, for example, you would do well to examine and present your findings within a context of voting patterns, rates of voter turnout, or similar statistics relevant to your research interest. Or, if you were doing evaluation research on an experimental morale-building program on an assembly line, probably statistics on absenteeism, sick leave, and so on would be interesting and revealing in connection with the data your own research would generate. Existing statistics, then, can often provide a historical or conceptual context within which to locate your original research.

Existing statistics can also provide the main data for a social scientific inquiry. In contrast to the structure of preceding discussions, I want to begin here with an illustration: Emile Durkheim's classic study, *Suicide* ([1897] 1951). Then we'll look at some of the special problems this method presents in terms of units of analysis, validity, and reliability. I'll conclude the discussion by mentioning some useful sources of data.

Studying Suicide

Why do people kill themselves? Undoubtedly every suicide case has a unique history and explanation, yet all such cases could no doubt be grouped according to certain common causes: financial failure, trouble in love, disgrace, and other kinds of personal problems. The French sociologist Emile Durkheim had a slightly different question in mind when he addressed the matter of suicide, however. He wanted to discover the environmental conditions that encouraged or discouraged it, especially social conditions.

The more he examined the available records, the more patterns of differences became apparent to Durkheim. All of these patterns interested him. One of the first things to attract his attention was the relative *stability* of suicide rates. Looking at several countries, he found suicide rates to be about the same year after year. He also discovered that a disproportionate number of suicides occurred in summer, leading him to hypothesize that temperature might have something to do with suicide. If this were the case, suicide rates should be higher in the southern European countries than in the temperate ones. However, Durkheim discovered that the highest rates were found in countries in the central latitudes, so temperature couldn't be the answer.

He explored the role of age (35 was the most common suicide age), gender (men outnumbered women around four to one), and numerous other factors. Eventually, a general pattern emerged from different sources.

In terms of the stability of suicide rates over time, for instance, Durkheim found the pattern was not *totally* stable. He found spurts in the rates during times of political turmoil, which occurred in several European countries around 1848. This observation led him to hypothesize that suicide might have something to do with "breaches in social equilibrium." Put differently, social stability and integration seemed to be a protection against suicide.

This general hypothesis was substantiated and specified through Durkheim's analysis of a different set of data. The different countries of Europe had radically different suicide rates. The rate in Saxony, for example, was about ten times that of Italy, and the relative ranking of various countries persisted over time. As Durkheim considered other differences in the various countries, he eventually noticed a striking pattern: Predominantly Protestant countries had consistently higher suicide rates than Catholic ones. The predominantly Protestant countries had 190 suicides per million population; mixed Protestant-Catholic countries, 96; and predominantly Catholic countries, 58 (Durkheim [1897] 1951:152).

Durkheim reasoned that some other factor, such as level of economic and cultural development, might explain the observed differences. If religion had a genuine effect on suicide, then the religious difference would have to be found *within* given countries. To test this idea, Durkheim first noted that the German state of Bavaria had both the most Catholics and the lowest suicide rates in that country, whereas heavily Protestant Prussia had a much higher suicide rate. Not content to stop there, however, Durkheim examined the provinces composing each of those states. Table 12-2 shows what he found.

As you can see, in both Bavaria and Prussia, provinces with the highest proportion of Protestants also had the highest suicide rates. Increasingly, Durkheim became confident that religion played a significant role in the matter of suicide.

Returning eventually to a more general theoretical level, Durkheim combined the religious findings with the earlier observation about increased suicide rates during times of political turmoil. Put most simply, Durkheim suggested that many suicides are a product of *anomie*, "normlessness," or a general sense of social instability and disintegration. During times of political strife, people might feel that the old ways of society were collapsing. They would become demoralized and depressed, and suicide was one answer to the severe discomfort. Seen from the other direction, social integration and solidarity—reflected in personal feelings of being part of a coherent, enduring social whole—would offer protection against depression and suicide. That was where the religious difference fit in. Catholicism, as a far more structured and integrated religious system, would give people a greater sense of coherence and stability than would the more loosely structured Protestantism.

From these theories, Durkheim created the concept of *anomic suicide*. More important, as you know, he added the concept of *anomie* to the lexicon of the social sciences. Please realize I have given you only the most superficial picture of Durkheim's classic study, and I think you'd enjoy looking through the original. In any event, this study gives you a good illustration of the possibilities for research contained in the masses of data regularly gathered and reported by government agencies.

Units of Analysis

As we've already seen in the case of *Suicide*, the unit of analysis involved in the analysis of existing statistics is often *not* the individual. Thus, Durkheim was required to work with political-geographical units: countries, regions, states, and cities. The same situation would probably appear if you were to undertake a study of crime rates, accident rates, disease, and so forth. By their nature, most existing statistics are *aggregated:* They describe groups.

The aggregate nature of existing statistics can present a problem, though not an insurmountable one. As we saw, for example, Durkheim wanted to determine whether Protestants or Catholics were more likely to commit suicide. None of the records available to him indicated the religion of those people who committed suicide, however. Ultimately, then, it was not possible for him to say whether Protestants committed suicide more often than Catholics, though he *inferred* as much. Because Protestant countries, regions, and states had higher suicides than Catholic countries, regions, and states, he drew the obvious conclusion.

TABLE 12-2
Suicide Rates in Various German Provinces, Arranged in Terms of Religious Affiliation

Religious Character of Province	Suicides per Million Inhabitants
Bavarian Provinces (1867–1875)*	
Less than 50% Catholic	
Rhenish Palatinate	167
Central Franconia	207
Upper Franconia	204
Average	192
50% to 90% Catholic	
Lower Franconia	157
Swabia	118
Average	135
More than 90% Catholic	
Upper Palatinate	64
Upper Bavaria	114
Lower Bavaria	19
Average	75
Prussian Provinces (1883–1890)	
More than 90% Protestant	
Saxony	309.4
Schleswig	312.9
Pomerania	171.5
Average	264.6
68% to 89% Protestant	
Hanover	212.3
Hesse	200.3
Brandenburg and Berlin	296.3
East Prussia	171.3
Average	220.0
40% to 50% Protestant	
West Prussia	123.9
Silesia	260.2
Westphalia	107.5
Average	163.6
28% to 32% Protestant	
Posen	96.4
Rhineland	100.3
Hohenzollern	90.1
Average	95.6

Note: The population below 15 years has been omitted.
Source: Adapted from Emile Durkheim, *Suicide* (Glencoe, IL: Free Press, [1897], 1951), 153.

There's danger in drawing this kind of conclusion, however. It is always possible that patterns of behavior at a group level do not reflect corresponding patterns on an individual level. Such errors are said to be due to an *ecological fallacy* (see Chapter 4). It was altogether possible, for example, that it was Catholics who committed suicide in the predominantly Protestant areas. Perhaps Catholics in predominantly Protestant areas were so badly persecuted that they were led into despair and suicide. Then it would be possible for Protestant countries to have high suicide rates without any Protestants committing suicide.

Durkheim avoided the danger of the ecological fallacy in two ways. First, his general conclusions were based as much on rigorous, theoretical deductions as on the empirical facts. The correspondence between theory and fact made a counterexplanation, such as the one I just made up, less likely. Second, by extensively retesting his conclusions in a variety of ways, Durkheim further strengthened the likelihood that they were correct. Suicide rates were higher in Protestant countries than in Catholic ones; higher in Protestant regions of Catholic countries than in Catholic regions of Protestant countries; and so forth. The replication of findings added to the weight of evidence in support of his conclusions.

Problems of Validity

Whenever you base your research on an analysis of data that already exist, you are obviously limited to what exists. Often, the existing data don't cover exactly what you're interested in, and your measurements may not be altogether valid representations of the variables and concepts you want to draw conclusions about.

Two characteristics of science are used to handle the problem of validity in analysis of existing statistics: *logical reasoning* and *replication.* As an example of logical reasoning, you'll recall that Durkheim could not determine the religion of persons who committed suicide. He did know the predominant religions of the regions whose suicides he studied, reasoning that most of the suicides in a predominantly Protestant region would be Protestants.

Replication can be a general solution to problems of validity in social research. Recall the earlier discussion of the interchangeability of indicators. Crying in sad movies isn't necessarily a valid measure of compassion, so if women cry more than men, that doesn't *prove* they're more compassionate. Neither is putting little birds back in their nests a valid measure of compassion, so that wouldn't *prove* women to be more compassionate. And giving money to charity could represent something other than compassion, and so forth. None of these things, *taken alone,* would prove that women were more compassionate than men. But if women appeared more compassionate than men by *all* these measures, that would create a weight of evidence in support of the conclusion. In the analysis of existing statistics, a little ingenuity and reasoning can usually turn up several independent tests of your hypothesis, and if all the tests seem to confirm it, then the weight of evidence supports the view you're advancing.

Problems of Reliability

The analysis of existing statistics depends heavily on the quality of the statistics themselves: Are they accurate reports of what they claim to report? This can be a substantial problem sometimes, because the weighty tables of government statistics are sometimes grossly inaccurate.

Because a great deal of the research into crime depends on official crime statistics, this body of data has come under critical evaluation. The results have not been too encouraging. Suppose, for purposes of illustration, that you were interested in tracing the long-term trends in marijuana use in the United States. Official statistics on the numbers of people arrested for selling or possessing it would seem to be a reasonable measure of use. Right? Not necessarily.

To begin, you face a hefty problem of validity. Before the passage of the Marihuana Tax Act in 1937, grass was legal in the United States, so arrest records would not give you a valid measure of use. But even if you limited your inquiry to the post-1937 era, you would still have problems of reliability, stemming from the nature of law enforcement and crime record keeping.

Law enforcement, for example, is subject to various pressures. A public outcry against marijuana, led perhaps by a vocal citizens' group, often results in a police "crackdown on drug trafficking"—especially if it occurs during an election or budget year. A sensational story in the press can have a similar effect. In addition, the volume of other business facing police affects marijuana arrests.

In tracing the pattern of drug arrests in Chicago between 1942 and 1970, Lois DeFleur (1975) has demonstrated that the official records present a far less accurate history of drug use than of police practices and political pressure on police. On a different level of analysis, Donald Black (1970) and others have analyzed the factors influencing whether an offender is actually arrested by police or let off with a warning. Ultimately, official crime statistics are influenced by whether specific offenders are well or poorly dressed, whether they are polite or abusive to police officers, and so forth. When we consider unreported crimes, sometimes estimated to be as much as ten times the number of crimes known to police, the reliability of crime statistics gets even shakier.

These comments concern crime statistics at a local level. Often it's useful to analyze national crime statistics, such as those reported in the FBI's annual *Uniform Crime Reports*. Additional problems are introduced at the national level. Different local jurisdictions define crimes differently. Also, participation in the FBI program is voluntary, so the data are incomplete.

Finally, the process of record keeping affects the records that are kept and reported. Whenever a law enforcement unit improves its record-keeping system—computerizing it, for example—the apparent crime rates always increase dramatically. This can happen even if the number of crimes committed, reported, and investigated does not increase.

Your first protection against the problems of reliability in the analysis of existing statistics is awareness—knowing that the problem may exist. Investigating the nature of the data collection and tabulation may enable you to assess the nature and degree of unreliability so that you can judge its potential impact on your research interest. If you also use logical reasoning and replication, as discussed previously, you can usually cope with the problem.

Sources of Existing Statistics

It would take a whole book just to list the sources of data available for analysis. In this section, I want to mention a few sources and point you in the direction of finding others relevant to your research interest.

Undoubtedly, the single most valuable book you can buy is the annual *Statistical Abstract of the United States*, published by the United States Department of Commerce. Unquestionably the single best source of data about the United States, it includes statistics on the individual states and (less extensively) cities as well as on the nation as a whole. Where else can you learn the number of work stoppages in the country year by year, residential property taxes of major cities, the number of water pollution discharges reported around the country, the number of business proprietorships in the nation, and hundreds of other such handy bits of information? To make things even better, Hoover's Business Press offers the same book in soft cover for less cost. The commercial version is entitled *The American Almanac* and shouldn't be confused with other almanacs that are less reliable and less useful for social scientific research. Better yet, you can buy the *Statistical Abstract* on a CD-ROM, making the search for and transfer of data quite easy.

Federal agencies—the Departments of Labor, Agriculture, Transportation, and so forth—publish countless data series. To find out what's available, go to your library, find the government documents section, and spend a few hours browsing through the shelves. You'll come away with a clear sense of the wealth of data available to your insight and ingenuity.

The latest development in access to existing statistics is the World Wide Web (discussed in Appendix B). Here are just a few Web sites to illustrate the richness of this new resource.

- Bureau of the Census
    http://www.census.gov/
- Bureau of Labor Statistics
    http://stats.bls.gov/blshome.html
- Department of Education
    http://www.ed.gov/
- Bureau of Transportation Statistics
    http://www.bts.gov/
- Federal Bureau of Investigation
    http://www.fbi.gov/
- Central Intelligence Agency
    http://www.ic.gov/
- State and Local Governments
    http://www.piperinfo.com/~piper/state/states.html
- The World Bank
    http://www.worldbank.org/

Suffering Around the World

IN 1992, the Population Crisis Committee, a nonprofit organization committed to combatting the population explosion, undertook to analyze the relative degree of suffering in nations around the world. Every country with a population of one million or more was evaluated in terms of the following ten indicators—with a score of 10 on any indicator representing the highest level of adversity:

Life expectancy
Daily per capita calorie supply
Percentage of the population with access to clean drinking water
Proportion of infant immunization
Rate of secondary school enrollment
Gross national product
Inflation
Number of telephones per 1,000 people
Political freedom
Civil rights

Here's how the world's nations ranked in terms of these indicators. Remember, high scores are signs of overall suffering.

Extreme Human Suffering:

93—Mozambique
92—Somalia
89—Afghanistan, Haiti, Sudan
88—Zaire
87—Laos
86—Guinea, Angola
85—Ethiopia, Uganda
84—Cambodia, Sierra Leone
82—Chad, Guinea-Bissau
81—Ghana, Burma
79—Malawi
77—Cameroon, Mauritania
76—Rwanda, Vietnam, Liberia
75—Burundi, Kenya, Madagascar, Yemen

High Human Suffering:

74—Ivory Coast
73—Bhutan, Burkina Faso, Central African Republic
71—Tanzania, Togo
70—Lesotho, Mali, Niger, Nigeria
69—Guatemala, Nepal

World statistics are available through the United Nations. Its *Demographic Yearbook* presents annual vital statistics (births, deaths, and other data relevant to population) for the individual nations of the world. Other publications report a variety of other kinds of data. Again, a trip to your library is the best introduction to what's available.

The amount of data provided by nongovernment agencies is as staggering as the amount your taxes buy. Chambers of commerce often publish data reports on business, as do private consumer groups. Ralph Nader has information on automobile safety, and Common Cause covers politics and government. And, as mentioned earlier, George Gallup publishes reference volumes on public opinion as tapped by Gallup Polls since 1935.

Organizations such as the Population Reference Bureau publish a variety of demographic data, U.S. and international, that a secondary analyst could use. Their *World Population Data Sheet* and *Population Bulletin* are resources heavily used by social scientists. Social indicator data can be found in the journal *SINET: A Quarterly Review of Social Reports and Research on Social Indicators, Social Trends, and the Quality of Life.*

My temptation is to continue listing data sources, but I suspect you've already gotten the idea. I suggest you visit the governmental documents section the next time you're at your college library or the next time you're surfing the Web. You'll be amazed by the data waiting for your analysis. The lack of funds to support expensive data collection is no reason for not doing good and useful social research.

The availability of existing statistics makes it possible to create some fairly sophisticated measures. The accompanying box on "Suffering Around the World" describes an analysis published by the Population Crisis Committee.

68—Bangladesh, Bolivia, Zambia
67—Pakistan
66—Nicaragua, Papua-New Guinea, Senegal, Swaziland, Zimbabwe
65—Iraq
64—Gambia, Congo, El Salvador, Indonesia, Syria
63—Comores, India, Paraguay, Peru
62—Benin, Honduras
61—Lebanon, China, Guyana, South Africa
59—Egypt, Morocco
58—Ecuador, Sri Lanka
57—Botswana
56—Iran
55—Suriname
54—Algeria, Thailand
53—Dominican Republic, Mexico, Tunisia, Turkey
51—Libya, Colombia, Venezuela
50—Brazil, Oman, Philippines

Moderate Human Suffering:

49—Solomon Islands
47—Albania
45—Vanuatu
44—Jamaica, Romania, Saudi Arabia, Seychelles, Yugoslavia (former)
43—Mongolia
41—Jordan

40—Malaysia, Mauritius
39—Argentina
38—Cuba, Panama
37—Chile, Uruguay, North Korea
34—Costa Rica, South Korea, United Arab Emirates
33—Poland
32—Bulgaria, Hungary, Qatar
31—Soviet Union (former)
29—Bahrain, Hong Kong, Trinidad and Tobago
28—Kuwait, Singapore
25—Czechoslovakia, Portugal, Taiwan

Minimal Human Suffering:

21—Israel
19—Greece
16—United Kingdom
12—Italy
11—Barbados, Ireland, Spain, Sweden
8—Finland, New Zealand
7—France, Iceland, Japan, Luxembourg
6—Austria, Germany
5—United States
4—Australia, Norway
3—Canada, Switzerland
2—Belgium, Netherlands
1—Denmark

■ HISTORICAL/COMPARATIVE ANALYSIS

In this final section of the chapter, we examine historical/comparative research, a method that differs substantially from those previously discussed, though it overlaps somewhat with field research, content analysis, and the analysis of existing statistics. It involves the use of historical methods by sociologists, political scientists, and other social scientists.

The discussion of longitudinal research designs in Chapter 4 notwithstanding, our examination of research methods so far has focused primarily on studies anchored in one point in time and in one locale, whether a particular small group or a nation. Although accurately portraying the main thrust of contemporary social scientific research, this focus conceals the fact that social scientists are also interested in tracing the development of social forms over time and comparing those developmental processes across cultures. So in this section, after describing some major instances of historical and comparative research in the past, I'll turn to the key elements of this method with the purpose of empowering you to use it.

Examples of Historical/Comparative Analysis

August Comte, who coined the term *sociologie*, saw that new discipline as the final stage in a historical development of ideas. With his broadest brush, he painted an evolutionary picture that took humans from a reliance on religion to metaphysics to science. With a finer brush, he portrayed science as evolving from the development of biology and the other natural sciences to the development of psychology and, finally, to the development of scientific sociology.

A great many later social scientists have also turned their attention to broad historical processes. Several have examined the historical progression of social forms from the simple to the complex, from rural-agrarian to urban-industrial societies. The U.S. anthropologist Lewis Morgan, for example, saw a progression from "savagery" to "barbarism" to "civilization" (1870). Robert Redfield, another anthropologist, has more recently written of a shift from "folk society" to "urban society" (1941). Emile Durkheim saw social evolution largely as a process of ever-greater division of labor ([1893] 1964). In a more specific analysis, Karl Marx examined economic systems progressing historically from primitive to feudal to capitalistic forms ([1867] 1967). All history, he wrote in this context, was a history of class struggle—the "haves" struggling to maintain their advantages and the "have-nots" struggling for a better lot in life. Looking beyond capitalism, Marx saw the development of socialism and finally communism.

Not all historical studies in the social sciences have had this evolutionary flavor, however. Some social scientific readings of the historical record, in fact, point to grand cycles rather than to linear progressions. No scholar better represents this view than Pitirim A. Sorokin. A participant in the Russian Revolution of 1917, Sorokin served as secretary to Prime Minister Kerensky. Both Kerensky and Sorokin fell from favor, however, and Sorokin began his second career—as an American sociologist.

Whereas Comte read history as a progression from religion to science, Sorokin (1937–1940) suggested that societies alternate cyclically between two points of view, which he called "ideational" and "sensate." Sorokin's sensate point of view defines reality in terms of sense experiences. The ideational, by contrast, places a greater emphasis on spiritual and religious factors. Sorokin's reading of the historical record further indicated that the passage between the ideational and sensate was through a third point of view, which he called the "idealistic." This latter combined elements of the sensate and ideational in an integrated, rational view of the world.

These examples indicate some of the topics historical/comparative researchers have examined. To get a better sense of what historical/comparative research entails, let's look at a few examples in somewhat more detail.

Weber and the Role of Ideas In his analysis of economic history, Karl Marx put forward a view of economic determinism. That is, he felt that economic factors determined the nature of all other aspects of society. For example, Marx's analysis showed that a function of European churches was to justify and support the capitalist status quo—religion was a tool of the powerful in maintaining their dominance over the powerless. "Religion is the sigh of the oppressed creature," Marx wrote in a famous passage, "the sentiment of a heartless world, and the soul of soulless conditions. It is the opium of the people" (Bottomore and Rubel [1843] 1956:27).

Max Weber, a German sociologist, disagreed. Without denying that economic factors could and did affect other aspects of society, Weber argued that economic determinism did not explain everything. Indeed, Weber said, economic forms could come from noneconomic ideas. In his research in the sociology of religion, Weber examined the extent to which religious institutions were the source of social behavior rather than mere reflections of economic conditions. His most noted statement of this side of the issue is found in *The Protestant Ethic and the Spirit of Capitalism* ([1905] 1958). Here's a brief overview of Weber's thesis.

John Calvin (1509–1564), a French theologian, was an important figure in the Protestant reformation of Christianity. Calvin taught that the ultimate salvation or damnation of every individual had already been decided by God; this idea is called *predestination*. Calvin also suggested that God communicated his decisions to people by making them either successful or unsuccessful during their earthly existence. God gave each person an earthly "calling"—an occupation or profession—and manifested their success or failure through that medium. Ironically, this point of view led Calvin's followers to seek proof of their coming salvation by working hard, saving their money, and generally striving for economic success.

In Weber's analysis, Calvinism provided an important stimulus for the development of capitalism. Rather than "wasting" their money on worldly comforts, the Calvinists reinvested it in their economic enterprises, thus providing the *capital* necessary for the development of capitalism. In arriving at this interpretation of the origins of capitalism, Weber researched the official doctrines of the early Protestant churches, studied the preachings of Calvin and other church leaders, and examined other relevant historical documents.

In three other studies, Weber conducted detailed historical analyses of Judaism ([1934] 1952) and the religions of China ([1934] 1951) and India ([1934] 1958). Among other things, Weber wanted to know why capitalism had not developed in the ancient societies of China, India, and Israel. In none of the three religions did he find any teaching that would have supported the accumulation and reinvestment of capital—strengthening his conclusion about the role of Protestantism in that regard.

Japanese Religion and Capitalism Weber's thesis regarding Protestantism and capitalism has become a classic in the social sciences. Not surprisingly, other scholars have attempted to test it in other historical situations. No analysis has been more interesting, however, than Robert Bellah's examination of the growth of capitalism in Japan during the late nineteenth and early twentieth centuries, entitled *Tokugawa Religion* (1957).

As both an undergraduate and a graduate student, Bellah had developed interests in Weber and in Japanese society. Given these two interests, it was perhaps inevitable that he would, in 1951, first conceive his Ph.D. thesis topic as "nothing less than an 'Essay on the Economic Ethic of Japan' to be a companion to Weber's studies of China, India, and Judaism: *The Economic Ethic of the World Religions*" (recalled in Bellah 1967:168). Originally, Bellah sketched his research design as follows:

■ Problems would have to be specific and limited—no general history would be attempted—since time span is several centuries. Field work in Japan on the actual economic ethic practiced by persons in various situations, with, if possible, controlled matched samples from the U.S. (questionnaires, interviews, etc.).

(1967:168)

Bellah's original plan, then, called for surveys of contemporary Japanese and Americans. However, he did not receive the financial support necessary for the study as originally envisioned. So instead, he immersed himself in the historical records of Japanese religion, seeking the roots of the rise of capitalism in Japan.

Over the course of several years' research, Bellah uncovered numerous leads. In a 1952 term paper on the subject, Bellah felt he had found the answer in the samurai code of Bushido and in the Confucianism practiced by the samurai class:

■ Here I think we find a real development of this worldly asceticism, at least equaling anything found in Europe. Further, in this class the idea of duty in occupation involved achievement without traditionalistic limits, but to the limits of one's capacities, whether in the role of bureaucrat, doctor, teacher, scholar, or other role open to the Samurai.

(QUOTED IN BELLAH 1967:171)

The samurai, however, made up only a portion of Japanese society. So Bellah kept looking at the religions among Japanese generally. His understanding of the Japanese language was not yet very good, but he wanted to read religious texts in the original. Under these constraints and experiencing increased time pressure, Bellah decided to concentrate his attention on a single group: Shingaku, a religious movement among merchants in the eighteenth and nineteenth centuries. He found that Shingaku had two influences on the development of capitalism. It offered an attitude toward work similar to the Calvinist notion of a "calling," and it had the effect of making business a more acceptable calling for Japanese. Previously, commerce had had a very low standing in Japan.

In other aspects of his analysis, Bellah examined the religious and political roles of the Emperor and the economic impact of periodically appearing emperor cults. Ultimately, Bellah's researches pointed to the variety of religious and philosophical factors that laid the groundwork for capitalism in Japan. It seems unlikely that he would have achieved anything approaching that depth of understanding if he had been able to pursue his original plan to interview matched samples of U.S. and Japanese citizens.

These examples of historical/comparative research should have given you some sense of the potential power in the method. Let's turn now to an examination of the sources and techniques used in this method.

Sources of Historical/Comparative Data

As we saw in the case of existing statistics, there is no end of data available for analysis in historical research. To begin, historians may have already reported on whatever it is you want to examine, and their analyses can give you an initial grounding in the subject, a jumping-off point for more in-depth research.

Ultimately, you'll usually want to go beyond others' conclusions and examine some "raw data" to draw your own conclusions. These data vary, of course, according to the topic under study. In Bellah's study of Tokugawa religion, raw data included the sermons of Shingaku teachers. When W. I. Tnomas and Florian Znaniecki (1918) studied the adjustment process for Polish peasants coming to the United States early in this century, they examined letters written by the immigrants to their families in Poland. (They obtained the letters through newspaper advertisements.) Other researchers have analyzed old diaries. Such personal documents only scratch the surface, however.

In discussing procedures for studying the history of family life, Ellen Rothman points to the following sources:

■ In addition to personal sources, there are public records which are also revealing of family history. Newspapers are especially rich in evidence on the educational, legal, and recreational aspects of family life in the past as seen from a local point of view. Magazines reflect more general patterns of family life; students often find them interesting to explore for data on perceptions and expectations of mainstream family values. Magazines offer several different kinds of sources at once: visual materials (illustrations and advertisements), commentary (editorial and advice columns), and fiction. Popular periodicals are particularly rich in the last two. Advice on many questions of concern to families—from the proper way to discipline children to the economics of wallpaper—fills magazine columns from the early nineteenth century to the present. Stories that suggest common experiences or perceptions of family life appear with the same continuity.

(1981:53)

Organizations generally document themselves, so if you're studying the development of some organization—as Bellah studied Shingaku, for example—you should examine its official documents: charters, policy statements, speeches by leaders, and so on. Once when I was studying the rise of a contemporary Japanese religious group—Sokagakkai—I discovered not only weekly newspapers and magazines published by the group but also a published collection of all the speeches given by the original leaders. I could, then, trace changes in recruitment patterns over time. At the outset, followers were enjoined to enroll all the world. Later, the emphasis shifted specifically to Japan. Once a sizable Japanese membership had been established, an emphasis on enrolling all the world returned (Babbie 1966).

Often, official government documents provide the data needed for analysis. To better appreciate the history of race relations in the United States, A. Leon Higginbotham, Jr. (1978) examined some 200 years of laws and court cases involving race. Himself the first African American appointed a federal judge, Higginbotham found that the law, rather than protecting African Americans, was the embodiment of bigotry and oppression. In the earliest court cases, there was considerable ambiguity over whether African Americans were indentured servants or, in fact, slaves. Later court cases and laws clarified the matter—holding African Americans to be something less than human.

The sources of data for historical analysis are too extensive to cover even in outline here, though I trust the few examples I've given you so far will enable you to find whatever resources you need. I want to conclude this section with a couple of cautions.

As you saw in the case of existing statistics, you can't trust the accuracy of records—official or unofficial, primary or secondary. Your protection lies in replication: In the case of historical research, it lies in corroboration. If several sources point to the same set of "facts," your confidence in them might reasonably increase.

At the same time, you need always be wary of bias in your data sources. If all your data on the development of a political movement are taken from the movement itself, you're unlikely to gain a well-rounded view of it. The diaries of well-to-do gentry of the Middle Ages may not give you an accurate view of life in general during those times. Where possible, obtain data from a variety of sources, representing different points of view. Here's what Bellah said regarding his analysis of Shingaku:

■ One could argue that there would be a bias in what was selected for notice by Western scholars. However, the fact that there was material from Western scholars with varied interests from a number of countries and over a period of nearly a century reduced the probability of bias.

(BELLAH 1967:179)

The issues raised by Bellah are important ones. As the box "Reading and Evaluating Documents" indicates, there is an art in knowing how to regard such documents and what to make of them.

In this box, the critical review that Ron Aminzade and Barbara Laslett urge for the reading of historical documents can serve you in more areas of your life than just the pursuit of historical/comparative research. Consider applying some of their questions with regard to presidential press conferences, advertising, or (gasp) college textbooks. None of these offers a direct view of reality; all have human authors and human subjects.

Analytical Techniques

I want to conclude this section of the chapter with some comments regarding the analysis of historical/comparative data. Because historical/comparative research is a qualitative method, there are no easily listed steps to follow in the analysis of historical data.

Max Weber used the German term *verstehen*—"understanding"—in reference to an essential quality of social research. He meant that the researcher must be able to take on, mentally, the circumstances, views, and feelings of those being studied to interpret their actions appropriately.

The historical/comparative researcher must find patterns among the voluminous details describing the subject matter of study. Often this takes the form of what Weber called *ideal types*: conceptual models composed of the essential characteristics of social phenomena. Thus, for example, Weber himself did considerable research on bureaucracy. Having observed numerous actual bureaucracies, Weber ([1925] 1946) detailed those qualities essential to bureaucracies in general: jurisdictional areas, hierarchically structured authority, written files, and so on. Weber did not merely list those characteristics common to all the actual bureaucracies he observed. Rather, he needed to understand fully the essentials of bureaucratic operation to create a theoretical model of the "perfect" (ideal type) bureaucracy.

Often historical/comparative research is informed by a particular theoretical paradigm. Thus Marxist scholars may undertake historical analyses of particular situations—such as the history of Latino minorities in the United States—to determine whether they can be understood in terms of the Marxist version of conflict theory. Sometimes, historical/comparative researchers attempt to replicate prior studies in new situations—for example, Bellah's study of Tokugawa religion in the context of Weber's studies of religion and economics.

Reading and Evaluating Documents

by Ron Aminzade and Barbara Laslett
University of Minnesota

THE purpose of the following comments is to give you some sense of the kind of interpretive work historians do and the critical approach they take toward their sources. It should help you to appreciate some of the skills historians develop in their efforts to reconstruct the past from residues, to assess the evidentiary status of different types of documents, and to determine the range of permissible inferences and interpretations. Here are some of the questions historians ask about documents:

1. Who composed the documents? Why were they written? Why have they survived all these years? What methods were used to acquire the information contained in the documents?
2. What are some of the biases in the documents and how might you go about checking or correcting them? How inclusive or representative is the sample of individuals, events, and so on, contained in the document? What were the institutional constraints and the general organizational routines under which the document was prepared? To what extent does the document provide

---

While historical/comparative research is often regarded as a qualitative rather than quantitative technique, this is by no means necessary. Historical analysts sometimes use *time-series* data to monitor changing conditions over time, such as data on population, crime rates, unemployment, infant mortality rates, and so forth. The analysis of such data sometimes requires sophistication, however.

Larry Isaac and Larry Griffin (1989) discuss the uses of a variation on regression techniques (see Chapter 17) in determining the meaningful breaking points in historical processes as well as for specifying the periods within which certain relationships occur among variables. Criticizing the tendency to regard history as a steadily unfolding process, the authors focus their attention on the statistical relationship between unionization and the frequency of strikes, demonstrating that the relationship has shifted importantly over time.

Isaac and Griffin raise several important issues regarding the relationship between theory, research methods, and the "historical facts" they address. Their analysis, once again, warns against the naive assumption that history as documented necessarily coincides with what actually happened.

This concludes our discussion of unobtrusive research methods. As you can see, social scientists have a variety of ways to study social life without having any impact on what they study.

■ MAIN POINTS

- Unobtrusive measures are ways of studying social behavior without affecting it in the process.
- Content analysis is a social research method appropriate for studying human communications. Besides being used to study communication processes, it may be used to study other aspects of social behavior.
- Units of communication, such as words, paragraphs, and books, are common units of analysis in content analysis.
- Standard probability sampling techniques are sometimes appropriate in content analysis.
- Manifest content refers to the directly visible, objectively identifiable characteristics of a communication, such as the specific words in a book, the specific colors used in a painting, and so forth.

more of an index of institutional activity than of the phenomenon being studied? What is the time lapse between the observation of the events documented and the witnesses' documentation of them? How confidential or public was the document meant to be? What role did etiquette, convention, and custom play in the presentation of the material contained within the document? If you relied solely upon the evidence contained in these documents, how might your vision of the past be distorted? What other kinds of documents might you look at for evidence on the same issues?

3. What are the key categories and concepts used by the writer of the document to organize the information presented? What selectivities or silences result from these categories of thought?
4. What sorts of theoretical issues and debates do these documents cast light on? What kinds of historical and/or sociological questions do they help to answer? What sorts of valid inferences can one make from the information contained in these documents? What sorts of generalizations can one make on the basis of the information contained in these documents?

- Latent content refers to the meanings contained within communications. The determination of latent content requires judgments on the part of the researcher.
- Coding is the process of transforming raw data—either manifest or latent content—into categories.
- Both quantitative and qualitative techniques are appropriate for interpreting content analysis data.
- A variety of government and nongovernment agencies provide aggregate data for studying aspects of social life.
- The ecological fallacy refers to the possibility that patterns found at a group level differ from those that would be found on an individual level; thus we can be misled when we analyze aggregated data for the purpose of understanding individual behavior.
- The problem of validity in connection with the analysis of existing statistics can often be handled through logical reasoning and replication.
- Existing statistics often have problems of reliability, so we must use them with caution.

- Social scientists can use historical/comparative methods to discover patterns in the histories of different cultures.
- An ideal type is a conceptual model composed of the essential qualities of a social phenomenon.

■ REVIEW QUESTIONS AND EXERCISES

1. In two or three paragraphs, outline a content analysis design to determine whether the Republican or the Democratic party is the more supportive of free speech. Be sure to specify units of analysis, sampling methods, and the relevant measurements.
2. Social scientists often contrast the sense of "community" in villages, small towns, and neighborhoods with life in large, urban societies. Try your hand at constructing an ideal type of community, listing its essential qualities.
3. Locate pictures from three non-American social settings on the Web. What social features do the different locations share in common? How do they differ? Include the pictures with

your report, either on paper or as Web addresses (URLs).

ADDITIONAL READINGS

Baker, Vern, and Charles Lambert. "The National Collegiate Athletic Association and the Governance of Higher Education." *Sociological Quarterly* 31, no. 3 (1990: 403–21). A historical analysis of the factors producing and shaping the NCAA.

Berg, Bruce L. *Qualitative Research Methods for the Social Sciences.* Boston: Allyn and Bacon, 1989. Contains excellent materials on unobtrusive measures, including a chapter on content analysis. While focusing on qualitative research, Berg shows the logical links between qualitative and quantitative approaches.

Evans, William. "Computer-Supported Content Analysis: Trends, Tools, and Techniques." *Social Science Computer Review* 14, No. 3 (1996): 269–79. Here's a review of current computer software for content analysis, such as CETA, DICTION, INTEXT, MCCA, MECA, TEXTPACK, VBPro, and WORDLINK.

Øyen, Else, ed. *Comparative Methodology: Theory and Practice in International Social Research.* Newbury Park, CA: Sage, 1990. Here are a variety of viewpoints on different aspects of comparative research. Appropriately, the contributors are from many different countries.

U.S. Bureau of the Census. *Statistical Abstract of the United States, 1996, National Data Book and Guide to Sources.* Washington, DC: U.S. Government Printing Office, 1996. This is absolutely the best book bargain available (present company excluded). Although the hundreds of pages of tables of statistics are not exciting bedtime reading—the plot is a little thin—it is an absolutely essential resource volume for every social scientist. This document is now also available on CD-ROM.

Webb, Eugene T., Donald T. Campbell, Richard D. Schwartz, Lee Sechrest, and Janet Belew Grove. *Nonreactive Measures in the Social Sciences.* Boston: Houghton Mifflin, 1981. A compendium of unobtrusive measures. Includes physical traces, a variety of archival sources, and observation. Good discussion of the ethics involved and the limitations of such measures.

Weber, Robert Philip. *Basic Content Analysis.* Newbury Park, CA: Sage, 1990. Here's an excellent beginner's book for the design and execution of content analysis. Both general issues and specific techniques are presented.

CHAPTER 13 *Evaluation Research*

What You'll Learn in This Chapter

Now you're going to see one of the most rapidly growing uses of social research: the evaluation of social interventions. You'll come away from this chapter able to judge whether social programs have succeeded or failed.

INTRODUCTION

TOPICS COMMONLY SUBJECTED TO EVALUATION RESEARCH

FORMULATING THE PROBLEM
Measurement
Experimental Designs
Quasi-Experimental Designs
Operationalizing Success/Failure
Qualitative Evaluations

THE SOCIAL CONTEXT
Logistical Problems
Some Ethical Issues
Use of Research Results

SOCIAL INDICATORS RESEARCH
The Death Penalty and Deterrence
Computer Simulation

MAIN POINTS

REVIEW QUESTIONS AND EXERCISES

ADDITIONAL READINGS

INTRODUCTION

You may not be familiar with *Twende na Wakati* ("Let's Go with the Times"), but it's the most popular radio show in Tanzania. It's a soap opera. The main character, Mkwaju, is a truck driver with some pretty traditional ideas about gender roles and sex. By contrast, Fundi Mitindo, a tailor, and his wife, Mama Waridi, have more modern ideas regarding the roles of men and women and, particularly, on the issues of overpopulation and family planning.

Twende na Wakati was the creation of Population Communications International (PCI) and other organizations working in conjunction with the Tanzanian government in response to two problems facing that country today: (1) a population growth rate over twice that of the rest of the world and (2) an AIDS epidemic particularly heavy along the international truck route, where more than a fourth of the truck drivers and over half the commercial sex workers were found to be HIV positive in 1991. The prevalence of contraceptive use was 11 percent (Rogers et al. 1996:5–6).

The purpose of the soap opera was to bring about a change in knowledge, attitudes, and practices (KAP) relating to contraception and family planning. Rather than instituting a conventional educational campaign, PCI felt it would be more effective to illustrate the message through entertainment.

Between 1993 and 1995, 108 episodes of *Twende na Wakati* were aired, aiming at the 67 percent of Tanzanians who listen to the radio. Eighty-four percent of the radio listeners reported listening to the PCI soap opera, making it the most popular show in the country. Ninety percent of the show's listeners recognized Mkwaju, the sexist truck driver, and only three percent regarded him as a positive role model. Over two-thirds identified Mama Wardi, a businesswoman, and her tailor husband as positive role models.

Surveys conducted to measure the impact of the show indicated it had affected knowledge, attitudes, and behavior. For example, 49 percent of the married women who listened to the show said they now practiced family planning, compared with only 19 percent of the nonlisteners. There were other impacts:

■ Some 72 percent of the listeners in 1994 said that they adopted an HIV/AIDS prevention behavior because of listening to *"Twende na Wakati,"* and this percentage increased to 82 percent in our 1995 survey. Seventy-seven percent of these individuals adopted monogamy, 16 percent began using condoms, and 6 percent stopped sharing razors and/or needles.

(Rogers et al. 1996:21)

We can judge the effectiveness of the soap opera because of a particular form of social science. *Evaluation research*—sometimes called *program evaluation*—refers to a research purpose rather than a specific research method. This purpose is to evaluate the impact of social interventions such as new teaching methods, innovations in parole, and a wide variety of such programs. Many methods—surveys, experiments, and so on—can be used in evaluation research.

Evaluation research is probably as old as general social research itself. Whenever people have instituted a social reform for a specific purpose, they have paid attention to its actual consequences, even if they have not always done so in a conscious, deliberate, or sophisticated fashion. In recent years, however, the field of evaluation research has become an increasingly popular and active research specialty, as reflected in textbooks, courses, and projects. The growth of evaluation research also indicates a more general trend in the social sciences. As a consequence, you'll likely read increasing numbers of evaluation reports, and as a researcher you'll likely be asked to conduct evaluations.

In part, the growth of evaluation research no doubt reflects social scientists' increasing desire to make an actual difference in the world. At the same time, we can't discount the influence of (1) increased federal requirements for program evaluations to accompany the implementation of new programs and (2) the availability of research funds to fulfill that requirement. Whatever the mixture of these influences, it seems clear that social scientists will be bringing their skills into the real world more than ever before.

In this chapter, we're going to look at some of the key elements in this form of social research. We'll start by considering the kinds of topics commonly subjected to evaluation, and then we'll move through some of the main operational aspects of it: measurement, study design, and execution. As you'll see, formulating questions is as important as answering them. Because it occurs within real life, evaluation research has special problems, some of which we'll examine. Apart from particular logistical problems, special ethical issues arise from evaluation research generally and in its specific, technical procedures. As you review reports of program evaluations, you should be especially sensitive to these problems.

Evaluation is a form of *applied* research—intended to have some real-world effect. It will be useful, therefore, to consider whether and how it is actually applied. As you'll see, the clear and obvious implications of an evaluation research project do not necessarily affect real life. They may become the focus of ideological, rather than scientific, debates. They may simply be denied out of hand, as for political reasons. Or, perhaps most typically, they are simply ignored and forgotten, left to warp on shelves and collect dust in bookcases across the land.

To conclude this chapter, I'm going to focus on a particular resource for large-scale evaluation—*social indicators research*. This type of research is also a rapidly growing specialty. Essentially it involves the creation of aggregated indicators of the "health" of society, similar to the economic indicators that give diagnoses and prognoses of economies.

■ TOPICS COMMONLY SUBJECTED TO EVALUATION RESEARCH

Most fundamentally, evaluation research is appropriate whenever some social intervention occurs or is planned. A *social intervention* is an action taken within a social context for the purpose of producing some intended result. In its simplest sense, evaluation research is a process of determining whether the intended result was produced.

The substantive topics appropriate to evaluation research are limitless. When the federal government abolished the selective service system, military researchers began paying special attention to the impact on enlistments. As individual states have liberalized their marijuana laws, researchers have sought to learn the consequences, both for marijuana use and for other forms of social behavior. Do no-fault divorce reforms increase the number of divorces, and are related social problems lessened or increased? Has no-fault automobile insurance really brought down insurance policy premiums?

A project evaluating the nation's driver education programs, conducted by the National Highway and Transportation Safety Administration (NHTSA), stirred up a controversy. Philip Hilts reports on its findings:

> ■ For years the auto insurance industry has given large insurance discounts for children who take drivers' education courses, because statistics show that they have fewer accidents.
>
> The preliminary results of a new major study, however, indicate that drivers' education does not prevent or reduce the incidence of traffic accidents at all.
>
> (HILTS 1981:4)

Based on an analysis of 17,500 young people in DeKalb County, Georgia (including Atlanta), the preliminary findings indicate that students who take driver training have just as many accidents and traffic violations as those who don't. Although the matter has not been fully resolved, the study has already revealed some subtle aspects of driver training.

First, it suggests that the apparent impact of driver education is largely a matter of self-selection. The kind of students who take driver education are less likely to have accidents and traffic violations—with or without driver training. Students with high grades, for example, are more likely to sign up for driver training, and they are also less likely to have accidents.

More startling, however, is the suggestion that driver training courses may actually *increase* traffic accidents! The existence of driver education may encourage some students to get their licenses earlier than if there were no such courses. In a study of ten Connecticut towns that discontinued driver training, it was found that about three-fourths of those who probably would have been licensed through their classes delayed getting licenses until they were 18 and older (Hilts 1981:4).

As you might imagine, the preliminary results have not been well received by those most closely associated with driver training. This matter was complicated, moreover, by the fact that the NHTSA study was also evaluating a new, more intensive training program—and the preliminary results showed the new program was effective.

Here's a very different example of evaluation research. Rudolf Andorka, a Hungarian sociologist, has been particularly interested in his country's shift to a market economy. Even before the dramatic events in Eastern Europe in 1989, Andorka and his colleagues had been monitoring the nation's "second economy"—jobs pursued outside the socialist economy. Their surveys have followed the rise and fall of such jobs and have examined their impact within Hungarian society. One conclusion was that "the second economy, which earlier probably tended to diminish income inequalities or at least improved the standard of living of the poorest part of the population, in the 1980s increasingly contributed to the growth of inequalities" (Andorka 1990:111).

As you can see, the questions appropriate to evaluation research are of great practical significance: Jobs, programs, and investments as well as beliefs and values are at stake. Let's now examine how these questions are answered—how evaluations are conducted.

■ FORMULATING THE PROBLEM

Several years ago, I headed an institutional research office that conducted research of direct relevance to the operation of the university. Often, we were asked to evaluate new programs in the curriculum. The following description is fairly typical of the problem that arose in that context, and it points to one of the key barriers to good evaluation research.

Faculty members would appear at my office to say they'd been told by the university administration to arrange for an evaluation of the new program they'd been given permission to try. This points to a common problem: Often the people whose programs are being evaluated aren't thrilled at the prospect. For them, an independent evaluation threatens the survival of the program and perhaps even their jobs.

The main problem I want to introduce, however, has to do with the purpose of the intervention to be evaluated. The question "What is the intended result of the new program?" often produced a rather vague response; for example, "Students will get an in-depth and genuine understanding of mathematics, instead of simply memorizing methods of calculations." Fabulous! And how could we measure that "in-depth and genuine understanding"? Often, I was told that the program aimed at producing something that could not be measured by conventional aptitude and achievement tests. No problem there; that's to be expected when we're innovating and being unconventional. What would be an unconventional measure of the intended result? Sometimes this discussion came down to an assertion that the effects of the program would be "unmeasurable."

There's the common rub in evaluation research: measuring the "unmeasurable." Evaluation research is a matter of finding out whether something is there or not there, whether something happened or didn't happen. To conduct evaluation research, we must be able to operationalize, observe, and recognize the presence or absence of what is under study.

Often, outcomes can be derived from published program documents. Thus, when Edward Howard and Darlene Norman (1981) evaluated the performance of the Vigo County Public Library in Indiana, they began with the statement of purpose previously adopted by the library's Board of Trustees.

- To acquire by purchase or gift, and by recording and production, relevant and potentially useful information that is produced by, about, or for the citizens of the community;

To organize this information for efficient delivery and convenient access, furnish the equipment necessary for its use, and provide assistance in its utilization; and

To effect maximum use of this information toward making the community a better place in which to live through aiding the search for understanding by its citizens.

(1981:306)

As the researchers said, "Everything that VCPL does can be tested against the Statement of Purpose." They then set about creating operational measures appropriate to each of the purposes.

While "official" purposes of interventions are often the key to designing an evaluation, this may not always be sufficient. Anna-Marie Madison (1992), for example, warns that programs designed to help disadvantaged minorities do not always reflect what the targets of the aid may need and desire.

- The cultural biases inherent in how middle-class white researchers interpret the experiences of low-income minorities may lead to erroneous assumptions and faulty propositions concerning causal relationships, to invalid social theory, and consequently to invalid program theory. Descriptive theories derived from faulty premises, which have been legitimized in the literature as existing knowledge, may have negative consequences for program participants.

(1992:38)

In setting up an evaluation, then, researchers must construct a research design that clearly specifies the appropriate outcomes of the program. Let's see some of the elements in such a design.

Measurement

This book's earlier discussions of measurement all apply to evaluation research. In the present case, it will be most useful to focus our attention on what should be measured.

Specifying Outcomes Clearly, a key variable for evaluation researchers to measure is the outcome or response variable. If a social program is intended to accomplish something, we must be able to measure that something. If we want to reduce prejudice, we need to be able to measure prejudice. If we want to increase marital harmony, we need to be able to measure that.

It is essential to achieve agreements on definitions in advance:

- The most difficult situation arises when there is disagreement as to standards. For example, many parties may disagree as to what defines *serious* drug abuse—is it defined best as 15% or more of students using drugs weekly, 5% or more using hard drugs such as cocaine or PCP monthly, students beginning to use drugs as young as seventh grade, or some combination of the dimensions of rate of use, nature of use, and age of user? . . . Applied researchers should, to the degree possible, attempt to achieve consensus from research consumers in advance of the study (e.g., through advisory groups) or at least ensure that their studies are able to produce data relevant to the standards posited by all potentially interested parties.

(Hedrick, Bickman, and Rog 1993:27)

Sometimes the definitions of a problem and a sufficient solution are defined by law or agency regulations; you must be aware of such specifications and accommodate them. Moreover, whatever the agreed-on definitions, you must also achieve agreement on how the measurements will be made. Because there would be different methods for estimating the percentage of students "using drugs weekly," for example, you'd have to be sure all the parties involved understood and accepted the method(s) you've chosen.

In the case of the Tanzanian soap opera, there were several outcome measures. In part, they wanted to improve knowledge about both family planning and AIDS. Thus, for example, one show debunked the belief that the AIDS virus was spread by mosquitoes and could be avoided by the use of insect repellant. Studies of listeners showed a reduction in that belief (Rogers et al. 1996:21).

PCI also wanted to change Tanzanian attitudes toward family size, gender roles, HIV/AIDS, and other related topics; the research indicated that the show had affected these as well. Finally, the progam aimed at affecting behavior. We've already seen that radio listeners reported changing their behavior with regard to AIDS prevention. They reported a greater use of family planning as well. However, because there's always the possibility of a gap between what people say they do and what they actually do, the researchers sought independent, confirming data.

Tanzania's national AIDS-control program had been offering condoms free of charge to citizens. In the areas covered by the soap opera, the number of condoms given out increased sixfold between 1992 and 1994. This far exceeded the increase of 1.4 times in the control area, where broadcasters did not carry the soap opera.

Measuring Experimental Contexts Measuring the dependent variables directly involved in the experimental program is only a beginning. As Henry Riecken and Robert Boruch (1974:120–21) point out, it is often appropriate and important to measure aspects of the context of an experiment. Though external to the experiment itself, these variables do affect it. Consider, for example, an evaluation of a program aimed at training unskilled people for employment. The primary outcome measure would be their success at gaining employment after completing the program. You would, of course, observe and calculate the subjects' employment rate, but you should also determine what has happened to the employment/unemployment rates of society at large during the evaluation. A general slump in the job market should be taken into account in assessing what might otherwise seem a pretty low employment rate for subjects. Or, if all the experimental subjects get jobs following the program, you should consider any general increase in available jobs. Combining complementary measures with proper control group designs should allow you to pinpoint the effects of the program you're evaluating.

Specifying Interventions Besides making measurements relevant to the outcomes of a program, you must measure the program intervention—the experimental stimulus. In part, this measurement will be handled by the assignment of subjects to experimental and control groups, if that's the research design. Assigning a person to the experimental group is the same as scoring that person yes on the stimulus, and assignment to the control group represents a score of no. In practice, however, it's seldom that simple.

Let's stick with the job-training example. Some people will participate in the program; others will not. But imagine for a moment what job-training programs are probably like. Some subjects will participate fully; others will miss a lot of sessions or fool around when they are present. So we may need measures of the extent or quality of participation in the program. And if the program is effective, we should find that those who participated fully have higher employment rates than those who participated less.

Other factors may further confound the administration of the experimental stimulus. Suppose you and I were evaluating a new form of psychotherapy that's designed to cure sexual impotence. Several therapists administer it to subjects composing an experimental group. We'll compare the recovery rate of the experimental group with that of a control group (a group receiving some other therapy or none at all). It might be useful to include the names of the therapists treating specific subjects in the experimental group, since some may be more effective than others. If this turns out to be the case, we must find out why the treatment worked better for some therapists than for others. What we learn will further develop our understanding of the therapy itself.

Specifying Other Variables It's usually necessary to measure the population of subjects involved in the program being evaluated. In particular, it's important to define those for whom the program is appropriate. If we're evaluating a new form of psychotherapy, it's probably appropriate for people with mental problems, but how should we define and measure mental problems more specifically? The job-training program mentioned previously is probably intended for people who are having trouble finding work, but a more specific definition would be needed.

This process of definition and measurement has two aspects. First, the population of possible subjects for the evaluation must be defined. Then, ideally, all or a sample of appropriate subjects should be assigned to experimental and control groups as warranted by the study design. Beyond defining the relevant population, however, you should make fairly precise measurements on the variables considered in your definition. For example, even though the randomization of subjects in the psychotherapy study would insure an equal distribution of those with mild and severe mental problems in the experimental and control groups, we'd need to keep track of the relative severity of different subjects' problems in case the therapy turns out to be effective only for those with mild disorders. Similarly, we should measure such demographic variables as gender, age, race, and so forth in case the therapy works only for women, the elderly, or whatever.

Second, in providing for the measurement of these different kinds of variables, you must continually choose whether to create new measures or to use ones already devised by other researchers. If your study addresses something that's never been measured before, the choice is easy. If not, you'll have to evaluate the relative worth of various existing measurement devices in terms of your specific research situations and purpose. Recall that this is a general issue in social research that applies well beyond evaluation research. Let's examine briefly the advantages of the two options.

Creating measurements specifically for a study can offer greater relevance and validity. If the psychotherapy we're evaluating aims at a specific aspect of recovery, we can create measures that pinpoint that aspect. We might not be able to find any standardized psychological measures that hit that aspect right on the head. However, creating our own measure will cost us the advantages to be gained from using preexisting measures. Creating good measures takes time and energy, both of which could be saved by adopting an existing technique. Of greater scientific significance, measures that have been used frequently by other researchers carry a body of possible comparisons that might be important to our evaluation. If the experimental therapy raises scores by an average of ten points on a standardized test, we'll be in a position to compare that therapy with others that had been evaluated using the same measure. Finally, measures with a long history of use usually have known degrees of validity and reliability, but newly created measures will require pretesting or will be used with considerable uncertainty.

As you can see, you must take measurement quite seriously in evaluation research. You must carefully determine all the variables to be measured and get appropriate measures for each. However, you need to realize that such decisions are typically not purely scientific ones. Evaluation researchers often must work out their measurement strategy with the people responsible for the program being evaluated. It usually doesn't make sense to determine whether a program achieves Outcome X when its purpose is to achieve Outcome Y. (Realize, however, that evaluation designs sometimes have the purpose of testing for unintended consequences.)

There is a political aspect to these choices, also. Because evaluation research often affects other people's professional interests—their pet program may be halted, or they may be fired or lose professional standing—the results of evaluation research are often argued about.

Let's turn now to some of the evaluation designs commonly employed by researchers.

Experimental Designs

Chapter 9 has already given you a good introduction to a variety of experimental designs that researchers use in studying social life. Many of these designs apply to evaluation research. By way of illustration, let's see how the classical experimental model might be applied to our evaluation of the new psychotherapy mentioned previously.

Because the therapy is designed to cure sexual impotence, we should begin by identifying a population of patients relevant to the therapy. This identification might be made by researchers experimenting with the new therapy. Let's say we're dealing with a clinic that already has 100 patients being treated for sexual impotence. We might take that existing identification-definition as a starting point, and we should maintain any existing assessments of the severity of the problem for each specific patient.

For purposes of the evaluation research, however, we'll need to develop a more specific measure of impotence. Maybe it will involve whether patients have sexual intercourse at all (within a specified time), how often they have intercourse, or whether and how often they reach orgasm. Alternatively, the outcome measure might be based on the assessments of independent therapists not involved in the therapy who interview the patients later. In any event, we'll need to agree on the measures to be used.

In the simplest design, we would assign the 100 patients randomly to experimental and control groups; the former would receive the new therapy, and the latter would be taken out of therapy altogether for the course of the experiment. Because ethical practice would probably prevent withdrawing therapy altogether from the control group, however, it's more likely that the control group would continue to receive their conventional therapy.

Having assigned subjects to the experimental and control groups, we need to agree on the length of the experiment. Perhaps the designers of the new therapy feel it ought to be effective within two months, and an agreement could be reached. The duration of the study doesn't need to be rigid, however. One purpose of the experiment and evaluation might be to determine how long it actually takes for the new therapy to be effective. Conceivably, then, an agreement could be struck to measure recovery rates weekly, say, and let the ultimate length of the experiment rest on a continual review of the results.

Let's suppose the new therapy involves showing pornographic movies to patients. We'd need to specify that stimulus. How often would patients see the movies, and how long would each session be? Would they see the movies in private or in groups? Should therapists be present? Perhaps we should observe the patients while the movies are being shown and include our observations among the measurements of the experimental stimulus. Do some patients watch the movies eagerly but others look away from the screen? We'd have to ask these kinds of questions and create specific measurements to address them.

Having thus designed the study, all we have to do is "roll 'em." The study is set in motion, the observations are made and recorded, and the mass of data is accumulated for analysis. Once the study has run its course, we can determine whether the new therapy had its intended—or perhaps some unintended—consequences. We can tell whether the movies were most effective for patients with mild problems or severe ones, whether they worked for young subjects but not older ones, and so forth.

This simple illustration should show you how the standard experimental designs presented in Chapter 9 can be used in evaluation research. Many, perhaps most, of the evaluations you'll read about in the research literature, however, won't look exactly like this illustration. Being nested in real life, evaluation research often calls for quasi-experimental designs. Let's see what this means.

Quasi-Experimental Designs

Quasi-experiments are distinguished from "true" experiments primarily by the lack of random assignment of subjects to an experimental and a control group. In evaluation research, it's often impossible to achieve such an assignment of subjects. Rather than forgo evaluation altogether in such instances, you can sometimes create and execute research designs that give some evaluation of the program in question. In this section, I'll describe some of these designs.

Time-Series Designs To illustrate the *time-series design*—studies of processes occurring over time—I'll begin by asking you to assess the meaning of some hypothetical data. Suppose I come to you with what I say is an effective technique for getting students to participate in classroom sessions of a course I am teaching. To prove my assertion, I tell you that on Monday, only four students asked questions or made a comment in class; on Wednesday I devoted the class time to an open discussion of a controversial issue raging on campus; and on Friday, when we returned to the subject matter of the course, eight students asked questions or made comments. In other words, I contend, the discussion of a controversial issue on Wednesday has doubled classroom participation. This simple set of data is presented graphically in Figure 13-1.

Have I persuaded you that the open discussion on Wednesday has had the consequence I say it has? Probably you'd object that my data don't prove the case. Two observations (Monday and Friday) aren't really enough to prove anything. Ideally I should have had two classes, with students assigned randomly to each, held an open discussion in only one, and then compared the two on Friday. But I don't have two classes with random assignment of students. Instead, I've been keeping a record of class participation throughout the semester for the one class. This record would allow you to conduct a time-series evaluation.

Figure 13-2 presents three possible patterns of class participation over time—both before and after the open discussion on Wednesday. Which of these patterns would give you some confidence that the discussion had the impact I contend it had?

If the time-series results looked like the first pattern in Figure 13-2, you'd probably conclude that the process of greater class participation had begun on the Wednesday before the discussion and had continued, unaffected, after the day devoted to the discussion. The long-term data seem to suggest that the trend would have occurred even without the discussion on Wednesday. The first pattern, then, contradicts my assertion that the special discussion increased class participation.

The second pattern contradicts my assertion by indicating that class participation has been bouncing up and down in a regular pattern throughout the semester. Sometimes it increases from one class to the next, and sometimes it decreases; the open discussion on that Wednesday simply came at a time when the level of participation was about to increase. More to the point, we note that class participation decreased again at the class following the alleged postdiscussion increase.

FIGURE 13-1
Two Observations of Class Participation: Before and after an Open Discussion

Only the third pattern in Figure 13-2 supports my contention that the open discussion mattered. As we see, the level of discussion before that Wednesday had been a steady four students per class. Not only did the level of participation double following the day of discussion, but it continued to increase further afterward. Although these data do not protect us against the possible influence of some extraneous factor (I might also have mentioned that participation would figure into students' grades), they do exclude the possibility that the increase results from a process of maturation (indicated in the first pattern) or from regular fluctuations (indicated in the second).

Nonequivalent Control Groups The time-series design just described involves only an "experimental" group; you'll recall the value to be gained from having a control group. Sometimes, when you can't create experimental and control groups by random assignment from a common pool, you can find an existing "control" group that appears similar to the experimental group. If an innovative foreign language program is being tried in one class in a large high school, for example, you may be able to find another foreign language class in the same school that has a very similar student population: one that has about the same composition in terms of grade in school, gender, ethnicity, IQ, and so forth. The second class, then, could provide a point of comparison. At the end

FIGURE 13-2
Three Patterns of Class Participation in a Longer Historical Perspective

of the semester, both classes could be given the same foreign language test, and you could compare performances. Here's how two junior high schools were selected for purposes of evaluating a program aimed at discouraging tobacco, alcohol, and drug use:

■ The pairing of the two schools and their assignment to "experimental" and "control" conditions was not random. The local Lung Association had identified the school where we delivered the program as one in which administrators were seeking a solution to admitted problems of smoking, alcohol, and drug abuse. The "control" school was chosen as a convenient and nearby demographic match where administrators were willing to allow our surveying and breath-testing procedures. The principal of that school considered the existing program of health education to be effective and believed that the onset of smoking was relatively uncommon among his students. The communities served by the two schools were very similar. The rate of parental smoking reported by the students was just above 40 percent in both schools.

(McAlister et al. 1980:720)

In the initial set of observations, the experimental and control groups reported virtually the same (low) frequency of smoking. Over the 21 months of the study, smoking increased in both groups, but it increased less in the experimental group than in the control group, suggesting that the program had an impact on students' behavior.

Multiple Time-Series Designs Sometimes the evaluation of processes occurring outside of "pure" experimental controls can be made easier by the use of more than one time-series analysis. This design is an improved version of the nonequivalent control group design just described. Carol Weiss has presented a useful example of this design:

■ An interesting example of multiple time series was the evaluation of the Connecticut crackdown on highway speeding. Evaluators collected reports of traffic fatalities for several periods before and after the new program went into effect. They found that fatalities went down after the crackdown, but since the series had had an unstable up-and-down pattern for many years, it was not certain that the drop was due to the program. They then compared the statistics with time-series data from four neighboring states where there had been no changes in traffic enforcement. Those states registered no equivalent drop in fatalities. The comparison lent credence to the conclusion that the crackdown had had some effect.

(1972:69)

Although this study design is not as good as one in which subjects are assigned randomly, it's nonetheless an improvement over assessing the experimental group's performance without any comparison. That's what makes these designs quasi-experiments instead of just fooling around. The key in assessing this aspect of evaluation studies is *comparability,* as the following example illustrates.

A growing concern in the poor countries of the world, rural development has captured the attention and support of many rich countries. Through national foreign assistance programs and through international agencies such as the World Bank, the developed countries are in the process of sharing their technological knowledge and skills with the developing countries. Such programs have had mixed results, however. Often, modern techniques do not produce the intended results when applied in traditional societies.

Rajesh Tandon and L. Dave Brown (1981) undertook an experiment in which technological training would be accompanied by instruction in village organization. They felt it was important for poor farmers to learn how to organize and exert collective influence within their villages—getting needed action from government officials, for example. Only then would their new technological skills bear fruit.

Both intervention and evaluation were attached to an ongoing program in which 25 villages had been selected for technological training. Two poor farmers from each village had been trained in new agricultural technologies. Then they had been sent home to share their new knowledge with their fellow villagers and to organize other farmers into "peer groups" who would assist in spreading that knowledge. Two years later, the authors randomly selected two of the 25 villages (subsequently called Group A and Group B) for special training and 11 others as controls. A careful comparison of demographic characteristics showed the experimental and control groups to be strikingly similar to each other, suggesting they were sufficiently comparable for the study.

The peer groups from the two experimental villages were brought together for special training in organization-building. The participants were given some information about organizing and making demands on the government, and they were also given opportunities to act out dramas similar to the situations they faced at home. The training took three days.

The outcome variables considered by the evaluation all had to do with the extent to which members of the peer groups initiated group activities designed to improve their situation. Six types were studied. "Active initiative," for example, was defined as "active effort to influence persons or events affecting group members versus passive response or withdrawal" (Tandon and Brown 1981:180). The data for evaluation came from the journals that the peer group leaders had been keeping since their initial technological training. The researchers read through the journals and counted the number of initiatives taken by members of the peer groups. Two researchers coded the journals independently and compared their work to test the reliability of the coding process.

Figure 13-3 compares the number of active initiatives by members of the two experimental groups with those coming from the control groups.

Chapter 13: Evaluation Research

FIGURE 13-3
Active Initiatives over Time

Source: Rajesh Tandon and L. Dave Brown, "Organization-Building for Rural Development: An Experiment in India," *Journal of Applied Behavior Science,* April–June 1981, p. 182.

Similar results were found for the other outcome measures.

Notice two things about the graph. First, there is a dramatic difference in the number of initiatives by the two experimental groups as compared with the eleven controls. This would seem to confirm the effectiveness of the special training program. Second, notice that the number of initiatives also increased among the control groups. The researchers explain this latter pattern as a result of contagion. Because all the villages were near each other, the lessons learned by peer group members in the experimental groups were communicated in part to members of the control villages.

This example illustrates the strengths of multiple time-series designs in situations where true experiments are inappropriate to the program being evaluated.

Operationalizing Success/Failure

Potentially, one of the most taxing aspects of evaluation research is determining whether the program under review succeeded or failed. The purpose of the foreign language program mentioned earlier may be to help students better learn the language, but how much better is enough? The purpose of the conjugal visit program at a prison may be to raise morale, but how high does morale need to be raised to justify the program?

As you may anticipate, there are almost never clear-cut answers to questions like these. This dilemma has surely been the source of what is generally called *cost/benefit analysis.* How much does the program cost in relation to what it returns in benefits? If the benefits outweigh the cost, keep the program going. If the reverse, junk it. That's simple enough, and it seems to apply in straightforward economic situations: If it cost you $20 to produce something and you can sell it for only $18, there's no way you can make up the difference in volume.

Unfortunately, the situations usually faced by evaluation researchers are seldom amenable to straightforward economic accounting. The foreign language program may cost the school district $100 per student, and it may raise students' performances on tests by an average of 15 points. Because the test scores can't be converted into dollars, there's no obvious ground for weighing the costs and benefits.

Sometimes, as a practical matter, the criteria of success and failure can be handled through competition among programs. If a different foreign language program costs only $50 per student and produces an increase of 20 points in test scores, it would undoubtedly be considered more successful than the first program—assuming that test scores were seen as an appropriate measure of the purpose of both programs and the less expensive program had no negative, unintended consequences.

Ultimately, the criteria of success and failure are often a matter of agreement. The people responsible for the program may commit themselves in advance to a particular outcome that will be regarded as an indication of success. If that's the case, all you need to do is make absolutely certain that the research design will measure the specified outcome. I mention this obvious requirement simply because researchers sometimes fail to meet it, and there's little or nothing more embarrassing than that.

Qualitative Evaluations

While I've laid out the steps involved in tightly structured, mostly quantitative evaluation research, you should know that evaluations can also be less structured and more qualitative. For example, Pauline Bart and Patricia O'Brien (1985) undertook in-depth interviews with both rape victims and women who had successfully fended off rape attempts; the researchers wanted to evaluate different possible ways to stop rape.

Sometimes even structured, quantitative evaluations can yield unexpected, qualitative results. Paul Steel is a social researcher specializing in the evaluation of programs aimed at pregnant drug users. One program he evaluated involved counseling by public health nurses, who warned pregnant drug users that continued drug use would likely result in underweight babies, whose skulls would be an average of 10 percent smaller than normal. In his in-depth interviews with program participants, however, he discovered that the program omitted one important piece of information: that undersized babies were a bad thing. Many of the young women Steel interviewed thought that smaller babies would mean easier deliveries.

In another program, a local district attorney had instituted what would generally be regarded as a progressive, enlightened program. If a pregnant drug user were arrested, she could avoid prosecution if she would (1) agree to stop using drugs and (2) successfully complete a drug rehabilitation program. Again, in-depth interviews suggested that the program did not always operate on the ground the way it did in principle. Specifically, Steel discovered that whenever a young woman was arrested for drug use, her fellow inmates would advise her to get pregnant as soon as she was released on bail. That way, she would be able to avoid prosecution (personal communication, November 22, 1993).

The most effective evaluation research is one that combines qualitative and quantitative components. While making statistical comparisons is useful, so is gaining an in-depth understanding of the processes producing the observed results—or preventing the expected results from appearing.

The evaluation of the Tanzanian soap opera, presented earlier in this chapter, employed several research techniques. I've already mentioned the listener surveys and data obtained from clinics. In addition, the researchers conducted numerous focus groups to probe more deeply into how the shows impacted listeners. Also, content analyses were done on the soap opera episodes themselves and on the many letters received from listeners. Both quantitative and qualitative analyses were undertaken (Swalehe et al. 1995).

■ THE SOCIAL CONTEXT

Many of the comments in previous sections have hinted at the possibility of problems in the actual execution of evaluation research projects. Of course, all forms of research can run into problems, but evaluation research has a special propensity for it, and I want to draw your attention to some of these difficult aspects so you can recognize them in the reports you read. We're going to look at some of the logistical problems that can hinder evaluation research and at some of the special ethical issues evaluation touches. Finally, I'll make a few comments about using evaluation research results.

Logistical Problems

In a military context, *logistics* refers to moving supplies around—making sure people have food, guns, and tent pegs when they need them. Here, I use it to refer to getting subjects to do what they're supposed to do, getting research instruments distributed and returned, and other seemingly unchallenging tasks. These tasks are more challenging than you might guess!

Motivating Sailors When Kent Crawford, Edmund Thomas, and Jeffrey Fink (1980) set out to find a way to motivate "low performers" in the U.S. Navy, they found out just how many problems can occur. The purpose of the research was to test a three-pronged program for motivating sailors who were chronically poor performers and often in trouble aboard ship. First, a workshop was to be held for supervisory personnel, training them in effective leadership of low performers. Second, a few supervisors would be selected and trained as special counselors and role models—people the low performers could turn to for advice or just as sounding boards. Finally, the low performers themselves would participate in workshops aimed at training them to be more motivated and effective in their work and in their lives. The project was to be conducted aboard a particular ship, with a control group selected from sailors on four other ships.

To begin, the researchers reported that the supervisory personnel were not exactly thrilled with the program.

> ■ Not surprisingly, there was considerable resistance on the part of some supervisors toward dealing with these issues. In fact, their reluctance to assume ownership of the problem was reflected by "blaming" any of several factors that can contribute to their personnel problem. The recruiting system, recruit training, parents, and society at large were named as influencing low performance—factors that were well beyond the control of the supervisors.
>
> (CRAWFORD, THOMAS, AND FINK 1980:488)

Eventually, the reluctant supervisors came around and "this initial reluctance gave way to guarded optimism and later to enthusiasm" (1980:489).

The low performers themselves were even more of a problem, however. The research design called for pre- and posttesting of attitudes and personalities, so that changes brought about by the program could be measured and evaluated.

■ Unfortunately, all of the LPs (Low Performers) were strongly opposed to taking these so-called personality tests and it was therefore concluded that the data collected under these circumstances would be of questionable validity. Ethical concerns also dictated that we not force "testing" on the LPs.

(CRAWFORD ET AL. 1980:490)

As a consequence, the researchers had to rely on interviews with the low performers and on the judgments of supervisors for their measures of attitude change. The subjects continued to present problems, however.

Initially, the ship's command ordered 15 low performers to participate in the experiment. Of the 15, however, one went into the hospital, another was assigned duties that prevented participation, and a third went over the hill (absent without leave). Thus, the experiment began with 12 subjects. But before it was completed, three more subjects completed their enlistments and left the Navy, and another was thrown out for disciplinary reasons. The experiment concluded, then, with 8 subjects. Although the evaluation pointed to positive results, the very small number of subjects warrants caution in any generalizations from the experiment.

The special, logistical problems of evaluation research grow out of the fact that it occurs within the context of real life. Although evaluation research is modeled after the experiment—which suggests that the researchers have control over what happens—it takes place within frequently uncontrollable daily life. Of course, the participant-observer in field research doesn't have control over what is observed either, but that method doesn't strive for control. If you realize the impact of this lack of control, I think you'll start to understand the dilemma facing the evaluation researcher.

Administrative Control As suggested in the previous example, the logistical details of an evaluation project often fall to program administrators. Let's suppose you're evaluating a "conjugal visit" program in which married prisoners are allowed periodic visits from their spouses during which they can have sexual relations. On the fourth day of the program, a male prisoner dresses up in his wife's clothes and escapes. Although you might be tempted to assume that his morale was greatly improved by escaping, that turn of events would complicate your study design in many ways. Perhaps the warden will terminate the program altogether, and where's your evaluation then? Or, if the warden is brave, he or she may review the files of all those prisoners you selected randomly for the experimental group and veto the "bad risks." There goes the comparability of your experimental and control groups. As an alternative, stricter security measures may be introduced to prevent further escapes, and the security measures may have a dampening effect on morale. So the experimental stimulus has changed in the middle of your research project. Some of the data will reflect the original stimulus; other data will reflect the modification. Although you'll probably be able to sort it all out, your carefully designed study has become a logistical snakepit.

Maybe you've been engaged to evaluate the effect of race relations lectures on prejudice in the army. You've carefully studied the soldiers available to you for study, and you've randomly assigned some to attend the lectures and others to stay away. The rosters have been circulated weeks in advance, and at the appointed day and hour, the lectures begin. Everything seems to be going smoothly until you begin processing the files: The names don't match. Checking around, you discover that military field exercises, KP duty, and a variety of emergencies required some of the experimental subjects to be elsewhere at the time of the lectures. That's bad enough, but then you learn that helpful commanding officers sent others to fill in for the missing soldiers. And whom do you suppose they picked to fill in? Soldiers who didn't have anything else to do or who couldn't be trusted to do anything important. You might learn this bit of information a week or so before the deadline for submitting your final report on the impact of the race relations lectures.

These are some of the logistical problems confronting evaluation researchers. You need to be familiar with the problems to understand why some research procedures may not measure up to the design of the classical experiment. As you read reports of evaluation research, however, you'll find that—my earlier comments notwithstanding—it is possible to carry out controlled social research in conjunction with real-life experiments.

Just as evaluation research has special logistical problems, it also raises special ethical concerns. Because ethical problems can affect the scientific quality of the research, we should look at them briefly.

Some Ethical Issues

Ethics and evaluation are intertwined in many ways. Sometimes the social interventions being evaluated raise ethical issues. Evaluating the impact of busing school children to achieve educational integration will throw the researchers directly into the political, ideological, and ethical issues of busing itself. It's not possible to evaluate a sex education program in elementary schools without becoming involved in the heated issues surrounding sex education itself, and the researcher will find it difficult to remain impartial. The evaluation study design will *require* that some children receive sex education—in fact, you may very well be the one who decides which children do. (From a scientific standpoint, you *should* be in charge of selection.) This means that when parents become outraged that their child is being taught about sex, you'll be directly responsible.

Now let's look on the "bright" side. Maybe the experimental program is of great value to those participating in it. Let's say that the new industrial safety program being evaluated reduces injuries dramatically. What about the control group members who were deprived of the program by the research design? The evaluators' actions could be an important part of the reason that a control group subject suffered an injury.

Sometimes the name of evaluation research has actually been a mask for unethical behavior. I've already discussed push-polls, which pretend to evaluate the impact of various political campaign accusations but intend to spread malicious misinformation. That's not the worst example, however.

In 1932, researchers in Tuskegee, Alabama, began a program of providing free treatment for syphilis to poor, black men suffering from the disease. Over the years that followed, several hundred men participated in the program. What they didn't know was that they were not actually receiving any treatment at all; the physicians conducting the study merely wanted to observe the natural progress of the disease. Even after penicillin was found to be an effective cure, the researchers still withheld the treatment. While there is no doubt unanimous agreement today as to the unethical nature of the study, this was not the case at the time. Even when the study began being reported in research publications, the researchers refused to acknowledge they had done anything wrong. When professional complaints were finally lodged with the U.S. Center for Disease Control in 1965, there was no reply (J. Jones 1981).

My purpose in these comments has not been to cast a shadow on evaluation research. Rather, I want to bring home the real-life consequences of the evaluation researcher's actions. Ultimately, all social research has ethical components, and we'll return to this topic in Chapter 18.

Use of Research Results

There's one more facts-of-life aspect of evaluation research that you should be aware of. Because the purpose of evaluation research is to determine the success or failure of social interventions, you might think it reasonable that a program would automatically be continued or terminated based on the results of the research.

Reality isn't that simple and reasonable, however. Other factors intrude on the assessment of evaluation research results, sometimes blatantly and sometimes subtly. As president, Richard Nixon appointed a blue-ribbon national commission to study the consequences of pornography. After a diligent, multifaceted evaluation, the commission reported that pornography didn't appear to have any of the negative social consequences often attributed to it. Exposure to pornographic materials, for example, didn't increase the likelihood of sex crimes. You might have expected liberalized legislation to follow from the research. Instead, the president said the commission was wrong.

Less dramatic examples of the failure to follow the implications of evaluation research could be listed endlessly. Undoubtedly every evaluation researcher can point to studies he or she conducted—studies providing clear research results and obvious policy implications—that were ignored. I want to discuss this issue a bit, since your own evaluation of research reports may depend in part on whether others make use of the findings.

There are three important reasons why the implications of the evaluation research results are not always put into practice. First, the implications may not always be presented in a way that the nonresearchers can understand. Second, evaluation results sometimes contradict deeply held beliefs. That was certainly true in the case of the pornography commission. If everybody *knows* that pornography is bad, that it causes all manner of sexual deviance, then it is likely that research results to the contrary will have little immediate impact. By the same token, people thought Copernicus was crazy when he said the earth revolved around the sun. Anybody could tell the earth was standing still. The third barrier to the use of evaluation results is *vested interests*. If I have devised a new rehabilitation program that I'm convinced will keep ex-convicts from returning to prison, and if people have taken to calling it "the Babbie Plan," how do you think I'm going to feel when your evaluation suggests the program doesn't work? I might apologize for misleading people, fold up my tent, and go into another line of work. But more likely, I'd call your research worthless and begin intense lobbying with the appropriate authorities to have my program continue.

In the earlier example of the evaluation of driver education, Philip Hilts reported some of the reactions to the researchers' preliminary results:

■ Ray Burneson, traffic safety specialist with the National Safety Council, criticized the study, saying that it was a product of a group (NHTSA) run by people who believe "that you can't do anything to train drivers. You can only improve medical facilities and build stronger cars for when the accidents happen. . . . This knocks the whole philosophy of education."

(1981:4)

By its nature, evaluation research takes place in the midst of real life, affecting it and being affected by it. Here's another example, well known to social researchers.

Rape Reform Legislation For years, many social scientists and other observers have noted certain problems with the prosecution of rape cases. All too often, it is felt, the victim ends up suffering almost as much on the witness stand as in the rape itself. Frequently she is portrayed by the defense lawyers as having encouraged the sex act and being of shady moral character; other personal attacks are intended to deflect responsibility from the accused rapist.

Criticisms such as these have resulted in a variety of state-level legislation aimed at remedying the problems. Cassie Spohn and Julie Horney (1990) were interested in tracking the impact of such legislation. The researchers summarize the ways in which new laws were intended to make a difference:

■ The most changes are: (1) redefining rape and replacing the single crime of rape with a series of graded offenses defined by the presence or absence of aggravating conditions; (2) changing the consent standard by eliminating the requirement that the victim physically resist her attacker; (3) eliminating the requirement that the victim's testimony be corroborated; and (4) placing restrictions on the introduction of evidence of the victim's prior sexual conduct.

(1990:2)

It was generally expected that such legislation would encourage women to report being raped and would increase convictions when the cases were brought to court. To examine the latter expectation, the researchers focused on the period from 1970 to 1985 in Cook County, Illinois: "Our data file includes 4,628 rape cases, 405 deviate sexual assault cases, 745 aggravated criminal sexual assault cases, and 37 criminal sexual assault

TABLE 13-1
Analysis of Rape Cases before and after Legislation

	Rape	
	Before ($N = 2252$)	After ($N = 2369$)
Outcome of case		
Convicted of original charge	45.8%	45.4%
Convicted of another charge	20.6	19.4
Not convicted	33.6	35.1
Median prison sentence in months		
For those convicted of original charge	96.0	144.0
For those convicted of another charge	36.0	36.0

cases." (1990:4) Table 13-1 shows some of what they discovered.

The researchers summarize these findings as follows:

■ The only significant effects revealed by our analyses were increases in the average maximum prison sentences; there was an increase of almost 48 months for rape and of almost 36 months for sex offenses. Because plots of the data indicated an increase in the average sentence before the reform took effect, we modeled the series with the intervention moved back one year earlier than the actual reform date. The size of the effect was even larger and still significant, indicating that the effect should not be attributed to the legal reform.

(1990:10)

In addition to the analysis of existing statistics, Spohn and Horney interviewed judges and lawyers to determine what they felt about the impact of the laws. Their responses were somewhat more encouraging.

■ Judges, prosecutors and defense attorneys in Chicago stressed that rape cases are taken more seriously and rape victims treated more humanely as a result of the legal changes. These educative effects clearly are important and should please advocates of rape reform legislation.

(1990:17)

This study demonstrates the importance of following up on social interventions to determine whether, in what ways, and to what degree they accomplish their intended results.

Preventing Wife Battering In a somewhat similar study, researchers in Indianapolis have focused their attention on the problem of wife battering, with a special concern for whether prosecuting the batterers can lead to subsequent violence. David Ford and Mary Jean Regoli (1992) set about to study the consequences of various options for prosecution allowed within the "Indianapolis Prosecution Experiment" (IPE).

Wife-battering cases can follow a variety of patterns, as Ford and Regoli summarize:

■ After a violent attack on a woman, someone may or may not call the police to the scene. If the police are at the scene, they are expected to investigate for evidence to support probable cause for a warrantless arrest. If it exists, they may arrest at their discretion. Upon making such an on-scene arrest, officers fill out a probable cause affidavit and slate the suspect into court for an initial hearing. When the police are not called, or if they are called but do not arrest, a victim may initiate charges on her own by going to the prosecutor's office and swearing out a probable cause affidavit with her allegation against the man. Following a judge's approval, the alleged batterer may either be summoned to court or be arrested on a warrant and taken to court for his initial hearing.

(1992:184)

What if a wife brings charges against her husband and then reconsiders later on? Many courts have a policy of prohibiting such actions, in the belief that they are serving the interests of the victim by forcing the case to be pursued to completion. In the IPE, however, some victims are offered the possibility of dropping the charges, if they so choose later in the process. In addition, the court offers several other options. Since wife battering is largely a function of sexism, stress, and an inability to deal with anger, some of the innovative possibilities in the IPE involve educational classes with anger-control counseling.

If the defendant admits his guilt and is willing to participate in an anger-control counseling program, the judge may postpone the trial for that purpose and can later dismiss the charges if the defendant successfully completes the program. Alternatively, the defendant may be tried and, if found guilty, be granted probation provided he participates in the anger-control program. Finally, the defendant can be tried and, if found guilty, given a conventional punishment such as imprisonment.

Which of these possibilities most effectively prevents subsequent wife battering? That's the question Ford and Regoli addressed. Here are some of their findings.

First, their research shows that men who are brought to court for a hearing are less likely to continue beating their wives, no matter what the outcome of the hearing. Simply being brought into the criminal justice system has an impact.

Second, women who have the right to drop charges later on are less likely to be abused subsequently than those who do not have that right. In particular, the combined policies of arresting defendants by warrant and allowing victims to drop charges provides victims with greater security from subsequent violence than do any of the other prosecution policies (Ford and Regoli 1992).

However, giving victims the right to drop charges has a somewhat strange impact. Women who exercise that right are more likely to be abused later than those who insist on the prosecution proceeding to completion. The researchers interpret this as showing that future violence can be decreased when victims have a sense of control supported by a clear and consistent alliance with criminal justice agencies.

■ A decisive system response to any violation of conditions for pretrial release, including of course new violence, should serve notice that the victim-system alliance is strong. It tells the defendant that the victim is serious in her resolve to end the violence and that the system is unwavering in its support of her interest in securing protection.

(FORD AND REGOLI 1992:204)

The effectiveness of anger-control counseling cannot be assessed simply. Policies aimed at getting defendants into anger-control counseling seem to be relatively ineffective in preventing new violence. The researchers note, however, that the policy effects should not be confused with actual counseling outcomes. Some defendants scheduled for treatment never received it. Considerably more information on implementing counseling is needed for a proper evaluation, and the analysis continues.

Moreover, the researchers caution that the results of their research point to general patterns, and that individual battered wives must choose courses of action appropriate to their particular situations and should not act blindly on the basis of the overall patterns. The research is probably more useful in what it says about ways of structuring the criminal justice system (giving victims the right to drop charges, for example) than in guiding the actions of individual victims.

Finally, the IPE offers an example of a common problem in evaluation research. Often, actual practices differ from what might be expected in principle. For example, the researchers considered the impact of different alternatives for bringing suspects into court: Specifically, the court can issue either a summons ordering the husband to appear in court or a warrant to have the husband arrested. The researchers were concerned that having the husband arrested might actually add to his anger over the situation. They were somewhat puzzled, therefore, to find no difference in the anger of husbands summoned or arrested.

The solution of the puzzle lay in the discrepancy between principle and practice:

■ Although a warrant arrest should in principle be at least as punishing as on-scene arrest, in practice it may differ little from a summons. A man usually knows about a warrant for his arrest and often elects to turn himself in at his convenience, or he is contacted by the warrant service agency and invited to turn himself in. Thus, he may not experience the obvious punishment of, say, being arrested, handcuffed, and taken away from a workplace.

(FORD 1989:9–10)

By now, you've seen the various scientific and nonscientific aspects of evaluation research that affect the scientific quality of the results. You should now be prepared to design evaluation studies and to evaluate the evaluations you'll be reading in the research literature. I want to conclude this chapter with a type of research that combines what you've learned about evaluation research and the analysis of existing data.

■ SOCIAL INDICATORS RESEARCH

Now let's consider a special form of evaluation research hinted at in the earlier discussion of existing statistics. Another rapidly growing field in social research involves the development and monitoring of *social indicators*, aggregated statistics that reflect the social condition of a society or social subgroup. Similar to the way economists use indexes such as gross national product (GNP) per capita as an indicator of a nation's economic development, we can monitor aspects of society.

If we wanted to compare the relative health conditions in different societies, we could compare their death rates (number of deaths per 1,000 population). Or, more specifically, we could look at infant mortality: the number of infants who die during their first year of life among every 1,000 births. Depending on the particular aspect of health conditions we were interested in, we could devise any number of other measures: physicians per capita, hospital beds per capita, days of hospitalization per capita, and so forth. Notice that intersocietal comparisons are facilitated by calculating per capita rates (dividing by the size of the population).

Before we go further with social indicators, recall from Chapter 12 the problems involved in existing statistics. In a word, they're often unreliable, reflecting their modes of collection, storage, and calculation. With this in mind, we'll look at some of the ways we can use social indicators for evaluation research on a large scale.

The Death Penalty and Deterrence

Does the death penalty deter capital crimes such as murder? This question is hotly debated every time a state considers eliminating or reinstating capital punishment and every time someone is executed. Those supporting capital punishment often argue that the threat of execution will keep potential murderers from killing people. Opponents of capital punishment often argue that it has no effect in that regard. Social indicators can help shed some light on the question.

If capital punishment actually deters people from committing murder, then we should expect to find murder rates lower in those states that have the death penalty than in those that do not. The relevant comparisons in this instance are not only possible, they've been compiled and published. Table 13-2 presents data compiled by William Bailey (1975) that directly contradict the view that the death penalty deters murderers. In both 1967 and 1968, those states with capital punishment had dramatically *higher* murder rates than those without capital punishment. Some people criticized the interpretation of Bailey's data, saying that most states have not used the death penalty in recent years, even when they had it on the books. That could explain why it hasn't seemed to work as a deterrent. Further analysis, however, contradicts this explanation. When Bailey compared those states that hadn't used the death penalty with those that *had*, he found no real difference in murder rates.

Another counterexplanation is possible, however. It could be the case that the interpretation given Bailey's data was *backward*. Maybe the existence of the death penalty as an option was a consequence of high murder rates: Those states with high rates instituted it; those with low rates didn't institute it or repealed it if they had it on the books. It could be the case, then, that instituting the death penalty would bring murder rates

TABLE 13-2
Average Rate per 100,000 Population of First- and Second-Degree Murders for Capital-Punishment and Non–Capital-Punishment States, 1967 and 1968

	Non–Capital-Punishment States		Capital-Punishment States	
	1967	1968	1967	1968
First-degree murder	.18	.21	.47	.58
Second-degree murder	.30	.43	.92	1.03
Total murders	.48	.64	1.38	1.59

Source: Adapted from William C. Bailey, "Murder and Capital Punishment," in William J. Chambliss, ed., *Criminal Law in Action.* Copyright © 1975 by John Wiley & Sons, Inc. Used by permission.

down, and repealing it would increase murders and still produce—in a broad aggregate—the data presented in Table 13-2. Not so, however. Analyses over time do not show an increase in murder rates when a state repeals the death penalty nor a decrease in murders when one is instituted.

Notice from the preceding discussion that it's possible to use social indicators data either for comparison across groups at one time or across some period of time. Often, doing both sheds the most light on the subject.

At present, work on the use of social indicators is proceeding on two fronts. On the one hand, researchers are developing ever more refined indicators—finding which indicators of a general variable are the most useful in monitoring social life. At the same time, research is being devoted to discovering the relationships among variables within whole societies.

Computer Simulation

One of the most exciting prospects for social indicators research lies in the area of *computer simulation.* As we begin compiling mathematical equations describing the relationships that link social variables to one another (for example, the relationship between growth in population and the number of automobiles), those equations can be stored and linked to one another in a computer. With a sufficient number of adequately accurate equations on tap, we could one day test the implications of specific social changes by computer rather than in real life.

Suppose a state contemplated doubling the size of its tourism industry, for example. We could enter that proposal into a computer simulation model and receive in seconds or minutes a description of all the direct and indirect consequences of the increase in tourism. We could know what new public facilities would be required, which public agencies such as police and fire departments would have to be increased and by how much, what the labor force would look like, what kind of training would be required to provide it, how much new income and tax revenue would be produced, and so forth, through all the intended and unintended consequences of the action. Depending on the results, the public planners might say, "Suppose we increased the industry only by half," and have a new printout of consequences immediately.

An excellent illustration of computer simulation linking social and physical variables is to be found in the research of Donella and Dennis Meadows and their colleagues at Dartmouth and Massachusetts Institute of Technology. They have taken as input data known and estimated reserves of various nonreplaceable natural resources (for example, oil, coal, iron), past patterns of population and economic growth, and the relationships between growth and use of resources. Using a complex computer simulation model, they have been able to project, among other things, the probable number of years various resources will last in the face of alternative usage patterns in the future. Going beyond the initially gloomy projections, such models also make it possible to chart out less gloomy futures, specifying the actions required to achieve them. Clearly, the value of computer simulation is not limited to evaluation research, though it can serve an important function in that regard. *Stella* is a microcomputer version of the "system dynamics" analysis program used by the Meadows and others. (See Donella Meadows et al. 1972; Donella Meadows, Meadows, and Randers 1992.)

This potentiality points to the special value of evaluation research in general. Throughout human history, we've been tinkering with our social arrangements, seeking better results. Evaluation research provides a means for us to learn right away whether a particular tinkering really makes things better. Social indicators allow us to make that determination on a broad scale; coupling them with computer simulation opens up the possibility of knowing how much we would like a particular intervention without having to suffer through it for real.

■ MAIN POINTS

- Evaluation research is a good example of applied research in social science.
- Evaluation research is especially appropriate whenever a social intervention is undertaken.
- A careful formulation of the problem, including relevant measurements and criteria of success or failure, is essential in evaluation research.
- Evaluation researchers typically use experimental or quasi-experimental designs.
- A time-series design involves the observation of an experimental group over time. It is a weak design in that something other than the experimental stimulus may explain any observed change.
- Evaluation research can involve both quantitative and qualitative data analyses.
- Evaluation research entails special logistical and ethical problems because it is embedded in the day-to-day events of real life.
- The implications of evaluation research won't necessarily be put into practice, especially if they conflict with official points of view.
- Social indicators are aggregated descriptions of populations. They can provide an understanding of broad social processes.
- Sometimes computer simulation models can be constructed to point to the possible results of social intervention without our having to experience those results in real life.

■ REVIEW QUESTIONS AND EXERCISES

1. Review the evaluation of the Navy low-performer program discussed in the chapter. Redesign the program and the evaluation to handle the problems that appeared in the actual study.
2. Take a minute to think of the many ways your society has changed during your own lifetime. Specify those changes as social indicators that could be used in monitoring the quality of life in your society.
3. The U.S. Bureau of Prisons engages in evaluation research into various aspects of prison operations. Locate one of their studies and write a short summary of the study design and the findings. See http://www.bop.gov/oreindex.html

■ ADDITIONAL READINGS

Bennet, Carl A., and Arthur A. Lumsdaine, eds. *Evaluation and Experiment.* New York: Academic Press, 1975. Packed with illustrative examples, this reader digs into several special aspects of evaluation research. About every problem you're likely to hit is discussed in the book.

Burstein, Leigh, Howard E. Freeman, and Peter H. Rossi, eds. *Collecting Evaluation Data: Problems and Solutions.* Beverly Hills, CA: Sage, 1985. Here's an excellent collection of varied evaluation research projects, with special attention paid to data-collection issues.

Chen, Huey-Tsyh. *Theory-Driven Evaluations.* Newbury Park, CA: Sage, 1990. Chen argues that evaluation research must be firmly based in theory if it is to be meaningful and useful.

Cunningham, J. Barton. *Action Research and Organizational Development.* Westport, CT: Praeger, 1993. This book urges researchers to bridge the gap between theory and action, becoming engaged participants in the evolution of organizational life and using social research to monitor problems and solutions.

Hedrick, Terry E., Leonard Bickman, and Debra J. Rog. *Applied Research Design: A Practical Guide.* Newbury Park, CA: Sage, 1993. This introduction to evaluation research is, as its subtitle claims, a practical guide, dealing straight-on with the compromises that must usually be made in research design and execution.

Rossi, Peter H., and Howard E. Freeman. *Evaluation: A Systematic Approach.* Newbury Park, CA: Sage, 1993. This thorough examination of evaluation research is an excellent resource. In addition to discussing the key concepts of evaluation research, the authors provide numerous examples that might be useful in guiding your own designs.

Walker, Robert, ed. *Applied Qualitative Research.* Hants, England: Gower, 1985. Whereas surveys and experiments are commonly used in evaluation research, this book demonstrates that qualitative methods are also appropriate. In a study of police-community relations in London, for example, both surveys and participant observations were used.

PART 4 Analysis of Data

14 Quantifying Data
15 Elementary Analyses
16 The Elaboration Model
17 Social Statistics

IN THIS part of the book, we'll discuss the analysis of quantitative data, and we'll examine the steps that separate observation from the final reporting of findings.

Chapter 14 is addressed to the quantification of the data collected through the modes of observation discussed in Part 3. We'll look at the powerful impact computers have had in this respect.

The first of several discussions on the logic of quantitative data analysis is presented in Chapter 15. We'll begin with an examination of methods of analyzing and presenting the data related to a single variable. Then we'll turn to the relationship between two variables and learn how to construct and read simple percentage tables. The chapter ends with a preview of multivariate analysis.

Chapter 16 describes the elaboration model of data analysis developed by Paul Lazarsfeld at Columbia University. The concluding theme in

Chapter 15, multivariate analysis, will be picked up again and developed further. Chapter 16 will present the logic of causal analysis through the use of percentage tables. The same logic will then be applied when we use other statistical techniques in subsequent chapters.

Chapter 17 provides an introduction to some of the more commonly used statistical methods in social science research, including an overview of some of the more advanced methods of multivariate analysis. Rather than merely showing how to compute statistics by these methods (computers can do that), I've attempted to place them in the context of earlier theoretical and logical discussions. Thus, you should come away from this chapter knowing when to use various statistical measures as well as how to compute them.

CHAPTER 14 Quantifying Data

What You'll Learn in This Chapter

Having amassed a volume of observations, you may find it useful to transform them into a form appropriate to computer analysis. Here you'll see the social scientist's answer to microscopes, lasers, and cyclotrons.

INTRODUCTION

COMPUTERS IN SOCIAL RESEARCH
Enter Computers
Microcomputers

CODING
Developing Code Categories

CODEBOOK CONSTRUCTION

CODING AND DATA ENTRY OPTIONS
Transfer Sheets
Edge-Coding
Direct Data Entry

Data Entry by Interviewers
Coding to Optical Scan Sheets
Direct Use of Optical Scan Sheets
Connecting with a Data Analysis Program

DATA CLEANING
Possible-Code Cleaning
Contingency Cleaning

MAIN POINTS

REVIEW QUESTIONS AND EXERCISES

ADDITIONAL READINGS

INTRODUCTION

What the microscope was to biology, what the telescope was to astronomy—that's what the computer has been to quantitative social research. Moreover, you're taking this course at a time when the computer's contribution to social science is still being discovered. This chapter will introduce you to that contribution.

The purpose of this chapter is to describe methods of converting social science data into a *machine-readable form*—a form that can be read and manipulated by computers and similar machines used in **quantitative analysis.** If you conducted a quantitative research project more or less parallel to reading the chapters of this book, your data at this point would be in the form of completed questionnaires, content analysis code sheets, or the like. In the stage covered in this chapter, those data would be recorded on microcomputer diskettes, hard drive, or some other device that can be read and analyzed by the computer.

Given the pace of computer development and dissemination today, it is difficult to anticipate the kind of equipment actually available to you. As a result, I'm going to provide you with an overview of several stages in the evolution of computers in social research. This way, I'll probably at least touch on whatever you have to work with. Moreover, it's useful to know about the earlier equipment and techniques, since they sometimes reveal the logic of data analysis more clearly than today's advanced equipment and techniques—in the same sense that you can learn the fundamentals of how an automobile works more easily from a VW Bug than from the latest Maserati.

By the end of this discussion, I think you will realize you've picked a great time to learn social research. The tools now available and those due in the near future make research more exciting than ever before.

COMPUTERS IN SOCIAL RESEARCH

For our purposes, the history of computing in social research began in France in 1801, about the same time the seeds of modern social science itself were germinating. That's the year Joseph-Marie Jacquard created a revolution in the textile industry that would affect the most unlikely corners of life.

To facilitate the weaving of intricate patterns, Jacquard invented an automatic loom that took its instructions from punched cards. As a series of cards passed through the loom's "reader," wooden pegs poked through the holes punched in the cards, and the loom translated that information into weaving patterns. To create new designs, Jacquard needed merely to punch the appropriate holes in new cards, and the loom responded accordingly.

The point to be recognized here is that *information* (for example, a desired weaving pattern) could be *coded* and *stored* in the form of holes punched in a card and subsequently *retrieved* by a machine that read the holes and took action based on the meaning assigned to those holes.

The next step in our selective computer history takes place in the United States, during the 1890 census. As you may know, the U.S. Constitution mandates a complete census of the nation's population every ten years, beginning with the 1790 enumeration of just under 4 million U.S. citizens. As the new nation's population grew, however, so did the task of measuring it. The 1880 census enumerated over 62 million population—but it took the Census Bureau *nine years* to finish its tabulations. Clearly, a technological breakthrough was required before the 1890 census was conducted. The bureau sought suggestions.

Herman Hollerith, a former Census Bureau employee, had an idea. Hollerith had worked on the 1880 census. As a young engineering instructor at MIT, he proposed to adapt the Jacquard card to the task of counting the nation's population. As local tallies were compiled, they would be punched into cards. Then a tabulating machine of Hollerith's creation would read the cards and determine the population counts for the entire nation.

Hollerith's system was tested in competition with other proposals and found to be the fastest. As a result, the Census Bureau rented $750,000 worth of equipment from Hollerith's new Tabulating Machine Company, and the 1890 population total was reported within six weeks. Hollerith's company, incidentally, continued to develop new equipment, merged with other pioneering firms, and was eventually renamed the International Business Machines Corporation: IBM. By the 1950s, punched cards—commonly called *IBM cards*—were being adapted for the storage and retrieval of social research data, and they're still used, although rarely, for that purpose.

Enter Computers

Most data analyses today are conducted with computers, ranging from large, mainframe computers to small, personal microcomputers. A computer can go beyond simple counting and sorting to perform intricate computations and provide sophisticated presentations of the results. Popular computer programs examine several variables simultaneously and can compute a variety of statistics. Data stored on diskettes, hard drives, or CD-ROMs can be read much faster than punched cards allow. Computers can calculate complex statistics a good deal faster and more accurately than people can. In fact, the original "computers" *were* human—rooms full of mathematical clerks calculating military ballistics. When machines took over that function, the machines were also called computers.

Many computer programs today serve specifically to analyze social science data. Appendix I of this book gives some information and instructions about the use of one of the most popular of these: SPSS. If you can get a sense of how SPSS works, you'll understand the general logic of using computer programs to carry out data analyses.

Alternatively, you may have some other computer program available to you: ABtab, AIDA, A.STAT, BMDP, CRISP, DAISY, Data Desk, DATA-X, Dynacomp, INTER-STAT, MASS, Micro-Case, Microquest, Microstat, Micro-SURVEY, Minitab, POINT FIVE, P-STAT, SAM, SAS, SNAP, STATA, STAT80, Statgraf, Statpak, StatPro, STATS PLUS, Statview, Survey Mate, SURVTAB, SYSTAT, and TECPACS, to name just a few. Whatever program you use, the basic logic of data storage and analysis is the same.

Up until the late 1970s, all computer analyses were perfomed on large, expensive computers—sometimes called mainframe computers—maintained by centralized computer centers, and some analyses still are. To make use of such facilities, you needed to supply the data for analysis and the instructions for the analysis you want. Your instructions might have been in the form of an SPSS setup, as mentioned previously. And you might have taken your data to the computer center in the form of cards or a magnetic tape.

Subsequently, two developments improved the process just described. Remote job entry systems placed card readers and printers near the researchers and allowed them to submit jobs and receive their results at locations some distance from the computer center.

Time sharing was a further advance. In a sense, computers have always operated on a time-sharing basis—several users sharing the same computer. Initially, however, computer facilities were shared in a serial fashion: The computer would run your job, then mine, then someone else's. More sophisticated computers, however, could perform several different tasks simultaneously. They could read my request, analyze yours, and print out someone else's all at the same time. In fact, the tremendous speed of computers made it possible to sandwich small operations (which may take only thousandths of a second) in the middle of larger jobs.

This capacity made it possible for computers to handle requests from hundreds of users simultaneously, often giving the impression that each one had the computer's complete attention. Such interactions with the computer typically involved computer terminals—typewriting devices that either printed on paper or displayed their operations on video monitors that looked like television screens.

The use of computer time sharing in social research became even more practical with the development of portable computer terminals no larger than small, portable typewriters. Such terminals communicated with the computer over standard telephone lines. Thus you could take a portable terminal home or on a trip around the world.

Early telecommunications required you to fit the telephone receiver into two rubber cups—

called an *acoustical coupler*—on the terminal. Today, however, *modems*—either built into the computer or contained in an external device—can be connected directly into a standard telephone jack. Once connected, anything you type on the terminal is transmitted over telephone lines to the computer. It does what you ask and sends the results back to your terminal.

Today, you're most likely familiar with time sharing in the form of international computer networks such as the Internet, CompuServe, America Online, and the World Wide Web. The current revision of this textbook, for example, involved countless electronic communications with colleagues around the world. Research and teaching examples were found in electronic forums. Portions of the manuscript were sent electronically for review and comment. Appendix B examines the evolving cyberspace in more detail.

More relevant to our current discussion, computer networks make it possible for a researcher sitting at home in California to get a copy of a data set maintained on a computer in Massachusetts and to analyze those data using a program maintained on a computer in Texas. The results of the analysis would be returned to the user in California, and the results could also be stored for examination by a colleague in Russia. Procedures like this will likely become commonplace early in your research career. And before the end of your career, you'll look back on all this as primitive.

Microcomputers

The most useful and exciting development to date has been the *microcomputer,* and you've probably had some personal experience with it. These machines are small, complete computers, not much larger than a typewriter (or even smaller). Operations are displayed on some type of video-display screen. Information is stored on diskettes, hard drives, or CD-ROMs.

The microcomputer revolution has progressed so rapidly that it's easy to lose sight of how much things have changed in a relatively short time. When I was a graduate student at the University of California at Berkeley during the 1960s, the Survey Research Center had an IBM 1620 computer, which occupied approximately the same space as six or seven refrigerators. Its memory capacity was 24K, or approximately 24,000 characters worth of information. The IBM 1620 served the needs of 30 to 40 active researchers, who published numerous books and articles each year.

Right now, I'm working on a battery-operated laptop microcomputer about the size of a metropolitan telephone directory. Its memory is 48 megabytes: *2,000 times as much memory* as the old 1620. The pocket computer I use to maintain addresses and phone numbers has a memory 83 times that of the IBM 1620. The wristwatch I'm wearing has one-twelfth the memory of the huge machine that served the needs of 30 to 40 researchers at the Survey Research Center not that long ago!

The IBM 1620 stored data on cards that held 80 bytes of information on magnetic tapes holding a few thousands of bytes. Most microcomputers today use hard drives that store data in the millions of bytes (megabytes) or even gigabytes (billions of bytes). For example, my laptop has a hard disk that stores 3 gigabytes.

Finally, the advent of CD-ROMs has vastly expanded the storage capacity of microcomputers. A small, thin disk can store hundreds of millions of bytes of data. The "ROM" in CD-ROM stands for *read-only memory,* meaning that you can retrieve data stored there by the manufacturer but you cannot write anything new to the disk. The new generation of optical CDs allows both reading and writing. The Census Bureau's *Statistical Abstract* CD-ROM is a good example of the value of this development to social researchers. Also of general use are encyclopedias such as MicroSoft's *Encarta.* Historical researchers are possibly the most blessèd, with volumes of materials easily available on different historical periods and on specific topics.

Now you have an overview of the role played by computers in social research. The remainder of this chapter will discuss the steps and options involved in converting data into forms amenable to computer analysis. I'll present the coding process and enumerate the several methods of transforming data into a machine-readable form.

CODING

For computers to work their magic, they must be able to read the data you've collected in your research. Moreover, computers are at their best with numbers. If a survey respondent tells you that he or she thinks the biggest problem facing Stowe, Vermont, today is "the disintegrating ozone layer," the computer can't understand that response. You must translate: a process called coding. The discussion of content analysis in Chapter 12 dealt with the coding process in a manner close to our present concern. Recall that the content analysis must develop methods of assigning individual paragraphs, editorials, books, songs, and so forth with specific classifications or attributes. In content analysis, the coding process is inherent in data collection or observation.

To conduct a quantitative analysis when other research methods are employed, you often must engage in a coding process after the data have been collected. For example, open-ended questionnaire items result in nonnumerical responses, which must be coded before analysis. Or a field researcher might wish to undertake a quantitative analysis based on qualitative field notes. You might wish, for example, to quantify the open-ended interviews you conducted with participants in some social event under study.

As with content analysis, the task here is to reduce a wide variety of idiosyncratic items of information to a more limited set of attributes composing a variable. Suppose, for example, that a survey researcher has asked respondents, "What is your occupation?" The responses to such a question would vary considerably. Although it would be possible to assign each separate occupation reported a separate numerical code, this procedure would not facilitate analysis, which typically depends on several subjects having the same attribute.

The occupation variable has many preestablished coding schemes, none of them very good. One such scheme distinguishes professional and managerial occupations, clerical occupations, semiskilled occupations, and so forth. Another scheme distinguishes among different sectors of the economy: manufacturing, health, education, commerce, and so forth. Still others combine both.

The occupational coding scheme chosen should be appropriate to the theoretical concepts being examined in the study. For some studies, coding all occupations as either white-collar or blue-collar might be sufficient. For others, self-employed and not self-employed might be sufficient. Or a peace researcher might wish to know only whether the occupation depended on the defense establishment or not.

Although the coding scheme ought to be tailored to meet particular requirements of the analysis, one general guideline should be kept in mind. If the data are coded to maintain a great deal of detail, code categories can always be combined during analysis that does not require such detail. (Appendix I describes how to do this in SPSS.) If the data are coded into relatively few, gross categories, however, there's no way during analysis to recreate the original detail. Thus, you would be well advised to code your data in somewhat more detail than you plan to use in the analysis.

Developing Code Categories

There are two basic approaches to the coding process. First, you may begin with a relatively well-developed coding scheme, derived from your research purpose. Thus, as suggested previously, the peace researcher might code occupations in terms of their relationship to the defense establishment. Or let's suppose you've been engaging in participant observation of an emerging religious cult. You've been keeping careful notes of the reasons new members have given for joining. Perhaps you've developed the impression that new members seem to regard the cult as a substitute for a family. You might then review your notes carefully—coding each new member's comments in terms of whether this aspect of the cult was mentioned. You might also code their comments in terms of their own family status: whether they have a family or not.

If you're fortunate enough to have assistance in the coding process, your task would be to refine your definitions of code categories and show your coders how to assign given responses to the proper categories. You should explain the meaning of the code categories you've developed and give several examples of each. To make sure your coders fully understand what you have in mind, you should code several cases. Then your coders should be asked to code the same cases, without knowing how you coded them, and you should compare your coders' work with your own. Any discrepancies will indicate an imperfect communication of your coding scheme to your coders. Even with perfect agreement between you and your coders, however, you should still *check-code* at least a portion of the cases throughout the coding process.

If you're not fortunate enough to have assistance in coding, you should still obtain some verification of your own reliability as a coder. Nobody's perfect, especially a researcher hot on the trail of a finding. In your study of an emerging cult, let's suppose you have the impression that people who do not have a regular family will be the most likely to regard the new cult as a family substitute. The danger is that whenever you discover a subject who reports no family, you'll unconsciously try to find some evidence in the subject's comments that the cult is a substitute for family. If at all possible, then, you should try to get someone else to code some of your cases to see if that person would make the same assignments you made. (Note how this relates to *intersubjectivity* in science.)

The second approach to coding is appropriate whenever you're not sure initially how your data should be coded; that is, you don't know what variables they represent among your subjects of study. Suppose, for example, that you've asked, "How do you feel about a woman's right to an abortion for any reason?" Although you might anticipate coding responses as being positive, negative, or neutral, it's unlikely you could anticipate the full range of variation in responses. In such a situation, it would be useful to prepare a list of perhaps 50 or 100 actual responses to this open-ended question. You could then review that list, noting the different dimensions those responses reflect. Perhaps you would find several of the positive responses contained references to civil liberties; perhaps a number of the negative responses referred to religious beliefs.

Once you have developed a coding scheme based on the list of 50 or 100 responses, you should make sure that each of the listed responses fits into one of the code categories. Then you would be ready to begin coding the remaining responses. If you have coding assistance, the previous comments regarding the training and checking of coders would apply here; if you do not, the comments on having your own work checked apply.

Like the set of attributes composing a variable, and like the response categories in a closed-ended questionnaire item, code categories should be both exhaustive and mutually exclusive. Every piece of information being coded should fit into *one and only one* category. Problems arise whenever a given response appears to fit equally into more than one code category, or when it fits into no category.

■ CODEBOOK CONSTRUCTION

The end product of the coding process is the conversion of data items into numerical codes. These codes represent attributes composing variables, which, in turn, are assigned card and column locations within a data file. A **codebook** is a document that describes the locations of variables and lists the code assignments to the attributes composing those variables. A codebook serves two essential functions. First, it is the primary guide used in the coding process. Second, it is your guide for locating variables and interpreting codes in your data file during analysis. If you decide to correlate two variables as a part of your analysis of your data, the codebook tells you where to find the variables and what the codes represent.

Figure 14-1 is a partial codebook created from two variables from the General Social Survey. Though there is no one right format for a codebook, I've presented some of the common elements in this example.

FIGURE 14-1
A Partial Codebook

POLVIEWS
We hear a lot of talk these days about liberals and conservatives. I'm going to show you a seven-point scale on which the political views that people might hold are arranged from extremely liberal—point 1—to extremely conservative—point 7. Where would you place yourself on this scale?
1. Extremely liberal
2. Liberal
3. Slightly liberal
4. Moderate, middle of the road
5. Slightly conservative
6. Conservative
7. Extremely conservative
8. Don't know
9. No answer

ATTEND
How often do you attend religious services?
0. Never
1. Less than once a year
2. About once or twice a year
3. Several times a year
4. About once a month
5. 2–3 times a month
6. Nearly every week
7. Every week
8. Several times a week
9. Don't know, No answer

There are several elements worth noting in the partial codebook illustrated in this figure. First, each variable is identified by an abbreviated variable name: *POLVIEWS, ATTEND*. We can determine the church attendance of respondents, for example, by referencing *ATTEND*. In this example, I've used the format established by the General Social Survey, which has been carried over into SPSS. Realize that other data sets and/or analysis programs might format variables differently. Some use numerical codes in place of abbreviated names, for example. You must, however, have *some* identifier that will allow you to locate and use the variable in question.

Next, every codebook should contain the full definition of the variable. In the case of a questionnaire, this would be the exact wordings of the questions asked, because, as we've seen, the wording of questions strongly influences the answers returned. In the case of *POLVIEWS*, you know that respondents were handed a card containing the several political categories and asked to pick the one that best fit them.

Your codebook will also indicate the attributes composing each variable. Thus in *POLVIEWS*, respondents could characterize their political orientations as "Extremely liberal," "Liberal," "Slightly liberal," and so forth. Finally, notice that each attribute also has a numeric label: "Extremely liberal" in *POLVIEWS* is code category "1", for example. These numeric codes are used in various manipulations of the data: For example, you might decide to combine categories 1 through 3 (all the "liberal" responses). It's easier to do this using code numbers than with lengthy names.

■ CODING AND DATA ENTRY OPTIONS

Years ago, all data entry took the form of manual keypunching, with cards either analyzed by unit-record equipment or read into computers for more complex analyses. All that has changed. Data are now typically keyed directly into data files stored on computer disks. As before, however, this is intimately related to coding, and there are several methods for effecting this link. Let's look at a few of these possibilities.

Transfer Sheets

The traditional method of data processing involves the coding of data and the transfer of code assignments to a *transfer sheet* or *code sheet*. Such sheets were traditionally ruled off in 80 columns, corresponding to the data card columns, but they can be adapted to other data configurations appropriate to the data entry method. (Figure 14-2 provides an illustration.) Coders write numbers corresponding to the desired code categories in the appropriate columns of the sheets. The code

FIGURE 14-2
A Partial Coding Transfer Sheet

01	02	03	04	05	06	07	08	09	10	71	72	73	74	75	76	77	78	79	80
0	0	1	3	7	8	9	3	1	1	4	5	2	1	1	7	8	7	1	2
0	0	2	4	2	4	2	4	1	2	2	2	5	1	1	2	8	2	2	2
0	0	3	5	6	1	2	3	1	1	1	3	6	2	1	3	9	2	2	3
0	0	4	6	3	4	4	2	2	1	1	4	1	0	3	6	0	4	2	1

sheets are then used for keying data into computer files. This is still a useful technique when particularly complex questionnaires or other data source documents are being processed.

Edge-Coding

Edge-coding is sometimes used to do away with the need for transfer sheets. The outside margin of each page of a questionnaire or other data source document is left blank or is marked with spaces corresponding to variable names or numbers. Rather than transferring code assignments to a separate sheet, the codes are written in the appropriate spaces in the margins. The edge-coded source documents are then used for data entry.

Direct Data Entry

If the questionnaires or other data collection forms have been adequately designed, you can often enter data directly into the computer without using separate code sheets or even edge-coding. A precoded questionnaire would contain indications of the columns and the codes to be assigned to questions and responses, and data could be entered directly. (See Appendix D of this book for an example of a precoded questionnaire.)

Data Entry by Interviewers

The most direct data entry method in survey research has already been discussed in Chapter 10: computer-assisted telephone interviewing, or CATI. As you'll recall, interviewers with telephone headsets sit at computer terminals, which display the questions to be asked, and type in the respondents' answers. In this fashion, data are entered directly into data files as soon as they are generated. Closed-ended data are ready for immediate analysis. Open-ended data can be entered as well, but they require an extra step.

Let's say the questionnaire asks respondents, "What would you say is the greatest problem facing the United States today?" The computer terminal would prompt the interviewer to ask that question. Then, instead of expecting a simple numerical code as input, it would allow the interviewer to type in whatever the respondent said: for example, "crime in the streets, especially the crimes committed by drug dealers." Subsequently, coders could sit at computer terminals, retrieving the open-ended responses one by one and assigning numerical codes as discussed earlier in this chapter.

Coding to Optical Scan Sheets

Sometimes data entry can be achieved effectively through the use of an *optical scanner*. This machine reads black pencil marks on a special code sheet and creates data files to correspond with those marks. (These sheets are frequently called *op-sense* or *mark-sense* sheets.)

Coders can transfer coded data to such special sheets by blacking in the appropriate spaces. The sheets are then fed into an optical scanner, and data files are created automatically.

Although an optical scanner provides greater accuracy and speed than manual data entry, it has disadvantages as well. Some coders find it difficult to transfer data to the special sheets. It can be difficult to locate the appropriate column, and once the appropriate column is found, the coder must search for the appropriate space to blacken.

Second, the optical scanner has relatively rigid tolerances. Unless the black marks are sufficiently black, the scanner may make mistakes. Further, you'll have no way of knowing when this has happened until you begin your analysis. And if the op-sense sheets are folded or mutilated, the scanner may refuse to read them at all.

Direct Use of Optical Scan Sheets

Sometimes you can use optical scan sheets a little differently to avoid the difficulties they present. Survey respondents can sometimes be asked to record their responses directly on such sheets. Either standard or specially prepared sheets can be provided with instructions on their use. To answer questions presented with the several answer categories, respondents can be asked to blacken the spaces provided beside the answers they choose. If such sheets are properly laid out, the optical scanner can read and enter the answers directly. This method may be even more feasible in recording experimental observations or in compiling data in a content analysis.

Connecting with a Data Analysis Program

Different computer programs structure data sets in different ways. In most cases, you'll probably use your data analysis program for data entry. SPSS, for example, will present you with a blank matrix of rows and columns. You can assign variable names to the columns and enter data for each case (such as survey respondent) on a separate line. Once you're finished, your data will be ready for analysis.

As an alternative, you can often create your data set using some other means (such as a spreadsheet or a word processor) and then import the data into the analysis program. In the case of SPSS, for example, a text file with data items separated by tabs (such as *datafile.dat*) can be imported and then can be saved in the SPSS (such as *datafile.sav*) format. Subsequently, you can load the data file as though it had been initially created through SPSS. Most other data-analysis programs have similar options.

■ DATA CLEANING

Whichever data-processing method you have used, you will now have a set of machine-readable data that supposedly represent the information collected in your study. The next important step is the elimination of errors: "cleaning" the data.

No matter how, or how carefully, the data have been entered, some errors are inevitable. Depending on the data-processing method, these errors may result from incorrect coding, incorrect reading of written codes, incorrect sensing of blackened marks, and so forth.

Two types of cleaning should be done: *possible-code* cleaning and *contingency* cleaning.

Possible-Code Cleaning

For any given variable, there is a specified set of legitimate attributes, translated into a set of possible codes. In the variable *gender*, there will be perhaps three possible codes: 1 for male, 2 for female, and 0 for no answer. If a case has been coded 7, say, in the variable assigned to gender, it's clear that an error has been made.

Possible-code cleaning can be accomplished in two different ways. First, as we've seen, many of the computer programs available for data entry today can check for errors as the data are being entered. If you tried to enter a 7 for gender in such programs, for example, the computer might "beep" and refuse the erroneous code. Other computer programs are designed to test for illegitimate codes in data files that weren't checked during data entry.

If you don't have access to these kinds of computer programs, you can achieve a possible-code cleaning by examining the distribution of responses to each item in your data set. Thus if you find your data set contains 350 people coded 1 on gender (for female), 400 people coded 2 (for male), and one person coded 7, you'll probably suspect the 7 is an error.

Whenever you discover errors, the next step is to locate the appropriate source document (for example, the questionnaire), determine what code should have been entered, and make the necessary correction.

Contingency Cleaning

Contingency cleaning is more complicated. The logical structure of the data may place special limits on the responses of certain respondents. For example, a questionnaire may ask for the number of children that women have had. All female respondents, then, should have a response coded (or a special code for failure to answer), but no male respondent should have an answer recorded (or should only have a special code indicating the question is inappropriate to him). If a given male respondent is coded as having borne three children, either an error has been made and should be corrected or your study is about to become more famous than you ever dreamed.

Although data cleaning is an essential step in data processing, you can safely avoid it in certain cases. Perhaps you'll feel you can safely exclude the very few errors that appear in a given item—if the exclusion of those cases will not significantly affect your results. Or, some inappropriate contingency responses may be safely ignored. If some men have received motherhood status, you can limit your analysis of this variable to women. However, you should not use these comments as rationalizations for sloppy research. "Dirty" data will almost always produce misleading research findings.

■ MAIN POINTS

- The quantification of data is necessary when statistical analyses are desired.
- The observations describing each unit of analysis must be transformed into standardized, numerical codes for retrieval and manipulation by machine.
- A given variable is assigned a specific identifier in the data storage medium: either a number or an abbreviated name.
- The attributes of a given variable are represented by numerical codes.
- A codebook is the document that describes the identifiers assigned to different variables and the codes assigned to represent different attributes.
- Data entry can be accomplished in a variety of ways. Increasingly, data are keyed directly into computer files.
- A transfer sheet is a special coding sheet on which numerical codes are recorded. These transfer sheets are then used for data entry.
- Edge-coding is an alternative to the use of transfer sheets. The numerical coding is done in the margins of the original documents—such as questionnaires—instead of on transfer sheets.
- Optical-scan sheets (op-sense or mark-sense sheets) may be used in some research projects to save time and money in data processing. These are the familiar sheets used in examinations, on which answers are indicated by black marks in the appropriate spaces. Optical scanners are machines that read the black marks and transfer the same information to data files.
- Possible-code cleaning refers to the process of checking to see that only those codes assigned to particular attributes—possible codes—appear in the data files. This process guards against one class of data-processing error.
- Contingency cleaning is the process of checking to see that only those cases that *should* have data on a particular variable do in fact have such data. This process guards against another class of data-processing error.

■ REVIEW QUESTIONS AND EXERCISES

1. Find out the data-processing facilities available to social researchers on your campus and describe how survey questionnaires might be processed using those facilities.

2. Create a codebook—with variable and code assignments—for the following questions in a questionnaire:
   a. Did you vote in the 1992 general election?
      ☐ Yes ⟶ *If yes*, whom did you vote for in the mayor's race?
         ☐ Smith   ☐ Brown
      ☐ No
   b. Do you generally consider yourself a Republican, a Democrat, an Independent, or something else?
      ☐ Republican
      ☐ Democrat
      ☐ Independent
      ☐ Other:____
   c. What do you feel is the most important problem facing this community today?
   d. In the spaces provided below, please indicate the three community problems that most concern you by putting a 1 beside the one that most concerns you, a 2 beside your second choice, and a 3 beside your third choice.
      ____ Crime
      ____ Traffic
      ____ Drug abuse
      ____ Pollution
      ____ Prejudice and discrimination
      ____ Recession
      ____ Unemployment
      ____ Housing shortage
3. Over the years, the General Social Survey (GSS) has tracked public opinion on the Equal Rights Amendment (ERA), reporting the percentages in favor and opposed. Your assignment is to discover some of the reasons respondents have given for their opinions. Begin by going to

   http://www.icpsr.umich.edu/gss/append/apdxindx.htm

   Look through the appendixes, find the one dealing with the coding of opinions on ERA, and copy out three reasons people gave for supporting the ERA and three reasons they gave for opposing it.

■ ADDITIONAL READINGS

Fielding, Nigel G., and Raymond M. Lee, eds. *Using Computers in Qualitative Research*. Newbury Park, CA: Sage, 1991. While computers are primarily associated with quantitative research, this set of articles shows how powerfully they can be used with qualitative methods.

Hall, Larry D., and Kimball P. Marshall. *Computing for Social Research: Practical Approaches*. Belmont, CA: Wadsworth, 1992. An excellent introduction to computer hardware and software, useful whether you continue in social research or not.

Heise, David, ed. *Microcomputers in Social Research*. Beverly Hills, CA: Sage, 1981. This special issue of *Sociological Methods and Research* examines the role of the microcomputer in several areas of social research, including anthropology, urban planning, social-psychophysiology, and simulations of social systems. Contains some how-to discussions also.

Madron, Thomas W., C. Neal Tate, and Robert G. Brookshire. *Using Microcomputers in Research*. Newbury Park, CA: Sage, 1985. This book examines many different ways in which social researchers can profit from microcomputers, including data gathering, analysis, and writing, to name a few.

Saris, Willem E. *Computer-Assisted Interviewing*. Newbury Park, CA: Sage, 1991. Here's an up-to-date review of the *CADAC* (computer-assisted data collection) options available to modern social researchers.

CHAPTER 15 *Elementary Analyses*

What You'll Learn in This Chapter
You'll come away from this chapter able to perform several simple though powerful ways to manipulate data in order to reach research conclusions.

INTRODUCTION

UNIVARIATE ANALYSIS

Distributions
Central Tendency
Dispersion
Continuous and Discrete Variables
Detail versus Manageability

SUBGROUP COMPARISONS
"Collapsing" Response Categories
Handling "Don't Knows"
Numerical Descriptions in Qualitative Research

BIVARIATE ANALYSIS

Percentaging a Table
Constructing and Reading Tables
Bivariate Table Formats

INTRODUCTION TO MULTIVARIATE ANALYSIS

MAIN POINTS

REVIEW QUESTIONS AND EXERCISES

ADDITIONAL READINGS

Chapter 15: Elementary Analyses

■ INTRODUCTION

Most social science analysis falls within the general rubric of **multivariate analysis**, and the bulk of Part 4 of this book is devoted to a variety of multivariate analyses. This term refers simply to the examination of several variables simultaneously. The analysis of the simultaneous association among age, education, and prejudice would be an example of multivariate analysis.

You should realize that *multivariate analysis* is a general term and is not a specific form of analysis. Specific techniques for conducting a multivariate analysis include factor analysis, smallest-space analysis, multiple correlation, multiple regression, and path analysis. The basic logic of multivariate analysis can best be seen through the use of simple tables, called **contingency tables** or *cross-tabulations*. Thus the present chapter is devoted to the construction and understanding of such tables.

Multivariate analysis cannot be fully understood without a firm understanding of even more fundamental analytic modes: univariate and bivariate analyses. The chapter, therefore, will begin with these.

■ UNIVARIATE ANALYSIS

Univariate analysis is the examination of the distribution of cases on only one variable at a time. We'll begin with the logic and formats for the analysis of univariate data.

Distributions

The most basic format for presenting univariate data is to report all individual cases: that is, to list the attribute for each case under study in terms of the variable in question. Let's take the General Social Survey data on attendance at religious services, *ATTEND*. Table 15-1 presents the results of an SPSS analysis of this variable.

Let's examine the table, piece by piece. First, if you look near the bottom of the table, you'll see that the sample being analyzed has a total of 1,500 cases. You'll also see that 17 of the 1,500 respondents either said they didn't know (DK) or gave no answer (NA) in response to this question. So our assessment of U.S. attendance at religious services during the two decades from 1973 to 1993 will be based on the 1,483 respondents who answered the question.

Go back to the top of the table now. You'll see that 224 people said they never went to religious services. This number in and of itself tells us nothing about religious practices. If the data we're examining were based on 3,000 respondents instead of 1,500, we could assume that about 448 people would have said they never attended religious services. Neither the 224 nor the 448 gives us an idea of whether the "average American" goes to church a little or a lot.

By analogy, suppose your best friend tells you he or she drank a six-pack of beer. Notice that your reaction to that statement would depend on whether the beer had been consumed in a month, a week, a day, or an hour. In the case of religious participation, similarly, we need some basis for assessing the 224 who never attend church.

If you were to divide 224 by the 1,483 who gave some answer, you would get 15.1 percent, which appears in the table as the "valid percent." So we see that 15 percent, or roughly one U.S. adult in seven, reports never attending religious services.

Lest you think that people in the United States are generally nonreligious, look through Table 15-1 and find the response category most often chosen: EVERY WEEK, with 19.8 percent of the respondents giving that answer. Add to that the 8 percent who report attending religious services more than once a week, and we find that over a fourth (27.8 percent) of U.S. adults say they attend religious services *at least* once a week.

Sometimes it's easier to see a **frequency distribution** in a graph. Figure 15-1 was created by SPSS from the GSS data on *ATTEND*.

Central Tendency

Beyond simply reporting marginals, you may choose to present your data in the form of summary **averages** or measures of *central tendency*. Your options in this regard are the **mode** (the most frequent attribute, either grouped or un-

Univariate Analysis

TABLE 15-1
GSS Attendance at Religious Services, 1973–1993

```
Attend     How Often R Attends Religious Services
                                                    Valid        Cum
Value Label           Value  Frequency   Percent   Percent     Percent
NEVER                   0       224       14.9      15.1         15.1
LT ONCE A YEAR          1       139        9.3       9.4         24.5
ONCE A YEAR             2       180       12.0      12.1         36.6
SEVRL TIMES A YR        3       194       12.9      13.1         49.7
ONCE A MONTH            4        84        5.6       5.7         55.4
2-3X A MONTH            5       136        9.1       9.2         64.5
NRLY EVERY WEEK         6       114        7.6       7.7         72.2
EVERY WEEK              7       294       19.6      19.8         92.0
MORE THN ONCE WK        8       118        7.9       8.0        100.0
DK,NA                   9        17        1.1     Missing
                      Total    1,500     100.0     100.0

Valid cases    1,483      Missing cases    17
```

FIGURE 15-1
Bar Chart of GSS ATTEND, 1973–1993

grouped), the arithmetic **mean**, or the **median** (the middle attribute in the ranked distribution of observed attributes). Here's how the three averages would be calculated from a set of data.

Suppose you're conducting an experiment that involves teenagers as subjects. They range in age from 13 to 19, as indicated in the following table:

Age	Number
13	3
14	4
15	6
16	8
17	4
18	3
19	3

Now that you've seen the actual ages of the 31 subjects, how old would you say they are in general, or on the average? Let's look at three different ways you might answer that question.

The easiest average to calculate is the *mode*, the most frequent value. As you can see, there were more 16-year-olds (eight of them) than any other age, so the modal age is 16, as indicated in Figure 15-2.

This figure also demonstrates the calculation of the *mean*. There are three steps: (1) multiply each age by the number of subjects who have that age, (2) total the results of all those multiplications, and (3) divide that total by the number of subjects. As indicated in Figure 15-2, the mean age in this illustration is 15.87.

The *median* represents the "middle" value: Half are above it, half below. If we had the precise ages of each subject (for example, 17 years and 124 days), we'd be able to arrange all 31 subjects in order by age, and the median for the whole group would be the age of the middle subject.

As you can see, however, we do not know precise ages; our data constitute "grouped data" in this regard: Three people who are not precisely the same age have been grouped in the category "13 years old," for example.

Figure 15-2 illustrates the logic of calculating a median for grouped data. Because there are 31 subjects altogether, the "middle" subject would be number 16 if they were arranged by age—15 teenagers would be younger and 15 older. Look at the bottom portion of Figure 15-2, and you'll see that the middle person is one of the eight 16-year-olds. In the enlarged view of that group, we see that number 16 is the third from the left.

Because we do not know the precise ages of the subjects in this group, the statistical convention here is to assume they are evenly spread along the width of the group. In this instance, the *possible* ages of the subjects go from 16 years and no days to 16 years and 364 days. Strictly speaking, the range, then, is 364/365 days. As a practical matter, it's sufficient to call it one year.

If the eight subjects in this group were evenly spread from one limit to the other, they would be one-eighth of a year apart from each other—a 0.125-year interval. Look at the illustration and you'll see that if we place the first subject half the interval from the lower limit and add a full interval to the age of each successive subject, the final one is half an interval from the upper limit.

What we've done, therefore, is calculate, hypothetically, the precise ages of the eight subjects—assuming their ages were spread out evenly. Having done this, we merely note the age of the middle subject—16.31—and that is the median age for the group.

Whenever the total number of subjects is an even number, of course, there is no middle case. In that case, you merely calculate the mean of the two values it falls between. Suppose there were one more 19–year-old, for example. The midpoint in that case would fall between number 16 and number 17. The median, in that case, would be calculated as $(16.31 + 16.44)/2 = 16.38$.

In the research literature, you will find both means and medians presented. Whenever means are presented, you should be aware that they are susceptible to extreme values: a few very large or very small numbers. Here's an example to illustrate why this is true.

In attempting to determine the well-being of a country's citizens, researchers use a variety of indicators. A country's *infant mortality rate (IMR)*—the percentage of infants who die during their first year of life, usually expressed as the number of deaths per 1,000 births—is one commonly used measure. Here are the 1991 IMRs for four countries, representing two quite different kinds of societies (Population Reference Bureau, 1993).

	Infant Mortality Rates, 1991
United Arab Emirates	25
Qatar	26
Netherlands	6.5
Belgium	9.9

The relatively high infant mortality rates in the United Arab Emirates and Qatar reflect the impoverished status of many families in these nations. In Belgium and the Netherlands, like other nations in Western Europe, we find much lower IMRs.

Economics represents another aspect of quality of life, and an easily available measure is the *per capita gross national product* of countries. The gross

Univariate Analysis 373

FIGURE 15-2
Three "Averages"

Age	Number
13	(3)
14	(4)
15	(6)
16	(8)
17	(4)
18	(3)
19	(3)

Mode = 16
Most frequent

Age	Number	
13	(3)	13 × 3 = 39
14	(4)	14 × 4 = 56
15	(6)	15 × 6 = 90
16	(8)	16 × 8 = 128
17	(4)	17 × 4 = 68
18	(3)	18 × 3 = 54
19	(3)	19 × 3 = 57

$\overline{492}$ ÷ 31 = 15.87
(Total) (Cases)

Mean = 15.87
Arithmetic average

Age	Number	
13	(3)	1–3
14	(4)	4–7
15	(6)	8–13
16	(8)	
17	(4)	22–25
18	(3)	26–28
19	(3)	29–31

Median = 16.31
Midpoint

14	15	16	17	18	19	20	21
16.06	16.19	16.31	16.44	16.56	16.69	16.81	16.94

national product (GNP) is the total value of all goods and services produced within a nation; dividing this by the population (the *mean* productivity of each citizen) yields an indication of the economic well-being of the citizens. The following table presents these data from the four countries under consideration (Population Reference Bureau, 1993).

GNP per Capita, 1991	
United Arab Emirates	$19,870
Qatar	$15,870
Netherlands	$18,560
Belgium	$19,300

In fact, as we can see, the highest GNP per capita is in the United Arab Emirates, and Qatar is not far behind Belgium and the Netherlands. The reason for this disparity lies in the *distribution* of income in the two oil-rich sheikdoms, where a few families have great wealth, which inflates the apparent average. Clearly, the mean is a misleading figure here; a measure such as *median family income* would provide a more accurate picture of the "average" citizen in the four countries.

Sometimes you'll find means presented where medians would be more appropriate because it's easier to arrive at the means. Notice that in this case all we need are the total GNP and the total population for each country: data that are commonly reported. To determine the median family income, on the other hand, we would need to survey a representative sample of families in each country, learn each family's income, and then calculate the median. While such surveys are common in developed countries, they are less common in the Third World.

Dispersion

Averages offer readers the special advantage of reducing the raw data to the most manageable form: A single number (or attribute) can represent all the detailed data collected in regard to the variable. This advantage comes at a cost, of course, because the reader cannot reconstruct the original data from an average. Summaries of the **dispersion** of responses can somewhat alleviate this disadvantage. The simplest measure of dispersion is the **range:** the distance separating the highest from the lowest value. Thus, besides reporting that our subjects have a mean age of 15.87, we might also indicate that their ages ranged from 13 to 19. A somewhat more sophisticated measure of dispersion is the *standard deviation.* The logic of this measure was discussed in Chapter 8 as the standard error of a sampling distribution.

There are many other measures of dispersion. In reporting intelligence test scores, for example, you might determine the *interquartile range,* the range of scores for the middle 50 percent of subjects, the second fourth, and so forth. If the highest one-fourth had scores ranging from 120 to 150, and if the lowest one-fourth had scores ranging from 60 to 90, you could report that the interquartile range was 120 to 90, or 30, with a mean score of, let's say, 102.

Continuous and Discrete Variables

The preceding calculations are not appropriate for all variables. To understand this, we must examine two types of variables: *continuous* and *discrete. Age* is a continuous, ratio variable; it increases steadily in tiny fractions instead of jumping from category to category as does a discrete variable such as *gender* or *military rank.* If discrete variables were being analyzed—a nominal or ordinal variable, for example—then some of the techniques discussed previously would not be applicable. Strictly speaking, medians and means should be calculated only for interval and ratio data, respectively (see Chapter 6). If the variable in question were *gender,* for example, raw numbers (23 of the cross-dressing outlaw bikers were women) or percentages (7 percent were women) would be appropriate and useful analyses. Calculating the mode would be a legitimate, though not very revealing, analysis, but reports of mean, median, or dispersion summaries would be inappropriate. Although researchers can sometimes learn something of value by violating rules like these, you should do so only with caution.

Detail versus Manageability

In presenting univariate—and other—data, you'll be constrained by two often conflicting goals. On the one hand, you should attempt to provide your reader with the fullest degree of detail regarding those data. On the other hand, the data should be presented in a manageable form. As these two goals often go directly counter to each other, you will find yourself continually seeking the best compromise between them. One useful solution is to report a given set of data in more than one form. In the case of age, for example, you might report the distribution of ungrouped ages *plus* the mean age and standard deviation.

As you can see from this introductory discussion of univariate analysis, this seemingly simple matter can be rather complex. The lessons of this section, in any event, will be important as we move now to a consideration of subgroup comparisons and bivariate analyses.

■ SUBGROUP COMPARISONS

Univariate analyses *describe* the units of analysis of a study and, if they are a sample drawn from some larger population, allow us to make descriptive inferences about the larger population. Bivariate and multivariate analyses are aimed primarily at explanation. Before turning to *explanation*, however, we should consider the case of subgroup description.

Often it's appropriate to describe subsets of cases, subjects, or respondents. Table 15-2, for example, presents income data for men and women separately. In addition, the table presents the ratio of women's median income to that of men, showing that women in the labor force earn a little over half what men earn.

In some situations, the researcher presents subgroup comparisons purely for descriptive purposes. More often, the purpose of subgroup descriptions is comparative: Women earn less than men. In the present case, it is assumed that there is something about being a woman that results in their lower incomes. When we compare incomes of African Americans and whites, a similar assumption is made. In such cases, the analysis is based on an assumption of *causality:* one variable causing another, as in *gender* causing *income.*

When the data shown in Table 15-2 were published by the Census Bureau in 1978, they added legitimacy to the growing outcry over the discrimination of women in the U.S. economy. Both

TABLE 15-2
Median Earnings of Year-Round, Full-time Civilian Workers with Earnings by Gender: 1967–1977

Year	Women	Men	Ratio of Women's to Men's Earnings
1977	$8,618	$14,626	.59
1976	8,622	14,323	.60
1975	8,449	14,175	.60
1974	8,565	14,578	.59
1973	8,639	15,254	.57
1972	8,551	14,778	.58
1971	8,369	14,064	.61
1970	8,307	13,993	.59
1969	8,227	13,976	.59
1968	7,763	13,349	.58
1967	7,503	13,021	.58

Source: Adapted from the U.S. Bureau of the Census, "Statistical Portrait of Women in the United States: 1978," Series P-23, No. 100, p. 73.

TABLE 15-3
Ratio of Women-to-Men Earnings among Year-Round, Full-time Workers: 1980–1993

	Ratio of Women's to Men's Median Year Earnings
1980	.64
1985	.66
1990	.71
1991	.70
1993	.65

Source: 1980 and 1985 figures based on hourly wages and taken from Michael W. Horrigan and James P. Markey, "Recent Gains in Women's Earnings: Better Pay or Longer Hours?" *Monthly Labor Review* (July 1990): 11–17. 1990–91 figures based on annual incomes and taken from U.S. Bureau of the Census, CPR Series P-60, No. 180, *Money Income of Households, Families, and Persons in the United States:* 1991 (Washington, DC: Government Printing Office, 1992). 1993 data are from U.S. Bureau of the Census *Statistical Abstract* of the United States, 1995 (CD-ROM CD-SA-95, April 1996): Table 742.

politics and research have focused on the issue ever since, though the discrepancy in male and female earnings has hardly been resolved.

The most recent statistics reflect some improvement but still show a distinct difference. As this is written, the average full-time, year-round female worker earns 66 cents for each dollar earned by her male counterpart. See Table 15-3 for the recent wage ratios.

Before moving on to the logic of bivariate, causal analysis, let's consider another example of

TABLE 15-4
Attitudes Toward the United Nations: "How is the UN doing in solving the problems it has had to face?"

	West Germany	Britain	France	Japan	United States
Very good job	2%	7%	2%	1%	5%
Good job	46	39	45	11	46
Poor job	21	28	22	43	27
Very poor job	6	9	3	5	13
Don't know	26	17	28	41	10

Source: "5-Nation Survey Finds Hope for U.N.," *New York Times*, June 26, 1985, p. 6.

TABLE 15-5
Collapsing Extreme Categories

	West Germany	Britain	France	Japan	United States
Good job or better	48%	46%	47%	12%	51%
Poor job or worse	27	37	25	48	40
Don't know	26	17	28	41	10

subgroup comparisons—one that will let us address some table-formatting issues.

"Collapsing" Response Categories

"Textbook examples" of tables are often simpler than you'll typically find in published research reports or in your own analyses of data, so this section and the next one address two common problems and suggest solutions.

Let's begin by turning to the data reported in Table 15-4, which reports data collected in a multinational poll conducted by the *New York Times*, CBS News, and the *Herald Tribune* in 1985, concerning attitudes about the United Nations. The question reported in Table 15-4 deals with general attitudes about the way the UN was handling its job.

Here's the question: How do people in the five nations reported on in Table 15-4 compare in their support for the kind of job the UN is doing? As you review the table, you may find there are simply so many numbers that it is hard for you to see any meaningful pattern.

Part of the problem with Table 15-4 lies in the relatively small percentages of respondents selecting the two extreme response categories: saying the UN is doing a *very* good or a *very* poor job. Although it might be tempting to merely read the second line of the table—those saying "good job"—that would be improper. Looking at only the second row, we would conclude that West Germany and the United States were the most positive (46 percent) about the UN's performance, followed closely by France (45 percent), with Britain (39 percent) less positive than any of those three and Japan (11 percent) the least positive of all.

This procedure is inappropriate in that it ignores all those respondents who gave the most positive answer of all: "very good job." In a situation like this, you should combine or "collapse" the two ends of the range of variation. In this instance, combine "very good" with "good" and "very poor" with "poor." If you were to do this in the analysis of your own data, it would be wise to add the raw frequencies together and recompute percentages for the combined categories, but in analyzing a published table such as this one, you can simply add the percentages as illustrated by the results shown in Table 15-5.

With the collapsed categories illustrated in Table 15-5, we can now rather easily read across the several national percentages who say the UN is doing at least a good job. Now the United States appears the most positive; Germany, Britain, and France are only slightly less positive and are nearly indistinguishable from one another; and Japan stands alone in its quite low assessment of the UN's performance. Although the conclusions to be drawn now do not differ radically from what we might have concluded from simply reading the second line of Table 15-4, we should note that Britain now appears relatively more supportive.

TABLE 15-6
Omitting the "Don't Knows"

	West Germany	Britain	France	Japan	United States
Good job or better	65%	55%	65%	20%	57%
Poor job or worse	35%	45%	35%	81%	44%

Here's the risk I'd like to spare you. Suppose you had hastily read the second row of Table 15-4 and noted that the British had a somewhat lower assessment of the job the UN was doing than was true of the Americans, the West Germans, and the French. You might feel obliged to think up an explanation for why that was so—possibly creating an ingenious psychohistorical theory about the painful decline of the once powerful and dignified British Empire. Then, once you had touted your "theory" about, someone else might point out that a proper reading of the data would show the British were actually not really less positive than the other three nations. Please realize this is not a hypothetical risk. It happens frequently, but it can be avoided by collapsing answer categories where appropriate.

Handling "Don't Knows"

Tables 15-4 and 15-5 illustrate another common problem in the analysis of survey data. It's usually a good idea to give people the option of saying "don't know" or "no opinion" when asking for their opinions on issues, but what do you do with those answers in analyzing the data?

Notice there is a good deal of variation in the national percentages saying "don't know" in this instance, ranging from only 10 percent in the United States to 41 percent in Japan. The presence of substantial percentages saying they don't know can confuse the results of a table like this one. For example, are the Japanese so much less likely to say the UN is doing a good job simply because so many didn't express any opinion?

Here's an easy way to recalculate percentages, with the "don't knows" excluded.

Look at the first column of percentages in Table 15-5: West Germany's answers to the question about the UN's performance. Notice that 26 percent of the respondents said they didn't know. This means that those who said "good" or "bad" job—taken together—represent only 74 percent (100 minus 26) of the whole. If we divide the 48 percent saying "good job or better" by .74 (the proportion giving any opinion), we can say that 65 percent "of those with an opinion" said the UN was doing a good or very good job (48%/.74 = 65%). Table 15-6 presents the whole table with the "don't knows" excluded.

Notice that these new data offer a somewhat different interpretation than the previous tables. Specifically, it would now appear that France and West Germany are the most positive in their assessments of the UN, with the United States and Britain a bit lower. Although Japan still stands out as lowest in this regard, it has moved from 12 percent up to 20 percent positive.

At this point, having seen three versions of the data, you may be asking yourself: Which is the *right* one? The answer depends on your purpose in analyzing and interpreting the data. For example, if it is not essential for you to distinguish "very good" from "good," it makes sense to combine them, because it's easier to read the table.

Whether to include or exclude the "don't knows" is harder to decide in the abstract. It may be a very important finding that such a large percentage of the Japanese had no opinion—if you wanted to find out whether people were familiar with the work of the UN, for example. On the other hand, if you wanted to know how people might vote on an issue, it might be more appropriate to exclude the "don't knows" on the assumption that they wouldn't vote or that they would divide their votes between the two sides of the issue.

In any event, the *truth* contained within your data is that a certain percentage said they didn't know and the remainder divided their opinions in whatever manner they did that. Often, it is appropriate to report your data in both forms—with and without the "don't knows"—so your readers can also draw their own conclusions.

Numerical Descriptions in Qualitative Research

Although this chapter deals primarily with quantitative research, you should realize that the discussions are also relevant to qualitative studies. The findings of in-depth, qualitative studies often can be verified by some numerical testing. Thus, for example, when David Silverman wanted to compare the cancer treatments received by patients in private clinics with those in Britain's National Health Service, he primarily chose in-depth analyses of the interactions between doctors and patients.

■ My method of analysis was largely qualitative and . . . I used extracts of what doctors and patients had said as well as offering a brief ethnography of the setting and of certain behavioural data. In addition, however, I constructed a coding form which enabled me to collate a number of crude measures of doctor and patient interactions.

(SILVERMAN 1993:163)

Not only did the numerical data fine-tune Silverman's impressions based on his qualitative observations, but his in-depth understanding of the situation allowed him to craft an ever more appropriate quantitative analysis. Listen to the interaction between qualitative and quantitative approaches in this lengthy discussion.

■ My overall impression was that private consultations lasted considerably longer than those held in the NHS clinics. When examined, the data indeed did show that the former were almost twice as long as the latter (20 minutes as against 11 minutes) and that the difference was statistically highly significant. However, I recalled that, for special reasons, one of the NHS clinics had abnormally short consultations. I felt a fairer comparison of consultations in the two sectors should exclude this clinic and should only compare consultations taken by a single doctor in both sectors. This subsample of cases revealed that the difference in length between NHS and private consultations was now reduced to an average of under 3 minutes. This was still statistically significant, although the significance was reduced. Finally, however, if I compared only *new* patients seen by the same doctor, NHS patients got 4 minutes more on the average—34 minutes as against 30 minutes in the private clinic.

(SILVERMAN 1993:163–64)

This example further demonstrates the special power that can be gained from a combination of approaches in social research. The combination of qualitative and quantitative analyses can be especially potent.

■ BIVARIATE ANALYSIS

In contrast to univariate analysis, subgroup comparisons constitute a kind of **bivariate analysis** in that two variables are involved. As we saw earlier, the purpose of univariate analysis is purely descriptive. The purpose of subgroup comparisons is also largely descriptive—independently describing the subgroups—but the element of *comparison* is added. Most bivariate analysis in social research adds another element: relationships among the variables themselves. Thus, univariate analysis and subgroup comparisons focus on describing the *people* (or other units of analysis) under study, and bivariate analysis focuses on the *variables*.

Notice, then, that Table 15-7 could be regarded as an instance of subgroup comparison: It independently describes the church attendance of men and women, as reported in the 1990 General Social Survey. It shows—comparatively and descriptively—that the women under study attend church more often than the men.

The same table, seen as an *explanatory* bivariate analysis, tells a somewhat different story. It suggests that the variable *gender* has an effect on the variable *church attendance*. The behavior is seen as a *dependent variable* that is partially determined by the *independent variable, gender*. Explanatory bivariate analyses, then, involve the "variable language" introduced in Chapter 1. In a subtle shift of focus, we are no longer talking about men and women as different subgroups but about *gender* as a variable: one that has an influence on other variables. The logic of interpreting Table 15-7 might be taken from Charles Glock's Comfort Hypothesis as discussed in Chapter 2:

TABLE 15-7
Church Attendance Reported by Men and Women in 1996

	Men	Women
Weekly	25%	34%
Less often	75	66
100% =	(901)	(1134)

Source: General Social Survey, National Opinion Research Center.

1. Women are still treated as second-class citizens in American society.
2. People denied status gratification in the secular society may turn to religion as an alternative source of status.
3. Hence, women should be more religious than men.

The data presented in Table 15-7 confirm this reasoning. Thirty-four percent of the women attend church weekly, as compared with 25 percent of the men.

Adding the logic of causal relationships among variables has an important implication for the construction and reading of percentage tables. One of the chief bugaboos for new data analysts is deciding on the appropriate "direction of percentaging" for any given table. In Table 15-7, for example, I've divided the group of subjects into two subgroups—men and women—and then described the behavior of each subgroup. That is the correct method for constructing this table.

Notice, however, that we could—however inappropriately—construct the table differently. We could first divide the subjects into different degrees of church attendance and then describe each of those subgroups in terms of the percentage of men and women in each. This method would make no sense in terms of explanation, however.

Table 15-7 suggests that your gender will affect your frequency of church attendance. Had we used the other method of construction, the table would suggest that your church attendance affects whether you are a man or a woman—which makes no sense. Your behavior cannot determine your gender.

A related problem complicates the lives of new data analysts. How do you *read* a percentage table? There is a temptation to read Table 15-7 as follows: "Of the women, only 34 percent attended church weekly, and 66 percent said they attended less often; therefore, being a woman makes you less likely to attend church frequently." This is *not* the correct way to read the table, however. The conclusion that *gender*—as a variable—has an effect on church attendance must hinge on a comparison between men and women. Specifically, we compare the 34 percent with the 25 percent and note that *women are more likely than men* to attend church weekly. The comparison of subgroups, then, is essential in reading an explanatory bivariate table.

In constructing and presenting Table 15-7, I have used a convention called *percentage down*. This term means that you can add the percentages down each column to total 100 percent. You read this form of table across a row. For the row labeled "weekly," what percentage of the men attend weekly? What percentage of the women attend weekly?

The direction of percentaging in tables is arbitrary, and some researchers prefer to percentage across. They would organize Table 15-7 so that "men" and "women" were shown on the left side of the table, identifying the two rows, and "weekly" and "less often" would appear at the top to identify the columns. The actual numbers in the table would be moved around accordingly, and each *row* of percentages would total 100 percent. In that case, you would read the table down a column, still asking what percentage of men and women attended frequently. The logic and the conclusion would be the same in either case; only the form would differ.

In reading a table that someone else has constructed, therefore, you need to find out in which direction it has been percentaged. Usually this will be labeled or be clear from the logic of the variables being analyzed. As a last resort, however, you should add the percentages in each column and each row. If each of the columns totals 100 percent, the table has been percentaged down. If the rows total 100 percent each, it has been percentaged across. The rule, then, is as follows:

1. If the table is percentaged down, read across.
2. If the table is percentaged across, read down.

FIGURE 15-3
Percentaging a Table

A. Some men and women who either favor (=) sexual equality or don't (≠) favor it.

B. Separate the men and the women (the independent variable).

Women   Men

C. Within each gender group, separate those who favor equality from those who don't (the dependent variable).

Women   Men

FIGURE 15-3
(continued)

D. Count the numbers in each cell of the table.

	Women	Men
=	8	6
≠	2	4

E. What percentage of the women favor equality?

80%

F. What percentage of the men favor equality?

60%

G. Conclusions

While a majority of both men and women favored sexual equality, women were more likely than men to do so.

Thus, gender appears to be one of the causes of attitudes toward sexual equality.

	Women	Men
Favor equality	80%	60%
Don't favor equality	20	40
Total	100%	100%

Percentaging a Table

Figure 15-3 reviews the logic by which we create percentage tables from two variables. I've used as variables *gender* and *attitudes toward equality for men and women.*

Here's another example. Suppose we're interested in learning something about newspaper editorial policies regarding the legalization of marijuana. We undertake a content analysis of editorials on this subject that have appeared during a given year in a sample of daily newspapers across

TABLE 15-8
Hypothetical Data Regarding Newspaper Editorials on the Legalization of Marijuana

Editorial Policy Toward Legalizing Marijuana	Community Size Under 100,000	Community Size Over 100,000
Favorable	11%	32%
Neutral	29	40
Unfavorable	60	28
100% =	(127)	(438)

the nation. Each editorial has been classified as favorable, neutral, or unfavorable toward the legalization of marijuana. Perhaps we wish to examine the relationship between editorial policies and the types of communities in which the newspapers are published, thinking that rural newspapers might be more conservative in this regard than urban ones. Thus, each newspaper (hence, each editorial) has been classified in terms of the population of the community in which it is published.

Table 15-8 presents some hypothetical data describing the editorial policies of rural and urban newspapers. Note that the unit of analysis in this example is the individual editorial. Table 15-8 tells us that there were 127 editorials about marijuana in our sample of newspapers published in communities with populations under 100,000. (*Note:* This cutting point is chosen for simplicity of illustration and does not mean that *rural* refers to a community of less than 100,000 in any absolute sense.) Of these, 11 percent (14 editorials) were favorable toward legalization of marijuana, 29 percent were neutral, and 60 percent were unfavorable. Of the 438 editorials that appeared in our sample of newspapers published in communities of more than 100,000 residents, 32 percent (140 editorials) were favorable toward legalizing marijuana, 40 percent were neutral, and 28 percent were unfavorable.

When we compare the editorial policies of rural and urban newspapers in our imaginary study, we find—as expected—that rural newspapers are less favorable toward the legalization of marijuana than urban newspapers. We determine this by noting that a larger percentage (32 percent) of the urban editorials were favorable than the rural ones (11 percent). We might note, as well, that more rural than urban editorials were unfavorable (60 percent compared to 28 percent). Note that this table assumes that the size of a community might affect its newspapers' editorial policies on this issue, rather than that editorial policy might affect the size of communities.

Constructing and Reading Tables

Before introducing multivariate analysis, let's review the steps involved in the construction of explanatory bivariate tables:

1. The cases are divided into groups according to their attributes of the independent variable.
2. Each of these subgroups is then described in terms of attributes of the dependent variable.
3. Finally, the table is read by comparing the independent variable subgroups with one another in terms of a given attribute of the dependent variable.

Let's repeat the analysis of gender and attitude on sexual equality following these steps. For the reasons outlined previously, *gender* is the independent variable; *attitude toward sexual equality* constitutes the dependent variable. Thus, we proceed as follows:

1. The cases are divided into men and women.
2. Each gender subgrouping is described in terms of approval or disapproval of sexual equality.
3. Men and women are compared in terms of the percentages approving of sexual equality.

In the example of editorial policies regarding the legalization of marijuana, *size of community* is the independent variable, and a *newspaper's editorial policy* the dependent variable. The table would be constructed as follows:

1. Divide the editorials into subgroups according to the sizes of the communities in which the newspapers are published.
2. Describe each subgroup of editorials in terms of the percentages favorable, neutral, or unfavorable toward the legalization of marijuana.
3. Compare the two subgroups in terms of the percentages favorable toward the legalization of marijuana.

Bivariate analyses typically have an explanatory causal purpose. These two hypothetical examples have hinted at the nature of causation as social scientists use it. I hope the rather simplified approach to causation employed in these examples will have a commonsense acceptability for you at this point. This rather superficial, commonsense view of causation will help you understand this chapter and Chapter 16, which will take a much closer look at causation. Together, these discussions should help you understand more fully the complex nature of causation.

Bivariate Table Formats

Tables such as the ones we've been examining are commonly called *contingency tables:* Values of the dependent variable are contingent on values of the independent variable. Although contingency tables are common in social science, their format has never been standardized. As a result, you'll find a variety of formats in research literature. As long as a table is easy to read and interpret, there's probably no reason to strive for standardization. However, there are several guidelines that you should follow in the presentation of most tabular data.

1. A table should have a heading or a title that succinctly describes what is contained in the table.
2. The original content of the variables should be clearly presented—in the table itself if at all possible or in the text with a paraphrase in the table. This information is especially critical when a variable is derived from responses to an attitudinal question, because the meaning of the responses will depend largely on the wording of the question.
3. The attributes of each variable should be clearly indicated. Though complex categories will have to be abbreviated, their meaning should be clear in the table and, of course, the full description should be reported in the text.
4. When percentages are reported in the table, the base on which they are computed should be indicated. It's redundant to present all the raw numbers for each category, since these could be reconstructed from the percentages and the bases. Moreover, the presentation of both numbers and percentages often confuses a table and makes it more difficult to read.
5. If any cases are omitted from the table because of missing data ("no answer," for example), their numbers should be indicated in the table.

■ INTRODUCTION TO MULTIVARIATE ANALYSIS

The logic of multivariate analysis is a main topic of Chapters 16 and 17. At this point, however, it will be useful to discuss briefly the construction of *multivariate tables:* those constructed from several variables.

We can construct multivariate tables on the basis of a more complicated subgroup description by following essentially the same steps outlined previously for bivariate tables. Instead of one independent variable and one dependent variable, however, we'll have more than one independent variable. Instead of explaining the dependent variable on the basis of a single independent variable, we'll seek an explanation through the use of more than one independent variable.

Let's return to the example of church attendance. Suppose we believed age would also affect such behavior: Glock's Comfort Hypothesis suggests that older people are more religious than younger people. As the first step in table construction, we would divide the total sample into subgroups based on the attributes of *both* independent variables simultaneously: younger men, older men, younger women, and older women. Then the several subgroups would be described in terms of the dependent variable, and comparisons would be made. Table 15-9, from an analysis of the 1973–93 General Social Survey data, is the result.

Following the convention presented here, this table has also been percentaged down, and therefore should be read across. The interpretation of this table warrants several conclusions.

1. Among both men and women, older people attend church more often than younger

384 Chapter 15: Elementary Analyses

TABLE 15-9
Multivariate Relationship:
Church Attendance, Gender, and Age

"How often do you attend religious services?"

	Under 40		40 and Older	
	Men	Women	Men	Women
About weekly*	24%	32%	33%	48%
Less often	76	68	67	52
100% =	(325)	(383)	(323)	(452)

*About weekly = "More than once a week," "Weekly," and "Nearly every week."

Source: A random sample of GSS respondents in 1973, 1983, and 1993.

TABLE 15-10
A Simplification of Table 15-9

	Percent Who Attend about Weekly	
	Men	Women
Under 40	24 (325)	32 (383)
40 and older	33 (323)	48 (452)

people. Among women, 32 percent of those under 40 and 48 percent of those 40 and older attend church weekly. Among men, the respective figures are 24 and 33 percent.

2. Within each age group, women attend more frequently than men. Among those respondents under 40, 32 percent of the women attend weekly, compared with 24 percent of the men. Among those 40 and over, 48 percent of the women and 33 percent of the men attend weekly.
3. As measured in the table, gender and age appear to have comparable effects on attendance at religious services.
4. Age and gender have independent effects on church attendance. Within a given attribute of one independent variable, different attributes of the second still affect behaviors.
5. Similarly, the two independent variables have a *cumulative* effect on behaviors. Older women attend the most often (48 percent), and younger men attend the least frequently (24 percent).

Chapter 16, on the *elaboration model*, will examine the logic of multivariate analysis in much greater detail. Before we conclude this section, however, it will be useful to note an alternative format for presenting such data.

Several of the tables presented in this chapter are somewhat inefficient. When the dependent variable, *church attendance*, is dichotomous (two attributes), knowing one attribute permits the reader to reconstruct the other easily. Thus, if we know that 32 percent of the women under 40 attend church weekly, then we know automatically that 68 percent attend less often. So reporting the percentages who attend less often is unnecessary. On the basis of this recognition, Table 15-9 could be presented in the alternative format of Table 15-10.

In Table 15-10, the percentages saying they attend church about weekly are reported in the cells representing the intersections of the two independent variables. The numbers presented in parentheses below each percentage represent the number of cases on which the percentages are based. Thus, for example, the reader knows there are 383 women under 40 years of age in the sample, and 32 percent of them attend church weekly. We can calculate from this that 123 of those 383 women attend weekly and that the other 260 younger women (or 68 percent) attend less frequently. This new table is easier to read than the former one, and it does not sacrifice any detail.

For another simple example of multivariate analysis, let's return to the issue of gender and income that was introduced earlier. As you'll recall, there has been a long-standing pattern of women in the labor force earning less than men, and many explanations have been advanced to account for that difference.

One explanation is that because of traditional family patterns, women as a group have participated less in the labor force and many only began working outside the home after certain child-rearing tasks were completed. Thus, women as a group will probably have less seniority at work than men, and income increases with seniority. A 1984 study by the Census Bureau shows

TABLE 15-11
Gender, Job Tenure, and Income (Full-time workers 21–64 years of age)

Years working with current employer	Average hourly income Men	Women	Women/Men ratio
Less than 2 years	$ 8.46	$6.03	.71
2 to 4 years	$ 9.38	$6.78	.72
5 to 9 years	$10.42	$7.56	.73
10 years or more	$12.38	$7.91	.64

Source: U.S. Bureau of the Census, Current Population Reports, Series P-70, No. 10, *Male-Female Differences in Work Experience, Occupation, and Earning, 1984* (Washington, DC: U.S. Government Printing Office, 1987): 4.

this reasoning to be *partly* true, as Table 15-11 shows.

Table 15-11 indicates, first of all, that job tenure does indeed affect income. Among both men and women, those with more years on the job earn more. This is seen by reading down the first two columns of the table.

The table also indicates that women earn less than men, regardless of job seniority. This can be seen by comparing average wages across the rows of the table, and the ratio of women-to-men wages is shown in the third column.

This analysis indicates that years on the job is an important determinant of earnings; it does not provide an adequate explanation for the pattern of women earning less than men. In fact, we see that women with 10 or more years on the job earn substantially less ($7.91/hour) than men with less than two years ($8.46/hour).

These data indicate that the difference between men's and women's pay is not merely a matter of men having more time on the job. But then there are other possible explanations for the difference: education, child-care responsibilities, and so forth.

The researchers who calculated Table 15-11 also examined some of the other variables that might reasonably explain the male/female difference in pay without representing gender discrimination. In addition to the number of years with current employer, the variables they considered included these:

- Number of years in the current occupation
- Total years of work experience (any occupation)
- Whether they have usually worked full time
- Marital status
- Size of city or town they live in
- Whether covered by a union contract
- Type of occupation
- Number of employees in the firm
- Whether private or public employer
- Whether they left previous job involuntarily
- Time spent between current and previous job
- Race
- Whether they have a disability
- Health status
- Age of children
- Whether they took an academic curriculum in high school
- Number of math, science, and foreign language classes in high school
- Whether they attended private or public high school
- Educational level achieved
- Percentage of women in the occupation
- College major

Each of the variables listed above might reasonably affect earnings and, if women and men differ in these regards, could account for female/male income differences. When *all* these variables were taken into account, the researchers were able to account for 60 percent of the discrepancy between the incomes of men and women. The remaining 40 percent, then, is a function of other "reasonable" variables and/or prejudice.

This latest illustration should give you a fuller view of the uses of multivariate analysis. At a superficial level, you have now been exposed to the entire process of data analysis. In this sense, Chapters 16 and 17 are a review—at a much deeper level—of material already covered.

MAIN POINTS

- Univariate analysis is the analysis of a single variable.
- The full original data collected with regard to a single variable are, in that form, usually impossible to interpret. Data reduction is the process of summarizing the original data to make them more manageable, all the while maintaining as much of the original detail as possible.
- A frequency distribution shows the number of cases having each of the attributes of a given variable.
- Grouped data are created through the combination of attributes of a variable.
- Averages (the mean, median, and mode) reduce data to an easily manageable form, but they do not convey the detail of the original data.
- Measures of dispersion give a summary indication of the distribution of cases around an average value.
- To undertake a subgroup comparison: (1) divide cases into the appropriate subgroups, (2) describe each subgroup in terms of a given variable, and (3) compare those descriptions across the subgroups.
- Bivariate analysis is nothing more than a different interpretation of subgroup comparisons: (1) divide cases into subgroups in terms of their attributes on some independent variable, (2) describe each subgroup in terms of some dependent variable, (3) compare the dependent variable descriptions of the subgroups, and (4) interpret any observed differences as a statistical association between the independent and dependent variables.
- To interpret bivariate percentage tables properly: (1) "percentage down" and "read across" or (2) "percentage across" and "read down" in making subgroup comparisons.
- Multivariate analysis is a method of analyzing the simultaneous relationships among several variables and may be used to understand the relationship between two variables more fully.
- While the topics discussed in this chapter are primarily associated with quantitative research, the logic and techniques involved can also be valuable to qualitative researchers.

REVIEW QUESTIONS AND EXERCISES

1. Construct and interpret a contingency table from the following information: 150 Democrats favor raising the minimum wage, and 50 oppose it; 100 Republicans favor raising the minimum wage, and 300 oppose it.
2. Using the data in the following table, construct and interpret tables showing the following:
   a. The bivariate relationship between age and attitude toward abortion
   b. The bivariate relationship between political orientation and attitude toward abortion
   c. The multivariate relationship linking age, political orientation, and attitude toward abortion

Age	Political Orientation	Attitude toward Abortion	Frequency
Young	Liberal	Favor	90
Young	Liberal	Oppose	10
Young	Conservative	Favor	60
Young	Conservative	Oppose	40
Old	Liberal	Favor	60
Old	Liberal	Oppose	40
Old	Conservative	Favor	20
Old	Conservative	Oppose	80

3. Your assignment is to create a simple bivariate percentage table from General Social Survey data. You can do this online, without having the data files in your possession. Begin by going to the Computer-assisted Survey Methods Program at the University of California at Berkeley:

   http://bravo.berkeley.edu/cgi-bin/hcsa?harc3

   Your first step is to select two variables you would like to analyze. You may already know some GSS variables' names, such as ABANY, CAPPUN, SEX, or GRASS. Or you can locate some variables using the "Browse Codebook" option.

Once you've identified two variables, choose the "Run Crosstabulation" option. Enter variable names for the horizontal and vertical variables, indicate that you want vertical percentaging, and indicate that you want the "Question Text."

Submit the table you create to your instructor.

ADDITIONAL READINGS

Cole, Stephen. *The Sociological Method: An Introduction to the Science of Sociology.* Boston: Houghton Mifflin, 1980. A readable introduction to analysis. Cole begins with the general question of what social scientific inquiry is and then illustrates with easily understood examples. He then presents a useful introduction of the elaboration model.

Davis, James. *Elementary Survey Analysis.* Englewood Cliffs, NJ: Prentice-Hall, 1971. An extremely well-written and well-reasoned introduction to analysis. In addition to covering the materials just presented in Chapter 15, Davis's book is well worth reading in terms of measurement, statistics, and the elaboration model.

Labovitz, Sanford, and Robert Hagedorn. *Introduction to Social Research.* New York: McGraw-Hill, 1981. Another useful introduction to analysis. Against the background of more general concerns for social scientific inquiry, the authors provide a very readable and useful introduction to elementary analyses in their Chapter 6. Like Cole and Davis, they then go on to a consideration of multivariate analysis and the elaboration model.

Weisberg, Herbert F. *Central Tendency and Variability.* Newbury Park, CA: Sage, 1992. Provides a more in-depth examination of levels of measurement and measures of central tendency.

Ziesel, Hans. *Say It with Figures.* New York: Harper & Row, 1957. An excellent discussion of table construction and other elementary analyses. Though many years old, this is still perhaps the best available presentation of that specific topic. It is eminently readable and understandable and has many concrete examples.

16 The Elaboration Model

What You'll Learn in This Chapter
This chapter will take you through the fundamental logic of multivariate analysis. Having seen this logic in action in the form of simple percentage tables, you'll then be prepared to make sense of more complex analytical methods.

INTRODUCTION

HISTORY OF THE ELABORATION MODEL

THE ELABORATION PARADIGM
Replication
Explanation
Interpretation
Specification
Refinements to the Paradigm

ELABORATION AND EX POST FACTO HYPOTHESIZING

MAIN POINTS

REVIEW QUESTIONS AND EXERCISES

ADDITIONAL READINGS

INTRODUCTION

Chapter 16 is devoted to a perspective on social scientific analysis that is referred to variously as the elaboration model, the interpretation method, the Columbia school, or the Lazarsfeld method. It has so many names because it aims at *elaborating* on an empirical relationship among variables in order to *interpret* that relationship in the manner developed by Paul Lazarsfeld while he was at Columbia University.

Researchers use the *elaboration model* to understand the relationship between two variables through the simultaneous introduction of additional variables. Though developed primarily through the medium of contingency tables, it may be used with other statistical techniques, as later chapters of this book will show.

I firmly believe that the elaboration model offers the clearest available picture of the logic of causal analysis in social research. Especially through the use of contingency tables, this method portrays the logical process of scientific analysis. Moreover, if you can comprehend fully the use of the elaboration model using contingency tables, you should greatly improve your ability to use and understand more sophisticated statistical techniques. The box "Why Do Elaboration?" by one of the elaboration model's creators, Patricia Kendall, provides another powerful justification.

HISTORY OF THE ELABORATION MODEL

The historical origins of the elaboration model can help you gain a realistic appreciation of scientific research in practice. During World War II, Samuel Stouffer organized and headed a special social research branch within the U.S. Army, already discussed in Chapter 1. Throughout the war, this group conducted a large number and variety of surveys among U.S. servicemen. Although the objectives of these studies varied somewhat, they generally focused on the factors affecting soldiers' combat effectiveness.

Several of the studies examined morale in the military. Because morale seemed to affect combat effectiveness, improving morale would make the war effort more effective. Stouffer and his research staff sought to uncover some of the variables that affected morale. In part, the group sought to confirm, empirically, some commonly accepted propositions, including the following:

1. Promotions surely affect soldiers' morale, so soldiers serving in units with low promotion rates should have relatively low morale.
2. Given racial segregation and discrimination in the South, African-American soldiers being trained in northern training camps should have higher morale than those being trained in the South.
3. Soldiers with more education should be more likely to resent being drafted into the army as enlisted men than those with less education.

Each of these propositions made sense logically, and common wisdom held each to be true. Stouffer decided to test each empirically. To his surprise, none of the propositions was confirmed.

First, as you'll recall, soldiers serving in the Military Police—where promotions were the slowest in the army—had fewer complaints about the promotion system than those serving in the Army Air Corps—where promotions were the fastest in the army. Second, African-American soldiers serving in northern training camps and those serving in southern training camps seemed to differ little if at all in their general morale. Third, less educated soldiers were more likely to resent being drafted into the army than those with more education.

As we saw in Chapter 1, rather than trying to hide the findings or just running tests of statistical significance and publishing the results, Stouffer asked, "Why?" He found the answer to this question within the concepts of *reference group* and *relative deprivation*. Put simply, Stouffer suggested that soldiers did not evaluate their positions in life according to absolute, objective standards, but rather on the basis of their relative position vis-à-vis others around them. The people they compared themselves with were in their reference group, and they felt relative deprivation if they didn't compare favorably in that regard.

Why Do Elaboration?

by Patricia L. Kendall
Department of Sociology, Queens College, CUNY

THERE ARE several aspects of a true controlled experiment. The most crucial are (a) creating experimental and control groups that are *identical* within limits of chance (this is done by assigning individuals to the two groups through processes of randomization: using tables of random numbers, flipping coins, etc.); (b) making sure that it is the *experimenter* who introduces the stimulus, not external events; and (c) waiting to see whether the stimulus has had its presumed effect.

We may have the hypothesis, for example, that attending Ivy League colleges leads to greater success professionally than attending other kinds of colleges and universities. How would we study this through a true experiment? Suppose you said, "Take a group of people in their 40s, find out which ones went to Ivy League colleges, and see whether they are more successful than those who went to other kinds of colleges." If that is your answer, you are wrong.

A true experiment would require the investigator to select several classes of high school seniors, divide each class at random into experimental and control groups, send the experimental groups to Ivy League colleges (regardless of their financial circumstances or academic qualifications and regardless of the desire of the colleges to accept them) and the control group to other colleges and universities, wait 20 years or so until the two groups have reached professional maturity, and then measure the relative success of the two groups. Certainly a bizarre process.

Sociologists also investigate the hypothesis that coming from a broken home leads to juvenile delinquency. How would we go about studying this experimentally? If you followed the example above, you would see that studying this hypothesis through a true experiment would be totally impossible. Just think of what the experimenter would have to do!

The requirements of true experiments are so unrealistic in sociological research that we are forced to use other, and less ideal, methods in all but the most trivial situations. We can study experimentally whether students learn more from one type of lecture than another, or whether a film changes viewers' attitudes. But these are not always the sorts of questions in which we are truly interested.

We therefore resort to approximations—generally surveys—that have their own shortcomings. However, the elaboration model allows us to examine survey data, take account of their possible shortcomings, and draw rather sophisticated conclusions about important issues.

Within the concepts of reference group and relative deprivation, Stouffer found an answer to each of the anomalies in his empirical data. Regarding promotion, he suggested that soldiers judged the fairness of the promotion system based on their own experiences relative to others around them. In the Military Police, where promotions were few and slow, few soldiers knew of a less qualified buddy who had been promoted faster than they had. In the Army Air Corps, however, the rapid promotion rate meant that many soldiers knew of less qualified buddies who had been promoted faster than seemed appropriate. Thus, ironically, the MPs said the promotion system was generally fair, and the air corpsmen said it was not.

A similar analysis seemed to explain the case of the African-American soldiers. Rather than comparing conditions in the North with those in the South, African-American soldiers compared their own status with the status of the African-American civilians around them. In the South, where discrimination was at its worst, they found that being a soldier insulated them somewhat from adverse cultural norms in the surrounding community. Whereas southern African-American civilians were grossly discriminated against and denied self-esteem, good jobs, and so forth, African-American soldiers had a slightly better status. In the North, however, many of the African-American civilians they encountered held well-paying defense jobs. And with discrimination less severe, being a soldier did not help one's status in the community.

Finally, the concepts of reference group and relative deprivation seemed to explain the anomaly of highly educated draftees accepting their induction more willingly than those with less education. Stouffer reasoned as follows:

1. A person's friends, on the whole, have about the same educational status as that person does.
2. Draft-age men with less education are more likely to engage in semi-skilled production-line occupations and farming than more educated men.
3. During wartime, many production-line industries and farming are vital to the national interest; workers in those industries and farmers are exempted from the draft.
4. A man with little education is more likely to have friends in draft-exempt occupations than a man with more education.
5. When each compares himself with his friends, a less educated draftee is more likely to feel discriminated against than a draftee with more education.
(1949:122–27)

Stouffer's explanations unlocked the mystery of the three anomalous findings. Because they were not part of a preplanned study design, he lacked empirical data for testing them, however. Nevertheless, Stouffer's logical exposition provided the basis for the later development of the elaboration model: understanding the relationship between two variables through the controlled introduction of other variables.

Paul Lazarsfeld and his associates at Columbia University formally developed the elaboration model in 1946. In a methodological review of Stouffer's army studies, Lazarsfeld and Patricia Kendall used the logic of the elaboration model to present hypothetical tables that would have proved Stouffer's contention regarding education and acceptance of induction had the empirical data been available (Kendall and Lazarsfeld 1950).

TABLE 16-1
Summary of Stouffer's Data on Education and Acceptance of Induction

	High Ed.	Low Ed.
Should not have been deferred	88%	70%
Should have been deferred	12	30
	100	100
	(1,761)	(1,876)

Source: Tables 16-1, 16-2, 16-3, and 16-4 are modified with permission of Macmillan Publishing Co., Inc., from *Continuities in Social Research: Studies in the Scope and Method of "The American Soldier"* by Robert K. Merton and Paul F. Lazarsfeld (eds.). Copyright 1950 by The Free Press, a Corporation, renewed 1978 by Robert K. Merton.

TABLE 16-2
Hypothetical Relationship between Education and Deferment of Friends

Friends Deferred?	High Ed.	Low Ed.
Yes	19%	79%
No	81	21
	100	100
	(1,761)	(1,876)

TABLE 16-3
Hypothetical Relationship between Deferment of Friends and Acceptance of One's Own Induction

	Friends Deferred?	
	Yes	No
Should not have been deferred	63%	94%
Should have been deferred	37	6
	100	100
	(1,819)	(1,818)

Kendall and Lazarsfeld began with Stouffer's data showing the positive association between education and acceptance of induction (see Table 16-1). Following Stouffer's explanation, they created a hypothetical table, compatible with the empirical data, to show that education was related to whether one had friends who were deferred. In Table 16-2, we note that 19 percent of those with high education reported having friends who were deferred, as compared with 79 percent among those with less education.

Stouffer's explanation next assumed that soldiers with friends who had been deferred would be more likely to resent their own induction than

TABLE 16-4
Hypothetical Data Relating Education to Acceptance of Induction through the Factor of Having Friends Who Were Deferred

	Friends Deferred		No Friends Deferred	
	High Ed.	Low Ed.	High Ed.	Low Ed.
Should not have been deferred	63%	63%	94%	95%
Should have been deferred	37	37	6	5
	100	100	100	100
100% =	(335)	(1,484)	(1,426)	(392)

those who had no deferred friends. Table 16-3 presents the hypothetical data that would have supported that assumption.

The hypothetical data in Tables 16-2 and 16-3 confirm linkages that Stouffer had specified in his explanation. First, soldiers with low education were more likely to have friends who were deferred than soldiers with more education. And, second, having friends who were deferred made a soldier more likely to think he should have been deferred. Stouffer had suggested that these two relationships would clarify the original relationship between education and acceptance of induction. Kendall and Lazarsfeld created a hypothetical table that would confirm Stouffer's explanation (see Table 16-4).

Recall that the original finding was that draftees with high education were more likely to accept their induction into the army as fair than those with less education. In Table 16-4, however, we note that level of education has no effect on the acceptance of induction among those who report having friends deferred: 63 percent among *both* educational groups say they should not have been deferred. Similarly, educational level has no significant effect on acceptance of induction among those who reported having no friends deferred: 94 and 95 percent say they should not have been deferred.

On the other hand, among those with high education the acceptance of induction is strongly related to whether or not one's friends were deferred: 63 percent versus 94 percent. And the same is true among those with less education. The hypothetical data in Table 16-4, then, support Stouffer's contention that education affected acceptance of induction only through the medium of having friends deferred. Highly educated draftees were less likely to have friends deferred and, by virtue of that fact, were more likely to accept their own induction as fair. Those with less education were more likely to have friends deferred and, by virtue of that fact, were less likely to accept their own induction.

Recognize that neither Stouffer's explanation nor the hypothetical data denied the reality of the original relationship. As educational level increased, acceptance of one's own induction also increased. The nature of this empirical relationship, however, was interpreted through the introduction of a third variable. The variable, deferment of friends, did not deny the original relationship; it merely clarified the mechanism through which the original relationship occurred. This, then, is the heart of the elaboration model and of multivariate analysis.

Having observed an empirical relationship between two variables, we seek to understand the nature of that relationship through the effects produced by introducing other variables. Mechanically, we accomplish this by first dividing our sample into subsets on the basis of the **control** or **test variable**. For example, having friends deferred or not is the control variable in our present example, and the sample is divided into those who have deferred friends and those who do not. The relationship between the original two variables is then recomputed separately for each of the subsamples. The tables produced in this manner are called the *partial tables*, and the relationships found in the partial tables are called the *partial relationships*. The partial relationships are then compared with the initial relationship discovered in the total sample.

THE ELABORATION PARADIGM

This section presents guidelines for understanding an elaboration analysis. To begin, we must know whether the test variable is *antecedent* (prior in time) to the other two variables or whether it is *intervening* between them, because these positions suggest different logical relationships in the multivariate model. If the test variable is intervening, as in the case of education, deferment of friends, and acceptance of induction, then the analysis is based on the model shown in Figure 16-1. The logic of this multivariate relationship is that the independent variable (educational level) affects the intervening test variable (having friends deferred or not), which in turn affects the dependent variable (accepting induction).

If the test variable is antecedent to both the independent and dependent variables, a very different model must be used (see Figure 16-2). Here the test variable affects both the "independent" and "dependent" variables. Realize, of course, that the terms *independent variable* and *dependent variable* are, strictly speaking, used incorrectly in the diagram. In fact, we have one independent variable (the test variable) and two dependent variables. The incorrect terminology has been used only to provide continuity with the preceding example. Because of their individual relationships to the test variable, the "independent" and "dependent" variables are empirically related to each other, but there is no causal link between them. Their empirical relationship is merely a product of their coincidental relationships to the test variable. (Subsequent examples will further clarify this relationship.)

FIGURE 16-1
Intervening Test Variable

Independent variable → Test variable → Dependent variable

FIGURE 16-2
Antecedent Test Variable

Test variable → "Independent" variable
Test variable → "Dependent" variable

TABLE 16-5
The Elaboration Paradigm

Partial Relationships Compared with Original	Test Variable Antecedent	Test Variable Intervening
Same relationship	Relication	Replication
Less or none	Explanation	Interpretation
Split*	Specification	Specification

*One partial is the same or greater, and the other is less or none.

Table 16-5 is a guide to the understanding of an elaboration analysis. The two columns in the table indicate whether the test variable is antecedent or intervening in the sense described previously. The left side of the table shows the nature of the partial relationships as compared with the original relationship between the independent and dependent variables. The body of the table gives the technical notations—replication, explanation, interpretation, and specification—assigned to each case. We will discuss each in turn.

Replication

Whenever the partial relationships are essentially the same as the original relationship, the term *replication* is assigned to the result, regardless of whether the test variable is antecedent or intervening. This means that the original relationship has been replicated under test conditions. If, in our previous example, education still affected acceptance of induction both among those who had friends deferred and those who did not, then we would say the original relationship had been replicated. Note, however, that this finding would not confirm Stouffer's explanation of the original relationship. Having friends deferred or not would not be the mechanism through which education affected the acceptance of induction.

To see what a replication looks like, turn back to Tables 16-3 and 16-4 for a minute. Imagine that our initial discovery was that having friends deferred strongly influenced how soldiers felt about being drafted, as shown in Table 16-3. Had we first discovered this relationship, we might have wanted to see whether it was equally true

Attending an Ivy League College and Success in Later Professional Life

by Patricia L. Kendall
Department of Sociology, Queens College, CUNY

PROBABLY THE main danger for survey analysts is that a relationship they hope is causal will turn out to be spurious. That is, the original relationship between X and Y is explained by an antecedent test factor. More specifically, the partial relationships between X and Y reduce to 0 when that antecedent test factor is held constant.

This was a distinct possibility in a major finding from a study carried out nearly 35 years ago. One of my fellow graduate students at Columbia University, Patricia Salter West, based her dissertation on questionnaires obtained by *Time Magazine* from 10,000 of its male subscribers. Among many of the hypotheses developed by West was that male graduates of Ivy League schools (Brown, Columbia, Cornell, Dartmouth, Harvard, University of Pennsylvania, Princeton, and Yale) were more successful in their later professional careers, as defined by their annual earnings, than those who graduated from other colleges and universities.

The initial four-fold table supported West's expectation.

Although I made up the figures, they conform closely to what West actually found in her study. Having attended an Ivy League school seems to lead to considerably greater professional success than being a graduate of some other kind of college or university.

But wait a minute. Isn't this a relationship that typically could be spurious? Who can afford to send their sons to Ivy League schools? Wealthy families, of course.[†] And who can provide the business and professional connections that could help sons become successful in their careers? Again, wealthy or well-to-do families.

In other words, the socioeconomic status of the student's family may explain away the apparent causal relationship. In fact, some of West's findings suggest that this might indeed be the case.

A third of those coming from families defined as wealthy, compared with 1 in 11 coming from less well-to-do backgrounds, attended Ivy

TABLE 1*

Later Professional Success (Y)	College Attended (X)	
	Ivy League College	Other College or University
Successful	1,300 (65%)	2,000 (25%)
Unsuccessful	700 (35%)	6,000 (75%)
Total	2,000 (100%)	8,000 (100%)

*I have had to invent relevant figures because the only published version of West's study contained no totals. See Ernest Havemann and Patricia Salter West, *They Went to College* (New York: Harcourt, Brace, 1952).

TABLE 2
Attendance at Ivy League Colleges According to Family Socioeconomic Status (SES)

College Attended (X)	Family SES (T)	
	High SES	Low SES
Ivy League colleges	1,500 (33%)	500 (9%)
Other colleges and universities	3,000 (67%)	5,000 (91%)
Total	4,500 (100%)	5,500 (100%)

for soldiers of different educational backgrounds. To find out, we would have made education our control or test variable.

Table 16-4 contains the results of such an examination, though it is constructed somewhat differently from what we would have done had we used education as the control variable. Nevertheless, we see in the table that having friends deferred or not still influences attitudes toward being drafted among those soldiers with high education and those with low education. (Compare columns 1 and 3, then 2 and 4.) This result represents a replication of the relationship between having friends deferred and attitude toward being drafted.

TABLE 3
Partial Relationships between X and Y with T Held Constant

Later success (Y)	High Family SES (T)		Low Family SES (T)	
	Ivy League College (X)	Other College (X)	Ivy League College (X)	Other College
Successful	1,000 (67%)	1,000 (33%)	300 (60%)	1,000 (20%)
Not successful	500 (33%)	2,000 (67%)	200 (40%)	4,000 (80%)
Total	1,500 (100%)	3,000 (100%)	500 (100%)	5,000 (100%)

League colleges. Thus there is a very high correlation between the two variables, X and T. (There is a similarly high correlation between family socioeconomic status [T] and later professional success [Y].)

The magnitude of these so-called marginal correlations suggest that West's hypothesis regarding the causal nature of having attended an Ivy League college might be incorrect; it suggests instead that the socioeconomic status of the students' families accounted for the original relationship she observed.

We are not done yet, however. The crucial question is what happens to the partial relationships once the test factor is controlled. These are shown in Table 3.

These partial relationships show that, even when family socioeconomic status is held constant, there is still a marked relationship between having attended an Ivy League college and success in later professional life. As a result, West's initial hypothesis receives support from the analysis she carried out.

Despite this, West has in no way proved her hypothesis. There are almost always additional antecedent factors that might explain the original relationship. Consider, for example, the intelligence of the students (as measured by IQ tests or SAT scores). Ivy League colleges pride themselves on the excellence of their student bodies. They may therefore be willing to award merit scholarships to students with exceptional qualifications but not enough money to pay tuition and board. Once admitted to these prestigious colleges, bright students may develop the skills—and connections—that will lead to later professional success. Since West had no data on the intelligence of the men she studied, she was unable to study whether the partial relationships disappeared once this test factor was introduced.

In sum, the elaboration paradigm permits the investigator to rule out certain possibilities and to gain support for others. It does not permit us to prove anything.

---

†Since she had no direct data on family socioeconomic status, West defined as wealthy or having high socioeconomic status those who supported their sons completely during all four years of college. She defined as less wealthy or having low socioeconomic status those whose sons worked their way through college, in part or totally.

Researchers frequently use the elaboration model rather routinely in the hope of replicating their findings among subsets of the sample. If we discovered a relationship between education and prejudice, for example, we might introduce such test variables as age, region of the country, race, religion, and so forth, to test the stability of the original relationship. If the relationship were replicated among young and old, among people from different parts of the country, and so forth, we would have grounds for concluding that the original relationship was a genuine and general one.

In the box "Attending an Ivy League College and Success in Later Professional Life," Patricia

FIGURE 16-3
The Facts of Life about Storks and Babies

I. BIRTHRATES OF TOWNS AND CITIES HAVING FEW OR MANY STORKS

H = Town or city with high birthrate
L = Town or city with low birthrate

NUMBER OF STORKS

Few	Many
L L L LL L LLL LH L L L LL LL	H H H L H H H H H H H H

II. CONTROLLING FOR RURAL (Towns) AND URBAN (Cities)

NUMBER OF STORKS

	Few	Many
Rural	H	H H H H H H H H H H H H H H H
Urban	L L L L LL L L L L L L L L L L L	L

Kendall, one of the founders of the elaboration model, recalls a study in which the researcher suspected an explanation but found a replication. Though the example is now a bit dated, the topic is still of vital interest to students: To what extent does your professional success depend on attending the "right" school?

Explanation

Explanation is the term used to describe a *spurious relationship:* an original relationship explained away through the introduction of a test variable. This requires two conditions: (1) The test variable must be antecedent to both the independent and dependent variables. (2) The partial relationships must be zero or significantly less than those found in the original. Several examples will illustrate this situation.

There is an empirical relationship between the number of storks in different areas and the birthrates for those areas. The more storks in an area, the higher the birthrate. This empirical relationship might lead one to assume that the number of storks affects the birthrate. An antecedent test explains away this relationship, however. Rural areas have both more storks and higher birthrates than urban areas. Within rural areas, there is no relationship between the number of storks and the birthrate; nor is there a relationship within urban areas.

Figure 16-3 illustrates how the rural/urban variable causes the apparent relationship between storks and birthrates. Part I of the figure shows the original relationship. Notice how all but one of the entries in the box for towns and cities with few storks have high birthrates; with one exception, all those in the box for towns and cities with few storks have low birthrates. In percentage form, we say that 93 percent of the towns and cities with many storks also had high birthrates, as contrasted with 7 percent of those with few storks. That's quite a large percentage point difference and represents a strong association between the two variables.

Part II of the figure separates the towns from the cities, the rural from urban areas, and examines storks and babies in each type of place separately. Now we can see that all the rural places have high birthrates, and all the urban places have low birthrates. Also notice that only one rural place had few storks and only one urban place had lots of storks.

Here's a similar example. There is a positive relationship between the number of fire trucks responding to a fire and the amount of damage done. If more trucks respond, more damage is done. One might assume from this fact that the fire trucks themselves cause the damage. However, an antecedent test variable, the size of the fire, explains away the original relationship. Large fires do more damage than small ones, and more fire trucks respond to large fires than to small ones. Looking only at large fires, we would see that the original relationship vanishes (or perhaps reverses itself); and the same would be true looking only at small fires.

Finally, let's take a real research example. There is an empirical relationship between the region of the country in which medical school faculty members attended medical school and their attitudes toward Medicare (Babbie 1970). To simplify matters, only the East and the South will be examined. Of faculty members attending eastern medical schools, 78 percent said they approved of Medicare, compared with 59 percent of those attending southern medical schools. This finding makes sense in view of the fact that the South seems generally more resistant to such programs than the East, and medical school training should presumably affect a doctor's medical attitudes. However, this relationship is explained away when we introduce an antecedent test variable: the region of the country in which the faculty member was raised. Of faculty members

TABLE 16-6
Region of Origin, Region of Schooling, and Attitude toward Medicare

		Percentage Who Approve of Medicare	
		Region in Which Raised	
		East	South
Region of Medical School Training	East	84	50
	South	80	47

Source: Earl R. Babbie, *Science and Morality in Medicine* (Berkeley: University of California Press, 1970): 181.

raised in the East, 89 percent attended medical school in the East and 11 percent in the South. Of those raised in the South, 53 percent attended medical school in the East and 47 percent in the South. Moreover, the areas in which faculty members were raised related to attitudes toward Medicare. Of those raised in the East, 84 percent approved of Medicare, as compared with 49 percent of those raised in the South.

Table 16-6 presents the three-variable relationship among region in which raised, region of medical school training, and attitude toward Medicare. Faculty members raised in the East are quite likely to approve of Medicare, regardless of where they attended medical school. Those raised in the South are relatively less likely to approve of Medicare, but, again, the region of their medical school training has little or no effect. These data indicate, therefore, that the original relationship between region of medical training and attitude toward Medicare was spurious; it was due only to the coincidental effect of region of origin on both region of medical training and on attitude toward Medicare. When region of origin is *held constant*, as we have done in Table 16-6, the original relationship disappears in the partials.

Interpretation

Interpretation is similar to explanation, except for the time placement of the test variable and the implications that follow from that difference. The earlier example of education, friends deferred, and acceptance of induction is an excellent illustration of interpretation. In terms of the elaboration model, the effect of education on acceptance of induction is not explained away; it is still a genuine relationship. In a real sense, educational differences *cause* differential acceptance of induction. The intervening variable, deferment of friends, merely helps to interpret the mechanism through which the relationship occurs. Thus an interpretation does not deny the validity of the original, causal relationship but simply clarifies the process through which that relationship functions.

Here's another example of interpretation. Researchers have observed that children from broken homes are more likely to become delinquent than those from intact homes. This relationship may be interpreted, however, through the introduction of supervision as a test variable. Among children who are supervised, delinquency rates are not affected by whether or not their parents are divorced. The same is true among those who are not supervised. It is the relationship between broken homes and the lack of supervision that produced the original relationship.

Specification

Sometimes the elaboration model produces partial relationships that differ significantly from each other. For example, one partial relationship is the same as or stronger than the original two-variable relationship, and the second partial relationship is less than the original and may be reduced to zero. This situation is referred to as **specification** in the elaboration paradigm. We have specified the conditions under which the original relationship occurs.

Now recall the study of the sources of religious involvement (Glock et al. 1967:92). It was discovered that among Episcopal church members, involvement decreased as social class increased. This finding is reported in Table 16-7, which examines mean levels of church involvement among women parishioners at different levels of social class.

Glock interpreted this finding in the context of others in the analysis and concluded that church involvement provides an alternative form of gratification for people who are denied gratification in the secular society. This conclusion explained why women were more religious than men, why old people were more religious than young people,

TABLE 16-7
Social Class and Mean Church Involvement among Episcopal Women

	Social Class Levels				
	Low 0	1	2	3	High 4
Mean involvement	.63	.58	.49	.48	.45

Source: Tables 16-7, 16-8, and 16-9 are from Charles Y. Glock, Benjamin B. Ringer, and Earl R. Babbie. *To Comfort and to Challenge* (Berkeley: University of California Press, 1967). Used with permission of the Regents of the University of California.
Note: Mean scores rather than percentages have been used here.

TABLE 16-8
Social Class and the Holding of Office in Secular Organizations

	Social Class Levels				
	Low 0	1	2	3	High 4
Percentage who have held office in a secular organization	46	47	54	60	83

Note: Percentages are used in this table.

TABLE 16-9
Church Involvement by Social Class and Holding Secular Office

	Mean Church Involvement for Social Class Levels				
	Low 0	1	2	3	High 4
Have held office	.46	.53	.46	.46	.46
Have not held office	.62	.55	.47	.46	.40

and so forth. Glock reasoned that people of lower social class (measured by income and education) had fewer chances to gain self-esteem from the secular society than people of higher social class. To illustrate this idea, he noted that social class was strongly related to the likelihood that a woman had ever held an office in a secular organization (see Table 16-8).

Glock then reasoned that if social class were related to church involvement only by virtue of the fact that lower-class women would be denied opportunities for gratification in the secular society, the original relationship should *not* hold among women who were getting gratification. As a rough indicator of the receipt of gratifica-

TABLE 16-10
Example of a Suppressor Variable

I: No Apparent Relationship between Attitudes toward Jews and Length of Time in the Union

	Less than four years	Four years or more
Percent who don't care if there are Jews on the union staff	49.2 (126)	50.5 (256)

II: In Each Age Group, Length of Time in Union Increases Willingness to Have Jews on Union Staff

		Length of Time in the Union	
Percent who don't care if there are Jews on the union staff	Age:	Less than four years	Four years or more
	29 years and under	56.4 (78)	62.7 (51)
	30–49 years	37.1 (35)	48.3 (116)
	50 years and older	38.4 (13)	56.1 (89)

Source: Adapted from Morris Rosenberg, *The Logic of Survey Analysis* (New York: Basic Books, 1968): 88–89. Used by permission.

tion from the secular society, he used as a variable the holding of secular office. In this test, social class should be unrelated to church involvement among those who had held such office.

Table 16-9 presents an example of a specification. Among women who have held office in secular organizations, there is essentially no relationship between social class and church involvement. In effect, the table specifies the conditions under which the original relationship holds: among those women lacking gratification in the secular society.

The term *specification* is used in the elaboration paradigm regardless of whether the test variable is antecedent or intervening. In either case, the meaning is the same. We have specified the particular conditions under which the original relationship holds.

Refinements to the Paradigm

The preceding sections have presented the primary logic of the elaboration model as developed by Lazarsfeld and his colleagues. Morris Rosenberg (1968) offers an excellent presentation of this paradigm and goes beyond it to suggest additional variations.

Rather than reviewing Rosenberg's comments, let's consider the logically possible variations. Some of these points are found in Rosenberg's book; others were suggested by it.

First, the basic paradigm assumes an initial relationship between two variables. It might be useful, however, in a more comprehensive model to differentiate between positive and negative relationships. Moreover, Rosenberg suggests using the elaboration model even with an original relationship of *zero*. He cites as an example a study of union membership and attitudes toward having Jews on the union staff (see Table 16-10). The initial analysis indicated that length of union membership did not relate to the attitude: Those who had belonged to the union less than four years were just as willing to accept Jews on the staff as those who had belonged for more than four years. The *age* of union members, however, was found to *suppress* the relationship between length of union membership and attitude toward Jews. Overall, younger members were more favorable to Jews than older members. At the same time, of course, younger members were not likely to have been in the union as long as the old members. Within specific age groups, however, those in the union longest were the most supportive of having Jews on the staff. Age, in this case, was a *suppressor variable*, concealing the relationship between length of membership and attitude toward Jews.

Second, the basic paradigm focuses on partials being the same or weaker than the original relationship but does not provide guidelines for specifying what constitutes a significant difference between the original and the partials. When you use the elaboration model, you'll frequently find yourself making an arbitrary decision about whether a given partial is significantly weaker than the original. This, then, suggests another dimension that could be added to the paradigm.

Third, the limitation of the basic paradigm to partials that are the same as or weaker than the original neglects two other possibilities. A partial relationship might be *stronger* than the original. Or, on the other hand, a partial relationship might be the reverse of the original—negative where the original was positive.

Rosenberg provides a hypothetical example of the latter possibility by first suggesting that a researcher might find working-class respondents in his study more supportive of the civil rights movement than middle-class respondents are (see Table 16-11). He further suggests that *race* might be a *distorter variable* in this instance, distorting the true relationship between class and attitudes. Presumably, African-American respondents would be more supportive of the movement than whites, but African Americans would also be overrepresented among working-class respondents and underrepresented among the middle class. Middle-class African-American respondents might be more supportive of the movement than working-class African Americans, however; and the same relationship might be found among whites. *Holding race constant*, then, the researcher would conclude that support for the civil rights movement was greater among the middle class than among the working class.

Here's another example of a distorter variable at work. When Michel de Seve set out to examine the starting salaries of men and women in the same organization, she was surprised to find the women receiving higher starting salaries, on the average, than their male counterparts. The distorter variable was time of first hire. Many of the women had been hired relatively recently, when salaries were higher overall than in the earlier years when many of the men had been hired (reported in E. Cook 1995).

All these new dimensions further complicate the notion of specification. If one partial is the same as the original, and the other partial is even stronger, how should you react to that situation? You've specified one condition under which the original relationship holds up, but you've also specified another condition under which it holds even more clearly.

Finally, the basic paradigm focuses primarily on dichotomous test variables. In fact, the elaboration model is not so limited—either in theory or in use—but the basic paradigm becomes more complicated when the test variable divides the sample into three or more subsamples. And the paradigm becomes more complicated yet when more than one test variable is used simultaneously.

I'm not saying all this to fault the basic elaboration paradigm. To the contrary, I want to impress on you that the elaboration model is not a simple algorithm—a set of procedures through which to analyze research. Rather, it is primarily a logical device for assisting the researcher in understanding his or her data. A firm understanding of the elaboration model will make a sophisticated analysis easier. However, it suggests neither which variables should be introduced as controls nor definitive conclusions about the nature of

TABLE 16-11
Example of a Distorter Variable (Hypothetical)

I: Working-Class Subjects Appear More Liberal on Civil Rights than Middle-Class Subjects

Civil Rights Score	Middle Class	Working Class
High	37%	45%
Low	63	55
100% =	100 (120)	100 (120)

II: Controlling for Race Shows the Middle Class to Be More Liberal than the Working Class

	Social Class			
	Blacks		Whites	
Civil Rights Score	Middle Class	Working Class	Middle Class	Working Class
High	70%	50%	30%	20%
Low	30	50	70	80
100% =	100 (20)	100 (100)	100 (100)	100 (20)

Source: Morris Rosenberg, *The Logic of Survey Analysis* (New York: Basic Books, 1968): 94–95. Used by permission.

elaboration results. For all these things, you must look to your own ingenuity. Such ingenuity, moreover, will come only through extensive experience. By pointing to oversimplifications in the basic elaboration paradigm, I have sought to bring home the point that the model provides only a logical framework. You'll find sophisticated analyses far more complicated than the examples used to illustrate the basic paradigm.

At the same time, if you fully understand the basic model, you'll understand other techniques such as correlations, regressions, and factor analyses a lot more easily. Chapter 17 will attempt to place such techniques as partial correlations and partial regressions in the context of the elaboration model.

■ ELABORATION AND EX POST FACTO HYPOTHESIZING

Before we leave the discussion of the elaboration model, we should look at it in connection with *ex post facto hypothesizing,* a form of fallacious reasoning. The reader of methodological literature will find countless references warning against it. But although the intentions of such injunctions are correct, inexperienced researchers can sometimes be confused about its implications.

When you observe an empirical relationship between two variables and then simply suggest a reason for that relationship, that is sometimes called ex post facto hypothesizing. You've generated a hypothesis linking two variables after their relationship is already known. You'll recall, from an early discussion in this book, that all hypotheses must be subject to disconfirmation. Unless you can specify empirical findings that would disprove your hypothesis, it's not really a hypothesis as researchers use that term. You might reason, therefore, that once you've observed a relationship between two variables, any hypothesis regarding that relationship cannot be disproved.

This is a fair assessment if you are doing nothing more than dressing up your empirical observations with deceptive hypotheses after the fact. Having observed that women are more religious than men, you should not simply assert that women will be more religious than men because of some general dynamic of social behavior and then rest your case on the initial observation.

The unfortunate spin-off of the injunction against ex post facto hypothesizing is in its inhibition of good, honest hypothesizing after the fact. Inexperienced researchers are often led to believe that they must make all their hypotheses before examining their data—even if that process means making a lot of poorly reasoned ones. Furthermore, they're led to ignore any empirically observed relationships that do not confirm some prior hypothesis.

Surely, few researchers would now wish that Sam Stouffer had hushed up his anomalous findings regarding morale among soldiers in the army. Stouffer noted peculiar empirical observations and set about hypothesizing the reasons for those findings. And his reasoning has proved invaluable to researchers ever since.

There is another, more sophisticated point to be made here, however. Anyone can generate hypotheses to explain observed empirical relationships in a body of data, but the elaboration model provides the logical tools for *testing* those hypotheses within the same body of data. A good example of this testing may be found in the earlier discussion of social class and church involvement. Glock explained the original relationship in terms of social deprivation theory. If he had stopped at that point, his comments would have been interesting but hardly persuasive. He went beyond that point, however. He noted that if the hypothesis was correct, then the relationship between social class and church involvement should disappear among those women who were receiving gratification from the secular society—those who had held office in a secular organization. This hypothesis was then subjected to an empirical test. Had the new hypothesis not been confirmed by the data, he would have been forced to reconsider.

These additional comments should further illustrate the point that data analysis is a continuing process, demanding all the ingenuity and perseverance you can muster. The image of a researcher carefully laying out hypotheses and then testing them in a ritualistic fashion results only in ritualistic research.

In case you're concerned that the strength of ex post facto proofs seems to be less than that of the traditional kinds, let me repeat the earlier assertion that "scientific proof" is a contradiction in terms. Nothing is ever *proved* scientifically. Hypotheses, explanations, theories, or hunches can all escape a stream of attempts at disproof, but none can be proved in any absolute sense. The acceptance of a hypothesis, then, is really a function of the extent to which it has been tested and not disconfirmed. No hypothesis, therefore, should be considered sound on the basis of one test—whether the hypothesis was generated before or after the observation of empirical data. With this in mind, you should not deny yourself some of the most fruitful avenues available to you in data analysis. You should always try to reach an honest understanding of your data, develop meaningful theories for more general understanding, and not worry about the manner of reaching that understanding.

■ MAIN POINTS

- The elaboration model is a method of multivariate analysis appropriate to social research.
- The elaboration model is primarily a logical model that can illustrate the basic logic of other multivariate methods.
- The basic steps in elaboration are as follows: (1) A relationship is observed to exist between two variables; (2) a third variable is held constant in the sense that the cases under study are subdivided according to the attributes of that third variable; (3) the original two-variable relationship is recomputed within each of the subgroups; and (4) the comparison of the original relationship with the relationships found within each subgroup provides a fuller understanding of the original relationship itself.
- An intervening control variable is one that occurs in time between the independent variable and the dependent variable.
- An antecedent control variable is one that occurs earlier in time than both the independent and the dependent variable.
- A zero-order relationship is the observed relationship between two variables *without* a third variable being held constant or controlled.
- A partial relationship is the observed relationship between two variables—within a subgroup of cases based on some attribute of the control variable. Thus, the relationship between age and prejudice among men only (that is, controlling for gender) would be a partial relationship.
- If a set of partial relationships is essentially the same as the corresponding zero-order relationship, this outcome is called a replication, regardless of whether the control variable is intervening or antecedent. This means, simply, that the originally observed relationship has been replicated within smaller subgroups and that the control variable has no influence on that original relationship.
- If a set of partial relationships is reduced essentially to zero when an antecedent variable is held constant, this outcome is called an explanation, meaning that the originally observed "relationship" was a spurious or ungenuine one. This outcome suggests that the control variable has a causal effect on each of the variables examined in the zero-order relationship, thus resulting in a statistical relationship between those two that does not represent a causal relationship in itself.
- If a set of partial relationships is reduced essentially to zero when an intervening variable is held constant, this outcome is called an interpretation, meaning that we have interpreted the manner in which the independent variable has its influence on the dependent variable: The independent variable influences the intervening variable, which, in turn, influences the dependent variable. In this instance, we conclude that the original relationship was a genuine causal relationship; we have shed further light on how that causal process operates.
- If one partial relationship is reduced (ideally to zero) and the other remains about the same as the original relationship (or is stronger), this outcome is called a specification, regardless of whether the control variable was intervening or antecedent. This means, simply, that

- we have specified the conditions under which the originally observed relationship occurs.
- A suppressor variable is one that conceals the relationship between two other variables.
- A distorter variable is one that causes an apparent reversal in the relationship between two other variables: from negative to positive or vice versa.
- Ex post facto hypothesizing refers to the development of hypotheses "predicting" relationships that have already been observed. This is invalid in science, since it is impossible to disconfirm such hypotheses. Of course, nothing prevents us from suggesting reasons that observed relationships may be the way they are; we simply should not frame those reasons in the form of "hypotheses." More important, one observed relationship and possible reasons for it may suggest hypotheses about other relationships that have not been examined. The elaboration model is an excellent logical device for this kind of unfolding analysis of data.

■ REVIEW QUESTIONS AND EXERCISES

1. In your own words describe the elaboration logic of
   a. Replication
   b. Interpretation
   c. Explanation
   d. Specification
2. Review the Stouffer-Kendall-Lazarsfeld example of education, friends deferred, and attitudes toward being drafted. Suppose they had begun with an association between friends deferred and attitudes toward being drafted, and then they controlled for education. What conclusion would they have reached?
3. Search the Web for a research report on the discovery of a spurious relationship. Give the Web address of the document and quote or paraphrase what was discovered.

■ ADDITIONAL READINGS

Glock, Charles, ed. *Survey Research in the Social Sciences.* New York: Russell Sage Foundation, 1967: Chapter 1. An excellent discussion of the logic of elaboration. Glock's own chapter in this book presents the elaboration model, providing concrete illustrations.

Lazarsfeld, Paul F. *The Varied Sociology of Paul F. Lazarsfeld.* Edited by Patricia L. Kendall. New York: Columbia University Press, 1982. Here's a collection of essays on the logic of social research by the principal founder of the elaboration model, edited by his cofounder.

Lazarsfeld, Paul, Ann Pasanella, and Morris Rosenberg, eds. *Continuities in the Language of Social Research.* New York: Free Press, 1972. An excellent and classic collection of conceptual discussions and empirical illustrations. Section II is especially relevant, though the logic of elaboration runs throughout most of the volume.

Merton, Robert K., James S. Coleman, and Peter H. Rossi, eds. *Qualitative and Quantitative Social Research.* New York: The Free Press, 1979. This collection of articles written in honor of Lazarsfeld illustrates the logic he brought to social research.

Rosenberg, Morris. *The Logic of Survey Analysis.* New York: Basic Books, 1968. The most comprehensive statement of elaboration available. Rosenberg presents the basic paradigm and goes on to suggest logical extensions of it. It is difficult to decide what is most important, this aspect of the book or the voluminous illustrations. Both are simply excellent, and this book serves an important instructional purpose.

CHAPTER 17 Social Statistics

What You'll Learn in This Chapter
Here you'll learn about a few simple statistics frequently used in social research. If you have an aversion to statistics, you may be pleasantly surprised.

INTRODUCTION

THE DANGER OF SUCCESS IN MATH

DESCRIPTIVE STATISTICS
Data Reduction
Measures of Association
Regression Analysis

OTHER MULTIVARIATE TECHNIQUES
Path Analysis
Time-Series Analysis
Factor Analysis

INFERENTIAL STATISTICS
Univariate Inferences
Tests of Statistical Significance
The Logic of Statistical Significance
Chi Square

MAIN POINTS

REVIEW QUESTIONS AND EXERCISES

ADDITIONAL READINGS

INTRODUCTION

It has been my experience over the years that many students are intimidated by statistics. Sometimes statistics makes them feel they're

- A few clowns short of a circus
- Dumber than a box of hair
- A few feathers short of a duck
- All foam, no beer
- Missing a few buttons on their remote control
- A few beans short of a burrito
- As screwed up as a football bat
- About as sharp as a bowling ball
- About four cents short of a nickel
- Not running on full thrusters*

Many people are intimidated by empirical research because they feel uncomfortable with mathematics and statistics. And indeed, many research reports are filled with unspecified computations. The role of statistics in social research is quite important, but it is equally important that you see this role in its proper perspective.

Empirical research is first and foremost a logical rather than a mathematical operation. Mathematics is merely a convenient and efficient language for accomplishing the logical operations inherent in good data analysis. *Statistics* is the applied branch of mathematics especially appropriate to a variety of research analyses.

I want to start this chapter with an informal look at one of the concerns I find people have when they approach statistics. I suspect this exercise will make it easier for you to understand and feel comfortable with the relatively simple statistics introduced in the remainder of the chapter. We'll be looking at two types of statistics: *descriptive* and *inferential*. **Descriptive statistics** is a medium for describing data in manageable forms. **Inferential statistics,** on the other hand, assists you in drawing conclusions from your observations; typically, this involves drawing conclusions about a population from the study of a sample drawn from it.

---

*Thanks to the many contributors to humor lists on the Internet.

THE DANGER OF SUCCESS IN MATH

Since I began teaching research methods that include at least a small amount of statistics, I've been struck by the large number of students who report that they are "simply no good at math." Just as some people are reported to be inherently tone-deaf and others unable to learn foreign languages, about 90 percent of my college students seemed to suffer from *congenital math deficiency syndrome* (CMDS). Some of its common symptoms are frustration, boredom, and drowsiness. I'm delighted to report that I have finally uncovered a major cause of the disease and have brewed up a cure. In the event that you may be a sufferer, I'd like to share it with you before we delve into the statistics of social research.

You may be familiar with the story of Typhoid Mary, whose real name was Mary Mallon. Mary was a typhoid carrier who died in 1938 in New York. Before her death, she worked as a household cook, moving from household to household and causing ten outbreaks of typhoid fever. Over 50 people caught the disease from her, and 3 of them died.

The congenital math deficiency syndrome has a similar cause. After an exhaustive search, I've discovered the culprit, whom I'll call Mathematical Marvin, though he has used countless aliases. If you suffer from CMDS, I suspect you've met him. Take a minute to recall your years in high school. Remember the person your teachers and your classmates regarded as a "mathematical genius." Getting *A*'s in all the math classes was only part of it; often the math genius seemed to know math better than the teachers.

Now that you have that math genius in mind, let me ask you a few questions. First, what was the person's gender? I'd guess he was probably male. Most of the students I've asked in class report that. But let's consider some other characteristics:

1. How athletic was he?
2. Did he wear glasses?
3. How many parties did he get invited to during high school?
4. If he was invited to parties, did anyone ever talk to him?

5. How often did you find yourself envying the math genius, wishing you could trade places with him?

I've been asking students (including some adult classes) these questions for several years, and the answers I've gotten are amazing. Marvin is usually unathletic, often either very skinny or overweight. He usually wears glasses, and he seems otherwise rather delicate. During his high school years, he was invited to an average (mean) of 1.2 parties, and nobody talked to him. His complexion was terrible. Almost nobody ever wanted to change places with him; he was a social misfit, more to be pitied than envied.

Here's the point of my report on Mathematical Marvin. As I've discussed Marvin with my students, it has become increasingly clear that most of them have formed a subconscious association between mathematical proficiency and Marvin's unenviable characteristics. Most have concluded that doing well in math and statistics would turn them into social misfits, which they regard as too high a price to pay.

Everything I've said about Mathematical Marvin represents a powerful stereotype that many people still seem to share, but I'd like you to realize that it's only a social stereotype, not a matter of biology. Women can excel in mathematics; attractive people can calculate as accurately as unattractive ones. Yet the stereotypes exercise a powerful influence on our behavior, as evidenced in the tragic examples of young women, for example, pretending mathematical impotence in the belief that they will be seen as less attractive if they are gifted in that realm.

So if you're one of those people who's "just no good at math," it's possible you carry around a hidden fear that your face will break out in pimples if you do well in statistics in this course. If so, you're going to be reading the rest of this chapter in a terrible state: wanting to understand it at least until the next exam and, at the same time, worrying that you may understand it too well and lose all your friends.

Before exposing you to any numbers, then, I want to assure you that the level of statistics contained in the rest of this chapter has been proved safe for humans. There has not been a single documented case of pimples connected to understanding *lambda, gamma, chi square,* or any of the other statistics discussed in the pages to follow. In fact, this level of exposure has been found to be *beneficial* to young social researchers.

By the way, uncovering Marvin can clear up a lot of mysteries. It did for me. (In my high school class, he didn't wear glasses, but he squinted a lot.) In the first research methods book I wrote, I presented three statistical computations and got one of them wrong. In the first edition of this book, I got a different one wrong. Most embarrassing of all, however, the first printing of the earlier book had a unique feature. I thought it would be fun to write a computer program to generate my own table of random numbers rather than reprinting one that someone else had created. In doing that, I had the dubious honor of publishing the world's first table of random numbers that *didn't have any nines!* It was not until I tracked Marvin down that I discovered the source of my problems, and statistics has been much more fun (and trouble-free) ever since. So enjoy.

■ DESCRIPTIVE STATISTICS

As I've already suggested, descriptive statistics is a method for presenting quantitative descriptions in a manageable form. Sometimes we want to describe single variables, and sometimes we want to describe the associations that connect one variable with another. Let's look at some of the ways to do these things.

Data Reduction

Scientific research often involves collecting large masses of data. Suppose we had surveyed 2,000 people, asking each of them 100 questions—not an unusually large study. We would now have a staggering 200,000 answers! No one could possibly read all those 200,000 answers and reach any meaningful conclusion about them. Thus, much scientific analysis involves the *reduction* of data from unmanageable details to manageable summaries.

TABLE 17-1
Partial Raw Data Matrix

	Gender	Age	Education	Income	Occupation	Political Affiliation	Political Orientation	Religious Affiliation	Importance of Religion
Person 1	1	3	2	4	1	2	3	0	4
Person 2	1	4	2	4	4	1	1	1	2
Person 3	2	2	5	5	2	2	4	2	3
Person 4	1	5	4	4	3	2	2	2	4
Person 5	2	3	7	8	6	1	1	5	1
Person 6	2	1	3	3	5	3	5	1	1

TABLE 17-2
Hypothetical Raw Data on Education and Prejudice

	Educational Level				
Prejudice	None	Grade School	High School	College	Graduate Degree
High	23	34	156	67	16
Medium	11	21	123	102	23
Low	6	12	95	164	77

To begin our discussion, let's look briefly at the raw data matrix created by a quantitative research project. Table 17-1 presents a partial data matrix. Notice that each row in the matrix represents a person (or other unit of analysis), each column represents a variable, and each cell represents the coded attribute or value a given person has on a given variable. The first column in Table 17-1 represents a person's gender. Let's say a "1" represents male and "2" represents female. This means that persons 1 and 2 are male, person 3 is female, and so forth.

In the case of age, person 1's "3" might mean 30–39 years old, person 2's "4" might mean 40–49. However age had been coded (see Chapter 14), the code numbers shown in Table 17-1 would describe each of the people represented there.

Notice that the data have already been reduced somewhat by the time a data matrix like this one has been created. If age had been coded as suggested previously, the specific answer "33 years old" has already been assigned to the category "30–39." The people responding to our survey may have given us 60 or 70 different ages, but we have now reduced them to 6 or 7 categories.

Chapter 15 discussed some of the ways of further summarizing univariate data: averages such as the mode, median, and mean and measures of dispersion such as the range, the standard deviation, and so forth. It's also possible to summarize the associations among variables.

Measures of Association

The association between any two variables can also be represented by a data matrix, this time produced by the joint frequency distributions of the two variables. Table 17-2 presents such a matrix. It provides all the information needed to determine the nature and extent of the relationship between education and prejudice.

Notice, for example, that 23 people (1) have no education and (2) scored high on prejudice; 77 people (1) had graduate degrees and (2) scored low on prejudice.

Like the raw-data matrix in Table 17-1, this matrix gives you more information than you can easily comprehend. If you study the table carefully, however, you will note that as education increases from "None" to "Graduate degree," there is a general tendency for prejudice to decrease, but no more than a general impression is possible. A variety of descriptive statistics permit the summarization of this data matrix, however. Selecting the appropriate measure depends initially on the nature of the two variables.

We'll turn now to some of the options available for summarizing the association between two variables. Each measure of association we'll discuss is based on the same model—*proportionate reduction of error* (PRE). To see how this model works, let's assume that I asked you to guess respondents' attributes on a given variable: for example, whether they answered yes or no to a given questionnaire item.

To assist you, let's first assume you know the overall distribution of responses in the total sample—say, 60 percent said yes and 40 percent said no. You would make the fewest errors in this process if you always guessed the *modal* (most frequent) response: yes.

Second, let's assume you also know the empirical relationship between the first variable and some other variable: say, *gender*. Now, each time I ask you to guess whether a respondent said yes or no, I'll tell you whether the respondent is a man or a woman. If the two variables are related, you should make fewer errors the second time. It is possible, therefore, to compute the PRE by knowing the relationship between the two variables: the greater the relationship, the greater the reduction of error.

This basic PRE model is modified slightly to take account of different levels of measurement—nominal, ordinal, or interval. The following sections will consider each level of measurement and present one measure of association appropriate to each. You should realize that the three measures discussed are only an arbitrary selection from among many appropriate measures.

Nominal Variables If the two variables consist of nominal data (for example, gender, religious affiliation, race), lambda (λ) would be one appropriate measure. Lambda is based on your ability to guess values on one of the variables: the PRE achieved through knowledge of values on the other variable.

Imagine this situation. I tell you that a room contains 100 people and I would like you to guess the gender of each person, one at a time. If half are men and half women, you will probably be right half the time and wrong half the time. But suppose I tell you each person's occupation before you guess that person's gender.

TABLE 17-3
Hypothetical Data Relating Gender to Employment Status

	Men	Women	Total
Employed	900	200	1,100
Unemployed	100	800	900
Total	1,000	1,000	2,000

What gender would you guess if I said the person was a truck driver? Probably you would be wise to guess "male"; although there are now plenty of women truck drivers, most are still men. If I said the next person was a nurse, you'd probably be wisest to guess "female," following the same logic. While you would still make errors in guessing genders, you would clearly do better than you would if you didn't know their occupations. The extent to which you did better (the proportionate reduction of error) would be an indicator of the association that exists between gender and occupation.

Here's another simple hypothetical example that illustrates the logic and method of lambda. Table 17-3 presents hypothetical data relating gender to employment status. Overall, we note that 1,100 people are employed, and 900 are not employed. If you were to predict whether people were employed, knowing only the overall distribution on that variable, you would always predict "employed," since that would result in fewer errors than always predicting "not employed." Nevertheless, this strategy would result in 900 errors out of 2,000 predictions.

Let's suppose that you had access to the data in Table 17-3 and that you were told each person's gender before making your prediction of employment status. Your strategy would change in that case. For every man, you would predict "employed," and for every woman, you would predict "not employed." In this instance, you would make 300 errors—the 100 men who were not employed and the 200 employed women—or 600 fewer errors than you would make without knowing the person's gender.

Lambda, then, represents the reduction in errors as a proportion of the errors that would have been made on the basis of the overall distribution. In this hypothetical example, lambda would equal .67; that is, 600 fewer errors divided by the 900 total errors based on employment status alone. In this fashion, lambda measures the statistical association between gender and employment status.

If gender and employment status were statistically independent, we would find the same distribution of employment status for men and women. In this case, knowing gender would not affect the number of errors made in predicting employment status, and the resulting lambda would be zero. If, on the other hand, all men were employed and none of the women were employed, by knowing gender you would avoid errors in predicting employment status. You would make 900 fewer errors (out of 900), so lambda would be 1.0—representing a perfect statistical association.

Lambda is only one of several measures of association appropriate to the analysis of two nominal variables. You could look at any statistics textbook for a discussion of other appropriate measures.

Ordinal Variables If the variables being related are ordinal (for example, social class, religiosity, alienation), gamma (γ) is one appropriate measure of association. Like lambda, gamma is based on your ability to guess values on one variable by knowing values on another. Instead of guessing exact values, however, gamma is based on the ordinal arrangement of values. For any given pair of cases, you guess that their ordinal ranking on one variable will correspond (positively or negatively) to their ordinal ranking on the other.

Let's say we have a group of elementary students. It would be reasonable to assume there is a relationship between their ages and their heights. We could test this by comparing every pair of students: Sam and Mary, Sam and Fred, Mary and Fred, and so forth. Then we would ignore all the pairs in which the students were the same age and/or the same height. We would then classify each of the remaining pairs (those who differed in both age and height) into one of two categories: those in which the oldest child was also the tallest ("same" pairs) and those in which the oldest child was the shortest ("opposite" pairs). So, if Sam was older and taller than Mary, the Sam-Mary pair would be counted as a "same." If Sam was older but shorter than Mary, then that pair would be an "opposite." (If they were the same age and/or same height, we would have ignored them.)

To determine whether age and height were related to one another, we would compare the number of same and opposite pairs. If the same pairs outnumbered the opposite pairs, we'd conclude that there was a *positive* association between the two variables—as one increases, the other increases. If there were more opposites than sames, we'd conclude that the relationship was a *negative* one. If there were about as many sames as opposites, we'd conclude that age and height were not related to each another, that they were *independent* of each other.

Here's a social science example to illustrate the simple calculations involved in gamma. Let's say you suspect that religiosity is positively related to political conservatism, and if Person A is more religious than Person B, you guess that A is also more conservative than B. Gamma is the proportion of paired comparisons that fits this pattern.

Table 17-4 presents hypothetical data relating social class to prejudice. The general nature of the relationship between these two variables is that as social class increases, prejudice decreases. There is a negative association between social class and prejudice.

Gamma is computed from two quantities: (1) the number of pairs having the same ranking on the two variables and (2) the number of pairs having the opposite ranking on the two variables. The pairs having the same ranking are computed as follows. The frequency of each cell in the table is multiplied by the sum of all cells appearing below and to the right of it—with all these products being summed. In Table 17-4, the number of pairs with the same ranking would be 200(900 + 300 + 400 + 100) + 500(300 + 100) + 400(400

TABLE 17-4
Hypothetical Data Relating Social Class to Prejudice

Prejudice	Lower Class	Middle Class	Upper Class
Low	200	400	700
Medium	500	900	400
High	800	300	100

TABLE 17-5
Gamma Associations among the Semantic Differentiation Items of the Sanctification Scale

	Useful	Honest	Superior	Kind	Friendly	Warm
Good	.79	.88	.80	.90	.79	.83
Useful		.84	.71	.77	.68	.72
Honest			.83	.89	.79	.82
Superior				.78	.60	.73
Kind					.88	.90
Friendly						.90

Source: Helena Znaniecki Lopata, "Widowhood and Husband Sanctification," *Journal of Marriage and the Family* (May 1981): 439–50.

+ 100) + 900(100) or 340,000 + 200,000 + 200,000 + 90,000 = 830,000.

The pairs having the opposite ranking on the two variables are computed as follows: The frequency of each cell in the table is multiplied by the sum of all cells appearing below and to the left of it—with all these products being summed. In Table 17-4, the numbers of pairs with opposite rankings would be 700(500 + 800 + 900 + 300) + 400(800 + 300) + 400(500 + 800) + 900(800) or 1,750,000 + 440,000 + 520,000 + 720,000 = 3,430,000. Gamma is computed from the numbers of same-ranked pairs and opposite-ranked pairs as follows:

$$gamma = \frac{same - opposite}{same + opposite}$$

In our example, gamma equals (830,000 − 3,430,000) divided by (830,000 + 3,430,000) or −.61. The negative sign in this answer indicates the negative association suggested by the initial inspection of the table. Social class and prejudice, in this hypothetical example, are negatively associated with one another. The numerical figure for gamma indicates that 61 percent more of the pairs examined had the opposite ranking than the same ranking.

Note that whereas values of lambda vary from 0 to 1, values of gamma vary from 1 to +1, representing the *direction* as well as the magnitude of the association. Because nominal variables have no ordinal structure, it makes no sense to speak of the direction of the relationship. (A negative lambda would indicate that you made more errors in predicting values on one variable while knowing values on the second than you made in ignorance of the second, and that's not logically possible.)

Table 17-5 is an example of the use of gamma in contemporary social research. To study the extent to which widows sanctified their deceased husbands, Helena Znaniecki Lopata (1981) administered a questionnaire to a probability sample of 301 widows. In part, the questionnaire asked the respondents to characterize their deceased husbands in terms of the following *semantic differentiation scale:*

			Characteristic				
Positive Extreme							Negative Extreme
Good	1	2	3	4	5	6	7	Bad
Useful	1	2	3	4	5	6	7	Useless
Honest	1	2	3	4	5	6	7	Dishonest
Superior	1	2	3	4	5	6	7	Inferior
Kind	1	2	3	4	5	6	7	Cruel
Friendly	1	2	3	4	5	6	7	Unfriendly
Warm	1	2	3	4	5	6	7	Cold

Respondents were asked to describe their deceased spouses by circling a number for each pair of opposing characteristics. Notice that the series of numbers connecting each pair of characteristics is an ordinal measure.

Next, Lopata wanted to discover the extent to which the several measures were related to each other. Appropriately, she chose gamma as the measure of association. Table 17-5 shows how she presented the results of her investigation.

The format presented in Table 17-5 is called a *correlation matrix*. For each pair of measures, Lopata has calculated the gamma. Good and Useful, for example, are related to each other by a gamma equal to .79. The matrix is a convenient way of presenting the intercorrelations among several variables, and you'll find it frequently in the research literature. In this case, we see that all the variables are quite strongly related to each other, though some pairs are more strongly related than others.

Gamma is only one of several measures of association appropriate to ordinal variables. Again, any introductory statistics textbook will give you a more comprehensive treatment of this subject.

Interval or Ratio Variables If interval or ratio variables (for example, age, income, grade point average, and so forth) are being associated, one appropriate measure of association is Pearson's product-moment correlation (r). The derivation and computation of this measure of association is complex enough to lie outside the scope of this book, so I'll make only a few general comments here.

Like both gamma and lambda, r is based on guessing the value of one variable by knowing the other. For continuous interval or ratio variables, however, it is unlikely that you could predict the *precise* value of the variable. But on the other hand, predicting only the ordinal arrangement of values on the two variables would not take advantage of the greater amount of information conveyed by an interval or ratio variable. In a sense, r reflects *how closely* you can guess the value of one variable through your knowledge of the value of the other.

To understand the logic of r, consider the way you might hypothetically guess values that particular cases have on a given variable. With nominal variables, we've seen that you might always guess the modal value. But for interval or ratio data, you would minimize your errors by always guessing the mean value of the variable. Although this practice produces few if any perfect guesses, the extent of your errors will be minimized.

In the computation of lambda, we noted the number of errors produced by always guessing the modal value. In the case of r, errors are measured in terms of the sum of the squared differences between the actual value and the mean. This sum is called the *total variation*.

To understand this concept, we must expand the scope of our examination. Let's look at the logic of **regression analysis** and return to correlation within that context.

Regression Analysis

At several points in this text, I have referred to the general formula for describing the association between two variables: $Y = f(X)$. This formula is read "Y is a function of X," meaning that values of Y can be explained in terms of variations in the values of X. Stated more strongly, we might say that X causes Y, so the value of X determines the value of Y. Regression analysis is a method of determining the specific function relating Y to X. There are several forms of regression analysis, depending on the complexity of the relationships being studied. Let's begin with the simplest.

Linear Regression The regression model can be seen most clearly in the case of a perfect linear association between two variables. Figure 17-1 is a scattergram presenting in graphic form the values of X and Y as produced by a hypothetical study. It shows that for the four cases in our study, the values of X and Y are identical in each instance. The case with a value of 1 on X also has a value of 1 on Y, and so forth. The relationship between the two variables in this instance is described by the equation $Y = X$; this is called the *regression equation*. Because all four points lie on a straight line, we could superimpose that line over the points; this is the *regression line*.

The linear regression model has important descriptive uses. The regression line offers a graphic

FIGURE 17-1
Simple Scattergram of Values of X and Y

FIGURE 17-2
A Scattergram of the Values of Two Variables with Regression Line Added (Hypothertical)

picture of the association between X and Y, and the regression equation is an efficient form for summarizing that association. The regression model has inferential value as well. To the extent that the regression equation correctly describes the general association between the two variables, it may be used to predict other sets of values. If, for example, we know that a new case has a value of 3.5 on X, we can predict the value of 3.5 on Y as well.

In practice, of course, studies are seldom limited to four cases, and the associations between variables are seldom as clear as the one presented in Figure 17-1.

A somewhat more realistic example is presented in Figure 17-2, representing a hypothetical relationship between population and crime rate in small- to medium-sized cities. Each dot in the scattergram is a city, and its placement reflects that city's population and its crime rate. As was the case in our previous example, the values of Y (crime rates) generally correspond to those of X (populations); and as values of X increase, so do values of Y. However, the association is not nearly as clear as it was for the case in Figure 17-1.

In Figure 17-2 we can't superimpose a straight line that will pass through all the points in the scattergram. But we can draw an approximate line showing the best possible linear representation of the several points. I've drawn that line on the graph.

If you've ever studied geometry, you'll know that any straight line on a graph can be represented by an equation of the form $Y = a + bX$, where X and Y are values of the two variables. In this equation, a equals the value of Y when X is 0, and b represents the slope of the line. If we know the values of a and b, we can calculate an estimate of Y for every value of X.

Regression analysis is a technique for establishing the regression equation representing the geometric line that comes closest to the distribution of points. This equation is valuable both descriptively and inferentially. First, the regression equation provides a mathematical description of the relationship between the variables. Second, the regression equation allows us to infer values of Y when we have values of X. Recalling Figure 17-2, we could estimate crime rates of cities if we knew their populations.

To improve your guessing, you construct a *regression line*, stated in the form of a regression equation that permits the estimation of values on one variable from values on the other. The general format for this equation is $Y' = a + b(X)$, where a and b are computed values, X is a given value on one variable, and Y' is the estimated value on the other. The values of a and b are computed to minimize the differences between actual values of Y and the corresponding estimates (Y') based on the known value of X. The sum of squared differences between actual and estimated values of Y is called the *unexplained variation* because it represents errors that still exist even when estimates are based on known values of X.

The *explained variation* is the difference between the total variation and the unexplained variation. Dividing the explained variation by the total variation produces a measure of the *proportionate reduction of error* corresponding to the similar quantity in the computation of lambda. In the present case, this quantity is the *correlation squared*: r^2. Thus, if $r = .7$, then $r^2 = .49$, meaning that about half the variation has been explained. In practice, we compute r rather than r^2, since the product-moment correlation can take either a positive or negative sign, depending on the direction of the relationship between the two variables. (Computing r^2 and taking a square root would always produce a positive quantity.) See any other standard statistics textbook for the *method* of computing r, although I anticipate that most readers using this measure will have access to computer programs designed for this function.

Even though the preceding discussion may have been more statistical than you find comfortable, social life is so complex that the simple linear regression model often does not sufficiently represent the state of affairs. As we saw in Chapter 15, it is possible, using percentage tables, to analyze more than two variables. As the number of variables increases, such tables become increasingly complicated and hard to read. But the regression model offers a useful alternative in such cases.

Multiple Regression Very often, social researchers find that a given dependent variable is affected simultaneously by several independent variables. Multiple regression analysis provides a means of analyzing such situations. This was the case when Beverly Yerg (1981) set about studying teacher effectiveness in physical education. She stated her expectations in the form of a multiple regression equation:

$F = b_0 + b_1 I + b_2 X_1 + b_3 X_2 + b_4 X_3 + b_5 X_4 + e$
F = Final pupil-performance score
I = Initial pupil-performance score
X_1 = Composite of guiding and supporting practice
X_2 = Composite of teacher mastery of content
X_3 = Composite of providing specific, task-related feedback
X_4 = Composite of clear, concise task presentation
b = Regression weight
e = Residual

(ADAPTED FROM YERG 1981:42)

Notice that in place of the single X variable in a linear regression, there are several X's, and there are also several b's instead of just one. Also, Yerg has chosen to represent a as b_0 in this equation but with the same meaning as discussed previously. Finally, the equation ends with a residual factor (e), which represents the variance in Y that is not accounted for by the X variables analyzed.

Beginning with this equation, then, Yerg calculated the values of the several b's to show the relative contributions of the several independent variables in determining final student-performance scores. She also calculated the multiple-correlation coefficient as an indicator of the extent to which all six variables predict the final scores. This follows the same logic as the simple bivariate correlation discussed earlier, and it is traditionally reported as a capital R. In this case, $R = .877$, meaning that 77 percent of the variance ($.877^2 = .77$) in final scores is explained by the six variables acting in concert.

Partial Regression In explaining the elaboration model, we paid special attention to the relationship between two variables when a third test variable was held constant. Thus, we might examine the effect of education on prejudice with age held constant, testing the independent effect of education. To do so, we would compute the tabular relationship between education and prejudice separately for each age group.

Partial regressions are based on this same logical model. The equation summarizing the relationship between variables is computed on the basis of the test variables remaining constant. As in the case of the elaboration model, the result may then be compared with the uncontrolled relationship between the two variables to clarify further the overall relationship.

Curvilinear Regression Up to now, we have been discussing the association among variables as represented by a straight line—though in more than two dimensions. The regression model is even more general than our discussion thus far has implied.

If you have a knowledge of geometry, you already know that curvilinear functions also can be represented by equations. For example, the equation $X^2 + Y^2 = 25$ describes a circle with a radius of 5. Raising variables to powers greater than 1 has the effect of producing curves rather than straight lines. And in empirical research, there is no reason to assume that the relationship among every set of variables will be linear. In some cases, then, curvilinear regression analysis can provide a better understanding of empirical relationships than can any linear model.

Recall, however, that a regression line serves two functions. It describes a set of empirical observations, and it provides a *general* model for making inferences about the relationship between two variables in the general population that the observations represent. A very complex equation might produce an erratic line that would indeed pass through every individual point. In this sense, it would perfectly describe the empirical observations. There would be no guarantee, however, that such a line could adequately predict new observations or that it in any meaningful way represented the relationship between the two variables in general. Thus, it would have little or no inferential value.

Earlier in this book, we discussed the need for balancing detail and utility in data reduction. Ultimately, researchers attempt to provide the most faithful, yet also the simplest, representation of their data. This practice also applies to regression analysis. Data should be presented in the simplest fashion (thus, linear regressions are most frequently used) that best describes the actual data. Curvilinear regression analysis adds a new option to the researcher in this regard, but it does not solve the problems altogether. Nothing does that.

Cautions in Regression Analysis The use of regression analysis for statistical inferences is based on the same assumptions made for correlational analysis: simple random sampling, the absence of nonsampling errors, and continuous interval data. Because social scientific research seldom completely satisfies these assumptions, you should use caution in assessing the results in regression analyses.

Also, regression lines—linear or curvilinear—can be useful for *interpolation* (estimating cases lying between those observed), but they are less trustworthy when used for *extrapolation* (estimating cases that lie beyond the range of observations). This limitation on extrapolations is important in two ways. First, you are likely to come across regression equations that seem to make illogical predictions. An equation linking population and crimes, for example, might seem to suggest that small towns with, say, a population of 1,000 should produce 123 crimes a year. This failure in predictive ability does not disqualify the equation but dramatizes that its applicability is limited to a particular range of population sizes. Second, researchers sometimes overstep this limitation, drawing inferences that lie outside their range of observation, and you'd be right in criticizing them for that.

The preceding sections have introduced you to some of the techniques for measuring associations among variables at different levels of measurement. Matters become slightly more complex when the two variables represent different levels of measurement. Though we aren't going to pursue this issue in this textbook, I have offered a

Measures of Association and Levels of Measurement

by Peter Nardi
Pitzer College

Note that this table itself is set up with the dependent variables in the rows and the independent variable in the columns, as tables are commonly organized. Also, notice that the levels of measurement are themselves an ordinal scale.

If you want to use an interval/ratio level variable in a crosstab, you must first recode it into an ordinal-level variable.

		Independent Variable		
		Nominal	Ordinal	Interval/Ratio
Dependent Variable	Nominal	Crosstabs Chi-square Lambda	Crosstabs Chi-square Lambda	
	Ordinal	Crosstabs Chi-square Lambda	Crosstabs Chi-square Lambda Gamma Kendall's tau Sommers' *d*	
	Interval/Ratio	Means *t*-test ANOVA	Means *t*-test ANOVA	Correlate Pearson *r* Regression *(R)*

box by Peter Nardi as a useful resource if you ever have to address such situations.

■ OTHER MULTIVARIATE TECHNIQUES

For the most part, this book has focused on rather rudimentary forms of data manipulation, such as the use of contingency tables and percentages. The elaboration model of analysis was presented in this form, as were the statistical techniques presented so far in this chapter.

In this section of the chapter, you're going to get a cook's tour of three other multivariate techniques used by social scientists. Don't worry about learning how to use any of these techniques. I simply want you to know enough about them so that you won't be at a complete loss if you run across them in a research report.

Each technique examined in this section will be presented from the logical perspective of the elaboration model. The three methods of analysis we'll examine are *path analysis, time-series analysis,* and *factor analysis,* but realize these are only a few of the many multivariate techniques used by social scientists.

Path Analysis

Path analysis is a *causal* model for understanding relationships between variables. Though based on regression analysis, it can provide a more useful graphic picture of relationships among several variables than other means can. Path analysis assumes that the values of one variable are caused by the values of another, so it is essential that independent and dependent variables be distinguished. This requirement is not unique to path analysis, of course, but path analysis provides a unique way of displaying explanatory results for interpretation.

Recall for a moment one of the ways I represented the elaboration model in Chapter 16

FIGURE 17-3
Diagramming the Religious Sources of Anti-Semitism

Source: Rodney Stark, Bruce D. Foster, Charles Y. Glock, and Harold E. Quinley, *Wayward Shepherds—Prejudice and the Protestant Clergy.* Copyright © 1971 by Anti-Defamation League of B'nai Brith. Reprinted by permission of Harper & Row, Publishers, Inc.

(Figure 16-1). Here's how we might diagram the logic of interpretation:

Independent Variable → Intervening Variable → Dependent Variable

The logic of this presentation is that an independent variable has an impact on an intervening variable which, in turn, has an impact on a dependent variable. The path analyst constructs similar patterns of relationships among variables, but the typical path diagram contains many more variables than shown in this diagram.

Besides diagramming a network of relationships among variables, path analysis also shows the strengths of those several relationships. The strengths of relationships are calculated from a regression analysis that produces numbers analogous to the partial relationships in the elaboration model. These *path coefficients,* as they are called, represent the strengths of the relationships between pairs of variables, with the effects of all other variables in the model held constant.

The analysis in Figure 17-3, for example, focuses on the religious causes of anti-Semitism among Christian church members. The variables in the diagram are, from left to right, (1) orthodoxy, or the extent to which the subjects accept conventional beliefs about God, Jesus, the biblical miracles, and so forth; (2) particularism, the belief that one's religion is the "only true faith"; (3) acceptance of the view that the Jews crucified Jesus; (4) religious hostility toward contemporary Jews, such as believing that God is punishing them or that they will suffer damnation unless they convert to Christianity; and (5) secular anti-Semitism, such as believing that Jews cheat in business, are disloyal to their country, and so forth.

To start with, the researchers who conducted this analysis proposed that secular anti-Semitism was produced by moving through the five variables: Orthodoxy caused particularism, which caused the view of the historical Jews as crucifiers, which caused religious hostility toward contemporary Jews, which resulted, finally, in secular anti-Semitism.

The path diagram tells a different story. The researchers found, for example, that belief in the historical role of Jews as the crucifiers of Jesus doesn't seem to matter in the process. And, although particularism is a part of one process resulting in secular anti-Semitism, the diagram also shows that anti-Semitism is created more directly by orthodoxy and religious hostility. Orthodoxy produces religious hostility even without particularism, and religious hostility generates secular hostility in any event.

One last comment on path analysis is in order. Although it is an excellent way of handling complex causal chains and networks of variables, you must realize that path analysis itself does not tell the causal order of the variables. Nor was the path diagram generated by computer. The researcher decided the structure of relationships among the variables and used computer analysis merely to calculate the path coefficients that apply to such a structure.

Time-Series Analysis

The various forms of regression analysis are often used to examine *time-series* data, representing changes in one or more variables over time. As I'm sure you know, U.S. crime rates have generally increased over the years. A time-series analysis of crime rates could express the long-term trend in a regression format and provide a way of testing explanations for the trend—such as population growth or economic fluctuations—and could permit forecasting of future crime rates.

In a simple illustration, Figure 17-4 graphs the larceny rates of a hypothetical city over time. Each dot on the graph represents the number of larcenies reported to police during the year indicated.

FIGURE 17-4
The Larceny Rates over Time in a Hypothetical City

Suppose we feel that larceny is partly a function of overpopulation. You might reason that crowding would lead to psychological stress and frustration, resulting in increased crimes of many sorts. Recalling the discussion of regression analysis, we could create a regression equation representing the relationship between larceny and population density—using the actual figures for each variable, with years as the units of analysis. Having created the best-fitting regression equation, we could then calculate a larceny rate for each year, based on that year's population density rate. For the sake of simplicity, let's assume that the city's population size (and hence density) has been steadily increasing. This would lead us to predict a steadily increasing larceny rate as well. These regression estimates are represented by the dashed regression line in Figure 17-4.

Time-series relationships are often more complex than this simple illustration suggests. For one thing, there can be more than one causal variable. For example, we might find that unemployment rates also had a powerful impact on larceny. We might develop an equation to predict larceny on the basis of both of these causal variables. As a result, the predictions might not fall along a simple, straight line.

Whereas population density was increasing steadily in the first model, unemployment rates rise and fall. As a consequence, our predictions of the larceny rate would similarly go up and down.

Pursuing the relationship between larceny and unemployment rates, we might reason that people do not begin stealing as soon as they become unemployed. Typically, they might first exhaust their savings, borrow from friends, and keep hoping for work. Larceny would be a last resort.

Time-lagged regression analysis could be used to address this more complex case. Thus, we might create a regression equation that predicted a given year's larceny rate based, in part, on the *previous* year's unemployment rate or perhaps on an average of the two years' unemployment rates. The possibilities are endless.

If you think about it, a great many causal relationships are likely to involve a time lag. Many of the world's poor countries survive by matching high death rates with equally high birth rates. It has been observed repeatedly, moreover, that when a society's death rate is drastically reduced—through improved medical care, public sanitation, and improved agriculture, for example—that society's birth rate drops sometime later on, but with an intervening period of rapid population growth. Or, to take a very different example, a crackdown on speeding on a state's highways is likely to reduce the average speed of cars. Again, however, the causal relationship would undoubtedly involve a time lag—days, weeks, or months, perhaps—as motorists began to realize the seriousness of the crackdown.

In all such cases, the regression equations generated might take many forms. In any event, the criterion for judging success or failure is the extent to which the researcher can account for the actual values observed in the dependent variable.

Factor Analysis

Factor analysis is a different approach to multivariate analysis than regression analysis. Its statistical basis is complex enough and different enough from the foregoing discussions to suggest a general discussion here.

Factor analysis is used to discover patterns among the variations in values of several variables. This is done essentially through the generation of artificial dimensions (factors) that correlate highly with several of the real variables and that are independent of one another. A computer must be used to perform this complex operation.

Let's suppose that a data file contains several indicators of subjects' prejudice. Each item should provide some indication of prejudice, but none will give a perfect indication. All of these items, moreover, should be highly intercorrelated empirically. In a factor analysis of the data, the researcher would create an artificial dimension that would be highly correlated with each of the items measuring prejudice. Each subject would essentially receive a value on that artificial dimension, and the value assigned would be a good predictor of the observed attributes on each item.

Suppose now that the same study provided several indicators of subjects' mathematical ability. It's likely that the factor analysis would also

TABLE 17-6
Factor Analysis: Delinquent Acts, Whites

Delinquent act	Property Offenses Factor I	Incorrigibility Factor II	Drugs/Truancy Factor III	Fighting Factor IV
Broke street light, etc.	.669	.126	.119	.167
Broke windows	.637	.093	.077	.215
Broke down fences, clothes lines, etc.	.621	.186	.186	.186
Taken things worth $2 to $50	.616	.187	.233	.068
Let air out of tires	.587	.243	.054	.156
Taken things worth over $50	.548	−.017	.276	.034
Thrown eggs, garbage, etc.	.526	.339	−.023	.266
Taken things worth under $2	.486	.393	.143	.077
Taken things from desks, etc., at school	.464	.232	−.002	.027
Taken car without owner's permission	.461	.172	.080	.040
Put paint on something	.451	.237	.071	.250
Disobeyed parents	.054	.642	.209	.039
Marked on desk, wall, etc.	.236	.550	−.061	.021
Said mean things to get even	.134	.537	.045	.100
Disobeyed teacher, school official	.240	.497	.223	.195
Defied parents to their face	.232	.458	.305	.058
Made anonymous telephone calls	.373	.446	.029	.135
Smoked marijuana	.054	.064	.755	−.028
Used other drugs for kicks	.137	.016	.669	.004
Signed name to school excuse	.246	.249	.395	.189
Drank alcohol, parents absent	.049	.247	.358	.175
Skipped school	.101	.252	.319	.181
Beat up someone in a fight	.309	.088	.181	.843
Fought—hit or wrestled	.242	.266	.070	.602
Percent of variance	**67.2**	**13.4**	**10.9**	**8.4**

Source: Morris A. Forslund, "Patterns of Delinquency Involvement: An Empirical Typology." Paper presented at the Annual Meeting of the Western Association of Sociologists and Anthropologists, Lethbridge, Alberta, February 8, 1980. The table above is adapted from page 10.

generate an artificial dimension highly correlated with each of those items.

The output of a factor analysis program consists of columns representing the several factors (artificial dimensions) generated from the observed relations among variables plus the correlations between each variable and each factor—called the *factor loadings*.

In the preceding example, it's likely that one factor would more or less represent prejudice, and another would more or less represent mathematical ability. Data items measuring prejudice would have high loadings on (correlations with) the prejudice factor and low loadings on the mathematical ability factor. Data items measuring mathematical ability would have just the opposite pattern.

In practice, however, factor analysis does not proceed in this fashion. Rather, the variables are input to the program, and a series of factors with appropriate factor loadings are the output. You must then determine the meaning of a given factor on the basis of those variables that load highly on it. The generation of factors, however, has no reference to the meaning of variables, only to their empirical associations. Two criteria are taken into account: (1) a factor must explain a relatively large portion of the variance found in the study variables, and (2) every factor must be more or less independent of every other factor.

Here's an example of the use of factor analysis. Many social researchers have studied the problem of delinquency. When you look deeply into the problem, however, you discover that there are many different types of delinquents. In a survey of high school students in a small Wyoming town, Morris Forslund (1980) set out to create a typology of delinquency. His questionnaire asked students to report whether they had committed a variety of delinquent acts. He then submitted their responses to factor analysis. The results are shown in Table 17-6.

As you can see in this table, the various delinquent acts are listed on the left. The numbers shown in the body of the table are the factor loadings on the four factors constructed in the analysis. You'll notice that Forslund has labeled the dimensions. I've bracketed the items on each factor that led to his choice of labels. Forslund summarizes the results as follows:

■ For the total sample four fairly distinct patterns of delinquent acts are apparent. In order of variance explained, they have been labeled: 1) Property Offenses, including both vandalism and theft; 2) Incorrigibility; 3) Drugs/Truancy; and 4) Fighting. It is interesting, and perhaps surprising, to find both vandalism and theft appear together in the same factor. It would seem that those high school students who engage in property offenses tend to be involved in both vandalism and theft. It is also interesting to note that drugs, alcohol and truancy fall in the same factor.

(1980:4)

Having determined this overall pattern, Forslund reran the factor analysis separately for boys and for girls. Essentially the same patterns emerged in both cases.

I think this example shows that factor analysis is an efficient method of discovering predominant patterns among a large number of variables. Instead of you and the researcher being forced to compare countless correlations—simple, partial, and multiple—to discover those patterns, factor analysis can be used for this task. Incidentally, this is a good example of a helpful use of computers.

Factor analysis also presents data in a form that can be interpreted by the reader or researcher. For a given factor, the reader can easily discover the variables loading highly on it, thus noting clusters of variables. Or, the reader can easily discover which factors a given variable is or is not loaded highly on.

But factor analysis also has disadvantages. First, as noted previously, factors are generated without any regard to substantive meaning. Often researchers will find factors producing very high loadings for a group of substantively disparate variables. They might find, for example, that prejudice and religiosity have high positive loadings on a given factor with education having an equally high negative loading. Surely the three variables are highly correlated, but what does the factor represent? All too often, inexperienced researchers will be led into naming such factors as "religio-prejudicial lack of education" or something similarly nonsensical.

Second, factor analysis is often criticized on basic philosophical grounds. Recall an earlier statement that to be legitimate, a hypothesis must be disconfirmable. If the researcher cannot specify the conditions under which the hypothesis would be disproved, the hypothesis is in reality either a tautology or useless. In a sense, factor analysis suffers this defect. No matter what data are input, factor analysis produces a solution in the form of factors. Thus if the researcher were asking, "Are there any patterns among these variables?" the answer always would be yes. This fact must also be taken into account in evaluating the results of factor analysis. The generation of factors by no means insures meaning.

My personal view of factor analysis is the same as that for other complex modes of analysis. It can be an extremely useful tool for the social science researcher. Its use should be encouraged whenever such activity may assist researchers in understanding a body of data. As in all cases, however, you must remain aware that such tools are only tools and never magical solutions.

This, then, completes our discussion of some of the additional analytical techniques commonly used by social scientists. I have only brushed the surface of each, and there are many other techniques I haven't touched on at all. My purpose has been to give you a preview of some of the techniques you may want to study in more depth later and to familiarize you with them in case you run across them in reading others' research reports.

■ INFERENTIAL STATISTICS

Many, if not most, social scientific research projects involve the examination of data collected from a sample drawn from a larger population.

A sample of people may be interviewed in a survey; a sample of divorce records may be coded and analyzed; a sample of newspapers may be examined through content analysis. Researchers seldom if ever study samples just to describe the samples per se; in most instances, their ultimate purpose is to make assertions about the larger population from which the sample has been selected. Frequently, then, you'll wish to interpret your univariate and multivariate sample findings as the basis for *inferences* about some population.

This section will examine the statistical measures used for making such inferences and their logical bases. We'll begin with univariate data and move to multivariate.

Univariate Inferences

The opening sections of Chapter 15 dealt with methods of presenting univariate data. Each summary measure was intended as a method of describing the sample studied. Now we'll use such measures to make broader assertions about the population. This section addresses two univariate measures: percentages and means.

If 50 percent of a sample of people say they have had colds during the past year, 50 percent is also our best estimate of the proportion of colds in the total population from which the sample was drawn. (This estimate assumes a simple random sample, of course.) It's rather unlikely, however, that *precisely* 50 percent of the population have had colds during the year. If a rigorous sampling design for random selection has been followed, however, we will be able to estimate the expected range of error when the sample finding is applied to the population.

Chapter 8 on sampling theory covered the procedures for making such estimates, so I'll only review them here. In the case of a percentage, the quantity

$$\sqrt{\frac{p \times q}{n}}$$

where p is a percentage, q equals $1 - p$, and n is the sample size, is called the *standard error*. As noted in Chapter 8, this quantity is very important in the estimation of sampling error. We may be 68 percent confident that the population figure falls within plus or minus one standard error of the sample figure; we may be 95 percent confident that it falls within plus or minus two standard errors; and we may be 99.9 percent confident that it falls within plus or minus three standard errors.

Any statement of sampling error, then, must contain two essential components: the *confidence level* (for example, 95 percent) and the *confidence interval* (for example, ±2.5 percent). If 50 percent of a sample of 1,600 people say they have had colds during the year, we might say we're 95 percent confident that the population figure is between 47.5 percent and 52.5 percent.

Recognize in this example that we've moved beyond simply describing the sample into the realm of making estimates (inferences) about the larger population. In doing so, we must take care in several ways.

First, the sample must be drawn from the population about which inferences are being made. A sample taken from a telephone directory cannot legitimately be the basis for statistical inferences about the population of a city.

Second, the inferential statistics assume simple random sampling, which is virtually never the case in sample surveys. The statistics assume sampling with replacement, which is almost never done—but this is probably not a serious problem. Although systematic sampling is used more frequently than random sampling, it, too, probably presents no serious problem if done correctly. Stratified sampling, because it improves representativeness, clearly presents no problem. Cluster sampling does present a problem, however, as the estimates of sampling error may be too small. Quite clearly, street-corner sampling does not warrant the use of inferential statistics. This standard error sampling technique also assumes a 100 percent completion rate. This problem increases in seriousness as the completion rate decreases.

Third, inferential statistics are addressed to sampling error only, not nonsampling errors. Thus, although we might state correctly that between 47.5 and 52.5 percent of the population (95 percent confidence) would *report* having colds during the previous year, we couldn't so confidently guess the percentage who had actually *had* them. Because nonsampling errors are probably larger than sampling errors in a respectable sample design, we need to be especially cautious in generalizing from our sample findings to the population.

Tests of Statistical Significance

There is no scientific answer to the question of whether a given association between two variables is significant, strong, important, interesting, or worth reporting. Perhaps the ultimate test of significance rests with your ability to persuade your audience (present and future) of the association's significance. At the same time, there is a body of inferential statistics to assist you in this regard, called *parametric tests of significance*. As the name suggests, parametric statistics are those that make certain assumptions about the parameters describing the population from which the sample is selected.

Although **tests of statistical significance** are widely reported in social scientific literature, the logic underlying them is rather subtle and often misunderstood. Tests of significance are based on the same sampling logic discussed elsewhere in this book. To understand that logic, let's return for a moment to the concept of sampling error in regard to univariate data.

Recall that a sample statistic normally provides the best single estimate of the corresponding population parameter, but the statistic and the parameter seldom correspond precisely. Thus, we report the probability that the parameter falls within a certain range (confidence interval). The degree of uncertainty within that range is due to normal sampling error. The corollary of such a statement is, of course, that it is *improbable* that the parameter would fall outside the specified range only as a result of sampling error. Thus, if we estimate that a parameter (99.9 percent confidence) lies between 45 percent and 55 percent, we say by implication that it is *extremely improbable* that the parameter is actually, say, 90 percent if our only error of estimation is due to normal sampling. This is the basic logic behind tests of significance.

The Logic of Statistical Significance

I think I can illustrate this logic of **statistical significance** best in a series of diagrams representing the selection of samples from a population. Here are the elements in the logic I'll illustrate:

1. Assumptions regarding the independence of two variables in the population study
2. Assumptions regarding the representativeness of samples selected through conventional probability sampling procedures
3. The observed joint distribution of sample elements in terms of the two variables

Figure 17-5 represents a hypothetical population of 256 people; half are women, half men. The diagram also indicates how each person feels about women enjoying equality to men. In the diagram, those favoring equality have open circles, those opposing it have their circles shaded in.

The question we'll be investigating is whether there is any relationship between gender and feelings about equality for men and women. More specifically, we'll see if women are more likely to favor equality than men, since they would presumably benefit more from it. Take a moment to look at Figure 17-5 and see what the answer to this question is.

The illustration in the figure indicates there is no relationship between gender and attitudes about equality. Exactly half of each group favors equality and half opposes it. Recall the earlier discussion of proportionate reduction of error. In this instance, knowing a person's gender would not reduce the "errors" we'd make in guessing his or her attitude toward equality. The table at the bottom of Figure 17-5 provides a tabular view of what you can observe in the graphic diagram.

Figure 17-6 represents the selection of a one-fourth sample from the hypothetical population. In terms of the graphic illustration, a "square" selection from the center of the population provides a representative sample. Notice that our sample

FIGURE 17-5
A Hypothetical Population of Men and Women Who Either Favor or Oppose Sexual Equality

	Women	Men
Favor equality	50%	50%
Oppose equality	50%	50%
	100%	100%

Legend	
♀	Woman who favors equality
♂	Man who favors equality
♀ (filled)	Woman who opposes equality
♂ (filled)	Man who opposes equality

contains 16 of each type of person: Half are men and half are women; half of each gender favors equality, and the other half opposes it.

The sample selected in Figure 17-6 would allow us to draw accurate conclusions about the relationship between gender and equality in the larger population. Following the sampling logic we saw in Chapter 8, we'd note there was no relationship between gender and equality in the sample; thus, we'd conclude there was similarly no relationship in the larger population—since we've presumably selected a sample in accord with the conventional rules of sampling.

Of course, real-life samples are seldom such perfect reflections of the populations from which they are drawn. It would not be unusual for us to have selected, say, one or two extra men who opposed equality and a couple of extra women who favored it—even if there was no relationship between the two variables in the population. Such

FIGURE 17-6
A Representative Sample

minor variations are part and parcel of probability sampling, as we saw in Chapter 8.

Figure 17-7, however, represents a sample that falls far short of the mark in reflecting the larger population. Notice it has selected far too many supportive women and too many opposing men. As the table shows, three-fourths of the women in the sample support equality, but only one-fourth of the men do so. If we had selected this sample from a population in which the two variables were unrelated to each other, we'd be sorely misled by the analysis of our sample.

As you'll recall, it's unlikely that a properly drawn probability sample would ever be as inaccurate as the one shown in Figure 17-7. In fact, if we actually selected a sample that gave us the results this one does, we'd look for a different explanation. Figure 17-8 illustrates.

Notice that the sample selected in Figure 17-8 also shows a strong relationship between gender

FIGURE 17-7
An Unrepresentative Sample

and equality. The reason is quite different this time. We've selected a perfectly representative sample, but we see that there is actually a strong relationship between the two variables in the population at large. In this latest figure, women are more likely to support equality than men: That's the case in the population, and the sample reflects it.

In practice, of course, we never know what's so for the total population; that's why we select samples. So if we selected a sample and found the strong relationship presented in Figures 17-7 and

FIGURE 17-8
A Representative Sample from a Population in Which the Variables Are Related

17-8, we'd need to decide whether that finding accurately reflected the population or was simply a product of sampling error.

The fundamental logic of tests of statistical significance, then, is this: Faced with any discrepancy between the assumed independence of variables in a population and the observed distribution of sample elements, we may explain that discrepancy in either of two ways: (1) we may attribute it to an unrepresentative sample, or (2) we may reject the assumption of independence. The logic and statistics associated with probability sampling methods offer guidance about the varying probabilities of varying degrees of unrepresentativeness (expressed as sampling error). Most simply put, there is a *high* probability of a *small* degree of unrepresentativeness and a *low* probability of a *large* degree of unrepresentativeness.

The *statistical significance* of a relationship observed in a set of sample data, then, is always expressed in terms of probabilities. Significant at the .05 level ($p \leq .05$) simply means that the probability of a relationship as strong as the observed one being attributable to sampling error alone is no more than 5 in 100. Put somewhat differently, if two variables are independent of one another in the population, and if 100 probability samples were selected from that population, no more than 5 of those samples should provide a relationship as strong as the one that has been observed.

There is, then, a corollary to confidence intervals in tests of significance, which represent the probability of the measured associations being due *only* to *sampling error*. This is called the **level of significance.** Like confidence intervals, levels of significance are derived from a logical model in which several samples are drawn from a given population. In the present case, we assume that there is no association between the variables in the population, and then ask what proportion of the samples drawn from that population would produce associations at least as great as those measured in the empirical data. Three levels of significance are frequently used in research reports: .05, .01, and .001. These mean, respectively, that the chances of obtaining the measured association as a result of sampling error are 5/100, 1/100, and 1/1,000.

Researchers who use tests of significance normally follow one of two patterns. Some specify in advance the level of significance they will regard as sufficient. If any measured association is statistically significant at that level, they will regard it as representing a genuine association between the two variables. In other words, they are willing to discount the possibility of its resulting from sampling error only.

Other researchers prefer to report the specific level of significance for each association, disregarding the conventions of .05, .01, and .001. Rather than reporting that a given association is significant at the .05 level, they might report significance at the .023 level, indicating the chances of its having resulted from sampling error as 23 out of 1,000.

Chi Square

Chi square (χ^2) is a frequently used test of significance in social science. It is based on the null hypothesis: the assumption that there is no relationship between the two variables in the total population. Given the observed distribution of values on the two separate variables, we compute the conjoint distribution that would be expected if there were no relationship between the two variables. The result of this operation is a set of *expected frequencies* for all the cells in the contingency table. We then compare this expected distribution with the distribution of cases actually found in the sample data, and we determine the probability that the discovered discrepancy could have resulted from sampling error alone. An example will illustrate this procedure.

Let's assume we're interested in the possible relationship between church attendance and gender of the members of a particular church. To test this relationship, we select a sample of 100 church members at random. We find our sample is made up of 40 men and 60 women and that 70 percent of our sample report having attended church during the preceding week, whereas the remaining 30 percent say they did not.

If there is no relationship between gender and church attendance, then 70 percent of the men in the sample should have attended church during the preceding week, and 30 percent should have stayed away. Moreover, women should have attended in the same proportion. Table 17-7 (Part I) shows that, based on this model, 28 men and 42 women would have attended church, with 12 men and 18 women not attending.

Part II of Table 17-7 presents the observed attendance for the hypothetical sample of 100 church members. Note that 20 of the men report having attended church during the preceding week, and the remaining 20 say they did not. Among the women in the sample, 50 attended church and 10 did not. Comparing the expected and observed frequencies (Parts I and II), we note that somewhat fewer men attended church than expected, whereas somewhat more women than expected attended.

Chi square is computed as follows. For each cell in the tables, the researcher (1) subtracts the expected frequency for that cell from the observed frequency, (2) squares this quantity, and (3) divides the squared difference by the expected frequency. This procedure is carried out for each

TABLE 17-7
A Hypothetical Illustration of Chi Square

I. Expected Cell Frequencies	Men	Women	Total
Attended church	28	42	70
Did not attend church	12	18	30
Total	40	60	100

II. Observed Cell Frequencies	Men	Women	Total
Attended church	20	50	70
Did not attend church	20	10	30
Total	40	60	100

III. (Observed − Expected)^2 ÷ Expected	Men	Women	
Attended church	2.29	1.52	$x^2 = 12.70$
Did not attend church	5.33	3.56	$p < .001$

cell in the tables, and the several results are added together. (Part III of Table 17-7 presents the cell-by-cell computations.) The final sum is the value of chi square: 12.70 in the example.

This value is the overall discrepancy between the observed conjoint distribution in the sample and the distribution we should have expected if the two variables were unrelated to one another. Of course, the mere discovery of a discrepancy does not prove that the two variables are related, since normal sampling error might produce discrepancies even when there was no relationship in the total population. The magnitude of the value of chi square, however, permits us to estimate the probability of that having happened.

Degrees of Freedom To determine the statistical significance of the observed relationship, we must use a standard set of chi square values. This will require the computation of the *degrees of freedom*, which refers to the possibilities for variation within a statistical model. Suppose I challenge you to find three numbers whose mean is 11. There is an infinite number of solutions to this problem: (11, 11, 11), (10, 11, 12), (−11, 11, 33), etc. Now, suppose I require that one of the numbers be 7. There would still be an infinite number of possibilities for the other two numbers.

If I told you one number had to be 7 and another 10, there would be only one possible value for the third. If the average of three numbers is 11, their sum must be 33. If two total 17, the third must be 16. In this situation, we say there are two degrees of freedom. Two of the numbers could have any values we choose, but once they are specified, the third number is determined.

More generally, whenever we are examining the mean of N values, we can see that the degrees of freedom is $N - 1$. Thus in the case of the mean of 23 values, we could make 22 of them anything we liked, but the 23rd would then be determined.

A similar logic applies to bivariate tables, such as those analyzed by chi square. Consider a table reporting the relationship between two dichotomous variables: gender (men/women) and abortion attitude (approve/disapprove). Notice that the table provides the marginal frequencies of both variables.

Abortion Attitude	Men	Women	Total
Approve			500
Disapprove			500
Total	500	500	1,000

Despite the conveniently round numbers in this hypothetical example, notice there are numerous possibilities for the cell frequencies. For example, it could be the case that all 500 men approve and all 500 women disapprove, or it could be just the reverse. Or there could be 250 cases in each cell. Notice there are numerous other possibilities.

Now the question is, How many cells could we fill in pretty much as we choose before the remainder are determined by the marginal frequencies? The answer is only one. If we know that 300 men approved, for example, then 200 men would have had to disapprove, and the distribution would need to be just the opposite for the women.

In this instance, then, we say the table has *one degree of freedom*. Now, take a few minutes to construct a three-by-three table. Assume you know the marginal frequencies for each variable, and see if you can determine how many degrees of freedom it has.

For chi square, the degrees of freedom are computed as follows: the number of rows in the table of observed frequencies, minus 1, is multiplied by the number of columns, minus 1. This may be written as $(r - 1)(c - 1)$. For a *three-by-three* table, then, there are *four degrees of freedom*.

In the example of gender and church attendance, we have two rows and two columns (discounting the *totals*), so there is one degree of freedom. Turning to a table of chi square values (see Appendix F), we find that for one degree of freedom and random sampling from a population in which there is no relationship between two variables, 10 percent of the time we should expect a chi square of at least 2.7. Thus, if we selected 100 samples from such a population, we should expect about 10 of those samples to produce chi squares equal to or greater than 2.7. Moreover, we should expect chi square values of at least 6.6 in only 1 percent of the samples and chi square values of 7.9 in only half a percent (.005) of the samples. The higher the chi square value, the less probable it is that the value could be attributed to sampling error alone.

In our example, the computed value of chi square is 12.70. If there were no relationship between gender and church attendance in the church member population and a large number of samples had been selected and studied, then we would expect a chi square of this magnitude in fewer than 1/10 of 1 percent (.001) of those samples. Thus, the probability of obtaining a chi square of this magnitude is less than .001, if random sampling has been used and there is no relationship in the population. We report this finding by saying the relationship is *statistically significant at the .001 level*. Because it is so improbable that the observed relationship could have resulted from sampling error alone, we're likely to reject the null hypothesis and assume that there is a relationship between the two variables in the population of church members.

Most measures of association can be tested for statistical significance in a similar manner. Standard tables of values permit us to determine whether a given association is statistically significant and at what level. Any standard statistics textbook provides instructions on the use of such tables, so we'll not pursue the matter further here.

Some Words of Caution Tests of significance provide an objective yardstick against which to estimate the significance of associations between variables. They help us rule out associations that may not represent genuine relationships in the population under study. The researcher who uses or reads reports of significance tests should remain wary of several dangers in their interpretation, however.

First, we have been discussing tests of *statistical significance;* there are no objective tests of substantive significance. Thus, we may be legitimately convinced that a given association is not due to sampling error, but we may be in the position of asserting without fear of contradiction that two variables are only slightly related to one another. Recall that sampling error is an inverse function of sample size—the larger the sample, the smaller the expected error. Thus, a correlation of, say, .1 might very well be significant (at a given level) if discovered in a large sample, whereas the same correlation between the same two variables would not be significant if found in a smaller sample. Of course this makes perfectly good sense if one understands the basic logic of tests of significance: In the larger sample, there is less chance that the correlation could be simply the product of sampling error. In both samples, however, it might represent an essentially zero correlation.

The distinction between statistical and substantive significance is perhaps best illustrated by those cases where there is *absolute certainty* that observed differences cannot be a result of sampling error. This would be the case when we observe an entire population. Suppose we were able to learn the ages of every public official in the United States and also the ages of every public official in Russia. For argument's sake, let's assume further that the average age of U.S. officials was 45 years old compared to, say, 46 for the Russian officials. Because we would have the ages of all officials, there would be no question of sampling error. We know with certainty that the Russian officials are older than their U.S. counterparts. At the same time, we would say that the difference was of no substantive significance. We'd conclude, in fact, that they were essentially the same age.

Second, lest you be misled by this hypothetical example, you should not calculate statistical significance on relationships observed in data collected from whole populations. Remember, tests of statistical significance measure the likelihood of relationships between variables being only a product of sampling error; if there's no sampling, there's no sampling error.

Third, tests of significance are based on the same sampling assumptions we used in computing confidence intervals. To the extent that these assumptions are not met by the actual sampling design, the tests of significance are not strictly legitimate.

While we have examined statistical significance here in the form of chi square, there are several other measures commonly used by social scientists. Analysis of variance and *t*-tests are two examples you may run across in your studies.

As is the case for most matters covered in this book, I have a personal prejudice. In this instance, it is against tests of significance. I don't object to the statistical logic of those tests, since the logic is sound. Rather, I'm concerned that such tests seem to mislead more than they enlighten. My principal reservations are the following:

1. Tests of significance make sampling assumptions that are virtually never satisfied by actual sampling designs.
2. They depend on the absence of **nonsampling errors,** a questionable assumption in most actual empirical measurements.
3. In practice, they are too often applied to measures of association that have been computed in violation of the assumptions made by those measures (for example, product-moment correlations computed from ordinal data).
4. Statistical significance is too easily misinterpreted as "strength of association," or substantive significance.

The concerns just expressed are underscored by a recent study (Sterling et al. 1995) examining the publication policies of nine psychology and three medical journals. As the researchers discovered, the journals were quite unlikely to publish articles that did not report statistically significant correlations among variables. They quote the following from a rejection letter:

■ Unfortunately, we are not able to publish this manuscript. The manuscript is very well written and the study was well documented. Unfortunately, the negative results translates into a minimal contribution to the field. We encourage you to continue your work in this area and we will be glad to consider additional manuscripts that you may prepare in the future.

(STERLING ET AL. 1995:109)

Let's suppose a researcher conducts a scientifically excellent study to determine whether X causes Y. The results indicate no statistically significant correlation. That's good to know. If we're interested in what causes cancer, war, or juvenile delinquency, it's good to know that a possible cause actually does *not* cause it. That knowledge would free researchers to look elsewhere for causes.

As we've seen, however, such a study might very well be rejected by journals. As such, other researchers will continue testing whether X causes Y, not knowing that previous studies found no causal relationship. This would produce many wasted studies, none of which would see publication and draw a close to the analysis of X as a cause of Y.

From what you've learned about probabilities, however, you can understand that if enough studies are conducted, one will eventually measure a statistically significant correlation between X and Y. If there is absolutely no relationship between the two variables, we would expect a correlation significant at the .05 level five times out of a hundred, since that's what the .05 level of significance means. If a hundred studies were conducted, therefore, we can expect five to suggest a causal relationship where there is actually none—and those five studies would be published!

There are, then, serious problems inherent in too much reliance on tests of statistical significance. At the same time—perhaps paradoxically—I would suggest that tests of significance can be a valuable asset to the researcher—useful tools for understanding data. Although many of my comments suggest an extremely conservative approach to tests of significance—that you should use them only when all assumptions are met—my general perspective is just the reverse.

I encourage you to use any statistical technique—any measure of association or any test of significance—on any set of data if it will help you understand your data. If the computation of product-moment correlations among nominal variables and the testing of statistical significance in the context of uncontrolled sampling will meet this criterion, then I encourage such activities. I say this in the spirit of what Hanan Selvin, another pioneer in developing the elaboration model, referred to as "data-dredging techniques." Anything goes, if it leads ultimately to the understanding of data and of the social world under study.

The price of this radical freedom, however, is the giving up of strict, statistical interpretations. You will not be able to base the ultimate importance of your finding solely on a significant correlation at the .05 level. Whatever the avenue of discovery, empirical data must ultimately be presented in a legitimate manner, and their importance must be argued logically.

■ MAIN POINTS

- Descriptive statistics are used to summarize data under study. Some descriptive statistics summarize the distribution of attributes on a single variable; others summarize the associations between variables.
- Descriptive statistics summarizing the relationships between variables are called measures of association.
- Inferential statistics are used to estimate the generalizability of findings arrived at through the analysis of a sample to the larger population from which the sample has been selected. Some inferential statistics estimate the single-variable characteristics of the population; others—tests of statistical significance—estimate the relationships between variables in the population.
- Many measures of association are based on a proportionate reduction of error (PRE) model. This model is based on a comparison of (1) the number of errors we would make in attempting to guess the attributes of a given variable for each of the cases under study—if we knew nothing but the distribution of attributes on that variable—and (2) the number of errors we would make if we knew the joint distribution overall and were told for each case the attribute of one variable each time we were asked to guess the attribute of the other.
- Lambda (λ) is an appropriate measure of association to be used in the analysis of two *nominal* variables. It also provides a clear illustration of the PRE model.
- Gamma (γ) is an appropriate measure of association to be used in the analysis of two *ordinal* variables.
- Pearson's product-moment correlation (r) is an appropriate measure of association to be used in the analysis of two *interval* or *ratio* variables.
- Regression analysis represents the relationships between variables in the form of equations, which can be used to predict the values of a dependent variable on the basis of values of one or more independent variables.
- The basic regression equation—for a simple linear regression—is of the form $Y = a + bX$. Y in this case is the value (estimated) of the dependent variable; a is some constant value; b is another numerical value, which is multiplied by X, the value of the independent variable.

- Regression equations are computed on the basis of a regression line: that geometric line representing, with the least amount of discrepancy, the actual location of points in a scattergram.
- A multiple regression analysis results in a regression equation, which estimates the values of a dependent variable from the values of several independent variables.
- A partial regression analysis examines the effects of several independent variables, but with each independent variable's effect expressed separately while the effects of all others are held constant.
- A curvilinear regression analysis permits the "best-fitting" regression line to be something other than a straight line. The curvature of the regression line is achieved by permitting the values of the independent variables to be raised to powers greater than 1—squared, cubed, and so forth.
- Time-series analysis involves the study of processes occurring over time, such as population growth or crime rates.
- Path analysis is a method of presenting graphically the networks of causal relationships among several variables. It illustrates graphically the primary "paths" of variables through which independent variables cause dependent ones.
- Path coefficients are standardized regression coefficients representing the partial relationships between variables.
- Factor analysis, feasible only by computer, is an analytical method of discovering the general dimensions represented by a collection of actual variables. These general dimensions, or factors, are calculated hypothetical dimensions that are not perfectly represented by any of the empirical variables under study but that are highly associated with groups of empirical variables.
- A factor loading indicates the degree of association between a given empirical variable and a given factor.
- Inferences about some characteristic of a population—such as the percentage of voters favoring Candidate A—must contain an indication of a confidence interval (the range within which the value is expected to be: for example, between 45 and 55 percent favor Candidate A) and an indication of the confidence level (the likelihood the value does fall within that range: for example, 95 percent confidence). Computations of confidence levels and intervals are based on probability theory and assume that conventional probability sampling techniques have been employed in the study.
- Inferences about the generalizability to a population of the associations discovered between variables in a sample involve tests of statistical significance. Most simply put, these tests estimate the likelihood that an association as large as the observed one could result from normal sampling error if no such association exists between the variables in the larger population. Tests of statistical significance, then, are also based on probability theory and assume that conventional probability sampling techniques have been employed in the study.
- Statistical significance must not be confused with substantive significance, the latter meaning that an observed association is strong, important, meaningful, or worth writing home to your mother about.
- The level of significance of an observed association is reported in the form of the probability that the association could have been produced merely by sampling error. To say that an association is significant at the .05 level is to say that an association as large as the observed one could not be expected to result from sampling error more than 5 times out of 100.
- Social researchers tend to use a particular set of levels of significance in connection with tests of statistical significance: .05, .01, and .001. This is merely a convention, however.
- Tests of statistical significance, strictly speaking, make assumptions about data and methods that are almost never satisfied completely by real social research. Despite this, the tests

can serve a useful function in the analysis and interpretation of data. You should be wary of interpreting the "significance" of the test results too precisely, however.

■ REVIEW QUESTIONS AND EXERCISES

1. In your own words, explain the logic of *proportionate reduction of error* (PRE) measures of associations.
2. In your own words, explain *partial regression analysis* in terms of the logic of elaboration analysis.
3. In your own words, distinguish between *measures of association* and *tests of statistical significance*.
4. This chapter has discussed the concept of statistical significance. Go to the Web and find at least three different disciplines (such as sociology or biology) that use this concept. Give the Web addresses of the materials that support your choices. *Hint:* Use one of the Web search engines to search for "statistical significance," using quotation marks around the phrase.

■ ADDITIONAL READINGS

Babbie, Earl, and Fred Halley. *Adventures in Social Research*. Newbury Park, CA: Pine Forge Press, 1995. This book introduces you to the analysis of social research data through SPSS for Windows. Several of the basic statistical techniques used by social researchers are discussed and illustrated.

Blalock, Hubert M., Jr. *Social Statistics*. New York: McGraw-Hill, 1979. Blalock's textbook has been a standard for social science students (and faculty) for decades. Tad Blalock's death was a loss to all social science.

Healey, Joseph F. *Statistics: A Tool for Social Research*. Belmont, CA: Wadsworth, 1990. An effective introduction to social statistics for the beginning student.

Jendrek, Margaret Platt. *Through the Maze: Statistics with Computer Applications*. Belmont, CA: Wadsworth, 1985. An innovative, practical introduction to social statistics. Jendrek explains the logic of various statistical techniques and then illustrates how the reader can calculate them with simple computer programs or through the use of systems such as SPSS.

Mohr, Lawrence B. *Understanding Significance Testing*. Newbury Park, CA: Sage, 1990. Here's an excellent and comprehensive examination of the topic: both the technical details of testing statistical significance and the meaning of such tests.

Schroeder, Larry D., David L. Sjoquist, and Paula E. Stephan. *Understanding Regression Analysis: An Introductory Guide*. Newbury Park, CA: Sage, 1986. If you wish to pursue regression as an analytical technique, this would be an excellent next step. The authors offer an understandable introduction to a complex topic.

PART 5

The Social Context of Research

18 The Ethics and Politics of Social Research
19 The Uses of Social Research

In the preceding chapters, we've seen that there are certain scientific goals and principles to be satisfied in research design and execution and certain practical, administrative constraints that require well-thought-out compromises. In Chapter 18, we'll see that ethical and political considerations also require compromises concerning what might otherwise seem perfect "scientific" practices. Though we've touched on ethical and logistical issues from time to time already, I want to focus on them fully now.

Chapter 19 aims at bringing the many topics of this book together into an integrated whole, while demonstrating the value of understanding social research for your future happiness and success. I've reviewed the relationships among theory, research, and statistics. I've suggested ways the materials you've learned in this book may be useful in nonresearch aspects of life. And I've concluded the chapter with a "consumer's guide" to help you separate the wheat from the chaff in the many social research studies you'll be reading about every day for the rest of your life. I think you'll also find the consumer's guide a useful review of the book, in the event that you have a final exam in your future. Good luck.

CHAPTER 18: The Ethics and Politics of Social Research

What You'll Learn in This Chapter

In this chapter, you'll see something of the social context within which social research is conducted. As you'll see, ethical and political considerations must be taken into account alongside scientific ones in the design and execution of research.

INTRODUCTION

ETHICAL ISSUES IN SOCIAL RESEARCH
Voluntary Participation
No Harm to the Participants
Anonymity and Confidentiality
Deceiving Subjects
Analysis and Reporting
Institutional Review Boards
A Professional Code of Ethics

TWO ETHICAL CONTROVERSIES
Trouble in the Tearoom
Observing Human Obedience

DISCUSSION EXAMPLES

THE POLITICS OF SOCIAL RESEARCH
Objectivity and Ideology
Politics with a Little "p"
Politics in Perspective

MAIN POINTS

REVIEW QUESTIONS AND EXERCISES

ADDITIONAL READINGS

■ INTRODUCTION

We have now just about completed our exploration of social scientific research methods. My purpose in this book has been to give you a realistic and useful introduction to doing social research. For this introduction to be fully realistic, it must present four main constraints on research projects: scientific, administrative, ethical, and political.

The preceding 17 chapters have focused on scientific and administrative constraints. We've seen that the logic of science suggests certain research procedures, but we've also seen that some scientifically appropriate designs wouldn't be administratively feasible: Some "perfect" study designs would be too expensive or take too long to execute. Throughout the book, therefore, we've dealt with workable compromises.

But what of the two other important considerations in doing research in the real world: *ethics* and *politics?* Because they are somewhat subtler and less obvious, I want to devote this chapter to them. Just as certain procedures are too impractical to use, others are either ethically prohibitive or politically difficult or impossible. Here's a story to show you what I mean.

Several years ago, I was invited to sit in on a planning session to design a study of legal education in California. The joint project was to be conducted by a university research center and the state bar association. The purpose of the project was to improve legal education by learning which aspects of the law school experience were related to success on the bar exam. Essentially, the plan was to prepare a questionnaire that would get detailed information about the law school experiences of individuals. People would be required to answer the questionnaire when they took the bar exam. By analyzing how people with different kinds of law school experiences did on the bar exam, we could find out what sorts of things worked and what didn't. The findings of the research could be made available to law schools, and ultimately legal education could be improved.

The exciting thing about collaborating with the bar association was that all the normally irritating logistical hassles would be handled. There would be no problem getting permission to administer questionnaires in conjunction with the exam, for example, and the problem of *nonresponse* could be eliminated altogether.

I left the meeting excited about the prospects for the study. When I told a colleague about it, I glowed about the absolute handling of the nonresponse problem. Her immediate comment turned everything around completely. "That's unethical. There's no law requiring the questionnaire, and participation in research has to be voluntary." The study wasn't done.

In retelling this story, it is obvious to me that requiring participation would have been inappropriate. You may have seen that before I told you about my colleague's comment. I still feel a little embarrassed over the matter. Yet, I have a specific purpose in telling this story about myself.

All of us consider ourselves ethical; not perfect perhaps, but more ethical than most of humanity. The problem in social research—and probably in life—is that ethical considerations are not always apparent to us. As a result, we often plunge into things without seeing ethical issues that may be apparent to others and may even be obvious to us when pointed out. When I reported back to the others in the planning group, for example, no one disagreed with the inappropriateness of requiring participation. Everyone was a bit embarrassed about not having seen it.

Any of us can immediately see that a study that requires the torturing of small children is unethical. I know you'd speak out immediately if I suggested we interview people about their sex lives and then publish what they said in the local newspaper. But, as ethical as you are, you'd totally miss the ethical issue in some other situations—not because you're bad, but because we all do that.

The first half of this chapter, then, deals with the ethics of social research. In part, I'll present some of the broadly agreed-on norms describing what's ethical and what's not. More importantly, however, my purpose is to *sensitize* you to the ethical component in research so that you'll look for it whenever you plan a study. Even when the ethical aspects of a situation are debatable, you should know there's something to argue about.

Political considerations in research are also subtle, ambiguous, and arguable. Notice that the law school example involves politics as well as ethics. Although social scientists have an ethical norm that participation in research should be voluntary, this norm clearly grows out of U.S. political norms protecting civil liberties. In other nations, the proposed study would not have been considered unethical at all.

In the second half of this chapter, we'll look at some cases of social research projects that were crushed or nearly crushed by political considerations. As with ethical concerns, there is often no "correct" take on a given situation. People of goodwill disagree. Again, however, my purpose is to assist you in becoming more sensitive to the political considerations involved without giving you a party line of what's politically acceptable or unacceptable.

■ ETHICAL ISSUES IN SOCIAL RESEARCH

In most dictionaries and in common usage, ethics is typically associated with morality, and both deal with matters of right and wrong. But what is right and what wrong? What is the source of the distinction? For individuals the sources vary. They may be religions, political ideologies, or the pragmatic observation of what seems to work and what doesn't.

Webster's New World Dictionary is typical among dictionaries in defining *ethical* as "conforming to the standards of conduct of a given profession or group." Although the idea may frustrate those in search of moral absolutes, what we regard as morality and ethics in day-to-day life is a matter of agreement among members of a group. And, not surprisingly, different groups have agreed on different codes of conduct. If you are going to live in a particular society, then, it's extremely useful for you to know what that society considers ethical and unethical. The same holds true for the social research community.

If you're going to do social scientific research, then you need to to be aware of the general agreements shared by researchers about what's proper and improper in the conduct of scientific inquiry. The section that follows summarizes some of the most important ethical agreements that prevail in social research.

Voluntary Participation

Social research often, though not always, represents an intrusion into people's lives. The interviewer's knock on the door or the arrival of a questionnaire in the mail signals the beginning of an activity that the respondent has not requested and one that may require a significant portion of his or her time and energy. Participation in a social experiment disrupts the subject's regular activities.

Social research, moreover, often requires that people reveal personal information about themselves—information that may be unknown to their friends and associates. And social research often requires that such information be revealed to strangers. Other professionals, such as physicians and lawyers, also require such information. Their requests may be justified, however, because the information is required for them to serve the personal interests of the respondent. Social researchers can seldom make this claim. Like medical scientists, they can only argue that the research effort may ultimately help all humanity.

A major tenet of medical research ethics is that experimental participation must be *voluntary*. The same norm applies to social research. No one should be forced to participate. This norm is far easier to accept in theory than to apply in practice, however.

Again, medical research provides a useful parallel. Many experimental drugs are tested on prisoners. In the most rigorously ethical cases, the prisoners are told the nature—and the possible dangers—of the experiment; they are told that participation is completely voluntary; and they are further instructed that they can expect no special rewards—such as early parole—for participation. Even under these conditions, it's often clear that volunteers are motivated by the belief that they will personally benefit from their cooperation.

When the instructor in an introductory sociology class asks students to fill out a questionnaire that he or she hopes to analyze and publish, students should always be told that their participation in the survey is completely voluntary. Even so, most students will fear that nonparticipation will somehow affect their grade. The instructor should therefore be especially sensitive to the implied sanctions and make special provisions to obviate them. For example, the instructor could leave the room while the questionnaires are being completed. Or, students could be asked to return the questionnaires by mail or to drop them in a box near the door just before the next course meeting.

This norm of voluntary participation, though, goes directly against a number of scientific concerns. In the most general terms, the scientific goal of *generalizability* is threatened if experimental subjects or survey respondents are all the kinds of people who willingly participate in such things. This orientation probably reflects more general personality traits; possibly, then, the results of the research will not be generalizable to all kinds of people. Most clearly, in the case of a descriptive survey, a researcher cannot generalize the sample survey findings to an entire population unless a substantial majority of the scientifically selected sample actually participates—the willing respondents and the somewhat unwilling.

As you may recall from Chapter 11, field research has its own ethical dilemmas in this regard. Very often, the researcher cannot even reveal that a study is being done, for fear that that revelation might significantly affect the social processes being studied. Clearly, the subjects of study in such cases are not given the opportunity to volunteer or refuse to participate.

Though the norm of voluntary participation is important, it is often impossible to follow it. In cases where you feel ultimately justified in violating it, it is all the more important that you observe the other ethical norms of scientific research, such as bringing no harm to the people under study.

No Harm to the Participants

Social research should never injure the people being studied, regardless of whether they volunteer for the study. Perhaps the clearest instance of this norm in practice concerns the revealing of information that would embarrass them or endanger their home life, friendships, jobs, and so forth. This norm is discussed more fully in the next section.

Because subjects can be harmed psychologically in the course of a study, the researcher must look for the subtlest dangers and guard against them. Quite often, research subjects are asked to reveal deviant behavior, attitudes they feel are unpopular, or demeaning personal characteristics such as low income, the receipt of welfare payments, and the like. Revealing such information usually makes them feel at least uncomfortable.

Social research projects may also force participants to face aspects of themselves that they don't normally consider. This can happen even when the information is not revealed directly to the researcher. In retrospect, a certain past behavior may appear unjust or immoral. The project, then, can be the source of a continuing, personal agony for the subject. If the study concerns codes of ethical conduct, for example, the subject may begin questioning his or her own morality, and that personal concern may last long after the research has been completed and reported. For instance, probing questions can injure a fragile self-esteem.

By now, you should have realized that just about any research you might conduct runs the risk of injuring other people somehow. There is no way for the researcher to insure against all these possible injuries. Yet, some study designs make such injuries more likely than others. If a particular research procedure seems likely to produce unpleasant effects for subjects—asking survey respondents to report deviant behavior, for example—the researcher should have the firmest of scientific grounds for doing it. If the research design is essential and also likely to be unpleasant for subjects, you will find yourself in an ethical netherworld and may find yourself forced to do some personal agonizing. Although agonizing has little value in itself, it may be a healthy sign that you have become sensitive to the problem.

Increasingly, the ethical norms of voluntary participation and no harm to participants have become formalized in the concept of "informed consent." Thus prospective subjects in a medical experiment will be presented with a discussion of the experiment and all the possible risks to themselves. They will be required to sign a statement indicating that they are aware of the risks and choose to participate anyway. While the value of such a procedure is obvious when subjects will be injected with drugs designed to produce physical effects, for example, it's hardly appropriate when a participant observer rushes to the scene of urban rioting to study deviant behavior. While the researcher in this latter case is not excused from the norm of not bringing harm to those observed, gaining informed consent is not the means to achieving that end.

Although the fact often goes unrecognized, subjects can be harmed by the analysis and reporting of data. Every now and then, research subjects read the books published about the studies they participated in. Reasonably sophisticated subjects can locate themselves in the various indexes and tables. Having done so, they may find themselves characterized—though not identified by name—as bigoted, unpatriotic, irreligious, and so forth. At the very least, such characterizations are likely to trouble them and threaten their self-images. Yet the whole purpose of the research project may be to explain why some people are prejudiced and others are not.

In one survey of churchwomen (Babbie 1967), ministers in a sample of churches were asked to distribute questionnaires to a specified sample of members, collect them, and return them to the research office. One of these ministers read through the questionnaires from his sample before returning them, and then delivered a hellfire and brimstone sermon to his congregation, saying that many of them were atheists and were going to hell. Even though he could not identify the respondents who gave particular responses, it seems certain that many respondents were personally harmed by the action.

Like voluntary participation, not harming people is easy in theory, but often difficult in practice. Sensitivity to the issue and experience with its applications, however, should improve the researcher's tact in delicate areas of research.

In recent years, social researchers have been getting greater support for abiding by this norm. Federal and other funding agencies typically require an independent evaluation of the treatment of human subjects for research proposals, and most universities now have human subject committees to serve this evaluative function. Although sometimes troublesome and inappropriately applied, such requirements not only guard against unethical research but can also reveal ethical issues overlooked by the most scrupulous of researchers.

Anonymity and Confidentiality

The clearest concern in the protection of the subjects' interests and well-being is the protection of their identity, especially in survey research. If revealing their survey responses would injure them in any way, adherence to this norm becomes all the more important. Two techniques—*anonymity* and *confidentiality*—assist you in this regard, although the two are often confused.

Anonymity A respondent may be considered anonymous when the researcher cannot identify a given response with a given respondent. This means an interview survey respondent can never be considered anonymous, since an interviewer collects the information from an identifiable respondent. (I assume here that standard sampling methods are followed.) An example of anonymity would be the mail survey in which no identification numbers are put on the questionnaires before their return to the research office.

As we saw in Chapter 10 on survey research, assuring anonymity makes it difficult to keep track of who has or hasn't returned the questionnaires. Despite this problem, there are some situations in which you may be advised to pay the necessary price. In one study of drug use among university students during the 1960s, I decided that I specifically did not want to know the identity of respondents. I felt that honestly assuring anonymity would increase the likelihood and accuracy of responses. Also, I did not want to be in the position of being asked by authorities for the names of drug offenders. In the few instances in which respondents volunteered their names, such information was immediately obliterated on the questionnaires.

Confidentiality In a confidential survey, the researcher can identify a given person's responses but essentially promises not to do so publicly. In an interview survey, for example, the researcher would be in a position to make public the income reported by a given respondent, but the respondent is assured that this will not be done.

You can use several techniques to insure better performance on this guarantee. To begin, interviewers and others with access to respondent identifications should be trained in their ethical responsibilities. As soon as possible, all names and addresses should be removed from questionnaires and replaced by identification numbers. A master identification file should be created that links numbers to names to permit the later correction of missing or contradictory information, but this file should not be available except for legitimate purposes. Whenever a survey is confidential rather than anonymous, it is the researcher's responsibility to make that fact clear to the respondent. Never use the term *anonymous* to mean *confidential*.

With few exceptions (such as surveys of public figures who agree to have their responses published), the information respondents give must at least be kept confidential. This is not always an easy norm to follow, since the courts have not recognized social research data as constituting the kind of "privileged communication" accepted in the case of priests and attorneys.

This unprotected guarantee of confidentiality came to a near disaster in 1991. Two years earlier, the Exxon *Valdez* supertanker had run aground near the port of Valdez in Alaska, spilling ten million gallons of oil into the bay. The economic and environmental damage was widely reported.

Less attention was given to the psychological and sociological damage suffered by residents of the area. There were anecdotal reports of increased alcoholism, family violence, and similar, secondary consequences of the disruptions caused by the oil spill. Eventually, 22 communities in Prince William Sound and the Gulf of Alaska sued Exxon for the economic, social, and psychological damages suffered by their residents.

To determine the amount of damage done, the communities commissioned a San Diego research firm to undertake a household survey in which residents would be asked very personal questions about increased problems being experienced in their families. The sample of residents were asked to reveal painful and embarrassing information, under the guarantee of absolute confidentiality. Ultimately, the results of the survey confirmed that a variety of personal and family problems had increased substantially following the oil spill.

When Exxon learned that survey data would be presented to document the suffering, they took an unusual step: They asked the court to subpoena the survey questionnaires! The court granted the defendant's request and ordered the researchers to turn over the questionnaires—with all identifying information. It appeared that Exxon's intention was to call survey respondents to the stand and cross-examine them regarding answers they had given interviewers under the guarantee of confidentiality. Moreover, many of the respondents were Native Americans, whose cultural norms made such public revelations all the more painful.

The seriousness of this issue is not limited to established research firms. Rik Scarce was a graduate student at Washington State University when he undertook participant observation among animal rights activists. In 1990, he published a book based on his research: *Ecowarriors: Understanding the Radical Environmental Movement*. In 1993, Scarce was called before a grand jury and asked to identify the activists he had studied. In keeping with the norm of confidentiality, the young researcher refused to answer the grand jury's questions and spent 159 days in the Spokane County jail.

Robert Boruch and Joe Cecil (1979) have examined the issue of confidentiality in depth and have suggested several techniques you can use to insure that subjects' identities will never become public. The most fundamental technique involves the removal of identifying information as soon as it's no longer necessary. For example, you may need to identify survey respondents initially so you could recontact them to verify that the interview was conducted and perhaps to get information that was missing in the original interview. Thus, knowing respondents' identities may be vital to quality control in data collection.

As soon as you've verified an interview and assured that you don't need any further information from the respondent, however, you can safely remove all identifying information from the interview booklet. Often, interview booklets are printed so that the first page contains all the identifiers—it can be torn off once the respondent's identification is no longer needed.

But suppose you had not yet removed the identifying information. What would you do, then, when the police or a court ordered you to provide them with the responses provided by your research subjects?

This is a real issue for practicing social researchers, even though they sometimes disagree about how to protect subjects. Harry O'Neill, the vice chair of The Roper Organization, for example, suggests the best solution is to avoid the ability to identify respondents with their responses:

■ So how is this accomplished? Quite simply by not having any respondent-identifiable information available for the court to request. In my initial contact with a lawyer-client, I make it unmistakably clear that, once the survey is completed and validated, all respondent-identifiable information will be removed and destroyed immediately. Everything else connected with the survey—completed questionnaires, data tapes, methodology, names of interviewers and supervisors—of course will be made available.

(O'NEILL 1992:4)

Board Chairman Burns Roper (1992:5) disagrees, saying that such procedures might raise questions about the validity of the research methods. Instead, Roper says that he feels he must be prepared to go to jail if necessary. (He notes that Vice Chair O'Neill has promised to visit him in that event.)

Happily, the Exxon *Valdez* case was settled before the court decided whether it would force survey respondents to testify in open court. Unhappily, the potential for disaster remains.

Deceiving Subjects

We've seen that the handling of subjects' identities is an important ethical consideration. Handling your own identity as a researcher can be tricky also. Sometimes it's useful and even necessary to identify yourself as a researcher to those you want to study. You'd have to be a master con artist to get people to participate in a laboratory experiment or complete a lengthy questionnaire without letting on that you were conducting research.

Even when you must conceal your research identity, as Randall Alfred did while studying the Church of Satan (Chapter 11), you need to consider the following. Because deceiving people is unethical, deception within social research needs to be justified by compelling scientific or administrative concerns. Even then, the justification will be arguable.

Sometimes researchers admit that they're doing research but fudge about why they're doing it or for whom. Suppose you've been asked by a public welfare agency to conduct a study of living standards among aid recipients. Even if the agency is looking for ways of improving conditions, the recipient-subjects are likely to fear a witch-hunt for "cheaters." They might be tempted, therefore, to give answers making them seem more destitute than they really are. Unless they provide truthful answers, however, the study will not produce accurate data that will contribute to an effective improvement of living conditions. What do you do? One solution would be to tell subjects that you're conducting the study as part of a university research program—concealing your affiliation with the welfare agency. Doing that improves the scientific quality of the study, but it raises a serious ethical issue in the process.

Lying about research purposes is common in laboratory experiments. Although it is difficult to conceal the fact you're conducting research, it's usually a simple—and sometimes appropriate—matter to conceal your purpose. Many experiments in social psychology, for example, test the extent to which subjects will abandon the evidence of their own observations in favor of the views expressed by others. Figure 18-1 shows the classic Asch experiment—frequently replicated by psychology classes—in which subjects are shown three lines of differing lengths (A, B, and C) and asked to compare them with a fourth line (D). Subjects are then asked, "Which of the first three lines is the same length as the fourth?"

You'd probably find it a fairly simple task: "B" is clearly the correct answer. Your job would be slightly complicated by the fact that several other "subjects" sitting beside you all agree that A is the same length as D! In reality, of course, the others in the experiment are all confederates of the researcher, told to agree on the wrong answer. The purpose would be to see if you'd give up your own judgment in favor of the group agreement. I think you can see it's a useful phenomenon to study and understand, and it couldn't be studied without deceiving the subjects. We'll examine a similar situation in the discussion of the Milgram experiment later in this chapter.

One solution researchers have found appropriate in such experiments is *debriefing* subjects following the experiment. Even though subjects can't be told the true purpose of the study prior to their participation in it, there's usually no reason they can't know afterward. Telling them the truth afterward may make up for having to lie to them at the outset. This must be done with care, however, making sure the subjects aren't left with bad feelings or doubts about themselves based on their performance in the experiment. If this seems complicated, it's simply the price we pay for using other people's lives as the subject matter for our research.

Analysis and Reporting

As a social researcher, then, you have many ethical obligations to your subjects of study. At the same time, you have ethical obligations to your colleagues in the scientific community; a few comments on these obligations are in order.

In any rigorous study, the researcher should be more familiar than anyone else with the technical shortcomings and failures of the study. You have an obligation to make such shortcomings known to your readers. Even though you may feel foolish admitting mistakes, you should do it anyway.

Negative findings should be reported if they are at all related to your analysis. There is an unfortunate myth in scientific reporting that only positive discoveries are worth reporting (and journal editors are sometimes guilty of believing this as well). In science, however, it is often as important to know that two variables are *not* related as to know that they are. Recall the earlier discussion of Stouffer's examination of attitudes toward the promotion system in the army. It was a mark of his caliber as a researcher that he insisted on

FIGURE 18-1
Asch Experiment: Lines of Differing Lengths

Ethical Issues in Research on Human Sexuality

by Kathleen McKinney
Department of Sociology, Illinois State University

WHEN STUDYING any form of human behavior, ethical concerns are paramount. This statement may be even more true for studies of human sexuality because of the topic's highly personal, salient, and perhaps threatening nature. Concern has been expressed by the public and by legislators about human sexuality research. Three commonly discussed ethical criteria have been related specifically to research in the area of human sexuality.

Informed Consent This criterion emphasizes the importance of both accurately informing your subject or respondent as to the nature of the research and obtaining his or her verbal or written consent to participate. Coercion is not to be used to force participation, and subjects may terminate their involvement in the research at any time. There are many possible violations of this standard. Misrepresentation or deception may be used when describing an embarrassing or personal topic of study because the researchers fear high rates of refusal or false data. Covert research, such as some observational studies, also violate the informed consent standard since subjects are unaware that they are being studied. Informed consent may create special problems with certain populations. For example, studies of the sexuality of children are limited by the concern that children may be cognitively and emotionally unable to give informed consent. Although there can be problems such as those discussed, most research is clearly voluntary, with informed consent from those participating.

Right to Privacy Given the highly personal nature of sexuality and society's tremendous concern with social control of sexuality, the right to privacy is a very important ethical concern for research in this area. Individuals may risk losing their jobs, having family difficulties, or being ostracized by peers if certain facets of their sexual

---

finding out *why* the MPs thought the system was fair and the air corpsmen didn't. Had he simply set the puzzling findings aside for later analysis, our understanding of reference groups and relative deprivation would have been held back.

Similarly, you must avoid the temptation to save face by describing your findings as the product of a carefully preplanned analytical strategy when that is not the case. Many findings arrive unexpectedly—even though they may seem obvious in retrospect. So you uncovered an interesting relationship by accident—so what? Embroidering such situations with descriptions of fictitious hypotheses is dishonest and tends to mislead inexperienced researchers into thinking that all scientific inquiry is rigorously preplanned and organized.

In general, science progresses through honesty and openness; ego-defenses and deception retard it. You can best serve other researchers—and scientific discovery as a whole—by telling the truth about all the pitfalls and problems you've experienced in a particular line of inquiry. Perhaps you'll save them from the same problems. The box entitled "Ethical Issues in Research on Human Sexuality" examines some of the ethical issues involved in a specific research arena.

Institutional Review Boards

The issue of research ethics in studies involving humans is now also governed by federal law. Any agency (such as a university or a hospital) wishing to receive federal research support must establish an "Institutional Review Board" (IRB), a panel of faculty (and possibly others) who review all research proposals involving human subjects to insure that their rights and interests are being protected.

lives are revealed. This is especially true for individuals involved in sexual behavior categorized as deviant (such as transvestism). Violations of right to privacy occur when researchers identify members of certain groups they have studied, release or share an individual's data or responses, or covertly observe sexual behavior. In most cases, right to privacy is easily maintained by the researcher. In survey research, self-administered questionnaires can be anonymous and interviews can be kept confidential. In case and observational studies, the identity of the person or group studied can be disguised in any publications. In most research methods, analysis and reporting of data should be at the group or aggregate level.

Protection from Harm Harm may include emotional or psychological distress, as well as physical harm. Potential for harm varies by research method; it is more likely in experimental studies where the researcher manipulates or does something to the subject than in observational or survey research. Emotional distress, however, is a possibility in all studies of human sexuality. Respondents may be asked questions that elicit anxiety, dredge up unpleasant memories, or cause them to evaluate themselves critically. Researchers can reduce the potential for such distress during a study by using anonymous, self-administered questionnaires or well-trained interviewers and by wording sensitive questions carefully.

All three of these ethical criteria are quite subjective. Violations are sometimes justified by arguing that risks to subjects are outweighed by benefits to society. The issue here, of course, is who makes that critical decision. Usually, such decisions are made by the researcher and often a screening committee that deals with ethical concerns. Most creative researchers have been able to follow all three ethical guidelines and still do important research.

The chief responsibility of an IRB is to insure that the risks faced by human participants in research are minimal. In some cases, the IRB may ask the researcher to revise the study design; in other cases, the IRB may refuse to approve a study. Where some minimal risks are deemed unavoidable, researchers are required to prepare an "informed consent" form, as we've seen, that describes those risks clearly, and subjects may participate in the study only after they have read the statement and signed it as an indication that they know the risks and voluntarily accept them.

Much of the impetus for the establishment of IRBs had to do with medical experimentation on humans, and many social science study designs are generally regarded as exempt from IRB review. An anonymous survey sent to a large sample of respondents would be an example. The guideline to be followed by IRBs, as contained in the federal Exemption Categories (45 CFR 46.101 [b]), asks whether the research "could reasonably place the subject at risk of criminal or civil liability or be damaging to the subject's financial standing or employability." Typically, this is not the case—especially given the norms of confidentiality.

A Professional Code of Ethics

Because ethical issues in social research are both important and ambiguous, most of the professional associations have created and published formal codes of conduct describing what is considered acceptable and unacceptable professional behavior. To illustrate, I've presented the code of conduct of the American Association for Public Opinion Research, since AAPOR is an interdisciplinary research association in the social sciences (see Figure 18-2).

FIGURE 18-2
Code of Conduct of the American Association for Public Opinion Research

CODE OF PROFESSIONAL ETHICS AND PRACTICES

We, the members of the American Association for Public Opinion Research, subscribe to the principles expressed in the following code.

Our goal is to support sound practice in the profession of public opinion research. (By public opinion research we mean studies in which the principal source of information about individual beliefs, preferences, and behavior is a report given by the individual himself or herself.)

We pledge ourselves to maintain high standards of scientific competence and integrity in our work, and in our relations both with our clients and with the general public. We further pledge ourselves to reject all tasks or assignments which would be inconsistent with the principles of this code.

THE CODE

I. *Principles of Professional Practice in the Conduct of Our Work*

  A. We shall exercise due care in gathering and processing data, taking all reasonable steps to assume the accuracy of results.

  B. We shall exercise due care in the development of research designs and in the analysis of data.

   1. We shall employ only research tools and methods of analysis which, in our professional judgment, are well suited to the research problem at hand.
   2. We shall not select research tools and methods of analysis because of their special capacity to yield a desired conclusion.
   3. We shall not knowingly make interpretations of research results, nor shall we tacitly permit interpretations, which are inconsistent with the data available.
   4. We shall not knowingly imply that interpretations should be accorded greater confidence than the data actually warrant.

  C. We shall describe our findings and methods accurately and in appropriate detail in all research reports.

II. *Principles of Professional Responsibility in Our Dealings with People*

  A. The Public:

   1. We shall cooperate with legally authorized representatives of the public by describing the methods used in our studies.
   2. We shall maintain the right to approve the release of our findings whether or not ascribed to us. When misinterpretation appears, we shall publicly disclose what is required to correct it, notwithstanding our obligation for client confidentiality in all other respects.

  B. Clients or Sponsors:

   1. We shall hold confidential all information obtained about the client's general business affairs and about the findings of research conducted for the client, except when the dissemination of such information is expressly authorized.
   2. We shall be mindful of the limitations of our techniques and facilities and shall accept only those research assignments which can be accomplished within these limitations.

  C. The Profession:

   1. We shall not cite our membership in the Association as evidence of professional competence, since the Association does not so certify any persons or organizations.
   2. We recognize our responsibility to contribute to the science of public opinion research and to disseminate as freely as possible the ideas and findings which emerge from our research.

  D. The Respondent:

   1. We shall not lie to survey respondents or use practices and methods which abuse, coerce, or humiliate them.
   2. We shall protect the anonymity of every respondent, unless the respondent waives such anonymity for specified uses. In addition, we shall hold as privileged and confidential all information which tends to identify the respondent.

Source: American Association for Public Opinion Research, *By-Laws* (May 1977). Used by permission.

■ TWO ETHICAL CONTROVERSIES

As you may already have guessed, the adoption and publication of professional codes of conduct have not totally resolved the issue of research ethics. Social scientists still disagree on some general principles, and those who seem to agree in principle debate specifics.

In this section, I'm going to describe briefly two research projects that have provoked ethical controversy and discussion in recent years. These are not the only two controversial projects that have been done; they simply illustrate ethical issues in the real world, and I thought you'd find them interesting and perhaps provocative. The first project studied homosexual behavior in public restrooms, and the second examined obedience in a laboratory setting.

Trouble in the Tearoom

As a graduate student, Laud Humphreys became interested in the study of homosexuality. He developed a special interest in the casual and fleeting homosexual acts engaged in by some non-homosexuals. In particular, his research interest focused on homosexual acts between strangers meeting in the public restrooms in parks, called "tearooms" among homosexuals. The result was the publication in 1970 of *Tearoom Trade.*

What particularly interested Humphreys about the tearoom activity was that the participants seemed to live "normal" lives otherwise, as family men and as accepted members of the community. They did nothing else that might qualify them as homosexuals. Thus, it was important to them that they remain anonymous in their tearoom visits. How would you study something like that?

Humphreys decided to take advantage of the social structure of the situation. Typically, the tearoom encounter involved three people: the two men actually engaged in the homosexual act and a lookout, called the "watchqueen." Thus, Humphreys began showing up at public restrooms, offering to serve as watchqueen whenever it seemed appropriate. Since the watchqueen's payoff was the chance to watch the action, Humphreys was able to conduct field observations as he would in a study of political rallies or jaywalking behavior at intersections.

To round out his understanding of the tearoom trade, Humphreys needed to know something more about the people who participated. Since the men probably would not have been thrilled about being interviewed, Humphreys developed a different solution. Whenever possible, he noted the license numbers of participants' cars and tracked down their names and addresses through the police. Humphreys then visited the men at their homes, disguising himself enough to avoid recognition, and announced that he was conducting a survey. In that fashion, he collected the personal information he couldn't get in the restrooms.

Humphreys's research provoked considerable controversy both within and outside the social scientific community. Some critics charged Humphreys with a gross invasion of privacy in the name of science. What men did in public restrooms was their own business and not Humphreys. Others were mostly concerned about the deceit involved—Humphreys had lied to the participants by leading them to believe he was only a voyeur-participant. People who felt that the tearoom participants, because they were doing their stuff in a public facility, were fair game for observation nonetheless protested the follow-up survey. They felt it was unethical for Humphreys to trace the participants to their homes and to interview them under false pretenses. Still others justified Humphreys's research. The topic, they said, was worth study. It couldn't be studied any other way, and they regarded the deceit to be essentially harmless, noting that Humphreys was careful not to harm his subjects by disclosing their tearoom activities.

The tearoom trade controversy, as you might imagine, has never been resolved. It is still debated, and it probably always will be, since it stirs emotions and contains ethical issues people disagree about. What do you think? Was Humphreys ethical in doing what he did? Are there parts of the research you feel were acceptable and other parts that were not? Whatever you feel in the matter, you are sure to find others who disagree with you.

Observing Human Obedience

The second illustration differs from the first in many ways. Whereas Humphreys' study involved participant observation, this study setting was in the laboratory. The first study was sociological, this one psychological. And where the first examined a form of human deviance, the study we're going to look at now examined conformity.

One of the more unsettling clichés to come out of World War II was the German soldier's common excuse for atrocities: "I was only following orders." From the point of view that gave rise to this comment, any behavior—no matter how reprehensible—could be justified if someone else could be assigned responsibility for it. If a superior officer ordered a soldier to kill a baby, the fact of the order was said to exempt the soldier from personal responsibility for the action.

Although the military tribunals that tried the war crime cases did not accept the excuse, social scientists and others have recognized the extent to which this point of view pervades social life. People often seem willing to do things they know would be considered wrong by others, *if* they can cite some higher authority as ordering them to do it. Such was the pattern of justification in the My Lai tragedy of Vietnam, when U.S. soldiers killed more than 300 unarmed civilians—some of them young children—simply because their village of My Lai was believed to be a Viet Cong stronghold. It appears less dramatically in day-to-day civilian life. Few would disagree that this reliance on authority exists, yet Stanley Milgram's study (1963, 1965) of the topic provoked considerable controversy.

To observe people's willingness to harm others when following orders, Milgram brought 40 adult men—from many different walks of life—into a laboratory setting designed to create the phenomenon under study. If you had been a subject in the experiment, you would have had something like the following experience.

You have been informed that you and another subject are about to participate in a learning experiment. Through a draw of lots, you are assigned the job of "teacher" and your fellow subject the job of "pupil." He's led into another room and strapped into a chair; an electrode is attached to his wrist. As the teacher, you're seated in front of an impressive electrical control panel covered with dials, gauges, and switches. You notice that each switch has a label giving a different number of volts, ranging from 15 to 315. The switches have other labels, too, some with the ominous phrases "Extreme-Intensity Shock," "Danger—Severe Shock," and "XXX."

The experiment runs like this. You read a list of word pairs to the learner and then test his ability to match them up. Since you can't see him, a light on your control panel indicates his answer. Whenever the learner makes a mistake, you're instructed by the experimenter to throw one of the switches—beginning with the mildest—and administer a shock to your pupil. Through an open door between the two rooms, you hear your pupil's response to the shock. Then you read another list of word pairs and test him again.

As the experiment progresses, you administer ever more intense shocks, until your pupil screams for mercy and begs for the experiment to end. You're instructed to administer the next shock anyway. After a while, your pupil begins kicking the wall between the two rooms and continues to scream. You are told to give the next shock. Finally, you read a list and ask for the pupil's answer—but there is no reply whatever, only silence from the other room. The experimenter informs you that no answer is considered an error and instructs you to administer the next higher shock. This continues up to the "XXX" shock at the end of the series.

What do you suppose you really would have done when the pupil first began screaming? When he began kicking on the wall? Or when he became totally silent and gave no indication of life? You'd refuse to continue giving shocks, right? Of the first 40 adult men Milgram tested, nobody refused to administer the shocks until the pupil began kicking the wall between the two rooms. Of the 40, 5 did so then. Two-thirds of the subjects, 26 of the 40, continued doing as they were told through the entire series—up to and including the administration of the highest shock.

As you've probably guessed, the shocks were phony, and the "pupil" was another experimenter. Only the "teacher" was a real subject in the experiment. You wouldn't have been hurting another person, even though you would have been led to think you were. The experiment was designed to test your *willingness* to follow orders, to the point of presumably killing someone.

Milgram's experiments have been criticized both methodologically and ethically. On the ethical side, critics have particularly cited the effects of the experiment on the subjects. Many seem to have personally experienced about as much pain as they thought they were administering to someone else. They pleaded with the experimenter to let them stop giving the shocks. They became extremely upset and nervous. Some had uncontrollable seizures.

How do *you* feel about this research? Do you think the topic was important enough to justify such measures? Can you think of other ways the researcher might have examined obedience?

■ DISCUSSION EXAMPLES

Research ethics, then, is an important though ambiguous topic. The difficulty of resolving ethical issues should not be an excuse for ignoring them. To sensitize yourself further to the ethical component in social research, I've prepared a list of real and hypothetical research situations. See if you can see the ethical component in each. How do you feel about it? Do you feel the procedures described are ultimately acceptable or unacceptable? It would be useful to discuss some of these with others in your methods course.

1. A psychology instructor asks students in an introductory psychology class to complete questionnaires that the instructor will analyze and use in preparing a journal article for publication.
2. After a field study of deviant behavior during a riot, law enforcement officials demand that the researcher identify those people who were observed looting. Rather than risk arrest as an accomplice after the fact, the researcher complies.
3. After completing the final draft of a book reporting a research project, the researcher-author discovers that 25 of the 2,000 survey interviews were falsified by interviewers—but chooses to ignore that fact and publish the book anyway.
4. Researchers obtain a list of right-wing radicals they wish to study. They contact the radicals with the explanation that each has been selected "at random" from among the general population to take a sampling of "public opinion."
5. A college instructor who wants to test the effect of unfair berating administers an hour exam to both sections of a specific course. The overall performance of the two sections is essentially the same. The grades of one section are artificially lowered, however, and the instructor berates them for performing so badly. The instructor then administers the same final exam to both sections and discovers that the performance of the unfairly berated section is worse. The hypothesis is confirmed, and the research report is published.
6. In a study of sexual behavior, the investigator wants to overcome subjects' reluctance to report what they might regard as shameful behavior. To get past their reluctance, subjects are asked: "Everyone masturbates now and then; about how much do you masturbate?"
7. A researcher studying dorm life on campus discovers that 60 percent of the residents regularly violate restrictions on alcohol consumption. Publication of this finding would probably create a furor in the campus community. Because no extensive analysis of alcohol use is planned, the researcher decides to ignore the finding and keep it quiet.
8. To test the extent to which people may try to save face by expressing attitudes on matters they are wholly uninformed about, the

researcher asks for their attitudes regarding a fictitious issue.
9. A research questionnaire is circulated among students as part of their university registration packet. Although students are not told they must complete the questionnaire, the hope is that they will believe they must—thus ensuring a higher completion rate.
10. A participant-observer pretends to join a radical, political group in order to study it and is successfully accepted as a member of the inner planning circle. What should the researcher do if the group makes plans for the following?
    a. A peaceful, though illegal, demonstration
    b. The bombing of a public building during a time it is sure to be unoccupied
    c. The assassination of a public official

■ THE POLITICS OF SOCIAL RESEARCH

As I've indicated earlier, both ethics and politics hinge on ideological points of view. What is unacceptable from one point of view will be acceptable from another. Though disagreements on political aspects of research resemble ethical ones, I want to distinguish ethical from political issues in two ways.

First, although ethics and politics are often closely intertwined, the ethics of social research deals mostly with the methods employed; political issues tend to center on the substance and use of research. Thus, for example, some critics raise ethical objections to the Milgram experiments, saying that the methods used harmed the subjects. A political objection would be that obedience is not a worthy topic for study: either that (1) we should not tinker with people's willingness to follow orders from higher authority or, from the opposite political point of view, that (2) the results of the research could be used to make people *more* obedient.

The second thing that distinguishes ethical from political aspects of social research is that there are no formal codes of accepted political conduct comparable to the codes of ethical conduct we've discussed earlier. Although some ethical norms have political aspects—for example, not harming subjects clearly relates to our protection of civil liberties—no one has developed a set of political norms that all social researchers accept.

The only partial exception to the lack of political norms is the generally accepted view that a researcher's personal political orientation should not interfere with or unduly influence his or her scientific research. It would be considered improper for you to use shoddy techniques or lie about your research as a way of furthering your political views.

Objectivity and Ideology

In Chapter 1, I suggested that social research can never be totally objective, since researchers are humanly subjective. Science, as a collective enterprise, achieves the equivalent of objectivity through intersubjectivity. That is, different scientists, having different subjective views, can and should arrive at the same results when they employ accepted research techniques. Essentially, this will happen to the extent that each can set personal values and views aside for the duration of the research.

The classic statement on objectivity and neutrality in social science is Max Weber's lecture, "Science as a Vocation" ([1925] 1946). In this talk, Weber coined the phrase "value-free sociology," urging that sociology, like other sciences, needed to be unencumbered by personal values if it was to make a special contribution to society. Liberals and conservatives alike could recognize the "facts" of social science, regardless of how those facts accorded with their personal politics.

Most, but not all, social scientists have agreed with this abstract ideal. Increasingly, Marxist and neo-Marxist scholars have argued that social science and social action cannot and should not be separated. Explanations of the status quo in society, they contend, shade subtly into defenses of that same status quo. Simple explanations of the social functions of, say, discrimination can easily become justifications for its continuance. By the same token, merely studying society and its ills without a commitment to making society more humane has been called irresponsible.

Quite aside from abstract disagreements about whether social science can or should be value-free, many have argued about whether particular research undertakings *are* value-free or whether they represent an intrusion of the researcher's own political values. Typically, researchers have denied the intrusion, and the denial has been challenged. Let's look at some examples of the controversies that have raged and continue to rage over this issue.

Social Research and Race Nowhere have social research and politics been more controversially intertwined than in the area of racial relations. Social scientists studied the topic for a long time, and often the products of the social research have found their way into practical politics. A few brief references should illustrate the point.

In 1896, when the U.S. Supreme Court established the principle of "separate but equal" as a means of reconciling the Fourteenth Amendment's guarantee of equality to African Americans with the norms of segregation, it neither asked for nor cited social science research. Nonetheless, it is widely believed that the Court was influenced by the writings of William Graham Sumner, a leading social scientist of his era. Sumner was noted for his view that the mores and folkways of a society were relatively impervious to legislation and social planning. His view has often been paraphrased as "stateways do not make folkways." Thus the Court ruled that it could not accept the assumption that "social prejudices may be overcome by legislation" and denied the wisdom of "laws which conflict with the general sentiment of the community" (Blaunstein and Zangrando 1970:308).

There is no doubt that Gunnar Myrdal's classic two-volume study (1944) of race relations in the United States had a significant impact on the topic of his research. Myrdal amassed a great deal of data to show that the position of African Americans directly contradicted U.S. values of social and political equality. Further, Myrdal did not attempt to hide his own point of view in the matter.

When the doctrine of "separate but equal" was overturned in 1954 (*Brown* v. *Board of Education of Topeka*), the new Supreme Court decision was based in part on the conclusion that segregation had a detrimental effect on African-American children. In drawing that conclusion, the Court cited a number of sociological and psychological research reports (Blaunstein and Zangrando 1970).

For the most part, social scientists in this century have supported the cause of African-American equality in the United States. Many have been actively involved in the civil rights movement, some more radically than others. Thus, social scientists have been able to draw research conclusions supporting the cause of equality without fear of criticism from colleagues. To recognize the solidity of the general social science position in the matter of equality, we need only examine a few research projects that have produced conclusions disagreeing with the predominant ideological position.

Most social scientists have—overtly, at least—supported the end of school segregation. Thus, an immediate and heated controversy was provoked in 1966 when James Coleman, a respected sociologist, published the results of a major national study of race and education. Contrary to general agreement, Coleman found little difference in academic performance between African-American students attending integrated schools and those attending segregated ones. Indeed, such obvious things as libraries, laboratory facilities, and high expenditures per student made little difference. Instead, Coleman reported that family and neighborhood factors had the most influence on academic achievement.

Coleman's findings were not well received by many of the social scientists who had been active in the civil rights movement. Some scholars criticized Coleman's work on methodological grounds, but many others objected hotly on the grounds that the findings would have segregationist political consequences. The controversy that raged around the Coleman report was reminiscent of that provoked earlier by Daniel Moynihan (1965) in his critical analysis of the African-American family in the United States.

Another example of political controversy surrounding social research in connection with race concerns the issue of IQ scores of African-American and white people. In 1969, Arthur Jensen, a Harvard psychologist, was asked to prepare an article for the *Harvard Educational Review* examining the data on racial differences in IQ test results (Jensen, 1969). In the article, Jensen concluded that genetic differences between African Americans and whites accounted for the lower average IQ scores of African Americans. Jensen became so identified with that position that he appeared on college campuses across the country discussing it.

Jensen's position has been attacked on numerous methodological bases. It was charged that much of the data on which Jensen's conclusion was based were inadequate and sloppy—there are many IQ tests, some worse than others. Similarly, it was argued that Jensen had not taken social-environmental factors sufficiently into account. Other social scientists raised other appropriate methodological objections.

Beyond the scientific critique, however, Jensen was condemned by many as a racist. He was booed and his public presentations were drowned out by hostile crowds. Jensen's reception by several university audiences was not significantly different from the reception received by abolitionists a century before.

Many social scientists limited their objections to the Moynihan, Coleman, and Jensen research to scientific, methodological grounds. The purpose of my account, however, is to point out that political ideology often gets involved in matters of social research. Although the abstract model of science is divorced from ideology, the practice of science is not.

Project Camelot Among social scientists Camelot is a household term in discussions of research and politics, frequently referenced with no further description. Irving Louis Horowitz (1967), a man who has criticized government agencies on occasion, said that Project Camelot "has had perhaps the worst public relations record of any agency or subagency of the U.S. government" (p. vi). What provoked such a stir?

On December 4, 1964, the Special Operations Research Office of American University sent an announcement to several social scientists about a project being organized around the topic of internal war within a nation. The announcement contained, in part, the following description:

■ Project *Camelot* is a study whose objective is to determine the feasibility of developing a general social systems model which would make it possible to predict and influence politically significant aspects of social change in the developing nations of the world. Somewhat more specifically, its objectives are:

First, to devise procedures for assessing the potential for internal war within national societies;

Second, to identify with increased degrees of confidence those actions which a government might take to relieve conditions which are assessed as giving rise to a potential for internal war.

(HOROWITZ, 1967:47)

Of course, few people are openly in favor of war, and most would support research aimed at ending or preventing war. By the summer of 1965, however, with the national debate on Vietnam gaining momentum, Camelot was being hotly argued in social science circles as a Department of Defense attempt to co-opt scientists into a counterinsurgency effort in Chile. Some claimed that the Defense Department intended to sponsor social scientific research aimed at putting down political and potentially revolutionary dissatisfaction in that volatile Latin-American nation. Whatever the motivations of the social scientists, it was feared that their research would be used to strengthen established regimes and thwart popular reformist and revolutionary movements in foreign countries.

Many social scientists who had agreed in principle to participate in the project soon felt they were facing a lesson learned decades before them by Robert Oppenheimer and some of the atomic scientists—that scientific findings can be used for purposes that the scientists themselves oppose.

Charges and countercharges were hurled around professional circles. Names were called, motives questioned. Old friendships ended. The Defense Department was roundly damned by all for attempting to subvert social research. Foreign relations with Latin America simultaneously chilled and got hot. Finally, under the cloud of growing criticism, Camelot was canceled and dismantled.

It is interesting to imagine what might have happened to Project Camelot had it been proposed to a steadfastly conservative and anticommunist social research community. I think there is no doubt that it would have been supported, executed, and completed without serious challenge or controversy. Certainly war per se was not the issue. There was no serious criticism when Sam Stouffer organized the research branch in the army during World War II to conduct research aimed at supporting the war effort, making U.S. soldiers more effective fighters. Ultimately science is neutral on the topics of war and peace, but scientists are not.

More recently Hamnett et al. have examined several research ethics as seen from the standpoint of the countries that U.S. researchers sometimes study. For example, they point out the following:

■ Governments in many parts of the Third World are increasingly making demands on cross-national researchers.... These range from restrictions on research not directly relevant to national development priorities to requirements for collaboration with host country institutions and scholars. The view that the exploitation of any national resource, including social or cultural data, should be of benefit to that country provides one rationale for such requirements.

(HAMNETT ET AL. 1984:6)

Politics with a Little "p"

Often social research is confounded by political ideologies. I would like you to recognize, however, that the "politics" of social research runs far deeper than this. Social research in relation to contested social issues simply cannot remain antiseptically objective. This is the case whenever differing ideologies are pitted against one another in a field of social science data. It pertains no less when people with conflicting self-interests confront one another.

Social researchers who have served as "expert witnesses" in court would probably agree that the scientific ideal of a "search for truth" seems hopelessly naive in a court of law. While expert witnesses technically do not "represent" either side in court, they are, nonetheless, engaged by only one side to appear, and their testimony tends to support the side of the party who pays for their time. This doesn't mean these witnesses will lie on behalf of their patrons, but the contenders in a lawsuit are understandably more likely to pay for expert testimony that supports their case than for testimony that attacks it.

Thus, as an expert witness, you appear in court only because your presumably scientific and honest judgment happens to coincide with the interests of the party paying you to testify. Once you arrive in court and swear to tell the truth, the whole truth, and nothing but the truth, however, you find yourself in a world foreign to the ideals of objective contemplation. Suddenly the norms are those of winning and losing. As an expert witness, of course, all you have to lose is respectability generally. Still, such stakes are high enough for most social scientists.

I recall one case in federal court when I was testifying on behalf of some civil service workers who had had their cost-of-living allowance (COLA) cut on the basis of research I thought was rather shoddy. I was engaged to conduct more "scientific" research that would demonstrate the injustice worked against the civil servants. I've described the research elsewhere (Babbie 1982: 232–43), so I won't repeat it here.

I took the stand, feeling pretty much like a respected professor and textbook author. In short order, however, I found I had moved from the academy to the hockey rink. Tests of statistical significance and sampling error were suddenly less relevant than a slap shot. At one point, an attorney from Washington lured me into casually agreeing that I was familiar with a certain, nonexistent professional journal. I was mortified and suddenly found myself shifting domains. Without really thinking about it, I now was less committed to being a friendly Mr. Chips and more aligned with ninja-professor. I would not be fully satisfied until I, in turn, could mortify the attorney, which I succeeded in doing.

Even though the civil servants got their cost-of-living allowance back, I have to admit I was also concerned with how I looked in front of the courtroom assemblage. I tell you this anecdote to illustrate the personal "politics" of human interactions involving presumably scientific and objective research. We need to realize that as human beings, social researchers are going to act like human beings, and we must take this into account in assessing their findings. It does not invalidate their research; it just needs to be taken into account.

Politics in Perspective

Certainly, social scientists must pay serious attention to both the ethical and the political dimensions of research. Moreover, there is a clear intersection between the two concerns. Whenever politicians or the public feel that social research is violating ethical or moral standards, they'll be quick to respond with remedies of their own. Moreover, the standards so defended may not be those of the research community. And even when researchers might support the goals of legislation, the means specified in law can hamstring research. By way of illustration, the accompanying box presents a bill passed by the Virginia Senate in 1995, aimed at perceived abuses in political polling.

The bill addressed a real issue—the potential impact of research funding on the objectivity of the researchers. If you recall an earlier discussion of push-polls, you'll recognize the potential dangers. At the same time, the detailed specifications of legislation such as this could create new problems while seeking to solve old ones. Routinely announcing the identity of the poll's sponsor, for example, can itself bias responses. (Respondents have the right to know the sponsor's identity after the interviewing is complete, and, of course, they have the right to refuse to participate altogether.)

There is a special concern among legislators for research on children. And while the social research norms discussed in this chapter would guard against bringing any physical or emotional harm to children, some of the restrictive legislation introduced from time to time borders on the actions of one particular Western city, which shall remain nameless. In response to concerns that a public school teacher had been playing new age music in class and encouraging students to meditate, the city council passed legislation stating that no teacher could do anything that would "affect the minds of students."

The role of politics and related ideologies is not unique to social research. The natural sciences have experienced and continue to experience similar situations. The preceding discussion has three main purposes in any textbook on the *practice* of social research.

First, you need to realize that science is not untouched by politics. Social science, in particular, is a part of social life. We study things that matter to people, things they have firm, personal feelings about, and things that affect their lives. Scientists are human beings, and their human feelings often show through in their professional lives. To think otherwise would be naive.

Second, science does proceed even under political controversy and hostility. Even when researchers get angry and call each other names, or when the research community comes under attack from the outside, the job of science gets done anyway. Scientific inquiry persists, studies are done, reports are published, and new things are learned. In short, ideological disputes do not bring science to a halt but rather make it more exciting.

Finally, I want you to make ideological considerations a part of the backdrop you create—a backdrop that will increase your awareness as you learn the various techniques of social science methods. Many of the established techniques of science function to cancel out or hold in check our human shortcomings, especially those we are unaware of. Otherwise, we might look into the world and never see anything but ourselves—our personal biases and beliefs.

Senate Bill No. 1126

February 24, 1995

A BILL to amend the Code of Virginia by adding a section numbered 24.2-1014.1, relating to political campaign telephone polls; penalties.

Patron–Robb

Introduced at the request of Governor

Referred to the committee on Privileges and Elections

Be it enacted by the General Assembly of Virginia:

1. That the code of Virginia is amended by adding a section numbered 2-1014.1 as follows:

§2-1014.1. Identifying persons responsible for certain telephone polls: penalties.

A. As used in this section, a "telephone poll" means a series of telephone calls made (i) to twenty-five or more telephone numbers in the Commonwealth, (ii) during the 180 days before a general or special election or during the ninety days before a primary, and (iii) information reflecting public opinion or preferences as to any candidate in the election or primary.

B. It shall be unlawful for any person to conduct a telephone poll unless he discloses, before the conclusion of each telephone call, information to identify the person who has authorized or is paying for the poll. The person conducting the telephone poll shall disclose the following identifying information:
  1. The name of the candidate if the poll is authorized by the candidate or his campaign committee;
  2. The name of the political party committee if the poll is authorized by a political party committee; or
  3. The name of the committee, group, or individual authorizing the poll if the poll is authorized by any person other than a candidate, his campaign committee, or political party committee. If the person being polled requests additional identifying information concerning the named committee, group, or individual, the person conducting the poll shall state the registration number provided by the State Board for any committee or person who has filed a statement of organization under §24.2-9098 or, if the committee or person has not been registered, the full name and residence address for an individual who has authorized or paid for the poll.

C. It shall be unlawful for any persons supervising the telephone poll to fail to provide to the persons making the telephone calls the identifying information required by this section.

D. It shall be unlawful for any persons to provide a false or fictitious name or address when providing the identifying information required under subsection B.

E. Any person violating any provision of this section shall be subject to a civil penalty not to exceed fifty dollars; and in the case of a willful violation, he shall be guilty of a Class I misdemeanor. The procedure to enforce the civil penalty in this section shall be as stated in §24.2-929. The violation of this section shall not void any election.

MAIN POINTS

- In addition to technical, scientific considerations, social research projects are likely to be shaped by administrative, ethical, and political considerations.
- What's ethically "right" and "wrong" in research is ultimately a matter of what people *agree* is right and wrong.
- Scientists agree that participation in research should normally be voluntary. This norm, however, can conflict with the scientific need for generalizability.
- Probably all scientists agree that research should not harm those who participate in it, unless they willingly and knowingly accept the risks of harm.
- Anonymity refers to the situation in which even the researcher cannot identify specific information with the individuals it describes.
- Confidentiality refers to the situation in which the researcher—although knowing which data describe which subjects—agrees to keep that information confidential.
- Although science is neutral on political matters, scientists are not.
- Even though the norms of science cannot force individual scientists to give up their personal values, the intersubjective character of science provides a guard against "scientific" findings being the product of bias only.

REVIEW QUESTIONS AND EXERCISES

1. Review the discussion of the Milgram experiment on obedience. See if you can design a study that would have accomplished the same purpose but would have avoided the ethical criticisms leveled at Milgram.
2. Suppose a researcher who is personally in favor of small families—as a response to the problem of overpopulation—wants to conduct a survey to determine why some people want many children and others don't. Discuss the personal-involvement problems he or she would face and how they might be avoided.
3. On the Web, locate an official document detailing the procedures for obtaining informed consent in research projects. Give the Web address of the document and quote or paraphrase one of the procedures discussed. *Hint:* Use one of the Web search engines to search for "informed consent," using quotation marks around the phrase.

ADDITIONAL READINGS

Boruch, Robert F., and Joe S. Cecil. *Assuring the Confidentiality of Social Research Data.* Philadelphia: University of Pennsylvania Press, 1979. The authors discuss the conflict between a researcher's need to identify respondents and their right to privacy—and shows techniques for resolving the conflict.

Bower, Robert T., and Priscilla de Gasparis. *Ethics in Social Research: Protecting the Interests of Human Subjects.* New York: Praeger, 1978. Provides an excellent overview of the ethical issues involved in social research and discusses the ways those issues are dealt with. It contains an extensive annotated bibliography.

Hamnett, Michael P., Douglas J. Porter, Amarjit Singh, and Krishna Kumar. *Ethics, Politics, and International Social Science Research.* Honolulu: University of Hawaii Press, 1984. Discussions of research ethics typically focus on the interests of the individual participants in research projects, but this book raises the level of the discussion to include the rights of whole societies.

Homan, Roger. *The Ethics of Social Research.* London: Longman, 1991. A thoughtful analysis of the ethical issues of social science research, by a practicing British social scientist.

Lee, Raymond. *Doing Research on Sensitive Topics.* Newbury Park, CA: Sage, 1993. This book examines the conflicts between scientific research needs and the rights of the people involved—with guidelines for dealing with such conflicts.

CHAPTER 19
The Uses of Social Research

What You'll Learn in This Chapter

You'll look over the territory we've covered together, reviewing the interrelations among the components of social research. You'll see how the things you've learned show up in everyday life, and you'll be empowered as a consumer.

INTRODUCTION

THEORY—DATA COLLECTION—ANALYSIS

EVERYDAY USES OF SOCIAL RESEARCH SKILLS

A CONSUMER'S GUIDE TO SOCIAL RESEARCH
Research Design
Measurement

Sampling
Experiments
Survey Research
Field Research
Analyzing Existing Statistics
Evaluation Research
Data Analysis
Data Reporting

CONCLUSION

■ INTRODUCTION

As you've probably gathered, we're getting very close to the conclusion of your venture into social research. I imagine some parts have been pretty simple for you, and others have been a bit more challenging—and some may have seemed more challenging than necessary. Whatever the balance of these materials for you, I'm pleased to report there's no new technical material in this chapter, meaning you've already covered everything you need to know in your introduction to social research. The purpose of this chapter is to bring things together and help you retain and use what you've already learned.

We'll begin by reviewing the introductory discussion of theory, data collection, and analysis. I think it will all make more sense to you now. Next, we'll look at some of the ways you may find yourself using social research techniques in your daily life. You may be surprised by the new abilities you've developed.

The chapter concludes with a set of guidelines for you as a *consumer* of social research. Even if you never conduct a complex research project, you will find yourself continually confronted with the research of others, and it's important to know how to separate the wheat from the chaff. This section of the chapter will also serve as a review of the book, and I think you'll be impressed at how much you know.

■ THEORY—DATA COLLECTION—ANALYSIS

Social research is an attempt to make sense of our social life. It's not the only way of making sense of things, of course. All of us, every day, try to see patterns in what goes on around us. We want to understand, and we want some ability to predict what will happen in the future. At the least we'd like some idea about the likely consequences of the various options available to us. We want to do what will produce the results we want.

In everyday life, people attempt to understand and predict on the basis of many strategies. In part, we simply get into habits, repeating behaviors that worked well in the past, hoping they'll keep working. As a society, we establish traditions for that same purpose. We may not understand *why* planting a fish at the base of a corn stalk makes it grow tall, but we do it because it works.

Many of the dietary traditions in various cultures of the world probably arose out of the observation that people died after eating tainted foods. Along the same lines, the Hindu sanction against eating beef probably arose as a way of ensuring that hungry farmers didn't kill their oxen—thereby unable to plow the fields in the future.

If you study the traditions of various societies, however, you'll tend to find explanations that attempt to make sense out of the prescribed and proscribed ways of doing things. Many of those explanations are religious, reporting supernatural intentions. Others may simply sound like silly superstitions to you. Whatever the tradition and the explanation for it, you'll find people quick to report anecdotal evidence to substantiate it. You may be told, for example, of people who died or suffered terribly shortly after breaking some taboo or otherwise parting with tradition.

Once traditional patterns have been established in practice and have been rationalized by religion or another system of belief, they are difficult to shake. Even when the conditions that originally produced the tradition change, the patterns may continue. For example, it made sense to have big families under certain agricultural conditions in the past, providing additional hands for planting and harvesting. Once established and justified, however, the pattern has been difficult to shake, even under conditions of overpopulation, hunger, and the depletion of resources.

Although people tend to contrast cultural traditions and science, it is useful to note some similarities. In particular, people want their individual and social behaviors to (1) make sense and (2) correspond with reality. If you lived on the slopes of an active volcano, it might make no sense to you to throw a bottle of gin into the crater, but to the traditional Hawaiians, placating *Madam Pele* is the only sensible action. And they will offer voluminous examples of danger being averted in just that fashion—as well as darker tales of what happened to those who annoyed the goddess of volcanoes.

The belief systems and anecdotal evidence of cultural traditions correspond roughly to the roles of theory and data analysis in social research. Scientists want things to make sense, and that's the role of theory. And in the realm of concrete, observed events, scientists demand that their theories be borne out in fact. Thus if a theory suggests women are more religious than men, a statistical analysis showing 40 percent of the men and 70 percent of the women attending church regularly would support the theory. Statistics indicating the same attendance rates by gender would seriously challenge it.

In our understandings of things in everyday life, we may "go wrong" in three related ways. First, we sometimes become so committed to our explanations that we may ignore the evidence of our observations. This is especially true of religious explanations, but deeply held political ideologies or loyalty to family can produce the same result. Second, we're often pretty casual about the analysis of patterns in everyday life. We tend to rely on anecdotes rather than rigorously analyze data. Thus, we recall a few vivid examples of times when the facts supported our explanations rather than calculate the percentages of times when that happened. Finally, in everyday life, there is no explicit link between our explanations and observations. Thus, we may cite "evidence" that is not logically related to the belief system we want to substantiate. Moving in the opposite direction, we are sometimes sloppy in arriving at explanations for a mass of unrelated experiences.

In social research, by contrast, theories are always fair game for testing and subject to disconfirmation. No theory is sacred, even though individual scientists sometimes lose sight of that, at least temporarily. And in place of anecdotes, we demand that theories be supported by unambiguous empirical evidence. Thus scientists of differing backgrounds and beliefs can all agree that 40 percent is 40 percent—and that it is smaller than 70 percent.

Study design, sampling, measurement, and data-collection techniques make it possible to develop evidence appropriate to our theoretical explanations, either confirming or contradicting our initial expectations. Those same research methods allow us to find patterns within a mass of observations, resulting perhaps in the establishment of abstract theories. You may recall our earlier discussions of deductive and inductive models of inquiry.

One of my aims in this book has been to sharpen your observation and reasoning in everyday life. Quite aside from the formal execution of research projects, you may find yourself thinking a bit more rigorously in general. You may notice more instances of people being illogical or observing inaccurately. And I'll bet you catch yourself more often going astray. This simply indicates that you've become more sensitive to the logic of inquiry and understanding—you've become a more critical thinker.

At the same time, you're probably going to find a surprising number of situations in which the specific skills of social research will help you. In the following section of this chapter, I want to suggest a few situations in which this may happen.

■ EVERYDAY USES OF SOCIAL RESEARCH SKILLS

In this section, I'm going to assume that you will not enter an occupation that involves social research per se, although I know you may be planning that. Even so, I intend to show how you may end up doing social research anyway. This is all the more likely to the extent that people around you learn you have some skills in this area.

There's a good chance, for example, that one day you'll participate in the design and execution of a survey. In a democracy, the practice of making decisions by voting is so deeply ingrained in us that we fall back on it automatically in situations of disagreement. Let the garden club members disagree on where to have their annual picnic, and someone will finally say, "Let's vote!"—and people are reluctant to disagree with that suggestion. Very often, such "voting" takes the form of a survey of members. Your abilities to design appropriate questions, to distribute and collect questionnaires effectively, and to process the results will assure a fair vote.

Perhaps you'll find yourself involved in a community issue: locating a toxic waste dump in the middle of a residential area, for example. You could use your knowledge of survey research to poll local residents to determine how they felt about the proposal. The mass media could publicize the results of the poll, and you might want to mention them in your conversations with public officials.

The close linkage between survey research and democracy makes it a common phenomenon in modern society, but that's only one of the ways you're likely to put your social research training into practice. Here's a very different example.

The work you've done on measurement, especially questionnaire design, may come in handy any time you have to deal with *forms*. Let's say you become a personnel director. You'll want job applicants to give you various information relevant to their possible hiring and placement. I know that in the past you've had to fill out forms that you found confusing and even stupid. Many forms are. However, it's not always easy to design a form that elicits the appropriate information in a way that works. I suspect you'll find that your training in this course will have strengthened your ability to design clear and useful forms.

Your skills as a participant-observer may very well be the most basic contribution of this course to your everyday life. You are a participant-observer in life—you've always been one. Now you can bring a little class to that role. You should be able to observe a bit more accurately than when you began, and you should be especially sensitive to the subjectivities that sometimes color what you see and think. In the course of learning social research, you may have become a more trustworthy witness. Certainly, you can become a more powerful "conversationalist" through your ability to listen to others and be interested in what they have to say.

I hope your training in qualitative research will empower you to recognize some of the more hidden aspects of social life. What people say is not always what they mean, and what they do may belie their beliefs and feelings. Your ability to look and listen for subtle nuances in human interactions should allow you to understand people a little better than you did before taking this course.

You may find what you've learned about content analysis useful in a variety of ways. Literary critics could profit from what you've learned, for example. Now, instead of simply "knowing what you like," you can look a bit more deeply into why. The same skills might be useful to lawyers reviewing the history of legislation on some topic. Advertising specialists might use content analysis techniques in discovering why some advertisements work and others don't.

Your training in the analysis of existing statistics can prove useful in a great many ways. Suppose you're considering jobs or schools in different regions of the country. It might be worth taking a few minutes to specify the variables most relevant to you: climate, cost of living, demographic characteristics, cultural facilities, and so on. Once you've determined what you most want, you can then find the data appropriate to rating the different locations you're considering.

You may want to keep the logic of experimentation and evaluation research always at your elbow in both your personal and professional life. Either rigorously or implicitly, you'll probably always be pursuing a variety of goals. Maybe you want to work more effectively, take more time off, earn more money, lose weight, fight less with your loved ones, or any number of other aims in life. People often blunder around their goals, but you can now get explicit about (1) what you want, (2) what you're doing to get it, and (3) whether what you're doing is producing the result. Don't be afraid to keep records of how things are working for you, although you may not want to tell everyone you're doing it.

Despite the occasional jokes about "mad scientists" and "nutty professors," there are some real advantages in bringing a scientific outlook into most aspects of your life. To the extent that this means being logical, observing accurately, and being rigorous in relating what you observe to what you understand, being scientific about life can benefit both you and the people around you.

■ A CONSUMER'S GUIDE TO SOCIAL RESEARCH

You may feel that some aspects of this course and this book weren't really appropriate for you. Aside from some of the simpler studies I've just mentioned, you may find it hard to believe right now that you'll ever engage in the execution of social research. You're probably right. On a per capita basis, there just aren't all that many social researchers in the world.

The chances are not good ($p < .001$) that you'll ever be responsible for designing and running a multistage, area probability survey of the nation's workforce for the purpose of determining whether there's a statistically significant relationship between gender and income among matched subsets of wage earners. But notice that you know basically what that means and could say something about the various steps involved in such a study: questionnaire design, sampling, data collection, calculating mean incomes for those employed full-time, part-time, and so on. Even if you needed to refer to this and other books to refresh your memory on some details, that's what professionals do all the time.

As a rough estimate, you now know more about social research than 99.98 percent of the world's population. (If this concerns you, tell all your friends to take this course.) Even if you aren't fully prepared to undertake major research projects on your own, you've become what is sometimes called the "informed consumer." Even if you never conduct a major project of your own, you can evaluate the social research of others. This is not an insignificant ability, because you're going to be exposed to social research every day for the rest of your life. You will read reports of research in newspapers and magazines; you will hear about it on television and radio; politicians and manufacturers will tell you what "research shows." You must, therefore, be able to separate the wheat from the chaff even if you never grow wheat on your own.

In this section of the book, I want to offer some consumer tips for you to use in reviewing reports of social research in the years to come. In part, these guidelines serve as a review of the territory we've covered in the book. It's fine for you to use this section as a review of the book, but realize that my primary purpose here is to strengthen your abilities to evaluate research rather than to design and execute it. As a consequence, I've skipped over several topics of the book, focusing only on those germane to consumer skills. I will organize the consumer's guide pretty much along the same lines as the rest of the book, however.

So, whenever you're confronted with what "research shows," here are some of the questions you might want to ask. Not all of these questions apply to all studies, but I think I've given you enough to choose from.

Research Design

- What was the purpose of the study: exploration, description, explanation, or a combination?
- Who conducted the research? Who paid for it? What motivated the study? If the study's conclusions happen to correspond to the interests of the sponsor or researcher, this doesn't disqualify the conclusions, but you'll want to be especially wary.
- What was the unit of analysis? Was it appropriate to the purpose of the study? Are the conclusions drawn from the research appropriate to the unit of analysis? For example, have the researchers studied cities and ended up with assertions about individuals?
- Is this a cross-sectional or longitudinal study? Be especially wary of longitudinal assertions being made on the basis of cross-sectional observations.
- If longitudinal data have been collected, be sure that comparable measurements have been made at each point in time. If survey data are involved, for example, have the same

questions been asked each time? If the report compares, say, crime or poverty rates, be sure they've been defined the same way each time. (Definitions of *poverty* frequently change, for example.)
- If a panel study has been conducted, check on the number of people who dropped out ("panel attrition") over the course of the study.

Measurement

- What are the names of the concepts under study?
- Has the researcher delineated different dimensions of the variable? Have those distinctions been kept straight in the analysis and reporting?
- What indicators—either qualitative or quantitative—have been chosen as measures of those dimensions and concepts? For each indicator, ask if it's a valid measure of what it's intended to measure. What else could the indicator be a measure of? Is it a reliable measure? Has the reliability been tested?
- What is the level of measurement of each variable: nominal, ordinal, interval, or ratio? And is it the appropriate level?
- Have composite measurements been used: indexes, scales, or typologies? If so, is it appropriate to the purpose of the study? Has it been constructed correctly?

Sampling

- Was it appropriate to study a sample, or should all elements have been studied? Remember, it's not always feasible to select a random sample.
- If sampling was called for, were probability sampling methods appropriate, or would a purposive, snowball, or quota sample have been appropriate? Has the appropriate sample design been used?
- What population does the researcher want to draw conclusions about?
- What is the researcher's purpose? If it is statistical description, then rigorous probability sampling methods are called for.
- If a probability sample has been selected, what sampling frame has been used? Does it appropriately represent the population that interests the researcher? What elements of the population have been omitted from the sampling frame, and what extraneous elements have been included?
- What specific sampling techniques have been employed: simple random sampling, systematic sampling, or cluster sampling? Has the researcher stratified the sampling frame prior to sampling? Have the stratification variables been chosen wisely? That is, are they relevant to the variables under study?
- How large a sample was selected? What was the completion rate; that is, what percent of the sample responded? Are there any likely differences between those who responded and those who didn't?
- Even assuming that the respondents are representative of those selected in the sample, what sampling error do you expect from a sample of this size?
- Has the researcher tested for representativeness: comparing the gender distribution of the population and of respondents, for example, or their ages, ethnicity, education, or income?
- Ultimately, do the individuals (or other units of analysis) studied represent the larger population from which they were chosen? That is, do conclusions drawn about the sample tell us anything about meaningful populations or about life in general?
- If probability sampling and statistical representation were not appropriate to the study, have subjects and observations been selected in such a way as to provide a broad overview of the phenomenon being examined? Has the researcher paid special attention to deviant or disconfirming cases?

Experiments

- What is the primary dependent variable in the experiment? What effect is the experimenter trying to achieve, for example?
- What is the experimental stimulus or stimuli?

- What other variables are relevant to the experiment? Have they been measured?
- For each variable, check carefully how it has been defined and measured. Consider potential problems of validity and reliability.
- Has a proper control group been used? Have subjects been assigned to the experimental and control groups through random selection or by matching? Has it been done properly? Has the researcher provided any evidence of the initial comparability of experimental and control group subjects? Have there been pre- and posttest measurements of the dependent variable? What is the chance of a placebo (or "Hawthorne") effect in the experiment? Has any attention been given to the problem? Does the study employ a double-blind design, for example?
- Are there any problems of internal validity: history, maturation, testing, instrumentation, statistical regression, selection biases, experimental mortality, ambiguous causal direction, diffusion or imitation, compensatory effects, rivalry, or demoralization?
- Regarding external validity, how has the experimenter insured that the laboratory findings will apply to life in the real world?

Survey Research

- Check all the relevant questions regarding sampling.
- What questions have been asked of respondents? What was the precise wording of the questions? Be wary of researchers who merely paraphrase the questions.
- If closed-ended questions have been asked, were the answer categories provided appropriate, exhaustive, and mutually exclusive?
- If open-ended questions were asked, how have the answers been categorized? Has the researcher guarded against his or her own bias creeping in during the coding of open-ended responses?
- Are all the questions clear and unambiguous? Could they have been misinterpreted by respondents? If so, could the answers given mean something other than what the researcher has assumed?
- Are respondents capable of answering the questions asked? If not, they may answer anyway, but their answers may not mean anything.
- Are any of the questions double-barreled? Look for conjunctions, such as *and* and *or*. Are respondents being asked to agree or disagree with two ideas, when they might like to agree with one and disagree with the other?
- Do the questions contain negative terms? If so, respondents may have misunderstood them and answered inappropriately. Is there a danger of social desirability in any of the questions? Is any answer so right or so wrong that respondents may have answered on the basis of what people would think of them?
- As a general rule, test all questionnaire items by asking yourself how you would answer. Any difficulty you might have in answering might also apply to others. Then, try to assume different points of view (for example, liberal vs. conservative, religious vs. unreligious) and ask how the questions might sound to someone with each point of view.
- If the researcher has conducted a secondary analysis of previously collected data, then determine the quality of the researchers who originally collected the data. Also, are the data available for analysis appropriate to the current purposes? Do the questions originally asked reflect adequately on the variables now being analyzed?
- The National Council on Public Polls has created a list of 20 questions to ask about polls, which have been reprinted in Appendix J of this book.

Field Research

- What are the main variables in this study? How have they been defined and measured? Do you see any problems of validity?
- How about reliability? Would another researcher, observing the same events, classify things the same?

- Is there any chance that the classification of observations has been influenced by the way those classifications will affect the research findings and/or the researcher's hypotheses?
- If descriptive conclusions have been drawn—for example, "the group's standards were quite conservative"—what are the implicit standards being used?
- How much can the study's findings be generalized to a broader sector of society? What claims has the researcher made in this regard? What is the basis for such claims?
- If people have been interviewed, how were they selected? Do they represent all appropriate types?
- How much did the researcher participate in the events under study? How might that participation have affected the events themselves?
- Did the researcher reveal his or her identity as a researcher? If so, what influence could that revelation have had on the behavior of those being observed?
- Does the research indicate any personal feelings—positive or negative—about those being observed? If so, what effect might this have on what was observed and the conclusions drawn from it?
- Has the researcher's own cultural identity or background clouded his or her interpretation of what has been observed?

Analyzing Existing Statistics

- Who originally collected the data being reanalyzed? Were there any flaws in the data-collection methods? What was the original purpose of data collection? Would that affect the data collected?
- What was the unit of analysis of the data? Is it appropriate to the current research question and the conclusions being drawn? Is there a danger of the ecological fallacy?
- When were the data collected? Are they still appropriate to present concerns?
- What are the variables being analyzed in the present research? Were the definitions used by the original researchers appropriate to present interests?

Evaluation Research

- What is the social intervention being analyzed? How has it been measured? Are there any problems of validity or reliability?
- Have the appropriate people (or other units of analysis) been observed?
- How has "success" been defined? Where would the success be manifested—in individuals, in organizations, in crime rates, or where? Has it been measured appropriately?
- Has the researcher judged the intervention a success or a failure? Is the judgment well founded?
- Who paid for the research, and who actually conducted it? Can you be confident of the researcher's objectivity? Did the sponsor interfere in any way?

Data Analysis

- Did the purpose and design of the study call for a qualitative or a quantitative analysis?
- Are any statistical techniques used in the analysis of data appropriate to the levels of measurement of the variables involved?
- Has the researcher undertaken all relevant analyses? Have all appropriate variables been examined? Could the correlation observed between two variables have been caused by a third, antecedent variable, making the observed relationship spurious?
- If tests of statistical significance were used, have they been interpreted correctly? Has statistical significance been confused with substantive significance?
- Does a particular research finding really make a difference? Does it matter? Is an observed difference between subgroups, for example, a large or meaningful one? Are there any implications for action? Not all findings need to have policy implications, but it's one yardstick to use in reviewing research.
- Has the researcher gone beyond the actual findings in drawing conclusions and implications?
- Are there logical flaws in the analysis and interpretation of data?

- Have the empirical observations of the study revealed new patterns of relationships, providing the bases for grounded theories of social life? Has the researcher looked for disconfirming cases that would challenge the new theories?

Data Reporting

- Has the researcher placed this particular project in the context of previous research on the topic? Does this research add to, modify, replicate, or contradict previous studies?
- In general, has the researcher reported the details of the study design and execution fully? Are there parts of the report that seem particularly vague or incomplete in the reporting of details?
- Has the researcher reported any flaws or shortcomings in the study design or execution? Are there any suggestions for improved research on the topic in the future?

■ CONCLUSION

Whether you actively pursue a career in social research or simply focus your skills on being an empowered consumer, I hope this venture into the rigorous study of society has conveyed some of its excitement. Social research offers a thrill of discovery second to none in science. After a long night of analyzing masses of data, finding a pattern, and finally seeing the logic of how people relate to one another, there is something special about walking outside into the waking dawn of society in action—stepping into the middle of what you now understand a little more clearly.

A similar satisfaction can be yours as a consumer of social research. As I've said, we all want to understand the world around us, and your new skills in social research can make you an active and critical consumer in what is sometimes called the "information society." You should be somewhat spared the frustration of contradictions in what the "experts" say. You'll be able to make some sense of professional disagreements and even judge which results are most appropriate to which situations and purposes in your life.

Finally, I trust you'll find that what you've learned here empowers you in making a difference in your society and world. As social life has become more complex, it has become easier and easier for individuals to feel ineffective in creating structures of humane relations. Increasingly, we have put up with imperfections, stood on the sidelines, and mourned the death of possibility. I invite you to set aside any reluctance to engage in the issues that matter to you. Take part. Now that you've sharpened your abilities to think critically and observe accurately, make them a contribution to the world you live in and those you share it with.

Appendixes

- **A** USING THE LIBRARY
- **B** SOCIAL RESEARCH IN CYBERSPACE
- **C** THE RESEARCH REPORT
- **D** GSS HOUSEHOLD ENUMERATION QUESTIONNAIRE
- **E** RANDOM NUMBERS
- **F** DISTRIBUTION OF CHI SQUARE
- **G** NORMAL CURVE AREAS
- **H** ESTIMATED SAMPLING ERROR
- **I** A LEARNER'S GUIDE TO SPSS
- **J** TWENTY QUESTIONS A JOURNALIST SHOULD ASK ABOUT POLL RESULTS

APPENDIX A: Using the Library

■ INTRODUCTION

Throughout this book I've been assuming that you'll be reading reports of social science research. In this appendix, I want to talk a little about how you'll find reports to read.

As I've indicated repeatedly, you live in a world filled with social science research reports. Your daily newspaper, magazines, professional journals, alumni bulletins, club newsletters—virtually everything you pick up to read may carry reports dealing with a particular topic. Usually, you'll pursue that interest through your library or the World Wide Web.

Today, there are two major approaches to finding library materials: the traditional paper route and electronically. Let's begin with the traditional method first and examine the electronic option afterward.

■ GETTING HELP

When you want to find something in the library, your best friend is the reference librarian, who is specially trained to find things in the library. Sometimes it's hard to ask people for help, but you'll do yourself a real service to make an exception in this case.

Some libraries have specialized reference librarians—for the social sciences, humanities, government documents, and so forth. Find the one you need and tell him or her what you're interested in. The reference librarian will probably put you in touch with some of the many available reference sources.

■ REFERENCE SOURCES

You've probably heard the expression *information explosion*. Your library is one of the main battlefields. Fortunately, a large number of reference volumes offer a guide to the information that's available.

Books in Print This volume lists all the books currently in print in the United States—listed separately by author and by title. Out-of-print books can often be found in older editions of *Books in Print*.

Readers' Guide to Periodical Literature This annual volume with monthly updates lists articles published in many journals and magazines. Because the entries are organized by subject matter, this is an excellent source for organizing your reading on a particular topic. Figure A-1 presents a sample page from the *Readers' Guide*.

In addition to these general reference volumes, you'll find a great variety of specialized references. A few are listed as examples.

- Sociological Abstracts
- Psychological Abstracts
- Social Science Index
- Social Science Citation Index
- Popular Guide to Government Publications
- New York Times Index
- Facts on File
- Editorial Research Reports
- Business Periodicals Index
- Monthly Catalog of Government Publications
- Public Affairs Information Service Bulletin
- Education Index
- Applied Science and Technology Index

FIGURE A-1
A Page from the Readers' Guide to Periodical Literature

128   READERS' GUIDE TO PERIODICAL LITERATURE

MUSIC—*cont.*
                 Study and teaching
   See also
   Guitar—Study and teaching
                 Themes, motives, etc.
   See also
   Automobiles in music
                 Theory
   See also
   Atonality
                 Japan
   The Japanese and Western music. L. Futoransky. il *The Courier (Unesco)* 40:38+ D '87
MUSIC, AMERICAN
   See also
   Jazz music
MUSIC, ELECTRONIC
   See also
   Computers—Musical use
   Musical instruments, Electronic
MUSIC AND STATE
   Viewpoint [government subsidies of opera] J. P. Poole. Opera News 52:4 F 13 '88
                 Soviet Union
   Gorbachev sets the beat for Soviet rock. il *U.S. News & World Report* 104:8-9 F 8 '88
MUSIC AND THE BLIND
   Call him Doc [D. Watson] F. L. Schultz. il pors *Country Journal* 15:44-53 F '88
MUSIC AND THE HANDICAPPED
   See also
   Guitarists, Handicapped
MUSIC CORPORATION OF AMERICA *See* MCA Inc.
MUSIC CRITICS AND CRITICISM
   See also
   Opera reviews
MUSIC FESTIVALS
                 Austria
   Bregenz. H. Koegler. il *Opera News* 52:38 F 13 '88
                 Germany (West)
   Bayreuth. J. H. Sutcliffe. il *Opera News* 52:36 Ja 30 '88
                 Great Britain
   Buxton. E. Forbes. *Opera News* 52:40-1 F 13 '88
                 Italy
   Torre del Lago (Puccini Festival) M. Hamlet-Mets. *Opera News* 52:38-40 F 13 '88
                 Pennsylvania
   Philadelphia [American Music Theater Festival] R. Baxter. *Opera News* 52:34 Ja 30 '88
MUSICAL COMEDIES, REVUES, ETC. *See* Musicals, revues, etc.
MUSICAL INSTRUMENTS, ELECTRONIC
   It's alive with the sound of—well, just about everything (Synclavier synthesizer) L. Helm. il *Business Week* p75 F 8 '88
MUSICAL INSTRUMENTS INDUSTRY
   See also
   New England Digital Corporation
MUSICALS, REVUES, ETC.
                 Choreography
   See Choreography
                 Reviews
                 Single works
   Anything goes
     Dance Magazine il 62:52-7 Ja '88. J. Gruen
   Cabaret
     Dance Magazine 62:73-4 Ja '88. H. M. Simpson
   The chosen
     The Nation 246:176 F 6 '88. T. M Disch
   Into the woods
     Dance Magazine 62:64 Ja '88. K. Grubb
   Oil City Symphony
     The Nation 246:175-6 F 6 '88. T. M. Disch
   The phantom of the opera
     Life il 11:88-92 F '88. M. Stasio
     Maclean's il 101:51 F 8 '88. L. Black
     New York il 21:89-90 F 8 '88. J. Simon
     The New Yorker 63:97-8 F 8 '88. M. Kramer
     Newsweek il por 111:68-70+ F 8 '88. J. Kroll
     Rolling Stone il p26 F 25 '88. D. Handelman
     Time il 131:83-4 F 8 '88. W. A. Henry
                 Stage setting and scenery
   High-tech magic: follow that gondola [Phantom of the opera] J. Kroll. il *Newsweek* 111:70 F 8 '88
                 Writing
   Changing the face of Broadway [A. Lloyd Webber] M. Stasio. il pors *Life* 11:88-92 F '88
MUSICIANS
   See also

   Drugs and musicians
   Rock musicians
MUSKE, CAROL, 1945-
   Skid [poem] *The New Yorker* 63:38 F 8 '88
MUSLIMS
   See also
   Islam
                 Afghanistan
   Beyond the Afghan stalemate. L. Komisar. il *The New Leader* 71:5-6 Ja 11-25 '88
                 Middle East
   The Islamic resurgence: a new phase? R. Wright. bibl f *Current History* 87:53-6+ F '88
MUTATION
   See also
   Transposons
MUTUAL FUNDS *See* Investment trusts
MUTUALISM (BIOLOGY) *See* Symbiosis
MUZIEKTHEATER (AMSTERDAM, NETHERLANDS)
   See Opera houses
MYASTHENIA GRAVIS
   Suzanne Rogers: "I looked at my face and thought, 'Who'd hire a freak?" A. W. Petrucelli. pors *Redbook* 170:104+F '88
MYCOBACTERIAL DISEASES
   See also
   Tuberculosis
MYCOTOXINS *See* Toxins and antitoxins

N

N. W. AYER & SON, INC.
   Ayer to the throne [Burger King ad campaign] B. Kanner. il *New York* 21:24+ F 29 '88
NADIS, STEVEN J.
   Robot observatories. il *Omni (New York, N.Y.)* 10:24+ Ja '88
NAEP *See* National Assessment of Educational Progress
NAKAGAMI, KENJI, 1946-
                 about
   Two contemporary writers. D. Palmé. *The Courier (Unesco)* 40:44 D '87
NAKED SHORT SELLING *See* Securities—Short selling
NANDINA
   Nandina does the unexpected. il *Southern Living* 23:50 Ja '88
NAPLES (ITALY)
                 Music
   See also
   Opera—Italy
NARCOTIC ADDICTS *See* Drug abuse
NARCOTICS LAWS AND REGULATIONS
   See also
   Boats in narcotics regulation
   Robots in narcotics regulation
                 Austria
   A five-year penalty call [Czech hockey legend J. Bubla serving prison sentence for smuggling heroin] J. Holland. il por *Maclean's* 101:6 F 8 '88
                 Colombia
   Battling the drug lords [Attorney General C. Hoyos murdered] E. Tolmie. il *Maclean's* 101:26 F 8 '88
   Day of the assassins [Attorney General C. Hoyos murdered] M. S. Serrill. il por *Time* 131:42 F 8 '88
   How cocaine rules the law in Colombia [assassination of Attorney General C. Hoyos] C. A. Robbins. il *U.S. News & World Report* 104:28-9 F 8 '88
   Murderers of Medellín [assassination of Colombia's Attorney General C. Hoyos] F. Willey. il *Newsweek* 111:33 F 8 '88
NARCOTICS TRADE
   See also
   Boats in narcotics regulation
   Narcotics laws and regulations
   Robots in narcotics regulation
   Teen drug dealers: uncovering the real story. W. White and K. Dickerson. il '*Teen* 32:36-9+ F '88
                 Panama
   The dictator in the dock [M. A. Noriega] N. Cooper. il por *Newsweek* 111:33 F 22 '88
   Drugs, money and death [cover story, special section] il pors map *Newsweek* 111:32-6+ F 15 '88
   More bad news for Noriega. N. Cooper. il por *Newsweek* 111:37 F 8 '88
   Noriega's money machine [aides testify before Senate subcommittee] M. S. Serrill. il *Time* 131:39-40 F 22 '88

Appendix A: Using the Library

FIGURE A-2
Sample Subject Catalog Card

```
                    1
              2
                ADOLESCENCE                    3
         301.43  Eagan, Andrea Boroff
    7       E      Why am I so miserable if these
                 are the best years of my life?  A
                 survival guide for the young woman;
                 with an introduction by Ellen
                 Frankfort.  Lippincott 1976
                   251p illus
              6
                                        4        5
```

Source: Lilian L. Shapiro, *Teaching Yourself in Libraries* (New York: H. W. Wilson, 1978), 3–4. Used by permission.

- A Guide to Geographic Periodicals
- General Science Index
- Biological and Agricultural Index
- Nursing and Applied Health Index
- Nursing Studies Index
- Index to Little Magazines
- Popular Periodical Index
- Biography Index
- Congressional Quarterly Weekly Report
- Library Literature
- Bibliographic Index

■ USING THE STACKS

For serious research, you should learn to use the stacks, where most of the library's books are stored. In this section, I'll give you some information about finding books in the stacks.

The Card Catalog

Your library's card catalog is the main reference system for finding out where books are stored. Each book is described on three separate 3-by-5 cards. The cards are then filed in three alphabetical sets. One set is arranged by author, another by title, and the third by subject matter.

If you want to find a particular book, you can look it up in either the author file or the title file. If you only have a general subject area of interest, you should thumb through the subject catalog. Figure A-2 presents a sample card in the card catalog.

1. Subject heading (always in capital letters)
2. Author's name (last name, first name)
3. Title of the book
4. Publisher
5. Date of publication
6. Number of pages in the book plus other information (such as whether the book contains illustrations)
7. Call number needed to find a nonfiction book on the library shelves; fiction generally found in alphabetical order by the author's name)

Library of Congress Classification

Here's a useful strategy to use when you're researching a topic. Once you've identified the call number for a particular book in your subject area, go to the stacks, find that book, and look over the other books on the shelves *near* it. Because the books are arranged by subject matter, this method will help you locate relevant books you didn't know about.

Alternatively, you may want to go directly to the stacks and look at books in your subject area. In most libraries, books are arranged and numbered according to a subject matter classification developed by the Library of Congress. (Some follow the Dewey decimal system.) The following is a selected list of Library of Congress categories.

Library of Congress Classifications (partial)

A	GENERAL WORKS	
B	PHILOSOPHY, PSYCHOLOGY, RELIGION	
	B-BD	Philosophy
	BF	Psychology
	BL-BX	Religion
C	HISTORY-AUXILIARY SCIENCES	
D	HISTORY (except America)	
	DA-DR	Europe
	DS	Asia
	DT	Africa
E-F	HISTORY (America)	
	E	United States
	E51–99	Indians of North America
	E185	Negroes in the United States
	F101–1140	Canada
	F1201–3799	Latin America
G	GEOGRAPHY-ANTHROPOLOGY	
	G-GF	Geography
	GC	Oceanology and oceanography
	GN	Anthropology
	GV	Sports, amusements, games
H	SOCIAL SCIENCES	
	H62.B2	*The Practice of Social Research*
	HB-HJ	Economics and business
	HM-HX	Sociology
J	POLITICAL SCIENCE	
	JK	United States
	JN	Europe
	JQ	Asia, Africa
	JX	International relations
K	LAW	
L	EDUCATION	
M	MUSIC	
N	FINE ARTS	
	NA	Architecture
	NB	Sculpture
	NC	Graphic arts
	ND	Painting
	NE	Engraving
	NK	Ceramics, textiles
P	LANGUAGE AND LITERATURE	
	RE	English language
	PG	Slavic language
	PJ-PM	Oriental language
	PN	Drama, oratory, journalism
	PQ	Romance literature
	PR	English literature
	PS	American literature
	PT	Germanic literature
Q	SCIENCE	
	QA	Mathematics
	QB	Astronomy
	QC	Physics
	QD	Chemistry
	QE	Geology
	QH-QR	Biology
R	MEDICINE	
	RK	Dentistry
	RT	Nursing
S	AGRICULTURE—PLANT AND ANIMAL INDUSTRY	
T	TECHNOLOGY	
	TA-TL	Engineering
	TR	Photography
U	MILITARY SCIENCE	
V	NAVAL SCIENCE	
Z	BIBLIOGRAPHY AND LIBRARY SCIENCE	

■ COMPUTERIZED LIBRARY FILES

In the years to come, you'll be finding library materials increasingly by computer. Your school may have already instituted such a system. While there are different computerized library systems, here's a typical example of how they work.

FIGURE A-3
A Research Summary from *Sociological Abstracts*

AU Kinloch-Graham-C.
TI The Changing Definition and Content of Sociology in Introductory Textbooks, 1894–1981.
SO International Review of Modern Sociology. 1984, 14, 1, spring, 89–103.
DE Sociology-Education; (D810300). Textbooks; (D863400).
AB An analysis of 105 introductory sociology textbooks published between 1894 & 1981 reveals historical changes in definitions of the discipline & major topics in relation to professional factors & changing societal contexts. Predominant views of sociology in each decade are discussed, with the prevailing view being that of a "scientific study of social structure in order to decrease conflict & deviance, thereby increasing social control." Consistencies in this orientation over time, coupled with the textbooks' generally low sensitivity to social issues, are explored in terms of their authors' relative homogeneity in age & educational backgrounds. 1 Table, 23 References. Modified HA.

Sitting at a computer terminal—in the library, at a computer lab, or at home—you can type the title of a book and in seconds see a video display of a catalog card. If you want to explore the book further, you can type an instruction at the terminal and see an abstract of the book. Someday soon, you'll be able to retrieve the whole book.

Alternatively, you might type a subject name and see a listing of all the books and articles written on that topic. You could skim through the list and indicate which ones you want to see.

Many college libraries now have access to the Educational Resources Information Center (ERIC). This computer-based system allows you to search through hundreds of major educational journals to find articles published in the subject area of your interest (within the field of education). Once you identify the articles you're interested in, the computer will print out their abstracts.

Of particular value to social science researchers, the publications *Sociological Abstracts* and *Psychological Abstracts* present summaries of books and articles—often prepared by the original authors—so that you can locate a great many relevant references easily and effectively. As you find relevant references, you can track down the original works and see the full details. The summaries are available in both written and computerized forms.

Figure A-3 contains the abstract of an article obtained in a computer search of *Sociological Abstracts*. I began by asking for a list of articles dealing with sociology textbooks. After reviewing the list, I asked to see the abstracts of each of the listed articles. Here's an example of what I received seconds later: an article by sociologist Graham C. Kinloch, published in the *International Review of Modern Sociology*.

In the event that some of the abbreviations used in Figure A-3 aren't immediately obvious, *AU* is author; *TI* is title; *SO* is the source or location of the original publication; *DE* indicates classification codes under which the abstract is referenced; and *AB* is the abstract. The computerized availability of resources such as *Sociological Abstracts* provides a powerful research tool for modern social scientists.

Developments in this arena are moving so fast that anything I write here will be out-of-date by the time this book is in your hands. Appendix B, which follows, looks at other aspects of social research in cyberspace.

■ ADDITIONAL READINGS

Bart, Pauline, and Linda Frankel. *The Student Sociologist's Handbook,* 3rd edition. Glenview, IL: Scott, Foresman, 1981. A survival kit for doing sociological research. Contains a step-by-step guide for writing research papers; chapters on periodicals, abstract and indexing services, bibliographies, bibliographical aids, and other secondary sources; and a complete guide to governmental and nongovernmental sources of data. Special section on sex roles and women's studies.

Becker, Leonard, and Clair Gustafson. *Encounter with Sociology: The Term Paper.* San Francisco: Boyd and Fraser, 1976. An excellent guide for writing term and research papers in the social sciences. Contains some good discussion of methodological issues to consider as well.

Gruber, James, Judith Pryor, and Patricia Berge. *Materials and Methods for Sociology Research.* New York: Neal-Schuman, 1980. This workbook offers a "hands-on," problem-oriented approach to the use of a wide variety of reference and research tools through individual chapters and assignments. Also available for political science, history, and other fields.

Li, Tze-chung. *Social Science Reference Sources: A Practical Guide.* Westport, CT: Greenwood Press, 1980. Lists and describes all types of reference materials, including data bases and archives as well as published sources. Organized into two parts: social sciences in general and by discipline.

Mark, Charles. *Sociology of America: A Guide to Information.* Detroit: Gale, 1976. An annotated bibliography covering all aspects of U.S. society: population, regional studies, ethnic groups, religion, work, stratification, the family, and so on. Includes sections on reference materials.

APPENDIX B: Social Research in Cyberspace

A new resource is rapidly becoming a powerful tool for social scientists. Soon it will be indispensable. Since the Internet, the World Wide Web, and other elements of the "information superhighway" are changing month by month, I'll simply cover some basics that may be useful for readers new to cyberspace. My aim is to orient you sufficiently for you to ask for help effectively.

I'll talk about three topics: email, gophers, and the World Wide Web.

■ EMAIL

The most common use of the Internet at present is as a substitute for telephone and postal services. Email is a hybrid of these two modes. Like a letter, you type out your communication on a computer. Then, rather than putting the letter in an envelope and mailing it, you send it over telephone lines. The recipient receives your message with his or her computer.

You'll need a computer account at your school or through some other provider to use email or any of the other systems described in this appendix. If you can't obtain an account through your school, you may want to consider joining a commercial online service such as America Online, Bitnet, CompuServe, Delphi, Genie, MCI Mail, Prodigy, or Sprintmail. While subscribers to the same commercial service can communicate easily with each other, they can also communicate with other portions of the Internet. I'll illustrate how this is done.

Once you're connected, you send messages comprising the following elements: a message (just like a note, memo, or letter), a title (a fairly short heading to identify the message, such as "Travel Plans") and the address where you want to send the message. Your own address will be attached automatically to all sent messages.

Let's look a little more carefully at the address. Each email address contains three basic elements:

<name> @ <server> . <type>

The name is usually fairly straightforward. Names are assigned when an account is opened. Mine is "babbie," for example. (What are the odds on that?) Thus an email address is typically a name at (@) a location.

The type of account is also fairly simple. A series of abbreviations indicate the type of installation providing the person access to the net. Some common types used in the United States are these:

edu	an educational institution
com	a commercial provider such as Compuserve or a company
org	a nonprofit organization, such as NPR
gov	a government office
net	a regional provider
bit	Bitnet

In place of these abbreviations, the address may be an international country abbreviation. Here are some examples:

ar	Argentina
au	Australia
ca	Canada
cn	China

de	Germany
eg	Egypt
fr	France
gh	Ghana
jp	Japan
mx	Mexico
sg	Singapore
uk	United Kingdom
za	South Africa

The middle portion of the address (the server, the local computer) varies greatly. For example, it's simply "aol" for America Online. An example of an America Online address might be

JDoe@aol.com

Compuserve uses a two-part account number in place of a name and "Compuserve" as the server. An example might be

76424.156@Compuserve.com

Some educational servers are pretty straightforward. For example, babbie@nexus.chapman.edu is mine at Chapman University. "Nexus" is the name given to the computer at Chapman that handles the email.

When people give their addresses, they tend to pronounce the "@" as "at" and call periods "dots." Hence, I would tell you my internet address is "babbie-at-nexus-dot-chapman-dot-e-d-u."

In addition to originating messages, most email systems make it easy for you to reply to a message you receive. When you do so, the computer automatically addresses your reply to the original sender and attaches your address as well. It may also automatically reprint the original message as a part of your reply, often identifying lines with ">" marks.

Including the original message (or part of it) can be used to remind the original sender of what you're responding to. Sometimes, you can break up the original message, interspersing your responses to the different parts of it. Here's a brief example:

Original message:
Pat:
Let's go to the movies Saturday night.
I'd prefer to go in your car if that's okay.
Let me know by Thursday.
Cheers, Jan

Automatic Reply Format:
>Pat:
>Let's go to the movies Saturday night.
>I'd prefer to go in your car if that's okay.
>Let me know by Thursday.
>Cheers, Jan

Edited Reply:
Jan:
>Let's go to the movies Saturday night.
　　Sure, that's great. What do you want to see?
>I'd prefer to go in your car if that's okay.
　　My car's in the shop. How about yours?
See ya, Pat

Since it's possible to reply to a reply, you may find yourself engaged in an unfolding conversation.

When replying to a message, it's generally a bad idea to resend the entire message you received. Just include those portions (if any) that are useful in framing your response. If you resend everything, you may make the recipient wade through a lengthy document looking for your comment. Excess verbiage also uses up net resources, not to mention your recipient's hard disk space.

In the evolving conventions of email, capital letters are used as the equivalent of shouting or emphasis and should be used sparingly. For example, you might say, "I MUST get a new computer before I go nuts," but putting your whole message in capitals is the equivalent of screaming.

Now and then, you may encounter capital letters that make no sense, such as BTW or IMHO. These are some of the abbreviations used in Internet culture. Here are only a few of those you may come across:

BTW	By the way
FYI	For your information
IMHO	In my humble opinion
IMNSHO	In my not so humble opinion
FAQ	Frequently asked questions
RTFM	Read the f——g manual

Because you can't communicate facial expressions or tones of voice in typed messages, some conventions have been developed to handle that lack. For example, you can include emotional references in your statements, such as "It really made my day <grin> when you reminded me the exam is Monday."

As a more creative solution, Internetters have been establishing an ever-growing set of *emoticons* to indicate emotions in print. Here are some examples. You need to tip your head 90 degrees to the left to get the point.

:-)	happy person
8-)	happy person with glasses
:-(	unhappy person
:-O	surprised person
:-p	person sticking out tongue

You can probably think up some new emoticons and introduce them to the world of the Internet.

```
   ---
  / ØØ \
    o
   \_/
```

■ MAILING LISTS

In addition to person-to-person email, you may find some of the thousands of electronic conversations useful. The most common of these go by the term *listserv*, though *listproc* and *majordomo* are major, alternate systems. There are several such mailing lists appropriate to social research methods.

For example, METHODS is a mailing list created for people teaching social research methods, though anyone can join. About 600 people from around the world belong as I write these words. Any of the subscribers can send a message to the list, and that message will appear in the mailboxes of all the other subscribers. If another subscriber wants to reply, that reply will also appear in the mailboxes of all subscribers. As a consequence, methods instructors have been able to discuss common problems and share solutions.

To subscribe to a mailing list, you send an email message to the computer that manages that list. In the case of METHODS, you do the following:

1. Send a message to: listserv@unm.edu
2. Do not put a title on the message
3. Send this message: subscribe methods Jane Doe but substitute your name for "Jane Doe."

You can send messages to methods@unm.edu after you've subscribed.

This is a standard format, although there are some variants and exceptions. To subscribe to any of the lists that follow, send a subscribing message by substituting "listserv" for the name of the list and use the name of the list in the body of the message, as illustrated in the case of METHODS. Then, you can send messages to the list using the given address.

There's no charge for subscribing to mailing lists. You don't have to participate in the conversations; you can just listen if you want. And you can unsubscribe any time. Here are some other mailing lists you might find interesting. (Please note that addresses have no breaks or spaces, even though here they might have line breaks.)

por@gibbs.oit.unc.edu
  public opinion research
social-theory@mailbase.ac.uk
  social theory
qualrs-l@uga.cc.uga.edu
  qualitative research
qual-software@mailbase.ac.uk
  software for qualitative social research
cjust-l@cunyvm.cuny.edu
  criminal justice discussion
demographic-list@coombs.anu.edu.au
  demography list out of Australia
  Note: send subscription to **majordomo@coombs.anu.edu.au** instead of to "listserv"
familysci@ukcc.uky.edu
  family science discussion
ipe@csf.colorado.edu
  international political economy discussion
ncs-l@umdd.umd.edu
  National Crime Survey discussion
qualnet@chimera.sph.umn.edu
  qualitative research discussion
socgrad@ucsd.edu
  sociology graduate student discussion
uncjin-l@albnyvm1
  United Nations Criminal Justice Information Network
sos-data@unc.edu
  social science data discussion

These are only a few of the mailing lists of interest to social researchers. Moreover, the number increases daily. In the spirit of a snowball sample, however, you'll find that subscribing to one list will bring you references to others, and if you subscribe to them as well, they'll bring further references. Without a doubt, there is more useful information available to you than you will be able to collect and read.

■ GOPHERS

Imagine that a friend of yours wrote a computer program or created a document that they wanted to share with you. Probably they would put a copy of the file on a disk and give it to you, so that you could load it into your computer. Now imagine that you have tens of thousands of friends around the globe doing just that. Obviously they can't put all those files on disks and send them to you. That's the function of *gophers*, which can execute a *file transfer protocol* (ftp).

Programs such as Turbogopher or MacIP are designed to connect you to computers around the world. All you need (other than an ftp program) is the address ("host name") of an available computer. Perhaps the computer at your school can be accessed via a gopher.

Since this is a little more involved than sending email or subscribing to a mailing list, you should get local assistance in connecting to a gopher site. Once you are connected with the distant computer, you'll find yourself looking at a directory of files available there. Your job is to select a file at the distant computer and copy it to your own. While it may require a little trial and error, you'll find the gopher program is designed to help you make the copies. (It will probably involve clicking a button labeled "Copy.")

The files available on computers around the world include text documents, computer games, check record programs, data analysis programs, and so forth. You won't be able to appreciate the volume and variety of materials available to you except by checking it out for yourself.

■ WORLD WIDE WEB

Perhaps the most exciting aspect of the net today is the World Wide Web. It's something like the network of ftp sites—sources of information scattered around the world—but you can access information much more easily, and the presentation format is much fancier.

To access the Web, you'll need a "browser" such as NetScape. The commercial online services such as American Online provide their own web browser. Then you can enter Web URL addresses (typically beginning, "http://") and go visit. As you'll discover, nearly every Web location will contain buttons you can click, which will take you to other, related locations.

For example, you can visit Chapman University by going to

http://www.chapman.edu/

Once there, you'll discover a variety of options, including a list of Chapman's academic programs. By clicking the "Wilkinson College" button, you'll be presented with, among other things, a list of the divisions composing the college. Click "Social Science" and then "Sociology." Now you'll be able to get a list of the department "Faculty." Click that and then "Babbie" to get a picture of this book's author. (Don't be fooled by the tie.)

If you had chosen "Political Science Department" instead of "Sociology," you would discover buttons that would take you to "The White House" or "The House of Representatives." This illustrates the interconnectedness of the various locations on the World Wide Web.

Here are just a few Web locations to get you started. Please be aware that these addresses may change. Happy Surfing!

Books
   gopher://ftp.std.com/11/obi/book
   http://www.bookwire.com/links/
      readingroom/readingroom.html
   http://www.elibrary.com/id/51/123/
      page_02.htm

China
    http://www.ihep.ac.cn:80/

Foundations

FEDIX—Federal Informational Exchange, Inc.
    http://web.fie.com/fedix/index.html

National Science Foundation
    http://cos.gdb.org/best/fedfund/nsf-intro.html

Searchable Index of Minority Scholarships & Fellowships
    http://web.fie.com/htbin/cashe.pl

Yahoo Listing of Foundations
    http://www.yahoo.com/Business_and_Economy/Organizations/Foundations/

Jokes
    http://www.misty.com/laughweb/lweb.html

Movie Reviews
    gopher://spinaltap.micro.umn.edu:70/11/fun/Movies

Newspapers

Asahi Shimbun (Japan)
    http://www.asahi.com/english/english.html

Chicago Sun Times
    http://www.suntimes.com/

Christian Science Monitor
    http://www.csmonitor.com/csmonitor/index.html

Hong Kong Standard
    http://www.hkstandard.com/

Houston Chronicle
    http://www.chron.com/fronts/chronicle/index.html

Iceland Daily News
    http://www.centrum.is/icerev/daily1.html

India World
    http://www.indiaworld.com/

Irish Times
    http://www.irish-times.com/

Jerusalem Post
    http://www.jpost.co.il/

Joong-ang Ilbo (Korea)
    http://168.126.70.2/home/ehome.html

New York Times
    http://www.nytimes.com/

New Zealand News
    http://nz.com/NZ/NZNewsArchive/

St. Petersburg Times (Russia)
    http://www.spb.su/times/183-184/index.html

San Jose Mercury News
    http://www.sjmercury.com/

Singapore Business Times
    http://www.asia1.com.sg/biztimes/

The Star (Maylaysia)
    http://www.jaring.my/~star/

Sydney Morning Herald
    http://www.smh.com.au:80/daily/

The Times of London
    http://www.the-times.co.uk/news/pages/home.html?000999

USA Today
    http://www.usatoday.com/

Yahoo (Reuters News Service)
    http://www.yahoo.com/headlines/current/news

News on the Net (connections to the world's new media)
    http://www.parsec.it/cgi-bin/w3-msql/newsnet/find.htm?p1=&p2=&p3=English&p4=&p5=news

Population Data

Florida State University
    gopher://gopher.fsu.edu:70/11/FSU/Popctr

Pennsylvania State University
    http://www.pop.psu.edu/

Princeton
    http://opr.princeton.edu/archive/archive.html

University of Michigan
    http://www.psc.lsa.umich.edu/index.html

World Fertility Survey Data
    ftp://lotka.princeton.edu

Public Opinion Data

Gallup Organization
    http://www.gallup.com/

General Social Survey at ICPSR
    http://www.icpsr.umich.edu/gss

Queen's College, Sociology Department
    http://www.soc.qc.edu/QC_Software/GSS.html

Roper Center, University of Connecticut
    http://www.lib.uconn.edu/RoperCenter/

Social Issues

Abortion
> http://www.yahoo.com/Society_and_Culture/Abortion_Issues/

Children
> http://www.yahoo.com/Society_and_Culture/Children/

Civil Rights
> http://www.yahoo.com/Society_and_Culture/Civil_Rights/

Crime
> http://www.yahoo.com/Society_and_Culture/Crime/

Disabilities
> http://www.yahoo.com/Society_and_Culture/Disabilities/

Feminism
> http://www.igc.apc.org./vsister/
> http://www.igc.apc.org/women/feminist.html
> http://english.hss.cmu.edu/Feminism.html
> http://www.undp.org/fwcw/dawl.htm

Gender Issues
> http://www.yahoo.com/Society_and_Culture/Gender_Issues/

Homelessness
> http://www.yahoo.com/Society_and_Culture/Homelessness/

Human Rights
> http://www.yahoo.com/Society_and_Culture/Human_Rights/

Hunger
> http://www.yahoo.com/Society_and_Culture/Hunger/
> http://www.thp.org/thp

Minorities
> http://www.yahoo.com/Society_and_Culture/Minorities/

Seniors
> http://www.yahoo.com/Society_and_Culture/Seniors/

Sexuality
> http://www.yahoo.com/Society_and_Culture/Sexuality/

Social Science Research Resources

Australian National University
> http://coombs.anu.edu.au/CoombsHome.html

Clearing House for Social Sciences & Social Issues
> http://www.lib.umich.edu/chouse/tree/social.html

Consortium for International EarthScience Information Network
> http://plue.sedac.ciesin.org/plue/ulysses

Corporate Information Database
> http://www.sec.gov/edgarhp.htm

Economic and Social Research Council Data Archive
> http://dawww.essex.ac.uk

Institute for Research in Social Science
> http://www.irss.unc.edu

Institute for Research in the Social Sciences
> http://www.cuesun.org/datasets/irss/irss.html

Inter-university Consortium for Political and Social Research
> http://www.icpsr.umich.edu

National Election Survey
> http://www.umich.edu/~nes

National Survey of Families & Households
> ftp://elaine.ssc.wusc.edu

Public Use Microdata Samples
> ftp://ftp.hist.umn.edu

Research for Social Science
> http://www.carleton.ca/~cmckie/research.html

Social Science Information Gateway
> http://sosig.esrc.bris.ac.uk/

Social Sciences Data Center
> http://www.lib.virginia.edu/socsci/

University of California, San Diego
> http://ssdc.ucsd.edu/

The Urban Information Center
> http://oseda.missouri.edu:80/uic/

WWW Virtual Library of Sociology
> http://www.w3.org/hypertext/DataSources/bySubject/Sociology/Overview.html

Yahoo—Social Science
> http://www.yahoo.com/Social_Science/

Yahoo—Society and Culture
> http://www.yahoo.com/Society_and_Culture/

State and Local Governments
    http://www.piperinfo.com/~piper/state/states.html

U.S. Government
Bureau of the Census
    http://www.census.gov/
Bureau of Labor Statistics
    http://stats.bls.gov/
Bureau of Transportation Statistics
    http://www.bts.gov/
Centers for Disease Control
    http://www.cdc.gov/
Central Intelligence Agency (CIA)
    http://www.ic.gov/
Department of Education
    http://www.ed.gov/
Environmental Protection Agency
    http://www.epa.gov/
Federal Bureau of Investigation
    http://www.fbi.gov/
House of Representatives
    http://www.house.gov/
National Center for Educational Statistics
    http://www.ed.gov/NCES
National Institutes of Health
    http://www.nih.gov/
White House
    http://www.whitehouse.gov/

World Factbook
    http://www.ic.gov/94fact/fb94toc/fb94toc.html

World History
    http://neal.ctstateu.edu/history/world_history/world_history.html

This list is not even the tip of the *tip* of the iceberg. If I could give you a complete listing of the Web sites relevant to social research, it would be out of date by the time my manuscript reached my publisher, let alone by the time it reached your hands. To give you a sense of how fast the Web is expanding, I'd like you to recall a time when you worked on a project that absolutely consumed you for days on end. You hardly thought about anything else while you were completing the project. Well, tonight, tens of thousands of individuals around the world are working with that level of passion on their Web sites and countless others are working at a less frantic pace. And they're doing it just for you.

■ ADDITIONAL READINGS

Cassell, James W. "Internet Data Archives for Sociologists." Paper presented to the American Sociological Association in New York City, August 19, 1996.

Ferrante, Joan, and Angela Vaughn. *Let's Go Sociology: Travels on the Internet.* Belmont, CA: Wadsworth, 1997. This is a student-oriented guide to about 500 URLs. Includes a brief intro to the Web.

Kardas, Edward P., and Tommy M. Milford. *Using the Internet for Social Science Research and Practice.* Belmont, CA: Wadsworth, 1996. As the title indicates, this introduction to the net focuses on the resources specifically relevant to social science research. It's loaded with Web sites and more, and an enclosed diskette makes it easier for you to use them.

Kurland, Daniel J. *The Net, the Web, and You.* Belmont, CA: Wadsworth, 1996. Here's a good introduction to the topics of this appendix, beginning with speech and then the printed word.

APPENDIX C: The Research Report

■ INTRODUCTION

This book has considered the variety of activities that compose the *doing* of social research. In this appendix, we'll turn to an often neglected subject: reporting the research to others. Unless research is properly communicated, all the efforts devoted to previously discussed procedures will go for naught.

Before proceeding further on this topic, I should suggest one absolutely basic guideline. Good social reporting requires good English (or Spanish or whatever language you use). Whenever we ask the figures "to speak for themselves," they tend to remain mute. Whenever we use unduly complex terminology or construction, communication is reduced. Every researcher should read and reread (at approximately three-month intervals) an excellent small book by William Strunk, Jr., and E. B. White, *The Elements of Style*.* If you do this faithfully, and if even 10 percent of the contents rub off, you stand a rather good chance of making yourself understood and your findings perhaps appreciated.

Scientific reporting has several functions you should keep in mind. First, the report communicates to an audience a body of specific data and ideas. The report should provide those specifics clearly and with sufficient detail to permit an informed evaluation. Second, the scientific report should be viewed as a contribution to the general body of scientific knowledge. While remaining appropriately humble, you should always regard your research report as an addition to what we know about social behavior. Finally, the report should serve the function of stimulating and directing further inquiry.

■ SOME BASIC CONSIDERATIONS

Despite these general guidelines, different reports serve different purposes. A report appropriate for one purpose might be wholly inappropriate for another. This section of this appendix deals with some of the basic considerations in this regard.

Audience

Before drafting your report, you must ask yourself who you hope will read it. Normally, you should make a distinction between scientists and general readers. If written for the former, you may make certain assumptions about their existing knowledge and may perhaps summarize certain points rather than explain them in detail. Similarly, you may appropriately use more technical language than would be appropriate for a general audience.

At the same time, you should remain always aware that any science is composed of factions or cults. Terms and assumptions acceptable to your immediate colleagues may only confuse other scientists. This applies in regard to substance as well as techniques. The sociologist of religion writing for a general sociology audience, for example, should explain previous findings in more detail

---

*Third ed. (New York: Macmillan, 1979). Here's another useful reference on writing: H. W. Fowler, *A Dictionary of Modern English Usage* (New York: Oxford University Press, 1983).

than would be necessary if he or she were addressing an audience of other sociologists of religion.

Form and Length of Report

I should begin this subsection by saying that my comments apply to both written and oral reports. Each form, however, affects the nature of the report.

It's useful to think about the variety of reports that might result from a research project. To begin, you may wish to prepare a short *research note* for publication in an academic or technical journal. Such reports should be approximately one to five pages long (typed, double-spaced) and should be concise and direct. In a short amount of space, you can't present the state of the field in any detail, so your methodological notes must be somewhat abbreviated as well. Basically, you should tell the reader why you feel a brief note is justified by your findings, then tell what those findings are.

Often, researchers must prepare reports for the sponsors of their research. These may vary greatly in length, of course. In preparing such a report, however, you should bear in mind the audience for the report—scientific or lay—and their reasons for sponsoring the project in the first place. It is both bad politics and bad manners to bore the sponsors with research findings that have no interest or value to them. At the same time, it may be useful to summarize how the research has advanced basic scientific knowledge (if it has).

Working papers or *monographs* are another form of research reporting. Especially in a large and complex project, you'll find comments on your analysis and the interpretation of your data useful. A working paper constitutes a tentative presentation with an implicit request for comments. Working papers can also vary in length, and they may present all of the research findings of the project or only a portion of them. Because your professional reputation is not at stake in a working paper, you should feel free to present tentative interpretations that you can't altogether justify—identifying them as such and asking for evaluations.

Many research projects result in papers delivered at professional meetings. Often, these serve the same purpose as working papers. You can present findings and ideas of possible interest to your colleagues and ask for their comments. Although the length of *professional papers* may vary depending on the organization of the meetings, I encourage you to say too little rather than too much. Although a working paper may ramble somewhat through a variety of tentative conclusions, conference participants should not be forced to sit through an oral unveiling of the same. Interested listeners can always ask for more details later, and uninterested ones can gratefully escape.

Probably the most popular research report is the *article* published in an academic journal. Again, lengths vary, and you should examine the lengths of articles previously published by the journal in question. As a rough guide, however, 25 typed pages is as good a length as any. A subsequent section on the organization of the report is primarily based on the structure of a journal article, so I shall say no more at this point, except to indicate that student term papers should follow this model. As a general rule, a term paper that would make a good journal article would also make a good term paper.

A *book*, of course, represents the most prestigious form of research report. It has all the advantages of the working paper—length, detail—but it should be a more polished document. Because publishing research findings as a book gives those findings an appearance of greater substance and worth, you have a special obligation to your audience. Although you will still hope to receive comments from colleagues, possibly leading you to revise your ideas, you must realize that other readers may be led to accept your findings uncritically.

Aim of the Report

Earlier in this book, we considered the different purposes of social research projects. In preparing your report, you should keep these different purposes in mind.

Some reports may focus primarily on the *exploration* of a topic of interest. Inherent in this aim is the tentativeness and incompleteness of the conclusions. You should clearly indicate to your audience the exploratory aim of the study and point to the shortcomings of the particular project. An important aspect of an exploratory report is to point the way to more refined research on the topic.

Most studies have a *descriptive* purpose, and the research reports from such studies will have a descriptive element. You should carefully distinguish for the reader those descriptions that apply only to the sample and those that apply to the population. You should give your audience some indication of the probable range of error in any inferential descriptions you make.

Many reports have an *explanatory* aim; you wish to point to causal relationships among variables. Depending on the probable audience for your report, you should carefully delineate the rules of explanation that lie behind your computations and conclusions. Also, as in the case of description, you must give your readers some guide to the relative certainty of your conclusions.

Finally, some research reports may *propose action*. For example, the researcher of prejudice may wish to suggest how prejudice may be reduced, on the basis of the research findings. This aim often presents knotty problems, however, because your own values and orientations may interfere with your proposals. Although it is perfectly legitimate for your proposals to be motivated by personal values, you must insure that the specific actions you propose are warranted by your data. Thus, you should be especially careful to spell out the logic by which you move from empirical data to proposed action.

■ ORGANIZATION OF THE REPORT

Although the organization of reports differs somewhat in terms of form and purpose, it is possible to suggest a general format for presenting research data. The following comments apply most directly to a journal article, but with some modification they apply to most forms of research reports.

Purpose and Overview

It's always helpful to the reader if you begin with a brief statement of the purpose of the study and the main findings of the analysis. In a journal article, this overview may sometimes be given in the form of an *abstract* or *synopsis*.

Some researchers find this difficult to do. For example, your analysis may have involved considerable detective work, with important findings revealing themselves only as a result of imaginative deduction and data manipulation. You may wish, therefore, to lead the reader through the same exciting process, chronicling the discovery process with a degree of suspense and surprise. To the extent that this form of reporting gives an accurate picture of the research process, I feel it has considerable instructional value. Nevertheless, many readers may not be interested in following your entire research account, and not knowing the purpose and general conclusions in advance may make it difficult for them to understand the significance of the study.

An old forensic dictum says, "Tell them what you're going to tell them; tell them; and tell them what you told them." You would do well to follow this dictum in the preparation of research reports.

Review of the Literature

Because every research report should be placed in the context of the general body of scientific knowledge, you must indicate where your report fits in that picture. Having presented the general purpose of your study, you should then bring the reader up to date on the previous research in the area, pointing to general agreements and disagreements among the previous researchers.

In some cases, you may wish to challenge previously accepted ideas. You should carefully review the studies that had led to the acceptance of those ideas, then indicate the factors that have not been previously considered or the logical fallacies present in the previous research.

When you're concerned with resolving a disagreement among previous researchers, you should organize your review of the literature around the opposing points of view. You should summarize the research supporting one view, then summarize the research supporting the other, and finally suggest the reasons for the disagreement.

To an extent, your review of the literature serves a bibliographical function for readers, indexing the previous research on a given topic.

This can be overdone, however, and you should avoid an opening paragraph that runs three pages, mentioning every previous study in the field. The comprehensive bibliographical function can best be served by a bibliography at the end of the report, and the review of the literature should focus only on those studies that have direct relevance to the present one.

Avoiding Plagiarism

Whenever you're reporting on the work of others, you must be clear about who said what. That is, you must avoid *plagiarism:* the theft of another's words and/or ideas—whether intentional or accidental—and the presentation of those words and ideas as your own. Because this is a common and sometimes unclear problem for college students, let's take a minute to examine it in some detail. Here are the main ground rules regarding plagiarism:

- You cannot use another writer's exact words without using quotation marks and giving a complete citation, which indicates the source of the quotation such that your reader could locate that quotation in its original context. As a general rule, taking a passage of eight or more words without citation is a violation of federal copyright laws.
- It's also not acceptable to edit or paraphrase another's words and present the revised version as your own work.
- Finally, it's not even acceptable to present another's *ideas* as your own—even if you use totally different words to express those ideas.

The following examples should clarify what is or is not acceptable in the use of another's work.

The Original Work

Laws of Growth

Systems are like babies: once you get one, you have it. They don't go away. On the contrary, they display the most remarkable persistence. They not only persist; they grow. And as they grow, they encroach. The growth potential of systems was explored in a tentative, preliminary way by Parkinson, who concluded that administrative systems maintain an average growth of 5 to 6 percent per annum regardless of the work to be done. Parkinson was right so far as he goes, and we must give him full honors for initiating the serious study of this important topic. But what Parkinson failed to perceive, we now enunciate—the general systems analogue of Parkinson's Law.

The System Itself Tends to Grow At 5 To 6 Percent Per Annum

Again, this Law is but the preliminary to the most general possible formulation, the Big-Bang Theorem of Systems Cosmology.

Systems Tend To Expand To Fill The Known Universe*

Now let's look at some of the *acceptable* ways you might make use of Gall's work in a term paper.

- **Acceptable:** John Gall, in his work *Systemantics,* draws a humorous parallel between systems and infants: "Systems are like babies: once you get one, you have it. They don't go away. On the contrary, they display the most remarkable persistence. They not only persist; they grow."**
- **Acceptable:** John Gall warns that systems are like babies. Create a system and it sticks around. Worse yet, Gall notes, systems keep growing larger and larger.*
- **Acceptable:** It has also been suggested that systems have a natural tendency to persist, even grow and encroach (Gall, 1975:12). [*Note:* This format requires that you give a complete citation in your bibliography.]

Here now are some *unacceptable* uses of the same material, reflecting some common errors.

- **Unacceptable:** In this paper, I want to look at some of the characteristics of the social sys-

---

*John Gall, *Systemantics: How Systems Work and Especially How They Fail* (New York: Quadrangle, 1975), 12–14. *Note:* Gall previously gave a full citation for Parkinson.

**John Gall, *Systemantics: How Systems Work and Especially How They Fail* (New York: Quadrangle, 1975), 12.

tems we create in our organizations. First, systems are like babies: once you get one, you have it. They don't go away. On the contrary, they display the most remarkable persistence. They not only persist; they grow. [It is unacceptable to directly quote someone else's materials without using quotation marks and giving a full citation.]

- **Unacceptable:** In this paper, I want to look at some of the characteristics of the social systems we create in our organizations. First, systems are a lot like children: once you get one, it's yours. They don't go away; they persist. They not only persist, in fact: they grow. [It is unacceptable to edit another's work and present it as your own.]
- **Unacceptable:** In this paper, I want to look at some of the characteristics of the social systems we create in our organizations. One thing I've noticed is that once you create a system, it never seems to go away. Just the opposite, in fact: they have a tendency to grow. You might say systems are a lot like children in that respect. [It is unacceptable to paraphrase someone else's ideas and present them as your own.]

Each of the preceding unacceptable examples is an example of plagiarism and represents a serious offense. Admittedly, there are some "gray areas." Some ideas are more or less in the public domain, not "belonging" to any one person. Or you may reach an idea on your own that someone else has already put in writing. If you have a question about a specific situation, discuss it with your instructor in advance.

I've discussed this topic in some detail because though you must place your research in the context of what others have done and said, the improper use of their materials is a serious offense. Mastering this matter, however, is a part of your "coming of age" as a scholar.

Study Design and Execution

A research report containing interesting findings and conclusions can be very frustrating when the reader can't determine the methodological design and execution of the study. The worth of all scientific findings depends heavily on the manner in which the data were collected and analyzed.

In reporting the design and execution of a survey, for example, you should always include the following: the population, the sampling frame, the sampling method, the sample size, the data-collection method, the completion rate, and the methods of data processing and analysis. Comparable details should be given if other methods are used. The experienced researcher can report these details in a rather short space, without omitting anything required for the reader's evaluation of the study.

Analysis and Interpretation

Having set the study in the perspective of previous research and having described the design and execution of it, you should then present your data. The following major section will provide further guidelines in this regard. For now, a few general comments are in order.

The presentation of data, the manipulations of those data, and your interpretations should be integrated into a logical whole. It's frustrating to the reader to discover a collection of seemingly unrelated analyses and findings with a promise that all the loose ends will be tied together later in the report. Every step in the analysis should make sense—at the time it is taken. You should present your rationale for a particular analysis, present the data relevant to it, interpret the results, then indicate where that result leads next.

Summary and Conclusions

Following the forensic dictum mentioned earlier, I believe it is essential to summarize the research report. You should avoid reviewing every specific finding, but you should review all the significant ones, pointing once more to their general significance.

The report should conclude with a statement of what you have discovered about your subject matter and where future research might be directed. A quick review of recent journal articles will probably indicate a high frequency of the concluding statement, "It is clear that much more research is needed." This is probably always a true conclusion, but it is of little value unless you can offer pertinent suggestions about the nature of that future research. You should review the particular shortcomings of your own study and suggest ways those shortcomings might be avoided.

■ GUIDELINES FOR REPORTING ANALYSES

The presentation of data analyses should provide a maximum of detail without being cluttered. You can accomplish this best by continually examining your report to see whether it achieves the following aims.

If you're using quantitative data, present them so the reader can recompute them. In the case of percentage tables, for example, the reader should be able to collapse categories and recompute the percentages. Readers should receive sufficient information to permit them to compute percentages in the table in the opposite direction from that of your own presentation.

You should describe all aspects of a quantitative analysis in sufficient detail to permit a secondary analyst to replicate the analysis from the same body of data. This means that he or she should be able to create the same indexes and scales, produce the same tables, arrive at the same regression equations, obtain the same factors and factor loadings, and so forth. This will seldom be done, of course, but if the report allows for it, the reader will be far better equipped to evaluate the report than if it does not.

If you're doing a qualitative analysis, you must provide sufficient details from your observations that your reader can create a sense of having been there with you. Presenting only those data that support your interpretations is not sufficient; you must also share with your reader those data that conflict with the way you've made sense of things. Ultimately, you should provide your reader with enough information that he or she might reach a different conclusion than you did—though you can hope your interpretation will make the most sense.

The reader, in fact, should be in position to replicate the entire study independently, whether it involves participant observation among heavy metal groupies, an experiment regarding jury deliberation, or any other kind of study. Recall that replicability is an essential norm of science generally. A single study does not prove a point; only a series of studies can begin to do so. And unless studies can be replicated, there can be no meaningful series of studies.

I have previously mentioned the importance of integrating data and interpretations in the report. A more specific guideline can be offered in this regard. Tables, charts, and figures, if any, should be integrated into the text of the report—appearing near that portion of the text discussing them. Sometimes students describe their analyses in the body of the report and place all the tables in an appendix. This procedure greatly impedes the reader, however. As a general rule, it is best to (1) describe the purpose for presenting the table, (2) present it, and (3) review and interpret it.

Draw explicit conclusions. Although research is typically conducted for the purpose of drawing general conclusions, you should carefully note the specific basis for such conclusions. Otherwise you may lead your reader into accepting unwarranted conclusions.

Point to any qualifications or conditions warranted in the evaluation of conclusions. Typically, you know best the shortcomings and tentativeness of your conclusions, and you should give the reader the advantage of that knowledge. Failure to do so can misdirect future research and result in a waste of research funds.

I will conclude with a point made at the outset of this appendix, because it is extremely important. Research reports should be written in the best possible literary style. Writing lucidly is easier for some people than for others, and it is always harder than writing poorly. You are again referred to the Strunk and White volume. Every researcher would do well to follow this procedure: Write. Read Strunk and White. Revise. Reread Strunk and White. Revise again. This will be a difficult and time-consuming endeavor, but so is science.

A perfectly designed, carefully executed, and brilliantly analyzed study will be altogether worthless unless you can communicate your findings to others. This appendix has attempted to provide some general and specific guidelines toward that end. The best guides are logic, clarity, and honesty. Ultimately, there is probably no substitute for practice.

APPENDIX D: GSS Household Enumeration Questionnaire

The National Opinion Research Center (NORC) at the University of Chicago is one of the primary social science research centers in the world. Its General Social Survey (GSS), moreover, has become a major source of social science data for researchers. You may have noticed that many of the examples in this book have been taken from the GSS. It is fitting, therefore, that we turn to the GSS for an example of an interview questionnaire. The following pages present the questionnaire used by interviewers in collecting basic demographic data about households selected in the sample. Questionnaires such as these are an important part of the scientific equipment used by social scientists. Just as a microscope is an appropriate instrument for observing cells and molecules and a telescope for observing distant planets and stars, a questionnaire such as this one is often the best instrument for observing the subject matter of social science.

GSS
AMERICA'S SOCIAL SURVEY

INTERVIEWER NAME

INTERVIEWER ID#

| | | | | | - | |

5325 NORC
JANUARY 1990

HOUSEHOLD ENUMERATION FOLDER
COMPLETE SAMPLING REPORT   HEF

INTRODUCTION:

Hello, I'm (YOUR NAME) from the National Opinion Research Center at the University of Chicago (SHOW ID CARD).

(We recently sent you a letter explaining that) Your household has been selected to take part in this year's GSS: America's Social Survey.

We've been conducting this study all over the country for more than fifteen years, learning about how people feel about issues like schools, crime, government spending, and the military. This year several households in your community will be participating in this important research.

First, I'd like to make sure that I have your street address described correctly. Is it (READ FROM ASSIGNMENT LABEL OR BOX BELOW: STREET NUMBER AND NAME, APARTMENT NUMBER OR OTHER DESCRIPTION OF HU.) IF EXACTLY THE SAME, CHECK BOX:

☐ (GO TO Q.1, P.2)

IF DIFFERENT IN ANY WAY, EXAMINE SEGMENT PRINTOUT AND RECONCILE. EXPLAIN THE DIFFERENCE HERE:

_____

_____

IF DIFFERENCE CAN'T BE RESOLVED, CALL YOUR FIELD MANAGER BEFORE CONTINUING.

BEGIN DECK 01

INTERVIEWER: STICK ASSIGNMENT LABEL HERE
OR
IF THIS IS A CASE YOU'RE ADDING
TO YOUR ASSIGNMENT AS A MISSED HU,
COPY INFORMATION FROM ORIGINAL LABEL

SURVEY **5325**   CASE#
PSU
SEG   PT **1**   LINE   BLK
LOCALITY
HU ADDRESS
HU DESCRIPTION
A, B, OR C   X OR Y

(CASE #)   01-06/
(PSU)   07-09/
(SEG)   10-12/
(PT)   13/
(LINE #)   14-23/
(A, B, or C)   24/
(X or Y)   25/
(INTID)   26-31/

HEF-2

TIME BEGAN: ___ AM / PM

1. Only one member of your household will be eligible for this survey. In order to scientifically select that person, first I need to list the names of the people who usually live here.

2. Please tell me the names of the people who usually live in this household. Let's start with the head of the household. LIST ON LINES 01-10 BELOW.

3. Have we forgotten anyone: such as babies or small children; roomers; people who usually live here, but are away temporarily—on business trips, vacations, at school, temporarily in a hospital, and so on?
   Yes ☐ LIST ADDITIONAL PERSONS ON LINES 01-10 BELOW.
   No ☐ GO TO Q.4.

4. Are there any people currently staying here—visitors, friends or relatives—who do not usually live here?
   Yes ☐ LIST VISITORS ON LINES 11-14 BELOW.
   No ☐ GO TO Q.5.

   AFTER QS. 1-4, ASK QS. 5-8 FOR EACH PERSON.

9. Are any of the people we have listed staying somewhere else right now?
   IF NO, CHECK BOX AND SKIP TO Q. 12 ☐
   IF YES, GO TO Q. 10 BELOW.

10. Who is staying somewhere else right now? CHECK (✓) LINE OF EACH PERSON WHO IS AWAY.

11. ASK FOR EACH PERSON CHECKED (✓) IN Q. 10:
    Where is (PERSON) staying right now: Is (PERSON) staying at another household; Is (he/she) traveling; Is (he/she) in some Institution or dormitory-like at college, or in a hospital or something; or what?
    CIRCLE CODE, FOLLOW INSTRUCTIONS

	First Name	Last name	5. What is (PERSON)'s relationship to (HEAD OF HOUSEHOLD)?	6. CODE SEX (ASK IF NOT OBVIOUS) M / F	7. How old was (HEAD/PERSON) on (his/her) last birthday?	8. IF 13 YRS OR OLDER ASK: Is (PERSON) now married, widowed, divorced, separated, or has (he/she) never been married? Ma Wi Di Se NM	10.	11. Another House-hold	Travel-ing	Insti-tution	Other DK
01			49 HEAD	50 1 2	51-52	53 1 2 3 4 5	54	1 CROSS OUT	2 LEAVE IN	3 CROSS OUT	55 4*
02			56	57 1 2	58-59	60 1 2 3 4 5	61	1 CROSS OUT	2 LEAVE IN	3 CROSS OUT	62 4*
03			63	64 1 2	65-66	67 1 2 3 4 5	68	1 CROSS OUT	2 LEAVE IN	3 CROSS OUT	69 4*
04		BEGIN DECK 03	07	08 1 2	09-10	11 1 2 3 4 5	12	1 CROSS OUT	2 LEAVE IN	3 CROSS OUT	13 4*

USUAL

VISITOR

05		14	1 15 2	16-17	1 2 3 4 18 5	19	1 CROSS OUT	2 LEAVE IN	3 CROSS OUT	20 4*
06		21	1 22 2	23-24	1 2 3 4 25 5	26	1 CROSS OUT	2 LEAVE IN	3 CROSS OUT	27 4*
07		28	1 29 2	30-31	1 2 3 4 32 5	33	1 CROSS OUT	2 LEAVE IN	3 CROSS OUT	34 4*
08		35	1 36 2	37-38	1 2 3 4 39 5	40	1 CROSS OUT	2 LEAVE IN	3 CROSS OUT	41 4*
09		42	1 43 2	44-45	1 2 3 4 46 5	47	1 CROSS OUT	2 LEAVE IN	3 CROSS OUT	48 4*
10		49	1 50 2	51-52	1 2 3 4 53 5	54	1 CROSS OUT	2 LEAVE IN	3 CROSS OUT	55 4*
11		56	1 57 2	58-59	1 2 3 4 60 5	61	1 CROSS OUT	2 LEAVE IN	3 CROSS OUT	62 4*
12		63	1 64 2	65-66	1 2 3 4 67 5	68	1 CROSS OUT	2 LEAVE IN	3 CROSS OUT	69 4*
13	BEGIN DECK 04	07	1 08 2	09-10	1 2 3 4 11 5	12	1 CROSS OUT	2 LEAVE IN	3 CROSS OUT	13 4*
14		14	1 15 2	16-17	1 2 3 4 18 5	19	1 CROSS OUT	2 LEAVE IN	3 CROSS OUT	20 4*

AFTER Q.8 FOR LAST PERSON 13 OR OLDER, ASK Q.9.

*PROBE FOR DETAILS AND CHECK INTERVIEWER MANUAL FOR HELP IF NECESSARY

IF MORE THAN 10 USUAL PERSONS AND/OR MORE THAN 4 VISITORS, USE A BLANK HEF FOR ADDITIONAL LISTING.

12. Now I'm going to scientifically select the one person in this household chosen for this study. By interviewing only the person picked in this way, we can be sure the views we find do accurately represent the views of the country as a whole.

STEP 1: ELIGIBLE PEOPLE: 18 OR OVER
         NAME NOT CROSSED OUT ON HOUSEHOLD ENUMERATION (P.2)

IF ONLY ONE ELIGIBLE PERSON, GO TO Q.13 AND MAKE APPOINTMENT TO INTERVIEW THAT PERSON.

IF MORE THAN ONE, CONTINUE WITH STEPS 2-6 BELOW.

STEP 2: LIST NAMES OF ELIGIBLE PEOPLE IN SUMMARY BOX, IN ORDER OF AGE.

SUMMARY BOX

LINE #	AGE	NAMES OF ELIGIBLE PERSONS
1 OLDEST (Not necessarily the head)		
2		
3		
4		
5		
6 YOUNGEST		

SAMPLING TABLE

NUMBER OF ELIGIBLE PERSONS LISTED ABOVE	INTERVIEW PERSON ON LINE NUMBER
	STICK SAMPLING PART OF ASSIGNMENT LABEL HERE. (If this is a "missed HU" added to your assignment, copy sampling numbers from original case.)
TWO	
THREE	
FOUR	
FIVE	
SIX OR MORE	

STEP 3: USE SAMPLING TABLE TO THE RIGHT TO SELECT WHICH ELIGIBLE PERSON TO INTERVIEW.

STEP 4: CIRCLE SELECTED R'S LINE # IN SUMMARY BOX.

STEP 5: PRINT SELECTED R'S NAME HERE: _____

STEP 6: ARRANGE TO INTERVIEW THIS PERSON. REQUEST PHONE AND MAILING INFORMATION (Qs.13 AND 14) TO HELP IN FOLLOW-UP.

13. If I have to talk with (SELECTED RESPONDENT), what phone numbers should I use?

Telephone number given: (___) _____
   AREA CODE   NUMBER

A. Code location of phone:
   In household..............................1 22/
   In home of neighbor.......................2
   Other (SPECIFY) _____...3

B. If no number given, code
   No phone..................................4
   Refused...................................5

14. If I have to mail a note to (SELECTED RESPONDENT), what would be the best mailing address to use?

| # AND STREET/BOX #/RFD # |
| POST OFFICE, TOWN |
| STATE   ZIP CODE |

IMMEDIATELY AFTER LEAVING THE HOUSEHOLD, FILL OUT A-D BELOW AND COMPLETE THE SAMPLING REPORT.

A. Date HEF administered: | 0 | __ | __ | 9 | 0 | 23-25/
                            MONTH   DAY   YEAR

B. Name of HEF informant: _____

C. List line number of HEF informant
   from Household Enumeration (P.2, Q.4)... | __ | 26-27/
   (If non-household informant, line # = 22)

D. Race of household (by observation)
   White.....................................1 28/
   Black/Negro...............................2
   American Indian...........................3
   Asiatic, Oriental.........................4
   Other, mixed, not able to observe.........5

E. List line number of selected respondent
   from Household Enumeration (P.2, Q.4)... | __ | 29-30/

THANK RESPONDENT FOR THEIR TIME AND HELP.

| TIME HEF ENDED: | ____ AM / PM |

| LENGTH OF TIME FOR HEF: | ____ MIN |

HEF-4 HEF-5
NON-INTERVIEW REPORT (NIR)

Name (if known): _____

Telephone number, (if available): _____

Please Circle Appropriate Code:

HEF not completed 1 31/
HEF complete/interview incomplete 2

1. Why were you unable to complete HEF/Interview at this address?   32-33/

   NOT AN HU: .... (Ans. Q.2) .01
     Condemned .... (Ans. Q.2) .02
     Demolished .... (Ans. Q.2) .03
     Place of business .... (Ans. Q.2) .04
     No such address/no such HU .... (Ans. Q.2) .05
     Group quarters .... (Ans. Q.2) .06
     Vacation cabin .... (Ans. Q.2) .07
     Not usable as permanent residence .... (Ans. Q.2) .08
     Transient use (less than one month) .... (Ans. Q.2) .09
     Not an HU for other reason .... (Ans. Q.2) .10
     Still under construction .... (Skip to Q.7) .11
   VACANT .... (Skip to Q.4) .12
   REFUSED .... (Skip to Q.4) .13
   BREAKOFF .... (Skip to Q.3) .14
   NOT HOME AFTER 4 CALLS .... (Skip to Q.5) .15
   RESPONDENT IS UNAVAILABLE FOR ENTIRE
     FIELD PERIOD .... (SKIP TO Q.6) .16
   LANGUAGE PROBLEM (SPECIFY LANGUAGE SPOKEN)
   TOO ILL (DESCRIBE SITUATION ON PAGE 7) .... (Skip to Q.7) .17
   OTHER (DESCRIBE SITUATION ON PAGE 7) .... (Skip to Q.7) .18

2. **IF NOT AN HU:**
   Describe the reason for this NIR fully, then go to Q.19.
                                                                34-35/

3. **IF NOT AT HOME AFTER 4 CALLS:**
   Why do you think it has been so hard to find the occupants of this housing unit at home?   36-37/

   A. Describe your efforts to obtain information about the occupants.   38-39/

4. **IF REFUSED OR BREAKOFF:**
   Did the respondent give the refusal?
   Yes .... (Ans. A) ... 1 40/
   No .... (Ans. B) ... 2
   DK, HEF not complete .... (Skip to Q.6) .. 8

   A. **IF YES:** Why did the respondent (refuse/breakoff)?   41-42/
      (Report verbatim remarks and reasons.)
                                                    (SKIP TO Q.6)   43-44/

   B. **IF NO:** Why were you unable to speak with
                the respondent?   (SKIP TO Q.6)

5. **IF TEMPORARILY UNAVAILABLE FOR THE ENTIRE PERIOD:**
   What is the reason for this status?   45-46/

   A. When will R be available?   47-48/

6. Was a follow-up letter sent to the respondent?
   Yes .... (Ans. A) ... 1 49/
   No .... (Ans. B) ... 2
   DK 8

   A. **IF YES:** Did you speak with R after receipt of letter?
      Yes .... (Ans. A) ... 1 50/
      No .... (Ans. B) ... 2
      DK 8

   B. **IF NO:** Why not?

ANSWER C.7 UNLESS NOT AN HU

7. Were you ever able to talk with someone at this HU (not necessarily a resident)?

NIR

```
            Yes....................................(GO TO Q.8) ....1  51/
            No............................................(Ans. A) ....2

         A. Why not?                                                       52-53/

      8. On any calls were there people in the HU who did not
         answer the door?
            Yes, definitely.......................................1  54/
            Suspect so............................................2
            No reason to think so.................................3

         ┌─────────────────────────────────────────────────────────┐
         │ ANSWER Qs 9-17 FROM INFORMATION OBTAINED BY OBSERVATION │
         │ AND/OR CONTACTS WITH HM MEMBERS, NEIGHBORS AND OTHER    │
         │ SOURCES.                                                │
         └─────────────────────────────────────────────────────────┘

      9. What is the estimated income of R's family? (NOTE: IF
         MULTIPLE FAMILIES AND R NOT DETERMINED, ESTIMATE FOR
         PRIMARY FAMILY.)
            Low...................................................1  55/
            Medium................................................2
            High..................................................3
            Don't know/unable to observe..........................8

     10. Were you able to complete the household listing?
            Yes.................................(Skip to Q.16) ....1  56/
            No................................(Ans. Qs. 11-20) ....2

     11. What is the race of the residents?
            White......................................(definitely) ....1  57/
            White........................................(probably) ....2
            Black......................................(definitely) ....3
            Black........................................(probably) ....4
            Hispanic..............................................5
            Asiatic/Oriental......................................6
            Other (DESCRIBE)......................................7
            Could not determine...................................8

     12. Estimate the number of adults living in the HU.
            # of adults:   ☐☐                                      58-59/

     13. Estimate the number of adult males living in the HU.
            # of adults:   ☐☐                                      60-61/

     14. Is there a married (or living as married) couple living
         in the HU?
            Yes...................................................1  62/
            No....................................................2
            Don't know............................................3

     15. What is your estimate of the age of the Household Head?
            Under 30..............................................1  63/
            30-64.................................................2
            65 or older...........................................3
            Don't know............................................8

     16. Type of structure.                                          64-65
            Trailer...............................................01
            Detached single family house..........................02
            2 family house, 2 units side by side..................03
            2 family house, 2 units one above the other..........04
            Detached 3-4 family house.............................05
            Rowhouse (3 or more units in an attached row).........06
            Apartment house (5 or more units,
              3 stories or less)..................................07
            Apartment house (5 or more units,
              4 stories or more)..................................08
            Apartment in a partly commercial structure............09
            Other (SPECIFY) _____               10

     17. Compared to house/apartments in the neighborhood,
         would you say the house/apartment was . .
            Far above average.....................................1  66/
            Above average.........................................2
            Average...............................................3
            Below average.........................................4
            Far below average.....................................5

     18. ADDITIONAL COMMENTS:
         _____

     19. Interviewer Name: _____

     20. Interviewer Number:     ☐☐☐ - ☐☐

     21. Enter Supervisor's name.
```

HEF-6
RECORD OF CALLS ON HOUSEHOLD

USE PENCIL

A. Day
M.1 Tu.2 W.3
Th.4 F.5 Sa.6
Su.7
B. Month
C. Date

D. Time
Pre3..1 3-6..2 Post 6..3
E. Type
Per..1 Tel..2 Mail..3
F. Outcome of Contact
If 35,37,45,47,82,92 Do G

		G. Refusal Description	H. Results/Reason for Refusal. Give verbatim reasons and explain in all circumstances.	I. Purpose of Contact	J. Int'r Initials
A. ⎵⎵ 32/R	D. ⎵ 37/R	G. M.....F | Age _____	H.	I. 41/R	J.
B. ⎵⎵ 33-34/R	E. ⎵ 38/R	Other char:		HEF.......1	
C. ⎵⎵ 35-36/R	F. ⎵⎵ 39-40/R	HEF Line # when complete _____		Quex.......2	
A. ⎵⎵ 42/R	D. ⎵ 47/R	G. M.....F | Age _____	H.	I. 51/R	J.
B. ⎵⎵ 43-44/R	E. ⎵ 48/R	Other char:		HEF.......1	
C. ⎵⎵ 45-46/R	F. ⎵⎵ 49-50/R	HEF Line # when complete _____		Quex.......2	
A. ⎵⎵ 52/R	D. ⎵ 57/R	G. M.....F | Age _____	H.	I. 61/R	J.
B. ⎵⎵ 53-54/R	E. ⎵ 58/R	Other char:		HEF.......1	
C. ⎵⎵ 55-56/R	F. ⎵⎵ 59-60/R	HEF Line # when complete _____		Quex.......2	
A. ⎵⎵ 62/R	D. ⎵ 67/R	G. M.....F | Age _____	H.	I. 71/R	J.
B. ⎵⎵ 63-64/R	E. ⎵ 68/R	Other char:		HEF.......1	
C. ⎵⎵ 65-66/R	F. ⎵⎵ 69-70/R	HEF Line # when complete _____		Quex.......2	

BEGIN DECK 02

A.	☐☐ 07/R	D.	12/R	G. M....F Age ____	H.	I. 16/R
B.	☐☐ 08-09/R	E.	13/R	Other char: ____		HEF......1
C.	☐☐ 10-11/R	F.	14-15/R	HEF Line # when complete ____		Quex......2
A.	☐☐ 17/R	D.	22/R	G. M....F Age ____	H.	I. 26/R
B.	☐☐ 18-19/R	E.	23/R	Other char: ____		HEF......1
C.	☐☐ 20-21/R	F.	24-25/R	HEF Line # when complete ____		Quex......2
A.	☐☐ 27/R	D.	32/R	G. M....F Age ____	H.	I. 36/R
B.	☐☐ 28-29/R	E.	33/R	Other char: ____		HEF......1
C.	☐☐ 30-31/R	F.	34-35/R	HEF Line # when complete ____		Quex......2
A.	☐☐ 37/R	D.	42/R	G. M....F Age ____	H.	I. 46/R
B.	☐☐ 38-39/R	E.	43/R	Other char: ____		HEF......1
C.	☐☐ 40-41/R	F.	44-45/R	HEF Line # when complete ____		Quex......2

47-48

STATUS CODES FOR OUTCOME (COLUMN F)

TEMPORARY   FINAL (Requires supervisor's approval)

HEF   QUEX   HEF   QUEX
31 No action   43 R not home/unavailable   10 No HU*   13 R does not speak English*
32 No one home/No answer/Busy 45 Temp refusal/breakoff   11 Vacant*   92 Refusal/breakoff*
35 Temporary refusal/breakoff 46 Appointment   12 HH speaks no English*   94 R absent entire field period*
36 Appointment   47 Broken appointment   82 Refusal/breakoff*   97 Other*
37 Broken appointment   49 Other   84 Not home/unavailable*   60 Ballot Quex only
38 HH not accessible   85 HH not accessible*   65 Ballot Quex & some, not all documents
39 Other   87 Other*   67 Ballot Quex & all documents

EVERYONE COMPLETE SAMPLING REPORT   USE CONTINUATION SHEET IF NECESSARY   *FILL OUT NIR

APPENDIX E *Random Numbers*

10480	15011	01536	02011	81647	91646	69179	14194	62590	36207	20969	99570	91291	90700
22368	46573	25595	85393	30995	89198	27982	53402	93965	34095	52666	19174	39615	99505
24130	48360	22527	97265	76393	64809	15179	24830	49340	32081	30680	19655	63348	58629
42167	93093	06243	61680	07856	16376	39440	53537	71341	57004	00849	74917	97758	16379
37570	39975	81837	16656	06121	91782	60468	81305	49684	60672	14110	06927	01263	54613
77921	06907	11008	42751	27756	53498	18602	70659	90655	15053	21916	81825	44394	42880
99562	72905	56420	69994	98872	31016	71194	18738	44013	48840	63213	21069	10634	12952
96301	91977	05463	07972	18876	20922	94595	56869	69014	60045	18425	84903	42508	32307
89579	14342	63661	10281	17453	18103	57740	84378	25331	12566	58678	44947	05585	56941
85475	36857	53342	53988	53060	59533	38867	62300	08158	17983	16439	11458	18593	64952
28918	69578	88231	33276	70997	79936	56865	05859	90106	31595	01547	85590	91610	78188
63553	40961	48235	03427	49626	69445	18663	72695	52180	20847	12234	90511	33703	90322
09429	93969	52636	92737	88974	33488	36320	17617	30015	08272	84115	27156	30613	74952
10365	61129	87529	85689	48237	52267	67689	93394	01511	26358	85104	20285	29975	89868
07119	97336	71048	08178	77233	13916	47564	81056	97735	85977	29372	74461	28551	90707
51085	12765	51821	51259	77452	16308	60756	92144	49442	53900	70960	63990	75601	40719
02368	21382	52404	60268	89368	19885	55322	44819	01188	65255	64835	44919	05944	55157
01011	54092	33362	94904	31273	04146	18594	29852	71585	85030	51132	01915	92747	64951
52162	53916	46369	58586	23216	14513	83149	98736	23495	64350	94738	17752	35156	35749
07056	97628	33787	09998	42698	06691	76988	13602	51851	46104	88916	19509	25625	58104
48663	91245	85828	14346	09172	30168	90229	04734	59193	22178	30421	61666	99904	32812
54164	58492	22421	74103	47070	25306	76468	26384	58151	06646	21524	15227	96909	44592
32639	32363	05597	24200	13363	38005	94342	28728	35806	06912	17012	64161	18296	22851
29334	27001	87637	87308	58731	00256	45834	15398	46557	41135	10367	07684	36188	18510
02488	33062	28834	07351	19731	92420	60952	61280	50001	67658	32586	86679	50720	94953
81525	72295	04839	96423	24878	82651	66566	14778	76797	14780	13300	87074	79666	95725
29676	20591	68086	26432	46901	20849	89768	81536	86645	12659	92259	57102	80428	25280
00742	57392	39064	66432	84673	40027	32832	61362	98947	96067	64760	64584	96096	98253
05366	04213	25669	26422	44407	44048	37397	63904	45766	66134	75470	66520	34693	90449
91921	26418	64117	94305	26766	25940	39972	22209	71500	64568	91402	42416	07844	69618
00582	04711	87917	77341	42206	35126	74087	99547	81817	42607	43808	76655	62028	76630
00725	69884	62797	56170	86324	88072	76222	36086	84637	93161	76038	65855	77919	88006
69011	65795	95876	55293	18988	27354	26575	08625	40801	59920	29841	80150	12777	48501
25976	57948	29888	88604	67917	48708	18912	82271	65424	69774	33611	54262	85963	03547
09763	83473	73577	12908	30883	18317	28290	35797	05998	41688	34952	37888	38917	88050
91567	42595	27958	30134	04024	86385	29880	99730	55536	84855	29080	09250	79656	73211
17955	56349	90999	49127	20044	59931	06115	20542	18059	02008	73708	83517	36103	42791
46503	18584	18845	49618	02304	51038	20655	58727	28168	15475	56942	53389	20562	87338
92157	89634	94824	78171	84610	82834	09922	25417	44137	48413	25555	21246	35509	20468
14577	62765	35605	81263	39667	47358	56873	56307	61607	49518	89656	20103	77490	18062
98427	07523	33362	64270	01638	92477	66969	98420	04880	45585	46565	04102	46880	45709
34914	63976	88720	82765	34476	17032	87589	40836	32427	70002	70663	88863	77775	69348
70060	28277	39475	46473	23219	53416	94970	25832	69975	94884	19661	72828	00102	66794
53976	54914	06990	67245	68350	82948	11398	42878	80287	88267	47363	46634	06541	97809
76072	29515	40980	07391	58745	25774	22987	80059	39911	96189	41151	14222	60697	59583
90725	52210	83974	29992	65831	38857	50490	83765	55657	14361	31720	57375	56228	41546
64364	67412	33339	31926	14883	24413	59744	92351	97473	89286	35931	04110	23726	51900
08962	00358	31662	25388	61642	34072	81249	35648	56891	69352	48373	45578	78547	81788
95012	68379	93526	70765	10592	04542	76463	54328	02349	17247	28865	14777	62730	92277
15664	10493	20492	38391	91132	21999	59516	81652	27195	48223	46751	22923	32261	85653
16408	81899	04153	53381	79401	21438	83035	92350	36693	31238	59649	91754	72772	02338
18629	81953	05520	91962	04739	13092	97662	24822	94730	06496	35090	04822	86774	98289
73115	35101	47498	87637	99016	71060	88824	71013	18735	20286	23153	72924	35165	43040
57491	16703	23167	49323	45021	33132	12544	41035	80780	45393	44812	12515	98931	91202
30405	83946	23792	14422	15059	45799	22716	19792	09983	74353	68668	30429	70735	25499
16631	35006	85900	98275	32388	52390	16815	69298	82732	38480	73817	32523	41961	44437
96773	20206	42559	78985	05300	22164	24369	54224	35083	19687	11052	91491	60383	19746
38935	64202	14349	82674	66523	44133	00697	35552	35970	19124	63318	29686	03387	59846
31624	76384	17403	53363	44167	64486	64758	75366	76554	31601	12614	33072	60332	92325
78919	19474	23632	27889	47914	02584	37680	20801	72152	39339	34806	08930	85001	87820

Appendix E: Random Numbers

03931	33309	57047	74211	63445	17361	62825	39908	05607	91284	68833	25570	38818	46920
74426	33278	43972	10119	89917	15665	52872	73823	73144	88662	88970	74492	51805	99378
09066	00903	20795	95452	92648	45454	09552	88815	16553	51125	79375	97596	16296	66092
42238	12426	87025	14267	20979	04508	64535	31355	86064	29472	47689	05974	52468	16834
16153	08002	26504	41744	81959	65642	74240	56302	00033	67107	77510	70625	28725	34191
21457	40742	29820	96783	29400	21840	15035	34537	33310	06116	95240	15957	16572	06004
21581	57802	02050	89728	17937	37621	47075	42080	97403	48626	68995	43805	33386	21597
55612	78095	83197	33732	05810	24813	86902	60397	16489	03264	88525	42786	05269	92532
44657	66999	99324	51281	84463	60563	79312	93454	68876	25471	93911	25650	12682	73572
91340	84979	46949	81973	37949	61023	43997	15263	80644	43942	89203	71795	99533	50501
91227	21199	31935	27022	84067	05462	35216	14486	29891	68607	41867	14951	91696	85065
50001	38140	66321	19924	72163	09538	12151	06878	91903	18749	34405	56087	82790	70925
65390	05224	72958	28609	81406	39147	25549	48542	42627	45233	57202	94617	23772	07896
27504	96131	83944	41575	10573	08619	64482	73923	36152	05184	94142	25299	84387	34925
37169	94851	39117	89632	00959	16487	65536	49071	39782	17095	02330	74301	00275	48280
11508	70225	51111	38351	19444	66499	71945	05422	13442	78675	84081	66938	93654	59894
37449	30362	06694	54690	04052	53115	62757	95348	78662	11163	81651	50245	34971	52924
46515	70331	85922	38329	57015	15765	97161	17869	45349	61796	66345	81073	49106	79860
30986	81223	42416	58353	21532	30502	32305	86482	05174	07901	54339	58861	74818	46942
63798	64995	46583	09785	44160	78128	83991	42865	92520	83531	80377	35909	81250	54238
82486	84846	99254	67632	43218	50076	21361	64816	51202	88124	41870	52689	51275	83556
21885	32906	92431	09060	64297	51674	64126	62570	26123	05155	59194	52799	28225	85762
60336	98782	07408	53458	13564	59089	26445	29789	85205	41001	12535	12133	14645	23541
43937	46891	24010	25560	86355	33941	25786	54990	71899	15475	95434	98227	21824	19585
97656	63175	89303	16275	07100	92063	21942	18611	47348	20203	18534	03862	78095	50136
03299	01221	05418	38982	55758	92237	26759	86367	21216	98442	08303	56613	91511	75928
79626	06486	03574	17668	07785	76020	79924	25651	83325	88428	85076	72811	22717	50585
85636	68335	47539	03129	65651	11977	02510	26113	99447	68645	34327	15152	55230	93448
18039	14367	61337	06177	12143	46609	32989	74014	64708	00533	35398	58408	13261	47908
08362	15656	60627	36478	65648	16764	53412	09013	07832	41574	17639	82163	60859	75567
79556	29068	04142	16268	15387	12856	66227	38358	22478	73373	88732	09443	82558	05250
92608	82674	27072	32534	17075	27698	98204	63863	11951	34648	88022	56148	34925	57031
23982	25835	40055	67006	12293	02753	14827	23235	35071	99704	37543	11601	35503	85171
09915	96306	05908	97901	28395	14186	00821	80703	70426	75647	76310	88717	37890	40129
59037	33300	26695	62247	69927	76123	50842	43834	86654	70959	79725	93872	28117	19233
42488	78077	69882	61657	34136	79180	97526	43092	04098	73571	80799	76536	71255	64239
46764	86273	63003	93017	31204	36692	40202	35275	57306	55543	53203	18098	47625	88684
03237	45430	55417	63282	90816	17349	88298	90183	36600	78406	06216	95787	42579	90730
86591	81482	52667	61582	14972	90053	89534	76036	49199	43716	97548	04379	46370	28672
38534	01715	94964	87288	65680	43772	39560	12918	86537	62738	19636	51132	25739	56947

Abridged from *Handbook of Tables for Probability and Statistics,* 2nd ed., edited by William H. Beyer (Cleveland: The Chemical Rubber Company, 1968). Used by permission of The Chemical Rubber Company.

APPENDIX F: Distribution of Chi Square

df	.99	.98	.95	.90	.80	.70	.50
1	.0³157	.0³628	.00393	.0158	.0642	.148	.455
2	.0201	.0404	.103	.211	.446	.713	1.386
3	.115	.185	.352	.584	1.005	1.424	2.366
4	.297	.429	.711	1.064	1.649	2.195	3.357
5	.554	.752	1.145	1.610	2.343	3.000	4.351
6	.872	1.134	1.635	2.204	3.070	3.828	5.348
7	1.239	1.564	2.167	2.833	3.822	4.671	6.346
8	1.646	2.032	2.733	3.490	4.594	5.528	7.344
9	2.088	2.532	3.325	4.168	5.380	6.393	8.343
10	2.558	3.059	3.940	4.865	6.179	7.267	9.342
11	3.053	3.609	4.575	5.578	6.989	8.148	10.341
12	3.571	4.178	5.226	6.304	7.807	9.034	11.340
13	4.107	4.765	5.892	7.042	8.634	9.926	12.340
14	4.660	5.368	6.571	7.790	9.467	10.821	13.339
15	5.229	5.985	7.261	8.547	10.307	11.721	14.339
16	5.812	6.614	7.962	9.312	11.152	12.624	15.338
17	6.408	7.255	8.672	10.085	12.002	13.531	16.338
18	7.015	7.906	9.390	10.865	12.857	14.440	17.338
19	7.633	8.567	10.117	11.651	13.716	15.352	18.338
20	8.260	9.237	10.851	12.443	14.578	16.266	19.337
21	8.897	9.915	11.591	13.240	15.445	17.182	20.337
22	9.542	10.600	12.338	14.041	16.314	18.101	21.337
23	10.196	11.293	13.091	14.848	17.187	19.021	22.337
24	10.856	11.992	13.848	15.659	18.062	19.943	23.337
25	11.524	12.697	14.611	16.473	18.940	20.867	24.337
26	12.198	13.409	15.379	17.292	19.820	21.792	25.336
27	12.879	14.125	16.151	18.114	20.703	22.719	26.336
28	13.565	14.847	16.928	18.939	21.588	23.647	27.336
29	14.256	15.574	17.708	19.768	22.475	24.577	28.336
30	14.953	16.306	18.493	20.599	23.364	25.508	29.336

continued

For larger values of df, the expression $\sqrt{2\chi^2} - \sqrt{2df - 1}$ may be used as a normal deviate with unit variance, remembering that the probability of χ^2 corresponds with that of a single tail of the normal curve.

Source: I am grateful to the Literary Executor of the late Sir Ronald A. Fisher, F.R.S., to Dr. Frank Yates, F.R.S., and to Longman Group Ltd., London, for permission to reprint Table IV from their book *Statistical Tables for Biological, Agricultural, and Medical Research* (6th Edition, 1974).

Appendix F: Distribution of Chi Square

			Probability				
df	.30	.20	.10	.05	.02	.01	.001
1	1.074	1.642	2.706	3.841	5.412	6.635	10.827
2	2.408	3.219	4.605	5.991	7.824	9.210	13.815
3	3.665	4.642	6.251	7.815	9.837	11.341	16.268
4	4.878	5.989	7.779	9.488	11.668	13.277	18.465
5	6.064	7.289	9.236	11.070	13.388	15.086	20.517
6	7.231	8.558	10.645	12.592	15.033	16.812	22.457
7	8.383	9.803	12.017	14.067	16.622	18.475	24.322
8	9.524	11.030	13.362	15.507	18.168	20.090	29.125
9	10.656	12.242	14.684	16.919	19.679	21.666	27.877
10	11.781	13.442	15.987	18.307	21.161	23.209	29.588
11	12.899	14.631	17.275	19.675	22.618	24.725	31.264
12	14.011	15.812	18.549	21.026	24.054	26.217	32.909
13	15.119	16.985	19.812	22.362	25.472	27.688	34.528
14	16.222	18.151	21.064	23.685	26.873	29.141	36.123
15	17.322	19.311	22.307	24.996	28.259	30.578	37.697
16	18.841	20.465	23.542	26.296	29.633	32.000	39.252
17	15.511	21.615	24.769	27.587	30.995	33.409	40.790
18	20.601	22.760	25.989	28.869	32.346	34.805	42.312
19	21.689	23.900	27.204	30.144	33.687	36.191	43.820
20	22.775	25.038	28.412	31.410	35.020	37.566	45.315
21	23.858	26.171	29.615	32.671	36.343	38.932	46.797
22	24.939	27.301	30.813	33.924	37.659	40.289	48.268
23	26.018	28.429	32.007	35.172	38.968	41.638	49.728
24	27.096	29.553	33.196	36.415	40.270	42.980	51.179
25	28.172	30.675	34.382	37.652	41.566	44.314	52.620
26	29.246	31.795	35.563	38.885	42.856	45.642	54.052
27	30.319	32.912	36.741	40.113	44.140	46.963	55.476
28	31.391	34.027	37.916	41.337	45.419	48.278	56.893
29	32.461	35.139	39.087	42.557	46.693	49.588	58.302
30	35.530	36.250	40.256	43.773	47.962	50.892	59.703

Appendix G: Normal Curve Areas

z	.00	.01	.02	.03	.04	.05	.06	.07	.08	.09
0.0	.0000	.0040	.0080	.0120	.0160	.0199	.0239	.0279	.0319	.0359
0.1	.0398	.0438	.0478	.0517	.0557	.0596	.0636	.0675	.0714	.0753
0.2	.0793	.0832	.0871	.0910	.0948	.0987	.1026	.1064	.1103	.1141
0.3	.1179	.1217	.1255	.1293	.1331	.1368	.1406	.1443	.1480	.1517
0.4	.1554	.1591	.1628	.1664	.1700	.1736	.1772	.1808	.1844	.1879
0.5	.1915	.1950	.1985	.2019	.2054	.2088	.2123	.2157	.2190	.2224
0.6	.2257	.2291	.2324	.2357	.2389	.2422	.2454	.2486	.2517	.2549
0.7	.2580	.2611	.2642	.2673	.2704	.2734	.2764	.2794	.2823	.2852
0.8	.2881	.2910	.2939	.2967	.2995	.3023	.3051	.3078	.3106	.3133
0.9	.3159	.3186	.3212	.3238	.3264	.3289	.3315	.3340	.3365	.3389
1.0	.3413	.3438	.3461	.3485	.3508	.3531	.3554	.3577	.3599	.3621
1.1	.3643	.3665	.3686	.3708	.3729	.3749	.3770	.3790	.3810	.3830
1.2	.3849	.3869	.3888	.3907	.3925	.3944	.3962	.3980	.3997	.4015
1.3	.4032	.4049	.4066	.4082	.4099	.4115	.4131	.4147	.4162	.4177
1.4	.4192	.4207	.4222	.4236	.4251	.4265	.4279	.4292	.4306	.4319
1.5	.4332	.4345	.4357	.4370	.4382	.4394	.4406	.4418	.4429	.4441
1.6	.4452	.4463	.4474	.4484	.4495	.4505	.4515	.4525	.4535	.4545
1.7	.4554	.4564	.4573	.4582	.4591	.4599	.4608	.4616	.4625	.4633
1.8	.4641	.4649	.4656	.4664	.4671	.4678	.4686	.4693	.4699	.4706
1.9	.4713	.4719	.4726	.4732	.4738	.4744	.4750	.4756	.4761	.4767
2.0	.4772	.4778	.4783	.4788	.4793	.4798	.4803	.4808	.4812	.4817
2.1	.4821	.4826	.4830	.4834	.4838	.4842	.4846	.4850	.4854	.4857
2.2	.4861	.4864	.4868	.4871	.4875	.4878	.4881	.4884	.4887	.4890
2.3	.4893	.4896	.4898	.4901	.4904	.4906	.4909	.4911	.4913	.4916
2.4	.4918	.4920	.4922	.4925	.4927	.4929	.4931	.4932	.4934	.4936
2.5	.4938	.4940	.4941	.4943	.4945	.4946	.4948	.4949	.4951	.4952
2.6	.4953	.4955	.4956	.4957	.4959	.4960	.4961	.4962	.4963	.4964
2.7	.4965	.4966	.4967	.4968	.4969	.4970	.4971	.4972	.4973	.4974
2.8	.4974	.4975	.4976	.4977	.4977	.4978	.4979	.4979	.4980	.4981
2.9	.4981	.4982	.4982	.4983	.4984	.4984	.4985	.4985	.4986	.4986
3.0	.4987	.4987	.4987	.4988	.4988	.4989	.4989	.4989	.4990	.4990

Abridged from Table I of *Statistical Tables and Formulas,* by A. Hald (New York: John Wiley & Sons, Inc., 1952). Used by permission of John Wiley & Sons, Inc.

APPENDIX H: Estimated Sampling Error

How to use this table: Find the intersection between the sample size and the approximate percentage distribution of the binomial in the sample. The number appearing at this intersection represents the estimated sampling error, at the 95 percent confidence level, expressed in percentage points (plus or minus).

Example: In the sample of 400 respondents, 60 percent answer yes and 40 percent answer no. The sampling error is estimated at plus or minus 4.9 percentage points. The confidence interval, then, is between 55.1 percent and 64.9 percent. We would estimate (95 percent confidence) that the proportion of the total population who would say yes is somewhere within that interval.

Binomial Percentage Distribution

Sample Size	50/50	60/40	70/30	80/20	90/10
100	10	9.8	9.2	8	6
200	7.1	6.9	6.5	5.7	4.2
300	5.8	5.7	5.3	4.6	3.5
400	5	4.9	4.6	4	3
500	4.5	4.4	4.1	3.6	2.7
600	4.1	4	3.7	3.3	2.4
700	3.8	3.7	3.5	3	2.3
800	3.5	3.5	3.2	2.8	2.1
900	3.3	3.3	3.1	2.7	2
1000	3.2	3.1	2.9	2.5	1.9
1100	3	3	2.8	2.4	1.8
1200	2.9	2.8	2.6	2.3	1.7
1300	2.8	2.7	2.5	2.2	1.7
1400	2.7	2.6	2.4	2.1	1.6
1500	2.6	2.5	2.4	2.1	1.5
1600	2.5	2.4	2.3	2	1.5
1700	2.4	2.4	2.2	1.9	1.5
1800	2.4	2.3	2.2	1.9	1.4
1900	2.3	2.2	2.1	1.8	1.4
2000	2.2	2.2	2	1.8	1.3

APPENDIX

A Learner's Guide to SPSS 6.1[1]

JEFFREY M. JACQUES, PH.D.*
Department of Sociology and Criminal Justice
Florida A&M University

■ INSTRUCTIONAL GOALS

By the time you complete this appendix and do all the suggested exercises, you will know:

- When to use SPSS
- How to use basic SPSS 6.1 files created by others
- Which basic SPSS commands to use when performing statistical analysis such as:
  1. Univariate analysis
  2. Scaling
  3. Bivariate analysis
  4. Multivariate analysis
- How to create your own SPSS files
- How to build basic SPSS system files
- How to build an enhanced SPSS system file

■ INTRODUCTION

This Learner's Guide has been developed specifically for students and faculty who have an interest in understanding how to approach data analysis using state-of-the-art microcomputer technology. We shall concentrate on how best to use the computer and the powerful statistical/analytic software of SPSS: The Statistical Package for the Social Sciences, Version 6.1. We only assume here that you have a basic understanding of how to use your computer—whether it be an IBM/MS–DOS compatible, an Apple Macintosh/PowerPC, or a Unix-based system—and the graphic user interface (GUI) common among computers with a Windows-like environment.

In this Learner's Guide we shall emphasize the basic approach and practical skills that any professional might be expected to use routinely during his or her career. We shall examine carefully how best to evaluate and understand data collected by others as well as how best to work with data you or I might collect. Additionally, as a sophisticated consumer, your knowledge of the procedures outlined below will better prepare you to interpret the analytic work reported by others. Most important, you will have developed the basic skills in how to approach data analysis by becoming the researcher—by using your skills, your computer, and the sophisticated software of SPSS.

Strange as it may seem, the best place to begin a discussion of when to use the computer is not at the computer. Nor is a discussion of the software the best approach. The best place to start is with a clear understanding of what you wish to find out. The computer and SPSS are simply tools that can be used to help you: (1) summarize your data, (2) create appropriate tables and graphs, (3) examine relationships among variables, (4) perform tests of statistical significance based on your hypotheses, and (5) develop fairly sophisticated models. Indeed, because the computer and SPSS are extremely fast, you will be able to examine data and relationships among variables in a variety of ways heretofore unimagined. The basic point is this: If you understand your research questions thoroughly, then

---

[1] In the text, I shall use SPSS to stand for SPSS 6.1. Most of the later versions use a similar interface while earlier versions use a command line interface typically hidden from the user. In any case, SPSS^X, SPSS, SPSS for Windows, SPSS for Windows95, or SPSS PC+ produce similar statistical outputs that require appropriate interpretations. By the way, all procedures were tested with SPSS Version 6.1 for Windows and SPSS for the Macintosh editions.

*My thanks to the people who critiqued earlier versions of this appendix. I would particularly like to thank my long-time colleague Emmit Hunt at Florida A&M University and Kenneth Jacques, a sociology major, at The Florida State University.

your computer and SPSS can be very helpful when it comes to manipulating large amounts of data, finding patterns, and testing hypotheses.

One or two comments about what this appendix will not do. This appendix will not make you an expert at using your computer system or SPSS. We assume here that you have developed basic expertise working with Windows, Windows95, MacOS, etc. Nor will you become an SPSS consultant—well, not at first. SPSS software includes hundreds of commands, procedures, and options within these procedures. What this Learner's Guide will do is to emphasize the most often used commands and procedures, outline how best to approach a research study by using your hardware and software, show you the basic commands of SPSS, and show you step by step how to use the computer and SPSS, Version 6.1 to facilitate the analysis of data.

The Example

To help illustrate each step of the analytic-computer process, we shall use the results from the General Social Survey,[2] most often called the GSS. The GSS has been an ongoing survey of social indicators of the American population since 1972. Since that time, data were collected by carefully trained interviewers from a national multistage probability sample of approximately 1,500 English-speaking persons, 18 years of age or over, who were living in noninstitutional settings within the continental United States. Thus, data have been collected from more than 30,000 American adults over a 23-year period. The publisher provides a subset of these samples: 300 cases for each of the years of 1973, 1978, 1983, 1988, and 1993. Thus, a total of 1,500 cases and more than 50 variables have been provided to all instructors who adopted this text. You can use your copy of this data set to follow the examples below. In addition, you can go beyond these examples and examine relationships among other variables found on this same data file. Doing the suggested exercises on this data set will improve your mastery of SPSS.

One continuing focus of the GSS surveys was abortion—how Americans view the conditions under which women have the right to obtain a legal abortion. It is a topic that provokes strong feelings on both sides of the issue. At one extreme, it is argued, "Americans with a conscience" believe that reproductive rights are "issues of life and death for women, not mere matters of choice. NOW supports access to safe and legal abortion, to effective birth control, to reproductive health and education. We oppose attempts to restrict these rights through legislation, regulation (like the gag rule) or Constitutional amendment."[3] Similarly, "Americans with a conscience," it is argued from the other side, believe that life begins at conception, that the developing fetus experiences sleep and wakefulness and awareness, and that it is morally and religiously abhorrent to take a life, particularly while that life is growing in the womb.[4]

While each group has eloquently stated their position, the overall research questions for us to explore include:

- How frequently are such views held? or Where do most Americans stand on the right of women to obtain a legal abortion?
- What are the descriptive characteristics of people associated with each position?
- Why do people hold these divergent attitudes?

Your previous work in research methods has included a discussion of the need to operationalize important concepts. The GSS survey research team at the National Opinion Research Center (NORC), University of Chicago, chose to operationalize Americans' attitudes toward legal abortion by including a total of seven questions. They included the following statement and questions:

Please tell me whether or not *you* think it should be possible for a pregnant woman to obtain a *legal* abortion:

1. If there is a strong chance of serious defect in the baby?
2. If she is married and does not want any more children?
3. If the woman's own health is seriously endangered by the pregnancy?

---

[2] Davis, James Allan, and Smith, Tom W. *General Social Surveys, 1972–1994*. Principal Investigator, James A. Davis; Director and Co-Principal Investigator, Tom W. Smith. NORC ed. Chicago: National Opinion Research Center, producer, 1994; Storrs, CT: The Roper Center for Public Opinion Research, University of Connecticut, distribution. 1 data file (32,380 logical records) and 1 codebook (1,073 pp).

[3] NOW statement on reproductive rights. National Organization for Women 10/83. Revised 1/95. http://www.now.org:80/general.html#Reproductive, May, 1996.

[4] See ProLife News at http://hebron.ee.gannon.edu/~frezza/AboutPLN.html, May, 1996, and related documents.

FIGURE 1
Working Model of Legal Abortion Attitude Study

- Year of Study
- Gender, Race, Age
- Religion & Attendance Patterns
- Education and Income
- Marital Status, Number of Children
- Political Party, Political Viewpoint

→ Attitudes Toward a Woman's Right to a Legal Abortion

4. If the family has a very low income and cannot afford any more children?
5. If she became pregnant as a result of rape?
6. If she is not married and does not want to marry the man?
7. If the woman wants it for any reason?[5]

To each of these statements, thousands of GSS respondents could answer: "Yes," "No," "Don't Know," or simply refuse to respond. Most people responded "Yes" or "No" to most questions. Thus it is possible to use these data to explore where most Americans stand on the issue of access to legal abortion services.

In addition to attitudes toward abortion and many other topical areas of interest (e.g., crime, welfare, government, etc.), the GSS survey team collected background information on respondents: income, occupational prestige, marital status, age, education, sex, race, family status and number of children, religious affiliation and church attendance patterns, and political party membership and political views. (Although the GSS includes more than 2000 variables, we shall restrict our analysis to these background variables and the seven attitude questions on abortion rights.) Thus we can describe the characteristics of Americans and their associated views toward legal abortion as well as attempt to explain why various attitudes are held.

Our study provides an opportunity to test the general hypothesis that in America, attitudes toward legal abortion can be explained, in part, by the life experiences and social categories of Americans. More specifically, we can examine the following questions:

1. What are the current views of Americans toward a woman's right to a legal abortion?
2. Were there significant changes in Americans' attitudes toward a woman's right to a legal abortion over the last two decades?

---
[5]This question was added in 1977. The previous six items were included in each survey year.

FIGURE 2
Initial Display Screen for SPSS 6.1

3. Are there significant differences among people from different racial groups, gender categories, age groups, or religious organizations on the variables used to measure attitudes toward legal abortion?
4. Are there significant differences between people with different familial experiences (e.g., marital status, having children) on the variables used to measure attitudes toward legal abortion?
5. Are there significant correlations between the variables of income or education with attitudes toward legal abortion?
6. Is there any substantial difference between how those who identify with the Democratic or Republican party view a woman's right of access to a legal abortion? What about self-described political views—conservatism or liberalism—and their relationship to attitudes toward a woman's right to a legal abortion?
7. What variable, or combinations of variables, are the best predictors of Americans' attitudes toward legal abortion?

A short summary of the model of this research project may be found in Figure 1. This model, and our research questions, will guide our examination of the GSS data set and our use of the computer via SPSS.

■ WORKING WITH THE GENERAL SOCIAL SURVEY (GSS) DATA

By now you have probably mastered the fundamentals of how to structure a research project, how to develop an instrument, and how to select your sample. Here's where you get a chance to start your examination of the data collected by the National Opinion Research Center and reported in the GSS.

Go ahead and boot your computer[6]—turn on the monitor, the CPU, and all related equipment. When the screen lights up, find and launch SPSS Version 6.1. After some time and a few clicks and clanks of the hard drive, your screen should look like that of Figure 2.

---

[6]If you are planning to use your college's computer lab, this is a good time to find out about your college's resources and which version of SPSS you will be using. If you don't know about your college's computer lab, ask your teacher or a fellow student. Then, get the help you need by telling the computer personnel what you plan to do. They will probably set up an account for you and give you documentation on how to use your college's system and how to access SPSS. Unfortunately, there is no single standard for all computer sites. So, take your time and find out.

FIGURE 3
Display Screen with GSS Loaded for SPSS

	year	abany	abdefect	abhlth	abnomore	abpoor	abrape	absingle
1	73	0	2	1	2	2	2	2
2	73	0	1	1	1	1	1	1
3	73	0	1	1	1	1	1	1
4	73	0	1	1	2	2	1	2
5	73	0	2	2	2	2	2	2
6	73	0	2	1	2	2	1	2
7	73	0	1	1	2	2	1	1

When you launch successfully SPSS 6.1, you will see a screen similar to that of Figure 2. It will have a menu bar with the typical options of "File," "Edit," etc. across the top, a row of icons that perform many of the same functions as those listed in the menu bar immediately below, and at least two layers of windows.[7] At the bottom you will see the status bar, which will provide changing information about what SPSS is doing. When SPSS is ready for your command(s), the status bar will report: "SPSS Processor is ready" in the lower left part of your SPSS window.

Most of the screen is reserved for your data, input or syntax window, and output window. For now, we'll work with two basic windows. In the foreground you will see a data editor window, which will display the "active file" or "working file" data in a series of rows—typically one row for each respondent—and a series of columns—typically one column for each variable (e.g., YEAR, SEX, RACE, etc.). In the background will be the output window for displaying textual outputs—the results of all commands you use. We'll examine this soon.

To load the GSS file, simply use your mouse to choose from the menu bar at the top of the screen:

File ➤
    Open . . .

and then choose from the selection box GSS7393s.sav if you wish to work with the smaller version (fewer variables as required by SPSS 6.1 for Windows Student Version), or GSS7393.sav if you choose to work with the larger file and any standard SPSS version. As illustrated in Figure 3, variable names (year, abany, abdefect, age, race, sex, etc.) appear at the top of each column and each row includes the response of each GSS respondent.

You can examine additional variables by using the arrow graphics at the end of the scroll bar at the bottom of the data editor display window, and you can examine additional respondents' data by using the arrows at the end of the scroll bar at the right of the display window. A simple press on any of the arrow graphics at each corner of the scroll bars will give a slightly different view of the data set. Try it. To get back to the original display, press the arrow at the opposite location of the same scroll bar or, from the menu bar, choose:

Data ➤
    Go to Case . . .

---

[7] The number of layers will depend on the preferences you set in the Preference option of the Edit menu.

and enter a 1 in the space provided. A simple press of the return key will bring the display to the first case of the data set.

■ WORKING WITH SOMEONE ELSE'S DATA

Initial Activities: Step 1

The first goal of working with someone else's data is to understand what has been provided. Most data sets come with a complete codebook—a complete listing of all the variables (what each variable name means, e.g., abany = "[O]btain a legal abortion: If the woman wants it for any reason"), the codes used for each attribute (e.g., 1 = "Yes," 2 = "No"), and how those who did not respond, or were not asked, were coded (e.g., 0 or blank for "Never Asked/Not Applicable," 8 for "Don't Know," or 9 "No answer").

When no such codebook is provided, you can see a roster of variables, one variable at a time, by using:

Utilities ➤
   Variables . . .

which will provide an information or dialogue box. In this dialogue box, the left-hand side will list all the variables in the working file and the associated variable information to its right. As you select each variable in its picker box by using your mouse and "clicking" on the variable of interest, the summary information will change at the right. Try it.

To get a complete list of all variables used by SPSS, you can create a dictionary of what is included in the data set by using the File Info subcommand. From the menu bar at the top of the screen, choose:

Utilities ➤
   File Info

and you will get a complete roster of all the variables in your active file written to the output window. Your output, in the output window, will include a report that will have a format similar to this:

```
ABANY    ABORTION IF WOMAN WANTS FOR ANY REASON          2
            Print Format: F1
            Write Format: F1
            Missing Values: 0, 8, 9

            Value     Label
                0 M   NAP
                1     YES
                2     NO
                8 M   DK
                9 M   NA
```

Pretty much what you would expect. The name of the variable is listed first (e.g., ABANY) and its corresponding label next ("ABORTION IF A WOMAN WANTS FOR ANY REASON"). The number to the far right is the variable position in the file—in this case, the variable ABANY is the second variable in this data set. Immediately below the variable label is a roster of how SPSS will handle the data when printed or written to another file (in both cases, "F1" indicates a numeric display one character wide). Missing values (e.g., 0, 8, 9) are those values that will be excluded when statistical summaries and analyses are calculated. More important, all values, and their associated labels, are listed next. A "0" is used for "Not Applicable," "1" for "Yes," and "2" for "No." Note that between the values and labels (e.g., 0, 8, and 9) is the capital letter "M" for "missing values" designation, again. You can now examine the remaining variables and clearly see what is included in this file.

Exercise 1: If you do have access to a computer, SPSS, and the GSS data set, try these commands (Utilities ➤ File Info) yourself. When the !Untitled Output Window is the front most active window, you can scroll—using the scroll bar at your far right—to see the dictionary for each of the variables. You can print a copy of this dictionary, assuming that you are connected to a printer, by choosing from the menu bar, File and then Print. This is always a good first step. If you do not have access to this equipment, look at the end of this appendix for a complete roster of GSS codebook information.

Basic Working and System Files   Now that we have the data entered into an active SPSS file we must tell the computer how to manipulate the data. This is where we will use SPSS commands that instruct SPSS what to do with the data in our GSS data set.

SPSS Commands   While you will be selecting most of your procedures from a menu system, you need to know how SPSS is generating the commands. Each time you select a menu item or its submenu component, SPSS is building an SPSS command. SPSS commands are composed of at least two parts—the first is the command name or keyword(s) (e.g., LIST, FREQUENCIES, etc.) while the second is the specifications (typically a list of your variables on which you wish to execute this command). Thus, SPSS generates, behind the scenes, appropriate information that it then processes using your data to know which file management or statistical procedures you wish to execute. For example, when we requested Utilities ➤ File Info we created a command, DISPLAY DICTIONARY,[8] which SPSS then executed to produce the roster of all variables and their elements.

Similarly, to produce a roster of the data actually in the file we could choose from the menu bar:

Statistics ➤
  Summarize ➤
    List Cases . . .

which would then bring up a dialog box like that of Figure 4.

All of this is used to produce a standard list output from an English-like command that actually looks something like this:

```
LIST VARIABLES = YEAR, SEX, RACE.
```

We'll have more to say about this later. But for now, it is important to remember that command names (i.e., LIST) come first, the subcommand of VARIABLES= follows closely, while the specifications or variable names (i.e., YEAR, SEX, RACE)—that which is specific about your study—follow immediately after the subcommand.

You say that you are using SPSS 6.1, so why bother to know this? Good question. You will find knowing how to structure SPSS commands is an important asset when we start working with complex commands that are not easily developed using the menu system. Similarly, if you make an error developing a command, you may find it easier to fix your errors using the syntax window than by trying to re-create complex commands using the menu system. In addition, SPSS is in fact writing these commands in this format to a separate file, typically titled spss.jnl, which you may find useful when you are working in a production environment. Speaking of a production environment, you can save your commands in a file for later use under a separate file name and then "reuse" them with different data that use the same variables or variable names as often as you wish.[9]

Data Cleaning and Error Checking: Step 2

Whether you plan to enter the data for this study yourself—to be discussed later—or are using data entered by others, it is always a good idea to check the veracity of the data. Most people take considerable care in entering the data

---

[8] If DISPLAY DICTIONARY is not listed on the !OUTPUT window and you are using the SPSS standard version, go to the

Edit ➤
  Preferences ➤
    Output . . .

and then select (place an X in the box by clicking on it) the box labeled "Display" in the "Command" options in the upper left corner.

[9] Alas, this option is not available if you are using the SPSS 6.1: Student Version.

FIGURE 4
LIST CASES Dialog Box

from any study. However, even the most careful data entry person will make a few errors—especially after entering several hundreds of data values.

One approach to error checking is to examine the data set directly. From the "File Info" command you have a roster of variables and labels for valid values and missing values. You can, with the LIST command, produce a roster of values for each and every variable. By checking both rosters you can identify data entry errors. For example, the attributes for the variable SEX has been assigned "1" for "Male" and "2" for "Female" as the only valid entries. Any values other than these would be due to data entry errors. Thus, a value of 3 entered for the variable of SEX would be an invalid value and should be changed to the correct value, when known, or to a standard missing value.

The LIST Command While this is only useful if you are working with a relatively small file, the LIST CASES command will list the values for each variable for each respondent. If you wish a complete listing of all the variables and the values for each person in the study, you would include the following commands. Choose, from the menu bar:

Statistics ➤
  Summarize ➤
    List Cases . . .

You will then be given a dialog box, as seen in Figure 4. Simply select the variables of interest to you—choose from those listed in the left box, press the ➤ button to transfer them to the Variable(s): box, and, when finished, press "OK." By default, SPSS 6.1 will give you a complete listing of all cases in your output window. To see all the results simply use the scroll bar at the right of the output window. Point the arrow of the mouse at the box in the scroll bar, hold the mouse button down, and then drag the mouse up to see earlier pages.

To restrict the number of cases—say, to 20 cases—simply choose the option in the lower left portion of the screen and enter 20 in the "First through" box. Then click the "OK" button. A typical output would look like Table 1.

A Better Approach: FREQUENCIES A better approach for checking data entry errors, as well as getting a first peek at the variables of interest, involves running the procedure, FREQUENCIES. This procedure will produce a summary table of values for each variable. Since you know from your codebook/dictionary the valid maximum and minimum values for each variable, any reported value(s) outside this range would indicate a data entry error.

TABLE 1
Output from LIST VARIABLES=YEAR, SEX, RACE Command

```
YEAR SEX RACE
 73   1    1
 73   2    1
 73   2    1
 73   2    1
 73   1    1
 73   2    1
 73   1    1
 73   2    1
 73   1    1
 73   2    1
 73   2    1
 73   1    1
 73   1    1
 73   1    1
 73   2    1
 73   1    1
 73   1    1
 73   2    1
 73   1    1
 73   2    1
Number of cases read:    20    Number of cases listed:   20
```

In SPSS 6.1, make sure that you have loaded an active file by going to the menu bar and selecting

Window ➤
   GSS7393s.sav. (or whatever your file name is)

This will bring the data set window to the foreground. Now, point and click the mouse at menu option:

Statistics ➤
   Summarize ➤
      Frequencies . . .

This will open a dialog box for the FREQUENCIES command where you can identify each of the variables of interest. Once you choose a variable of interest, press the ➤ button [10] in the middle of the dialog box to move the selected variable to the "Variable(s):" box. See Figure 5.

Repeat this for as many variables with which you wish to work. A simple press of the "OK" button will force SPSS 6.1 to write the results to your !OUTPUT window. (Click on the "!output" window, or select it from the window command of the menu bar, to see these results.) See Table 2 for an example of a typical output window.

Alternately, you can type in the syntax window [11] the FREQUENCIES command. It is easy to enter. Minimally, it consists of:

```
FREQUENCIES VARIABLES=variable_name(s).
```

---

[10] Alternately, you can double-click on the variable name and SPSS will transfer it to the Variable(s) box for processing.

[11] The syntax window is simply a third window. It provides an opportunity to key-in SPSS commands by by-passing the menu system—which is used to generate these same commands. It is often much more efficient to use the syntax window than the menu system. If no syntax window is open and you are using the SPSS 6.1 standard version, do:

Edit ➤
   Preferences . . .

and then click on the box "Open a syntax window at start-up to run SPSS commands."

FIGURE 5
FREQUENCIES Dialog Box

```
┌─────────────────────────────────────────────┐
│                 Frequencies                  │
│                                              │
│  abdefect  ▲    Variable(s):      ┌──────┐  │
│  abhlth    ▓       year      ▲    │  OK  │  │
│  abnomore  ▓       sex            └──────┘  │
│  abpoor    ▓       race           ┌──────┐  │
│  abrape   ▶▶       abany          │Paste │  │
│  absingle                         └──────┘  │
│  age                              ┌──────┐  │
│  anomia5   ▼                 ▼    │Reset │  │
│                                   └──────┘  │
│                                   ┌──────┐  │
│                                   │Cancel│  │
│                                   └──────┘  │
│                                   ┌──────┐  │
│                                   │ Help │  │
│                                   └──────┘  │
│  ☒ Display frequency tables                  │
│         ┌─────────┐ ┌───────┐ ┌────────┐    │
│         │Statistics│ │Charts.│ │Format..│    │
│         └─────────┘ └───────┘ └────────┘    │
└─────────────────────────────────────────────┘
```

You can identify each variable name.[12]

`FREQUENCIES VARIABLES= YEAR SEX RACE.`

and then execute the command. This command will create the same results and write them to your !OUTPUT window.

In either case, a comparison between the values reported in the value column of each table and the values listed in your dictionary will enable you to capture invalid entries.

If you do find a data entry error, here's how to find and fix an error fast. Let's assume that your Frequencies procedure produced a table for the variable of SEX with mostly "1"s—"males," and "2"s—"females," and one "3." You know that the value of "3" is an invalid value and you wish to change the data in the file. Just select the first cell under the variable name SEX in the Data Editor window. Now, from the menu bar, choose:

Edit ➤
  Search For Data . . .

and enter the value 3 in the text box titled:"Search." A simple press on the button "Search Forward" would identify the offending entry and place you in the appropriate row and cell. If you know the correct value, type over the incorrect value in the Data Editor window and "Save" the corrected information. If you don't know the correct value, enter an appropriate missing value (e.g., 0, 8, or 9—that which is defined as a missing value in the codebook or dictionary). Fast, simple, and neat.

Whichever SPSS version you have chosen to use, the output should confirm that all the values recorded for the variables are appropriate.

Take a minute and examine closely Table 2. It provides a quick "first look" at the pattern of response across the 1,500 sampled Americans as reported in this GSS data subset. The file includes an equal number of respondents/cases (i.e., 300 cases) from each year of study (i.e., 1973, 1978, 1983, 1988, and 1993); more white respondents than any other racial designation—88% were "white," 9.7% reported "Black" and 2.3% reported "Other"; and more female than male respondents—590 were male (39.3%) while 910 were female (60.7%). All these variables had no missing data.

---

[12]Or you may be able to use the FREQUENCIES command and the keyword, ALL, by writing the command line in the "!untitled syntax" window. This command substitutes for naming each and every variable in your active file. Then run the command.

TABLE 2
Typical FREQUENCIES Output

```
YEAR        GSS YEAR FOR THIS RESPONDENT
                                              Valid      Cum
Value Label              Value  Frequency  Percent  Percent  Percent

                           73      300      20.0     20.0     20.0
                           78      300      20.0     20.0     40.0
                           83      300      20.0     20.0     60.0
                           88      300      20.0     20.0     80.0
                           93      300      20.0     20.0    100.0
                                 -------  -------  -------
                         Total    1500     100.0    100.0

Valid cases    1500    Missing cases     0
- - - - - - - - - - - - - - - - - - - - - - - - - - - - - - - -

SEX         RESPONDENTS SEX
                                              Valid      Cum
Value Label              Value  Frequency  Percent  Percent  Percent

MALE                       1       590      39.3     39.3     39.3
FEMALE                     2       910      60.7     60.7    100.0
                                 -------  -------  -------
                         Total    1500     100.0    100.0

Valid cases    1500    Missing cases     0
- - - - - - - - - - - - - - - - - - - - - - - - - - - - - - - -

RACE        RACE OF RESPONDENT
                                              Valid      Cum
Value Label              Value  Frequency  Percent  Percent  Percent

WHITE                      1      1320      88.0     88.0     88.0
BLACK                      2       146       9.7      9.7     97.7
OTHER                      3        34       2.3      2.3    100.0
                                 -------  -------  -------
                         Total    1500     100.0    100.0

Valid cases    1500    Missing cases     0
- - - - - - - - - - - - - - - - - - - - - - - - - - - - - - - -

ABANY       ABORTION IF WOMAN WANTS FOR ANY REASON
                                              Valid      Cum
Value Label              Value  Frequency  Percent  Percent  Percent

YES                        1       448      29.9     38.1     38.1
NO                         2       728      48.5     61.9    100.0
NAP                        0       300      20.0   Missing
DK                         8        22       1.5   Missing
NA                         9         2        .1   Missing
                                 -------  -------  -------
                         Total    1500     100.0    100.0

Valid cases    1176    Missing cases   324
```

FIGURE 6
CROSTABS Dialog Box

Of these same 1,500 cases, 1,176 answered the question on "Abortion for any reason" with "valid" responses (responding either "Yes"—448 or "No"—728) while two respondents did not answer, 22 "Didn't know," and 300 were classified as "Not Applicable"—NAP. Thus, of all 1,500 respondents, 29.9% said "Yes" while 48.5% said "No;" of those who gave a valid response, 38.1% said "Yes" while 61.9% said "No." SPSS nicely provides both ways of looking—including and excluding missing cases—at the response pattern.

One More Approach: Crosstabs The CROSSTABS procedure is useful for creating tabular displays of two variables at a time. This is especially important when you wish to confirm that the respondents had consistent patterns across a set of descriptive variables. For example, we noted earlier that for the variable of ABANY, 300 cases were classified "NAP" and treated as missing. We may use the SPSS procedure, CROSSTABS, to find out if there is a pattern.

Using SPSS 6.1, choose:

Statistics ➤
  Summarize ➤
    Crosstabs . . .

which opens a dialog box like that of Figure 6.

Select ABANY and press the ➤ key on top and closest to the keyword "Row(s)." Scroll down so you can select YEAR and press the ➤ key nearest the word column. A press on the OK button will produce a table like that of Table 3.

Or, the CROSSTAB command may be entered from the syntax window:

```
CROSSTABS TABLES=varlist BY varlist
```

For looking at the ABANY response pattern by YEAR, the minimal CROSSTABS command becomes:

```
CROSSTABS TABLES=ABANY BY YEAR
```

Using either procedure produces a table. Note that in the lower right hand corner of Table 3, 1,176 cases are reported. Not surprisingly, 448 "Yes" and 728 "No" responses were recorded—look across the rows of the table. Similarly slightly less than 300 responses were noted for each of the listed years—look down each column—labeled 78,

TABLE 3
Typical CROSSTABS Output: ABANY BY YEAR

```
ABANY   ABORTION IF WOMAN WANTS FOR ANY REASON
 by  YEAR   GSS YEAR FOR THIS RESPONDENT

                    YEAR                         Page 1 of 1
            Count |
                  |
                  |
                  |               Row
                  |    78|    83|    88|    93| Total
  ABANY     ------+------+------+------+------+
              1   |   109|    99|   104|   136|   448
  YES            |      |      |      |      |   38.1
                  +------+------+------+------+
              2   |   185|   198|   186|   159|   728
  NO              |      |      |      |      |   61.9
                  +------+------+------+------+
           Column     294    297    290    295   1176
           Total     25.0   25.3   24.7   25.1  100.0

  Number of Missing Observations:   324
```

83, 88, and 93. All this is consistent with our earlier FREQUENCIES run. But note that there is no column for 1973, even though 1973 was listed earlier. Thus, the 300 cases we found as "NAP" when we ran the FREQUENCIES command have been identified as occurring in 1973—the missing year of the data.

There are other useful crosstabs when searching for incongruities in the data. Let's assume that we are interested in the joint distribution of race by sex over the life of the study, as well as looking at race and sex for each year. To start with we would choose:

Statistics ➤
  Summarize ➤
    Crosstabs . . .

(If there are entries in the Row(s) and Column(s) boxes, press reset.) Now, select the variable of SEX for Row(s) and RACE for Column(s). A press of OK will produce a table similar to the first table in Table 6. Most (88%) of the respondents were white with more than half of these being "FEMALE"—910 versus 590 for "MALE."

Return to your CROSSTABS dialog box and now, in the bottom entry box, choose the variable YEAR. A press of the "OK" button produces a series of tables—one for each year. See Table 4. By inspection of each year (i.e., YEAR GSS YEAR FOR THIS RESPONDENT, Value = 73, 78, 83, 88, or 93) we can see that each table includes 300 cases (as we would expect from what we learned from the FREQUENCIES run) and that the distribution of these data is pretty consistent across the years. This completes Table 4. Take a minute and review it carefully.

One more use of CROSSTABS should be noted. When more than one variable has been used to measure the same concept, or related concepts, we have an opportunity to check the reliability, and thus the veracity, of these variables and make a judgment about the entire data set. We have that opportunity here: Data were collected about educational background using two variables—(1) number of years of education, and (2) earned degree. Using the complete 1972–1994 GSS data set, it is interesting to examine this joint distribution. See Table 5.

Each row indicates the number of years of completed education (i.e., 0 through 20 years) while each column reports the highest earned degree (i.e., less than H.S., High School, Junior College, Bachelor, and Graduate degrees). Of the 31,664 randomly sampled respondents, 31,510 answered queries on both variables—number of years of education and highest earned degree. Just as we could find using FREQUENCIES, respondents more often reported 12 years of education (32.7%) than any other year, with 16 years of education being second most common (10.4%). Not surprisingly, the most often reported earned degree was earning a high school diploma (51.4%). Inspection of

TABLE 4
Typical CROSSTABS Output: RACE, SEX, AND YEAR*

```
SEX    RESPONDENTS SEX   by   RACE   RACE OF RESPONDENT

                    RACE                         Page 1 of 1
             Count |
                   |WHITE    BLACK    OTHER
                   |                            Row
                   |    1 |      2 |      3 | Total
     SEX     ------+--------+--------+--------+
               1   |   532 |     49 |      9 |   590
         MALE     |        |        |        |  39.3
             ------+--------+--------+--------+
               2   |   788 |     97 |     25 |   910
       FEMALE     |        |        |        |  60.7
             ------+--------+--------+--------+
             Column   1320      146       34     1500
             Total    88.0      9.7      2.3    100.0

Number of Missing Observations:  0
-------------------------------------------------------------------
SEX    RESPONDENTS SEX   by   RACE   RACE OF RESPONDENT
Controlling for..
YEAR   GSS YEAR FOR THIS RESPONDENT   Value = 73

                    RACE                         Page 1 of 1
             Count |
                   |WHITE    BLACK    OTHER
                   |                            Row
                   |    1 |      2 |      3 | Total
     SEX     ------+--------+--------+--------+
               1   |   119 |      9 |      1 |   129
         MALE     |        |        |        |  43.0
             ------+--------+--------+--------+
               2   |   149 |     20 |      2 |   171
       FEMALE     |        |        |        |  57.0
             ------+--------+--------+--------+
             Column    268       29        3      300
             Total    89.3      9.7      1.0    100.0

SEX    RESPONDENTS SEX   by   RACE   RACE OF RESPONDENT
Controlling for..
YEAR   GSS YEAR FOR THIS RESPONDENT   Value = 78

                    RACE                         Page 1 of 1
             Count |
                   |WHITE    BLACK    OTHER
                   |                            Row
                   |    1 |      2 |      3 | Total
     SEX     ------+--------+--------+--------+
               1   |    99 |     12 |      1 |   112
         MALE     |        |        |        |  37.3
             ------+--------+--------+--------+
               2   |   172 |     15 |      1 |   188
       FEMALE     |        |        |        |  62.7
             ------+--------+--------+--------+
             Column    271       27        2      300
             Total    90.3      9.0       .7    100.0
```
----
*Partial Output - 1983, 1988, and 1993 not included in this table.

TABLE 5
CROSSTABS Output: EDUCATION BY DEGREE

DEGREE BY EDUCATION

Count	LT HIGH SCHOOL 0	HIGH SCHOOL 1	JUNIOR COLLEGE 2	BACHELOR 3	GRADUATE 4	Row Total
EDUC 0	90	1				91 / 0.3
1	31					31 / 0.1
2	71					71 / 0.2
3	164					164 / 0.5
4	234					234 / 0.7
5	292	1				293 / 0.9
6	474					474 / 1.5
7	668					668 / 2.1
8	1967	8				1975 / 6.3
9	1132	133				1265 / 4
10	1552	191				1743 / 5.5
11	1638	380		1		2019 / 6.4
12	297	10004	2	3	3	10309 / 32.7
13	56	2266	37	1		2360 / 7.5
14	26	2054	778	16	6	2880 / 9.1
15	12	899	263	42	6	1222 / 3.9
16	7	190	71	2863	135	3266 / 10.4
17	2	32	13	515	243	805 / 2.6
18		18	5	212	593	828 / 2.6
19		4	1	66	280	351 / 1.1
20	1	9	2	47	402	461 / 1.5
Column Total	8714 / 27.7	16190 / 51.4	1172 / 3.7	3766 / 12	1668 / 5.3	31510 / 100

Number of Missing Observations: 154

the body of the table indicates that 10,004 of the 31,510 respondents completed 12 years of education and earned a high school diploma. No surprises here. Similarly, those who held a degree from a junior college (N=1,172) most often had 14 years of education (778 of the 1,172 respondents) while those with a baccalaureate degree (N=3,766) typically reported 16 years of education (2,863 of the 3,766 respondents). Such data make sense and support our assessment of reliability.

But clearly some of the response patterns do not make logical sense. A few respondents reported 15, 16, or 17 years of education but never earned a degree: That is, 12 people reported 15 years of education, 7 people reported 16 years of education, and 2 people reported 17 years of education, but none of these same people reported earning any educational degree(s). Additional data incongruities should be examined. While some respondents may have earned a H.S. diploma early with only 10 or 11 years of school—perhaps earning a H.S. degree via a GED program—it is unlikely that those eight people who had completed only eight years of school had, in fact, earned a H.S. diploma. It is even more unlikely that the five respondents who reported 11, 12, or 13 years of education earned a baccalaureate degree. While most people reported their education in a reliable manner, some people likely "fudged" their educational information. You may find these respondents and change their data to a missing code or, as you will learn later, simply tell SPSS to ignore these respondents.

Exercise 2: Why not take some time, load your SPSS file, and try the summarize commands of FREQUENCIES and CROSSTABS. After you re-create the tables noted above, try other variables, commands, and optional subcommands. When using the CROSSTABS command, make sure that you examine carefully the joint distribution of DEGREE and EDUCation. Which data appear reasonable? Which data appear unreasonable? Why? If you find some errors, make appropriate corrections and save your file using a new file name.

Useful Descriptive Statistics: Step 3

The third step when working with files prepared by others is to develop a clear picture of who were the respondents. Thus, a brief demographic descriptive profile should be gleaned from the data. There are several SPSS procedures that are very efficient tools for this purpose—some of which you have begun to master already. They include FREQUENCIES, DESCRIPTIVES, and CROSSTABS. You have mastered the procedures FREQUENCIES and CROSSTABS so that you could find errors in the data set. Now, we can use these same procedures to develop a clear description of the characteristics of the respondents.

The use of the FREQUENCIES procedure takes a moment of thought. It is a powerful procedure that will list all values of each variable as well as all possible summary statistics (i.e., measures of central tendency—mean, median, mode, measures of dispersion—range, variance, standard error, and the shape of the distribution—skewness and kurtosis). This is at once an asset as well as a liability. While it makes sense to make such calculations for interval-level variables (e.g., age, number of years of completed education, etc.), it makes less sense for ordinal-level variables (e.g., degree, church/synagogue attendance) and no sense for nominal-level variables with three or more categories (e.g., race, religion, etc.).

Thus, while you can ask SPSS to compute such summary descriptive statistics for each and every numeric variable—even variables that use numerals as descriptive codes, SPSS assumes that you have the sophistication to know when to use each summary statistic. Here's a rule of thumb based on the earlier text discussion of levels of measurement:

If the Variable Is Measured at the	Then Use the Measure(s) of Central Tendency of:
NOMINAL LEVEL	MODE & reported percents
ORDINAL LEVEL	+ MEDIAN
INTERVAL & RATIO LEVEL	+ MEAN, Standard Dev

Now, to execute the Frequencies command, choose:

Statistics ➤
    Summarize ➤
        Frequencies . . .

TABLE 6
SUMMARY STATS: STANDARD FREQUENCIES

```
FREQUENCIES VARIABLES=,race,sex, relig, marital.*
```

SEX   RESPONDENTS SEX

Value Label	Value	Frequency	Percent	Valid Percent	Cum Percent
MALE	1	590	39.3	39.3	39.3
FEMALE	2	910	60.7	60.7	100.0
		------	------	------	
	Total	1500	100.0	100.0	

Valid cases   1500   Missing cases   0

RACE   RACE OF RESPONDENT

Value Label	Value	Frequency	Percent	Valid Percent	Cum Percent
WHITE	1	1320	88.0	88.0	88.0
BLACK	2	146	9.7	9.7	97.7
OTHER	3	34	2.3	2.3	100.0
		------	------	------	
	Total	1500	100.0	100.0	

Valid cases   1500   Missing cases   0

RELIG   RS RELIGIOUS PREFERENCE

Value Label	Value	Frequency	Percent	Valid Percent	Cum Percent
PROTESTANT	1	910	60.7	60.7	60.7
CATHOLIC	2	392	26.1	26.2	86.9
JEWISH	3	36	2.4	2.4	89.3
NONE	4	124	8.3	8.3	97.6
OTHER	5	36	2.4	2.4	100.0
NA	9	2	.1	Missing	
		------	------	------	
	Total	1500	100.0	100.0	

Valid cases   1498   Missing cases   2

MARITAL   MARITAL STATUS

Value Label	Value	Frequency	Percent	Valid Percent	Cum Percent
MARRIED	1	886	59.1	59.1	59.1
WIDOWED	2	132	8.8	8.8	68.0
DIVORCED	3	164	10.9	10.9	78.9
SEPARATED	4	49	3.3	3.3	82.2
NEVER MARRIED	5	267	17.8	17.8	100.0
NA	9	2	.1	Missing	
		------	------	------	
	Total	1500	100.0	100.0	

Valid cases   1498   Missing cases   2

FIGURE 7
FREQUENCIES:STATISTICS Dialog Box

Frequencies: Statistics

Percentile Values
- ☐ Quartiles
- ☐ Cut points for [10] equal groups
- ☐ Percentile(s):
  - Add
  - Change
  - Remove

Central Tendency
- ☒ Mean
- ☒ Median
- ☒ Mode
- ☒ Sum

☐ Values are group midpoints

Dispersion
- ☒ Std. deviation   ☒ Minimum
- ☒ Variance   ☒ Maximum
- ☒ Range   ☒ S.E. mean

Distribution
- ☒ Skewness
- ☒ Kurtosis

[Continue] [Cancel] [Help]

FIGURE 8
FREQUENCIES:FORMAT Dialog Box

Frequencies: Format

Order by
- ⦿ Ascending values
- ○ Descending values
- ○ Ascending counts
- ○ Descending counts

☐ Display index
☒ Display value labels

Page Format
- ○ Standard
- ○ Condensed
- ⦿ Best fit
- ○ Suppress tables with more than [10] categories

[Continue] [Cancel] [Help]

---

and select each of the nominal-level variables (e.g., RACE, SEX, MARITAL, RELIG). Your output should look like that of Table 6.

When working with interval-level variables, add summary statistics. Following standard practice, choose:

Statistics ➤
  Summarize ➤
    Frequencies . . .

A press of the STATISTICS . . . command button at the bottom of the FREQUENCIES dialog box presents a roster of summary statistics options. See Figure 7.

Select all the statistics of interest. When finished, press the "Continue" button (it will return you to the original dialog box) and then the "OK" button. Your output should look like that of Table 7. In addition to the standard frequencies distribution, you now have appropriate summary statistics with which to, well, summarize the data.

Here's an interesting wrinkle. If you had asked for a variable with many values (e.g., age or income), you would have had pages of output for each variable. SPSS provides a useful solution to this problem—a FORMAT dialog box. It may be selected from the lower right corner of the FREQUENCIES dialog box (Figure 8).

TABLE 7
FREQUENCIES WITH SUMMARY STATS

```
FREQUENCIES VARIABLES = EDUC DEGREE/STATISTICS=ALL

EDUC      HIGHEST YEAR OF SCHOOL COMPLETED
```

				Valid	Cum
Value Label		Value	Frequency	Percent	Valid Percent	Cum Percent
		0	4	.3	.3	.3
		1	1	.1	.1	.3
		2	2	.1	.1	.5
		3	9	.6	.6	1.1
		4	13	.9	.9	1.9
		5	12	.8	.8	2.7
		6	22	1.5	1.5	4.2
		7	25	1.7	1.7	5.9
		8	89	5.9	5.9	11.8
		9	56	3.7	3.7	15.6
		10	77	5.1	5.1	20.7
		11	94	6.3	6.3	27.0
		12	519	34.6	34.7	61.7
		13	104	6.9	6.9	68.6
		14	137	9.1	9.2	77.8
		15	54	3.6	3.6	81.4
		16	156	10.4	10.4	91.8
		17	36	2.4	2.4	94.2
		18	44	2.9	2.9	97.1
		19	22	1.5	1.5	98.6
		20	21	1.4	1.4	100.0
DK		98	2	.1	Missing	
NA		99	1	.1	Missing	
		Total	1500	100.0	100.0	

```
Mean        12.369     Std err        .082     Median      12.000
Mode        12.000     Std dev       3.180     Variance    10.113
Kurtosis      .975     S E Kurt       .126     Skewness     -.318
S E Skew      .063     Range       20.000     Minimum       .000
Maximum     20.000     Sum      18517.000

Valid cases   1497     Missing cases      3

DEGREE    RS HIGHEST DEGREE
```

					Valid	Cum
Value Label		Value	Frequency	Percent	Valid Percent	Cum Percent
LT HIGH SCHOOL		0	390	26.0	26.0	26.0
HIGH SCHOOL		1	781	52.1	52.1	78.2
JUNIOR COLLEGE		2	61	4.1	4.1	82.2
BACHELOR		3	183	12.2	12.2	94.5
GRADUATE		4	83	5.5	5.5	100.0
NA		9	2	.1	Missing	
		Total	1500	100.0	100.0	

```
Mean         1.191     Std err        .029     Median       1.000
Mode         1.000     Std dev       1.119     Variance     1.253
Kurtosis      .387     S E Kurt       .126     Skewness     1.093
S E Skew      .063     Range        4.000     Minimum       .000
Maximum      4.000     Sum       1784.000
Valid cases   1498     Missing cases      2
```

TABLE 8
FREQUENCIES WITH SUMMARY STATS CONDENSED FORMAT

```
FREQUENCIES VARIABLES=age/format=onepage/statistics=all.
```

AGE   AGE OF RESPONDENT

Value	Freq	Pct	Cum Pct	Value	Freq	Pct	Cum Pct	Value	Freq	Pct	Cum Pct
18	9	1	1	42	32	2	54	66	20	1	87
19	21	1	2	43	30	2	56	67	14	1	88
20	22	1	3	44	25	2	58	68	19	1	89
21	23	2	5	45	19	1	59	69	7	0	90
22	35	2	7	46	22	1	61	70	15	1	91
23	38	3	10	47	27	2	62	71	16	1	92
24	32	2	12	48	18	1	64	72	10	1	92
25	38	3	15	49	27	2	66	73	13	1	93
26	45	3	18	50	20	1	67	74	14	1	94
27	49	3	21	51	21	1	68	75	14	1	95
28	29	2	23	52	16	1	69	76	7	0	96
29	43	3	26	53	19	1	71	77	11	1	96
30	38	3	28	54	25	2	72	78	13	1	97
31	37	2	31	55	22	1	74	79	5	0	98
32	27	2	33	56	17	1	75	80	5	0	98
33	38	3	35	57	18	1	76	81	6	0	98
34	31	2	37	58	20	1	77	82	8	1	99
35	38	3	40	59	18	1	79	83	5	0	99
36	37	2	42	60	18	1	80	84	2	0	99
37	35	2	45	61	17	1	81	85	3	0	99
38	26	2	46	62	19	1	82	86	3	0	100
39	31	2	48	63	19	1	84	87	3	0	100
40	33	2	51	64	15	1	85	89	2	0	100
41	23	2	52	65	16	1	86				

M I S S I N G   D A T A

Value	Freq	Value	Freq	Value	Freq
99	7				

Mean	43.759	Std err	.445	Median	40.000
Mode	27.000	Std dev	17.197	Variance	295.729
Kurtosis	-.728	S E Kurt	.127	Skewness	.537
S E Skew	.063	Range	71.000	Minimum	18.000
Maximum	89.000	Sum	65332.000		

Valid cases   1493   Missing cases   7

TABLE 9
SUMMARY STATS: DESCRIPTIVES

```
DESCRIPTIVES VARIABLES=,race,sex, relig, marital.

Number of valid observations (listwise) =      1486.00
```

Variable	Mean	Std Dev	Minimum	Maximum	Valid N	Label
CHILDS	1.95	1.84	0	8	1497	NUMBER OF CHILDREN
SIBS	3.98	3.16	0	26	1498	NUMBER OF BROTHERS AN
EDUC	12.37	3.18	0	20	1497	HIGHEST YEAR OF SCHOO
AGE	43.76	17.20	18	89	1493	AGE OF RESPONDENT

Once displayed, choose the "Best Fit" option. SPSS produces a single-page summary output, as seen in Table 8. Note the differences between Table 6 and Table 7—the inclusion of summary statistics; then examine closely the difference between these two tables and Table 8—the format of the output. In constructing the output for the variable of AGE, SPSS produced a condensed three-column format on a single page.

In these FREQUENCIES commands, we have specified which variables we wish to use rather than using the expression: FREQUENCIES VARIABLES=ALL in the syntax window. This is appropriate since we wish to have summary statistics computed only when the variable of interest was measured at the metric level (e.g., age, education, etc.).

Sometimes it is not necessary to report data using frequency distributions; rather, the summary statistics may be sufficient. You have two quick ways of producing such summaries. First, you can continue to use the FREQUENCIES command, just unselect "Display frequency tables." A click of the mouse in the box to the left of this subcommand will instruct SPSS to not display the table but still report all selected summary statistics.

A second SPSS alternative to summarize interval-level variables is to use the DESCRIPTIVES . . . command.

Statistics ➤
   Summarize ➤
      Descriptives . . .

You will see the standard dialog selection box. You can choose which variables and which summary statistics you wish to have SPSS calculate. Which summary statistics? Well, a click on the Options . . . button will enable you to select all appropriate summary statistics—basically from the same roster as that found in the FREQUENCIES command.

Note that DESCRIPTIVES may be much more efficient and produce the same results[13] as found in the FREQUENCIES command. See Table 9.

Note also that if you are not completely familiar with your data set there is some danger in using this command. For example, you may not know if a value was not declared as a missing value and that value, as well as all the respondents who chose that value, were included in the calculations of the reported summary statistics. This is the case for the variables of INCOME, which uses coded values for income intervals, and the code of 13 for those persons who "refused" to answer the question. Similarly, the variable of PARTYID uses an ordinal scale of valid values that range from 0—"Strong Democrat" through 6—"Strong Republican." Unfortunately for the unsuspecting, the value 7 is not classified as missing and is used to indicate "Other Party." Thus, I recommend that you run your FREQUENCIES commands first, examine carefully all parts of the output, and then use the DESCRIPTIVES command to summarize appropriately selected variables.

Other Useful Statistical Descriptive Measures You have already mastered CROSSTABS. But here are some additional uses, especially when you are working with longitudinal data. For example, a roster of the demographic variable of sex by year is important. We know that there will be differences—at least due to sampling error. Comparing

---

[13] Okay, for those who look carefully, there are some minor differences in the reported summary statistics. This is due to rounding-off procedures.

TABLE 10
CROSSTABS OUTPUT: SEX BY YEAR

```
CROSSTABS
 /TABLES= sex BY year
 /CELLS= COUNT COLUMN
 /STATISTICS.

SEX   RESPONDENTS SEX  by  YEAR  GSS YEAR FOR THIS RESPONDENT

                   YEAR                                  Page 1 of 1
           Count  |
           Col Pct|
                  |                                        Row
                  |   73|    78|    83|    88|    93|    Total
   SEX    --------+------+------+------+------+------+
            1     |  150|   128|   135|   122|   119|    654
       MALE       | 50.0|  42.7|  45.0|  40.7|  39.7|   43.6
                  +------+------+------+------+------+
            2     |  150|   172|   165|   178|   181|    846
       FEMALE     | 50.0|  57.3|  55.0|  59.3|  60.3|   56.4
                  +------+------+------+------+------+
           Column   300    300    300    300    300    1500
           Total   20.0   20.0   20.0   20.0   20.0   100.0

         Chi-Square               Value          DF         Significance
     -------------------        ---------       ----        ------------

     Pearson                     8.27965          4            .08185
     Likelihood Ratio            8.25918          4            .08253
     Mantel-Haenszel test for    6.26385          1            .01232
        linear association

     Minimum Expected Frequency -  130.800

     Number of Missing Observations:  0
```

differences is facilitated by using percents. We can request CROSSTABS to provide cell counts and percentages (percents based on row totals, column totals, or total sample size) in the CROSSTABS display dialog box.

Following our usual practice, choose:

Statistics ➤
  Summarize ➤
    Crosstabs . . .

which opens a dialog box like that of Figure 6. Now, press the "Cells" button along the bottom of this dialog box. From here select the "Observed" option in "Counts" and the "Column" option in "Percentages."[14] See Figure 9.

A press of the "Continue" button returns us to the crosstabs dialog box. We can now select the "statistics" button and choose the "chi square" option in the upper left portion of this dialog box. A press of "Continue" and then "OK" runs the CROSSTABS procedure and produces an output like that of Table 10.

---
[14]If you have access to the syntax window, you can enter the command:
  CROSSTABS
   /TABLES= sex BY year
   /CELLS= COUNT COLUMN
   /STATISTICS.
quickly and easily. Go ahead and execute this command to get the same results without going through so many menu steps.

FIGURE 9
CROSSTABS Cell Display Dialog Box

Crosstabs: Cell Display

Counts
- ☒ Observed
- ☐ Expected

Percentages
- ☐ Row
- ☒ Column
- ☐ Total

Residuals
- ☐ Unstandardized
- ☐ Standardized
- ☐ Adj. standardized

[Continue] [Cancel] [Help]

FIGURE 10
MEANS Dialog Box

Means

Dependent List: age, educ

Layer 1 of 1

Independent List: year

Variables: abany, abdefect, abhlth, abnomore, abpoor, abrape, absingle, aged, anomia5, anomia6, anomia7

[OK] [Paste] [Reset] [Cancel] [Help] [Options...]

Note that below each table cell count is the reported percentage for that column. Of the 300 sampled respondents in 1973, 50% were male and 50% were female. In 1978 42.7% of the GSS sampled respondents were male while 57.3% were female. (Examine Table 10 for the remaining years.) Thus, there were some differences in the distribution of sex across the sampled years; however, these differences were not large enough—chi square$_{(4\,df)}$ = 8.27965, p = .082—to be considered statistically significant.

The final procedure of interest useful in summarizing these demographic comparisons is the procedure MEANS. It is particularly useful when you wish to use the average value to summarize variables such as age, educational years, and so on. It is found in the menu bar under:

Statistics ➤
  Compare Means ➤
    Means . . .

which brings forward the Means dialog box as seen in Figure 10.

A press of the "OK" button executes the MEANS procedure. We can now examine the output. See Table 11 for any trend in the demographic variables of age or education over the life of the study.

We could have just as easily entered the MEANS command in the syntax window. It takes the form of:

MEANS TABLES= vr_list BY var_list.

or

MEANS TABLES= AGE, EDUC BY YEAR.

This follows the standard SPSS format and enables a simple comparison of averages across each category of the independent variable—in this case we are using YEAR as though it were an independent variable. Thus, as seen in Table 11, the average age of all the sample respondents was 44.4, while the average ages of 43.7, 42.6, 43.9, 46.1, and 45.5 years were found for the 1973, 1978, 1983, 1988, and 1993 sample years, respectively. Thus, there was not a large difference in the average ages across the study years. See Table 11.

Some differences do appear across the years on other variables, however. For example, the variable of EDUC, the number of years of education, does change over the years—increasing from 11.5 years in 1973 to 13.06 years by 1993. Using the MEANS command and the subcommand STATISTICS enables examining the data using ANOVA and testing for LINEARITY. The typical adult American was more likely to have completed high school and attended college than in earlier years.

The great advantage in using CROSSTABS and MEANS over FREQUENCIES is that you not only get the summary totals for all respondents (e.g., look at the "Total" column and row line on the CROSSTABS output and the "Summaries For Entire Population" row on the MEANS output), but you also get information for each attribute of your "independent" variable.

Indeed, CROSSTABS and MEANS are sufficiently powerful to include several levels of variables. You can enter these levels in the appropriate dialog box if you are using the menu bar or by entering additional BY keywords directly into the command. For example, you might wish to know the religious affiliation of respondents for each study year by race and sex. Here's a simple embellishment of the CROSSTABS command:

CROSSTABS TABLES=RELIG BY YEAR BY RACE BY SEX.

Or, you may wish to know the average level of educational attainment of the respondents for each study year by sex within each race category. Your MEANS procedure becomes:

MEANS TABLES=EDUC BY YEAR BY RACE BY SEX.

You may include up to four levels of control using the BY keyword. Of course, the more BY keywords, the more complex the output and the fewer cases in any unique cell. This does give you a brief picture, however, of the power of SPSS.

Well, as the saying goes, this is "just a first look" about retrieving data set demographic statistics and how to use the basic tabular summary and simple comparative procedures of SPSS.

Exercise 3: Take some time, load your SPSS file, and try the commands of FREQUENCIES, CROSSTABS, and MEANS. After you re-create the tables noted above, try other variables, commands, and optional subcommands.

Some Useful Graphic Techniques While statistical tables are solid communication devices for those interested in social science data, graphic presentations of such data often make a visceral impact on the reader. SPSS has a wealth of graphic options, some of which exist within statistical commands—e.g., FREQUENCIES—while others may be accessed through the graphic routines. Most graphics are best created, not surprisingly, from the graph menu:

Graphs ➤

From here you can choose from a variety of graph types, including bar, line, area, hi-lo, scatterplots, etc. In addition, most of these have a variety of additional choices; there are three choices of bar and line charts, two for area charts and four for scatterplots. Within each of these choices you control the types of data with which you are working—summaries across a single variable, comparing variables, etc. I think you get the point. One of the great advances of

TABLE 11
SUMMARY STATS: MEANS AGE EDUCATION BY YEAR

```
-> MEANS
->     TABLES=age BY year
->     /TABLES= educ  BY year
->     /CELLS MEAN STDDEV COUNT
->     /FORMAT= LABELS
->     /STATISTICS ANOVA LINEARITY.
```

- - Description of Subpopulations - -

Summaries of   AGE   AGE OF RESPONDENT
By levels of   YEAR   GSS YEAR FOR THIS RESPONDENT

Variable	Value	Label	Mean	Std Dev	Cases
For Entire Population			44.3728	17.4967	1494
YEAR	73		43.7215	16.9727	298
YEAR	78		42.6333	17.8177	300
YEAR	83		43.8930	17.7199	299
YEAR	88		46.1342	18.2645	298
YEAR	93		45.4916	16.5402	299

Total Cases = 1500
Missing Cases = 6 or   .4 Pct

- - Description of Subpopulations - -

Summaries of   EDUC   HIGHEST YEAR OF SCHOOL COMPLETED
By levels of   YEAR   GSS YEAR FOR THIS RESPONDENT

Variable	Value	Label	Mean	Std Dev	Cases
For Entire Population			12.3031	3.1409	1498
YEAR	73		11.5251	3.0159	299
YEAR	78		12.0133	3.4262	300
YEAR	83		12.5800	3.0988	300
YEAR	88		12.3344	2.9461	299
YEAR	93		13.0600	2.9988	300

Total Cases = 1500
Missing Cases = 2 or   .1 Pct

- - Analysis of Variance - -

Dependent Variable   EDUC   HIGHEST YEAR OF SCHOOL COMPLETED
   By levels of   YEAR   GSS YEAR FOR THIS RESPONDENT

Value	Label	Mean	Std Dev	Sum of Sq	Cases
73		11.5251	3.0159	2710.5619	299
78		12.0133	3.4262	3509.9467	300
83		12.5800	3.0988	2871.0800	300
88		12.3344	2.9461	2586.5552	299
93		13.0600	2.9988	2688.9200	300

Within Groups Total   12.3031   3.1021 14367.0637   1498

Source	Sum of Squares	d.f.	Mean Square	F	Sig.
Between Groups	401.3422	4	100.3355	10.4267	.0000
Linearity	344.4543	1	344.4543	35.7951	.0000
Dev. from Linearity	56.8879	3	18.9626	1.9706	.1165
	R = .1527	R Squared = .0233			
Within Groups	14367.0637	1493	9.6229		
	Eta = .1649	Eta Squared = .0272			

SPSS 6.1 over earlier versions has been the addition of powerful graphic capabilities. We'll illustrate only a few here. You can try these, and others, too.

Perhaps a good place to start is with the descriptive data on education. We can create, at first, a simple graph and then improve upon presenting the changes in educational achievement we noted earlier. The command sequence:

Graphs ➤
    Bar . . .

begins the process. Choosing within this dialog box the options of "simple" and "Summaries for groups of cases" are the default choices—how convenient. A press of the "Define" button lists the variables from which we may choose and how we wish to display the results—what the bars represent and how to display the data. See Figure 11 for the dialog box and selections. A press on the "Titles . . ." yields an opportunity to key in an appropriate title and de-selecting, in the "Options . . ." button; "display groups defined by missing data" will complete the bar graph. (If you miss these options, you can further modify the graph once it is displayed.)

A more complex bar graph may be seen in Figure 12. Let's work with the variables of degree and year since we are interested in tracing the changes in educational achievement over the last 20 years. We will again choose

Graphs ➤
    Bar . . .

but here we shall select the icon for "Stacked bars." A press of the "Define" button gives us the opportunity to select—bar represents—"N of cases," the "category axis:" defined by the variable of YEAR and "defined stacks by:" DEGREE. Again, entering a "Title . . ." and eliminating the inclusion of missing data from the "Options . . ." buttons are no problem. Once displaced, we can further improve on the graphic appeal by choosing to make each bar three-dimensional—choose from the menu bar:

Carousel ➤
    Edit . . .

then, from the new menu bar:

Attributes ➤
    Bar Style

and then 3D-effect.

A click of the mouse button on the "Apply All" button and the stacked bar chart will include an interesting 3-D look. Finally, we can reduce the amount of white space at the top of each bar by setting the axis display limit between 0 and 350 with 50 for major divisions and tick marks—labels listed on the vertical axis. This is accomplished in:

Chart ➤
    Axis

Now choose scale and then change the appropriate values. When finished, it will look like Figure 12—actually it will look better on the screen than in print.

From this graph it is easy to see that since 1973, the number of Americans who had yet to earn at least a high school diploma decreased substantially over the last twenty years. In addition, by 1993, the number of Americans earning a baccalaureate degree was substantially greater than those in earlier years. Such graphs make a visually strong case when you "look at data" and when you need to present your findings to others.

Of course, you are expected to know which graphs are appropriate for which data types—bar charts for categorical data (race or sex status), histograms for continuous data (age), scatterplots for two continuous variables (income and degree), and so on. Since you can easily modify the chart, add titles, determine the number of tick marks, use the grid lines, use labels rather than values of the variables, add footnotes, determine what to do with missing values, etc., you should examine several ways to graphically summarize data—you can present the data as simply or as complicated as you wish by combining multiple variables. So, do the exercise below.

FIGURE 11
Bar Graph Dialog Boxes and Bar Graph

Exercise 4: Take some time, go ahead and load the data set, and try various graphic routines and options within each. After you re-create these simple bar graphs, try other techniques by choosing from the gallery options alternate graphic types with the "Replace" button.

Well, what have we found out about the GSS respondents, and therefore most Americans, across the last 20-odd years?

For most years, the typical respondents were white (88%), female (60.7%), and Protestant (60.7%). A substantial minority, 31%, of the respondents were members of other faiths—typically, Catholic(26.2%)—while few (8.3%) reported no religious membership. They attended church—typically on a monthly basis. While the average age was 44 years old, most adult respondents were between the ages of 27 and 61. Most respondents were married in each of the sampled years, although proportionately fewer Americans were married in 1993 (52.5%) than in 1973 (60.7%). They had a median family income, in 1986 dollars, of $24,000 per year, approximately, across the study years. Finally, they typically defined their political views as "moderate." You say that you don't see how I know this. Try running the procedures outlined above with the background variables included in our data file. Now, compare your results with mine.

Before You Run the Race, Make Sure It's Worth the Effort: Step 4

We now have a brief look at the respondents and how they answered each of the demographic questions of interest. A reasonable social scientist would want to convince himself/herself that the data set is, in fact, reasonably representative of the population from which it was selected. This is especially true when you are working with data col-

FIGURE 12
Stacked Bar Graph

Earned Degrees of Americans by Years: GSS 73-93

RS HIGHEST DEGREE
- GRADUATE
- BACHELOR
- JUNIOR COLLEGE
- HIGH SCHOOL
- LT HIGH SCHOOL

GSS YEAR FOR THIS RESPONDENT

lected by others. Using some of these same demographic variables, we can compare the distribution of our GSS subset to the larger data set. For example, I know from examining the GSS codebook and original file [15] the number and proportion of women and men in each of the survey years. In 1993, 57.3% of the 1,606 respondents were women and 42.7% were men. If our data subset sampling procedure were exactly on target, then we would have expected to find 172 women (57.3% * 300) and 128 men (42.7% * 300) in our subsample. We have already noted that the number of men and women in our 1993 subsample was 186 women and 114 men. Are these differences between what we would expect to find and what we in fact found likely due to sampling error, or do they reflect a bias in the sampling process? Read on. . . .

We can use SPSS to examine this question.

Data ➤
  Select Cases . . . ➤
    If

and select just those cases from the 1993 sample by entering the expression: YEAR = 93. SPSS will indicate all other cases are to be excluded (note the slash drawn through the row numbers to the left of each row) from further analysis—at least until you reselect "all cases" from the same menu. Now, select

Statistics ➤
  Nonparametric Tests ➤
    Chi square . . .

You should see a dialog box, albeit incomplete, like that of Figure 13.

---
[15] See earlier Davis and Smith reference.

FIGURE 13
Chi-Square Test Dialog Box

Just choose the variable SEX from the variable list and then choose the "Values:" option within the "Expected Values" box. In this box, enter 128 and press the "Add" button. Then enter 172 and press the "Add" button again. (Note that these values must be entered in the appropriate order—since men have a coded value of "1" while women have a code of "2," the expected number of men must be entered before the expected number of women.) Your chi-square test dialog box should now look exactly like that of Figure 13. A press on the "OK" button is all that is needed to invoke the SPSS command. The results—chi square$_{(1\ df)}$ = 2.6708, sig = .1022—indicate no significant difference between our GSS subsample and the total 1993 data set on the variable of sex.

Of course you could write in the syntax window the following commands:

```
TEMPORARY.
SELECT IF (YEAR EQ 93).
NPAR TEST
 /CHISQUARE = sex
 /EXPECTED = 128 172
 /MISSING ANALYSIS.
```

and then run them, directly producing the same tabular results.

Why not try these calculations yourself. A quick trip to the library will give you access to the complete GSS codebook. Choose one or two other demographic variables and make your own comparison between our subsample data and the larger data set. Then, if you have Internet skills, examine *Census* summary statistics and compare the original GSS demographic variables distribution to *Census* summary statistics for 1980 and 1990. What do you conclude about the veracity of the GSS?

Making a Class Act Work for You: COMPUTE, IF, and RECODE

All of us like to work with data that are easy to use and easy to understand. Data transformation commands are useful tools in "fixing" data values. What needs to be fixed? Well, here are some examples. When doing data entry we sometimes take the easy way out and use coded values for class intervals rather than entering the actual values. NORC personnel are no different. For example, they chose for the variable of income to enter a 5 for all respondents whose total family income was between $5,000 through $5,999 rather than the actual amount. These codes may be easily entered but they are less easy to interpret.

We may find that it is to our advantage to change the codes of some variables rather than use the original codes entered by others or us—for example, changing the coding of a variable that is a dichotomy (e.g., SEX) from "1" and "2" to "0" and "1" since the values "0" and "1" are preferable when interpreting mean scores. Additionally, we may wish to more easily summarize a variable with many attributes by aggregating several attributes into just a few categories. Finally, we may wish to create new variables from those already in our study so that we can better target answers to our research questions (e.g., combining the two variables of RACE and SEX into a single variable of RACE-SEX). Below is a brief discussion of some useful data transformation commands.

Converting Coded Values to Useful and Real Values: RECODE RECODE is a simple procedure that enables us to convert easily the current values of any variable to new values. It has a standard SPSS form:

```
RECODE varname (old value = new value)... (old value = new value).
```

We can, for example, RECODE the variable of SEX with the command:

```
RECODE SEX (2=0).
```

or RECODE the variable of RACE:

```
RECODE RACE (2=0).
```

or do both at the same time:

```
RECODE SEX, RACE (2=0).
```

Converting variables such as SEX or RACE to a dichotomy of codes "0" (for "Female" or "Black") and "1" (for "Male" or "White") will enhance our calculating and reporting of statistical findings.[16] Mean values calculated on "0" and "1" will yield a value that can be interpreted as the proportion of respondents that were coded "1." Read on. Right now, let's return to the RECODE procedure.

Those whose code on the variable of SEX or RACE was "2" are now assigned a value of "0." (To exclude those who were neither African American nor white can be accomplished with a MISSING VALUES command—the value "3" can be declared as a missing value):

```
MISSING VALUES RACE (3).
```

Those persons coded "3" can then be excluded easily from most further analyses.[17]

While it may not be apparent from this example, you may RECODE several variables with the same statement. Using our GSS survey, we can tell SPSS to treat all variables that measured abortion attitudes similarly:

```
RECODE abany,abdefect,abhlth,abnomore,abpoor,abrape,absingle (0=99)(1=1)(2=0)(ELSE=99).
```

Those who were coded in the original data set with a value of "0" will now have a code of "99." Those coded with a "1" = "Yes" will retain the value, those with a value of "2" = "No" will now have a code of "0," and those with any other code, "ELSE," will have a value of "99." Now, if we reassign the missing values from "0" to "99" with the command

```
MISSING VALUES abany,abdefect,abhlth,abnomore,abpoor,abrape,absingle (99).
```

all respondents coded "99" who did not answer these questions will be treated as missing. Those persons who answered "Yes" will continue to have a coded value of "1" while those who answered "No" will have a coded value of "0." (This will become more meaningful when we examine the issue of developing a scale of the items used to measure abortion.)

It is often useful or necessary to RECODE values to "true" values. The original values of INCOME, for example, went from 1 through 13 with 1 through 12 indicating valid values. A value of 1 indicated total family income of less than $1,000, a 2 indicated $1,000 through $2,999, etc. One of the nice facilities of SPSS is the ability to easily reassign

---

[16] We could have just as easily coded the variables of SEX as "0" for "Male" and "1" for "Female" or the variable of RACE as "0" for "White" and "1" for "Black." The only impact will be in how we describe and interpret the analysis.

[17] If you wish to keep the current variable of RACE and create a new variable, such as NRACE, just add the expression INTO NRACE. Thus your command should look like this:
```
RECODE RACE (1=1)(2=0)(3=3) INTO NRACE.
```

the entered values of our data file to some other, more appropriate, data values. Rather than continue to work with these coded values of "1," "2," "3," etc., we can have SPSS store the "true" values. What are the "true" values? Well, if we take the average of each class interval:

$$(\$1,000 + \$2,999) / 2 \sim \$2,000$$
$$(\$3,000 + \$3,999) / 2 \sim \$3,500$$
$$(\$4,000 + \$4,999) / 2 \sim \$4,500$$

and choose a reasonable beginning (say, $500) and ending (say, $40,000) values, then we can have SPSS store the "true" values rather than the entered coded values.[18] This is accomplished with the RECODE command. The format of this RECODE command is:

```
RECODE INCOME (1=500)(2=2000)(3=3500)(4=4500)(5=5500)
              (6=6500)(7=7500)(8=9000)(9=12500)(10=17500)
              (11=22500)(12=40000)(13=0).
```

Note the standard form of the expressions used above (i.e., use of blanks, open and closed parentheses, and equal signs). Note also that no commas were used. These subcommands would be entered into the syntax window and then executed.

Several other options exist when working with the RECODE command and old values. For example, you could RECODE a range of values—say, (2 THRU 4=2)—in a single command segment rather than listing each of these values separately. If I am interested in combining the MARITAL statuses of divorced, separated, and widowed into one category—"previously married"—I could key:

```
RECODE MARITAL (2,3,4 = 2).
```

or, I could have used

```
RECODE MARITAL (2 thru 4 = 2).
```

and then changed the value labels—the labels assigned to each attribute—by entering in the syntax window the command:

```
VALUE LABELS MARITAL 1 "Married" 2 "Previously Married".
```

If you wish to use the dialog boxes in SPSS, then the Recode command will be found by choosing:

Transform ➤
  Recode ➤
    "Into same variables . . ."

from the menu bar. Then choose the variable of SEX. Press on the "Old and New Values . . ." button at the bottom of the dialog box. When the new dialog box appears, enter the old value of "2" and the new value "0" in their appropriate text boxes. Click on the "Add" button and 2 → 0 appears in the "Old — New" box. A click on the "Continue" button returns to the previous dialog box; a press on the OK button with your mouse will execute the Recode command. In a minute or two you will see the changed data in the Data Editor window—all those who had a value of "2" are now coded as "0" for this variable. By clicking on the variable name MARITAL in the data editor window you will be able to change the value labels as listed above.

More complex recoding requires just a little more work. The variable of RACE may serve as a good example. Here we wish to recode the variable so that we are working with a "dummy" variable—using the "0" for "African Americans" and "1" for "White"— and exclude all others. Since we are treating the values quite differently we shall, in this example, create a new variable, NRACE, using the codes as noted above. Thus, choose from the menu bar:

---

[18]The NORC staff were nice enough to recognize this problem and have included an additional variable, REALINC. It not only uses midpoint values but takes into account the effect of time by standardizing family income to 1986 dollars across all respondents who were included in the 1973–1993 surveys.

FIGURE 14
RECODE Variable Dialog Box

Recode into Different Variables dialog showing Numeric Variable → Output with "race --> ?", Output Variable Name "NRACE", Label "New Race Variable".

Recode into Different Variables: Old and New Values dialog showing Old → New mappings: 1 --> 1, 2 --> 0, 3 --> SYSMIS.

Transform ▶
  Recode ▶
    "Into different variables . . ."

and then select the variable of RACE. In the "Output Variable" box, type the name of the new variable, NRACE, and its label, "New Race Variable." Now press the "Change" button. As before, a press of the "Old and New Values . . ." button brings up the new screen (Figure 14).

Enter a "1" in "Old Value," and a "1" in "New Value," and press the "Add" button. (A 1 → 1 will appear in the "Old → New:" box.) Enter a "2" in the "Old Value" and a "0" in the "New Value" boxes and press the "Add" button again. Finally, enter "3" in the "Old Value" and choose, in the "New Value" box, the "System-missing" option. Press the "Add" button. The second part of Figure 14 should be your guide.

(To include a value label for these newly assigned values—for example, in the variable of SEX, the value of "0"—double-click on the variable name, SEX, or NRACE in the data editor window. [If you would rather work with NRACE, you will find the variable, NRACE, added at the end of your list of variables in the data editor window.] A variable dialog box, like that seen in Figure 15, will appear. Simply choose the option, "Labels . . .", and enter, for the variable of SEX, a "0" in the "Value:" box and "FEMALE" in the "LABEL" box. A simple press of the "Add" button, "Continue" button, and then the "OK" button will change the value labels assigned to the variable of SEX. Executing the FREQUENCIES command will convince you that the change in data values and labels has been made successfully.)

Working with Valid Values and Creating New Variables: COMPUTE and IF Commands We already noted the use of the RECODE procedure to transform and store a coded value into a "true" value as well as create a new variable with many of the same values of another variable. Well, we can sometimes do this more efficiently with the COMPUTE and IF procedures. When we are working with interval and ratio level data, the COMPUTE statement will enable us

FIGURE 15
DEFINE Variable Dialog Box

to manipulate the data in the variable with all the typical mathematical operators. We can add (+), subtract (−), multiply values (*), and divide (/) values and variables. In addition, there is a large array of functions, including: (1) arithmetic functions (e.g., round to nearest integer, take the square root, etc.), (2) statistical functions (e.g., sum the values stored in several variables, calculate the mean across several variables, etc.), (3) logical functions (test to see if a value is in a specific range of values), and more. The simple format of the COMPUTE procedure is:

```
COMPUTE targetvariable = oldvariable operator oldvariable.
```

For example:

```
COMPUTE ABORTION = abany + abdefect + abhlth +  abnomore + abpoor + abrape + absingle.
```

   This procedure statement tells SPSS to create a new variable, ABORTION, and store in this new variable the sum total of values for each respondent in ABANY, ABDEFECT, ABHLTH, etc.
   You may be wondering what happens to people who did not answer all the questions. You will recall that we have declared MISSING VALUES for all these variables. When SPSS encounters a value previously defined as missing for the old variable (e.g., ABANY, ABDEFECT, etc.) it assigns the target variable (e.g., ABORTION) as missing, too. Therefore, those who did not respond to all the abortion rights questions will be treated as missing values. This makes logical sense since you do not know what their overall scale score would be unless you knew how each person responded to each and every one of the items.
   If, however, you wished to include all people who answered at least five of the seven questions, then you could use the expression:

```
COMPUTE ABORTION = SUM.5(abany, abdefect, abhlth, abnomore, abpoor, abrape, absingle).
```

FIGURE 16
COMPUTE Variable Dialog Box

```
┌─────────────────────────────────────────────────────────────┐
│                       Compute Variable                       │
│   Target Variable:    Numeric Expression:                    │
│   ┌──────────────┐    ┌──────────────────────────────────┐   │
│   │ abortion     │ =  │ abany + abdefect + abhlth +      │   │
│   └──────────────┘    │ abnomore + abpoor + abrape +     │   │
│   ┌──────────────┐    │ absingle                         │   │
│   │ Type&Label...│    └──────────────────────────────────┘   │
│   └──────────────┘                                           │
│   ┌──────────┐  ▶  ┌──────────────────┐  Functions:  ┌──┐   │
│   │ abany    │▲    │ + < > 7 8 9      │              │▲ │   │
│   │ abdefect │     │ - <= >= 4 5 6    │  ABS(numexpr)    │   │
│   │ abhlth   │     │ * = ~= 1 2 3     │  ANY(test,value,value,...)│
│   │ abnomore │     │ / & | 0 .        │  ARSIN(numexpr)  │   │
│   │ abortion │     │ ** ~ ( ) Delete  │  ARTAN(numexpr)  │   │
│   │ abpoor   │     └──────────────────┘              └──┘   │
│   │ abrape   │                                               │
│   │ absingle │     ┌─────┐                                  │
│   │ age      │     │ If..│                                  │
│   │ anomia5  │▼    └─────┘                                  │
│   └──────────┘   ┌────┐ ┌──────┐ ┌─────┐ ┌──────┐ ┌─────┐   │
│                  │ OK │ │Paste │ │Reset│ │Cancel│ │Help │   │
│                  └────┘ └──────┘ └─────┘ └──────┘ └─────┘   │
└─────────────────────────────────────────────────────────────┘
```

or, even better,

```
COMPUTE ABORTION = MEAN.5(abany, abdefect, abhlth, abnomore, abpoor, abrape, absingle).
```

If you wish to use the dialogue process,[19] go ahead and try the

Transform ➤
  Compute

option. You will see a new dialog box with the variables at the left and all the operational and mathematical functions listed. (The functions will be in a scroll box.) You will be able to create this command by typing a new variable name in the appropriate text box—"Target Variable." Now, select the variable (e.g., ABANY), then the function ("+"), and then select the next variable (e.g., ABDEFECT). Repeat the process until all the variables have been selected. Press "OK" and SPSS will add this variable to your variable list. See Figure 16.

If you created this new summary variable, you might wish to give it a variable label. This is simple. From the syntax window, use the expression:

```
VARIABLE LABELS
 ABORTION 'SUM OF ALL ANSWERS TO EACH ABORTION QUESTION'.
```

or, from the dialog box, choose the "Type&Label" button. (Since this is an index and each of the values has a meaning, there is no need to use the VALUE LABELS command.)

Before we conclude this section, it is interesting to note that you can combine the COMPUTE command with IF statements to create new variables and assign appropriate values. The IF command enables you to use a logical expression—that is, a test condition—before you assign a value to a target variable. It takes the form of:

```
IF (logical expression) targetvariable = value.
```

Logical expressions test to see if a condition is true. You may use, for example, such phrases as RACE EQ 1. This logical expression contains a variable name, RACE; a logical operator, EQ (equal, or =); and a test value, 1. If the first part of the command is "true," then the second part of the command (targetvariable = value) is performed. More on this later.

---

[19]If you are using the Student Version with the GSS, you will have to make room for each and every new variable. (Remember, the Student Version is limited to 50 variables.) Simply select variables that you are not going to use. Now, choose Edit from the menu bar and then cut. SPSS will eliminate these variables and you will now have the necessary room with which to work.

Appendix I: A Learner's Guide to SPSS 6.1

For now, it is important to note that you may work with several logical expressions and have several logical expressions linked to each other as long as you include the appropriate logical operator(s) such as: AND, OR, NOT. Additionally, you have several alternate operators available. They include:

```
EQ or =  Equal to                NE or      Not equal to
LT or <  less than               LE or <=   Less than or equal to
GT or >  greater than            GE or >=   greater than or equal to
```

Here's one example. Let us assume that we wish to create a new variable that combines the variables of RACE and SEX. That is, we wish to be able to work with a variable that identifies African-Am. males, African-Am. females, white males, and white females. We can combine our COMPUTE and IF statement to create this new variable (RACESEX) by using the original values for RACE and SEX and using the command set of:

```
COMPUTE RACESEX=9.
IF (RACE EQ 1 AND SEX EQ 1)RACESEX=1.
IF (RACE EQ 1 AND SEX EQ 2)RACESEX=2.
IF (RACE EQ 2 AND SEX EQ 1)RACESEX=3.
IF (RACE EQ 2 AND SEX EQ 2)RACESEX=4.
```

The COMPUTE statement first creates a new variable, RACESEX, and assigns everyone a value of "9." The IF statements then check the RACE and SEX value codes for each respondent. If a respondent was white (RACE EQ 1) and male (SEX EQ 1), then his RACESEX code would be "1"; if the respondent was African-Am. (RACE EQ 2) and female (SEX EQ 2), then her RACESEX code would be reassigned from a value of "9" to the value of "4." Similarly, if the respondent was white (RACE EQ 1) and female (SEX EQ 2), then she would have her RACESEX code reassigned to the value of "2." Only where both conditions were true would SPSS change the assigned value of "9" to some other value.

To help keep track of this new variable and its values, we can use our labeling procedures:

```
VARIABLE LABELS   RACESEX, 'RACE AND SEX IDENTIFIER'.
VALUE LABELS      RACESEX  1 'WH-MALE' 2 'WH-FEMALE'
                           3 'AA-MALE' 4 'AA-FEMALE'.
```

and our MISSING VALUES procedure:

```
MISSING VALUES   RACESEX (9).
```

Of course, you would want to check any earlier RECODE changes made to these variables (i.e., have you already changed the coded values of RACE and/or SEX?) so that these statements use the most current and correct codes.

You now know how to better improve your data set by RECODEing variable values to their "true" value, treating dichotomies as 0 and 1 to improve interpretations, COMPUTE new variables, and create new variables with COMPUTE and IF statements. Once you get these values and variables just as you wish, make sure that you SAVE the file by using the "Save As" option in the File menu. Just use the dialog box to give it a new file name and you will have a saved copy—with all relevant changes—on your disk as well as the original file.

Exercise 5: Here's your chance to modify or create additional variables with which you wish to work. Take a few moments. Identify which variables are coded values that should really be changed to "true" values. If you are conducting your own study, then think back to your study goals. Ask yourself what combination of variables, if any, are needed to more adequately examine your hypotheses. Now, go ahead and use your RECODE, COMPUTE, and IF statements to make the necessary changes. Then, go ahead and label these, when necessary. Last, but not least, make sure that you save these changes in a new file that you can use later.

Developing a Scale   You may be wondering why we spent so much time on how to use the data transformation commands of RECODE, COMPUTE, IF, and MISSING VALUES. We did so because we are interested in developing an appropriate scale that will give us a reliable measure of respondents' attitudes toward the right of women to obtain a legal abortion.

Our first step in developing such a scale is to use these recoded items and examine the typical response patterns. To do this, we can use the menu bar and select the appropriate procedures, or, in the syntax window, we can run the procedures you mastered earlier, RECODE, MISSING VALUES, and DESCRIPTIVES with the commands:

```
RECODE abany,abdefect,abhlth,abnomore,abpoor,abrape,absingle (0=99)(1=1)(2=0)(ELSE=99).

MISSING VALUES abany,abdefect,abhlth,abnomore,abpoor,abrape,absingle (99).

DESCRIPTIVES
  VARIABLES = abany,abdefect,abhlth,abnomore,abpoor,abrape,absingle.
```

Or, better,

```
DESCRIPTIVES
  VARIABLES =abdefect,abhlth,abnomore,abpoor,abrape,absingle/MISSING = LISTWISE /SORT = MEAN (D).
```

Thus, our first look at our variable of interest, attitudes toward the right of women to obtain a legal abortion, lists all items. The "mean" value, given that we have now recoded the variable values to 0 and 1, tells us the proportion of persons who said "yes" to each of the questions. Thus, most respondents supported the right of a women to obtain an abortion if: (1) her health is seriously endangered (91%), (2) she was raped (83%), or (3) there is a strong chance of serious defect in the baby (82%). Clearly, there is much less agreement on abortion rights when other reasons are considered. We'll have more to say about these results later. For now, see Table 12.

Our DESCRIPTIVES analysis was only a reasonable first step. Since we are interested in a stable summary variable to measure abortion rights, we shall need to explore creating a scale or index. The principles of creating scales and indices are discussed elsewhere in this text. We recall from that discussion that all items should: (1) have sufficient data for all variables, (2) be logically related, (3) be reasonably correlated, and (4) be sufficiently diverse in their response pattern. Finally, (5) an index should have a sufficient range of scores. For our data, we recognize that we meet several of these criteria. There are two glaring exceptions. First, as we noted earlier, the item querying Americans that used the variable "any reason"—ABANY—was not asked in 1973. This explains why the number of cases fell substantially from 1,500 cases. ABANY will not be part of this scale, although it could be used in other analyses and other scales measuring abortion attitudes from 1978 through 1993. Second, there is more than 90% agreement among Americans about the right of access to an abortion for women whose health is endangered. ABHLTH will be excluded from this analysis, too.

SPSS provides a procedure called RELIABILITY[20] for testing the internal consistency of any scale. We can execute the RELIABILITY procedure[21] with the following basic commands:

```
RELIABILITY VARIABLES =
    abdefect,abnomore,abpoor,abrape,absingle
    /SCALE (abortion) =
    abdefect,abnomore,abpoor,abrape,absingle
    /SUMMARY means corr total
    /STATISTICS descriptive corr scale.
```

---

[20] If you are limited to the SPSS for Windows, Student Version, you will not be able to run the RELIABILITY procedure. You will, however, be able to run DESCRIPTIVES and CORRELATIONS. Use these procedures to choose the best combination of items for your scale.

[21] To use the RELIABILITY procedure correctly, we must first make sure that all the variables are coded in the same direction. Let's assume that you are studying political attitudes and you ask people to respond to ten statements, as was done in the 1985 GSS survey, using the options of "Strongly Agree, Agree, Disagree, and Strongly Disagree." In entering the data you assign a code of 1 for Strongly Agree, 2 for Agree, etc. You now recognize that some of the items were phrased in a positive direction while others were phrased in a negative direction. For example,

  Taking everything into account, the world is getting better.
  The public has little control over what politicians do in office.

Clearly these two statements are in opposite directions. Thus, each item must be coded so that a higher score indicates a greater belief in the variable of interest. If you "Strongly Agree" to the first statement, then you should have a high score (4) rather than a low score (1) as entered. We can RECODE this first item so that the code of 1 indicates "Strongly Disagree" while the code of 4 indicates "Strongly Agree." The second item is already coded in the correct direction—if you "agreed" to this statement, it would indicate that you felt that you had little control, rather than a lot of control; "disagree" responses would indicate greater political efficacy. Thus, using the RECODE facility, we can instruct SPSS to make the values assigned to each variable indicate a higher level of agreement. The RECODE statement is:

RECODE ITEM1 (1=4)(2=3)(3=2)(4=1).

Now higher scores on each variable indicate a belief in greater control of the political system. Thus, you may now run the RELIABILITY procedure with confidence.

TABLE 12
SUMMARY STATS:DESCRIPTIVES

```
-> RECODE abany,abdefect,abhlth,abnomore,abpoor,abrape,absingle
->      (0=99)(1=1)(2=0)(ELSE=99).
-> MISSING VALUES abany,abdefect,abhlth,abnomore,abpoor,abrape,absingle (99) .
-> DESCRIPTIVES
->   VARIABLES = abany,abdefect,abhlth,abnomore,abpoor,abrape,absingle.

Number of valid observations (listwise) =     1076.00
Valid
Variable       Mean    Std Dev   Minimum   Maximum    N    Label
ABANY          .38      .49        0         1      1176  ABORTION IF WOMAN WAN
ABDEFECT       .82      .39        0         1      1481  STRONG CHANCE OF SERI
ABHLTH         .91      .28        0         1      1483  WOMANS HEALTH SERIOUS
ABNOMORE       .44      .50        0         1      1478  MARRIED—WANTS NO MOR
ABPOOR         .49      .50        0         1      1482  LOW INCOME—CANT AFFO
ABRAPE         .83      .37        0         1      1471  PREGNANT AS RESULT OF
ABSINGLE       .45      .50        0         1      1479  NOT MARRIED


-> DESCRIPTIVES VARIABLES = abdefect,abhlth,abnomore,abpoor,abrape,absingle
->   /MISSING = LISTWISE /SORT = MEAN (D).

Number of valid observations (listwise) =     1374.00


Variable       Mean    Std Dev   Minimum   Maximum   Label

ABHLTH         .91      .29        0         1      WOMANS HEALTH SERIOUSLY END
ABRAPE         .83      .37        0         1      PREGNANT AS RESULT OF RAPE
ABDEFECT       .82      .39        0         1      STRONG CHANCE OF SERIOUS DE
ABPOOR         .51      .50        0         1      LOW INCOME—CANT AFFORD MOR
ABNOMORE       .47      .50        0         1      MARRIED—WANTS NO MORE CHIL
ABSINGLE       .46      .50        0         1      NOT MARRIED
```

*Note the differences between these two commands. The first produces a simple descriptive listing for each variable in the order listed on the command. The second produces the same statistics but eliminates all those persons who missed any question, sorts the variables by mean score, and prints the results in descending order. Note also that the variable, ABANY, was not included in the second DESCRIPTIVES command since the question was not asked in 1973.

Or, after several iterations of finding the "best variables," the complete command becomes:

```
-> RELIABILITY VARIABLES =
->      abdefect,abnomore,abpoor,abrape,absingle
->      /SCALE (abortn1) =
->      abdefect,abnomore,abpoor,abrape,absingle,
->      /SCALE (abortn2) =
->      abnomore,abpoor,abrape,absingle,
->      /SCALE (abortn3) =
->      abnomore,abpoor,absingle,
->      /SUMMARY means corr total
->      /STATISTICS descriptive corr scale..
```

This will produce a complete RELIABILITY output like that of Table 13. Note that the output is divided into four major sections. The first section is a complete list of each of the declared variables to be included in the scale. In addition, you will find the mean, standard deviation and number of cases summary—just as we did with the DESCRIPTIVES command. Since all our data are coded 0 and 1, the mean values are simply the proportion of respondents who scored "high" or "yes" on each item.

You have probably noticed that the number of cases was substantially reduced from our initial 1,500 (Americans who responded between 1973 and 1993) to 1,391 cases. Any respondent who did not have a value of 0 or 1 was treated as a missing case. All those respondents who did not respond to one or more items were excluded from this analysis.

The second section reports a simple correlation matrix of all items and summarizes the scale statistics. If all five items were included, then the summary scale mean and standard deviation values, the item means and standard deviation values, and inter-item correlation statistics would be reported correctly. That is, if we kept all five items and added all the values of each item, our scale mean would be 3.06 with a standard deviation of 1.82. These reported data and summary statistics will become more useful when you complete the item selection process.

The third section, item-total statistics, is most important when building a scale or index. It helps you to identify which items or variables are contributing to your overall internal consistency score. Notice especially the column titled "alpha if item deleted." Notice also the computed and reported alpha (internal consistency) value (i.e., alpha = .8558) reported in the last section of the output. Now, return to the last column of section 3. Examine the variable of ABDEFECT. If this item, ABDEFECT, was deleted from the scale, the alpha value would improve to .8578. Thus, SCALE (abortn2) is created and run without the variable of ABDEFECT in the equations. ABDEFECT is suppressing the internal consistency value, which will improve to .8578 and may be omitted from all remaining iterations. We continue this process of eliminating variables until the reported value of alpha cannot be improved by eliminating any additional variables. Thus, in the final section, the final and "best"—most internally consistent—scale includes the three items of:

```
1.    ABNOMORE    MARRIED—WANTS NO MORE CHILDREN
2.    ABPOOR      LOW INCOME—CANT AFFORD MORE CHILDREN
3.    ABSINGLE    NOT MARRIED
```

Note that in our final iteration, the alpha value was .9065. This would be considered a reasonably reliable scale since its internal consistency alpha value is beyond .9. Our mean additive scale score for this scale across the 1,391 respondents who answered all the questions about the rights of women to obtain a abortion is 1.42 with a standard deviation of 1.37. Average inter-item correlation was .7637—a relatively high figure further reflecting consistency in response across the three selected items.

I now know, at least tentatively, which items to include in my scale. A simple COMPUTE statement can be used to create an additive ABORTION index value for each respondent with the expression:

```
COMPUTE abortion=SUM.3(abnomore,abpoor,absingle).
```

or, even better, with an average computation across these three items:

```
COMPUTE abortion=MEAN.3(abnomore,abpoor,absingle).[22]
```

We shall include anyone who answered all three items—since there are so few items with which to work. It should be pointed out that with so few items we have a restricted range of possible scale values. A three dichotomous items scale produces a maximum of four unique values whether you sum the values of each item or calculate the mean score across the three items for each respondent. If we used all five of the best legal abortion items, the number of possible unique values becomes six (because those who said "No" to each question would have a scale score of "0"). This expression would be:

```
COMPUTE abortion=MEAN.5(abdefect,abnomore,abpoor,abrape,absingle).
```

---

[22] If SPSS creates the variable in your Data Editor window but no data appear, choose
Transform ➤
  Run Pending Transformations

TABLE 13
RELIABILITY

```
->  RELIABILITY VARIABLES =
->      abdefect,abnomore,abpoor,abrape,absingle
->      /SCALE (abortn1) =
->      abdefect,abnomore,abpoor,abrape,absingle,
->      /SCALE (abortn2) =
->      abnomore,abpoor,abrape,absingle,
->      /SCALE (abortn3) =
->      abnomore,abpoor,absingle,
->      /SUMMARY means corr total
->      /STATISTICS descriptive corr scale..

****** Method 2 (covariance matrix) will be used for this analysis ******
  R E L I A B I L I T Y   A N A L Y S I S   -   S C A L E   (A B O R T N 1)
                        Mean         Std Dev       Cases
  1.   ABDEFECT        .8160          .3877       1391.0
  2.   ABNOMORE        .4615          .4987       1391.0
  3.   ABPOOR          .5018          .5002       1391.0
  4.   ABRAPE          .8267          .3786       1391.0
  5.   ABSINGLE        .4565          .4983       1391.0
Correlation Matrix
              ABDEFECT    ABNOMORE    ABPOOR    ABRAPE    ABSINGLE
ABDEFECT       1.0000
ABNOMORE        .4025      1.0000
ABPOOR          .4061       .7552     1.0000
ABRAPE          .6159       .4010      .4252    1.0000
ABSINGLE        .4129       .7873      .7487     .4043    1.0000

            N of Cases =      1391.0
                                                      N of
Statistics for      Mean       Variance    Std Dev   Variables
     Scale         3.0625       3.3004      1.8167       5

Item Means          Mean      Minimum    Maximum    Range    Max/Min   Variance
                   .6125       .4565      .8267     .3702    1.8110     .0367
Inter-item
Correlations        Mean      Minimum    Maximum    Range    Max/Min   Variance
                   .5359       .4010      .7873     .3863    1.9634     .0274

Item-total Statistics
                Scale         Scale      Corrected
                Mean         Variance      Item-         Squared      Alpha
               if Item       if Item       Total        Multiple    if Item
               Deleted       Deleted    Correlation    Correlation   Deleted
ABDEFECT       2.2466         2.4967       .5334         .4152       .8578
ABNOMORE       2.6010         1.9767       .7666         .6848       .7990
ABPOOR         2.5607         1.9817       .7587         .6425       .8014
ABRAPE         2.2358         2.5113       .5382         .4186       .8568
ABSINGLE       2.6060         1.9756       .7685         .6797       .7985

Reliability Coefficients      5 items
Alpha =    .8558          Standardized item alpha =    .8524
```

(continued)

TABLE 13
RELIABILITY (continued)

```
        R E L I A B I L I T Y   A N A L Y S I S   -   S C A L E   (A B O R T N 2)

  Item-total Statistics
              Scale        Scale      Corrected
              Mean        Variance     Item-         Squared        Alpha
              if Item     if Item     Total         Multiple       if Item
              Deleted     Deleted     Correlation   Correlation    Deleted
  ABNOMORE    1.7850      1.3286       .7998         .6840          .7754
  ABPOOR      1.7448      1.3355       .7880         .6420          .7808
  ABRAPE      1.4198      1.8884       .4469         .2018          .9065
  ABSINGLE    1.7901      1.3314       .7974         .6775          .7765

  Reliability Coefficients    4 items
  Alpha =   .8578             Standardized item alpha =   .8504


        R E L I A B I L I T Y   A N A L Y S I S   -   S C A L E   (A B O R T N 3)
  ABSINGLE       .7873         .7487       1.0000

          N of Cases =       1391.0
                                                       N of
  Statistics for      Mean    Variance    Std Dev   Variables
       Scale         1.4198    1.8884     1.3742        3

  Item Means          Mean    Minimum    Maximum    Range     Max/Min    Variance
                      .4733    .4565      .5018     .0453     1.0992      .0006
  Inter-item
  Correlations        Mean    Minimum    Maximum    Range     Max/Min    Variance
                      .7637    .7487      .7873     .0386     1.0516      .0003

  Item-total Statistics
              Scale        Scale      Corrected
              Mean        Variance     Item-         Squared        Alpha
              if Item     if Item     Total         Multiple       if Item
              Deleted     Deleted     Correlation   Correlation    Deleted
  ABNOMORE     .9583       .8716       .8248         .6823          .8563
  ABPOOR       .9180       .8882       .7954         .6328          .8810
  ABSINGLE     .9633       .8756       .8197         .6751          .8605

  Reliability Coefficients    3 items
  Alpha =   .9065             Standardized item alpha =   .9065
```

*Note this is a subset of the complete run. You may wish to run the procedure yourself to see the complete listing.

or we could calculate the average score across all five items for each respondent who answered at least four out of the five items with the expression:

COMPUTE abortion=MEAN.4(abdefect,abnomore,abpoor,abrape,absingle).

In the "real world" of social research, you would want to calculate findings using a variety of sets of indices and check to make sure that each index led you to similar conclusions. For our illustrative work here, we shall use the three-item scale.

We now may examine more closely Americans' attitudes toward a legal abortion and how they have changed over these twenty-one years; we may determine what relationships exist, if any, between this summary scale and other variables such as those listed in our initial hypotheses—sex, race, education, political attitudes, etc. We can then examine the "best fit" multivariate model.

Exercise 6: Here's your chance to create a scale or index. You may wish to run the same items, or you may wish to use other items that are logically related to each other (i.e., the five life satisfaction items). In either case, identify which variables need RECODEing, if any, and do it. Then, run the RELIABILITY procedure and determine the "best" scale. Once you find your "best" scale, go ahead and use your COMPUTE command to implement the scale for each case in your study.

A Closer Look at Summarizing the Variable of Interest: Attitudes Toward Legal Abortion

We have the opportunity to summarize our newly created variable, ABORTN3. A good place to start is with our standby, FREQUENCIES. Once we enter our COMPUTE statement:

```
COMPUTE abortion=MEAN.3(abnomore,abpoor,absingle).
```

we can enter the usual command sequence of:

Statistics ➤
  Summarize ➤
    Frequencies . . .

A press of the STATISTICS . . . command button at the bottom of the FREQUENCIES dialog box presents a roster of summary statistics options that we can select. Now, press the "CHARTS . . ." button and select "Bar Charts." A click on "Continue" and "OK" buttons will produce a table and chart like that of Figure 17.

While most Americans are in clear agreement about the legal rights of women to abortion access in issues of health of the mother, rape, and birth defect of the unborn, Americans are clearly divided on the remaining criteria. Thus, most Americans either accepted all (37.7%), or rejected all (42.9%) of the remaining criteria for legal access—legal access based on (1) poverty, (2) marital status, and (3) choice of married women. Relatively few (18.1%) Americans fell in between these two extreme positions. Similarly, the summary statistics of mean (.46) and standard deviation (.458) show clearly the degree of disagreement among Americans. See Figure 17.

Exercise 7: Here's your chance to create a scale or index. You may wish to run the same items, or you may wish to use other items that are logically related to each other. In either case, identify which variables need RECODEing, if any, and do it. Then, run the RELIABILITY procedure and determine the "best" scale. Once you find your "best" scale, go ahead and use your COMPUTE command to implement the scale for each case in your study.

Working with Valid Cases In looking at the tabular displays and summary statistics we have produced so far, it is probably clear to you that not everyone answered all the questions of interest. We know from the RELIABILITY procedure that 61 people did not answer at least one of the three useful items about abortion. Additionally, if you ran the FREQUENCIES, CROSSTABS, MEANS, or DESCRIPTIVES commands on other variables you have noted that they too had "missing cases." For example, while only a few respondents did not report their age or years of education, income data, REALINC, was less likely to be reported—116 missing observations. For our data set, one-third of the cases were missing on the variable of political views—POLVIEWS. Thus, we shall have to omit some people and/or some variables from further analysis.

At this point, let's assume that you are interested in those persons who were either African American or white, and responded to the questions on abortion.

To select a subset of cases, you can use the menu bar. Choose the:

Data ➤
  Select Cases . . .

option. Once chosen from the menu, a Select Cases dialog box will appear. From here you can choose logical conditions for each variable. Just choose the option, "If condition is satisfied." and then press the "If" button. A new dialog box will appear where you can create the expression—for example:

```
((RACE EQ 1 OR RACE EQ 2) AND
NOT SYSMIS(ABORTION))
```

FIGURE 17
Summary of Abortion Attitudes—3-Item Index

```
Bar Chart
```

```
                    ABORTN3   WOMEN'S RIGHT TO A LEGAL ABORTION-3 ITEM

                                                       Valid     Cum
        Value Label               Value  Frequency  Percent   Percent   Percent

                                   .00      643       42.9      44.7      44.7
                                   .33      147        9.8      10.2      54.9
                                   .67      107        7.1       7.4      62.3
                                  1.00      542       36.1      37.7     100.0
                                    .        61        4.1    Missing
                                         -------    -------   -------
                                 Total    1500      100.0     100.0

        Hi-Res Chart  # 9:Bar chart of women's right to a legal abortion-3 items

            Mean         .460      Std err      .012    Median       .333
            Mode         .000      Std dev      .458    Variance     .209
            Kurtosis   -1.810      S E Kurt     .129    Skewness     .168
            S E Skew     .065      Range       1.000    Minimum      .000
            Maximum     1.000      Sum       662.333

            Valid cases  1439      Missing cases   61
```

or

`((race = 1 or race = 2) and not SYSMIS(abortion))` [23]

which is equivalent to commands you would type in the syntax window, such as:

```
SELECT IF (RACE EQ 1 OR RACE EQ 2).
SELECT IF NOT MISSING(abortion).
```

You can add additional parameters as you see fit. Once you decide on the final selection criteria, implement the file command and save this new subset of data under its own file name using the "Save As . . ." option in the File menu.

Exercise 8: If you are working with the GSS, then this is your chance to reduce substantially the cost of using SPSS as well as improve response time. Go ahead and create a new system file with just those cases of interest.

Now that we have created the subset of data with which we shall work, we can run the tabular and summary statistics we noted before, thus getting a clearer picture of the characteristics of people in our analysis. I encourage you to rerun these earlier procedures with the selected cases across all your variables in your or our GSS study.

---

[23] This assumes that you have saved a file with the new variable "ABORTION."

Exercise 9: After creating this modified file, execute the descriptive procedures in a variety of ways. Try further work with the graphics options. Remember to first consider the level of measurement of each variable, and then determine the most appropriate statistics and graphing techniques.

Bivariate Analysis

Now that we know that we may have faith in the reliability of our scale, we can begin to explore several of the research questions we listed earlier.

- Are there significant changes over the last two decades in Americans' attitudes toward legal abortion?
- Are there significant differences among people from different racial groups, gender categories, or religious groups on the variables used to measure attitudes toward legal abortion?
- Are there significant differences between people with different familial experiences (e.g., marital status, having children) on the variables used to measure attitudes toward legal abortion?

A useful analytic tool to address these questions is the CROSSTABS procedure. The general format of the CROSSTABS command in SPSS is:

```
CROSSTABS TABLES= varlist, varlist BY varlist...varlist/CELLS list
```

To this command, we will add the statistics option, which has the form:

```
/STATISTICS list.
```

Thus, if we wished to examine the relationship between the variables of legal abortion rights and change over time, religion, race, or sex we could do so with the following command sequence:

```
CROSSTABS TABLES= ABORTN3 BY YEAR, RELIG, RACE, SEX, RACESEX
 /CELLS COUNT, COLUMN
 /STATISTICS CHISQ, LAMBDA, GAMMA, ETA, CORR.
```

Alternately, we could simply select:

Statistics ➤
   Summarize ➤
      Crosstabs . . .

and then enter the appropriate variables, choose the Statistics option and appropriate bivariate summary statistics, and run the routine.

In either case, in addition to producing standard contingency tables that will list: (1) each variable, related values, and labels; (2) the number of cases for each value of each variable; and (3) the number of cases for each intersection of the variable pair, this CROSSTABS procedure will produce important summary statistics of: chi square, lambda, eta, gamma, and Pearsonian r.

The chi-square measure will enable us to test if the observed differences in the sample are sufficiently large for us to conclude that such differences exist in the population. Table 14 includes one of these outputs, attitudes toward legal abortion by year. The data illustrates well that there has been a significant change over the years—with a higher proportion of respondents supporting the rights of access to a legal abortion among the 1973 (43.4%) and 1993 (42.3%) respondents than at other times (35.1%, 31.4%, and 37.5% in 1978, 1983, and 1988, respectively).

When you are examining variables where there are relatively few cases for certain attributes and you are using the crosstabs command, it is often prudent to aggregate such categories and reassign the value labels. Here I recommend the following:

```
RECODE ABORTN3 (0=0)(.3 THRU .7 = 1)(1=2).
VALUE LABEL ABORTN3 0 "AGAINST" 1 "SOMETIMES" 2 "FOR".
```

and for the variable of religion:

```
RECODE RELIG (3 THRU 5=3).
VALUE LABEL RELIG 1 'PROTESTANT' 2 'CATHOLIC' 3 'JEW/NONE/OTHER'.
```

TABLE 14
Abortion Attitudes by Year

```
-> TITLE "BIVARIATE STATISTICS".
-> GET FILE="Jeff's HD:SPSS 6.1:GSS7393s.sav".
-> RECODE abany,abdefect,abhlth,abnomore,abpoor,abrape,absingle
->        (0=99)(1=1)(2=0)(ELSE=99).
-> MISSING VALUES abany,abdefect,abhlth,abnomore,abpoor,abrape,absingle (99) .
-> COMPUTE abortn3=MEAN.3(abnomore,abpoor,absingle).
-> VARIABLE LABEL ABORTN3 "WOMEN'S RIGHT TO A LEGAL ABORTION-3 ITEMS".
-> SELECT IF ((race  = 1 or race  = 2) AND NOT SYSMIS(ABORTN3)).
-> CROSSTABS TABLES= ABORTN3 BY YEAR
->    /CELLS COUNT, COLUMN
->    /STATISTICS CHISQ, LAMBDA, GAMMA, ETA, CORR.
```

```
                    YEAR                                    Page 1 of 1
           Count |
           Col Pct|
                  |                                          Row
                  |    73|    78|    83|    88|    93| Total
ABORTN3    -------+------+------+------+------+------+
              .00 |   114|   120|   142|   132|   116|   624
                  |  39.6|  42.1|  49.5|  48.5|  42.3|  44.4
                  +------+------+------+------+------+
              .33 |    26|    37|    24|    27|    29|   143
                  |   9.0|  13.0|   8.4|   9.9|  10.6|  10.2
                  +------+------+------+------+------+
              .67 |    23|    28|    31|    11|    13|   106
                  |   8.0|   9.8|  10.8|   4.0|   4.7|   7.5
                  +------+------+------+------+------+
             1.00 |   125|   100|    90|   102|   116|   533
                  |  43.4|  35.1|  31.4|  37.5|  42.3|  37.9
                  +------+------+------+------+------+
           Column     288    285    287    272    274   1406
           Total     20.5   20.3   20.4   19.3   19.5  100.0
```

```
     Chi-Square                         Value        DF         Significance
--------------------                   --------      ----       ------------
Pearson                                29.30427       12            .00355
Likelihood Ratio                       29.91794       12            .00287
Mantel-Haenszel test for                 .90135        1            .34242
 linear association
Minimum Expected Frequency -   20.506
     Approximate
       Statistic                    Value      ASE1      Val/ASE0    Significance
--------------------                --------  --------   --------    ------------
Lambda :
   symmetric                         .03053    .01508    2.00405
   with ABORTN3  dependent           .01407    .01963     .71166
   with YEAR     dependent           .04204    .01691    2.43871
Goodman & Kruskal Tau :
   with ABORTN3  dependent           .00705    .00311                 .00308 *2
   with YEAR     dependent           .00523    .00186                 .00347 *2
Gamma                                -.02961    .03183    -.93031
Pearson's R                          -.02533    .02696    -.94936     .34260 *4
Spearman Correlation                 -.02434    .02700    -.91220     .36182 *4
Eta
   with ABORTN3  dependent           .08191
   with YEAR     dependent           .06736
*2 Based on chi-square approximation
*4 VAL/ASE0 is a t-value based on a normal approximation, as is the significance
Number of Missing Observations:   0
```

Since persons of the Jewish faith and those classified as "Other" religions had similar attitudes toward abortion as those with "No" religious affiliation, you may wish to combine them into a single category. Now, execute the command:

```
CROSSTABS TABLES= ABORTN3 BY RELIG
 /CELLS COUNT, COLUMN
 /STATISTICS CHISQ, LAMBDA, GAMMA, ETA, CORR.
```

The output becomes much easier to read and interpret. See Table 15. While more people were opposed to women having access to a legal abortion than were "for" such access, attitudes varied according to religious beliefs, although not quite as skewed as the public may believe. Both in the case of Protestants (47.6%) and Catholics (50.1%), more respondents were "against" such legal access while those who were of other faiths, or had no report of other religious memberships (68.5%), were much more likely to report that they were "for" the right of such legal access. These differences were statistically reliable and likely reflect an important basis for differences of opinions.

The statistics lambda, gamma, eta, and Pearsonian r values are all measures of association. The use of each depends on the level of measurement of each variable. Use the following table to help you decide which measure(s) of association is most appropriate for your study:

Dependent Variable Level of Measurement	Independent Variable Level of Measurement		
	Nominal	Ordinal	Interval/Ratio
Nominal	Lambda	Lambda	Lambda
Ordinal	Lambda	Gamma	Gamma
Interval/ratio	Eta	Eta/Gamma	Pearson's r

Note: Some people argue that you can treat ordinal-level variables that are not very skewed and that have relatively few categories as interval-level data—"metric-level data"—and use Pearson's r values.

In the current table, ABORTN3 BY RELIG, the variable of religious affiliation was measured at the nominal level and the variable of abortion attitudes may be treated as measured at the ordinal or interval level. Thus, you could argue reasonably that knowledge of respondents' religion reduces our errors in predicting attitudes toward abortion more than 20% (i.e., Gamma = .22 reduction in error; Eta, with Abortion as the dependent variable = .247 ~ 6.1% reduction in error). We will have more to say about this idea later.

One of the nicer features of using SPSS is the power it gives you to examine variable relationships using dependent, independent, and control variables. For example, you may be interested in comparing attitudes toward abortion by race controlling for sex—that is, comparing black and white men with each other and then comparing black and white women with each other. This could be accomplished easily by substituting the current CROSSTABS command with:

```
CROSSTABS TABLES=ABORTN3 BY RACE BY SEX.
    (Don't forget optional CELL and STATISTICS commands.)
```

Note that the intervening or control variable, in this case SEX, must be listed after an additional BY keyword. (You may have up to four levels of control variables or a maximum of five BY keywords.) This command will produce a separate table for males and for females where each table will enable you to compare black and white respondents' abortion attitude scores for that sex attribute. Of course, you could easily compare all four groups with the RACESEX variable.

```
CROSSTABS TABLES=ABORTN3 BY RACESEX.
```

And then you might wish to examine the RACESEX variable for each year as well as across all years with the command:

```
CROSSTABS TABLES=ABORTN3 BY RACESEX/ABORTN3 BY RACESEX BY YEAR.
```

Pretty easy; pretty neat. . . .

TABLE 15
Abortion Attitudes by Religious Affiliation

```
\\\\\\ - see previous tables for preliminary commands
-> TEMPORARY.
-> RECODE ABORTN3 (0=0)(.3 THRU .7 = 1)(1=2).
-> VALUE LABEL ABORTN3 0 "AGAINST" 1 "SOMETIMES" 2 "FOR".
-> RECODE RELIG (3 THRU 5=3).
-> VALUE LABEL RELIG 1 'PROTESTANT' 2 'CATHOLIC' 3 'JEW/NONE/OTHER'.
-> CROSSTABS TABLES= ABORTN3 BY RELIG
->   /CELLS COUNT, COLUMN
->   /STATISTICS CHISQ, LAMBDA, GAMMA, ETA, CORR.

ABORTN3   WOMEN'S RIGHT TO A LEGAL ABORTION-3 ITEM
by  RELIG  RS RELIGIOUS PREFERENCE

                   RELIG                            Page 1 of 1
           Count  |
           Col Pct|PROTESTA CATHOLIC JEW/NONE
                  |NT                /OTHER    Row
                  |      1 |      2 |      3 | Total
ABORTN3    -------+--------+--------+--------+
             .00  |    408 |    183 |     31 |   622
      AGAINST    |   47.6 |   50.1 |   17.1 |  44.3
           -------+--------+--------+--------+
            1.00  |    154 |     69 |     26 |   249
      SOMETIMES  |   17.9 |   18.9 |   14.4 |  17.7
           -------+--------+--------+--------+
            2.00  |    296 |    113 |    124 |   533
         FOR     |   34.5 |   31.0 |   68.5 |  38.0
           -------+--------+--------+--------+
           Column      858      365      181    1404
            Total     61.1     26.0     12.9   100.0

         Chi-Square                  Value         DF       Significance
---------------------------       ----------      ----      ------------
Pearson                             88.39841        4         .00000
Likelihood Ratio                    89.34234        4         .00000
Mantel-Haenszel test for            45.00578        1         .00000
    linear association

Minimum Expected Frequency -    32.100

Approximate
    Statistic               Value      ASE1      Val/ASE0   Significance
---------------------       --------   --------  --------   ------------
Lambda :
    symmetric                .07003     .00873    7.62296
    with ABORTN3  dependent  .11893     .01494    7.62296
    with RELIG    dependent  .00000     .00000
Goodman & Kruskal Tau :
    with ABORTN3  dependent  .04023     .00767               .00000 *2
    with RELIG    dependent  .01934     .00432               .00000 *2

Gamma                        .21985     .04025    5.28859

Pearson's R                  .17910     .02586    6.81646    .00000 *4
Spearman Correlation         .14230     .02660    5.38305    .00000 *4
Eta :
    with ABORTN3  dependent  .24712
    with RELIG    dependent  .18107

*2 Based on chi-square approximation
*4 VAL/ASE0 is a t-value based on a normal approximation, as is the significance

Number of Missing Observations:  2
```

FIGURE 18
T-Test Dialog Box

Exercise 10: Now go ahead and run the appropriate CROSSTABS procedures on the data for other variables. Go ahead and try it out. Then, take a few moments and think about how best to interpret what your outputs mean and the similarities and/or differences between the results across the different survey years.

Our variable of interest, ABORTION, provides us with the opportunity to use two other related hypotheses testing measures—the T-test and ANOVA or Analysis of Variance. The T-test is used to compare the mean values of a dependent variable (e.g. ABORTION) when there are only two attributes of an independent variable (e.g., SEX, or as we have done here, RACE). The T-test may be invoked from the menu bar with:

Statistics ➤
  Compare Means ➤
    Independent Samples T-test . . .

which will produce a dialog box like that of Figure 18. Once you select each and every dependent variable used to measure respondents' attitudes toward abortion and place them in the "Test Variable(s):" box, a simple click on the independent variable, SEX, will produce:

sex(? ?)

SPSS is asking for you to indicate the values that will define the two groups. A press of the "Define Groups . . ." will bring the subdialog box—as seen in the second part of Figure 18. Selecting the original values of "1" and "2" will complete the building of the T-test expression. A press of "Continue" and then "OK" will invoke the T-tests. See Figure 18.

The procedure statement for invoking the T-test directly from the syntax window is straightforward. It takes the form:

```
T-TEST GROUPS = varname (val1,val2)
   /VARIABLES = varlist.
```

TABLE 16
Abortion Attitudes by Sex

```
\\\\\\ - see previous tables for preliminary commands
-> TEMPORARY.
-> RECODE ABORTN3 (0=0)(.3 THRU .7 = 1)(1=2).
-> VALUE LABEL ABORTN3 0 "AGAINST" 1 "SOMETIMES" 2 "FOR".
-> RECODE RELIG (3 THRU 5=3).
-> VALUE LABEL RELIG 1 'PROTESTANT' 2 'CATHOLIC' 3 'JEW/NONE/OTHER'.
-> T-TEST
->     GROUPS=sex(1 2)
->     /VARIABLES = abortn3.


t-tests for Independent Samples of SEX      RESPONDENTS SEX
                           Number
   Variable               of Cases      Mean        SD      SE of Mean
   -----------------------------------------------------------------
   ABORTN3  WOMEN'S RIGHT TO A LEGAL ABORTION-3 ITEM

   MALE                      561       .4973      .456        .019
   FEMALE                    845       .4406      .457        .016
   -----------------------------------------------------------------

           Mean Difference = .0567

           Levene's Test for Equality of Variances: F= .031   P= .860


              t-test for Equality of Means                         95%
   Variances  t-value     df      2-Tail Sig    SE of Diff      CI for Diff
   -----------------------------------------------------------------
   Equal       2.28      1404       .023         .025         (.008, .106)
   Unequal     2.28      1201.05    .023         .025         (.008, .106)
```

After the procedure name, the word GROUPS must appear if you wish to run a test of independent samples. (The keyword PAIRS is used when working with related samples.) Since a T-TEST can compare only two groups at a time, you are asked to specify which two values of an independent variable are appropriate. The VARIABLES keyword provides you an opportunity to list which dependent variable(s) you wish to test. For example, in our study, the following T-TEST procedure works well:

T-TEST GROUPS = SEX(1,2)/VARIABLES = ABORTION.

or, we can test all the items as well as the summary scale score with the command:

T-TEST GROUPS = SEX(0,1)
  /VARIABLES=abany abdefect abhlth abnomore abpoor abrape absingle.

That is, SPSS is to execute the T-test on each of our ABORTION items as well as our index scale score by comparing males and females. Note that no STATISTICS subcommand is needed. See Table 16.

The output from the T-TEST procedure is segmented by variables and types of information. For each dependent variable, SPSS reports descriptive statistics (number of cases, mean, etc.) for each grouping in the first part of the output. An F-value is then calculated. It will help you to determine which T-test value to use. The average difference on the three-item abortion index variable between males and females was .0567. Test for equality of variances is reported next. (If the F-value is not significant, then use the pooled variance T-value.) For our study, there was a significant difference between female and male mean values (T-value $_{[1,404\ df]}$ = 2.28, sig = .023), although this difference is numerically not large (.0567). For these respondents, you can run each of the specific abortion questions. In addition, you can now run the T-test procedure for the variable of RACE, if you wish, by simply substituting the variable name SEX with RACE. But, what if you wish to compare all four race/sex categories?

If you wish to compare more than two groups at the same time, then you will need to use the Analysis of Variance, ANOVA, procedure. SPSS has several such procedures. The procedure that best fits our needs here is called ONEWAY. Not surprisingly, it is a one-way analysis of variance test. In addition to calculating appropriate sums of squares and F-values, it will report tests for homogeneity of variance, allow you to make a priori contrast comparisons of any combination of groups, and make a posteriori comparisons as well:

Statistics ➤
   Compare Means ➤
      Oneway ANOVA . . .

which will bring forward an ANOVA dialog box like that of Figure 19.

Once you choose ABORTN3 as the "Dependent List:" variable and RACESEX as the "Factor" or independent variable, you will have to "Define the Range . . .". See the second dialog box. This is where you would enter the values of 1—"Minimum:" and 4 "Maximum:". A press on the "Continue" button returns to the original dialog box with the values of 1 and 4 present next to variable of RACESEX.

For the sake of illustration, let us assume that we wish to compare the race-sex groups (black male, black female, white male, and white female) on our ABORTION variable. Additionally, we wish to test the hypothesis that black females and white females were different from one another. Finally, we would like to find out if there are any other differences. Thus, we shall use the subcommands of "Contrasts . . ." for the a priori comparison of African-American females with white females. A press on the "Contrasts . . ." button produces the third dialog box in Figure 19. For each of the RACESEX attributes a value in the "Coefficients:" box must be keyed. These values must be keyed in the same order as the attributes and must, when completed, total to 0.000. Thus, to select the two female groups for a priori comparison, one must enter the values of 0, 1, 0, −1.

To select the multiple comparison procedure across all RACESEX categories, select the "Post Hoc . . ." button and then select the "Duncan's multiple range test." A press of the "Continue" button returns the original One-Way dialog box. A press of "OK" executes the ANOVA procedure. Finally, additional important summary statistics and labels may be requested from the "Options . . ." button. Choose both available summary statistics and choose also the display label option.

Here is the general format, if you wish to enter this command via the syntax window:

```
ONEWAY varlist BY varname (min,max)
   /CONTRASTS wt wt wt wt
   /RANGES test
   /FORMAT LABELS
   /STATISTICS list.
```

Or, the procedure command would look like this:

```
ONEWAY ABORTION BY RACESEX (1,4)
   /CONTRAST= 0 1 0 -1
   /RANGES=DUNCAN
   /FORMAT LABELS
   /STATISTICS ALL
   /MISSING ANALYSIS.
```

Table 17 illustrates this output. First, SPSS produces the standard analysis of variance F-test table. Then, for each group, it produces summary descriptive information (e.g., counts, mean, standard deviation, etc.).

The second section of the output reports the contrasts. These are basically T-tests. Several contrasts may be run at any one time. Here we were just interested in running African-American females vs. white females. Note that a reliable difference was found.

The third section of the output reports the tests for homogeneity of variance. To help determine how much confidence you can have in your F-value, tests for homogeneity of variances are performed. (Generally, if these are significant, then you cannot have a great deal of faith in your direct ANOVA output.)

FIGURE 19
One-Way ANOVA Dialog Box

The final section of the ONEWAY output is the a posteriori comparisons. Our procedure indicated that we wished to run the DUNCAN test. Note the organization of the summary table and the placement of stars where homogeneous subsets were found.

Quite a clearer pattern emerges when examining the variable of marital status. Those persons whose current marital status was "Never Married" (mean on abortion scale = .5638) were quite different from both of the other aggregates (those persons "Married," mean = .4458 or "Previously Married," mean = .4254). See Table 18. These differences were statistically reliable: $F(2,1401) = 7.9381$; sig = 0004. (We cannot determine directly from this output if these observed abortion attitude scale differences of "Never Married" persons vs. the other groups were due to marital status differences or, perhaps, age. This is an interesting question requiring multivariate techniques—to be explored soon.)

TABLE 17
Abortion Attitudes by Race and Sex

```
\\\\\\ - see previous tables for preliminary commands
ONEWAY ABORTION BY RACESEX (1, 4)
  /CONTRAST= 0 1 0 -1
  /RANGES=DUNCAN
  /FORMAT LABELS
  /STATISTICS ALL
  /MISSING ANALYSIS .

             - - - - O N E W A Y - - - - -

     Variable  ABORTN3    WOMEN'S RIGHT TO A LEGAL ABORTION-3 ITEM
     By Variable  RACESEX    RACE AND SEX IDENTIFIER

                          Analysis of Variance

                          Sum of        Mean              F        F
      Source        D.F.  Squares      Squares          Ratio    Prob.
Between Groups        3    2.0909       .6970           3.3444   .0186
Within Groups      1402  292.1771       .2084
Total              1405  294.2681

                          Standard    Standard
Group       Count   Mean  Deviation    Error     Minimum  Maximum   95 Pct Conf Int for Mean

WH-MALE      513   .4964    .4584       .0202     .0000   1.0000    .4567  TO    .5362
WH-FEMAL     750   .4529    .4600       .0168     .0000   1.0000    .4199  TO    .4859
AA-MALE       48   .5069    .4402       .0635     .0000   1.0000    .3791  TO    .6348
AA-FEMAL      95   .3439    .4251       .0436     .0000   1.0000    .2573  TO    .4305

Total       1406   .4633    .4576       .0122                       .4393  TO    .4872

       Fixed Effects Model            .4565       .0122                     .4394  to    .4871

       Random Effects Model                       .0302                     .3671  to    .5595

Random Effects Model - estimate of between component variance     1.808E-03

     Variable  ABORTN3    WOMEN'S RIGHT TO A LEGAL ABORTION-3 ITEM
     By Variable  RACESEX    RACE AND SEX IDENTIFIER

Contrast Coefficient Matrix

          WH-MALE      AA-MALE
              WH-FEMAL     AA-FEMAL

Contrast 1    .0   1.0     .0   -1.0
```

TABLE 17
Abortion Attitudes by Race and Sex *(continued)*

			Pooled Variance Estimate				Separate Variance Estimate		
	Value	S. Error	T Value	D.F.	T Prob.	S. Error	T Value	D.F.	T Prob.
Contrast 1	.1090	.0497	2.193	1402.0	.028	.0467	2.333	123.6	.021

Levene Test for Homogeneity of Variances

```
Statistic    df1    df2      2-tail Sig.
 7.7343       3    1402         .000
```

```
   Variable  ABORTN3     WOMEN'S RIGHT TO A LEGAL ABORTION-3 ITEM
By Variable  RACESEX     RACE AND SEX IDENTIFIER
```

Multiple Range Tests: Duncan test with significance level .05

The difference between two means is significant if
  MEAN(J)-MEAN(I) >= .3228 * RANGE * SQRT(1/N(I) + 1/N(J))
  with the following value(s) for RANGE:

```
Step      2     3     4
RANGE   2.78  2.92  3.01
```

(*) Indicates significant differences which are shown in the lower triangle

```
                    A W
                    A H W A
                    - - H A
                    F F - -
                    E E M M
                    M M A A
                    A A L L
                    L L E E

Mean        RACESEX
.3439       AA-FEMAL
.4529       WH-FEMAL    *
.4964       WH-MALE     *
.5069       AA-MALE
```

TABLE 18
Abortion Attitudes by Marital Status

```
-> TITLE "BIVARIATE STATISTICS".
-> GET
->    FILE="Jeff's HD:SPSS 6.1:GSS7393s.sav".
-> EXECUTE.
-> RECODE abany,abdefect,abhlth,abnomore,abpoor,abrape,absingle
->    (0=99)(1=1)(2=0)(ELSE=99).
-> MISSING VALUES abany,abdefect,abhlth,abnomore,abpoor,abrape,absingle (99).
-> COMPUTE abortn3=MEAN.3 (abnomore,abpoor,absingle).
-> VARIABLE LABEL ABORTN3 "WOMEN'S RIGHT TO A LEGAL ABORTION-3 ITEMS".
-> SELECT IF ((race = 1 or race = 2) AND NOT SYSMIS(ABORTN3)).
-> RECODE MARITAL (1=1)(2,3,4 = 2)(5=3).
-> VALUE LABELS MARITAL
->    1 "Married" 2 "Prev-Married" 3 "Nev-Married".
-> ONEWAY
->    abortn3 BY MARITAL(1 3)
->    /RANGES=DUNCAN
->    /HARMONIC NONE
->    /FORMAT LABELS
->    /STATISTICS ALL
->    /MISSING ANALYSIS .
```

- - - - - O N E W A Y - - - - -

Variable   ABORTN3   WOMEN'S RIGHT TO A LEGAL ABORTION-3 ITEM
By Variable MARITAL   MARITAL STATUS
Analysis of Variance

```
                           Sum of       Mean        F       F
     Source       D.F.    Squares      Squares    Ratio   Prob.
Between Groups      2     3.2936       1.6468    7.9381   .0004
Within Groups    1401   290.6446        .2075
Total            1403   293.9382
```

```
                            Standard   Standard
Group     Count    Mean    Deviation    Error    Minimum  Maximum   95 Pct Conf Int for Mean

Married     833   .4458     .4562       .0158     .0000   1.0000    .4148   TO   .4768
Prev-Mar    315   .4254     .4542       .0256     .0000   1.0000    .3750   TO   .4757
Nev-Marr    256   .5638     .4548       .0284     .0000   1.0000    .5078   TO   .6198

Total      1404   .4627     .4577       .0122     .0000   1.0000    .4388   TO   .4866

Fixed Effects Model       .4555        .0122                                 .4389  to   .4867

Random Effects Model                   .0416                                 .2838  to   .6417

Random Effects Model - estimate of between component variance    3.633E-03
```

TABLE 18
Abortion Attitudes by Marital Status (*continued*)

```
Variable  ABORTN3      WOMEN'S RIGHT TO A LEGAL ABORTION-3 ITEM
  By Variable  MARITAL    MARITAL STATUS

Levene Test for Homogeneity of Variances

    Statistic      df1        df2      2-tail Sig.
      .1903         2        1401         .827

- - - - O N E W A Y - - - - -

    Variable  ABORTN3      WOMEN'S RIGHT TO A LEGAL ABORTION-3 ITEM
  By Variable  MARITAL    MARITAL STATUS

Multiple Range Tests:  Duncan test with significance level .05

The difference between two means is significant if
  MEAN(J)-MEAN(I)  >= .3221 * RANGE * SQRT(1/N(I) + 1/N(J))
  with the following value(s) for RANGE:

Step       2      3
RANGE    2.78   2.92
(*) Indicates significant differences which are shown in the lower triangle

                     P   N
                     r   M   e
                     e   a   v
                     v   r   -
                     -   r   M
                     M   i   a
                     a   e   r
                     r   d   r

   Mean      MARITAL
   .4254     Prev-Mar
   .4458     Married
   .5638     Nev-Marr      *   *
```

Appendix I: A Learner's Guide to SPSS 6.1

Exercise 11: Here's your chance to run appropriate T-TEST and ONEWAY procedures. Take a few minutes and try them on your data or on the data for any specific year of respondents.

In addition to comparing ascribed status groups (e.g., males vs. females, African-Am. vs. whites), we indicated an interest in determining the relationship, if any, between attitudes toward abortion and the explanatory variables of socioeconomic status and political philosophy. We noted two general research questions.

- Are there significant correlations between the variables of income, age, or education with attitudes toward legal abortion?
- Is there any substantial difference between how those who identify with the Democratic or Republican parties view a woman's right of access for a legal abortion? What about self-described political views—conservatism or liberalism—and their relationship to attitudes toward a woman's right to a legal abortion?

Testing for significant associations between variable sets is easy with SPSS. You have several options, including the command CORRELATION. From the menu bar select:

Statistics ➤
  Correlate ➤
    Bivariate . . .

These choices invoke the bivariate correlation dialogue boxes as seen in Figure 20.

To test this first correlate question, simply select the variables of abortn3 age, educ, degree, realinc, etc. from the picker box and make sure that each of the following have been selected: (1) Pearson (correlation coefficient), (2) Two-tailed (test of significance),[24] (3) and Display actual significance levels. A click on the "Options . . ." brings forward the window in which you can select: (1) Means and standard deviations and (2) "Exclude cases pairwise." This final optional choice will include as many cases as possible for each variable. If you had chosen "listwise," the variable with the least number of actual cases (POLVIEWS) would serve as the standard for the maximum number of cases available—fewer than 1,000 cases for each variable pair would then be used.

The format of the CORRELATION command, when using the syntax window, is straightforward:

```
CORRELATION varlist WITH varlist.
```

or

```
CORRELATION age educ realinc abortn3.
```

or we can take advantage of several options and get a more complete output with the command:

```
CORRELATION
    /VARIABLES= abortn3 age educ degree realinc partyid polviews
    /PRINT=TWOTAIL SIG
    /STATISTICS DESCRIPTIVES
    /MISSING=PAIRWISE.
```

SPSS will provide the usual summary statistics and, more important, Pearson's "Correlation Coefficients" values, the number of valid cases, and the level of statistical significance for each pair. In this case, I have requested two-tailed tests of significance. The report is printed in matrix format so that you or I can inspect the correlations between not only my variable of interest (abortn3) and explanatory variables, but also the correlations between each pair of explanatory variables. In addition, by including the STATISTICS subcommand, SPSS will provide a list of the mean and standard deviation values for each variable. See Table 19.

From these data (reading the first column of results from Table 19) it is clear that there is a significant, albeit small, correlation between the variable of attitudes toward legal access to abortion and age (r = −.0814)—the higher the age of respondents, the less willing to support access to a legal abortion; educational attainment as measured by the number of years of completed schooling (r = .2286) or the earned degree (r = .1972)—the greater the education, the more willing to support access; and income (r = .1196) standardized on 1986 dollar values.

---

[24] If you have hypothesized the direction of the relationship between variable pairs, then change this option to "One-tailed" test of significance.

FIGURE 20
Bivariate Correlation Dialog Box

[Bivariate Correlations dialog box showing variables list (partyid, polviews, race, relig, satcity, satfam, satfrnd) and selected Variables (abortn3, age, educ, degree, realinc). Correlation Coefficients: ☒ Pearson ☐ Kendall's tau-b ☐ Spearman. Test of Significance: ● Two-tailed ○ One-tailed. ☒ Display actual significance level. Buttons: OK, Paste, Reset, Cancel, Help, Options...]

[Bivariate Correlations: Options dialog box. Statistics: ☒ Means and standard deviations, ☐ Cross-product deviations and covariances. Missing Values: ● Exclude cases pairwise, ○ Exclude cases listwise. Buttons: Continue, Cancel, Help]

Examining the relationship between political party affiliation (PARTYID), political liberalism/conservatism (POLVIEWS), and abortion attitudes takes only a second or two longer. Here you must recall that NORC personnel used the values of 0 through 6 for "Strong Democrat" to "Strong Republican." They used also a value of "7" to indicate "other party" affiliation. You will need to recode the value "7" to a missing value before adding these variables to your "/VARIABLES=" roster and invoking the CORRELATION procedure. (No such problem exists with the variable POLVIEWS.)

Some will be surprised to find that there is no large correlation ($r = -.0517$, $p = .054$) between the level of political party identification and attitude toward abortion. However, political views, at least as was measured by the degree of self-identified liberalism (i.e., measured on a seven-point scale from extremely liberal—"1"—to extremely conservative—"7") was significantly correlated ($r = -.2211$; $p\ .001$) with the attitude toward the right of women to obtain a legal abortion—those with greater levels of self-described conservatism held less "liberal" views on the right of access to a legal abortion.

In examining the table further it is important to note that almost all of the socioeconomic explanatory variables were significantly correlated with each other: for example, the variables of EDUC and DEGREE ($r = .8571$), REALINC and DEGREE ($r = .3766$), AGE and EDUC ($r = -.2228$). This is what one would reasonably expect. See the remaining matrix items in Table 19. Finally, on some of these variables and variable pairs (e.g., ABORTN3 with REALINC and POLVIEWS) there were many missing cases—the number of cases falls from 1,406 cases to 1,196 cases and 944 cases, respectively. Thus, we now know that considerable care would be required to include all these variables in any multivariate model.

Appendix I: A Learner's Guide to SPSS 6.1

TABLE 19
Bivariate Correlations Output

```
-> TITLE "BIVARIATE STATISTICS".
-> GET FILE="Jeff's HD:SPSS 6.1:GSS7393s.sav".
-> EXECUTE.
-> RECODE abany,abdefect,abhlth,abnomore,abpoor,abrape,absingle
->       (0=99)(1=1)(2=0)(ELSE=99).
-> MISSING VALUES abany,abdefect,abhlth,abnomore,abpoor,abrape,absingle (99) .
-> COMPUTE abortn3=MEAN.3(abnomore,abpoor,absingle).
-> VARIABLE LABEL ABORTN3 "WOMEN'S RIGHT TO A LEGAL ABORTION-3 ITEMS".
-> SELECT IF ((race  = 1 or race  = 2) AND NOT SYSMIS(ABORTN3)).
-> RECODE PARTYID(7=9).
-> CORRELATIONS
->      /VARIABLES= abortn3 age educ degree realinc partyid polviews
->      /PRINT=TWOTAIL SIG
->      /STATISTICS DESCRIPTIVES
->      /MISSING=PAIRWISE .
```

Variable	Cases	Mean	Std Dev
ABORTN3	1406	.4633	.4576
AGE	1400	43.3371	17.0944
EDUC	1404	12.4224	3.1384
DEGREE	1404	1.2066	1.1207
REALINC	1300	30600.3038	25983.5471
PARTYID	1386	2.6890	1.9900
POLVIEWS	944	4.1970	1.3392

- - Correlation Coefficients - -

	ABORTN3	AGE	EDUC	DEGREE	REALINC	PARTYID	POLVIEWS
ABORTN3	1.0000 (1406) P= .	-.0814 (1400) P= .002	.2286 (1404) P= .000	.1972 (1404) P= .000	.1196 (1300) P= .000	-.0517 (1386) P= .054	-.2211 (944) P= .000
AGE	-.0814 (1400) P= .002	1.0000 (1400) P= .	-.2228 (1398) P= .000	-.1387 (1398) P= .000	-.0902 (1296) P= .001	.0427 (1380) P= .113	.1175 (939) P= .000
EDUC	.2286 (1404) P= .000	-.2228 (1398) P= .000	1.0000 (1404) P= .	.8571 (1402) P= .000	.3604 (1298) P= .000	.1012 (1384) P= .000	-.0592 (943) P= .069
DEGREE	.1972 (1404) P= .000	-.1387 (1398) P= .000	.8571 (1402) P= .000	1.0000 (1404) P= .	.3766 (1300) P= .000	.1006 (1384) P= .000	-.0593 (944) P= .069
REALINC	.1196 (1300) P= .000	-.0902 (1296) P= .001	.3604 (1298) P= .000	.3766 (1300) P= .000	1.0000 (1300) P= .	.1059 (1282) P= .000	.0117 (875) P= .730
PARTYID	-.0517 (1386) P= .054	.0427 (1380) P= .113	.1012 (1384) P= .000	.1006 (1384) P= .000	.1059 (1282) P= .000	1.0000 (1386) P= .	.2813 (937) P= .000
POLVIEWS	-.2211 (944) P= .000	.1175 (939) P= .000	-.0592 (943) P= .069	-.0593 (944) P= .069	.0117 (875) P= .730	.2813 (937) P= .000	1.0000 (944) P= .

(Coefficient / (Cases) / 2-tailed Significance)   " . " is printed if a coefficient cannot be computed

Just as there are graphic forms and summary statistics for describing a single distribution, SPSS provides procedures for producing scatterplots as well as summary correlation/regression statistics. In SPSS 6.1, you can produce attractive scatterplots. Here's how. From the menu choose:

Graphs ➤
    Scatter . . .

From the Scatterplot dialog box choose:

Simple

and then press the "Define" button. From the Simple Scatterplot dialog box choose which variables you wish to plot in the usual manner; for example, choose DEGREE for the Y-Axis and EDUC for the X-Axis. A click on the "OK" button will produce an appropriate scatterplot similar to that of the first part of Figure 21.

To create a new graph, reselect from the menu bar:

Graphs ➤
    Scatter . . .

and "Define." To remove the variable "DEGREE," select it and then press the left arrow button to its left. Now, select the variable ABORTN3 and press the right arrow key for the Y-Axis variable selection. A press of the "OK" button will complete the process and invoke the creation of the new graph. (You can try additional sets of variables, at your convenience.)

Running the REGRESSION procedure will produce similar summary CORRELATION measures as well as the values for appropriate prediction equations. You don't know how to do this? Read on.

Regression Analysis

While examining correlation values is important, it is only part of the story. It is also important to be able to express the mathematical relationship between, and among, variables. The SPSS REGRESSION procedure provides useful tools to examine such relationships. It may be invoked from the menu bar by selecting:

Statistics ➤
    Regression . . . ➤
        Linear . . .

(While several options have been provided, here we shall concentrate on the most often used standard, simple linear regression.) When the Linear Regression dialog box appears, like that of Figure 22, choose ABORTN3 for your "Dependent:" variable and "EDUC" for your "Independent(s):" variable.

Choosing the "Statistics . . ." option provides an opportunity to produce summary descriptive statistics, too.

Of course, you could have just as easily entered the commands directly in the syntax window. The command would look like this:

```
REGRESSION VARIABLES = ABORTN3 EDUC
    /DESCRIPTIVES MEAN STDDEV CORR SIG N
    /STATISTICS COEFF OUTS CI R ANOVA
    /DEPENDENT abortn3
    /METHOD=ENTER educ.
```

In either case, there are no surprises here. The format of the REGRESSION command is consistent with the procedures just discussed. Once the command name is given, and the optional subcommands entered, the keywords DEPENDENT and METHOD enable you to identify your dependent variable and independent variable, respectively. (We will have more to say about these commands in the next section of this Learner's Guide.) Of course, SPSS will assume you know enough about the levels of measurement of these variables so that the variables you include and the statistics computed are meaningful.

The output will look like that of Table 20. The output is divided into several major parts. The first part is a simple summary of descriptive statistics while the second part reports the bivariate correlation statistics. The third part

FIGURE 21
Scatterplot of Degree on Education; and Attitudes Toward a Legal Abortion on Educational Achievement

FIGURE 22
Dialog Box for Linear Regression

reports how well the variables are correlated (Multiple R = .22856), how much of the variation in the dependent variable was accounted for by the independent variable(s) (R-Squared = .05224), and whether or not these values are statistically significant by using a standard ANOVA table (F $_{(1, 1402\, df)}$ = 77.27953, Signif F = .000).

The final part of the output provides the estimates for making a prediction. In this case, your model for predicting ABORTN3 scale scores from knowledge of EDUC would be:

```
Predicted abortn3 values = -.049880 +.033330 * EDUC
```

Such a model would reduce our errors in predicting abortion scale scores by slightly more than 5%. Other variables, such as church/synagogue ATTENDance may have more explanatory power. Try one or more.

To draw a linear line on your scatterplot graph, simply calculate the appropriate predicted values for abortion scale scores, plot the points, and then connect them on the graph. That is, choose simple values for education (e.g., "0" years of education, then "20" years of education) and calculate predicted abortion values (e.g., -.05 and .617, respectively). Thus, as you might expect, those with little education were, as a group, estimated to have very little support for legal access while those with more education were, as a group, estimated to have higher levels of support for legal abortion access.

Exercise 12: Bivariate correlation procedures are particularly useful when you are beginning to look for relationships among variable pairs. Take a few minutes and try these procedures on other variables or on your data set.

Multivariate Statistics Using Regression Analysis

The best known and most widely used multivariate technique is multiple regression. It is simply the logical extension of the simple linear model that we encountered earlier. The REGRESSION procedure is a powerful tool that works well with two, three, or more independent variables. It can be used to find the best linear fit among several

TABLE 20
Regression Output

```
-> TITLE "BIVARIATE STATISTICS".
-> GET FILE="Jeff's HD:SPSS 6.1:GSS7393s.sav".
-> EXECUTE.
-> RECODE abany,abdefect,abhlth,abnomore,abpoor,abrape,absingle
->     (0=99)(1=1)(2=0)(ELSE=99).
-> MISSING VALUES abany,abdefect,abhlth,abnomore,abpoor,abrape,absingle (99) .
-> COMPUTE abortn3=MEAN.3(abnomore,abpoor,absingle).
-> VARIABLE LABEL ABORTN3 "WOMEN'S RIGHT TO A LEGAL ABORTION-3 ITEMS".
-> SELECT IF ((race  = 1 or race  = 2) AND NOT SYSMIS(ABORTN3)).
-> REGRESSION
->    /DESCRIPTIVES MEAN STDDEV CORR SIG N
->    /MISSING LISTWISE
->    /STATISTICS COEFF OUTS CI R ANOVA
->    /CRITERIA=PIN(.05) POUT(.10)
->    /NOORIGIN
->    /DEPENDENT abortn3
->    /METHOD=ENTER educ  .
```

* * * *   M U L T I P L E   R E G R E S S I O N   * * * *

Listwise Deletion of Missing Data

```
             Mean    Std Dev   Label

ABORTN3      .464      .458    WOMEN'S RIGHT TO A LEGAL ABORTION-3 ITEM
EDUC       12.422     3.138    HIGHEST YEAR OF SCHOOL COMPLETED

N of Cases =  1404

Correlation, 1-tailed Sig:

            ABORTN3         EDUC

ABORTN3      1.000          .229
                .           .000

EDUC          .229         1.000
             .000            .
```

* * * *   M U L T I P L E   R E G R E S S I O N   * * * *

Equation Number 1   Dependent Variable..   ABORTN3   WOMEN'S RIGHT TO A LEGAL A

   Descriptive Statistics are printed on Page   2

Block Number 1. Method: Enter   EDUC

Variable(s) Entered on Step Number 1..   EDUC   HIGHEST YEAR OF SCHOOL COMPLETED

```
Multiple R            .22856       Analysis of Variance
R Square              .05224                       DF      Sum of Squares     Mean Square
Adjusted R Square     .05157       Regression       1            15.35050        15.35050
Standard Error        .44569       Residual      1402           278.48774          .19864

                                   F =      77.27953       Signif F =  .0000
```

------------------------------ Variables in the Equation ------------------------------

```
Variable              B         SE B     95% Confdnce Intrvl B        Beta         T     Sig T

EDUC              .033330     .003791     .025892       .040767      .228564    8.791   .0000
(Constant)        .049880     .048577    -.045411       .145171                 1.027   .3047
```

End Block Number   1   All requested variables entered.

independent or explanatory variables and a single dependent variable, as long as each of these variables can be treated as though they were measured at the metric level. This is not a problem with most of our variables (e.g., EDUC, AGE, and CHILDS). Other explanatory variables we shall have to RECODE to reflect a dichotomy using the values of 0 and 1 for SEX and RACE. (This is often referred to as creating a "dummy" variable.)

```
RECODE RACE (2=0).
VAR LABELS RACE "Proportion White".
RECODE SEX (2=0).
VAR LABELS SEX "Proportion Male".
```

All these variables may be treated as interval-level variables.

With only a little more energy, we can create from other important nominal-level variables (e.g., religion and marital status) other appropriate dichotomous variables that use our standard values of 0 and 1. Here are the appropriate commands for creating variables for each religion:

```
COMPUTE PROTEST=0.
IF (RELIG EQ 1)PROTEST=1.
COMPUTE CATHOLIC=0.
IF (RELIG EQ 2)CATHOLIC=1.
COMPUTE JEWISH=0.
IF (RELIG EQ 3)JEWISH=1.
COMPUTE OTHR=0.
IF (RELIG EQ 5)OTHR=1.
```

Now, people who reported a typical religious affiliation, or for that matter an atypical religious membership, will have a code of 1 for that "religion." See above. If they were not a member of that religion, they will have a code of 0. Note that the attribute "NONE" appears to be missing. Actually, it will be included in each of the other values and serve as the reference point for each variable. Simple enough.

Similarly, separate variables for each marital status attribute may be created with the command sequence:

```
COMPUTE married=0.
IF (marital eq 1)married=1.
COMPUTE widow=0.
IF (marital eq 2)widow=1.
COMPUTE divorce=0.
IF (marital eq 3)divorce=1.
COMPUTE separat=0.
IF (marital eq 4)separat=1.
```

Note that those coded as "Never Married" do not have a separate variable but are, again, included in the analysis as a reference point.

You may recall from our earlier analysis that the average scores on these abortion items were not related, in a linear manner, to the year in which the survey was taken. Thus it would be inappropriate to include a single variable, "YEAR." Rather, we can create a series of four variables from the five years of study. While which year we use as a reference point is arbitrary, it is often easiest to interpret findings if you know which attribute was associated with the lowest score. If you recall, those persons responding in 1988 had the lowest average ABORT3 score. It makes logical sense to not include it as a separately listed variable. Here are the commands:

```
COMPUTE YR73=0.
IF (YEAR EQ 73)YR73=1.
COMPUTE YR78=0.
IF (YEAR EQ 78)YR78=1.
COMPUTE YR88=0.
IF (YEAR EQ 88)YR88=1.
COMPUTE YR93=0.
IF (YEAR EQ 93)YR93=1.
```

Certainly easy enough. . . .

Appendix I: A Learner's Guide to SPSS 6.1

Once all nonmetric level variables have been handled in this manner, we can implement the REGRESSION procedure. The general form of a more complete REGRESSION procedure for SPSS is:

```
REGRESSION
 /CRITERIA = DEFAULTS PIN(value) POUT(value)
 /DESCRIPTIVES=DEFAULTS VARIANCE COV SIG N
 /VARIABLES = varlist
 /STATISTICS = DEFAULTS CHA HISTORY
 /DEPENDENT = variable
 /method (single option of FORWARD, STEPWISE, etc.)
 /RESIDUALS=DEFAULTS
 /SCATTERPLOT (select temporary variable names).
```

As you can see, SPSS provides a great deal of options and is extremely versatile. It can be used to find the best predictors of any interval level variable. Here's one way to run it with our data.

```
REGRESSION
 /DESCRIPTIVES
 /STATISTICS=DEFAULTS CHA HISTORY
 /VARIABLES= ABORTN3,
    RACE,SEX,AGE,
    EDUC,
    MARRIED TO SEPARAT
    CHILDS,
    PROTEST TO OTHR
    ATTEND,
    YR73 TO YR93
    PARTYID
 /DEPENDENT=ABORTN3
 /STEPWISE
 /RESIDUALS
 /SCATTERPLOT(*PRED,*RESID).
```

This command is not that difficult to decipher since it is an embellishment upon the bivariate example noted above. First, the DESCRIPTIVES keyword will, again, produce means and standard deviation values for each variable as well as a zero-order correlation matrix of all the variables listed in the VARIABLES= statement. Of course, if you wish, you could request SPSS to compute and display the values for variance (use the option, VARIANCE), and the covariance matrix (use the option, COV), as well as other related statistics.

The VARIABLES=[25] specification enables you to specify which variables are included in your run. There is nothing really new here since all listed variables must be spelled as they were spelled earlier when they were declaring. See above. Additionally, you will note that we used the TO convention to identify all the variables we just created; from MARRIED to SEPARATed, from PROTEST (Protestant) to OTHR (other religious affiliation), and from YR73 to YR93. Since these variables are contiguous we can use the TO convention rather than listing each one.

The DEPENDENT= specification subcommand is the easiest of all REGRESSION subcommands. It enables you to identify which variable is to be treated as the dependent variable. You therefore see the variable name ABORTN3. That's all there is to using it.

Optionally, we can request that the REGRESSION procedure be run as an ENTER, FORWARD, BACKWARD, REMOVE, or STEPWISE procedure. Basically, the ENTER command enters all the variables simultaneously while the FORWARD subcommand causes SPSS to enter all the independent variables one at a time and check the F-value and criterion (PIN) tests. The BACKWARD subcommand enters all the variables at once and then begins removing the least powerful explanatory variables one at a time. The STEPWISE subcommand enters each independent variable one at a time, starting with the most powerful predictor, and then finds the second best predictor, the third best predictor, etc., on each new step. In the STEPWISE procedure, entry of an additional independent variable is based on the value of the partial correlation coefficients—those with the largest partial correlation coefficients are entered

---

[25] You may have noticed that I did not include the variables of DEGREE or POLVIEWS. DEGREE was well correlated with EDUC so I have already included the important information. By not including POLVIEWS I do not exclude all the 1973 data. If you wish to include POLVIEWS, recognize that your analysis will be restricted to 1978 and later data.

first. Additional predictor variables are entered, or are removed if they are no longer useful, until all the variables are in the equation or the limits set in the CRITERIA subcommand (default is .05 for entry of any variable) have been reached. Each entry of a new independent variable is treated as a new step, and all equation summary statistics—assuming the STATISTICS subcommand is present (e.g., Multiple R, R-squared, ANOVA, etc.), equation coefficients (e.g., slope, BETA values, significance, etc.), and summary data of those variables not in the equation (e.g., partial correlations, significance, etc.)—are recalculated. See Table 21.

The STATISTICS keyword can cause SPSS to output more than those statistics outlined above. By including the option CHA, a summary of R^2 CHAnges is printed as well as the F-value and significance level. The HISTORY option prints a final summary report at the end of all the steps.

Many researchers argue that it is essential to examine the residuals in order to make sure that they have not violated several of the basic multiple regression statistical assumptions. Well, SPSS is particularly strong in helping you to summarize and identify the RESIDUALS. This is accomplished by outputs that include histograms, normal probability plots, outliers, and test for the residuals.

You may be interested in having SPSS produce a scatterplot using the predicted values and the residual values as variables, or for that matter a variety of other scatterplots. That's exactly what you get with the SCATTERPLOT subcommand. See Table 21.

As you can see, REGRESSION is an enormously powerful procedure that provides a substantial amount of information. The first part of the output lists summary descriptive statistics for each variable across all cases for which there were data on all variables—thus we have 1,363 cases out of the 1,500 sampled cases for whom we have data on each and every variable in our data set. Simple mean and standard deviation values are reported here. Note that by choosing carefully descriptive SPSS variable names for each of the dummy variables, we did not need to enter variable labels and are easily able to interpret the meaning of these summary stats (i.e., .594 of the 1,363 respondents were MARRIED, .083 were WIDOWed, etc.).

The second part of the standard output is a simple correlation matrix where the Pearson r values for each variable pair are presented. The correlation between ABORTN3 and RACE—proportion white—was .045; between ABORTN3 and SEX—proportion male—was .059; etc.

The heart of the REGRESSION output begins in the third section by reporting what is happening on each step of the analysis. Part three was designed to first list summary information and then summary statistics—particularly useful statistics such as "Multiple R," R-Squared, significance levels, etc. for the variables included in the equation at this step of the analysis. You ask which variables? They are listed in the section titled "Variables in the Equation." In addition to the values of the slopes, "b" and standardized slopes, "Beta," T-value, and significance value will be reported for each variable. The last major section of part three—either to its right or immediately following—will report a roster of "Variables not in the Equation." Useful information included here are the values for partial correlations—the correlation between each variable and the dependent variable given that other variables have been entered earlier, and related statistics. In the STEPWISE method you will have an additional page of part three output for each significant variable to be entered into the predictive equation. Once all variables, or all significant variables, have been entered, the typical end statement of part 3 will appear "End Block Number 1 PIN = .050 Limits reached."

Parts 4 and 5, when requested, provide a simple summary of what happened at each step and a calculation for the Durban-Watson test, which checks for problems of multicollinearity among the explanatory variables. As noted earlier, a series of graphs summarizing a variety of calculations are then provided.

If you remember, way back at the beginning of this Appendix, we said that we were interested in finding the best predictors of attitudes toward the rights of women to obtain a legal abortion across the last 20 years of American history. We herein reported the STEPWISE method and standard CRITERIA for independent variable entry and removal across the 1,500 cases—well, across the 1,363 cases for whom we had data on each variable. While we had many independent variables in our original research model (see Figure 1 and our VARIABLES= list in Table 21), only a few variables were found to be "good"—in this case, significant beyond .05—predictors. Not surprisingly, the best predictor (r = −.335)—and entered on step one of the REGRESSION procedure—was church ATTENDance. It was entered first and explained approximately 11% of the variation in the abortion index scores for our data set. See part 3 of Table 21. Next, the variable of EDUCation—number of years of education—was entered since it had the largest partial correlation value (partial r = .258) of all variables yet to be entered into the equation. Note that the report on step 2, both variables, ATTEND and EDUC, are "Variables in the Equation." Education accounted for another

TABLE 21
Multiple Regression Output

```
     * * * *   M U L T I P L E   R E G R E S S I O N   * * * *

Listwise Deletion of Missing Data

          Mean    Std Dev  Label

ABORTN3    .464    .458    WOMEN'S RIGHT TO A LEGAL ABORTION-3 ITEM
RACE       .898    .303    Proportion White
SEX        .397    .489    Proportion Male
AGE      43.337  17.067    AGE OF RESPONDENT
EDUC     12.415   3.135    HIGHEST YEAR OF SCHOOL COMPLETED
MARRIED    .594    .491
WIDOW      .083    .276
DIVORCE    .110    .313
SEPARAT    .032    .177
YR73       .201    .401
YR78       .205    .404
YR88       .199    .399
YR93       .189    .392
CHILDS    1.944   1.837    NUMBER OF CHILDREN
PROTEST    .611    .488
CATHOLIC   .262    .440
JEWISH     .023    .151
OTHR       .021    .142
ATTEND    3.856   2.696    HOW OFTEN R ATTENDS RELIGIOUS SERVICES
PARTYID   2.684   1.989    POLITICAL PARTY AFFILIATION

N of Cases =    1363

Correlation:

          ABORTN3  RACE    SEX    AGE    EDUC   MARRIED WIDOW  DIVORCE SEPARAT  YR73   YR78   YR88   YR93

ABORTN3   1.000    .045   .059  -.082   .228   -.050   -.063   .016   -.031    .061  -.004  -.030   .029
RACE       .045   1.000   .040   .031   .104    .131    .005  -.013   -.130    .000   .015  -.008  -.041
SEX        .059    .040  1.000  -.016   .056    .075   -.151  -.041   -.005    .038  -.029  -.036  -.009
AGE       -.082    .031  -.016  1.000  -.223    .010    .456   .007   -.031   -.035  -.005   .038   .053
EDUC       .228    .104   .056  -.223  1.000    .000   -.165  -.012   -.041   -.098  -.089   .057   .105
MARRIED   -.050    .131   .075   .010   .000   1.000   -.364  -.426   -.221    .079   .049  -.068  -.055
WIDOW     -.063    .005  -.151   .456  -.165   -.364   1.000  -.106   -.055   -.038  -.001   .030  -.018
DIVORCE    .016   -.013  -.041   .007  -.012   -.426   -.106  1.000   -.064   -.059  -.010   .030   .052
SEPARAT   -.031   -.130  -.005  -.031  -.041   -.221   -.055  -.064   1.000    .012  -.021  -.008   .018
YR73       .061    .000   .038  -.035  -.098    .079   -.038  -.059    .012   1.000  -.254  -.250  -.242
YR78      -.004    .015  -.029  -.005  -.089    .049   -.001  -.010   -.021   -.254  1.000  -.253  -.245
YR88      -.030   -.008  -.036   .038   .057   -.068    .030   .030   -.008   -.250  -.253  1.000  -.241
YR93       .029   -.041  -.009   .053   .105   -.055    .018   .052    .018   -.242  -.245  -.241  1.000
```

TABLE 21
Multiple Regression Output (continued)

	CHILDS	PROTEST	CATHOLIC	JEWISH	OTHR	ATTEND	PARTYID				
CHILDS	-.159	-.086	-.062	.331	-.210	.241	.121	.006	.087	.072	.024	-.001	-.075
PROTEST	-.095	-.130	-.067	.122	-.088	.009	.076	.040	-.042	-.069	.035	-.006	.059
CATHOLIC	-.080	.135	-.013	-.065	-.021	.047	-.016	-.060	.004	-.063	-.029	.013	-.066
JEWISH	.171	.052	.043	.012	.157	.029	-.047	.023	-.028	.043	-.031	-.004	-.038
OTHR	.034	-.002	.052	-.009	.068	-.007	-.044	.015	.032	.005	-.009	.019	.022
ATTEND	-.335	-.084	-.102	.142	.043	.118	.039	-.069	-.055	-.019	-.047	.018	.001
PARTYID	-.048	.217	.000	.047	.097	.040	.049	-.036	-.042	-.051	-.024	.034	.048

	CHILDS	PROTEST	CATHOLIC	JEWISH	OTHR	ATTEND	PARTYID
ABORTN3	-.159	-.095	-.080	.171	.034	-.335	-.048
RACE	-.086	-.130	.135	.052	-.002	-.084	.217
SEX	-.062	-.067	-.013	.043	.052	-.102	.000
AGE	.331	.122	-.065	.012	-.009	.142	.047
EDUC	-.210	-.088	-.021	.157	.068	.043	.097
MARRIED	.241	.009	.047	.029	-.007	.118	.040
WIDOW	.121	.076	-.016	-.047	-.044	.039	.049
DIVORCE	.006	.040	-.060	.023	.015	-.069	-.036
SEPARAT	.087	-.042	.004	-.028	.032	-.055	-.042
YR73	.072	-.069	.063	.043	.005	-.019	-.051
YR78	.024	.035	-.029	-.031	-.009	-.047	-.024
YR88	-.001	-.006	.013	-.004	.019	.018	.034
YR93	-.075	.059	-.066	-.038	.022	.001	.048
CHILDS	1.000	.030	.076	-.072	-.029	.130	-.035
PROTEST	.030	1.000	-.747	-.194	-.182	.090	.102
CATHOLIC	.076	-.747	1.000	-.092	-.086	.146	-.063
JEWISH	-.072	-.194	-.092	1.000	-.022	-.080	-.100
OTHR	-.029	-.182	-.086	-.022	1.000	.004	-.003
ATTEND	.130	.090	.146	-.080	.004	1.000	.062
PARTYID	-.035	.102	-.063	-.100	-.003	.062	1.000

TABLE 21
Multiple Regression Output (continued)

```
* * * *   M U L T I P L E   R E G R E S S I O N   * * * *

Equation Number 1    Dependent Variable..   ABORTN3      WOMEN'S RIGHT TO A LEGAL A

  Descriptive Statistics are printed on Page    3

Block Number  1.  Method: Stepwise    Criteria   PIN  .0500   POUT  .1000

Variable(s) Entered on Step Number  1..    ATTEND      HOW OFTEN R ATTENDS RELIGIOUS SERVICES

Multiple R             .33507                           Analysis of Variance
R Square               .11227     R Square Change     .11227                 DF    Sum of Squares   Mean Square
Adjusted R Square      .11162     F Change         172.12338    Regression    1          32.01918      32.01918
Standard Error         .43131     Signif F Change     .0000     Residual   1361         253.17948        .18602

                                                       F =    172.12338       Signif F =  .0000

------------------ Variables in the Equation ------------------    ------------ Variables not in the Equation ------------

Variable         B           SE B         Beta         T     Sig T    Variable     Beta In   Partial   Min Toler    T       Sig T

ATTEND       -.056865      .004334      -.335067    -13.120  .0000    RACE         .017070   .018053   .993004     .666     .5056
(Constant)    .683212      .020392                   33.503  .0000    SEX          .025167   .026572   .989611     .980     .3271
                                                                      AGE         -.035766  -.037578   .979967   -1.387     .1657
                                                                      EDUC         .243421   .258111   .998112    9.853     .0000
                                                                      MARRIED     -.011147  -.011749   .986126    -.433     .6649
                                                                      WIDOW       -.049664  -.052671   .998499   -1.945     .0520
                                                                      DIVORCE     -.007412  -.007848   .995227    -.289     .7723
                                                                      SEPARAT     -.049527  -.052487   .996982   -1.938     .0528
                                                                      YR73         .054412   .057740   .999623    2.133     .0331
                                                                      YR78        -.020224  -.021441   .997777    -.791     .4292
                                                                      YR88        -.023547  -.024987   .999662    -.922     .3568
                                                                      YR93         .029040   .030822   .999998    1.137     .2557
                                                                      CHILDS      -.117541  -.123689   .983027   -4.597     .0000
                                                                      PROTEST     -.064968  -.068672   .991839   -2.538     .0112
                                                                      CATHOLIC    -.031951  -.033550   .978773   -1.238     .2159
                                                                      JEWISH       .145301   .153723   .993629    5.737     .0000
                                                                      OTHR         .035338   .037506   .999985    1.384     .1665
                                                                      PARTYID     -.026903  -.028498   .996138   -1.051     .2933
```

TABLE 21
Multiple Regression Output *(continued)*

Equation Number 1   Dependent Variable..   ABORTN3   WOMEN'S RIGHT TO A LEGAL A

Variable(s) Entered on Step Number 2..   EDUC   HIGHEST YEAR OF SCHOOL COMPLETED

Multiple R	.41402			Analysis of Variance
R Square	.17141	R Square Change	.05914	DF Sum of Squares Mean Square
Adjusted R Square	.17019	F Change	97.07194	Regression 2 48.88631 24.44316
Standard Error	.41684	Signif F Change	.0000	Residual 1360 236.31235 .17376

F = 140.67269   Signif F = .0000

------------ Variables in the Equation ------------

Variable	B	SE B	Beta	T	Sig T
EDUC	.035535	.003607	.243421	9.853	.0000
ATTEND	-.058661	.004193	-.345645	-13.990	.0000
(Constant)	.248983	.048279		5.157	.0000

------------ Variables not in the Equation ------------

Variable	Beta In	Partial	Min Toler	T	Sig T
RACE	-.009465	-.010300	.981363	-.380	.7042
SEX	.010373	.011316	.985968	.417	.6766
AGE	.022438	.023736	.927216	.875	.3816
MARRIED	-.009912	-.010813	.984239	-.399	.6902
WIDOW	-.009386	-.010160	.970420	-.375	.7080
DIVORCE	-.011044	-.012102	.993266	-.446	.6555
SEPARAT	-.040068	-.043917	.995283	-1.621	.1053
YR73	.078945	.086295	.988573	3.193	.0014
YR78	.001037	.001134	.990174	.042	.9667
YR88	-.037423	-.041039	.994919	-1.514	.1302
YR93	.003627	.003962	.987178	.146	.8839
CHILDS	-.067301	-.071544	.936374	-2.644	.0083
PROTEST	-.042877	-.046713	.983454	-1.724	.0849
CATHOLIC	-.025101	-.027270	.976604	-1.006	.3147
JEWISH	.108746	.117522	.967728	4.363	.0000
OTHR	.018835	.020643	.993466	.761	.4467
PARTYID	-.050451	-.055068	.987189	-2.033	.0422

TABLE 21
Multiple Regression Output *(continued)*

```
Equation Number 1    Dependent Variable..    ABORTN3    WOMEN'S RIGHT TO A LEGAL A

Variable(s) Entered on Step Number   5..    CHILDS    NUMBER OF CHILDREN

Multiple R            .43876                                  Analysis of Variance
R Square              .19251         R Square Change   .00441                          DF      Sum of Squares    Mean Square
Adjusted R Square     .18954         F Change        7.41702   Regression              5            54.90433        10.9808
Standard Error        .41196         Signif F Change   .0065   Residual             1357           230.29433         .16971

                                                                F =    64.70431       Signif F =  .0000

------------ Variables in the Equation ------------     ----------- Variables not in the Equation -----------

Variable         B        SE B       Beta        T      Sig T   Variable   Beta In  Partial  Min Toler     T       Sig T

EDUC          .032054    .003711   .219575    8.638    .0000    RACE      -.016743  -.018424  .913577   -.679     .4975
YR73          .087604    .028076   .076752    3.120    .0018    SEX        .002065   .002277  .918604    .084     .9332
CHILDS       -.017136    .006292  -.068795   -2.723    .0065    AGE        .043774   .044729  .843097   1.649     .0994
JEWISH        .309085    .075079   .102310    4.117    .0000    MARRIED   -.004969  -.005321  .882664   -.196     .8447
ATTEND       -.055325    .004202  -.325989  -13.167    .0000    WIDOW      .002285   .002492  .901188    .092     .9269
(Constant)    .287772    .052608              5.470    .0000    DIVORCE   -.006802  -.007534  .920891   -.277     .7815
                                                                SEPARAT   -.032248  -.035652  .920792  -1.314     .1892
                                                                YR78       .026233   .027988  .910547   1.031     .3027
                                                                YR88      -.017851  -.019217  .919743   -.708     .4792
                                                                YR93       .025104   .026957  .915214    .993     .3209
                                                                PROTEST   -.019816  -.021475  .916521   -.791     .4291
                                                                CATHOLIC  -.018794  -.020547  .920982   -.757     .4493
                                                                OTHR      -.020339  -.022563  .916636    .831     .4061
                                                                PARTYID   -.038016  -.041730  .911633  -1.538     .1243

End Block Number   1    PIN =    .050 Limits reached.
```

TABLE 21
Multiple Regression Output (*continued*)

```
* * * *   M U L T I P L E   R E G R E S S I O N   * * * *

Equation Number 1     Dependent Variable..    ABORTN3    WOMEN'S RIGHT TO A LEGAL A

                Summary table
                -------------

Step  MultR  Rsq   AdjRsq  F(Eqn)   SigF  RsqCh  FCh      SigCh      Variable  BetaIn  Correl
1     .3351  .1123 .1116   172.123  .000  .1123  172.123  .000   In: ATTEND    -.3351  -.3351    HOW OFTEN R ATTENDS RELIGIOUS
2     .4140  .1714 .1702   140.673  .000  .0591  97.072   .000   In: EDUC       .2434   .2284    HIGHEST YEAR OF SCHOOL COMPLE
3     .4276  .1829 .1811   101.369  .000  .0114  19.033   .000   In: JEWISH     .1087   .1711
4     .4337  .1881 .1857   78.654   .000  .0052  8.771    .003   In: YR73       .0729   .0609
5     .4388  .1925 .1895   64.704   .000  .0044  7.417    .007   In: CHILDS    -.0688  -.1592    NUMBER OF CHILDREN

* * * * * * * * * * * * * * * * * * * * * * * * * * * * * *

Residuals Statistics:

           Min       Max      Mean    Std Dev    N
*PRED     -.0763    1.1887    .4657    .2019    1388
*RESID   -1.0165    1.0763   -.0008    .4113    1388
*ZPRED   -2.6908    3.6101    .0090   1.0056    1388
*ZRESID  -2.4674    2.6127   -.0019    .9985    1388

Total Cases =     1406

Durbin-Watson Test =   1.86825
```

TABLE 21
Multiple Regression Output (*continued*)

Histogram
Dependent Variable: WOMEN'S RIGHT TO A LEGAL

Std. Dev = 1.00
Mean = -.00
N = 1388.00

Scatterplot
Dependent Variable: WOMEN'S RIGHT TO A LEGAL

6% of the variation in our abortion index. Note also that SPSS output provides access to important comparative (use of Beta) and equation (use of "B" or slope) information at the left of each table. Summary stats (e.g., partial r, t statistics, significance level, etc.) are provided to the right under the heading of "Variables not in the Equation" for all those variables yet to be included in our "best predictors" model. The variable of JEWISH added 1% while the variables of YR73 and number of CHILDren, when entered sequentially, accounted for an additional .5% of explained variation each. All the remaining variables (e.g., sex, race, political party identification, etc.) did not add substantially to accurately predicting attitudes toward abortion, once these five variables were identified. Thus, our "best" predictor model accounted for slightly less than 20% of the variation in how our sampled Americans responded to our legal access to abortion index.

Our best simple equation, based on these respondents, becomes:

```
Predicted value of Abortion Index Value = .288 + .032*EDUC
                                        + .088*YR73
                                        - .017*CHILD
                                        + .309*JEWISH
                                        - .055*ATTEND
```

Thus, higher education, being Jewish, and being a 1973 respondent were associated with greater support for legal access to abortion services, while having more children and attending church more regularly were associated with less support for legal access to such services. To calculate the predicted value of support of such services from knowledge of these variables, simply substitute in the equation with the value for the variable (e.g., if respondent's number of years was 12, then multiply 0.32 by 12; if respondent was not in the 1973 sample, then enter a 0 for YR73). Complete the process and then do the math to calculate a value. A single value will provide an indication of where people with similar characteristics would fall on this index.

However, examining the residuals indicates a need for some further work before finalizing the "best" equation. Of course, another form of this abortion scale—with additional or different items or perhaps across different years—might have produced different findings. . . .

Exercise 13: If you are a hearty soul, this is your chance to try a multiple regression run. Simply follow your instincts and try the REGRESSION procedure using the minimum REGRESSION commands. Then, go ahead and try some of the options listed earlier. Don't worry, you can't hurt the computer or damage the software. Once you've mastered this command, try variations: Try it on the GSS 1983 or 1993 data set only, use different explanatory variables, substitute DEGREE for EDUC and add POLVIEWS. You might even wish to see how well the regression equation built with your GSS 1988 sample "fits" the GSS 1993 sample data—just how good are models built on earlier data sets for predicting more recent attitudes? Or try other item sets (e.g., Life Satisfaction five-item scale or attitudes toward expenditures on national problems such as drugs, education, environment, etc.). In any case, feel free to explore! Examine Table 22 to see the complete list of the commands I used in this Learner's Guide. It will serve as a beginning reference for your independent work.

■ WORKING WITH DATA YOU COLLECT

Here's a postscript designed explicitly for those of you who wish to work with your own data, raw data, or data that must be imported from other files. If you are working on your own research project you have probably collected more data than you know what to do with. The question here is to find a way to effectively transfer the data so that you may work with them effectively using SPSS.

The reality of doing social research includes not only the design and implementation of good research methods and data collection techniques, but also the management and analysis of the collected data. With the use of your computer, and SPSS, you shall be able to manage the data in a fast, efficient, and cost-effective manner.

Getting the Data to the Computer: Step 1

SPSS 6.1 provides a Data Editor window that will enable you to enter your data into an SPSS file with all the appropriate labels and formats. If you have created a data file using Excel or another spreadsheet program, or word processing software, you can tell SPSS to read these files, too.

TABLE 22
Summary of Command Files

```
TITLE "BIVARIATE STATISTICS".
GET
   FILE="Jeff's HD:SPSS 6.1:GSS7393s.sav".
EXECUTE.

RECODE abany,abdefect,abhlth,abnomore,abpoor,abrape,absingle
      (0=99)(1=1)(2=0)(ELSE=99).
MISSING VALUES abany,abdefect,abhlth,abnomore,abpoor,abrape,absingle (99) .
COMPUTE abortn3=MEAN.3(abnomore,abpoor,absingle).
VARIABLE LABEL ABORTN3 "WOMEN'S RIGHT TO A LEGAL ABORTION-3 ITEMS".

COMPUTE RACESEX=9.
IF (RACE EQ 1 AND SEX EQ 1)RACESEX=1.
IF (RACE EQ 1 AND SEX EQ 2)RACESEX=2.
IF (RACE EQ 2 AND SEX EQ 1)RACESEX=3.
IF (RACE EQ 2 AND SEX EQ 2)RACESEX=4.
VARIABLE LABELS   RACESEX, 'RACE AND SEX IDENTIFIER'.
VALUE LABELS    RACESEX  1 'WH-MALE' 2 'WH-FEMALE'
                              3 'AA-MALE' 4 'AA-FEMALE'.
MISSING VALUES     RACESEX (9).

SELECT IF ((race  = 1 or race  = 2) AND NOT SYSMIS(ABORTN3)).

CROSSTABS TABLES= ABORTN3 BY YEAR
 /CELLS COUNT, COLUMN
 /STATISTICS CHISQ, LAMBDA, GAMMA, ETA, CORR.

TEMPORARY.
RECODE ABORTN3 (0=0)(.3 THRU .7 = 1)(1=2).
VALUE LABEL ABORTN3 0 "AGAINST" 1 "SOMETIMES" 2 "FOR".
RECODE RELIG (3 THRU 5=3).
VALUE LABEL RELIG 1 'PROTESTANT' 2 'CATHOLIC' 3 'JEW/NONE/OTHER'.
CROSSTABS TABLES= ABORTN3 BY YEAR, RELIG,RACE,SEX, RACESEX
 /ABORTN3 BY RACESEX BY YEAR
 /CELLS COUNT, COLUMN
 /STATISTICS CHISQ, LAMBDA, GAMMA, ETA, CORR.

T-TEST
    GROUPS=sex(1 2)
    /VARIABLES= abortn3.

T-TEST
    GROUPS=sex(1 2)
    /VARIABLES=abany abdefect abhlth abnomore abpoor abrape absingle abortn3.
    /CRITERIA=CIN(.95) .

ONEWAY
   abortn3 BY racesex(1 4)
    /CONTRAST= 0 1 0 -1
    /RANGES=DUNCAN
    /HARMONIC NONE
    /FORMAT LABELS
    /STATISTICS ALL
    /MISSING ANALYSIS .
```

TABLE 22
Summary of Command Files (continued)

```
RECODE MARITAL (1=1)(2,3,4 = 2)(5=3).
VALUE LABELS MARITAL
   1 "Married" 2 "Prev-Married" 3 "Nev-Married".
ONEWAY
   abortn3 BY MARITAL(1 3)
     /CONTRAST= 0 1 0 -1
     /RANGES=DUNCAN
     /HARMONIC NONE
     /FORMAT LABELS
     /STATISTICS ALL
     /MISSING ANALYSIS .

RECODE PARTYID(7=9).
CORRELATIONS
     /VARIABLES= abortn3 age educ degree realinc partyid polviews
     /PRINT=TWOTAIL SIG
     /STATISTICS DESCRIPTIVES
     /MISSING=PAIRWISE .

REGRESSION VARIABLES = ABORTN3 EDUC
     /DESCRIPTIVES MEAN STDDEV CORR SIG N
     /STATISTICS COEFF OUTS CI R ANOVA
     /DEPENDENT abortn3
     /METHOD=ENTER educ   .


TITLE "MULTIVARIATE STATISTICS".
GET
   FILE="Jeff's HD:SPSS 6.1:GSS7393s.sav".
EXECUTE.

RECODE abany,abdefect,abhlth,abnomore,abpoor,abrape,absingle
      (0=99)(1=1)(2=0)(ELSE=99).
MISSING VALUES abany,abdefect,abhlth,abnomore,abpoor,abrape,absingle (99)  .
COMPUTE abortn3=MEAN.3(abnomore,abpoor,absingle).
VARIABLE LABEL ABORTN3 "WOMEN'S RIGHT TO A LEGAL ABORTION-3 ITEMS".

SELECT IF ((race  = 1 or race  = 2) AND NOT SYSMIS(ABORTN3)).

RECODE RACE (2=0).
VAR LABELS RACE "Proportion White".
RECODE SEX (2=0).
VAR LABELS SEX "Proportion Male".

COMPUTE PROTEST=0.
IF (RELIG EQ 1)PROTEST=1.
COMPUTE CATHOLIC=0.
IF (RELIG EQ 2)CATHOLIC=1.
COMPUTE JEWISH=0.
IF (RELIG EQ 3)JEWISH=1.
COMPUTE OTHR=0.
IF (RELIG EQ 5)OTHR=1.
```

TABLE 22
Summary of Command Files (*continued*)

```
COMPUTE married=0.
IF (marital eq 1)married=1.
COMPUTE widow=0.
IF (marital eq 2)widow=1.
COMPUTE divorce=0.
IF (marital eq 3)divorce=1.
COMPUTE separat=0.
IF (marital eq 4)separat=1.

COMPUTE YR73=0.
IF (YEAR EQ 73)YR73=1.
COMPUTE YR78=0.
IF (YEAR EQ 78)YR78=1.
COMPUTE YR88=0.
IF (YEAR EQ 88)YR88=1.
COMPUTE YR93=0.
IF (YEAR EQ 93)YR93=1.

RECODE PARTYID(7=9).

REGRESSION
 /DESCRIPTIVES
 /STATISTICS=DEFAULTS CHA HISTORY
 /VARIABLES= ABORTN3,
    RACE,SEX,AGE,
    EDUC,
    MARRIED TO SEPARAT
    YR73 TO YR93
    CHILDS,
    PROTEST TO OTHR
    ATTEND,
    PARTYID
 /DEPENDENT=ABORTN3
 /STEPWISE
 /RESIDUALS
 /SCATTERPLOT(*PRED,*RESID).
```

It's not hard to do, but several steps are required. Taking prudent care at this point is to your advantage. An example will help. Let us assume that you are conducting your own study of attitudes toward abortion and you select 20 people to respond to your survey. Let us assume further that you restrict your study to examining the impact of ascribed status characteristics (e.g., gender, race, and age) on abortion attitudes as measured by the GSS. Your questionnaire might look like Table 23.

You now have several options in creating a data file. Here are three of the many options available to you. First, you may use the traditional SPSS approach of a standard structured text file. Second, you might use any of the standard spreadsheet software packages (e.g., Excel, Lotus 1-2-3, Quatro Pro, etc.) for your data entry task. Third, you may use the Data Editor feature of SPSS. Each alternative has its strengths and weaknesses. The best data entry procedure is to find what is easiest and most comfortable for you. Here we shall emphasize working with the Data Editor window of SPSS, so let's just scan the other techniques first.

If You Plan to Work with a Standard Text File . . . If you are planning to use a standard fixed file format that may be created with any standard text editor or word processor, just remember that each record or line in the file represents each respondent. The number of "columns" you use on each record is determined by the number of variables and the width of each variable. Thus, if you plan to follow the GSS convention, the first six "columns" of each record or

TABLE 23
Output from Display Command

```
                                                          I.D. #____
                        STUDENT SURVEY

Hello, my name is Jeff Jacques and I am a student enrolled in Research Methods. As
part of the course requirement I am conducting a brief study of student attitudes
toward abortion.  Please take a moment and consider when, in your judgment, a woman
should have the right to obtain a legal abortion.
You do not need to put your name on this survey--all information is anonymous. Just
take a few moments and CIRCLE the most appropriate answer.

Please CIRCLE whether or not you think it should be possible for a pregnant woman to
obtain a legal abortion:

  1. If there is a strong chance of serious       1.Yes     2.No     9. Don't Know
     defect in the baby?
  2. If she is married and does not want          1.Yes     2.No     9. Don't Know
     any more children?
  3. If the woman's own health is                 1.Yes     2.No     9. Don't Know
     seriously endangered by the pregnancy?
  4. If the family has a very low income          1.Yes     2.No     9. Don't Know
     and cannot afford any more children?
  5. If she became pregnant as a result           1.Yes     2.No     9. Don't Know
     of rape?
  6. If she is not married and does not           1.Yes     2.No     9. Don't Know
     want to marry the man?
  7. If the woman wants it for any reason?        1.Yes     2.No     9. Don't Know

Background Items
  8. Sex                         1. Male       2. Female
  9. Race                        1. Black      2. White        3. Other
 10. Date of Birth               19____

Thanks for your help!
```

line will contain the IDNUMBER for each and every respondent—starting with 960001. Each question on abortion uses only one column, so all respondents' answers to question number 1, "If there is a strong chance of serious defect in the baby?" shall be recorded in the seventh column for every respondent. (That's why the file is sometimes called a fixed format file.) Similarly, column 8 will be used to record respondents' answers to question 2, "If she is married and does not want any more children?" See Table 24.

You may be asking yourself how one would know what to enter for each value of each variable. You will find in Table 25 a copy of a codebook based on a subset of the GSS questionnaire and the questionnaire we created in Table 23. If you plan to use this data entry method, then examine closely Table 25. Note that the data for most variables required only one column, but IDNUMBER and year of birth, YRBIRTH, required more than one column. We therefore assigned the first six columns to IDNUMBER and four columns, 16–19, to YRBIRTH. Each record (or line of Table 24) contained the data for each variable in the same columnar format. Because we have such a consistent file structure, we will be able to tell SPSS how to read the variables and how to tell which variables are single-digit numbers and which require more than a single digit or column.

In the TABLE 5 subset of variables from the GSS, I have included information about the actual GSS format on this codebook. The original GSS codebook will serve as a good example for your work. You would find that the complete data set, the physical location of each variable (i.e., beginning and ending column number), what each variable was called, and the description of each variable name and values would be consistent with the information provided in Table 25 for our subset of variables.

Appendix I: A Learner's Guide to SPSS 6.1

TABLE 24
Text File of My Survey

```
                    1         2
          12345678901234567890 1
```

```
9600012222222111931
9600021111111121965
9600031122222321969
9600041111111111931
9600051122122121955
9600061122122121919
9600071111111121949
9600081111122121948
9600091111111121959
9600101100120221961
9600111111111221969
9600122222122121920
9600131122112121928
9600141121112121926
9600152222222121923
9600161111111111913
9600171122112121931
9600181222122111973
9600191111111121971
9600201121112121958
```

Note that these data are the same as those presented earlier.

If You Plan to Work with a Spreadsheet File . . . If you plan to use a spreadsheet package, then enter the data so that each row contains all the data for each respondent and each column contains a variable. We might use column A for IDNUMBER, column B for the first question about a "Serious defect in the baby," column C for the second question, "She does not want any more children," etc. If we use row 1 for the variable names, then data for the first respondent will begin in row 2, data for the second respondent will begin in row 3, etc. Thus, the fourth respondent's answer to question 3—a "Yes," which was coded as a value of 1—will be found in cell D5. Similarly, all the responses to each item by each respondent may be placed in their appropriate cell locations.

Once you enter all the data, make sure that you Save the file for further use. Typically, this command can be found under the File menu on most spreadsheet applications.

Using SPSS Version 6.1 Data Editor First, make sure that the Data Editor Window—the window with the rows and columns—is in the foreground. If we use this short survey data set, you can begin entering the responses made by the first person in row 1 (e.g., 960001 for the IDNUMBER). (As soon as you begin to type, the values you type will appear in the data editor bar, and with a press of the tab key, the top of the column will change from "var" to "var00001" and the row number 1 will be darkened.) You are now ready to enter the data for the respondents' answer to the first question on abortion, "Serious defect in the baby." Just enter the value 2 in the second column. (Again, the column label at the top will change—"var" will change to "var00002.") You continue this process of entering data until all the data for each variable for the first respondent are entered. When you are ready to enter the data for the second respondent, simply use the arrow keys or the scroll bars to find the cell located at "var00001" and row 2. Or make this cell the active cell by moving the mouse to point to it and then click on it. Now, enter the data for the second respondent as you did the first; enter 9600002, tab key, 1, tab key, 1, etc. Simply continue this process until all the data have been entered. By the way, if you make an error, just choose the cell in which the error occurs and re-enter the correct data. The old data will be replaced with the correct data.

Once all the data have been entered, make sure that you save the data. Take your mouse, point at the word File, click the mouse button, and choose Save Data. Type an appropriate file name (e.g., MYDATA.SAV) and you will be able to access these data when you are ready to begin your analysis.

TABLE 25
My Variable Codebook

GSS VARIABLE NAME	GSS QUEST'N NO.	DESCRIPTION	CODES/VALUES Survey	My REC/COL'S	GSS FORMAT VALUES	MISSING
IDNUMBER		Identifier squence	960001-96XXXX	1-6	1-6	
ABDEFECT	206A	If there is a strong chance of serious defect in the baby		7-13	780	8. Don't know
ABNOMORE	206B	If she is married and does not want any more children	All items used the following categories: 1. Yes 2. No		781	9. No answer BK. NA
ABHLTH	206C	If the woman's own helath is seriously endangered by the pregnancy			782	
ABPOOR	206D	If the family has a very low income and cannot afford any more children.			783	
ABRAPE	206E	If she became pregnant as a result of rape.			784	
ABSINGLE	206F	If she is not married and does not want to marry the man.			785	
ABANY	206G	The woman wants it for any reason.			786	
SEX	20	Sex	1. Male 2. Female	14	109	
RACE	21	Race	1. White 2. African American 3. Other	15	110	9
YRBIRTH	9	Date of Birth/AGE		16-17	92-93	9. No answer

GSS format for RECords and COLumns were based on The General Social Surveys, 1972-1994 Cumulative Codebook, 1995, Storrs, CT: The Roper Center for Public Opinion Research, 1995.

Exercise 14: If you are working on a new project, you need to determine how you will complete your data entry activity. Choose and implement any one of the three methods noted above. In addition, with whichever method you choose, you should develop a codebook for your study—even if you do not need to list beginning and ending physical locations. You may use the codebook format of Table 25. When you finish developing a complete codebook, enter your data.

Finding Out about Your Computer Site: Step 2

If you are planning to use your college's computer lab, this is a good time to find out about your college's resources and which version of SPSS you will be using. If you don't know about your college's computer lab, ask your instructor or a friend. Then, get the help you need by telling the computer personnel what you plan to do; that is, that you plan to enter data, create files, and use SPSS to perform the analysis. They will probably set up an account for you and give you documentation on how to use your college's system, including how to create a file, how to enter data into a file, how to correct any data entry errors, and—most important—how to access and use SPSS.

Unfortunately, there is no single standard for all computer sites or a single standard for all text editors, word processors, and spreadsheets. If you have yet to master these applications, you will have to get help from colleagues and university personnel. Just remember, if you are not using the SPSS Data Editor system, your goal is to get the data set created so that every card image, record, or line of data in the data file represents the responses from one respondent and that every response for the same variable is entered in the same fields or columns across all the respondents' records. Careful data entry takes time and effort. But, it will save you hours when you reach the data analysis stage. Take the time to do it right, and don't be reluctant to talk to the necessary people.

Reading the Data with SPSS Commands: Step 3

Now that you know the major parts of an SPSS command and how variable names are defined correctly, let's get started by telling the computer how to read your data. Indeed, until you give SPSS the essential information on how to read your data file, you will not be able to manipulate any of your variables or produce even the simplest reports.

If You Worked with a Spreadsheet File . . .   If you entered the data into any standard spreadsheet file with the variable names in the first row and saved it as a Lotus 1-2-3 or an Excel file, then choose:

File ➤
   Open . . .

and select your data file from the picker box, remembering to select "Read variable names" from the spreadsheet option box, or a simple expression in the syntax window, such as:

```
GET TRANSLATE /FILE "MYSTUDY.XLS"[26]
     /TYPE XLS /FIELDNAMES.
```

Either set of steps will read your data successfully and create an "active" SPSS file. GET TRANSLATE tells SPSS that it should go out and retrieve the data from another file. /FILE "MYSTUDY.XLS" indicates the file's name and /TYPE XLS indicates, not surprisingly, the file type—in this case an Excel file. (There are many file types SPSS may read successfully but not all types are available in all versions of SPSS. So check the documentation that came with your version.) Finally, the specification /FIELDNAMES makes it clear to treat the first row in the spreadsheet file as variable names rather than data; the data will begin in the second read row. (Simply remember to choose the "Spreadsheet Options: Read variable Names" box if you are using the menu bar approach.)

Once you execute this command and have the Data Editor window as the active window, you can save all the variable names and the data in a single SPSS system file. The command is straightforward:

File ➤
   Save Data . . .

---

[26] By the way, if you are using the Macintosh and plan to use your word processor, make sure that "smart quotes" is turned off.

or

```
SAVE OUTFILE = 'filename'.
```

or

```
SAVE OUTFILE = 'MYSTUDY.SAV'.
```

Just run this command with the correct file name, and extension where needed. We'll be able to retrieve all the data and appropriate variable names from SPSS in all future work.

If You Worked with a Standard Data File . . .   For fixed formatted text files, the information on how to read the data is processed through the menu items of:

File ➤
  Read ASCII Data . . .

Not surprisingly, a dialog box will ask you to identify the file with your data. (Note that "Fixed" file type is the default and already selected for you.) Once the data file has been identified, a "Define Fixed Variables" dialog box appears. From the codebook, simply key in the variable name (e.g., IDNUMBER, ABDEFECT, etc.), "Start column:" (e.g., 1, 7, 8), and, if more than one column is needed, "End column:" (e.g., 6). (You do one variable at a time.) A press of the Add button builds the DATA LIST command; a press of "OK" executes the DATA LIST command to read the file using your newly entered format.

Did I say the DATA LIST command? The SPSS menu/dialog system is simply creating a DATA LIST command. If you wish to enter it directly in the syntax window, your DATA LIST command would look like this:

```
DATA LIST FILE="MYSTUDY"
 / IDNUMBER 1-6
     ABDEFECT 7, ABHLTH 8, ABNOMORE 9, ABPOOR 10,
     ABRAPE 11, ABSINGLE 12, ABANY 13,
     RACE 14, SEX 15, YRBIRTH 16-19.
```

If, however you were reading the 1994 version of the GSS and you wished to examine similar variables, then your command would be:

```
DATA LIST FILE="MYSTUDY"
 /1 IDNUMBER 1-6
  AGE 92-93, SEX 109, RACE 110
  ABDEFECT ABHLTH ABNOMORE ABPOOR ABRAPE ABSINGLE ABANY
  780-786.
```

In both cases, the words DATA LIST are the procedure name, and are, therefore, required—that's how SPSS knows how to read the data file. The FILE="MYSTUDY"[27] identifies the data file name you used. This enables SPSS to keep track of where to find the data. The /1 tells SPSS to read the first record. If you have a multi-record data set such that /2 would indicate to SPSS to read the second record, /10 would indicate that SPSS should read the tenth record, and so on.

In either case where the DATA LIST command is appropriate, I have identified the column(s) where SPSS may find each variable. For example, in our short classroom survey answers to ABDEFECT may be found in column 7, answers to ABHLTH may be found in column 8, etc. Note that I left a single blank between the variable name (e.g., ABDEFECT) and the column (i.e., 7) where the data for that variable may be found. (Without a blank between the variable name and the variable column identifier, SPSS would not know that I had finished the variable name and was trying to indicate the column locations of the values. Look again at the other variables used to gather data on attitudes toward abortion.)

If the variable took more than a single column, I followed the variable name with a space, then the beginning column number, a dash, and then the ending column number. For example, the variable of year of birth, YRBIRTH,

---

[27] It's always a good idea to check with your computer site on how best to reference data files, especially if you are using a different SPSS version and/or a different hardware platform.

was entered as a four-digit field in columns 16 and 19 with the expression YRBIRTH 16-19. Similarly, IDNUMBER used six columns, one through six. I used the expression IDNUMBER 1-6.

If you need more than one record to complete your DATA LIST command—that is, to list all your variables and column identifiers—just start on the next record and skip at least one space. SPSS continues working with the same procedure command.

If your study includes data values with a decimal point but you used a text editor where you chose not to enter decimal points, we can tell SPSS to store these data as a real number (e.g., values that include a decimal point) by modifying our DATA LIST command record to read:

```
VARIABLENAME column number (2)
```

The (2) tells SPSS to place a decimal point two columns from the right-most value. For example, student grade point average (GPA) may have been part of your study. It might be declared with:

```
GPA 11-13 (2)
```

SPSS will read the values from columns 11 through 13 (e.g., 250, 300, 350, etc.) and convert them to real numbers (e.g., 2.50, 3.00, 3.50, etc.) by placing a decimal point in the appropriate place.

Similarly, SPSS can handle alphabetic values for a variable (e.g., STATE). In the parentheses you simply place an A. The (A) follows the column identifiers for that variable. Using the postal service two-character abbreviations for STATE (e.g., CA for California, FL for Florida, etc.), we can define the variable name and characteristics with:

```
STATE 20-21 (A)
```

Thus, STATE would be read as alpha-numeric characters from columns 20 through 21 of each record of the data file.

You will find, however, that declaring and using alphabetic values will limit your ability to manipulate and analyze the data. So, try to use only numeric values when creating your data file.

Here is another way to create the DATA LIST command for our short classroom study. These records are precisely equivalent to our earlier SPSS DATA LIST command.

```
DATA LIST FILE="MYSTUDY"
 / IDNUMBER 1-6
     ABDEFECT ABHLTH ABNOMORE ABPOOR ABRAPE ABSINGLE ABANY
     7-13,
     RACE 14, SEX 15, YRBIRTH 16-19.
```

SPSS is smart enough to figure out that it needs to equally divide all the variables with the number of columns available. In this case, SPSS will assign the data stored in column 7 to ABDEFECT, the data stored in column 8 to ABHLTH, the data stored in column 9 to ABNOMORE, etc. Alternately, if we were flexible, we might have used the expression:

```
    ABORT1 TO ABORT7 7-13,
```

When you have a large number of variables, all of which cover the same type(s) of information and each variable has the same column width, then you may use the TO convention.

Once you run your DATA LIST procedure, you can save all the variable names in the usual manner.

If You Worked with the Data Editor Window in SPSS 6.1 . . .   If you are working in SPSS 6.1, then you can easily convert "var00001" or "var00002" to a more meaningful variable name:

- Move the mouse so that the pointer is at var00001. (Note that the arrow is replaced with a + sign.)
- Double-click the mouse button.
- In the Define Variable dialog box, type the new name, e.g. IDNUMBER. (We'll examine the other options listed in this dialog box shortly.)
- Point and click on the "OK" button.

You should now see IDNUMBER rather than var00001 as the header for the first column. Repeat each of the steps listed above so that you are using reasonable descriptive variable names for each variable in your study. Remember the simple rules for variable names. Include every variable. Each variable name must: (1) be unique, (2) start with an alphabetic character, (3) have no more than eight characters, and (4) not use a reserved keyword (e.g., EQ, ALL, LE, etc.) or have as part of its name reserved special characters.

Once you make these changes, you can save all the descriptive variable names and the data in a single SPSS file. The process is straightforward—choose

File ➤
   Save Data . . .

Exercise 15: If you are working on your own project or have to analyze someone else's data, then this is the time to try to create appropriate variable names. Take a few minutes and do so now. After doing the activities outlined above, SAVE the work using the appropriate procedures.

SPSS with a Little Class: Step 4

From this point you can begin to examine the data set with the typical SPSS commands used for descriptive summaries. But, before you do this, you may wish to add a little class.

To help you and the reader more clearly and fully understand what he or she is looking at, it is useful to label each of the variables and associated values—particularly those variables that may not be clearly understood. While the reader may have no trouble figuring out that the variable name RACE stands for respondent's race, or SEX stands for the respondent's sex, the reader may not be clear what the variable names of ABDEFECT, ABNOMORE mean. Similarly, when procedures are executed and results displayed for categorical variables such as sex, a value of 1 or 2 is not very meaningful unless you know that 1 is a code for "Male" and 2 is a code for "Female." SPSS will print out on your output the label for each variable name and each value when you use the appropriate optional commands.

If you wish to use the standard SPSS 6.1 interface to accomplish this task, recall from our earlier discussion of variable names that we noted that you could change any variable name with another by double-clicking the current variable name listed at the top of the column of the Data Editor window. In doing so, a "Define Variable" dialog box was activated. In addition to giving you the opportunity to change the variable name, it presented an opportunity to "Change Settings" including "Labels." By pointing at and clicking the mouse on the "Labels" button, you can enter the variable label and associated value labels, one at a time. In this version of SPSS, you may enter a variable label up to 120 characters long—although most of the time SPSS will only report the first 50 or so characters. So choose your variable labels carefully so that you and any reader of your output will find it easy to understand the variable under study.

To assign a label for a value in any variable, simply use this dialog box, enter a value in the "Value:" text box, and enter a label in the "Value Label" text box. Click on the "Add" button. The value label is added to the list. Repeat this procedure to add additional values and their associated labels. When you complete all the entries for this variable, then click on the "Continue" button, click "OK," and repeat these steps for the next variable.

Let us assume that you have a number of variables that use the same Value Labels (e.g., all the abortion questions use "1" for "YES" and "2" for "NO"). SPSS provides a nice option for this situation in that you can use templates. Simply select each of the continuous variables in the data window by pointing the mouse at the first variable, holding the mouse button down, and dragging across the other similarly structured variables. Now, choose:

DATA ➤
   Templates . . .

A template dialog box should now be open. Simply point and click your mouse on the "DEFINE" button. Then enter the Value Labels as you did above, remembering to point and click on the "Add" button, or press the ALT-A keys simultaneously, as you complete each value label. In the Apply box, activate the "Value labels" option. Voilá.

Alternately you could be using the following commands from the syntax window:

```
VARIABLE LABELS varname 'label'.
```

For example, the following statements may be used for our survey of attitudes toward legal abortion:

```
VARIABLE LABELS IDNUMBER, 'RESPONDENT ID'
 /ABDEFECT  'STRONG CHANCE OF SERIOUS DEFECT'
 /ABHLTH    'WOMANS HEALTH SERIOUSLY ENDANGERED'
 /ABNOMORE  'MARRIED-WANTS NO MORE CHILDREN'
 /ABPOOR    'LOW INCOME-CANT AFFORD MORE CHILDREN'
 /ABRAPE    'PREGNANT AS RESULT OF RAPE'
 /ABSINGLE  'NOT MARRIED'
 /ABANY     'ABORTION IF WOMAN WANTS FOR ANY REASON'
 /RACE      'RACE OF RESPONDENT'
 /SEX       'SEX OF RESPONDENT'.
```

Note that the command name, VARIABLE LABELS, is needed only once and the specifications—variable names and labels—are spaced properly. All the variable labels are identified by the variable name used in the DATA LIST command, a comma, and then the label for each is enclosed in single quote marks. So that SPSS may separate each variable from another, a slash "/" is placed at the beginning of each new variable label. So that SPSS knows that it is finished with the VARIABLE LABELS command, a period (.) is placed at the end of the last variable label.

As we have indicated, you can help the reader master the material more quickly by labeling not only the variable name, but also the values for certain variables. While it is not necessary to label every value for every variable (i.e., variables such as YRBIRTH or AGE require no value label since the numeric values are self-evident), such variables as RACE or SEX, which use coded values, should be labeled. Similarly, whenever you use codes for response categories—1 for "Yes," 2 for "No," etc., such as we did for our seven attitude questions—you should report what these value codes mean. This may be easily accomplished with the command:

```
VALUE LABELS varname, value 'label' value 'label'...value 'label'.
```

For example, returning to our short classroom study, here are several forms of the value label command:

```
VALUE LABELS RACE,     1 'WHITE'      2 'AFRICAN-AM'
                       3 'OTHER'
 /SEX,                 1 'MALE'       2 'FEMALE'
 /ABDEFECT TO ABANY    1 'YES'        2 'NO'
                       8 'DONT KNOW'  9 'NA'.
```

Note that the command name, VALUE LABELS, begins in column 1 and is followed by a space, the specifications of a variable name, its value, a single quote mark, the label, and then an ending single quote mark. Additional values and labels for the same variable follow the same format. Note also that when all the values and their labels for the variable have been entered, then for each new variable a slash "/" is entered. The values and the value labels then follow in the same manner.

By the way, when several variables use the same values and labels for each value, you may list all the variable names together, and then their values and labels. Of course, the use of the TO convention can be very helpful when several variables are listed one right after the other (e.g., ABDEFECT TO ABANY 1 'YES' 2 'NO', etc.).

What to Do When You Don't Know—MISSING VALUES: Step 5

Let's face it. Not everyone will answer every question. Some people are reluctant to tell you how much money they make or when they were born. When this occurs, or when you don't know what the valid value should be, you can tell the computer to ignore it. (Remember, we indicated in our codebook what we would do when we did not have a valid response.) Now, here's our chance to tell SPSS which variables will have which MISSING VALUES. It follows the usual command format of the procedure commands.

In SPSS 6.1, the "Missing Values . . . " command is part of the "Define Variable" and template dialog boxes. You would access this command just as you did the "Value Labels" command noted above.

Alternately, you could enter the following commands in the syntax window:

```
MISSING VALUES varname (value).
```

Here's the SPSS command for our study on attitudes toward legal abortion:

```
MISSING VALUES ABDEFECT TO ABANY (0 8 9)
    /RACE, YRBIRTH (9) .
```

It is important to note that when we have several contiguous variables, one right after another, all that have the same missing value, we can use the TO convention. Also note that when we change the value we shall choose as missing, a slash is placed between the value and the next variable name. Of course, we use the exact variable name that we assigned in our earlier statements.

Why use a MISSING VALUES command? Well, remember the FREQUENCIES output. Compare the columns and VALID PERCENT in tables that have "missing data." SPSS is smart enough to know to omit the person who did not answer the question before it computes each of these VALID PERCENTS. Similarly SPSS is also smart enough to know that the CUMulative PERCENT column should contain only those values based on valid responses.

Again, it is your responsibility to remember to save your work on a regular basis—especially after making substantive changes to your data file. All data and associated variable definitions, value labels, and missing values will be accessed automatically when you remember to save your data file.

Exercise 16: Here's your chance to help others read your results more easily. (Actually, it will probably help you remember what each variable name and value mean, too.) Take a few minutes and develop appropriate VARIABLE LABELS and VALUE LABEL procedures for your study. Then, check the veracity of the data with the LIST and FREQUENCIES procedures. Once you have convinced yourself that you are working with a valid data set, create a new SPSS SYSTEM FILE.

■ CONCLUSIONS

Don't despair. It's not that hard. If you have been doing the exercises and working with the GSS data, then you have probably mastered many of the basics. If you have just looked through this appendix, then go back to the first page and start reading the text and doing the exercises.

This is a good time to point out the steps we took in working with our GSS data set. Indeed, these steps are equally applicable to just about any study.

1. Know your research questions and specify your hypotheses in light of the data you collected.
2. Specify the information and statistical procedures you need to use.
3. Develop a codebook—either an original or use your DISPLAY command.
4. Build the data file and command files to create an SPSS file, if necessary.
5. Check and/or clean the data.
6. Enhance your SPSS file.
7. Run your SPSS descriptive procedures.
8. Develop and test your scale.
9. Rerun your descriptive procedures with just those cases to be included in your final analysis.
10. Run your SPSS bivariate procedures.
11. Run your SPSS multivariate procedures.

Perhaps most important, take a few moments after each step and consider what you did, how it relates back to your study, and what patterns you can discover among the variables.

I would be remiss if I didn't point out that we have only scratched the surface of SPSS. If you would like to read more about this package, I recommend the SPSS manuals. If you are going to use SPSS in any continuing way, you will find them extremely useful. I know that I have.

TABLE 26
Display Dictionary of All Variables

```
08 Jun 96 SPSS 6.1 for the Power Macintosh                                Page 1

-> SET
->     FORMAT=F8.2 PRINTBACK=ON ERRORS=ON MESSAGES=OFF HEADER=BLANK
->     BOX=X'13141516171819111211C1D' HISTOGRAM=X'1F' BLOCK=X'1E' WIDTH=80
->     LENGTH=59 JOURNAL "Jeff's HD:SPSS 6.1:Jeff" JOURNAL ON WORKSPACE=512 .

-> GET
->     FILE="Jeff's HD:SPSS 6.1:gss".

-> EXECUTE .

-> DISPLAY DICTIONARY.


List of variables on the working file

Name                                                                    Position

YEAR        GSS YEAR FOR THIS RESPONDENT                                    1
            Print Format: F2
            Write Format: F2

ID          RESPONDENT ID NUMBER                                            2
            Print Format: F4
            Write Format: F4

AGE         AGE OF RESPONDENT                                               3
            Print Format: F2
            Write Format: F2
            Missing Values: 0, 98, 99

            Value     Label

               98 M   DK
               99 M   NA

ATTEND      HOW OFTEN R ATTENDS RELIGIOUS SERVICES                          4
            Print Format: F1
            Write Format: F1
            Missing Values: 9

            Value     Label

                0     NEVER
                1     LT ONCE A YEAR
                2     ONCE A YEAR
                3     SEVRL TIMES A YR
                4     ONCE A MONTH
                5     2-3X A MONTH
                6     NRLY EVERY WEEK
                7     EVERY WEEK
                8     MORE THN ONCE WK
                9 M   DK,NA
```

TABLE 26
Display Dictionary of All Variables (continued)

```
CHILDS     NUMBER OF CHILDREN                                    5
           Print Format: F1
           Write Format: F1
           Missing Values: 9

           Value     Label

               8     EIGHT OR MORE
               9 M   NA

DEGREE     RS HIGHEST DEGREE                                     6
           Print Format: F1
           Write Format: F1
           Missing Values: 7, 8, 9

           Value     Label

               0     LT HIGH SCHOOL
               1     HIGH SCHOOL
               2     JUNIOR COLLEGE
               3     BACHELOR
               4     GRADUATE
               7 M   NAP
               8 M   DK
               9 M   NA

EDUC       HIGHEST YEAR OF SCHOOL COMPLETED                      7
           Print Format: F2
           Write Format: F2
           Missing Values: 97, 98, 99

           Value     Label

              97 M   NAP
              98 M   DK
              99 M   NA

FINRELA    OPINION OF FAMILY INCOME                              8
           Print Format: F1
           Write Format: F1
           Missing Values: 8, 9

           Value     Label

               1     FAR BELOW AVERAGE
               2     BELOW AVERAGE
               3     AVERAGE
               4     ABOVE AVERAGE
               5     FAR ABOVE AVERAGE
               8 M   DK
               9 M   NA
```

TABLE 26
Display Dictionary of All Variables (*continued*)

```
INCOME      TOTAL FAMILY INCOME                                    9
            Print Format: F2
            Write Format: F2
            Missing Values: 0, 98, 99

            Value     Label

              0  M    NAP
              1       LT $1000
              2       $1000 TO 2999
              3       $3000 TO 3999
              4       $4000 TO 4999
              5       $5000 TO 5999
              6       $6000 TO 6999
              7       $7000 TO 7999
              8       $8000 TO 9999
              9       $10000 - 14999
             10       $15000 - 19999
             11       $20000 - 24999
             12       $25000 OR MORE
             13       REFUSED
             98  M    DK
             99  M    NA

MARITAL     MARITAL STATUS                                        10
            Print Format: F1
            Write Format: F1
            Missing Values: 9

            Value     Label

              1       MARRIED
              2       WIDOWED
              3       DIVORCED
              4       SEPARATED
              5       NEVER MARRIED
              9  M    NA

MAWORK      MOTHERS EMPLOYMENT SINCE MARRIAGE                     11
            Print Format: F1
            Write Format: F1
            Missing Values: 0, 8, 9

            Value     Label

              0  M    NAP
              1       YES
              2       NO
              8  M    DK
              9  M    NA
```

TABLE 26
Display Dictionary of All Variables (*continued*)

```
MEMNUM      NUMBER OF MEMBERSHIPS                                  12
            Print Format: F2
            Write Format: F2
            Missing Values: -1, 98, 99

            Value     Label

              -1 M    NAP
              98 M    DK
              99 M    NA

PAPRES16    FATHERS OCCUPATIONAL PRESTIGE SCORE (1970)             13
            Print Format: F2
            Write Format: F2
            Missing Values: 0

            Value     Label

               0 M    DK,NA,NAP

PARTYID     POLITICAL PARTY AFFILIATION                            14
            Print Format: F1
            Write Format: F1
            Missing Values: 8, 9

            Value     Label

               0      STRONG DEMOCRAT
               1      NOT STR DEMOCRAT
               2      IND,NEAR DEM
               3      INDEPENDENT
               4      IND,NEAR REP
               5      NOT STR REPUBLICAN
               6      STRONG REPUBLICAN
               7      OTHER PARTY
               8 M    DK
               9 M    NA

POSTLIFE    BELIEF IN LIFE AFTER DEATH                             15
            Print Format: F1
            Write Format: F1
            Missing Values: 0, 8, 9

            Value     Label

               0 M    NAP
               1      YES
               2      NO
               8 M    DK
               9 M    NA
```

TABLE 26
Display Dictionary of All Variables (*continued*)

```
PRESTIGE    RS OCCUPATIONAL PRESTIGE SCORE   (1970)                    16
            Print Format: F2
            Write Format: F2
            Missing Values: 0

            Value    Label

                0 M  DK,NA,NAP

RACE        RACE OF RESPONDENT                                          17
            Print Format: F1
            Write Format: F1

            Value    Label

                1    WHITE
                2    BLACK
                3    OTHER

REALINC     FAMILY INCOME IN CONSTANT $                                 18
            Print Format: F6
            Write Format: F6
            Missing Values: 0, 999999, 999998

            Value    Label

                0 M  NAP
           999998 M  DONT KNOW
           999999 M  NA

REGION      REGION OF INTERVIEW                                         19
            Print Format: F1
            Write Format: F1
            Missing Values: 0

            Value    Label

                0 M  NOT ASSIGNED
                1    NEW ENGLAND
                2    MIDDLE ATLANTIC
                3    E. NOR. CENTRAL
                4    W. NOR. CENTRAL
                5    SOUTH ATLANTIC
                6    E. SOU. CENTRAL
                7    W. SOU. CENTRAL
                8    MOUNTAIN
                9    PACIFIC

RELIG       RS RELIGIOUS PREFERENCE                                     20
            Print Format: F1
            Write Format: F1
            Missing Values: 8, 9
```

TABLE 26
Display Dictionary of All Variables (*continued*)

```
              Value     Label
                1       PROTESTANT
                2       CATHOLIC
                3       JEWISH
                4       NONE
                5       OTHER
                8 M     DK
                9 M     NA

SEX           RESPONDENTS SEX                                          21
              Print Format: F1
              Write Format: F1

              Value     Label

                1       MALE
                2       FEMALE

SIBS          NUMBER OF BROTHERS AND SISTERS                           22
              Print Format: F2
              Write Format: F2
              Missing Values: 98, 99

              Value     Label

               98 M     DK
               99 M     NA

SIZE          SIZE OF PLACE IN 1000S                                   23
              Print Format: F4
              Write Format: F4
              Missing Values: -1

              Value     Label

               -1 M     NOT ASSIGNED

TVHOURS       HOURS PER DAY WATCHING TV                                24
              Print Format: F2
              Write Format: F2
              Missing Values: -1, 98, 99

              Value     Label

               -1 M     NAP
               98 M     DK
               99 M     NA

ZODIAC        RESPONDENTS ASTROLOGICAL SIGN                            25
              Print Format: F2
              Write Format: F2
              Missing Values: 0, 98, 99
```

TABLE 26
Display Dictionary of All Variables (*continued*)

```
            Value    Label

              0 M    NAP
              1      ARIES
              2      TAURUS
              3      GEMINI
              4      CANCER
              5      LEO
              6      VIRGO
              7      LIBRA
              8      SCORPIO
              9      SAGITTARIUS
             10      CAPRICORN
             11      AQUARIUS
             12      PISCES
             98 M    DK
             99 M    NA

ABANY       ABORTION IF WOMAN WANTS FOR ANY REASON                26
            Print Format: F1
            Write Format: F1
            Missing Values: 0, 8, 9

            Value    Label

              0 M    NAP
              1      YES
              2      NO
              8 M    DK
              9 M    NA

ABDEFECT    STRONG CHANCE OF SERIOUS DEFECT                       27
            Print Format: F1
            Write Format: F1
            Missing Values: 0, 8, 9

            Value    Label

              0 M    NAP
              1      YES
              2      NO
              8 M    DK
              9 M    NA

ABHLTH      WOMANS HEALTH SERIOUSLY ENDANGERED                    28
            Print Format: F1
            Write Format: F1
            Missing Values: 0, 8, 9

            Value    Label

              0 M    NAP
              1      YES
              2      NO
              8 M    DK
              9 M    NA
```

TABLE 26
Display Dictionary of All Variables (*continued*)

```
ABNOMORE   MARRIED—WANTS NO MORE CHILDREN                              29
           Print Format: F1
           Write Format: F1
           Missing Values: 0, 8, 9

           Value     Label

             0 M     NAP
             1       YES
             2       NO
             8 M     DK
             9 M     NA

ABPOOR     LOW INCOME—CANT AFFORD MORE CHILDREN                        30
           Print Format: F1
           Write Format: F1
           Missing Values: 0, 8, 9

           Value     Label

             0 M     NAP
             1       YES
             2       NO
             8 M     DK
             9 M     NA

ABRAPE     PREGNANT AS RESULT OF RAPE                                  31
           Print Format: F1
           Write Format: F1
           Missing Values: 0, 8, 9

           Value     Label

             0 M     NAP
             1       YES
             2       NO
             8 M     DK
             9 M     NA

ABSINGLE   NOT MARRIED                                                 32
           Print Format: F1
           Write Format: F1
           Missing Values: 0, 8, 9

           Value     Label

             0 M     NAP
             1       YES
             2       NO
             8 M     DK
             9 M     NA
```

TABLE 26
Display Dictionary of All Variables (*continued*)

```
AGED        SHOULD AGED LIVE WITH THEIR CHILDREN                    33
            Print Format: F1
            Write Format: F1
            Missing Values: 0, 8, 9

            Value     Label

              0 M     NAP
              1       A GOOD IDEA
              2       A BAD IDEA
              3       DEPENDS
              8 M     DK
              9 M     NA

ANOMIA5     LOT OF THE AVERAGE MAN GETTING WORSE                    34
            Print Format: F1
            Write Format: F1
            Missing Values: 0, 8, 9

            Value     Label

              0 M     NAP
              1       AGREE
              2       DISAGREE
              8 M     DK
              9 M     NA

ANOMIA6     NOT FAIR TO BRING CHILD INTO WORLD                      35
            Print Format: F1
            Write Format: F1
            Missing Values: 0, 8, 9

            Value     Label

              0 M     NAP
              1       AGREE
              2       DISAGREE
              8 M     DK
              9 M     NA

ANOMIA7     OFFICIALS NOT INTERESTED IN AVERAGE MAN                 36
            Print Format: F1
            Write Format: F1
            Missing Values: 0, 8, 9

            Value     Label

              0 M     NAP
              1       AGREE
              2       DISAGREE
              8 M     DK
              9 M     NA
```

TABLE 26
Display Dictionary of All Variables (*continued*)

```
CAPPUN     FAVOR OR OPPOSE DEATH PENALTY FOR MURDER                    37
           Print Format: F1
           Write Format: F1
           Missing Values: 0, 8, 9

           Value     Label

             0 M     NAP
             1       FAVOR
             2       OPPOSE
             8 M     DK
             9 M     NA

CONEDUC    CONFIDENCE IN EDUCATION                                      38
           Print Format: F1
           Write Format: F1
           Missing Values: 0, 8, 9

           Value     Label

             0 M     NAP
             1       A GREAT DEAL
             2       ONLY SOME
             3       HARDLY ANY
             8 M     DK
             9 M     NA

CONLEGIS   CONFIDENCE IN CONGRESS                                       39
           Print Format: F1
           Write Format: F1
           Missing Values: 0, 8, 9

           Value     Label

             0 M     NAP
             1       A GREAT DEAL
             2       ONLY SOME
             3       HARDLY ANY
             8 M     DK
             9 M     NA

CONPRESS   CONFIDENCE IN PRESS                                          40
           Print Format: F1
           Write Format: F1
           Missing Values: 0, 8, 9

           Value     Label

             0 M     NAP
             1       A GREAT DEAL
             2       ONLY SOME
             3       HARDLY ANY
             8 M     DK
             9 M     NA
```

TABLE 26
Display Dictionary of All Variables (*continued*)

```
COURTS      COURTS DEALING WITH CRIMINALS                        41
            Print Format: F1
            Write Format: F1
            Missing Values: 0, 8, 9

            Value     Label

              0 M     NAP
              1       TOO HARSH
              2       NOT HARSH ENOUGH
              3       ABOUT RIGHT
              8 M     DK
              9 M     NA

GRASS       SHOULD MARIJUANA BE MADE LEGAL                       42
            Print Format: F1
            Write Format: F1
            Missing Values: 0, 8, 9

            Value     Label

              0 M     NAP
              1       LEGAL
              2       NOT LEGAL
              8 M     DK
              9 M     NA

HAPPY       GENERAL HAPPINESS                                    43
            Print Format: F1
            Write Format: F1
            Missing Values: 0, 8, 9

            Value     Label

              0 M     NAP
              1       VERY HAPPY
              2       PRETTY HAPPY
              3       NOT TOO HAPPY
              8 M     DK
              9 M     NA

HELPFUL     PEOPLE HELPFUL OR LOOKING OUT FOR SELVES             44
            Print Format: F1
            Write Format: F1
            Missing Values: 0, 8, 9

            Value     Label

              0 M     NAP
              1       HELPFUL
              2       LOOKOUT FOR SELF
              3       DEPENDS
              8 M     DK
              9 M     NA
```

TABLE 26
Display Dictionary of All Variables (*continued*)

```
HIT        EVER PUNCHED OR BEATEN BY ANOTHER PERSON                45
           Print Format: F1
           Write Format: F1
           Missing Values: 0, 8, 9

           Value     Label

             0 M     NAP
             1       YES
             2       NO
             8 M     DK
             9 M     NA

HITOK      EVER APPROVE OF MAN PUNCHING ADULT MALE                 46
           Print Format: F1
           Write Format: F1
           Missing Values: 0, 8, 9

           Value     Label

             0 M     NAP
             1       YES
             2       NO
             8 M     DK
             9 M     NA

NATCRIME   HALTING RISING CRIME RATE                               47
           Print Format: F1
           Write Format: F1
           Missing Values: 0, 8, 9

           Value     Label

             0 M     NAP
             1       TOO LITTLE
             2       ABOUT RIGHT
             3       TOO MUCH
             8 M     DK
             9 M     NA

NATDRUG    DEALING WITH DRUG ADDICTION                             48
           Print Format: F1
           Write Format: F1
           Missing Values: 0, 8, 9

           Value     Label

             0 M     NAP
             1       TOO LITTLE
             2       ABOUT RIGHT
             3       TOO MUCH
             8 M     DK
             9 M     NA
```

TABLE 26
Display Dictionary of All Variables (*continued*)

```
NATEDUC    IMPROVING NATIONS EDUCATION SYSTEM                      49
           Print Format: F1
           Write Format: F1
           Missing Values: 0, 8, 9

           Value     Label

             0 M     NAP
             1       TOO LITTLE
             2       ABOUT RIGHT
             3       TOO MUCH
             8 M     DK
             9 M     NA

NATENVIR   IMPROVING & PROTECTING ENVIRONMENT                      50
           Print Format: F1
           Write Format: F1
           Missing Values: 0, 8, 9

           Value     Label

             0 M     NAP
             1       TOO LITTLE
             2       ABOUT RIGHT
             3       TOO MUCH
             8 M     DK
             9 M     NA

NATFARE    WELFARE                                                 51
           Print Format: F1
           Write Format: F1
           Missing Values: 0, 8, 9

           Value     Label

             0 M     NAP
             1       TOO LITTLE
             2       ABOUT RIGHT
             3       TOO MUCH
             8 M     DK
             9 M     NA

OWNGUN     HAVE GUN IN HOME                                        52
           Print Format: F1
           Write Format: F1
           Missing Values: 0, 8, 9

           Value     Label

             0 M     NAP
             1       YES
             2       NO
             3       REFUSED
             8 M     DK
             9 M     NA
```

TABLE 26
Display Dictionary of All Variables (*continued*)

```
POLHITOK   EVER APPROVE OF POLICE STRIKING CITIZEN                    53
           Print Format: F1
           Write Format: F1
           Missing Values: 0, 8, 9

           Value      Label

             0 M      NAP
             1        YES
             2        NO
             8 M      DK
             9 M      NA

POLVIEWS   THINK OF SELF AS LIBERAL OR CONSERVATIVE                   54
           Print Format: F1
           Write Format: F1
           Missing Values: 0, 8, 9

           Value      Label

             0 M      NAP
             1        EXTREMELY LIBERAL
             2        LIBERAL
             3        SLIGHTLY LIBERAL
             4        MODERATE
             5        SLGHTLY CONSERVATIVE
             6        CONSERVATIVE
             7        EXTRMLY CONSERVATIVE
             8 M      DK
             9 M      NA

PORNINF    MATERIALS PROVIDE INFO ABOUT SEX                           55
           Print Format: F1
           Write Format: F1
           Missing Values: 0, 8, 9

           Value      Label

             0 M      NAP
             1        YES
             2        NO
             8 M      DK
             9 M      NA

PORNOUT    MATERIALS PROVIDE OUTLET                                   56
           Print Format: F1
           Write Format: F1
           Missing Values: 0, 8, 9

           Value      Label

             0 M      NAP
             1        YES
             2        NO
             8 M      DK
             9 M      NA
```

TABLE 26
Display Dictionary of All Variables (*continued*)

```
PORNRAPE   MATERIALS LEAD TO RAPE                              57
           Print Format: F1
           Write Format: F1
           Missing Values: 0, 8, 9

           Value     Label

               0 M   NAP
               1     YES
               2     NO
               8 M   DK
               9 M   NA

RACLIVE    ANY OPP. RACE IN NEIGHBORHOOD                       58
           Print Format: F1
           Write Format: F1
           Missing Values: 0, 8, 9

           Value     Label

               0 M   NAP
               1     YES
               2     NO
               8 M   DK
               9 M   NA

SATCITY    CITY OR PLACE R LIVES IN                            59
           Print Format: F1
           Write Format: F1
           Missing Values: 0, 8, 9

           Value     Label

               0 M   NAP
               1     VERY GREAT DEAL
               2     GREAT DEAL
               3     QUITE A BIT
               4     A FAIR AMOUNT
               5     SOME
               6     A LITTLE
               7     NONE
               8 M   DK
               9 M   NA

SATFAM     FAMILY LIFE                                         60
           Print Format: F1
           Write Format: F1
           Missing Values: 0, 8, 9

           Value     Label

               0 M   NAP
               1     VERY GREAT DEAL
               2     GREAT DEAL
               3     QUITE A BIT
```

TABLE 26
Display Dictionary of All Variables (*continued*)

```
                 4      A FAIR AMOUNT
                 5      SOME
                 6      A LITTLE
                 7      NONE
                 8  M   DK
                 9  M   NA

SATFIN      SATISFACTION WITH FINANCIAL SITUATION                    61
            Print Format: F1
            Write Format: F1
            Missing Values: 8, 9

            Value      Label

                 1      SATISFIED
                 2      MORE OR LESS
                 3      NOT AT ALL SAT
                 8  M   DK
                 9  M   NA

SATFRND     FRIENDSHIPS                                              62
            Print Format: F1
            Write Format: F1
            Missing Values: 0, 8, 9

            Value      Label

                 0  M   NAP
                 1      VERY GREAT DEAL
                 2      GREAT DEAL
                 3      QUITE A BIT
                 4      A FAIR AMOUNT
                 5      SOME
                 6      A LITTLE
                 7      NONE
                 8  M   DK
                 9  M   NA

SATHEALT    HEALTH AND PHYSICAL CONDITION                            63
            Print Format: F1
            Write Format: F1
            Missing Values: 0, 8, 9

            Value      Label

                 0  M   NAP
                 1      VERY GREAT DEAL
                 2      GREAT DEAL
                 3      QUITE A BIT
                 4      A FAIR AMOUNT
                 5      SOME
                 6      A LITTLE
                 7      NONE
                 8  M   DK
                 9  M   NA
```

TABLE 26
Display Dictionary of All Variables (*continued*)

```
SATHOBBY   NON-WORKING ACTIVITIES, HOBBIES                    64
           Print Format: F1
           Write Format: F1
           Missing Values: 0, 8, 9

           Value      Label

               0 M    NAP
               1      VERY GREAT DEAL
               2      GREAT DEAL
               3      QUITE A BIT
               4      A FAIR AMOUNT
               5      SOME
               6      A LITTLE
               7      NONE
               8 M    DK
               9 M    NA

SATJOB     JOB OR HOUSEWORK                                   65
           Print Format: F1
           Write Format: F1
           Missing Values: 0, 8, 9

           Value      Label

               0 M    NAP
               1      VERY SATISFIED
               2      MOD. SATISFIED
               3      A LITTLE DISSAT
               4      VERY DISSATISFIED
               8 M    DK
               9 M    NA

XMOVIE     SEEN X-RATED MOVIE IN LAST YEAR                    66
           Print Format: F1
           Write Format: F1
           Missing Values: 0, 8, 9

           Value      Label

               0 M    NAP
               1      YES
               2      NO
               8 M    DK
               9 M    NA
```

APPENDIX J: Twenty Questions a Journalist Should Ask about Poll Results*

SHELDON R. GAWISER

G. EVANS WITT

For journalists and for pollsters, questions are the most frequently used tool for gathering information. Here are 20 questions for the journalist to ask the pollster before reporting poll results. This publication is designed to help the working journalist do a thorough, professional job covering polls; it is not a primer on how to conduct a public opinion survey.

This work is about polls that are "scientific." A number of the questions will help you decide whether or not a poll is a "scientific" one worthy of coverage—or an unscientific survey that may be entertaining, but meaningless.

Of the scientific polls, the Gallup Poll is probably the best known and one of the oldest. There are many other excellent surveys conducted by reputable firms, as well.

The unscientific surveys are less well-known, if quite widespread. There are 900-number call-in polls, man-on-the-street surveys, shopping mall polls, and even the classic toilet tissue poll featuring pictures of the candidates on each sheet.

The major distinguishing difference between scientific and unscientific polls is who picks the respondents for the survey. In a scientific poll, the pollster identifies and seeks out the people to be interviewed. In an unscientific poll, the respondents usually "volunteer" their opinions, selecting themselves for the poll.

The results of the well-conducted scientific poll can provide a reliable guide to the opinions of many people in addition to those interviewed—even the opinions of all Americans. The results of an unscientific poll tell you nothing more than simply what those respondents say.

With these 20 questions in hand, the journalist can seek the facts to decide just how to handle every poll that comes across the news desk each day.

1. Who did the poll? What polling firm, research house, political campaign, corporation, or other group conducted the poll? This is always the first question to ask.

If you don't know who did the poll, you can't get the answers to all the other questions listed here. And if the person providing poll results can't or won't tell you who did it, serious questions must be raised about the reliability and truthfulness of the results being presented.

In most cases, reputable polling firms will provide you with the information you need to evaluate the survey. And because reputation is important to a quality firm, a professionally conducted poll will avoid many errors.

2. Who paid for the poll and why was it done? You must know who paid for the survey, because that tells you—and your audience—who thought these topics were important enough to spend money finding out what people think. And that goes to the whole issue of why the poll was done.

Polls usually are not conducted for the good of the world. They are conducted for a reason—either to gain helpful information or to advance a particular cause.

---

*Published as a brochure by the National Council on Public Polls and reprinted here with permission.

It may be the news organization wants to develop a good story. It may be the politician wants to be re-elected. It may be that the corporation is trying to push sales of its new product. Or a special interest group may be trying to prove that its views are the views of the entire country.

All are legitimate reasons for doing a poll.

The important issue for you as a journalist is whether the motive for doing the poll creates such serious doubts about the validity of the poll results that the results should not be publicized.

An example of suspect polls are private polls conducted by a political campaign. These polls are conducted solely to help the candidate win—and for no other reason. The poll may have terrifically slanted questions or a strange sampling methodology, all with a tactical campaign purpose. For example, the campaign may be testing out new slogans or a new stance on a key issue or a new attack on the opponent.

But since accurately gauging the general public's sentiments is not the goal of the candidate's poll, the results should be reported with great care.

Likewise, reporting on a survey by a special interest group is tricky. For example, an environmental group trumpets a poll saying the American people support strong measures to protect the environment. That may be true, but the poll may have been conducted for a group with definite views. That may have swayed the question wording, the timing of the poll, the group interviewed, and the order of the questions. You should examine the poll to be certain that it accurately samples public opinion—and does not simply push a single viewpoint.

3. How many people were interviewed for the survey? This is another basic piece of information you should have. Because polls give approximate answers, the more people interviewed in a scientific poll, the smaller the error due to the size of the sample, all other things being equal.

However, a common trap to avoid is that "more is automatically better." It is absolutely true that the more people interviewed in a reliable survey, the smaller the sampling error—all other things being equal. But, other factors may be more important in judging the quality of a survey.

4. How were those people chosen? The key reason that some polls reflect public opinion accurately and other polls are unscientific junk is how the people were chosen to be interviewed.

In scientific polls, the pollster uses a specific method for picking respondents. In unscientific polls, the person picks himself to participate.

The method pollsters use to pick interviewees relies on the bedrock of mathematical reality: when the chance of selecting each person in the target population is known, then and only then do the results of the sample survey reflect the entire population. This is called a random sample or a probability sample. This is the reason that interviews with 1000 American adults can accurately reflect the opinions of more than 185 million American adults.

Most scientific samples use special techniques to be economically feasible. For example, some sampling methods for telephone interviewing do not just pick randomly generated telephone numbers. Only telephone exchanges that are known to contain working residential numbers are selected—to reduce the number of wasted calls.

But even a random sample cannot be purely random in practice since some people don't have phones, refuse to answer, or aren't home.

5. What area: nation, state, or region—or what group: teachers, lawyers, Democratic voters, etc.— were these people chosen from? Although the results of probability samples can be projected to represent the larger population from which they were selected, the characteristics of the larger population must be specified, for example, you should know if a sample represents all people in the United States or just those in one state or one city. In another example, the case of telephone samples, the population is that of people living in households with telephones. For most purposes, telephone households may be similar to the general population. But, if you were reporting a poll on what it was like to be poor or homeless, this would not be the appropriate sample. Remember, the use of a scientific sampling technique does not mean that the correct population was interviewed.

It is absolutely critical to know from which group the interviewees were chosen.

For example, a survey of business people can reflect the opinions of business people—but not of all adults. Only if the interviewees were chosen from among all American adults can the poll reflect the opinions of all American adults.

Political polls are especially sensitive to this issue.

In pre-primary and pre-election polls, how the people are chosen as the base for poll results is critical. A poll of all adults, for example, is not very useful on a primary race where only 25 percent of the registered voters actually turn out. So look for polls based on registered voters, "likely voters," previous primary voters, and such. These distinctions are important and should be included in the story.

One of the most variable aspects of polling is trying to figure out who actually is going to vote.

6. Are the results based on the answers of all the people interviewed? One of the easiest ways to misrepresent the results of a poll is to report the answers of only a subgroup. For example, there is usually a substantial difference between the opinions of Democrats and Republicans on campaign-related matters. Reporting the opinions of only Democrats in a poll purported to be of all adults would substantially misrepresent the results.

Poll results based on Democrats must be identified as such and should be reported as representing only Democratic opinions.

Of course, reporting on just one subgroup can be exactly the right course. In polling on a Republican primary contest, it is the opinions of the Republicans who can vote in the primary that count—not those of Democrats who cannot vote in that GOP contest.

7. Who should have been interviewed and was not? You ought to know how many people refused to answer the survey or were never contacted.

The non-response rate is the percentage of people contacted who should have been interviewed, but were not. They may have refused attempts to interview them. Or interviews may not have been attempted if people were not home when the interviewer called.

The results of a survey should be judged very differently if the 100 convention delegates interviewed were a random sample of 1000 delegates as compared to their being the only 100 out of the 1000 willing to participate. The same potential for distorted results occurs if some of the delegates who were in the sample were never actually contacted.

8. When was the poll done? Events have a dramatic impact on poll results. Your interpretation of a poll should depend on when it was conducted relative to key events. Even the freshest poll results can be overtaken by subsequent events. The President may have given a stirring speech to the nation, the stock market may have crashed, or an oil tanker may have sunk, spilling millions of gallons of crude on beautiful beaches.

Poll results that are several weeks or months old may be perfectly valid as history, but are not always newsworthy.

9. How were the interviews conducted? There are three main possibilities: in person at home, by telephone, or by mail.

Most surveys are now conducted by telephone, with the calls made from a central interviewing center. However, some surveys are still conducted by sending interviewers into people's homes to conduct the interviews.

Some surveys are conducted by mail. In scientific polls, the pollster picks the people to receive the mail questionnaires. The respondent fills out the questionnaire and returns it.

Mail surveys can be excellent sources of information, but it takes weeks to do a mail survey, meaning that the results cannot be as timely as a telephone survey. And mail surveys can be subject to other kinds of errors, particularly low response rates. In many mail surveys, more people fail to participate than do. This makes the results suspect.

Surveys done in shopping mails, in stores or restaurants or on the sidewalk may have their uses for their sponsors, but publishing the results in the media is not among them. These "man in the street" approaches may yield interesting human interest stories, but they should never be treated as if they represent a public opinion poll.

10. Is this a dial-in poll, a mail-in poll, or a subscriber coupon poll? If the poll you are looking at is a dial-in, mail-in, or coupon poll, don't report the results because the respondents are self-selected. These pseudo-polls have no validity. Remember, the purpose of a poll is to draw conclusions about the population, not about the sample. In these pseudo-polls there is no way to project the results to any larger group. Scientific polls usually show different results than pseudo-polls.

The 900-number dial-in polls may be fine for deciding whether or not Larry the Lobster should be cooked on Saturday Night Live or even for dedicated fans to express their opinions on who is the greatest quarterback in the National Football League, but they have only entertainment value. There is no way to tell who actually called in, how old they are, or how many times each person called.

Never be fooled by the number of responses. In some cases, a few people call in thousands of times. Even if 500,000 calls are tallied, no one has any real knowledge of what the results mean. If big numbers impress you, remember that the *Literary Digest's* non-scientific sample of 12,000,000 people said Landon would beat Roosevelt.

The subscriber coupon polls are just as bad. In these cases, the magazine or newspaper includes a coupon to be mailed in with the answers to the questions. Again, there is no way to know who responded and how many times. These results are not projectable even to the subscribers of the publication that includes the coupon.

11. What is the sampling error for the poll results? Interviews with a scientific sample of 1000 adults can accurately reflect the opinions of more than 185 million American adults. That means interviews attempted with all 185 million adults—if such were possible—would give approximately the same results as a well-conducted survey.

But what happens if another carefully done poll of 1000 adults gives slightly different results from the first survey? Neither of the polls is "wrong." This range of results is called the error due to sampling, often called the margin of error.

This is not an "error" in the sense of making a mistake. Rather, it is a measure of the possible range of approximation in the results because a sample was used.

Pollsters express the size of the uncertainty caused by using a sample at a "confidence level." This means a sample is likely to be within so many points of the results one would have gotten if an interview was attempted with the entire target population. They usually say this with 95% confidence.

Thus, for example, a "3 percentage point margin of error" in a national poll means that if the attempt was made to interview every adult in the nation with the same questions in the same way at about the same time as the poll was taken, the poll's answers would fall within plus or minus 3 percentage points of the complete count result 95% of the time.

Please note that this does not address the issue of whether or not people cooperate with the survey, or if the questions are understood, or if any other methodological issue exists. The sampling error is only the portion of the potential error in a survey introduced by using a sample rather than the entire population. Sampling error tells us nothing about the refusals or those consistently unavailable for interview; it also tells us nothing about the biasing effects of a particular question wording or the bias a particular interviewer may inject into the interview situation.

Remember that the sampling error margin applies to each figure in the results—it is at least 3 percentage points plus or minus for each one. Thus, in a poll question matching two candidates for President, both figures are subject to sampling error.

This raises one of the thorniest problems in the presentation of poll results. For a horse-race poll, when is one candidate really ahead of the other?

Certainly, when the gap between the two candidates is more than twice the error margin—6 percentage points in our example—you can say with confidence that the poll says Candidate A is leading Candidate B.

And just as certainly, if the gap between the two candidates is less than error margin then you should not say that one candidate is ahead of the other. Then, the race is "close"; the race is "roughly even"; or there is "little difference between the candidates."

And bear in mind that when subgroup results are reported—women or blacks, or young people—the sampling error margin for those figures is greater than for results based on the survey as a whole.

12. What other kinds of mistakes can skew poll results? The margin of sampling error is just one source of inaccuracy in a poll and not necessarily the greatest source of error; we use it because it's the only one that can be quantified. Question phrasing and ordering are also a likely source of flaws. That's why you need to examine poll questions for bias.

You should always ask if the poll results have been "weighted." This process is usually used to account for unequal probabilities of selection and to correct demographics in the sample. However, you should be aware that a poll can also be unduly manipulated by weighing to produce some desired result.

And there are other possible sources of error. These include issues such as inadequate interviewer training and supervision, data processing errors, and other operational problems. Professional polling operations are less subject to these problems than volunteer-conducted polls, which are usually less trustworthy.

13. What questions were asked? You must find out the exact wording of the poll questions. Why? Because the very wording of questions can make major differences in the results.

Perhaps the best test of any poll question is your reaction to it. On the face of it, does the question seem fair and unbiased? Does it present a balanced set of choices? Would people you know be able to answer the question?

On sensitive questions—such as abortion—the complete wording of the question should probably be included in your story. But at the very least, you must have the exact wording as you are preparing the story.

It may well be worthwhile to compare the results of several different polls from different organizations on these sensitive questions. In that case, you should be careful to compare both the results and the exact wording of the questions.

14. In what order were the questions asked? Sometimes the very order of the questions can have an impact on the results. Often that impact is intentional; sometimes, it is not. The impact of order can often be subtle.

During troubled economic times, for example, if people are asked what they think of the economy before they are asked their opinion of the president, the presidential popularity rating will probably be lower than if you had reversed the questions. And in good economic times, the opposite is true.

In political polls, campaign consultants often ask a series of questions about various issue positions of the candidates—or various things that could be said about the candidates. After these questions are asked, the horse-race question is asked, usually for the second time in the pole. This second horse-race question is then examined to see if the questions about issues and positions swayed any opinions. This may be a good way to test issues. It is a poor way to test the candidates' true standings in the public's mind.

What is important here is whether the questions that went before the important question affect the results. If the poll asks questions about abortion just before a question about an abortion ballot measure, those previous questions could sway the results.

15. What other polls have been done on this topic? Do they say the same thing? If they are different, why are they different? Results of other polls—a candidate's opponent, public polls, media polls, or whatever—should be used to check and contrast poll results you have in hand.

If the polls differ, first check the timing of when the interviewing was done. The different poll results may demonstrate a swing in public opinion.

If the polls were done about the same time, and no other factor seems to explain the disagreement, go to each poll sponsor and ask for an explanation of the differences. Conflicting polls often make good stories.

16. So, the poll says the race is all over. What now? No matter how good the poll, no matter how wide the margin, no matter how big the sample, a pre-election poll does not show that one candidate has the race "locked up." Things change—often and dramatically in politics.

17. Was the poll part of a fund-raising effort? This is another example of a pseudo-poll. An organization sends out a survey form to a large list of people. The last question usually asks for a contribution from the respondent. He or she is expected to send money to support the organization or pay for tabulating the survey.

The people who respond to these types of surveys are likely to be those who agree with the organization's goals. Also, the questions are usually loaded and the results meaningless.

This technique is used by a wide variety of organizations from political parties and special-interest groups to charitable organizations. Again, if the poll in question is part of a fund-raising pitch, pitch it—in the waste basket.

18. So I've asked all the questions. The answers sound good. The poll is correct, right? Usually, yes. However, remember that the laws of chance alone say that the results of one poll out of 20 may be skewed away from the public's real views just because of sampling error.

19. With all these potential problems, should we ever report poll results? Yes. Because reputable polling organizations consistently do good work. In spite of the difficulties, the public opinion survey, correctly conducted, is still the best objective measure of the state of the views of the public.

20. Is this poll worth reporting? If the poll was conducted correctly, and you have been able to obtain the information outlined here, your news judgment and that of your editors should be applied to polls, as it is to every other element of a story.

Bibliography

Alfred, Randall. 1976. "The Church of Satan." Pp. 180–202 in *The New Religious Consciousness,* edited by Charles Glock and Robert Bellah. Berkeley: University of California Press.

Almond, Gabriel, and Sidney Verba. 1963. *The Civic Culture.* Princeton, NJ: Princeton University Press.

Anderson, Andy B., Alexander Basilevsky, and Derek P. J. Hum. 1983. "Measurement: Theory and Techniques." Pp. 231–87 in *Handbook of Survey Research,* edited by Peter H. Rossi, James D. Wright, and Andy B. Anderson. New York: Academic Press.

Anderson, Martin. 1978. *Welfare: The Political Economy of Welfare Reform in the United States.* Stanford, CA: Hoover Institution Press.

Anderson, Walt. 1990. *Reality Isn't What It Used to Be: Theatrical Politics, Ready-to-Wear Religion, Global Myths, Primitive Chic, and Other Wonders of the Postmodern World.* San Francisco: Harper & Row.

Andorka, Rudolf. 1990. "The Importance and the Role of the Second Economy for the Hungarian Economy and Society." *Quarterly Journal of Budapest University of Economic Sciences* 12, (2): 95–113.

Aneshensel, Carol S., Rosina Becerra, Eve Fielder, and Roberleigh Schuler. 1989. "Participation of Mexican American Female Adolescents in a Longitudinal Panel Survey." *Public Opinion Quarterly* 53:548–62.

Asch, Solomon. 1958. "Effects of Group Pressure upon the Modification and Distortion of Judgments." Pp. 174–83 in *Readings in Social Psychology,* 3rd ed., edited by Eleanor E. Maccoby, et al. New York: Holt, Rinehart & Winston.

Asher, Ramona M., and Gary Alan Fine. 1991. "Fragile Ties: Sharing Research Relationships with Women Married to Alcoholics." Pp. 196–205 in *Experiencing Fieldwork: An Inside View of Qualitative Research,* edited by William B. Shaffir and Roberta A. Stebbins. Newbury Park, CA: Sage.

Auster, Carol J. 1985. "Manuals for Socialization: Examples from Girl Scout Handbooks 1913–1984." *Qualitative Sociology* 8(4): 359–367.

Babbie, Earl. 1966. "The Third Civilization." *Review of Religious Research,* Winter, pp. 101–21.
———. 1967. "A Religious Profile of Episcopal Churchwomen," *Pacific Churchman,* January, pp. 6–8, 12.
———. 1970. *Science and Morality in Medicine.* Berkeley: University of California Press.
———. 1982. *Social Research for Consumers.* Belmont, CA: Wadsworth.
———. 1985. *You Can Make a Difference.* New York: St. Martin's Press.
———. 1986. *Observing Ourselves: Essays in Social Research.* Belmont, CA: Wadsworth.
———. 1990. *Survey Research Methods.* Belmont, CA: Wadsworth.
———. 1994. *The Sociological Spirit.* Belmont, CA: Wadsworth.

Babbie, Earl, and Fred Halley. 1995. *Adventures in Social Research: Data Analysis Using SPSS for Windows.* Newbury Park, CA: Pine Forge Press.

Bailey, William C. 1975. "Murder and Capital Punishment." In *Criminal Law in Action,* edited by William J. Chambliss. New York: Wiley.

Baker, Vern, and Charles Lambert. 1990. "The National Collegiate Athletic Association and the Governance of Higher Education." *Sociological Quarterly* 31 (3): 403–21.

Ball-Rokeach, Sandra J., Joel W. Grube, and Milton Rokeach. 1981. "Roots: The Next Generation—Who Watched and with What Effect." *Public Opinion Quarterly* 45:58–68.

Banfield, Edward. 1968. *The Unheavenly City: The Nature and Future of Our Urban Crisis.* Boston: Little, Brown.

Bart, Pauline, and Linda Frankel. 1986. *The Student Sociologist's Handbook.* Morristown, NJ: General Learning Press.

Bart, Pauline, and Patricia O'Brien. 1985. *Stopping Rape: Successful Survival Strategies.* New York: Pergamon.

Beck, E. M., and Stewart E. Tolnay. 1990. "The Killing Fields of the Deep South: The Market for Cotton and the Lynching of Blacks, 1882–1930." *American Sociological Review* 55 (August): 526–39.

Bednarz, Marlene. 1996. "Push polls statement." Report to the AAPORnet listserv, April 5 [On-line]. Available: mbednarz@umich.edu

Belenky, Mary Field, Blythe McVicker Clinchy, Nancy

Rule Goldberger, and Jill Mattuck Tarule. 1986. *Women's Ways of Knowing: The Development of Self, Voice, and Mind.* New York: Basic Books.

Bellah, Robert N. 1957. *Tokugawa Religion.* Glencoe, IL: Free Press.

———. 1967. "Research Chronicle: Tokugawa Religion." Pp. 164–85 in *Sociologists at Work,* edited by Phillip E. Hammond. Garden City, NY: Anchor Books.

———. 1970. "Christianity and Symbolic Realism." *Journal for the Scientific Study of Religion* 9:89–96.

———. 1974. "Comment on the Limits of Symbolic Realism." *Journal for the Scientific Study of Religion* 13:487–89.

Beniger, James. 1996. "NIC Questionnaire, Pre-Post Shifts." Report to the AAPORNET listserv, January 31 [On-line]. Message-ID: <Pine.SUN.3.91.960131050554.2202A-100000 @almaak.usc.edu>. Reach Beniger at beniger @rcf.usc.edu

Bennet, Carl A., and Arthur A. Lumsdaine, eds. 1975. *Evaluation and Experiment.* New York: Academic Press.

Benton, J. Edwin, and John L. Daly. 1991. "A Question Order Effect in a Local Government Survey." *Public Opinion Quarterly* 55:640–42.

Berg, Bruce L. 1989. *Qualitative Research Methods for the Social Sciences.* Boston: Allyn and Bacon.

Berger, Joseph, Morris Zelditch, Jr., and Bo Anderson, eds. 1989. *Sociological Theories in Progress.* Newbury Park, CA: Sage.

Beveridge, W. I. B. 1950. *The Art of Scientific Investigation.* New York: Vintage Books.

Beyer, Judith E. 1981. "Interpersonal Communication as Perceived by Nurse Educators in Collegial Interactions." *Nursing Research,* March–April, pp. 111–17.

Bian, Yanjie. 1994. *Work and Inequality in Urban China.* Albany: State University of New York Press.

Black, Donald. 1970. "Production of Crime Rates." *American Sociological Review* 35 (August): 733–48.

Blair, Johnny, Shanyang Zhao, Barbara Bickart, and Ralph Kuhn. 1995. *Sample Design for Household Telephone Surveys: A Bibliography 1949–1995.* College Park: Survey Research Center, University of Maryland.

Blalock, Hubert M., Jr. 1979. *Social Statistics.* New York: McGraw-Hill.

Blau, Peter M., ed. 1975. *Approaches to the Study of Social Structure.* New York: Free Press.

Blaunstein, Albert, and Robert Zangrando, eds. 1970. *Civil Rights and the Black American.* New York: Washington Square Press.

Bobo, Lawrence, and Frederick C. Licari. 1989. "Education and Political Tolerance: Testing the Effects of Cognitive Sophistication and Target Group Effect." *Public Opinion Quarterly* 53:285–308.

Bohrnstedt, George W. 1983. "Measurement." Pp. 70–121 in *Handbook of Survey Research,* edited by Peter H. Rossi, James D. Wright, and Andy B. Anderson. New York: Academic Press.

Bolstein, Richard. 1991. "Comparison of the Likelihood to Vote among Preelection Poll Respondents and Nonrespondents." *Public Opinion Quarterly* 55:648–50.

Boruch, Robert F., and Joe S. Cecil. 1979. *Assuring the Confidentiality of Social Research Data.* Philadelphia: University of Pennsylvania Press.

Botein, B. 1965. "The Manhattan Bail Project: Its Impact in Criminology and the Criminal Law Process." *Texas Law Review* 43:319–31.

Bottomore, T. B., and Maximilien Rubel, eds. [1843] 1956. *Karl Marx: Selected Writings in Sociology and Social Philosophy.* Translated by T. B. Bottomore. New York: McGraw-Hill.

Bower, Robert T., and Priscilla de Gasparis. 1978. *Ethics in Social Research: Protecting the Interests of Human Subjects.* New York: Praeger.

Bradburn, Norman M., and Seymour Sudman. 1988. *Polls and Surveys: Understanding What They Tell Us.* San Francisco: Jossey-Bass.

Breuer, Josef, and Sigmund Freud. [1895] 1957. "Studies in Hysteria." In *The Standard Edition of the Complete Psychological Works of Sigmund Freud,* Vol. 2, edited and translated by James Strachey. London: Hogarth Press.

Brownlee, K. A. 1975. "A Note on the Effects of Nonresponse on Surveys." *Journal of the American Statistical Association* 52 (227): 29–32.

Burstein, Leigh, Howard E. Freeman, and Peter H. Rossi, eds. 1985. *Collecting Evaluation Data: Problems and Solutions.* Beverly Hills, CA: Sage.

Campbell, Donald, and Julian Stanley. 1963. *Experimental and Quasi-Experimental Designs for Research.* Chicago: Rand McNally.

Carmines, Edward G., and Richard A. Zeller. 1979. *Reliability and Validity Assessment.* Beverly Hills, CA: Sage.

Carpini, Michael X. Delli, and Scott Keeter. 1991. "Stability and Change in the U.S. Public's Knowledge of Politics." *Public Opinion Quarterly* 55:583–612.

Casley, D. J., and D. A. Lury. 1987. *Data Collection in Developing Countries.* Oxford: Clarendon Press.

Census Bureau. See U.S. Bureau of the Census.

Chafetz, Janet. 1978. *A Primer on the Construction and Testing of Theories in Sociology.* Itasca, IL: Peacock.

———. 1988. *Feminist Sociology.* Itasca, IL: Peacock.

Chen, Huey-Tsyh. 1990. *Theory-Driven Evaluations.* Newbury Park, CA: Sage.

Coffey, Amanda, and Paul Atkinson. 1996. *Making Sense of Qualitative Data: Complementary Research Strategies.* Thousand Oaks, CA: Sage.

Cole, Stephen. 1980. *The Sociological Method: An Introduction to the Science of Sociology.* Boston: Houghton Mifflin.

———. 1992. *Making Science: Between Nature and Society.* Cambridge, MA: Harvard University Press.

Coleman, James. 1966. *Equality of Educational Opportunity.* Washington, DC: U.S. Government Printing Office.

Collins, G. C., and Timothy B. Blodgett. 1981. "Sexual Harassment . . . Some See It . . . Some Won't." *Harvard Business Review,* March–April, pp. 76–95.

Comstock, Donald. 1980. "Dimensions of Influence in Organizations." *Pacific Sociological Review,* January, pp. 67–84.

Converse, Jean M. 1987. *Survey Research in the United States: Roots and Emergence, 1890–1960.* Berkeley: University of California Press.

Converse, Jean M., and Stanley Presser. 1986. *Survey Questions: Handcrafting the Standardized Questionnaire.* Newbury Park, CA: Sage.

Cook, Elizabeth. 1995. Communication to the METHODS listserv, April 25, from Michel de Seve (T120@music.ulaval.ca) to Cook (EC1645A@american.edu) [On-line].

Cook, Thomas D., and Donald T. Campbell. 1979. *Quasi-Experimentation: Design and Analysis Issues for Field Settings.* Chicago: Rand McNally.

Cooper, Harris M. 1989. *Integrating Research: A Guide for Literature Reviews.* Newbury Park, CA: Sage.

Cooper-Stephenson, Cynthia, and Athanasios Theologides. 1981. "Nutrition in Cancer: Physicians' Knowledge, Opinions, and Educational Needs." *Journal of the American Dietetic Association,* May, pp. 472–76.

Coser, Lewis. 1956. *The Functions of Social Conflict.* New York: Free Press.

Craig, R. Stephen. 1992. "The Effect of Television Day Part on Gender Portrayals in Television Commercials: A Content Analysis." *Sex Roles* 26 (5/6): 197–211.

Crawford, Kent S., Edmund D. Thomas, and Jeffrey J. Fink. 1980. "Pygmalion at Sea: Improving the Work Effectiveness of Low Performers." *The Journal of Applied Behavioral Science,* October–December, pp. 482–505.

Cunningham, J. Barton. 1993. *Action Research and Organizational Development.* Westport, CT: Praeger.

Dale, Angela, Sara L. Arber, and Michael Procter. 1988. *Doing Secondary Analysis.* Boston: Allen & Unwin.

Davis, Fred. 1973. "The Martian and the Convert: Ontological Polarities in Social Research." *Urban Life* 2 (3): 333–43.

Davis, James A. 1971. *Elementary Survey Analysis.* Englewood Cliffs, NJ: Prentice-Hall.

———. 1985. *The Logic of Causal Order.* Beverly Hills, CA: Sage.

———. 1992. "Changeable Weather in a Cooling Climate atop the Liberal Plateau: Conversion and Replacement in Forty-Two General Social Survey Items, 1972–1989." *Public Opinion Quarterly* 56:261–306.

Davis, James Allan, and Tom W. Smith. 1990. *General Social Surveys, 1972–1990: Cumulative Codebook* [machine-readable data file]. Principal Investigator, James A. Davis; Director and Co–Principal Investigator, Tom W. Smith. NORC ed. Chicago: National Opinion Research Center [producer]. Storrs, CT: The Roper Center for Public Opinion Research, University of Connecticut [distributor]. One data file (26,265 logical records) and 1 codebook (909 p.).

DeFleur, Lois. 1975. "Biasing Influences on Drug Arrest Records: Implications for Deviance Research." *American Sociological Review,* February, pp. 88–103.

Dillman, Don A. 1978. *Mail and Telephone Surveys: The Total Design Method.* New York: Wiley.

Donald, Marjorie N. 1960. "Implications of Nonresponse for the Interpretation of Mail Questionnaire Data." *Public Opinion Quarterly* 24:99–114.

Douglas, Jack. 1985. *Creative Interviewing.* Beverly Hills, CA: Sage.

Doyle, Sir Arthur Conan. [1891] 1892. "A Scandal in Bohemia." First published in *The Strand,* July 1891. Reprinted in *The Original Illustrated Sherlock Holmes.* Secaucus, NJ: Castle, pp. 11–25.

Duncan, Greg J., with Richard D. Coe, et al. 1984. *Years of Poverty, Years of Plenty: The Changing Fortunes of American Workers and Families.* Ann Arbor: Survey Research Center Institute for Social Research, University of Michigan.

Durkheim, Emile. [1893] 1964. *The Division of Labor in Society.* Translated by George Simpson. New York: Free Press.

———. [1897] 1951. *Suicide.* Glencoe, IL: Free Press.

Einstein, Albert. 1940. "The Fundamentals of Theoretical Physics." *Science,* May 24, p. 487.

Elder, Glen H., Jr., Eliza K. Pavalko, and Elizabeth C. Clipp. 1993. *Working with Archival Data: Studying Lives.* Newbury Park, CA: Sage.

Ellison, Christopher G., and Darren E. Sherkat. 1990. "Patterns of Religious Mobility among Black Americans." *Sociological Quarterly* 31 (4): 551–68.

Emerson, Robert M., ed. 1988. *Contemporary Field Research.* Boston: Little, Brown.

Feick, Lawrence, F. 1989. "Latent Class Analysis of Survey Questions That Include Don't Know Responses." *Public Opinion Quarterly* 53:525–47.

Festinger, L., H. W. Reicker, and S. Schachter. 1956. *When Prophecy Fails.* Minneapolis: University of Minnesota Press.

Fielding, Nigel G., and Raymond M. Lee, eds. 1991.

Using Computers in Qualitative Research. Newbury Park, CA: Sage.

Ford, David A. 1989. "Preventing and Provoking Wife Battery through Criminal Sanctioning: A Look at the Risks." September, unpublished.

Ford, David A., and Mary Jean Regoli. 1992. "The Preventive Impacts of Policies for Prosecuting Wife Batterers." Pp. 181–208 in *Domestic Violence: The Changing Criminal Justice Response,* edited by E. S. Buzawa and C. G. Buzawa. New York: Auburn.

Forslund, Morris A. 1980. "Patterns of Delinquency Involvement: An Empirical Typology." Paper presented at the Annual Meeting of the Western Association of Sociologists and Anthropologists, Lethbridge, Alberta, February 8.

Foschi, Martha, G. Keith Warriner, and Stephen D. Hart. 1985. "Standards, Expectations, and Interpersonal Influence." *Social Psychology Quarterly* 48 (2): 108–17.

Freeman, Linton C. 1968. *Elementary Applied Statistics.* New York: Wiley.

Funkhouser, G. Ray. 1973. "The Issues of the Sixties: An Exploratory Study." *Public Opinion Quarterly* 37:62–75.

Gallup, George. 1984. "Where Parents Go Wrong," *San Francisco Chronicle,* December 13, p. 7.

Gallup, George, Jr., Burns Roper, Daniel Yankelovich, et al. 1990. "Polls that Made a Difference." *Public Perspective,* May–June, pp. 17–21.

Gamson, William A. 1992. *Talking Politics.* New York: Cambridge University Press.

Garant, Carol. 1980. "Stalls in the Therapeutic Process." *American Journal of Nursing,* December, pp. 2166–67.

Gee, Wilson. 1950. *Social Science Research Methods.* New York: Appleton-Century-Crofts.

Gilder, George. 1990. "The Nature of Poverty." Pp. 658–63 in *The American Polity Reader,* edited by A. Serow, W. Shannon, and E. Ladd. New York: Norton.

Glaser, Barney, and Anselm Strauss. 1967. *The Discovery of Grounded Theory.* Chicago: Aldine.

Glazer, Myron. 1972. *The Research Adventure: Promise and Problems of Field Work.* New York: Random House.

Glock, Charles, ed. 1967. *Survey Research in the Social Sciences.* New York: Russell Sage Foundation.

Glock, Charles Y., and Rodney Stark. 1967. *Christian Beliefs and Anti-Semitism.* New York: Harper & Row.

Glock, Charles Y., Benjamin B. Ringer, and Earl R. Babbie. 1967. *To Comfort and to Challenge.* Berkeley: University of California Press.

Goffman, Erving. 1961. *Asylums: Essays on the Social Situation of Mental Patients and Other Inmates.* Chicago: Aldine.

———. 1963. *Stigma: Notes on the Management of a Spoiled Identity.* Englewood Cliffs, NJ: Prentice-Hall.

———. 1974. *Frame Analysis.* Cambridge, MA: Harvard University Press.

Gold, Raymond L. 1969. "Roles in Sociological Field Observation." Pp. 30–39 in *Issues in Participant Observation,* edited by George J. McCall and J. L. Simmons. Reading, MA: Addison-Wesley.

Gould, Julius, and William Kolb. 1964. *A Dictionary of the Social Sciences.* New York: Free Press.

Goyder, John. 1985. "Face-to-Face Interviews and Mailed Questionnaires: The Net Difference in Response Rate." *Public Opinion Quarterly* 49:234–52.

Graham, Laurie, and Richard Hogan. 1990. "Social Class and Tactics: Neighborhood Opposition to Group Homes." *Sociological Quarterly* 31 (4): 513–29.

Greg, J. Duncan. 1984. *Years of Poverty, Years of Plenty: The Changing Fortunes of American Workers and Families.* Ann Arbor: University of Michigan Press.

Grimes, Michael D. 1991. *Class in Twentieth-Century American Sociology: An Analysis of Theories and Measurement Strategies.* New York: Praeger.

Groves, Robert M. 1990. "Theories and Methods of Telephone Surveys." Pp. 221–40 in *Annual Review of Sociology* (Vol. 16), edited by W. Richard Scott and Judith Blake. Palo Alto, CA: Annual Reviews.

Gubrium, Jaber F., and David Silverman, eds. 1989. *The Politics of Field Research: Sociology beyond Enlightenment.* Newbury Park, CA: Sage.

Habermas, Jurgen. 1971. *Knowledge and Human Interests.* Boston: Beacon Press.

Hall, Larry D., and Kimball P. Marshall. 1992. *Computing for Social Research: Practical Approaches.* Belmont, CA: Wadsworth.

Hamnett, Michael P., Douglas J. Porter, Amarjit Singh, and Krishna Kumar. 1984. *Ethics, Politics, and International Social Science Research.* Honolulu: University of Hawaii Press.

Healey, Joseph F. 1990. *Statistics: A Tool for Social Research.* Belmont, CA: Wadsworth.

Hedrick, Terry E., Leonard Bickman, and Debra J. Rog. 1993. *Applied Research Design: A Practical Guide.* Newbury Park, CA: Sage.

Hein, Jeremy. 1993. "Refugees, Immigrants, and the State." *Annual Review of Sociology* 19:43–59.

Heise, David R. 1981. "Foreward: Special Issue on Microcomputers and Social Research." *Sociological Methods and Research* 9 (4): 395–96.

Hempel, Carl G. 1952. "Fundamentals of Concept Formation in Empirical Science." *International Encyclopedia of United Science II,* no. 7.

Heritage, Johen, and David Greatbatch. 1992. "On the Institutional Character of Institutional Talk." In *Talk at Work,* edited by P. Drew and J. Heritage. Cambridge, England: Cambridge University Press.

Higginbotham, A. Leon, Jr. 1978. *In the Matter of Color: Race and the American Legal Process.* New York: Oxford University Press.

Hilts, Philip J. 1981. "Values of Driving Classes Disputed," *San Francisco Chronicle,* June 25, p. 4.

Hirschi, Travis, and Hanan Selvin. 1973. *Principles of Survey Analysis.* New York: Free Press.

Homan, Roger. 1991. *The Ethics of Social Research.* London: Longman.

Homans, George C. 1974. *Social Behavior: Its Elementary Forms.* New York: Harcourt Brace Jovanovich.

Hoover, Kenneth R. 1992. *The Elements of Social Scientific Thinking.* New York: St. Martin's Press.

Horowitz, Irving Louis. 1967. *The Rise and Fall of Project Camelot.* Cambridge, MA: MIT Press.

Horrigan, Michael W., and James P. Markey. 1990. "Recent Gains in Women's Earnings: Better Pay or Longer Hours?" *Monthly Labor Review,* July, pp. 11–17.

"How the Poll Was Conducted." 1995. *New York Times,* October 1, p. 15.

Howard, Edward N., and Darlene M. Norman. 1981. "Measuring Public Library Performance." *Library Journal,* February, pp. 305–8.

Howell, Joseph T. 1973. *Hard Living on Clay Street.* Garden City, NY: Doubleday Anchor.

Hughes, Michael. 1980. "The Fruits of Cultivation Analysis: A Reexamination of Some Effects of Television Watching." *Public Opinion Quarterly* (Fall): 287–302.

Humphreys, Laud. 1970. *Tearoom Trade: Impersonal Sex in Public Places.* Chicago: Aldine.

Hunt, Morton. 1985. *Profiles of Social Research: The Scientific Study of Human Interactions.* New York: Basic Books.

Hyman, Herbert H., with Eleanor Singer. 1991. *Taking Society's Measure: A Personal History of Survey Research.* New York: Russell Sage Foundation.

Isaac, Larry W., and Larry J. Griffin. 1989. "A Historicism in Time-Series Analyses of Historical Process: Critique, Redirection, and Illustrations from U.S. Labor History." *American Sociological Association* 54 (December): 873–90.

Iversen, Gudmund R. 1991. *Contextual Analysis.* Newbury Park, CA: Sage.

Jackman, Mary R., and Mary Scheuer Senter. 1980. "Images of Social Groups: Categorical or Qualified?" *Public Opinion Quarterly* 44: 340–61.

Jasso, Guillermina. 1988. "Principles of Theoretical Analysis." *Sociological Theory* 6: 1–20.

Jendrek, Margaret Platt. 1985. *Through the Maze: Statistics with Computer Applications.* Belmont, CA: Wadsworth.

Jensen, Arthur. 1969. "How Much Can We Boost IQ and Scholastic Achievement?" *Harvard Educational Review* 39: 273–74.

Johnson, Jeffrey C. 1990. *Selecting Ethnographic Informants.* Newbury Park, CA: Sage.

Johnston, Hank. 1980. "The Marketed Social Movement: A Case Study of the Rapid Growth of TM." *Pacific Sociological Review,* July, pp. 333–54.

Jones, James H. 1981. *Bad Blood: The Tuskegee Syphilis Experiments.* New York: Free Press.

Jones, Stephen R. G. 1990. "Worker Independence and Output: The Hawthorne Studies Reevaluated." *American Sociological Review* 55 (April): 176–90.

Kahane, Howard. 1992. *Logic and Contemporary Rhetoric.* Belmont, CA: Wadsworth.

Kalton, Graham. 1983. *Introduction to Survey Sampling.* Newbury Park, CA: Sage.

Kaplan, Abraham. 1964. *The Conduct of Inquiry.* San Francisco: Chandler.

Kasl, Stanislav V., Rupert F. Chisolm, and Brenda Eskenazi. 1981. "The lmpact of the Accident at Three Mile Island on the Behavior and Well-Being of Nuclear Workers." *American Journal of Public Health,* May, pp. 472–95.

Kasof, Joseph. 1993. "Sex Bias in the Naming of Stimulus Persons." *Psychological Bulletin* 113 (1): 140–63.

Kendall, Patricia L., and Paul F. Lazarsfeld. 1950. "Problems of Survey Analysis." Pp. 133–96 in *Continuities in Social Research: Studies in the Scope and Method of "The American Soldier,"* edited by Robert K. Merton and Paul F. Lazarsfeld. New York: Free Press.

Kiecolt, E. Jill, and Laura E. Nathan. 1985. *Secondary Analysis of Survey Data.* Beverly Hills, CA: Sage.

Kish, Leslie. 1965. *Survey Sampling.* New York: Wiley.

Krueger, Richard A. 1988. *Focus Groups.* Newbury Park, CA: Sage.

Kuhn, Thomas. 1970. *The Structure of Scientific Revolutions.* Chicago: University of Chicago Press.

Kvale, Steinar. 1996. *InterViews: An Introduction to Qualitative Research Interviewing.* Thousand Oaks, CA: Sage.

Labovitz, Sanford, and Robert Hagedorn. 1981. *Introduction to Social Research.* New York: McGraw-Hill.

Lazarsfeld, Paul F. 1955. "Foreword." In *Survey Design and Analysis,* by Herbert Hyman. New York: Free Press.

———. 1959. "Problems in Methodology." In *Sociology Today,* edited by Robert K. Merton. New York: Basic Books.

———. 1982. *The Varied Sociology of Paul F. Lazarsfeld.* Edited by Patricia L. Kendall. New York: Columbia University Press.

Lazarsfeld, Paul, Ann Pasanella, and Morris Rosenberg, eds. 1972. *Continuities in the Language of Social Research.* New York: Free Press.

Lazarsfeld, Paul F., and Morris Rosenberg, eds. 1955. *The Language of Social Research.* New York: Free Press.

Lee, Raymond. 1993. *Doing Research on Sensitive Topics.* Newbury Park, CA: Sage.

Lever, Janet. 1986. "Sex Differences in the Complexity of Children's Play and Games." Pp. 74–89 in *Structure and Process,* edited by Richard J. Peterson and Charlotte A. Vaughan. Belmont, CA: Wadsworth.

Levin, Jack, and James Spates. 1970. "Hippie Values: An Analysis of the Underground Press." *Youth and Society* 2:59–72. [Reprinted in M. Patricia Golden, ed. 1976. *The Research Experience.* Itasca, IL: Peacock.]

Liebow, Elliot. 1967. *Tally's Corner.* Boston: Little, Brown.

Literary Digest. 1936a. "Landon, 1,293,669: Roosevelt, 972,897." October 31, pp. 5–6.

———. 1936b. "What Went Wrong with the Polls?" November 14, pp. 7–8.

Lofland, John. 1995. "Analytic Ethnography: Features, Failings, and Futures." *Journal of Contemporary Ethnography* 24 (1): 30–67.

Lofland, John, and Lyn H. Lofland. 1995. *Analyzing Social Settings: A Guide to Qualitative Observation and Analysis.* Belmont, CA: Wadsworth.

Lopata, Helena Znaniecki. 1981. "Widowhood and Husband Sanctification." *Journal of Marriage and the Family,* May, pp. 439–50.

MacLaine, Shirley. 1983. *Out on a Limb.* New York: Bantam Books.

Madison, Anna-Marie. 1992. "Primary Inclusion of Culturally Diverse Minority Program Participants in the Evaluation Process." *New Directions for Program Evaluation,* no. 53, pp. 35–43.

Madron, Thomas Wm., C. Neal Tate, and Robert G. Brookshire. 1985. *Using Microcomputers in Research.* Newbury Park, CA: Sage.

Marshall, Catherine, and Gretchen B. Rossman. 1995. *Designing Qualitative Research.* Thousand Oaks, CA: Sage.

Martin, David W. 1991. *Doing Psychology Experiments.* Monterey, CA: Brooks/Cole.

Marx, Karl. [1867] 1967. *Capital.* New York: International Publishers.

———. [1880] 1956. *Revue Socialist,* July 5. Reprinted in *Karl Marx: Selected Writings in Sociology and Social Philosophy,* edited by T. B. Bottomore and Maximilien Rubel. New York: McGraw-Hill.

Maxwell, Joseph A. 1996. *Qualitative Research Design.* Thousand Oaks, CA: Sage.

McAlister, Alfred, Cheryl Perry, Joel Killen, Lee Ann Slinkard, and Nathan Maccoby. 1980. "Pilot Study of Smoking, Alcohol, and Drug Abuse Prevention," *American Journal of Public Health,* July, pp. 719–21.

McCall, George J., and J. L. Simmons, eds. 1969. *Issues in Participant Observation.* Reading, MA: Addison-Wesley.

McGrane, Bernard. 1994. The Un-TV and the 10 mph Car: Experiments in Personal Freedom and Everyday Life. Fort Bragg, CA: The Small Press.

McIver, John P., and Edward G. Carmines. 1981. *Unidimensional Scaling.* Newbury Park, CA: Sage.

Meadows, Dennis, et al. 1973. *The Dynamics of Growth in a Finite World.* Cambridge, MA: Wright-Allen.

Meadows, Donella H., Dennis L. Meadows, and Jørgen Randers. 1992. *Beyond the Limits: Confronting Global Collapse, Envisioning a Sustainable Future.* Post Mills, VT: Chelsea Green.

Meadows, Donella, Dennis L. Meadows, Jørgen Randers, and William W. Behrens, III. 1972. *The Limits to Growth.* New York: Universe Books.

Menard, Scott. 1991. *Longitudinal Research.* Newbury Park, CA: Sage.

Merton, Robert K. 1938. "Social Structure and Anomie." *American Sociological Review* 3:672–82.

———. 1957. *Social Theory and Social Structure.* Glencoe, IL: Free Press.

Merton, Robert K., James S. Coleman, and Peter H. Rossi, eds. 1979. *Qualitative and Quantitative Social Research.* New York: Free Press.

Meyer, H. J., and E. J. Borgatta. 1959. *An Experiment in Mental Patient Rehabilitation.* New York: Russell Sage Foundation.

Michael, M., W. T. Boyce, and A. J. Wilcox. 1984. *Biomedical Bestiary: An Epidemiologic Guide to Flaws and Fallacies in the Medical Literature.* Boston: Little, Brown.

Milgram, Stanley. 1963. "Behavioral Study of Obedience." *Journal of Abnormal Social Psychology* 67:371–78.

———. 1965. "Some Conditions of Obedience and Disobedience to Authority." *Human Relations* 18:57–76.

Miller, Delbert. 1991. *Handbook of Research Design and Social Measurement.* Newbury Park, CA: Sage.

Mitchell, Richard G., Jr. 1991. "Secrecy and Disclosure in Field Work." Pp. 97–108 in *Experiencing Fieldwork: An Inside View of Qualitative Research,* edited by William B. Shaffir and Robert A. Stebbins. Newbury Park, CA: Sage.

Mohr, Lawrence B. 1990. *Understanding Significance Testing.* Newbury Park, CA: Sage.

Morgan, David L., ed. 1993. *Successful Focus Groups: Advancing the State of the Art.* Newbury Park, CA: Sage.

Morgan, Lewis H. 1870. *Systems of Consanguinity and Affinity.* Washington, DC: Smithsonian Institution.

Moskowitz, Milt. 1981. "The Drugs That Doctors Order." *San Francisco Chronicle,* May 23, p. 33.

Moynihan, Daniel. 1965. *The Negro Family: The Case for National Action.* Washington, DC: U.S. Government Printing Office.

Myrdal, Gunnar. 1944. *An American Dilemma.* New York: Harper & Row.

Naisbitt, John. 1982. *Megatrends: Ten New Directions Transforming Our Lives.* New York: Warner Books.

Naisbitt, John, and Patricia Aburdene. 1990. *Megatrends 2000: Ten New Directions for the 1990's,* 1st ed. New York: Morrow.

Nicholls, William L., II, Reginald P. Baker, and Jean Martin. Forthcoming. "The Effect of New Data Collection Technology on Survey Data Quality."

O'Neill, Harry W. 1992. "They Can't Subpoena What You Ain't Got." *AAPOR News* 19 (2): 4, 7.

Øyen, Else, ed. 1990. *Comparative Methodology: Theory and Practice in International Social Research.* Newbury Park, CA: Sage.

Parsons, Talcott. 1951. *The Social System.* Glencoe, IL: Free Press.

Parsons, Talcott, and Edward A. Shils. 1951. *Toward a General Theory of Action.* Cambridge, MA: Harvard University Press.

Payne, Charles M. 1995. *I've Got the Light of Freedom: The Organizing Tradition and the Mississippi Freedom Struggle.* Berkeley: University of California Press.

Perinelli, Phillip J. 1986. "Nonsuspecting Public in TV Call-In Polls." *New York Times,* February 14, letter to the editor.

Perlman, David. 1984. "Fluoride, AIDS Experts Scoff at Nelder's Idea." *San Francisco Chronicle,* September 6, p. 1.

Petersen, Larry R., and Judy L. Maynard. 1981. "Income, Equity, and Wives' Housekeeping Role Expectations." *Pacific Sociological Review,* January, pp. 87–105.

Polivka, Anne E., and Jennifer M. Rothgeb. 1993. "Redesigning the CPS Questionnaire." *Monthly Labor Review* 116 (9): 10–28.

Plutzer, Eric, and John F. Zipp. 1996. "Identity Politics, Partisanship, and Voting for Women Candidates." *Public Opinion Quarterly* 60:30–57.

Population Communications International. 1996. *International Dateline* [February]. New York: Population Communications International.

Population Reference Bureau. 1980. "1980 World Population Data Sheet." (Poster prepared by Carl Haub and Douglas W. Heisler. Washington, DC: Population Reference Bureau.

Population Reference Bureau. 1993. "1993 World Population Data Sheet." Washington, DC: Population Reference Bureau.

Powell, Elwin H. 1958. "Occupation, Status, and Suicide: Toward a Redefinition of Anomie." *American Sociological Review* 23:131–39.

Presser, Stanley, and Johnny Blair. 1994. "Survey Pretesting: Do Different Methods Produce Different Results?" Pp. 73–104 in *Sociological Methodology 1994,* edited by Peter Marsden. San Francisco, CA: Jossey-Bass.

Ransford, H. Edward. 1968. "Isolation, Powerlessness, and Violence: A Study of Attitudes and Participants in the Watts Riots." *American Journal of Sociology* 73:581–91.

Rasinski, Kenneth A. 1989. "The Effect of Question Wording on Public Support for Government Spending." *Public Opinion Quarterly* 53:388–94.

Ray, William, and Richard Ravizza. 1993. *Methods Toward a Science of Behavior and Experience.* Belmont, CA: Wadsworth.

Redfield, Robert. 1941. *The Folk Culture of Yucatan.* Chicago: University of Chicago Press.

Reinharz, Shulamit. 1992. *Feminist Methods in Social Research.* New York: Oxford University Press.

Riecken, Henry W., and Robert F. Boruch. 1974. *Social Experimentation: A Method for Planning and Evaluating Social Intervention.* New York: Academic Press.

Ritzer, George. 1988. *Sociological Theory.* New York: Knopf.

Roberts, Jane. 1974. *Seth Speaks.* New York: Bantam Books.

Roethlisberger, F. J., and W. J. Dickson. 1939. *Management and the Worker.* Cambridge, MA: Harvard University Press.

Rogers, Everett M., Peter W. Vaughan, Ramadhan M. A. Swalehe, Nagesh Rao, and Suruchi Sood. 1996. "Effects of an Entertainment-Education Radio Soap Opera on Family Planning and HIV/AIDS Prevention Behavior in Tanzania." Report presented at a technical briefing on the Tanzania Entertainment-Education Project, Rockefeller Foundation, New York, March 27.

Roper, Burns. 1992. ". . . But Will They Give the Poll Its Due?" *AAPOR News* 19 (2): 5–6.

Rosenberg, Morris. 1968. *The Logic of Survey Analysis.* New York: Basic Books.

Rosenthal, Robert, and Leonore Jacobson. 1968. *Pygmalion in the Classroom.* New York: Holt, Rinehart & Winston.

Rothman, Ellen K.. 1981. "The Written Record." *Journal of Family History,* Spring, pp. 47–56.

Rubin, Herbert J., and Riene S. Rubin. 1995. *Qualitative Interviewing: The Art of Hearing Data.* Thousand Oaks, CA: Sage.

Rule, James B. 1989. "Rationality and Non-rationality in Militant Collective Action." *Sociological Theory* 7 (Fall): 145–60.

Sacks, Jeffrey J., W. Mark Krushat, and Jeffrey Newman. 1980. "Reliability of the Health Hazard Appraisal." *American Journal of Public Health,* July, pp. 730–32.

Sanders, William B. 1994. *Gangbangs and Drive-bys: Grounded Culture and Juvenile Gang Violence.* New York: Aldine De Gruyter.

Saris, Willem E. 1991. *Computer-Assisted Interviewing.* Newbury Park, CA: Sage.

Bibliography

Scarce, Rik. 1990. *Ecowarriors: Understanding the Radical Environmental Movement.* Chicago: Noble Press.

Schifiett, Kathy L., and Mary Zey. 1990. "Comparison of Characteristics of Private Product Producing Organizations and Public Service Organizations." *Sociological Quarterly* 31 (4): 569–83.

Schroeder, Larry D., David L. Sjoquist, and Paula E. Stephan. 1986. *Understanding Regression Analysis: An Introductory Guide.* Newbury Park, CA: Sage.

Schwartz, Norbert, Bärbel Knäuper, Hans-J. Hippler, Elisabeth Noelle-Neumann, and Leslie Clark. 1991. "Rating Scales: Numeric Values May Change the Meaning of Scale Labels." *Public Opinion Quarterly* 55:570–82.

"See How They Ran." *Public Opinion,* 1984. October–November, pp. 38–40.

Segalman, Ralph, and David Marsland. 1989. *Cradle to Grave: Comparative Perspectives on the State of Welfare.* New York: St. Martin's Press.

Shaffir, William B., and Robert A. Stebbins, eds. 1991. *Experiencing Fieldwork: An Inside View of Qualitative Research.* Newbury Park, CA: Sage.

Shanks, J. Merrill, and Robert D. Tortora. 1985. "Beyond CATI: Generalized and Distributed Systems for Computer-Assisted Surveys." Prepared for the U.S. Bureau of the Census, First Annual Research Conference, Reston, VA, March 20–23.

Shaver, Kelly G. 1985. *The Attribution of Blame: Causality, Responsibility, and Blameworthiness.* New York: Springer-Verlag.

Sheatsley, Paul F. 1983. "Questionnaire Construction and Item Writing." Pp. 195–230 in *Handbook of Survey Research,* edited by Peter H. Rossi, James D. Wright, and Andy B. Anderson. New York: Academic Press.

Sheehan, Susan. 1976. *A Welfare Mother.* New York: Mentor.

Shostak, Arthur, ed. 1977. *Our Sociological Eye: Personal Essays on Society and Culture.* Port Washington, NY: Alfred.

Silverman, David. 1993. *Interpreting Qualitative Data.* Newbury Park, CA: Sage.

Smith, Andrew E., and G. F. Bishop. 1992. *The Gallup Secret Ballot Experiments: 1944–1988.* Paper presented at the annual conference of the American Association for Public Opinion Research, St. Petersburg, FL, May.

Smith, Eric R. A. N., and Peverill Squire. 1990. "The Effects of Prestige Names in Question Wording." *Public Opinion Quarterly* 54:97–116.

Smith, Joel. 1991. "A Methodology for Twenty-First Century Sociology." *Social Forces* 70 (1): 1–17.

Smith, Tom W. 1990. "The First Straw? A Study of the Origins of Election Polls." *Public Opinion Quarterly* 54:21–36.

Sorokin, Pitirim A. 1937–1940. *Social and Cultural Dynamics,* 4 vols. Englewood Cliffs, NJ: Bedminster Press.

Spohn, Cassie, and Julie Horney. 1990. "A Case of Unrealistic Expectations: The Impact of Rape Reform Legislation in Illinois." *The Criminal Justice Policy Review* 4 (1): 1–18.

Srole, Leo. 1956. "Social Integration and Certain Corollaries: An Exploratory Study." *American Sociological Review* 21:709–16.

Steel, Paul. 1993. Private communication, November 22, at the University of New Mexico.

Sterling, T. D., W. L. Rosenbaum, and J. J. Weinkam. 1995. "Publication Decisions Revisited: The Effect of the Outcome of Statistical Tests on the Decision to Publish and Vice Versa." *The American Statistician* 49 (1): 108–12.

Stouffer, Samuel A., and Jackson Toby. 1951. "Role Conflict and Personality." Pp. 481–96 in *Toward a General Theory of Action,* edited by Talcott Parsons and Edward A. Shils. Cambridge, MA: Harvard University Press.

Stouffer, Samuel. [1937] 1962. "Effects of the Depression on the Family." Reprinted in *Social Research to Test Ideas,* by Samuel A. Stouffer. New York: Free Press.

Stouffer, Samuel, et al. 1949, 1950. *The American Soldier,* 3 vols. Princeton, NJ: Princeton University Press.

Straits, Bruce C. 1990. "The Social Context of Voter Turnout." *Public Opinion Quarterly* 54:64–73.

Strang, David, and James N. Baron. 1990. "Categorical Imperatives: The Structure of Job Titles in California State Agencies." *American Sociological Review* 55 (August): 479–95.

Sudman, Seymour. 1983. "Applied Sampling." Pp. 145–94 in *Handbook of Survey Research,* edited by Peter H. Rossi, James D. Wright, and Andy B. Anderson. New York: Academic Press.

Swafford, Michael. 1992. "Soviet Survey Research—the 1970's vs. the 1990's." *AAPOR News* 19 (3): 3–4.

Swalehe, Ramadhan, Everett M. Rogers, Mark J. Gilboard, Krista Alford, and Rima Montoya. 1995. "A Content Analysis of the Entertainment-Education Radio Soap Opera 'Twende na Wakati' (Let's Go with the Times) in Tanzania." Arusha, Tanzania: Population Family Life and Education Programme (POFLEP), Ministry of Community Development, Women Affairs, and Children, November 15.

Takeuchi, David. 1974. "Grass in Hawaii: A Structural Constraints Approach." M.A. thesis, University of Hawaii.

Tan, Alexis S. 1980. "Mass Media Use, Issue Knowledge and Political Involvement." *Public Opinion Quarterly* 44:241–48.

Tandon, Rajesh, and L. Dave Brown. 1981. "Organization-Building for Rural Development: An Experiment in India." *Journal of Applied Behavioral Science,* April–June, pp. 172–89.

Thomas, W. I., and Florian Znaniecki. 1918. *The Polish Peasant in Europe and America.* Chicago: University of Chicago Press.

Thomson, Bill. 1996. "Letter on Push Polling." Letter posted May 29 to the AAPORnet listserv [On-line]. Available: billt@pos.org

Tiano, Susan. 1994. *Patriarchy on the Line: Labor, Gender, and Ideology in the Mexican Maquila Industry.* Philadelphia, PA: Temple University Press.

Tourangeau, Roger, Kenneth A. Rasinski, Norman Bradburn, and Roy D'Andrade. 1989. "Carryover Effects in Attitude Surveys." *Public Opinion Quarterly* 53:495–524.

Tuckel, Peter S., and Barry M. Feinberg. 1991. "The Answering Machine Poses Many Questions for Telephone Survey Researchers. *Public Opinion Quarterly* 55:200–17.

Turk, Theresa Guminski. 1980. "Hospital Support: Urban Correlates of Allocation Based on Organizational Prestige." *Pacific Sociological Review,* July, pp. 315–32.

Turner, Jonathan. 1974. *The Structure of Sociological Theory.* Homewood, IL: Dorsey.

Turner, Jonathan H., ed. 1989. *Theory Building in Sociology: Assessing Theoretical Cumulation.* Newbury Park, CA: Sage.

Turner, Jonathan H., and Alexandra R. Maryanski. 1988. "Is 'Neofunctionalism' Really Functional?" *Sociological Theory* 6 (Spring): 110–21.

Turner, Stephen Park, and Jonathan H. Turner. 1990. *The Impossible Science: An Institutional Analysis of American Sociology.* Newbury Park, CA: Sage.

United Nations. 1995. *Human Development Report 1995,* New York: United Nations Development Program. [Summarized in Population Communication International. 1996. *International Dateline,* February, pp. 1–4.]

U.S. Bureau of the Census. 1975. *Historical Statistics of the United States: Colonial Times to 1970.* Washington, DC: U.S. Government Printing Office.
1987. *Current Population Reports, Series P-70, No. 10, Male-Female Differences in Work Experience, Occupation, and Earning, 1984.* Washington, DC: U.S. Government Printing Office.
1987. *Statistical Abstract of the United States.* Washington, DC: U.S. Government Printing Office.
1992. *Statistical Abstract of the United States.* Washington, DC: U.S. Government Printing Office.
1992. *CPR Series P-60, No. 180, Money Income of Households, Families, and Persons in the United States: 1991.* Washington, DC: U.S. Government Printing Office.
1993. *Current Population Reports, Series P23–185, Population Profile of the United States.* Washington, DC: U.S. Government Printing Office.
1993. *Statistical Abstract of the United States, 1993, National Data Book and Guide to Sources.* Washington, DC: U.S. Government Printing Office.
1996. *Statistical Abstract of the United States, 1995.* CD-ROM CD-SA-95, issued April.

U.S. Department of Health and Human Services. 1992. *Survey Measurement of Drug Use.* Washington, DC: U.S. Government Printing Office.

U.S. Department of Labor (Bureau of Labor Statistics). 1978. "The Consumer Price Index: Concepts and Content over the Years." Report 517.

Veroff, Joseph, Shirley Hatchett, and Elizabeth Douvan. 1992. "Consequences of Participating in a Longitudinal Study of Marriage." *Public Opinion Quarterly* 56:325–27.

Votaw, Carmen Delgado. 1979. "Women's Rights in the United States." United States Commission on Civil Rights, Inter-American Commission on Women. Washington, DC: Clearinghouse Publications.

Wagner-Pacifici, Robin. 1995. *Discourse and Destruction: The City of Philadelphia versus MOVE.* Chicago: University of Chicago Press.

Walker, Jeffery T. 1994. "Fax Machines and Social Surveys: Teaching an Old Dog New Tricks." *Journal of Quantitative Criminology* 10 (2): 181–88.

Walker Research. 1988. *Industry Image Study,* 8th ed. Indianapolis, IN: Walker Research.

Walker, Robert, ed. 1985. *Applied Qualitative Research.* Hants, England: Gower.

Wallace, Walter. 1971. *The Logic of Science in Sociology.* Chicago: Aldine.

Wallace, William A. 1972. *Causality and Scientific Explanation.* Ann Arbor: University of Michigan Press.

Webb, Eugene, et al. 1966. *Unobtrusive Measures: Nonreactive Research in the Social Sciences.* Chicago: Rand McNally.

Weber, Eugene J., Donald T. Campbell, Richard D. Schwartz, and Lee Sechrest. 1981. *Nonreactive Measures in the Social Sciences.* Boston: Houghton Mifflin.

Weber, Max. [1905] 1958. *The Protestant Ethic and the Spirit of Capitalism.* Translated by Talcott Parsons. New York: Scribners.
[1925] 1946. "Science as a Vocation." Pp. 129–56 in *From Max Weber: Essays in Sociology,* edited and translated by Hans Gerth and C. Wright Mills. New York: Oxford University Press.
[1934] 1951. *The Religion of China.* Translated by Hans H. Gerth. New York: Free Press.
[1934] 1952. *Ancient Judaism.* Translated by Hans H. Gerth and Don Martindale. New York: Free Press.

[1934] 1958. *The Religion of India*. Translated by Hans H. Gerth and Don Martindale. New York: Free Press.
Weber, Robert Philip. 1990. *Basic Content Analysis*. Newbury Park: Sage.
Weisberg, Herbert F. 1992. *Central Tendency and Variability*. Newbury Park, CA: Sage.
Weiss, Carol. 1972. *Evaluation Research*. Englewood Cliffs, NJ: Prentice-Hall.
Weiss, Carol H., and Eleanor Singer. 1988. *Reporting of Social Science in the National Media*. New York: Russell Sage Foundation.
Weitzman, Eber, and Matthew Miles. 1995. *Computer Programs for Qualitative Data Analysis*. Newbury Park, CA: Sage.
Wellman, David. *The Union Makes Us Stronger: Radical Unionism on the San Francisco Waterfront,* Cambridge, MA: Cambridge University Press, 1995.
Wells, Richard H., and J. Steven Picou. 1981. *American Sociology: Theoretical and Methodological Structures*. Washington, DC: University Press of America.
Wharton, Amy S., and James N. Baron. 1987. "So Happy Together? The Impact of Gender Segregation on Men at Work." *American Sociological Review* 52 (October): 574–87.
White, Ralph. 1951. *Value-Analysis: The Nature and Use of the Method*. New York: Society for the Psychological Study of Social Issues.
Wolcott, Harry F. 1995. *The Art of Fieldwork*. Walnut Creek, CA: AltaMira Press.
Wolf, Daniel R.. 1990. *The Rebels: A Brotherhood of Outlaw Bikers*. Toronto: University of Toronto Press.
Wolf, Daniel R. 1991. "High-Risk Methodology: Reflections on Leaving an Outlaw Society." Pp. 211–13 in *Experiencing Fieldwork: An Inside View of Qualitative Research*, edited by William B. Shaffir and Robert A. Stebbins. Newbury Park, CA: Sage.
Yammarino, Francis J., Steven J. Skinner, and Terry L. Childers. 1991. "Understanding Mail Survey Response Behavior: A Meta-analysis." *Public Opinion Quarterly* 55:613–39.
Yankelovich, Daniel. 1981. "Stepchildren of the Moral Majority." *Psychology Today,* November, pp. 5–10.
Yerg, Beverly J. 1981. "Reflections on the Use of the RTE Model in Physical Education." *Research Quarterly for Exercise and Sport,* March, pp. 38–47.
Yinger, J. Milton, et al. 1977. *Middle Start: An Experiment in the Educational Enrichment of Young Adolescents*. London: Cambridge University Press.
York, James, and Elmer Persigehl. 1981. "Productivity Trends in the Ball and Roller Bearing Industry," *Monthly Labor Review,* January, pp. 40–43.
Ziesel, Hans. 1957. *Say It with Figures*. New York: Harper & Row.

Glossary

attributes Characteristics of persons or things. See *variables* and Chapter 1.

average An ambiguous term generally suggesting typical or normal. The *mean, median,* and *mode* are specific examples of mathematical *averages.* See Chapter 15.

bias (1) That quality of a measurement device that tends to result in a misrepresentation of what is being measured in a particular direction. For example, the questionnaire item "Don't you agree that the president is doing a good job?" would be *biased* in that it would generally encourage more favorable responses. See Chapter 6 for more on this topic. (2) The thing inside you that makes other people or groups seem consistently better or worse than they really are. (3) What a nail looks like after you hit it crooked. (If you drink, don't drive.)

binomial variable (1) A variable that has only two attributes is binomial. Gender would be an example, having the attributes *male* and *female*. (2) The advertising slogan used by the Nomial Widget Co.

bivariate analysis The analysis of two variables simultaneously, for the purpose of determining the empirical relationship between them. The construction of a simple percentage table or the computation of a simple correlation coefficient would be examples of *bivariate analyses.* See Chapter 15 for more on this topic.

Bogardus social distance scale A measurement technique for determining the willingness of people to participate in social relations—of varying degrees of closeness—with other kinds of people. It is an especially efficient technique in that several discrete answers may be summarized without losing any of the original details of the data. See Chapter 7.

census (1) An enumeration of the characteristics of some population. A *census* is often similar to a survey, with the difference that the *census* collects data from *all* members of the population and the survey is limited to a sample. (2) What sober-minded folks always want to bring you to.

cluster sample (1) A multistage sample in which natural groups (*clusters*) are sampled initially, with the members of each selected group being subsampled afterward. For example, you might select a sample of U.S. colleges and universities from a directory, get lists of the students at all the selected schools, then draw samples of students from each. This procedure is discussed in Chapter 8. See also *area probability sample.* (2) Pawing around in a box of macadamia nut clusters to take all the big ones for yourself.

codebook (1) The document used in data processing and analysis that tells the location of different data items in a data file. Typically, the codebook identifies the locations of data items and the meaning of the codes used to represent different attributes of variables. See Chapter 14 for more discussion and illustrations. (2) The document that cost you 38 boxtops just to learn that Captain Marvelous wanted you to brush your teeth and always tell the truth. (3) The document that allows CIA agents to learn that Captain Marvelous wants them to brush their teeth.

coding The process whereby raw data are transformed into standardized form suitable for machine processing and analysis. See Chapters 13 and 14.

coefficient of reproducibility (1) A measure of the extent to which a scale score allows you to reconstruct accurately the specific data that went into the construction of the scale. See Chapter 7 for a fuller description and an illustration. (2) Fecundity.

cohort study A study in which some specific group is studied over time although data may be collected from different members in each set of observations. A study of the occupational history of the class of 1970, in which questionnaires were sent every five years, for example, would be a cohort study. See Chapter 4 for more on this topic (if you want more).

conceptualization (1) The mental process whereby fuzzy and imprecise notions (*concepts*) are made more specific and precise. So you want to study *prejudice.* What do you *mean* by *prejudice?* Are there different kinds of prejudice? What are they? See Chapter 5, which is all about *conceptualization,* and Chapter 6 about its pal, *operationalization.* (2) Sexual reproduction among intellectuals.

confidence interval   (1) The range of values within which a population parameter is estimated to lie. A survey, for example, may show 40 percent of a sample favoring Candidate A (poor devil). Although the best estimate of the support existing among all voters would also be 40 percent, we would not expect it to be exactly that. We might, therefore, compute a *confidence interval* (such as from 35 to 45 percent) within which the actual percentage of the population probably lies. Note that we must specify a *confidence level* in connection with every *confidence interval*. See Chapters 8 and 17. (2) How close you dare to get to an alligator.

confidence level   (1) The estimated probability that a population parameter lies within a given *confidence interval*. Thus, we might be 95 percent *confident* that between 35 and 45 percent of all voters favor Candidate A. See Chapters 8 and 17. (2) How sure you are that the ring you bought from a street vendor for ten dollars is really a three-carat diamond.

conflict paradigm   An approach to understanding social life that focuses on attempts by individuals or groups to dominate each other or avoid being dominated. Consider a football game, for example.

construct validity   The degree to which a measure relates to other variables as expected within a system of theoretical relationships. See Chapter 5.

content validity   The degree to which a measure covers the range of meanings included within a concept. See Chapter 5.

contingency question   A survey question intended for only *some* respondents, determined by their responses to some other question. For example, all respondents might be asked whether they belong to the Cosa Nostra, and only those who said yes would be asked how often they go to company meetings and picnics. The latter would be a *contingency question*. See Chapter 10 for illustrations of this topic.

contingency table   (1) A format for presenting the relationships among variables—in the form of percentage distributions. See Chapter 15 for several illustrations of it and for guides to doing it. (2) The card table you keep around in case your guests bring their seven kids with them to dinner.

control group   (1) In experimentation, a group of subjects to whom no experimental stimulus is administered and who should resemble the experimental group in all other respects. The comparison of the *control group* and the experimental group at the end of the experiment points to the effect of the experimental stimulus. See Chapter 9. (2) American Association of Managers.

control variable   A variable that is held constant in an attempt to clarify further the relationship between two other variables. Having discovered a relationship between education and prejudice, for example, we might hold gender constant by examining the relationship between education and prejudice among men only and then among women only. In this example, gender would be the *control variable*. See Chapter 16 to find out how important the proper use of control variables is in analysis.

criterion-related validity   The degree to which a measure relates with some external criterion. For example, the validity of the college board is shown in their ability to predict the college success of students. See Chapter 5.

cross-sectional study   A study based on observations representing a single point in time. Contrasted with a *longitudinal study*.

deduction   (1) The logical model in which specific expectations of *hypotheses* are developed on the basis of general principles. Starting from the general principle that all deans are meanies, you might anticipate that this one won't let you change courses. This anticipation would be the result of *deduction*. See also *induction* and Chapters 2 and 3. (2) What the Internal Revenue Service said your good-for-nothing moocher of a brother-in-law technically isn't. (3) Of a duck.

dependent variable   (1) A variable assumed to *depend* on or be caused by another (called the *independent variable*). If you find that income is partly a function of amount of formal education, income is being treated as a *dependent variable*. (2) A wimpy variable.

descriptive statistics   Statistical computations describing either the characteristics of a sample or the relationship among variables in a sample. *Descriptive statistics* merely summarize a set of sample observations, whereas *inferential statistics* move beyond the description of specific observations to make inferences about the larger population from which the sample observations were drawn.

dichotomous variable   A variable having only two categories. Also called *binomial variable*.

dimension   A specifiable aspect or facet of a concept.

discourse analysis   The analysis of communications or conversations such as those occurring in an interview, with special attention given to the speaker's intent and how the communication is structured.

dispersion   The distribution of values around some central value, such as an *average*. The *range* is a simple example of a measure of *dispersion*. Thus, we may report that the *mean* age of a group is 37.9, and the range is from 12 to 89.

ecological fallacy   Erroneously drawing conclusions about individuals based solely on the observation of groups.

EPSEM   Equal probability of selection method   A sample design in which each member of a population has the same chance of being selected into the sample. See Chapter 8.

external invalidity Refers to the possibility that conclusions drawn from experimental results may not be generalizable to the "real" world. See Chapter 9 and also *internal invalidity*.

external validation The process of testing the *validity* of a measure, such as an index or scale, by examining its relationship to other, presumed indicators of the same variable. If the index really measures *prejudice*, for example, it should correlate with other indicators of prejudice. See Chapter 7 for a fuller discussion of this topic and for illustrations.

face validity (1) That quality of an indicator that makes it seem a reasonable measure of some variable. That the frequency of church attendance is some indication of a person's religiosity seems to make sense without a lot of explanation. It has *face validity*. (2) When your face looks like your driver's license photo (rare).

factor analysis A complex algebraic method for determining the general dimensions or factors that exist within a set of concrete observations. See Chapter 17 for more details on this topic.

frequency distribution (1) A description of the number of times the various attributes of a variable are observed in a sample. The report that 53 percent of a sample were men and 47 percent were women would be a simple example of a *frequency distribution*. Another example would be the report that 15 of the cities studied had populations under 10,000, 23 had populations between 10,000 and 25,000, and so forth. (2) A radio dial.

functionalism A paradigm that focuses on the functions served by the elements making up a whole system or organism. Thus, one of the functions of higher education is to keep young people out of the job market.

generalizability (1) That quality of a research finding that justifies the inference that it represents something more than the specific observations on which it was based. Sometimes this involves the *generalization* of findings from a sample to a population. Other times, it is a matter of concepts: If you discover why people commit burglaries, can you *generalize* that discovery to other crimes as well? (2) The likelihood that you will ever be a general.

Guttman scale (1) A type of composite measure used to summarize several discrete observations and to represent some more general variable. See Chapter 7. (2) The device Louis Guttman weighs himself on.

Hawthorne effect A term coined in reference to a series of productivity studies at the Hawthorne plant of the Western Electric Company in Chicago, Illinois. The researchers discovered that their presence affected the behavior of the workers being studied. The term now refers to any impact of research on the subject of study. See Chapter 9.

hypothesis An expectation about the nature of things derived from a theory. It is a statement of something that ought to be observed in the real world if the theory is correct. See *deduction* and also Chapters 2 and 4.

hypothesis testing The determination of whether the expectations that a hypothesis represents are, indeed, found to exist in the real world. See Chapters 2 and 4.

idiographic An approach to explanation in which we seek to exhaust the idiosyncratic causes of a particular condition or event. Imagine trying to list all the reasons why you chose to attend your particular college. Given all those reasons, it's difficult to imagine your making any other choice. By contrast, see *nomothetic*.

independent variable (1) A variable with values that are not problematical in an analysis but are taken as simply given. An *independent variable* is presumed to cause or determine a *dependent variable*. If we discover that religiosity is partly a function of gender—women are more religious than men—*gender* is the *independent variable* and *religiosity* is the dependent variable. Note that any given variable might be treated as independent in one part of an analysis and dependent in another part of it. *Religiosity* might become an *independent variable* in the explanation of crime. (2) A variable that refuses to take advice.

index A type of composite measure that summarizes several specific observations and represents some more general dimension. Contrasted with *scale*. See Chapter 7.

indicator An observation that we choose to consider as a reflection of a variable we wish to study. Thus, for example, attending church might be considered an *indicator* of religiosity.

induction (1) The logical model in which general principles are developed from specific observations. Having noted that Jews and Catholics are more likely to vote Democratic than Protestants are, you might conclude that religious minorities in the United States are more affiliated with the Democratic party and explain why. This would be an example of *induction*. See also *deduction* and Chapters 2 and 3. (2) The culinary art of stuffing ducks.

inferential statistics The body of statistical computations relevant to making inferences from findings based on sample observations to some larger population. See also *descriptive statistics* and Chapter 17. Not to be confused with infernal statistics, a characterization sometimes invoked by frustrated statistics students.

informant Someone well versed in the social phenomenon that you wish to study and who is willing to tell you what he or she knows. If you were planning participant observation among the members of a religious sect, you would do well to make friends with someone who already knows about them—possibly a member of the sect—who could give you some background information about them. Not to be confused with a *respondent*.

interactionist paradigm An approach to understanding social life that focuses on the ways people interact with each other in the search for meaning. Consider two people having a conversation, trying to reach an agreement, for example.

internal invalidity Refers to the possibility that the conclusions drawn from experimental results may not accurately reflect what went on in the experiment itself. See Chapter 9 and also *external invalidity*.

internal validation The process whereby the individual items composing a composite measure are correlated with the measure itself. This provides one test of the wisdom of including all the items in the composite measure. See also *external validation* and Chapter 7.

interpretation A technical term used in connection with the elaboration model. It represents the research outcome in which a *control variable* is discovered to be the mediating factor through which an *independent variable* has its effect on a *dependent variable*. See Chapter 16.

intersubjectivity That quality of science (and other inquiries) whereby two different researchers, studying the same problem, arrive at the same conclusion. Ultimately, this is the practical criterion for what is called *objectivity*. We agree that something is "objectively true" if independent observers with different subjective orientations conclude that it is "true." See Chapter 2.

interval measure A level of measurement describing a variable whose attributes are rank-ordered and have equal distances between adjacent attributes. The Fahrenheit temperature scale is an example of this, since the distance between 17 and 18 is the same as that between 89 and 90. See also *nominal measure, ordinal measure,* and *ratio measure*.

interview A data-collection encounter in which one person (an interviewer) asks questions of another (a *respondent*). Interviews may be conducted face-to-face or by telephone. See Chapter 10 for more information on interviewing as a method of survey research.

judgmental sample (1) A type of *nonprobability sample* in which you select the units to be observed on the basis of your own *judgment* about which ones will be the most useful or representative. Another name for this is *purposive sample*. See Chapter 8 for more details. (2) A sample of opinionated people.

latent content (1) As used in connection with content analysis, the underlying meaning of communications as distinguished from their *manifest content*. See Chapter 12. (2) What you need to make a latent.

level of significance (1) In the context of *tests of statistical significance*, the degree of likelihood that an observed, empirical relationship could be attributable to sampling error. A relationship is *significant* at the .05 level if the likelihood of its being only a function of sampling error is no greater than 5 out of 100. See Chapter 17. (2) Height limits on outdoor advertising.

Likert scale A type of composite measure developed by Rensis Likert in an attempt to improve the levels of measurement in social research through the use of standardized response categories in survey *questionnaires*. *Likert* items are those using such response categories as strongly agree, agree, disagree, and strongly disagree. Such items may be used in the construction of true *Likert scales* as well as other types of composite measures. See Chapter 7.

longitudinal study A study design involving the collection of data at different points in time, as contrasted with a *cross-sectional study*. See also Chapter 4 and *cohort study, panel study,* and *trend study*.

macrotheory A theory aimed at understanding the "big picture" of institutions, whole societies, and the interactions among societies. Karl Marx's examination of the class struggle is an example of *macrotheory*. By contrast, see *microtheory*.

manifest content (1) In connection with content analysis, the concrete terms contained in a communication, as distinguished from *latent content*. See Chapter 12. (2) What you have after a manifest bursts.

matching In connection with experiments, the procedure whereby pairs of subjects are *matched* on the basis of their similarities on one or more variables, and one member of the pair is assigned to the experimental group and the other to the *control group*. See Chapter 9.

mean (1) An *average*, computed by summing the values of several observations and dividing by the number of observations. If you now have a grade point average of 4.0 based on 10 courses, and you get an *F* in this course, your new grade point (mean) average will be 3.6. (2) The quality of the thoughts you might have if your instructor did that to you.

median (1) Another *average*, representing the value of the "middle" case in a rank-ordered set of observations. If the ages of five men are 16, 17, 20, 54, and 88, the *median* would be 20. (The *mean* would be 39.) (2) The dividing line between safe driving and *exciting* driving.

microtheory   A theory aimed at understanding social life at the intimate level of individuals and their interactions. Examining how the play behavior of girls differs from that of boys would be an example of *microtheory*. By contrast, see *macrotheory*.

mode   (1) Still another *average*, representing the most frequently observed value or attribute. If a sample contains 1,000 Protestants, 275 Catholics, and 33 Jews, *Protestant* is the *modal* category. See Chapter 14 for more thrilling disclosures about averages. (2) Better than apple pie à la median.

multivariate analysis   The analysis of the simultaneous relationships among several variables. Examining simultaneously the effects of age, gender, and social class on religiosity would be an example of *multivariate analysis*. See Chapters 15, 16, and 18.

nominal measure   A level of measurement describing a variable the different attributes of which are *only* different, as distinguished from *ordinal, interval,* or *ratio measures*. Gender would be an example of a nominal measure.

nomothetic   An approach to explanation in which we seek to identify a few causal factors that generally impact a class of conditions or events. Imagine the two or three key factors that determine which colleges students choose, such as proximity, reputation, and so forth. By contrast, see *idiographic*.

nonprobability sample   A sample selected in some fashion other than any suggested by probability theory. Examples include *judgmental (purposive)*, *quota,* and *snowball samples*. See Chapter 8.

nonsampling error   (1) Those imperfections of data quality that are a result of factors other than sampling error. Examples include misunderstandings of questions by respondents, erroneous recordings by interviewers and coders, and keypunch errors. (2) The mistake you made in deciding to interview everyone rather than selecting a sample.

null hypothesis   (1) In connection with *hypothesis testing* and *tests of statistical significance*, that *hypothesis* that suggests there is no relationship among the variables under study. You may conclude that the variables are related after having statistically rejected the *null hypothesis*. (2) An expectation about nulls.

objectivity   Doesn't exist. See *intersubjectivity*.

operational definition   The concrete and specific definition of something in terms of the *operations* by which observations are to be categorized. The *operational definition* of "earning an *A* in this course" might be "correctly answering at least 90 percent of the final exam questions." See Chapter 6.

operationalization   (1) One step beyond *conceptualization*. *Operationalization* is the process of developing *operational definitions*. (2) Surgery on intellectuals.

ordinal measure   A level of measurement describing a variable with attributes you can *rank-order* along some dimension. An example would be *socioeconomic status* as composed of the attributes *high, medium, low*. See also *nominal measure, interval measure,* and *ratio measure*.

panel study   A type of *longitudinal study*, in which data are collected from the same sample (the *panel*) at several points in time. See Chapter 4.

paradigm   (1) A model or framework for observation and understanding, which shapes both what we see and how we understand it. The *conflict paradigm* causes us to see social behavior one way, the *interactionist paradigm* causes us to see it differently. (2) $0.20.

path analysis   (1) A form of *multivariate analysis* in which the causal relationships among variables are presented in graphic format. See Chapter 17. (2) Watching your step along a horse trail.

PPS   Probability proportionate to size   (1) This refers to a type of multistage *cluster sample* in which clusters are selected, not with equal probabilities (see *EPSEM*) but with probabilities proportionate to their sizes—as measured by the number of units to be subsampled. See Chapter 8. (2) The odds on who gets to go first: you or the 275-pound fullback.

probability sample   The general term for a sample selected in accord with probability theory, typically involving some random-selection mechanism. Specific types of *probability samples* include *area probability sample, EPSEM, PPS, simple random sample,* and *systematic sample*. See Chapter 8.

probe   A technique employed in interviewing to solicit a more complete answer to a question. It is a nondirective phrase or question used to encourage a respondent to elaborate on an answer. Examples include "Anything more?" and "How is that?" See Chapter 10 for a discussion of interviewing.

purposive sample   See *judgmental sample* and Chapters 8 and 11.

qualitative analysis   (1) The nonnumerical examination and interpretation of observations, for the purpose of discovering underlying meanings and patterns of relationships. This is most typical of field research and historical research. See Chapter 11. (2) A classy analysis.

quantitative analysis   (1) The numerical representation and manipulation of observations for the purpose of describing and explaining the phenomena that those observations reflect. See Chapter 14 especially, and also the remainder of Part 4. (2) A BIG analysis.

questionnaire   A document containing questions and other types of items designed to solicit information appropriate to analysis. *Questionnaires* are used primarily in survey research and also in experiments, field research, and other modes of observation. See Chapters 6 and 10.

quota sample A type of nonprobability sample in which units are selected into the sample on the basis of prespecified characteristics, so that the total sample will have the same distribution of characteristics assumed to exist in the population being studied. See Chapter 8.

randomization A technique for assigning experimental subjects to experimental and *control groups* randomly. See Chapter 9.

range (1) A measure of *dispersion*, composed of the highest and lowest values of a variable in some set of observations. In your class, for example, the *range* of ages might be from 17 to 37. (2) Recreation area for deer and antelope.

ratio measure A level of measurement describing a variable the attributes of which have all the qualities of *nominal*, *ordinal*, and *interval measures* and in addition are based on a "true zero" point. Age would be an example of a *ratio measure*.

reductionism (1) A fault of some researchers: a strict limitation (reduction) of the kinds of concepts to be considered relevant to the phenomenon under study. (2) The cloning of ducks.

regression analysis (1) A method of data analysis in which the relationships among variables are represented in the form of an equation, called a *regression equation*. See Chapter 17 for a discussion of the different forms of *regression analysis*. (2) What seems to happen to your knowledge of social research methods just before an exam.

reification The process of regarding things that are not real as real.

reliability (1) That quality of measurement method that suggests that the same data would have been collected each time in repeated observations of the same phenomenon. In the context of a survey, we would expect that the question "Did you attend church last week?" would have higher reliability than the question "About how many times have you attended church in your life?" This is not to be confused with *validity*. (2) Quality of repeatability in untruths.

replication Generally, the duplication of an experiment to expose or reduce error. It is also a technical term used in connection with the elaboration model, referring to the elaboration outcome in which the initially observed relationship between two variables persists when a *control variable* is held constant. See Chapter 16. See also Chapter 1 and *intersubjectivity*.

representativeness (1) That quality of a sample of having the same distribution of characteristics as the population from which it was selected. By implication, descriptions and explanations derived from an analysis of the sample may be assumed to represent similar ones in the population. *Representativeness* is enhanced by *probability sampling* and provides for *generalizability* and the use of *inferential statistics*. See Chapter 8. (2) A noticeable quality in the presentation-of-self of some members of the U.S. Congress.

respondent A person who provides data for analysis by responding to a survey *questionnaire*.

response rate The number of people participating in a survey divided by the number selected in the sample, in the form of a percentage. This is also called the completion rate or, in self-administered surveys, the return rate: the percentage of *questionnaires* sent out that are returned. See Chapter 10.

sampling frame That list or quasi-list of units composing a population from which a sample is selected. If the sample is to be *representative* of the population, it is essential that the *sampling frame* include all (or nearly all) members of the population. See Chapter 8.

sampling interval The standard distance between elements selected from a population for a sample. See Chapter 8.

sampling ratio The proportion of elements in the population that are selected to be in a sample. See Chapter 8.

scale (1) A type of composite measure composed of several items that have a logical or empirical structure among them. Examples of *scales* include Bogardus social distance, Guttman, Likert, and Thurstone scales. Contrasted with *index*. See also Chapter 7. (2) One of the less appetizing parts of a fish.

secondary analysis (1) A form of research in which the data collected and processed by one researcher are reanalyzed—often for a different purpose—by another. This is especially appropriate in the case of survey data. Data archives are repositories or libraries for the storage and distribution of data for *secondary analysis*. (2) Estimating the weight and speed of an opposing team's linebackers.

semantic differential A questionnaire format in which the respondent is asked to rate something in terms of two, opposite adjectives (e.g., rate textbooks as "boring" or "exciting"), using qualifiers such as "very," "somewhat," "neither," "somewhat," and "very" to bridge the distance between the two opposites.

simple random sample (1) A type of *probability sample* in which the units composing a population are assigned numbers. A set of random numbers is then generated, and the units having those numbers are included in the sample. Although probability theory and the calculations it provides assume this basic sampling method, it is seldom used, for practical reasons. An equivalent alternative is the *systematic sample* (with a random start). See Chapter 8. (2) A random sample with a low IQ.

snowball sample   (1) A *nonprobability sampling* method often employed in field research. Each person interviewed may be asked to suggest additional people for interviewing. See Chapter 11. (2) Picking the icy ones to throw at your methods instructor.

specification   Generally, the process through which concepts are made more specific. It is also a technical term used in connection with the elaboration model, representing the elaboration outcome in which an initially observed relationship between two variables is replicated among some subgroups created by the *control variable* and not among others. In such a situation, you will have *specified* the conditions under which the original relationship exists: for example, among men but not among women. See Chapter 16.

statistical significance   (1) A general term referring to the unlikeliness that relationships observed in a sample could be attributed to sampling error alone. See *tests of statistical significance* and Chapter 17. (2) How important it would really be if you flunked your statistics exam. I mean, you could always be a poet.

stratification   The grouping of the units composing a population into homogeneous groups (or strata) before sampling. This procedure, which may be used in conjunction with *simple random, systematic,* or *cluster sampling,* improves the *representativeness* of a sample, at least in terms of the stratification variables. See Chapter 8.

systematic sample   (1) A type of *probability sample* in which every *k*th unit in a list is selected for inclusion in the sample—for example, every 25th student in the college directory of students. You compute *k* by dividing the size of the population by the desired sample size; *k* is called the *sampling interval.* Within certain constraints, *systematic sampling* is a functional equivalent of *simple random sampling* and usually easier to do. Typically, the first unit is selected at random. See Chapter 8. (2) Picking every third one whether it's icy or not. See *snowball sample (2).*

test variable   See *control variable.*

tests of statistical significance   (1) A class of statistical computations that indicate the likelihood that the relationship observed between variables in a sample can be attributed to sampling error only. See *inferential statistics* and Chapter 17. (2) A determination of how important statistics have been in improving humankind's lot in life. (3) An examination that can radically affect your grade in this course and your grade point average as well.

theory   A systematic explanation for the observations that relate to a particular aspect of life: juvenile delinquency, for example, or perhaps social stratification or political revolution.

Thurstone scale   A type of composite measure, constructed in accord with the weights assigned by "judges" to various indicators of some variables. See Chapter 7.

trend study   A type of *longitudinal study* in which a given characteristic of some population is monitored over time. An example would be the series of Gallup Polls showing the political candidate preferences of the electorate over the course of a campaign, even though different samples were interviewed at each point. See Chapter 4.

typology   (1) The classification (typically nominal) of observations in terms of their attributes on two or more variables. The classification of newspapers as liberal-urban, liberal-rural, conservative-urban, or conservative-rural would be an example. See Chapter 7. (2) Apologizing for your neckwear.

units of analysis   The *what* or *whom* being studied. In social science research, the most typical units of analysis are individual people. See Chapter 4.

univariate analysis   The analysis of a single variable, for purposes of description. *Frequency distributions, averages,* and measures of *dispersion* would be examples of *univariate analysis,* as distinguished from *bivariate* and *multivariate analysis.* See Chapter 15.

validity   A term describing a measure that accurately reflects the concept it is intended to measure. For example, your IQ would seem a more *valid* measure of your intelligence than would the number of hours you spend in the library. Though the ultimate *validity* of a measure can never be proven, we may agree to its relative validity on the basis of *face validity, criterion validity, content validity, construct validity, internal validation,* and *external validation.* This must not be confused with *reliability.* See Chapter 5.

variables   Logical groupings of *attributes.* The variable *gender* is made of up of the attributes *male* and *female.*

weighting   (1) A procedure employed in connection with sampling whereby units selected with unequal probabilities are assigned weights in such a manner as to make the sample *representative* of the population from which it was selected. See Chapter 8. (2) Olde English for hanging around for somebody who never gets there on time.

Index

Abortion rights, 106–109, 171, 185–186
Abstract, A17
ABtab, 360
Academic performance, African Americans and, 451–452
Acoustical coupler, 361
Actions, as points of focus, 100
Active initiative, 343–344
Adams, John, 255
Administrative control, 347–348
Administrative costs, 149
African Americans, 79, 117–118
   academic performance and, 451–452
   crime rates and, 96–97
   equality and, 451–452
   law and, 328–329
   prejudice against, 233–235, 239–240, 251
   as soldiers, discrimination and, 390–392
   street-corner life and, 300–301
   syphilis and, 348
   undernourishment of children and, 80
Age
   Comfort Hypothesis and, 55
   political liberalism and, 103
Aggregated statistics, 320
Aggregates, social regularity and, 28–29
Aging, time dimension and, 105
AIDA, 360
AIDS, 17, 77–78, 334, 337–338
Alexander, Lamar, 249
Alfred, Randall, 299–300, 442
Alienation, 108, 168
Almond, Gabriel, 275
The American Almanac, 323
American Association for Public Opinion Polling, 257
American Association for Public Opinion Research (AAPOR), Code of Conduct of, 445, 446
American Institute for Scientific Information, 127
American Institute of Public Opinion, 194
American Sociological Review (ASR), 65, 127, 255
America Online, 361, A8, A11
Aminzade, Ron, 329, 330

Analysis. *See also specific type*
   research project design and, 110
   research proposal and, 112
   social research and, 443–444
Analysis of variance, 430
Analytical files, 295
Analytic ethnography, 282
Analytic induction, 316
Analyzing, interviewing process and, 293
Analyzing Social Settings, 284, 293, 294
Andorka, Rudolf, 336
Aneshensel, Carol S., 103
Anomia, 125
   origins of, 126–127
Anomic suicide, 320
Anomie, 124–125, 320
Anonymity, social research and, 440–441
Anti-Semitism, 416–417
Appearance, survey interviewing and, 265
Application, research project design and, 110
Arithmetic mean, 371, 372
Asch experiment, 49, 443
Asher, Ramona, 101
Aspects, 296
Association
   example of, 82–83
   linking measurement and, 79–83
   measures of, 407–411, 415
   between variables, 32–33
Association for Public Opinion Research, 256
A.STAT, 360
ATLAS/ti, 296
Attitudes, measurement of, 5–6
Attributes, 30–31
   mutually exclusive, 141–142
Attribution process, 246
Audience, research report and, A15–A16
Auster, Carol, 314, 315
Authority, inquiry and, 19–20
Averages, 370–374
Axioms, theory construction and, 52

Babbie, Earl R., 397, 440
Bailey, William, 352

Balir, Johnny, 272
Ball-Rokeach, Sandra, 251
Baron, James, 177
Bart, Pauline, 345
Base, 315
Beatles, 312
Belenky, Mary Field, 48
Bellah, Robert, 288, 327–328, 329
Benton, J. Edwin, 157
Berg, Bruce, 167, 310, 314, 315, 317
Beveridge, W. J. B., 54
Bian, Yanjie, 101
Bias
   questionnaires and, 152–153
   sampling, conscious and unconscious, 198–200
   selection, internal invalidity and, 242
Bigotry, 29, 328
Binomial sampling distribution, 205–210
Bishop, G. F., 150
Bitnet, A8
Bivariate analysis, 10, 378–383, A80–A95
   explanatory, 378
Bivariate relationship, index items and, 171–174
Black, Donald, 322
Blair, Johnny, 159
Blaue, Peter, 49
Blodgett, Timothy, 225
BMDP, 360
Bogardus social distance scale, 182–183
Bollen, Kenneth, 172
Bolstein, Richard, 262
Bonney, Charles, 74
Books in Print, A2
Borg, Marian J., 270
Boruch, Robert, 338, 442
Brown, L. Dave, 343
Brown v. Board of Education of Topeka, 451
Browser, A11
Budget, research proposal and, 112
Burneson, Ray, 349
Bush, George, 51
Bushido, 327

Calvin, John, 326–327
Calvinism, 9, 327
Camelot, 452–453

Index

Campbell, Donald, 239–241, 244–245, 252
Candy Poll, 258
CAPI (computer-assisted personal interviewing), 260
Capitalism, 327–328
Capital punishment, deterrence and, 352–353
Card catalog, A4
Carmines, Edward, 133–134
Carolina Observer, 255
Carpini, Michael, 101
Carrier, 29
Case study, 280, 282
  one-shot, 239–240, 241
CASI (computer-assisted self-interviewing), 260
CATI (computer-assisted telephone interviewing), 259–260, 270–271
Causal analysis, 4
Causality
  correlation and, 74–75
  criteria for, 73–77
Causal reasoning, 18
  faulty, statistical analysis and, 77–78
Causal time-order, internal invalidity and, 242
Causation, 4–5, 33, 69
  in natural sciences, 69
Cause(s)
  field research and, 298
  necessary and sufficient, 76–77
  questionable, 79
CBS News, 376
CD-ROM, 361
Cecil, Joe, 442
Central tendency, univariate analysis and, 370–374
Central tendency theorem, 209
Channel, 90
Channeling, 90–91
Chaos theory, 50
Characteristics, as points of focus, 97–100
Child abuse, 298
Childers, Terry, 262
Chisholm, Rupert, 250
Chi square, 427–431
  distribution of, A34–A35
Christian Beliefs and Anti-Semitism, 82
Christianity, 326
Church attendance, gender and, 378–379
Church of Satan, 299–300, 442
The Civic Culture, 275
Civil law, 310
Clay Street, 304
Clinton, Bill, 51, 72, 76, 192
Closed-ended questions, 148
Cluster, 220
Cluster sampling, 313
  multistage, 219–226
  illustration of, 226–227
Clymer, Adam, 256
Codebook, construction of, 363–364
Code sheet, 364–365
Coding
  computers and, 362–363
  conceptualization and, 314–315
  content analysis and, 313–317
  numerical, 315
  options for, 364–366
Coefficient of reproducibility, 187
Cofta, 296
Cohort study, 102, 105
Coleman, James, 451–452
College performance, 145
Collins, G. C., 225
Comfort Hypothesis, 55–56, 378, 383
Commercials, television, gender stereotyping in, 317–318
Common Cause, 324
Comparability, 343
Comparative conclusion, 172
Comparison, bivariate analysis and, 378
Compassion, 116, 118–120, 121, 122
Compensation, internal invalidity and, 243
Compensatory rivalry, internal invalidity and, 243
Competency, of respondents, 149
Complete observer, 287
Complexity, 50
Composite measurement, 145
  of variables, 168
Compuserve, 361, A8
Computer-assisted personal interviewing (CAPI), 260
Computer-assisted self-interviewing (CASI), 260
Computer-assisted telephone interviewing (CATI), 259–260, 270–271
Computerized library files, A5–A6
Computerized self-administered questionnaire (CSAQ), 260
Computer-Mediated Dialog Simulation, 296
Computer Programs for Qualitative Data Analysis, 297
Computers
  coding and, 362–363
  field research and, 296–297
  social research and, 359–361
Computer simulation, 353–354
Comte, Auguste, 43, 47, 48, 325
Conceptions, 118–120
Concepts, 118–120
  clarification of, 122–124
  operationalization of, 81
  theory construction and, 52
Conceptual entrapment, process of, 123

Conceptualization, 86, 116, 118, 120, 139
  creation of code categories and, 314–315
  example of, 124–127
  measurement and, 5
  research project design and, 108
Conclusion
  comparative, 172
  hasty, 79
  tentative, 97
Confidence interval, sampling and, 202, 209, 421
Confidence level, sampling and, 202, 209, 421
Confidentiality, social research and, 441–442
Conflict paradigm, 4, 44–45
Confucianism, 327
Congenital math deficiency syndrome (CMDS), 405
Conjecture, 75
Consent, informed, 444
Consequences, field research and, 298
Conservatism, 128–129, 170, 174, 176
Constructs, 119
Construct validity, 133–134
Content
  latent, 313–314
  manifest, 313–314
Content analysis, 108, 308
  coding in, 313–317
  illustration of, 317–318
  sampling in, 310–313
  strengths and weaknesses of, 318–319
  topics appropriate to, 309–310
Content validity, 133–134
Context, 296
  social, 273, 346–352
Contingency cleaning, 367
Contingency questions, 155–156
Contingency tables, 383
Continuous variable, 374
Control
  administrative, 347–348
  survey interviewing and, 267–268
Control group
  classical experiment and, 235–236
  nonequivalent, 341–342
  posttest-only design, 245
Control variable, 10
Cook, E., 400
Cook, Thomas, 240–241, 252
Cooley, Charles Horton, 45, 246
Coordination, survey interviewing and, 267–268
Correlation, causality and, 74–75
Correlation matrix, 410–411
Correlation squared, 413
Coser, Lewis, 45
Cost/benefit analysis, 345

Cost-of-living allowance (COLA), 453
Counting, coding and, 315
Cox, James, 193
Craig, R. Stephen, 317–318
Crawford, Kent, 346
Crime rates, African Americans and, 96–97
Crime statistics, 322–323
Criminal law, 310
CRISP, 360
Criteria
  for causality, 73–77
  for measurement quality, 129–136
Criterion-related validity, 133–134
Cross-referencing, 296
Cross-sectional study, 100–101, 105
Cumulative effect, 384
Current Population Survey (CPS), 149
Curvilinear regression, 414

DAISY, 360
Daly, John, 157
Danish Data Archives, 275
Dannemiller, James E., 272
Darwin, Charles, 28, 44
Darwinism, social, 44
Data
  empirical, collection of, 81
  qualitative, 36–38, 280
  quantitative, 36–38
    multiple indicators and, 167
  supplemental source of, 319
  time-series, 330
Data analysis, 24–25, 26, 458–459, 464–465
  guidelines for reporting, A20–A21
  indexes and scales and, 167
  qualitative, 297–299
    content analysis and, 315–317
  quantitative, 9
  social research and, 2–3
Data analysis program, connecting with, 366
Data archives, 275
Data cleaning, 366–367
Data collection, 24–25, 26, 458–459
  through mail, 258–259
  research proposal and, 112
Data Desk, 360
Data entry
  direct, 365
  by interviewers, 365
  options for, 364–366
Data processing
  qualitative, 294–297
  research project design and, 109–110
Data reduction, descriptive statistics and, 406–407
Data-reduction devices, 167
Data reporting, 465
DATA-X, 360

Davis, Fred, 287
Davis, James, 102
Davis, Miles, 4
Death penalty, deterrence and, 352–353
Debriefing, 443
Deception, social research and, 442–443
Deduction, induction compared, 54–60
Deductive logic, 54–55
Deductive method, 4, 283
Deductive model, traditional, 80–82
Deductive theory, 35–36
  construction of, 60–63
  example of, 61–63
Definitions, 122
  descriptive research and, 128–129
  nominal, 122
  operational, 122, 124
  real, 122
  reality and, 122
DeFleur, Lois, 322
Degrees of freedom, 428–429
Dehumanization, 73
Delinquency, 52, 53–54, 81–82, 419–420
Delphi, A8
Demeanor, survey interviewing and, 265
Demographic Yearbook, 324
Demoralization, internal invalidity and, 243
Dependent variable, 7, 188, 378, 393
  classical experiment and, 234
Deprivation
  Comfort Hypothesis and, 55–56
  relative, 389–390
Depth, field research and, 313
Description
  numerical, qualitative research and, 378
  social research and, 91–92, 128
Descriptive statistics, 405, 406–415, A53–A61
  data reduction and, 406–407
  measures of association and, 407–411
  regression analysis and, 411–415
de Seve, Michel, 400
Designing, interviewing process and, 292
Detail, univariate analysis and, 374–375
Determinism
  economic, 326
  social science and, 69–71
Deterrence, death penalty and, 352–353
Deviant cases, 195
Dewey, Thomas E., 193–194
Dichotomous variable, 210, 234
Dickson, W. J., 235
Differences, 297
Dillman, Don, 262, 269
Dimensions, 120–121, 141, 184
Direct observables, 119
Direct observation, 280

Disconfirmability, 53
Discrete variable, 374
Discrimination, 5, 450
  African-American soldiers and, 390–392
Dispersion, univariate analysis and, 374
Disproportionate sampling, 224–226
Dissimilarities, 297
Distorter variable, 400
Distribution
  sampling, 203–205
    binomial, 205–210
  univariate analysis and, 370
Distributive justice, 61
Documents, reading and evaluating, 330–331
Dole, Robert, 72, 76, 192
"Don't knows", 377–378
Double-barreled questions, 149, 150–151
Double-blind experiment, 236–237
Douvan, Elizabeth, 102
Doyle, Arthur Conan, 60
DragonDictate, 296
Driver training, traffic accidents and, 335–336
Drug use, 345–346
Dunlap, Riley, E., 56
Durkheim, Emile, 8, 47, 59–60, 124–125, 127, 308, 319–322, 326
Dynacomp, 360

Ecological fallacy, 96–97
Economic determinism, 326
The Economic Ethic of the World Religions, 327
Economic reductionism, 97
Ecowarriors: Understanding the Radical Environmental Movement, 441
Edge-coding, 365
Education, 31–34
Egalitarianism, gender-based, 87
Elaboration
  ex post facto hypothesizing and, 401–402
  reasons for doing, 390
Elaboration model, 10–11, 384
  history of, 389–392
Elaboration paradigm, 393–401
  explanation and, 396–397
  interpretation and, 397–398
  refinements to, 399–401
  replication and, 393–396
  specification and, 398–399
Electronic surveys, 259–260
Element, sampling and, 200–201
The Elements of Style, A15
Email, A8–A10
Emergent analysis, 282–283
Empirical data, collection of, 81
Employed, 141–142

Employment status, 141
　gender and, 408–409
Encounters, field research and, 284
Ends, 52
Entities, 90
Environmental activism, 119
Episodes, field research and, 284
Epistemology, 18
EPSEM samples, 200
Equality, African Americans and, 451–452
Equal Rights Amendment (ERA), 4
Errors, of reasoning, 77–79
Eskenazi, Brenda, 250
Essential questions, 167
Ethical controversies, 447–449
Ethics
　evaluation research and, 348
　field research and, 302–303
　professional code of, 445–446
　sexuality research and, 444–445
　social research and, 11, 38–39, 438–446
Ethnicity, juvenile delinquency theory and, 52
Ethnograph, 296, 297
Ethnography, 282
Ethnomethodology, 46
Evaluation research, 9, 25, 251, 334–335, 464
　ethics and, 348
　problem formulation and, 336–346
　qualitative, 345–346
　results of, 348–352
　social context and, 273, 346–352
　topics commonly subjected to, 335–336
Evidence, weight of, 134
Evolution, 44
Exceptions, social regularity and, 28
Exchange paradigm, 48–49, 61
Existing statistics
　analyzing, 308–309, 319–324, 464
　sources of, 323–324
Expectations communication model, 246
Expectations-states theory, 246
Expected frequencies, 427
Experiment(s), 7–8, 462–463
　basic design of, diagram of, 235
　classical, 233–237
　double-blind, 236–237
　illustration of, 245–248
　laboratory, 249
　"natural", 249–251
　subject selection and, 237–239
　topics appropriate to, 233
　variations on design of, 239–245
Experimental design, evaluation research and, 339–340
Experimental group, 235–236
Experimental method, strengths and weaknesses of, 251–252

Experimental mortality, internal invalidity and, 242
Explained variation, 413
Explanation
　elaboration paradigm and, 396–397
　idiographic, 34–35
　idiographic and nomothetic models of, 71–73
　nomothetic, 34–35
　social research and, 92, 128
Explanatory analysis, 4
Explanatory bivariate analysis, 378
Exploration, social research and, 90–91
Ex post facto hypothesizing, 401–402
External invalidity, 7, 240, 244
　sources of, 244–245
External validation, index validation and, 180
Extrapolation, 414
Extra questions, 167
Extremes, variations between, 140
Exxon *Valdez*, 441, 442

Face validity, 133, 170
Fact, theory construction and, 51
Factor analysis, 418–420
Factor loadings, 419
Fallacy
　ecological, 96–97
　gambler's, 21
　individualistic, 97
False dilemma, 79
Familiarity with questionnaire, survey interviewing and, 265–266
Family, as unit of analysis, 94
Family income, median, 374
Federal Bureau of Investigation (FBI), 323
Feinberg, Barry, 269
Feminism, 6
Feminist paradigm, 47–48
Festinger, Leon, 101
Field research, 8, 63, 108, 280, 463–464
　ethics in, 302–303
　illustrations of, 299–302
　preparing for, 289–290
　qualitative data processing and, 294–297
　recording observations and, 293–294
　relations to subjects and, 287–289
　roles of observer and, 286–287
　strengths and weaknesses of, 303–305
　topics appropriate to, 283–285
Files, field research and, 295–296
File transfer protocol (ftp), A11
Final sampling unit, 201
Fine, Gary, 101
Fink, Jeffrey, 346
Finkel, Steven E., 270
Fisher, Patricia, 130

Fit, 131
Focus group, 90, 248–249
Follow-up mailings, 261
Fool's experiment, 28
Forbes, Steve, 249
Ford, David, 350–351
Forslund, Morris, 419–420
Foschi, Martha, 246
Fourteenth Amendment, 451
Free will, 69
Frequencies, field research and, 298
Functionalist paradigm, 3–4
Fuzzy logic, 50

Gall, John, A18
Gallup, George, 193–194, 196, 210, 255, 324
Gallup Poll, 91, 101, 103, 147, 150, 210, 256, 275, 324, A139
Gambler's fallacy, 21
Gamma, 409–411
Gamson, William, 249
Garfinkel, Harold, 46
Gender
　attitudes toward sexual equality and, 382
　church attendance and, 378–379
　Comfort Hypothesis and, 55
　employment status and, 408–409
　sexual equality and, 422–427
Gender-based egalitarianism, 87
Gender Empowerment Measure (GEM), 181–182
Gender-related Development Index (GDI)181
Gender stereotyping, television commercials and, 317–318
Generalizability, 87, 237, 244, 439
Generalized understanding, 93
General Social Survey (GSS), 6, 9, 92, 126, 152, 159, 185, 363–364, 378, 383, A22
Genie, A8
Girl Scouts, 314, 315
Glaser, Barney, 63, 283
Glaser, Barry, 316
Glock, Charles, 55, 57–58, 82, 275, 378, 383, 398
Goffman, Erving, 63, 282
Good citizenship, 285
Gophers, A11
Gore, Al, 249
Grade point average (GPA), 145, 260
Graham, George, 80
Gramm, Phil, 249
Graphics COPE, 296
Greatbatch, David, 46
Griffin, Larry, 146, 330
Gross national product (GNP), 372–374
Grounded theory, 63, 283
　code development and, 314

Index

Groups
 field research and, 284
 social scientific research and, 93–94
Grube, Joel, 251
GSS household enumeration questionnaire, A22–A31
Guterbok, Thomas M., 270
Guttman, Louis, 185
Guttman scaling, 185–187

Habermas, Jurgen, 281
Haley, Alex, 251
Hamnett, Michael P., 453
Happiness, 86
Harding, Warren, 192–193
Harm, protection from, 38, 439–440, 445
Harris Poll, 147, 150–151, 256, 275
Hart, Stephen, 246
Harvard Business Review, 225
Harvard Educational Review, 452
Hasty conclusion, 79
Hatchett, Shirley, 102
Hawthorne effect, 236, 286
Health Hazard Appraisal (HHA), 132
Hein, Jeremy, 73
Hempel, Carl, 122
Herald Tribune, 376
Heritage, Johen, 46
Hermeneutics, 281–282
Higginbotham, A. Leon, Jr., 328
Hilts, Philip, 349
Hirschi, Travis, 75
Historical/comparative analysis, 308, 325–330
 examples of, 325–328
 sources of, 328–329
 techniques of, 329–330
History, internal invalidity and, 241
Hite, Shere, 256
"Hite Reports", 256
HIV, 334
Hollerith, Herman, 359–360
Holmes, Sherlock, 60, 73
Hologram, social research, 1–12
Homans, George, 48–49
Homosexuality, 447
Horney, Julie, 349–350
Horowitz, Irving Louis, 452
Housing unit, 271
Howard, Edward, 336
Howell, Joseph, 304
Human inquiry
 ordinary, 18–19
 science and, 3
Human suffering, worldwide, 324–325
Humphreys, Laud, 447, 448
Husserl, Edmund, 281
HyperResearch, 296
Hypotheses
 empirical testing of, 81
 hints for stating, 56–57

null, 57, 427
 theoretical, derivation of, 81
 theory construction and, 52
Hypothesis testing, 4
Hypothesizing, ex post facto, 401–402

IBM, 360
IBM 1620, 361
IBM cards, 360
Ideal types, 329
Ideology, social research and, 450–453
Idiographic approach, 281
Idiographic explanation, 34–35
Idiographic model, of explanation, 71–73
Idiosyncracy, 34
Illogical reasoning, 20–21
Income, family, median, 374
Independent variable, 7, 188, 378, 393
 classical experiment and, 234
In-depth interview, 282
Indexes, 6, 87, 167
 bivariate relationships among items, 171–174
 construction of, 170–182
 handling missing data and, 177–178
 item selection for, 170–171
 multivariate relationships among items, 174–176
 vs. scales, 167–170
 scoring, 176–177
 status of women and, 181–182
 validating, 178–181
Indianapolis Prosecution Experiment (IPE), 350–351
Indicators, 120–121
 "cause" and "effect", 172–173
 interchangeability of, 121–122, 132
 multiple, quantitative data and, 167
 single or multiple, 145–146
Indirect observables, 119
Individualistic fallacy, 97
Individuals, social scientific research and, 93
Induction
 analytic, 316
 deduction compared, 54–60
 illustration of, 56–58
Inductive logic, 55
Inductive method, 4, 283
Inductive theory, 35–36
 construction of, 63–64
Infant mortality rate (IMR), 372
Inferential statistics, 405, 420–431
 chi square and, 427–431
 logic of statistical significance and, 422–427
 tests of statistical significance and, 422
 univariate inferences and, 421–422
Informants, 194
 selecting for sampling, 196–197

Information, 359
Informed consent, 444
"Innovator", 52
Inquiry
 authority and, 19–20
 errors in, 20–21
 human
  ordinary, 18–19
  science and, 3
 qualitative, terminology of, 280–283
 tradition and, 19
Institutional review board (IRB), 444–445
Instrumentation, internal invalidity and, 242
Intellectual measure, religious involvement and, 55
Intellectual sophistication, 168
Intelligence, African Americans and, 452
Intensity, relative, 183–184
Intensity structure, 168
Interactionist paradigm, 4
Interchangeability, of indicators, 121–122, 132
Interference, social regularity and, 28
Internal invalidity, 7, 240–241
 sources of, 240–244
International Business Machines Corporation, 360
International Review of Modern Sociology, A6
Internet, 296, 361, A8–A14
Interpolation, 414
Interpretation
 elaboration paradigm and, 397–398
 social research and, 2–3
Interpretivism, 281
INTER-STAT, 360
Intersubjectivity, 299
Inter-University Consortium for Political and Social Research, 275
Interval measures, 143
Interval variable, 411
Interviewer, data entry by, 365
Interviewing
 computer-assisted, 259–260
 in-depth, 282
 qualitative, 290–293
Interview survey, 264–268
Intext, 296
Introspection, 299
Invalidity, 7
 external, 240, 244
  sources of, 244–245
 internal, 240–241
  sources of, 240–244
Isaac, Larry, 146, 330
Item analysis, index validation and, 179–180
Ivy League college, attendance at, success in life and, 394–395

Jacobson, Lenore, 246
Japanese religion, 327–328
Jasso, Guillermina, 61
Jefferson, Thomas, 255
Jensen, Arthur, 452
Job-related depression, 177
Johnson, Jeffrey, 197
Judaism, 327
Judgmental sampling, 194, 195
Justice, distributive, 61
Juvenile delinquency, 52, 53–54, 81–82, 419–420

Kahane, Howard, 78, 79
Kaplan, Abraham, 51, 119–120
Karolinska Institute, 275
Kasl, Stanislav, 250
Kasof, Joseph, 153
Keeter, Scott, 101
Kendall, Patricia, 389, 390, 391, 394–396
Kerensky, Alexander, 326
Kiecolt, E. Jill, 275
Kings Crew MC, 301–302
Kinloch, Graham C., A6
Kish, Leslie, 200
Knowledge, attitudes, and practices (KAP), 334
Krueger, Richard, 248
Krushat, W. Mark, 132
Kuhn, Thomas, 42–43
Ku Klux Klan, 152
Kurzweil Voice, 296
Kvale, Steinar, 281, 290, 292
Kwalitan, 296

Laboratory experiment, 249
Labor force, 128–129
Lambda, 408–409, 413
Landon, Alf, 192–193, 257
Language, of variables, 29–34
Larceny rates, time-series analysis and, 417–418
Laslett, Barbara, 329, 330
Latent content, 313–314
LaVey, Anton, 299–300
Law, theory construction and, 51–52
Lazarsfeld, Paul, 73, 132, 389, 391, 399
Legislation, rape reform, 349–350
Leon, Joseph J., 105
Lever, Janet, 48
Liberalism, 86, 108, 116, 170
 age and, 103
Library, A2–A6
Library files, computerized, A5–A6
Library of Congress classifications, A4–A5
Liebow, Elliot, 282, 300–301
Lifestyles, field research and, 284
Likert, Rensis, 183
Likert scale, 148, 183–184
Linear regression, 411–413
Linton, Ralph, 45–46, 47

listproc, A10
listserv, A10
Literary Digest, 192–193, 212, 257, 268, A142
Literature review, A17–A18
 research proposal and, 112
Lofland, John, 75, 95, 282–283, 284, 288, 292, 293, 294, 298, 302
Lofland, Lyn, 75, 95, 284, 288, 292, 293, 294, 298, 302
Logic
 of causal social research, 7
 deductive, 54–55
 fuzzy, 50
 inductive, 55
 of probability sampling, 197–200
 of sampling, 6–7
 of statistical significance, 422–427
Logical reasoning, 322
Logical systems, 52–60
Logic and Contemporary Rhetoric, 78
Logistics, 346–348
Longitudinal study, 101–103, 105
 approximating, 103–104
Lopata, Helena Znaniecki, 410
LSD, 104
Lugar, Richard, 249
Lynching, 71–72, 118, 309

Machine-readable form, 359
MacIP, A11
MacLaine, Shirley, 90
Macrotheory, 43
Madison, Anna-Marie, 337
Magnitudes, field research and, 298
Mailing lists, A10–A11
majordomo, A10
Mallon, Mary, 405
Manageability, univariate analysis and, 374–375
Manifest content, 313–314
Marihuana Tax Act, 322
Marijuana, 63–64, 74, 92, 104, 155, 335, 382
Marital satisfaction, 134
Mark-sense sheet, 365
Marshall, Catherine, 120, 286, 287
Marx, Karl, 4, 44–45, 255, 326
Marxism, 450
MASS, 360
Matching, 238–239
Matrix questions, 156–157
Maturation, internal invalidity and, 241–242
Maxwell, Joseph, 73
McGrane, Bernard, 46
MCI Mail, A8
McKinney, Kathleen, 444
Mead, George Herbert, 45, 48, 246, 299
Meadows, Dennis, 353–354
Meadows, Donella, 353–354
Mean(s), 52, 371, 372

Measurement, 116, 462
 of anything that exists, 116–127
 composite, 145
 conceptualization and, 5
 criteria for, 129–136
 evaluation research and, 337–339
 example of, 82–83
 levels of, 141–145, 415
  implications of, 143–145
 linking association and, 79–83
 qualitative, 2
 quantitative, 2
 reliability and, 129–133
 research proposal and, 112
 social research and, 2
 validity and, 133–134
Measures
 of association, 407–411, 415
 composite, of variables, 168
 interval, 143
 nominal, 142
 ordinal, 142–143, 168
 ratio, 143
Median, 371, 372
Median family income, 374
Medium, 90
 neutral, 264
Megatrends 2000, 309
Melevin, Paul T., 258
Merton, Robert, 27, 52, 125
Methodology, 18
MicroCase, 360
Microcomputers, social research and, 361
Microquest, 360
Microstat, 360
Micro-SURVEY, 360
Microtheory, 43
Midtown Manhattan Mental Health Study, 127
Miles, Matthew, 297
Milgram, Stanley, 448
Miller, Delbert, 262
Minitab, 360
Minnesota Multiphasic Personality Inventory (MMPI), 133
Mitchell, Richard, 150
Modal, 408
Mode, 370, 372
Modem, 361
Modern view, 21–22
Monographs, A16
Morgan, David, 249
Morgan, Lewis, 326
Motorcycle gangs, 301–302
MOVE civil rights group, 72, 84
Moynihan, Daniel, 452
Multiple regression, 413
Multiple time-series design, 342–345
Multistage cluster sampling, 219–226
 illustration of, 226–227
Multivariate analysis, 370, 383–385

Multivariate relationship, index items and, 174–176
Multivariate tables, 383
Multivariate techniques, 415–420
Murder, capital punishment and, 353
Mutually exclusive, 141–142, 148
My Fair Lady, 246
My Lai, 448
Myrdal, Gunnar, 451

Nader, Ralph, 324
"Naive realism", 21
Nardi, Peter, 415
Nathan, Laura, 275
National Council on Public Polls, 463
National Geographic, 17
National Health Service, 378
National Highway and Transportation Safety Administration (NHTSA), 335–336, 349
National Opinion Research Center (NORC), 6, 126, 159, A22
National Safety Council, 349
National Science Foundation, 69
"Natural" experiment, 249–251
Natural sciences, causation in, 69
Natural selection, 44
Necessary cause, 76–77
Negation, questionnaires and, 152
Neutral medium, 264
Newman, Jeffrey, 132
New York Times, 210, 221, 256, 376
Nixon, Richard, 348
Nominal definition, 122
Nominal measures, 142
Nominal variable, 57, 408–409
Nomothetic approach, 281
Nomothetic explanation, 34–35
Nomothetic model, of explanation, 71–73
Nonequivalent control group, 341–342
Nonprobability sampling, 194–197
Nonreactive research, 308
Nonsampling error, 430
Normal curve, 207
Normal curve areas, A36
Norman, Darlene, 336
Norms, 297
Norwegian Social Science Data Services, 275
Null hypothesis, 57, 427
Numbers, random, A32–A33
Numerical coding, 315
Numerical description, qualitative research and, 378

Obedience, observing, 448–450
Objective, research proposal and, 112
Objectivity, 3
  rational, 49–51
  social research and, 450–453
O'Brien, Patricia, 345

Observables
  direct, 119
  indirect, 119
Observation, 116
  direct, 280
  inaccurate, 20
  participant, 8, 280, 282
  quantification and, 37
  recording, 293–294
  research project design and, 109
  selective, 20
  social research and, 2–3
  theory construction and, 51
  traditional model of science and, 53–54
  units of, 93
Observation unit, 202
One-group pretest-posttest design, 240, 241
O'Neill, Harry, 442
One-shot case study, 239–240, 241
Open-ended questions, 148
Operational definition, 122, 124
Operationalization, 5–6, 86, 116, 139
  choices in, 139–146
  of concepts, 81
  illustrations of, 146–147
  research project design and, 109
  traditional model of science and, 53
  variable names and, 130–131
Opinions, measurement of, 6
Oppenheimer, Robert, 452
Oppression, 122, 328
Op-sense sheet, 365
Optical scanner, 365–366
Optical scan sheet
  coding to, 365–366
  direct use of, 366
Ordinality, response categories and, 183
Ordinal measures, 142–143, 168
Ordinal variable, 409–411
Organism, 47
Organizational measure, religious involvement and, 55
Organizations
  field research and, 284
  social scientific research and, 94
Orientations, as points of focus, 100
Origin of the Species, 44
Outlaw bikers, 301–302
Overgeneralization, 20

Panel attrition, 103
Panel study, 102–103, 105
Paradigms, 3–4, 51
  conflict, 4, 44–45
  elaboration. *See* Elaboration paradigm
  exchange, 48–49, 61
  feminist, 47–48
  functionalist, 3–4
  interactionist, 4

rational-choice, 49
social science, 42–51
Parameter(s)
  population, 207
  sampling and, 202
Parametric tests of significance, 422
Parker, Charlie, 4
Partial regression, 414
Partial relationships, 392
Partial tables, 392
Participant observation, 8, 280, 282
Participant-observer, roles of, 286–287
Participation, voluntary, 38–39, 438–439
Path analysis, 415–417
Path coefficients, 416
Payne, Charles, 71
Pearson's product-moment correlation, 411
Percentaging tables, 381–382
Perinelli, Philip, 199–200
Periodicity, 214–215
Perot, Ross, 141, 192
Personal interviewing, computer-assisted, 260
Phenomenology, 281
Picou, J. Steven, 65
Plagiarism, research report and, A18–A19
Plutzer, Eric, 72
POINT FIVE, 360
Points of focus, 89, 97–100
Political party affiliation, 116, 141
Politics, social research and, 450–454
Polling, 256–257
Polling companies, 147
Polls
  predicting presidential election outcomes, 193
  results of, questioning, A139–A144
Population
  research project design and, 109
  sampling and, 201, 210–213
Population Bulletin, 324
Population Communications International (PCI), 181, 334
Population Crisis Committee, 324
Population parameter, 207
Population Reference Bureau, 324, 372, 374
Pornography, 348
Positivism, 24
  early, 43–44
Possible-code cleaning, 366–367
Postmodern view, 22–24
Post-positivism, 24
Posttesting, classical experiment and, 234–235
Posttest-only control group design, 245
Postulates, theory construction and, 52
Powell, Elwin, 125
Powerlessness, 124

Index

Practices, field research and, 284
Precision, measurement quality and, 129
Precoding, 159
Predestination, 326
Prediction, 19
Prejudice, 5, 31–34, 86, 108, 117–118, 122, 152, 168, 183
  against African Americans, 233–235, 239–240, 251
  religiosity and, 82
  social class and, 409
Premodern view, 21
Presser, Stanley, 159
Pretesting
  classical experiment and, 234–235
  of questionnaires, 159
Primary sampling unit, 201
Principles, 51
Principles of Survey Analysis, 75
Privacy, right to, 444–445
Probabilistic causal model, 71
Probabilistic reasoning, 18
Probability proportionate to size (PPS) sampling, 222–224
Probability sampling, 192, 237
  logic of, 197–200
Probability sampling theory, 202–203
Probing, for responses, 266–267
Problem, research proposal and, 112
Problem formulation, evaluation research and, 336–346
Processes, field research and, 298
Prodigy, A8
Professional code of ethics, 445–446
Professional papers, A16
Program evaluation, 334
Project Camelot, 452–453
Proportionate reduction of error (PRE), 408, 413
Propositions, theory construction and, 52
The Protestant Ethic and the Spirit of Capitalism, 326
Protestant reformation, 326
Provincialism, 78
P-STAT, 360
Psychological Abstracts, A6
Psychological reductionism, 97
Public opinion polling, 256–257
Purposive sampling, 194, 195
Pygmalion, 246
Pygmalion effect, 246

Qualitative data, 36–38, 280
Qualitative data analysis, 297–299
  content analysis and, 315–317
Qualitative data processing, 294–297
Qualitative evaluation, 345–346
Qualitative inquiry, terminology of, 280–283
Qualitative interviewing, 290–293
Qualitative measurement, 2
Qualitative research, numerical descriptions in, 378

Quantification, observations and, 37
Quantitative analysis, 9, 280
Quantitative data, 36–38
  multiple indicators and, 167
Quantitative measurement, 2
Quasi-experimental design, 340–345
Questionable cause, 79
Questionnaires, 147–148
  acceptable response rates and, 261–262
  biased items/terms and, 152–153
  case study, 262–264
  construction of, 153–162
  follow-up mailings and, 261
  formats for respondents and, 154–155
  general format for, 153–154
  GSS household enumeration, A22–A31
  instructions in, 158–159
  monitoring returns and, 260–261
  negative items and, 152
  ordering items in, 157–158
  pretesting, 159
  sample, 160–163
  self-administered, 147, 158, 257–264
    computerized, 260
  self-mailing, 259
  standardized, 8
Questions, 147–148
  closed-ended, 148
  contingency, 155–156
  double-barreled, 149, 150–151
  essential, 167
  extra, 167
  guidelines for asking, 147–153
  matrix, 156–157
  open-ended, 148
  relevancy of, 151
Quota frame, 196
Quota matrix, 238
  illustration of, 239
Quota sampling, 193, 194, 196, 238

Race
  as distorter variable, 400
  social research and, 451–452
Radcliffe-Brown, Alfred, 126
Random-digit dialing, 203, 269, 270
Randomization, 237–238
Random numbers, A32–A33
  using table of, 214–215
Random sample, 312
  simple, 216
Random sampling, 192, 421
  simple, 213
Random selection, 203
Range, of variation, 139–140
Rank order, 142
Rape reform legislation, 349–350
Rasinski, Kenneth, 152
Rather, Dan, 90
Ratio measures, 143
Rational-choice paradigm, 49

Rational objectivity, 49–51
Ratio variable, 411
Raw data matrix, 407
Reader's Guide to Periodical Literature, A2–A4
Read-only memory, 361
Reagan, Ronald, 78, 80
Real definition, 122
Reality
  definitions and, 122
  views of, 21–24
Reasoning
  causal, 18
    statistical analysis and, 77–78
  errors of, 77–79
  illogical, 20–21
  logical, 322
  probabilistic, 18
Reasons have reasons, 70–71
Recall, 104
Record keeping, coding and, 315
Redfield, Robert, 326
Reductionism, 97
  economic, 97
  psychological, 97
Reference group, 389–390
Reference group theory, 27
Regoli, Mary Jean, 350–351
Regression analysis, 411–415, A95–A97
  cautions in, 414–415
  time-lagged, 418
Regression line, 411, 413
Rehabilitation, 9
Reicker, Henry, 101
Reification, 122
Reinharz, Shulamit, 309
Relationship(s)
  bivariate, index items and, 171–174
  causal, criteria for, 73–75
  field research and, 284
  multivariate, index items and, 174–176
  partial, 392
  spurious, 396
  statistical significance of, 426–427
  between variables, 32–33
Relative deprivation, 389–390
Relative intensity, 183–184
Relevancy, of questions, 151
Reliability, 155
  analyzing existing statistics and, 322–323
  coding and, 313
  field research and, 304–305
  measurement quality and, 129–133
  survey research and, 274
  validity compared, 135–136
Religion
  Comfort Hypothesis and, 55
  Japanese, 327–328
  suicide rates and, 59–60, 96–97, 125, 320

Religiosity, 108, 116, 157, 168, 170, 174
  prejudice and, 82
Replication, 322
  elaboration paradigm and, 393–396
  of inquiry, 20
Reporting
  interviewing process and, 293
  social research and, 443–444
Representativeness, sampling and, 200, 225
Representative sample, 199, 424, 426
Reproducibility, coefficient of, 187
Research
  evaluation. *See* Evaluation research
  field. *See* Field research
  nonreactive, 308
  social. *See* Social research
  social indicators, 335, 352–354
  survey. *See* Survey research
  unobtrusive, 8–9, 308–309
Research note, A16
Research process, 107
Research project. designing, 105–111
Research proposal, 89, 111–112
  elements of, 112
Research report, A15–A21
  organization of, A17–A20
Research subjects
  deceiving, 442–443
  no harm to, 38, 439–440, 445
Research workers, reliability of, 133
Respondents, 196
  compentency of, 149
  formats for, 154–155
  willingness of, 149–150
Response categories, "collapsing", 376–377
Responses
  probing for, 266–267
  recording exactly, 266
Response set, 157
Review, research project design and, 110–111
Riecken, Henry, 338
Right to privacy, 444–445
Ringer, Benjamin, 55, 57
Ritual, 55
Rivalry, internal invalidity and, 243
Roberts, Jane, 90
Roethlisberger, F J., 235
Rokeach, Milton, 251
Role(s), 46
  field research and, 284
Role theory, 45–46
Roosevelt, Franklin Delano, 193, 257
Roots, 251
Roots: The Next Generation, 251
Roper, Burns, 442
Roper Center for Public Opinion Research, 275
Roper Organization, 442
Roper Poll, 147, 256, 275

Rosenberg, Morris, 95, 399, 400
Rosenthal, Robert, 246
Rossman, Gretchen, 120, 286, 287
Rothman, Ellen, 328
Rubin, Herbert, 290, 292
Rubin, Riene, 290, 292
Ruby Ridge, 72
Rules, breaking, 46

Sacks, Jeffrey, 132
Sailors, motivating, 346–347
SALT (Systemic Analysis of Language Transactions), 296
SAM, 360
Sample
  EMPSEM, 200
  modification to, 219
  random, 312
    simple, 216
  representative, 199, 424, 426
  selecting, 219
  self-weighting, 224
  systematic, 312
  unrepresentative, 425
Sampling, 2, 87, 192, 462
  cluster, 313
    multistage, 219–227
  concepts and terminology, 200–202
  content analysis and, 310–313
  design types, 213–218
  disproportionate, 224–226
  history of, 192–194
  illustration of, 219
  judgmental, 194, 195
  logic of, 6–7
  nonprobability, 194–197
  probability, 192, 237
    logic of, 197–200
  probability proportionate to size, 222–224
  probability theory, 202–203
  purposive, 194, 195
  quota, 193, 194, 196, 238
  random, 192, 421
    simple, 213
  research project design and, 109
  snowball, 194, 195–196
  stratified, 216–218, 313
  systematic, 213–216
    implicit stratification in, 218
Sampling bias, conscious and unconscious, 198–200
Sampling distribution, 203–205
  binomial, 205–210
Sampling error, 202, 427
  estimated, A37
Sampling frame, 201–202, 210–213, 219
Sampling ratio, 219
Sampling unit, 201
Samurai, 327
Sanders, William, 92
San Francisco Chronicle, 77

Santa Claus, 221
SAS, 360
Satanists, 299–300
Scales, 6, 87, 167
  construction of, 182–187
  vs. indexes, 167–170
  semantic differentiation, 410
Scale types, Guttman scaling and, 185–186
Scaling techniques, 169
Scarce, Rik, 441
Scattergram, 411, 412
Schachter, Stanley, 101
Schedule, research proposal and, 112
Scholastic Aptitude Test, 133
School segregation, 451
Science
  human inquiry and, 3
  traditional model of, 52–54
  wheel of, 59
Science Citation Index, 127
Scientific orientation(s), 173, 177
  bivariate relationships among, 174
  trivariate relationships among, 175, 176
Scientific orientation index, validation of, 181
Scientific theory, 25
Secondary analysis, 274–276
Secondary sampling unit, 201
Segregation, 451
Selection bias, internal invalidity and, 242
Selective observation, 20
Self-administered questionnaire, 147, 158, 257–264
  computerized, 260
Self-concept, 246
Self-interviewing, computer-assisted, 260
Self-mailing questionnaire, 259
Self-weighting sample, 224
Selvin, Hanan, 75
Semantic differential, 184–185
Semantic differentiation scale, 410
Sentimentality, 119
Settlements, field research and, 284
Sex education, 348
Sexual equality, gender and, 382, 422–427
Sexual harassment, 225
Sexual impotence, 339–340
Sexuality research, ethical issues in, 444–445
Shaffir, William, 288
Shakespeare, William, 45, 312
Shanks, J. Merrill, 271
Shaw, George Bernard, 246
Silverman, David, 79, 134, 378
Similarities, 297
Simmel, Georg, 44–45
Simple random sample, 216
Simple random sampling (SRS), 213

SINET: A Quarterly Review of Social Reports and Research on Social Indicators, Social Trends, and the Quality of Life, 324
Skinner, Steven, 262
Smith, Andrew, 150
Smith, Joel, 37
Smith, Tom, 255
SNAP, 360
Snowball sampling, 194, 195–196
Social artifacts, social scientific research and, 94–95
Social class, 30
   Comfort Hypothesis and, 55
   juvenile delinquency theory and, 52
   prejudice and, 409
Social context, 273, 346–352
Social Darwinism, 44
Social evolution, 44, 326
Social indicators, 352
Social indicators research, 335, 352–354
Social intervention, 335
Social regularity, 25–28
   aggregate, 28–29
   exceptions to, 28
   interference and, 28
Social research
   causal language of, 4
   computers in, 359–361
   consumer's guide to, 461–465
   in cyberspace, A8–A14
   definitions and, 128–129
   description and, 91–92, 128
   design, 5, 461–462
   dialectics of, 34–38
   ethical issues in, 11, 38–39, 438–446
   everyday uses of, 459–461
   explanation and, 92, 128
   exploration and, 90–91
   hologram, 1–12
   politics of, 450–454
   purposes of, 89, 90–92
   race and, 451–452
   theory and, 64–65
   time dimension and, 100–104
   uses of, 12
Social science
   determinism and, 69–71
   foundations of, 24–34
   paradigms, 42–51
Social Science Citation Index, 127
Social statistics, 11
Social systems theory, 47
Social theory, 25
   research and, 64–65
   structure of, 51–52
Social worlds, field research and, 284
Socioeconomic status (SES), 122, 124, 168
Sociological Abstracts, A6
Sociologie, 325
Socrates, 54–55

Sokagakkai, 328
Solomon four-group design, 244–245
Sonar Professional, 296
Sorokin, Pitirim, A., 326
Specification, 264
   elaboration paradigm and, 298–399
Specificity, field research and, 313
Spencer, Herbert, 44, 47
Split-half method, 132
Spock, Benjamin, 14
Spohn, Cassie, 349–350
Sprintmail, A8
Spurious relationship, 396
Srole, Leo, 125, 126
Srole scale, 126
Stability, suicide rates and, 319–320
Standard deviation, 208
Standard error, 207–208, 421
Standardized questionnaire, 8
Stanley, Julian, 239–241, 244–245, 252
Stark, Rodney, 82
STAT80, 360
STATA, 360
Statements, 147–148
Statgraf, 360
Static-group comparison, 240, 241
Statistical Abstract CD-ROM, 361
Statistical Abstract of the United States, 147, 323
Statistical analysis, faulty causal reasoning and, 77–78
Statistical Package for Social Sciences (SPSS), version 6.1
   bivariate analysis, A80–A95
   commands, A44
   COMPUTE, IF, RECODE, A66–A72
   CROSSTAB procedure, A49–A53
   data cleaning and error checking, A44–A45
   data editor, A114–A116
   data editor window, A118–A119
   descriptive statistics, A53–A61
   developing scales, A72–A78
   FREQUENCIES procedure, A45–A49
   getting data to computer, A109–A112
   graphic techniques, A61–A66
   initial display screen, A41
   learner's guide to, A38–A138
   LIST command, A45
   missing values, A120–A121
   multivariate statistics using regression analysis, A97–A109
   reading data, A116
   regression analysis, A95–A97
   spreadsheet file, A114, A116–A117
   standard data file, A117–A118
   standard text file, A112–A113
   summarizing variable of interest, A78
   working and system files, A44
   working with general social survey data, A41–A43
   working with valid cases, A78–A80

Statistical regression, internal invalidity and, 242
Statistical significance, 8
   logic of, 422–427
   tests of, 422
Statistics, 405
   aggregated, 320
   descriptive. *See* Descriptive statistics
   existing
      analyzing, 308–309, 319–324, 464
      sources of, 323–324
   inferential. *See* Inferential statistics
   social, 11
StatPro, 360
STATS PLUS, 360
Status, 46
Statview, 360
Stebbins, Robert, 288
Steel, Paul, 345–346
Stein, Gertrude, 22
Stella, 353–354
Stereotypes, 5
Stereotyping, gender, television commercials and, 317–318
Stimulus-response theory, 264
Stouffer, Samuel, 27, 389–391, 393, 443, 453
Stratification, 219
   multistage cluster sampling and, 222
   systematic sampling and, 218
Stratified sampling, 216–218, 313
Strauss, Anselm, 63, 283, 316
Structural functionalism, 47
The Structure of Scientific Revolutions, 42
Structures, field research and, 298
Strunk, William, Jr., A15
The Study of Man, 47
Study population, 201, 219
Subcultures, field research and, 284
Subgroups, comparisons of, 375–378
Subjectivity, 3, 50–51
Subjects. *See also* Research subjects
   available, sampling and, 194–195
   field research and, 287–289
   research proposal and, 112
Substantive significance, 8
Success/failure, operationalizing, 345
Sufficient cause, 76–77
Suicide, 319–320
   anomic, 320
   religion and, 59–60, 96–97, 125, 320
Suicide, 124, 126, 319
Sumner, William Graham, 451
Supervision, 81
Suppressed evidence, 79
Suppressor variable, 399
Survey interviewer, role of, 264–265
Survey interviewing, 264–268
   rules for, 264–267
Survey Mate, 360
Survey research, 8, 255–256, 463. *See also* Questionnaires

comparison of methods, 271–272
electronic, 259–260
strengths and weaknesses of, 272–274
telephone, 268–271
topics appropriate to, 256–257
Survey Research Center, 361
Survey Sampling, 200
SURVTAB, 360
Syllogism, 54–55
Symbolic interactionism, 45
Symbolic realism, 288
Synopsis, A17
Syphilis, 348
SYSTAT, 360
Systematic sample, 312
Systematic sampling, 213–216
 implicit stratification in, 218

Tables
 bivariate formats for, 383
 constructing and reading, 382–383
 contingency, 383
 multivariate, 383
 partial, 392
 percentaging, 381–382
Tabulating Machine Company, 359–360
Takeuchi, David, 63
Tally's Corner, 282, 300
Tally sheet, 316
Tandon, Rajesh, 343
Tautology, 82
TDE (touchtone data entry), 260
Tearoom Trade, 447
TECPACS, 360
Telephone cues, 270
Telephone interviewing, computer-assisted, 259–260
Telephone survey, 268–271
Television commercials, gender stereotyping in, 317–318
Television violence, 309
 recording sheet for, 311
Tentative conclusion, 97
Testing, internal invalidity and, 242
Test-retest method, 132
Tests of statistical significance, 422
 parametric, 422
Textpack, 296
Thematizing, interviewing process and, 292
Theoretical hypotheses, derivation of, 81
Theory, 3, 24, 26, 52, 106, 458–459
 central tendency, 209
 chaos, 50
 construction of, 80–81
 deductive, 35–36
  construction of, 60–63
  example of, 61–63
 expectations-states, 246
 grounded, 63, 283

code development and, 314
inductive, 35–36
 construction of, 63–64
reference group, 27
role, 45–46
scientific, 25
social, 25
 research and, 64–65
 structure of, 51–52
social systems, 47
stimulus-response, 264
traditional model of science and, 53
Thinking topics, 284
Thomas, Edmund, 346
Thomas, W. I., 328
Three Mile Island nuclear accident, 250–251
Thurstone scaling, 183
Tiano, Susan, 35
Time dimension
 aging and, 105
 research design and, 100–104
Time-lagged regression analysis, 418
Time-series analysis, 417–418
Time-series data, 330
Time-series design, 341
 multiple, 342–345
Time sharing, 360
Tokugawa Religion, 327
Tolstoy, Leo, 312
Top Grade, 296
Tortora, Robert, 271
Total variation, 411
Touchtone data entry (TDE), 260
Tradition, inquiry and, 19
Traffic accidents, driver training and, 335–336
Transcribing, interviewing process and, 292
Transfer sheet, 364–365
Trend study, 101–102, 105
Triviality, 27–28
Truman, Harry S, 194
t-test, 430
Tuckel, Peter, 269
Turbogopher, A11
Turner, Jonathan, 52
Twende na Wakati, 334
Typhoid Mary, 405
Typologies, 6, 87, 167, 187–189

Understanding, 19
 generalized, 93
Unemployed, 128, 141–142
Unidimensionality, scale and index construction and, 170
Uniform Crime Reports, 323
United Nations, 6, 324, 376–377
United States Census, 91
United States Census Bureau, 127, 131, 133, 149, 256, 268, 271, 359, 361, 375, 384

United States Center For Disease Control, 348
United States Decennial Census, 256
United States Defense Department, 452–453
United States Department of Agriculture, 271
United States Department of Labor, 131
United States Supreme Court, 451
Units of analysis, 5, 89, 92–97
 analyzing existing statistics and, 320–322
 content analysis and, 310–312
 ecological fallacy and, 96–97
 reductionism and, 97
Units of observation, 93
Univariate analysis, 9–10, 370–375
 central tendency and, 370–374
 detail vs. manageability and, 374–375
 dispersion and, 374
 distributions and, 370
 variables and, 374
Universals, 297
Unobtrusive measures, 308–309
Unrepresentative sample, 425
URL, A11

Valencia, Jocelyn, 258
Validation
 external, 180
 indexes and, 178–181
Validity, 155
 analyzing existing statistics and, 322
 classical experiment and, 234–235
 coding and, 313
 construct, 133–134
 content, 133–134
 criterion-related, 133–134
 face, 133, 170
 field research and, 303–304
 measurement quality and, 133–134
 reliability compared, 135–136
 survey research and, 274
Values, 30
Variable names, importance of, 130–131
Variables, 3, 30–31
 bivariate analysis and, 378
 causality among, criteria for, 73–75
 composite measures of, 168
 control, 10
 dependent, 7, 188, 378
  classical experiment and, 234
 dichotomous, 210, 234
 distorter, 400
 elaboration paradigm and, 393
 independent, 7, 188, 378
  classical experiment and, 234
 interval, 411
 language of, 29–34
 nominal, 57, 408–409
 ordinal, 409–411
 ratio, 411

relationship between, 32
relationships among, 3
sampling and, 202
stratified sampling and, 217
suppressor, 399
theory construction and, 52
univariate analysis and, 374
Variation
　explained, 413
　between extremes, 140
　index items and, 170–171
　range of, 139–140
　total, 411
VBPro, 296
Verba, Sidney, 275
Verifying, interviewing process and, 293
Veroff, Joseph, 102
Verstehen, 329
Vested interests, 349
Violence, television, 309
　recording sheet for, 311
Virginia Senate Bill No. 1126, 455
Voice Capture, 272–273
Voice recognition (VR), 260

Voluntary participation, 38–39, 438–439
VR (voice recognition), 260

Waco, 72
Wagner-Pacifici, Robin, 72, 94
Walker, Jeffery, 270
Walker Research, 270
Wallace, Walter, 59
War and Peace, 312
Warner, William Lloyd, 126
Warriner, G. Keith, 246
Washington, George, 255
Watson, Dr., 60
Webb, Eugene, 308–309
Weber, Max, 8–9, 326–327, 329, 450
Webster's New World Dictionary, 438
Weighting, 224–226
Weight of evidence, 134
Weiss, Carol, 343
Weitzman, Eben, 297
Wellman, David, 35
Wells, Ida B., 309
Wells, Richard H., 65
West, Patricia Salter, 394–395
Wharton, Amy, 177

When Prophecy Fails, 101
White, E. B., A15
Wife battering, 350–352
Wilder, Douglas, 270
WinWord, 296
Witnesses, 282
Wolcott, Harry, 78
Wolf, Daniel, 301–302
Women, status of, indexing, 181–182
Women's Ways of Knowing, 48
Working papers, A16
World Population Data Sheet, 324
World statistics, 324
World Wide Web, 361
　as source of statistics, 323, A11–A14

Yammarino, Francis, 262
Yankelovich Poll, 256, 275
Yerg, Beverly, 413
Yinger, Milton, 239

Zeller, Richard, 133–134
Zhang, Ray, 37
Zipp, John, 72
Znaniecki, Florian, 328